Social Sciences

# DOES NOT CIRCULATE

# Educational Systems
# of Africa

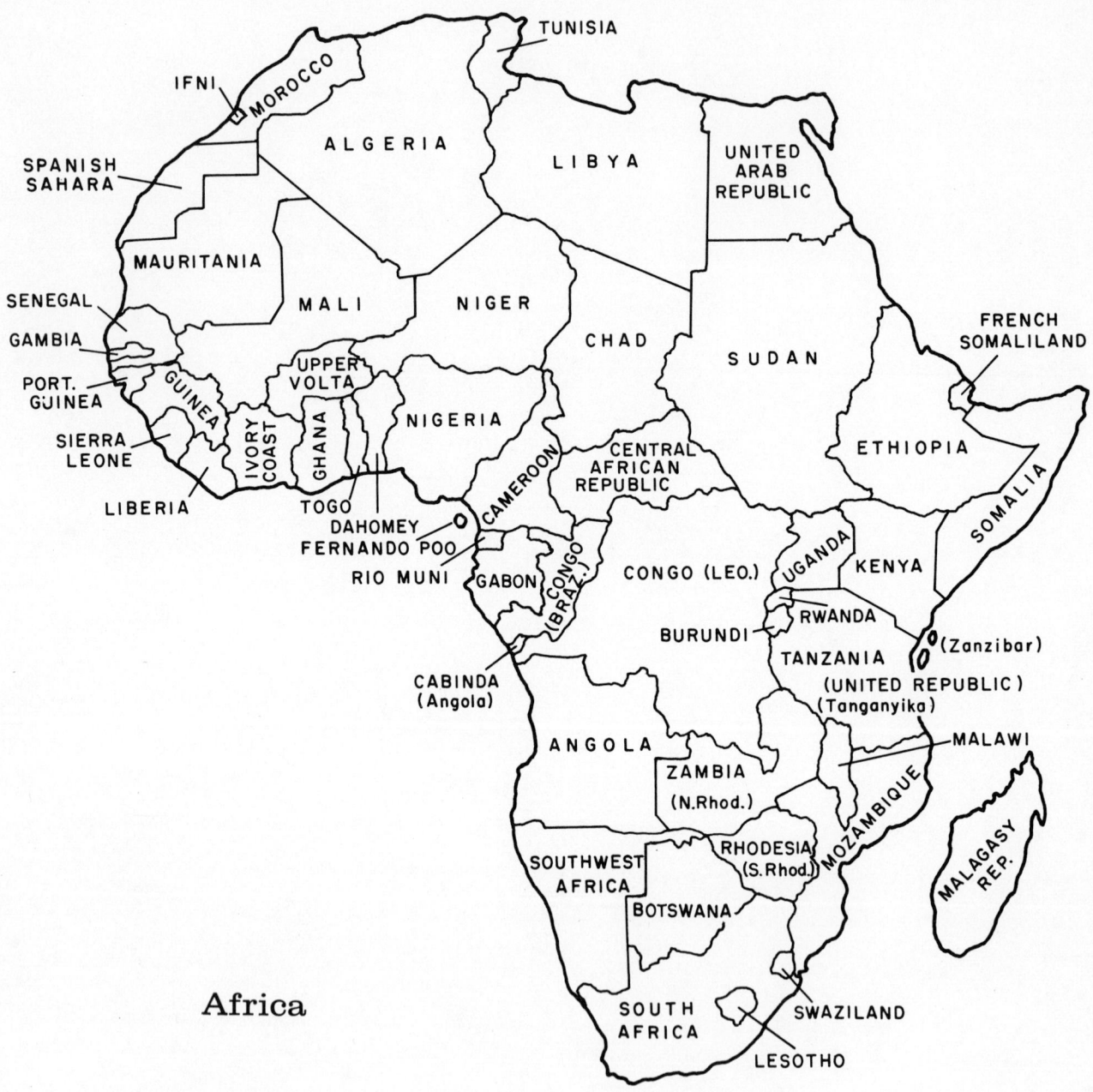

Africa

# Educational Systems
# of Africa

*Interpretations for Use
in the Evaluation of
Academic Credentials*

## Martena Sasnett
and
## Inez Sepmeyer

# University of California Press

Berkeley and Los Angeles

University of California Press
Berkeley and Los Angeles, California

Cambridge University Press
London, England

# P R E F A C E

## RESPONSE TO AN INCREASING NEED

With the dramatic mobility of individuals trekking between countries for various educational enterprises, the need to understand the educational systems of the world becomes greater every year.

As student populations began an accelerated flow from country to country after World War II, admissions officers in schools, colleges and universities were the first large professional group to be faced with the need for interpreting "foreign" education. Now, in the United States alone, the task of evaluating academic credentials from abroad is an enormous undertaking. In 1965, each of the 82,000 foreign students[1] who came to study in U.S. colleges and universities had sent ahead one to four credentials to be evaluated for admissions. Multiply this on a global scale, and one may recognize the world-wide imperative of having information on a student's previous educational milieu.

One section of the world about which little has been known in the educational field has been Africa. During recent years more than six thousand African students have come to the United States for study, many selected under the African Scholarship Program of American Universities (ASPAU).[2] The U.S. Department of State has been offering more and more

---

[1] *Open Doors*, 1965 (New York:  Institute of International Education).

[2] 75 Mt. Auburn Street, Cambridge, Massachusetts 02138.

v

opportunities to African grantees. U.S. professors have been commuting

to Africa to advise on the setting up of new institutions. Ques-

tions about the academic training of Africans have mounted.

The International Training and Research Program of the Ford

Foundation, sensitive to international educational needs, provided

a grant to the University of California, Los Angeles, in 1964 for the

compilation of this volume  It constitutes the first step in a 6-part

revision and expansion of Educational Systems of the World,[1] a

reference work prepared in 1952 for use in the evaluation of foreign

credentials.

For an admissions officer, the items of major importance about a

foreign educational system are: the number of years of study, the entrance

requirements for the various phases of training, the length of programs,

curricular content, the types of examinations, the grading system, the

exact names of certificates, diplomas and degrees awarded and the approx-

imate levels of achievement they represent. Those are the raw data which

form the basis for judging academic eligibility of overseas students.

Faced with an overwhelming amount of paper work, the admissions officer

has come to value brevity in presentation of such data, and a style

which permits him to assimilate information readily.

At the request of those who have found helpful the format of

Educational Systems of the World, the material here set forth is also

in a telegraphic style of reporting. All statements are cut to a bare

minimum of words with the purpose of spotlighting salient facts and

---

[1]Martena Tenney Sasnett, Educational Systems of the World: Interpretations for Use in the Evaluation of Foreign Credentials (Los Angeles:
University of Southern California Press, 1952). Out of print.

reducing reading time. To the layman the material may appear deceptively simple because of this form of presentation. To the initiated, it is not. An analogy can be made to the doctor who reads an X-ray film, or the scientist who interprets a slide under his microscope; the professional knowledge brought to it illuminates the subject.

Up to the present time it is still difficult to amass the specific type of data here presented because Ministries of Education reports are primarily statistical, dealing with the number of schools, classes, students, teachers, diplomas awarded, and other numerical factors. The usual articles on education, though extremely informative, treat of philosophy and methodology or are scholarly critiques on some aspect of the system. As various professional groups the world around seek to serve each other's needs in the coming years, it is hoped that the raw-data type of information will become more readily available since it is the "bare bones" of an educational system which permits it to be viewed without bias of any sort.

There are expanding audiences for raw data studies. Thousands of teachers and professors now shuttle between countries on academic assignments. Administrative personnel from education, business and industry travel back and forth across oceans to set up new curricular patterns and training programs. These individuals are requiring knowledge of the educational systems in which they are to carry on some creative endeavor. The field of comparative education grows rapidly and demands increasing information on education in other countries. Political scientists, economists, sociologists and historians are today closely studying the educational matrix, recognizing that a country's culture, politics, economics and national history are largely rooted in the seedbed of education.

THIS VOLUME:  ITS SCOPE AND PRESENTATION

Forty-four educational patterns of Africa are depicted in chart

and outline in this presentation.  (All countries on the African con-

tinent are included except Egypt which is slated for inclusion in Educa-

tional Systems of the Middle East.)

For an over-all picture, one simple continental map of Africa is

presented, with geographic area maps which carry brief statistics.  In

the past decade, maps of Africa have become quickly outmoded.  Smith

Hempstone, in reporting from Nairobi, Kenya to the Chicago Daily News on

July 8, 1964, wrote:

> The former British Protectorate of Nyasaland has done its bit to
> make the map of Africa obsolete by changing its name to Malawi
> when it attained independence Monday.  The new African states have
> been giving cartographers fits over the last seven years with their
> penchant for assuming new names.  About a dozen of Africa's 35
> independent nations have adopted new names.  Other changes are
> likely.

Thereafter, Southern Rhodesia dropped "Southern," Northern Rhodesia became

Zambia, Bechuanaland took the name Botswana, and Basutoland became the

Kingdom of Lesotho!

Efforts to match statistics from a group of encyclopedias for

the geographic area maps disclosed that there are frequent, though minor,

differences in reporting on population and square miles.  Pamphlets

received from the Washington Embassies and the African Ministries often

quoted still other figures.  The best that could be done was to give

each nation the benefit of the latest and highest figures.  Paul Hoffman

of the United Nations Special Fund has noted that "there are no reliable

statistics on underdeveloped countries."  The editor of the Worldmark

Encyclopedia of the Nations has pointed out that in most countries the

collection of basic data is a recent development; that methods of collecting vary from country to country; and that years during which collection
is made are not the same, so that total figures do not reflect a continental situation at any one time.  This is particularly true of Africa,
so the figures presented here should be accepted in that light.

For those intrigued by comparative statistics, one of the most
unique presentations on the new countries of Africa has been made by
Wattenberg and Smith[1] covering:  area, population, density per square
mile, percentage of illiteracy, number of cinemas, number of doctors
available, passenger automobiles available, mileage of surfaced roads,
and per capita annual income.

To condense a few figures into one cogent statistical statement
on Africa, one could not improvise any sentence more startling than one
sent from Roscoe Drummond in Uganda to the Los Angeles Times, May 26,
1965:  "Here is a turbulent continent spanning one-fourth of the surface
of the earth on which 200 million Africans in 37 newly-created states -
one-third of the entire United Nations - have won control of their own
destiny in 10 nerve-wracking years."

So that the users of this volume might have a larger frame of
reference for the educational picture, each national study herein is
prefaced with a brief historical statement.  Superficial in coverage,
it is, however, an attempt to provide a thumbnail sketch of each country's
background.  Since each national study stands alone, nowhere in the volume

---

[1]Ben Wattenberg and Ralph Lee Smith, The New Nations of Africa
(New York:  Hart Publishing Co., 1963), pp. 458-461.

are there any generalities about the African continent.  The following

analysis, therefore, might make some of the single studies more meaning-

ful to the reader:

> Persons familiar with Africa often speak of "Africa, South of the
> Sahara" and distinguish the area from "Africa, North of the Sahara."
> This reflects the fact that the two areas are profoundly different.
> . . . The Northern coast of Africa has been in touch with European
> civilization since antiquity, and the cities of North Africa have
> suffered successive invasions that brought with them elements of
> European and Middle Eastern culture . . . By contrast, "Africa
> South of the Sahara," has had little contact with European civil-
> ization.  Particularly, very little is known of the pre-colonial
> history of large areas of tropical Africa because few historical
> records exist.  Africa, north of the Sahara, has had a very long
> experience with dynastic government, and with governmental admin-
> istration on the pattern of Europe and the Middle East.  By con-
> trast, in tropical Africa, the tribe long remained the principal
> political unit.[1]

Those familiar with Africa know also that the spelling of African

names reveals many inconsistencies.  A few comments from Russell Warren

Howe's fascinating article, "How to S-p-e-1-1 an African Name," describes

well some of the orthographical problems faced by any who report on

Africa:

> One of the legacies which colonial rule has left behind in Africa
> is a bewildering inconsistency in the spellings and pronunciations
> of African place and personal names. . . . Five of the six colonial
> powers which organized Africa into its present administrative div-
> isions enforced their own orthographical eccentricities on the
> lexicon they found in their domains.  Members of the Kwanyama tribe
> of Angola, governed by Portugal, are known as the Cuanhama.  If
> Angola had been French, they would have been the Couaniama; if
> Spanish, the Cuañama; if German, the Kuaniama; if Italian, the
> Coaniama; in the local Latin Mass, they are the Cvaniama. . . .
> The British, not sure in the nineteenth century why e is not pro-
> nounced in words as it is in the alphabet itself, still write Fante
> (for Fanti).  The Germans, whose w is pronounced like the English
> v, made Rwanda into Ruanda; using ch where most Western languages
> use k, they made Togo's second city Anecho.  The French, having no

---

[1]Ibid., p. 257.

consonant for <u>w</u>, turned Dwala, the main city of Kamerun, into
Douala, and Bwake, the second city of the Ivory Coast, into Bouaké,
which leads most visitors to give these bi-syllabic names three
syllables. Wagadugu, the Voltaic capital, becomes a dizzy Ouagadougou,
on its home ground. Spain brought in its accented ñ for ny-sounds.
To complete the Babelian nightmare, countries changed hands without
always changing spellings, with the result that new pronunciations
developed that were even further removed from the original oral form.[1]

African names in this volume have been recorded precisely as they came

from original sources without staff attempts at transliteration.

Spellings like "Centre" and other deviations from American

orthography, uses of hyphens, apostrophes, and quotation marks - all

have been copied exactly from the materials presented so as not to vio-

late national usages. For instance, some countries hyphenate School-

Leaving Certificate; others do not. Some countries use the form

Teacher's College; others use Teachers' College; still others use

Teachers College. Therefore, in all matters of recording, each country

is <u>sui generis</u>.

The charts which precede each national study in this volume show

in simple graphic form the various levels of education and the lengths

of programs. The age levels indicated on the far left-hand ladders take

the stipulated Ministry of Education minimum entry age as the criterion.

But, in actuality, the age of entry to elementary schooling throughout

Africa is a variable matter, for a variety of reasons. Thus, it is not

uncommon for some 15-17 year olds to be graduated from elementary school

in certain situations, or for those of university age to be starting

secondary technical training. Two or three charts have been made for

---

[1]Russell Warren Howe, "How to S-p-e-l-l an African Name," <u>Africa
Report</u>, January 1964, p. 3.

some countries where significant changes in the educational structures

have occurred.  Charts bearing no date labels represent current standards.

All others are dated.  Where educational reforms over a period of years

could be more suitably depicted on one chart, only the affected areas

have been charted anew.  Single and double asterisks found on charts at

the secondary level denote the period at which important examinations

are taken.  Explanations of these examinations, indicated by similar

asterisks, are found in the body of the outline.  Double asterisks rep-

resent the point at which a student may take an examination which, if

successfully completed, will usually make him eligible for entrance into

a university.

Data reported for each educational system revolve around curri-

cular offerings, the examinations required, and the certificates, diplomas

and degrees awarded at the various stages in the educational process.

Unless otherwise labeled, education offered by the government is being

described  Since the secondary examinations listed in the individual

studies are of key importance to college and university admissions offi-

cers, there are supplementary treatments of the major examinations in

Appendixes B, C, D, E, F, G.

As many changes and variations in an educational system as could

be identified over the past decades are recorded in the studies.  Where

projected plans for the future seemed more than tentative, they have been

included.

In this volume the first attempt has been made to present full-

scale condensations of higher educational offerings.  For the well-established institutions, such as those in South Africa, university bulletins are readily available. But for some of the institutions which are newly developing or moving from missionary sponsorship to government control, only preliminary mimeographed sheets were available. In several cases, material had to be especially prepared.

As an important part of the volume, recommendations on the granting of credit on African credentials and proposals for academic placement of students in U S. institutions are offered in Appendix H. These recommendations are approved by the Council on the Evaluation of Foreign Student Credentials, which represents the major professional agencies concerned with international educational exchange. Since each institution in the United States is autonomous in setting its standards for admission and placement, these recommendations can only state the consensus of past experience in institutions with generally high standards. They may be subject to change as more information about an educational system becomes available or larger numbers of African students provide greater dependability of information on academic performance. Institutions in a position to set lesser standards should take into consideration other indices of aptitude.

The bibliography which completes this volume is selected. Due to the unexpected proportions of this book, it seemed unwise to duplicate large sections of  excellent bibliographies already available in published form. Some general books on Africa are included among the materials dealing strictly with education, since an educational system can only come alive when one becomes familiar with the nation's cultural heritage. Two books are especially recommended for background reading, both are avail-

able in paperback:  Paul Bohannan's <u>Africa and Africans</u> and <u>Continuity</u>

<u>and Change in African Cultures</u>, edited by William R. Bascom and Melville

J. Herskovitz.

The major task for those who prepare a raw data study is one of

faithful reporting.  This demands maximum accuracy in the use of all

educational nomenclature and terminology.  One of the most serious mat-

ters now confronting evaluators of academic credentials in the United

States is the trend among those in other parts of the world to translate

their educational systems into American terms in attempts to be helpful.

Although we are now being forced to consider certain "equivalences" of

academic credentials on a world scale, we must recognize that any trans-

lation of one educational system into the terms of another succeeds only

in distorting the system under review.  Strictly speaking, there are no

"equivalences" of certificates, diplomas and degrees around the world.

Each document needs to be interpreted in its own light.  The greatest

service we can render our students and each other is to set forth our

country's educational system with its <u>own</u> authentic terminology and with

<u>literal</u> translations of academic documents.  It is always more effective

to let the uniqueness of a system stand alone, and offer an "interpreta-

tion" by <u>additional data describing content of courses and rigorousness</u>

<u>of examinations</u>.  It is the <u>level of work accomplished</u> which is the major

concern of every admissions officer and every educator and all efforts

at interpretation should be directed to that end.

Terminology, of course, is one of the major stumbling blocks in becoming acquainted with "foreign" systems. Even such words as "primary" and "elementary," which in the United States for instance are used interchangeably without violation of educational meaning, have special connotations in certain countries and in most nations one or the other term has preferential use. Words like "college" or "higher technical institute" in some countries denote schools at the secondary level. "Bachelor's" degrees are awarded at the close of secondary education in some nations. "Honors" degrees at the university level are sometimes awarded after an additional year of study following a bachelor's degree; others are not. Some higher degrees are earned by a specified number of years of study; others are attained after a lapse of time by a payment of fees. The list of variations is long and complex.

Several of the above-mentioned usages are exemplified in the African systems. African education has been divided mainly between British and French patterns. Belgian and Italian forms of education have played a smaller role. Spanish and Portuguese patterns still continue in the African provinces of Spain and Portugal. In reporting the distinctive features of each African system, a diligent attempt has been made to reproduce the national terminology with exactness. Liberal use is made of nomenclature in the national languages themselves with English translations juxtaposed. This treatment was preferred to a single glossary which proves impractical when dealing with so many different countries.

A simple example of the need for literalistic translations rather than loose general ones might be taken from the Cameroun study: technical colleges (collèges techniques) offering 5-year programs need to be identified separately from colleges of technical instruction (collèges d'enseignement technique) offering 4-year programs.  It would be easy

indeed to refer to <u>all</u> of these secondary schools as "technical colleges"

without making any distinction, thus blurring the type and length of

training offered in each.  It is difficult to be alert to both linguistic

and educational variations in meaning as we seek to interpret other sys-

tems of education.

It is worth noting that in almost all African countries, through-

out all levels of education, terms are rapidly changing.  Some of the

nations, for example, in developing their own indigenous sytems have

made a special point of changing the wording from "primary" to "elemen-

tary," or vice versa, in an effort to eradicate colonial classifications.

Traditional words like "standards" to denote certain years of study are

in some cases being replaced by the word "grades," or as in the case of

Uganda merely by denoting "Primary I, Primary II," and so on.  Roman

numerals used in labeling years of study are now in some instances being

transposed to Arabic figures.  Names of schools and higher institutions

are subject to change also, as governments take over more and more of

the missionary schools, or as training programs alter their character.

It is hoped that the staff has measurably succeeded in recording

these seemingly small yet significant variations as they have come through

from African sources in the prepared materials, printed reports and diver-

sity of pamphlets and catalogues.  But even educators, Ministry officials

and those who write commission reports and university bulletins are not

infallible.  So ingrained is the habit of using traditional phrases which

have been in educational parlance for many years that most of the French-speaking countries were still prone to printed and written references to

Part I and Part II of the French <u>Baccalauréat</u> with the assumption that

the outsider would know that the <u>Examen Probatoire</u> replaced Part I of

the <u>Baccalauréat</u> in September 1962 and became slated for withdrawal in

1965. English-speaking countries were found to have numerous printed

and written references to the Cambridge Oversea (or "Overseas" as it was

frequently reported) School Certificate although the Cambridge Local

Examinations Syndicate dropped the word "Oversea" (it was never Overseas)

from the title of this Certificate in 1961.

Mention is made of such matters not to call attention unkindly to

such small inaccuracies which often confounded the staff and led to addi-

tional correspondence for checking details, but merely to focus on the

future need for as scrupulous accuracy as possible when communicating

educational matters across national boundaries.


CONTRIBUTORS TO THIS VOLUME AND ITS PREPARATION

Contacts with those capable of gathering data in the African

countries were established through many professional channels.

It was through Ruth Sloan, director of Ruth Sloan Associates,

responsible for the pioneering book, <u>The Educated African</u>,[1] that the

project directors were given an introduction to Raymond Smyke, Special

Assistant for Africa, World Confederation of Organizations of the Teach-

ing Profession (WCOTP, 1330 Mass. Ave. N.W., Washington, D.C. 20005).

---

[1]Helen Kitchen (ed.), <u>The Educated African</u>, compiled by Ruth Sloan
Associates (New York: Frederick A. Praeger, 1962).

Aware of the problems of acquiring educational information from Africa
due to cultural ferment, the changing of Ministries of Education personnel
in the newly-independent nations, the overburdening of all Ministry officials, and the ceaseless requests from overseas, Mr. Smyke offered the
services of his African representatives. The offer was accepted, and
thus the directors availed themselves of an unusual opportunity to have
contacts in twenty African nations with teachers or administrators
who were operating in the indigenous systems.

Contacts for the complicated Nigerian study came through Wendell
P. Jones, UCLA Associate Professor of Education who, as educational consultant in Nigeria for several years, was acquainted with educational
officials in the various Nigerian Ministries of Education. R. Stanley
Gex of Eastern Michigan University, US/AID Chief of Party at the Somali
Teacher Training Institute in Mogadiscio, was helpful in procuring information for the study on Somalia; T. Noel Stern, Professor of Political
Science at the Southeastern Massachusetts Technological Institute, for
the study on Guinea. For assistance on the Malawi report, credit is due
John A. Carpenter, Director of the Center for Intercultural Education at
the University of Southern California.

Staff members of the American Friends of the Middle East (AFME,
1607 New Hampshire Avenue, N.W., Washington 9, D.C.) have played significant roles: Virgil Crippin, Vice-President in charge of Programs,
opened the way for contacts with AFME overseas offices; Leo Fraenkel,
former AFME representative in Tunisia and Morocco, was responsible for
most of the data on these countries; Dorothy LaGuardia, Head of Educational

Placement  Service in the Washington office, arranged for the checking

of the Algerian study; and the AFME librarians put their facilities at

the disposal of the project directors.

Africa specialist, Betty George, in the International Division

of the U.S. Office of Education, shared her information on French Equa-

torial Africa with the project directors; Ellen Doherty, Research Assist-

ant in the Comparative Education Branch of the U.S. Office of Education

provided supplementary information on Spain.  Lily von Klemperer, Coun-

selor at the Institute of International Education (IIE, 809 United Nations

Plaza, New York 17) shared her extensive bibliography listings at the

inception of the project and subsequently has tendered advice.  Gordon

Hagberg, Director of IIE's East Africa Regional Office in Nairobi, pro-

vided the staff services of Donald Schramm and Lloyd Sherman in gathering

needed data on Kenya.

Interest and cooperation have been shown by the staff members of

the African-American Institute (AAI, 345 East 46th Street, New York 17,

and 1346 Connecticut Avenue, N.W., Washington 6, D.C.):  William L.

Gaines, director of Educational Programs; Helen Kitchen, editor of the

valuable journal, Africa Report, and Julien Engel, head of the French-

Speaking Areas Program.

Margaret Gillett, Associate Professor in the Institute of Educa-

tion, McDonald College of McGill University of Canada, former visiting

Registrar at Haile Selassie I University, provided a wealth of materials

on education in Ethiopia.  Vera L. Zollberg, Instructor in the Sociology

and Anthropology Department of St. Xavier College, Chicago, who with her husband, a political scientist, spent two years in Africa studying several educational and political systems, provided major data on Mali and the Ivory Coast.  Hope Diffenderfer, whose husband is with the US/AID program in Sierra Leone, prepared the Sierra Leone materials with the collaboration of the Ministry of Education.

In the Washington embassies, officials have been helpful.  Special publications were loaned or acquired from overseas by Laura Tucker, Cultural Attaché and Student Adviser, Embassy of the Republic of Liberia, Maurice Le Flem, Cultural Attaché, Embassy of the Republic of Gabon, Louis Navega, Second Secretary, Embassy of Portugal, Carlos M. Fernandez-Shaw and Vizconde de Priego, Cultural Counselors, Embassy of Spain, and the Secretariat of the Embassy of the Central African Republic.  Also, important educational information was supplied by Edouard Morot-Sir, Cultural Counselor, Embassy of France, Mustapha Mzabi, Cultural Attaché, Embassy of Morocco, Mohamed Aberkane, Counselor, Embassy of Algeria, and J. Pongo, Chargé d'Affaires a.i., Embassy of the Republic of the Congo .(Léopoldville).  Alioune A. N'Doye, Chargé d'Affaires a.i., Embassy of Sénégal, was the intermediary for the materials sent by WCOTP representative, M'Baye Mbengue.  Johannes C. van Rooy, Cultural Attaché, South African Embassy, gave names and addresses of sources for data-gathering.  Mutwakil Amin, former Cultural Attaché of the Sudan Embassy, accepted full responsibility for information on his country's educational system through his close affiliations with Khartoum.

The full listing of contributors is included in Appendix A.  It is somewhat long since in many situations the task of data-gathering in

a country required several persons. Also, numerous African schools,
higher institutions and organizations were individually solicited by the
U.S. project staff for special information. In spite of its length, the
list does not begin to cover the large number of persons who, unknown to
the U.S. staff, gave helpful information to the key African contacts, nor
could there be included the many unidentified Ministry officials who
checked the studies at the request of the national representatives.

For those who carried the major responsibility for collecting
data, an honorarium was provided. Reimbursement for airmail postage was
made to all contributors.

The U.S. staff members chosen for the project had all had previous relationships in international education: Louise Prugh, former
Executive Secretary of the UCLA Council on International Students, who
had traveled widely in Africa and taught in a secondary school in Nigeria;
Barbara Garlick, a resident French linguist from England; Janyce Anker,
former foreign credentials evaluator in the UCLA Office of Admissions;
and Vicky Sapriel, French educated in North Africa, formerly Administrative
Assistant in the UCLA French Department, whose language proficiency also
included Arabic and Italian, who was selected as bibliographer.

Having several staff members with French facility has meant that
correspondence with French-speaking countries could readily be carried on,
and translations of a large body of French materials were expedited.
Marina Preussner and Marilyn Parrish, dissertation typists, chosen to
make the study press-ready, were also bi-lingual. Marina Preussner was
responsible for the lay-out and editorial work in the manuscript.

The project directors have been fortunate in being able to call

upon the language skills of James Lazarus, a UCLA doctoral candidate.
He was capable of translating the extensive Afrikaans bulletins of the
Universities of Pretoria, Stellenbosch, Potchestroom, and Orange Free
State. So far as the directors can ascertain this is the first time
that the offerings of these Afrikaans universities have been translated
into English. A. Mayore Dias, UCLA Associate in Spanish and Portuguese,
aided in the Portuguese translations.

Those in the UCLA Office of Admissions, Foreign Division, who
have greatly supported the project staff with a variety of services are:
Alice McCutcheon, Ruth Coleman, Belva Fouser, Irene Holland, Mary Jannis.
Miss Fouser has carried special responsibilities for the photocopying of
enormous amounts of materials for overseas checking, conferences and
reports. Elizabeth Butler, Librarian in the African Studies Center, has
kept the staff informed of relevant materials. Lorraine Mathies, Librarian in the UCLA Education Library, has cooperated in many helpful ways.

Procedures for the creation of the studies by the U.S. staff members have been as follows:

1. Collection of data on African education from all available
   printed sources - books, pamphlets, UNESCO publications,
   educational journals, Embassy brochures, encyclopedias, newspaper educational supplements - as background information
   for the materials sent from Africa.

2. Systematization of materials from direct African sources,
   and inclusion of relevant background data.

3.  After the first skeletal outline of each study was made,
    many letters were sent back to Africa to fill in the gaps in
    information:  to the main contact; to separate schools, ask-
    ing for timetables of subjects studied; to higher institu-
    tions, asking for course descriptions; to examining bodies
    asking for clarification of certain matters; and so on.

4.  The new information was added.

5.  Each completed study was sent directly to the country's
    Ministry of Education, for corrections and additions, or to
    the key contact for final checking with the Ministry.  In
    situations where education is still segregated, the European
    and African sections were sent to appropriate sources.

6.  The final changes were incorporated in preparation for the
    typescript.

To launch the project, data-request sheets in the national language were provided to each potential contributor.  It was discovered
that, for the most part, the data requested was not available in published
form, partly because of the type of material required, and partly because
the most current information had not yet reached print.  Too, in Africa,
Ministries of Education information seldom ranges the full educational
scene.  Various types of training such as vocational, technical and agricultural are frequently under separate Ministries, government departments,
or independent agencies; data from these sources are sometimes difficult
to secure.  Thus it developed that most of the information for the studies
was especially prepared by the African contacts from numerous sources,

sometimes under considerable difficulty. In many countries, the contributors had to travel to secure information. E. Bennett Caulley,
Director of the WCOTP African Regional Office in Accra, and J.W.A.
Sackeyfio of the Ghana Ministry of Education traveled extensively to
uncover the data requested.

Throughout the year and a half in which the project has been
operating, news media have carried daily accounts of the political tur-
moil in Africa. The revolutionary changes affecting almost every African
country have had repercussions in the Ministries of Education and the
teaching profession. During the serious rebellion in the Congo (Leopoldville) it seemed hopeless to expect that information might be prepared
and sent out to the directors. But even at the height of the fighting,
the WCOTP representative, Basile Mabusa, compiled and mailed out the
requested data. In other situations also, where crises have been less
acute but tensions have been the order of the day, those involved in the
project have labored to fulfill their commitments.

Since the start of the enterprise, personal liaison has been made
with many of the African informants. The professional duties of Raymond
Smyke have taken him frequently to Africa. He has been able to discuss
the undertaking with his representatives. In the summer of 1964, the
Office of U.S. Programs and Services of the Department of State gave an
African travel grant to William Strain, Associate Registrar for Admis-
sions at Indiana University, Chairman of the Council on Evaluation of
Foreign Credentials, and Editor of the AACRAO World Education Series.
In the course of his tour he conferred with several contributors to the

volume. Clifford Prator, UCLA Professor of English, Vice Chairman of
the Department of English and Supervisor of the English as a Second
Language Program, on a trip to Africa was also in touch with some of the
data-gatherers. Wendell Jones during two trips to Africa met with
Nigerian Ministry of Education officials whom he had recommended.

The project has been undergirded by two Advisory Committees: one
national, one on the UCLA campus. The national Committee was constituted
of representatives from agencies and organizations who met in Washington,
D.C., February 11, 1964, at a specially-called conference for users and
producers of information on foreign educational systems. (A listing of
the National Advisory Committee is included in Appendix J.) Members of
the local Committee were: Benjamin E. Thomas, Acting Director, African
Studies Center and Professor of Geography; Wendell P. Jones, Associate
Professor of Education; Hassan Nouty, Associate Professor of French;
Clifford Prator, Professor of English as a Second Language; and J. Wesley
Robson, Professor of Philosophy and Admissions Officer.

As may be seen, this volume represents a very large corporate
endeavor. That a work of such proportions could have been compiled as
a first effort attests to the thoroughness and dedication of the numerous
contributors.

At the start of the project it might have been assumed that
because of the rapid changes taking place on the African continent the
study would have little more than fleeting relevance. The final product,
however, seems to reveal its more permanent nature: not only does it
present an up-to-date picture, with future trends, but it will serve in

an historical sense to preserve data on the many changes in African

education during the recent decades which already are being expunged

from the resource materials of new regimes.

## RESEARCH IN RELATION TO THE PROJECT

To round out the project on education in Africa, a research

study on the academic performance of African students in U.S. institu-

tions was considered.  However, the lack of uniformity in record-keeping

in U.S. colleges and universities, and the expense involved in such

an undertaking, made a national study impractical.  But records on the

African students under the ASPAU Program were uniform and fairly com-

plete, so it was decided to carry out a research study on a sampling of

these students.

The investigation has been under the supervision of Lee Wilcox,

Assistant Director of Admissions, University of Minnesota, and co-chair-

man of the AACRAO Committee on Research in International Education.  In

August 1965, David Henry and Richard Moll of the African Scholarship

Program of American Universities opened the files of the agency to the

research team.  Janyce Anker of the project staff was sent to Cambridge

for data-gathering.  She was joined in the work by a former ASPAU staff

member, Marissa Chorlian.

The results of the investigation, prepared by Mr. Wilcox, are

presented in Appendix I.  While it was generally known in educational

circles that the performance of these students was outstanding due to

careful selection through field screening, the research statistics

underscore previous information.  Admittedly, this is a biased picture,
not typical of the majority of Africans who come under many other types
of sponsorship or who make their way alone by part-time employment and
part-time study.  It does, however, point up the fact that field screening is of great advantage both to student and institution.  This fact is
being widely recognized, and overseas centers in various areas of the
world are now being developed for this purpose.

The UCLA Office of Admissions, Foreign Division, has run a study
on its African students as part of its annual statistical check-up on
the performance of overseas students.  These findings play a significant
role in the annual review of the minimum entry requirements from all countries sending students to the University of California.

## SUMMARY OBSERVATIONS

Returning from one of several trips to Africa, Harold C. Case,
President of Boston University, stated in a press interview:  "Next to
nationalism, the greatest urge in Africa is for education."  He voices
the impression of all who have viewed this continent at close range.

As we seek to get an overview of education in Africa, David G.
Scanlon, Professor of Education, Columbia University Teachers College,
draws the picture into focus for us:

> In retrospect, it is possible to divide the history of African edu-
> cation into four periods.  The first:  that period in which the
> coming-of-age ceremonies, the rites of passage, provided the prin-
> cipal education of the African child.  Although weakened by the
> pressure of westernization, these rites continue today to hold
> varying degrees of importance in many parts of Africa.  The intro-
> duction of Western education by European missionaries in the late

19th century marked the opening of the second period. This education was carried on almost exclusively by religious groups until the close of World War I. During the third period - the interbellum era - the metropolitan powers undertook to provide financial and professional assistance for the education of Africans. The final period, beginning at the close of World War II, saw the emergence of a renewed interest in African education, and plans were drawn by all the colonial powers for its extension. The result was an unprecedented expansion of African educational facilities through the decade of the 1950s. Resting heavily on the policies developed by the colonial powers, African education could truly be said to be in the "take-off" stage of development. Today, African educators are reexamining the basic organization of their educational systems and the philosophical foundations on which they rest.[1]

In writing of educational planning, Robert Jacobs, Professor of Education and Coordinator of International Programs, Southern Illinois University, directs our attention to the challenges faced by developing nations as they pioneer new ways:

> There is little dispute concerning the important role which education must play in the total development of a society. Education must not only produce the trained manpower required for industrial progress, political development, and social advance; it must also create an adequate social base to undergird developmental aims - adequate in terms of values, attitudes, and motivations, as well as skills to support modern national objectives. An expensive, new irrigation system contributes little to increased agricultural production if the farmers in the affected area refuse to accept the new and hold to old, traditional ways of farming; health clinics and immunization centers do little to eliminate disease if those who could be served are suspicious of these innovations and continue to patronize the witch doctor; a new highway will not open a formerly isolated area if the old footpaths and cart trails continue to be used in preference to the new product of road engineering skill. Illiteracy, ignorance, and superstition are perhaps the most formidable barriers which education must remove.[2]

---

[1] David G. Scanlon (ed.), _Traditions of African Education_ (New York: Bureau of Publications, Teachers College, Columbia University), pp. 2-3.

[2] Robert Jacobs, "The Interdisciplinary Approach to Educational Planning," _Comparative Education Review_, VIII, No. 1 (June 1964), 17.

These comments singularly spotlight Africa as the majority of its
nations seek to move from a type of colonial education designed solely
for the elite toward education for the many, and ultimately for the
masses. One cannot study many of the frank reports of the Ministries of
Education and Commissions without learning that African educators are
well aware of these factors enumerated by Dr. Jacobs and are striving
their utmost to meet these challenges.

Picking up a pamphlet at random, one may see the phrase, "formal
education and economic development are parallel" from the Congo (Brazzaville); or a booklet from Liberia where one may read, "Education is the
most important single factor in achieving rapid economic development and
technological progress and in creating a social order founded on the
values of freedom, justice and equality of opportunity for all."[1] Similar ideas are found explicit in materials from most of the African nations.

In May 1961 the Conference of African States on the Development
of Education in Africa, held in Addis Ababa, gave the first great impetus
and direction to planning for African education as a whole. Called by
UNESCO and ECA (Economic Commission for Africa), the conference was
attended by representatives from thirty-two tropical African countries
and three North African states. A twenty-year plan, 1960-1980, was
approved and the cost of financing estimated. Recommended aims for
enrollment were summarized as:

---

[1] *Annual Report to the Legislature of the Republic of Liberia
for the year October 1, 1963 to September 30, 1964*, p. 91.

### Percentage of Attendance by:

|           | 1961-62      | 1965-66      | 1970-71      | 1980-81       |
|-----------|--------------|--------------|--------------|---------------|
| Primary   | 40 per cent  | 51 per cent  | 71 per cent  | 100 per cent  |
| Secondary | 3 per cent   | 9 per cent   | 15 per cent  | 23 per cent   |
| Higher    | .2 per cent  | .2 per cent  | .4 per cent  | 2 per cent    |

Cost of the program for tropical Africa was estimated as rising from $590 million in 1961 to more than $1 billion in 1965 and $2.6 billion in 1980. The African nations agreed to increase the 3 per cent investment in education from national income to 4 per cent by 1965, 5 per cent by 1970, and 6 per cent by 1980. These plans were approved by UNESCO, the Economic and Social Council, the General Assembly of the United Nations (UN Resolution A/RES/1717(XVI)), and the Economic Council for Africa.

A Paris conference was called by UNESCO and ECA in March 1962 to discuss implementation of the Addis Ababa Plan during 1962 and 1963. Thirty-six African states and territories were represented, thirty-one by their Ministers of Education. The educational programs of these nations came under intensive scrutiny, along with financial and other matters. A series of recommendations were adopted, the most urgent of which were that priority be given to secondary education, the training of primary and secondary school teachers, the teaching of English and French, and research on African languages. (There are reported to be more than 600 languages spoken on the African continent.)

This Paris meeting established a permanent vehicle of inter-African and international cooperation: a "Conference of Ministers of Education" of the African countries committed to the Addis Ababa Plan,

to convene biennially for review of the programs initiated under the Plan.
The March 1964 Abidjan meeting was the first session of this Conference.

To carry forward Paris recommendations, a meeting was held in
Tananarive, July 1962, on "Adaptation of the General Secondary Curriculum
in Africa." Forty-five participants from 29 countries were present, most
of whom were Ministry of Education officers. Guidelines were set down
for revisions of syllabi and methods of teaching in the natural and social
sciences, fine arts, languages, and physical education. Long-term research and the need for innovations were recognized. A special recommendation was made for the constitution of an African committee of experts,
under the sponsorship of UNESCO, to spearhead such developments.

On the heels of this meeting concerned with secondary education,
came the September 1962 Tananarive meeting on higher education. This
Conference on the Development of Higher Education in Africa, under the
auspices of UNESCO and ECA, confronted the need to pool and concentrate
resources for university training, allowing other institutions at the
higher level to develop according to national demands. The conference
designated 32 key universities. Plans were proposed for increasing enrollment at the higher educational level from 31,000 in 1961-62 to 274,000
in 1980 for Middle Africa, and from 134,000 to 365,000 students in North
Africa. Special need for increased enrollments in the fields of agriculture, fishery and forestry were emphasized. Attention was given to the
adaptation and Africanization of curricula to meet the requirements of
African life and future socioeconomic developments. Cost of higher
educational financing was estimated to rise from $100 million in 1965 to
more than $500 million in 1980.

Beyond these meetings, so briefly sketched above, are the 1964 gatherings on Adult Literacy, on Scientific and Natural Resource Development, and other UNESCO activities undergirding a full range of educational advancement.

Booklets and reports on the many UNESCO conferences and undertakings may be secured from the Publications Center, 317 East 34th Street, New York, N. Y. 10016. Those interested in learning how well the African nations have been meeting the goals set for themselves in the Development Decade, 1960-1970, may become informed of the remarkable progress through a report by James Avery Joyce, British barrister and Consultant to UNESCO: "Priorities in African Education."[1]

To empathize with the African nations in their problems of educational planning, one must know the hierarchy of planning levels which is found in most of the newly developing countries:

1. Planning at the national level.

2. Planning at the Ministry of Education level.

3. Planning at the departmental level within the Ministry of Education.

4. Planning at the school or institutional level.

5. Planning at the classroom level.[2]

Herein lies the enormity of the planning enterprise itself, let alone the complexities of implementation.

---

[1] _Saturday Review_, August 16, 1964, pp. 55-58.

[2] Robert Jacobs, _ibid_., p. 20.

For planning at the national level, several nations have called in teams of scholars from other countries to evaluate their educational systems and make recommendations. One of the most searching studies on education in Nigeria carried out by a nine-member team, analyzes the country's needs up to 1980. This investigation, called generally "The Ashby Report,"[1] was handed to the Nigerian government on the eve of independence. This report has remained somewhat of a classic because the approach was unorthodox. The team stated:

> We could have approached this task by calculating what the coun-
> try can afford to spend on education, and by proposing cautious,
> modest, and reasonable ways in which the educational system might
> be improved within the limits of the budget.
>
> We have unanimously rejected this approach to our task. The
> upsurge of Africa is so dramatic and so powerful that proposals
> which to-day appear to be reasonable and sensible will in a very
> few years appear to be short-sighted and timid. . . .
>
> To approach our task, therefore, we have to think of Nigeria
> in 1980: a nation of some 50 million people, with industries,
> oil, and a well developed agriculture; intimately associated with
> other free African countries on either side of its borders; a
> voice to be listened to in the Christian and Moslem worlds; with
> its traditions in art preserved and fostered and with the begin-
> nings of its own literature; a nation which is taking its place
> in a technological civilisation, with its own airways, its organs
> of mass-communication, its research institutes.
>
> Millions of the people who will live in this Nigeria of 1980
> are already born. Under the present educational system more than
> half of them will never go to school. Like people elsewhere, their
> talents will vary from dullness to genius. Somehow, before 1980,
> as many talented children as possible must be discovered and edu-
> cated if this vision of Nigeria is to be turned into reality. This
> is a stupendous undertaking. It will cost large sums of money.
> The Nigerian people will have to forego other things they want so
> that every available penny is invested in education. Even this
> will not be enough. Countries outside Nigeria will have to be
> enlisted to help with men and money. Nigerian education must for
> a time become an international enterprise.

---

[1] *Investment in Education: The Report of the Commission on Post-School Certificate and Higher Education in Nigeria*, Federal Ministry of Education, Nigeria, 1960. Price 5/.

It is on this level of thinking that we make our recommendations. We have, of course, taken every precaution to save needless
expenditure, but our proposals remain massive, expensive and uncon-
ventional. To accomplish them all would undoubtedly be beyond the
present resources of the Federal and Regional Governments. But a
way must be found. To the best of our belief nothing less than
these proposals will suffice for Nigeria's development. To enter-
tain any more modest programme is to confess defeat.[1]

Looking through the telescope pointed at the year 1980 by the Ashby team

one sees not only the challenge to Nigeria but similar challenges to many

other African countries as they break with colonial educational patterns

and create indigenous ones adapted to local needs.

"Adaptation to local needs" is a phrase which occurs again and

again in African materials. It is the rallying cry of educational offi-

cials; it will turn out to be the hallmark of their success.

It is interesting to follow government recommendations in Nigeria,

based on the Ashby Report, because the "local needs" set forth for Nigeria

are the "local needs" in almost every African country. Briefly excerpted,

they state:

> The foundations of technological education must be laid in the
> primary schools if progress is to be assured. For this reason,
> the Federal Government fully endorses the proposal that manual
> training and handicraft lessons must be an integral part of the
> primary school curriculum. . . .
> The content of secondary school education is of particular
> interest to the Government. Obligatory manual subjects must be
> introduced. Vocational training must be increased. Agricultural
> education must be expanded in all secondary schools . . .
> More science laboratories must be built and equipped. Com-
> mercial education must be made available to an increasing number
> of girls in schools built and equipped for the purpose. . . .
> The Federal Government recognises that existing facilities for
> the training of technicians at the post-school certificate level
> are inadequate to meet the demands of our expanding economy. It

---

[1] Ibid., p. 3.

is therefore proposed that they should be enlarged so that about
5,000 technicians may be produced per annum in technical institutes
in the Federation as a whole. . . . Federal grants will be given to
Regions for the expansion of Technical Institutes and for the recruitment of suitably qualified teachers to promote scientific and
technical education as a basis for economic and general development. . . . Commercial courses at post-secondary institutions designed to promote commercial enterprises that meet the needs of
the country will also be supported by Federal grants.

Government is perturbed about the existing state of agricultural education in the country and the dearth of Nigerian recruits
into the agricultural services. There will be consultation between
the Federal Government and Regions to devise means of making agricultural careers attractive and bringing to bear on the day to day
practice of the farmers the fruits of agricultural research. With
the improvement of these conditions the Government will encourage
secondary schools throughout the Federation to add streams for
agricultural education and to recruit well-qualified teachers for
that purpose.[1]

In East Africa, an attempt to meet "local needs" at the univer-

sity level is reported by Crane Haussamen, U.S. Minister and Permanent

Representative to UNESCO:

At Tanzania's University College, the creation of new curricula to
meet local needs applies to many courses. Literature, for instance,
is not taught as the history of literature. The works studied are
immediately related to the student's background. Since most of
them come from the country, an entire course is devoted to poetry
in rural life. This poetry, which dominates their childhood, is
thereby placed in an objective environment providing a more mature
perspective. The law school has created ad hoc programs answering
the government's requirements of the moment. If the administration
says: "We need diplomats," the University College extemporizes to
produce them; later on there are specialized courses to compensate
for early deficencies.[2]

Educational vision is not lacking in Africa, nor expertise in

high places, but those within and observers without agree that the grim

---

[1]Federation of Nigeria, Educational Development, 1961-70, Sessional Paper No. 3 of 1961 (Lagos:  Federal Government Printer, 1961),
pp. 5-7.

[2]"When Foreign Student Scholarships are Misused," Saturday
Review, August 21, 1965, pp. 62-63.

factors of shortages of money, teaching staffs, appropriate syllabi and
textbooks have been, and will continue to be, major drawbacks to achievement of goals.

For physical plants alone, the sums needed for building are stag-
gering. A single statement in a report from a Central African country
mirrors a similar picture of present conditions throughout the continent:
"Class accommodations vary from the very modern to what is known as the
'primitive wattle-and-daub' or its equivalent." To update inadequate
structures and erect new ones, equipping them with facilities for the
scientific and technical training urgently required, will tax any nation's
educational budget.

Teacher training and recruitment present one of the serious concerns of the nations. As the African countries assumed independence,
thousands of expatriate teachers returned to their European homelands.
Though expatriate teachers still form a significant part of the teaching
corps in Africa, and though teacher training programs are being expanded
and revised, the shortage of teachers is extremely grave. Usually throughout Africa it has been the less well-endowed students who entered teacher
training after failing to meet the standards for full secondary "academic
programs." While this still will obtain for several years, strenuous
efforts are being made to recruit a higher quality of student and to lure
more promising youth into the teaching field. In order to conserve the
skills of its university graduates, Ethiopia has adopted the policy of
requiring all Haile Selassie I University graduates to teach for one year
in the provinces before assuming their professional careers. Throughout

Africa, all kinds of devices are being used to balance supply with demand, and improvisations will continue indefinitely until each nation finds its educational equilibrium.[1]

The matter of appropriate teaching materials will also be a problem for the next several decades. All schooling for Africans has been European-oriented. Africanization of syllabi and texts, greatly needed, will challenge the finest African intellects. The only danger here may be the wide swing of the pendulum to a certain provincialism which seems to take over for a period following liberation due to intense nationalistic feelings; this has been noted in educational quarters in other parts of the world where colonial patterns have been supplanted.

The contributions of African universities in fostering research, conferences, programs, colloquia, and institutes "organized in Africa, on and for Africa" ("organisés en Afrique, sur et pour l'Afrique") are summarized in a speech by Vincent Monteil, Professor in the Faculty of Letters at the University of Dakar, to the General Assembly of the Association of Universities Using Entirely or Partially the French Language.[2] Here one may see enumerated the varied attempts during the past ten years to study, perpetuate, and nourish the African culture.

There is no doubt that one of the major thrusts of African

---

[1] For a cogent survey of the teaching profession in Africa, see Handbook for Raising Teacher Status in Africa (Washington, D.C.: World Confederation of Organizations of the Teaching Profession), June 1964.

[2] Compte Rendu de la Première Réunion de l'Assemblée Générale, Association des Universités Entièrement ou Partiellement de Langue Française (Paris: La Sorbonne), 24-28 Avril 1963, pp. 124-126.

Ministries of Education in the years ahead will be toward the preparation

of national examinations for the conclusion of secondary education.  The

West African Examinations Council is a transitional move to create an

examining body to serve regional needs.  This Council consists of:   2

members representing the Universities of Cambridge and London; 4 members

each nominated by the governments of Nigeria and Ghana; 3 members nomi-

nated by the government of Sierra Leone; 2 members nominated by the gov-

ernment of the Gambia; and 15 members elected by the Local Committees

(3 from each region of Nigeria, 1 from the Federal Territory of Lagos,

3 from Ghana, and 1 each from Sierra Leone and the Gambia).  The elected

members represent primarily the interests of secondary schools.  The

University of Cambridge Local Examinations Syndicate has collaborated

with the Council in developing examinations adapted to African needs

and in awarding certificates; by 1965 the major responsibility for award-

ing of certificates was transferred to the Council.

The Sudan, Algeria, Tunisia, Morocco, Mali and Guinea have created

their own final secondary examinations.  This will inevitably be the

trend, and rightly so.  The most difficult task for the Ministries will

not be the expert preparation and administration of the examinations,

demanding as this will be, but the gaining of recognition around the

world for the credentials representing these examinations.  Many years

of student performance in foreign academic situations will be required

before the certificates awarded on new national examinations can be fully

accredited.

Of necessity, experimentation and change will be the order of

the day as nation-building continues in Africa. The details of phasing
in and out various programs, of adding and subtracting years for certain
areas of training, of upgrading technical programs, of lowering university entrance standards so that more students can be accommodated - these
and other matters previously mentioned will engage African educators in
the immediate future.

Meanwhile, even as the best of educational adaptations take place,
distortions in the social pattern occur. Countries which have measurably
increased the primary educational training find that hundreds of primary
school-leavers, unable to pass on through the present narrow bottleneck
in secondary education, flock to the cities, fail to find work, engage
in juvenile crimes, participate in riots and become a political threat.
Secondary school-leavers who cannot find career possibilities also become
social problems. There are those who return from higher training overseas and are frequently unable to place their talents; others become dis-
enchanted with the positions they do find.

In appraising the African scene, Waldemar A. Nielsen, president
of the African-American Institute, has stated: "These new nations, full
of hope and expectation, are trembling on the razor edge between progress
and calamity. They need our understanding. They also need our positive
help."

The United States is attempting to help: by opening its college
and university doors to those Africans qualified for higher educational

training, by sending its educators to share educational experience, by
establishing private agencies to contribute to African cultural and educational activities, by appropriating government funds for professional
training of Africans in the United States and for sending experts to
Africa to work with the people, by giving philanthropic grants to make
possible special projects.

This volume, undergirded by philanthropic funds, represents a
U.S.-African enterprise, mutually executed, and now mutually helpful.
With the educational flux in Africa, it can be only a point of departure,
but it is an earnest of the desire of admissions officers in the United
States to understand with some definitiveness the present educational
patterns in Africa so that educational exchange between our continents
may be facilitated.

The members of the U.S. staff extend sincere thanks to The Ford
Foundation and Mr. Melvin Fox of the International Training and Research
Program for the project grant; to the University of California, Los
Angeles, for sponsorship of the undertaking and to the concerned University
officials for administering the fund. Deep appreciation is expressed to
all those in Africa and the United States who have contributed so willingly
to the volume. The members of the staff themselves have felt privileged
to be responsible for the creation of the final instrument. They believe
that the bonds of cooperation forged during the past year and a half give
promise of incresingly fruitful relationships between United States and
African educational officials in the years ahead.

# CONTENTS

## F R E N C H - S P E A K I N G   E Q U A T O R I A L   A F R I C A

## C E N T R A L   A F R I C A

## S P A N I S H   A F R I C A . . . . . . . . . . . . . . .   997

## P O R T U G U E S E   A F R I C A . . . . . . . . . . . . .   1004

## S O U T H E R N   A F R I C A

# NORTH AFRICA

2

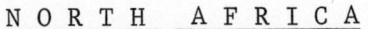

N O R T H   A F R I C A

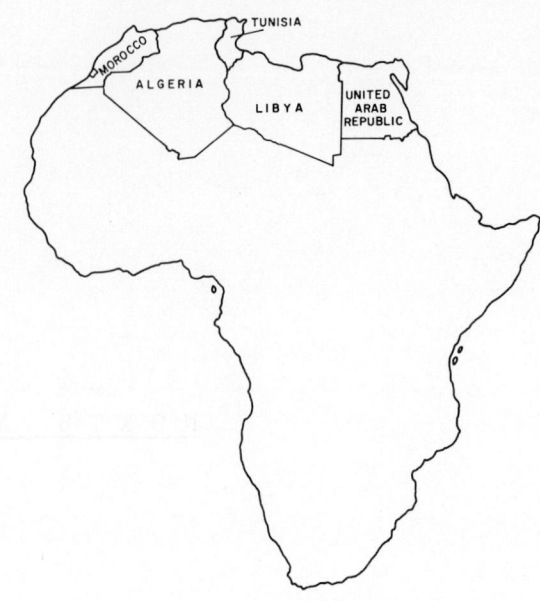

| Country and Capital | Area (sq. miles) | Est. Population | Independence Dates or Political Status | Official Language(s) |
|---|---|---|---|---|
| DEMOCRATIC AND POPULAR REPUBLIC OF ALGERIA<br>Algiers | 952,198 | 11,020,000 | 5 July 1962 | Arabic and French |
| KINGDOM OF LIBYA<br>Beyda (formerly: Tripoli and Benghazi) | 680,000 | 1,244,000 | 24 December 1951 | Arabic and English |
| KINGDOM OF MOROCCO<br>Rabat | 171,305 | 13,320,000 | 2 March 1956 | Arabic and French |
| REPUBLIC OF TUNISIA<br>Tunis | 63,362 | 4,300,000 | 20 March 1956 | Arabic and French |

UNITED ARAB REPUBLIC

(To be a part of a subsequent volume, EDUCATIONAL SYSTEMS OF THE MIDDLE EAST.)

DEMOCRATIC AND POPULAR REPUBLIC OF ALGERIA

Agriculture and Vocational Training

Nat'l Sch. of Com.

Nat'l Sch. of Agric.

Nat'l School of Eng.

Secondary Vocational and Technical Education

School of Arch. and Fine Arts

Collège d'Enseignement Général

Tech.Tch.Tr.

Higher Teacher Train.

Teacher Training

Medicine

Pharmacy

Dentistry

Arts

Sciences

Law and Econ.

Pol. St.

Arab. St.

SECONDARY EDUCATION

PRIMARY EDUCATION

Nursery School

HIGHER EDUCATION — SECONDARY — ELEMENTARY

** *   7 6 5 4 3 2 1

| Year of Schooling | Student's Age |
|---|---|
| 20 | 26 |
| 19 | 25 |
| 18 | 24 |
| 17 | 23 |
| 16 | 22 |
| 15 | 21 |
| 14 | 20 |
| 13 | 19 |
| 12 | 18 |
| 11 | 17 |
| 10 | 16 |
| 9 | 15 |
| 8 | 14 |
| 7 | 13 |
| 6 | 12 |
| 5 | 11 |
| 4 | 10 |
| 3 | 9 |
| 2 | 8 |
| 1 | 7 |
|  | 6 |
|  | 5 |
|  | 4 |
|  | 3 |
|  | 2 |

Compulsory education: 6-14 years of age

School year: October-June

Grading: 0-20

20 Perfect

10/20 Pass

4

DEMOCRATIC AND POPULAR REPUBLIC OF ALGERIA
(République Algérienne Démocratique et Populaire)


Independence:   July 5, 1962.


BACKGROUND


Algeria was known as the Barbary Coast in classical times.  Briefly,
the country's historical periods are:

The Phoenician Period:  Founding of Carthage, 914 B.C.  Phoenicians
occupied only coastal areas.

The Roman Period:  Romans inhabited the northern portion in 106 B.C.
This occupation lasted 5 centuries.

The Vandal Period (429-533):  In the 5th century, from the time of the
conquest of the Roman Empire by the German barbarians, a part of the
Vandal hordes took over the eastern part of Algeria.

The Byzantine Period (533-647):  From the middle of the 6th century, the
Byzantines dominated the Berbers.

Arrival of the Arabs and Islamization:  In 647 the Arabs arrived, bringing with them their cultural, linguistic, and religious traditions which
were taken over by the Berbers.

The Turkish Period (1518-1830):  Algeria became a vassal state of the
Ottoman Turkish Empire.

French Occupation (1830-1962):  In July, 1830 France occupied Algiers
and gradually extended its conquest over all of Algeria.  With the
French occupation some 800,000 people of European background settled in
Algeria, half of whom were non-French (Spanish, Italian, Maltese, and
others).  15,000 Algerian Jews were politically integrated into the group.

Reconquest of Independence (1954-1962):  On November 1, 1954, a war of
national liberation was declared which terminated in the Proclamation of
Algerian Independence, July 5, 1962.  By Spring of 1956, almost one-
fourth of the schools were destroyed, damaged or closed.  At independence,
the majority of Europeans left.  Of the present population of almost 12
million, 99% are Moslems:  where formerly the proportion of Europeans to
indigenous Algerian Moslems was 1 to 9, it is now approximately 1 to 200.

National language:   Arabic.

Up to independence, education was largely separate for Europeans,
Moslems and others (mixed).   Segregation in primary schools was officially
abolished in 1949.   Up to 1949 the French government aided elementary
schools for Europeans and elementary schools for Moslems which included
instruction in French.

Private schools for Europeans were run from nursery through secondary
education by lay teachers and various Catholic and Protestant religious
missions.   In southern Algeria Christian mission schools were established
by the White Brothers and Sisters.

Private schools by the Society of Reformist Ulema were established in
1936.   Traditional and Islamic subjects offered were:   Arabic, Arithmetic,
Geometry, Geography, History, Science, Morals.   Special lessons in Arabic,
Arab History and Islam provided for students attending French schools.

General secondary schools were established in 1958:   lycée at Tlemcen,
collège at Orleansville, Lycée for Girls at Kouba (Algiers).

Students in metropolitan-type lycées followed a 7-year secondary program
leading to the French Baccalauréat Parts I and II.

For baccalauréat examinations a 1946 provision was introduced so that
Algerian candidates might be exempted from the foreign language requirement:   literary Arabic was to be counted as the first language and a
dialect of Arabic as the second language.

In 1951 experimental secondary education for Moslems was started with 3
lycées d'enseignement franco-musulman; another was established in 1954.
Curriculum included subjects of both cultures and was preparatory to
entrance into the Institute of Higher Islamic Studies of the University
of Algiers.   During rebellion activities these schools were closed, but
the institutions at Algiers, Tlemcen, and Constantine became normal
schools for training teachers of Arabic.   The Diplôme de fin d'études
d'enseignement franco-musulman (as the first part of the Franco-Muslim
Secondary School Leaving Certificate) was awarded at the close of the
6-year program; the second part of the Franco-Muslim Certificate was
awarded at the close of the 7-year program.

Previous to independence the school programs were identical to those of
France.   September 1962, the Ministry of National Education (which later
became the Ministry of National Guidance) was created.   It started the
Algerianization of elementary and secondary programs toward the creation
of a national education.   Arabic to be the language of instruction.
Approved private Arabic schools to be integrated with public school
system.   The National University to be reopened.

From 1962 to 1965, primary enrollment went from 600,000 students to
1,400,000.   Secondary enrollment from 35,000 to  110,000.   Higher
Education from 600 to 7,000.

The French Cultural Mission, which is quite extensive, presently runs
schools from pre-primary through secondary education mainly for French
children, but all of them include Algerian children.


## PRESENT SYSTEM


## PRIMARY EDUCATION

Entry age:       6 years.

6-year program in <u>écoles primaires élémentaires</u>.

Before independence the language of instruction was French.  From
October 1, 1962 teaching of Arabic became compulsory.  Schedule from
1962-63:  7½ hrs. per week; from 1963-64, 10 hrs. per week.

Weekly hours of languages:        1st yr.:  15 hrs. Arabic.
                                  2nd, 3rd, 4th yrs.:  10 hrs. Arabic,
                                                       15 hrs. French.
                                  5th-8th yrs:  10 hrs. Arabic, 20 hrs. French.

Morals and Civics are taught by the <u>arabophone</u> teachers in accord with
Islamic values.

History and Geography are centered around the Maghreb, Africa  and the
Arab world, the Africo-Asian countries and the world in general.

Training in Arithmetic and Sciences has been increased from 3 hrs. 45 min.
to 5 hrs. per week from the 2nd to 4th years; from 6½ hrs. to 10 hrs. per
week for the 5th to 8th years.

<u>Certificat d'études primaires élémentaires</u> awarded at close of program.


## SECONDARY EDUCATION

Entrance requirements:           Competitive examination at the close of the
                                 6th year of primary education.

4-year programs in <u>collèges d'enseignement général</u> leading to the award
of a <u>Brevet d'études du premier cycle</u>.

7-year programs in <u>lycées classiques arabes</u>, <u>lycées classiques et
modernes</u>, and <u>lycées techniques</u>.

Before 1962, Arabic was taught as a foreign language.  Since October 1, 1962, the following schedule has been introduced in the <u>lycées classiques arabes</u>, <u>C.E.G.</u>, and <u>lycées classiques et modernes</u>:

| | |
|---|---|
| 1st and 2nd yrs: | 8 hrs. per week |
| 3rd yr: | 7 hrs. per week |
| 4th yr: | 6 hrs. per week |
| 5th yr: | 5 hrs. per week |
| 6th and 7th yrs: | 4 hrs. per week |

Algerianization of Literature, History, Geography and Philosophy in all programs.

The Ministry of National Guidance by decree of November 23, 1963, created a specifically Algerian <u>baccalauréat</u> examination:  <u>Baccalauréat algérien de l'enseignement secondaire</u>.  It consists of 2 parts:  <u>examen probatoire</u> and <u>examen du baccalauréat</u>.  There are 2 series of options:  a <u>série transitoire</u> in which tests are worked out according to the new programs, and a <u>série normale</u> according to the old system.

## Examen Probatoire

Taken at the close of 6th year of secondary education.  Consists of compulsory written tests.

Eligibility:   Average grade of 10/20, or at least 8/20 (on recommendation of special Jury decision).

Candidates may choose from the following 5 tests (<u>série normale</u>):

        Série Normale Lettres
        Série Normale Moderne I
        Série Normale Moderne II
        Série Normale Technique T
        Série Normale Technique T'

Candidates who have not followed the training which would prepare them for the <u>série normale</u> may choose from the following tests (<u>série transitoire</u>):

        Série Transitoire Lettres
        Série Transitoire Sciences (Moderne I)
        Série Transitoire Mathématiques (Moderne II)
        Série Technique T
        Série Technique T'

## Coefficients and Lengths of Tests - Séries Normales

| Subjects | LETTRES Coef. | Time | MODERNE I Coef. | Time | MODERNE II Coef. | Time | TECH. T Coef. | Time | TECH. T' Coef. | Time |
|---|---|---|---|---|---|---|---|---|---|---|
| Arabic | 5 | 3 | 3 | 3 | 3 | 3 | 3 | 3 | 4 | 3 |
| French | 4 | 3 | 2 | 3 | 2 | 3 | 2 | 3 | 3 | 3 |
| History and Geography | 3 | 2 | 1 | 1 | 1 | 1 | 1 | 1 | 2 | 1 |
| Mathematics | 3 | 2.5 | 5 | 3 | 6 | 3 | 4 | 3 | 3 | 2.5 |
| Phys. Scs. | 2 | 2 | 5 | 3 | 5 | 3 | 3 | 3 | 2 | 2 |
| Nat. Scs. | - | - | 2 | 2 | - | - | - | - | - | - |
| Mec. Const. | - | - | - | - | - | - | 4 | 4 | - | - |
| Economics | - | - | - | - | - | - | - | - | 2 | 3 |
| Marketing | - | - | - | - | - | - | - | - | 1 | 1 |
| | 17 | | 18 | | 17 | | 17 | | 17 | |
| 2nd optional language | 1 | 2 | 1 | 2 | 1 | 2 | 1 | 2 | 2 | 2 |

## Coefficients and Lengths of Tests - Séries Transitoires

| Subjects | LETTRES Coef. | Time | MODERNE I Coef. | Time | MODERNE II Coef. | Time | TECH. T Coef. | Time | TECH. T' Coef. | Time |
|---|---|---|---|---|---|---|---|---|---|---|
| French | 5 | 3 | 3 | 3 | 3 | 3 | 3 | 3 | 4 | 3 |
| Arabic or Lang. 1 | 4 | 3 | 2 | 3 | 2 | 3 | 2 | 3 | 3 | 3 |
| History and Geography | 3 | 2 | 1 | 1 | 1 | 1 | 1 | 1 | 2 | 2 |
| Mathematics | 3 | 2.5 | 5 | 3 | 6 | 3 | 4 | 3 | 3 | 2.5 |
| Phys. Scs. | 2 | 2 | 5 | 3 | 5 | 3 | 3 | 3 | 2 | 2 |
| Nat. Scs. | - | - | 2 | 2 | - | - | - | - | - | - |
| Mec. Const. | - | - | - | - | - | - | 4 | 4 | - | - |
| Economics | - | - | - | - | - | - | - | - | 2 | 3 |
| Marketing | - | - | - | - | - | - | - | - | 1 | 1 |
| | 17 | | 18 | | 17 | | 17 | | 17 | |
| 2nd optional language | 1 | 2 | 1 | 2 | 1 | 2 | 1 | 2 | 2 | 2 |

** Baccalauréat

Taken at the close of the 7th year.  Consists of written tests, oral
and practical work and a physical education test.

Eligibility:   Average grade of 10/20, or at least 8/20 (on recommendation
               of special Jury decision).

Candidate may choose from the following 5 tests (<u>série normale</u>):

        Série Normale Philosophie
        Série Normale Sciences Expérimentales
        Série Normale Mathématiques Elémentaires
        Série Normale Technique T
        Série Normale Technique T'

Candidates who have not followed the training which would prepare them for the <u>série normale</u> may choose from the following tests (<u>série transitoire</u>):

        Série Transitoire Philosophie
        Série Transitoire Sciences Expérimentales
        Série Transitoire Mathématiques Elémentaires
        Série Transitoire Technique T
        Série Transitoire Technique T'

## Coefficients and Lengths of Tests - Séries Normales

| Written | PHIL. Coef. | PHIL. Time | EXP. SCS. Coef. | EXP. SCS. Time | MATH. ELEM. Coef. | MATH. ELEM. Time | TECH. T Coef. | TECH. T Time | TECH. T' Coef. | TECH. T' Time |
|---|---|---|---|---|---|---|---|---|---|---|
| Philosophy | 6 | 4 | 6 | 3 | 3 | 3 | 3 | 3 | 3 | 4 |
| Islamic Phil. | 2 | 3 | - | - | - | - | - | - | - | - |
| Language | 2 | 2 | 1 | 2 | 1 | 2 | 1 | 2 | 3 | 2 |
| History and Geography | 2 | 3 | - | - | - | - | - | - | 3 | 3 |
| Mathematics | 2 | 3 | 3 | 2 | 7 | 3 | 5 | 3 | 4 | 3 |
| Phys. Scs. | 2 | 3 | 4 | 3 | 6 | 3 | 4 | 3 | - | - |
| Nat. Scs. | 2 | 2 | 3 | 2 | 1 | 1 | - | - | - | - |
| Mech. Const. | - | - | - | - | - | - | 4 | 5 | - | - |
| Economics | - | - | - | - | - | - | - | - | 5 | 3 |
|  | 18 | | 17 | | 18 | | 17 | | 18 | |
| **Oral and Pract.** | | | | | | | | | | |
| 2nd Lang. | - | - | - | - | - | - | - | - | 1 | - |
| Islamic Phil. | 1 | - | 1 | - | 1 | - | 1 | - | 1 | - |
| History and Geography | - | - | 1 | - | 1 | - | 1 | - | - | - |
| Prac. Tech. | - | - | - | - | - | - | 2 | 5 | - | - |
|  | 19 | | 19 | | 20 | | 21 | | 20 | |
| Phys. Ed. | 1 | | 1 | | 1 | | 1 | | 1 | |

## Coefficients and Lengths of Tests - Séries Transitoires

| Written | PHIL. Coef. | Time | EXP. SCS. Coef. | Time | MATH. ELEM. Coef. | Time | TECH. T Coef. | Time | TECH. T' Coef. | Time |
|---|---|---|---|---|---|---|---|---|---|---|
| Philosophy | 8 | 4 | 6 | 3 | 3 | 3 | 3 | 3 | 3 | 4 |
| Arabic or |  |  |  |  |  |  |  |  |  |  |
| Lang. 1 | 2 | 2 | 1 | 2 | 1 | 2 | 1 | 2 | 3 | 2 |
| History and |  |  |  |  |  |  |  |  |  |  |
| Geography | 2 | 3 | - | - | - | - | - | - | 3 | 3 |
| Mathematics | 2 | 3 | 3 | 2 | 7 | 3 | 5 | 3 | 4 | 3 |
| Phys. Scs. | 2 | 3 | 4 | 3 | 6 | 3 | 4 | 3 | - | - |
| Nat. Scs. | 2 | 2 | 3 | 2 | 1 | 1 | - | - | - | - |
| Mech. Const. | - | - | - | - | - | - | 4 | 5 | - | - |
| Economics | - | - | - | - | - | - | - | - | 5 | 3 |
|  | 18 |  | 17 |  | 18 |  | 17 |  | 18 |  |

| Oral and Pract. |  |  |  |  |  |  |  |  |  |  |
|---|---|---|---|---|---|---|---|---|---|---|
| 2nd Lang. | 1 | - | - | - | - | - | - | - | 2 | - |
| History and |  |  |  |  |  |  |  |  |  |  |
| Geography | - | - | 2 | - | 2 | - | 2 | - | - | - |
| Prac. Tech. | - | - | - | - | - | - | 2 | 5 | - | - |
|  | 19 |  | 19 |  | 20 |  | 21 |  | 20 |  |
| Phys. Ed. | 1 |  | 1 |  | 1 |  | 1 |  | 1 |  |

Grading:  0-20        Très Bien      20-16
                      Bien           16-14
                      Assez Bien     14-12
                      Passable       12-10

The grade given to each test is multiplied by the coefficient assigned to the subject (see above).

The total of the points obtained by each candidate is:  the sum of the tests multiplied by their coefficients divided by the sum of the co-efficients.


## BEN BADIS INSTITUTE

Secondary school.  Established by the Society of Reformist Ulema, 1947.

In addition to secondary courses, students can read Muslim law and learn French.  After 2 years students can qualify for work toward degree of Doctor of Muslim Law, or continue for another 2 years at the Institute.

## HIGHER EDUCATION

## UNIVERSITY OF ALGIERS, Algiers

Composed of the Preparatory School of Medicine and Pharmacy, established
in 1849, and the four Higher Schools of Medicine, Law, Letters and
Science established in 1879; in 1905 these combined to form the University.
In 1909 the name of the University of Algiers was given to the institution and granted same status as French universities.  Closed Spring
1962.  Functioning normally 1963.

Entrance requirements:          Baccalauréat complet, or equivalent. Special
                                entrance examinations for students over 21
                                years of age.

### Faculties:

        Letters
        Science
        Law and Economics
        Medicine and Pharmacy

### Institutes of the University:

        Institute of Commercial Training
        Institute of Dental-Stomatology (under Faculty of Medicine)
        Institute of Ethnology
        Institute of General Biochemistry and Biochemistry of Food
        Institute of Arabic Studies (formerly Institute of Higher
          Islamic Studies)
        Institute of Hygiene and Overseas Medicine
        Institute of Legal Studies, Oran and Constantine
        Institute of Meteorology and World Physics
        Institute of Nuclear Research
        Institute of Oriental Studies
        Institute of Philosophical Studies
        Institute of Physical Education and Sport
        Institute of Political Studies (under Faculty of Law)
        Institute of Psychometry and Biometry
        Institute of Saharan Research
        Institute of Solar Energy
        Institute of Town Planning
        Institute of Trachoma and Tropical Ophthalmology
        Institute of University Studies for Workers
        Centre of Administrative Training
        Astronomical Observatory of Algiers, Bouzaréa

Faculté des Lettres (Faculty of Letters)

Entrance examination:          Certificat d'études littéraires générales
                               (Certificate of general literary studies).

4-year program.  Certificate awarded at end of each year.

Licence de philosophie (Philosophy)

General History of Philosophy
Special course in Psychology
General Philosophy and Logic
Moral Philosophy and Sociology

Licence de psychologie (Psychology)

Psychology with Psycho-Pathology
Psychology of Social Life
Psychology of Children and Adolescents
(4th certificate prepared for in the Science Faculty)

Licence d'études classiques (Classical Studies)

Greek
Latin
French Literature
Grammar and Philology

Licence de lettres modernes (Modern Letters)

French Literature
French Grammar and Philology
Foreign Literature

Choice of:  Phonetics, Modern and Contemporary History, General Geography,
            Philology of the living foreign language chosen for Foreign
            Literature.

Licence de lettres d'arabe (Arab Letters)

Arab Literature
Arab Grammar and Philology
Civilization
Foreign Literature

## Licence d'histoire (History)

Ancient History
Medieval History
Modern and Contemporary History
Geography

## Licence de géographie (Geography)

General Geography
Regional Geography
Modern and Contemporary History
Ancient and Medieval History

## Licence d'histoire de l'art (History of Art)

History of Ancient Art
Prehistoric Archeology
Arts and Civilization of Islam

## Licence de languages modernes (Modern Languages)

English
German
Italian
Spanish
Portuguese
Certificate of American Literature and Civilization

## Special Certificates

Prehistory of Africa
Ancient History of North Africa
History and Civilization of Western Muslim Countries
Contemporary History of North Africa
Geography of North Africa
Higher Studies in Muslim Orient
Higher Studies in Semitic Languages
Higher Studies in Berber
Phonetics
Sociology and Ethnography of North Africa
Aesthetics
General Linguistics

Diplomas in Higher Studies

    Philosophy
    Classical Languages and Literature
    Arabic
    History
    Geography
    Living Foreign Language and Literature

Doctorats

    Doctorat de 3ème cycle
    Doctorat de l'Université d'Alger
    Doctorat d'Etat

## Faculté des Sciences (Faculty of Science)

### Licence ès sciences

1st cycle (at least 1 year):

    One of 3 preparatory certificates of higher studies:

    General and Physical Mathematics (M.G.P.)
    Mathematics, Physics and Chemistry (M.P.C.)
    Physics and Chemistry and Natural Science (S.P.C.N.)

2nd cycle:  5 other certificates of higher studies, at least 3 belonging
          to different groups, at least 1 chosen from a list determined
          by the Ministry of National Education.

#### Mathematical Sciences

Math. I, Electricity or Thermodynamics and Physical or Optional
Mechanics, Math. II, General Mechanics, optional certificate.

#### Applied Mathematics

Math. I, Mathematical Techniques of Physics, General Mechanics,
Electricity, Optics, Thermodynamics and Physical Mechanics, 2
optional certificates.

#### Physics (Honours Physics I)

Mathematical Techniques of Physics, Optical Electricity, Thermodynamics and Mechanics.

#### Physics (Honours Physics II)

Mathematical Techniques of Physics, Electrotechniques or Electronics,
one optional certificate.

#### Physics (Honours Chemistry)

General Chemistry I, Experimental Physics or Electricity, Organic Chemistry, Mineral Chemistry.

#### Natural Sciences (Honours Biology)

Botany, Zoology, General Geology, General Biology, Microbiological Biochemistry and Vegetal Physiology, Animal Physiology.

#### Natural Sciences (Honours Earth Sciences)

Botany, Zoology, General Geology, General Biology, Historical Geology, Mineralogy or Animal Physiology, or an optional certificate.

#### Chemistry-Physiology

Experimental or Electrical Physics, General Chemistry I, Microbiological Chemistry and Vegetal Physiology, Animal Physiology, Organic Chemistry.

Degrees:

Physics:         Electronics, Optics, Electricity, Thermodynamics and Physical Mechanics (T.M.P.), Solar Energy, Experimental Physics.

Chemistry:       General Chemistry I, General Chemistry II, Organic Chemistry, Mineral Chemistry, Applied Chemistry, Industrial Analytical Chemistry.

Chemist's Diploma of the University of Algiers (1st and 2nd years).

Mathematics:     Math. I, Math. II, General Mechanics, Astronomy, Advanced Astronomy, Mathematical Methods of Physics.

Natural Sciences: Zoology, General Biology, Microbiological Biochemistry and Vegetal Physiology (B.M.P.V.), Advanced Zoology, Advanced Botany, Animal Physiology, General Psycho-Physiology, Comparative Psycho-Physiology, General Geology, Historical Geology.

Courses will be organized for preparation of the agrégation (qualification for lycée teaching).


Doctorat de troisième cycle - Theoretical Physics, Nuclear Physics.

Faculté de Droit et des Sciences Economiques (Faculty of Law and Economic Sciences)

4-year program.

After 2 years, student receives Bachelier; after 4 years, the Licence.

### Institute of Political Studies

Object:    To coordinate and complete instruction in the Faculties of Law and Arts in economic, administrative and social subjects; to teach methods of work and display and to initiate pupils into concrete problems of administration and social life.

Admittance by normal requirements for Faculty of Law (baccalauréat).

Instruction includes courses, conferences and practical work.

Period of study over 2 or 3 years. Students must have a sufficient grade for conference work, and pass examinations in course work at the end of each year.

### Diploma awarded.

The course may be audited (free of charge) and a Certificate de scolarité (certificate of attendance) may be awarded for good work.

The Institute also organizes conferences designed to form and help officials and civil servants.

Faculté Mixte de Médecine et de Pharmacie (Joint Faculty of Medicine and Pharmacy)

## Medical Studies

6 years plus a thesis.

Examinations:    1st year - Examination A and B.
                 2nd through 5th years - yearly examination.
                 6th year - 3 examinations in Clinical Medicine, Surgery and Obstetrics.

## Dental Surgery

5 years.

Examinations:   1st year - Examination A and special materials (1st and
                            2nd part).
                2nd year - 1st and 2nd parts.
                3rd year - 1st and 2nd parts.
                4th year - final yearly examination.
                5th year - diploma examination.

Diploma awarded by the Institute of Dental-Stomatology under the control
of the Faculty.


Pharmacy

Probationary period (1 year) plus 4 years.

Examinations:   Probationary examination.
                1st year - final yearly examination.
                2nd year - 1st and 2nd parts.
                3rd year - yearly examination.
                4th year - 1st and 2nd parts.

Second part of 4th-year examination confers the title of pharmacien.


Midwifery

Entrance examination under the control of the Department of Public Health.

3 years.

Examinations:   1st-year examination under the control of the Department
                of Public Health.
                2nd year - yearly examination.
                3rd year - yearly examination.

Diploma awarded.


Certificats d'études spéciales (Special Certificates)

        Industrial Medicine
        Legal Medicine
        Hygiene and Sanitary and Social Proceedings
        Ophthalmology
        O.R.L.
        Stomatology
        Neuro-Psychiatry
        Anaestheology
        Gynecology and Obstetrics
        Pneumo-Phtisiology
        Electro-Radiology

<u>Institute of Dental-Stomatology</u>

Comprises: (1)  Center of Jaw-facial and Reparative Surgery
          (2)  Dental School for Dental Surgeons and preparation
               of doctors for specialization in Stomatology.
          Also projected is a School of Prosthetics.

(1)  Center of Jaw-facial Surgery

     Part of the Mustapha Hospital.  Students in Dental Surgery in
     the 3rd, 4th and 5th years attend twice a week for courses on
     their program.  Attend bedside conferences and make regular
     observations on patients.  Follow operations on television.

(2)  Dental School

     Emphasis on the medical specialization.  Program includes:
     traumatic lesions of the face, infectious lesions of the mouth
     cavity, pathology of the facial bones and mouth, salivary
     glands, temporomaxillary deformations of the face.  All dental
     complications.

<u>SEPARATE UNIVERSITY INSTITUTES</u>

<u>Institute of Arabic Studies</u>

Branches in Constantine and Tlemcen.

2-year program.

Completion of 1st year:    <u>Brevet d'arabe</u>
                           <u>Brevet de berbère</u>

Completion of 2nd year:    <u>Diplôme d'arabe</u>
                           <u>Diplôme de berbère</u>

<u>Institute of Legal Studies, Oran</u>

First 2 years of study of Law, preparing for the <u>Certificat de capacité</u>
<u>en droit</u>.

<u>Institute of Meteorology and Global Physics</u>  (Not now operating)

Established in 1873.  Laboratories and offices located at the University.
Other stations where measurements and recordings are taken include the
Observatory of Tamanrasset, geophysical center.

Training in:    Meteorology, Gravimetry, Seismology, Terrestrial
                Magnetism and Aerology.
Minimum of Licence for entrance.
Research in cooperation with the International Union of Geodesy and
Geophysics.


## Institute of Nuclear Research

Scientific training in Nuclear Physics for research personnel in
industry, medicine, agriculture, and chemistry.  Licence to enter.


## Institute of Philosophical Studies

Functions mainly as liaison between several disciplines.  It does not
sponsor any teaching different from that done by professors who
collaborate in 3 licences:  Philosophy, Psychology, Sociology.

It oversees the 3 laboratories related to the Faculty of Letters:
Experimental Psychology, Child Psychology, Sociology.


## Institute of Psychometry and Biometry

Established in 1945.  Under supervision of Department of Physiology in
the Joint Faculty of Medicine and Pharmacy.

At present, one year of instruction in preparation for the Diplôme
d'opérateur psychotechnicien which is required for personnel selection
in administrative services.

Theoretical instruction in Physiology, Psycho-Physiology, General and
Applied Psychology, Statistics, Industrial Psychology, Techniques of
Industrial Methods and Legislation.  Also demonstrations, practical work
and conducted visits.   Research program not now operating.


## Institute of Saharan Research

Established in 1937 to coordinate and intensify research in all areas
related to the Saharan countries.

Most students are those registered in the faculties of the University,
especially those in the fields of geography preparing for advanced
studies or for theses of the 3rd cycle.  Some foreign students are
accepted.

Institute of Solar Energy (Not now operating)

Established in 1959.  Practical and theoretical studies.  Research in
cooperation with other Mediterranean countries in the utilization of
solar energy.  Minimum of a Licence to carry on research.

Solar stations at Bouzaréah and Ouargla.

Certificat d'énergie solaire awarded.


Institute of Town Planning

Affiliated with Faculties of Law and Letters.

Eligibility:    Registration in any Faculty.
                1st part of baccalauréat - examen probatoire.
                Pupils from any state School of Architecture.
                Officials or administrative agents of civil or public
                    service whose work deals with town planning.
                Special examination of credentials and experience.

Technical and administrative sections.

At present 2 years of study.  Courses may be taken by correspondence,
but personal attendance at examinations is obligatory.

Instruction in:        History of Town Planning            )
                       Human Geography                     )
                       Climatology and Cosmography         )
                       Map-reading                         )
                       Utilization of Aerial Photographs   )   common
                       Demography                          )   subjects
                       Sociology                           )
                       Urban Surveys                       )

                       Ideas of Administrative Law         )
                       Town Planning Legislation           )
                       Hygiene Legislation                 )   administrative
                       Municipalism                        )

                       Principles of Urban Composition     )
                       Presentation of Urban Planning      )
                       Housing Problems                    )   technical
                       The Art of the Urban Engineer       )

Both oral and practical examinations at the end of each year.

In the common subjects:  10/20 for each oral.

Students who do not gain the minimum marks in 3 orals can be admitted to the following year, but must make up the other courses.

Final examination is a discussion of a dissertation in a public session.

Marking:  10-12     Passable       Pass
          12-14     Assez Bien     Fairly Good
          15-17     Bien           Good
          18-20     Très Bien      Very Good

Diplôme de l'Institut d'Urbanisme awarded.  The title of lauréat may be awarded for "Very Good" after a further examination by the Dissertation Jury.


## Institute of Higher Studies for Workers

Training at a scientific and technical level for those already professionally employed.

Entrance requirements:            Baccalauréat (Elementary Mathematics or Mathematics and Technics).

Courses:  Advanced Mathematics, 2 hrs. weekly.
          Advanced Physics, 1½ hrs. weekly.

No diploma awarded, but an attestation of examination results.


## VOCATIONAL AND TECHNICAL EDUCATION

### PRIMARY VOCATIONAL AND AGRICULTURAL

State-run.  Vocational training in Carpentry, Automobile Engineering, Arts and Crafts in apprenticeship centers, complementary and evening classes.

Agriculture  in Rural Vocational Centers.  2-year special courses for those over 14 years of age.


### SECONDARY VOCATIONAL AND AGRICULTURAL

Entrance requirements:            Certificat d'études primaires élémentaires, or completion of classe de cinquième.

State-run.  Schools for Construction and Machine Tool Techniques, and Automobile Engineering, Woodworking.

Collège d'Enseignement Agricole:    4-year program.

Agricultural schools at Phillipeville, Guelma, Tizi-Ouzou, Ain Temouchent:
2-year courses.

Agriculture offered at Experimental Centers in Algiers.  Special training in tree culture (especially olive, fig, cork), live-stock raising,
basic agricultural techniques.

School of Horticulture at Jardin d'Essai, Algiers, and School of Home
Economics at El Biar:  instruction at lower level.

School for maritime apprenticeship.


## LOWER TECHNICAL TRAINING

Apprenticeship centers for students holding Certificate of Primary
Studies.

3-year program leading to Certificat d'aptitude professionnelle in one
of several fields.


## SECONDARY TECHNICAL

Secondary technical education is provided in the technical (industrial
and commercial) collèges of Algiers, Constantine, Bone; and in
technical streams of lycées and collèges.

Collège in Oran:          Technical (industrial and commercial) stream.

Maison-Carrée lycée:      Stream preparing for technical baccalauréat and
                          preliminary examination for surveyors.

Lycées and collèges of:   Algiers, Oran, Sidi-bel-Abbes, Tlemcen, Mascara,
                          Philippeville, all offer combined economics and
                          commercial streams.
                          Algiers and Oran also prepare pupils for the
                          National School of Engineering (Civil Engineer-
                          ing).

Special subjects in industrial streams:

> Fitting and machine tools, locksmithing, iron-working, boiler-
> making, carpentry and joinery, welding, cabinet-making, pattern-
> making, auto-mechanics, electricity.  Also, according to need,
> foundry work, building and public works, refrigeration, house
> painting, decorative painting, leatherwork.

## ECOLE NATIONALE PROFESSIONNELLE, Dellys

Industrial school.  Acquired status of a national vocational school, 1950.

Training technicians for:   Precision engineering, public works and
                            building, electricity, refrigeration.

Together with the industrial streams of Algiers, Oran, Bone and
Maison-Carrée, it prepares students for technical baccalauréat.


## NATIONAL SCHOOL OF AGRICULTURE, Maison-Carrée

Established from an agricultural school founded in 1918.  Formerly under
the control of the Ministry of Agriculture, now under the Ministry of
Education.

Entrance requirements:          Baccalauréat, Diploma of Secondary Agri-
                                cultural Studies, or special examination.

3-year program.

Diploma in Agricultural Engineering awarded.


## HIGHER SCHOOL OF COMMERCE, Algiers

2-year program.

Diploma of Higher Commercial Studies awarded.


## ECOLE NATIONALE D'ARCHITECTURE ET DES BEAUX-ARTS, Algiers (National School of Architecture and Fine Arts)

### Architecture Section

Entrance requirements:          17-30 years of age, baccalauréat.

Length of program:    5 years.

<u>TIMETABLE</u>
(Hours per week)

| Subjects | 1st yr. | 2nd yr. | 3rd yr. | 4th yr. | 5th yr. |
|---|---|---|---|---|---|
| Architecture Workshop | 20 | 20 | 20 | 28 | 24 |
| Elements of Stress | - | - | 4 | - | - |
| Interior Design | - | - | - | 4 | - |
| History of Arch. | 4 | 4 | - | - | - |
| Graphic and Plastic Production | 4 | 4 | - | - | - |
| Mathematics | 4 | - | - | - | - |
| Descriptive Geometry and Perspective | 4 | - | - | - | - |
| Statics, Resistance of Materials | - | 4 | 4 | - | - |
| Elements of Construction | 4 | 4 | - | - | - |
| Technical Physics | - | 4 | 4 | - | - |
| Economics, Sociology | - | - | 4 | - | - |
| City Planning | - | - | - | 4 | 8 |
| Topography, Measurements | - | - | - | - | 4 |
| Law, Professional Life, Worker's Organization | - | - | - | - | 4 |
| Construction Sciences | - | - | 4 | 4 | - |
| | 40 | 40 | 40 | 40 | 40 |

<u>Diplôme d'état</u> awarded.


<u>Fine Arts Section</u>

Entrance requirements:        At least 25 years of age, presentation of
                              personal dossier, competitive examination.

Length of program:    5 years.

Subjects offered (40 hrs. per week):

   Drawing, Painting, Sculpture, Decoration, Archeology and History
   of Art, Ceramics, Bookbinding, Illuminating, Miniature Painting,
   Calligraphy, Wood Decorating, Mosaics.

<u>Certificat d'aptitude à la formation artistique supérieure</u> awarded at
close of 5 years.  After 5 years:  <u>Diplôme national des beaux-arts</u>.

ECOLE NATIONALE POLYTECHNIQUE or ECOLE NATIONALE D'INGENIEURS (National
  School of Engineering)

Attached to the University of Algiers.  Offers advanced technical
training.

Entrance requirements (from 1963):

| | |
|---|---|
| to 1st year: | Competitive examination in Mathematics, Physics, Chemistry, Arabic French. Scientific level is that of the baccalauréat (Elementary Mathematics). |
| to 2nd year: | Competitive examination in Mathematics, Physics, Chemistry, Drawing, Arabic, French. The level of Mathematics, Physics and Chemistry is that of the Certificat d'études supérieures de M.P.C.  Those having completed the Propédeutique M.G.P. or M.P.C. (see Faculty of Science, University of Algiers) are excused from the scientific examination. |

4-year program.

Curriculum:

1st yr:   Same theoretical and practical courses for all students.
          Mathematics, Physics and Chemistry of the M.P.C. program,
          Technology, Drawing, Workshop.

2nd yr:   Scientific orientation for all students in Mathematics,
          Statistics, Mechanics, Resistance of Materials, Technology,
          Theory and Practice, Drawing.

3rd and   Specialization in one of the following sections:  Civil,
4th yrs:  Electrical, Mechanical, Chemical.  In October 1963, Public
          Works, Electrotechnics, Electronics, Oil-Chemistry were added.

Apprenticeship work from 2nd year.

Studies prepare for Certificats d'études supérieures.


PRIVATE AND TECHNICAL TRAINING

Private associations, municipalities and chambers of commerce have
established training courses, with the help of the technical education
authorities in:  Banking, Commerce, Dressmaking, and other fields.

ECOLE SUPERIEURE DE COMMERCE (Higher School of Commerce), Algiers

Attached to the University of Algiers. Advanced training for administrative positions in commerce, economics, and finance. Also provides access to various professions: professorat, expertise-comptable, and others.

Entrance requirements:        Competitive examination. Candidate must be 17 years of age and offer a level of study corresponding to the Baccalaureat complet, or equivalent.

Preparatory Section (1 year of training for the competitive examination): Open to those who have passed the Examen Probatoire. Those holding the Brevet d'enseignement commercial are eligible for admission on review of their student books.

3-year program of theoretical and practical studies. Apprenticeship from end of 2nd year. Promotions on basis of yearly examinations.

Curriculum:

1st yr:    Economics and Sociology
           Economic Geography
           Civil Law, Commercial Law, Moslem Law
           Technique of written and oral expression
           Financial Management and Bookkeeping
           Financial Mathematics and Statistics
           Two compulsory languages:  Arabic and English

2nd yr:    Economics and Sociology
           Economic Geography
           Commercial Law and Applications, Public Law, Moslem Law
           Business Organization
           Written and Oral Reports
           Psychosociology
           Financial Management and Bookkeeping
           Financial Mathematics and Statistics
           First Language
           Option A:  Financial Management and Bookkeeping
           Option B:  Second Language

3rd yr:    The Nation and Economic Problems
           Comparative and International and Commercial Law, Social Law
           Human Relations in Business
           Insurance, Financial Management and Bookkeeping
           Financial Economics and Fiscal Laws
           Banking and Credit
           Organization and Techniques of Distribution
           First Language

Diplôme d'études supérieures commerciales, administratives et financières (D.E.S.C.A.F.) awarded.

Center of Higher Studies, open to School graduates and those with Licence, offering Advanced Accounting Techniques and Business Management.

## TEACHER EDUCATION

### P R E - I N D E P E N D E N C E

### TRAINING OF ELEMENTARY SCHOOL TEACHERS

Men trained at normal schools located in Oran, Constantine or Bouzaréa in Algiers.  Women trained at normal schools located in Oran, Constantine or Miliano in Algiers.

Entrance requirements:          Brevet élémentaire or Brevet d'études du premier cycle and competitive examination.

4-year program.

Some teachers had no teacher training, holding only B.E.P.C. or Baccalauréat Part I or Diploma from Franco-Moslem lycées.  For those holding B.E.P.C. a 3-month training program offered a Certificat de culture générale et professionnelle.

### TRAINING OF SECONDARY SCHOOL TEACHERS

Trained at University of Algiers or at institutions in France.

### S I N C E   I N D E P E N D E N C E

Due to the leaving of 80% of the French teaching staff at the time of independence, recruitment of teachers has been handled by massive local recruiting (by examination) from all levels of education (monitors from the primary level).  Monitors and instructors have also been recruited from several Middle Eastern countries.

To train the new teachers, programs have been initiated for training of monitors and of educational counselors.  Each educational counselor to be taught to supervise 50-75 beginners.

### TRAINING OF MONITORS

4-8 weeks of training sessions for monitors.  In 1962-63, 5,500 attended such sessions; by 1963-64, more than 9,000.

Pedagogical sessions:  more than 120 pedagogical sessions held every week for the monitors under the supervision of the educational counselors.

By fulfilling a professional and cultural training program, monitors are permitted access to the staff of instructors.

Formation professionnelle:    by means of seminars, practice teaching, and
                              apprenticeship.

Formation culturelle:         by means of evening courses in the Centres
                              de Formation culturelle et Professionnelle,
                              by correspondence and radio courses.

Certificat de culture générale et professionnelle awarded.


TRAINING OF ARABIC-SPEAKING TEACHERS

Due to Arabization of school curriculum training of Arabic-speaking
teachers has had emphasis since 1962.  Six sections for classical Arabic
were created in Teacher Training Colleges and in 5 classical Arabic
secondary schools.  Arabic teachers for secondary schools trained at the
Institute of Arabic Studies.

3-year program, with practice teaching in 3rd year.

Certificate of Ability in Teaching Arabic in Public Secondary Schools
awarded.


TEACHER TRAINING COLLEGES (Ecoles Normales):

There are 2 types:  Ecole Normale d'Instructeurs and Ecole Normale
d'Instituteurs.

Ecoles Normales d'Instructeurs:    Recruitment from the level of the 2nd
                                   year of secondary education.

                                   4-year program.

Ecoles Normales d'Instituteurs:    Recruitment from the end of the 3rd
                                   year of secondary education.

                                   4-year program, leading to C.F.E.N.

Algerian Certificate of Proficiency in Teaching (C.A.E.P.) awarded.


ECOLE NORMALE NATIONALE D'ENSEIGNEMENT PROFESSIONNEL, Algiers

The various programs for training teachers for technical education are
as follows:

Professeurs d'enseignement général (Professors of General Education):

     P.E.G. Lettres
     P.E.G. Sciences

Entrance requirements:     More than 20 years of age, less than 45
                           years by December 31 of the examination
                           year. Baccalauréat or Brevet supérieur de
                           capacité.

Duration of course:        1 year.

Professeurs d'enseignement technique théorique (Professors of Technical
    Education):

    P.E.T.T. Secrétariat (Secretarial)
    P.E.T.T. Comptabilité (Accounting)
    P.E.T.T. Dessin Mécanique (Mechanical Design)
    P.E.T.T. Dessin Bâtiment (Building Design)

    Secretarial and Accounting programs:

    For preparatory sections (sections préparatoires):

    Entrance requirements:     More than 18 years of age, less than 25
                               years by December 31 of the examination
                               year. B.E.P.C. or C.A.P. (sténo-dactylo-
                               graphe, aide-comptable, employé de bureau)
                               or equivalent.

    Duration of course:        1 year.

    For pedagogy sections (sections de formation pédagogique):

    Entrance requirements:     More than 20 years of age, less than 45
                               years by December 31 of the examination
                               year. Brevet de technicien, Baccalauréat
                               technique économique, Brevet professionnel,
                               B.E.C. de la spécialité.

    Duration of course:        1 year.

    Mechanical and Building Design programs:

    Entrance requirements:     More than 20 years of age, less than 45
                               years by December 31 of the examination
                               year. Baccalauréat mathématique et tech-
                               nique, Diplôme d'élève bréveté du Lycée
                               Technique d'Etat de Dellys, Brevet pro-
                               fessionnel de dessinateur, Brevet d'en-
                               seignement industriel.

    Duration of course:        2 years.

Professeurs techniques adjoints (Assistant Professors of Technical
    Education):

    P.T.A. Mécanique Générale (General Mechanics)

P.T.A. Mécanique Auto (Auto Mechanics)
P.T.A. Electricité (Electricity)
P.T.A. Maçonnerie (Masonry)
P.T.A. Menuiserie (Carpentry)
P.T.A. Forge-Serrurerie (Blacksmith-locksmith trades)
P.T.A. Plomberie Sanitaire (Plumbing)
P.T.A. Couture Industrielle (Industrial Dressmaking)

Entrance requirements:    More than 20 years of age, less than 45
                          years by December 31 of the examination
                          year.  Candidates must have carried on
                          their profession for a minimum of 2 years.

Duration of course:       1 year.

### Professeurs d'Enseignement Ménager (Professors of Home Economics):

Entrance requirements:    More than 20 years of age, less than 45
                          years by December 31 of examination year.
                          Baccalauréat, Brevet d'enseignement social,
                          Brevet d'enseignement commercial.

Candidates are admitted to a preparatory class before being
admitted into the normal section.

### Professeurs d'Enseignement Social (Professors of Social Study):

Entrance requirements:    More than 20 years of age, less than 45
                          years by December 31 of the examination
                          year.  Baccalauréat, Brevet supérieur
                          d'études commerciales, Brevet d'enseigne-
                          ment social, Brevet d'enseignement
                          commercial.

Duration of course:       1 year.

### ECOLE NORMALE SUPERIEURE (Higher Teacher Training College), Algiers

Training of secondary school teachers.

Entrance requirements:    To 1st year:
                          Baccalauréat or a diploma recognized as
                          equivalent by the University of Algiers,
                          competitive examination.

                          To 2nd year:
                          Limited openings to candidates who have
                          distinguished records for the Certificat
                          propédeutique.

To 3rd year:
2 <u>Certificats ès lettres d'enseignement</u> or
3 <u>Certificats ès sciences d'enseignement</u>.

Competitive examination:

<u>Science Section</u>

Group I    Option:  Mathematics, Physical Sciences.

   (a)  Written tests:
Mathematics composition (program of the elementary
  mathematics class)
  4 hrs., coefficient 6.
Physics composition
  3 hrs., coefficient 2.

   (b)  Oral tests:
Mathematics (program of the elementary mathematics class)
  coefficient 5.
Physics (program of the elementary mathematics class)
  coefficient 4.
Chemistry (program of the elementary mathematics class)
  coefficient 2.

Group II   Option:  Experimental Sciences.

   (a)  Written tests:
Physical Sciences composition (program of the experimental
  sciences class)
  4 hrs., coefficient 6.
Natural Sciences composition (program of the experimental
  sciences class)
  3 hrs., coefficient 4.
General Culture
  3 hrs., coefficient 2.

   (b)  Oral tests:
Mathematics (program of the experimental sciences class)
  coefficient - to be assigned.
Physical Sciences (program of the experimental sciences
  class)
  4 hrs., coefficient - to be assigned.
Natural Sciences (program of the experimental sciences
  class)
  coefficient 4.

<u>Technical Sciences Section</u>

   (a)  Written tests:
Mathematics composition (program of the elementary
  mathematics and technical mathematics classes)
  4 hrs., coefficient 5.

Physics composition (program of the elementary mathematics and technical mathematics classes)
   4 hrs., coefficient 4.
Industrial Drawing (program of the technical mathematics
   class)
   4 hrs., coefficient 3.

(b) Oral tests:
Mathematics (program of the elementary mathematics and
   technical mathematics classes)
   coefficient 3.
Technology (program of the technical mathematics class)
   coefficient 3.
Physics (program of the elementary mathematics and
   technical mathematics class)
   coefficient 5.

## Letters Section

Option:    Arabic Language and Literature.

(a) Written tests:
Literary or philosophical dissertation
   4 hrs., coefficient 6.
Literary commentary
   3 hrs., coefficient 3.
Grammatical commentary
   2 hrs., coefficient 3.

(b) Oral tests:
Explication of text
   coefficient 5.
History
   coefficient 3.
Geography
   coefficient 3.

Option:    French Language and Literature.

The written and oral tests are the same as those for the
option above.  They are of the same duration of time and
are affected by the same coefficients.

* * *

3-year program, for those entering the first year.

Students are registered and pursue regular courses in one of the two
Faculties of the University, Letters or Sciences, to work for Certificats de licence d'enseignement.

At the Ecole Normale Supérieure they follow complementary courses which reinforce their university studies and give them teaching methods suitable to their particular disciplines.

In the 2nd and 3rd years there are special courses in Psychology and Pedagogy, in Arabic for those who will teach in the section arabe and in French for the others.

In the 3rd year the students have practice teaching, under supervision, in pilot lycées.

In addition to the diploma of licence granted to the students by the University Faculties, the Ecole Normale Supérieure awards a Diplôme de sortie, giving graduates the privilege of being probationary professors (professeurs stagiaires) in secondary schools.

After a year of teaching tests are given for a Certificat de fin de stage. On successful completion, student receives a Certificat d'aptitude de l'enseignement secondaire.

Graduates are required to serve as professors for at least 5 years after leaving the Ecole.


## ADULT EDUCATION

### CENTRE NATIONAL D'ALPHABETISATION

Work school for adult education with 752 centers for professional and cultural studies.

Preparing for:          Certificat d'études adultes
                        Brevet élémentaire

Baccalauréat (projected) with final examination:  Examen de promotion sociale d'entrée aux facultés.

34

KINGDOM OF LIBYA

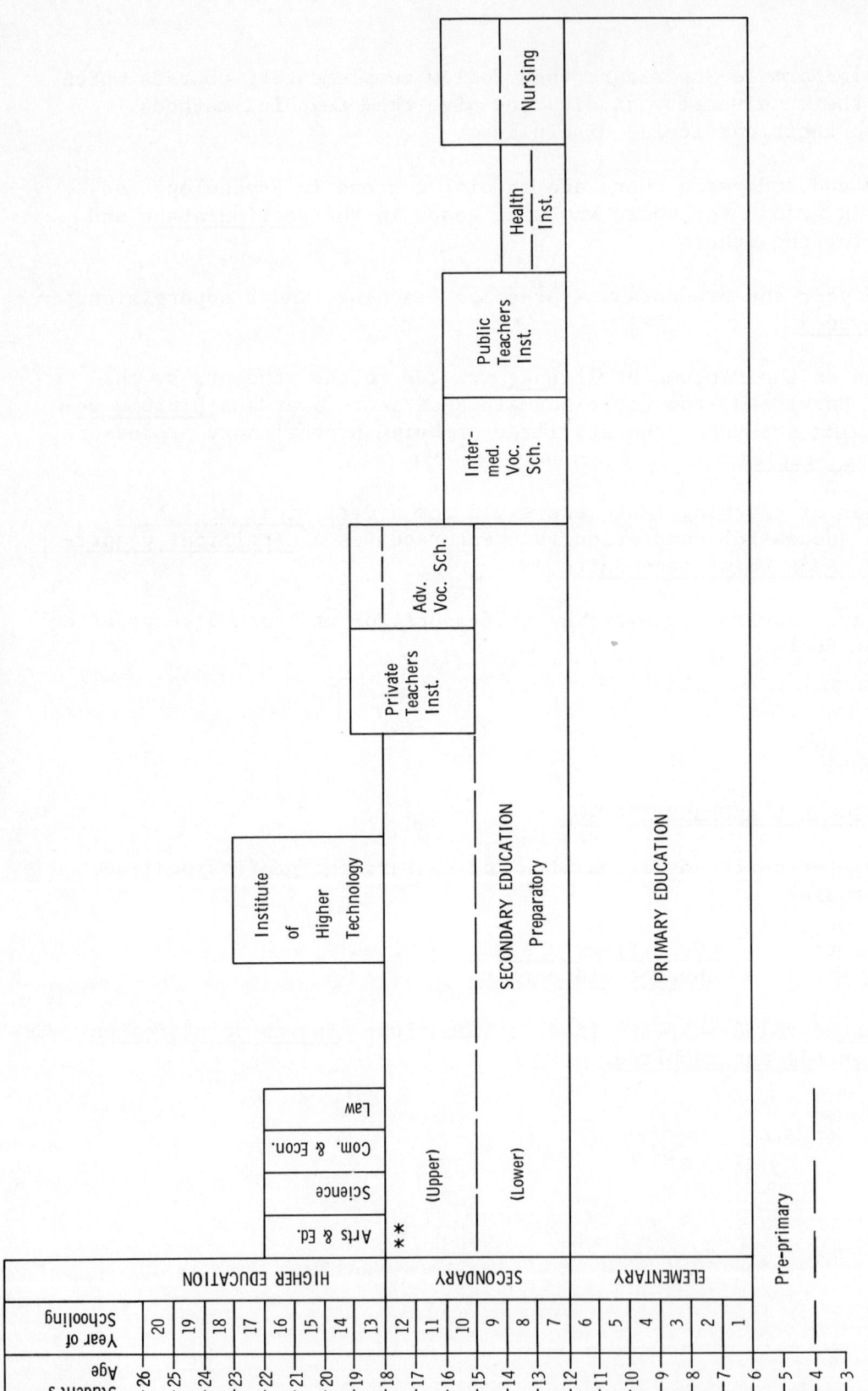

Compulsory education: through Primary education (not enforced)

School year:  October – May (6-day week)  (Friday, the "week-end")

Secondary grading:  100% with 50% passing grade

KINGDOM OF LIBYA

Independence:  December 24, 1951.


## BACKGROUND

Federated Kingdom of 3 autonomous provinces:  Tripolitania, Cyrenaica, Fezzan.

Tripolitania, best developed of the provinces, with its capital of Tripoli, has two-thirds of the Libyan population.  Fezzan, separated from Tripolitania by 600 miles of desert; Sebha, capital city.  Province mostly desert except for the Kufra and Homra oases.  Cyrenaica, eastern province, separated from Tripolitania by Syrte Desert; Benghazi, capital city.

In north, Arabs and Berbers; in south, Teda and Bornu; in west, Taureg. There are small groups of Italians, Greeks, Maltese, and Jews.

In 46 B.C. Tripolitania became part of the Roman Empire.  From 1 A.D. to the 3rd century, Libya enjoyed peace and prosperity.  In the middle of the 4th century Barbarians swept the country, causing anarchy.  In 643, the Arabs came from Egypt to Libya.  In the 10th  century, Libya was governed from Cairo.

In 1510, Tripoli was taken by Spaniards.  In 1531, Turkish occupation. From 1551 to 1912 Libya was under Ottoman rule.  In 1911 Italians declared war on Turkey.  Tripoli and Benghazi occupied.  1912-31, Italian rule.

In 1934 Libya became official name of Italian colony formed by the Union of Cyrenaica and Tripolitania; incorporated into metropolitan kingdom of Italy, 1939.  1939-45, World War II; desert war in Libya, 1940-42.

From 1943-51 Cyrenaica and Tripolitania were under British administration; Fezzan under French.  September 13, 1947, Italy relinquished its rights. Future status of Libya referred to U.N.  November 21, 1949, on resolution of U.N. General Assembly Libya to become independent and sovereign state not later than January 1, 1952.

December 24, 1951, first king of United Kingdom of Libya elected, Idris I. Capital alternating between Tripoli and Benghazi.  December 1962, administrative center of country designated as Beyda (al Baida)

## EDUCATION - PRE-INDEPENDENCE

### Turkish Period

Religious schooling, in mosques, for boys; no public education for girls.
1904, French and Italian schools for boys opened by Roman Catholic Church;
separate schools for girls. French and Italian, principal languages,
Arabic subsidiary. An Arts and Crafts school for orphans.

### Italian Period

Koranic, elementary Arab and Italian schools.

Koranic: religion, reading, writing, arithmetic. Completion of elementary
studies led to Islamic institutes such as Ahmad Pasha College, Zavia Mizran
College or Asmari Institute (all under government control).

1935, School of Islamic Studies (for boys) offering 3-year junior and 4-year
senior programs. Senior program - 2 divisions: (a) teacher-training;
(b) preparation of judges, administrators, and religious officials. Entrance
requirements: 12 years of age and 5 years of primary school. Language of
instruction: Arabic.

Elementary Arab schools: 5-year course of Arabic, religion, and other subjects. School Leaving Certificate leading to Higher Islamic School.

Italian schools: elementary and secondary courses in Italian primarily for
foreign students; limited number of Libyan students admitted.

Arts and Crafts School expanded to include primary training, followed by
4-year vocational course in carpentry, pottery, leatherwork, fashioning of
brass, tailoring, shoemaking, bookbinding.

Agricultural School established in Sidi Masri (suburb of Tripoli).

1936, Training Center for Nurses established, admitting girls from Italian
primary school. 3-year course taught by specialists in eye diseases, internal ailments, first aid, mid-wifery.

### British administration

1943, school for boys, 6-13 years of age. Instruction in Italian and
Arabic. Primary schools for girls: usually primary subjects, with Koran,
handwork, embroidery and drawing. Teachers had completed 5th grade in
Italian primary school.

Under British, 11-year system: primary school, 6 years; secondary, 5 years.
Secondary education started in full sense only in 1947.

1948, Teacher-training centers for men and women, Tripoli. Women's Training
College, 1950.

## Independence

According to Constitution adopted by National Assembly in 1951, free education at all stages:  primary, secondary, technical, and teacher training. Compulsory education at primary level.  By Education Act of 1952, each of 3 provinces responsible for establishing all levels of education, except university.

1954, secondary stage divided into 2 stages:  2 years' preparatory, 3 years' secondary.  1956, reorganized - 12-year system:  6-3-3 plan.


## PRESENT SYSTEM

### PRE-PRIMARY EDUCATION

Entry age:  approximately 4 years.

2-year kindergarten and nursery schools.  Some private kindergartens attached to primary schools.


### PRIMARY EDUCATION

Entry age:  6 years.

6-year program.  (Initially, 5 years.  Koranic schools, 4-year program). Program same in 3 provinces, urban and rural.  Government schools for boys, and for girls.  Some rural schools, coeducational; private schools, boys, and coeducational).

### PRIMARY PROGRAM
(45-minute periods per week)

| Subjects                          | Years: | 1  | 2  | 3  | 4  | 5  | 6  |
|-----------------------------------|--------|----|----|----|----|----|----|
| Koran and Religion                |        | 3  | 3  | 4  | 4  | 3  | 3  |
| Arabic                            |        | 12 | 12 | 10 | 9  | 9  | 9  |
| Singing and Music                 |        |    |    | 1  | 1  | 1  | 1  |
| Arithmetic                        |        | 6  | 6  | 6  | 6  | 5  | 5  |
| Practical Geometry                |        |    |    |    |    | 1  | 1  |
| History and Civics                |        |    |    | 1  | 2  | 2  | 3  |
| Geography                         |        |    |    | 2  | 2  | 2  | 2  |
| Elementary Natural Science        |        | 3  | 3  | 2  | 2  | 2  | 2  |
| Hygiene                           |        |    |    |    |    | 1  | 1  |
| Drawing                           |        | 3  | 3  | 2  | 2  | 2  | 2  |
| Gardening and/or Home Economics   |        | 3  | 3  | 2  | 2  | 2  | 1  |
| Physical Education                |        | 6  | 6  | 6  | 6  | 6  | 6  |
|                                   |        | 36 | 36 | 36 | 36 | 36 | 36 |

Promotion from one class to another on total passing grade calculated as
25% of year's work, 75% of final examination.

Primary School Certificate (Ashahada El Abdidayiyah) awarded at close of
6-year program.


SECONDARY EDUCATION

Entrance requirements:          Primary School Certificate, and entrance
                                examination.

6-year program, 2 stages:       Preparatory - 3 years.
                                Secondary   - 3 years.

In some cases, preparatory courses attached to primary schools, others to
secondary schools.

Prior to 1961, preparatory program was 2 years. At end of 2nd year, student took public examination for "preparatory certificate." Another 2
years, student took public examination for "general secondary certificate,"
permitting him to take an orientation course of 1 year (scientific, mathematics, literary). Public examination at the close of this final year for
"special secondary certificate" admitting student to university, college,
or higher institute.

3-year preparatory program:     Religion, Arabic, English, Mathematics,
                                Physics, Science, Geography, History. Civics,
                                Drawing, Sports, Hygiene, practical work
                                (boys: Handcrafts and Horticulture; girls,
                                Needlework and Domestic Science).

3-year secondary program:       1st-year curriculum common to all: Arabic,
                                English, French, Religion, History, Geography,
                                Physics, Chemistry, Drawing, Mathematics,
                                Libyan Society, practical hobbies, Physical
                                Education, and Games.

                                2nd year, student chooses between literary
                                and scientific curriculum.

    Literary (2 years):         Religion, Arabic, English, French, History,
                                Geography, Philosophy, Sociology, Physical
                                Education, practical work, and additional
                                classes in field of specialization.

    Scientific (2 years):       Religion, Arabic, English, French, Mathe-
                                matics, Physics, Chemistry, Biology, practical
                                work, Physical Education, and additional
                                courses in field of specialization.

## UPPER SECONDARY PROGRAM
### (Periods per week)

| Subjects | Common studies 1st yr: | Arts section 2nd & 3rd yrs. | Science section 2nd & 3rd yrs. |
|---|---|---|---|
| Arabic | 6 | 8 | 5 |
| English | 6 | 7 | 5 |
| French | 4 | 5 | 4 |
| Koran and Religion | 2 | 2 | 2 |
| History | 2 | 2 | |
| Geography | 2 | 2 | |
| Mathematics | 4 | | $7^{++}$ |
| Physics | 2 | | 3 |
| Chemistry | 2 | | 3 |
| Biology | | | 3 |
| Study of Society | 2 | | |
| Elementary Philosophy | | 2 | |
| Elementary Sociology | | 2 | |
| Drawing | 1 | | |
| Practical Work | 2 | 2 | 2 |
| Physical Education | 2 | 2 | 2 |
| Additional courses | | $3^{+}$ | $3^{+++}$ |
| | 37 | 37 | 30 |

$^{+}$Arabic, English, History, or Geography
$^{++}$Including Mechanics
$^{+++}$Mathematics, Physics, Chemistry, or Biology

For the year, final examinations count 75% of total work, term work only 25%. (Only half of students expected to pass.)

Student failing 3 subjects must repeat total year's work (subjects failed and subjects passed). Student failing 2 subjects may study during summer and take supplementary examinations in September. Student failing 1 subject is permitted to enter next class. If he fails subject 2 successive years, he must repeat all subjects studied during 2nd year.

In final examination, under Ministry of Education, student must obtain prescribed minimum mark in each subject:
> 20 out of 40 - Arabic
> 16 out of 40 - 1st foreign language
> 12 out of 30 - 2nd foreign language
and 50% of total marks obtainable in all subjects.

In scientific section, those receiving 67% or higher are given scholarships to study abroad.

**On successful examinations, General Secondary Education Certificate awarded.

## HIGHER EDUCATION

## THE LIBYAN UNIVERSITY, Benghazi

Opened 1956-57.

January 26, 1956, Faculty of Arts and Education established as a nucleus of the University. A year later, Faculty of Science and Faculty of Commerce and Economics added. 1962, Faculty of Law.

Women accepted, 1958-59. Subsidies paid to all students.

Entrance requirements:

General Secondary Education Certificate (and total marks obtained in subjects pertinent to pursuit of studies in Faculty chosen).

For Faculty of Science, student must be graduated from Scientific section; for Faculty of Law, from the Literary section; for the Faculty of Arts and Education, priority given to those from Literary section.

2 types of students:  internal or regular students
external or associate students

Majority are regular students. External students are subject to same rules and regulations applied to regular students but are not required to attend classes; most external students are employees.

Student teachers must be regular and internal students in order to participate in student teaching program.

4-year programs for B.A. or B.Sc. degree.

## Faculty of Arts and Education

## Bachelor's degree (B.A. and B.Ed.) (General)

Undergraduate work leading to above degrees offered in 5 academic departments.
- (1) Arabic Department:  Studies relative to Arabic Language Arts and Literature
- (2) English Department:  Studies relative to English Language and Literature
- (3) Department of History:  Historical studies

(5)  Department of Sociology:  Sociological studies  )   After 1963,
     Department of Philosophy: Philosophical studies )   1 Department

In addition to the courses offered by the 5 academic departments and the
Department of Education, the Faculty offers courses in modern languages
other than English, and ancient languages.

Preliminary year:  general program.

In 2nd year, student chooses his specialization from 5 specializations,
corresponding to the previous academic departments and 6 introductory
courses offered in preliminary year.

Beginning with the 3rd year, students in all specializations provided
with uniform educational programs.  Student teaching, 4th year (once a
week).

### PRELIMINARY YEAR COMMON CURRICULUM

| Subjects | Hours per week |
|---|---|
| Arabic Language and Literature | 5 |
| English Language and Literature | 5 |
| History | 2 |
| Geography | 3 |
| Philosophy | 3 |
| Sociology | 3 |
| | 21 |

Specializations for 3 years in each department, with hours devoted to
each subject.

(1)  Arabic Department

| | Subjects | Hours per week |
|---|---|---|
| 2nd yr: | Islamic Studies | 2 |
| | Grammar and Etymology | 2 |
| | Literature Texts and Prosody | 4 |
| | Intellectual and Literature in North Africa and Andalusia | 2 |
| | Rhetorics | 1 |
| | Tutorial | 2 |
| | Translation of texts from the studies of the Orientalists | 2 |
| | English Language | 2 |
| | Turkish or Persian Language | 2 |
| | Islamic Philosophy | 2 |
| | A historical subject (chosen by the Department) | 2 |
| | | 23 |

| 3rd yr: | Literature and Texts | 3 |
|---|---|---|
| | Intellectual and Literary Life in North Africa and Andalusia | 1 |
| | Grammar and Etymology | 2 |
| | Philology | 1 |
| | Rhetorics | 2 |
| | Islamic Studies | 1 |
| | Turkish or Persian Language | 2 |
| | Tutorial | 1 |
| | History of Abbasid Dynasty | 2 |
| | English Language | 2 |
| | Educational Psychology | 2 |
| | Education and Methods of Teaching | 2 |
| | | 21 |

| 4th yr: | Literature and Texts | 3 |
|---|---|---|
| | Literary Criticism | 2 |
| | Comparative Literature | 1 |
| | Grammar and Etymology | 2 |
| | Islamic Studies | 1 |
| | Tutorial | 1 |
| | English Language | 2 |
| | Turkish or Persian Language | 2 |
| | Special Methods of Teaching | 1 |
| | Philosophy of Education and Educational Supervision | 2 |
| | Educational Psychology | 1 |
| | | 18 |

## (2) English Department

| | Subjects | Hours per week |
|---|---|---|
| 2nd yr: | Language | 4 |
| | Shakespeare and Poetry | 2 |
| | Prose | 2 |
| | Criticism | 2 |
| | British Life and Thought | 1 |
| | Tutorial and Library | 2 |
| | Arabic Language, Texts and Translation | 5 |
| | History | 2 |
| | Second European Language (French, German or Italian) | 2 |
| | | 22 |

| 3rd yr: | History of Literature | 2 |
|---|---|---|
| | Drama | 2 |
| | Prose | 2 |
| | Poetry | 2 |
| | British Life and Thought | 1 |

| | | |
|---|---|---|
| | Language and Practical Criticism | 1 |
| | Tutorial and Library | 2 |
| | Arabic | 3 |
| | Second European Language (French, German, or Italian) | 2 |
| | Educational Psychology | 2 |
| | Education and Methods of Teaching | 1 |
| | | 21 |

| | | |
|---|---|---|
| 4th yr: | History of Literature | 2 |
| | Drama | 2 |
| | Prose | 2 |
| | Poetry | 2 |
| | 20th Century Literature and Practical Criticism | 2 |
| | Language and Tutorial | 2 |
| | Arabic | 2 |
| | Second European Language (French, German, or Italian) | 1 |
| | Special Methods of Teaching | 1 |
| | Philosophy of Education and Educational Supervision | 2 |
| | Educational Psychology | 1 |
| | | 19 |

(3)  Department of History

| | Subjects | Hours per week |
|---|---|---|
| 2nd yr: | Ancient History and Archaeology of Libya | 2 |
| | Ancient History of the East | 2 |
| | Greek History | 2 |
| | Roman History | 2 |
| | Hellenistic Period | 2 |
| | History of Byzantine Empire | 2 |
| | Geography | 3 |
| | English Language | 2 |
| | Arabic Language | 2 |
| | Tutorial | 2 |
| | | 21 |

| | | |
|---|---|---|
| 3rd yr: | History of Islamic Libya | 2 |
| | History of the Abbasid Dynasty | 2 |
| | History of North Africa and Andalusia | 2 |
| | Medieval History of Europe | 2 |
| | Islamic Civilization and Texts | 2 |
| | Relations between East and West in Middle Ages | 2 |
| | Geography | 2 |
| | English Language | 2 |

|  | | Hours |
|---|---|---|
| | Tutorial | 2 |
| | Educational Psychology | 2 |
| | Education and Methods of Teaching | 1 |
| | | 21 |
| 4th yr: | Modern History of Libya | 2 |
| | Modern Arab History | 2 |
| | Modern History of Europe | 2 |
| | History of the 19th and the Beginning of the 20th Centuries | 2 |
| | Geography | 2 |
| | English Language | 2 |
| | Tutorial | 2 |
| | Special Methods of Teaching | 1 |
| | Philosophy of Education and Educational Supervision | 2 |
| | Educational Psychology | 1 |
| | | 18 |

**(4) Department of Geography**

| | Subjects | Hours per week |
|---|---|---|
| 2nd yr: | Physical Geography | 4 |
| | Geography of Africa | 2 |
| | Geography of North and Latin America | 2 |
| | Physical Anthropology and Social Geography | 3 |
| | Islamic History of Libya | 2 |
| | Cartography | 2 |
| | Social Anthropology | 3 |
| | Arabic Language | 2 |
| | English Language | 1 |
| | Tutorial | 2 |
| 3rd yr: | Geomorphology | 2 |
| | Regional Geography of Eurasia and Australia | 3 |
| | Economic Geography | 3 |
| | Tutorial and Geographical Texts | 2 |
| | English Language | 2 |
| | Political Economy | 3 |
| | History | 2 |
| | Education and Methods of Teaching | 1 |
| | Educational Psychology | 2 |
| | | 20 |
| 4th yr: | Geography of Libya | 2 |
| | Political Geography | 3 |
| | Geography of Transportation | 2 |
| | Tutorial | 1 |
| | History | 2 |

| | |
|---|---|
| Libyan Society | 2 |
| English Language | 2 |
| Philosophy of Education and Educational Supervision | 2 |
| Educational Psychology | 1 |
| Special Methods of Teaching | 1 |
| | 18 |

## (5) Department of Philosophy

| | Subjects | Hours per week |
|---|---|---|
| 2nd yr: | Islamic Theological Philosophy and Texts (I'LM Al-Kalam) | 3 |
| | Greek Philosophy and Medieval Philosophy (with texts) | 3 |
| | Formal Logic | 2 |
| | General and Physiological Psychology | 2 |
| | Social Research and Statistics | 2 |
| | Society Structure and Systems | 2 |
| | Social Anthropology | 2 |
| | Social Services and Institutions | 2 |
| | Tutorial (Development of Culture and Civilization) | 1 |
| | Arabic Language | 2 |
| | English Language | 2 |
| | | 23 |
| 3rd yr: | Philosophers of Islam | 3 |
| | History of Modern Philosophy | 2 |
| | Ethics | 2 |
| | Methodology in Science | 2 |
| | Social Psychology | 1 |
| | Rural Sociology | 1 |
| | Schools of Sociology | 2 |
| | Demography | 2 |
| | Educational Psychology | 1 |
| | Tutorial | 2 |
| | Education and Methods of Teaching | 2 |
| | Ancient or Modern Language (Greek, Latin, English, French, German, Italian) | 2 |
| | | 22 |
| 4th yr: | Islamic Mysticism and Texts | 2 |
| | History of Contemporary Philosophy and Texts | 3 |
| | Aesthetics | 1 |
| | Metaphysics | 2 |
| | Mental Health | 1 |

| | |
|---|---|
| Libyan Society | 1 |
| Social and Political Theories and Systems | 2 |
| Industrial and Urban Sociology | 2 |
| Field Studies | 1 |
| Philosophy of Education and Educational Supervision | 2 |
| Educational Psychology | 1 |
| Ancient or Modern Language (Greek, Latin, English, French, German or Italian) | 1 |
| Special Methods of Teaching | 1 |
| | 20 |

## Faculty of Science (located in Tripoli)

## Bachelor of Science (B.Sc.) (General)

1st yr:   Choice of any 1 of the following groups of subjects:

    Group    I:   Pure Mathematics, Applied Mathematics, Physics, Chemistry
    Group   II:   Pure Mathematics, Geology, Physics, Chemistry
    Group  III:   Physics, Chemistry, Botany, Zoology
    Group   IV:   Chemistry, Geology, Botany, Zoology
    Group    V:   General Mathematics, Physics, Chemistry, Zoology
    Group   VI:   General Mathematics, Physics, Chemistry, Geology
    Group  VII:   General Mathematics, Physics, Chemistry, Botany

2nd yr:   Choice of any 1 of the groups:

    Group    I:   Pure Mathematics, Applied Mathematics, Physics
    Group   II:   Pure Mathematics, Physics, Chemistry
    Group  III:   Chemistry, Botany, Zoology
    Group   IV:   Botany, Zoology, Geology
    Group    V:   Chemistry, Zoology, Geology
    Group   VI:   General Mathematics, Physics, Geology
    Group  VII:   Chemistry, Botany, Geology

3rd and   Choice of any 1 of the combinations of subjects:
4th yrs:

    (1)   Pure Mathematics, Physics
    (2)   Applied Mathematics, Physics
    (3)   General Mathematics, Physics
    (4)   Chemistry, Physics
    (5)   Chemistry, Botany
    (6)   Chemistry, Zoology
    (7)   Botany, Zoology
    (8)   Botany, Geology
    (9)   Zoology, Geology

(10)  Physics, Geology
(11)  Chemistry, Geology
(12)  Physics, Astronomy
(13)  Pure Mathematics, Astronomy
(14)  Applied Mathematics, Astronomy

| | Subjects | Hours per week | |
|---|---|---|---|
| | | Theoretical | Practical |
| 1st yr: | Pure Mathematics | 4 | 4 |
| | Applied Mathematics | 4 | 4 |
| | General Mathematics | 3 | 5 |
| | Physics | 3 | 5 |
| | Chemistry | 3 | 5 |
| | Botany | 3 | 5 |
| | Zoology | 3 | 5 |
| | Geology | 3 | 5 |
| | English Language | 2 | - |
| | | 28 | 38 |
| 2nd yr: | Pure Mathematics | 5 | 4 |
| | Applied Mathematics | 5 | 4 |
| | General Mathematics | 4 | 5 |
| | Physics | 4 | 5 |
| | Chemistry | 4 | 5 |
| | Botany | 4 | 5 |
| | Zoology | 4 | 5 |
| | Geology | 4 | 5 |
| | | 34 | 38 |
| 3rd yr: | Pure Mathematics | 5 | $2\frac{1}{2}$ |
| | Applied Mathematics | 5 | $2\frac{1}{2}$ |
| | General Mathematics | 5 | 6 |
| | Physics | 1 | 10 |
| | Chemistry | 5 | 10 |
| | Botany | 5 | 10 |
| | Zoology | 5 | 10 |
| | Mathematical Statistics | 5 | 10 |
| | Astronomy | 5 | 10 |
| | Geology | 5 | 10 |
| | | 50 | 81 |
| 4th yr: | Pure Mathematics | 5 | $2\frac{1}{2}$ |
| | Applied Mathematics | 5 | $2\frac{1}{2}$ |
| | General Mathematics | 5 | 6 |
| | Physics | 5 | 10 |
| | Chemistry | 5 | 10 |

| | | |
|---|---|---|
| Botany | 5 | 10 |
| Zoology | 5 | 10 |
| Geology | 5 | 10 |
| Mathematical Statistics | 5 | 10 |
| Astronomy | 5 | 10 |
| | 50 | 81 |

## Faculty of Commerce and Economics

### Bachelor of Commerce and Economics (B.Com. and Econ.) (General)

| | Subjects | Hours per week | |
|---|---|---|---|
| | | Theoretical | Tutorial |
| 1st yr: | Business Administration | 2 | 1 |
| | Accountancy | 3 | 1 |
| | Law (Introduction) | 2 | - |
| | Economic History | 2 | - |
| | Economics | 2 | 1 |
| | Economic Geography | 2 | - |
| | Arabic Society | 2 | - |
| | English Language | 4 | - |
| | Modern European Language | 2 | - |
| | | 21 | 3 |
| 2nd yr: | Accountancy | 3 | 1 |
| | Financial and Pure Mathematics | 3 | 1 |
| | Economics | 2 | 1 |
| | Law (Obligations) | 2 | - |
| | Public Administration | 2 | - |
| | Business Administration | 2 | 1 |
| | English Language | 4 | - |
| | Modern European Language | 2 | 1 |
| | | 20 | 4 |
| 3rd yr: | (A) Department of Economics | | |
| | Statistics | 2 | 1 |
| | Public Finance | 2 | - |
| | Commercial Law | 3 | - |
| | Types and Systems of Government | 2 | - |
| | International Economy | 3 | 1 |
| | Economic Analysis | 2 | - |
| | Agriculture and Industrial Economy | 3 | - |
| | Personal Management and Industrial Relationship | 3 | - |
| | Marketing | 2 | - |
| | English Language | 1 | - |
| | | 23 | 2 |

## (B)  Department of Commerce

| | | |
|---|---|---|
| Statistics | 2 | 1 |
| Marketing | 2 | - |
| Public Finance | 2 | - |
| Commercial Law | 3 | - |
| International Economy | 3 | 1 |
| Cost Accountancy | 3 | 1 |
| Companies Accountancy | 2 | - |
| Applied Accountancy | 2 | - |
| Personnel Management and Industrial Relationship | 3 | 1 |
| English Language | 1 | - |
| | 23 | 4 |

4th yr:

## (A)  Department of Economics

| | | |
|---|---|---|
| Theory of Employment | 2 | - |
| Development of Economic Thought | 2 | 1 |
| Applied Economy | 2 | - |
| Statistics | 2 | 1 |
| Modern Economic Problems | 2 | 1 |
| International Relations and Problems | 2 | - |
| Public International Law | 2 | - |
| Tax Legislations | 2 | - |
| English Language | 1 | - |
| Social Economy | 2 | - |
| | 19 | 3 |

## (B)  Department of Commerce

| | | |
|---|---|---|
| Financial Management | 2 | - |
| Insurance | 2 | - |
| Companies Accountancy | 2 | 1 |
| Auditing | 3 | 1 |
| Applied Accountancy | 2 | - |
| Maritime Law | 1 | - |
| Tax Legislations | 2 | - |
| Administrative Control | 2 | 1 |
| Social Economy | 2 | - |
| English Language | 1 | - |
| | 19 | 3 |

## Faculty of Law

### Bachelor of Law (LL.B.) (General)

|          | Subjects                                    | Hours per week |
|----------|---------------------------------------------|:---:|
| 1st yr:  | Introduction to Law Studies                 | 3 |
|          | Political Economy                           | 3 |
|          | Political Systems and Constitutional Law    | 3 |
|          | Islamic Law                                 | 2 |
|          | Roman Law                                   | 2 |
|          | History of Law                              | 1 |
|          | Arabic History                              | 2 |
|          | A Foreign Language                          | 3 |
|          | Tutorial                                    | 3 |
|          |                                             | 22 |
| 2nd yr:  | Civil Law                                   | 4 |
|          | Procedure and Criminal Law                  | 3 |
|          | Public International Law                     | 3 |
|          | Political Economy                           | 3 |
|          | Islamic Law                                 | 3 |
|          | Administrative Law                          | 2 |
|          | Social Law                                  | 2 |
|          | A Study with Foreign Language               | 2 |
|          | Tutorial                                    | 2 |
|          |                                             | 24 |
| 3rd yr:  | Civil Law                                   | 3 |
|          | Jurisprudence                               | 3 |
|          | Mercantile Law                              | 3 |
|          | Criminal Law                                | 2 |
|          | Administrative Law                          | 2 |
|          | Public Finance and Taxation                 | 3 |
|          | Social Law                                  | 2 |
|          | Islamic Law                                 | 2 |
|          | A Study with Foreign Language               | 2 |
|          | Tutorial                                    | 2 |
|          |                                             | 24 |
| 4th yr:  | Civil Law                                   | 4 |
|          | Procedure of Criminal Law                   | 3 |
|          | Mercantile Law                              | 3 |
|          | Civil Procedure and Education               | 2 |
|          | Principles of Doctrine                      | 2 |
|          | Maritime Law                                | 2 |
|          | A Study with Foreign Language               | 2 |
|          | Tutorial                                    | 2 |
|          |                                             | 23 |

4th year student may choose any of the following subject groups in addition
to subjects listed above:

| | | Hours per week |
|---|---|:---:|
| (1) | Insurance Regulations and Outer Space Law | 2 |
| (2) | Criminology and Special Criminal Law | 2 |
| (3) | Local Administration and Public Administration | 2 |
| (4) | International Organization, Regional Conventions, Diplomatic Corps, and Consular Corps | 2 |


## RELIGIOUS EDUCATION

Previous to 1960, schools divided into following sections:  Primary, 4;
years; Secondary, 5 years; Advanced, 4 years; Specialization sections,
2 and 5 years.

Present levels:
  (1)  Pre-elementary (includes the Koranic schools) (775 schools)
  (2)  Elementary
  (3)  Secondary
  (4)  University

Administered and supervised by a religious authority semi-independent of
the Ministry of Education and the Department of Education in the province.

Similar to government schools in curricula and regulations, but emphasis
on study of Arabic language and Muslim Law.


## MOSLEM UNIVERSITY OF MUHAMMED IBN ALI ES-SENUSSI

Established, November 1952.  The religious school (Zavia) of Zaghboub is
the nucleus of the  University.

The Nazarat of Education of the Provincial Government supervised and administered the University until 1955 when, by royal decree, the University
became an independent body.

1956, several institutes established in the Kingdom.  1960-61, the organization re-formed and made into 1 university.


Faculties:

        Theology                          Arabic Language
        Moslem Jurisprudence

4-year programs.

The University also comprises the following institutes:

    The Institute of Arabic Calligraphy
    The Institute of Research
    The Institute of Quaanic Readings
    The Institute of Adult Education

## VOCATIONAL AND TECHNICAL EDUCATION

Started last 2 years of British administration.

Short vocational training courses.  2 technical schools established in Tripolitania and Cyrenaica.  In Benghazi (Cyrenaica), 2-year program for woodworking, metal, leather, textile workers; admission on primary school certificate.  2 agricultural schools:  Magdalena School of Agriculture, Cyrenaica, and Sidi Mesri School of Agriculture.

Presently, commercial schools, technical and industrial schools, agricultural schools, handicrafts school, applied engineering school, fundamental education center.  (6 at intermediate level; 5 at advanced level.)

## INTERMEDIATE LEVEL SCHOOLS

Training artisans and skilled workers.

Entrance requirements:                  Primary School Certificate.

Programs:  2-year vocational (such as Mother and Child Welfare Institutes)
           3-year vocational - technical and commercial schools
           4-year agricultural schools

## ADVANCED LEVEL SCHOOLS

Training highly skilled workers and assistant technicians.

Entrance requirements:                  Preparatory Certificate (3 years secondary education)

Programs:  1 year - such as Health Inspector's Institute
           2 year - Nursing School
           3 year - advanced teacher training instituted (see TEACHER
                EDUCATION)
           4 year - applied engineering school (established 1957-58)

Intermediate and advanced levels are usually combined in 1 institute.

## INSTITUTE OF HEALTH OFFICERS AND INSPECTORS

Established 1957 by Ministry of Health jointly with World Health Organization and UNICEF to train health officials for rural areas.

2 sections:     (a)  Health Officers
                (b)  Inspectors


## INSTITUTE OF HIGHER TECHNOLOGY, Tripoli

Established in collaboration with UNESCO.

Entrance requirements:              Graduation from secondary school from mathematics and scientific program.

4 courses:     Civil Engineering
               Electrical Engineering
               Mechanical Engineering
               Food Technology

Programs:  5 years.

B.Sc. degrees awarded in specialty.


## TEACHER EDUCATION

Started last 2 years of British administration.

In Tripolitania, in addition to short courses for in-service teachers, a training section established in secondary school in Tripoli, 1948.  1950, teacher training center at Sidi Hesri in Tripoli for boys.  Teacher training center for girls opened in Tripoli, October 1950.

In Cyrenaica, teacher training section in Benghazi secondary school, 1950. At Marsa Susa (Appolonia), 1950, holiday training course for teachers holding positions:  history, geography, physical education, handicrafts, Arabic, and English.

2 types of teacher training:  Public Institutes, training class teachers
                              for primary schools
                              Private Institutes, training subject teachers
                              for preparatory schools

PUBLIC TEACHER TRAINING INSTITUTES

Entrance requirements:        Primary School Certificate, not less than
                              14 years of age, not more than 18 years
                              of age, medical examination, personality
                              examination (through interview).

4-year program.   (7 government schools for boys; 3 for girls.)

### Teacher Training Program
#### (Periods per week)

| Subjects                                                              | Years: 1 | 2  | 3  | 4  |
|-----------------------------------------------------------------------|----------|----|----|----|
| Arabic Language and Songs                                             | 10       | 10 | 8  | 8  |
| Arabic Handwriting                                                    | 2        | 2  | 1  | 1  |
| Religion and Koran                                                    | 4        | 4  | 3  | 3  |
| Foreign Language                                                      | 5        | 5  | 3  | 3  |
| History                                                               | 2        | 2  | 2  | 2  |
| Geography                                                             | 2        | 2  | 2  | 1  |
| Civics                                                                | 1        | 1  | -  | -  |
| Arithetic and Algebra                                                 | 3        | 2  | -  | -  |
| Algebra                                                               | -        | -  | 2  | 2  |
| Geometry                                                              | 2        | 2  | 1  | -  |
| Geometry and Trigonometry                                             | -        | -  | -  | 2  |
| General Science and Hygiene                                           | 3        | 4  | -  | -  |
| Physics                                                               | -        | -  | 2  | 1  |
| Chemistry                                                             | -        | -  | 2  | -  |
| Biology                                                               | -        | -  | 2  | -  |
| School and Public Health                                              | -        | -  | -  | 1  |
| Education and Psychology                                              | -        | -  | 2  | 2  |
| Methods of Teaching                                                   | -        | -  | 2  | 3  |
| Practical Teaching and Criticism*                                     | -        | -  | 5  | 5  |
| Drawing and Manual Training (boys)                                    | 4        | 4  | 4  | 4  |
| Drawing and Art Training (girls) and Home Economics and Needlework    | 4        | 4  | 4  | 4  |
| Physical Education                                                    | 2        | 2  | 2  | 1  |
|                                                                       | 40       | 40 | 41 | 41 |

*A day is devoted to practical teaching every week; in addition, 3 con-
tinuous weeks for the 4th year students in primary schools.

Examinations on the material taught in all subjects during final academic
year.  On successful completion, student awarded Public Teaching Diploma.

Graduate must remain in teaching profession for a period of at least 6
years from date of receiving diploma.

## PRIVATE TEACHER TRAINING INSTITUTES

From 1954 when secondary education divided into 2 stages, with lower preparatory stage, there became a need for teacher training institutes to
prepare teachers for this lower secondary level.  (For upper secondary,
trained at University.)

First teacher training institute established 1954-55 to train preparatory
teachers.  3 institutes by 1964.

Entrance requirements:              Completion of preparatory secondary
                                    program, medical examination, person-
                                    ality examination (through interview).

4-year program:  1st year, general studies.

                 Remaining 3 years, students offered 3 specializations:
                 (a)  Arabic Language and Religion
                 (b)  Scientific - Science and Mathematics
                 (c)  Literary - Social Studies, Literature and Foreign
                      Language

                 1961, 2 other specializations added:

                 (d)  Physical Education
                 (e)  Arts Education

### Program for Men's and Women's Special Institutes for Teachers
(Periods per week)

| Subjects | General Studies | Arabic Language 2 | 3 | 4 | Social Studies 2 | 3 | 4 | Science and Mathematics 2 | 3 | 4 |
|---|---|---|---|---|---|---|---|---|---|---|
| Religion and Koran | 1 | 5 | 4 | 3 | 7 | 5 | 4 | 6 | 5 | 4 |
| Arabic Language | 7 | 12 | 10 | 10 | - | - | - | - | - | - |
| Foreign Language | 6 | 6 | 3 | 3 | 10 | 8 | 9 | 5 | 4 | 3 |
| History | 2 | - | - | - | 5 | 2 | 3 | - | - | - |
| Geography | 2 | - | - | - | 5 | 2 | 3 | - | - | - |
| Introduction to Philosophy | 2 | 4 | 4 | 3 | 4 | 4 | - | - | - | - |
| Elementary Sociology | 4 | - | - | - | - | - | - | - | - | - |
| Physics ) Chemistry ) Science Biology, Botany) Zoology ) | 5 | - | - | - | - | - | - | 11 | 6 | 6 |
| Algebra ) Mathematics Geometry ) | 2 2 | - | - | - | - | - | - | 9 | 6 | 7 |
| Drawing | 2 | - | - | - | - | - | - | - | - | - |
| Manual Training and Farming (Boys) | 3 | - | - | - | - | - | - | - | - | - |

| Subjects | General Studies | Arabic Language | | | Social Studies | | | Science and Mathematics | | |
|---|---|---|---|---|---|---|---|---|---|---|
| | | 2 | 3 | 4 | 2 | 3 | 4 | 2 | 3 | 4 |
| Home Economics and Needlework (Girls) | 3 | - | - | - | - | - | - | - | - | - |
| Principles of Education and Psychology | - | - | 3 | 4 | - | 3 | 4 | - | 3 | 4 |
| Spec. Methods of Teaching | - | - | 2 | 3 | - | 2 | 3 | - | 2 | 2 |
| School and Social Hygiene | - | - | 1 | 1 | - | 1 | 1 | - | 1 | 1 |
| Practice Teaching+ | - | - | 6 | 6 | - | 6 | 6 | - | 6 | 6 |
| Art Education | - | 3 | 1 | 1 | 3 | 1 | 1 | 3 | 1 | 1 |
| Physical Education and Games | 2 | 2 | 2 | 2 | 2 | 2 | 2 | 2 | 2 | 2 |
| | 36 | 36 | 36 | 36 | 36 | 36 | 36 | 36 | 36 | 36 |

+1 full day per week is for applied education; in addition to 3 continuous weeks for the last year students in preparatory schools.

Private Teaching Diploma awarded (on successful completion of examinations).

Graduate must remain in teaching profession for a period of at least 6 years from date of receiving diploma.

## ADULT EDUCATION

Focuses on combating illiteracy.

In 1958, 150 schools in Tripolitania offering adult education courses; 20 centers established in Fezzan Province.

Presently, classes in literacy and fundamental education in more than 250 schools.

## TRAINING CENTER FOR FUNDAMENTAL EDUCATION

Established with aid of UNESCO, 1957. 1958, raised to level of a national institute for the whole of Libya.

3-year course: Adult Education, Methods of Teaching Literacy, Health and Hygiene, Rural Occupations, general cultural subjects.

## OTHER EDUCATION

State runs boarding schools for orphans and bedouin children.

## CENTERS FOR CARE OF MOTHERS AND CHILDREN

Instruction of an elementary type given in such subjects as:  Nursing, First Aid, Public Health, Contagious Diseases, Anatomy, Physiology, Obstetrics, etc.

## FOREIGN-OPERATED SCHOOLS

Franco-Libyan School, Tripoli, established 1956.

Shell Oil, Dutch School.

American petroleum companies school in Naura-Geogimpopoli, outside Tripoli.

Whellus Air Base schools for children of Base personnel, kindergarten through high school - discontinued at closing of Base.

British Army School.

57 church-oriented Italian schools.

## TRIPOLI COLLEGE

Established 1957 as an Anglo-Libyan venture.  School has added 1 Form per annum.  Kindergarten through 10th Form.

5th Form, end of Junior School (age 11).
6th, 7th, 8th, 9th and 10th Forms - "High" School:  5-year course.

Main courses offered at 6th Form:

| | |
|---|---|
| Geography | English (Language and Literature) |
| History | Arabic |
| Social Science | General Science |
| French | Mathematics (Arithmetic, Algebra, |
| Religion | Geometry) |
| Art | Needlework |
| Crafts | Physical Education |

7th Form:  Physics, Chemistry and Biology replace General Science.

8th Form:  Continues same studies.

9th Form:   Trigonometry added
            Breakdown of Physics or History
            Breakdown of Chemistry and Biology

10th Form:  At close of 10th Form all students take General Certificate of
            Education examination.

Language of instruction:  English, except for the Arabic and Islamic Religion
                          classes.

KINGDOM OF MOROCCO

Enseignement général de type marocain (Moroccan type)

Enseignement général de type Français (French type).

Medicine ** 6
Letters
Science
Law
Pol. 1st.
Socio.
Engineering
Agriculture
Statistics
Admin.

Lycée or Collège (2nd Cycle)

Higher Islamic Ed.

Teacher Train. College

Enseignement Long (Long Course) (1st Cycle)

Teacher Tr.

Enseignement Moyen (Short Course)

Continued Vocational

Cours d'observation
Cours moyen
Cours élémentaire
Préparatoire

Collège d'Enseignement Général
Collège d'Enseignement Technique

Classe d'orientation
Cours moyen
Classe Primaire
Cours élémentaire
Préparatoire

SECONDARY EDUCATION
PRIMARY EDUCATION

Nursery School

| Student's Age | Year of Schooling | | |
|---|---|---|---|
| 26 | 20 | | HIGHER EDUCATION |
| 25 | 19 | | |
| 24 | 18 | | |
| 23 | 17 | | |
| 22 | 16 | | |
| 21 | 15 | | |
| 20 | 14 | | |
| 19 | 13 | | |
| 18 | 12 | | SECONDARY |
| 17 | 11 | | |
| 16 | 10 | | |
| 15 | 9 | | |
| 14 | 8 | | |
| 13 | 7 | | |
| 12 | 6 | | |
| 11 | 5 | | ELEMENTARY |
| 10 | 4 | | |
| 9 | 3 | | |
| 8 | 2 | | |
| 7 | 1 | | |
| 6 | | | |
| 5 | | | |
| 4 | | | |
| 3 | | | |

** T 1 2 3 4 5 6 7 8 9 10 11
** 6 5 4 3 2 1 2 1 2 1

Compulsory education: 7-13 years of age (Implementation up to each school district)

School Year: October 1 – June 30

Secondary grading: 0-20

10/20 Pass Mark

(See grading for Baccalauréats under SECONDARY EDUCATION)

KINGDOM OF MOROCCO

(Royaume du Maroc)

Independence:  March 2, 1956.

## BACKGROUND

Morocco has been termed Kingdom of the West:  Al-Mamlaka al-Maghrabiya.
Thirty percent of the population live in cities and towns; one half of
the population is under 20 years of age.

Arab tribes are distributed mostly along the Atlantic coastal plain;
Berbers are in the middle plains of the Atlas, the Sous Valley, and in
northern regions of the Rif.  Approximately 395,000 Europeans live in
Morocco, one-third in Casablanca.  100,000 Jews live mainly in urban
centers.

Classical Arabic is the written and official language.  French and
Spanish are widely spoken, as is Maghribi Arabic, a Moroccan dialect.
Principal Berber dialects spoken in mountain areas by about one-third of
the people are:  Zenatiya, Tamazirt, and Tashelit.

The earliest inhabitants of Morocco were Berbers.  Invaders in ancient
times were in succession:  the Phoenicians, Carthaginians, Romans (1st
century B.C.), Vandals (5th century A.D.), and Byzantines (6th century).
682, Arabs conquered North Africa.  788, Berber tribes were united and
the Islamic faith and Arabic language were taken over.  Berbers overthrew the last Moorish dynasty in 974.

Muslim sect of Almoravids governed Morocco, 1055; conquered by Almohade
sect, 1147.  By 1269 the Marinid dynasty ruled.  This was the period
when the great mosques and colleges were built and art and philosophy
flourished.  From 1578 to 1603 th Sa'adi dynasty began a golden age.
The final dynasty, the Filali, continued to the present times.

Trade with France and other European powers was extensive during the 18th
and 19th centuries.  1844, France conquered Algerian and Moroccan armies
at Isly.  In 1860, Spain, in agreement with France, occupied north
Morocco.  April 7, 1906, the Act of Algeciras, signed by France, Spain,
Germany, the United Kingdom, the United States, and other powers established

commercial equality in Morocco and authorized a French-Spanish police force in the ports of Morocco.

1912-1956, the French and Spanish Protectorate established over Morocco was administered in 4 sections:  France governing the main portion; two portions ruled by Spain; one by an international commission.  Rif War between 1921 and 1926; Moroccans defeated by French and Spanish forces. In 1934, Plan of Reforms submitted to French government.  During World War II, on November 8, 1942, U.S. troops landed in Morocco, and from 1944-45 Moroccan troops campaigned for liberation of France.

After the war, Morocco pressed for independence.  Franco-Moroccan agreement of March 2, 1956, provided independence.  Along with the French and Spanish zones of Morocco, Tangier (formerly a British territory, later ruled by a consortium of nations in 1906, and an international zone from 1923) was incorporated into the new country.  On independence, sovereignty was given to central government, and steps were taken to begin to unify a diverse people .

Education before 1912 was conducted in Koranic schools under mosques supervised by the ancient Karouin (Qarawiyine) University Mosque, Fez, and the Ben Youssef University Mosque, Marrakesh.  Teaching was almost entirely religious:  Theology, Arabic literature, Muslim law and grammar necessary to the reading of texts, mathematics, astronomy, geography. Higher Islamic studies were also given in mosques to train the theologian, the judge in the Islamic law system (kadi), the notary and scholar (alem); this education continues today.

After 1930, modern educational practice was introduced alongside the traditional schooling.  French educational system inaugurated and European children followed metropolitan French primary and secondary school programs.

Muslim private education was established under the Protectorate, giving educational training that would prepare for French Baccalauréat, a Moroccan Baccalauréat, or train for clerkships and junior technical positions in business.  All subjects taught in Arabic;  French as a second language.

Most Moroccan Jewish children attended schools established by the Alliance Universelle Israélite, an organization recognized by the Protectorate government in 1915.  Similar to French school courses; some taught in Hebrew, others in Arabic.  Most of these schools are now being absorbed by the Ministry of Education to unify Moroccan education.

Schools at close of Protectorate:

| | |
|---|---|
| Moslem: | Primary, secondary, private. |
| European: | Primary, secondary, private. |
| Jewish: | Franco-Israelite, Universal Jewish Alliance. |
| Others: | Normal, lower technical, upper technical. |

In 1956, government began a national literacy campaign, and 10,000
voluntary instructors taught 250,000 adults to read and write.  In 1957
adult illiteracy still exceeded 85% in some areas.  In 1957, there was
a reform of secondary education:  unification ot timetables and curricula;
a new secondary teacher training school.  In 1958, a Secondary Education
Division was formed, combining Muslim and European educational services;
54 secondary schools of European or Moroccan type were established.  An
Educational Research Center was founded.

May, 1957, Moroccan and French governments signed an agreement establishing a French University and Cultural Mission (Mission Universitaire et
Culturelle Française - MUCF).  Under this agreement the French government
continues to control and operate certain elementary and secondary schools
and provide other educational services in Morocco.  1959-60, over 600 new
schools were constructed.

In 1962, all eligible children were able to enter primary school for the
first time.

In 1964 there were 1,150,000 pupils in primary schools; 130,000 in
secondary schools; 8,000 in the two Moroccan universities.

The present attempt is to make uniform the three types of state education:
national, French, Islamic, so as to give all citizens a common outlook and
abolish the "traditionalist" and "modern" differences.

In the administration of national education, Morocco is divided into 10
Ministerial "Delegations":  Beni-Mellal, Casa-Prefecture, Casa-Blanca
Province, Agadir, Marrakesh, Oujda, Fez, Meknes, Rabat, Tetouan.


## PRESENT SYSTEM


## PRE-PRIMARY EDUCATION

Nursery schools for children from 4 years of age.


## PRIMARY EDUCATION

Entry age:        6-7 years of age.  No child 14 years of age or more can
                  attend primary school (école primaire).

5-year program.

Arabic instead of French as language of instruction in the first 2 years.
Upper 3 grades, half of subjects taught in Arabic, and the other half in
French.  Greater emphasis given to purely Moroccan subjects.

In general, primary education is divided into 3 segments:

cours préparatoire (CP)          1st year.

cours élémentaire (CE)           1st year and 2nd year:  2nd and 3rd
                                 years.

cours moyen (CM)                 1st year and 2nd year:  4th and 5th
                                 years.

Classes primaires (primary classes) in connection with the French lycées
are numbered from the beginning year, 11, 10, 9, 8, 7.

Prior to 1960, Islamic education had only 3-year program.

Primary school program includes:  Arabic and French languages, Islamic
Religion, Arithmetic, Elementary Geometry, Moroccan History and Geography,
Physical Education.

As of October 1958, necessary to provide 30 hours of instruction in
classical Arabic during 1st year and 15 hours each in French or classical
Arabic for remaining years.

5-year Plan 1960-64:

    All classes in first 2 years, on half time (15 hrs. a week).
    Remaining grades, 30 hrs. a week.
    Students over 14 years of age who have already had 7 years of
        school not to be continued in primary school.
    At end of 5 years, 80% to continue in secondary education; others
        to have 2 years of terminal studies, including instruction in
        agriculture, hand crafts, housekeeping.  On graduation could
        enter public or private trade schools.

In addition to public schools, primary schools run by MUCF, Alliance
Universelle Israélite, and other special institutions.  Private Arabic-
language elementary schools.

National examination in 5th year, Certificat d'études primaires (C.E.P.).


SECONDARY EDUCATION

Entrance examination required in addition to C.E.P.:  examen d'entrée
dans les classes d'observation.  C.E.P. not administered to Arabic and
and special school students.

Four types of secondary education:

    New Moroccan Public School Education (enseignement général de type
        marocain).

Traditional French Lycée Education (<u>enseignement général de type français</u>).

Arabic School Education (traditional and modern)
   (<u>enseignement traditionnel</u> - emphasizing classical Islamic studies)
   (<u>enseignement moderne</u> - secular subjects as contrasted with the traditional).

Special Schools.

Reformed system of secondary education begun in 1957:  6 years of secondary education, divided into 2 equal cycles:  1st cycle, general education, taken by all.  2nd cycle, 5 specialized sections:

Section A - Classical Letters (Arabic and Islamic Sciences).

Section B - Modern Letters (Study of a second living language and economic and social subjects).

Section C - Science (with emphasis on Experimental Sciences).

Section D - Science (with emphasis on Mathematics).

Section E - Technical instruction.

Moslem secondary education system, by 1958:

5 provincial <u>lycées</u>.
6 <u>collèges</u> for boys.
2 <u>collèges</u> for girls.
16 <u>collèges</u> (one-half of secondary program only).

After the merger of the European schools and Moslem schools, October 1958, to form the Division of Education for the Second Degree, students were receiving education in:

13 <u>lycées</u> located in Agadir, Azrou, Casablanca, Fez, Kenitra, Marrakesh, Meknes, Oujda, Rabat, Tetuan.
17 <u>collèges</u> located in Casablanca, al-Jadida, Fez, Khouribga, Meknes, Oujda, Rabat, Settat, Sidi-Kacem, Tangier, Tetuan.
24 first-cycle <u>collèges</u> located in Alhucemas, Arcila, Beni Mellal, Berkane, Casablanca, Chaouen, al-Jadida, Al-Ksar al-Kebir, Khemisset, Kenitra, Ksar-es-Souk, Larache, Nador, Ouezzane, Safi, Sefrou, Taroudant, Taza, Marrakesh, Meknes, Oujda.

1960, Secondary Education Reform:

3 branches:

6 years of pre-university work (<u>enseignement long</u>), terminating in Moroccan <u>baccalauréat</u>.
(Under the Division of Education of the Second Degree)

6 years of commercial or industrial studies, terminating in commercial or industrial <u>brevets</u> (for middle level, commercial and industrial employment).
(Under Division of Education of the Second Degree)

3 years of training for industry, agriculture and commerce
(enseignement moyen), terminating in professional certificates.
(Under Division of Technical Education) - See program under
TECHNICAL EDUCATION.

In 1962, 7-year secondary program inaugurated.

Classe d'observation (or cours d'observation) created in October 1963,
inserted at the beginning of secondary education in which student's
abilities might be judged.  1962-63, slower students placed in classe
d'observation.  October 1963 and October 1964, best students were
admitted directly to 1st year of secondary education (50% in 1963, 33%
in 1964).  By October 1965, classe d'observation compulsory for all
lycée students.


## NEW MOROCCAN PUBLIC SECONDARY EDUCATION

Entrance requirements:          C.E.P. and examen d'entrée dans les
                                classes d'observation.

Entrance examination covers 3 subjects:  1 test in classical Arabic, 1
test in Arithmetic, 1 test in French.

7-year program, enseignement long (long course), including the classe
d'observation:

|  |  |  |
|---|---|---|
| Premier cycle<br>(1st cycle) | - Classe d'observation      )<br>- Première année secondaire )<br>- Deuxième année secondaire<br>- Troisième année secondaire | tronc commun |
| Second cycle<br>(2nd cycle) | - Quatrième année secondaire<br>- Cinquième année secondaire<br>- Sixième année secondaire | |

First cycle:    4 years of general education in line with Moroccan
                needs.

Classe d'observation:    10 hrs. Arabic, 10 hrs. French, 8 hrs. Arith-
                         metic, 2 hrs. Physical Education.


### TIMETABLE
(Hours per week)

#### 1st Cycle - Long Course

| Subjects | 1st yr. | 2nd yr. | 3rd yr. |
|---|---|---|---|
| Arabic Language  and Letters    )<br>Civic and Religious Instruction ) | 9 | 9 | 9 |

| | | | |
|---|---|---|---|
| French | 6 | 6 | 5 |
| 2nd Foreign Language | | | 5 |
| History and Geography | 3 | 3 | 3 |
| Mathematics | 6 | 6 | 5 |
| Natural Sciences | 2 | 2 | 2 |
| Drawing | 1 | 1 | 1 |
| Physical Education | 2 | 2 | 2 |
| | 29 | 29 | 32 |

<u>Certificat d'études secondaires musulmanes</u> (<u>C.E.S.M.</u>) awarded on successful examination at close of program.


<u>Second cycle</u>:     3 years.  Student specializes in a chosen field, which will determine the type of final secondary examination he will take.

Selection is made from the following programs:

Letters (lettres arabes)
Modern Letters (lettres modernes)
Experimental Sciences (sciences expérimentales)
Mathematics (mathématiques)
Economics (économique)
Industrial (industriel)    - See under VOCATIONAL AND
Commercial (commercial)    - TECHNICAL EDUCATION

French, language of instruction in Moroccan <u>lycées</u>, with exception of specifically Arabic subjects, such as Islamic Religion, Arabic languages, Grammar and History.  30 hrs. a week.

1st cycle, 9 hrs. in Arabic.  2nd cycle, 4 hrs. (except in courses specializing in Arabic Literature, 10 hrs.).

3rd language begun in 3rd year.  Students studying 3 languages by their 3rd year:  Classical Arabic, French, and the "first" foreign language - English (preferred), Spanish or German.


<u>TIMETABLE</u>
(Hours per week)

2nd Cycle - Long Course

| Subjects | 4th yr. | 5th yr. | 6th yr. |
|---|---|---|---|
| LETTRES ORIGINELLES (L.O.) | | | |
| Arabic Language and Letters    )<br>Civic and Religious Instruction ) | 12 | 12 | 11 |
| French | 5 | 5 | 3 |
| 2nd Foreign Language | 4 | 4 | 3 |

| LETTRES ORIGINELLES (L.O.) - cont'd | 4th yr. | 5th yr. | 6th yr. |
|---|---|---|---|
| History and Geography | 4 | 4 | 4 |
| General Philosophy | | | 6 |
| Islamic Thought | | | 1 |
| Mathematics | 2 | 2 | |
| Physics and Chemistry | 2 | 2 | 2 |
| Natural Sciences | | 1 | |
| Physical Education | 2 | 2 | 2 |
| | 31 | 32 | 32 |

LETTRES MODERNES (L.M.)

| | 4th yr. | 5th yr. | 6th yr. |
|---|---|---|---|
| Arabic Language and Letters )<br>Civic and Religious Instruction ) | 9 | 9 | 7 |
| French | 6 | 5 | 4 |
| 2nd Foreign Language | 5 | 5 | 4 |
| History and Geography | 5 | 5 | 5 |
| General Philosophy | | | 7 |
| Islamic Thought | | | 1 |
| Mathematics | 2 | 2 | 2 |
| Physics and Chemistry | 2 | 2 | |
| Natural Sciences | | 1 | |
| Physical Education | 2 | 2 | 2 |
| | 31 | 31 | 32 |

SCIENCES EXPERIMENTALES (S.E.)

| | 4th yr. | 5th yr. | 6th yr. |
|---|---|---|---|
| Arabic Language and Letters )<br>Civic and Religious Instruction ) | 5 | 4 | 2 |
| French | 4 | 3 | |
| 2nd Foreign Language | 3 | 3 | 2 |
| History and Geography | 2 | 2 | 2 |
| General Philosophy | | | 3 |
| Islamic Thought | | | 1 |
| Mathematics | 6 | 6 | 8 |
| Physics and Chemistry )<br>Mechanics and Electricity ) | 6 | 6 | 8 |
| Natural Sciences | 2½ | 3 | 4 |
| Drawing | 1 | 1 | |
| Physical Education | 2 | 2 | 2 |
| | 31½ | 30 | 32 |

MATHEMATIQUES (S.M.)

| | 4th yr. | 5th yr. | 6th yr. |
|---|---|---|---|
| Arabic Language and Literature )<br>Civic and Religious Instruction ) | 4 | 4 | 2 |
| French | 4 | 3 | |
| 2nd Foreign Language | 3 | 3 | 2 |
| History and Geography | 2 | 2 | 2 |
| General Philosophy | | | 2 |
| Islamic Thought | | | 1 |

| MATHEMATIQUES (S.M.) - cont'd | 4th yr. | 5th yr. | 6th yr. |
|---|---|---|---|
| Mathematics | 8 | 8 | 11 |
| Physics and Chemistry ) Mechanics and Electricity ) | 6 | 6 | 8 |
| Natural Sciences | | 1 | |
| Graphic Theory and Technique | 3 | 3 | 3 |
| Physical Education | 2 | 2 | 2 |
| | 32 | 32 | 33 |

ECONOMIQUE (E.)

| | 4th yr. | 5th yr. | 6th yr. |
|---|---|---|---|
| Arabic Language and Literature ) Civic and Religious Instruction ) | 5 | 5 | 3 |
| French | 4 | 4 | 2 |
| 2nd Foreign Language | 4 | 4 | 3 |
| History and Geography | 5 | 5 | 5 |
| General Philosophy | | | 4 |
| Islamic Thought | | | 1 |
| Mathematics | 6 | 4 | 4 |
| Physics and Chemistry | 3 | 3 | 2 |
| Natural Sciences | | 2 | 2 |
| Merchandising | 1 | 1 | |
| Introductory Economics ) Political Economy ) | 2 | 2 | 2 |
| Law | | | 2 |
| Typing in French | | 1 | 1 |
| Physical Education | 2 | 2 | 2 |
| | 32 | 33 | 33 |

At the close of the 2nd cycle a student takes an examination for the Moroccan Baccalaureate (Baccalauréat Marocain).  Failing in June, he may take the examination again in October.

Moroccan Baccalaureate examination:

  As of June 1963, 5 programs (séries), formerly 3:

  Letters (originelles)
  Modern Letters
  Mathematics
  Experimental Sciences
  Economics

In addition to written examinations, each program has orals in 2 foreign languages (with a coefficient of 2 for each).

To compute the average grade of a baccalaureate examination, a coefficient (fixed according to the importance of the subject) is used to multiply the grade earned by the student in that subject.  The sum of the multiplications of earned grades is divided by the sum of the coefficients.

Grading scale:

16, 17, 18, 19, 20 - Très Bien (very good)
14, 15          - Bien (good)
12, 13          - Assez Bien (above average)
10, 11          - Passable (pass)

| Coefficients | Letters (Originelles) | Modern Letters | Mathematics | Experimental Sciences | Economics |
|---|---|---|---|---|---|
| Islamic Law | 6 | | | | |
| Arabic Dissertation | 4 | 6 | | | |
| 1st Foreign Lang. | 2 | 4 | | | 2 |
| 2nd Foreign Lang. | 2 | 3 | 2 | 2 | 3 |
| Philosophy | 5 | 6 | 2 | 2 | 2 |
| History-Geography | 3 | 3 | 2 | 2 | 3 |
| Physics-Chemistry | 2 | | 6 | 6 | 2 |
| Arabic | | | 2 | 2 | 4 |
| Mathematics | | 2 | 8 | 6 | 5 |
| Technical Drawing | | | 3 | | |
| Natural Science | | | | 6 | |
| Elementary Economics | | | | | 3 |

(For an example of the use of coefficients in computing Baccalaureate grade, see following section, FRENCH LYCEE EDUCATION.)

**On completion of successful examinations, student awarded Moroccan Baccalaureate (Baccalauréat Marocain). The University of Rabat controls the baccalaureate examination. French authorities have recognized the Moroccan Baccalaureate as equivalent to the former examen probatoire de fin de classe (previously French Baccalaureate Part I).

Courses in Economics, Business and Social Science in certain lycées lead to specialized baccalauréat diplomas.

3-year short course (enseignement moyen), prefaced by the classe d'observation, has 6 sections: general, commercial, agricultural, industrial masculine, industrial feminine, normal. (For sample programs, see VOCATIONAL AND TECHNICAL EDUCATION.)

FRENCH LYCEE EDUCATION

7-year program, 2 cycles.

Language of instruction:      French throughout.

2 main categories of French lycées: Standard and Technical.

     Standard lycées:      Prepare students for university.
                                2 main programs:
                                (1) Classical, featuring Latin and Greek.

(2)   Modern, featuring classical Arabic,
      colloquial Arabic.  (Most Moroccans choose
      modern program, with classical Arabic as
      1st language, begun in 1st year.  2nd
      language begun in 3rd year.)

Technical lycées:   Prepare students for employment or higher
                    technical training.  1st and 2nd grades known
                    as "orientation classes."
                    5 more years ending in technical baccalaureate.
                    (For program description, see VOCATIONAL AND
                    TECHNICAL EDUCATION.)


## MUCF-controlled Lycées:

Lycée Descartes, Rabat
Lycée Gourand, Rabat
Lycée Lyautey, Casablanca
Lycée Technique, Casablanca
Lycée Paul Valéry, Meknes
Lycée de  Jeunes Filles, Oujda
Lycée Victor Hugo, Marrakesh
Lycée Regnault, Tangier
Lycée Mixte, Fez


## Moroccan Public Secondary Schools with French Lycée Programs:

Lycée de  Jeunes Filles (Lalla Aicha), Rabat
Lycée Omar Khayam, Rabat
Lycée El Laymoune, Rabat
Lycée Abdel Malek As-Saadi, Kenitra
Lycée Moulay Ismale, Meknes
Lycée Moulay Sliman, Fez
Lycée Mixte de Khouribga
Collège de Souk El Arba du Gharb
Lycée Omar Ibn el Aziz, Oujda
Lycée Al Khawaizmy, Casablanca
Collège Ibn Toumert, Casablanca
Lycée de  Jeunes Filles, Casablanca
Lycée Ibn Khaldoun, El Jadida
Collège Idrissi, Safi
Lycée Ibn Abbas, Marrakesh
Lycée Youssef ben Tachfin, Agadir


## Program of Standard lycées:

First cycle    - 4 years.  Concludes with national examination,
                 Brevet d'études du premier cycle (B.E.P.C.).

Particularly important for those students not
continuing further education since it opens the
way to technical schools and to lower level
administrative jobs.

Second cycle   - 3 years.  Concludes with Baccalauréat de l'enseignement secondaire.  Examinations given at close of
2nd and 3rd years.
In the final year of study, student chooses one of
three fields for specialization:
(a)  Philosophy (Humanities)
(b)  Experimental Sciences
(c)  Mathematics

Baccalaureate examinations:   Both written and oral.

Up to 1965, at close of 6 years of secondary study, a student took the
first baccalaureate examination:  called Part I up to 1962, became
probationary examination (examen probatoire de fin de classe) to 1965
and was then suppressed.  Examination covered Mathematics, Physics-
Chemistry, French, 1st foreign language, 2nd foreign language, Physical
Education.

A student failing the written examination (less than 10/20) but receiving a minimum of 7/20 was required to sit for the oral examination.  If
he failed the oral examination he might try again.  If successful, he
might start the final lycée year.

** For the final baccalauréat (called Part II up to 1965), the student is
examined in all subjects, but the marks in his field of specialization
carry more weight in the final grade.

Grading scale for baccalaureate examinations:

| | |
|---|---|
| 10, 11 | Passable (pass) |
| 12, 13, 14 | Assez Bien (above average) |
| 15, 16, 17 | Bien (good) |
| 18, 19, 20 | (Très Bien (very good) |

Variance in coefficients (between former Bac. Part I and examen
probatoire):

| Subjects | Former Bac. Part I | Examen Probatoire |
|---|---|---|
| French | 6 | 4 |
| Mathematics | 8 | 4 |
| Sciences | 7 | 4 |
| History and Geography | 3 | 2 |
| 1st Foreign Language | | |
| - Written | 2 | 2 |
| - Oral | 2 | 1 |
| 2nd Foreign Language | 3 | 2 |
| Physical Education | 1 | 1 |

Example of the use of coefficients in computing over-all grade:

| Subjects | Grade | | Coefficient | | Product | Average |
|----------|-------|---|-------------|---|---------|---------|
| French | 15 | x | 4 | = | 60 | |
| Mathematics | 11 | x | 4 | = | 44 | |
| Sciences | 13 | x | 4 | = | 52 | |
| History and Geography | 12 | x | 2 | = | 24 | |
| 1st Foreign Language | 14 | x | 3 | = | 42 | |
| 2nd Foreign Language | 13 | x | 2 | = | 26 | |
| Physical Education | 12 | x | 1 | = | 12 | |
| | | | 20 | | 260 | 13 |

Coefficients for final Baccalaureate:

| Subjects | Philosophy | Mathematics | Experimental Sciences |
|----------|------------|-------------|-----------------------|
| Philosophy | 7 | 5 | 4 |
| Physics-Chemistry | 3 | 7 | 4 |
| Mathematics | 1 | 8 | 4 |
| Natural Sciences | 2 | 2 | 4 |
| History-Geography | 3 | 3 | 3 |
| 1st Foreign Language | 2 | 2 | 2 |
| Physical Education | 1 | 1 | 1 |

## ARABIC SCHOOL EDUCATION

Traditional education being given modern content.

Children from 5 years up attend Koranic schools (msids).

Old system:     3 cycles.

        1st cycle:     3 years with first degree certificate (Taoural-Aouel).

        2nd cycle:     4 years with certificate of first degree; at close of 6th year, certificate of 2nd degree

        3rd cycle:     Arts Section )  3 years ending with higher
                         Law Section  )  diploma (alemiya)

Reform:     1st cycle - 5-year course to replace 3-year.
Establishment of rural schools.
1960 Plan that eventually all primary students to be enrolled in regular state system.

Reform, secondary level:

        6-year course divided in 2 phases.

        General culture - 3 years.

3-year pre-specialization:
   Literary Section, preparing for Faculty of Letters.
   Juridical Section, preparing for Faculty of Law and
      Sharia Faculty.
   Scientific Section, preparing for Faculty of Sciences
      and future Faculty of Medicine.

Transitional program created October, 1959, for final year of training for entrance to University of Rabat. Not considered necessary by 1964, when Baccalaureate was awarded at successful completion of all secondary studies.

Private schools offering a first cycle secondary program were established by late 1940's following the French lycée pattern but with instruction entirely in Arabic. After 1956 independence, 2nd cycle program offered, terminating in a Baccalaureate in Arabic. The 4 lycées with this program are:

   Lycée Mohammed V, Rabat
   Lycée Baladia, Casablanca
   Lycée El Azhar, Casablanca
   Lycée Nahda, Sale

Many Moroccan public secondary schools have now begun to offer an Arabic section with instruction entirely in Arabic; these sections are called enseignement originel. Arabic language Baccalaureate certificates are certified by the University of Rabat.


## SPECIAL SCHOOLS

In addition to the schools of the Alliance Universelle Israélite, now being unified with the Moroccan educational system, there are several foreign schools in Tangier: Spanish elementary school; Italian lycées; and the American School of Tangier (private, incorporated under the State of Delaware), offering kindergarten and 12 grades.

Also, several American elementary and high schools on military bases in Morocco.


## HIGHER EDUCATION

### UNIVERSITY OF MOHAMMED V, Rabat

The University, established December 21, 1959, brought together the Institute of Advanced Moroccan Studies, founded 1912, the Center of Legal Studies at Rabat, founded 1920, and the Faculty of Science, inaugurated 1940.

Faculties:

>   Faculté des Lettres et des Sciences Humaines (Humanities)
>   Faculté des Sciences Juridiques, Economiques et Sociales (Law)
>   Faculté des Sciences Mathématiques, Physiques et Naturelles
>       (Sciences)
>   Faculté de Médecine et de Pharmacie (Medicine and Pharmacy)

Also forming part of the University are the following Institutes and
Schools:

>   Institut d'Etudes Politiques
>   Institut de Sociologie
>   Ecole Mohammadia d'Ingénieurs
>   Ecole Marocaine d'Administration
>   Ecole des Statistiques
>   Ecole Normale Supérieure

Entrance requirements:          Baccalauréat or equivalent diploma.

There is a preparatory year required for entrance to the Faculties of
Letters, Sciences, and Medicine: année propédeutique.  The Faculty of
Law is the exception where students who hold the baccalauréat or an
equivalent diploma can register directly in its first year.

The courses of the program of the propédeutique are generally taken in
the lycées rather than in the faculties where only the licences, the
diploma of higher studies (D.E.S.) and the doctorat degrees are prepared.

After each successful university year, a Certificat d'études supérieures
is awarded.  With requisite number of certificates, student is awarded
degree of licence in his specialization.  Examination at close of each
year; student must pass to be eligible for further study.

Post-graduate degree of Diplôme d'études supérieures (D.E.S.) after
successful completion of 2 years of post-licence study.  Doctorat after
at least 3 years of study after diplôme.  M.D. awarded after 6 years of
study, comprising the preparatory year and a 5-year program.


Faculté des Lettres et des Sciences Humaines

Under Protectorate known as Institut des Hautes Etudes Marocaines
(I.H.E.M.).  Highest diploma available was Diplôme d'arabe classique
after 2 years of study.

First year of preparatory studies: année propédeutique.  Subsequently,
students must prepare 3 certificates out of 5 in their fields of study.

Faculty prepares for the following diplomas:

> Licence ès lettres:  3 years.
> Diplôme d'études supérieures ès lettres (D.E.S.):  2 years
>     after licence.
> Doctorat ès lettres:  3 years after D.E.S.

Diplomas in the following areas:

| | |
|---|---|
| History | Arabic Literature |
| Geography | French Literature |
| Philosophy | English Literature |
| | Spanish Literature |

Previous to 1963 the Faculty had a French program, controlled and staffed
by the University of Bordeaux, offering Philosophy, Literature, History
and Geography.  Program required 4 certificats for the licence, including
a preparatory year (année propédeutique).  The Moroccan program only
required 3 certificats.


## Faculté des Sciences Juridiques, Economiques et Sociales (Faculté de Droit)

Branches in Fez and Casablanca.

Faculty prepares for the following diplomas:

(1)  Legal Sciences (Sciences Juridiques)

> Licence en sciences juridiques:  3 years.
> Diplôme d'études supérieures en sciences juridiques:  2 years
>     after the licence.
> Doctorat en sciences juridiques:  3 years at least after the
>     diplôme.

(2)  Economic Sciences (Sciences Economiques)

> Licence en sciences économiques:  3 years.
> Diplôme d'études supérieures en sciences économiques:  2 years
>     after the licence.
> Doctorat en sciences économiques:  3 years after the D.E.S.

Capacité en droit diploma:       Non-university level, 2-year course for
                                 graduates of first secondary school cycle.
                                 Arabic and French sections.  Graduates
                                 eligible for clerical work in offices of
                                 lawyers and notaries public.

Faculté des Sciences Mathématiques, Physiques et Naturelles

First year of preparatory studies: année propédeutique. Subsequently, students must prepare 3 certificates out of 5 for their fields of study.

Faculty prepares for the following diplomas:

>   Licence ès sciences: 3 years.
>   Diplôme d'études supérieures ès sciences: 2 years after the
>       licence.
>   Doctorat ès sciences: 3 years after the D.E.S.

Each diploma includes the fields: Physics, Mathematics, Natural Sciences.

Certificates awarded in:

| | |
|---|---|
| Algebra | Zoology |
| Mathematics I and II | Animal Physiology |
| General Mechanics | General Biology |
| Mathematic Techniques of | Botany |
|    Physics, Electricity, | General Geology |
|    Electronics, Optics | Historical Geology |
| Thermodynamics | Vegetable Biochemistry |
| Organic Chemistry | Microbiology |
| Systematic Chemistry | Physiology |
| General Chemistry I and II | |

Candidates prepared for the following teaching degrees:

>   Mathematics
>   Physics I
>   Chemistry
>   Natural Sciences (Biological Sciences)
>   Natural Sciences (Earth Sciences)

2 Research Institutes attached to Faculty of Sciences:

Sharifian Scientific Institute

>   Conducts research in Zoology, Entomology, Flowering and Flowerless Plants, Physical Geography, Geology and Paleontology.

Institute of Terrestrial Physics and Meteorology

>   Conducts research in Geophysics, Terrestrial Magnetism, Seismology, Meteorology, Ocean Swells and the Ionosphere.

## Faculté de Médecine et de Pharmacie

Inaugurated in 1962.  Previously students with first 4 years completed in France returned to Morocco for 5th and 6th years at a Casablanca Hospital.  1963, 1st year preparing for French degrees.

First year of preparatory studies:  année propédeutique.  Subsequent 5-year program.

Pre-medical:  2 semesters.

    Examination A - Physics, Chemistry, Biology.
    Examination B - Anatomy and Histology.

## Docteur en médecine (M.D.)

6 years.

Pharmacy program being planned.

## Institut d'Etudes Politiques

Allied to Faculty of Law.

Institute offers the following diplomas:

    Licence ès sciences politiques:  3 years.
    Diplôme d'études supérieures ès sciences politiques:  2 years after licence.
    Doctorat ès sciences politiques:  3 years at least after D.E.S.

Institute has 2 divisions:

## Centre d'Etudes de Développement Economique et Social (C.E.D.E.S.), in Rabat and Casablanca

Study Center for Economic and Social Development.

Entrance requirements:  Baccalauréat, or special examination.

2-year course, dealing with economic and sociological subjects with reference to developing countries.  Students mostly high officials of Ministries, senior grade army officers, etc.

## Centre de Préparation à l'Administration (C.P.A.E.), Casablanca

Training Center for Business Management.

Entrance requirements:    Licence en droit, a diplôme of one of the Grandes Ecoles de France (university level technical schools), or pass a special entrance examination.

2-year course, study of business management for private and public corporations.  The certificat which the school issues after a final examination, to those entering with a licence or a diplôme, is recognized in France.

Students entering C.P.A.E. by examination (if they have neither a licence in law nor a diploma from a Grande Ecole in France) at the close of 2 years of study and final examination will receive a brevet.

Students may also attend lectures without registration.  They do not qualify for examinations or diplomas.


## Institut de Sociologie

Offers a program to students who are registered in the Faculty of Law or Faculty of Letters.

First 3-year program, 1964-65.  2 sections:  French and Arabic Languages.

Licence awarded:  3 certificats.


## Ecole Marocaine d'Administration

Under the supervision of the Ministry of Civil Service, for the purpose of the formation of Moroccan civil servants.

Entrance requirements:    Baccalauréat, or competitive examination for students and government employees who have reached the baccalauréat level.

3-year program, with annual examinations.

Diplôme de l'Ecole Nationale d'Administration awarded.


## Ecole Mohammadia d'Ingénieurs

Founded in 1960 with help of UNESCO.  Integrated into University, 1962. First graduating class, June 1964.  Begun in 1959 as the Ecole Préparatoire d'Ingénieurs (E.P.I.) to prepare the first pupils for the future Ecole Mohammadia. The E.P.I. gave 4 years' secondary study (3rd, 2nd, 1st and terminal classes). Pupils sat for the Baccalauréat mathématiques. Program: based essentially on Mathematics (16 hrs. per week), Physics and Chemistry (12 hrs. per week) and Industrial Design. The first pupils of the Ecole Mohammadia d'Ingénieurs (E.M.I.) were all graduates of E.P.I.

Entrance requirements:  Baccalauréat mathématiques or technique.
          From October 1964 entry examination for
          holders of Baccalauréat mathématiques only.
          Must have excellent knowledge of French.
          16-20 years.

4 sections:  Public Works, Mines, Electro-technology, Mechanics
      (Architecture planned).
      In each, laboratory and workshop practice each day.

Originally 3-year program (40 hrs. per week) envisaged, then increased to 4-year program (42 hrs. per week).

1st yr: General orientation year concentrating on Special Mathematics. At end of the year, 2-month period spend in industry, the mines or construction yards for career orientation (stage de vocation).

### WEEKLY TIMETABLE - 1st YEAR

| Subjects | Hours |
|---|---|
| English | 2 |
| Arabic | 1 |
| Mathematics | 8 |
| Physics - Electricity | 2 |
|    Thermodynamics | 1 |
|    Geometric Optics | 1 |
| Chemistry | 2 |
| General Mechanics | 2 |
| Material Resistances | 1 |
| Descriptive Geometry | 1 |
| Manufacturing Technology | 1 |
| Technical Design and | |
|   Construction Technology | 6 |
| Lab. work - Physics | 1½ |
|     Chemistry | 1½ |
| Workshop | 4 |

2nd yr: First year of specialization. 2-month training period taken abroad, particularly in France, at end of the year (stage de confirmation).

3rd yr:    Practical and specialized instruction now more important than
           theory.  2-month period at end of year organized by students
           themselves, in Morocco or abroad, in the chosen field.

4th yr:    Last year concentrated on projects, economic studies,
           industrial law, social questions, role of the man in charge,
           etc.  Within 6 months of graduation and being employed, a
           thesis must be presented on some aspect of the business the
           student is employed in.  If successful, candidate receives
           the Diplôme d'ingénieur d'état.

## TIMETABLES - 2nd, 3rd, 4th YEARS

| Public Works | 2nd yr. | 3rd yr. | 4th yr. |
|---|---|---|---|
| Economic Sciences | 1 | - | - |
| Industrial Legislation | - | - | 1 |
| O.S.T. | - | 1 | 1 |
| English | 2 | 2 | 2 |
| Arabic | 2 | 1 | - |
| Mathematics | 4 | 2 | - |
| Rational Mechanics | 2 | 1 | - |
| Fluid Mechanics | 2 | 1 | - |
| Oscillatory Physics | 1 | - | - |
| Electronics | - | 1 | 1 |
| Electrotechnology | 2 | 2 | - |
| Graphic and Graphstatistical Integration-Diagrams | 2 | - | - |
| Material Resistances | 4 | 2 | 2 |
| General and Applied Geology | - | 2 | 2 |
| Construction Materials | 2 | - | - |
| Hydraulics and Hydrology | 2 | 2 | 2 |
| Ground Mechanics | - | 2 | - |
| Reinforced Concrete | - | 2 | 2 |
| Metal Construction - Bridges | - | 2 | 3 |
| Roads and Embankings | 2 | 2 | - |
| Bridges in Reinforced Concrete | - | - | 2 |
| Railways | - | - | 2 |
| Maritime Works | - | - | 2 |
| General Construction Procedures | - | 2 | - |
| Topography | 2 | 2 | - |
| Air Bases | - | - | 1 |
| Architecture and Urbanism | 4 | 2+2 | 2+3 |
| Supervised Projects | 4 | - | 6 |
| Practical Work - Ground Mechanics | - | 4 | - |
| Geology | - | 1 | - |
| Topography | 2 | - | - |
| Electrotechnology | - | 2 | 2 |

| Mines | 2nd yr. | 3rd yr. | 4th yr. |
|---|---|---|---|
| Economic Sciences | 1 | - | - |
| Industrial Legislation | - | - | 2 |
| O.S.T. | - | 1 | 1 |
| English | 2 | 2 | 2 |
| Arabic | 1 | 1 | - |
| Mathematics | 4 | 2 | - |
| Rational Mechanics | 2 | 2 | - |
| Fluid Mechanics, Applied Hydraulics | - | 1 | - |
| Oscillatory Physics | 1 | - | - |
| Thermodynamics and Thermal Machines | - | 2 | - |
| Material Resistances | 2 | 2 | - |
| Chemistry | 2 | 1 | - |
| Electronics | - | 1 | 1 |
| Electrotechnology | 2 | 2 | - |
| Crystallography | 1 | - | - |
| Mineralogy | 1 | - | - |
| Petrography | 1 | - | - |
| Tectonics and Stratigraphy | - | 1 | - |
| General Geology | 2 | - | - |
| Applied Geology | - | 1 | 1 |
| Moroccan Geology | - | - | 2 |
| Preparation of Ores | - | 2 | - |
| General Metallurgy | 2 | - | - |
| Iron Metallurgy | - | 2 | 2 |
| Specialized Metallurgy | - | - | 2 |
| Exploitation of Mines | 4 | 6 | 4 |
| Mine Machinery | - | 1 | - |
| Topography | 2 | 1 | 1 |
| Mining Legislation and Economy | - | - | 2 |
| Business Management and Statistics | - | - | 1 |
| Chemical Engineering | - | - | 1 |
| Lab. Work - Chemistry | 1 | 1 | - |
| Metallurgy | 1 | 1 | 2 |
| Mineralogy/Petrography | 2 | - | - |
| Preparation of Ores | - | 1 | - |
| Crystallography - Practical Work | 1 | - | - |
| Practicals, Workshops, etc. | | | |
| - Topography | 1 | 1 | 1 |
| Exploitation of Mines | 2 | 4 | 10 |
| Electrical, Mechanical and Thermal Workshops | 2 | 2 | - |
| Geology | - | - | - |
| | | | |
| Mechanics | | | |
| Economic Sciences | 1 | - | - |
| Industrial Legislation | - | - | 1 |
| O.S.T. | - | 1 | 1 |

| Mechanics (cont'd) | 2nd yr. | 3rd yr. | 4th yr. |
|---|---|---|---|
| English | 1 | 2 | 2 |
| Arabic | 1 | 1 | - |
| Mathematics | 4 | 2 | 1 |
| Rational Mechanics | 2 | 2 | - |
| Fluid Mechanics | 2 | - | - |
| Oscillatory Physics | 1 | - | - |
| Thermodynamics, Thermal Machines | 1 | - | 2 |
| Material Resistances | 3 | 2 | 1 |
| Applied Hydraulics, Hydraulic Machines | - | 2 | 2 |
| Chemistry | 1 | - | - |
| Electronics | - | 1 | - |
| Electrotechnology | 2 | 2 | 2 |
| Aerodynamics | - | - | 1 |
| Metal Physics | ½ | ½ | - |
| Metallurgy and Iron Metallurgy | ½ | 1 | 1 |
| Technology of Elaboration | 1 | 1 | - |
| Technology of Execution | 1 | - | - |
| Design and Projects | 4 | 4 | 6 |
| Graphic and Graphstatistical Integration, Diagrams | 2 | | |
| Mechanical Constructions, Machine Device Calculations, Lifting Devices | 2 | 2 | 1 |
| Machine-Tools | - | 1 | - |
| Machinery with Alternative Movements: | | | |
|   Applied Cinematics | - | 1 | - |
|   Piston Machinery | - | 1 | - |
| Industrial Heating | - | 1 | - |
| Turbo-Machines with Compressible Fluids | - | 1 | - |
| Turbo-Compressors | - | - | 2 |
| Internal Combustion and Explosive Motors | - | - | 1 |
| Metallic Constructions | - | - | 2 |
| Construction, Installation and Organization of Factories | - | - | 1 |
| Servomechanics | - | - | 1 |
| Locomotive Rolling Stock | - | - | 8 1-hr. lessons |
| Physics of Elastic Vibrations | - | - | 1 |
| Lab. Work - Metallurgy | 1 | 1 | 1 |
|         Industrial Electricity | 2 | 1 | 2 |
|         Electronics | - | - | 2 |
|         Thermics and Machine Testing | - | 2 | 1 |
|         Metrology | 1 | 1 | 1 |
| Workshops - Electrical Applications and Installations | 2 | 1 | 2 |
|         Mechanics | 4 | 4 | 4 |

| Electro-Technology | 2nd yr. | 3rd yr. | 4th yr. |
|---|---|---|---|
| Economic Sciences | 1 | - | - |
| Industrial Legislation | - | - | 1 |
| O.S.T. | - | 1 | 1 |
| English | 1 | 2 | 2 |
| Arabic | 2 | 1 | - |
| Mathematics | 4 | 3 | 1 |
| Rational Mechanics | 2 | 1 | - |
| Material Resistances | 2 | 2 | - |
| Oscillatory Physics | 1 | - | - |
| Thermodynamics, Thermal Machines | - | 1 | 1 |
| Chemistry | 1 | - | - |
| Metallurgy | - | 1 | - |
| Fluid Mechanics, Applied Hydraulics | - | 1 | 1 |
| Turbines | - | - | 1 |
| Electrotechnology | 3 | 4 | 3 |
| Electrical Measures | 2 | 1 | - |
| Machine Testing | - | 2 | 2 |
| Electrical Equipment | 2 | - | - |
| Electrical Machine Construction | - | 2 | 4 |
| Plans | 2 | 2 | - |
| Electronics | 2 | 2 | - |
| Industrial Electronics | - | - | 2 |
| Servomechanisms | - | - | 1 |
| Nuclear Physics | - | - | 1 |
| Feeble Currents (Telephony) | - | - | 1 |
| Production and Distribution of Electricity | - | - | 1 |
| Electro-Chemistry, Electrometallurgy | - | - | 1 |
| Telecommunications | - | - | 1 |
| Diverse Applications | - | - | 2 |
| Projects, Reports | weekly | weekly | 4 |
| Electrical Traction | - | - | 15 1-hr. lessons |
| Physics of Elastic Vibrations | - | - | 1 |
| Lab. Work - Electrical Measures | 2 | 2 | 2 |
|     Electronics | 2 | 2 | 2 |
|     Heavy Machines | 4 | 4 | 2 |
| | | (6 sessions given to chemistry) | |
|     Metrology | - | - | 2 |
|     Chemistry | - | 6 4-hr. sessions | - |
| Workshops - Electricity | 4 | 2 | 2 |
|     Mechanics | 2 | 2 | - |

Grading:  Average of 12/20 to pass into each higher year.  Only the
          principal specialist subjects examined at end of each
          specialist year.  These examination grades plus grades during
          the year of these subjects and grades during the year of all
          other subjects taken to find average grade for the whole year.

          Examinations are given again in October for those with any
          subjects below 10/20 (if average 12/20 or more).

          13/20 average is required in final examination as an average
          over the whole 4 years to be awarded Diplôme d'ingénieur.

Certificates awarded:

          Diplôme d'ingénieur        - 4 years plus 6 months in industry
                                       with a thesis.
          Diplôme d'ancien élève     - Awarded if final average is between
                                       12/20 and 13/20.
          Certificat de scolarité    - Awarded if final average is between
                                       11/20 and 12/20.

Holders of the Diplôme d'ancien élève and the Certificat de scolarité may
sit for the general 4th-year examination twice more (consecutively or non-
consecutively) in order to gain a Diplôme d'ingénieur.


## Institut National de Statistique et d'Economie Appliquée

Prepares engineers (noted in first division) and technical assistants
(noted in second division) in statistics.

Entrance requirements:                    First division: Baccalauréat (séries
                                          mathématiques, or sciences experimen-
                                          tales, or mathématiques et technique),
                                          or equivalent.
                                          Second division:  Competitive examina-
                                          tion for those having completed the
                                          5th year of secondary studies, séries
                                          mathématiques or sciences expérimentales.

First division (applied engineering):  3-year program.  First 2 years, 28
   hours of courses with examinations, weekly.  Third year, 25 hours of
   courses with examinations and group work.
Diplôme d'ingénieur d'application awarded.

Second division:  1-year program.  30 hours of courses with examinations, weekly.
Diplôme d'adjoint technique de la statistique awarded.


## Ecole Nationale d'Agriculture

Entrance requirements:            Baccalauréat.

4-year program.
Diploma of Engineer in Agriculture awarded.

QARAWIYINE (Al-Quarawiyin or El-Quaraouiyyine) UNIVERSITY, Fez

Higher Islamic education.  Ancient Moroccan university, founded in 859
by a lady named Fatima Oumm El Banine.  Oldest in the world.

During the Middle Ages students from Europe came to study Medicine,
Science, and Letters.  Up to the 1930's the university was still employing the old master-disciple system of teaching.

Reorganization of university-level studies begun in 1960 with establishment of Faculty of Ec-Charia (Islamic Law) in Fez.  First licence awarded
in 1963.

In October 1963, Moroccan government reorganized the institution into a
modern university under the direct supervision of the Ministry of
National Education and added 2 faculties.  Faculties now are:

>           Faculty of El-Chaira (Islamic Law), Fez
>           Faculty of Arabic Studies, Marrakesh (dealing with the source
>              of Islamic Law)
>           Faculty of Ossol Din (Theology), Tetuan

Entrance requirements:        Baccalauréat or equivalent.

Each faculty offers 4 degrees:

>           El Ijaza supérieur (3 years of studies, licence)
>           Takhsis (2 years of study after El Ijaza, diploma of higher
>              studies)
>           Alimia (Ph.D. of the university)
>           Alimia (Ph.D. of the State)


OTHER HIGHER ISLAMIC EDUCATION

Offered at Ben Youssef University, Marrakesh, and Islamic Studies
Centers in Tetuan, Meknes, Taroudant, al-Jadida, Chaouen, Nador,
Alhucemas, Larache, and Al-Ksar al-Kebir.


VOCATIONAL AND TECHNICAL EDUCATION

ENSEIGNEMENT MOYEN (Short course - vocational)

3-year middle course, based on the classe d'observation.

Moroccan

6 sections:

> General - qualifies to enter regional teacher training colleges for
> primary education.  Use of Arabic as language of
> instruction.
> Industrial (masculine)
> Industrial (feminine)
> Commercial
> Agriculture
> Normal

## TIMETABLE
### (Hours per week)

INDUSTRIAL (Masculine)

| Subjects | 1st yr. | 2nd yr. | 3rd yr. | 4th yr. |
|---|---|---|---|---|
| Arabic | 5 | 4 | 4 | 1 |
| French | 5 | 3 | 2½ | 1 |
| History and Geography | 2 | 2 | 2 | - |
| Mathematics | 5 | 3 | 3 | 2 |
| Physics/Chemistry | 2 | 2 | - | - |
| Mechanics/Electricity | - | 1 | 3 | 2 |
| Natural Sciences | 1 | - | - | - |
| Physical Education | 2 | 2 | 2 | - |
| Law | - | - | ½ | - |
| Practical Work | 13 | 18 | 18 | 24 |
| Industrial Drawing | 4 | 4 | 4 | 3 |
| Technology | 1 | 1 | 1 | 3 |
| Directed Activities | - | - | - | 4 |
|  | 40 | 40 | 40 | 40 |

INDUSTRIAL (Feminine)

| Subjects | 1st yr. | 2nd yr. | 3rd yr.+ Dressmak. | Hairdress. | Combined |
|---|---|---|---|---|---|
| Arabic | 5 | 4 | 4 | 4 | 4 |
| French | 5 | 3 | 2½ | 2½ | 2½ |
| History and Geography | 2 | 2 | 1 | 1 | 1 |
| Mathematics | 5 | 3 | 2 | 2 | 2 |
| Natural Sciences, Anatomy, Hygiene | 1 | 1 | ½ | ½ | 1 |
| Theory of Child Care | - | 1 | 1 | 1 | 1 |
| Nutrition | 1 | ½ | - | - | - |

+"Social" section discontinued in 1962.

INDUSTRIAL (Feminine) - cont'd.

| | 1st yr. | 2nd yr. | 3rd yr. Dressmak. | 3rd yr. Hairdress. | 3rd yr. Combined |
|---|---|---|---|---|---|
| Domestic Science | 1 | ½ | ½ | ½ | 2 |
| Physical Education | 2 | 2 | 2 | 2 | 2 |
| Law | - | - | ½ | ½ | ½ |
| Drawing | 2 | 2 | 3 | 2 | 2 |
| Technology | 1 | 1 | 1 | 2 | 1 |
| Practical Work (Cutting, Dressmaking, Knitting, Child Care, etc.) | 13 | 16 | 19 | 22 | 12 |
| Practical Work (Cooking, House-keeping, etc.) | 2 | 3 | 2 | - | 8 |
| | 40 | 39 | 40 | 40 | 39 |

COMMERCIAL

| Subjects | 1st yr. | 2nd yr. | 3rd yr. Secret. | 3rd yr. Acctg. |
|---|---|---|---|---|
| Arabic | 6 | 6 | 6 | 6 |
| French | 5 | 5 | 5 | 5 |
| History and Geography | 2 | 2 | 2 | 2 |
| Commercial Mathematics | 4 | 3 | 2 | 4 |
| Commerce | 2 | 1 | 1 | 1 |
| Accounting | 2 | 3 | - | 4 |
| Practical Work (Commerce, Accounting) | 2 | 3 | - | 3 |
| Commercial Correspondence (Bilingual) | - | 2 | 3 | 2 |
| Classification of Business Materials | - | 1 | 1 | - |
| Practical Secretarial Work | - | - | 3 | - |
| Arabic Typing | 3 | 3 | 4 | 2 |
| French Typing | 3 | 3 | 4 | 2 |
| Writing | 1 | 1 | - | - |
| Administrative Organization | - | - | ½ | ½ |
| Applied Science (boys) | 1 | 1 | - | - |
| Homemaking Education (girls) | 2 | 2 | - | - |
| Physical Education | 2 | 2 | 2 | 2 |
| Work Laws | - | - | ½ | ½ |
| Boys | 33 | 36 | 34 | |
| Girls | 34 | 37 | 34 | |

AGRICULTURE

| Subjects | 1st yr. | 2nd yr. | 3rd yr. |
|---|---|---|---|
| Arabic | 5 | 4 | 4 |
| French | 5 | 3 | 2½ |
| Law and Accounting | - | - | ½ |
| Mathematics | 4 | 4 | 4 |
| Geography | - | 2 | 1 |
| Geology | - | 1 | 1 |
| Botany | 2 | 1 | 1 |
| Zoology | 1 | 1 | 1 |
| Physics | 1 | 2 | 2 |
| Chemistry | 2 | 2 | 1 |
| Drawing | 1 | 1 | 1 |
| General Agriculture, and Special | 2 | 2 | 1 |
| Zootechnics | 1 | 1 | 1 |
| Arboriculture/Horticulture | 2 | 2 | 1 |
| Plant Protection | - | - | 1 |
| Forestry | - | - | 1 |
| Agricultural Economics | - | - | 1 |
| Rural Engineering | - | - | 1 |
| Workshop | 4 | 4 | 4 |
| Practical Agricultural Work | 8 | 8 | 8 |
| Physical Education | 2 | 2 | 2 |
| | 40 | 40 | 40 |

Certificat d'enseignement technique (C.E.T.) awarded at close of programs.

Continued vocational course: 1-3 year program, stemming from the Industrial short course.


French

Short program:

        Enseignement général
        Enseignement technique
                Technique mathématique (TM)
                Technique économique (TE)
                Brevet économique commercial (BEC)
                Brevet économique industriel (BEI)

Brevet d'études du premier cycle (B.E.P.C.) awarded
Certificat d'aptitude professionnelle (C.A.P.) awarded.

TECHNICAL LYCEES, MOROCCAN:

Offer courses similar to Experimental Sciences and Mathematics programs of enseignement long, but include training in Applied Sciences.

Technical Baccalaureate awarded.

Standard Moroccan lycée program during first 3 grades of technical lycée. Practical program of technical secondary education offered, ending in Diplôme de technicien (Mechanic, Electrician, Accountant, Secretarial).


COLLEGE IBN WAFID DU FOUARAT, Kenitra

Technical agricultural lycée.

| | |
|---|---|
| Entrance requirements: | To the first cycle:<br>Students from primary school who have been admitted to the examen d'entrée dans les classes d'observation (1 test in classical Arabic, 1 test in Arithmetic, 1 test in French). |
| | To the second cycle:<br>Students from the collèges and the lycées d'enseignement général and oriented to agriculture. Orientation test required of all. |

7-year program.

| | | |
|---|---|---|
| First cycle: | Classe d'observation ) | |
| | Première A.S.            ) | tronc commun |
| | Deuxième A.S. | |
| | Troisième A.S. | |
| | -------------------- | |
| Second cycle: | 4° T.A. | |
| | 5° T.A. | |
| | 6° T.A. | |


TIMETABLE
(Hours per week per year)

TRONC COMMUN

Classe d'observation

| | |
|---|---|
| Arabic Language and Islamic Training | 10 |
| French | 8 |
| Mathematics | 8 |
| Introduction to History | 1 |

Introduction to Geography                          1
Physical Education                                 3
                                                  ─────
                                                  31 hours

Première année secondaire

Arabic Language and Ismalic Training          9
French                                         6
Mathematics                                    6
History/Geography                              3
Natural Sciences                               2
Physical Education                             3
Drawing, Singing and Manual Training           1
                                              ─────
                                              30 hours

## TECHNICAL AGRICULTURAL PROGRAM

| General Studies | 2nd yr. | 3rd yr. | 4th yr. | 5th yr. | 6th yr. |
|---|---|---|---|---|---|
| Arabic | 4 | 4 | 5 | 4 | 4 |
| French | 4 | 2½ | 4 | 4 | 4 |
| Law/Accounting | - | ½ | - | - | - |
| Mathematics | 4 | 4 | 5 | 5 | 5 |
| Geography | 1 | 1 | 2 | 3 | 3 |
| Geology | 1 | 1 | - | - | - |
| Botany | 1 | 1 | 4 | 4 | 4 |
| Zoology | 1 | 1 | - | - | - |
| Physics | 2 | 2 | 2 | 2 | 2 |
| Chemistry | 2 | 1 | 2 | 2 | 2 |
| Industrial Drawing | 1 | 1 | - | - | - |

Technical Theoretical Studies

| | 2nd yr. | 3rd yr. | 4th yr. | 5th yr. | 6th yr. |
|---|---|---|---|---|---|
| Agriculture (General and Special) | 1 | 1½ | 2 | 2 | 2 |
| Animal Care | 1 | 1 | - | - | - |
| Tree and Plant Care | 2 | 1 | 2 | 2 | 2 |
| Plant Protection | 1 | 1 | - | - | - |
| D.R.S. | - | ½ | - | - | - |
| Agricultural Econ. | - | 1 | - | - | - |
| Rural Engineering | - | 1 | 2 | 2 | 2 |

Practical Training

| | 2nd yr. | 3rd yr. | 4th yr. | 5th yr. | 6th yr. |
|---|---|---|---|---|---|
| Workshop | 4 | 4 | 2 | 2 | 2 |
| Practical Agric. Work | 8 | 8 | 6 | 6 | 6 |
| Physical Education | 2 | 2 | 2 | 2 | 2 |
| | 40 | 40 | 40 | 40 | 40 |

<u>Certificat d'enseignement technique agricole</u> (<u>C.E.T.A.</u>) awarded at close
of first cycle.

<u>Baccalauréat technique agricole</u> or <u>Diplôme de technicité agricole</u> awarded
at close of full 7-year program.

TECHNICAL LYCEES, FRENCH:

1st and 2nd years:  Orientation classes.
5 more years ending in <u>Technical Baccalaureate</u>.

2 programs:

    (1)  Mathematics:    including French Composition, Mathematics,
                         Physical Science, History or Geography, a
                         modern foreign language, Mechanical Construction,
                         Physical Education.

    (2)  Economics:      including French Composition, Mathematics, Sta-
                         tistical Mathematics or Economic Problems,
                         Physical Science or Marketing Techniques,
                         History or Geography, 1st modern foreign
                         language and 2nd modern foreign language.
                         (Technical economics program offered only at the
                         Lycées Moulay, Sliman, Fez.)

Also offer:  6-year practical program of technical secondary culminating
in <u>Brevet d'enseignement industriel</u> (<u>B.E.I.</u>) (General Mechanic, Auto
Mechanic, Lathe Operator, Milling Machine Operator, Electrician, Drafts-
man), and <u>Brevet d'enseignement commercial</u> (<u>B.E.C.</u>).

<u>HIGHER TECHNICAL EDUCATION</u>

See Ecole Mohammadia d'Ingénieurs, under University of Mohammed V.

<u>TEACHER EDUCATION</u>

<u>ELEMENTARY SCHOOL TEACHERS</u>

3 years, secondary school, and 1 year of teacher training at one of the
28 regional schools.

Certificat d'aptitude pédagogique (C.A.P.) degré élémentaire awarded at close of program.


## SECONDARY SCHOOL TEACHERS

Trained at Ecole Normale Supérieure (Teacher Training College), Rabat.

Entrance requirements:          Baccalauréat.

All students take 1 preparatory year before working for certificats.


### Professorat

Arabic Literature        )
History and Geography     )    taught in Arabic

2-year course in either subject, which in addition to Psychology and Pedagogy are all taught in the Teacher Training College.

Graduates entitled to teach in classe d'observation and first 3 grades of lycée (first cycle).


### Licence

Faculté des Lettres:      Arabic section
                          French section

Faculté des Sciences:     French section

4-year program. Licence programs are similar to those in the Faculté des Lettres or Faculté des Sciences of the University. Students must pass examinations which cover propédeutique and 3 certificats. There are additional courses in Psychology and Pedagogy.

At close of program, licence is awarded and the certificate of teaching, Certificat d'aptitude pédagogique à l'enseignement secondaire (C.A.P.E.S.). Graduates are entitled to teach in second cycle of lycées.

Some of the graduates may prepare for a competitive examination, agrégation. On successful completion, title of agrégé conferred.


## ADDITIONAL TEACHER TRAINING PROGRAMS

The Iraqi government has established a teacher-training institute in Casablanca for training secondary school history and geography teachers. Exclusively Arabic.

United Arab Republic has established a teacher-training institute in
Rabat specializing in secondary school Mathematics and Science.
Exclusively Arabic.


SPECIAL EDUCATION

Education for children between 6 and 14 who have never been to school:
20 hours of instruction a week for 4 years.  (Instructors, primary
school teachers or those having completed 1 year secondary education.)

Literacy courses at basic-education centers, as well as vocational,
recreational and fundamental-education activities.  Instruction in
housekeeping, hygiene, civics, care of animals, food preparation,
manual crafts and arts.

94

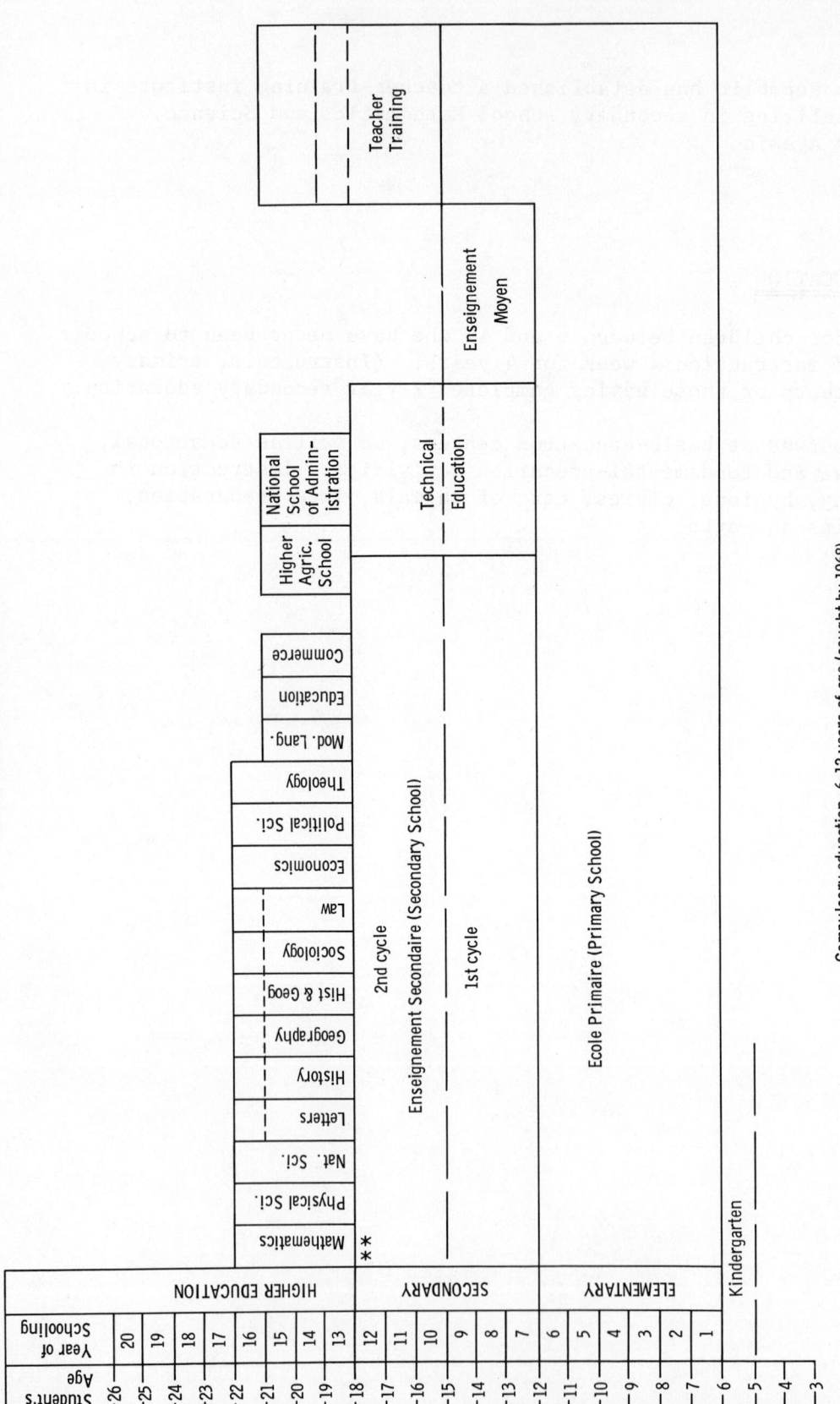

REPUBLIC OF TUNISIA

| Student's Age | Year of Schooling | | |
|---|---|---|---|
| 26 | | | |
| 25 | 20 | | |
| 24 | 19 | | |
| 23 | 18 | | HIGHER EDUCATION |
| 22 | 17 | | |
| 21 | 16 | | |
| 20 | 15 | | |
| 19 | 14 | | |
| 18 | 13 | | |
| 17 | 12 | | SECONDARY |
| 16 | 11 | | |
| 15 | 10 | | |
| 14 | 9 | | |
| 13 | 8 | | |
| 12 | 7 | | |
| 11 | 6 | | ELEMENTARY |
| 10 | 5 | | |
| 9 | 4 | | |
| 8 | 3 | | |
| 7 | 2 | | |
| 6 | 1 | | |
| 5 | | | Kindergarten |
| 4 | | | |
| 3 | | | |

Mathematics **
Physical Sci.
Nat. Sci.
Letters
History
Geography
Hist & Geog.
Sociology
Law
Economics
Political Sci.
Theology
Mod. Lang.
Education
Commerce

Higher Agric. School
National School of Administration

2nd cycle

1st cycle

Enseignement Secondaire (Secondary School)

Ecole Primaire (Primary School)

Technical Education

Enseignement Moyen

Teacher Training

Compulsory education: 6-12 years of age (sought by 1968)

School year: October 1-June 30, 3 terms

Secondary Grading: 20/20 Perfect    20/16  Très Bien
                   10/20 Passing     16/14  Bien
                                     14/12  Assez Bien
                                     12/10  Passable

Twice yearly examinations: June and October

REPUBLIC OF TUNISIA


Independence:  March 20, 1956.


BACKGROUND


From 1574 to 1881, Tunisia was annexed to the Turkish Ottoman Empire.
Following the Treaty of Bardo, 1881, and the Convention of Marsa, 1883,
France established a Protectorate.

Protectorate ended with independence, March 1956, and on July 25, 1956,
the country was officially proclaimed Republic of Tunisia.

The country is divided into 3 areas because of geographic conditions:
northern, the source of most of Tunisia's agricultural production;
central, with the coastal plains for cattle grazing; southern, bordering
on the Sahara,with semi-nomadic peoples with their grazing herds.

Tunisia is more of an Arab than an African country; 95% of population is
Moslem.  Islam is the official religion.  Arabic is the official
language but French is widely used and taught in the schools.


# E D U C A T I O N   P R E - I N D E P E N D E N C E


Kuttab, small Koranic schools attached to mosques gave students traditional
Islamic training. Students went from Kuttab to Zitouna University.

Zitouna University (Islamic) with annexes for higher Islamic studies
attempted "modernization," 1870.

Sadiqi College, founded in 1870 as a pilot secondary school, stressing
Arabic and Islamic studies.

Under French Protectorate, education primarily for French children in
Tunisia.  Four kinds of schools:

      (1)  French:  system totally integrated with that of France.
      (2)  Special Franco-Arab system especially for indigènes.
      (3)  "Modern Koranic schools":  established by private initia-
           tive at turn of century, designed as substitutes of Kuttab,
           offering Arabic and Islamic studies, Arithmetic, History,
           French, and Hygiene.

(4)   Traditional Zitouna schools.

Centers for Professional Training (3 years, secondary).
Institut des Hautes Etudes, and 2 teacher-training schools (1 for men,
1 for women).


# I N D E P E N D E N C E

## Ten-Year Plan of Educational Reform

Modern Koranic schools and Zitouna annexes integrated with national system.

June 1958, compulsory primary education (sought in 10 years).

7th year of primary education eliminated.  1st two years, Arabic; 3-6
years, 10 hours instruction a week in Arabic, 15 in French.

Secondary education:

3-year intermediate program (terminal) replacing Centers for Professional
Training.  Practical program.

6-year preparatory program, following the traditional preparatory-school
pattern, but with greater emphasis on the Natural Sciences.  Admittance
to either type of secondary school based on competitive examination.

Old Zitouna secondary system to be abolished by 1965.  A new university
to be built around Institut des Hautes Etudes and the 2 teacher-training
schools.

Major objectives of the Ten-Year Plan accomplished by 1964.  Regarding
the two final objectives listed above:  the old Zitouna secondary system
has been abolished, and Tunis University is being built around the
Faculté des Lettres and the 2 teacher-training schools.


## KINDERGARTEN

Sometimes a short period of kindergarten before primary education.


## PRIMARY EDUCATION

Students enter école primaire (primary school) at 6 years of age.

6 grades.

All primary schools, urban and rural, have same basic curriculum (under
control of Secretary of State for National Education).

First 2 years:  15 hours of instruction per week.
Next 4 years:  25 hours per week.  14 hours in French, 10 hours in Arabic, 1 hour Physical Education.

School time spread over 5 days in the week.  During Ramadan (fasting month), total weekly classes reduced.

Closed for approximately 3 months in summer.  Total vacation and holidays, approximately 150 days.

Language of instruction:     Arabic exclusively in first 2 years.  Also increasingly used in last 4 years, especially for new subjects with Tunisian emphasis:  Civics, Koran, Religious Islamic Instruction, study of environment, observation of natural facts.

History and Geography of Tunisia and the Maghreb taught at the elementary level.

Subjects:     Language instruction (a)  Arabic (all grades)
                                   (b)  French (3rd to 6th grades)

Arithmetic (in Arabic for first 2 grades, in French for grades 3-6)

Practical subjects:
Manual dexterity given by Arabic teacher (first 2 grades)
Practical exercises and knowledge of everyday facts (given by the French teacher, 3-6 grades)
Drawing (given by the French teacher, 3-6 grades)
Singing (in Arabic, all grades)
Physical Education (given by French teacher, 3-6 grades)

Study of environment (in Arabic):
Observation of nature (3rd and 4th grades)
Geography (5th and 6th grades)

Moral and Social education (in Arabic):
Koran and Morals (all grades)
History and Civics (5th and 6th grades)

Certificat de fin d'études primaires (Certificate of Primary Studies) awarded after 6 years and passing of comprehensive examination.  All children aged 12 or over are eligible for this examination.


SECONDARY EDUCATION

3 types of schools:    Tunisian Government Schools
                       Private Schools

> French Government Schools (owned and managed by
> Mission Universitaire et Culturelle Française, a
> section of the French Embassy in Tunis). These
> schools include both primary and secondary level
> French and Tunisian students.

Under new plan, two distinct branches:

    (1)   Terminal intermediate education (3 years).
    (2)   Secondary education (6 years).

Terminal intermediate education (enseignement moyen) for those who have
completed elementary school at an advanced age (14-16, or 17 years) or
those who do not have the intellectual and practical aptitudes for long-
range secondary studies. (See description under VOCATIONAL AND TECHNICAL
EDUCATION).

Admission examination for terminal intermediate education and 6-year
education, is the same.

Secondary education, 6-year program: 2 cycles. System of orientation
at two successive levels. Standardization of curricula for all secondary
schools accomplished by October 1963.

Two cycles:    First cycle - 1st, 2nd and 3rd years:

> 1st year, general program (tronc commun). All students
> take Languages, Mathematics, Science, History and Geo-
> graphy, Manual Training, Drawing.
>
> Psychological aptitude tests at end of 1st year direct
> students to one of 3 programs: General, Economics, Technical.
>
> 2nd and 3rd years, curriculum varies a little according
> to program chosen.
>
> A brevet is awarded by headmaster of school at end of
> 3rd year.
>
> Second cycle - 4th, 5th and 6th years:
>
> Divided into 2 periods: 4th and 5th years, 3 standard
> programs with various fields of specialization; and
> terminal year, more specialization.
>
> Second cycle prepared students for Baccalaureate of
> Secondary Education (Baccalauréat de l'enseignement
> secondaire).

Fields of specialization:

(1)  General program (enseignement secondaire général)

    (a)  Modern Languages (emphasis on Arabic and French languages)

(b)  Classical Languages (emphasis on Arabic Literature and Islamic Thought)
(c)  Sciences
(d)  Mathematics
(e)  Teachers College section (Diploma of Completion of Pedagogic Studies awarded on completion, not baccalauréat)

(2)  Economics program (enseignement secondaire économique)

(a)  Economics, leading to baccalauréat
(b)  Commerce
   i.  Accounting   ) leading to degree in Commercial Studies
  ii.  Secretarial  ) entitling holder to enter High School of Business and Commerce

(3)  Technical program (enseignement secondaire technique) (See TECHNICAL EDUCATION)

(a)  Mathematics
(b)  Industrial (boys) - Diploma of Industrial Education (5 years) and a Diploma of Technician (6 years) offering in following fields:
              Electronics
              Radio-Electricity
              Topography
              Bridges and Construction
              Building Trades
              Mechanics
        Entitle students to enter National Technical Institute.

   Industrial (girls)- Dressmaking, Needlework, etc.


Laboratory and field work:

In second cycle (4th, 5th and 6th years), practical work (travaux pratiques, T.P.) introduced into study of science. Direct observation on materials distributed and explained by professors, then notes made with accompanying sketch. Also includes work in laboratories.

4th, 5th years, 7 hours per week for science students in lectures and T.P. 6th year, 11 hours per week.

Students also make field trips and visit industries employing basic sciences.

At close of 5th year, examinations for examen probatoire taken (1st part of baccalaureate). During 6th year, major field of student's specialization stressed, qualifying him for higher education.

## 1st Cycle - GENERAL PROGRAM (Option Générale)
### (Hours per week per year)

| Subjects | 1st year | 2nd year | 3rd year |
|---|---|---|---|
| Language and Letters (Arabic) | 8 | 6 | 6 |
| Language and Letters (French) | 6 | 5 | 5 |
| 2nd Foreign Language | | 4 | 4 |
| History and Geography | 2 | 2 | 2 |
| Civic and Religious Instruction | 1 | 1 | 1 |
| Mathematics | 3 | 3½ | 3½ |
| Natural Sciences (course/prac. wk.) | 3 (1+2) | 2 (1+1) | 2 (1+1) |
| Physical Education | 2 | 2 | 2 |
| Music | | 1 | 1 |
| Manual Training | 3 | 2 | 2 |
| Drawing | 2 (1+1) | 1 | 1 |
| | 30 | 29½ | 29½ |

## 2nd Cycle - GENERAL PROGRAM - 4th Year

| | Let.Mod. | Let.Clas. | Sc. | Math. | Norm. |
|---|---|---|---|---|---|
| Language and Letters (Arabic) | 5 | 5 | 4 | 4 | 5 |
| Language and Letters (French) | 5 | 4 | 4 | 4 | 5 |
| 2nd Foreign Language | 5 | 4 | 4 | 4 | 3 |
| History and Geography | 3 | 3 | 2 | 2 | 2 |
| Civic and Religious Instruction | 1 | 2 | 1 | 1 | 1½ |
| Mathematics | 3 | 3 | 4 | 6 | 3 |
| Natural Science | 1 | 1 | 1½ | | 1 |
| Physical Education | 2 | 2 | 2 | 2 | 2½ |
| Music | | | | | 1½ |
| Manual Training | 1 | 1 | 1 | 1 | 3 |
| Drawing | 1 | 1 | 1 | 1 | 1 |
| Penmanship | | | | | ½ |
| Physical Sciences (course/prac. wk.) | 3 | 3 | 5½ | 5 | 3 |
| | 30 | 29 | 30 | 30 | 32 |

## 2nd Cycle - GENERAL PROGRAM - 5th Year

| | Let.Mod. | Let.Clas. | Sc. | Math. | Norm. |
|---|---|---|---|---|---|
| Language and Letters (Arabic) | 5 | 5 | 4 | 4 | 5 |
| Language and Letters (French) | 5 | 4 | 4 | 4 | 5 |
| 2nd Foreign Language | 5 | 4 | 4 | 4 | 3 |
| History and Geography | 3 | 3 | 3 | 2 | 2 |
| Civic and Religious Instruction | 1 | 2 | 1 | 1 | 1½ |
| Mathematics | 3 | 3 | 4 | 6 | 3 |
| Natural Sciences | 1 | 1 | 1½ | | 1 |
| Physical Sciences (course/prac. wk.) | 3 | 3 | 5½ | 5 | 3 |

|                                    | Let.Mod. | Let.Clas. | Sc. | Math. | Norm. |
|------------------------------------|----------|-----------|-----|-------|-------|
| Physical Education                 | 2        | 2         | 2   | 2     | 2½    |
| Music                              |          |           |     |       | 2     |
| Manual Training                    | 1        | 1         | 1   | 1     | 3     |
| Drawing                            | 1        | 1         | 1   | 1     | 1     |
|                                    | 30       | 29        | 31  | 30    | 32    |

## 2nd Cycle - GENERAL PROGRAM - 6th Year

|                                         | Let.Mod. | Let.Clas. | Sc. | Math. | Norm. |
|-----------------------------------------|----------|-----------|-----|-------|-------|
| Language and Letters (Arabic)           | 3        | 3         |     |       | 2     |
| Language and Letters (French)           | 1        | 1         |     |       | 2     |
| 2nd Foreign Language                    | 3        | 3         | 2   | 2     | 2     |
| History and Geography                   | 3        | 3         | 3   | 3     | 3     |
| Civic and Religious Instruction         |          |           |     |       |       |
| Mathematics                             | 2        | 2         | 7   | 11    | 2½    |
| Natural Sciences                        | 2        | 2         | 4   | 2     | 1½    |
| Physical Sciences (course/prac.wk.)     | 3        | 3         | 7   | 7     | 2½    |
| Physical Education                      | 2        | 2         | 2   | 2     | 2½    |
| Music                                   |          |           |     |       | 2     |
| Manual Training                         |          |           |     |       | 2     |
| Drawing                                 |          |           |     |       | 1     |
| Philosophy                              | 7        | 7         | 4   | 4     | 5     |
| Study of Islamic Thought                | 2        | 3         |     |       | 2     |
|                                         | 28       | 29        | 29  | 31    | 30    |

## 1st Cycle - ECONOMICS PROGRAM (Option Economique)
### (Hours per week per year)

| Subjects                                | 1st year   | 2nd year | 3rd year |
|-----------------------------------------|------------|----------|----------|
| Language and Letters (Arabic)           | 8          | 6        | 6        |
| Language and Letters (French)           | 6          | 5        | 5        |
| 2nd Foreign Language                    |            | 4        | 4        |
| History and Geography                   | 2          | 2        | 2        |
| Civic and Religious Instruction         | 1          | 1        | 1        |
| Mathematics                             | 3          | 3½       | 3½       |
| Natural Sciences (course/prac.wk.)      | 3 (1+2)    | 2        | 2        |
| Physical Education                      | 2          | 2        | 2        |
| Manual Training                         | 3          |          |          |
| Drawing                                 | 2          | 1        | 1        |
| Commerce and Accounting                 |            | 2        | 2        |
| Shorthand/Typing                        |            | 3        | 3        |
|                                         | 30         | 31½      | 31½      |

## 2nd Cycle - ECONOMICS PROGRAM - 4th Year

|                                           | Economics | Secretarial | Accounting |
|-------------------------------------------|-----------|-------------|------------|
| Language and Letters (Arabic)             | 4         | 4           | 3          |
| Language and Letters (French)             | 4         | 4           | 3          |
| 2nd Foreign Language                      | 4         | 4           | 3          |
| History and Geography                     | 3         | 2           | 2          |
| Civic and Religious Instruction           | 1         |             |            |
| Mathematics                               | 4         | 1           | 2          |
| Physical Sciences (course/prac.wk.)       | 3         | 1+          | 2+         |
| Physical Education                        | 2         | 2           | 2          |
| Drawing                                   | 1         | 1           | 1          |
| Commerce and Accounting                   | 2         | 6           | 8          |
| Commercial Law                            |           | 1           | 1          |
| Political Economy                         | 1         | 1           | 1          |
| Shorthand/Typing                          | 2         | 5           | 2          |
| Selling                                   |           | 1           | 1          |
|                                           | 31        | 33          | 31         |

+Sciences and Merchandising

## 2nd Cycle - ECONOMICS PROGRAM - 5th Year

|                                           | Economics | Secretarial | Accounting |
|-------------------------------------------|-----------|-------------|------------|
| Language and Letters (Arabic)             | 4         | 4           | 2          |
| Language and Letters (French)             | 4         | 4           | 2          |
| 2nd Foreign Language                      | 4         | 4           | 2          |
| History and Geography                     | 3         |             |            |
| Civic and Religious Instruction           | 1         |             |            |
| Mathematics                               | 4         | 1           | 4          |
| Physical Sciences (course/prac.wk.)       | 3         |             |            |
| Physical Education                        | 2         | 2           | 2          |
| Drawing                                   | 1         | 2           | 1          |
| Commerce and Accounting                   | 2         | 6           | 12         |
| Commercial Law                            | 1         | 1           | 1          |
| Political Economy                         | 2         | 1           | 1          |
| Shorthand/Typing                          |           | 6           | 3          |
| Selling                                   |           | 1           |            |
| Organization                              | 1         |             |            |
|                                           | 32        | 32          | 30         |

### 2nd Cycle - ECONOMICS PROGRAM - 6th Year

|                                      | Economics | Secretarial | Accounting |
|--------------------------------------|-----------|-------------|------------|
| Language and Letters (Arabic)        | 2         | 4           | 2          |
| Language and Letters (French)        |           | 4           | 2          |
| 2nd Foreign Language                 | 3         | 4           | 2          |
| History and Geography                | 4         |             |            |
| Mathematics                          | 4         |             | 4          |
| Physical Sciences (course/prac.wk.)  | 3         |             |            |
| Physical Education                   | 2         | 2           | 2          |
| Drawing                              |           | 1           |            |
| Philosophy                           | 5         |             |            |
| Commerce and Accounting              | 2         | 4           | 12         |
| Commercial Law                       | 1         | 1           | 4          |
| Political Economy                    | 2         | 2           | 2          |
| Shorthand/Typing                     |           | 10          | 2          |
| Selling                              |           | 2           |            |
| Organization                         | 1         |             |            |
| Legislation of Work                  | 1         |             |            |
|                                      | 30        | 34          | 32         |

** Baccalauréat de l'enseignement secondaire awarded at close of 6th year.
Written and oral examinations for this national diploma; June and October
sittings. Modelled on French examination; recognized by University of
Paris.

If student's average for whole year is below 10/20, student must repeat
entire year.

Student's average grade for baccalauréat computed on coefficient system.
Each subject assigned a numerical value according to its significance.
Specific grade multiplied by coefficient: totals added, sum divided by
sum of coefficients.

French baccalauréat at close of 7-year program.


### HIGHER EDUCATION

### UNIVERSITY OF TUNIS

Founded on March 31, 1960. The University is a composite of previously
existing institutions:

(a) Institute of Higher Studies:

Founded in 1945 under technical direction of University of Paris.
Faculties of Law, Science, Arabic, History, Sociology.

(b)  Bourguiba School of Modern Languages:

Founded by U.S. Government to teach English, partly financed by a
Ford Foundation grant.  Courses in English, Arabic, French, Italian,
Spanish, Russian, German, Serbo-Croatian.

(c)  Ez-Zitouna University:

Founded in 18th century, as a center of Islamic studies.  Students
direct from lower Koranic schools took courses in Religion, Philosophy, Astronomy, Rhetoric, Literature, History and Geography of
the Muslim world, graduated with title Ulema.

(d)  Training College for Secondary School Teachers

(e)  School of Higher Legal Studies

(f)  Center of Economic Studies

(g)  School of Fine Arts

(h)  National School of Administration


Present University structure:

Faculties:

    Mathematical, Physical and Natural Sciences
    Letters and Sociology
    Law and Political and Economic Science
    Ez-Zitouna of Theology and Religious Sciences
    Medicine and Pharmacy (mixed):  hospital, clinic, maternity,
      nursing school (projected).

Institutes:

    National Technical Institute
    Art Institute
    Research Institutes and Centers:
      Institute of Atomic Physics
      Center of Economic and Social Studies and Research
      Research Center on Problems of the Arid Zone
    Faculty of Science, laboratories:
      Mathematics
      Physics
      Chemistry
      Animal Biology
      Geology
      Pharmacology
      Physiology and Nutrition
      Plant Chemistry
      Experimental Medicine

Faculty of Letters:
   Center of English and North-American Studies
   Center of Social Science Studies
   Center of Geographical Studies
   Center of Historical Studies

Grandes Ecoles:

   Higher Teachers' College
   Normal School for Associate Professors
   Bourguiba Institute of Modern Languages
   Higher School of Commercial Studies
   School of Higher Legal Studies
   School of Fine Arts (since 1962 no longer part of the University)

University emphasizes sciences and training of higher administrative personnel.  Close association between teaching and research.

Research Institutes provide laboratory and library facilities.

Institute of Atomic Physics awards a Certificat d'études supérieures de physique nucléaire with the licence ès sciences.

Center of Economic and Social Studies and Research has 3 sections: Economic Studies, Social Studies and Geographical Studies.  Organizes seminars and discussions.

Research Center on Problems of the Arid Zone works closely with the Department of Agriculture.

School year:   October 1 - June 30, including examination period.

Entrance requirements:          Certified copy of Tunisian baccalaureate of secondary education.  French baccalaureate accepted after certification.  Minimum 10/20 or passable.

One Certificat d'études supérieures earned annually, with grade of 10/20 or higher on examination, taken in June or repeated in October.  Grading is severe at University level.

Graduation with the licence conditional upon obtaining requisite number of certificats.  Usually 4 (one for each school year), although Faculty of Sciences requires from 5 to 7.

Licence ès sciences mathématiques

Duration of course:   4 years.

1 <u>Certificat d'études supérieures préparatoires</u> (preparatory)
    includes Mathematics, Physics and Chemistry.

5 <u>Certificats</u>:    Analysis and Analytical Geometry
                    Physics (Electrical, or Optical, or Thermodynamics
                       and Mechanical Physics)
                    Algebra and Integral Calculus
                    Calculus and Differential Geometry, or Mechanics,
                     or Numerical Calculus, or Algebra, or Probabi-
                     lities, or Astronomy

## <u>Licence ès-sciences physiques (in Physics)</u>

Duration of course:    4 years.

To become a <u>licencié en sciences physiques</u>, the student must obtain:

(a)   A <u>Certificat d'études supérieures préparatoires de physique</u>

|  | Course work | Exercises | Practical work | |
|---|---|---|---|---|
| Physics | 4 | 2 | 4 | (hours |
| Mathematics | 3 | 2 | 4 | weekly) |
| Chemistry | 2 | 1 | 1½ | |

| Examination: | | Coefficient |
|---|---|---|
| Written test - | Physics | 2 |
| | Mathematics | 1 |
| | Chemistry | 1 |
| Practical test- | Physics | 2 |
| | Mathematics | 1 |
| | Chemistry | 1 |
| Oral test - | Physics | 2 |
| | Mathematics | 1 |
| | Chemistry | 1 |

(b)   6 <u>Certificats d'études supérieures</u> of the second cycle

    (1)   Mathematical techniques of Physics
          2-hr. course work and 4-hr. practical work weekly.
          Examination:  2 written tests     Coefficient 1 each
                       Oral interrogation   Coefficient 2

    (2)   Electricity

    (3)   Optics

    (4)   Thermodynamics and Physical Mechanics

    (5)   Electronics or Nuclear Physics, or Mathematical Physics, or
          Spectrometry, or Physical Chemistry, or an approved option.

(6) Systematic Chemistry or Organic Chemistry or Mineral Chemistry - for each of these certificates:
    3 hrs. course work, 4 hrs. practical work and 1 hr. supervised work weekly.

| Examination: | | |
|---|---|---|
| Written test | Coefficient 2 | |
| Practical test | Coefficient 1.5 | |
| Oral interrogation | Coefficient 2 | |

## Licence ès sciences physiques (in Chemistry)

Duration of course:    4 years.

1 Certificat préparatoire - includes Chemistry, Physics, Mathematics.

6 Certificats:    General Chemistry I
                  Organic Chemistry
                  Experimental Physics
                  Mineral Chemistry
                  General Chemistry II
                  Analytical and Industrial Chemistry, or Applied
                      Chemistry, or an approved option

## Licence ès sciences naturelles (in Biological Sciences)

Duration of course:    4 years.

1 Certificat préparatoire - includes Animal Biology, Plant Biology,
    Chemistry, Mathematics, Physics, and Geology.

4 Certificats:    Zoology and Animal Biology
                  Botany
                  Biochemistry and Animal and Plant Physiology
                  General Geology

## Licence ès sciences naturelles (in Earth Sciences)

Duration of course:    4 years.

1 Certificat préparatoire - includes Animal Biology, Plant Biology,
    Chemistry, Mathematics, Physics, Geology.

4 Certificats:    Zoology and Animal Biology
                  Botany
                  General Geology
                  Historical and Applied Geology

## Licence ès sciences naturelles (in Physiological Chemistry)

Duration of course:     4 years.

    1 Certificat préparatoire - includes Animal Biology, Plant Biology,
        Chemistry, Mathematics, Physics, Geology.

    5 Certificats:     Systematic Chemistry
                Organic Chemistry
                General Chemistry II
                Analytical and Industrial Chemistry
                Animal Biology

## Troisième cycle

Duration of course:     2 years.

This may be taken after completion of the Certificat d'études supérieures préparatoires (1st cycle) and the work leading to the licence (2nd cycle), and is designed to give a deeper knowledge of a specialty and to teach students methods of research.  It is open to students entitled to the licence or already holding the title.

## Diplômes

The Faculty also prepares students for diplomas in higher studies in three specialties:

    Diplôme d'études supérieures de mathématiques
    Diplôme d'études supérieures de sciences physiques
    Diplôme d'études supérieures de sciences naturelles

## Faculty of Letters and Sociology

## Licence ès-lettres arabes

Duration of course:     3 to 4 years.

    4 Certificats:     Islamic Civilization and Methodology
                Arab Grammar and Philology
                Arab Literature
                Foreign Language and Literature

## Licence ès-lettres anglaises

Duration of course:     3 to 4 years.

To become a <u>licencié ès-lettres anglaises</u>, the student must obtain

4 <u>Certificats</u>:    Initiation and Methodology
                        English and North American Civilization
                        English Grammar and Philology
                        English and North American Literature

## <u>Certificat d'études supérieures d'initiation et de méthodologie</u>

5 hrs. course work and 6 hrs. practical work weekly.

| Examination: | | <u>Coefficient</u> |
|---|---|---|
| Written - | Theme (prose translation) | 2 |
| Oral - | Oral translation | 1 |
| | Grammatical commentary | 1 |
| | Geography and History of English-speaking peoples | 1 |
| | Pronunciation test | 1 |

## <u>Certificat d'études supérieures de civilisation anglaise et nord-américaine</u>

4 hrs. course work and 7 hrs. practical work weekly.

| Examination: | | <u>Coefficient</u> |
|---|---|---|
| Written - | Composition on a question in the program | 2 |
| | Translation into French | 2 |
| Oral - | Question on English Civilization | 1 |
| | Question on North American Civilization | 1 |
| | Interrogation on a special study made by student during stay abroad | ½ |
| | Second modern language | 1 |

## <u>Certificat d'études supérieures de grammaire et de philologie anglaises</u>

4 hrs. course work and 5 hrs. practical work weekly.

| Examination: | | <u>Coefficient</u> |
|---|---|---|
| Written - | Theme (prose translation) | 2 |
| Oral - | Study of an Old English text | 1 |
| | Study of a Middle English or Renaissance text | 1 |

## <u>Certificat d'études supérieures de littérature anglaise et nord-américaine</u>

4 hrs. course work and 3 hrs. practical work weekly.

| Examination: | Coefficient |
|---|---|
| Written - Literary dissertation (in English) | 2 |
| Literary study of a 16th or 17th century text | 1 |
| Literary study of a modern text (English or American) | 1 |
| History of Literature | 1 |

## Licence d'histoire

Duration of course:     3 to 4 years.

4 Certificats:     Ancient History
Medieval History
Modern and Contemporary History
Geography (Historical)

## Licence de géographie

Duration of course:     3 to 4 years.

4 Certificats:     Physical Geography
Human Geography
Regional Geography
History (Geographical)

## Licence d'histoire et de géographie

Duration of course:     3 to 4 years.

4 Certificats:     Ancient and Medieval History
Modern and Contemporary History
General Geography
Regional Geography

## Licence de sociologie

Duration of course:     3 to 4 years.

4 Certificats:     General Sociology
Social Psychology
Sociology and Economic Geography
Islamic and Maghreb Sociology

## Faculty of Law and Political and Economic Sciences

### Licence en droit

Duration of course:    4 years.

To become a licencié en droit, the candidate must pass an examination at the end of each of the 4 years.

1st, 2nd and 3rd years:    7 subjects, comprising 13 hrs. course work and 2 sessions of practical work weekly.

4th year:    10 subjects of which 5 are specialist subjects from each special section. 18 to 19 hrs. course work and 2 sessions of practical work weekly.

4 Certificats:

1st yr:    Civil Law, Constitutional Law and Political Institutions, Political Economics, History of Institutions of the Moslem World, Moslem Law (sources), Moslem Law (personal statutes), International Institutions.

2nd yr:    Civil Law, Administrative Law, Political Economics, General Penal Law and Criminology, Moslem Law (obligations), History of Institutions of the Mediterranean World, Financial Institutions.

3rd yr:    Civil Law, Commercial Law, Penal Law and Procedure, Law of Property and Goods, Industrial Law and Social Security, Fiscal Science and Technique.

4th yr:    General subjects:
International Private Law, Commercial Law, Business Accountancy and Fiscal Policy, Civil Law, Methods of Execution, Administrative Legal Business.

Private Law:
General Principles of Private Law, Special Penal Law, Maritime Law, Insurance Law.

Public Law and Political Science:
Large Public Services, Public Liberties or Method of Political Science, History of Political Ideas, International Public Law.

Administrative:
Large Public Services, Public Accountancy, Administrative Methods of Public Services, Financial Economics in International Public Law.

| Examinations: | | Coefficient |
|---|---|---|
| For each year: | 2 written tests | 1 each |
| | Oral - all subjects except those in the 2nd written examination | 1 each |

## Licence ès-sciences économiques

Duration of course:    4 years.

4 Certificats d'études supérieures économiques at yearly intervals.
The last certificate includes a certain number of choice subjects.

## Licence en administration des entreprises

Duration of course:    4 years.

4 Certificats:

1st and 2nd yrs:    The first 2 certificats in the Licence ès-sciences économiques are taken.

3rd and 4th yrs:    Certificat d'études supérieures générales d'administration des entreprises and the Certificat d'études supérieures spécialisées d'administration des entreprises, the last including specialized choice subjects.

## Capacités

There is a corresponding capacité for each licence; may be admitted after 5 years secondary and the baccalauréat is not required.  Course of study over 2 years.  If a mean grade of over 12/20 is obtained, candidate with the capacité may be exempted from the baccalauréat to take the licence.

## Preparatory courses for Aptitude à la profession d'avocat

(a)  The role of the lawyer in judiciary organization.
(b)  Principles and techniques of penal and civil procedure.
(c)  Rules of practice and professional morals.

## Ez-Zitouna Faculty of Theology and Religious Sciences

## Licence de théologie

Duration of course:    4 years.

4 <u>Certificats</u>, the 1st-year <u>certificat</u> being the same as for the <u>Licence ès-sciences religieuses</u>.

## Licence ès-sciences religieuses

Duration of course:    4 years.

4 <u>Certificats</u>, the 1st-year <u>certificat</u> being the same as for the <u>Licence en théologie</u>.

## Diplôme zeitounien de prédication et d'orientation religieuses

Duration of course:    3 years.

An examination is given at the end of each year.

## Ecole Normale Supérieure (Higher Teachers' College)

Duration of course:    3 years.

Entrance requirements:        Entrance examination for candidates with <u>baccalauréat</u> and at least 24 years of age.

Courses:  Arab Letters, History, Geography, Mathematics, Physics-Chemistry, Natural Sciences, English.
In addition to these teacher-training courses, students also take courses in various faculties of the University.

Graduate awarded <u>licence</u> in his specialty.

## Ecole Normale des Professeurs-Adjoints (Normal School for Associate Professors)

Duration of course:    2 years.

Entrance requirements:        <u>Baccalauréat</u>, <u>Brevet industriel définitif</u>, <u>Brevet d'enseignement commercial</u> (2nd part), or equivalents. Entrance examination, and at least 24 years of age.

Trains teachers to teach commercial, industrial and technical subjects in first cycle of secondary education, and in terminal intermediate education.

Sections:        Arab Letters (History and Geography, or Civic and Religious
                 Instruction), French Letters, English Letters, Mathematics,
                 Science, Commercial Teaching, Mechanical Manufacture,
                 Electrotechniques.

Certificat d'aptitude au professeur adjoint granted, with a practical
professional probationary period.


## Institut Bourguiba des Langues Vivantes (Bourguiba Institute of Modern Languages)

Duration of course:    4 years.

Practical training school, teaching modern languages to nationals and to
those unacquainted with Arabic.  Also a research center to perfect
modern methods of language teaching and a center of audio-visual material
for teaching.

Open without special conditions to university, grandes écoles, lycées and
collèges students, and to members of the Tunisian government.

Languages taught:       Arabic, English, French, Italian, Spanish, Russian,
                        Yugoslav, German.

Diplôme de l'Institut Bourguiba des Langues Vivantes awarded, also a
Brevet d'études pratiques en langue arabe for a more intensive course.

Note:     For graduate study in the United States, work taken should be
          further reinforced with study at an English-language institute.


## Ecole Supérieure d'Etudes Commerciales (Higher School of Commercial Studies)

Prepares candidates for examinations leading to the magistracy and the Bar.

Entrance by examination open to those with baccalauréat or one of the
following diplomas:  Tahcil moderne, Diplôme supérieur d'arabe, Diplômes
du Collège Sadiki, Al Alymia (Section Juridique).


## ECOLE SUPERIEURE D'AGRICULTURE DE TUNIS (Higher Agricultural School of Tunis)

Established October 17, 1898, as Ecole Coloniale d'Agriculture de Tunis
(E.C.A.T.).  Present name adopted at time of the country's independence.
School under the supervision of the State Department of Agriculture.

Original 2-year program supplemented by a 3rd year, October 1947.

Sections:        (a)  Scientific
                 (b)  Technical

Admission on qualification:    Provisional admission with baccalauréat,
                               Elementary Mathematics or Experimental
                               Sciences series.

Admission after probatory examination:  Baccalauréat candidates, Philo-
                               sophy series are obliged to have passed
                               competitive probationary examination in
                               Mathematics.

Admission by competitive examination:  Is open only to students holding
                               the Diplôme du Collège Secondaire d'Agri-
                               culture of Maghrane.
                               The level of examination corresponds to
                               those of baccalauréat Elementary Mathematics
                               and Experimental Sciences.
                               Tests are written and carry the following
                               value:

| Obligatory examinations | | Length of Examination | Coefficient |
|---|---|---|---|
| Mathematics | | 3 hrs. | 4 |
| General Culture | | 3 hrs. | 3 |
| General Biology | | | |
|   Animal | $1\frac{1}{2}$ ) | 3 hrs. | 3 |
|   Vegetable | $1\frac{1}{2}$ ) | | |
| Physics | | 3 hrs. | 2 |
| Chemistry | | 3 hrs. | 2 |
| Geography | | 2 hrs. | 1 |
| Optional: English | | 2 hrs. | - |

  (The optional examination entitles student an increase in
  points equal to the number of points exceeding the average.)

Program:

1st yr:  General program (considered an année propédeutique)

   Mathematics:       Analysis, algebra, probabilities and statistics.

   Physics:           Meteorology, electrotechnology, thermodynamics,
                      optics, atomic physics.

   Chemistry:         General, mineral, organic.

   Vegetal Biology:   Morphology, histology and biology of pharma-
                      ceutical plants and cryptograms, systematic
                      botany, vegetal physiology.

Animal Biology:      General morphology, histology, cellular physio-
                     logy, cellular multiplication, tissue differenti-
                     ation, sexual reproduction, general physiology,
                     systematic zoology, vertebrates and invertebrates.

Genetics:            Laws of hybridization, chromosome theory of
                     heredity, factors of heredity, variation of
                     living matter.

Geology:             Petrography (sedimentary rocks chiefly), minera-
                     logy, actual phenomena, stratigraphy, paleontology.

Technical courses in addition to above basic courses:

Rural Engineering:   Applied mechanics

Agricultural machinery

Zootechnology:       Anatomy and physiology of domestic animals,
                     principals of selection, nutrition.

2nd yr:

Agriculture:         General agriculture, special agriculture of shrubs
                     of complex cultivation.

Viticulture:         Biology of the vine, study of the vine-plant,
                     constitution and maintenance of a vineyard,
                     comparative grape growing.

Horticulture and Arboriculture:  Cultivation of pot-herbs, fruit
                     trees, ornamental plants.

Technology:          Oil-works, dairy farming, miller's trade.

Rural Engineering:   Applied mechanics and resistance of materials,
                     hydraulics.

Improvement and selection of cultivated plants:  Genetic evolution,
                     bases of scientific improvement of vegetables,
                     botanical material of selection, hybridization,
                     genetics applied to the production of seeds.

Botanical Pathology:  Diseases of vegetal cryptograms - mycoses
                     (fungi), means of control.

Chemistry and Agricultural Chemistry:  Analytic chemistry, biological
                     chemistry, qualititative analysis.  Experiments
                     with agricultural materials, formation of agri-
                     cultural soils, properties, improvement of soils:
                     amendments and manure.

Agricultural Entomology:  Study of the species useful and injurious
                     to agriculture.  Biological, systematic means of
                     control.

Pedology:            Properties of soils, soil of Tunisia.

TUNISIA 117

| Zootechnics: | Anatomy and physiology, productions, management of herds. |
| Microbiology: | General microbiology, application to agriculture, to technology, and to hygiene. |
| Bioclimatology: | Production of fodder - physiology and multiplication of fodder-plants. |

3rd yr: Program slanted to agricultural problems of Tunisia and Mediterranean countries.

| Agronomy: | Special agriculture, agricultural cultivation. |
| Forestry: | Ecology of forest species, cultivation of wood and especially forests of corktrees, restocking, retimbering. |
| Technology: | Industrial fermentations, wine making in the warm countries, brewery, vinegar making, distillery. |
| Topography: | Elements of geodosy and geography, topographical problems. |
| Economic Sciences: | Political economy, legislation, rural economy, agricultural accounting. |
| Zootechnics: | Veterinary medicine. |
| Rural Geography: | Natural Tunisian milieu, human milieu, great agricultural regions and productions. Problem of orientation and clearings. Agriculture compared in Mediterranean countries. |
| Rural Engineering: | Agricultural improvements - irrigation, sanitation, drainage, conservation of water and sun. |

Agricultural Machinery

Classwork augmented with practical experience and excursions under supervision of professors.

Written and oral examinations at end of each course. At close of each year a student's classification established by marks obtained for examinations, affected by coefficient attached to the importance of each subject.

Graduation from 1st year to 2nd year: at least average 11/20.
Graduation from 2nd year to 3rd year: at least average 12/20 over the 2 years.
Minimum required to obtain Diplôme: 13/20. (This is obtained by the totals of 3 years' work multiplied by the respective coefficients, 4, 5 and 5, and divided by 14.)

Diplôme d'Ingénieur E.S.A.T. awarded by the Secretary of State for Agriculture.

A certificate for the course of study is awarded by the Director of the
School to those pupils who have not fulfilled the necessary conditions for
a Diploma.


ECOLE NATIONALE D'ADMINISTRATION (National School of Administration)

Duration of course:        3 years.

Under supervision of the Secretary of State of the Presidency.  Formerly
the Tunisian School of Administration.

Provides specialized administrative and political training.

Entrance by examination open to holders of baccalauréat or Tahcil.


VOCATIONAL AND TECHNICAL EDUCATION

Until 1943, technical education rudimentary.  Vocational training given
in workshops attached to primary schools.  Muslim girls' primary schools
taught traditional crafts.

Collège Emile Loubet for boys, established 1898.
Collège Paul Cambon for girls, established 1914.
3 industrial schools for boys.

Between 1943 and 1945 vocational training centers opened (13 for boys, 10
for girls).  1945 independent Technical Education Department established
and technical colleges founded at Sfax, Susa and Bizerte.  By 1957, 50
vocational training centers.

Vocational training centers offer following special subjects:

Boys:   Fitting, Machine-Tool Making, Automobile Mechanics, Foundry Work,
        Lathe Work, Electricity, Locksmithing, Sheet Iron Work, Plumbing,
        Cabinet Making, Damascening, Leather-Work, Agricultural Rural
        Crafts, Reinforced Concrete Work, Masonry, Printing, Carving,
        Book-Binding.

Girls:  Cutting, Sewing, Embroidery, Carpet-Weaving, Chebka-Weaving,
        Lace-Making.


INTERMEDIATE EDUCATION (Enseignement Moyen)

Former vocational training centers being converted into Collèges Moyens.

Students enter after 6 years of primary education. Candidates admitted up to 16 years of age. 17-year candidates may be admitted to the industrial section with special authorization.

3-year general education program with vocational training. Students may choose: (a) General, (b) Commercial, or (c) Industrial.

General Course:

The number of weekly hours the same for the 3 years.

Arabic Language, 5 hrs., French Language, 5 hrs., English, 3 hrs., History and Geography, 2 hrs., Civics and Religion, 2 hrs., Mathematics, 4 hrs., Science, 3 hrs., Drawing, 2 hrs., Workshop, 2 hrs., Physical Education, 2 hrs. Total: 30 hrs.

Commercial Course:

Number of weekly hours in first 6 subjects of General Course are same in 1st year. Science is cut to 2 hrs. in first 2 years, omitted in 3rd year. Drawing, 2 hrs. in first 2 years, omitted in 3rd year. Physical Education, 2 hrs. throughout 3 years. Typing (Arabic and French), 4 hrs. in first 2 years, 3 hrs. in 3rd year. Shorthand, 3 hrs. in 2nd and 3rd years. 2nd and 3rd years: 1 hr. Commercial Correspondence each year; 1 hr. of Labor Legislation each year. Total, 31 hrs., 1st year; 33 hrs., 2nd year; 33 hrs., 3rd year.

Industrial Course:

Consecutive figures indicate weekly hours in 1st, 2nd and 3rd years. Arabic Language, 4, 3, 3. French, 4, 3, 3. English, none. History and Geography, 1, 1, 1. Civics and Religion, 1, 1, $\frac{1}{2}$. Mathematics, 4, $4\frac{1}{2}$, $4\frac{1}{2}$. Science, $1\frac{1}{2}$, $2\frac{1}{2}$, $2\frac{1}{2}$. Drawing, 4, 4, 4. Workshop, 17, 18, 18-20. Physical Education, 1, 1, 0. Labor Legislation, 0, 0, 1. Technology, $2\frac{1}{2}$, $2\frac{1}{2}$, $2\frac{1}{2}$. Totals per week, 40, $40\frac{1}{2}$, 40-42.

Boys and girls work separately in this course. 1 hr. of Home Economics is added for girls in the 1st year, also Hygiene and Baby Training (1, 2, 1) are included. These subjects replacing Technology which is reduced to 1, 1, 1.

Certificate awarded upon successful examinations according to chosen field.

Extension of course to a 4th year in all sections may be authorized. 4th year will be mainly practical training.


TECHNICAL SECONDARY PROGRAM

Technical secondary programs, (a) Mathematics, (b) Industrial, given in secondary lycées. 6-year program for boys. 5-year program for girls.

## TECHNICAL PROGRAM (Option Technique)
### (Hours per week per year)

### T E C H N I C A L

#### Mathematics

| Subjects | Year 1 | 2 | 3 | 4 | 5 | 6 |
|---|---|---|---|---|---|---|
| Language and Letters (Arabic) | 8 | 6 | 6 | 4 | 4 | - |
| Language and Letters (French) | 6 | 5 | 4 | 4 | 4 | - |
| 2nd Foreign Language | - | 2 | 2 | 2 | 2 | 2 |
| History and Geography | 2 | 2 | 2 | 2 | 2 | 3 |
| Civic and Religious Instruction | 1 | - | - | - | - | - |
| Mathematics | 3 | 3½ | 3½ | 6 | 6 | 9 |
| Natural Sciences (course/practical work) | (1+2) | 1 | 2 | - | - | - |
| Physical Sciences (course/practical work) | | 2 | 2 | 5 | 5 | 7 |
| Physical Education | 2 | 2 | 2 | 2 | 2 | 2 |
| Workshop and Practical Works | 3 | (8+1) | (11+1) | 8 | 6 | 6 |
| Drawing | 2 | 4 | 4 | 4 | 4 | 4 |
| Technology | - | - | 2 | 3 | 3 | 3 |
| Philosophy | - | - | - | - | - | 3 |
| | 30 | 36½ | 41½ | 40 | 38 | 39 |

### I N D U S T R I A L

#### Electronics

| | 1 | 2 | 3 | 4 | 5 | 6 |
|---|---|---|---|---|---|---|
| Language and Letters (Arabic) | 8 | 6 | 6 | 2 | 2 | 2 |
| Language and Letters (French) | 6 | 5 | 4 | 2 | 2 | 2 |
| 2nd Foreign Language | - | 2 | 2 | - | - | - |
| History and Geography | 2 | 2 | 2 | 2 | - | - |
| Civic and Religious Instruction | 1 | - | - | - | - | - |
| Mathematics | 3 | 3½ | 3½ | 6 | 4 | 5 |
| Natural Sciences (course/practical work) | (1+2) | 1 | 2 | - | - | - |
| Physical Sciences | - | 2 | 2 | - | - | - |
| Electrotechnology | - | - | - | 4 | 4 | 6 |
| Mechanics and Resistance of Materials | - | - | - | 3 | 3 | 3 |
| Physical Education | 2 | 2 | 2 | 1 | 1 | 1 |
| Workshop and Practical Works | 3 | (8+1) | (11+1) | 14 | 14 | 8 |
| Electrical Measurements | - | - | - | 3 | 4 | 6 |
| Drawing | (1+1) | 4 | 4 | 3* | 4* | 3* |
| Technology | - | - | 2 | 1 | 1 | 1 |

*Technical Drawing and Technology of Construction

## Electronics (cont'd)

| Subjects | Year 1 | 2 | 3 | 4 | 5 | 6 |
|---|---|---|---|---|---|---|
| Special Technology | - | - | - | 3 | 3 | 3 |
| Industrial Organization | - | - | - | - | 1 | - |
| Economics - Legislation | - | - | - | - | 1 | - |
| | 30 | 36½ | 41½ | 44 | 44 | 40 |

## Radio-Electricity

| Subjects | 1 | 2 | 3 | 4 | 5 | 6 |
|---|---|---|---|---|---|---|
| Language and Letters (Arabic) | 8 | 6 | 6 | 2 | 2 | 2 |
| Language and Letters (French) | 6 | 5 | 4 | 2 | 2 | 2 |
| 2nd Foreign Language | - | 2 | 2 | - | - | - |
| History and Geography | 2 | 2 | 2 | 2 | - | - |
| Civic and Religious Instruction | 1 | - | - | - | - | - |
| Mathematics | 3 | 3½ | 3½ | 6 | 4 | 5 |
| Natural Sciences (course/practical work) | (1+2) | 1 | 2 | - | - | - |
| Physical Sciences | - | 2 | 2 | 4* | 3* | 3* |
| Electrotechnology | - | - | - | 3 | 3 | 4 |
| Radio-Electricity | - | - | - | 4 | 4 | 4 |
| Physical Education | 2 | 2 | 2 | 1 | 1 | 1 |
| Workshop and Practical Works | 3 | (8+1) | (11+1) | 10 | 12 | 8 |
| Electrical Measurements | - | - | - | 3 | 3 | 6 |
| Drawing | (1+1) | 4 | 4 | 3** | 3** | 3** |
| Technology | - | - | 2 | 1 | 1 | 1 |
| Special Technology | - | - | - | 3 | 3 | 3 |
| Industrial Organization | - | - | - | - | 1 | - |
| Economics and Legislation | - | - | - | - | 1 | - |
| | 30 | 36½ | 41½ | 44 | 43 | 42 |

*Applied Sciences
**Technical Drawing and Technology of Construction

## Mechanics

| Subjects | 1 | 2 | 3 | 4 | 5 | 6 |
|---|---|---|---|---|---|---|
| Language and Letters (Arabic) | 8 | 6 | 6 | 2 | 2 | 2 |
| Language and Letters (French) | 6 | 5 | 4 | 2 | 2 | 2 |
| 2nd Foreign Language | - | 2 | 2 | - | - | - |
| History and Geography | 2 | 2 | 2 | 2 | - | - |
| Civic and Religious Instruction | 1 | - | - | - | - | - |
| Mathematics | 3 | 3½ | 3½ | 6 | 4 | 5 |
| Natural Sciences (course/practical work) | (1+2) | 1 | 2 | - | - | - |
| Physical Sciences | - | 2 | 2 | - | - | - |
| Electrotechnology | - | - | - | 2 | 2 | - |
| Mechanics and Resistance of Materials | - | - | - | 4 | 3 | 3 |

## Mechanics (cont'd)

| Subjects | Year 1 | 2 | 3 | 4 | 5 | 6 |
|---|---|---|---|---|---|---|
| Physical Education | 2 | 2 | 2 | 1 | 1 | 1 |
| Workshop and Practical Works | 3 | (8+1) | (11+1) | 16 | 18 | 18 |
| Drawing | 2 | 4 | 4 | 6* | 5* | 5* |
| Technology | - | - | 2 | 1 | 2 | 1 |
| Special Technology | - | - | - | 1 | 1 | 1 |
| Industrial Organization | - | - | - | - | 1 | - |
| Economics - Legislation | - | - | - | - | 1 | - |
| | 30 | 36½ | 41½ | 43 | 42 | 38 |

*Technical Drawing and Technology of Construction

## Topography (Surveying)

| | | | | | | |
|---|---|---|---|---|---|---|
| Language and Letters (Arabic) | 8 | 6 | 6 | 2 | 2 | 2 |
| Language and Letters (French) | 6 | 5 | 4 | 2 | 2 | 2 |
| 2nd Foreign Language | - | 2 | 2 | - | - | - |
| History and Geography | 2 | 2 | 2 | 2 | 1 | 1* |
| Civic and Religious Instruction | 1 | - | - | - | - | - |
| Mathematics | 3 | 3½ | 3½ | 6 | 5 | 5 |
| Natural Science (course/practical work) | (1+2) | 1 | 2 | - | - | - |
| Physical Sciences | - | 2 | 2 | - | - | - |
| Electricity | - | - | - | 2 | 2 | - |
| Cosmography | - | - | - | - | 1 | 2 |
| Physical Education | 2 | 2 | 2 | 1 | 1 | 1 |
| Workshop and Practical Works | 3 | (8+1) | (11+1) | 12 | 12 | 12 |
| Drawing | (1+1) | 4 | 4 | 6** | 6** | 6** |
| Technology | - | - | 2 | - | - | - |
| Topography (Surveying) | - | - | - | 2 | 2 | 2 |
| Numerical Calculus | - | - | - | 2 | 2 | 2 |
| Mechanics and Resistance of Materials | - | - | - | 3 | 3 | 4 |
| Industrial Organization | - | - | - | - | 1 | - |
| Economics - Legislation | - | - | - | 1 | 1 | - |
| | 30 | 36½ | 41½ | 41 | 41 | 41 |

*Cartography
**Technical Drawing and Technology of Construction

## Building

| | | | | | | |
|---|---|---|---|---|---|---|
| Language and Letters (Arabic) | 8 | 6 | 6 | 2 | 2 | 2 |
| Language and Letters (French) | 6 | 5 | 4 | 2 | 2 | 2 |
| 2nd Foreign Language | - | 2 | 2 | - | - | - |

## Building (cont'd)

| Subjects | Year 1 | 2 | 3 | 4 | 5 | 6 |
|---|---|---|---|---|---|---|
| History and Geography | 2 | 2 | 2 | 2 | - | - |
| Civic and Religious Instruction | 1 | - | - | - | - | - |
| Mathematics | 3 | 3½ | 3½ | 6 | 4 | 5 |
| Natural Sciences (course/practical work) | (1+2) | 1 | 2 | - | - | - |
| Physical Sciences | - | 2 | 2 | - | - | 3* |
| Electricity | - | - | - | 1 | 1 | - |
| Geology | - | - | - | - | 1 | 1 |
| Physical Education | 2 | 2 | 2 | 1 | 1 | 1 |
| Workshop and Practical Works | 3 | (8+1) | (11+1) | 16 | 18 | 8 |
| Drawing | 2 | 4 | 4 | 5** | 6** | 5** |
| Technology | - | - | 2 | 1 | 1 | - |
| Technology of Specialty | - | - | - | 1 | 1 | - |
| Topography (Surveying) | - | - | - | - | - | 2 |
| Architecture | - | - | - | - | - | 2 |
| Stereotomy | - | - | - | - | - | 2 |
| Measurement (building and works of art) | - | - | - | - | - | 2 |
| General Construction | - | - | - | 1 | 1 | 2 |
| Mechanics and Resistance of Materials | - | - | - | 3 | 3 | 4 |
| Organization of Timber-Yards | - | - | - | 1 | 1 | - |
| Economics - Legislation | - | - | - | 1 | 1 | - |
| | 30 | 36½ | 41½ | 43 | 43 | 40 |

*Applied Sciences

**Industrial Design and Technology of Construction

## Bridges and Highways

| Subjects | Year 1 | 2 | 3 | 4 | 5 | 6 |
|---|---|---|---|---|---|---|
| Language and Letters (Arabic) | 8 | 6 | 6 | 2 | 2 | 2 |
| Language and Letters (French) | 6 | 5 | 4 | 2 | 2 | 2 |
| 2nd Foreign Language | - | 2 | 2 | - | - | - |
| History and Geography | 2 | 2 | 2 | 2 | - | - |
| Civic and Religious Instruction | 1 | - | - | - | - | - |
| Mathematics | 3 | 3½ | 3½ | 6 | 4 | 5 |
| Natural Sciences (course/practical work) | (1+2) | 1 | 2 | - | - | - |
| Physical Sciences | - | 2 | 2 | - | - | 3* |
| Electricity | - | - | - | 1 | 1 | - |
| Physical Education | 2 | 2 | 2 | 1 | 1 | 1 |
| Workshop and Practical Works | 3 | (8+1) | (11+1) | 12 | 12 | 11 |
| Drawing | (1+1) | 4 | 4 | 6** | 6** | 7** |

*Applied Sciences

**Technical Drawing and Technology of Construction

Bridges and Highways (cont'd)

| Subjects | Year 1 | 2 | 3 | 4 | 5 | 6 |
|---|---|---|---|---|---|---|
| Technology | - | - | 2 | - | - | - |
| Technology (works of art) | - | - | - | 1 | 1 | - |
| Architecture | - | - | - | - | - | 1 |
| Stereotomy | - | - | - | - | - | 1 |
| Measurement and Project (works of art and building) | - | - | - | 1 | 2 | 5 |
| General Construction | - | - | - | - | - | 2 |
| Transportation | - | - | - | 2 | 2 | - |
| Mechanics and Resistance of Materials | - | - | - | 4 | 4 | 4 |
| Topography | - | - | - | 2 | - | - |
| Accounting | - | - | - | - | 1 | - |
| Legislation and Organization of Practical Works | - | - | - | - | 1 | - |
|  | 30 | 36½ | 41½ | 42 | 39 | 44 |

Girls (all specialties) - 5-year program

| Subjects | 1 | 2 | 3 | 4 | 5 |
|---|---|---|---|---|---|
| Language and Letters (Arabic) | 8 | 6 | 6 | 2 | 2 |
| Language and Letters (French) | 6 | 5 | 4 | 2 | 2 |
| 2nd Foreign Language | - | 2 | 2 | - | - |
| History and Geography | 2 | 2 | 2 | 2 | - |
| Civic and Religious Instruction | 1 | - | - | - | - |
| Mathematics | 3 | 3½ | 3½ | 2 | 1 |
| Natural Sciences (course/practical work) | (1+2) | 2 | 2 | - | - |
| Applied Sciences | - | - | - | 1 | 1 |
| Physical Education | 2 | 2 | 2 | 2 | 2 |
| Workshop and Practical Work | 3 | (8+1) | (11+1) | 18 | 24* |
| Drawing | 2 | 4 | 4 | 5 | 5 |
| Technology | - | - | 2 | 1 | 1 |
| Housekeeping Instruction | - | - | - | 3 | 2 |
| Economics - Legislation | - | - | - | 1 | 1 |
|  | 30 | 35½ | 39½ | 39 | 41 |

*History of Art

Technical Baccalauréat awarded at close of 6-year program.

TEACHER EDUCATION

TRAINING OF TEACHERS FOR PRIMARY SCHOOL INSTRUCTION (Instituteurs)

Teacher-candidates are chosen from students who have completed the 1st cycle of secondary education (usually the general program).  Selection by school authorities, with concurrence of parents.

Candidates then proceed through the 2nd cycle of secondary education ("normal" division).  When the candidate finishes his 6th year of secondary education, he is awarded the Diplôme de fin d'études normales, divided into 2 parts (like the baccalaureate).  First part at end of 5th year, second part at end of 6th year.

Candidate then enters Ecole Normale d'Instituteurs (Teacher Training School for Primary School Teachers) for 1 year of training.

3 sections:    (a) for bilingual teachers, (b) for Arabic language teachers, and (c) for French language teachers.

Theoretical training in General Psychology, Child Psychology, Sociology and Ethics.
Practical training through practice teaching in various classes for 9 months.
Theoretical training alternated with periods of practical work.

Diplôme de fin de stage awarded to candidate on graduation.

Some Ecoles Normales d'Instituteurs offer a 3-year secondary program, identical with the "normal" division of lycée.  Preference for one program or the other depends on local circumstances.


Moniteurs

Moniteurs are teacher helpers in primary schools whose appointment is regarded as an emergency measure caused by withdrawal of many French teachers during recent years.  Moniteurs are taken from graduates of Enseignement Moyen (Terminal Intermediate Course).

1-year program offered in a special, separate section of the Ecole Normale d'Instituteurs.  1 year, practical training.

Moniteurs may be authorized by school authorities to pursue 2 extra years of study entitling them to full-scale primary school teacher standing.


TRAINING OF TEACHERS FOR ENSEIGNEMENT MOYEN (Terminal Intermediate Program)

In French.

Graduates of secondary education with 2nd part of baccalauréat trained at Ecole Normale de Professeurs Adjoints.

2-year program, university level studies.

A section préparatoire (preparatory instruction) in this school covers the same program as the 2nd cycle of secondary education and replaces it wherever indicated.

Certificat d'aptitude au professorat adjoint (C.A.P.A.) awarded at close of 2-year program.


TRAINING OF TEACHERS FOR SECONDARY EDUCATION

6-year program ("long" program or lycée).


Ecole Normale Supérieure

Open to candidates holding two parts of the baccalauréat.

Main function of the School, located in Tunis, is to supervise practical training during a 3-year program.  Candidates are full-time students at one of the sections of the University of Tunis.  (The section will depend on the candidates' specialization:  future teacher of literature will attend Faculté des Lettres; teacher of physics, the Faculté des Sciences, etc.)

Teacher's licence made up of 4 certificats.

Most students are boarders at the Ecole Normale Supérieure.


Centre National de Formation Pédagogique (National Pedagogical Training
    Center

Attached to the Ecole Normale Supérieure.

University licenciés must take 2 additional years at this Centre before they are authorized to start as independent lycée teachers.  Program consists of more Psychology and Pedagogy, and practical work at lycées (students serving as teacher-helpers).

Certificat d'études supérieures de psycho-pédagogie awarded.

EAST   AFRICA

E A S T   A F R I C A

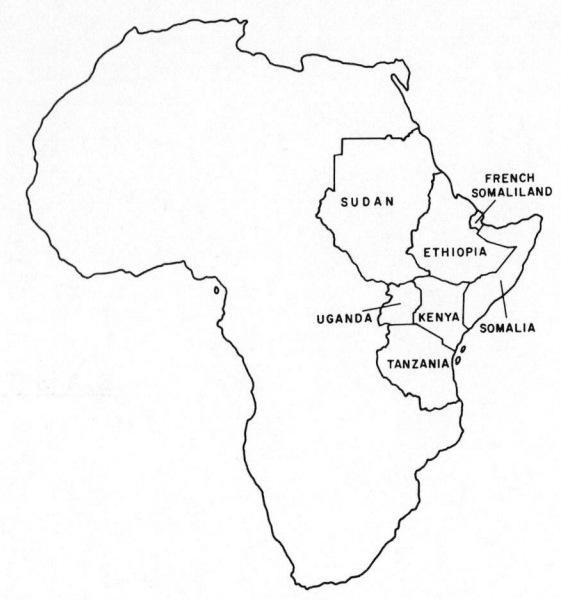

| Country and Capital | Area (sq. miles) | Est. Population | Independence Dates or Political Status | Official Language(s) |
|---|---|---|---|---|
| EMPIRE OF ETHIOPIA<br>Addis Ababa | 400,000 | 22,000,000 | About 2,000 years* | English |
| *Conquered by Italy in 1935-36, but liberated by British forces in 1941.) | | | | |
| REPUBLIC OF KENYA<br>Nairobi | 224,960 | 8,676,000 | 12 December 1963 | English |
| REPUBLIC OF SOMALIA<br>Mogasdiscio | 246,135 | 2,400,000 | 1 July 1960 | English and Italian |
| FRENCH SOMALILAND<br>Djibouti | 8,494 | 81,000 | French Overseas Territory | French |
| REPUBLIC OF THE SUDAN<br>Khartoum | 967,500 | 12,831,000 | 1 January 1956 | English |
| THE UNITED REPUBLIC OF TANZANIA<br>Dar es Salaam | | | Merged: April 26, 1964.  Changed name: October 29, 1964 | English |
| Formerly: Republic of Tanganyika<br>(Dar es Salaam) | 362,688 | 9,538,000 | (9 December 1961) | |
| and Zanzibar<br>(Zanzibar Town) | 640 | 165,253 | (10 December 1963) | |
| UGANDA | 93,981 | 6,845,000 | 9 October 1962 | English |

129

EMPIRE OF ETHIOPIA
(Revision 1959-60)

Prior to 1959-60

Secondary: XII, XI, X, IX

Middle School (Elementary): VIII, VII, VI, V

Primary: IV, III, II, I

In-serv. Tech. Tr. | Voc. Bldg. Tr.
Civil Avia.
Naval & Air Cadet Tr. | Army Cadets
Police Cadets | Tele.
Sani-tar.
Hosp. Pharm. | Voc.
Lab Tech.
Nurses Tr. | Dress.
Sec.
Agric. | Hand. T.T.
Tech. Sch. | C.S. Tchr. Tr.
Com. Sch.
Tchr. Tr.
(Post Primary)
Theol. Sec.

Defense Colleges
Sch. of Soc. Wk.
A. & M. Arts Col.
Building Inst.
Public H Col.
Engineering
Science
Arts **

UPPER SECONDARY (Academic)

LOWER SECONDARY

PRIMARY EDUCATION

Kindergarten

| Student's Age | Year of Schooling | | |
|---|---|---|---|
| 26 | 20 | HIGHER EDUCATION | |
| 25 | 19 | | |
| 24 | 18 | | |
| 23 | 17 | | |
| 22 | 16 | | |
| 21 | 15 | | |
| 20 | 14 | | |
| 19 | 13 | | |
| 18 | 12 | | |
| 17 | 11 | SECONDARY | |
| 16 | 10 | | |
| 15 | 9 | | |
| 14 | 8 | | |
| 13 | 7 | | |
| 12 | 6 | ELEMENTARY | |
| 11 | 5 | | |
| 10 | 4 | | |
| 9 | 3 | | |
| 8 | 2 | | |
| 7 | 1 | | |
| 6 | | | |
| 5 | | Kindergarten | |
| 4 | | | |
| 3 | | | |

Revision with shorter secondary program and new divisions between primary and secondary instituted in a few pilot schools. However, 1960-1963, most schools still operated on primary (4 years), middle school (4 years) and secondary (4 years) with above secondary programs stemming from 8-year primary-middle school training.

130

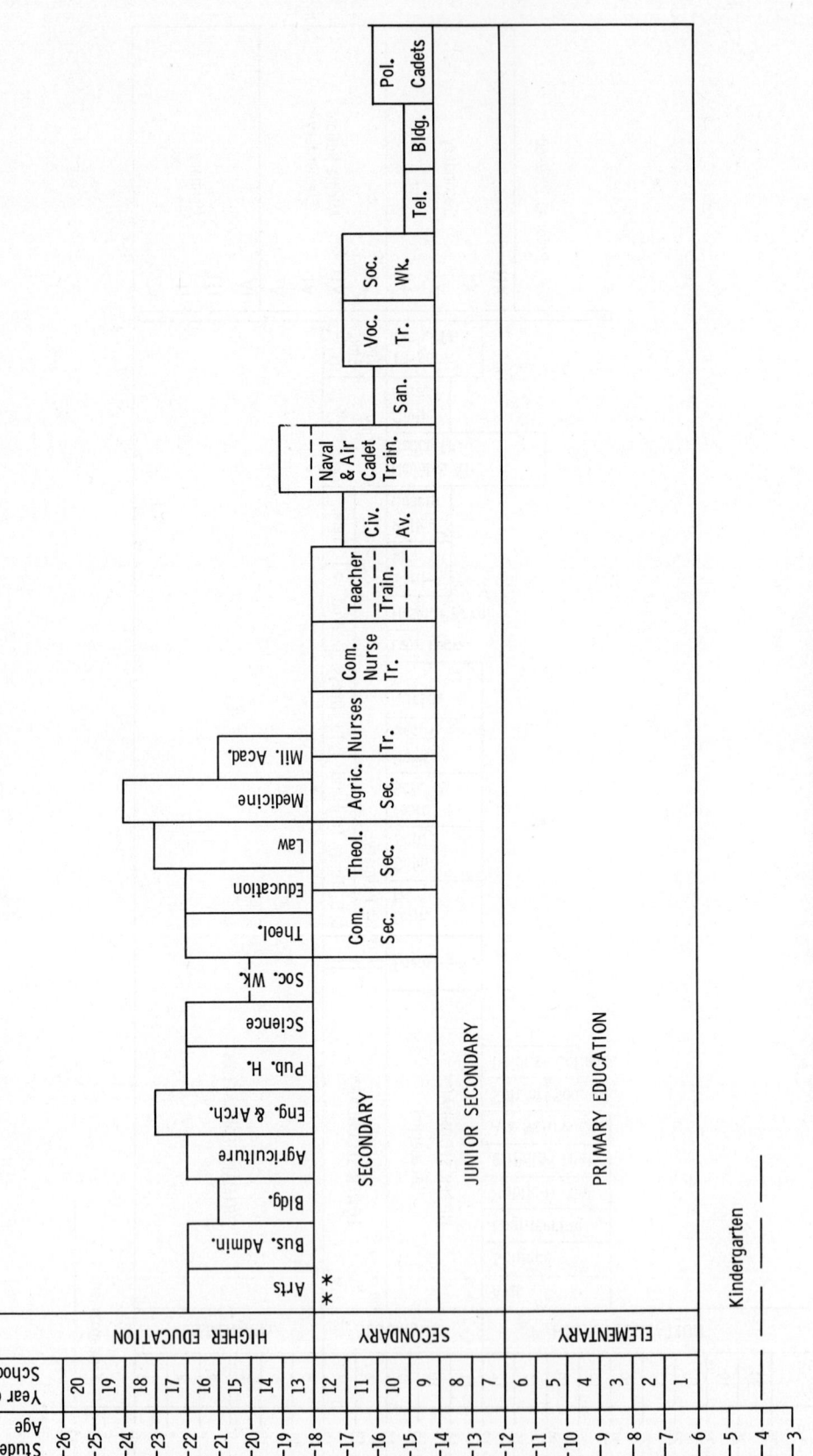

EMPIRE OF ETHIOPIA
(Revisions from 1963)

Compulsory education: Through primary education (not enforced).

School year: September–July.  3 terms.

Secondary Grading:  A – Excellent – 4 grade points
                    B – Very Good – 3 grade points
                    C – Average – 2 grade points
                    D – Below Average – 1 grade point
                    F – Failing – 0 grade point

An overall average of 1.5 grade points
is required for promotion.

EMPIRE OF ETHIOPIA

Independent for about 2,000 years.

## BACKGROUND

Politically the country is composed of 13 provinces including Eritrea (formerly a federated territory) which became a province in 1963.  Educationally, there are 13 plus Addis Ababa.  Educational statistics take special account of Addis Ababa, since most of the schools are there, but politically the city is in the province of Shoa.

Several millenia B.C. Cushitic people settled in Ethiopia; ancestors of the Beja in northeast of country, the Sidama south of the high plateau, and the nomadic Sankalis, Gallas, and Somalis on plains of the plateau.

During the first millenium Semites from southern Arabia mingled with Cushitic people and settled in Gojjam, Shoa, and Begemdir, founding Ethiopia as the Kingdom of Aksum.

The Amharas, highland people of mixed Semitic-Hamitic origin, have given the country its rulers and most of governing officials.  They constitute, together with the Tigreans, one-third of the population.  Nilotic tribes live in west along the Sudan border.  The non-indigenous population includes 50,000 Yemenite Arabs, and some Indians, Armenians, Greeks, and Italians.

Christianity was introduced into Ethiopia in the 4th century.  Subsequently, when the Muslims conquered Egypt, the Coptic Christian community in northeast Africa was threatened in the 7th century.

By 928, the Aksumite dynasty had declined.  Then the Zagwe dynasty became dominant; by 1260, the Aksumite dynasty regained the throne.  From 1314-44 Ethiopia had control of Muslim principalities in east and south.  Muslims returned in 16th century almost conquering the kingdom 1527-43.

During the 18th and 19th centuries the country was divided among several rival princes.  Central authority was achieved in 1855 under Emperor Theodore.  1869-85 Italy seized Assab, Massawa, Sahatti.  1886 Italian armies defeated at Aduwa by Emperor Menelik II.  By 1900 Ethiopia achieved control over Banadir (formerly Italian Somaliland).  France and the U.K. obtained Somali coastal enclaves through purchase and a series of protectorate treaties with local chieftains.

Menelik died, 1913.  1916, Ras Tafari of Shoa selected as heir apparent and head of government, and on November 2, 1930, crowned Emperor Haile Sellassie. Italy conquered Ethiopia 1935-36.  Emperor fled, returned during World War II, 1941, with aid of British armed forces.  By UN decision, the former territory of Eritrea was federated to Ethiopia in 1952, and in November 1962 was incorporated into the Empire of Ethiopia.

70 or more languages are spoken (mostly of the Hamitic-Semitic language family).  Amharic is official national language, spoken by 40%-50% of population.  The official second language is English, even though the most common European language in Eritrea is Italian.
Tigre is spoken in extreme north; Harari, in Harar Province.

Language of the Cushitic people includes Gallinya (or Galla), spoken in south-central part; Sidamo spoken in southwest; Agau, Beja (or Bedawiye), and Somali. Languages of the Nilotic group almost as numerous as the tribes.

Before the 19th century,education was the sole responsibility of the Coptic Church.  By middle of the 19th century, Roman Catholic and Protestant missionaries, mostly French, began to develop education.  Toward the end of the 19th century,Swedish Protestants and Italian Catholics began to open schools in Eritrea, then an Italian colony.

1906, the first government school was founded in Addis Ababa (still functioning as Menelik II School), designed primarily for teaching foreign languages.  First French mission school for boys, 1907, by the Frères de Saint-Gabriel; reorganized in 1912 with assistance of the Alliance Française.  Franciscan Sisters started school for small girls.

April 1925, Tafari Makonnen School created in Addis Ababa.  1927, schools at Dessie, Gore, Lekemt, Dire Dawa, and Jigjiga; in Addis Ababa, St. George's School giving primary instruction in French, with separate sections for boys and girls.

1930, Haile Sellassie I Grammar School founded at Addis Ababa, as a polytechnic school with primary sections, a Professional Department, a Department of Apprenticeship, Department of Medicine, and a Normal School. Girls' School, same year.

1935, School for Orphans, 2 more primary schools with instruction in French; a Military Academy in Holleta.  Throughout the provinces other schools created.

During 1936-41  Italian occupation all schools closed to Ethiopians; in some cases the schools being used for Italian children (Tafari Makonnen School became Liceo Vittorio Emanuel).  Orthodox Church managed to carry on some schools.

In 1941, new educational system built.  Ministry of Education created; Menelik II and Tafari Makonnen School for boys and Itegue Menen School for girls re-established, and a technical and a commercial school initiated. Elementary schools founded in Addis Ababa and provincial centers.

July 1943, the first high school, Haile Sellassie I Secondary School,
established.  Central and provincial Boards of Education constituted, 1947.
Uniform curriculum at elementary and secondary levels for entire country
developed over a period of years.

Before 1959, educational structure was:  4 years elementary, 4 years
middle school, 4 years secondary.  Between 1959-61 the Imperial Ethiopian
Ministry of Education and Fine Arts studied means of improving elementary
through secondary education.  Proposal of 1961, set in motion in pilot
schools:  6 years elementary, 2 years junior secondary, 3 years senior
secondary.  March 1969 revision:  6 years elementary, 2 years junior
secondary, 4 years secondary.

N.B.:       Ethiopia operates on an ETHIOPIAN CALENDAR in variance with the
            GREGORIAN CALENDAR; thus 7 years must be added to the Ethiopian
            Calendar (E.C.).

            Example:       Ethiopian Calendar       Gregorian Calendar
                                  1935                      1942
                                  1950                      1957

            From September 11 through December, there is a disparity of
            8 years.

## PRESENT SYSTEM

Government Schools are operated mainly by the Ministry of Education, but
include schools operated by the Ministry of Public Health, Ministry of
Agriculture, Ministry of Public Works and Communications, Ministry of
Posts, Telegrams and Telegraphs, Ministry of Commerce and Industry which
give specialized pre- or in-service training.  The Imperial Body Guard runs
a Cadets School; the Imperial Army, the Genet Military Academy, and the
Harar Military College; the Imperial Air Force, the Haile Sellassie Aviation School, and the Debre Zeit Technical School.

Mission Schools are schools operated by Christian Missions with or without
assistance from the government.  The assistance may be in the form of land,
building, or staff.  Some of the schools sponsored by religious organizations are private schools.

Private Schools are schools operated by some private person or institution
or religious organization with or without assistance from government
agencies.

Community Schools are schools established through community initiative and
by means of government assistance in the form of staff, building, or land.
These schools include some government schools converted into community

schools.  The purpose of these schools is to implement the Proclamation on
Fundamental and Adult Education, and to promote community participation in
the National Education Program.

Church Schools are schools maintained and operated by the Ethiopian Orthodox Church Administration.  In most cases these schools teach reading,
writing, and religion but some follow the Ministry of Education Curriculum.

## PRE-SCHOOL EDUCATION

A few kindergartens have been opened in some government and private schools.
Among these, the Gabre-Mariam School (Lycée Franco-Ethiopien), the Itegue
Menen Girls School, the English School, and the Nazareth School in Addis
Ababa.

## ELEMENTARY EDUCATION

Entry age:  6-7 years.  (Older boys and girls with no previous formal
            education may sometimes be admitted.)

6-year program.  Language of instruction:  Amharic.

Program composed of academic and non-academic subjects:

| Academic: | Amharic | Non-academic: | Health Education |
|---|---|---|---|
| | Arithmetic | | Agriculture |
| | Social Studies | | Arts and Crafts |
| | Natural Science | | Home Making |
| | English | | Physical training |
| | Music | | and games |
| | Morals | | |

### SUGGESTED TIME ALLOTMENT IN PERIODS PER WEEK
#### (one period = 40 minutes)

| Subjects | I | II | III | IV | V | VI |
|---|---|---|---|---|---|---|
| Amharic | 5-8 | 5-8 | 5 | 5 | 5 | 5 |
| Arithmetic | 5 | 5 | 5 | 5 | 5 | 5 |
| Social Studies | - | 1 | 3-4 | 3-4 | 4 | 4 |
| Natural Science | - | - | 3-4 | 4 | 6 | 6 |
| English (10 min. daily) | (same) | 5 | 5 | 6 | 6 |
| Music (15 min. daily) | (same) | 1 | 1 | 1 | 1 |
| Morals | 1 | 1 | 1 | 1 | 1 | 1 |
| Health Educ. (15 min. daily) | (same) | 1-2[+] | 1-2[+] | 1 | 1 |
| Agriculture | 2 | 2 | 1[+] | 1[+] | 1 | 1 |
| Arts and Crafts | 5 | 5 | 2-3[+] | 2-3[+] | 1 | 1 |

| | | | | | | |
|---|---|---|---|---|---|---|
| Home Making | - | - | (2-3)[++] | (2-3)[++] | 2 | 2 |
| Physical training and games | 5 | 5 | 3-4 | 3-4 | 2-3 | 2-3 |
| | 28-31 | 29-32 | 30-35 | 31-35 | 35-36 | 35-36 |

[+]May be increased or decreased according to age group.
[++]For big girls only.

First 4 years of course are a unit, may be regarded as "community education" --the academic subjects fulfilling the minimum education for the older boys and girls who are entering school at ages of 11-12 years. To give the maximum amount of practical experiences the non-academic subjects are especially organized. At end of 4 years, older boys and girls can return to community to work or attend a vocational school for 1 year. With this core 4-year unit, the younger pupil will have a chance to complete elementary education in 2 more years with a foundation for later education.

At end of 4 years, a general examination is given; it is designed to serve as an achievement test for the older pupils leaving school, and a diagnostic test for those continuing 5th and 6th grades.

Final examination is given by Ministry of Education at end of 6th year. On basis of this test and school records, students are promoted.

Elementary School Leaving Certificate awarded.

## SECONDARY EDUCATION

### JUNIOR SECONDARY

2-year program: Grades VII-VIII.

Language of instruction: English.

Program, general in character, in terms of "areas of study"--an academic core of work (Amharic, Mathematics, Science, and Social Studies) as a basis for the program but with emphasis on guidance and vocational education.

### JUNIOR SECONDARY SCHOOL TIMETABLE
(40-min. periods per week per year)

| ACADEMIC Subjects | Gr.7 | Gr.8 | NON ACADEMIC Subjects | Gr.7 | Gr.8 | GUIDANCE & VOCATIONAL Subjects | Gr.7 | Gr.8 |
|---|---|---|---|---|---|---|---|---|
| Amharic | 3 | 3 | Moral & Cultural | 2 | 2 | Gen. Guid. | 2 | 2 |
| English | 14 | 12-14 | | | | Tech. Ed. | 2 | - |
| Mathematics | 4 | 4 | Health & Phys. Ed. | 2 | 2 | Agric. Ed. | 2 | 2 |

| Science   | 4  | 4  |   |   | Home Making |   |   |
|-----------|----|----|---|---|-------------|---|---|
| History   | 3  | 3  |   |   | (Girls)     | - | 2 |
| Geography | 2  | 2  |   |   | Com. Ed.    | - | 2 |
|           | 30 | 30 | 4 | 4 |             | 6 | 6 |

Guidance and Vocational subjects:

| General Guidance: | Agriculture: | Technical: |
|-------------------|--------------|------------|
| Personal Health (Growth & Development) | Gardening | Woodworking |
| Public Health | Poultry | Electricity |
| Nutrition | Livestock | Metal Working |
| Safety & First Aid | Crop Production | |
| Mental Health | Field Trips | |

At the close of the 2-year program, tests set by the Ministry of Education
to assess levels of academic achievement as well as the interest and ability
of the student.  Headmaster and staff play an important role in assessing
student's interest and ability, particularly as exhibited through the
guidance and vocational program he has followed.


## SECONDARY

Schools offer academic, agricultural, theological, commercial, health, technical and vocational, police service, and teacher education programs.

Academic, agricultural, theological and commercial sections prepare for
university entrance.

Intensive study of Mathematics and Science in the secondary program.

Mathematics:   Arithmetic, algebra, geometry, trigonometry.

Physics:       Mechanics and properties of matter, heat, light, sound,
               magnetism and electricity, astronomy, the atom.

Chemistry:     Nature of matter, physical states of matter, units of
               measurement, and introduction to gases; water and solutions,
               structure of matter and chemical calculations, the alkali
               metals, the halogens, acids, bases and salts, ionization,
               types of chemical reactions, common characteristics of gases,
               nitrogen family, carbon and silicon and their compounds,
               glass, sulfur and its compounds, colloids, alkaline earth
               metals, boron and aluminum, copper, silver and gold, zinc,
               cadmium, mercury, tin and lead, iron, cobalt, and nickel;
               osmium, iridium, platinum, nuclear reactions, radioactivity,
               artificial transmutations, compounds of carbon, foods, soaps
               and medicines, plant foods, fuels, rubber and plastics, tex-
               tiles, paper; chemistry in everyday life.

## SUGGESTED PERIOD ALLOTMENTS FOR ACADEMIC SUBJECTS
(Periods per week)

| Subjects | Year | 1 | 2 | 3 | 4 |
|---|---|---|---|---|---|
| Amharic | | 3-4 | 3-4 | 3-4 | 3-4 |
| English | | 8-10 | 8-10 | 7-8 | 7-8 |
| Mathematics | | 5 | 5 | 5 | 5 |
| General Science | | 6 | 6 | 5 | 5 |
| Chemistry or | | | | | |
| Physics or | | | | | |
| Biology | | - | - | 2-3 | 2-3 |
| Geography | | 4-5 | 4-5 | 4 | 4 |
| History | | 3 | 3-4 | 3-4 | 3 |
| French | | 3-4 | 3-4 | 4 | 4 |
| | | 32-37 | 32-38 | 34-38 | 34-37 |

Non-academic subjects: At least 1 period per day for supervised games and/or physical training.
2-3 periods per week to each of the following: Home Economics, Music and Art, Handicraft or Shopwork.
1-2 periods per week to Moral Instruction.

At close of program, final examinations given for the national Ethiopian School Leaving Certificate (E.S.L.C.) (which serves as a qualifying entrance examination for the Haile Sellassie I University), and the General Certificate of Education of London University. Until 1963, the London G.C.E. taken as a matter of course by all twelfth graders.

Grading (according to the schedule of the Ethiopian School Leaving Certificate):

| | | |
|---|---|---|
| 100-75 | Excellent | A |
| 75-60 | Very Good | B |
| 59-50 | Good | C |
| 49-40 | Pass | D |
| 39-0 | Fail | F |

The Gabre Mariam School (Lycée Franco-Ethiopien) presents a few candidates annually for the French Baccalauréat.

Each major foreign community has established schools for children of its own citizens with instruction in the national language. However, some Ethiopians attend these schools.

Private, religious, and foreign schools:

| | |
|---|---|
| The English School | Nazareth School |
| The General Wingate Secondary School | The Mennonite School |
| The American School | Ethiopian Evangelical College |
| The German School | Licheyo Scientifico |
| The Greek School | Instituto Technico |
| The Israeli School | Aviamento Professionale |
| Scuola Italiana | Dekmare |
| St. Joseph's School | Camboni College |
| The Gabre Mariam School | Asmara |

### SECONDARY TIMETABLE - THE GENERAL WINGATE SCHOOL
(Periods per week)

| Subjects | 9a | 9b | 9c | 10a | 10b | 10c | 11a | 11b | 11c |
|---|---|---|---|---|---|---|---|---|---|
| Amharic | 4 | 4 | 4 | 4 | 4 | 4 | 5 | 5 | 5 |
| English | 10 | 10 | 10 | 7 | 7 | 11 | 5 | 5 | 10 |
| French | 4 | 4 | 4 | 4 | 4 | - | 5 | 5 | - |
| History | 3 | 3 | 3 | 4 | 4 | 4 | 5 | 5 | 5 |
| Geography | 4 | 4 | 4 | 5 | 5 | 5 | 5 | 5 | 5 |
| Mathematics | 6 | 6 | 6 | 6 | 6 | 6 | 6 | 6 | 6 |
| Physics | 2 | 2 | 2 | 3 | 3 | 3 | 3 | 3 | 3 |
| Chemistry | 2 | 2 | 2 | 3 | 3 | 3 | 3 | 3 | 3 |
| Biology | 2 | 2 | 2 | 3 | 3 | 3 | 3 | 3 | 3 |
| Religion | 3 | 3 | 3 | 2 | 2 | 2 | 2 | 2 | 2 |
| Phys. Ed. | 3 | 3 | 3 | 2 | 2 | 2 | 1 | 1 | 1 |
| Lecture | 1 | 1 | 1 | 1 | 1 | 1 | 1 | 1 | 1 |
| Headmaster's Class | 1 | 1 | 1 | 1 | 1 | 1 | 1 | 1 | 1 |

12th Grade:   Each subject gets 5 classes:  Amharic, English Language, Mathematics 'A' (these 3 are compulsory for all), and up to 5 selected from the following:  English Literature, French Geography, History, Mathematics 'B', Physics, Chemistry, Biology, General Science.

Add 2 Phys. Ed., 1 Religious Instruction, 1 Headmaster's Class, 1 general lecture for the whole school.

Total:  45 periods per week.

## HIGHER EDUCATION

## HAILE SELLASSIE I UNIVERSITY, Addis Ababa

Higher education in Ethiopia began with the founding of the University College of Addis Ababa (Faculties of Arts, and Science) on March 20, 1950. Within the next decade were added: a School of Social Work, a Geophysical Observatory, a Forestry Research Institute, an Extention Division. First U.C.A.A. degrees awarded in 1954.

The initial unit was followed by:

    College of Agriculture, Alemaya, 1951
    College of Engineering, Addis Ababa, 1953
    Building College, Addis Ababa, 1954
    Public Health College, Gondar, 1954
    Theological College, 1960

February 1961, an Imperial Charter brought together the Faculties and other higher educational units into Haile Sellassie I University.

At inauguration ceremonies, December 18, 1961, the Emperor's Guenet Leul Palace was donated as the main campus of the University.

First students received Baccalaureate degrees July, 1962.

1962, Faculty of Education established; 1963, Faculty of Law, Institute of Ethiopian Studies, College of Business Administration, and Creative Arts Center; 1964, Faculty of Medicine.

Entrance requirements (before 1965):

Degree programs:   Ethiopian School Leaving Certificate in at least 5 subjects at "Good" (50-59.9%) Level. Passes must include:
    (a)  The 3 compulsory subjects in
         Group I:   English Language
                    Amharic
                    Mathematics A

    (b)  At least 1 paper from each of
         Group II: History
                   Geography
                   English Literature
                   French
                   Geez
                   Economics
         and
         Group III: General Science
                    Biology
                    Physics
                    Chemistry
                    Mathematics B
                    Bookkeeping (acceptable for admission
                       to Business Administration only).

Alternatively, a candidate may present at least 5 passes, including English Language, and Mathematics at ordinary (O) level in the General Certificate of Education or at credit standard in the Cambridge School Certificate.

In addition to these basic passes, the various Colleges and Faculties have special requirements.

Diploma Programs:

Building Engineering:     Completion of 11th grade with good standing in Mathematics, Science, and English Language.

Elementary Teachers:      Open to teachers or administrators who have had at least 2 years of successful experience in the schools.

Junior Secondary          Completion of 12th grade with an E.S.L.C. pass
Teachers:                 of at least 50% in English Language and at least 60% in the subject to be taught.  Candidates must also be recommended by their School Directors.

Social Work:              Passes in E.S.L.C. at "Good" level in 5 subjects including English Language and Amharic.

Physical Education:  Completion of 12th grade with an E.S.L.C. pass (40%) in English Language and Amharic, as well as a 50% pass in General Science or one of the basic sciences; alternatively, completion of 12th grade in a teacher training school and one post-secondary vacation course of the Faculty of Education.

Certificate Programs:

Year of General Studies:  Passes of 40% in 5 subjects, including
(eliminated 1964)    English Language, in the E.S.L.C.

University Extension:     Passes in English Language in the E.S.L.C. or equivalent examination.


Admission to the following sections of the University depends both on meeting the academic requirements and a satisfactory personal interview:

    College of Agriculture
    Building College
    Public Health College
    School of Social Work
    Theological College

Entrance requirements (after 1965):

Degree programs:    Grade point average of 2.0 in <u>Ethiopian School Leaving Certificate</u> (i.e. a 'C' average in 5 subjects of which Amharic, English Language and Mathematics 'A' are compulsory, with no 'F' in any one of the compulsory subjects. The 2 additional subjects chosen from the following groups:

Group I:    English Literature, French, Ge'ez, History, Geography, Economics, Bookkeeping (for Business Administration only).

Group II:    Mathematics 'B', General Science, Physics, Chemistry, Biology.

Faculties of Arts and Theology:  At least one of the 2 optional subjects must be from Group I.

Faculties of Science, Engineering and Agriculture:  The 2 optional subjects must be from Group II.

Faculty of Education and Colleges of Business Administration and Public Health:  The 2 additional subjects can be from both Groups I and II, chosen in any manner.

Faculty of Law:  Students accepted only after a minimum of 2 years of university training.

Faculty of Medicine:  Students accepted only after a minimum of 2 years of university training.

Alternate requirements to the degree programs in the Faculties and Colleges of Agriculture, Business Administration, Education, Engineering, Public Health, and Theology:  Completion of 12th grade in certain secondary schools with an academic average above the percentile rank designated for the school attended, and approval of the chosen faculty or college.

Diploma Programs:

Building:    Completion of 12th grade with passes at 'C' level in the E.S.L.C. in Mathematics 'A' and either English Language or a science subject. A test and interview. (Alternatively, completion of 12th grade with an academic average above the percentile rank designated for the school attended. A test and an interview.) A limited number of graduates from recognized technical schools with 'C' level in English Language, Mathematics and General Science are accepted on the basis of a test and interview.

Education (Junior Secondary):  A pass in English in E.S.L.C.; a pass in 2 other subjects commonly taught in junior secondary school, with a 'C' average; an interview.

Education (Elementary School Director and Supervisors):  Completion of the 12th grade in teacher-training or other secondary school, 2 or more years of successful teaching in elementary school, and an interview.

Education (Physical Education):  A pass at 'C' level in General Science or one of the basic sciences and passes in English and 1 other subject, physical fitness certificate, letter of recommendation from candidates secondary school Director.

Social Work:  5 passes in the E.S.L.C. with a 'C' average including English Language and Amharic.  (Alternatively, completion of the 12th grade in certain secondary schools with an academic average above the percentile rank designated for the school attended.)

Theology:  Completion of the 12th grade of academic secondary school with a pass in English Language preferably at 'C' level in the E.S.L.C.  (Alternatively, completion of the 12th grade in certain secondary schools with an academic average above the percentile rank designated for the school attended.) Certificate from the Bishop of the candidate's diocese or head of his religious order.

Special Entrance Qualifications:

Agriculture:  Students from the Agricultural Schools at Ambo and Jimma who have passed special examinations conducted by the College of Agriculture.

Education:  Graduates of the 12th grade program of the University Laboratory School may be admitted upon recommendation of their teachers.

Teachers recommended by the Selection Committee of the Elementary Teachers Diploma Course.

Engineering:  A limited number of well-qualified graduates from the Technical School.

Theology:  Students who have passed a special examination in Christian Religious Knowledge arranged by the university may offer this in place of one of the non-compulsory subjects in the E.S.L.C.

Degree requirements:      Total credit-hour requirement for a bachelor's
                          degree is 130.
                          (A credit is defined as one lecture or recitation,
                          or 2-3 hours of laboratory work for the duration
                          of a semester.)

Minimum credit hours per semester taken by a regular student is 15;
maximum, 18.

Grading system:      A = 100-90      Excellent
                     B = 89-80       Good
                     C = 79-70       Average
                     D = 69-60       Passing
                     F = below 60    Failing

## College of Agriculture

4-year program leading to a B.Sc.(Agric.) degree in the following fields:

    General Agriculture
    Agricultural Economics and Business
    Agricultural Engineering Technology
    Animal Sciences
    Plant Sciences

Graduates from the Agricultural Schools at Jimma and Ambo who do not have
Ethiopian School Leaving Certificates are eligible to apply for admission;
a good secondary school record in English Language, Mathematics, and
Science is required.

## Faculty of Arts

4-year program leading to a B.A. degree.

Departments of:

    Philosophy                              History
    Ethiopian Languages and Literature      Geography
    European Languages                      Sociology
    English                                 Economics
    Public Administration                   Political Science

The first year provides for general education.  Specialization begins in the
2nd year when student chooses his major.

## Building College

3-year diploma course.

In addition to the entrance requirements listed above for students from the 11th grade, students who have graduated from the Vocational Schools may also apply for admission.

Certificate courses for Building Foremen and Building Workmen are also provided.

## College of Business Administration

4-year program leading to the B.Com. degree.

Major departments are Commerce and Accounting. Courses also given in Personnel Administration, Finance, Marketing and Managerial Control.

Special program in Secretarial Science begun in 1964.

## Faculty of Education

4-year program leading to the B.A. (Ed.) degree, with majors in English, Amharic, Geography, or History, and the B.Sc. (Ed.) degree, with a major in Mathematics.

Diploma courses are available as follows:

Junior Secondary Teachers:     In Mathematics, General Science, and
    (2-year course)            Social Studies (either Geography or
                               History)
Physical Education Teachers
Elementary Teachers (given in the summer)

Special 2-week intensive refresher course for elementary school teachers of English, beginning September 1963.

## College of Engineering

5-year program leading to a B.Sc. (Eng.) degree in Architecture and in the following fields of Engineering: Civil, Electrical, and Mechanical. High grades in Mathematics and Science are required of candidates.

First year given in the Faculty of Science, common to all students. Those passing transfer to the College of Engineering for another year of pre-Engineering. Specialization, 3rd year.

## Public Health College

Training for Health Officers.

4-year course for Public Health Officers leading to a <u>B.P.H.</u> degree.

## Faculty of Science

4-year program leading to the B.Sc. degree in the following fields:

    Mathematics and Physics
    Biology and Chemistry
    Chemistry
    Pharmacy (transferred to Faculty of Medicine, 1964)
    Chemistry and Geology

First year, basic course for all students.  Specialization, 2nd year.

## Faculty of Medicine

6-year program, operating in conjunction with the American University of Beirut.  4-year course in Pharmacy is offered at H.S.I.U. in this Faculty.

## School of Social Work

2-year diploma course.

Graduates are employed as field workers in Family Welfare, Medical Social Work, Probation Work, School Social Work, Group Work, Rehabilitation, Community Development and Social Research.

## Theological School of the Holy Trinity

4-year program in Theology leading to the B.Th. degree.

4-year diploma course for those who do not qualify for the baccalaureate.

## University Extension

Formally instituted, 1962.  (Prior to this date, extension work was carried on by the different colleges under one form or another for more than 10 years.)

Classes in Addis Ababa, Asmara, Debre Zeit, Harar, Massawa. Gondar, Jimma.  In Addis Ababa, adults may attend classes of the Faculties of Arts and Science and the Colleges of Business Administration, Engineering, and Building.

Offerings:        (a)  Degree courses in Arts and Business
                  (b)  Diploma courses
                  (c)  High school level courses
                  (d)  Correspondence for high school level students
                  (e)  Informal education

Entrance requirements:              Degree students:

                                    Ethiopian School Leaving Certificate in at
                                    least 5 subjects which must include English
                                    Language, Amharic, and Mathematics "A".

                                    Certificate and Diploma students:

                                    Candidate must have attended the 12th grade
                                    and must pass the English and a general
                                    knowledge entrance examination.

Programs of study:

(1)  Degree program

     For a Bachelor's degree in Arts and Business, a student must have
     successfully completed 140 credits, with a minimum of C average,
     having included in the program the following core subjects:

          Amharic                          Introduction to Philosophy
          English                          Introduction to Economics
          Introduction to Sociology        Introduction to Geography
          History of World Civilization and Ethiopian Studies

(2)  Certificate and Diploma programs

     Executive Secretarial Development Course        3 semesters
     Certificate program in Law                      2½ years
     Diploma program in Law                          3 years
     Diploma program for developing Junior Accountants  5 semesters
     Diploma in Political Science and Government      6 semesters
     Diploma in Economics                            3 years
     Diploma in Education for Junior Secondary
        School Teachers                              60 credits

     An Extension Intermediate Certificate awarded to those who have
     completed a total of 72 college credits (equivalent to 2 years of
     college work).


Correspondence Department - University Extension

Secondary education and college level instruction.

Entrance requirements:

    College level:      Pass, Ethiopian School Leaving Certificate in at
                          least 5 subjects. Passes should include English,
                          Mathematics, and Amharic.  The rest selected from:

| Group I<br>(for courses in fields of Art) | Group II<br>(for courses in fields of Science) |
|---|---|
| History | General Science |
| Geography | Biology |
| English Literature | Physics |
| Economics | Chemistry |
| French | Advanced Mathematics |
| | Bookkeeping (for those admitted<br>in Business Administration only) |

College level offerings:

    Economics
    Economic Development
    English Grammar and Composition
    World History (Western Civilization I, and II)
    Comparative Government (Political Science)
    Sociology (Man and Society)

Entrance requirements:

    Secondary level:    All who have reached 8th grade level (junior
                          secondary) are eligible.

Secondary level offerings:

    English 9th grade I, and II
    English 10th grade I, and II
    English 11th grade I
    English 12th grade I, and II
    Language usage
    Mathematics:
        Elementary Algebra I, and II
        Advanced Algebra I, and II (1st and 2nd semester of 2nd year
          high school algebra)
        Plane Geometry I, and II
        Trigonometry
    General Science I, and II
    Biology
    Chemistry I, and II, and III
    Physics I, and II
    Geography:
        World Geography I, and II
    History:
        World History I, and II
    Economics

<u>Year of General Studies</u> (eliminated 1964)

Provided background for those who have finished 12th grade but do not meet the admissions requirements for a degree program. Successful completion of this program led to first year entrance to a degree course.


<u>Institute of Ethiopian Studies</u>

For the promotion and undertaking of research in all fields relating to Ethiopia. Institute also offers a certain number of lectures and seminars for advanced students.


## VOCATIONAL AND TECHNICAL EDUCATION

COMMERCIAL TRAINING:

Courses offered in Commercial School, Addis Ababa, and in commercial sections of following secondary schools: Lycée Gabre Mariam, Ecole Ste. Marie, and Teferi Mekonnen (all, Addis Ababa), Haile Sellassie I (Gondar), Woizero Sihin (Dessie).

Entrance requirements:   Junior secondary training.

4-year program.

Courses:
>            General:  Amharic, English, French, Morals, Current Affairs.
>            Special:  Bookkeeping, Accounting, Typing, Shorthand, General
>                      Office Practice.

Students may sit for <u>Royal Society of Arts</u> examination, or enter for commercial subjects in the <u>General Certificate of Education</u> examination.


COMMERCIAL SCHOOL, Addis Ababa

Entrance requirements:   Over 16 years of age, successful passing of the
>                         <u>Eighth Grade General Examination</u> with a high
>                         percentile, a good knowledge of the English
>                         language, and aptitude for commercial training.

Courses divided into 3 main categories:

(1)  Language:  Amharic and English.
(2)  Skill Subjects:  Amharic and English Typing, Shorthand, Book-
>              keeping, Commercial Arithmetic, and Business Training.
(3)  Contributory Subjects;  Social Sciences, Physical Education, and
>              Morals.

Every student takes the same courses in the first 2 years; 3rd and 4th years specialize in Accounting or Secretarial Studies.

## TIMETABLE
### (45-min. periods per week)

| Subjects | 1st Year | 2nd Year |
|----------|----------|----------|
| Amharic | 5 | 3 |
| English | 10 | 10 |
| Amharic Typing | 4 | 3 |
| English Typing | 4 | 3 |
| Bookkeeping | 5 | 4 |
| Comm. Arithmetic | 5 | 4 |
| Business Training | 4 | 4 |
| Physical Education | 2 | |
| Shorthand | | 4 |
| Morals | 1 | 1 |
| Social Sciences | | 4 |
| Total | 40 | 40 |

Specialization: Accounting

| Subjects | 1st Year | 2nd Year |
|----------|----------|----------|
| Amharic | 3 | 3 |
| English | 10 | 10 |
| Amharic Typing | 3 | 3 |
| English Typing | 3 | 3 |
| Accounting | 7 | 7 |
| Comm. Mathematics | 5 | 5 |
| Business Training | 3 | 3 |
| Social Sciences | 5 | 5 |
| Morals | 1 | 1 |
| Total | 40 | 40 |

Specialization: Secretarial Studies

| Subjects | 1st Year | 2nd Year |
|----------|----------|----------|
| Amharic | 3 | 3 |
| English | 10 | 10 |
| Amharic Typing | 4 | 4 |
| English Typing | 4 | 4 |
| Shorthand | 7 | 7 |
| Comm. Arithmetic | 2 | 2 |

| | | |
|---|---|---|
| Business Training | 4 | 4 |
| Social Sciences | 5 | 5 |
| Morals | 1 | 1 |
| Total | 40 | 40 |

Grading:   Passing grade, 50%.  In each course:  20% of the semester mark
           for class work, 80% for final examination.
           First semester is worth 40% and the second 60% of the year's mark.

Examinations:

           Besides the regular school examinations and the Ethiopian School
           Leaving Certificate examinations, the Commercial School students
           are given the Royal Society of Arts of London examinations.
           These examinations include English, Bookkeeping, Shorthand, and
           Typing and come in 3 stages, I, II, and III.  Exceptional
           students may take Stage I examinations in 3rd year, and Stage II
           and III in 4th year.  Due to difficulty of examinations most
           students sit only for Stage I in the 4th year.


TECHNICAL AND VOCATIONAL TRAINING:

Training at:

           Technical School (Addis Ababa)
           Vocational Trade School (Asmara)
           Technical Secondary (Debre Zeit)
           Civil Aviation School (Addis Ababa)
           Tele-Institute Technical Education (Addis Ababa)
           Instituto Tecnico Butego (Asmara - Eritrea)
           Atse Yohanis Technical Secondary (Mekele)
           Woizero Sihin Technical Secondary (Dessie)
           Haile Sellassie I Technical Secondary (Gondar)


TECHNICAL SCHOOL, Addis Ababa

Entrance requirement:       Junior secondary training.  (Those who have passed
                            the Secondary School Leaving examination also
                            accepted.)

4-year program.

Academic subjects include:  Amharic, Science, Mathematics, Morals,
Mechanical Drawing.

General course in basic skills, 1st year:  Electricity, Woodwork, Metalwork.

Specialization from 2nd year in a trade chosen from:  Surveying, Foundry,
Forging and Welding, Arts and Crafts, Drafting (mech. and architect.),
Cabinet Making, Automechanics, Sheet Metal Work, Machines, Radio, Electricity.

## VOCATIONAL TRADE SCHOOLS

Entrance requirements:   Junior secondary training.

3-year program.

Basic general course of Amharic, Mathematics, Science, Mechanical Drawing, Physical Education, Workshop Practice.

Specialization, 2nd and 3rd years in one of the following:  Woodwork and Masonry, Forging, Welding, Machine Shop, Sheet Metal, Auto Shop, Electric Shop.

## DEBRE ZEIT TECHNICAL SECONDARY SCHOOL

Entrance requirements:   High score in junior secondary performance.

5-year program.

General subjects:  English, Amharic, Mathematics, Geography and History, Religious Instruction, Physical Education.

Technical training in:  Technical Drawing, Engineering Science, Woodwork, Metalwork.

Students may sit for Cambridge Overseas School Certificate examination.

## BUILDING TRADES SCHOOL

Entrance requirements:   Completion of 4th grade and at least 16 years of age, special entrance examination.  (Those with junior secondary training exempt from examination.)

Instruction in Amharic.

4-year practical program.

Divisions:  Carpentry, Plumbing, Masonry, Electrical Installation.

## IMPERIAL BOARD OF TELECOMMUNICATIONS TRAINING COURSES

Entrance requirements:  Junior secondary or academic secondary.

1-year program.

Graduates employed by Board.

CIVIL AVIATION SCHOOL

Entrance requirements:    Some higher secondary training.

3-year program.

Courses in:  Electronics, Radio, Meteorology, Aircraft Maintenance.


AGRICULTURAL TRAINING:

Training offered in:
        Agricultural and Forestry School, Ambo (Shoa Province)
        Jimma Agricultural Technical School (Kaffa Province)
        Atse Yohanis Agricultural section (Mekele)
        Woizero Sihin Agricultural section (Dessie)
        Haile Sellassie I Agricultural section (Gondar)

Programs at Ambo Agricultural and Forestry School and Jimma Agricultural
Technical School:  4-year general course, preparing for University training in agriculture.


AMBO AGRICULTURAL AND FORESTRY SCHOOL

| | |
|---|---|
| 1st year (9th grade): | Amharic, English, Arithmetic, General Science, Agriculture, Hygiene. |
| 10th grade: | World History, Biology added. |
| 11th grade: | Algebra, Chemistry added. |
| 12th grade: | Physics, Geometry, Economic Geography, Ethiopian History, and Farming Practice added. |

4-year program in Forestry:  general course and special forestry subjects.
Forest Ranger Diploma awarded at close of 2-year training; Forestry Engineer
Diploma at close of 4-year training.


JIMMA AGRICULTURAL TECHNICAL SCHOOL

Operated under contract with Oklahoma State University.

4-year high school program.

Entrance requirements:    Completion of the British Eighth Grade Leaving
                          Examination with the score in the 95th percentile
                          or above.

Academic program is combined with practical classroom and laboratory work
in Animal and Plant Sciences.

Academic subjects:  4 years of English, 3 years of Mathematics, 1 year each in General Science, Biology, Chemistry, and Physics, plus 3 years of Amharic.

Agricultural courses go more into depth than do conventional agricultural courses in the U.S. (according to Director of Instruction and Research from Oklahoma State University):  Animal Nutrition, Poultry, Dairy, and Beef Husbandry, Advanced Field Crops, Soils, Coffee Production, Shop, and Tractor Operation.


HEALTH TRAINING:

Programs at secondary levels, under Ministry of Public Health, in collaboration with national and international organizations and technical assistance programs.

Courses offered at:
     Red Cross School of Nursing (Addis Ababa)
     Princess Tshai Hospital Nurse Training (Addis Ababa)
     Empress Zauditu Hospital Nurse Training (Addis Ababa)
     Itege Menen School of Nursing (Asmara)
     Tafari Makonnen School of Nursing (Lekempt)
     Menelik II Hospital (Addis Ababa)
          (1)  X-ray Technician Course
          (2)  Dressers Course
     Public Health Training Centre (Gondar)

Hospital courses range up to 4 years.  Students recruited from higher grades of academic secondary.

Public Health Training Centre trains community nurses (women) and sanitarians (men).  Students recruited from junior secondary; must pass special medical examination.

     Nurses:    2-year program, and 1-year supervised field work.
                (English, Anatomy, Physiology, Microbiology, Psychology,
                Sociology, Nutrition, Hygiene, Diseases, Drugs, Midwifery,
                Infant and Child Care, related subjects, Nursing Studies.)

     Sanitarians:  1-year program, and 1 year supervised field work.
                (Sanitation, Public Health Education, Insect Control,
                English, Mathematics, Chemistry, Physics, Anatomy, and
                Statistics.)


MALARIA ERADICATION TRAINING SCHOOL

Entrance requirements:    Completion of 9th grade secondary school, 18-25
                          years of age, special entrance examination.

6-month program for men only.

5 years devoted to a work project required.

SERVICE TRAINING:

12 police training centers and Aba Dina Police Staff College, Addis Ababa.

Imperial Naval Petty Officer School, Massawa

Imperial Ethiopian Air Force Ground School, Debre Zeit

Cadet School for the Imperial Guard (outside Addis Ababa)

Military Colleges, Holleta and Harar


## TEACHER EDUCATION

First program started in 1944 with 2 classes in the Menelik II School, Addis Ababa.  Later, Teacher Training School established with its own premises.  3-year course leading to a diploma in teaching.
Later, other teacher training schools established in Addis Ababa and other provincial centers.

Secondary school teachers trained at the University.

Elementary and junior secondary teachers trained at:
    Teacher Training School, Harar
    Haile Sellassie I Day School, Addis Ababa
    Teacher Training School, Asmara
    Itegue Menen Girls' School, Addis Ababa
    Community Teacher Training School, Debre Berhan
    Theological Teacher Training School, Addis Ababa
    Mekane Yesus Theological Seminary (Swedish Evangelical Mission)
    Arts and Crafts Teacher Training School, Addis Ababa
    Atse Yohanie Teacher Training section, Mekele  ) Closed 1964. Students
    Woizero Sihin Teacher Training section, Dessie ) sent to Tchr. Tr. Sch.,
    Norwegian Lutheran Teacher Training, Yirga Alem         Asmara


## TEACHER TRAINING SCHOOL, Harar

Originally established in Addis Ababa.

Entrance requirements:   Junior secondary training.

4-year academic secondary course with strong bias toward Pedagogy; practice teaching at model elementary school.

Students prepared for <u>Ethiopian School Leaving Certificate</u> examination.

Qualified as primary and junior secondary school teachers.

## HAILE SELLASSIE I DAY SCHOOL

Entrance requirements:   Junior secondary training.

1-year program on methods of teaching primary school subjects.

Curriculum:      Basic academic courses:  Amharic, Mathematics, Science,
                 Social Studies.  Psychology, Education, Music, Art, Health,
                 Shopwork, Physical Education, Practice Teaching.

4-year program:  Basic academic courses, and Psychology, History of
                 Education, Teaching Methods, Statistics, Practice Teaching.

1-year course in school administration for school directors and inspectors.

Students from 4-year program sit for <u>E.S.L.C.</u> examination.

## EMPRESS MENEN GIRLS' SCHOOL, Addis Ababa

Program for girls, similar to Haile Sellassie I Day School.

4-year academic course and Domestic Science training.

Students eligible for <u>E.S.L.C.</u> and <u>G.C.E.</u> examinations.

## TEACHER TRAINING INSTITUTE, Asmara

Opened 1943.

1-2 year program for training elementary school teachers.

Entrance requirements:   For admission to "3rd year," candidates must have
                         successfully completed Grade 10 in any of secondary
                         schools in the Empire.  For admission to "4th year,"
                         candidates must have completed Grade 11.

<u>TIMETABLE</u>
(Hours per week)

| Subjects | 3rd Year | 4th Year |
|----------|----------|----------|
| Amharic  | 5        | 4        |
| English  | 6        | 6        |

| | | |
|---|---|---|
| Mathematics | 5 | 5 |
| General Science | 6 | 6 |
| History | 2 | 2 |
| Geography | 3 | 3 |
| Educational Psychology | 2 | 2 |
| School Administration and Classroom Management | 1 | 2 |
| History and Philosophy of Education | 1 | 1 |
| Statistics | | 1 |
| Methodology | 1 | 2 |
| Audio-visual Aids | 1 | 1 |
| Handcraft | 1 | 1 |
| Physical Education | 1 | 1 |
| Health Education | 1 | 1 |
| | 36 | 38 |

<u>Certificates</u> issued by the Ministry of Education, Imperial Government of Ethiopia.


COMMUNITY TEACHER TRAINING SCHOOL, Debre Berhan

Training of community school teachers (work in rural primary schools).

Entrance requirements:   Junior secondary training.

2-year program and supervised field work.

Curriculum:     Mathematics, Science, Social Studies, Morals, Health and
                Sanitation, Literacy Methods, School Administration, Methods
                of Teaching, Agriculture, Blacksmithing, Carpentry, Brick-
                making, Pottery, Arts and Crafts, Sports.


ARTS AND CRAFTS TEACHER TRAINING SCHOOL, Addis Ababa

4-year program.

1st year:       General course:  Amharic, English, Mathematics, Science,
                Morals, Mechanical Drawing, Teaching Methods, Shop Management.
                Development of basic skills in handling electrical tools,
                Woodwork, and Metalwork.

Final 3 years: Arts and Crafts courses:  Leather Crafts, Ceramics, Basketry,
                Weaving, Fibrework, Rug-weaving, Carving, Painting, Sculpture,
                Drama and Puppetry, Classroom Art and Art History.
                Educational Psychology, Methods of Teaching Arts and Crafts,
                Practice Teaching.

**N.B.** Ethiopian University Service

> Program, introduced Fall 1964, requires that all Ethiopian degree
> students spend 1 year teaching in the provinces before they are
> awarded their degrees. This service was considered not only a
> national necessity to relieve the shortage of teachers, but also a
> means of repaying the country for the entirely free education given
> to students, from primary school through college. (This may explain
> a gap in the chronology of some transcripts in the future.)

## SPECIALIZED EDUCATION

### SCHOOL OF FINE ARTS

Entrance requirements:   Junior secondary training, not more than 25 years
                         of age, presentation of art work.

4-year program.

Curriculum:   History of Art, Psychology of Art, Figure Drawing, Anatomy,
              Modelling, Life Painting, Composition, Etching, Lithography.

Specialization in Commercial Art, Painting, or Sculpture.

### SCHOOL OF MUSIC

Students from elementary and secondary school, university and other programs.

Part-time instruction.

### ADULT EDUCATION

General literacy programs, and training in Health and Social Welfare in
rural areas.

Centers first established at Tabasse and Shano with a clinic, instruction in
child care, Amharic lessons, and agricultural demonstrations. Now more than
100 community centers for "community education."

All primary schools in provinces covering grades 1-4 are considered "community
schools" where instruction is given to adults as well as to children.
Teachers for these centers trained at Debre Berhan and Dessie.

Evening adult classes in many schools throughout the country.

158

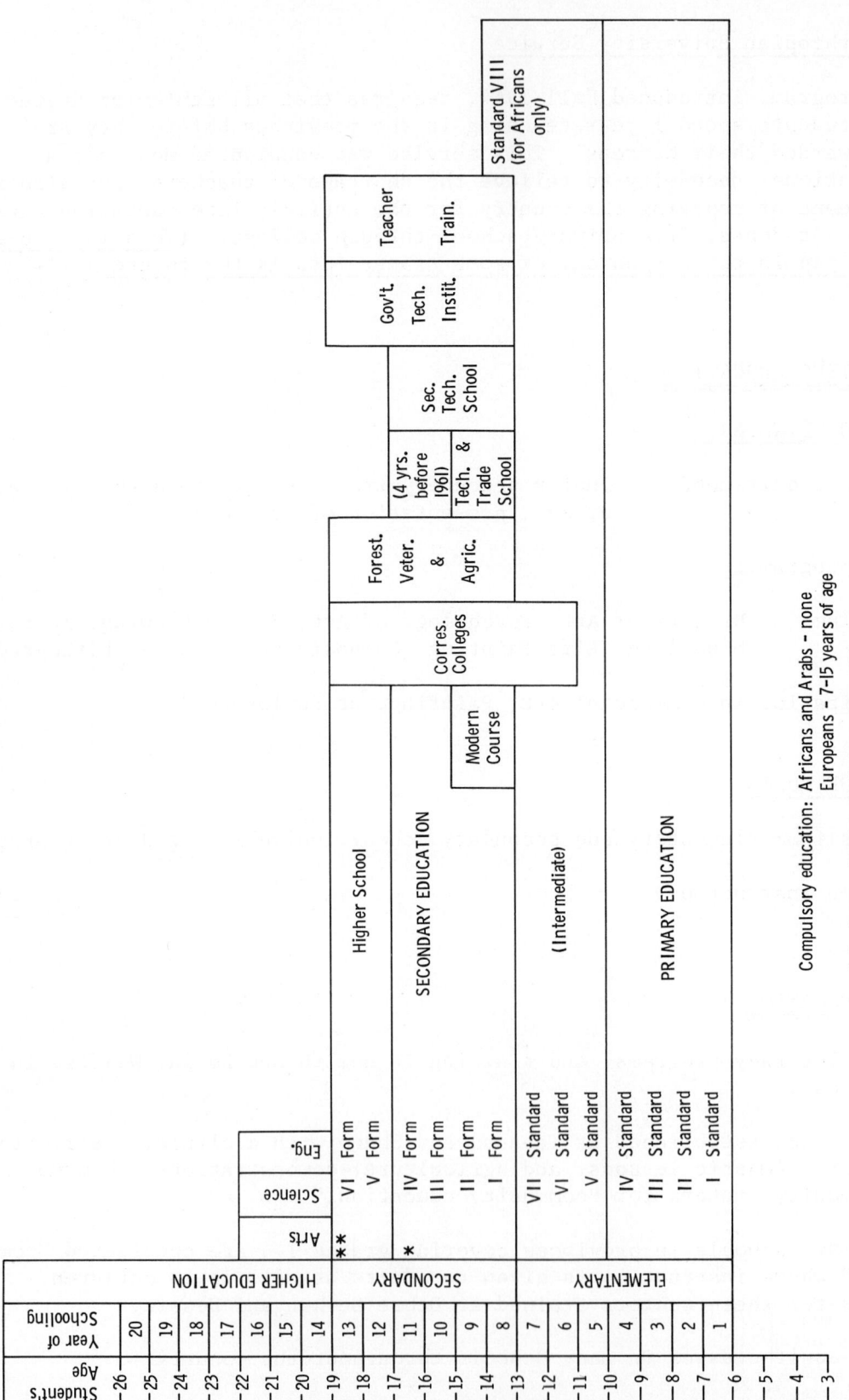

REPUBLIC OF KENYA
(Through 1962)

Compulsory education: Africans and Arabs – none
                     Europeans – 7–15 years of age

School year: January–Early December. 3 terms

Grading: Primary and secondary – numerical rank

1–9 School Certificate & General Certificate of Education
    (See SECONDARY EDUCATION)

159

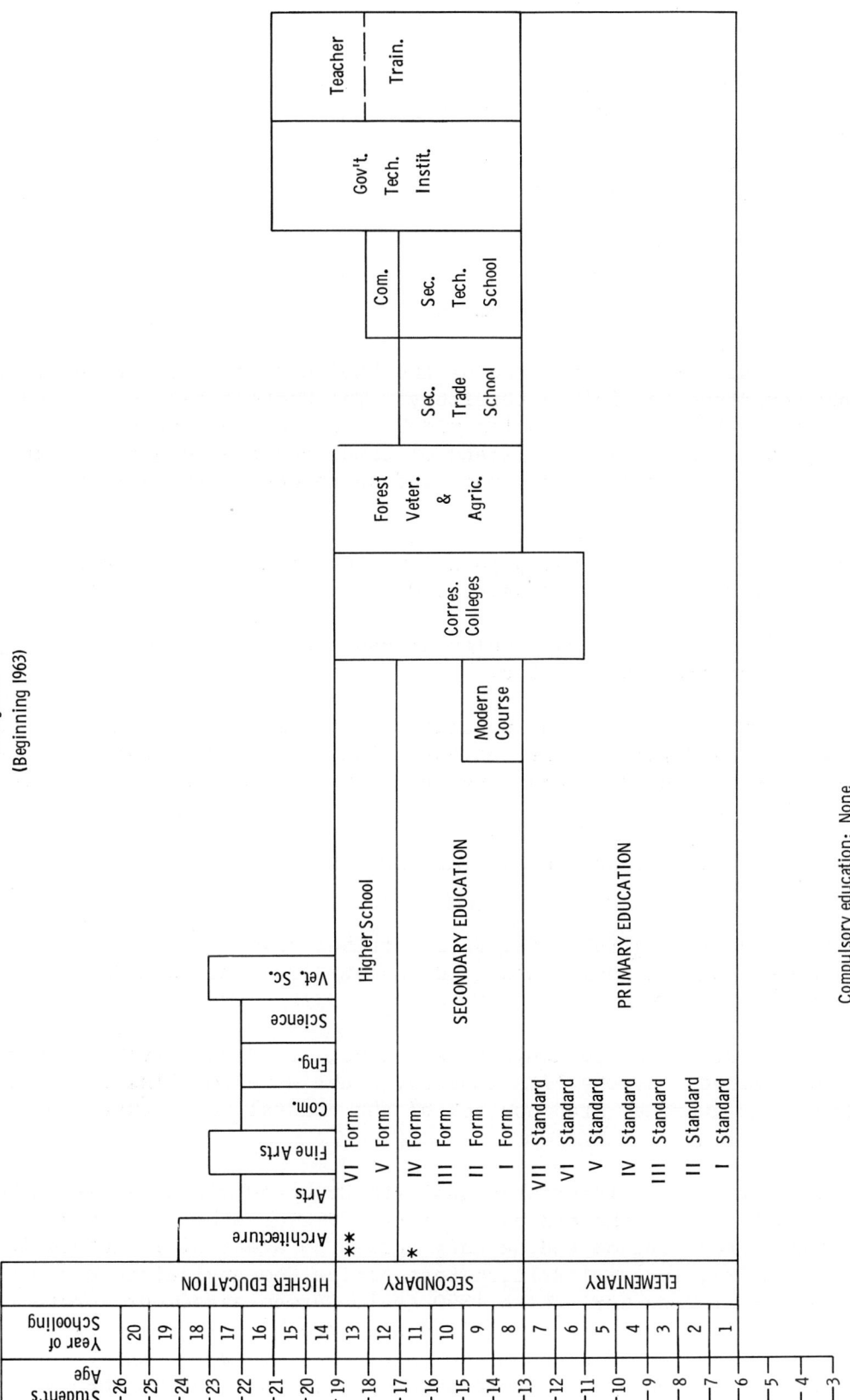

REPUBLIC OF KENYA
Integrated
(Beginning 1963)

Compulsory education: None

School year: January–Early December. 3 terms.

Grading: Primary and Secondary – numerical rank

1–9 Cambridge School Certificate & General Certificate of Education
(See SECONDARY EDUCATION)

REPUBLIC OF KENYA

Independence:   December 12, 1963.


## BACKGROUND


Until independence, Kenya consisted of the "Colony" and the "Protectorate."
The Colony comprised the inland territory.  The Protectorate comprised a
coastal strip of territory ten miles wide to the northern branch of the
Tana River, Mau, Kipini and the Island of Lamu, and the adjacent islands
between the Umba and Tana Rivers (mainland dominions of the Sultan of
Zanzibar.

African peoples form 97% of the population.  Europeans number approximately
66,000, Asians, 178,000, and Arabs, 39,000.

Africans are divided into 4 main cultural and linguistic groups:   Bantu,
Nilotic, Nilo-Hamitic, and Hamitic.

Of the Bantu tribes (over 70% of population), the most important are the
Kikuyu, Kamba, and Baluhya.  The largest tribe, the Kikuyu, numbering over
1 million, lives north of Nairobi and has played a major role in the development of the country.

Of the Asians, mostly Hindu and Muslim, there are 31 separate cultural
groups.

Official language is English.  Almost all tribes have their own language.
Swahili is the lingua franca.  Among the Asians, Gujerati and Punjabi is
spoken.

Portuguese explorers visited Kenya coast, 1498.  Trading posts were subsequently established.  By the 17th century, Arabs were settling in the coastal
area.  There was eventual Arab control of the coastal belt, extending into
19th century.

Exploration of the Kenya interior began with European missionaries, Rebman
and Kraft, 1849-50, and the discovery of Lake Victoria by John Speke, 1858.
In 1886, the United Kingdom and Germany agreed on areas of influence in
East Africa.  1887, Imperial British East Africa Company gained a concession
from the Sultan of Zanzibar.  With 1890 Anglo-German agreement, protection
of the Sultan's holdings on the mainland was arranged (later coastal Protectorate).  1895, the United Kingdom took over the Imperial British East
Africa Company, and declared a Protectorate over Kenya (known then as
British East Africa).

December 1901, railroad finished between Mombasa and Lake Victoria, which
subsequently brought many European and Asian settlers.  1902, boundary
between Kenya and Uganda shifted west (200 miles) to present position.
1920, Protectorate became Crown Colony, excepting the coastal strip which
became the Kenya Protectorate.

By treaty, July 15, 1924, Great Britain ceded to Italy the Juba River and
a strip from 50-100 miles wide on the British side of the River.  Cession,
June 29, 1925.  Northern boundary of Kenya defined with an agreement with
Ethiopia, 1947 (superseding original 1908 agreement).

Following European and Asians struggles for political power between World
Wars I and II, a third force developed with African nationalism.  With the
eruption of the Mau Mau movement, October 1952, a state of emergency was
declared, lasting until 1959.

The "Lytelton" multi-racial constitution, 1954, and the "Lenox-Boyd" constitution, November 1957, were attempts to give increased African representation to parity with Europeans in the Legislative Council.  The
"Macleod" constitution of February 1960 (Lancaster House Conference,
London), providing an African-elected majority in the Legislative Council,
brought advancement toward self-government.

Constitutional Conference in London, 1962, established a constitutional
framework including both political parties.  As a result of national elections under this constitution, May 1963, Kenya became internally self-
governing, June 1.  Independent, December 12, 1963.  On October 8, 1963,
the Sultan of Zanzibar ceded the "coastal strip" to Kenya with effect from
December 12, 1963.  December 12, 1964, Kenya became a republic.

From 1895-1911, missions carried the burden of African education.  1911,
Education Department established, which subsidized approved mission schools
and started its own system with the opening of primary schools.

By 1913, government technical school established in Machakos, providing
technical and teacher training.  1926, first secondary school.

Under the British rule, systems of education at primary and secondary
levels were for each of the four communities (European, Asian, African and
Arab), with its own facilities and standards.

Major reforms in education began in 1950; the Ministry of Education was
charged by the Educational Ordinance of 1952 with all educational responsibility of the Colony.  System established:

    Public:  (1)  Government-financed schools and colleges.

             (2)  Aided schools (owned and run by "managers" approved
                  by the Ministry).

                  (a)  Christian missions managed by missionary agencies.
                  (b)  Non-Christian managements approved on basis of
                       race, religion or sect.

## EDUCATION PREVIOUS TO 1963

## N O N - A F R I C A N   E D U C A T I O N

### European

European children until 1960 attended private European primary and secondary schools in Kenya, going for higher education either to South Africa or the United Kingdom.  Some Europeans, however, have attended the Polytechnic College (former Royal Technical College), taking major Governmental in-service technical training along with Africans and Asians.

Compulsory education for children between 7 and 15 years (repealed as of 1963).

Girls and boys attend separate day and also boarding schools.

### Primary School

Standards I through VII

   16 government schools; 8 grant-aided; 12 private schools.

   Certificate awarded:  Kenya European Preliminary Certificate.

### Secondary School

Forms I through IV ; Higher School Forms V - VI.

   Until 1953 all secondary training was academic (grammar).  Thereafter 3-year Modern classes introduced offering:  Woodcraft, Domestic Science, and Commercial Courses.  In private schools, these classes usually extensions to primary schools.

   European secondary schools multiracial beginning 1960.

   1963, 7 aided secondary schools; 7 unaided schools.

   Government secondary schools:

      Prince of Wales School (1932) includes Higher School
      Duke of York School includes Higher School
      Kenya Girls' High School includes Higher School
      Eldoret Secondary School
      Limuru Secondary School
      Mombasa Secondary School
      Delamare High School, Nairobi
      Francis Scott School      )
      Nakuru Girls' High School)  Closed 1962

1960 policy set by Boards of Governors (appointed autonomous members) of former European schools admitted pupils of other races, establishing successful integration.

Entrance requirements:   <u>Kenya European Preliminary Certificate</u>

Courses offered:         English, History, Geography, Mathematics, Physics, Chemistry, Biology, Zoology, Domestic Science[+], Economics, Arts, Physical Education, Languages: Latin, French, Spanish, German, Greek, Afrikaans[+].

Certificates awarded:    [*]<u>Cambridge School Certificate</u>, and <u>General
(at close of Form IV)    Certificate of Education</u>.

(at close of Form VI)    [**]<u>Cambridge Higher School Certificate</u>

   [+]Courses offered only to School Certificate standards.

Future of general secondary education for Europeans after independence 1963 dependent upon the future of the Kenya European farmer.


<u>Asian</u>

Comprises Indians, Goans, and others.

Between 1937 and 1949, Government secondary schools reached 39 (14 government, 12 aided, 12 unaided) and primary schools reached 121 (32 government, 87 aided, 2 unaided). 1961-63, 3 new primary and 2 new secondary Government schools added. <u>Higher School Certificate</u> work extended to another secondary school in Nairobi.

3 Asian teacher training colleges admitted mainly Africans, 1963 (2 in Nairobi, 1 in Mombasa).

Until integration and independence, the Asian community provided their own schools, grant-aided by the Kenya Government, and further assisted by the Aga Khan's Ismaili group.

Asian population mostly in urban areas allowed children to attend primary day schools. Separate schooling for boys and girls.

Compulsory education for Asians between 7 and 15 in Mombasa, Kisumu, and Nairobi until 1963 repeal.


<u>Primary School</u>

Standards I through VII.

Language of instruction:  English.

Certificate awarded:      <u>Kenya Asian Preliminary Certificate</u>.

## Secondary Schools

Forms I through IV.  Higher School Forms V-VI.

Government Secondary Schools

      Duke of Gloucester School - Nairobi
         (formerly Indian Secondary School (1930)) - Higher School
      Central High School - Thika
      Highway Secondary School                  - Higher School
      Eastleigh Secondary School  (1963)
      Ngara Secondary School for Girls
      Duchess of Gloucester School for Girls

Secondary education is offered mostly in day schools.

      Modern Schools          Forms I and II

      Secondary Modern courses introduced in most secondary schools and at
      top of certain primary schools, for those not suited for academic
      training.  (Discontinued, 1964.)

      Grammar Schools         Forms I through IV

      Entrance requirements:  <u>Kenya Asian Preliminary Certificate</u>

      Courses offered:        (See EUROPEAN secondary courses, p.163,
                               substituting following languages:
                               Hindi, Punjabi, Gujerati, Urdu (all
                               only to School Certificate level)).

      Certificates awarded:   *<u>Cambridge School Certificate</u> and <u>General</u>
      (at close of Form IV)   <u>Certificate of Education</u> (Grammar Schools).

                              <u>Leaving Certificate</u> (Modern courses)

      (at close of Form IV)   **<u>Cambridge Higher School Certificate</u>

## Secondary Technical Schools

      Technical High School - Nairobi
      Mombasa Institute of Muslim Education
      Technical High School - Mombasa

Certificates awarded:    *Cambridge School Certificate

City and Guilds of London Institute Royal
Society of Arts

No compulsory education for Arab children. Growing interest in the
education of girls. Arab students sharing Asian facilities in Kenya
as well as in the United Kingdom.

## Primary School

Standards I through VII.

Separate schools for boys and girls in Mombasa. Mostly day schools.
3 aided primary schools in addition to Government schools.

Training similar to that in Asian and European systems.

Certificate awarded:    Kenya Asian Preliminary Certificate.

## Secondary School

Forms I through IV - V (Academic)
Forms 1, 2              (Modern Course)

Entrance requirements:   Kenya Asian Preliminary Certificate.

Arab Boys' Secondary School

Secondary training up to School Certificate.

Courses offered:   (See EUROPEAN secondary courses, page 163,
substitution Arabic for other languages.)

Certificates awarded:    Cambridge School Certificate and General
School Certificate of Education (Academic).

Leaving Certificate (Modern course)

No Higher School course at Arab Secondary School, but those qualified
proceeded to higher studies at the Allidina Visram High School, Mombasa.
Arab girls attended Asian secondary schools.

## Secondary Technical Training

In Mombasa Technical Institute of Muslim Education, courses in various
trades leading to the City and Guilds Examination and also technical and
Commercial courses leading to the G.C.E.

# A F R I C A N   E D U C A T I O N

The establishment of a Kenya Education Department in 1911 initiated financial aid to mission primary schools and the opening of the first government secondary school, 1926.  Between 1934 and 1948, the government sought aid for primary schools from district councils, while expanding secondary training.

10-year plan for development of education, 1948, was followed by educational reforms and advances from 1950 through 1960.  As of 1961 there was no compulsory education but efforts were made to provide primary and intermediate training for all African children in urban areas.

As of 1963:   3,839 primary schools (6 government, 3,708 aided, 125 unaided).
2,055 intermediate schools (12 government, 2,028 aided,
15 unaided).
100 secondary schools (1 government, 85 aided, 14 unaided).
38 teacher training centers (36 aided, 2 unaided).

Boarding schools catering to boys and girls separately.

## Primary School

Primary and intermediate education administered through 36 District Education Boards.

Standards I - IV (to achieve vernacular literacy)
Standards V - VIII Intermediate (abolished as of 1963)

Courses offered:            Religious Instruction, English, Vernacular (Reading, Writing, Language Work), Swahili, History and Civics, Geography, Mathematics, Nature Study and Science, Gardening, Agriculture, Health Education, Physical Education, Music, Arts and Crafts, Needlework and Domestic Science.

Certificate awarded:        Kenya African Preliminary Certificate.

Certificate examination, written in English, taken at end of Intermediate course.

Certificate served as "Leaving Examination" and also as a means of selection for secondary school.

During the period of 1961-63, considerable expansion of primary education, especially in the intermediate section.

## Secondary School

Responsibility for secondary education lay with the voluntary agencies, whether they were churches or autonomous Boards of Governors.  In 1958, all government secondary schools were placed under Boards of Governors.

Entrance requirements:  Kenya African Preliminary Certificate.

Forms I, II, III, IV, and in a few selected schools, V and VI.

Certificates awarded:  Cambridge School Certificate and
(at close of Form IV)  General Certificate of Education.

(at close of Form VI)  Cambridge Higher School Certificate.

## Technical and Trade Schools

Entrance requirements:  Kenya African Preliminary Certificate.

3 - 4 year courses offered.

## Teacher Training Schools

Entrance requirements:  8 years primary education or Kenya African Preliminary Certificate.

2-year course.

Certificates awarded:  T4 Certificate for those having completed 8-year primary training.

T3 Certificate for those having passed the Kenya Preliminary Examination.

In addition, 2-year course for those having received secondary education up to School Certificate standard.

Certificates awarded:  K.T.1 Certificate (qualifying as teachers) for those who passed the School Certificate Examination.

T2 Certificate (qualifying as Assistant Teachers Grade I) for those who did not pass the School Certificate Examination.

## PRESENT SYSTEM

Beginning 1963, Kenya integrated its educational system, combining the 4 previously separate systems. Multi-racial enrollment in all former private schools. Introduction of combined Primary-Intermediate course, becoming "universal 7-year primary." The previous African system of Primary (Standards I through IV) and Intermediate (Standards V through VIII) began to be gradually phased out.

## PRIMARY EDUCATION

Entry age:  6 years.

Universal 7-year program, Standards I - VII.

Language of instruction:  English (beginning from the commencement of the primary course if teachers are available.)

### UNIVERSAL 7-YEAR PRIMARY SCHOOLS

#### TIMETABLE
(In districts where changes have been effected)

| Subjects | Lower Primary (30-minute period) | | | Upper Primary (40-minute period) | |
|---|---|---|---|---|---|
|  | I | II | III | IV-V | VI-VII |
| Religious Instruction | 4 | 4 | 4 | 4 | 4 |
| Vernaculars +(Reading, Writing, Language Work) | 10 | 9 | 5 | - | - |
| English | 4 | 4 | 7 | 7 | 7 |
| Second Language | - | - | - | 3 | 3 |
| Geography | - | - | 2 | 3 | 3 |
| History | - | - | 2 | 3 | 3 |
| Mathematics | 6 | 5 | 5 | 5 | 5 |
| Nature Study and Science | 1 | 1 | 2 | 2 | 2 |
| Health Education | - | - | - | 1 | 1 |
| Agriculture | - | - | - | 2 | 2 |
| Art and Craft, Needlework and Domestic Science | 4 | 4 | 4 | 5 | 5 |
| Music | 1 | 1 | 1 | 1 | 1 |
| Physical Education (incl. Health Education in Primary I, II, and III) | 5 | 5 | 5 | 3 | 3 |
| Gardening | - | 2 | 2 | - | - |
|  | 35 | 35 | 39 | 39 | 39 |

+Swahili, Arabic, Hindi, Punjabi, Gujerati, Urdu

Certificate awarded:     Kenya Preliminary Certificate
Taken at end of new full 7-year primary course.
Examination written in English.

Certificate serves as "Leaving Examination" and
also means of selection for Secondary School.
(1964, additional paper added for Secondary entry
selection.)

## SECONDARY EDUCATION

Gradually becoming integrated, from 1963.

Originally the majority of secondary training was in boarding schools
(separate for boys and girls). Between 1961-63, the number of secondary
institutions increased by 237 (by concentrating on "day" rather than
boarding schools).

Strathmore College of Arts and Science, Nairobi, established in 1961 by
Opus Dei Foundation with advanced secondary classes preparing students
for Higher School Certificate and university entrance. 1961, 9 Fifth
forms added to 7 secondary schools including Strathmore College. By 1963
there were 13 secondary schools with Sixth forms preparing for Higher
School Certificate. Africans took this examination for the first time in
1962. Narok Secondary School established in 1962 with assistance of U.S.
Agency for International Development.

Entrance requirements:  Kenya Preliminary Certificate.

Secondary courses:

Forms I through IV - Preparing for Cambridge School Certificate.
Form VI - Preparing for Higher School Certificate.


### NEW DAY SECONDARY SCHOOLS
(Integrated)

#### TIMETABLE
(40 periods per week; 40 minutes each)

| Subjects | Forms I and II |
|---|---|
| English | 9 |
| History | 3 |
| Geography | 3 |
| Mathematics | 7 |
| Science (Physics and Chemistry) | 6 |

+Swahili/French                    3
 Physical Education                2
 Art/Handwork/Music                3
 Current Affairs                   1
 Religious Instruction             3
                                  ──
                                  40

### Forms III and IV
(Examples of School Certificate Subjects)

| Subjects | Arts Bias | Science Bias |
|---|---|---|
| English Language | 6 | 6 |
| English Literature | 3 | - |
| History | 3 | 3 |
| Geography | 3 | 3 |
| Mathematics | 7 | 7 |
| General Science | 6 | - |
| Physics-with-Chemistry | - | 6 |
| Biology | - | 3 |
| +Swahili/French | 3 | 3 |
|  | 31 | 31 |

This leaves 9 spare periods into which can be fitted such subjects as:
Physical Education (2), Religious Instruction (3), Music (2), Art (2),
Handwork (2), Current Affairs (1), and Library (1).

+(and other languages: Arabic, Hindi, Punjabi, Gugerati, Urdu).

*University of Cambridge Joint Examination for the School Certificate and
General Certificate of Education at close of program. (For details, see
Appendix B.)

## HIGHER SCHOOL CERTIFICATE PROGRAM

2-year course preparing for university entrance.

Entrance requirements:     1st or 2nd class pass in Cambridge School Cer-
                           tificate.

## HIGHER SCHOOL CERTIFICATE COURSE (FORMS V - VI)
(40-minute periods per week)

| Subjects | Periods | |
|---|---|---|
| **Science Course** | | |
| Mathematics | 10 ) | |
| Physics | 10 ) | Major |
| Chemistry | 10 ) | Subjects |
| Biology | 10 ) | |
| Economics and Art | 5 and 6) | Other Subjects |

or

| Subjects | Periods | |
|---|---|---|
| **Arts Course** | | |
| English | 10 ) | |
| History | 10 ) | Major |
| Geography | 10 ) | Subjects |
| Mathematics | 10 ) | |
| Economics and Art | 5 and 6) | Other |
| Bible Knowledge | ) | Subjects |
| Economics and Public Affais | ) | |
| Latin | ) | |
| French | ) | |

**University of Cambridge Joint Examination for the Higher School Certificate and General Certificate of Education. (For details, see Appendix B.)

## HIGHER EDUCATION

## UNIVERSITY OF EAST AFRICA

### University College, Nairobi

Founded as the Royal Technical College of East Africa in 1954, incorporating the Ghandi Memorial Academy. It became the Royal College in 1961, the second inter-territorial University College, and was admitted into special relation with the University of London, teaching for degrees of the university. (Up to 1963, some students trained for Higher School Certificate work preceding degree courses.)

Following the University of East Africa Act of 1962, the Federal University of East Africa was inaugurated in 1963. The same year, the Royal College ceased to accept students for the London degree. The 3 constituent colleges of the University of East Africa are: Makerere University College in Uganda; the University College, Dar es Salaam in Tanzania, and the University College, Nairobi. Each of these University Colleges teaches for University of East Africa degrees. (Examinations for London degrees held until students having entered before 1963 complete their courses.)

## Minimum Entrance Requirements:

    I.    Applicable through February 1965:

either    (A)    Passes obtained at 1 or more of the following levels:

        (1)    Credit standard of the Cambridge School Certificate
        (2)    Ordinary level of an approved General Certificate of Education
        (3)    Subsidiary standard of the Cambridge Higher School Certificate
        (4)    Principal subjects standard of the Cambridge Higher School Certificate
        (5)    Advanced level of an approved General Certificate of Education.

        At least 2 of the 5 passes must be at one of the levels specified in (4) and (5).

or    (B)    4 passes obtained at one or more of the levels specified in (1) and (5) above, of which at least 3 must be at one of the levels specified in (4) and (5).

        (For Mature-Entry Scheme, see below )

    II.    Revised as of March 1965:

        (A)    A candidate must hold a School Certificate or General Certificate of Education containing at least 5 passes (from an approved list) taken prior to the sitting of Higher School Certificate.

        (1)    Approved list of subjects for School Certificate:

        English Language, English Literature, French, Latin, Luganda, Swahili, Physics, Chemistry, Physics with Chemistry, General Science, Mathematics, History, Geography, Biology, Religious Knowledge, and Art.

        (2)    Approved list of subjects for Higher School Certificate:

        English Literature, Geography, Geology, History, Ancient History, Economics, Economic History, Religious

Knowledge, Latin, French, Pure Mathematics, Applied
Mathematics, Mathematics (Pure and Applied), Physics,
Chemistry, Biology, Music, Art, Botany, Zoology.

Note:   Where a candidate is offering Biology, he may not take
either Botany or Zoology as the other subject combinations,
for purpose of admission into the university.

Similarly, where a candidate is offering Mathematics (Pure
and Applied) as a subject, he may not take Pure Mathematics
or Applied Mathematics as the other subjects for purposes
of admission into the university.

(B)   A candidate must hold the following qualifications:

   (1)   2 principal level passes taken at the same sitting.
   (2)   1 principal level pass plus 3 subsidiary passes taken
         at the same sitting (General Paper being counted as a
         subsidiary subject)
   (3)   1 principal level pass at "D" grade or higher plus 2
         subsidiary passes taken at the same sitting (the Gen-
         eral Paper being excluded as a subsidiary subject).
   (4)   2 principal passes not taken at the same sitting pro-
         vided that they are both of "C" grade or higher.

(C)   All school candidates who take the Cambridge Higher School
Certificate examination shall have sat the General Paper in
that examination and shall produce certificates from their
schools to the effect that they have followed a course of
general studies in preparation for the General Paper.

(D)   Mature Age Entry Scheme

Conditions:

   (1)   Candidates must be 25 years of age, or older, on July
         1 of the year in which entry is desired.  They must have
         completed their formal school education at least 5
         years before the date of application.

   (2)   They must be able to show that they have attended Extra-
         Mural classes or Residential courses (recommendations
         from the Extra-Mural Class Tutor or Resident Tutor are
         necessary), or that they have attended a residential
         course in an Adult Education college (recommendation
         from the principal of the college is necessary), or
         that they have a recommendation from a person accept-
         able to the university that they are qualified to
         profit from university education.

(3)  If they have complied with above conditions, they
     must take a special entrance examination (a general
     paper and an essay).

Faculties:

|            |            |
|------------|------------|
| Arts       | Commerce   |
| Science    | Veterinary Science |
| Engineering | Art and Architecture |

Institute of Adult Studies

Degrees awarded:

| Faculty | Degree | Duration of Course (years) |
|---------|--------|----------------------------|
| Arts | B.A. | 3 |
|  | M.A. | 1 |
|  | Ph.D. | 2 |
| Science | B.Sc. | 3 |
|  | M.Sc. | 1 |
|  | Ph.D. | 2 |
|  | D.Sc. |  |
|  | Dip. in Meteorology | 1 |
| Engineering | B.Sc. (Eng.) | 3 |
|  | M.Sc. (Eng.) | 1 |
|  | Ph.D. (Eng.) |  |
|  | D.Sc. (Eng.) |  |
|  | M.Sc. (Agric. Eng.) | 2 |
| Commerce | B.Com. | 3 |
| Veterinary Science | B.V.Sc. | 4 |
| Art and Architecture | Dip. in Fine Arts | 4 |
|  | B.Arch. | 5 |
| Institute of Adult Studies | Certificate of Adult Studies | 1 |

DEGREE PATTERNS IN THE FACULTIES OF ARTS AND SCIENCE:

Under the University of East Africa only 1 first degree is offered in each
of the Faculties of Arts and Science, viz. Bachelor of Arts (B.A.) and
Bachelor of Science (B.Sc.).  Each involves 3 years of study after entry

at Higher School Certificate level.  Honours gained by attaining required
standard, whatever the pattern of B.A. or B.Sc. curriculum.

The following are patterns that may be followed:

either (A)  3-2-2 Degree Pattern (Type X)

>3 subjects in 1st year, a continuation with 2 of the same
>into 2nd and 3rd years.

>Example in Science Faculty:

>1st yr:    Botany, Zoology, Chemistry
>2nd yr:    Botany and Zoology
>3rd yr:    Botany and Zoology

or     (B)  3-2-1 Degree Pattern (Type Y)

>3 subjects in 1st year, a continuation with 2 of the same
>into 2nd year, and only 1 of the 2 into the 3rd year.

>Example in Arts Faculty:

>1st yr:    English, Geography and Economics
>2nd yr:    English and Economics
>3rd yr:    English

or     (C)  3-1-1 Degree Pattern (Type Z)

>3 subjects in the 1st year, a continuation with 1 of these
>into the 2nd and 3rd years.

>Example in Arts Faculty:

>1st yr:    English, Mathematics and Economics
>2nd yr:    Economics
>3rd yr:    Economics

Patterns offered by various departments and regulations attaching to them
may be found under relevant faculties.

## Faculty of Arts

Entrance requirements:                University's minimum entrance require-
                                      ments.

                                      For admission to B.A. degree course,
                                      candidates must have at least 2 principal
                                      level passes at the Higher School Certifi-
                                      cate (or its equivalent) and 3 credits at
                                      School Certificate level in subjects
                                      approved by the Faculty Board.  A credit
                                      in English Language is essential.

Departments:

                Economics                History
                English                  Mathematics
                Geography


Bachelor of Arts

Duration of course:   3 years.

While the Department of English offers both the 3-2-2 and 3-2-1 degree
patterns (Type X and Type Y respectively), those of Mathematics, History
and Geography offer the 3-2-2 (Type X).  Economics offers both the 3-2-2
(Type X) and 3-1-1 (Type Z).  Proposed 3-1-1 in Mathematics.

Political Science introduced 1964-65 and offered as 1st year Arts course.
Students taking Economics in 2nd and 3rd years may offer 1 paper in Political Science.

Subjects:       Applied Mathematics, Economics, English, Geography,
                History, Mathematics, Political Science, Pure Mathematics,
                Religious Studies, Sociology.

If Mathematics is studied during 1st year, then neither Applied Mathematics
nor Pure Mathematics may be included in the same curriculum.

Courses in 3 subjects must be studied during the 1st year.  Thereafter,
the curriculum must conform to either Type X, Type Y or Type Z.


Economics

    1st yr:     Elements of Economics, African Economic Problems, Introduc-
                tion to Political Theory and Institutions.

    2nd and     (3-2-2)  Principles of Economics, Applied Economics, Eco-
    3rd yrs:    nomic History and either Elementary Statistical Method or
                Agricultural Economics.

    2nd and     (3-1-1)  Final examination consists of 8 papers of which 4
    3rd yrs:    will be same as prescribed for 3-2-2-degree.  Remaining 4
                papers from following:

                Advanced Economic Statistics, Problems of Economic Develop-
                ment, Administrative Organization, Accounting, Advanced
                Agricultural Economics, Application of Economic Statistics,
                Social Economics, Economics of Modern Industry, International
                Economics, Politics and Government with special reference to
                Africa.

## English

1st yr:       Verse and Drama, Prose and Comprehension.

2nd and       (3-2-2)   Poetic Tradition from 1798 to Present, the Novel
3rd yrs:      in 19th and 20th Centuries, Shakespeare and Development of
              Drama, English Language and Usage.

2nd and       (3-2-1)   In addition to the 4 courses above, 2 of the fol-
3rd yrs:      lowing required:

              Early Poetic Traditions, Satire:  A General Study of the
              Genre, Critical Theory and Application.  Study of Litera-
              ture includes Study of American and African Literature.

## Geography:

1st yr:       B.A. and B.Sc.
              Major Environments of the World, East Africa, Practical
              Geography.

2nd yr:       B.A. and B.Sc.
              Principles of Physical Geography, East Africa, Practical
              Geography, Seminars.

3rd yr:       B.A. and B.Sc.
              Principles of Biogeography, Africa, Practical Geography,
              Seminars.

              Optional subjects:  Geomorphology and Hydrology, North
              America, The Great World Powers, The Indian Ocean Basin
              and its Borderlands, Settlement Geography.

## History:

1st yr:       History of Africa (2 papers).

2nd and       (3-2-2)   The Emergence of Modern International Society
3rd yrs:      since 1763, Constitutional Development in the Commonwealth,
              East and Central Africa since 1700.

Final Examination includes 1 paper on each course, including the 1st
year course.

Mathematics:   (Same as in Science Faculty).  B.A. and B.Sc.

## Examinations:

University examinations are held in all subjects at end of 1st and 3rd
years of study for the degree.  An examination is also held at the end
of the 2nd year (for curriculum Type Y) in the subject which is being
discontinued thereafter.

## Degree awarded:

B.A. awarded with 1st class or 2nd class honours (Upper or Lower Division)
or as pass degree.

Postgraduate Studies:

Facilities in all departments for the degrees of Master of Arts (1 year minimum) and Doctor of Philosophy of Arts (additional 2 years).

Eligibility:    B.A. degree from any recognized university.


Faculty of Science

Entrance requirements:                  (discontinued, February 1965)
                                        University's minimum entrance require-
                                        ments:

                                        Candidates must offer at least 2 prin-
                                        cipal level passes at the Higher School
                                        Certificate (or its equivalent) and 3
                                        credits at School Certificate level.

                                        In order to read any subject in the
                                        Faculty of Science for full 3-year degree
                                        course, 1 of the following entrance sub-
                                        ject combinations must be satisfied:

(a)  Botany:

either    Principal level passes in Botany (or Biology) and Chemistry
or        Principal level passes in Zoology and Chemistry with credit
          level Botany
or        Principal level passes in Chemistry and Physics or Mathe-
          matics, with credit level Botany
or        Principal level pass in Botany or Biology with credit level
          Chemistry, Physics and Mathematics.

(b)  Chemistry:

Principal level passes in Chemistry and Mathematics or
Physics or Biology.

(c)  Geography:

Credit level Geography.

(d)  Geology:                  Part I

either    Principal level Physics with credit level Chemistry
or        Principal level Chemistry with credit level Physics.

                               Part II

B.Sc. (General) in appropriate subjects.

(e)  Mathematics:

Principal level Mathematics or principal level Pure Mathematics.

      (f)   Meteorology (Postgraduate course only)

either      An Honours degree in Mathematics or Physics.
or          An Honours degree in Mathematics and Physics.

      (g)   Zoology:

either      Principal level passes in Chemistry and Zoology (or Biology)
or          Principal pass in 1 of these 2 subjects and credit level pass
             in the other.

Departments:

| | |
|---|---|
| Botany | Mathematics |
| Chemistry | Meteorology |
| Geography | Physics |
| Geology | Zoology |

## Bachelor of Science

Duration of course:   3 years.

Faculty offers 3-2-2 degree pattern (Type X) in all the departments except Meteorology which is presently offered only as a postgraduate course. (Type Z) 3-1-1 degree proposed for Department of Mathematics.

Subjects:     Anatomy, Applied Mathematics, Botany, Chemistry, Geography, Geology, Mathematics, Physics, Physiology, Pure Mathematics, Zoology.

If Mathematics is studied during 1st year, then neither Applied Mathematics nor Pure Mathematics may be included in the same curriculum.

Courses in 3 subjects must be studied during the 1st year.  Thereafter, the curriculum must conform to either Type X, Type Y or Type Z.

Curriculum:

Botany:   Comparative Morphology, Life Histories and Taxonomy of Principal Division of the Plant Kingdom, Plant Physiology, Mycology and Plant Pathology, Angiosperm Taxonomy, Plant Anatomy, Plant Geography and Ecology, Cytogenetics and Evolution.

Chemistry:   The department offers 2 courses:

Course A  is designed as the 1st year of a continuous 3-year course for students wishing to read Chemistry as 1 of the 2 final examination subjects in the degree.  As part of entry qualifications students should have principal level Mathematics (or its equivalent) or alternatively should read Mathematics for at least 1 year of degree course.

Course B   is designed as a complete 1-year course for students wishing to
read Chemistry in 1st year of degree only.  While principal level
Chemistry is desirable for entry, provision can be made for entry
without this qualification.  This course does not normally allow
entry to 2nd year in Chemistry.  It must be taken with 2 other
1st year subjects in which student is eligible to proceed to full
3-year course.

Each course comprises broad survey of whole field of Chemistry - Inorganic,
Physical and Organic - over the 3 or 1-year period.  In final year of 3-year
course some more specialized topics may be covered.

Geography:       (Same as in Faculty of Arts).    B A. and B.Sc.

Geology:         The department offers a B.Sc. (General degree within the
                 3-2-2 pattern (see M.Sc. degree below).

   1st yr:       General Principles of Geology, with day excursions and
                 annual field course.

   2nd yr:       Mineralogy, Paleontology, Structural Geology, and interpre-
                 tation of geological maps.

   3rd yr:       Petrology, Stratigraphy, Economic Geology and Mineralogy,
                 with emphasis on East African aspects.

N.B. Emphasis placed on laboratory and field work.  Students encouraged to
     obtain additional practical experience during the long vacations.

In addition to these, the Department of Geology offers courses to students
in Architecture and Civil Engineering Departments.

   Geology for Civil Engineers:

        General Principles of Geology with emphasis on applications to
        Civil Engineering, such as courses of economic materials and
        problems connected with the location of reservoirs, dams, tunnels
        and foundations.  Selected local excursions.

   Geology for Architects:

        Sources and uses of local building stones.

Mathematics:

   1st yr:       Mathematics IA        )  for those with principal level
                 Applied Mathematics   )  passes in Mathematics

                 Mathematics IB - for those with School Certificate Mathe-
                                  matics and therefore not qualified to read
                                  beyond 1st year in degree course.

Mathematics IA is divided into 3 sections:

Techniques (1):  Calculus, Complex Numbers, Differential Equations, and other topics.

Techniques (2):  Vector Calculus, Functions of Several Variables, and other topics.

and          Introduction to Pure Mathematics:  Basic Ideas of Modern Mathematics.

All IA students must take Techniques (1);  students may choose between Techniques (2) and Introduction to Pure Mathematics.  All students taking Applied Mathematics I must take both Introduction to Pure Mathematics and Techniques (2), the latter being then regarded as part of their Applied Mathematics course.  Students proceeding to Mathematics II must take Introduction to Pure Mathematics but they may do so as part of 2nd year course.

At present, Applied Mathematics offered only in 1st year. Students wishing to enroll for Applied Mathematics I must take Pure Mathematics I as well.

2nd and      (3-2-2 pattern)  (Type X)
3rd yrs:      Desirable but not essential that students pursuing 2nd and 3rd year Mathematics take both Pure and Applied Mathematics as 1st year subjects.

Students taking Part II Mathematics must complete courses in following subjects, normally in 2nd year:  Techniques (3), Real Variable, Introduction to Topology, Lebesgue Measure and Integral, Modern Algebra.

The 3rd year will consist of a course in Complex Variable and such further courses in Analysis, Algebra, Topology, Statistics, Numerical Analysis or Applied Mathematics as may be prescribed by Department.

(Type Z) 3-1-1 pattern for Mathematics proposed.

Meteorology:  Department offers training at postgraduate level only (1965).

Physics:

   Course A:  3-year course for students with principal level Physics and principal level Mathematics.  Pure Mathematics must be 1 of 3 first-year subjects.

   Course B:  Self-contained 1-year course in Physics for students requiring background knowledge in this subject.  It is open to students who have passed School Certificate Physics

at credit level and have principal level Mathematics or
principal level Physics and credit level Mathematics.
Students taking this course cannot proceed with Physics
beyond the 1st year.

Zoology:

| | |
|---|---|
| 1st yr:<br>(Part I) | An introductory study of the phylla of living animals. Introduction to Mammalian Physiology, Vertebrate Embryology and Ecology. |
| | A terrestrial field course (at end of 1st year course, and is compulsory for all students proceeding to 2nd year). |
| 2nd and<br>3rd yrs:<br>(Part II) | A more detailed study of the Animal Kingdom with special courses in: Comparative Physiology, Ecology, Cellular Biology, Genetics and Evolution, Entomology, and Parasitology. |
| | During the 1st year of Part II, students attend a Marine Biology course organized in association with the East African Marine Fisheries Research Organization, Zanzibar (Tanzania). |

Examinations:

University examinations are held in all subjects at end of 1st and 3rd
years of study for the degree.  An examination is also held at the end
of the 2nd year (for curriculum Type Y) in the subject which is being discontinued thereafter.

Degree awarded:

B.A. awarded with first class or second class honours (Upper or Lower
Division) or as pass degree.

Postgraduate Studies and Higher Degrees:

Faculty has facilities for graduate work and most departments have special
research interests.

Master of Science

Offered in Geology and Mathematics.

Eligibility:          B.Sc. degree.

Duration of course:   1 year.

## Master of Arts

Offered in Mathematics.

Duration of course:  1 year.


## Doctor of Philosophy

Eligibility:              M.Sc. degree (of not less than 2 years' standing).

Duration of course:  2 years.


## Doctor of Science

Eligibility:              B.Sc. degree (of not less than 10 years' standing).


## Diploma in Meteorology

Duration of course:  1 year.


## Faculty of Engineering

Entrance requirements:                    (discontinued, February 1965)
                                          University's minimum entrance require-
                                          ments.

   (I)  Candidates for Civil, Electrical, and Mechanical branches
       of Engineering must offer at least 2 principal level passes
       at the Higher School (or its equivalent) and 3 credits at
       School Certificate level.  The passes should be as follows:

either      Principal level passes in Physics and Mathematics (Pure and
           Applied combined) with either principal or credit level
           Chemistry.

or          Principal level passes in Physics and Pure and Applied Math-
           ematics (as separate subjects), with either principal or
           credit level Chemistry.

  (II)  Land Surveying.

    (a)  Candidates for Land Surveying must satisfy 1 of the
        following:

      (i)  B.Sc. degree in Faculty of Science, with Mathe-
           matics, Physics or Geography as major subjects.

(ii)  B.A. degree in Faculty of Arts, with Mathematics and Geography as major subjects.

(iii)  Principal level passes in Pure Mathematics, Applied Mathematics and Physics at 1 or more sittings in Higher School Certificate (or its equivalent), and a credit in English Language at School Certificate level.

(iv)  Principal level passes in Pure and Applied Mathematics (as combined subjects), and Physics, and Geography or Chemistry at subsidiary level, and 1 credit in English Language at School Certificate level.

(v)  1st Professional examination of the Royal Institution in Chartered Surveyors.

(b)  Candidates offering option (a) (ii) required to complete qualifying courses for 2nd and 3rd years of study (other than 2nd and 3rd year courses in subjects taken as major subjects for either degrees in Faculties of Arts and Science) as prescribed under Surveying and Photogrammetry. Candidates must also complete requirements of 1st year study not completed in curriculum in Faculties of Arts and Science.

Candidates offering options (a) (iii), (iv) must satisfy requirements of 1st, 2nd and 3rd years of study for degree as prescribed under Surveying and Photogrammetry.

Departments:

Civil Engineering                  Mechanical Engineering
Electrical Engineering             Land Surveying and Photogrammetry

Bachelor of Science in Engineering

Duration of course:  3 years.

Departments of Civil, Electrical and Mechanical Engineering

Curriculum:

1st yr:   Common 1st year for all 3 departments.

Mathematics, Strength of Materials, Theory of Structures, Theory of Machines, Applied Heat, Mechanics of Fluids, Electrical Engineering I, Electrical Engineering II, Engineering Drawing.

(Candidates examined in 7 of the courses studied.)

Civil Engineering:

  2nd yr:  Mathematics, Theory of Structures and Stress Analysis, Survey-
           ing, Mechanics of Fluids, Soil Mechanics and Geology, and 1 of
           the following:

           Public Health and Highway Engineering, Architectural Engineering,
           Electrical Engineering, and any other provided course.

  3rd yr:  Theory of Structures, Mechanics of Fluids and Surveying, Soil
           Mechanics, a Civil Engineering project, and 1 of the following:

           Highway Engineering, Public Health Engineering, Architectural
           Engineering, Hydrology and Water Engineering, Mathematics, any
           other approved course.

  Honours: In addition to above courses, candidates must complete the
           following:

           1 course not already offered during 1st year chosen from the
           following:

           Highway Engineering, Public Health Engineering, Architectural
           Engineering, Hydrology and Water Engineering, Mathematics,
           and in addition

  either   another of the courses listed immediately above and not already
           offered in the 1st year

  or       advanced course of study in any 1 of the subjects in candidate's
           3rd year of study.

Mechanical Engineering:

  2nd yr:  Mathematics, Properties and Strength of Materials, Applied
           Thermodynamics, Mechanics of Fluids, Theory of Machines,
           either Electrical Engineering or Materials Science, Engineering
           Technology and Practice.

  3rd yr:  Strength of Materials, Theory of Machines, Fluid Dynamics,
           Applied Thermodynamics, a Mechanical Engineering project.

  Honours: In addition to above courses, candidates must complete the
           following:

           Mathematics and 1 course from the following:

           Production Engineering and Metrology, Advanced Stress Analysis,
           Elasticity, Air-conditioning, Advanced Thermodynamics and Heat
           Transfer, Servo Mechanisms, Vibration Engineering, Ideal Fluid
           Flow, Boundary Layer Theory, and any other approved course.

Electrical Engineering:

  2nd yr:  Mathematics, an Electrical Engineering project, and any 4 of
           the following:

Power System Analysis, Electrical Machines, Theory and Measurements, Electrical Control Systems, Electronics Theory, Applied Electronics, Telecommunications.

(Candidates examined in any 4 of the 5 subjects studied.)

3rd yr: Mathematics, Electrical Theory, Electrical Instruments, Electrical Power and Machines, Electronics and Telecommunications, Mechanical Engineering.

Honours: In addition to above courses, candidates must complete the following:

1 course chosen from the following:

Advanced Power System Analysis and Machines, Advanced Measurements and Control, Advanced Electronics and Telecommunications.

## Surveying and Photogrammetry Department

Curriculum:

1st yr: Qualifying courses for 1st year are:

Mathematics I, Physics (Special Course), Photogrammetry I, Law and Land Registration I, Cartography I, Surveying I.

In addition, student must attend satisfactorily courses in Principles of Engineering and English.

Credit in any qualifying course not obtained unless 4 of the following courses are completed in same academic year:  Mathematics I, Surveying I, Photogrammetry I, Land Registration I, Cartography I.

2nd yr: Mathematics II, Surveying II, Astronomy I, Land Registration II, Photogrammetry II, Cartography II.

In addition, student must attend satisfactorily a course in Town Planning.

Credit in any qualifying course not obtained unless 4 such courses completed in same academic year.

3rd yr: Mathematics III, Geodesy and Geophysics, Photogrammetry III, Astronomy II.

3 of the above courses must be completed in the same academic year.

## Examinations:

University Examinations are held at end of 1st and 3rd years of study for the degree.

Conditions of Honours Classification:

A candidate who has:

     (1)  maintained consistently high standard throughout degree course,

     (2)  submitted a thesis on suitable subject in the Geodetic Sciences,

and  (3)  obtained the aggregate pass-mark prescribed for honours degree awards will be eligible for a degree with honours in 1st or 2nd class.

Degree awarded:

B.Sc. Eng. awarded with 1st class or 2nd class honours (Upper or Lower Division) or as pass degree.

Postgraduate Studies and Higher Degrees:

Faculty has facilities for postgraduate studies and research.

Master of Science in Engineering

Eligibility:          B.Sc. Engineering or Diploma of Engineering of University College, Nairobi.

Duration of course:  1 year minimum.

Doctor of Philosophy in Engineering

Eligibility:          M.Sc. Engineering (of not less than 2 years standing).

                      Approved course of special study or research on some subject connected with the science of Engineering.

                      Must submit for approval outstanding published work on some subject(s) connected with the Mathematical, Physical, Natural, or Applied Sciences.

Doctor of Science in Engineering

Eligibility:          B.Sc. Engineering (of not less than 6 years' standing).

Master of Science (Agricultural Engineering)

Offered jointly by the Faculty of Agriculture, Makerere University College, and the Faculty of Engineering, University College, Nairobi.

Eligibility:              Holders of either B.Sc. Engineering or B.Sc. Agricul-
                          ture from any recognized university.

                          Candidates with 1st degree in Agriculture must provide
                          evidence of competence in Mathematics.

Duration of course:  2 years.

Curriculum:

1st yr:   (a)  Candidates with B.Sc. Agriculture attend University College,
               Nairobi, taking following subjects:

               Mathematics, Strength of Materials, Theory of Machines,
               Applied Heat, Mechanics of Fluids, Electrical Engineering,
               Engineering Drawing.

          (b)  Candidates with B.Sc. Engineering attend Makerere University
               College, taking following subjects:

               Principles of Agriculture, Principles of Agriculture Eco-
               nomics, Crop Husbandry and Farm Mechanization, Soil Science,
               Farm Classes.

          (c)  Qualification examinations given to each category of candi-
               dates at end of 1st year.  Research project undertaken
               (including vacation periods).

2nd yr:   Residence required at either University College, Nairobi, or at
          Makerere University College, depending on nature of research.

          Candidate attends tutorials and lectures in Advanced Agricultural
          Engineering and in subject of specialization, completing work on
          research project.

## Faculty of Commerce

Entrance requirements:                    (discontinued February 1964)
                                          University's minimum entrance require-
                                          ments.

                                          Candidates must have at least 2 prin-
                                          cipal level passes in any subjects
                                          regularly taught at school.

                                          Department of Domestic Science:  Candi-
                                          dates must have at least 5 credits at
                                          School Certificate level, 1 of which must
                                          be English Language.  Preference given to
                                          candidates having studied at least 1
                                          science subject up to School Certificate
                                          level.

Departments::

> Accountancy            Law and Government
> Business Administration  Domestic Science

Bachelor of Commerce

Duration of course:  3 years.

In first 2 years of the course, all subjects common to students qualifying
as Business Administrator or Accountant.  Specialization occurs in the 3rd
year at the end of which students will have:

either    (a)  Graduated in Business Administration
or        (b)  Graduated, having completed sufficient accountancy to be
               exempt from Intermediate Examination of the Association of
               Certified and Corporate Accountants.  Accountancy graduates
               after finding employment, complete studies for the final
               examination of the A.C.C.A.

Curriculum:

1st yr:   Development of Law and Government, Economics (Elements of Eco-
          nomics and African Economic Problems), Elementary Statistical
          Method and Sources, English Economic History (1776-1950).

2nd yr:   Accountancy I, Mercantile Law, Business Administration I, Prin-
          ciples of Economics, Applied Economics, Economics of Modern
          Industry, Problems of Economic Development.

3rd yr:   Students may select either of the following options:

          Business Administration Option:

          Business Administration II, Industrial Law (2 terms), Management
          Seminar (1 term), Principles of Marketing (1½ terms), Labor Rela-
          tions (1½ terms), Principles of Economics, Applied Economics,
          Economics of Modern Industry, Problems of Economic Development.

          Accountancy Option:

          Accountancy II, Costing, Taxation, Auditing, Principles of Eco-
          nomics, Applied Economics, Economics of Modern Industry, Problems
          of Economic Development.

Examinations:

1st yr:   All subjects.

2nd yr:   Mercantile Law, Business Administration I (for those electing
          Accountancy Option), Accountancy I (for Business Administration
          Option).

3rd yr:   All subjects.

Degree awarded:

B.Com. awarded with 1st class or 2nd class honours (Upper or Lower Division) or as pass degree.

## Department of Domestic Science

Duration of course:   3 years leading to the Certificate of the School of Education of Manchester University.

Subjects:   Principles and Practice of Education, English, Housecraft (Foods and Nutrition, Textiles and Clothing, Housewifery), Science (Biology with some Physiology, Physics, Chemistry), Applied Science (Laundry Chemistry, Food Chemistry, Household Appliances), Art related to Housecraft, Home Management.

Examinations:

Housecraft Part I of Manchester University taken towards end of 2nd year.
Housecraft Part II of Manchester University taken at end of 3rd year.
Teaching Practice final - term 8.

## Faculty of Veterinary Science

Entrance requirements:                    (discontinued February 1965)
University's minimum entrance requirements.

Candidates must offer at least 2 principal level passes at the Higher School Certificate (or its equivalent) in Biology and Chemistry. In addition, candidates should have Physics, either at principal or subsidiary level.

Departments:

Veterinary Anatomy (including Histology)
Physiology (including Biochemistry and Pharmacology)
Pathology
Animal Husbandry
Clinical Studies

## Bachelor of Veterinary Science

Duration of course:   4 years.

Curriculum (compulsory subjects):

1st yr:  Classical Veterinary Anatomy and Histology, Classical Physiology
         and Biochemistry.

2nd yr:  Applied Anatomy and Histology, Applied Physiology and Biochem-
         istry, Pharmacology, Animal Husbandry (including animal handling),
         Introduction to Microbiology, General Pathology.

3rd yr:  Microbiology (Bacteriology, Virology and Parasitology), Special
         Pathology and Histopathology, Introduction to Clinical Studies,
         Principles of General Preventive Medicine.

4th yr:  Veterinary Medicine and Infectious Medicine, Surgery, Reproduc-
         tory Medicine and Obstetrics, Clinical Exercises, Public Health.


Examinations:

1st yr:  Anatomy and Histology, Physiology and Biochemistry.

2nd yr:  Applied Physiology and Biochemistry, Applied Physiology with
         Embryology, Pharmacology, Animal Husbandry.

3rd yr:  Microbiology, Pathology and Histopathology.

4th yr:  Medicine (including questions on Public Health), Surgery, Repro-
         duction.


## Postgraduate Studies in Veterinary Science

Research studies being conducted in:  Department of Physiology, Department
of Anatomy, Department of Pathology.

Regulations for Higher Degrees to be published during academic year, September, 1965.


## Faculty of Art and Architecture

Departments:

         Art                        Land Development
         Architecture

### Department of Art

Entrance requirements:  An approved School Certificate (or its equivalent)
                        with at least 5 credits, 1 of which must be in
                        English Language.  In addition, candidates may be
                        required to sit an entrance examination.

Diploma in Fine Arts (E.A.)

Duration of course:  4 years.

The diploma is awarded after successful study in following subjects:
General Studies or Graphic Design or Painting.

Curriculum:     Life Drawing, General Drawing, Painting, Basic Design,
                Design, Graphic Design, Sculpture and Ceramics, History
                of Art.

Examinations:

1st yr:     1st Examination (all courses).

2nd, 3rd    Diploma in Fine Arts - General Studies
and  4th    Diploma in Fine Arts - Graphic Design
   yrs:     Diploma in Fine Arts - Painting

## Department of Architecture

Entrance requirements:              Minimum of 5 credits in the School Cer-
                                    tificate (or its equivalent).  5 credits
                                    must include:

    (i)  English Language

  (ii)  1 of the following subjects:

| G.C.E. "O" level | C.O.S. Certificate |
|---|---|
| Pure Mathematics | Mathematics |
| Applied Mathematics | Mechanics |
| Physics | Physics |

 (iii)  Any 3 other subjects from the remainder of a
          specialized list below:

| G.C.E. Subjects | C.S.C. Subjects |
|---|---|

### Group I

| | |
|---|---|
| General Science | General Science |
| Chemistry | Chemistry |
| Physics with | Physics with Chemistry |
|   Chemistry | Biology |
| Geology | Botany |
| Botany or Zoology | |

### Group II

| | |
|---|---|
| Art or Music | Art or Music |

## Group III

| | |
|---|---|
| Latin | Latin |
| Greek | Greek |
| French | French |
| German | German |
| Italian | Spanish |
| Spanish or Russian | |

## Group IV

| | |
|---|---|
| History | History |
| English Economic History | |
| British Constitution | |
| Ancient History | |

## Group V

| | |
|---|---|
| English Literature | English Literature |
| Religious Knowledge | Religious Knowledge |

## Group VI

| | |
|---|---|
| Geography | Geography |

## Group VII

Economics

Candidates having attended a course in Architecture in another approved institution may be admitted to the course but are not eligible to be awarded a degree of the University of East Africa unless they have completed a minimum period of 2 years full-time study in the Department.

(The Department is considering one "A" level entry requirement.)


## Bachelor of Architecture

Duration of course:  5 years.

Curriculum:   Physics of Buildings, Elements of Construction, Techniques of Expression, Appreciation of Architecture, Practice of Architecture, Design of Buildings, Course work.

(Course work includes Studio and Laboratory work and Tutorial exercises.  5th year Studio work comprises a Thesis Design based on a realistic program of students' own devising, with working drawings, report and model or perspective.)

Examinations:

1st yr:   Physics of Building, Elements of Construction, Practice of Arch-
(Part I)  itecture, Appreciation of Architecture, Design of Buildings,
          Course work.

2nd yr:   (Sessional examination only).  Title of papers same as above.

3rd yr:   Physics of Building, Elements of Construction, Practice of
(Part II) Architecture, Appreciation of Architecture, Design of Buildings,
          Course work.

4th yr:   Title of papers same as in Part II.
(Part III)

5th yr:   Thesis examination.
(Part IV)

B. Arch. awarded either with pass or with Honours (no subdivision in this
category).  Honours may be awarded a candidate having shown outstanding
ability and whose Thesis Design is of exceptional merit.


Master's Degree in Architecture to be introduced in near future.


## Department of Land Development

Entrance requirements:   Minimum entrance requirements are as follows:

             (a)  For those offering General Certificate of Educa-
                  tion:

                  (i)    Passes at ordinary level at 1 sitting in at
                         least 5 subjects including English Language
                         and Mathematics.
       or         (ii)   Passes at ordinary level at not more than 2
                         sittings in at least 6 subjects, including
                         English Language and Mathematics.
       or         (iii)  Passes in 1 subject at advanced level and
                         4 other subjects at ordinary level, to be
                         obtained at not more than 3 sittings and
                         to include English Language and Mathematics.
       or         (iv)   Passes in 2 subjects at advanced level and
                         2 other subjects at ordinary level, to in-
                         clude English Language or English Literature
                         and Mathematics.
       or         (v)    Passes in 4 subjects, including at least 3
                         at advanced level to include an English
                         subject and either Mathematical or Science
                         subject.

> (b)  For those offering a School Certificate:
>
>    Passes at credit standard in 5 subjects including English Language and Mathematics.
>
> (c)  Other examinations of equivalent standard which may be accepted by the R.I.C.S.

As of 1965, students in this department take the professional examinations of the Royal Institution of Chartered Surveyors in 1 of 2 sections:  Quantity Surveying Section or General Section.

Degree courses may be introduced in the future.

Curriculum and scheme of examinations:

(a)  Quantity Surveying

   Intermediate Examination (after 2 years and 2 terms)

      Elementary Surveying
      Building Construction and Draughtsmanship
      Principles of Structural Design
      Building Services
      Quantities I
      Principles of Law
      Economics

   Final Examination - Part I (1 year after passing Intermediate Exam.)

      Building Construction
      Building Services
      Principles of Law of Contract
      Analysis of Prices
      Specification
      Arbitration

   Final Examination - Part II (after 2 years practical experience)

      Building Economics and Cost Planning
      Quantities
      Professional Practice and Procedure

(b)  General

   1st Examination (after 1 year and 2 terms)

      Elementary Surveying
      Building Construction
      Elements of English Law
      Law of Property
      Economics

Intermediate Examination (taken 1 year after passing 1st Examination)

    Building Construction
    Principles of Town and Country Planning
    Local Government Law
    Law of Property
    Principles of Valuation
    National and Local Taxation

Final Examination (taken 2 years after passing Intermediate Exam.)

    Maintenance and Repair of Buildings
    Administrative Law
    Valuation
    Essay or Report
    Option subject - either:

        (a)  Estate Management
    or  (b)  Town and Country Planning
    or  (c)  Building Construction

## Institute of Adult Studies

### Department of Residential Adult Education

Entrance requirements:    Adults with sufficient command of English language
                          to take part in discussion and write regular essays.
                          Preference given to candidates able to bring mature
                          experience to bear on the subjects of study; may be
                          private students or sponsored by their employers.

Courses offered:

  (i)   Problem-centered short courses of 3 weeks concentrating on:  Sociol-
        ogy, Economics and Politics of East Africa.
  (ii)  8 to 10-week course of similar content.  Both courses intended for
        leaders and potential leaders in Industry, Commerce, Government and
        other forms of public service.
 (iii)  Small 1-year course leading either to new Certificate of Adult
        Studies or  to Mature Age entry to the University of East Africa.
        Students selected may have attended previous short course.

### Department of Extra-Mural Studies

This department is responsible for the extension work of the College.
Resident tutors, local graduates recruited on part-time basis, based in
major towns.  From Nairobi, Mombasa, Nakuru and Kisumu they cover the

surrounding areas.  Local facilities used for conducting 3 forms of work:
Organization and instruction of sessional weekly evening lectures and
tutorials; residential and non-residential "1-day" and "week-end" schools;
single public lectures.

Courses offered in each area are of the following types:

  (i)  Classes in liberal subjects as series of tutorials with emphasis
       on discussion and participation.
 (ii)  Classes in more formal academic subjects at various levels aiding
       adult students studying privately for public examinations.
(iii)  Courses for special professional bodies such as Trade Unionists,
       local Government workers, bankers and agricultural workers.

Subjects which have been taught include:

English Language, English Literature, Economics, History, Science, Geography, Mathematics, Law, International Affairs, Business Management, Government, Industrial Relations, Sociology, French, Swahili.

Attendance at any of the above courses and a recommendation from the resident tutor are 2 of the desirable qualifications of adult students sitting the University's Mature Age entry examination.  Prospective students are normally required to be adults no longer attending any full-time school.

## VOCATIONAL AND TECHNICAL EDUCATION

Approximate entry standards for training:

    (1)  Operatives:  Some primary education.
    (2)  Craftsmen:  Complete primary education.
    (3)  Technicians:  4 years of secondary education.
    (4)  Senior Technicians:  6 years of secondary education.
    (5)  Technologists:  University education.

## CRAFT CLUBS OR RURAL TRAINING CENTRES

Intended for boys and girls having left formal schooling at Primary IV.
Practical craft "hobby" training consists of simple building (boys), and
Domestic Science (girls).

Youth clubs and rural training centers sometimes prepare boys for passing
Labor Department's Trade Test.

## TRADE SCHOOLS

For many years the government prepared students for self-employment in
various crafts at artisan-industrial training centers.  Instruction was
7 to 8 hours a day, 5 days a week.  Four-fifths of training in workshops.

| | |
|---|---|
| Kabete Trade School | 1948 |
| Thike Trade School | 1949 |
| Sigaalagala Trade School | 1950 |
| Kwale (Coast) Trade School | 1954 |
| Machakos Trade School | 1958 |
| Mawego Trade School | 1962 |
| Eldoret Trade School | 1963 |
| Meru Trade School | 1963 |

Entrance requirements:          Kenya Preliminary Examination.
                                (Post Primary VIII).  (VII new system).

Duration of course:  2 years as of 1961 (formerly 3 to 4 years).

Courses:

 (i)  Academic subjects (limited).
(ii)  Trade courses:  Carpentry, Building, Plumbing, Electric Wiring,
      Painting and Decorating, Fitting, Turning, Sheet Metal Work, Mech-
      anics, General Garage Work, Blacksmithing, Welding, Pre-secretarial,
      Shoemaking, Tailoring, etc.

Emphasis turning to electrical and mechanical trades with oversupply of
building craftsmen.  Technical teacher training for trade schools progressing.

Certificates awarded:          General Certificate of Education, "O" level.

                               Grade III Government Trade Test (Labor Depart-
                               ment).
                               (Grade II test follows 1 additional year's
                                training.)

1964 Proposals:

    (1)  In order to expand scope of secondary education, a variety of
         vocational subjects should be added to the general academic
         syllabus in following manner:

         Conversion of present 2-year trade and technical schools into a
         4-year secondary trade school, each specializing in the follow-
         ing industries or crafts:  Building Trades, Tailoring, Metal Work,
         Electrical and Mechanical Engineering.

         Schools offering technical subjects in 2 streams (after years
         1 and 2, common to all):

         Stream A - Preliminary course qualifying students for work at a
                    technical college preparing for City and Guilds

<u>Technician Certificate</u>.

Stream B - Work leading to <u>Intermediate City and Guilds Craft</u>
Examination (and beyond); also school's own certification of workshop activities.

Standard of teaching in these proposed schools to be raised to
levels of secondary school standards.

(2)  To expand the 4 present secondary technical schools offering
courses for higher technological studies.


## SECONDARY TECHNICAL SCHOOLS

3 broadly-based schools offering secondary education with technical and
commercial bias leading to <u>General Certificate of Education</u>, ordinary
level.

Nakuru Secondary Technical School
(Began as a technical course in the Kabete Technical and Trade
School.  Predominantly African.  Boarding School.)

Technical High School, Nairobi.
Technical High School, Mombasa.
(Both day schools.  Predominantly Asian.)

Entrance requirements:                    Kenya Preliminary Examination.


## TYPICAL SECONDARY TECHNICAL SCHOOL
### TIMETABLE
(40 minutes per period)

| Subjects | F O R M S | | | |
|---|---|---|---|---|
|  | I | II | III | IV |
| English | 8 | 6 | 6 | 6 |
| Mathematics | 6 | 6 | 6 | 6 |
| Physics | 4 | 4 | 4 | 4 |
| Chemistry | 4 | 4 | 4 | 4 |
| Geography | 4 | 4 | 4 | 4 |
| Technical Drawing | 3 | 3 | 3 | 3 |
| Building or Engineering Science | 9 | 9 | 9 | 9 |
| +Workshop Practice | 9 | 9 | 9 | 9 |
| Survey | - | 4 | 4 | 4 |

+Workshop includes:  Metalwork, Woodwork, Masonry, Bricklaying, Plumbing, Carpentry.

| | | | | |
|---|---|---|---|---|
| Physical Education | 2 | 2 | 2 | 2 |
| Current Affairs | 1 | 1 | 1 | 1 |
| Religious Knowledge | 1 | 1 | 1 | 1 |
| Total | 51 | 53 | 53 | 53 |

(Includes 7½ hours of private study)

Commercial subjects in some schools:  Bookkeeping, Shorthand, and Typing.


Certificates awarded:          *Cambridge School Certificate
                                General Certificate of Education
                                City and Guilds of London Institute
                                Royal Society of Arts


## MOMBASA INSTITUTE OF MUSLIM EDUCATION (M.I.O.M.E.)

Originally established to raise the educational and economic standard of
Muslims in Kenya, Tanganyika and Zanzibar (Tanzania).  Since 1963, admission
has been open to students of all races.

Secondary technical training at 2 levels:

(1)  Cambridge School Certificate Secondary Course

Equal status to ordinary secondary school (grammar) course.

Entrance requirements:        Kenya Preliminary Certificate pass in
                               year immediately preceding year of entry.

Duration of course:  4 years.

(a)  Secondary Commercial Course (Commerce or Accountancy):

4-YEAR CAMBRIDGE SCHOOL CERTIFICATE COURSE (COMMERCIAL)

| Subjects | 1st yr. | 2nd yr. | 3rd yr. | 4th yr. |
|---|---|---|---|---|
| English | 9 | 9 | 9 | 9 |
| Mathematics | 7 | 8 | 8 | 8 |
| Geography | 9 | 6 | 6 | 6 |
| History | 8 | 4 | 4 | 4 |
| Commerce | - | 4 | 4 | 3 |
| Accounts | 2 | 3 | 3 | 4 |
| Typing | - | 4 | 3 | 4 |
| Statistics | - | 2 | 3 | 2 |
| Commercial Math. | 4 | 3 | 3 | 3 |
| Civics | 4 | - | - | - |
| Religion | 2 | 2 | 2 | 2 |
| Total | 45 | 45 | 45 | 45 |

(b)   Secondary Technical Course:

### 4-YEAR CAMBRIDGE SCHOOL CERTIFICATE COURSE (TECHNICAL)

| Subjects | 1st yr. | 2nd yr. | 3rd yr. | 4th yr. |
|---|---|---|---|---|
| English | 9 | 9 | 9 | 9 |
| Mathematics | 7 | 8 | 8 | 8 |
| Chemistry | 5 | 5 | 5 | 5 |
| Physics | 5 | 5 | 5 | 5 |
| Drawing | 5 | 5 | 5 | 5 |
| Workshop | 8 | 8 | 8 | 8 |
| Technology | 3 | 3 | 3 | 3 |
| Civics | 1 | - | - | - |
| Religion | 2 | 2 | 2 | 2 |
| Totals | 45 | 45 | 45 | 45 |

*Cambridge School Certificate awarded.

(2)   City and Guilds of London Institute Courses
National Certificate (Union of Lancashire and Cheshire Institutes)
Courses

Entrance requirements:    2 years academic secondary education.

Modern course (to 1963) and pass M.I.O.M.E. entrance examination in Mathematics and English.

Duration of course:  4½ years, full time.

### MECHANICAL COURSE+

| Subjects | Pre. (1 term) | 1st yr. | 2nd yr. | 3rd yr. | 4th yr. |
|---|---|---|---|---|---|
| English | 8 | 6 | 5 | 5 | 7 |
| Mathematics | 6 | 5 | 5 | 5 | 5 |
| Engineering Science | 5 | 4 | 5 | 5 | 5 |
| Physics | - | 2 | 2 | 4 | 5 |
| Drawing | 5 | 5 | 5 | 3 | 5 |
| Workshop | 13 | 13 | 13 | 13 | 13 |
| Technology | 3 | 3 | 3 | 3 | 3 |
| Electrical Technology | 2 | 4 | 5 | 5 | - |
| Civics | 1 | 1 | - | - | - |
| Religion | 2 | 2 | 2 | 2 | 2 |
| Totals | 45 | 45 | 45 | 45 | 45 |

ELECTRICAL COURSE[+]

| Subjects | Pre. (1 term) | 1st yr. | 2nd yr. | 3rd yr. | 4th yr. |
|---|---|---|---|---|---|
| English | 8 | 6 | 5 | 5 | 7 |
| Mathematics | 6 | 5 | 5 | 5 | 5 |
| Engineering Science | 5 | 5 | 5 | 5 | - |
| Physics | 2 | 2 | 2 | 4 | 5 |
| Drawing | 5 | 5 | 5 | 3 | 2 |
| Workshop | 8 | 8 | 8 | 8 | 8 |
| Technology | 4 | 5 | 7 | 5 | 8 |
| Electrical Technology | 3 | 5 | 5 | 5 | 5 |
| Electrical Lab. | - | - | - | 3 | 3 |
| Civics | 2 | 2 | 1 | - | - |
| Religion | 2 | 2 | 2 | 2 | 2 |
| Totals | 45 | 45 | 45 | 45 | 45 |

[+]Pattern of Examinations for City and Guilds and
National Certificate:

City and Guilds of London Institute (C. and G.)
National Certificate of the Union of Lancashire and
   Cheshire Institute (U.L.C.I.)

Mechanical Engineering:
   Pre M:    Internal
     1 M:    U.L.C.I.   Mech. Eng. Craft Practice
     2 M:    U.L.C.I.   G.2  General Engineering
     3 M:    C. & G.    Mech. Eng. Craft Practice I
             U.L.C.I.   Ordinary National Certificate
             U.L.C.I.   Technician Course
     4 M:    U.L.C.I.   Ordinary National Certificate
             U.L.C.I.   Technician Course
             C. & G.    Mech. Eng. Craft Practice II

Electrical Engineering:
   Pre E:    Internal
     1 E:    U.L.C.I.   1st year Electrical Installation
     2 E:    U.L.C.I.   2nd year Electrical Installation
             U.L.C.I.   Ordinary National Certificate
     3 E:    U.L.C.I.   Technician Course
             C. & G.    Electrical Installation Course "B"
     4 E:    U.L.C.I.   Ordinary National Certificate
             U.L.C.I.   Electrical Installation Course "C"

Ordinary National Certificate (U.L.C.I.) awarded at close of program on
successful examination of U.L.C.I.

<u>City and Guilds of London Institute Certificates</u> (according to level and specialty) awarded at close of program on successful examinations.

Trade courses previously held at the Coast Technical School have been transferred to the Mombasa Technical Institute. These courses will eventually be re-organized to become secondary technical courses.

<u>THE KENYA POLYTECHNIC, Nairobi</u>

This technical college opened in 1961 with following functions:

> To prepare students for university entrance and higher education by way of G.C.E. "A" level courses.

> To provide pre-employment training by way of full-time commercial and secretarial course.

> To provide instruction for apprentices and learners already employed in commerce and industry. This part-time training (day-release and evening classes) linked with practical, on-the-job experience produces skilled technicians.

The following are courses either already established or to be made available in the future:

I.  <u>Preliminary Technical Courses</u>

(1) Extra-Mural Section (at Kabete Technical and Trade School):

2-year full-time program.

Entrance requirements:        2-year vocational trade course.

Curriculum:        Engineering and Building, English, Mathematics, Science, Technical Drawing, Workshop Technology, Workshop Practice.

Award:        Successful students qualify for admission to technician courses at Polytechnic.

(2) Day-release and Engineering Section:

2-year part-time program, 1 day and 1 evening per week.

Entrance requirements:        <u>K.P.E. Certificate</u> and employment in industry.

Curriculum:        English, Mathematics, Technical Drawing, Elementary Science (intermediate school stage for artisans).

Award:                    Government Trade Certificate or possible admis-
                          sion to technician courses.

(3)  Evening Classes:

Same requirements, curriculum and award as above.

Time required:  3 evenings per week.


II.  Full-time Courses

Entrance requirements:                    Cambridge School Certificate,
                                          Grade 1 or 2.

(1)  General Certificate of Education (Advanced level)

Duration of course:  2 years (30 hours per week).

2 alternative Science courses:
  (i)  Pure and Applied Mathematics, Physics, Chemistry.
 (ii)  Biology, Physics, Chemistry and Supplementary Mathematics.

Course qualifies for university entrance.

(2)  Higher City and Guilds of London Institute

Duration of course:  Additional 2 years (30 hours per week).

(3)  Commercial Courses

Duration of course:  1-year program (30 hours per week).

Leading to examination of Royal Society of Arts (Group Certificate) or Pitman's Commercial and Secretarial Certificates.


III.  Part-time Courses

Instruction for apprentices and learners already employed is available in the following courses:

(1)  Engineering Department

General Engineering, Motor Vehicle Mechanics, Mechanical, Electrical, Telecommunications.

(2)  <u>Civil Engineering and Building Department</u>

General Construction, Construction Technician, General Building, Building and Civil Engineering, Surveying.

(3)  <u>Science Department</u>

G.E.C. "O" level; G.C.E. "A" level (see above), Laboratory Assistant, Science Laboratory Technician.

(4)  <u>Commercial Department</u>

Shorthand and Typewriting, Bookkeeping and Commerce, Secretaries, Accountancy, Insurance, Road Transport.

(5)  <u>Miscellaneous Courses</u>

Printing, Institution Management, Technical Teacher Training.

The above courses are offered in the following part-time arrangements:

Sandwich Courses:

For technicians in employment.  Entry with standard <u>School Certificate</u> or completion of suitable preliminary course.

Attendance in alternate terms full time, with day-release in most cases for intermediate terms.  When not in attendance and during vacations, in-service training with employers.

Full time:   30 hours per week.
Day-release:  6 hours per week.
(Telecommunications Technicians attend full time up to intermediate stage, 1 year and sandwich thereafter.)

Duration of course:  2½ years to <u>Ordinary Certificate/Diploma</u>, followed by 2 years to Higher Certificate.

Day-Release Courses:

An alternative to sandwich courses for locally-based craft employees.

Attendance 1 full day and 1 or 2 evenings (i.e., 8 or 10 hours per week).

Duration of course:  2 years to intermediate stage.  4 years to full course.

Part-time Evening Courses:

For those employed and not able to obtain release for daytime study.

Attendance 2 - 2½ hour evening classes.

Grouped courses:  6 - 8 hours per week.

Duration of course:  Each stage takes 1 year and completion of full course
                     may take up to 5 years.


G O V E R N M E N T   T R A I N I N G
   (Administration, Professional and Extension Services.  Governmental
   departments other than the Ministry of Education.)

Some courses at higher levels available for staff of all races.  Predominant aim of these Government schools to train African professional and
administrative staff for public service.  Instruction in full-time courses
given at both post-primary and post-secondary levels.


AGRICULTURAL AND VETERINARY TRAINING:

(1)  Junior Ranks of Extension Service

     These levels mainly trained at Embu Agricultural School.

     Entrance requirements:              Kenya Preliminary Examination
                                         Post-Standard VII or Form II

     Course:   1 year up-grading course preparing for Assistant Agricul-
               tural/Veterinary Instructor.

(2)  Technician Grade

     Entrance requirements:              General Certificate of Education,
                                         ordinary level, or School Certifi-
                                         cate

     Course:   2 year program leading to Certificate in Agriculture -
               Agricultural/Veterinary Assistant.

               2-year course includes:  Crop and Animal Husbandry, Survey
               for Farm Planning, other agricultural subjects and Mathe-
               matics.  Practical work on school farms.

     Training courses also given at Matuga and Kapenguria Agricultural
     Schools.

(3)  <u>Diploma Grade of Extension Service</u>

This level trained at Egerton and Siriba Agricultural Colleges.

These 2 institutions both provide training in agriculture, foresty and veterinary courses at diploma level.  (Above programs to be concentrated at Egerton).

Siriba also trains teachers in agriculture.

Field officers trained for:  Departments of Agriculture, Veterinary Service, Forestry, Farm Managers, Technical Salesmen, commercial firms.


<u>Egerton Agricultural College, Moro</u>
   (Government School)

|  |  |
|---|---|
| Entrance requirements: | <u>School Certificate</u> (1st or 2nd class). <br> (Agricultural Science courses offered in only a few secondary schools as examination subjects for <u>Cambridge School Certificate</u> syllabus.  "Agricultural Principles and Practice" approved by the Syndicate, as developed at Chavakali Secondary School, Kakamega district.) |

Courses:  For Assistant Agricultural/Live Stock Officers.

2-year program (30 hours per week).  Preceded by 7 to 9 months practical work.

Subjects studied:     Agriculture             )
                      Animal Husbandry        )     All
                      Forestry                )     with
                      Dairying                )     Field
                      Engineering Technology  )     Practice
                         (Mechanical Farming)
                         (This course leads to
                          variation of Agricul-
                          ture Diploma)

Certificate awarded:  <u>Diploma</u> (Egerton Diploma accepted as entry for university degree courses in East Africa, Britain, Australia).

1964 proposal:  Egerton keeps best students for 3½-year course preparing students for Senior Assistant Agricultural/Live Stock Officers.

(4) <u>Full Professional Agricultural or Veterinary Officer</u>

    Entrance requirements:           Agriculture degree from Makerere
                                     or Veterinary Science degree from
                                     University College, Nairobi, plus
                                     postgraduate work.

(5) <u>Livestock Overseer</u>

    Livestock Improvement Centre Schools
      (8 schools operated by Department of Veterinary Services)

    Entrance requirements:           <u>Kenya Preliminary Examination</u>

    Duration of course:  2 years.

    Subjects offered:     All practical aspects of selective breeding,
                              care and nutrition of cattle, sheep and poultry.

(6) <u>Forest Rangers</u>

      <u>Kenya Forest School, Londiani</u>

      Entrance requirements:        <u>Kenya Preliminary Examination</u> or
                                     <u>School Certificate</u> (lower standard
                                     than required by Egerton).

      Course:  1-year program for Rangers.

In addition to field staff positions in the above services, training at
School Certificate level is also offered in the Departments of Water,
Land and Surveys, Geological and other associated Departments.

<u>POLICE TRAINING:</u>

<u>Police Training School, Kiganjo</u>

Entrance requirements:           Standard VIII (VII)

Courses:       6-month training for Constables.
                3-month training for Inspectors.

<u>MEDICAL TRAINING:</u>

Medical Training Centre at Kenyatta National Hospital, Nairobi (formerly
King George V Hospital).

Basic technical education given at Kenya Polytechnic, and specialized courses provided at Medical Training Centre.

I.  Post-Primary:

   Entrance requirements:                    Standard VII

   Courses:   2 - 4-year programs for:
              Hospital Assistants, Graded Dressers, Health Assistants, Assistant Midwives, Assistant Health Visitors, Darkroom and Entomological Assistants, etc.

              Hospital Assistants:

              Recruited from male and female "dressers" (having worked at least 6 months at a hospital) and given 4 years training.

              End of 1st year  -  Preliminary
              End of 3rd year  -  Final examination of Nurses and Mid-wives Council of Kenya, receiving title of "Assistant Nurse."
              End of 4th year  -  Internal examination qualified for "Hospital Assistant."

              Health Assistants: (Male only)

              9 weeks of lectures given on Hygiene, Sanitation, Communicable Diseases.  Sent for 18 months for practical experience under direction of European Health Inspector.

              Internal examination follows final 9-week course of lectures.

              Dark Room Assistants:

              2-year training of lectures and practical work in X-ray Department of Kenyatta National Hospital.

II.  Post School Certificate:

   Entrance requirements:                    School Certificate
                                             (Training at secondary level given those wishing career in the Medical Department.)

   Courses:   3 - 4-year programs in following:
              Assistant Health Inspectors, Assistant Radiographers, Dispensers, Laboratory Assistants, Orthopaedic Assistants.

<u>Graduate Medical Course</u> (Makerere College, Uganda)

In association with the Mulago Hospital (internationally recognized medical qualifications).  No graduate training in Kenya.


<u>ADMINISTRATIVE TRAINING</u>:


<u>Kenya Institute of Administration, Lower Kabete</u>

"Africanization" programs provide intensive courses for administrative work in:
            Clerical, executive and administrative levels for central
            government, provincial administration and local government.

Preparing Africans for many positions.  Consists largely of up-grading or specially training experienced men.  In some cases the original school qualifications would be below what is now required for direct entry.

<u>Clerical</u> Level

Entrance requirements:                  Form IV or "failed <u>School Certificate</u>"

Courses:  Up-grade existing clerks, inside or outside government service.

<u>Executive</u> Level

Entrance requirements:          <u>School Certificate</u>

Courses:  3-months training for middle grade executives.

<u>District Assistants</u>

Entrance requirements:          <u>School Certificate</u>

Courses:  For Junior Administrative grade in provincial Administration.
            (Local government training similar.)

<u>District Officers</u>

Entrance requirements:          University graduates (in future)

Courses:  Some candidates up-graded from district assistants.

Senior Administrators

Entrance requirements:          University graduates

Courses:  In-service training appropriate to Institute of Public Admin-
          istration.

1964 Proposals:  Add courses for lay magistrates and basic secretarial
                 training.


O T H E R   G O V E R N M E N T   D E P A R T M E N T A L   T R A I N I N G
    (Ministry of Works, Departments of Co-operation and Community Development)

Lowest level of field services (clerks and artisans)

Entrance requirements:          Standard VII


Technical level

Entrance requirements:          School Certificate

Courses train:     Technicians and Laboratory Assistants,  Junior Officers
                   in Co-operatives, Community Development, Senior Clerks,
                   Storekeepers, Ministry of Works trainees for Inspector-
                   ate, Assistant Quantity Surveyors and Assistant (sub-
                   professional) grades throughout the Departments.


Professional level

Entrance requirements:          University graduates.

Courses train:     Engineers, Quantity Surveyors, Surveyors, Professional
                   Accountants, etc.

                   (These grades come from professional courses at the
                   University College, Nairobi.)


PROFESSIONAL SCHOOLS

Not confined to government employees.

Self-contained professional schools all in some way related to the Kenya
Government and include the following:

Kenya School of Law

(1)  For School Certificate holders:

   Course:   Complete academic training for students entering legal
             profession by way of articles (recognized by law under
             Advocates Act).

(2)  For university graduates:

   Course:   1-year postgraduate practical training for students having
             completed Law degree at University College, Dar es Salaam.

Training expected also to include courses for: Law clerks, lay magistrates, certain members of public services and employed persons from
industry and commerce.

Kenya Government Secretarial College

Commercial training (Candidates must be in government employ).

Entrance requirements:              Completion of 4 years secondary train-
                                    ing (students having taken but not
                                    necessarily passed School Certificate
                                    examination).

Duration of course:  1 year full time.
                     (3 terms, 3½ months each)

### TIMETABLE

| Subjects | Hours per week |
|----------|:--------------:|
| Typing | 10 |
| Shorthand | 11 |
| English | 6 |
| Secretarial Duties | 1 |
| General Knowledge | 1 |
| Current Affairs | 1 |
|  | 30 |

Other special courses and some evening classes offered.

## CORRESPONDENCE COURSES

These schools are all privately owned and operated, mostly based in the
United Kingdom.  Under the Education Act they are required to be registered.  The Ministry of Education maintains close relations with these
colleges, requiring an "efficient" standard of all recognized institutions.

Correspondence Colleges include the following:

> British Tutorial College
> International Correspondence School
> Wolsey Hall
> East African Correspondence College
> Rapid Results College

Courses available:        Forms I - IV and School Certificate, through
Higher School Certificate examinations.


# I N D U S T R I A L   A N D   C O M M E R C I A L   T R A I N I N G
### (Private Institutions and Public Utilities)

Several private industrial firms, the East African Common Services Organization and public utilities have established a range of training for
students.  They are recruited largely from Standard VII and in smaller
numbers from School Certificate holders.

The Kenya Ministry of Education programs are, in most cases, the base of
technical education upon which more specialized training is built.
Courses range from 3-year residential programs to in-service instruction.

Programs include:
- (a)  In-service training for semi-skilled operatives
- (b)  Foreman training
- (c)  Artisan apprenticeship
- (d)  Clerical training
- (f)  Technician and Commercial training, Accountancy, etc. in associa-
       tion with a technical institute
- (g)  Professional training associated with universities in East Africa
       and overseas
- (h)  Management training in-service.


## PUBLIC UTILITIES AND EAST AFRICA COMMON SERVICE ORGANIZATIONS

### East African Railways and Harbours

Mechanical Department Apprentice:  Post-primary entry.

5-year course:   1-day each week through entire period.

English, Arithmetic, Elementary Geometry, History, Geography, and Current Events; (1st year) First Aid.

Trainee Drivers:   Post-primary entry, Kenya Preliminary Certificate.

5-year course:   General instruction throughout entire 5 years similar to above course.  First 2 years at Railway Training school.

## East Africa Postal and Telecommunications Training School

School Certificate required for 2-year course.

## East Africa Power and Lighting Training School

School Certificate required for 3 - 4 year course.

## East Africa School of Co-operation

6 - 7 month course.

Training courses also provided by private firms:

East African Airways
East African Tobacco Company
Bata Shoe Company
Nyanza Textiles
Kenya Farmers' Union
Gailey and Roberts Technical School

East Africa Cargo Handling
  Training School
Most oil companies
Large banks
Some plantation companies

## TEACHER EDUCATION

Since 1955, teacher training in Kenya has been area of greatest educational development.  Colleges managed by voluntary agencies:  Churches, Missions, or Boards of Governors.  1963, aided schools - 38; unaided - 2.  Plans to amalgamate smaller colleges into total of 15 - 20 colleges, each with approximately 250 students and large specialist staff.

Boys and girls trained separately; mixed training increasing.

At end of 2-year course of academic knowledge, principles of education and psychology students take written and practical examinations set internally, moderated by Education inspectorate.

Kenya teaching profession includes all 4 races; training colleges attended by:

| | |
|---|---|
| Africans | Greatest majority |
| Asians | Moderate numbers |
| Arabs | Very few |
| Europeans | None (Graduates with overseas training only) |

As of 1965, in addition to free tuition and board, cash and clothing allowances given to all teacher training candidates.

As of 1963, teachers trained at following levels:

| Entrance Requirements and Training | Grade[+] | Teaching Area | Certificate Designation | |
|---|---|---|---|---|
| | | | Formerly | 1963 |
| Kenya Preliminary Exam (after 8 years) plus 2 years training. (after 7 years' Full Primary, November 1965) | Assistant Grade II | Teaching (lower) Full Primary | T 3 | P 3 |
| 2-years Secondary or Cambridge School Certificate (failed) plus 2 years training | Assistant Grade I | Teaching Assistant (upper) Full Primary | T 2 | P 2 |
| Cambridge School Certificate (passed) or equivalent, plus 2 years training | Teacher | Teaching Full Primary | T 1 | P 1 |

N.B.  1964 proposal to provide vacation courses to up-grade former untrained P 4 teachers.

Any teacher obtaining advanced academic qualifications becomes eligible for promotion to higher grade.

[+]These grades no longer used.

| Entrance Requirements and Training | Grade | Teaching Area | Certificate |
|---|---|---|---|
| Higher School Certificate (passed) | Master | Secondary Schools and Training Colleges | S 1+ |
| General Certificate of Education "A" plus 2 years' training | | | |
| School Certificate plus 3 years' training | Master | | S 1+ |
| Degree plus 1-year University (Diploma) or B.Ed. (3 years) Degree University (planned) | Graduate Teachers | | |

+N.B.  The new level S 1 (above) was introduced in 1963 at Kenya Central Teachers' College and Highridge Training College, Nairobi (mixed classes, 1965). The course replaces former 2-year Undergraduate Diploma of Education program previously offered at Institute of Education at Makerere College.

Most teacher training colleges offer a 2-year program of 35 weeks each year. During these 2 years, a total of 12 weeks is spent on teaching practice. Courses covered are essentially the same for all grades of teachers. Instruction given at all levels according to previous academic qualifications.

The time devoted to each subject varies, but the following is representative:

## TYPICAL TEACHER TRAINING COLLEGE
### (2 years)

### TIMETABLE

| Subjects | Periods per week (40 minutes each) |
|---|---|
| English | 6 |
| Mathematics | 6 |
| Education (including Psychology for P 1 and P 2 trainees both years) | 8½ |

Science[+] (including Agriculture) and
    Nature Study/Rural Science                  4
Swahili[++] and other languages             3
History                                          3
Geography                                 3
Arts and Crafts                     3
Music                                      3
Religious Knowledge                3
Physical Education                 3
                             Total       $45\frac{1}{2}$

[+]Women students take Domestic Science for 4 hours per week instead of Swahili and the Agricultural application of Science.

[++]Teachers specialize in 1 language:  English, Swahili, Arabic, Hindi, Punjabi, Gujerati, Urdu.

218

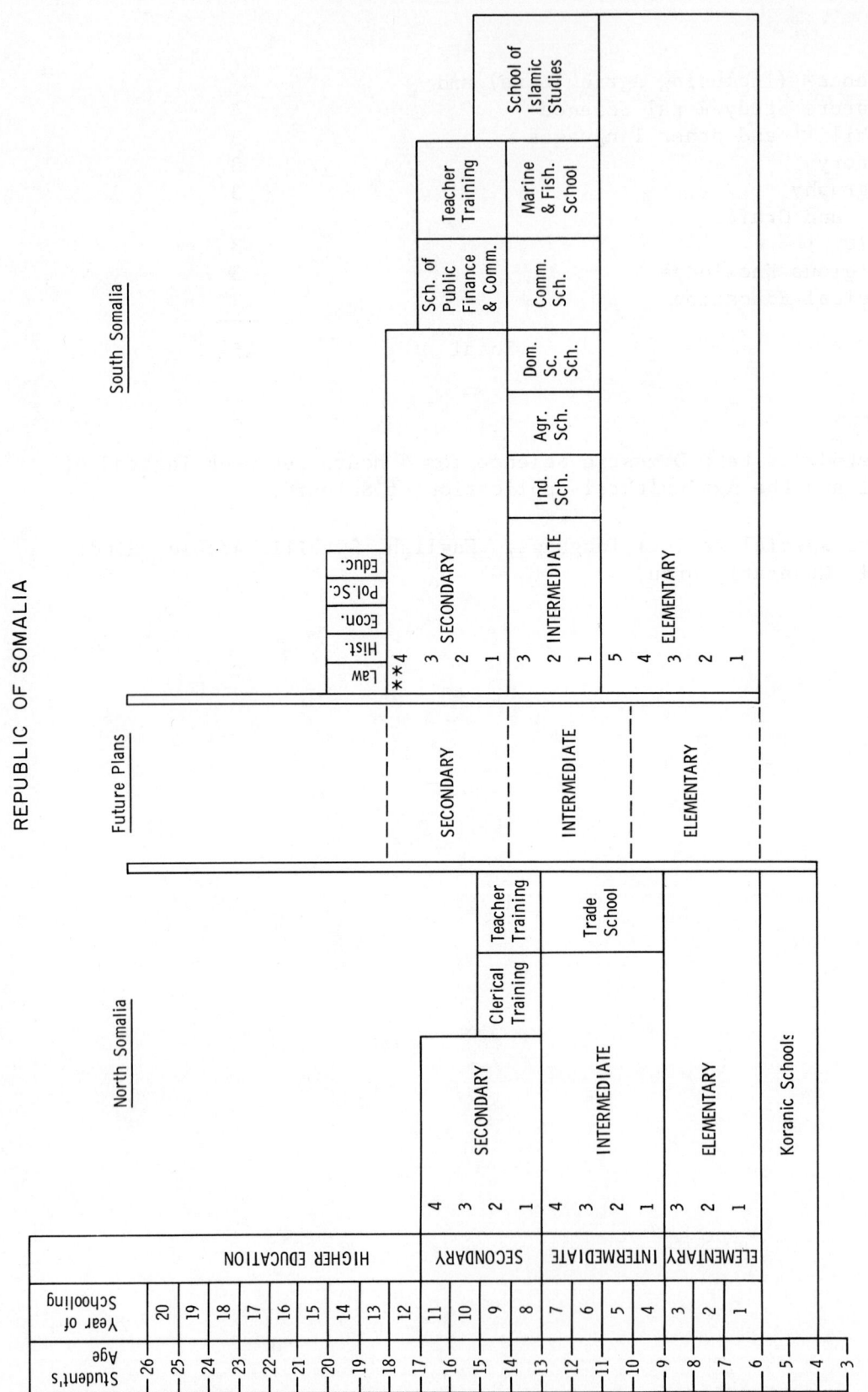

REPUBLIC OF SOMALIA

South Somalia

Future Plans

North Somalia

Compulsory education: None

School year: July 15 to May 5

REPUBLIC OF SOMALIA


Independence:  July 1, 1960.



BACKGROUND


Somalis are Hamitic people with Cushitic culture; came from Middle East;
intermingled with the Galla (also Hamitic) and the Bantu.

Two main groups:  the Samaale (which includes the Darod, Ishaak, Hawiye,
and Dir tribes), who are nomadic and semi-nomadic, and form 80% of the
population; and the Sab (which includes the Rahanwein, Dighil and other
tribes).  The Somalis are Moslems.  The Bantu-speaking negroid groups
live along the two rivers.  Non-Somali population consists of approximately
30,000 Arabs (mostly from Yemen), 1200 Indians and Pakistanis, and 500
Italians.

Languages:  Italian, Somali, Arabic, and English.

Ancient Egyptians visiting Somalis for incense and herbs called it "The
Land of Aromatics."

10th century, Arabs from Yemen and the Hadhramaut settled along coast
where Merka, Brava and Mogadishu are presently located.

15th and 16th centuries, Portuguese explorers tried unsuccessfully to
gain a foothold.

18th century, Sultan of Oman controlled main coastal areas; by latter half
of 19th century, Sultan of Zanzibar inherited control.

Italian explorers came in the latter part of the 19th century.  British
forces took Aden, 1839.  1861, Viceroy of India gave the anchorages of
Kismayu, Brava, Merka and Mogadishu to Sultan of Zanzibar.  1875, Egyptians
controlled some of northern centers.  1884-86, British signed some
Protectorate treaties with Somali chiefs of northern areas.  1885, Italian
expansion; 1889, Italian Protectorate over northern areas.  1892, Sultan
of Zanzibar transferred his jurisdiction over Merka, Brava, Mogadishu, and
Uarsceik to Italy.  Direct Italian control, 1908, over area known as
Italian Somaliland.

"Holy Wars," 1899-1920.  1925, British government transferred Jubaland to
Italy.  During Italo-Ethiopian conflict, 1934-36, Somalia was a staging
area.  1936-41, British colonial  government had unified administration
over British Somaliland and the Ogaden (Somali-inhabited section of
Ethiopia).

1940-41, Italian troops occupied British Somaliland but were defeated.
British conquered Italian Somaliland, and retained authority until 1950,
when Italian Somaliland became United Nations Trust Territory on April 1st.

November, 1949, U.N. General Assembly, with Italian approval, passed
resolution that Somalia would receive independence by 1960.  May 1956,
first all-Somali government established.  June 20, 1961, new constitution.

When Italy agreed to give independence to its Trusteeship Territory, July
1, 1960, United Kingdom gave its Protectorate independence, June 26, 1960,
so that the two Somali territories might join in a united Somali Republic,
July 1, 1960.

Nation has no underline language.  The two proposals, one based on Roman
characters, one on Arabic characters, have not been acted upon due to
political and religious matters.


EDUCATION - PRE-INDEPENDENCE


E X - I T A L I A N   S O M A L I L A N D


Under Italian rule (1885-1941), Catholic mission schools established.
British occupation (1941-50) brought emphasis on secular education.
1952, during Trusteeship period, 5-Year Education Plan initiated.

By 1961:

5-year primary programs (most children leaving after 2 years
due to need for them on the land).

Three 3-year lower secondary schools, established 1950 and 1959.

One 4-year secondary school, established 1953.
School of Public Finance and Commerce (upper secondary), 1958,
developed from School of Politics and Administration, established
1950-51.

Higher Institute of Economics and Law, established in Mogadiscio,
1954; later became University Institute of Somalia, and gained
university status in 1960.

Teacher Training Institute, established 1953.  3-year program.

School of Islamic Studies, established 1953, lower secondary
level (4-year program).

# EX - BRITISH SOMALILAND

First government schools established 1898-1908; discontinued due to hostilities. 1937-39, further attempts failed.

10% of population had Koranic education.

By 1961:

> 3-year primary programs, with vocational bias.
>
> 4-year intermediate school programs (Liberal Arts emphasis).
>
> 2 secondary schools, established 1953, 1959.
>
> Trade school, established 1952; integrated with Public Works Department. 3-year post-intermediate school training.
>
> Teacher Training Center, 2-year program for elementary school teachers.

## EDUCATION - AFTER INDEPENDENCE

### NORTH SOMALIA
(ex-British Somaliland)

## PRE-PRIMARY EDUCATION

## KORANIC SCHOOLS

1964, 189 Koranic schools in north.

2-year course.

Program: Arabic, the Holy Koran, Elementary Arithmetic.

Not a part of official government system, but a pre-requisite for admission to elementary school.

## ELEMENTARY EDUCATION

1964, 90 elementary schools in north, occasionally co-educational.

Entry age:     approximately 6 years.

Language of instruction:     Arabic. English usually introduced in 2nd year of elementary school.

Length of course:      3 years.

Program:  Arabic, Arithmetic, Arts and Crafts, English, Hygiene, Local
          Affairs, Physical Education.


INTERMEDIATE EDUCATION

1964, 17 intermediate schools in north.  Girls only 10% of total enrollment.

Language of instruction:      English.

Length of course:      4 years.

Program:  Arabic, English, the Koran, Mathematics, Science, Geography,
          History, Art, Physical Education.

          Local variations, e.g., Domestic Science in girls' schools,
          Woodworking, Mechanics and other industrial arts in boys'
          schools where teachers and facilities are available.


SECONDARY EDUCATION

Language of instruction:      English.

Length of course:      4 years in 2 general secondary schools, Sheikh
                       Secondary School and Amoud Secondary School, both
                       for boys only.

                       Shorter course in special secondary schools (see under
                       VOCATIONAL AND TECHNICAL EDUCATION, and TEACHER
                       EDUCATION).

Program:  British system.  Arabic, the Koran, English (including Literature),
          Chemistry, Physics, Mathematics, Geography, History.

Certificate awarded:  General Certificate of Education (G.C.E.).[+]


HIGHER EDUCATION

None.  Graduates of secondary school may enter University Institute of
Somalia, Mogadiscio, but handicapped because of use of Italian.

Scholarships awarded to Great Britain and other English-speaking countries.


[+]For Regulations and Syllabuses for the University of London General
   Certificate of Education Examination held overseas, write the
   Secretary, School Examinations Department, University of London,
   Senate House, Malet Street, London, W.C. 1.

## VOCATIONAL AND TECHNICAL EDUCATION

### TRADE SCHOOL, Hargeisa

Established 1952.  Intermediate level.

Length of course:      4 years, followed by 2-year apprenticeship with
                       Public Works Department.

Program:   Intermediate studies with trade subjects, Carpentry, Joinery,
           Auto Mechanics.

Prepare for Intermediate City and Guilds Examination (U.K.).

### CLERICAL TRAINING CENTER, Hargeisa

Secondary level.  Courses for in-service clerks and new recruits from
intermediate schools.

Length of course:      2 years.

Program:   English, Arithmetic, Typing, Local Accounting, Office
           Procedure.

### RURAL SCIENCE TRAINING

Courses run for junior staff of Department of Natural Resources who have
completed intermediate schooling.

Program:   English, Arithmetic, Science subjects connected with natural
           resources.

## TEACHER EDUCATION

### TEACHER TRAINING CENTER, Amoud

Secondary level.

Length of course:      1 year at present.  Originally 2 years.  Plans for
                       3-year course in the future.

Prepares elementary school teachers.

Teachers for intermediate and secondary school sent to Sudan, Lebanon or
Great Britain.

<u>TEACHER TRAINING CLASS FOR GIRLS</u>, Hargeisa

Secondary level.  2-year course held at Hargeisa Girls' Intermediate
School.  Prepares elementary school teachers.

6-month courses also offered for Koranic school teachers working with
nomads.

Program:  Arabic, Arithmetic, Hygiene, Livestock Improvement, Soil
          Preservation.

Teacher promotion examinations also available.


<u>ADULT EDUCATION</u>

Courses given in Arabic, Arithmetic, English.  Limited program because
of lack of teachers.


S O U T H   S O M A L I A
(ex-Italian Somaliland)

<u>PRE-PRIMARY EDUCATION</u>

<u>KORANIC SCHOOLS</u>

Attendance at Koranic schools not pre-requisite for entry to elementary
schools in south.  About 10 times as many Koranic schools in south as in
north.


<u>ELEMENTARY EDUCATION</u>

1964, 175 elementary schools in south.  Proportion of boys and girls,
approximately 4 to 1.

Entry age:       approximately 6 years.

Language of instruction:       Arabic first 2 years, Italian class 3
                               onwards.

Length of course:     5 years.

Certificate awarded:  <u>Licenza di scuola elementare</u>.

## INTERMEDIATE EDUCATION

1964, 14 intermediate schools in south, including vocational and technical training schools.

2 types of general lower secondary schools: scuola media italiane and scuolia media inferiore della Somalia.

Entrance requirements:          Examination open to holders of Licenza
                                di scuola elementare.

Language of instruction:        Italian.  English to be gradually introduced
                                and to become eventually the language of
                                instruction.

Length of course:       3 years.

### TIMETABLE FOR LOWER SECONDARY SCHOOL
(Hours per week)

| Subjects | 1 | 2 | 3 |
|---|---|---|---|
| Italian | 4 | 4 | 4 |
| Arabic | 5 | 5 | 4 |
| Religion | 2 | 2 | 2 |
| English | | | |
| History, Geography, Civics | 3 | 3 | 4 |
| Mathematics | 4 | 5 | 5 |
| Drawing | 3 | 2 | 2 |
| Hygiene | 1 | 1 | 1 |
| Physical Training | 2 | 2 | 2 |

Certificate awarded:  Licenza di scuola media, awarded on examination.

## SCUOLA DI DISCIPLINE ISLAMICHE (School of Islamic Studies), Mogadiscio

Established 1952.  Purpose to train judges (khadis) to administer Islamic law and to prepare religious leaders.  Intermediate level.

Entrance requirements:          Entrance examination open to holders of
                                Licenza di scuola elementare.

Length of course:       4 years.  First 2 years general education, last 2
                        Religion or Jurisprudence, according to speciali-
                        zation.

                        2-year course for teachers of Arabic and Religion.

## TIMETABLE FOR SCHOOL OF ISLAMIC STUDIES
(Hours per week)

| Subjects | 1 | 2 | 3 | 4 |
|---|---|---|---|---|
| Life of the Prophet | 1 | - | - | - |
| Koran | 2 | 1 | 3 | 3 |
| Law | 5 | 5 | 5 | 5 |
| Theology and Dogma | 1 | 1 | - | - |
| Arabic | | | | |
|   Grammar and Syntax | 5 | 5 | 5 | - |
|   Composition | 2 | 2 | 2 | - |
|   Reading | 1 | 1 | 1 | 1 |
|   Dictation | 2 | 2 | 1 | 1 |
|   Memorization | 1 | 1 | 1 | 1 |
| History of Arabic | | | | |
|   Literature | - | - | - | 2 |
| Religious History | - | - | 1 | 1 |
| Traditions | - | - | 2 | 2 |
| Ethics | - | - | 1 | 1 |
| Rhetoric | - | - | - | 4 |
| Hygiene | 1 | 1 | - | - |
| Italian | 2 | 2 | 2 | 2 |
| Calligraphy | 1 | 1 | 1 | 1 |
| Drawing | 1 | 1 | - | - |
| Geography and | | | | |
|   Political History | 2 | 2 | 2 | 2 |
| Mathematics | 3 | 3 | 3 | 3 |
| Physical Training | 1 | 1 | 1 | 1 |

Diploma awarded on results of examination.


## SCUOLA FEMMINILE DI ECONOMIA DOMESTICA (Domestic Science School), Mogadiscio

Entrance requirements:     Licenzia di scuola elementare, or the certificate of the primary school for adults, or
passing of special entrance examination.

Length of course:    3 years.  Intermediate level.

Program:  Italian, General Culture, Arabic, Mathematics, Drawing, Hygiene,
Child Care, Housework, Domestic Economy, Practical Activities,
Physical Education.

Diploma awarded on results of examination.

## SECONDARY EDUCATION

1964, 6 secondary schools in south.  New Russian-built school has laboratories for Biology, Chemistry, Physics, Geography, and Music.

Entrance requirements:        <u>Licenza di scuola media</u>.


## LICEO SCIENTIFICO ITALIANO

Secondary school exactly equivalent to Italian type.  Curriculum emphasizes Mathematics and Sciences, and includes a modern language.

Length of course:    5 years.

Certificate awarded:  <u>Maturità scientifica</u>, leads on to higher education in any Italian-speaking countries.


## SCUOLA MEDIA SUPERIORE DELLA SOMALIA

Upper General Secondary school of Somali type.

Length of course:    4 years.

### TIMETABLE FOR UPPER SECONDARY SCHOOL (Somali type)
#### (Hours per week)

| Subjects | 1 | 2 | 3 | 4 |
|---|---|---|---|---|
| Italian | 3 | 3 | 3 | 3 |
| Arabic | 3 | 3 | 3 | 3 |
| Religion and Islamic Subjects | 1 | 1 | 1 | 1 |
| English | 3 | 3 | 3 | 3 |
| History, Geography, Civics | 3 | 3 | 4 | 3 |
| Mathematics | 6 | 5 | 4 | 3 |
| Physics | - | 3 | 2 | 2 |
| Chemistry and Natural Sciences | 4 | 4 | 4 | 3 |
| History of Science | - | - | 2 | 3 |
| Drawing and History of Art | 2 | 2 | 2 | 3 |
| Physical Training | 2 | 2 | 2 | 2 |

**<u>Diploma</u> awarded.

## HIGHER EDUCATION

### ISTITUTO UNIVERSITARIO DELLA SOMALIA, Mogadiscio

University Institute of Somalia established 1954 as the Higher Institute of Legal, Economic and Social Studies. University status, 1960. Linked with University of Rome, which grants graduates 2 years of credit towards their degree.

>       Institute of Law and Economics
>       School of Statistics
>       Statistics and Sociology Research Center
>       School of Islamic Studies (including Department of Law)

Entrance requirements:          <u>Diploma</u> from upper secondary school, school of politics and administration, or certificate from normal or vocational school (requiring later supplementary examinations).

Length of course:     2 years.

Language of instruction:        Italian.

Program: Law, History, Economics, Political Science, Education.


## VOCATIONAL AND TECHNICAL EDUCATION

### SCUOLA DI AVVIAMENTO PROFESSIONALE A TIPO INDUSTRIALE (Industrial School), Mogadiscio

Entrance requirements:          <u>Licenza di scuola elementare</u>, or pass entrance examination.

Length of course:     3 years at intermediate level.

Language of instruction:        Italian.

Program: General subjects and specialized instruction in following sections: Auto Mechanics, Carpentry, Building, Electricity, Radio Engineering and Telecommunications.

<u>Diploma</u> awarded in specialty. Final examination includes a practical project in specialty.

## INDUSTRIAL SCHOOL TIMETABLE OF GENERAL SUBJECTS
### (Hours per week)

| Subjects | 1 | 2 | 3 |
|---|---|---|---|
| Italian and Civics | 4 | 4 | 3 |
| Arabic | 2 | 2 | 2 |
| History and Geography | 2 | 2 | 1 |
| Mathematics | 5 | 4 | 3 |
| Physics and Chemistry | - | 2 | 1 |
| Art and Design | 4 | 5 | - |
| Hygiene | 1 | 1 | - |
| Physical Education | 2 | 2 | 2 |

1st year:    15-18 hours given to specialty.
2nd year:    15 hours.
3rd year:    23-25 hours.

Grading:    Average mark over whole year determines passage to next class.

School assisted by International Labour Office and maintains close working relations with various industrial firms in the country through the Mogadiscio Chamber of Commerce.


## SCUOLA PROFESSIONALE AGRARIA (Agricultural School), Genale

Temporarily situated at Mogadiscio.  Close contact with Agricultural Center at Genale.

Entrance requirements:         Licenza di scuola elementare and pass entrance examination.

Length of course:    3 years at intermediate level.

Language of instruction:         Italian.

## AGRICULTURAL SCHOOL TIMETABLE
### (Hours per week)

| Subjects | 1 | 2 | 3 |
|---|---|---|---|
| Italian | 4 | 4 | 3 |
| Arabic | 1 | 1 | 1 |
| Geography | 2 | 1 | 1 |
| History | 1 | 1 | 1 |
| Mathematics | 4 | 4 | 3 |
| Freehand and Geometrical Drawing | 2 | 2 | - |
| Biology | 4 | 3 | - |
| Chemistry and Mineralogy | 2 | 1 | 1 |

| | | | |
|---|---|---|---|
| Physics | 2 | - | - |
| Human Hygiene | 1 | - | - |
| Zootechnics--Diet and Hygiene of Cattle | - | 2 | 3 |
| Agriculture | - | 3 | 3 |
| Agricultural Mechanics | - | 1 | 1 |
| Agricultural Pathology and Entomology | - | 2 | 2 |
| Land Surveying and Rural Building | - | - | 3 |
| Draughtsmanship | - | - | 1 |
| Agricultural Industries | - | - | 1 |
| Political and Rural Economy | - | 1 | 3 |
| Practical Work | 10 | 9 | 9 |
| Physical Training | 1 | 1 | 1 |

Grading:  Promotion dependent on average of year's marks.

Diploma awarded on results of examination.

Practical training given at experimental centers established by Inspectorate of Agriculture and Zootechnics.  Graduates can take refresher courses at the school or at various specialized centers or institutes in Somalia.


SCUOLA PROFESSIONALE MARITTIMA E DI PESCA (Marine and Fishery School), Mogadiscio

Entrance requirements:          Licenza di scuola elementare, and must be at least 12 years.

Length of course:     3 years for  a) apprentice ship's carpenters' section

b) apprentice masters' section

1-year course for those passing final examination of apprentice masters' section, in fisheries.

Language of instruction:     Italian.

Program:  3-year course general subjects:
Italian and Civics, English, Arabic, History, Geography, Mathematics, Physics, Drawing.

Plus technical and vocational subjects in chosen section.

1-year fisheries course:
Marine Biology (2h), Technology of Fishing (5h), Ships' Engines (2h), Legal, Economic and Social Aspects of Fisheries (3h), Practical Fishing (16h).

Diploma awarded on results of examination at end of 3 years.

School maintains relations with private fishing firms, mainly on coast of Nijertini (Gulf of Aden).

## SCUOLA DI AVVIAMENTO COMMERCIALE (Commercial School), Mogadiscio

Entrance requirements:          Licenza di scuola elementare.

Length of course:     3 years at intermediate level.

Language of instruction:          Italian.

Program:  Religion, Italian, History and Civics, Geography, English, Arabic, Mathematics, Science and Hygiene, Commercial Products, Shorthand and Typing, Drawing and Calligraphy, Bookkeeping and Accountancy, Physical Training.

Diploma awarded on results of final examination.

## SCHOOL OF PUBLIC FINANCE AND COMMERCE, Mogadiscio

Established in 1950 as School of Politics and Administration which gave 3-year course to men with some experience in government, politics or commerce.

Subjects taught:  Public Finance, History, Civil Law, Public Law, Geography, Arabic, Italian, Mathematics.

Best graduates offered 18 months of preparation in Italy and returned to responsible administrative posts.

1958, converted into a School of Public Finance and Commerce at level of upper secondary school.

Entrance requirements:          Licenza di scuola media.

Length of course:     3 years.

Program:  History of Civilization, Public Law, International Law, U.N., Islamic Institutions, Private Law, Criminal Law, Political Economy, Finance, Bookkeeping, State Accounting, Organization of Somaliland, Political and Economic Geography, Arabic, Italian, Mathematics, Science, General Geography.

Diploma awarded.

TEACHER EDUCATION

SCUOLA MAGISTRALE (Teacher Training College), Mogadiscio

Entrance requirements:        Licenza di scuola media.

Length of course:     3 years, upper secondary level.

Language of instruction:        Italian.

Program:  Italian, Arabic, Religion and Islamic Law, History, Geography
          and Civics, Education, Psychology and Practice Teaching,
          Mathematics, Physics, Chemistry, Biology, General Geography,
          Agriculture, Drawing, Hygiene, Physical Training, English.
          No laboratory or audio-visual equipment.

Diploma awarded.  Students may teach at primary level.


NATIONAL TEACHER EDUCATION CENTER, Afgoi

Established 1963, built by US/AID.  Links with Eastern Michigan University.

Entrance requirements:        Licenza di scuola media, and pass admission
                              examination consisting of interview and
                              ability test in Arabic and English.

Length of course:     3 years, upper secondary level.

                      Special 4th year of training for selected students
                      to prepare for service in intermediate schools.

Language of instruction:        English.

Program:  Arabic, Religion, English, Mathematics, Science, Social Science,
          Art, Music, Psychology, Methods of Teaching, Practice Teaching.

Students teach at primary level after 3-year course, at intermediate level
after special 4th-year training.

In-service training:    3-month courses at Mogadiscio for untrained teachers
                        (incaricati) and teachers with no diploma but with
                        at least 4 years' experience (coadiutori).

                        9-month course for coadiutori to make qualified
                        teachers of them.

                        7-month course for recruiting teachers of English.

                        6-week refresher course in English for graduates of
                        the Magistrale.

                        2-month course in Arabic and English for elementary
                        school teachers.

<u>SCHOOL OF ISLAMIC STUDIES</u>, Mogadiscio

Offers 2-year course for teachers of Arabic and Religion.

<u>UNIVERSITY INSTITUTE OF SOMALIA</u>, Mogadiscio

Faculty of Education offers higher education courses for students from the <u>Magistrale</u>.

<u>ADULT EDUCATION</u>

3 courses for 6 months each provided for illiterate adults.  On completion, at the level of the elementary School Leaving Certificate.

Begun in 1950.  9 hours of class work per week.

Program:  Arabic, Italian, Arithmetic, Civics, Geography, Hygiene.

## <u>FUTURE PLANS</u>

Unification is the major problem.  1965, gradual start towards a unified program of 4 years' primary, 4 years' intermediate, and 4 years' secondary. English eventually to be the language of instruction.  1964, English being taught as a foreign language in classes 2 and 3 of intermediate school in the South as initiation of change-over from Italian.

Two new technical institutes are planned, to be provided by Czechoslovakia and the Federal Republic of Germany.

Recent curricula conferences in the Ministry of Education have led to tentative decision to do away with the external <u>G.C.E.</u> examination.

FRENCH SOMALILAND

Teacher Training

Vocational and Technical Training

SECONDARY EDUCATION
(1st cycle)

PRIMARY EDUCATION

Cours moyen

Cours élémentaire

Préparatoire

3
4
5
6

2
1
2
1

Compulsory education: None

School year: October – June

Secondary grading: 0-20

10/20 Pass Mark

| Student's Age | Year of Schooling | | |
|---|---|---|---|
| 26 | 20 | | SECONDARY EDUCATION |
| 25 | 19 | | |
| 24 | 18 | | |
| 23 | 17 | | |
| 22 | 16 | | |
| 21 | 15 | | |
| 20 | 14 | | |
| 19 | 13 | | |
| 18 | 12 | | |
| 17 | 11 | | |
| 16 | 10 | | |
| 15 | 9 | | |
| 14 | 8 | | |
| 13 | 7 | | |
| 12 | 6 | | |
| 11 | 5 | | ELEMENTARY |
| 10 | 4 | | |
| 9 | 3 | | |
| 8 | 2 | | |
| 7 | 1 | | |
| 6 | | | |
| 5 | | | |
| 4 | | | |
| 3 | | | |

FRENCH SOMALILAND

## BACKGROUND

French Somaliland, an Overseas Territory of France, is a small enclave
with a population of 81,000 inhabitants.  Somalis, 24,000; Arabs, 3,000;
Danakil, 30,500;  Europeans and others, 23,500.

France signed a treaty with Danakil chiefs in 1862.  Influx of Europeans
when the Suez Canal was opened in 1869.  Other treaties with Danakil and
Issa chiefs, 1884-85.

Construction of railroad to Addis Ababa completed in 1917, linking
central Ethiopia with the Coast.  In 1946, Somaliland became a French
Overseas Territory, and achieved internal autonomy in 1956.  In the 1958
referendum it elected to remain a French Overseas Territory.

The country is administered by an executive council of 8 members, of
which the French-appointed Governor is President.  The Territory is
divided into districts:  Djibouti, Tadjoura, Dakhil, Ali Sabieh.  It is
represented in the French Parliament by one deputy and one senator.

The educational system was created by the decree of April 12, 1913.  First
public primary education in Djibouti, 1923.  In 1932, schools founded in
Tadjoura, 1940 in Dikhil.  Secondary, vocational and technical education
developed after 1952.

The educational system follows the French, and depends directly on the
Ministry of National Education in Paris.  By 1964, 16 public schools, 11
private schools.

## PRESENT SYSTEM

## PRIMARY EDUCATION

Entry age:      6 years.

5-year program.

Language of instruction:      French.

Program:  French, Reading, Arithmetic, History, Geography, Writing,
          Hygiene, Crafts.

<u>Certificat d'études primaires élémentaires</u> awarded at close of program.


## SECONDARY EDUCATION

Entrance by examination:     <u>Examen d'entrée en sixième</u>.

1 <u>lycée</u>, with first cycle of secondary education:  4-year program.

<u>Brevet d'études du premier cycle</u> (<u>B.E.P.C.</u>) awarded at close of program.


## HIGHER EDUCATION

None.


## VOCATIONAL AND TECHNICAL EDUCATION

### CENTRE DE FORMATION PROFESSIONNELLE, Djibouti

Entrance requirements:     <u>C.E.P.E.</u> or <u>examen d'entrée en sixième</u>.

4 sections:   Fitting (<u>ajustage</u>), Carpentry (<u>menuiserie</u>), Bookkeeping
              (<u>comptabilité</u>), Secretarial training (<u>secrétariat</u>).

3-year programs, divided into 2 parts:

    General:  Covering the basic desciplines (French, Mathematics,
          Science, History and Geography) - 10 to 12 hours per week.

    Specialized:  According to the particular requirements of each pro-
          fession (Technology, Industrial Design, Workshop, or Typing,
          Shorthand, Commerce, Commercial Correspondence, Bookkeeping,
          Commercial Arithmetic, etc.), 20 to 22 hours per week.

<u>Certificat d'aptitude professionnelle</u> awarded to fitters and carpenters.

<u>Certificat d'aptitude professionnelle d'aide-comptable</u> to bookkeepers.

<u>Certificat d'aptitude professionnelle de secrétaire sténo-dactylo</u> to
stenographers.


## TEACHER EDUCATION

One teacher-training program to prepare students to be assistant
teachers (<u>instituteurs-adjoints</u>).

237

REPUBLIC OF THE SUDAN

| Student's Age | Year of Schooling | | |
|---|---|---|---|
| 26 | 19 | HIGHER EDUCATION | Agriculture ** |
| 25 | 18 | | Arts Honours |
| 24 | 17 | | Arts General |
| 23 | 16 | | Economics |
| 22 | 15 | | Econ.-Soc. Studies |
| 21 | 14 | | Econ. Honours |
| 20 | 13 | | Soc. Anthr. Hon. |
| 19 | 12 | SECONDARY | Pol. Science Hon. |
| 18 | 11 | | Engineering |
| 17 | 10 | | Architecture |
| 16 | 9 | | Civil Law |
| 15 | 8 | INTERMEDIATE | Sharia Law |
| 14 | 7 | | Medicine |
| 13 | 6 | | Veterinary Science |
| 12 | 5 | | Science |
| 11 | 4 | ELEMENTARY | Science Honours |
| 10 | 3 | | Pharmacy |
| 9 | 2 | | |
| 8 | 1 | | |
| 7 | | | |
| 6 | | | |
| 5 | | | |
| 4 | | | |
| 3 | | | |

Higher Teacher Training Institute

Teacher Training Colleges

Teacher's College of Mabrouka

Sub-grade Elementary School

Higher Vocational School

Post-Intermediate Trade School

Technical Intermediate Schools

Khartoum Technical Institute

Technical Secondary School

Fine and Applied Arts

Shamb. Inst. of Agric.

Forest.

Pub. H.

Pub. Admin.

Commercial Secondary School

Academic Secondary School

Intermediate School

Elementary School

Compulsory education: None

School year: early July–mid-March or early April. 3 terms

Grading: Elementary and Intermediate: pass mark 50%

Secondary: 1 – 8 (see Secondary Education)

REPUBLIC OF THE SUDAN


Independence:   January 1, 1956.


## BACKGROUND


The Sudan is composed of several distinct segments:   the northern zone
with the Libyan desert on the west, and the Arabian desert on the east,
separated by the valley of the Nile; the central zone with large fertile
areas, including the rainlands of Kassala and Tokar; the Gezira plain and
the southern equatorial belt.

Over two-thirds of the north and central sections are composed of Arabic-
speaking Moslems, the intellectual, governing elite.   South of the 12th
parallel, semi-nomadic groups with 32 separate languages and about 250
dialects are more closely allied to Central Africa.   Government is intro-
ducing here Arabic and Arabized culture.

The Sudanese are composed of Arabs (40% of population), Nilotic peoples
(20%), Western tribesmen (14%), Beja (including the Hadendowa or "Fuzzy-
Wuzzies") (6%), Nuba (Arab Negroid) (5.5%), Nilo-Hamitic peoples including
Ethiopians (5%) and Sudanese peoples, a Negroid group (5%).   Other ethnic
groups are West Africans, Greeks, Egyptians, Italians, Armenians, Lebanese-
Syrians, Englishmen, and Indians.

Significant events have taken place in the northern part of the country;
southern part, until the 20th century, remained in tribal isolation.

The Sudan was under foreign rule for long periods of time:   Egypt, Rome,
Byzantium, the Arabs, the Turks, and finally the British.

From 1500-1820, a loose confederation of tribes, ruled by the "Black Sul-
tans" of the Funj dynasty, controlled a large part of northern and central
Sudan.

Ottoman Viceroy of Egypt brought country under Turko-Egyptian rule, 1820-
1885.

1885-1898, the Sudan became independent under Mahdist control.

January 19, 1899 Condominium Agreement, placed the Sudan under joint Anglo-
Egyptian administration.   Complete reorganization of the government along
English lines.   From 1899-1954 known as Anglo-Egyptian Sudan.

1953, New Nationalist Union Party to prepare country for self-determination
in 3 years.

New Republic of Sudan, under a British-type parliamentary government, proclaimed January 1, 1956.  1958, military dictatorship.

During the Mahdiyya, prior to the Anglo-Egyptian Condominium (1899-1956), education was religious in nature, in the traditional Islamic schools, Khalwa (Koran schools).  The Mosque (Masid) was the seat of learning and the Imam or Fekih (Koran teacher) taught the Koran, Arabic, and Theology.

By 1924 present educational system took shape, patterned on British system.

In 1936 inauguration of Graduates' General Congress (private body) increased the number of schools.

In 1898, only 2 primary schools in Sudan.  By the end of 1900, 7 primary schools were in operation.  By the end of 1903, Gordon College had 149 pupils (of whom 58 were Egyptians and Syrians).  In 1921, 9000 pupils were in primary and elementary schools.

Prior to 1957, schools of Roman Catholic and Protestant missions had done nearly all of the educating.  in 1957, Christian mission schools nationalized in 3 southern provinces.  Syllabi now provided by government. 1961, Sudan's first Ten Year Plan.

By 1961, there were 2375 primary schools, 171 intermediate schools, 49 secondary schools, 22 vocational and technical schools, and 6 teacher training schools.

The 1000 sub-grade village primary schools offering training in reading, writing, and arithmetic and (in the North) the Koran.  Previously operated as Christian village schools in the South and Koran religious schools in the North; now operated municipally by councils (almost one-half government-aided).  Eventually, these schools are to be up-graded to regular elementary level.

Education administered by the Ministry of Education (headquarters in Khartoum).  Each of the 9 provinces (Khartoum, Kassala, Kordofan, Northern, Blue Nile, Darfur in north; Bahr-al-Ghazal, Upper Nile, and Equatoria in south) has a Province Education Officer in charge of the area.

<u>PRESENT SYSTEM</u>

# P U B L I C   E D U C A T I O N

## ELEMENTARY EDUCATION

Entry age:  7 years.  Language of instruction:  Arabic.

Sub-grade elementary school (al-Awwaliyah al-sughrā) offers 3-year incomplete primary program.  Government attempting to upgrade these schools to elementary status.

Complete elementary school (al-Awwaliyah) offers <u>4-year program</u>.  Language of instruction:  Arabic.
  Subjects:  Arabic, Elements of Arithmetic, Religion, General
             Knowledge, Nature Studies.

At close of 4-year program, competitive examination:  <u>Intermediate</u>
<u>Entrance Examination</u>.


## INTERMEDIATE EDUCATION

4-year program in intermediate school (al-Wustā).  Anglo-Saxon literary bias.  English, compulsory subject, 10 hours.  Language of instruction: Arabic.


### INTERMEDIATE CURRICULUM
(45-minute periods per week)

| Subjects | 1st Year | 2nd Year | 3rd Year | 4th Year |
|---|---|---|---|---|
| Arabic | 9 | 9 | 9 | 9 |
| English | 10 | 10 | 10 | 10 |
| Mathematics | 6 | 6 | 6 | 6 |
| Religion | 3 | 3 | 3 | 3 |
| Geography | 4 | 4 | 3 | 3 |
| History | 2 | 2 | 2 | 2 |
| Physical Education | 2 | 2 | 2 | 1 |
| | 36 | 36 | 35 | 34 |

At close of program, <u>Intermediate School Final Examinations</u> are taken. On successful examinations, <u>Intermediate School Leaving Certificate</u> is awarded.


## SECONDARY EDUCATION

General secondary school (al-thānawiyah).

Entrance requirements:  <u>Intermediate School Leaving Certificate</u>.
                        Maximum age for entrance, 16½ years.

 3 types of schools:  Academic Secondary, Technical Secondary, Commercial
                      Secondary.

Competitive examinations for entrance to academic secondary schools.
Best candidates attend government or government-aided secondary schools.
Less qualified go to private secondary schools.  Lowest passers usually
attend commercial and technical secondary schools.

4-year program.  Language of instruction:  English.

## ACADEMIC SECONDARY CURRICULUM
(Hours per full academic year, 33 weeks)

| Subjects | 1st Year | 2nd Year | 3rd Year | 4th Year |
|---|---|---|---|---|
| Arabic Language and Literature | 132 | 132 | 132 | 132 |
| Art | 88 | 88 | 44 | 44 |
| English Language and Literature | 176 | 176 | 176 | 176 |
| Geography | 66 | 66 | 88 | 88 |
| History | 66 | 66 | 66 | 88 |
| Mathematics[+] (basic and higher) | 132 | 132 | 132 | 132 |
| Science[++] (Physics, Chemistry, Biology) | 88 | 88 | 132 | 132 |
| Religion (Islam for Muslims, Christianity for Christians) | 66 | 66 | 66 | 66 |
| General Education | 22 | 22 | -- | 22 |
| Physical and Military Training | 88 | 88 | 88 | 44 |
|  | 924 | 924 | 924 | 924 |

[+]Allocation of Math. Periods:  1st yr., 2 Arith.; 2 Algebra; 2 Geometry.
2nd yr.:  2 Arith. (or 1 Arith., 1 Trig.); 2 Algebra; 2 Geometry.
3rd and 4th yrs.:  1 Arith., 1 Trig.; 2 Algebra; 1 Geometry.

[++]One-third of hours allotted to laboratory work.

Technical Secondary Schools:  All the above subjects are studied, together
with such technical subjects as technical drawing and engineering.

Commercial Secondary Schools:  All the above subjects are studied, together with commercial subjects.

2 Secondary Schools for Girls, Khartoum and Omdurman:  The above curricu-
    lum includes Home Economics, Needlework, and Cookery.

All schools offer year's end examination in March.  At close of 2nd year
pupil selected for 3rd year "stream" according to his attainments in
major subjects:  Arabic, English, Mathematics, and Science.


## Syllabus for Elementary Mathematics

### 1st Year

Arithmetic:  Prime numbers and prime factors, expression of numbers in
index forms, laws of indices, square and cube roots by
the prime factor method, H.C.F. and L.C.M., problems on
H.C.F. and L.C.M.  The four rules, fractions and decimals,
metric system, problems on fractions and decimals.  Simple
areas and volumes, area of rectangle, land measurement,
areas of walls of rooms, surface areas of cuboids, volumes
of cuboids, volume of material required for boxes.  Simple
practice.  Simple direct and inverse variation.  Simple
graphs, including travel graphs.

Algebra:  Algebraic symbols and notation.  Algebraic expressions,
meaning of "term," "like term," "unlike term."  Simple multiplication and division.  Meaning of brackets, insertion
and removal of brackets.  Simple formulae, construction of
formulae, substitution in and use of formulae.  Directed
numbers, H.C.F. and L.C.M.  Simple equations.  Fractions.
Simultaneous equations, solutions by substitution and
addition and subtraction.  Graphs, axes, coordinates,
scales.  Solution of simultaneous equations by graphs.

Geometry:  Theorems up to and including those on parallelograms.
First six constructions.

### 2nd Year

Arithmetic:  Rate, ratio and proportion.  Rateable value.  Taxes.
Assets and liabilities.  Harder direct and inverse variations.  Multiplying factors.  Proportion and proportioned
parts.  Percentage.  Percentage change.  Percentage gain
and loss.  Simple interest, inverse cases using the formula averages.  Simple mixtures.  Graphs.

Algebra:  Factors - single term - relation between $(X+Y)$ and $(X-Y)$.
Binomial products.  Products by inspection.  Expansions of
$(x+y)^2$ and $(x-y)^2$.  Factorization by grouping and inspection.  Meaning of a "perfect square."  How to complete a
square.  Solution of quadratic equations by factorization,
completing the square, graphs.  Problems involving the use
of quadratic equations using the formula.

| Geometry: | Inequalities. Theorems on Areas leading to Theorem of Pythagoras and the extensions. Apollonius' Theorem. Intercept theorems. Loci. Constructions, 7, 8, 9. |

## 3rd Year

| Arithmetic: | Use of square root tables. Tables of reciprocals, tables of squares. Indices. Logarithms - properties of logarithms, bar logarithms, problems involving use of logarithms. Compound interest. Compound interest by formula and by calculation. Inverse problems on compound interest. Harder percentage gain and loss and mixtures. |

| Algebra: | Theory of logarithms (to tie up with the work in Arithmetic). Indices. Surds. Simultaneous equations - one linear, one quadratic. The Remainder Theorem. Graphs. |

| Geometry: | All theorems on the circle. Constructions 10 to 18. |

## 4th Year

| Arithmetic: | Mensuration of cylinder, cone, prism, pyramid. Specific gravity. Relative velocity. Problems on races, etc. Revision. |

| Algebra: | Harder graphs. Ratio , Proportion, and Variation. Progressions - Arithmetic and Geometric Revision. |

| Geometry: | Similar triangles. Rest of the constructions. Revision. |

Trigonometry given at different times in different schools. Some start it in 2nd year and avoid the use of logarithms; others teach it the 3rd year when logarithms are used.

## Syllabus for Additional Mathematics

All 3rd year Mathematics classes are set, on the basis of attainment in the final 2nd year examinations, into "Additional" and "Elementary" classes. Subsequent study is handled in two ways:
1. "Additional" classes begin Calculus and Coordinate Geometry for 2 periods a week initially, and Mechanics and Trigonometry are added as soon as possible. The other 4 weekly periods are spent on "Elementary" work which is covered faster than in "Elementary" classes. By the end of the 2nd term of 4th year, both Elementary and Additional Mathematics are covered for the School Certificate Examination.
2. "Elementary" work is covered as far as possible in 3rd year. Additional Mathematics is studied in 4th year.

Paper I:

## Algebra

Simple surds.  Use of the binomial theorem for a positive integral
index.

## Three-dimensional Geometry

Parallel lines, parallel planes, normal at a plane angle between a
line and a plane, angle between two planes.  Forms of the cube, rectangular block, pyramid tetrahedron, prism, wedge, circular cone,
sphere, and circular cylinder.

Locus of points in 2 or 3 dimensions.

## Applied Geometry

Solution of triangles by the use of the sine and cosine rules and
trigonometrical tables.

Constructions, using straight edge and compasses only:
  a)  bisection of angles and straight lines.
  b)  construction of perpendiculars to straight lines, of an
      angle equal to a given angle, and of angles of $60^\circ$, $45^\circ$, and
      $30^\circ$.
  c)  simple cases of the construction from sufficient data of
      triangles, quadrilaterals, and circles, including circum-
      scribed and inscribed circles of a triangle.
  d)  division of straight lines into a given number of equal parts
      or into parts in any given proportion.

Scale drawing.

Simple problems in three dimensions soluble by analysis into plane
figures.

## Formal Trigonometry

Definitions of sine, cosine, and tangent of angles between $0^\circ$ and
$360^\circ$.  The sine, cosine, and tangent formulae for the solution of a
triangle.

The formulae for the area of a triangle.
Graphs of simple trigonometrical functions.
Functions of compound angles.
Functions of multiple angles.
Simple identities.
Simple equations for angles between $0^\circ$ and $360^\circ$.

Paper II:

### Analytical Geometry (rectangular axes only)

The straight line.
The circle.

### Calculus

Gradient of a line, gradient of a curve; increment notation; gradient of a function; differentiation from first principles; differentiation of the functions $x^n$ and their sums and differences for all values of n; approximations; increasing and decreasing functions; turning points; points of inflexion; maxima and minima.
Applications to gradients of graphs; rates of increase; linear kinematics.
Integration; as opposite of differentiation; as a summation; indefinite and definite integrals; area under a graph.
Applications to plane areas; volumes of solids of revolution; linear kinematics.

### Mechanics

Dynamics
    Kinematics of a particle moving in a straight line; its graphical treatment; velocity and distance-time graphs; acceleration and velocity-time graph; displacement and velocity-time graph. Formulae for motion with uniform acceleration.
    Newton's Laws of Motion; definition of a force; the acceleration of a falling body; difference between mass and weight of a body; energy: kinetic and potential; momentum; work; power. Problems involving easy applications of the principles of the conservation of linear momentum (including inelastic collisions) and energy.
    Simple examples on motion of connected bodies.
    Elementary study of projectiles.

Statics
    Composition and resolution of forces; triangle of forces; Lami's theorem.
    Parallel forces; moments.
    Action and reaction; weight; center of gravity; centers of gravity of familiar uniform bodies; centers of gravity of uniform laminae.
    Machines; the lever, the inclined plane; pulleys--simple pulleys, systems of pulleys, the differential wheel and axle, Weston's differential pulley; the screw; gear wheels. Efficiency, velocity ratio, and mechanical advantage of a machine. The law of a machine.
    Friction; limiting friction, sliding friction, and angle of friction. Simple problems on sliding friction.

## Secondary Examinations

**At the end of the 4-year program, boys and girls sit for the <u>Joint Examination for the Sudan School Certificate and the General Certificate of Education</u> (G.C.E.) (London Examinations).

<u>The Sudan School Certificate  Examination</u> is the successor to the <u>Cambridge School Certificate Examination</u>.    Until 1962, the examination was conducted in collaboration with the University of Cambridge Local Examinations Syndicate.    Since 1962, the Sudan Examinations Council has worked independently in conducting the <u>School Certificate Examinations</u>, however the Cambridge Local Examinations Syndicate sends representatives to help the Council in the supervision of marking, grading, and the preparation of results.

## Subjects of the Examination and Conditions for the Award of Certificates

Subjects grouped as follows:

    I.   Compulsory Subjects for entry for the School Certificate.
        (1)  English Language
        (2)  Arabic[+] (or a classical or modern European language other than English)

    II.   General Subjects.
        (3)  English Literature
        (4)  Religious Knowledge (Islamic)
        (5)  Religious Knowledge (Christian)

    III.   Social Subjects.
        (6)  History
        (7)  Geography

    IV.   Mathematical Subjects.
        (8)  Mathematics
        (9)  Additional Mathematics

    V.  (a)  Science Subjects.
        (10)  General Science
        (11)  General Science (Second Subject)
        (12)  Biology

      (b)  Commercial Subjects
        (13)  Accounts
        (14)  Commercial Subjects

[+]Special Syllabus (Arabic Special) for candidates from Rumbek and Juba.  Other candidates may not offer Special Arabic except by permission of the Secretary.

VI.   (15)   Art
      (16)   Cookery
      (17)   Needlework

## Choice of Subjects

All candidates must enter and sit for six, seven, eight, or nine subjects.
These must include English Language and Arabic (or, by approval of the
Secretary, an acceptable alternative), and at least one subject from each
of the 3 groups II, III, IV, V, and VI.

## Conditions for the Award of a School Certificate

All requirements for the Certificate must be met at one and the same
examination.  Candidates must reach a satisfactory general standard as
judged by their performance in their best 6 subjects.  Subject to this
requirement, School Certificates are awarded to those who:

   either (a)  Pass in at least 6 subjects (including English Language
               and Arabic) with credit in at least 1 of them;

   or (b)  Pass in 5 subjects (including English Language and
           Arabic) with credit in at least 2 of them.

(A School Certificate in Division 1, 2, 3 may be awarded to a candidate
who fails to satisfy the special requirement in either, but not both, of
the subjects English Language and Arabic while satisfying the other
conditions.)

## Classification of Successful Candidates for the School Certificate

3 Divisions.  Division attained is noted on the Certificate.

### First Division School Certificate

Pass in 6 or more subjects, which must include at least 1 subject
from each of 3 of the groups II, III, IV, V, VI.

Pass with credit in at least 5 of these subjects, including English
Language and Arabic.

Reach a high general standard as judged by their performance in
their best 6 subjects.

### Second Division School Certificate

Pass in 6 or more subjects, which must include English Language and
Arabic and at least 1 subject from each of 3 of the groups II, III,
IV, V, VI.

Pass with credit in at least 4 of these subjects.

Reach a certain general standard as judged by their performance in their best 6 subjects.

Third Division School Certificate

The remaining successful candidates.

Conditions for the Award of a General Certificate of Education (G.C.E.) on the Results of the Joint Examination, in and after 1959

A General Certificate of Education is issued to candidates who do not qualify for a School Certificate but pass with credit in one or more subjects. Passes with credit will be recorded as General Certificate of Education ordinary level passes.

Candidates who enter and sit for but do not obtain a School Certificate are considered for the award of a General Certificate of Education. Candidates who do not enter for a School Certificate but who enter and sit for one or more subjects are also considered for the award of a General Certificate of Education. Neither English Language nor Arabic will be a compulsory subject for the award of a General Certificate of Education.

The General Certificate of Education includes a statement that the holder, while not qualifying for the award of a Sudan School Certificate, attained the standard of the G.C.E. ordinary level pass in the subject or subjects indicated in the certificate.

Grading System in the Joint Examination for the Sudan School Certificate and General Certificate of Education

School Certificates and General Certificates of Education awarded as a result of the Joint Examination[+] will show subject grades from Grade 1 to Grade 8 and both will indicate in which subjects candidates gained a G.C.E. ordinary level pass.

```
        1 - Outstanding      ----Pass at G.C.E. Ord. Level
        2 - Very Good        ----  "   "    "     "     "
        3 - Credit           ----  "   "    "     "     "
        4 - Credit           ----  "   "    "     "     "
        5 - Credit           ----  "   "    "     "     "
        6 - Credit           ----  "   "    "     "     "
        7 - Pass
        8 - Pass
        9 - Failure
```

[+]For booklet with detailed syllabuses for examination, send for REGU- LATIONS (Joint Examination for the Sudan School Certificate and General Certificate of Education) through the Secretary, Sudan Examination Council, P.O. Box 938, Khartoum, Sudan. Charge of 15 piastres or 3 s.

SUDAN                                                                    249

## Entrance to Higher Education

On the basis of the above examinations, those satisfying certain minimum
requirements are admitted to Khartoum University (see Higher Education);
Others go to Khartoum Technical Institute (see Technical Education) or
Shambat Institute of Agriculture and Teacher Training Colleges (see
Teacher Education) or study abroad.

(Only about half of secondary pupils reach the standard required for
entrance to the University of Khartoum.)

## N O N - G O V E R N M E N T   E D U C A T I O N

All non-government schools, whether they are ahlia (national private) or
foreign community institutions, are subject to the provisions of the non-
government schools' regulations.  Since 1959, Secondary School Inspectors
of the Ministry of Education have inspected non-government secondary
schools.  Provincial Education Officers have inspected elementary and
intermediate schools.

Outstanding non-government schools:
      Khartoum Secondary School
      Coptic College
      Comboni College
      Catholic Mission Sisters School
      Anglican Cathedral's Unity High School for Girls
      American Mission School in Khartoum North
      Afhad Schools
      Beit-al-Amana

## MISSIONARY SCHOOLS

9 American Mission Schools:
      Kindergarten (mixed)
      Elementary (boys)
      Elementary (girls)
      Intermediate (boys)
      Intermediate (girls)
      Secondary (boys)
      Secondary (girls)

13 Catholic Mission Schools:
      Kindergarten (boys)
      Kindergarten (girls)
      Elementary (boys)
      Elementary (girls)
      Intermediate (boys)
      Intermediate (girls)
      Secondary (boys)
      Secondary (girls)

In these mission schools, both Christian and Muslim boys and girls are in attendance. Islamic religion is taught to Muslim boys and girls. Also Arabic studies are introduced in addition to the foreign languages.

## BISHOP GWYNNE COLLEGE

Founded at Yei, 1945; moved to Mundri, 1948. Trains students to serve the Episcopal Church in the Sudan, the Church of Christ in the Upper Nile, and other Evangelical Churches, as ordained pastors and lay workers. It also gives courses in Scripture Teaching to teachers in the Ministry of Education.

General Bible Course:
  (a) Correspondence course
  (b) Bible Training course (April-December)

Pastoral Courses:
  3-year training for those to serve in Christian Church as pastors, or prepare for ordination as Priests or Presbyters.
  Candidates must have either a Secondary School Certificate, or an Intermediate School Certificate, or have passed the Yei V.T.T.C. course, or have passed the Bible Training course at Mundri with good marks.

Courses in Scripture Teaching:
  By arrangement with the Ministry of Education, Intermediate Masters may study for the Certificate of Proficiency in Religious Knowledge, University of London, which qualifies them to specialize in Scripture Teaching in intermediate schools. 12-month course, supplemented by lectures on Methods of Teaching.
  Selected Masters may also study for Diploma in Theology, University of London, which will qualify them to teach Scriptures at secondary level. 2-year course supplemented by lectures on Methods of Teaching.

## FOREIGN COMMUNITY SCHOOLS

4 Greek, 5 Indian, and 1 Armenian schools teaching programs similar to those of their home country.

The Goethe Institute, which is a branch of the West German Cultural Mission, has the main purpose of teaching the German language.

## FOREIGN SCHOOLS

Most important of the schools run by friendly countries are those run by the United Arab Republic. 19 such schools:
        Primary (boys)
        Primary (girls)
        Preparatory (boys)

                    Preparatory (girls)
                    Secondary (boys)
                    Secondary (girls)

7 other schools following the Egyptian syllabus:
          Kindergarten and Primary (boys)
          Kindergarten and Primary (girls)
          Preparatory (boys)
          Preparatory (girls)

Khartoum Branch, Cairo University, largest of all non-government institutions.  Established in 1955 with the purpose of promoting cultural
relations with the United Arab Republic.  Day and evening classes.  University comprises the following colleges:
          College of Arts (4 departments:  Arabic Language, Geography,
            History, Social Studies)
          College of Law
          College of Commerce (specializing in Commerce and Accountancy)


## FRENCH-SUDANESE SCHOOLS

2 schools under the French-Sudanese title, having a mixture of French-
Sudanese supervision.  Kindergarten and elementary sections; 1 developing
an intermediate and secondary level.


## HIGHER EDUCATION

### UNIVERSITY OF KHARTOUM, Khartoum

Founded as Gordon Memorial College, 1899, operating as primary school in
1902.  By 1913 raised to secondary school level with courses for teachers,
engineers and quadis; post-secondary, 1938.
In 1945 became institution of higher learning; recognized by University
of London, 1947.
In 1924 Kitchener School of Medicine was opened.
In 1951, Gordon Memorial College and the Kitchener School of Medicine were
joined, to become the University College of Khartoum, affiliated with the
University of London; students were awarded external degrees from University of London.
On July 24, 1956, the University of Khartoum became an independent university awarding its own degrees.

Entrance requirements:    Minimum entrance requirements must be obtained
                          at one and the same examination (see specific
                          listings below) but a candidate who has gained
                          the minimum entrance requirements at one exami-
                          nation may obtain the Faculty requirements at
                          any other examination (see under each Faculty).

EITHER     (i)    A <u>Sudan School Certificate</u> with credits obtained on one and the same occasion in at least five subjects which must be chosen from an approved list of subjects[+] and which must include either English or Arabic or another approved language.[++] If the language pass is in a language other than English, candidates will be required to pass an Entrance Examination in English.[+++]

OR    (ii)    A <u>Cambridge School Certificate</u> with credits obtained on one and the same occasion in at least five subjects which must be chosen from an approved list of subjects[+] and must include either English or Arabic or another approved language.[++] If the language pass is in a language other than English candidates will be required to pass an Entrance Examination in English.[+++]

OR    (iii)    A <u>General Certificate of Education</u> of one of the Schools Examining Bodies of England and Wales with passes at the ordinary level obtained on one and the same occasion in five subjects from the approved list of subjects,[+] and must include either English or Arabic or another approved language.[++] If the language pass is in a language other than English, candidates will be required to pass an Entrance Examination in English.[+++]

OR    (iv)    An <u>Egyptian Secondary School Certificate</u> with at least 60 percent in the aggregate and not less than 50 percent in each of six subjects, and must include the English language. Candidates will be required to pass an Entrance Examination in English.[+++]

OR    (v)    A <u>Greek Gymnasium Certificate</u> with 70 percent in not less than seven subjects from an approved list of subjects and must include the English language. Candidates will be required to pass an Entrance Examination in English.[+++]

OR    (vi)    Any other qualification which the Senate of the University holds to be equivalent. Candidates may be required by the Senate to pass an Entrance Examination in English.[+++]

[+]<u>The Approved List of Subjects</u>

The subjects in which a credit or equivalent (i.e. a pass at ordinary level or with 70 percent) is admissible are:

Arabic, English, French, German, Italian, Latin, English Literature, History, Geography, Commercial Subjects, Economics, General Science, Additional General Science, Botany, Chemistry, Physics, Physics with Chemistry, Elementary Math., Additional Math., Technical Drawing, Religious Knowledge, Philosophy.

In special circumstances, Arts or Homecraft or Accountancy may be added to the list.

++Approved Languages

The approved languages are:

Arabic, English, French, German, and Italian.

+++Regulations for the Special Entrance Examination in English

2 papers (2 hours each) and oral examination.
Paper I, essay of 300-400 words.
Paper II, 3 questions: on vocabulary, on grammar, on dictation.
Standard necessary, equivalent to Sudan School Certificate requirements.

Faculties: Agriculture, Arts, Economic and Social Studies, Engineering, Law, Medicine, Science, Veterinary Sciences, Pharmacy (added 1964).

The language of instruction is English except for Arabic and Islamic Studies.

Degrees Awarded

| Faculty | Degree | Duration of Course |
|---|---|---|
| Agriculture | B.Sc. (Agriculture) | 5 years |
| Arts | B.A. (Honours) | 5 years |
| (Arabic, History, Geography, English, Philosophy) | B.A. (General) | 4 years |
| Economic and Social Studies | B.Sc. (Economics) | 4 years |
| | B.Sc. (Economics and Social Studies) | 4 years |
| | B.Sc. (Honours in Economics) | 5 years |
| | B.Sc. (Honours in Social Anthropology) | 5 years |
| | B.Sc. (Honours in Political Science) | 5 years |
| Engineering and Architecture | B.Sc. (Engineering) | 6 years |
| | B.Sc. (Architecture) | 6 years |

| Law | LL.B. (Civil) | 5 years |
| | LL.B. (Sharia) | 4 years |
| Medicine | M.B., B.S. | 6 years |
| Science | B.Sc. (General) | 4 years |
| (Pure and Applied | B.Sc. (Honours) | 5 years |
| Mathematics, | | |
| Physics, Chemistry, | | |
| Botany, Zoology) | | |
| Veterinary Science | B.V.Sc. | 5 years |

## Master's Degrees

Master of Arts (M.A.)
Master of Laws (LL.M.)
Master of Science (M.Sc.)
Master of Science in Agriculture (M.Sc. Agric.)
Master of Science in Economic and Social Studies (M.Sc. Econ.)
Master of Science in Engineering (M.Sc. Eng.)
Master of Science in Architecture (M.Sc. Arch.)
Master of Veterinary Science (M.V.Sc.)

Requirements: Every candidate proceeding to the Master's degree is
required to:

(a) Submit a dissertation embodying the results of his
work and research and/or take a written and/or oral
examination

OR

(b) Take a written examination with/or without an oral
examination.

The normal qualification for proceeding to the Master's degree is an
Honours Degree or its equivalent. A candidate who holds another qualification may be required to pass a qualifying examination.

A candidate for the Master's degree must, after admission, pursue under
the direction and supervision of a member of the University staff,
appointed by the Senate on the recommendation of the Research Committee,
an approved course of advanced study and research, extending over a
period of not less than six terms, or two years.

## Degree of Doctor of Philosophy (Ph.D.)

The degree of Doctor of Philosophy is awarded in the Faculties of
Agriculture, Arts, Economic and Social Studies, Engineering and
Architecture, Law, Medicine, Science, and Veterinary Science.

Requirements:

A candidate applying for registration for the Ph.D. must have previously obtained an Honours Degree or a Master's Degree of University of Khartoum or an equivalent qualification, or such other suitable qualification as the Senate may specially approve.

After admission a candidate for the Ph.D. degree must pursue, under the direction of a supervisor appointed by the Senate on the recommendation of the Research Committee, an approved course of advanced study and research extending over a period of not less than nine terms, or three years, or such shorter period as may be approved by the Senate in each individual case.

After completing his course of study, every candidate must submit a thesis which must comply with the following conditions:

(a)  The greater portion of the work submitted therein must have been done subsequently to the registration of the student as a candidate for the Ph.D. degree.

(b)  It must form a distinct contribution to the knowledge of the subject and afford evidence of originality, shown either by the discovery of new facts or by the exercise of independent critical power.

(c)  The literary presentation must be satisfactory, and if not already published in an approved form, it must be suitable for publication either as submitted or in an abridged form.

(d)  A candidate must submit the title of his thesis or dissertation for approval at least six months before the date on which he proposes to present himself for examination, on the prescribed entry form for the examination.

If the thesis is adequate the examiners shall examine the candidate orally, and at their discretion by printed papers for practical examinations or by both methods, on the subject of the thesis and, if they see fit, on subjects relevant thereto.

## Other Doctor's Degrees

The University awards the degree of Doctor of Letters (D.Litt.), Doctor of Laws (LL.D.), and Doctor of Science (D.Sc.).

## Faculty of Agriculture

Entrance requirements:  By selection from those who have completed the Preliminary Course in Botany, Chemistry, and Zoology in the Faculty of Science where the students are to proceed towards a degree in Agriculture.

Students entering the Faculty of Agriculture for a degree in Agricultural Engineering, will be drawn from those who have completed successfully the 1st and 2nd year courses leading to the B.Sc. Engineering degree in the Faculty of Engineering; these students must comply with the regulations governing admission to the Faculty of Engineering.

The course leading to the B.Sc. (Agriculture), not less than three years duration for students entering from the Intermediate Course of the Faculty of Science, and not less than four years duration for students entering from the Preliminary Course of the Faculty of Science.

## Examinations required for degree

B.Sc. Agriculture

Part I

a.  Four-year course candidates

Agricultural Botany I
General Chemistry
Zoology

b.  Three-year course candidates

Agricultural Biochemistry I
Agricultural Botany II
Agricultural Engineering
Introduction to Agriculture
Soil Science I

Part II

a.  Four-year course candidates

Agricultural Biochemistry I
Agricultural Botany II
Agricultural Engineering
Animal Husbandry I and Crops Husbandry
Economics
Soil Science I

b.  Three-year course candidates

Agricultural Biochemistry II
Agricultural Botany III
Crop Production I
Economics of Agricultural Production
Entomology
Soil Science II

Part III
      a.   Four-year course candidates

                Agricultural Biochemistry II
                Agricultural Botany III
                Crop Production I
                Entomology
                Soil Science II

      b.   Three-year course candidates

                Agricultural Organization
                Animal Production
                Animal Husbandry
                Crop Production II
                Crop Production III

Part IV
        Four-year course only

                Agricultural Economics
                Animal Husbandry II
                Animal Production - Vet. Hygiene
                Crop Production II
                Crop Production III

## Faculty of Arts

Entrance requirements:    For those with a Sudan School Certificate or a Cambridge School Certificate, a G.C.E., or a Greek Certificate, a credit or its equivalent (i.e. a pass at ordinary level or with 70 percent) in at least three of the following subjects, at least one subject being taken from each group:

| Group A | Group B |
|---|---|
| Arabic | Geography |
| English Language | History |
| English Literature | Math. or Add. Math. |
| French | Philosophy |

For those with Egyptian Secondary School Certificates (Arts Section), with at least 60% in the aggregate, and not less than 50% in each of six subjects including English Language.

For those with Indian or Pakistani Intermediate Certificates, a pass in an Intermediate Examination in Arts.

Exemptions:     Exemption from the First Year Course and Preliminary
                Examination granted to applicants who have a <u>G.C.E.</u> with
                <u>not less than five passes</u>, provided that:

    (i)   One of the passes is in Arabic or English.
    (ii)  At least two passes are at advanced level from the
following list of subjects:  Arabic, English or
English Literature, French, Geography, History,
Philosophy.
    (iii) The same subject may not be offered at both ordinary
and  advanced levels.
    (iv) Where one pass is not in English the applicant passes
an entrance examination in English.

## Examinations required for degrees

## Curriculum

Preliminary Year for B.A. General and Honours:
    4 subjects:  Arabic, English, plus two of the following:
        Geography, History, Philosophy, Pure Mathematics.

Intermediate Year for B.A. General and Honours:
    3 subjects, one of which must be either Arabic or English,
chosen from:
        Arabic, Economics, English, Geography, History,
Philosophy, Political Science, Pure Mathematics,
Social Anthropology.

Third and Fourth Years for B.A. General:
    2 subjects from those taken in the Intermediate Year.

Third, Fourth and Fifth Years for B.A. Honours:
    Normally 2 cognate subjects from those taken in the Inter-
mediate Year for two years and one of these two for the Fifth
Year.

Preliminary Examination:
    4 subjects selected from above.

Intermediate Examination:
    3 subjects selected from above.

Third Year Sessional Examination:
    2 subjects selected from above.

B.A. General Examination:
    2 subjects selected from above.

B.A. Honours Examination Part I:
    2 subjects selected from above.

B.A. Honours Examination Part II:
    1 subject selected from above.


## Faculty of Economic and Social Studies

Entrance requirements:    For those with Sudan or Cambridge School Certifi-
                          cates, G.C.E., or Greek Certificates, a credit
                          or its equivalent (i.e. a pass at ordinary level
                          or with 70%) in at least three of the following
                          subjects:

                                  Accountancy or Commercial Subjects
                                  Economics
                                  English Language
                                  English Literature
                                  Geography
                                  History
                                  Math. or Additional Math.
                                  Philosophy

                          For those with the Egyptian Secondary School
                          Certificate, a Certificate (Arts Section) with
                          at least 60% in each of the six subjects includ-
                          ing English Language.

                          For those with Indian or Pakistani Intermediate
                          Certificates, a pass in an Intermediate Exami-
                          nation in Arts.


Exemptions:    Exemption from the First Year Course and Preliminary
               Examination granted to applicants who have a G.C.E. with
               not less than five passes, provided that:

    (i)    One of the passes is in Economics.
    (ii)   At least two passes are at advanced level from the
           following list of subjects:  British Constitution,
           Commerce, Economics, English or English Literature,
           Geography, History or Economic History, Mathematics,
           Philosophy.
    (iii)  The same subject may be offered at both ordinary and
           advanced levels.
    (iv)   Where one pass is not in English the student passes
           an entrance examination in English.

Examinations required for degrees

Curriculum

    Preliminary Year (for all degrees):
       4 subjects:    Economics and English, plus two of the following subjects: Business Administration, Geography, History, Mathematics, Philosophy.

    Intermediate Year (for all degrees):
       3 subjects, provided that:
           (i)  At least two subjects are taken from the following: Business Administration, Economics, Political Science, Social Anthropology.
          (ii)  At most one subject is chosen from the following: Geography, History, Philosophy.
        (iii)  11 subjects offered (except for Political Science and Social Anthropology) have been taken in the Preliminary Year.
        (iv)  Students taking Business Administration also take Economics.

    Third and Fourth Year (for B.Sc. Economics):
       1 subject:    Economics, provided that it has been taken in the Intermediate Year.

    Third and Fourth Year (for B.Sc. in Economics and Social Studies and B.Sc. Honours Part I in Political Science and Social Anthropology):
       2 subjects:    (provided that they have been taken in the Intermediate Year) in any one of the following combinations:
             Economics and Business Administration
             Economics and Geography
             Economics and History
             Economics and Philosophy
             Economics and Political Science
             Economics and Social Anthropology
             Political Science and Geography
             Political Science and History
             Political Science and Philosophy
             Political Science and Social Anthropology
             Social Anthropology and Geography
             Social Anthropology and History
             Social Anthropology and Philosophy

    Fifth Year (for B.Sc. Honours (Economics) and Part II Honours in Political Science and Social Anthropology):
       One subject

    Preliminary Examination:
       4 subjects selected from above.

Intermediate Examination:
    3 subjects selected from above.

Third Year Sessional Examination:
    2 subjects selected from above.


## B.Sc. (Economics) and B.Sc. (Economic and Social Studies) Examination

Candidates for the B.Sc. (Economics) degree examined in one subject, Economics.

Candidates for the B.Sc. (Economic and Social Studies) degree examined in two subjects selected from above.


## B.Sc. Honours Examination, Part I in Political Science and Social Anthropology

Candidates examined in all the papers prescribed for the B.Sc. Honours Examination, Part I.


## B.Sc. Honours (Economics) Examination

Candidates for this examination shall belong to one of the following "Special Subject " groups:

    (a)  Economic Theory
    (b)  Monetary Economics
    (c)  International Trade
    (d)  Statistics
    (e)  Any other "Special Subject" group which may be arranged


## B.Sc. Honours Examination, Part II in Political Science and Social Anthropology

Candidates examined in all the papers prescribed for the B.Sc. Honours Economics and the B.Sc. (Honours) Examination in Political Science and Social Anthropology.


## Faculty of Engineering and Architecture

Entrance requirements:    By selection from those who have completed the
  (Engineering)        two years Intermediate Course in Mathematics
                     (Pure and Applied), Physics and Chemistry in the
                     Faculty of Science.

At the end of the Preliminary Year in the Faculty
of Science candidates will be earmarked by tests
agreed upon between the two faculties.

Entrance requirements:        By selection from those who have completed the
  (Architecture)              Preliminary Year Course in Mathematics (Pure and
                              Applied), Physics and Chemistry in the Faculty
                              of Science.

## Examinations required for degrees

The course leading to the degree of B.Sc. (Engineering), not less than
four years duration; and that leading to the degree of B.Sc. (Architecture), not less than five years duration.  This is in addition to the two
years Intermediate Course in the Faculty of Science (engineers) and the
Preliminary Year Course in the Faculty of Science (architects) referred
to above.

## B.Sc. Engineering

First Year Examination:
    Electrical Engineering I
    Engineering Drawing
    Engineering Technology
    Pure and Applied Mathematics I
    Strength of Material and Metallurgy
    Surveying I

Second Year Examination:
    Electrical Engineering II
    Mechanics of Fluids I
    Pure and Applied Mathematics II
    Theory and Design of Structures I
    Theory of Machines and Machine Elements
    Thermodynamics I

Third Year Examination:
    (a)  Civil Engineering
            Geology
            Mechanics of Fluids II
            Pure and Applied Mathematics III
            Soil Mechanics
            Strength and Elasticity of Materials
            Surveying II
            Theory and Design of Structures II

    (b)  Electrical Engineering
            Electrical Machines I
            Electrical Measurements
            Electrical Power I
            Electronics and Telecommunications

                 Mechanics of Fluids II
                 Pure and Applied Mathematics III
                 Theory of Machines II
                 Thermodynamics II

   (c)   Mechanical Engineering
                 Heat Transfer
                 Machine Design I
                 Mechanics of Fluids II
                 Pure and Applied Mathematics III
                 Strength and Elasticity of Materials
                 Theory of Machines II
                 Thermodynamics II
                 Workshops Technology

B.Sc. (Engineering) Final Examination:
   (a)   Civil Engineering
                 Applied Hydraulic and Irrigation Design
                 Civil Engineering:
                     (i)  Soil Mechanics and Foundation
                    (ii)  Highway and Municipal Engineering
                 Engineering Economics and Organization
                 Theory and Design of Structures III
                 Theory of Elasticity and Vibrations

   (b)   Electrical Engineering
                 Electrical Machines II
                 Electrical Power II
                 Electronics
                 Hydraulic Machines
                 Industrial Management
                 Telecommunications

   (c)   Mechanical Engineering
                 Heat Engines and Apparatus
                 Hydraulic Machines
                 Industrial Management
                 Machine Design II
                 Power Stations
                 Theory of Machines III
                 Thermodynamics III

Beginning 1963-64:
   (a)   Civil Engineering
                 Applied Hydraulics and Irrigation Design
                 Elasticity and Vibrations
                 Engineering Economics and Organization
                 Soil Mechanics and Geology
                 Surveying II
                 Theory and Design of Structures II

      (b)   Electrical Engineering
           Electrical Machines
           Electrical Power
           Electronics
           Engineering Economics and Organization
           Fluid Dynamics
           Heat Engines
           Telecommunications

      (c)   Mechanical Engineering
           Elasticity and Vibrations
           Electrical Power
           Engineering Economics and Organization
           Fluid Dynamics
           Heat Engines and Refrigeration
           Theory and Design of Machines

## B.Sc. Architecture

Intermediate Examination:
(1) Studio work consisting of (a) Design and (b) Construction
(2) 3 subjects as follows:
    Architecture:
      (a) Architectural Presentation
      (b) Building Construction
      (c) History of Architecture I
      (d) Theory of Design I
    Mathematics
    Physics

First Year Examination:
(1) Studio work consisting of (a) Design and (b) Construction, to be completed during the session
(2) 6 subjects as follows:
    History of Architecture II
    Strength of Materials
    Surveying
    Theory of Design II
    Theory of Structures I
    Building Construction II

Second Year Examination:
(1) Studio work, consisting of (a) Design and (b) Construction, to be completed during the session
(2) 6 subjects as follows:
    Architectural Climatology
    Building Construction III
    History of Architecture III
    Services I
    Theory of Design III
    Theory of Structures II

Third Year Examination:
    (1)    Studio work consisting of (a) Design and (b) Construction
    (2)    6 subjects as follows:
            Architectural Climatology II
            Building Construction IV
            History of Architecture IV
            Quantity Surveying
            Services II
            Theory of Structures III

B.Sc. (Architecture) Final Examination:
    (1)    Thesis Design:
            Part 1:  Investigation and Report
            Part 2:  Design, including model
            Part 3:  Structural Solution
    (2)    2 subjects as follows:
            Professional Practice
            Theory of Structures IV

## Faculty of Law (Civil Law)

Entrance requirements:    For those with Sudan or Cambridge School Certificates, credits or equivalent (i.e. a pass at ordinary level or with 70%) in six subjects including English Language and Arabic.

OR

A Grade I Sudan School Certificate (or an equivalent grade in other recognized certificates) and credits in five subjects including English Language and Arabic.

For those with Egyptian Secondary School Certificate (either Arts or Scientific Section) with at least 60% in the aggregate and not less than 50% in each individual subject including English Language.

The Faculty may require candidates to take an entrance examination and/or to attend an interview by a Selection Board.

## Faculty of Law (Sharia)

Entrance requirements:    For those with Sudan or Cambridge School Certificates, G.C.E., or Greek Certificates, a credit or its equivalent (i.e. a pass at the ordinary level

or with 70%) in five subjects including Arabic
and Religious Knowledge.

For those with Egyptian Secondary School Certificates a Certificate (Art Section) with at least
60% in the aggregate and not less than 50% in
each of six subjects including English Language.

## Requirements for degrees

1.   Bachelor of Laws (Civil)

     Preliminary Examination:
          General Introduction to Law
          Criminal Law and Procedure
          Sharia or Comparative Law I

     Intermediate Examination:
          Sharia or Comparative Law II
          Elements of Law of Contract
          Constitutional Law

     Third Year Examination:
          Law of Tort
          Law of Personal Property
          Mercantile Law Part I

     Final Examination Part I:
          Public International Law
          Land Law
          Civil and Criminal Procedure
          Mercantile Law Part II

     Final Examination Part II:
          Jurisprudence
          Conflict of Law
          Equity
          Law of Evidence

2.   Bachelor of Laws (Sharia)

     Preliminary Examination:
          Fiqh-Ibadat and Hudud
          Tafsir-Ibadat and Hudud
          Hadith el Ahkam
          Tawhid
          Adab Bahth and Mustalah
          Criminal Law and Procedure

     Intermediate Examination:
          Fiqh-Muamalat
          Tafsir-Muamalat

Hadith-Muamalat
Tarikh al Tashri'
Usul al Fiqh
Contract and Civil Procedure

Final Examination Part I:
      Fiqh-Ahwal Shakhsia
      Tafsir-Ahwal Shakhsia
      Hadith-Ahwal Shakhsia
      Usul al Fiqh
      Siyassa Sharia' and Tarikh al Gada

Final Examination Part II:
      Murafaat
      Ahwal Shakhsia
      Tawthiqat and Layha
      Tafsir

## Faculty of Science (Biology)

Entrance requirements:        For those with Sudan or Cambridge School Certifi-
                              cates, G.C.E., or Greek Certificate, credits or
                              equivalent (i.e. pass at ordinary level or with
                              70%) in the following subjects:

                              (a)  Elementary Mathematics
                              (b)  Either General Science or Physics with
                                   Chemistry or Chemistry or Botany
                              (c)  Either Additional General Science or
                                   Biology or Physics or Additional Mathe-
                                   matics

                              For those with Egyptian Secondary School Certifi-
                              cates, a Certificate (Scientific Section) with at
                              least 60% in the aggregate and not less than 50%
                              in each of six subjects, and which must include
                              Elementary Mathematics and two Science subjects.

                              For those with Indian or Pakistani Intermediate
                              Certificates, a pass in an Intermediate Exami-
                              nation in Science or Medicine.

## Faculty of Science (Mathematics)

Entrance requirements:        For those with Sudan or Cambridge School Certifi-
                              cates, G.C.E., or Greek Certificates, credits or
                              equivalents (i.e. pass at ordinary level or with

70%) in the following subjects:

     (a)   Elementary Mathematics
     (b)   Additional Mathematics
     (c)   Either General Science or Additional
          General Science or Biology or Botany
          or Chemistry or Chemistry with Physics
          or Physics.

For those with Egyptian Secondary School Certificates, a Certificate (Scientific Section) with at least 60% in the aggregate and not less than 50% in each of six subjects, and which must include Elementary Mathematics, Additional Mathematics, and one Science subject.

For those with Indian or Pakistani Intermediate Certificates, a pass in an Intermediate Examination in Science or Medicine.

Exemption:     As of April, 1964 admission requirements to University waived for candidates to Faculty of Science for those who obtain a Sudan School Certificate with 5 or more credits or distinction in Science subjects and a pass in English or Arabic.

## Examinations required for degrees

Preliminary Examination:
    (i)  Chemistry and Physics and two subjects from Botany, Geography, and Zoology.

              OR

   (ii)  Applied Mathematics, Chemistry , Physics, Pure Mathematics.

              OR

 (iii)  Applied Mathematics, Geography, Physics, Pure Mathematics.

Intermediate Examination:
   3 subjects chosen from the following combinations:
       Botany, Chemistry, Zoology
  or  Botany, Geography, Geology
  or  Chemistry, Geology, Zoology
  or  Botany, Geography, Zoology
  or  Chemistry, Mathematics, Physics
  or  Geography, Mathematics, Physics
  or  Chemistry, Geology, Physics
  or  Applied Mathematics, Physics, Pure Mathematics
  or  Geology, Mathematics, Physics

Third Year Sessional Examination:
  2 subjects chosen from the following combinations:
          Botany, Zoology
  or    Chemistry, Botany
  or    Chemistry, Geology
  or    Chemistry, Mathematics
  or    Chemistry, Physics
  or    Chemistry, Zoology
  or    Geography, Botany
  or    Geography, Geology
  or    Geography, Mathematics
  or    Geography, Physics
  or    Geography, Zoology
  or    Geology, Botany
  or    Geology, Physics
  or    Geology, Zoology
  or    Mathematics, Physics

## B.Sc. General Examination and Part I Honours Mathematics

Candidates examined in 2 subjects chosen from above.  Part I Honours
Mathematics candidates write six papers in Mathematics.

## B.Sc. Honours Examination

Candidates examined in one of the following subjects:
        Botany, Chemistry, Geography, Geology, Mathematics, Physics,
        and Zoology.

## Faculty of Medicine

Entrance requirements:          By selection from those who have completed the
                                one-year Preliminary Course in Chemistry, Physics,
                                Botany, and Zoology in the Faculty of Science.

                                Candidates who have a credit or equivalent (i.e.
                                pass at ordinary level in G.C.E. or 70%) in
                                English Language in the School Certificate (or
                                equivalent) will be given preference in selection
                                for the Faculty of Medicine.

## Requirements for degrees

The course, not less than six years duration, the first of which
shall be spent in the Faculty of Science and the remaining five in
the Faculty of Medicine.

First Examination is the Preliminary Examination in Science in the
Faculty of Science.

Second Examination for Medical Degrees:
    Anatomy
    Physiology (including Elementary Pharmacology)
    Biochemistry (including Organic and Physical Chemistry)

Third Examination for Medical Degrees:
    Pathology
    Bacteriology and Parasitology
    Forensic Medicine and Toxicology
    Public Health

Final Examination for Medical Degrees:
    Medicine and Therapeutics
    Surgery
    Gynaecology
    Obstetrics

Post-graduate diplomas in Gynaecology and Obstetrics.


Faculty of Pharmacy

Entrance requirements:      By selection from those who have completed the
                            one-year Preliminary Course in Chemistry, Physics,
                            Botany, and Zoology in the Faculty of Science.


Requirements for degree

The course leading to the Bachelor of Pharmacy (B.Pharm.), not less
than five years, the first of which is spent in the Faculty of
Science.

Curriculum

First year:
    Chemistry, Physics, Botany, Zoology (in accordance with
    preliminary syllabus of Faculty of Science).

Second Year:
    History of Pharmacy, Pharmaceutics, Inorganic, Organic and
    Physical Chemistry, Biochemistry, Physiology, Elementary Anatomy,
    (including Histology), and Pharmacognosy.

Third Year:
    Pharmaceutics, Pharmaceutical Chemistry, Pharmacology, and
    Pharmacognosy.

Fourth Year:
    Pharmaceutics (including Forensic Pharmacy), Pharmaceutical
    Chemistry, Pharmacology (including Toxicology), and Pharma-
    cognosy.

Fifth Year:
    Pharmaceutics, Pharmaceutical Chemistry (including Analytical
    Chemistry), Pharmacology, Pharmacognosy, and short courses on
    aspects of the Practice of Pharmacy (including Business Adminis-
    tration, Public Health, First Aid, Organization of Retail or
    Hospital Pharmacy or Industrial Pharmaceutical Laboratory).

To fulfill degree requirements, students must:
  (i)    Pass Part I Examination (Preliminary Examination in Science
         (Biological Course) in Faculty of Science).
  (ii)   Pass Part II and Part III Examinations.
  (iii)  Complete period of practical training in a Retail or Hospital
         Pharmacy or in an Industrial Pharmaceutical Laboratory.

Part II Examination:[+]
    Pharmaceutics:  2 two-hour papers, 2 practical examinations,
                    1 oral examination.
    Pharmaceutical Chemistry:  2 three-hour papers, 2 practical
                    examinations, 1 oral examination.
    Pharmacology:   2 three-hour papers, 1 practical examination,
                    1 oral examination.
    Pharmacognosy:  1 three-hour paper, 1 practical examination,
                    1 oral examination.

Part III Examination:[+]
    Pharmaceutics:  3 three-hour papers (1 in Forensic Pharmacy),
                    2 practical examinations, 1 oral examination.
    Pharmaceutical Chemistry:  2 three-hour papers, 2 practical
                    examinations, 1 oral examination.
    Pharmacology:   2 three-hour papers, 1 practical examination,
                    1 oral examination.
    Pharmacognosy:  2 three-hour papers, 1 practical examination, 1
                    oral examination.
    Practice of Pharmacy:  1 three-hour paper, 1 oral examination.

[+]Also, assessment of candidate's course work.


## Faculty of Veterinary Science

Admission to the Faculty of Veterinary Science is by selection from those
who have completed the one-year Preliminary Course in Chemistry, Physics,
Botany, and Zoology in the Faculty of Science.

Requirements for degree

The course leading to the degree of B.V.Sc., not less than five years, the first year of which is spent in the Faculty of Science.

Part I Examination:
     2 subjects:   Animal Husbandry I
                   Chemistry

Part II Examination:
     2 subjects:   Anatomy (including Histology and Embryology)
                   Physiology, Biochemistry, and Pharmacology

Part III Examination:
     4 subjects:   Microbiology
                   Parasitology
                   Pathology
                   Animal Husbandry II

Part II Examination:
     4 subjects:   Preventive Medicine and Veterinary Public Health
                   Animal Husbandry III
                   Veterinary Medicine and Toxicology
                   Surgery, Obstetrics, and Gynaecology


COMMERCIAL EDUCATION

Secondary commercial schools prepare pupils for:
     1.  Commercial Occupations
     2.  Sudan School Certificate enabling holder to enter Khartoum Technical Institute.

Subjects:  Arabic, English, Mathematics, History, Geography, Commercial Bookkeeping, Commercial Arithmetic, Typing, Shorthand.
           (No Science or Art.)

Vocational subjects carried to standard of School Certificate and are accepted by Faculties of Arts and Economics of University of Khartoum. One-third of teaching time is given to vocational subjects and practice.

Selected students with School Certificate proceed to 3-year post-secondary course of School of Commerce of Khartoum Technical Institute. This leads to Intermediate Examinations of Association of Chartered and Corporate Accountants. Examination for equivalent Ordinary Level Certificate in Commerce and the Senior Diploma of Khartoum Technical Institute taken at end of second year.

## TECHNICAL EDUCATION

## TECHNICAL INTERMEDIATE SCHOOLS (al-sinā'iyah al-Wustā)

Warsha or Workshop Schools.

Entrance requirements:   Graduation from 4-year elementary school.

4-year program:   Courses in Carpentry, Metal Work, Practical Drawing,
Workshop Technology, Science, General Subjects, leading
to School Leaving Certificate.

Also night classes.

## POST-INTERMEDIATE TRADE SCHOOLS

For holders of Intermediate School Leaving Certificate not academically
eligible for secondary level at Khartoum Technical Institute.

3-year program:   Engineering and Building Trade courses.
Courses in Machine Engineering, Civil Engineering,
Motor-Vehicle Mechanics, Electrical Installations,
Carpentry and Joinery, Furniture Making, Bricklaying,
Plumbing, Sanitation.

### TYPICAL CURRICULUM
(Periods per 6-day week)

| Subject | 1st Year | 2nd Year | 3rd Year |
|---|---|---|---|
| Practical Shop Work (Auto Mechanics, Building Trades, Machine Shop, Electrical) | 21 | 21 | 21 |
| Shop Technology | 2 | 2 | 2 |
| Applied Science | 4 | 4 | 4 |
| General Drawing | 4 | - | - |
| Mathematics | 4 | 4 | 4 |
| Arabic and General Education | 3 | 3 | 3 |
| English | 4 | 4 | 4 |
| Applied Drawing | - | 4 | 4 |
| | 42 | 42 | 42 |

Graduates awarded the City and Guilds Intermediate Certificate.

## KHARTOUM SENIOR TRADE SCHOOL

Senior Trade School established in 1960 in collaboration with Dunwoody Industrial Institute of Minneapolis, Minnesota.

Entrance requirements:   Graduation from post-intermediate trade school and entrance examination.

2-year program, in the fields of Electronics, Metal Trades, Carpentry, Masonry, and Plumbing.

### TYPICAL WEEKLY SCHEDULE
#### (Periods per day)

|  | Subject | Periods |
|---|---|---|
| 1st Day | Workshop | 7 |
| 2nd Day | Mathematics | 2 |
|  | Drawing | 4 |
| 3rd Day | Workshop | 7 |
| 4th Day | English | 2 |
|  | Trade Technology | 3 |
|  | Mechanics | 2 |
| 5th Day | Workshop | 7 |
| 6th Day | Trade Technology | 2 |
|  | Mathematics | 2 |
|  | Mechanics | 1 |
|  | English | 2 |

On successful completion of program, students awarded the City and Guilds Final Certificate.

## TECHNICAL SECONDARY SCHOOL (al-sinā'iyah al-thānawiyah)

Connected with Khartoum Technical Institute.

Entrance requirements:   Graduation from intermediate technical school.

(See program listed below under the Institute's School of Engineering.) Academic subjects and Mechanical, Electrical, and Civil Engineering, Textile Manufacture, Commerce.

## KHARTOUM TECHNICAL INSTITUTE

Composed of 4 Schools (School of Engineering, School of Commerce, School of Fine and Applied Arts, Girls' Secretarial School), and Department of Further Education.  Language of instruction:  English.

Entrance requirements:    School Leaving and/or School Certificate.  Institute recognized by the Lancashire and Cheshire Association of Technical Colleges.

## School of Engineering

For holders of School Leaving Certificate:
5-year programs in Mechanical, Automobile, and Electrical Engineering.  Upon successful completion, students receive Ordinary National Certificate Senior Diploma.

5-year building programs in Bricklaying, Plumbing, and Carpentry. Upon successful completion students receive Ordinary National Certificate Senior Diploma.

With 2 additional years training, students in Building, and Civil, Mechanical, or Electrical Engineering receive a Higher National Certificate Advanced Diploma.

For holders of School Certificate:
2-year program for surveyors, leading to Intermediate Examinations of Royal Institute of Chartered Surveyors (Inter. R.I.C.S.)

2-year program in Building, and Mechanical and Electrical Engineering, leading to Ordinary National Certificate Senior Diploma.

## School of Fine and Applied Arts

For holder of School Leaving Certificate, 4-year program leading to a School Certificate.

With additional 3-years training, graduates receive an Art Diploma (Painting, Pottery, or Sculpture).

## School of Commerce

For holders of Commercial Secondary School Certificate, 3-year program leading to Intermediate Examination of the Association of Chartered and Corporate Accounts (Inter. A.C.C.A.).

## Girls' Secretarial School

Started in 1958.

For holders of <u>School Certificate</u>, 2-year program in secretarial subjects leading to <u>Secretarial Diploma</u>.

For holders of <u>Intermediate Certificate</u>, 3-year course of general education with Arabic, English, and Typewriting leading to a <u>Typist's Certificate</u>.

## Department of Further Education

The Further Education (or Evening Studies) Department is for those lacking sufficient formal education.

Part-time, day and evening classes in clerical and bookkeeping subjects.

Preparation for the <u>School Certificate</u> and Civil Service Examination.

Preparation for Elementary Crafts (Bricklaying, Carpentry, Building, Electricity, Automobile Mechanics, Diesel Building, Welding, Fitting, Turning), and for <u>City and Guilds Certificate and National Certificate</u>.

## PROFESSIONAL HIGHER EDUCATION

### SHAMBAT INSTITUTE OF AGRICULTURE, Khartoum North

Founded 1954.

Entrance requirement:    School Certificate.

2-year program in Agriculture and Animal Husbandry.

Upon successful completion of studies, <u>Certificate in Agriculture</u> awarded.

### INSTITUTE OF PUBLIC ADMINISTRATION, Khartoum

Established by the Resolution of March 12, 1960, to train the employees of the government and quasi-government organizations in the skills of administration.  Independent Institute annexed to the Ministry of Finance and Economics.

Presently located on the premises of the University of Khartoum.

Candidates are chosen and nominated by their employing departments.  They must have no less than 5-6 years of experience in the Service; no less than 10 years before retirement.  No academic qualifications essential, but usually a minimum educational standard of graduation from secondary school.  Persons must fall into one or more of the following categories:

  (a) They assume some responsibility for supervision.
  (b) They have the authority and ability to change methods, or at least recommend them to senior personnel.
  (c) They have shown potential for rising in the Service on the basis of merit.
  (d) They evidence that they can assume higher responsibilities in the future.

2 programs, each 3 months duration, 1960:

  Introduction to Public Administration (including a 1-hour per week session in the Structure and Function of Ministries and Departments)
  Financial Administration and Budgeting
  Personnel Administration
  Organization and Management
  Economics for Administrators and the Economy of Sudan

  Administrative Communication
  Methods of Supervision
  Human Relations
  Introduction to the Social Sciences
  Correctional Administration (for Prison and Police Officers)
  Theory and Practice of Auditing
  Accountancy as a Tool of Management (for Accountants)
  Statistics

Initiated as a joint undertaking in technical cooperation between the Republic of the Sudan and the United Nations.

From 1961-62, training on three levels:
    Level 1:  For senior personnel (Professional and Administrative)
    Level 2:  Middle-Management personnel (Executive)
    Level 3:  Clerical personnel (Clerical and Manipulative)

    Level 1 Course:  University graduates with a minimum of 3 years experience in public service.
                     Non-graduates with a minimum of 5 years experience.

      Syllabus:
            Seminar in Public Administration - 10 weeks, 48 hours.
            Seminar in Economic and Social Development
                                        - 10 weeks, 48 hours.
            Seminar in Economic and Social Development Planning
                                        - 10 weeks, 48 hours.
            Seminar in Executive Development - 5 weeks, 32 hours.
            Seminar in Administrative Management
                                        - 5 weeks, 32 hours.

<u>Level 2 Course</u>:   Graduates of secondary school, or the equivalent
in education and a minimum of 3 years experience.
Others who do not meet educational standard, but
have a minimum of 5 years experience in government
service and are recommended by superiors.

Flexible syllabus in terms of the number of hours.  Basic
courses usually include:
  Essentials of Government Administration
  Personnel Procedures
  Budgeting and Accounting
  Supervision
  Elementary Statistics and the Recording of Data
  Office Methods and Procedures
  Internal Communications

<u>Level 3 Course</u>:   Officers in the lower clerical grades and in the
manipulative classifications.

4 months duration, full time.

Appreciable portion of syllabus in on-the-job training of a
practical nature.

## FOREST RANGERS' COLLEGE, Khartoum

Established August 1946 as a Forest Rangers' School.  Raised to the
status of a college, 1960.

Entrance requirements:   (a)  Not less than 20 years of age, nor more
                              than 30.
                         (b)  Minimum educational qualifications:
                              completed and passed 4th year secondary
                              school.
                         (c)  Sound knowledge of English (both written
                              and spoken) and Mathematics.
                         (d)  Physical fitness, alertness, intelligence,
                              and keenness of observation.
                         (e)  Desire for living and working out-of-doors
                              and a natural ability to handle tools and
                              instruments.

College has one class running at a time.  Class consists up to 25 students.  Each class recruited according to the needs of the Department of
Forestry for staff.

2-year program.
Further recruitment may vary from 1-3 years according to Department needs.

Course divided into 4 terms, interspersed by 3 instructional tours to the
Fung, Southern, Western, and other parts of the Sudan.  Each of these 7
parts of the course lasts an average of 3-5 months.  No vacation periods.

Examinations held at the close of each term.  Final examination in all subjects at the end of course.

Pass mark is 50% of the aggregate obtainable.  Honours marks is 75%. Certificate awarded to successful candidates.

## Curriculum

Mathematics (General, Elementary Geometry, Mensuration, Elements
  of Trigonometry)
Botany
Sylviculture
Forest Protection
Meteorology
Surveying
Geology and Soil
Forest Engineering
Forest Management
Practical Courses (Nursery work at Khartoum, sylvicultural operations
  in Gebel Bouser sunt forest, 3-months treks)
Valuation
Ecology
Utilization of Produce
Mensuration
Forest Hygiene
Accounts Records
Soil Conservation and Land Management
Forest Policy and Forest Law


## SCHOOL OF HYGIENE, Khartoum

Training for public health officers.

Entrance requirements:    Candidate must have completed secondary
                          education and have obtained at least Grade III
                          of the Sudan School Certificate, or its equiva-
                          lent:  Cambridge, Tawgihia, etc.

3-year program:   1st year training in Khartoum Technical Institute;
                  2 final years in School of Hygiene.

| First Year: | Subjects | Hours |
|---|---|---|
| | Brick work | 123 |
| | Masonry | 70 |
| | Carpentry | 123 |
| | Decorating | 70 |
| | Technical Drawing | 173 |
| | Drainage | 180 |
| | Sewerage and Drainage | 123 |
| | Surveying | 30 |

| Building Construction | 180 |
|---|---|
| Total hrs. for W/shop and Theoretical | 1072 |
| Practical Work in the Provinces | 275 |
| | 1347 |

| Second Year: | Lecture Hours | Practice Hours | Lab. |
|---|---|---|---|
| P.H. Administration | 20 | 20 | |
| Anatomy and Physiology | 25 | 5 | |
| Elementary Bacteriology | 25 | 10 | 20 |
| Entomology and Control of Pests | 80 | 70 | 10 |
| Parasitology | 25 | 20 | 10 |
| Water | 60 | 20 | 5 |
| Waste Matter Disposal | 80 | 30 | 5 |
| | 315 | 175 | 50 |
| Total Hours | 540 | | |
| Practical Work | 865 | | |
| | 1405 | | |

| Third Year: | | | |
|---|---|---|---|
| Food | 100 | 40 | 10 |
| Housing | 60 | 30 | |
| Prevention and Control of Diseases | 75 | 20 | 15 |
| Hygiene in Relation to: Schools, Barracks, Factories, etc. | 30 | 30 | 5 |
| Port and Quarantine Control | 20 | 20 | |
| Sanitary Law | 25 | 10 | |
| Vital Statistics | 20 | 5 | |
| Relations between P.H. and Councils | 20 | 10 | |
| Health Education | 20 | 15 | |
| Mental Health | 15 | | |
| | 385 | 180 | 30 |
| Total Hours | 595 | | |
| Practical Work | 885 | | |
| | 1480 | | |

Practical work is done in the Khartoum municipalities and other provinces which provide good practical material, e.g. Gezira Irrigated Area, Port Sudan.

There is a board of studies to control the syllabus of training, and a Board of Examination approved by the Royal Society of Health to conduct the final examination and make final recommendations. Those who pass are awarded the Diploma of Public Health Inspectors by the Royal Society of Health and become Public Health Officers.

## NURSES' TRAINING COLLEGE

3-year program leading to a <u>Diploma in Nursing</u>.


## TEACHER EDUCATION

### Sub-grade Teachers

3 centers for training sub-grade teachers. Teachers recruited from 4th year intermediate graduates. From time to time, groups of them are selected to attend courses during the holidays, after 4 years of teaching. The rest are transferred to elementary schools.

### Elementary School Teachers

7 centers for training elementary school teachers (4 for men, 3 for women) (tadrib madarrisī al-madāris al-awwaliyah). Students recruited from elementary schools. Those passing successfully final examinations are given 2-year course of training (one center in south offers 3 years of training).

### Intermediate School Teachers

Teacher training colleges for teachers in intermediate schools (tadrib mudarrisī al-madāris al-wustā). 2 Intermediate Teacher Training Centers.


INSTITUTES OF EDUCATION FOR BOYS:

### INSTITUTE OF EDUCATION, Bakht-er-Ruda at Dueim

Principal educational institution with branches in various parts of the country. Founded in 1934 to train elementary teachers for rural areas, now covers elementary, intermediate, secondary, and agricultural education. Each branch has a vice-principal responsible to the principal of Bakht-er-Ruda.

Teaching in Arabic.

Institute is composed of the following Colleges:

1. Teachers' Training College
   For training intermediate schoolmasters. <u>Sudan School Certificate</u> for entrance, or equivalent.

2. Teachers' Training College
   For training elementary schoolmasters who have successfully completed 2 years in Training College.

3.  Teachers' College of Mabrouka
    Special intermediate school which qualifies its students
    to join Elementary Teachers' Training College for elementary
    school teachers.

Institute has 2 other branches, in Shendi and Dilling, training elementary
schoolmasters.

Refresher courses for selected teachers.

Entrance requirements:   Sudan School Certificate plus 2 years teaching
                         as trainees.

18-months course.

## Intermediate Teacher Training College Program

Academic training:   Student teachers choose 3 subjects of the following
                     groups:
                     (i)   Arabic, General Science
                     (ii)  History, Mathematics (Arith., Algebra, Geometry,
                           Trigonometry)
                     (iii) English, Geography

                     and one activity:
                     (i)   Rural Education
                     (ii)  Art and Handwork
                     (iii) Physical Education

                     Compulsory education courses:
                         History and Philosophy of Education, survey
                         course in Methods, Class Management, and
                         Educational Psychology.  Practice Teaching.

                     These subjects covered in 8-months program.  10
                     periods of 40 minutes are allotted to each subject
                     per 6-day week.

## Rural Education Study

Class work in:  Soil, Agriculture, Horticulture, and Stock.  Practical work in the fields, in the nursery, in the dairy and poultry
farms.

## Art and Handwork Study

96 periods for the total course divided into 3 subjects:  Fine Art,
Handwork, and Method.

First term:
    Fine Art:  Drawing, Painting, Sculpture, Clay Modelling,
              Pottery, Calligraphy, Fabric-Printing, Graphic
              Design.
    Handwork:  Folk Handwork, Crafts for Children, Bookbinding,
              Carpentry.
    Method:  Techniques for teaching Art.

Second term:
    Teaching practice, research, essays, and term papers.

## Physical Education Study

Practical side:
    Gymnastics:  Swedish, Vaulting, and Agility
    Games:  Major:  Football, Basketball, Volleyball, Tennis,
              Table Tennis, Badminton, Handball
          Minor:  Rounders, Postball, and Recreative Games
    Athletics:  Sprints, High Jumping, Pole Vaulting, etc.
          Shot Putting, Discus, Hammer and Javelin Throwing.

Theoretical side:
1. Methods of P.E.
2. Elementary Study of Anatomy and Physiology
3. Theory of P.E.
4. Rules of Games and Athletics

**Intermediate Teachers Training College Certificate** awarded at close of successful program.

## MARIDI INSTITUTE

Similar to Bakht-er-Ruda, training elementary schoolmasters for Southern Provinces. Same syllabi, but teaching done in English.

## INSTITUTES OF EDUCATION FOR GIRLS:

3 Institutes for mistresses for elementary schools in Northern Sudan: Wad Medani, Omdurman, and Dilling. One in South at Yei.

Each northern Institute comprises:
1. A complete intermediate school
2. Mistresses' section
3. Elementary school
4. Refresher course

Syllabi equivalent to 1st and 2nd year in secondary school with addition of Sewing, Needlework, Physical Training, etc.

Refresher courses held 3 times a year for Institute graduates, 8-10 weeks. Mistresses return every 4 years for further instruction.

Girls in intermediate school training with special art abilities are sent to Khartoum Technical Institute for special training in Fine Arts.


CO-EDUCATIONAL INSTITUTE:

HIGHER TEACHER TRAINING INSTITUTE, Omdurman

Founded in 1962 as a joint project of the Sudan Government, Ministry of Education, and the United Nations Special Fund, acting through UNESCO as its executing agency. Basic document of the project is a Plan of Operations agreed between the Sudan Government and the United Nations for a five-year period beginning in January, 1962 and ending in December, 1966. At the end of the period the project will be handed over to the Sudan Government for unassisted administration.

Training for secondary school teachers. Co-educational, residential.

Entrance requirement:        Minimum of Grade 2 in the Sudan School Certifi-
                             cate, with 5 credits. Entry is competitive.

Students are admitted on entry to Arts or Science, in accordance with the distribution of their School Certificate results.

4-year program. Higher academic subjects and professional training at university level.

First 2 years, with Education and English Language (Practical) = approximately to intermediate level, University of Khartoum, or the advanced level of the British General School Certificate.

Final 2 years = approximately to the pass degree standard of the University of Khartoum.

Students opt for 3 subjects in the first 2 years; two of these in 3rd year; one of them in the 4th year.

Education is taken throughout all 4 years. Subjects are selected in closely related fields, e.g. Arabic, English and History, or Mathematics, Physics, and Chemistry.

All science programs carry a full load of practical laboratory work.

First graduates to teach in secondary schools in 1965.

Major courses in operation:

| Science | | | Arts | | |
|---|---|---|---|---|---|
| Math. | Math. | Physics | History | Arabic | Geography |
| Physics | Chemistry | Math. | Geography | History | Arabic |
| Chemistry | Biology | Math. | English | History | Arabic |
| | | | English | English | Arabic |

Supervised Teaching-practice takes place in the 1st, 3rd, and 4th years. The national language is Arabic, but the language of instruction at secondary and higher levels is English.

The final award of the Institute is the Secondary Teachers' Diploma of the H.T.T.I. (Higher Teacher Training Institute), Sudan Ministry of Education.


## ISLAMIC EDUCATION

Supervised by Department of Religious Affairs.

3-levels government-operated instruction for boys only: 4-year intermediate, 4-year secondary,and higher Islamic studies. Entrance to 4-year intermediate program after graduation from secular government elementary school. Higher Institute in Khartoum.


## PUBLIC SERVICE EXAMINATION

Examination to decide the suitability of candidates for the Sudan Public Service.

Examination level:  4th year secondary school standard. (A considerable number of candidates do not normally come from secondary school.)

Subjects grouped as follows:
    (a)  Compulsory subjects:
           English Language
           Arabic
           Mathematics
    (b)  Optional subjects:
           Arabic Literature
           Geography
           History
           Office Practice
           Bookkeping
           Typewriting (Arabic or English)
           Arabic (Special Paper for the South)

Choice of subjects:
    All candidates, except Southerners, must sit for all 3 compulsory
    subjects, and any 2 optional subjects.  Southerners should sit for
    English Language and Mathematics together with any 3 optional sub-
    jects.

(Syllabus for Examination may be obtained from the Secretary, Sudan
Examinations, P.O. Box 938, Khartoum.)

## ADULT EDUCATION

Adult education introduced in 1939.  Aims to create the right family and
community environment for those leaving elementary schools.

Laubach approach.  There are literary campaigns in all Provinces.

The Gezira Scheme lays emphasis on community development, public health.
Women study primarily cooking, sewing, home hygiene.

The Community Development Training Center at Shendi under UNESCO management trains adult education officers, literary officers, women welfare
officers, and village workers.

There are artisan classes in the Gezira offering training for builders and
carpenters.  19 classes for workers' education with lectures on History,
Geography, Economics, etc.

## NEW PLAN FOR EDUCATION

The following plan has been submitted to the Council of Ministers for
approval.  Its implementation will take some time as it involves great
changes in buildings, curriculum, and teacher training.

    1.   The present educational ladder to be abolished.

    2.   6-year primary stage; age of entrance, 6 years.

    3.   4-year general secondary stage
       (a)  Vocational Academic
       (b)  Technical
       (c)  Girls' Secondary

    4.   4-year senior secondary stage
       (a)  Academic Secondary for Boys
       (b)  Academic Secondary for Girls
       (c)  Technical Secondary
       (d)  Vocational Secondary
       (e)  Vocational Secondary (Agriculture, Commerce, and Home
           Economics for Girls)

287

THE UNITED REPUBLIC OF TANZANIA
(Tanganyika Through 1961)

| Student's Age | Year of Schooling | | | |
|---|---|---|---|---|
| 26 | 20 | HIGHER EDUCATION | NONE | |
| 25 | 19 | | | |
| 24 | 18 | | | |
| 23 | 17 | | | |
| 22 | 16 | | | |
| 21 | 15 | | | |
| 20 | 14 | ** VI Form | HIGHER SCHOOL | Gov't Technical Institute |
| 19 | 13 | V Form | | |
| 18 | 12 | * IV Form | ACADEMIC SECONDARY SCHOOL | Technical & Commercial Training |
| 17 | 11 | III Form | | |
| 16 | 10 | II Form | | |
| 15 | 9 | I Form | | |
| 14 | 8 | VIII Standard | MIDDLE SCHOOL | |
| 13 | 7 | VII Standard | | |
| 12 | 6 | VI Standard | | |
| 11 | 5 | V Standard | | |
| 10 | 4 | IV Standard | PRIMARY SCHOOL | |
| 9 | 3 | III Standard | | |
| 8 | 2 | II Standard | | |
| 7 | 1 | I Standard | | |
| 6 | | | | |
| 5 | | | | |
| 4 | | | | |
| 3 | | | | |

(Grade I) Teacher Training (Grade II)

Agric./Vet. & Forestry

On-the-job training

Building & Engineering Trade Schools

Compulsory education: None

School year: February – November (2 terms, 4½ months each)

Secondary grading: 1-9 School Certificate and General Certificate of Education (See SECONDARY EDUCATION)

# THE UNITED REPUBLIC OF TANZANIA
### (Tanganyika—Beginning 1962)

On-the-job training

Building & Engineering Trade Schools

Field & Vet. Assistants

Agric./Vet. & Forestry

Gov't. Tech. Institute

Technical & Commercial Training

(Grade IA) Teacher Training (Grade I)

(Grade II)

HIGHER SCHOOL

ACADEMIC SECONDARY SCHOOL

PRIMARY SCHOOL

| Student's Age | Year of Schooling | | | |
|---|---|---|---|---|
| 26 | 20 | HIGHER EDUCATION | | |
| 25 | 19 | | | |
| 24 | 18 | | | |
| 23 | 17 | | | |
| 22 | 16 | | | |
| 21 | 15 | | | |
| 20 | 14 | Arts ** | Science | Law / Form VI |
| 19 | 13 | | | Form V |
| 18 | 12 | SECONDARY | * | Form IV |
| 17 | 11 | | | Form III |
| 16 | 10 | | | Form II |
| 15 | 9 | | | Form I |
| 14 | 8 | ELEMENTARY | | Standard VIII |
| 13 | 7 | | | Standard VII |
| 12 | 6 | | | Standard VI |
| 11 | 5 | | | Standard V |
| 10 | 4 | | | Standard IV |
| 9 | 3 | | | Standard III |
| 8 | 2 | | | Standard II |
| 7 | 1 | | | Standard I |
| 6 | | | | |
| 5 | | | | |
| 4 | | | | |
| 3 | | | | |

Compulsory education: None

School year: January – December (3 terms)

Secondary grading: 1–9 School Certificate and
General Certificate of Education
(See SECONDARY EDUCATION)

THE UNITED REPUBLIC OF TANZANIA


April 26, 1964, Tanganyika and Zanzibar united into a sovereign state,
the United Republic of Tanganyika and Zanzibar.  The country adopted
the name of TANZANIA, October 29, 1964.

The educational patterns of the 2 countries are presented SEPARATELY
because of a need for the historical development of the systems, and
more importantly, because "education is not a union matter in the
Republic of Tanzania," according to information received by the editors
from the Ministry of Education, Dar es Salaam.  The Ministry in Dar es
Salaam regretted its inability to send current educational changes in
Tanzania (Tanganyika) before this study went to press.




R E P U B L I C   O F   T A N G A N Y I K A


Became independent dominion in the British Commonwealth, December 9, 1961.



BACKGROUND


Africans constitute 98% of the population.  There are more than 120 varying tribal groups.  Main tribes are:  Sukuma, the largest (approximately
1,125,000), Masai, Nyamwezi, Haya, Aloof, Makonde, Gogo.

English is the official language; Swahili is spoken by everyone.

Trade between Arabs and peoples of East Africa is traced back to the
first century A.D.  Arab rule in Tanganyika lasted until German and
British explorers arrived about 1840.

After 1884, the country became a colony of German East Africa until 1918.
At the Peace Treaty of Versailles, Britain was given a mandate under the
League of Nations to administer Tanganyika as of 1919.  Following World
War II, the British assumed United Nations Trusteeship of Tanganyika,
1947.  With the growth of the TANU Party (Tanganyika African National
Union), political activity increased.  The British Colonial Governor
approved the African proposals for independence, 1960.

Pre-independence, the majority of schools were still built and managed
by mission organizations, in most cases grant-aided by the government.
After 1925, all educational institutions, both government and voluntary
agency, conformed to the standards and policy of the Education Department.

General secondary education in Tanganyika started in 1933 at Tabora Central
School where Standards IX and X took pupils to entrance examination into
Makerere College.  Tabora became full secondary (Standards IX through XII)
in 1939.  Makerere College raised standard of entry at this time to
Standard XII, School Certificate level.

Previous to 1962, the educational system was subdivided on an ethnic basis:
African (including Somalis and Arabs); European; Indian and "other non-
natives" (including Goans and others).

10-Year Plan (1947-1956) put into effect after World War II.

| | |
|---|---|
| 4 levels of instruction: | 4-year Village Schools<br>2-year District Primary Schools<br>2-year Pre-secondary Course<br>4-year Secondary Course |
| 1950 revision: | District Schools developed into<br>4-year Middle Schools |
| | 1959, all District and Pre-secondary<br>School Courses replaced by Middle<br>Schools |

5-Year Plan (1957-1961) expanding all areas of instruction.

| | |
|---|---|
| 1961 goal: | Higher School Certificate required<br>for all Government-sponsored can-<br>didates to Makerere College |

## Non-African Education

| | |
|---|---|
| European | Secondary education was established follow-<br>ing the termination in 1954 of an arrange-<br>ment whereby Kenya admitted Tanganyika<br>students to Government secondary schools. |
| | St. Michael's and St. George's School<br>opened 1959, offering full secondary<br>education. |
| Indian | Secondary education was started between<br>1933-1939.  Education up to School Certifi-<br>cate level provided at 7 Government schools,<br>7 assisted schools.  2 largest Government<br>schools offered Higher School Certificate<br>courses. |

Other Non-natives          Secondary education available at 4 assisted
(including Goans)          schools and up to School Certificate standard.

Educational institutions other than the Technical Institute at Dar es
Salaam attended by children of more than 1 race:

St. Joseph's Secondary School, Dar es Salaam (for all races)
Katoka Preparatory School, Bukoba
His Highness the Aga Khan Schools (opened for Africans)

(The 1st 2 schools offering School Certificate;
 the Aga Khan Schools providing Higher School Certificate training.)


## African Education

African system largely post-World War II creation.  Plans for development
and expansion of African education under the 10- and 5-Year Plans generated
an enrollment which tripled between 1947 and 1959.

System 1947-1961:  Three 4-year cycles

Primary            4-years
Middle             4-years
Secondary          4-years

Under centrally enacted (African) Education Ordinance, all secular education for Africans (except training courses conducted by various departments
of the Government, adult education, and clubs for children) to be administered by the Director of Education with advice of Central Advisory
Committee on African Education.

2 Categories of schools differing in standard were governed by the
Ordinance and supervised by the Department:

Part I of the Register of African Schools.

Fully recognized schools, having attained standards
desired by the Department, regarded as the African
Education System.

| Maintained | A | Schools managed by: | Central Government |
|---|---|---|---|
| Maintained | B | Schools managed by: | Native Authority |
| Assisted or Aided | C | Schools managed by: | Voluntary Agencies (Christian Missions) |
| Un-Aided | D | Schools managed by: | Various Agencies (Schools with common standard, curriculum, examinations, licensed or certificated teachers and subject to Government inspection) |

Part II of the Register of African Schools

> Subgrade Schools, employing untrained teachers,
> providing secular instruction equivalent to 1st
> 2 years of the primary course.

These were Group 1 of so-called 'Bush Schools' operated mostly by
Christian Missions.  No fees required.  Untrained teachers with
Standard VIII schooling.  2 Primary years taught with or without
religious instruction.

Students transferring to Part I schools entered before Standard III.

These schools developed under popular pressure for more education,
continuing only until sufficient trained teachers and Part I Primary
schools were available.  Most of them were run by Christian bodies
but a considerable number were started by TANU, later handed over
for operation by parents' associations.

Group 2 of Bush Schools provided religious, but minimum of secular,
education.  Not supervised by the Department.


Integrated Education

Government Paper No. 1, 1960 provided for "integrated system of education,"
inaugurated January 1962.



SYSTEM THROUGH 1964


PRIMARY EDUCATION

Entry age:   Between 6 and 10 years.

Co-educational day schools.

From 1962, 8-year elementary program.

Through 1961, 4-year primary program, Standards I-IV.   (Followed by 4-year
Middle School - see next section).

> Double sessions for Standards I and II.
>     (Children attended only part of day, necessitated by shortage
>      of qualified teachers.)

> Single sessions for Standards III and IV.
>     (Single sessions progressively introduced under 5-Year Plan.

Subjects in 4-year course:          (Periods, 30 minutes each)
                                    Arithmetic, Language (Reading, Writing,
                                    Composition), General Knowledge (Geography,
                                    Nature Study, Hygiene and Citizenship),
                                    English (Standards III-IV).  Also, Hand-
                                    work (gardening in season), Religious In-
                                    struction, Physical Education and Singing
                                    in some schools.  (1961, English and
                                    Swahili both compulsory from Standard I.)

New International Primary School opened in Dar es Salaam, 1963.  Supported
by British Government, United States Government and private sources.  1st
such institution in East Africa, catering to students from Tanganyika and
all foreign countries.  International orientation of education provided so
that students might enter secondary study in other parts of the world.

After 1962, local authorities accepted responsibility for primary schools.

Entrance from Primary to Middle Schools on basis of short written examination as well as on teachers' reports.


Middle Schools

Discontinued in 1962 when the 4-year Middle School program became part of
the new 8-year elementary scheme.

Middle School program:  Standards V-VIII.

Day schools either co-educational or segregated.
Boarding schools - separate for boys and girls.

Formal and academic methods redirected to training of a practical nature,
reflecting the life of the area in which each school was located.

        Biases:       Agriculture       - rural areas
                      Animal Husbandry  - pastoral localities
                      Commercial or
                        Industrial      - urban areas
                      Homecraft         - Girls' schools

Language of instruction:  English (beginning Standard VIII).

Subjects in 4-year course:

                Arithmetic and Practical Geometry, Swahili, English,
                General Knowledge (Geography, History, Civics and
                Current Affairs), General Science, (boys' schools -
                Health Science, Biology and Agricultural Science;
                girls' schools - Health Science, Agriculture and
                Animal Husbandry, of a light type); Handcraft

(boys' schools - Woodwork, Tinsmithery, Drawing, local crafts and simple building work); Homecraft (girls' schools); Religious Instruction.

1958, former Territorial Standard VIII Certificate examination replaced by General Entrance Examination.

General Entrance Examination taken after 3½ years of Middle School includes:

2 papers in English, 2 papers in Arithmetic and Practical Geometry, 1 paper in General Knowledge, 1 paper in General Science/Domestic Science.

Upon results of these tests pupils selected for entry to:

(1)   Secondary Schools
(2)   Grade II Teacher Training courses
(3)   Rural medical aids
(4)   Trade Schools

The best students are candidates for admission to the 5 territorial secondary schools (selecting pupils from all parts of the territory). Other students are selected for the provincial and multi-provincial secondary schools and for various training centers.

Pass in this examination also leads to selection for direct employment in the Tanganyika Subordinate Service as:

Clerks, agricultural instructors, employment with Police Force, Forest Department, Army, Navy or Prison Department.

School-Leaving Certificate awarded to pupils not taking or not having passed the General Entrance Examination, providing satisfactory performance has been attained.


SECONDARY EDUCATION

Aim of General Secondary Schools, not to prepare for particular career.

Secondary school fees abolished, 1963.

Most secondary institutions are boarding schools.  By 1962, some 70 secondary schools; 40 in rural areas.

5 Territorial Secondary Schools:
    Tabora Boys' Government Secondary School
    Tabora Girls' Secondary School

St. Francis' College (Pugu)
St. Andrew's College (Minaki)
Marian Girls' College (near Morogoro)

1st 4 schools offer Higher School.

Secondary Course - Forms I-IV (Standards IX-XII)

| | |
|---|---|
| Language of instruction: | English (except in Swahili courses and where English cannot be arranged in religious instruction). |
| Subjects in 4-year course: | English; Mathematics (Arithmetic, Algebra and Geometry, Trigonometry - Standard XII); Science (Biology, Physics, Chemistry or Domestic Science); History and Civics; Geography; Swahili; Religious Instruction; Art and/or Handwork. |
| | Physical Training and Singing normally performed outside classroom hours. |
| | Some schools offer Agriculture, Current Affairs. French and German additional languages (1961). |

5-Year Plan suggested technical and/or commercial subjects be included in curriculum. Secondary technical course introduced at Technical Institute in Dar es Salaam, 1961.

After 1st 2 years in secondary Forms I and II (Standards IX and X) selection again made on results of Territorial Standard X Examination. Places then allocated for:

> Form III (Standard XI) - continuation in secondary school
> Grade I Teacher Training
> Medical training, veterinary training, clerical course, survey course, meteorological course, post office training school, railway and policewomen training courses.

### LUTHERAN SECONDARY SCHOOL ILBORU, ARUSHA (1964-65)

TIMETABLE: FORMS I-IV
For Cambridge School Certificate
(40-minute periods per week)

| Subjects | I and II | III and IV |
|---|---|---|
| English | 9 | 9 |
| Swahili | 2 | 2 |
| Geography | 4 | 4 |

| | | |
|---|---|---|
| Biology | 3 | 3 |
| Bible Knowledge | 2 | 2 |
| History | 4 | - |
| Elementary Mathematics | 7 | - |
| Physics | 3 | - |
| Chemistry | 3 | - |

At the beginning of Form III, students begin specializing. In addition to the 5 "basic" subjects listed above, each pupil may choose 1 of the following combinations:

|     |                          | Periods |
|-----|--------------------------|---------|
| (A) | Physics                  | 4       |
|     | Chemistry                | 4       |
|     | Mathematics              | 4       |
|     | Additional Mathematics   | 3       |

or

|     |                      |   |
|-----|----------------------|---|
| (B) | English Literature   | 3 |
|     | History              | 4 |
|     | Elements of Commerce | 4 |
|     | Commercial Arithmetic| 3 |
|     | Health Science       | 2 |

The 2nd combination of subjects "B" usually taken by those not capable of continuing in Advanced Mathematics, Physics and Chemistry requiring good grounding in Mathematics. It is also selected by those intending to specialize on the Arts side in Forms V and VI.

This mission secondary school has recently extended its 4 years of academic classes to include Higher School courses - Forms V and VI.

*   *   *

*University of Cambridge Joint Examination for the School Certificate and General Certificate of Education at close of Form IV (Standard XII).+

+For Regulations booklet of the University of Cambridge Local Examinations Syndicate, write the Secretary, Syndicate Buildings, Cambridge. Price, 1 shilling.

Successful candidates qualify for Higher School Certificate training or are given a choice of further training in government department courses. (Through 1961 they entered preliminary courses at Makerere College, Uganda; Royal Technical College, Kenya; and beginning in 1959, Form V in 4 secondary schools in Tanganyika, preparing for Higher School Certificate.) Qualification for government bursary for preliminary course either at Makerere or Royal College: good 1st or 2nd class pass in Cambridge School Certificate, with a minimum of 5 credits, including English Language.)

## HIGHER SCHOOL CERTIFICATE PROGRAM

2-year course, Forms V and VI, preparing for university entrance.

Entrance requirements:   1st and 2nd class pass in Cambridge School Certificate or equivalent.

Science Course:   Biology, Mathematics, Physics, Chemistry, Additional Mathematics

Arts Course:   English, Geography, History and Economics

When entering Form V, students select 2 or 3 principal subjects with 1 or 2 subsidiary subjects which they study for 2 years.

Some of the possible subject combinations taken at this level are:

>   Science:   Biology, Chemistry and Geography
>   Physics, Chemistry, Biology and Subsidiary Mathematics
>   Mathematics, Physics, Chemistry
>   Pure Mathematics, Applied Mathematics, Physics, Subsidiary Chemistry.

>   Arts:   History, Geography and Economics
>   History, Economics and English
>   History, Geography and Bible
>   History, English and Bible

1 paper that rates as a subsidiary subject is required of all students - Arts and Science alike. This "General Paper" consists of a number of questions on various subjects.

The candidate selects 2 questions on which he writes compositions necessitating ability to present material logically and with clarity of thought.

**University of Cambridge Joint Examination for the Higher School Certificate and General Certificate of Education at close of program.[+]

[+]For Regulations booklet of the University of Cambridge Local Examinations Syndicate, write the Secretary, Syndicate Buildings, Cambridge. Price 1 sh.

(See Appendix B for subjects of examination and conditions of award.)

## HIGHER EDUCATION

## UNIVERSITY OF EAST AFRICA

### University College, Dar es Salaam

The University College, Dar es Salaam is 1 of 3 constituent colleges of the University of East Africa.  Others are at Nairobi, Kenya, and at Kampala, Uganda.

Entrance requirements:

(1)  General Regulations

    (i)  Candidates must have completed a full secondary course.

    (ii)  Candidates must be recommended by the Head of their schools as suitable for further education at the University College, Dar es Salaam.

    (iii)  Undergraduates admitted to the College expected to complete a course of study leading to final award at the College if place in such a course is accepted by them.

(2)  Regulations for Direct Entry to Degree Courses

Minimum Entrance requirements are:

either    5 passes obtained at 1 or more of the following:

    (i)  Credit standard of Cambridge School Certificate;

    (ii)  Ordinary level of an approved General Certificate of Education;

    (iii)  Subsidiary standard of Cambridge Higher School Certificate;

    (iv)  Principal subject standard of Cambridge Higher School Certificate;

    (v)  Advanced level of an approved General Certificate of Education.

At least 2 of the 5 passes must have been passed at the levels specified under either (iv) or (v) above.

or    (i)  Credit standard of Cambridge School Certificate;

    (ii)  Ordinary level of an approved General Certificate of Education

     (iii)    Subsidiary standard of Cambridge Higher School Certificate;

     (iv)    Principal subject standard of Cambridge Higher School Certificate;

     (v)    Advanced level of an approved General Certificate of Education.

At least 3 of the 4 passes must have been passed at the levels specified under either (iv) or (v) above.

All candidates must possess either a credit in English Language in the Cambridge Overseas School Certificate or a pass at Ordinary level in the General Certificate of Education or a pass in English Literature at Subsidiary level in the Higher School Certificate Examination or their equivalent.  Applicants who cannot offer either of these qualifications but are otherwise fully qualified for admission may be admitted if they pass a special university entrance examination in English.

## Mature-Age Entry Scheme

Conditions:

(a)    Candidates must be 25 years of age, or older, on July 1 of the year in which entry is desired.  They must have completed their formal school education at least 5 years before the date of application.

(b)    They must be able to show that they have attended Extra-Mural classes or Residential courses (recommendations from the Extra-Mural Class Tutor or Resident Tutor are necessary), or that they have attended a residential course in an Adult Education college (recommendation from the principal of the college is necessary), or that they have a recommendation from a person acceptable to the university that they are qualified to profit from university education.

Degree courses for which Mature-Age students are normally eligible are:

    Bachelor of Arts
    Bachelor of Science
    Bachelor of Education
    Bachelor of Commerce
    Bachelor of Laws

Admission to the professional schools is considered unlikely.

## Faculties:

        Law
        Arts and Social Science
    Department of Extra-Mural Studies
    Institute of Public Administration

| Faculty | Degree | Duration of course |
|---------|--------|--------------------|
| Law | LL.B. | 3 yrs. |
| Arts and Social Science | B.A. | 3 yrs. |

## General and Honours degree programs

The College has not introduced a departmental system or distinction between general and honours degree programs.

Honours standing is awarded on basis of performance in these degrees, not on basis of specialist courses.

## Faculty of Law

Subjects for degree include:

1st yr. (Intermediate):   Introduction to Law, Legal Systems of East Africa, Law of Contract, Criminal Law.

2nd yr. (Part I):   Law of Torts, Land Law, Public Law, Law of Evidence and Interpretation.

3rd yr. (Part II):   With Faculty approval, students allowed to select 4 of the following subjects: Jurisprudence, Law of Associations, Family Law, Conflict of Laws, Public International Law, Constitutional Law, and Succession and Trusts.

Examination required for degree:

The University Examination for the LL.B. degree consists of 3 main parts:

(1)   Intermediate Examination taken at end of 1st year of study. Students required to offer for the examination all the 4 subjects studied during 1st year.

No exemptions from any subject of the Intermediate Examination in Laws. For admission a candidate must:

(a)   have satisfied the General Requirements for admission to a degree course prescribed for students of University of East Africa.

(b)   have been registered as a student of the University of East Africa.

(c)   have pursued an approved course of study in the Faculty of Law of the University College, Dar es Salaam extending over not less than 1 academic year.

(2)  To be admitted to <u>Part I of the LL.B. Examination</u> a candidate must:

  (a)  have passed the Intermediate Examination in Laws.

  (b)  have pursued an appropriate course of study at the University College, Dar es Salaam.

(3)  To be admitted to <u>Part II of the LL.B. Examination</u> a candidate must:

  (a)  have passed Part I of the Examination.

  (b)  have pursued an appropriate course of study at the University College, Dar es Salaam.

<u>Degree awarded</u>:

Bachelor of Laws (LL.B.) - 3 yrs.

From 1965, there will be opportunity for a Law option within the B.A. degree so that Law and Social Sciences may be studied together.

## <u>Faculty of Arts and Social Science</u>

There is an Education option with the B.A. degree.  (Graduates wishing to teach will not have to return to college for a teacher's diploma.)

Subjects for degree include:

1st yr:       3 subjects chosen from the following:

Economics, Education, Geography, History, Language and Linguistics, Literature, and Political Science.

Linguistics (in French and Swahili) introduced in 1964.

2 examination papers in each subject at end of 1st year.

2nd and
3rd yrs:  (1)  In the 2nd and 3rd years, students continue to study 2 of their 3 1st-year subjects (see paragraph 3 below).

They take 5 examination papers in each subject at the end of the 3rd year.  Oral examinations held at discretion of examiners.

(2)  Education is not included as a <u>full</u> subject in the 2nd and 3rd years.  All students who take Education in the 1st year  continue with their other 2 subjects and take the Education option in each subject as well as vacation teaching practice.

(3)  The 5 examination papers in each subject include 4 compul-
     sory papers and 1 other chosen from a list of options.
     These options include:

     (a)  papers from within the subjects;
     (b)  papers in Education, and
     (c)  suitable papers from other subjects.

     Most students choose their optional papers from within
     their 2 main subjects or from Education.  Those who choose
     an option from outside their 2 main subjects may do so only
     after consultation with the Dean and the consent of the
     professors concerned.

## Degree awarded:

Bachelor of Arts (B.A.) - 3 yrs.

## Faculty of Science

Discontinued, 1964.

Special entrance requirements:      In addition to general entrance
                                    requirements, a candidate must offer
                                    passes at principal level in 2 of
                                    the following subjects:  Botany,
                                    Chemistry, Mathematics, Physics,
                                    Zoology.

Subjects for degree include:

1st yr:  Any of the 3 following subjects:

         Botany                Chemistry
         Education             Mathematics
         Physics               Zoology

2nd and
3rd yrs: 2-year course in any of the 2 subjects taken during the 1st
         year other than Education.

## Degree awarded:

Bachelor of Science (B.Sc.) - 3 yrs.

## Department of Extra-Mural Studies

This Department makes both university and pre-university education available to men and women outside the College who are not full-time university students. Among these some may later gain admission to the College under the Mature Age Entry Scheme.

Resident tutors of the Department in various areas of Tanzania organize and give a variety of courses. Part-time lecturers are employed when available in the region.

## Institute of Public Administration

The Institute is run by the College in conjunction with the Government of Tanzania.

Purpose:        Promotion of the social, economic and political progress of the peoples of Tanzania and other African countries.

                Opportunities given for study of and training in:

                        Principles of and techniques of public administration in general.

                        Patterns and procedures appropriate to Africa.

Courses:        3-9 months of training for both government administrative officers and for district magistrates.

## VOCATIONAL AND TECHNICAL EDUCATION

### G O V E R N M E N T   T R A I N I N G
### (Department of Education)

Publicly-provided training.

3 levels of technical training:

                Rural Crafts
                Trade Schools and Secondary Technical Schools
                Technical Institutes and Colleges

### RURAL CRAFTS CENTRES

Artisan level training offered in small centres:
                Simple building, Community development, Agricultural training.

Successful courses in artisan training at the Prison, Dar es Salaam.

Kilimanjaro Native Co-operative Union College (Chagga coffee growers)
(K.N.C.U.) provides more academic training in:

                    Domestic Science; Commercial Courses.


## TRADE SCHOOLS AND SECONDARY TECHNICAL SCHOOLS

Initial training for craftsmen.   Semi-professional level.

2 large Trade Schools:

    Ifunda in Southern Highlands

    Moshi in Northern Province

| | |
|---|---|
| Entrance requirements: | Post-standard VIII. |
| Program: | 3-year courses, followed by 2 years on-the-job training. |
| Courses: | Craft training in allied trades associated with the building and engineering industries: |
| | Engineering mechanic, carpenter, bricklayer, painter, plumber, electrician. |
| | Courses designed to provide knowledge of several trades in addition to specialities. |
| Building Trades: | Specialization in 1 of 5 trades throughout course, with training in subordinate subjects. |
| Engineering Trades: | 1 long lesson per week in each of 5 trades: |
| 1st yr: | Welding, sheetmetal work, blacksmithing, fitting and auto-electric work. |
| 2nd and 3rd yrs: | Specialization in:  General motor vehicle mechanics (both petrol and diesel engines) as main trade; and study 1 of the 5 trades as subordinate or secondary trade. |

Each class divided into 5 groups, each taking different subordinate
trade.


## COLLEGE OF COMMERCE K.N.C.U., Moshi, Northern Province.

Private institution financed by Kilimanjaro Native Co-operative Union.

K.N.C.U offers variety of commercial courses at same or lower level as
Dar es Salaam Institute.  Interracial basis.

1958  -    Full-time and part-time day classes.
           Part-time evening classes for office workers.

1959  -    Two 2-year Post-Standard X courses:

           General Commercial course in:  English, Bookkeeping, Commerce,
           Arithmetic, Stenography, Commercial Law, Geography.

           Course to train secretaries for co-operative unions.

           Post-Standard VIII courses:

           1-year preliminary course in preparation for higher courses.
           1-year Hotel and Catering course.
           6-month part-time Secretarial course.
           1-year Retail Distribution course (1960).


## TECHNICAL COLLEGES AND INSTITUTES

## TECHNICAL INSTITUTE, Dar es Salaam

Founded, 1958.

Interracial institution offering sub-professional technical and commercial
training at secondary and post-secondary levels for both sexes.

Most daytime classes preempted for government students taking in-service
or pre-service training.

1958  -    3 different courses in commercial and clerical subjects.

           1-year full-time clerical training (pre-service for government
           employees).

           Full-time, short intensive in-service courses (government
           employees).

           Part-time evening courses, commercial and clerical subjects.

1959  -    Full-time day courses offered:

           Junior Engineer's course

           Entrance requirements:  School Certificate or equivalent.

Program:   3-year sandwich course (2 years at Institute, 1
           intervening year on job).

           Internal examinations and employment in public works
           or water development sections of government.

### 1-Year Secretarial course

Entrance requirements:  School Certificate or equivalent and
                        pass in English.

Program:   English, Shorthand and Typing for employment as
           stenographers, personal secretaries or reporters.

### 1-Year Clerical course

Entrance requirements:  Post-Standard X.

Program:   English, Swahili, Arithmetic, Typing, Office and
           General Accounts Procedure and Bookkeeping.

### 6-Month Foremanship course

For employees of Public Works Department.

All commercial courses designed to prepare students for examinations of
the Royal Society of Arts, London.   (See Appendix,

### Evening Courses (Expanded in 1963 to aid in Africanization).

Entrance requirements:   Standard X or pass in prescribed entrance exam-
                         ination in English and Arithmetic.

                         For Shorthand (Beginners):
                         Completion of Standard XII or pass in English
                         entrance examination.

#### Commercial courses:

           Shorthand, Typing, Commerce, Commercial Arithmetic
           and Bookkeeping.
           (Prepares students for Royal Society of Arts Exam-
             inations.)

#### Technical courses:

           Building, Motor Mechanics, Mechanical Engineering
           and Radio.
           (Prepares students for City and Guilds Examinations,
             London;   See Appendix,

Academic courses:

> English, Physics, Chemistry, Mathematics, Geography, and Economic History.
>
> (Prepares students for <u>General Certificate of Education Examination</u>.)
>
> Secondary Technical and Secondary Commercial courses introduced in 1962.

English courses:

> Offered for full-time students and also for pupils of other schools preparing for School Certificate examination.
>
> Offered for those wishing to bring a School Certificate "pass" in English language up to mark of "credit."
>
> (Prepares for Royal Society of Arts examinations.)

Art courses:

> Painting and Drawing.

1964 - Institute offering solid technical training for industry and commerce providing full-time modern technical and commercial courses.

## GOVERNMENT TRAINING
### (Administration, Professional and Extension Services)

### AGRICULTURAL AND VETERINARY SERVICES

New agricultural college at Morogoro, 1964.

### Natural Resources School, Tengeru, Arusha

This school provides training courses leading to employment in the Agriculture, Veterinary and Forest Departments.

(1)  Junior ranks of extension services (Agriculture)

Entrance requirements:   At or below Standard VIII.

Program:                 3 years.

(Discontinued, 1959).

(Ag. 2)  Field Assistants (Agriculture)

        Entrance requirements:  Standard X (to be raised to Standard XII School Certificate level).

        Program:  1-year on farm followed by 2-year course.

        (Course also offered at Ukuriguru School.)

        Curriculum:  1st year - English, Mathematics, Biology, Civics, Surveying and Soil Science. Other subjects apply to either Agriculture or Forestry.

        Practical work, feature of course.

(Vet. 2)  Field Assistants (Veterinary). Program similar to one above, training for veterinary services.

(Ag. 3)  Field Officer (Diploma level)

        Entrance requirements:  (Good) School Certificate level.

        Program:  2½ to 3½ years.

        (As of 1963, Senior Field Assistants sent overseas for training. The best return to become Field Officers.)

(Vet. 3)  Veterinary practitioners (Diploma level) trained by promotion from Veterinary Assistants or are recruited from abroad.

(4)  Professional Agriculture or Veterinary Officer

        Entrance requirements:  Degree plus some post-graduate work via agriculture degree from Makerere, or Veterinary Science degree from Royal College.

MEDICAL SERVICES

(1)  Junior Auxiliaries

Entrance requirements:  Standard VIII (minimum)

Program:  2 to 3 years.

Qualifying for:  Assistant Nurse, Graded Dresser, Darkroom Assistant, Health Assistant, etc.

(2)   Auxiliary Technical Jobs

     Entrance requirements:   School Certificate (Form IV) minimum.

     (a)   Qualifying for:   Registered Nurses, Radiography Assistants, Physiotherapy Assistants, Laboratory Assistants, Dispensers, etc.

     (b)   Qualifying for:   Medical Assistants (to Medical Officer).

     Training:   Up-grading courses with more clinical than nursing content.

Dar es Salaam Training Centre (Rockefeller Grant)

     Entrance requirements:   School Certificate or equivalent.

     Program:   4 years.

     Qualifying for:   "Rural Medical Practitioners" (rural G.P.'s)

     Best Medical Assistants up-graded to this level.

(3)   Graduate Level

     Makerere Degree in Medicine (associated with Mulago Hospital).

     Offers internationally recognized medical qualification.

ADMINISTRATION

Courses of intensive training for "Africanization."

(1)   Clerical

     Entrance requirements:   Form IV or "failed" School Certificate.

     Course:   Up-grading of clerks inside or outside of government.

(2)   Executive

     Entrance requirements:   School Certificate or equivalent.

     Course:   For Middle-grade executives.

(3)   District Assistants

     Entrance requirements:   School Certificate or equivalent.

     (Junior Administrative grade in provincial administration. Local government training similar.)

(4)  District Officers

Entrance requirements:    Graduates (when possible).

(In past have been often up-graded from District level.)

(5)  Senior Administrators

Entrance requirements:    Graduates

Courses:                  In-service training, appropriate to
                          Institutes of Public Administration.


O T H E R   D E P A R T M E N T A L   T R A I N I N G
(Ministry of Works, Departments of Co-operation and Community Development)

(1)  Standard VIII Entry
Artisans, lowest level of field services, clerks.

(2)  School Certificate Entry
Sub-professional jobs throughout the Departments.

Qualifies for:            Technical and Laboratory Assistants, junior
                          officers in Co-operatives, community develop-
                          ment, etc.
                          Senior clerks, store-keepers, Ministry of
                          Works trainees for Inspectorate and Assist-
                          ant (sub-professional grades in all Depart-
                          ments).

(3)  Graduate Entry

Eventually drawn from Professional Courses at Royal College.

Qualifies for:            Engineers, Quantity Surveyors, Surveyors,
                          Professional Accountants, etc.

On smaller scale, courses for special and junior positions for work as
the following:
Game rangers, water bailiffs, forest rangers,  etc.

# INDUSTRIAL AND COMMERCIAL TRAINING
## (Private Institutions and Public Utilities)

## PUBLIC UTILITIES

East African Railways and Harbours
(Locomotive Training Centre, Railway Workshops, Dar es Salaam)

Training provided for:   Artisans, technicians, clerical grades,
inspectors, station staff, catering staff,
engineering students, others.

## PRIVATE FIRMS

East African Power and Lighting and TANESCO, Dar es Salaam.

East African Tobacco Company.

In-service training, Dar es Salaam.

Shell Company          Artisan training, Dar es Salaam.

Banks                  Training at clerical and School Certificate
entry; associated with professional examina-
tions.

Trainees attached temporarily to United
Kingdom branches or training centres.

Coffee, sisal and other plantations; agricultural and processing
enterprises; co-operatives; milling.

Local and in-service training for:

Field supervisors, assistant estate managers,
secretarial, clerical and accounting work,
some artisan and technical training.

Most boys and girls at Standard VIII level recruited for above
opportunities.

Artisan training usually requires trade school qualification.

## TEACHER EDUCATION

1st normal classes for African teachers started in 1916, attached to
Government Central School, Dar es Salaam.  Mission schools also trained
their own teachers.

As of 1960:    30 training colleges for Africans
               1 for Indians
               1 for non-natives (including Goans).

               Grade II and Grade I Training Colleges for African teachers.

               Post-School Certificate training for Africans and Indians
               at different colleges.

               No teacher training for Europeans.  (European schools
               recruited teachers overseas.)

1959, Asian teacher training centre started, discontinued, 1962.


## PREVIOUS TO 1961

In terms of qualifications, following categories of teachers employed in
Part I of Register of African Schools:

| | |
|---|---|
| Grade II | Vernacular teachers in Primary and Middle Entrance schools. |
| | Entrance requirements:  Standard VIII. |
| | 2-year training. |
| Grade I | Teaching Middle Schools and Grade II training centres. |
| | Entrance requirements:  Standard X. |
| | 2-year training. |
| Untrained Secondary School Leavers | Teaching technical and vocational students and at other non-primary schools. (Comparatively small number.) |
| Non-Graduate Teachers | Holding:  Makerere Undergraduate Diploma in Education, or another recognized diploma or certificate. |
| | Teaching in secondary schools. |
| Trained and Untrained University Graduates | Teaching in secondary schools. |


## TRAINING COURSES

Only Grade II, Grade I, in-service courses and refresher courses provided
in Tanganyika.

Higher teacher-training courses obtained outside East Africa or Diploma
in Education at Makerere, Uganda.

Government Teacher Training College, Mpouapona (Mpwapwa) (provided by
5-Year Plan), St. Andrews Teacher Training Centre, Korogwe, and others.

Curriculum:                English, Swahili, General Knowledge, General
                           Science, Mathematics, Education and Teaching
                           Methods.
                           (Courses for both Grade I and Grade II Certifi-
                             cates.)

Examinations:              Both written and practical portions, latter of
                           more weight.

   Grade II Examination - 4 papers:
                           School Organization
                           English (including composition)
                           Swahili
                           Civics

   Grade I Examination - 5 papers:

                           1  Professional paper
                              Principles of Education
                              School Organization
                              Method and Special Method
                           2 English papers
                           1 Civics
                           1 Swahili (language and method)

Language of instruction: English (since 1958).
                           Examinations in English with exception of
                           Swahili paper.

Promotion possible from 1 grade to next.

Grade II teachers might obtain Grade I certificates; Grade I teachers
with required abilities or qualifications might be promoted to master,
and masters to position of education officer.

Teachers employed under Part I of the Register of African Schools must
be registered in Part I of the Register of Teachers.

   Requirement:            Teacher's Certificate or license to teach and
                           fulfillment of prescribed conditions.

                           Certificates granted those completing training.
                           Licenses granted to holders of diploma, degree,
                           or certificate qualifying for grant of license.

Teachers employed under Part II of the Register of African Schools must
be registered in Part II of the Register of Teachers.

Requirement:              Permit to teach, granted to those having com-
                          pleted Standard VIII and fulfilled prescribed
                          condition.

## IN-SERVICE COURSES

Provided for:             Male Grade II agriculture instructors and hand-
                          work teachers for Middle schools.

                          African women Grade II domestic science teachers
                          for girls' Middle schools.

## REFRESHER COURSES

For African teachers of all grades, held at provincial and teacher-training
centres.

Special courses for school supervisors - 2 weeks.

Up-grading courses permit Grade II-certificated teachers who subsequently
pass Standard X examination to become Grade I.

Government Teacher Training College, Mpwapwa.

Training:                 Primary, Middle school teachers.
                          School supervisors and Headmasters.
                          (Special in-training course - 9 months)

Planned also as center of research and publication; to develop into
territorial institute of education.

## BEGINNING 1962

Previous length of courses varied in African, Asian and European schools
to integrated system of education.

## 3 Levels of teacher training:

Grade II          Primary School Teachers (Teaching Standards I - VIII).
                  Entrance requirements:  8 year Primary school
                                          (Standard VIII)
                  2-year training.

| Grade I | Teaching Middle and Lower Forms of Secondary. |
|---------|-----------------------------------------------|
| | Entrance requirements: Post Standard X training. |
| | 2-year training. |

| Grade IA | Teaching Middle and Lower Forms of Secondary. |
|----------|-----------------------------------------------|
| | Entrance requirements: Post School Certificate. |
| | 2-year training. |

## Post-Higher School Certificate training with at least 2 principal subjects.

Entrance requirements:  Higher School Certificate

Undergraduate Diploma offered at Makerere University College, Uganda (Institute of Education).

Diploma holders might teach in Secondary Schools up to School Certificate.


## Graduate Teachers

Entrance requirements:   General or Honours Degree studied in English or Diploma in Fine Arts from recognized University.

Program:                 1 academic year (26 weeks).

Graduate teachers trained mainly at the Institute of Education at University of East Africa, Uganda.


## ADULT EDUCATION

1961, classes in reading and writing in Swahili for those over 14 years of age.  Courses in Arithmetic, Agriculture, and Community Development added later.

Kiryukoni (Kivukoni) College for Political Science and Economics, Dar es Salaam, established in 1960 under TANU and its trade union affiliate, patterned after Ruskin College, Oxford, England.  Leadership program training for district officers and others.

# THE UNITED REPUBLIC OF TANZANIA
## (Zanzibar)

| Student's Age | Year of Schooling | | | |
|---|---|---|---|---|
| 26 | 20 | HIGHER EDUCATION | None | |
| 25 | 19 | HIGHER EDUCATION | None | |
| 24 | 18 | HIGHER EDUCATION | None | |
| 23 | 17 | HIGHER EDUCATION | None | |
| 22 | 16 | HIGHER EDUCATION | None | |
| 21 | 15 | HIGHER EDUCATION | None | |
| 20 | | | ** | VI Form |
| 19 | 14 | SECONDARY | ** | VI Form |
| 18 | 13 | SECONDARY | | V Form |
| 17 | 12 | SECONDARY | * | IV Form |
| 16 | 11 | SECONDARY | | III Form |
| 15 | 10 | SECONDARY | | II Form |
| 14 | 9 | SECONDARY | | I Form |
| 13 | 8 | ELEMENTARY | | VIII Standard |
| 12 | 7 | ELEMENTARY | | VII Standard |
| 11 | 6 | ELEMENTARY | | VI Standard |
| 10 | 5 | ELEMENTARY | | V Standard |
| 9 | 4 | ELEMENTARY | | IV Standard |
| 8 | 3 | ELEMENTARY | | III Standard |
| 7 | 2 | ELEMENTARY | | II Standard |
| 6 | 1 | ELEMENTARY | | I Standard |
| 5 | | | | Pre-primary – Koranic schools |
| 4 | | | | |
| 3 | | | | |

Teacher Training

SECONDARY EDUCATION

PRIMARY EDUCATION

Compulsory education: None

School Year: March–December (From 2nd term, mid-June—mid-September, 1964, Standards I–VI not in session on Saturdays)

Secondary Grading: 75% highest, rarely given

34% lowest passing

(For grading on secondary school certificates, see SECONDARY EDUCATION)

# Z A N Z I B A R

Independence:  December 10, 1963.
April, 1964, united with Tanganyika as a sovereign state.


## BACKGROUND - TO 1964

Population of Arabs, Africans, Indians, Europeans.  99% of people in
Zanzibar are Moslems.

1503, island of Zanzibar was annexed by the Portuguese.  Arabs conquered
Mombasa on the Kenya mainland in 1698.  Arabian sheiks governed the territories of Zanzibar, Pemba and other small islets, together with the
mainland strip in Kenya until 1861.

Sultanate of Zanzibar was proclaimed British Protectorate in 1890.  Constitutional government established in 1897.  Placed under the Colonial
Office, 1914.

December 10, 1963, Sultan Jamshid signed a transfer of this coastal mainland to Kenya.  The revolution of January 1964 overthrew the Sultan.

There have been Koranic schools since the 10th century.  Before the 20th
century, secular education was in mission schools or in schools established
by the Indians for their children.  Government education initiated in 1905.

After Education Commission was established in 1920 to revise educational
policy, men's teacher training school and commercial and industrial school
for boys were created.  In 1933, women trained as teachers; 1944, 2-year
training course in Teacher Training School was established.

1935, secondary school for boys replaced former commercial school which
offered 4-year course leading to Cambridge Overseas Certificate.  1947,
government secondary school for girls was established.

St. Joseph's Convent School became full-time coeducational private secondary school, 1947.

Ismaili Khoja community started private secondary classes, 1940.  Became
full-time private secondary school for boys, 1947.  This school (Aga Khan
Secondary School) was given a grant-in-aid, becoming coeduational in 1959.

Higher School Certificate classes were opened for boys and girls in 1959
in Government secondary school for boys.  When moving into new buildings
in 1959, the school changed its name to King George VI School.

The institute of Muslim Education at Mombasa opened in 1950 with facilities for technical and vocational training for boys.  Students entered
from Standard VIII of primary school.  4-year courses in Electronics, Motor

and Radio Mechanics, Welding, leading to City and Guilds of London Institute intermediate examination.  In 1963, Mombasa, in the mainland strip, transferred to Kenya (see above).

1956, government secondary technical school established.  Dressmaking courses for girls, 1953, broadened to include other domestic training, 1959, with the opening of the Lady Rankine Domestic Science Centre serving government girls' secondary school and providing adult classes in Domestic Science courses.

1959, there was an economic and financial depression due to decline of world clove market.

All schools teaching secular subjects (except a few primary schools) were government schools or were government-aided.

No separate education for European children; most were sent to mainland after 7 years of age, or to England for schooling.


## PRESENT SYSTEM


### PRE-PRIMARY EDUCATION

Koranic schools.

Entry age:              6 years.  Students remain 1 or more years.


### GOVERNMENT PRIMARY EDUCATION

Entry age:          6 years.

8-year program:     Standards I - VIII.  Standards I - VI, free.

Language of instruction:  Kiswahili, but gradually replaced by English
                          in Standards VII and VIII.

Curriculum (identical in urban and rural schools):

                    Religion, Arabic, Kiswahili, English, Arithmetic.
                    History, Geography, Hygiene, Nature Study, Handicraft, Needlework, Art, and practical activities.

Examination at close of 8-year program, determining whether student will go into government or government-aided school.

Pupils awarded Leaving Certificate on completion of the primary school course.

## SECONDARY EDUCATION

Entrance requirements:     Secondary school entrance examination conducted
                           by the Ministry of Education and National Culture
                           on completion of the primary school course.

Students selected for admission into Form I (1st year of secondary course)
by the Ministry of Education and National Culture on the basis of the
entrance examination.

Language of instruction: English.

*4-year program (Forms I-IV), leading to the Cambridge School Certificate
Examination and General Certificate of Education (G.C.E.).

2 additional years of training (Forms V and VI), leading to the Cambridge
Higher School Certificate Examination.

For the first 4 years all students take instruction in Science, Arts, and
some students, in technical subjects.  The minimum number of subjects
studied for the Cambridge School Certificate level is 6, the maximum, 8.

Forms V and VI only in Lumumba College.


## LUMUMBA COLLEGE

### TIMESCHEDULE
(Hours per week per year)

| Subjects | Form I | Form II | Form III | Form IV | Form V | Form VI |
|---|---|---|---|---|---|---|
| English | 6 2/3 | 6 2/3 | 8 | 8 | 5 1/3 | 5 1/3 |
| History | 2 | 2 | 2 2/3 | 2 2/3 | 5 1/3 | 5 1/3 |
| Geography | 2 | 2 | 2 2/3 | 2 2/3 | 5 1/3 | 5 1/3 |
| Swahili | 2 | 2 | 2 | 2 | | |
| Gujarati | 2 | 2 | 2 | 2 | | |
| Arabic | 3 1/3 | 2 1/3 | 3 1/3 | 3 1/3 | | |
| Mathematics | 4 | 4 | 4 | 4 | 10 2/3 | 6 |
| Physics | 2 2/3 | 2 2/3 | 2 2/3 | 2 2/3 | 5 1/3 | 5 1/3 |
| Chemistry | 2 | 2 | 2 2/3 | 2 2/3 | 5 1/3 | 5 1/3 |
| Biology | 2 | 2 | 2 2/3 | 2 2/3 | 5 1/3 | 5 1/3 |
| Art | 1 1/3 | 1 1/3 | 2 2/3 | 2 2/3 | | |
| General Engineering | | | | | 2 | 2 |
| Technical Drawing | 2 | 2 2/3 | 2 2/3 | 2 2/3 | | |
| Woodwork | 2 | 2 2/3 | 2 2/3 | 2 2/3 | | |
| Metal work | 2 | 2 2/3 | 2 2/3 | 2 2/3 | | |

Mathematics:          In the first 3 years, course includes Arithmetic, Algebra and Plane Geometry; in 4th year, Arithmetic, is replaced by Plane Trigonometry.

Science:          Laboratory work forms important part in the teaching of science.

Forms V and VI:     Besides General English, students may select any 1 of the following combinations of 3 subjects:

    (i)   History, English, Geography
   (ii)   English, Geography, Mathematics
  (iii)   Physics, Chemistry, Biology
   (iv)   Physics, Chemistry, Mathematics
    (v)   Physics, Geography, Mathematics

Students selecting (iii) above take a year's course in Mathematics (subsidiary level); all other subjects lead to principal level Higher School Certificate Examination (or "A" level, General Certificate of Education). 4 hours a week are devoted to subsidiary Mathematics in Form V.

Promotion from 1 Form to another is automatic; however, students take examinations (2-3 in a year) and the results, subject by subject, are recorded in their files.

Grading scale:     Lowest passing grade in each subject is 34% marks.

**Grading scale on University of Cambridge (Local Examination Syndicate) School Certificate, and Higher School Certificate, Examinations:**

Attainment in a subject is indicated by a grade:

Grade 1 - highest
Grade 9 - lowest

Only Grades 1-8 recorded on Certificates.

Grade 1)
2)  Very Good

3)
4)  Pass-with-Credit      G.C.E. Ordinary Level Pass
5)
6)

7)
8)  S.C. Subject Pass

## School Certificates and General Certificates of Education

School Certificates are awarded in 3 Divisions (of which Division 1 is the highest, and Division 3 the lowest) to candidates who satisfy certain conditions as stated in the regulations for the examination.

General Certificates of Education are awarded to candidates who do not qualify for a School Certificate but who reach Grade 6 (or better) in at least 3 subjects.

Subject names:    Any of the following subject names are in the form indicated on the right.

| Name of subject as it appears in the Regulations | Abbreviation used on the Certificate |
|---|---|
| Islamic Religious Knowledge | ISLAMIC RELIG KNOWLEDGE |
| Hindi (or Urdu or Bengali or Tamil) as a 1st Language | HINDI (or URDU or BENGALI or TAMIL)  A |
| Hindi (or Urdu or Bengali or Tamil) as a 2nd Language | HINDI (or URDU or BENGALI or TAMIL)  B |
| Additional Mathematics | ADDITIONAL MATHS. |
| General Science (including Practical) | GENERAL SCIENCE W PRACT |
| Additional Science | ADDITIONAL GENERAL SCIENCE |
| Physics-with-Chemistry | PHYSICS W CHEMISTRY |
| Needlework and Dressmaking | NEEDLEWORK/DRESSMAKING |
| Geometrical and Mechanical Drawing | GEOM & MECH DRAWING |
| Geometrical and Building Drawing | GEOM & BUILDING DRAWING |
| Principles of Accounts | PRINC OF ACCOUNTS |
| Engineering Workshop Practice | ENGINEERING WRK PRACT. |

## Higher School Certificate

Candidates who have attended for at least 2 years a post-School Certificate Course in a school recognized by the Syndicate are eligible for the award
**of a Higher School Certificate.

They are required to take, at 1 and the same examination:

    (i)   the General Paper
    (ii)  2 principal subjects
    (iii) either a 3rd principal subject or 2 subsidiary subjects
          and to reach the standard of performance laid down in the
          regulations for the examination.

For the purpose of exemption from University Entrance and Intermediate examinations and from the preliminary or other examinations of professional bodies:

a Pass at principal standard = a Pass at advanced level
in a subject of the Higher      in a subject of the Syndicate's
School Certificate              General Certificate of Education

a Pass at a subsidiary level = a Pass at an ordinary level
    (H.S.C.)                        (G.C.E.)

Principal level gradings:   A pass in a principal level subject is indicated by the abbreviation PRINC, followed by 1 of the 5 grades - A, B, C, D, E,- of which A is the highest and E the lowest.

Subject names:   Any of the following subject names which may appear are in the form indicated on the right:

Name of subject as it appears in       Abbreviation used on the Certificate
        the Regulations

Economic and Public Affairs            ECON & PUBLIC AFFAIRS

French (or Spanish) Prescribed
            Texts
    History, Geography, Life           FRENCH (or SPANISH) LITERATURE
    and Institutions

Physics-with-Chemistry                 PHYSICS W CHEMISTRY

                MATHEMATICS (principal level)

MATHEMATICS PRI/APPD indicates that the candidate passed in Applied Mathematics at principal level but could alternatively have been awarded a pass in Mathematics at principal level.

MATHEMATICS PRI/PURE indicates that the candidate passed in Pure Mathematics at principal level but could alternatively have been awarded a pass in Mathematics at principal level.


HIGHER EDUCATION

None.  Students usually go either to University College of East Africa (Makerere), Uganda, or Royal College, Nairobi, Kenya, or to foreign universities.

## TEACHER EDUCATION

Seyyid Khalifa Teacher Training College (for men) and Seyyida Manu Teacher Training College (for women) integrated into a co-educational training institution known as Nkrumah College.

Students admitted to Teacher Training College on completion of 4 years of secondary education (after 8 years of primary education).

Language of instruction:  English.

2-year program for training primary school teachers.

Curriculum:

(1)  Academic subjects:    English
                           Mathematics
                           History and Civics  )
                           Geography           )  Taught as Social Studies
                           Arabic and Religion
                           Swahili
                           Health Science
                           Nature Study
                           Arts and Crafts
                           Physical Education

      The aim is to consolidate the students' knowledge of the subjects so as to enable them to teach them with ease in all classes in primary schools.

(2)  Professional subjects:

                           Theory of Education (General Principles)
                           Infant (Junior) method
                           Methods of teaching the various subjects
                           School Organization
                           Supervised teaching practice

Promotion from 1 year to the next is almost automatic.  A student is deferred only if it is found that he or she will benefit by doing so or is so weak that he or she is not likely to cope with work in the next class.

Each student has to sit for the College final examination at the end of the 2-year course.  To pass the teacher's certificate examination, a student has to score minimum marks of 40% in each subject and an aggregate of 50% in all subjects.

The student must obtain at least a "C" mark in teaching practice.
(The highest grade is given in very special cases only.  This is very
 infrequent.)
Successful candidates are awarded the Primary Teacher's Certificate.

324

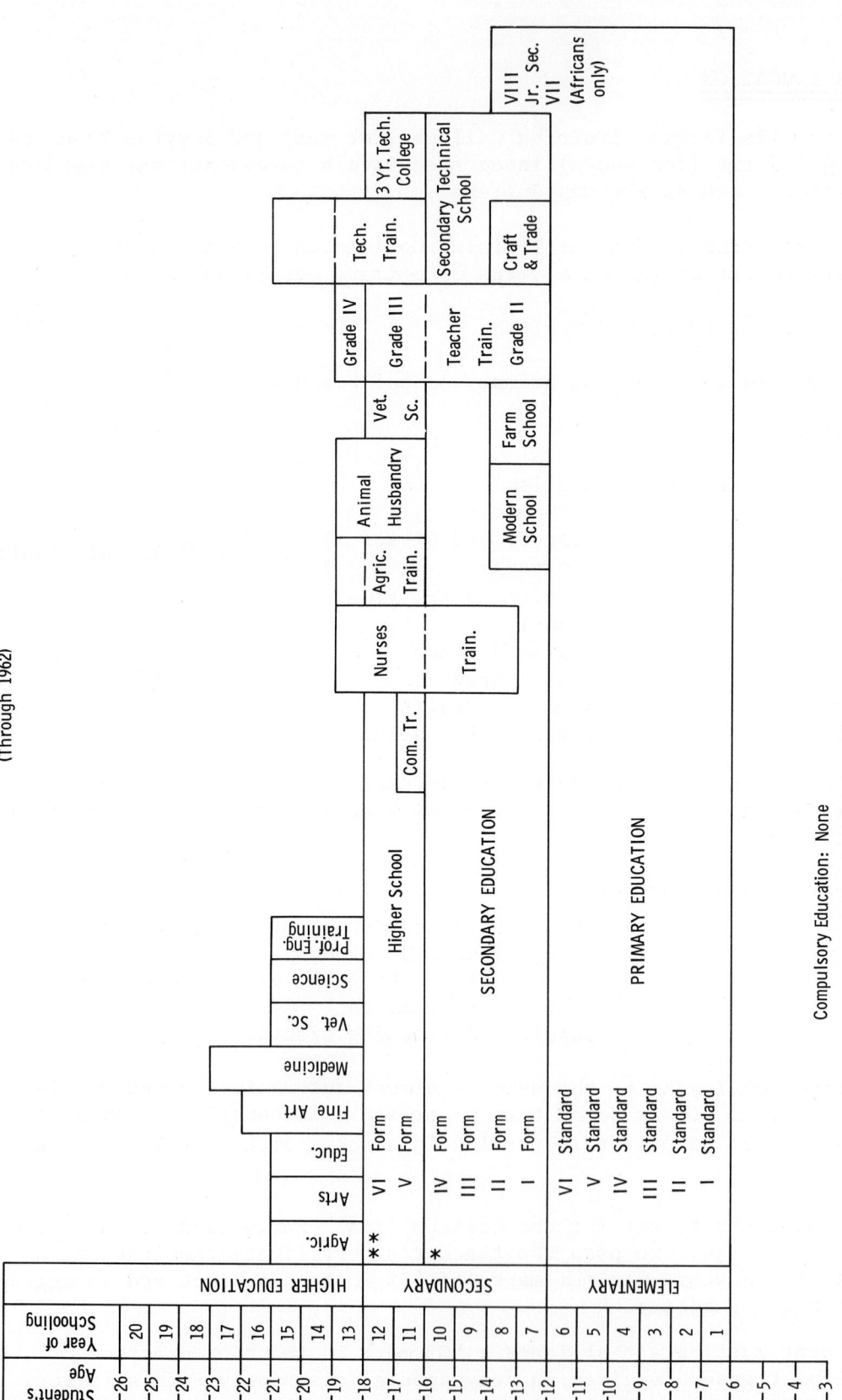

U G A N D A
(Through 1962)

Compulsory Education: None

School Year: Late January–Early December.
(University) July–March.

Grading: 1–9 Cambridge School Certificate and General Certificate of Education
(See SECONDARY EDUCATION)

U G A N D A

From 1963

(Incorporating Proposals to 1968)

HIGHER EDUCATION

Agric.

Arts

Educ.

Fine Art

Medicine

Soc. Sc.

Science

** VI Form

V Form

Higher School

* IV Form

III Form

II Form

I Form

SECONDARY EDUCATION

VII Primary

VI Primary

V Primary

IV Primary

III Primary

II Primary

I Primary

PRIMARY EDUCATION

Nurses Training

Proposed Secondary Schools
Home Econ. )
Tech. & Com. ) Bias
Agric. )

Com. (Adv.)

Agric. & Vet. Sc.

Farm Schools

Technical Colleges

Technical Schools

Proposed Diploma Course

Teacher Training Gr. II (phasing out)

| Student's Age | Year of Schooling | |
|---|---|---|
| 26 | 20 | HIGHER EDUCATION |
| 25 | 19 | |
| 24 | 18 | |
| 23 | 17 | |
| 22 | 16 | |
| 21 | 15 | |
| 20 | 14 | |
| 19 | 13 | |
| 18 | 12 | SECONDARY |
| 17 | 11 | |
| 16 | 10 | |
| 15 | 9 | |
| 14 | 8 | |
| 13 | 7 | ELEMENTARY |
| 12 | 6 | |
| 11 | 5 | |
| 10 | 4 | |
| 9 | 3 | |
| 8 | 2 | |
| 7 | 1 | |
| 6 | | |
| 5 | | |
| 4 | | |
| 3 | | |

Compulsory Education: None

School Year: Late-January-Early December. (University) July-March

Grading: 1-9 Cambridge School Certificate and General Certificate of Education. (See SECONDARY EDUCATION).

UGANDA

Independence:    October 9, 1962.


## BACKGROUND


98% of Uganda's population is African.   The non-native groups are Asian (Indian and Goan) and European.   80% of the inhabitants are engaged in farming cotton, coffee, and sugar.

The tribes in the center and south speak Luganda and are composed of Buganda and Bunyore people.   In the northern province, the nomadic Karamo-jong tribe speaks languages belonging to Sudaman, Hamitic, Nilotic, and Nilo-Hamitic people who immigrated into Uganda around 1000 A.D.

Traders arrived in Zanzibar in 1844, and the Buganda kingdom came under the control of Arabs and native Moslems.   1890, the first European explorers came; Buganda fell under the control of the British East Africa Company.

Uganda became a British Protectorate in 1894.   Subsequently, it was put under Civil Administration, 1899.   During the 1920's, executive and legis-lative councils were established; also, the first Department of Education, to assist mission schools.   After World War II, the first Africans were appointed to the Legislative Council, 1945.

1961, internal self-government and ministerial system were established, and independence from British was gained October 9, 1962 under the Queen and former Governor General.   In 1963, the National Assembly voted to re-place the Queen as head of state, creating the new office of President. The office of Governor General was abolished.

Until 1956, Uganda's educational system was on a religious and racial basis: African, European, and Asian.   Common schools after 1956 were opened to children of all races and denominations and Africans were admitted to former Asian and European schools at all levels.   English, the medium of instruc-tion.

European education has been confined to primary schools, with children going to Kenya for secondary training.   Secondary school leavers have taken university education in Britain and South Africa.

The majority of schools are still provided and managed by voluntary agen-cies:   Protestant and Catholic missions and, to a lesser extent, the Uganda Muslim Educational Association.   (The Aga Khan schools have been non-racial well before independence in Uganda, Kenya, and Tanzania.) There are also secular private schools and an increasing number of Local Authority primary schools. Government maintains a number of institutions largely at post-primary level.

Earliest African secondary schools were started by missions in 1902. (First girls' secondary school established at Gayaza in 1925.) Some provinces offered no secondary training until after 1945.

In 1921, government technical school started at Makerere, later confining instruction to post-secondary courses until 1928. Then, technical training taken over by government-owned Kampala Technical School. In 1938, Makerere became an institution of higher education.

In 1961, Ministry and Department of Education integrated, becoming Ministry of Education.


## PRESENT SYSTEM


Education integration started in 1957; accelerated on independence, 1962.

Schools are mostly interracial. Exceptions occur where some are predominantly Asian or European. Remainder of schools are completely African or predominantly African. Government or government-aided schools.

Some of the 1963 proposals for changes in the educational system have been put into effect; others are expected to be implemented by 1968.


## PRIMARY EDUCATION

Entry age:  6 years.

8-year program:     6 primary and 2 junior secondary (I through VIII).

Previous to 1962:   European: Primary I through VI
                    Asian:    Primary I through VI or VII
                    African:  Primary I through VI and
                              Primary VII-VIII (junior secondary)

Language of instruction:     Vernacular:  Primary I through IV
                             English:     Primary V through VIII


## JUNIOR SECONDARY COURSE

Considered part of primary school VII and VIII. Many junior secondary schools are boarding schools, separate for boys and girls. Some schools add a 3rd year for terminal training.

Entrance requirements:        Selective, from those having completed 6-year primary course and passed Primary School Leaving Examination.  (Before 1963, students sometimes permitted extra year when failing secondary entrance.)

2-year curriculum:            Religious Knowledge, English, Mathematics, Vernacular, History, Geography, General Science, Physical Education, Art, Handcrafts, Needlework, Home Economics, Civics, Music.

Examination (prepared and graded by Ministry of Education) for candidates to senior secondary entrance: English, History, Geography, Mathematics.

Certificate awarded:          Junior Secondary School Leaving Certificate.

Certificate qualifies also for primary teacher training colleges, technical and trade schools, and specialized departmental courses.

Planned by 1968:              7-year program (which means elimination of junior secondary and primary school training) which will prepare students for choice of a different secondary program.

Asian Education:              As a result of Asian school system reorganization, 1956-1963, junior secondary course transferred to primary schools.  Aims and curriculum virtually the same as those in African schools.

## SENIOR SECONDARY EDUCATION

Gradually becoming integrated.  Asians predominant in 7 government schools. Most of senior secondary training in boarding schools (predominantly African).  Separate schools for boys and girls.

Entrance requirements:        Junior Secondary School Leaving Certificate, Grade I or II.

## SENIOR SECONDARY COURSE

Forms I through IV:           Leading to University of Cambridge Joint Examination for the School Certificate and General Certificate of Education.  (Deviation from British and West African 5-year secondary system.)

Forms V and VI:             <u>Leading to University of Cambridge Joint
                            Examination for the Higher School Certificate
                            and General Certificate of Education.</u>


<u>TYPICAL SENIOR SECONDARY CURRICULUM:  FORMS I-IV</u>
                  For Cambridge School Certificate
                  (40-50 minute periods per week)


<u>FORMS I and II</u>                  <u>FORM III</u>                    <u>FORM IV</u>
                        <u>Arts course</u>      <u>Science Course</u>

Biology                 Biology         Biology             Student
English                 English         English
Fine Arts               Geography       Geography           continues
General Science         Mathematics     Mathematics
Geography               History         Chemistry           his
History                 Literature      Physics
Literature                                                  subjects
Mathematics
Bible Knowledge


Additional periods per week are filled with any number of the following
subjects:  Physical Education, Vernacular (Luganda, Swahili, Urdu, Gujerati),
French, Art, Craft, Music, Civics.

Some schools also offer Additional Mathematics and Agricultural Biology.


\*<u>University of Cambridge Joint Examination for the School Certificate and
General Certificate of Education</u> at close of program.[+]

(See Appendix B for subjects of examination and conditions of award.)

Holders of the School Certificate are prepared for teacher training colleges,
posts in civil service, industry and commerce, and for the Higher School
Certificate course.

        <u>N.B.</u>   Previous to 1960, students with Cambridge Overseas School
               Certificate admitted to 2-year pre-degree course at the
               University College of East Africa (Makerere).  After 2-year
               preparatory program at Makerere, students sat for the Uni-
               versity of London Preliminary Examinations, which qualified
               for university degree courses.


[+]For <u>Regulations</u> booklet of the University of Cambridge Local Examinations
Syndicate, write The Secretary, Syndicate Buildings, Cambridge.
Price 1 sh.

HIGHER SCHOOL CERTIFICATE PROGRAM

2-year course preparing for university entrance.

Entrance requirements:       1st or 2nd class pass in <u>Cambridge School Certificate</u>.

HIGHER SCHOOL CERTIFICATE COURSE:  FORMS V-VI<br>(40-minute periods per week)

<u>Subjects</u>             <u>Periods</u>

<u>Science Course</u>

| | | |
|---|---|---|
| Mathematics | 10 | ) |
| Physics | 10 | ) |
| Chemistry | 10 | ) Major subjects |
| Biology | 10 | ) |
| Economics and Art | 5 and 6 | ) Other subjects |

or

<u>Arts Course</u>

| | | |
|---|---|---|
| English | 10 | ) |
| History | 10 | ) |
| Geography | 10 | ) Major subjects |
| Mathematics | 10 | ) |
| Economics and Art | 5 and 6 | ) Other subjects |

**<u>University of Cambridge Joint Examination for the Higher School Certificate and General Certificate of Education</u> at close of program.+

(See Appendix B for subjects of examination and conditions of award.)

<u>Planned by 1968</u>:   7-year <u>Primary School Leaving Certificate</u> will qualify students for a choice of 4 secondary programs:

High Schools:  6 years (<u>Cambridge School Certificate</u> and <u>Higher School Certificate</u>).

Secondary Schools:  Starting with 3 years, extending to 4 years. (Replacing Rural Trade, Homecraft, Secondary Modern, and most Farm Schools.)  Bias as follows:

   (a)  Agricultural

+For <u>Regulations</u> booklet of the University of Cambridge Local Examinations Syndicate, write The Secretary, Syndicate Buildings, Cambridge. Price 1 sh.

(b)  Technical
(c)  Commercial
(d)  Home Economics

Leading to <u>Uganda Secondary Leaving Certificate</u>.

Farm Schools:  4 years (<u>Certificate</u>).

Technical Schools:  4 years (<u>First Craft Certificate of City and
Guilds of London Institute</u>).


<u>HIGHER EDUCATION</u>


<u>UNIVERSITY OF EAST AFRICA</u>

<u>Makerere University College, Kampala</u>

Makerere University College is one of three constituent colleges of the
University of East Africa.  Others are at Nairobi, Kenya, and at Dar es
Salaam, Tanzania.

Makerere School was established in 1921 as government-operated technical,
trade and secondary school.  August 1922, title changed to College, and
Mengo Hospital Medical School was incorporated into it under the Educational
Department of Uganda administration.  At the same time, courses in Arts,
Science, Medicine, Agriculture, Education, and Veterinary Science advanced
their standards and a School of Fine Arts was established.

In 1938, the institution gained the status of an independent college
governed by a Council with representatives from all the East African
Territories, to which Kenya and Tanganyika (Tanzania) contributed
financially.  Women were first admitted to the college in 1945.

Upon recommendations of the Asquith Commission 1945, it was decided that
the college should become the inter-territorial center of university
studies in East Africa.  In 1949, the institution became the University
College of East Africa with "special relationship" with the University of
London, offering Faculties of Arts, Science, Agriculture, Education,
Medicine, and Veterinary Science.  Examinations for General Degrees in
Arts and Science first held in 1953.

Until 1960, the first 2 years at Makerere were devoted to Higher School
Certificate work.  1961, new policy eliminated pre-degree courses when
Higher School Certificate classes started in selected secondary schools.
1962, Faculty of Veterinary Science transferred to the University College,
Nairobi.

1963, University of East Africa became independent, awarding its own
degrees (E.A.), also awarded by constituent colleges of Kenya and Tanzania.
The same year the Licentiateship in Medicine and Surgery became the M.B.,
Ch.B. (E.A.) Degree and the Faculty of Social Science was established.

General entrance requirements:

    <u>either</u>    A.   5 passes at 1 or more of the following levels:

        (i)   Credit standard of the <u>Cambridge School Certificate</u> (C.S.C.)

        (ii)  Ordinary level of an approved <u>General Certificate of Education</u> (G.C.E.)

     (iii)  Subsidiary standard of the <u>Cambridge Higher School Certificate</u> (H.S.C.)

      (iv)  Principal subject standard of the <u>Cambridge Higher School Certificate</u> (H.S.C.)

       (v)  Advanced level of an approved <u>General Certificate of Education</u> (G.C.E.)

At least 2 of the 5 passes must be at 1 of the levels specified in (iv) or (v).

    <u>or</u>      B.   4 passes obtained at 1 or more of the levels specified in (i) to (v), of which at least 3 must be at 1 of the levels specified in (iv) and (v).

The subjects in which passes are obtained under Schemes A or B must have been chosen from the approved list,[+] which includes the following:

| Level | | Subject |
|---|---|---|
| | II | English Literature |
| I | | English Language |
| I | II | Geography |
| | II | Geology |
| I | II | History |
| I | II | Ancient History |
| I | II | Economic History |
| I | II | British Constitution |
| I | II | Economics |
| I | | Logic |
| I | II | Religious Knowledge |
| I | | Greek Literature in Translation |

[+]<u>Notes</u>:    (a)  Level I means the level specified in (i), (ii), and (iii).

            (b)  Biology may not be included with Botany or Zoology.

            (c)  Mathematics (Pure and Applied) may not be included with Pure Mathematics or Applied Mathematics at Level II.

|   |    |                                 |
|---|----|---------------------------------|
| I | II | Latin                           |
| I | II | Greek                           |
| I | II | French                          |
| I | II | Pure Mathematics                |
| I |    | Additional Pure Mathematics     |
| I | II | Applied Mathematics             |
|   | II | Mathematics (Pure and Applied)  |
| I | II | Physics                         |
| I | II | Chemistry                       |
| I |    | Physics-with-Chemistry          |
| I |    | General Science                 |
| I |    | Additional General Science      |
| I | II | Botany                          |
|   | II | Zoology                         |
| I | II | Biology or General Biology      |
| I | II | Music                           |
| I | II | Art                             |
|   |    | Any other approved language     |

## Mature-Age Entry Scheme

### Conditions:

(a) Candidates must be 25 years of age, or older, on July 1 of the year in which entry is desired. They must have completed their formal school education at least 5 years before the date of application.

(b) They must be able to show that they have attended Extra-Mural classes or Residential courses (recommendations from the Extra-Mural Class Tutor or Resident Tutor are necessary), or that they have attended a residential course in an Adult Education college (recommendation from the principal of the college is necessary), or that they have a recommendation from a person acceptable to the university that they are qualified to profit from university education.

(c) If they have complied with above conditions, they must take a special entrance examination (a general paper and an essay).

Degree courses for which Mature-Age students are normally eligible are:

Bachelor of Arts
Bachelor of Science
Bachelor of Education
Bachelor of Commerce
Bachelor of Laws

Admission to the professional schools such as Medicine, Agriculture, Veterinary Science, Engineering and Architecture is considered unlikely.

Faculties:

        Arts
        Science
        Education
        Social Sciences
        Agriculture
        Medicine

School of Fine Art
Department of Extra-Mural Studies
East African School of Librarianship

Degrees and Diplomas Awarded:

New degrees and diplomas granted by University of East Africa (1963)
designated by "E.A.".

University of London degrees awarded to students entering before July
1962. Last London examinations conducted March 1965.

| Faculty | Degree | Duration of Course |
|---|---|---|
| Agriculture | B.Sc. (Agric.) | 3 yrs. |
| Arts | B.A. (Gen.) London | 3 yrs. |
| | B.A. (Hons.) London | 3 yrs. |
| | B.Sc. (Econ.) London | 3 yrs. |
| | B.A. (E.A.) | 3 yrs. |
| | Certificate in Religious Studies | 2 yrs. |
| Education | B.Ed. | 3 yrs. |
| | Diploma in Education | 1 yr. |
| Medicine | M.B., Ch.B. (E.A.) | 5 yrs. (1963) |
| | Licentiateship in Medicine and Surgery (E.A.) | 5 yrs. (prior to 1963) |
| Science | B.Sc. (Gen.) London | 3 yrs. |
| | B.Sc. (Spec.) London | 3 yrs. |
| | B.Sc. (E.A.) | 3 yrs. |
| Social Sciences | Diploma in African Studies | 1 yr. |
| | Diploma in Social Work Non-graduate | 2 yrs. |
| | Graduate | 1 yr. |
| School of Fine Art | Diploma in Fine Art (E.A.) | 4 yrs. |

| Extra-Mural Studies | Certificate of Adult Studies | 1 yr. (1965) |
| --- | --- | --- |
| East African School of Librarianship | Diploma | 2 yrs. |
| | Certificate | 6 months |

## Higher Degrees:

### Master's Degree (E.A.) - 1 year minimum

Master of Science in Agriculture - M.Sc. (Agriculture)
Master of Arts - M.A.
Master of Arts in African Studies - M.A. (African Studies)
Master of Arts in Education - M.A. (Ed.)
Master of Science - M.Sc.

### Doctor's Degree (E.A.) - 2 years minimum

Doctor of Philosophy (Ph.D.) in following Faculties:

    Arts
    Science
    Social Sciences

Doctor of Literature (D.Litt) in following Faculties:

    Arts
    Social Sciences

Doctor of Science (D.Sc.)

## Faculty of Agriculture

Entrance requirements:     Passes in Chemistry and Biology or Botany and Zoology.  At least one must be at advanced level.

Departments:    Agriculture
                Agricultural Biology
                Agricultural Chemistry

Subjects for degree include:  Botany, Chemistry, Principles of Agriculture, Zoology, Animal Physiology and Nutrition, Crop Botany, Principles of Agricultural Economics, Social Science, Agricultural Economics, Animal Production, Crop Management, and Farm Management.

Examinations required for degrees:

> First examination:  Botany, Chemistry, Principles of Agriculture, Zoology.
>
> B.Sc. (Agriculture) Part I examination:  Animal Physiology and Nutrition, Crop Botany, Principles of Agricultural Economics, Soil Science.
>
> B.Sc. (Agriculture) Part II examination:  Agricultural Economics, Animal Production, Crop Production, Farm Management.

Degrees awarded:

> Bachelor of Science (Agriculture), B.Sc. (Agric.) - 3 yrs.

Higher degree:

> Holders of B.Sc. (Agriculture) can study for Master of Science in Agriculture (E.A.).

Faculty of Arts and Social Sciences

The Faculties collaborate for the B.A. degree.

Entrance requirements for B.A. degree:

> Credit in English at Cambridge School Certificate,
>
> or  Pass at principal or subsidiary standard at Higher School Certificate in English,
>
> or  Pass in a special university entrance examination in English.

1.  Faculty of Arts

| Departments: | English | Mathematics |
|---|---|---|
|  | Geography | Religious Studies |
|  | History |  |

Examinations required for degrees:

For the first year examination any 3 of the following subjects may be offered:  Economics, English, Geography, History, Mathematics, Political Science, Religious Studies, and Sociology.

For the final examination:
> either  (i)  Any 2 of the above subjects,
> or  (ii)  Any 1 of the above subjects, excluding Political Science.

Degrees awarded:

       Bachelor of Arts - B.A. (General)      3 yrs.[+]
       Bachelor of Arts - B.A. (Honours)      3 yrs.[+]
       Bachelor of Science - B.Sc. (Economics)   3 yrs.[+]

Degrees of the University of East Africa:

       B.A. (in collaboration with the Faculty of Social Sciences)
       Diploma in Drama - 1 yr.
       M.A.
       Ph.D.
       D.Litt.
       College Certificate in Religious Studies    2 yrs. undergraduate

2.   Faculty of Social Sciences

       Departments:          Economics
                            Political Science and Public Administration
                            Sociology
                            East African Institute of Social Research

Faculty is also responsible for graduate work in African Studies.

Subjects for B.A. degree include:  Applied Mathematics, Economics, Political Science, Pure Mathematics, Religious Studies and Sociology.

Examinations required for degrees:

  For the B.A. degree, same requirements as Faculty of Arts.

  For the M.A. degree (Arts and Social Sciences), the examination consists of a dissertation, or of two or more written papers, or of a dissertation together with a written paper or papers.

Degrees awarded:

       Same as Faculty of Arts, plus:

          Diploma in Social Work          3 yrs.
             Non-graduate           2 yrs.
             Graduate              1 yr.

          Diploma in Social Studies
             Non-graduate           2 yrs.
             Graduate             6-9 mos.

[+]London degrees for students entering before 1962.

Higher degrees in Faculties of Arts and Social Sciences:

| | | |
|---|---|---|
| Master of Arts (M.A.): | Minimum period of study | 1 yr. |
| M.A. in African Studies | | 2 yrs. |
| Diploma | | 1 yr. |

Doctor of Philosophy (Ph.D.): A Bachelor of Arts (B.A.) of the University or any person admitted to the B.A. status may be expected to be registered as a candidate for M.A. (1 yr.) after which he will be admitted to the Ph.D. course.

Examinations required for degrees:

Ph.D. degree:   A candidate for the degree shall be required to submit a thesis embodying the results of his special study or research.

D.Litt. degree:   A candidate for the degree shall be required to submit an outstanding published work on some subject or subjects connected with Language, Literature, Philosophy, Mathematics, History, Geography, Economics, Political Science, Theology or Comparative Religion, or Sociology, and which falls within the scope of these studies as they are represented in the University. The works submitted shall be accompanied by a declaration that they have not been submitted for a degree in any other university.

## Faculty of Education

Entrance requirements:   (1)   For B.Ed. degree (instituted in 1963), 2 of the following subjects at advanced level:

English Literature, Geography, History, Ancient History, Economic History, British Constitution, Religious Knowledge, Pure Mathematics, Applied Mathematics, Mathematics (Pure and Applied), Physics, Chemistry, Botany, Zoology, Biology.

(2)   Diploma in Education - 1 yr. graduate course.

A General or Honours Degree studied in English,

or   A Diploma in Fine Art from a recognized university.

General University requirements.

Departments:              Education
                          Language Method
                          Educational Psychology

Courses:

   1st year:     All students take Education plus 2 other subjects
                          chosen from the following lists:

|                    A                    |                    B                    |
|-----------------------------------------|-----------------------------------------|
| Physics                                 | History                                 |
| Chemistry                               | English                                 |
| Botany          ) taken                 | Mathematics                             |
| Zoology         ) together              | Geography                               |
| Mathematics                             | Religious Knowledge                     |
| Geography                               |                                         |

   2nd year:     Education and 1 subject already taken in the 1st year
                          from the following list:

| Botany                                  | Mathematics                             |
|-----------------------------------------|-----------------------------------------|
| Zoology                                 | Geography                               |
| Chemistry                               | History                                 |
| Physics                                 | English                                 |

   3rd year:     Same subjects continued.   The Education course
                          includes:

| Philosophy of Education                 | Comparative Education                   |
|-----------------------------------------|-----------------------------------------|
| Contemporary Issues in                  | Individual Study of a                   |
|    Education              |    Special Education      |
|                                         |    Problem                |

Examinations required for degrees:

   1st year:     All students take Education and 2 other subjects chosen
                          from below:

|                    A                    |                    B                    |
|-----------------------------------------|-----------------------------------------|
| Physics                                 | History                                 |
| Chemistry                               | English                                 |
| Botany                                  | Mathematics                             |
| Zoology                                 | Geography                               |
| Mathematics                             | Religious Knowledge                     |
| Geography                               |                                         |

The subjects in the above lists will be studied in the
Faculties of Arts or Science and the courses and
examination will be identical with those for students
in those Faculties.

2nd year:        Students take Education and 1 subject studied in the
                 1st year.  Two written examinations in Education.

3rd year:        Same subjects as second year.  The final examination
                 will consist of the papers required by the Faculties
                 of Arts or Science in the subject other than Education,
                 together with 4 papers in Education, and an evaluation
                 of Practical Teaching.

Degrees awarded:

   Bachelor of Education (B.Ed.)                    3 yrs.
   Diploma in Education (Graduate)                  1 yr.

Higher degrees:

   A Bachelor of Education (B.Ed.) holder may take a Master Degree in
   Education (M.Ed.) - minimum 1 yr.
   Required:  Minimum 5 yrs. practical teaching.


Faculty of Medicine

Entrance requirements:        Passes required in 3 of the following:

                              Physics, Chemistry, and either Biology or
                              Zoology.  2 of these must be at advanced
                              level.

Departments:      Anatomy                        Medical Microbiology
                  Medicine                       Physiology
                  Obstetrics and Gynaecology     Preventive Medicine
                  Paediatrics                    Surgery
                  Pathology

Curriculum:

   Anatomy:       140 lecture hours, 450 practical work hours in 4 terms.

                  A seminar of 40 hours a year in Applied Anatomy
                  during terms 5-16.

   Physiology:    4 terms, 680 hours of instruction.

                  40 hours a year in Clinical Physiology and Biochemistry
                  during terms 5-16.

Behavioural and Social Sciences (Preventive Medicine):

                  40 lectures on Normal Psychology for 4 terms.

Pharmacology: 120 hours with Applied Pharmacology in medical wards during terms 13-16.

Microbiology: 2 years, 180 hours of practical and theory work.

Pathology: 230 hours.

Forensic Medicine:

20 hours lecture - demonstration.

Preventive Medicine:

Lecture course for 4 terms, 160 hours lecture during terms 5-16 and a 10-weeks' residential course.

Surgery: 160 hours, with weekly instruction in Surgical Pathology and Applied Anatomy and Physiology.

Obstetrics and Gynaecology:

40 hours to 2 terms of clinical instruction and community aspects of Obstetrics and Gynaecology co-operation with Department of Preventive Medicine.

Paediatrics and Child Health:

340 hours with more lectures in terms 12-16.

Medicine: 110 lectures during first 2 years. 1 year devoted to clinical instruction and Applied Anatomy and Physiology during terms 5 and 8 and 15-16 in Pharmacology, with 40 more lectures of 1 hour duration.

Examinations required for M.B., Ch.B. degrees:

Anatomy, Physiology and Biochemistry, Pharmacology, Pathology, Forensic Medicine, Microbiology, Paediatrics, Preventive Medicine, Medicine and Therapeutics, Obstetrics and Gynaecology, Surgery.

Degrees awarded:

Licentiateship in Medicine and Surgery (E.A.) - Before 1963
M.B., Ch.B. Degree (E.A.)            5 yrs.

Faculty of Science

Entrance requirements:        Passes in 2 of the following subjects:

Biology, Botany, Chemistry, Geography, Mathematics, Physics, Zoology, as specified

in General Entrance Requirements, A (iv)
and (v).   (See page 7).

Advanced level passes required for Pure
Mathematics and Applied Mathematics.

Departments:          Botany                         Mathematics
                      Chemistry                      Physics
                      Geography (including Geology)   Zoology

Subjects for degree include:   Applied Mathematics, Botany, Chemistry,
                               Geography, Geology, Mathematics, Physics,
                               Pure Mathematics, Zoology, Economics,
                               Anatomy and Physiology.

Examinations required for degrees:

   For the 1st year examination, 3 of the following subjects may be
   offered:          Botany, Chemistry, Geography, Geology, Mathematics,
                     Pure Mathematics, Applied Mathematics, Physics,
                     Zoology.

   For the final examination a candidate must offer:
   either     (i)   2 of the subjects:  Botany, Chemistry, Geography,
                    Mathematics, Physics, Zoology,
   or         (ii)  1 of the subjects:  Botany, Chemistry, Geography,
                    Mathematics, Physics.

   M.Sc. degree:    The examination for the degree shall consist of 2 or
                    more written papers, or of a dissertation, or of a
                    dissertation with 1 or more written papers.

   Ph.D. degree:    A candidate for the degree shall be required to submit
                    a thesis embodying the results of his special study
                    or research.

   D.Sc.:           A candidate for the degree shall be required to submit
                    an outstanding published work on some subject or sub-
                    jects connected with the mathematical, physical,
                    natural or applied sciences, and falling within the
                    scope of the studies represented in the University.
                    All works submitted shall be accompanied by a decla-
                    ration that they have not been submitted for a degree
                    in any other university.

Degrees awarded:

   Bachelor of Science (B.Sc.)                  3 yrs.

Higher degrees:

   Holders of B.Sc. degree from any recognized university may study for
   advanced degrees:  M.Sc., Ph.D., D.Sc.

Master of Science (M.Sc.)              1 yr.(minimum)


School of Fine Art

Entrance requirements:     The General University Entrance Requirements
                           for degree courses are not applicable.
                           Candidates must satisfy a general educational
                           requirement and pass special entrance exami-
                           nation in Art.

              (1)  General:

                   Candidates should hold a School Certificate
                   with 5 credits (including 1 in English
                   Language), or an approved equivalent.

              (2)  Entrance examination - 4 sections:

                   (a)  A painted composition, a set subject
                        or a composition modelled in clay.
                   (b)  A drawing in any black-and-white medium
                        from a living model.
                   (c)  An essay describing any craft.
                   (d)  A design with a simple geometric basis
                        will be supplied.  The candidate must
                        copy and complete the design to a
                        larger scale.

Subjects:      General, Painting, Modelling and Sculpture, Illustration,
               Print Making.

Syllabus for Diploma in Fina Art (E.A.):

               Objective Study, Life Drawing, Basic Design, Design,
               Illustration and Print Making, Painting, Modelling,
               Sculpture and Ceramics, History of Art.

Examinations required for diploma:

     1st year:      All of the following courses:

                    History of Art            Critical Essay
                    Life Drawing              Design
                    Objective Study           Modelling
                    Painting                  Print Making

     2nd year:      All of the following courses:

                    History of Art            Critical Essay
                    Life Drawing              Design
                    Objective Study           Print Making
                    Painting                  Modelling

Candidates who successfully pass the 2nd year examination will qualify for the award of an <u>Intermediate
Fine Art Certificate</u>.

For candidates pursuing final degree, years 3 and 4 offer the following
choices:

<u>3rd year</u>:        General

Life Drawing                    Modelling[+]
Painting[+]                     History of Art
Print Making[+]                 Critical Essay
Design[+]

[+]A combination of only 2 of these examinations is
  necessary.

Painting

Life Drawing                    Critical Essay
Techniques and Methods          History of Art
Painting

Modelling

Life Drawing                    Critical Essay
Modelling                       History of Art
Techniques and Methods

Illustration and Print Making

Life Drawing                    Techniques and
Print Making and                   Methods
   Illustration                 Critical Essay
                                History of Art

<u>4th year</u>:        General

Life Drawing
Painting <u>or</u> Print Making <u>or</u> Illustration <u>or</u> Modelling
   <u>or</u> Ceramics
Practical examination in alternative subject
A thesis

Painting:  Modelling and Sculpture:  Engraving and
              Illustration

Life Drawing
Presentation of major work
Practical examination in alternative subject
A thesis

Before graduation, students required to write a thesis.

Diplomas awarded:

Diploma in Fina Art (E.A.)    4 yrs.

Holders of the Diploma in Fine Art (E.A.) are admitted to a 1-yr. Graduate Diploma in Education Course.


## Department of Extra-Mural Studies

The Department began activities in 1953 and expanded programs in Tanganyika (Tanzania) and Kenya until the latter two countries incorporated the work into their own University Colleges by 1963.

The programs are multi-racial for all whose knowledge of English is sufficient to permit their benefiting from attendance.  The main work of the Department is providing regular classes of 5 weeks' to 2 years' duration, meeting once or twice weekly.  There are both resident and non-resident courses, including the following:

| | |
|---|---|
| Literature | Political and Social Sciences |
| English | Natural Science |
| French | Philosophy |
| History | Psychology |
| Geography | Art |
| Agriculture | Music |

Subjects depend upon desire of the students and availability of qualified tutors.


## Certificate in Adult Studies (Initiated 1965)

Entrance requirements:          21 years of age or over.
                                Written examination.

2 types of program offered:     Full-time residential course, 1 yr.

                                Evening classes, non-residential, 2-3 yrs.
                                (Examination may be taken in 2 parts)

Examinations:  4 papers as follows:

                                English, Development of the Modern World,
                                Social Science (3 hrs. each).

                                General Essay (1½ hrs.).

East African School of Librarianship

Certificate Course, Library Assistants (6 mos.)

Subjects:        Organization, Technical Processes, Services to Readers.

Diploma Course, Librarians (2 yrs.)

Syllabus to be prescribed.


VOCATIONAL AND TECHNICAL EDUCATION

G O V E R N M E N T   T E C H N I C A L   T R A I N I N G   (Department of
                                                            Education)

Publicly-provided training.

3 levels of technical training:

    Rural Crafts Centres
    Trade Schools and Secondary Technical Schools
    Technical Institutes and Colleges


RURAL CRAFTS CENTRES or RURAL TRADE SCHOOLS

Village craft schools:    Housebuilding and furniture making
Agricultural schools:     Cultivation of small holdings, rearing of
                          poultry and cattle, etc.

Boys:    3-year course in post-primary training at handyman or artisan
         level in village crafts and agriculture.

         25% of school time spent in classroom instruction on following
         subjects:
                          English
                          Arithmetic
                          Drawing
                          Care and use of tools or Crop and Animal Husbandry

Girls:   2-year course for primary school leavers in Homecraft and
         Vocational Centres.

Curriculum:    Practical Training in Household Management, Child Care,
               Needlework, Dressmaking, etc.  Also includes English,
               Arithmetic, Religion, Physical Training.

               2 centers offer more advanced courses in Handicrafts and
               Dressmaking; training for School Matron and Caterer.  3-year
               vocational courses.

TRADE SCHOOLS and SECONDARY TECHNICAL SCHOOLS

2 technical schools.
10 senior secondary technical schools - craft or "modern" syllabus
                                   (G.C.E. 'O' level)

Older form of Kampala Technical Institute operated along lines of trade
school before reorganization in 1962.

| 3-year courses in following trades: | Brickwork, Woodwork, Motor Vehicle Maintenance, Machine Shop Engineering, Foundry Work, Plumbing and Pipe Fitting, Electrical Installation, Boat-building, Painting and Decorating, Shoemaking and Tailoring. |
|---|---|
| Trade course, entry requirements: | 3-year junior secondary training. Students with only 6 or 7 years previous training required to take 2-yr. pre-technical course offered at most technical schools. |

Curriculum:    English, Arithmetic, Science, History, Geography, Arts and
               Handicrafts.

Uganda Junior Technical Certificate examination at conclusion of 3rd year
for trade training students.  Practical examinations conducted by teachers
and trade testing officers.  (This certificate serves as School Leaving
Certificate whose standard in various subjects qualifies students for
senior trade course or technical teacher training at the Institute.  Not
professional diploma.)

Following 3-year trade course, 1-yr. apprenticeship allowed by employers
for apprentices to acquire further technical education.

In 1963, 5 existing technical schools converted into senior secondary
schools.  The 5 remaining schools expanded enrollment, providing 4-year
Craft courses leading to City and Guilds Intermediate Certificate (in
future to be known as First Craft Certificate).

1963 proposals:
  (a)  To accept success in Certificate examinations after 4-year
       Craft courses in place of former Ministry of Works Trade tests.

  (b)  To close or transform all existing trade schools into proposed
       new type of secondary school (with technical bias); to incorpo-
       rate agriculture and craft education in one school wherever
       possible.

  (c)  To establish full-time courses equivalent to apprenticeship.

TECHNICAL COLLEGES

1 Technical College in each of the 4 provinces and 1 Central Government
Technical College in Kampala.  All prepare for First Craft Examination,
City and Guilds.


Professional Engineering Section

Entrance requirements:          Higher School Certificate

Program - 3 yrs:      Mechanical Engineering, Electrical Engineering,
                      Civil Engineering.

A diploma is awarded.


Technicians Section

Entrance requirements:          School Certificate

Program:  3 yrs.

Training for:         Mechanical and Electrical engineers
                      Building and Civil engineers
                      Laboratory technicians
                      Tele-communications technicians


Advanced Craft Training Section

Entrance requirements:          Craft  level  training.  (Candidates from the
                                4 up-country technical schools with a craft
                                level qualification.)

Courses offered:      Motor Vehicle Mechanics      Carpentry and Joinery
                      Electrical Installation      Concrete Block Work
                      Machine Shop Engineering


UGANDA TECHNICAL COLLEGE, Kampala   (Formerly Kampala Technical Institute)

Established in 1921 as Kampala Technical School with training for Building,
Motor Vehicle, and Tailoring students (virtually a trade school).  In 1953
it was moved to Kyambogo and combined with the School of Building and Civil
Engineering, the Muljibhai Madhvani School of Commerce, the School of
Mechanical and Electrical Engineering, and the School of Science and
Mathematics.

Entrance was at Form IV (School Certificate level), preparing for both
G.C.E. ordinary level and advanced level examinations.  The Engineering
School trained for Ordinary and Higher Certificates of City and Guilds.
Close relationship with Loughborough Technical College, England, was
maintained where students completed Diploma of Technology.

In 1962, the Institute was reorganized and upgraded with assistance from UNESCO.   In 1965, it became the Uganda Technical College when courses were provided for higher technical training of technologists, technicians and skilled craftsmen.   Courses are conducted in association with the University of Strathclyde, Scotland, leading to graduate membership in the major British engineering institutions.   New course for the Uganda Diploma in Engineering initiated in 1965.

The Uganda Technical College has been approved to conduct courses preparing students for Technician or Higher Technician status, leading to the award of Technician Diplomas in Mechanical and Electrical Engineering, and Building and Civil Engineering of the City and Guilds of London Institute.[+]

In the Technician Diploma courses, students later intending to specialize in either Mechanical or Electrical Engineering take the same basic subjects during the first 2 years.   In 3rd year, there are certain optional subjects for the final examination.   This also applies to the Technician Diploma Course in Building and Civil Engineering.   Courses for Higher Technician Diplomas, specializing in the separate fields of Electrical Engineering, Civil Engineering, Mechanical Engineering and Building, will be started if the demand arises.

Examinations set by City and Guilds are in 2 stages.   Students required to take at one time all papers relevant to each stage of the course, and must pass in all subjects of 1st stage before proceeding to 2nd stage.

Students required to have passed Cambridge School Certificate in appropriate subjects or to have attained an equivalent qualification.


Department of Civil Engineering and Building

Diploma in Civil Engineering Course

3-year, full-time course.   Professional level.

Entrance requirements:          Candidates should be

either  (a)  Holders of either a City and Guilds Technician Certificate in Mechanical Engineering or Technician Diploma in 'Mechanical and Electrical' Engineering or Technician Diploma in 'Building and Civil Engineering; or an Ordinary National Certificate or Diploma in Mechanical Engineering.

or      (b)  Holders of a Higher School Certificate with Mathematics and Physics at principal level, and English and 2 other subjects at credit level, or an equivalent G.C.E. at advanced and ordinary levels.

[+]Current prospectus may be obtained from City and Guilds of London Institute, 76 Portland Place, London, W1.

Courses:

    1st year:        Mathematics                     Applied Mechanics
                          Principles of Electricity    Heat, Light and Sound
                          Applied Chemistry             Engineering Workshops
                          English and Liberal Studies

    2nd and 3rd
         years:      Subjects selected from:

Mechanics of Fluids        Surveying
Hydraulics                   Geology and Soil
Strength of Materials and    Mechanics
   Theory and Structures    Civil Engineering
Theory and Design of        Construction
   Structures               Mathematics
                                   Liberal Studies

## Ordinary Technician Diploma in Building and Civil Engineering Course

3-year, full-time course.

This course supersedes the 3-year, full-time course leading to City and Guilds Ordinary Certificate in Building conducted by this Department. Last enrollment June, 1963, ending June 1966.

Students prepared for City and Guilds Ordinary Technician Diploma in Building and Civil Engineering.

Entrance requirements:       Cambridge School Certificate with
                                Mathematics, Science and English,

               or      a certificate of equivalent standard.

Courses:

Mathematics                     Elementary Quantity
Geometry                        Surveying
Building Construction         Industrial Orientation
Mechanics, Physics and Chemistry  English and General
Structures                     Studies
Surveying and Levelling       Workshop Technology and
Properties of Materials        Practice

College examinations at end of 1st year.

City and Guilds examinations at end of 2nd and 3rd years.

## East Africa Institute of Architects' Building Technicians Certificate Course

3-year, full-time course.

Entrance requirements:        Cambridge School Certificate in appropriate
                              subjects,

                    or   certificate of equivalent standard.

Students entering course eligible for Probationer class of membership of
East Africa Institute of Architects (E.A.I.A.) and upon passing exami-
nations are eligible for Building Technician class of membership of
E.A.I.A.

Courses:

    1st and 2nd    Courses common to City and Guilds Ordinary Diploma
       years:      in Building course.

    3rd year:      Specializes in technique of architectural draughts-
                   manship and work of subprofessional grade required
                   by technicians in architects' and government offices.

Examinations at end of 3-year course for E.A.I.A. in following:

        Physics of Building         Techniques of Expression
        Elements of Construction    Supervision of Buildings

Oral examination and a Survey Testimony of Study also required.

    Candidates holding City and Guilds Ordinary Certificate in
    Building exempt from examinations in Physics of Building
    and Elements of Construction.


Advanced Building Craft Courses

9-month, full-time course.

Entrance requirements:        Candidates should hold City and Guilds
                              Craft Certificate and be in employment
                              appropriate to the course.

Courses:

    Craft Theory, Associated Subjects and Craft Practice required by
    City and Guilds; other subjects relevant to the craft.

Examination:   City and Guilds of London Institute Advanced Craft
               Certificate


Painters and Decorators Course

1½ year, full-time course.

Prepares students for City and Guilds Advanced Craft Certificate in
Painters and Decorators Work.

Part-Time Courses

3-year, part-time day basis.

(1)   Measurement and Estimating of Builders Work

Course (if demand for it arises) designed for Technicians in
Building Industry and in offices of Quantity Surveyors.

Leads to City and Guilds examinations.   (3 year, part-time day basis.)

Entrance requirements:   Employment in appropriate work.

Good knowledge of building construction,
architects' detail and layout drawings,
and mathematics.

Examinations:   1st year: 'City and Guilds' Builders' Quantities I

2nd year: 'City and Guilds' Builders' Quantities II,
Section A.

3rd year: 'City and Guilds' Builders' Quantities II,
Section B.

or   City and Guilds of London Institute Certificate, Builders Quantities II, Section C.


(2)   Geology, Soil Mechanics and Foundations

Course (if demand for it arises) designed for Technicians in
Building, Civil Engineers and Architects, and to acquaint students
with Soil Engineering. (1-year, part-time day basis.)

Entrance requirements:   Employment in building, civil engineering or
architectural fields and holders of Ordinary
Certificate of City and Guilds.

No examination at end of course.


Department of Electrical Engineering

Diploma in Electrical Engineering Course

3-year, full-time course.  Professional level.

Entrance requirements:        Candidates should be

either   (a)  Holders of a City and Guilds Technician
Certificate in Electrical Engineering; or an
Ordinary National Certificate or Diploma in

Electrical Engineering.  Good final examination results required.

or    (b)   Holders of Higher School Certificate with
Mathematics and Physics at principal level,
and English and 2 other subjects at credit
level; or an equivalent G.C.E. at 'A' and
'O' levels.

The 1st year of the course will be common with courses for Diploma in
Mechanical Engineering and Diploma in Civil Engineering.

| | | |
|---|---|---|
| 1st year: | Mathematics | Applied Mechanics |
| | Principles of Electricity | Heat, Light and Sound |
| | Applied Chemistry | Engineering Workshops |
| | English and Liberal Studies | |

2nd and 3rd    Subjects selected from:
years:
Mathematics                     Testing Methods
Mechanical Technology           Electric Utilization
Electrical Engineering          Electrical Supply
Advanced Electrical             Liberal Studies
   Engineering

## Ordinary Technician Diploma in 'Mechanical and Electrical' Engineering Course

The original City and Guilds Ordinary Certificate course in Electrical
Engineering has been operating since 1959.  Present courses finish in
June 1966.

These courses replaced by City and Guilds Ordinary Technician Diploma
course in 'Mechanical and Electrical' Engineering.

See Department of Mechanical Engineering for details of this course.

## Telecommunication Technicians Course

9-month, full-time.  Students then expected to be employed in industry,
returning to the College for sandwich course of 2 periods of full-time
attendance, each about 13 weeks, spread over 2 years duration.

Entrance requirements:          Cambridge School Certificate or equivalent
                                qualification.  Preference to those with
                                credits in Mathematics, Science, and English.

Course leads to City and Guilds of London Institute Telecommunication
Technician Certificates.

In addition to main subjects of course, other electrical engineering subjects are studied along with a full range of experimental work.


Electrical Installation Work Course

(1)   Course 'B', 4-month, full-time.

      Entrance requirements:   Uganda Junior Technical Certificate in this subject.

      Course:   Students prepared for City and Guilds examination in Electrical Installation Work.


(2)   Course 'C', 1-year, full-time.

      Entrance requirements:   City and Guilds Electrical Installation Work Certificate.

      Course:   Students prepared for City and Guilds final examination.


Department of Mechanical Engineering

Diploma in Mechanical Engineering Course

3-year, full-time course.   Professional level.

Entrance requirements:          Candidates should be

            either   (a)   Holders of a City and Guilds Technician Certificate in Mechanical Engineering or Technician Diploma in 'Mechanical and Electrical' Engineering; or an Ordinary National Certificate or Diploma in Mechanical Engineering.   Good final examination results required.

            or       (b)   Holders of a Higher School Certificate with Mathematics and Physics at principal level, and English and 2 other subjects at credit level; or an equivalent G.C.E. at 'A' and 'O' levels.

The 1st year of the course will be common with courses for the Diploma in Electrical Engineering and the Diploma in Civil Engineering.

      1st year:     Mathematics                 Applied Mechanics
                    Principles of Electricity   Heat, Light and Sound
                    Applied Chemistry           Engineering Workshops
                    English and Liberal Studies

| 2nd and 3rd years: | Subjects selected from: | |
|---|---|---|
| | Mechanics of Fluids | Motive Power Engineering |
| | Mechanics of Machines | Engineering Design |
| | Properties and Strength of Materials | Electrotechnology |
| | Applied Thermodynamics | Mathematics |
| | Ventilation, Air Conditioning and Refrigeration | Liberal Studies |

## Ordinary Technician Diploma in 'Mechanical and Electrical' Engineering Course

3-year, full-time course.

Entrance requirements:     Cambridge School Certificate with credits in Mathematics, Science and English, or other equivalent qualification.

The original City and Guilds Ordinary Certificate course in Mechanical Engineering operating since 1959 will finish in June 1966 for the 1963 intake.

These courses replaced by City and Guilds Ordinary Technician Diploma course in 'Mechanical and Electrical' Engineering.

Course subjects:

| 1st and 2nd years: | Mathematics | Engineering Drawing |
|---|---|---|
| | Mechanical Engineering Science | Workshop Technology |
| | Electrical Engineering Science | Workshop Practice |
| | Physics and Chemistry | Industrial Orientation |
| | | English and General Studies |

| 3rd year: | Mathematics | Automobile Engines and Prime Movers |
|---|---|---|
| | Engineering Drawing | Workshop Practice |
| | Mechanical Engineering | Industrial Orientation |
| | Electrical Engineering | English and General Studies |
| | Power Production | |

Examinations held at end of each year as follows:

| 1st year: | College examination |
|---|---|
| 2nd year: | City and Guilds, 1st examination |
| 3rd year: | City and Guilds, 2nd examination |

## Motor Vehicle Mechanics Work Course

4-month, full-time course.

Entrance requirements:          Uganda Junior Technical Certificate in this
                                work.

Course:    Leads to City and Guilds examination Motor Vehicle Mechanics
           Work.


## Foundry Practice and Patternmaking Course

1st part of course common to both trades; later specialization.

City and Guilds examination in either Patternmaking or Foundry Practice.


## Department of Science and Mathematics

Provides teaching for the whole College in Science and Mathematics.


## Higher School Certificate in Science Subjects and Mathematics Course

2-year, full-time course.

Entrance requirements:          School Certificate with at least good credit
                                standard in relevant subjects.

Following curricula are available:

|  | | |
|---|---|---|
| (1) | Physics ) | Principal |
|  | Mathematics ) | level |
|  | Chemistry ) | |
|  | General Paper ) | Subsidiary |
|  | Technical Drawing ) | level |
| (2) | Physics ) | Principal |
|  | Pure Mathematics ) | level |
|  | Applied Mathematics ) | |
|  | General Paper ) | Subsidiary |
|  | Technical Drawing ) | level |
| or | Chemistry ) | |


## Science Laboratory Technicians Certificate Course

1-year, full-time course.

Entrance requirements:       <u>School Certificate</u> with credits in Science subjects and Mathematics, or an equivalent <u>G.C.E.</u>, '0' level.

Course:    General training in Laboratory Techniques and the associated Arts and Sciences.

Most candidates expected to be sponsored by employers, but private candidates also accepted.

Examination:   <u>City and Guilds Laboratory Technicians' Certificate</u>.


## Science Laboratory Technicians Advanced Certificate Course

Sandwich course:  3  12-weekly periods of attendance.

Entrance requirements:       <u>City and Guilds Science Laboratory Technicians Certificate</u>


## School Certificate (Technical) Course

4-year course.

Course finished as of 1965.

Subjects formerly taught:

|  |  |  |
|---|---|---|
| English | | Technical Drawing |
| Mathematics | | Building Construction |
| Physics | or | Engineering Workshop Theory |
| Chemistry | | and Practice |
| Geography | | |


## English and Liberal Studies Section

This section provides teaching in English and Liberal Studies in all departments and sections of the College.


## Industrial Ceramics Section

3-year, full-time course.

Entrance requirements:       <u>Junior Secondary Leaving Certificate</u>. (Higher qualifications desirable.)

Course:    In addition to industrial methods of manufacture, artistic
           ceramic projects, procurement and preparation of clay, etc.,
           Mathematics, Science and English are studied during each year
           of the course.

Examinations held annually.


## Women's Studies Section

This section conducts courses in Dressmaking for young women.

Course prepared for City and Guilds examination in Dressmaking.


# G O V E R N M E N T   A G R I C U L T U R A L   T R A I N I N G
## (Within Department of Education)

## FARM SCHOOLS

8 schools as of 1959.

Entrance requirements:          Junior Secondary Leaving Certificate

Length of course:    2 years.

Only Wairaka Farm School developed successful results.

1963 proposals:     Closing of former farm schools to be reorganized
                    into 4 inter-denominational farm schools.

New farm schools (patterned after Wairaka model).

Entrance requirements:          Primary VII

Course:    4 years providing technical training (Agriculture and General
           Education).


## AGRICULTURE IN OTHER SCHOOLS

A.    Primary Schools

      1963 proposal:          To provide practical Rural Science and Geography
                              courses to stimulate interest in Agriculture.

B.    Secondary Schools

      1963 proposals: (1) Curriculum in new high schools (4 years) to
                          include for both boys and girls a course in
                          Agricultural Biology at a School Certificate

level (supplying candidates for higher standards
of agricultural education).

(2) New secondary school (3 years) with agricultural
bias offering Farming Principles, Techniques of
Crop Production, and Animal Care.


# G O V E R N M E N T   A G R I C U L T U R A L   T R A I N I N G
## (Within Ministry of Agriculture)

Agricultural training, apart from that given within the Department of
Education (secondary schools and Faculty of Agriculture, Makerere University College), is provided at the following levels:


## AGRICULTURAL COLLEGES

Previously called "Farm Institutes."  Bukalasa and Arapai established in
1956.

Aim to provide:        Sound farming practice and management.

                       Field staff for Department of Agriculture and
                       Department of Veterinary Services and Animal
                       Industry.

                       Teaching staff for District Farm Institutes.

                       Teachers of Agriculture equipped to teach up to
                       School Certificate level and at teacher training
                       colleges.

Entrance requirements:         Originally Junior Secondary Leaving Certi-
                               ficate.  Later extended to School Certificate
                               level.

Length of courses:     2-year course leading to Certificate.

                       3-year course leading to Diploma (comparable to
                       National Diploma of Agriculture in the United
                       Kingdom).

                       5-year course (planned) post-School Certificate
                       training for East African Diploma of Agriculture.

Language of instruction:       English.

2-year course common to all students.  Specialization begins for those
students entering government service, either Department of Agriculture or
Department of Veterinary Services and Animal Industry.

Curriculum:     English, Arithmetic and General Knowledge throughout course.

Structure of soils, plants, and animals     1 term

Development and function of soils, plants,
and animals                                 1 term

Soil science, crop husbandry, animal
husbandry, farm management, and farm
economics                                   3 terms

Disease or pests of plants and animals,
deficiencies in soils and the cure,
control and prevention                      1 term

Practical Work:
Demonstration in laboratory or on farm, field training
and actual work on the farm.

## DISTRICT FARM INSTITUTES

Established 1959.  Gradually expanding into all districts of the country.
Short, practical courses of improved farming for practicing farmers and
others engaged in community development, co-operative and other forms of
rural improvement.

Length of courses:  2-3 weeks to a year.

1963 proposals:     Strengthening of staff and general expansion of
                    these vitally productive farm institutes.

## G O V E R N M E N T   T R A I N I N G
### (Professional, Administrative, and Extension Services)

## UGANDA SCHOOL OF VETERINARY SCIENCES

(1)  Certificate Course

Entrance requirements:   Candidates should have attempted Cambridge
                         School Certificate, preferably with passes
                         in Biology and Mathematics.

Program:  2 years.

(2)  Diploma in Animal Husbandry

Entrance requirements:   Completion of Certificate course and passing
                         of Science through the 2-year course.

Program:  1 year.

## MEDICAL SERVICES

(1) <u>Post-Standard VIII (or X)</u>

Junior Auxiliaries.   2-3 year course.

Training for Assistant Nurse, Assistant Health Visitor, Graded Dresser, and other medical assistantships.

(2) <u>School Certificate Entry</u>

(a) Form IV education requiring technical training for:

Radiography Assistants   )
Laboratory Assistants    )     3-year course
Dispensers               )

(b) Grade:  Medical Assistants.  (Original training, nursing syllabus only.)

1962, course 3 years including clinical training qualifying for simple duties of a medical officer.  Course started at Mbale.

(3) <u>Graduate Entry</u>

Makerere University College degree course.  (Associated with Mulago Hospital.)

Internationally recognized medical qualification.

## NURSES TRAINING

2 courses offered at Mulago Hospital, Kampala.

(1) <u>Uganda Certificated Nurses</u>

Entrance requirements:   Minimum of 9 years of schooling.
Program:  2 years, 9 months.

(2) <u>Uganda Registered Nurses</u>

Entrance requirements:   <u>Cambridge School Certificate</u> or equivalent.
Program:  3 years.
Syllabus: Similar to that of the General Council of Nursing for England and Wales.

## ADMINISTRATION

Intensive training and upgrading for qualified candidates for clerical executive, and administrative positions, and for central, provincial, and local government administration.

Courses offered at Nsamizi College (Court training) and Makerere University College, Department of Politics (course in Public Administration).

(1) Clerical Level

   Entrance requirements:   Form IV or failed School Certificate.

   Existing clerks (in or outside government) are upgraded.

(2) Executive Level

   Entrance requirements:   School Certificate.
   Training for middle grade executives.

(3) District Assistants

   Entrance requirements:   School Certificate.

   Training for Junior Administrative Grade in provincial administration and local government.

(4) District Officers

   Entrance requirements:   University graduates (when possible).
                            Some trainees train from District Assistant experience.

(5) Senior Administrators

   Entrance requirements:   Degree or experience.


UGANDA FISHERY SCHOOL

Opened 1964.

Program:  2 years.


OTHER  DEPARTMENTAL  TRAINING
   (Ministry of Works, Departments of Co-operation and Community Development)

(1) Standard VIII Entry

   Artisans, lowest level of field services, clerks.

(2) School Certificate Entry

   Technical and laboratory assistants, junior officers in co-operatives, community development, etc.

Senior clerks, store-keepers, Ministry of Works trainees for
inspectorate and assistant (sub-professional) grades in all Departments.

On smaller scale there are courses for special and junior positions
for work as the following:  Game rangers, water bailiffs, forest
rangers.  (Forest Department - Nyabyeya Forest School offers 2-year
course for School Certificate students, including academic studies
as well as research and practical work.)

The Department of Survey, Lands and Mines offers following courses
at secondary or secondary continuation level:

    (a)  5-year course for School Certificate students leading to
          qualifications as Assistant Surveyor or Surveyor.

    (b)  Plane Tabler courses for Junior Secondary III Certificate
          students.

(3)  Graduate Entry

Training for Engineers, Quantity Surveyors, Surveyors, professional
Accountants, etc.

These grades will come from professional courses planned at the
Royal College, Kenya.

C O M M E R C I A L   T R A I N I N G

DEPARTMENT OF PROFESSIONAL STUDIES

(1)  Advanced Level Course

Entrance requirements:  Cambridge School Certificate, Grade I or II
or equivalent, with credit in English and
Mathematics.

Candidates taking Economic Geography must
have passed at credit level in Geography.

Program:  English, Economics, General Principles of Law, Accountancy
or Economic Geography.

Length of course:  1 year.

Final qualification:  General Certificate.

(2)  Ordinary Certificate in Business Studies

Entrance requirements:

either (a) A General Certificate of Education (G.C.E.
ordinary level) in English and 2 other subjects from Mathematics, Geography, History,

Science, Commerce and a language other than
English.

<u>or</u>    (b)    A pass in some other approved examination
or equivalent standard as in (a).

Subjects:        Structure of Commerce, English, Accounting, Economic
Geography, Principles of English Law, Elements of
Statistics.

(3)    <u>Part-Time Evening Courses</u>

Starting September 1965.

Intermediate Accountants (ACCA)
Bankers (IOB)
Secretaries (CIS and CS)
Final Secretaries (CIS and CS)

(4)    <u>Diploma in Office Management</u>

(a)    Stenographic Course

Entrance requirements:    <u>Cambridge School Certificate</u> with
credit in English.

Subjects:        English, Shorthand, Typewriting, Commerce,
Principles of Accounts, Arithmetic, Office
Organization and Methods.

Length of course:    1 year.

(b)    Business Training Course

Entrance requirements:    <u>Cambridge School Certificate</u> with
credit in English.

Subjects:        As above, but without Shorthand.

Length of course:    1 year.

1963 proposals:    To include Commercial Studies section in new
secondary schools (3 years) offering 2-year course
preceded by 1 year of general education.

To offer in the part-time evening classes at Uganda
Technical College courses leading to 'A' level of the
Associated Examining Board, and final examinations of
professional bodies such as the Institute of Chartered
Secretaries.

To transfer commercial courses leading to Intermediate
Examination of the Association of Certified and

Corporate Accountants, presently held at Nakawa, to Uganda Technical College.

To offer facilities to train audio (dicta)-typists.

# I N D U S T R I A L   A N D   C O M M E R C I A L   T R A I N I N G
## (Private Institutions and Public Utilities)

## PUBLIC UTILITIES

Uganda Electricity Board, Jinga. All main grades. Higher training available through supplemental U.K. training centers.

## PRIVATE FIRMS

East African Tobacco Company, Jinga. In service training with higher courses offered by U.K. centers and attachments.

Banks. Training offered at clerical, School Certificate and professsional examination entry; U.K. branches provide temporary attachments or training.

Kilembe Copper Mine. In-service training offered.

Uganda Company. Estate managers, technical and commercial staff given in-service training.

Uganda Development Corporation. Certain grades of training for Uganda Hotels (sub-section).

Uganda Sugar Plantations.

Coffee, Sisal and Other Plantations. Agricultural and Processing Enterprises. Co-operatives. Milling. Local and in-service training offered for assistant estate managers, secretarial, clerical and accounting work. Some artisan and technical training.

Most boys and girls recruited for above training after Standard VIII. Artisan training usually requires trade school qualification. School Certificate necessary for commercial work taken in nearest technical institute.

## TEACHER EDUCATION

Teaching is the largest employment opportunity for qualified Africans. Profession includes Africans, Asians and Europeans. Training provided by voluntary agencies and government.

TRAINING FOR PRIMARY SCHOOL TEACHERS

By 1961, 26 recognized Primary Teacher Training Colleges:  1 Muslim (government-operated in conjunction with Muslim Education Association), 15 Roman Catholic, 10 Protestant.

Grade I.  Vernacular Teachers

Teaching Primary 1 and 2.

Entrance requirements:  6-year Primary School.

Course:  1-year program qualifying to teach in vernacular.

(No recruitment at Grade I level since 1958.)

Grade II.  Primary School Teachers

Teaching Primary 1 through 6.

Entrance requirements:  Junior Secondary (Primary 8).
(Prior 1961 entry:  6-year Primary.)

Length of course:  4 years.

2 years of general subjects similar to primary school syllabus and 2 years teaching methods.

Every student has 12 weeks of supervised teaching practice.

Grade III.  Junior Secondary Teachers

Teaching Primary 7 and 8.

4 Junior Secondary Training Colleges:  Central Government College, Kyambogo (trains majority), Shimoni Government College, 1 Protestant, 1 Roman Catholic.

Entrance requirements:  General Certificate of Education
            or  Cambridge School Certificate
                (12 years of schooling)

Course:  2-year program.

<u>Junior Secondary School Training College</u>

<u>TYPICAL TIMETABLE</u>
(2-year course)

| <u>Subjects</u> | <u>Hours per Week</u> |
|---|---|
| Education[+] | 2 |
| English (as foreign language) | 4 |
| Mathematics | 4 |
| Physical Education[++] | 2 |
| Bible Knowledge (Religion) | 1 |
| Blackboard Work, Visual Aids | 2 |
| Electives: | |
|     Art | |
|     Civics | 4 |
|     Music | |
| Geography, General Science or History | 4 |
| Total | 23 |

[+]Minimum of 11 weeks of supervised teaching practice in professional studies period.

[++]4 hours per week at advanced level.

In addition to stress in English and Mathematics, specialist courses may be studied in following:

| <u>Group A</u> | <u>Group B</u> |
|---|---|
| Geography | Art |
| History | Civics |
| Science | Music |

1963 proposals for Primary School Teacher Training:

> To reduce 31 to 18 Primary and Junior Secondary Teacher Training colleges.

> To expand Kyambogo Training Centre (present School Certificate entry) Primary Teacher Training.

> To reduce 4-year training to 3-year program when all colleges require School Certificate entry.

> To extend in-service training at Nakawa Centre in use of English as teaching medium.

<u>TRAINING FOR SECONDARY SCHOOL TEACHERS</u>

Grade IV. <u>Secondary School Teachers</u>

> Teaching Senior Secondary Forms I and II.

Entrance requirements:   Grade III Teachers' Certificate.

Length of course:        1-year training program offered out-
                         standing Primary teachers for up-grading
                         to Secondary School teaching.

Grade V.   Secondary School Teachers

Teaching up to School Certificate level.

Entrance requirements:   Higher School Certificate and at least
                         2 examinations at principal level.

Length of course:        2-year Undergraduate Diploma in
                         Education formerly offered at Makerere
                         College.

Above course being phased out as of 1963 with emphasis on Graduate
Teacher Training (see below).

1963 proposals for Secondary School Teacher Training:

        To introduce a 1-year Diploma Course at Higher School
        Certificate entry at Kyambogo Training College,
        teaching lower forms of High Schools.

        To initiate a 1-year course operated jointly by Uganda
        Technical College (Kampala Technical Institute) and
        Kyambogo Training College for training craftsmen and
        technicians in teaching methods.

        To expand commercial teacher training in the same
        manner.

## TRAINING FOR GRADUATE TEACHERS

(1)   Degree Course in Faculty of Education.
      B.Ed. (3 years) with B.A. or B.Sc.

(2)   1-year Graduate Course leading to Diploma in Education.

(See Makerere University College, Faculty of Education.)

## TRAINING FOR HOME ECONOMICS TEACHERS

Kyambogo and Nsube Training Colleges:

Entrance requirements:        Junior Secondary Schooling

                          or  Primary Teachers Certificate.

Length of course:          1-year supplementary courses for selected
                           primary teachers (following 4-year basic course).
                           3 years for junior secondary entrants.

Course:          Training as Home Economics specialists (Needlework and
                 Dressmaking, etc.).

Graduates teach in secondary modern schools as of 1963.

1963 proposals:          After entry standard into Teacher Training Colleges
                         is raised to School Certificate level, students to
                         transfer to the Home Economics College after 2-year
                         basic course for 1-year special course in Home
                         Economics.

                         To initiate a 3-year course at the Home Economics
                         Training College designed to train teachers for
                         Secondary Schools and High Schools.

# ENGLISH-SPEAKING

# WEST AFRICA

372

# ENGLISH-SPEAKING WEST AFRICA

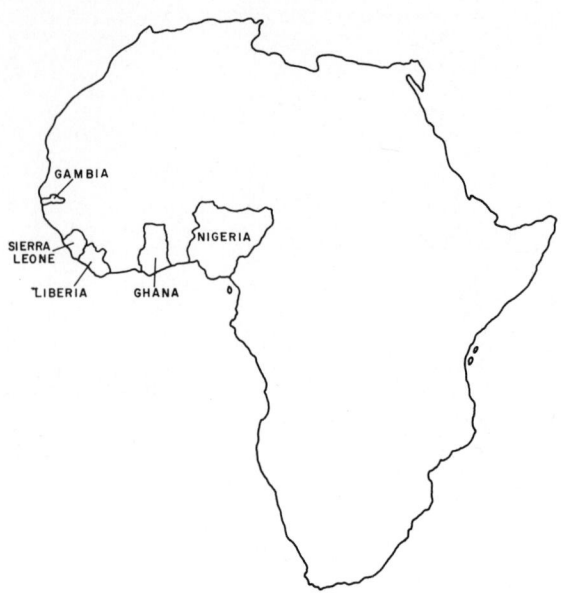

| Country and Capital | Area (sq. miles) | Est. Population | Independence Dates or Political Status | Official Language |
|---|---|---|---|---|
| THE GAMBIA<br>Bathurst | 4,011 | 316,000 | 18 February 1965 | English |
| REPUBLIC OF GHANA<br>Accra | 92,100 | 7,148,000 | 6 March 1957 | English |
| REPUBLIC OF LIBERIA<br>Monrovia | 42,990 | 1,290,000 | 26 July 1847 | English |
| FEDERATION OF NIGERIA<br>Lagos | 356,669 | 35,952,000 | 1 October 1960 | English |
| SIERRA LEONE<br>Freetown | 27,925 | 2,260,000 | 27 April 1961 | English |

THE GAMBIA

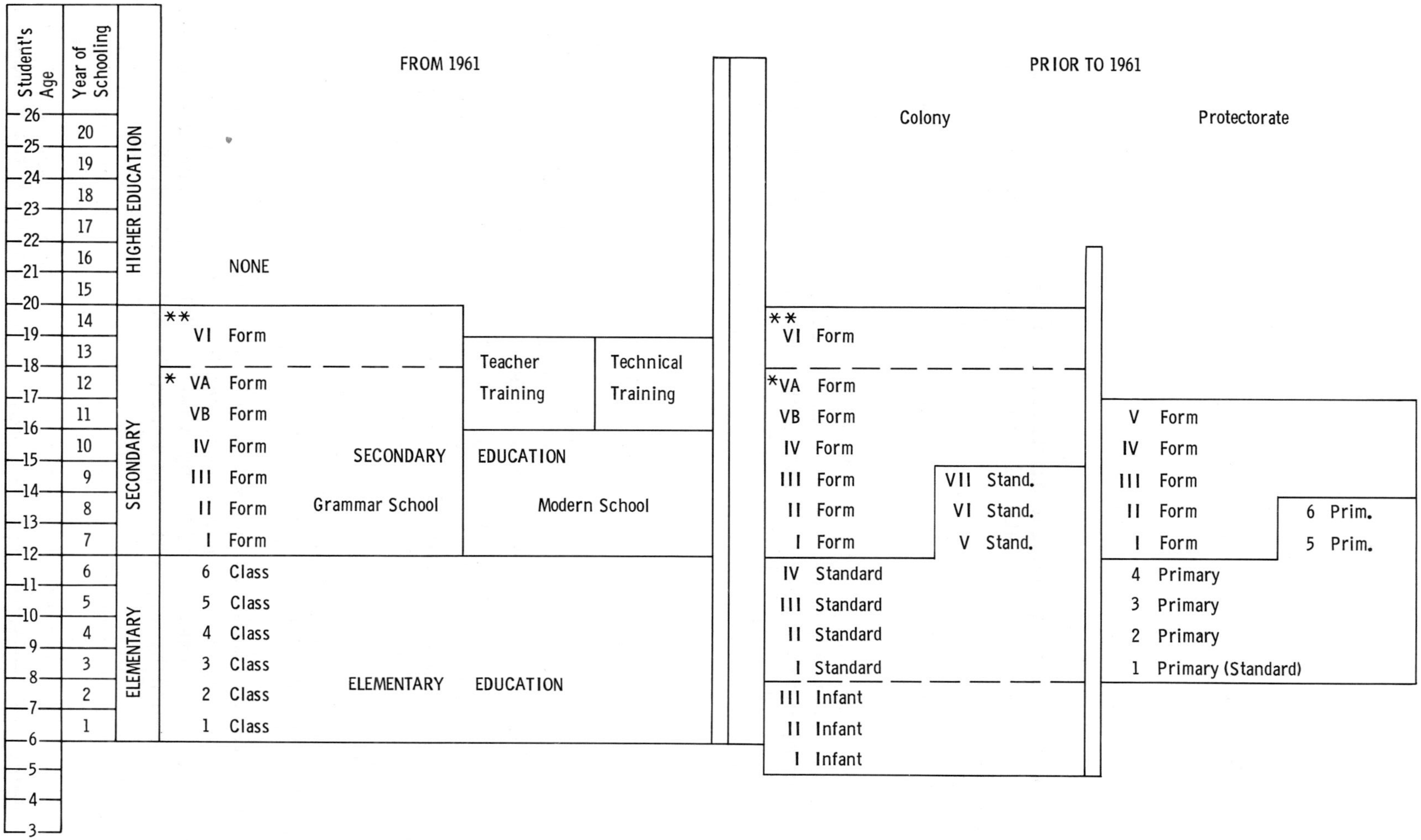

| Student's Age | Year of Schooling | | | |
|---|---|---|---|---|
| | | HIGHER EDUCATION | SECONDARY | ELEMENTARY |

Student's Age: 26 25 24 23 22 21 20 19 18 17 16 15 14 13 12 11 10 9 8 7 6 5 4 3
Year of Schooling: 20 19 18 17 16 15 14 13 12 11 10 9 8 7 6 5 4 3 2 1

**FROM 1961**

NONE

** VI Form
* VA Form
VB Form
IV Form
III Form
II Form
I Form

Teacher Training
Technical Training
SECONDARY EDUCATION
Grammar School
Modern School

6 Class
5 Class
4 Class
3 Class
2 Class
1 Class

ELEMENTARY EDUCATION

**PRIOR TO 1961**

*Colony*

** VI Form
*VA Form
VB Form
IV Form
III Form
II Form
I Form

VII Stand.
VI Stand.
V Stand.

IV Standard
III Standard
II Standard
I Standard
III Infant
II Infant
I Infant

*Protectorate*

V Form
IV Form
III Form
II Form
I Form

4 Primary
3 Primary
2 Primary
1 Primary (Standard)

6 Prim.
5 Prim.

Compulsory education:- None

School year: September – July

Grading: Primary, 100% with 40% passing
Secondary, 100% with 45% passing
(For secondary certificates, see SECONDARY EDUCATION)

373

THE GAMBIA

Independence:  February 18, 1965

## BACKGROUND

Before full internal self-government in 1963, the Gambia consisted of the
"Colony" (29 sq. miles) at the mouth of the Gambia River, and the "Protectorate" (3,974 sq. miles), a narrow strip of land along both banks
of the Gambia River for 300 miles, defined in 1902.  The "Colony" was
composed of the island of St. Mary, with Bathurst, the capital, and the
adjacent mainland district of Kombo St. Mary.

Only 10% of the population have been living in the "Colony," but educational facilities have been superior.  The former "Protectorate" area is rural,
with 4 main divisions, 35 sub-divisions, each governed by a Native Authority under a chief.  Principal tribes in the "Protectorate" have been the
Mandinga (35%), Fula, Jola, and Serahuli.  Mandinga and Serahuli are
mainly Moslems; the majority of the Jola have traditional African religion.
Small Christian population.

Portuguese navigators discovered the Gambia River and established settlements in the 15th century.  British dominant in early 17th century; Gambia
governed as part of Sierra Leone until 1843 and was one of the West African
Settlements from 1866-1888.  Received own government, 1888, and by 1902
the "Protectorate" was established in its present boundaries.

Internal self-government 1962, under an agreement reached at a constitutional conference in London, July 1961; independence, February 18, 1965.
The "Colony" now called the Mainland, and the "Protectorate," the Provinces.

## Education in the "Colony," previous to 1961

The Society of Friends (Quakers) opened a primary school in Bathurst and
one in Kombo St. Mary in 1821.  These were handed over to the Wesley
Methodist Mission which came in 1824; by 1841, 3 Methodist primary schools.
By 1860, schools opened by Anglican and Roman Catholic missions.

Until 1930, education through religious missions.  Independent Education
Department established 1930.  1945, government took over primary education
in Bathurst from the missions, although schools retained religious affiliation.  Education Ordinance of 1947 put major responsibility for education
in government hands.

In 1947, 3 infant schools, 5 primary schools, 4 mission secondary schools. By 1957, 4 infant schools, 11 primary schools. Student entered infant school at 5 years of age. 3-year program. At 8 years, entered primary school for 4-year course, Standards I-IV.

Senior primary school of 3 years (Standards V-VII) for those not accepted into secondary school. Domestic Science Center for senior primary girls. Arts and Crafts Center for senior primary boys.

Secondary education: 1 boys' school, 1 girls' school in Bathurst, operated by Methodist Mission. 1 boys' school, 1 girls' school operated by Roman Catholic Mission.

West African School Certificate examination, at close of secondary program.

School of Science at Bathurst, founded 1949 by government and missions as joint enterprise, offering courses in biology at School Certificate level, for students from secondary school; and courses for junior staffs of Medical Departments.

1958, modern secondary school opened at Crab Island. This brought together all post-primary classes with exception of Catholic Schools.

1958, new Gambia High School incorporated 2 Methodist High Schools and the Government Science School into one independent, non-denominational secondary school for the territory.

1963, Secondary Modern School (Latrikunda) opened in Kombo St. Mary.

Technical School, Bathurst, offering courses in Carpentry, Masonry, Motor Fitting, Electrical Trades. Government Clerical School offering Arithmetic, English, Bookkeeping, Shorthand, Typing.

Teacher-training in Yundum College. 2 or 3-year course. Refresher courses for teachers during vacation.

Minimum entrance requirements: Old Standard VII School Leaving Certificate or the new Government Secondary IV Certificate. A written test in English, Arithmetic, Civics (including Geography, History) and interview for all those not holding the West African School Certificate or higher academic qualification was required.

Curriculum: Teaching of English, Handwriting, Use of Textbooks, and subjects of local or rural interest.

Education in the "Protectorate," previous to 1961

By 1947, 9 small village primary schools (5 run by Native Authorities, 4 by missions).

30 village schools; 22 owned by the districts, 6 operated by Roman Catholics, 1 by Anglican mission, 1 by Methodist mission and a district authority.  Smaller schools taught in the vernacular, but no texts in vernacular.

Many Koranic schools outside the accredited system.  Only 2% of school-age children in schools; more than half of these in first 2 years of primary school.

Students entered primary school at 8 years of age.  4-year program.  Only post-primary course at Armitage school, established 1927 as boarding school for sons and relatives of chiefs.  Provided post-primary course of 5 years open to all boys completing Standard IV in Protectorate schools.


PRESENT SYSTEM


ELEMENTARY EDUCATION

Entry age:  6 years.

6-year program.

Prior to 1961, Colony had primary program of Infants I, II, III and Standards I, II, III, IV with post-primary Standards V, VI, & VII.  Prior to 1961, Protectorate had primary program of 4 years, with 6 years at some mission schools; with a post-primary of Forms 1-5 (Armitage).

Subjects:          English and Speech, Handwriting, Arithmetic, Religion,
                   Rural Science, Domestic Subjects, History, Geography,
                   Drawing, Handicrafts, Physical Education, Music, and
                   Health Education.

There is no formal certificate issued at the end of the primary school course.  During the last year, all children between 11-12+ years sit for the Common Entrance Examination which is held either in March or April. The result of this examination determines the type of secondary school to which child is admitted.  The examination is set and marked by the West African Examination Council.


SECONDARY EDUCATION

4 schools provide a 6-year course leading to the School Certificate Examination (renamed the West African General Certificate of Education in 1965).

They are Gambia High School, St. Augustine's Secondary School, St. Joseph's Secondary School (in Bathurst), and Armitage School (in the Provinces).

Armitage School in Georgetown formerly provided a 5-year course for pupils from rural schools. As of 1964, became secondary grammar school. Plans to enter first candidates for G.C.E. in June 1966.

## SECONDARY MODERN SCHOOLS

Crab Island School and Latrikunda School are Secondary Modern Schools, providing 4-year course. Fourth year is semi-vocational in character. Offers Government Secondary Four Examination with tests in English, Arithmetic, Civics, Woodwork, Crafts, and Domestic Subjects. Prepares for Stage 1 examinations in Arithmetic, English, History of the British Commonwealth, Geography, and commercial subjects of the Royal Society of Arts.

### SECONDARY MODERN CURRICULUM (CRAB ISLAND SCHOOL)
#### (45-minute periods per week)

| Subjects | 1st Year | 2nd Year | 3rd Year |
|---|---|---|---|
| English | 7 | 5 | 5 |
| Arithmetic | 5 | 5 | 4 |
| Social Studies[+] | 6 | 4 | 5 |
| Home Economics[++] | 3 | 4 | 5 |
| Craft[+++] | 4 | 5 | 5 |
| Physical Education | 2 | 2 | 2 |
| Religion | 3 | 3 | 3 |
| Civics | 1 | 1 | 1 |

The fourth year is specialized:

V1 Academic course (Boys and Girls)
V2 A&B Commercial course (Boys and Girls)
V3 A&B Craft course (Boys only)
V4 Agricultural course (Boys only)
V5 A&B Home Economics course (Girls only)

#### Fourth Year (Specialized)

| | V1 | V2 A&B | V3 A&B | V4 | V5 A&B |
|---|---|---|---|---|---|
| English | 7 | 7 | 6 | 7 | - |

| Arithmetic | 7 | 7 | 6 | 7 | 7 |
| Social Studies[+] | 7 | 4 | 6 | 4 | 7 |
| Home Economics[++] | - | - | - | - | 9 |
| Craft[+++] | - | - | 9 | - | - |
| Physical Education | 1 | 1 | 1 | 1 | 1 |
| Religion | 3 | 3 | 3 | 3 | 3 |
| Civics | 1 | 1 | 1 | 1 | 1 |
| French | 3 | - | - | - | - |
| Commercial | - | 8 | - | - | - |
| Agriculture | - | - | - | 9 | - |

[+]Social Studies includes History, Geography, and Science for the 1st, 2nd, and 3rd years.
In the 4th year V3 A&B does Science, History, and Geography; the other sets do only Geography and History.

[++]Home Economics includes Nursing, Mothercraft, Laundry, Needlework, and Cookery.

[+++]Craft includes Woodwork, Bookbinding, Metal Work, and Technical Drawing. Art is taken in the 1st, 2nd, and 3rd years only.

VI takes external examinations with the Royal Society of Arts (London).


Mathematics Syllabus

Secondary Modern Schools:

Length, money, weight, time, liquid measure. Use of ruler, simple scales and drawings, calendar. Revision of HCF, LCM, HCD. Fractions, decimals, metric system, averages, simple interest. Percentages, ratio and proportion, areas of rectangle, triangle, and circle. Time and distance problems, relative speeds, hire purchase, block graphs, line graphs. Area of parallelogram, trapezium, volume of cube, rectangular cuboid, and prism. Transposition of equations, negative numbers, square and cube roots. Gross and net profit, stocks and shares.

Secondary Grammar Schools:

English and metric systems of weights and measures. Addition, subtraction, multiplication, and division applied to numerical calculation, fractions and decimals, proportion and proportional parts; calculation of averages, percentage, simple interest and compound interest; profit and loss. Problems on speed. Graphs and their simple application.

Elementary algebraic operations; formulae expressing arithmetical generalization; change of subject of a formula; factors, fractions. The use of fractional and negative indices and the elementary theory of logarithms. Calculations by logarithms to base 10 with the use of four-figure tables. Solution of linear equations involving not more than two unknowns and quadratic equations involving only one quadratic, involving two unknowns. The use of the remainder theorem; ratio, and proportion; variation. Arithmetical and finite geometrical progressions.

Bisection of angles and of straight lines. Construction of perpendiculars to straight lines. Construction of angles of $60^\circ$, $45^\circ$, and $30^\circ$. Construction of parallels to a given straight line. Simple cases of the construction from sufficient data of triangles and quadrilaterals. Division of straight lines into a given number of equal parts or into parts in any given proportions.

Construction of a triangle equal in area to a given polygon. Construction of tangents to a circle and of common tangents to two circles. Construction of circumscribed, inscribed, and escribed circles of a triangle.

Simple cases of the construction of circles from sufficient data. Construction of a square equal in area to a given polygon. Construction of a fourth proportional to three given straight lines and a mean proportional to three given straight lines and a mean proportional to given straight lines. Construction of regular figures of 3, 4, 6, or 8 sides in or about a given circle.


SECONDARY GRAMMAR SCHOOLS

6-year program:        English Language and Literature, History, Geography,
                       Mathematics, Classical and Modern Languages, Natural
                       Science, Handicrafts, Domestic Subjects, Religion,
                       Music, Physical Education, Art, Commerce, Agricultural
                       Science.


Secondary Examinations

Prior to 1965, students took the Joint Examination for the School Certificate and General Certificate of Education in Gambia, Ghana and Sierra Leone.[+] After 1965, only General Certificate of Education Examination.


[+]For booklet with detailed syllabuses for examination, send for REGULATIONS AND SYLLABUSES (University Press, Oxford; price, 5 shillings). (See Appendix D for basic information.)

Prior to 1965, two types of certificate awarded:

The <u>School Certificate</u> of the West African Examinations Council awarded to candidates who satisfied conditions for the award of a <u>full</u> Certificate.

The <u>General Certificate of Education</u> of the West African Examinations Council awarded to candidates who entered for the full Certificate and who gained at least one credit but did not qualify for the award of a <u>School Certificate</u>.

<u>School Certificate</u> eliminated, 1965.  Thereafter, only <u>G.C.E.</u> awarded, without any restrictions regarding minimum entry or subject grouping.

Grading scale:  1-9.

| | |
|---|---|
| 1 | - Excellent |
| 2 | - Very Good |
| 1-6 | - Pass with Credit |
| 7-8 | - Pass |
| 9 | - Failure |

Subject Groups, prior to 1965:

I.   Languages:  English Language, Latin, Greek, French, German, Italian, Ewe, Fante, Ga, Twi, Arabic.

II.   General subjects:  English Literature, Bible Knowledge, Islamic Religious Knowledge, History, Geography.

III.   Mathematical subjects:  Mathematics, Additional Mathematics.

IV.   Science subjects:  General Science, Additional General Science, Physics, Chemistry, Biology, Agricultural Science.

V.   Arts and Crafts:  Art, Music, Woodwork, Metalwork, Needlework and Dressmaking, Cookery, General Housecraft.

VI.   Technical and commercial subjects:  Technical Drawing, Commercial Subjects, Health Science.

Regulations prior to 1965:  Candidates for the Joint Examination for the School Certificate and General Certificate of Education of the West African Examinations Council must sit for not less than 6 or not more than 9 subjects.  These must include subjects chosen from at least 3 of the Groups I, II, III, IV, V, and VI.  All requirements must be satisfied at one and the same examination.

To qualify for the certificate, candidates must:

(a)   Reach a satisfactory general standard as judged by their aggregate performance in their best 6 subjects, and either

(b)   Pass in at least 6 subjects, with credit in at least one of them, or

(c)   Pass in 5 subjects, with credits in at least 2 of them.

Successful candidates placed in the following Divisions (Division indicated on the School Certificate):

First Division Certificates awarded for:

(i) Pass in 6 or more subjects, drawn from not less than 3 of the Groups I through VI.

(ii) Pass with credit in at least 5 of these subjects, which must include credits in subjects drawn from at least 2 of the Groups I through IV.  And

(iii) Reach a high general standard as judged by their performance in their best 6 subjects.

Second Division Certificates awarded for:

(i) Pass in 6 or more subjects drawn from not less than 3 of the Groups I through VI.

(ii) Pass with credit in at least 4 subjects.  And

(iii) Reach a certain general standard as judged by their performance in their best 6 subjects.

A General Certificate of Education is awarded to candidates who:

(a) Enter for a full School Certificate.  And

(b) Pass with credit in at least 1 of the subjects offered.

Candidates who satisfy the conditions for the award of a School Certificate will receive a combined School Certificate and General Certificate of Education on which it will be made clear that in subjects in which they gained Grade 6 or better they achieved a G.C.E. pass at ordinary level.

Certificates awarded to successful candidates will show the standards attained:
                    Excellent
                    Very Good
                    Credit
                    Pass
in all the subjects in which the holder has passed.  Credit in a subject of the Joint Examination for the School Certificate and General Certificate of Education of the West African Examinations Council is equivalent to pass at ordinary level in the corresponding subject of the General Certificate of Education Examination (it is the lowest standard generally recognized for exemption from other examinations).

New standards from 1965:  Candidates will receive General Certificates of Education in respect of such subjects as they can pass.  (Performance at the old School Certificate level will be recorded on their Certificates.)

One school (Gambia High School) has post-certificate (Sixth Form) classes which prepare pupils for the advanced level subjects of the University of **London General Certificate of Education.  Open to pupils who obtain 5 or more credits in School Certificate.

## VOCATIONAL AND TECHNICAL EDUCATION

### COMMERCIAL TRAINING

Clerical courses at Crab Island School (see timetable under SECONDARY EDUCATION).

### GOVERNMENT CLERICAL SCHOOL

In Colony, evening classes in commercial subjects began in 1944. 1949 these classes reorganized as Government Clerical School. Closed in 1960. Reopened 1963. Courses in Typing, Shorthand, Bookkeeping.

1 course for clerks having passed Government Entrance Examination: 6 months. Clerical Assistant's Course, shorter period.

Students also receive instruction in English, Arithmetic, Civics, and attend lectures on Functions of Government.

### TECHNICAL SCHOOL, Bathurst

Established 1959.
Courses in Basic Engineering Practice, Carpentry and Joining. (Masonry, a 3-year course, has been dropped.)

Entrance requirements: 4 years of secondary school and aptitude test.

Basic Mechanical Training: 18 months. All practical: 6-day week, 6
    hours per day.

Carpentry: 2-year Basic Training. (Previous to 1963, 3-year course.)
    Full-time practical work. 6-day week, 6 hours per day.

Apprentices Day Release Course: 18 months. 2 days per week, 6 hours
    per day.

City and Guilds Intermediate Certificate Courses: 18 months.

    (a)  2 evenings per week (1 hour Engineering, 1 hour Mathematics).
    (b)  3 days per week, 6 hours per day. Mathematics, Engineering,
         English (2 hours each), Theory.

National Certificate Course: 3 days per week, 6 hours per day.

Upgrading Courses of Older Employees: 2-3 months. (Full-time on release of
    normal job. Practical workday, 6 hours.

TEACHER EDUCATION

YUNDUM COLLEGE

Located 16 miles from Bathurst.

Before 1942, training courses were held intermittently. In 1942 the
government started the training of Gambian teachers overseas, first at
Achimota College in Ghana (then the Gold Coast) and later in Fourah Bay
College, Sierra Leone.

1949, Teacher Training Center opened at Georgetown. 1952, Center transferred to Yundum becoming teacher training college.

Duration of training has varied. In pre-1942 era, it lasted 18 months.
Between 1942 and 1957, those trained overseas or locally had a course
lasting from 6 months to 3 years.

2-year course for those who have completed secondary school; 3-year course
for others.

Minimum entrance requirements:       Old Standard School Leaving Certificate,
                                     New Government Secondary IV Certificate,
                                     or the completion of Form Four of
                                     secondary grammar school.

Those with the West African School Certificate and above normally teach in
the junior forms of secondary grammar schools and in secondary modern
schools. Most of the others teach in primary or infant schools.

## TIMETABLE
### (45-minute periods a week)

| Subject | Pre | 1B | 1A | 2B | 2A |
|---|---|---|---|---|---|
| Mathematics | 6 | 5 | 5 | 5 | 5 |
| English | 9 | 7 | 7 | 7 | 7 |
| Geography | 5 | 2 | 3 | 3 | 3 |
| History | 5 | 3 | 3 | 3 | 3 |
| Science | 5 | - | - | - | - |
| Library | 2 | - | - | - | - |
| Music | 1 | 1 | 1 | 1 | 1 |
| Current Affairs | 1 | 1 | 1 | 1 | 1 |
| Education | - | 4 | 4 | 3 | 3 |
| Hygiene | - | 1 | 1 | 1 | 1 |
| Physical Education | 1 | 1 | 1 | 1 | 1 |
| Wood/Home Ec./Art | - | 3 | 3 | 3 | 3 |
| Rural Science | - | 3 | 3 | 3 | 3 |
| Tutorials | - | - | - | 1 | 1 |

## ADULT EDUCATION

The government sponsors Homecraft courses, Community Development Schemes
based on self-help basis, and a School for the Blind where Agriculture
and Crafts are taught.

There is also a privately run Adult Literacy Class in Bathurst.

REPUBLIC OF GHANA

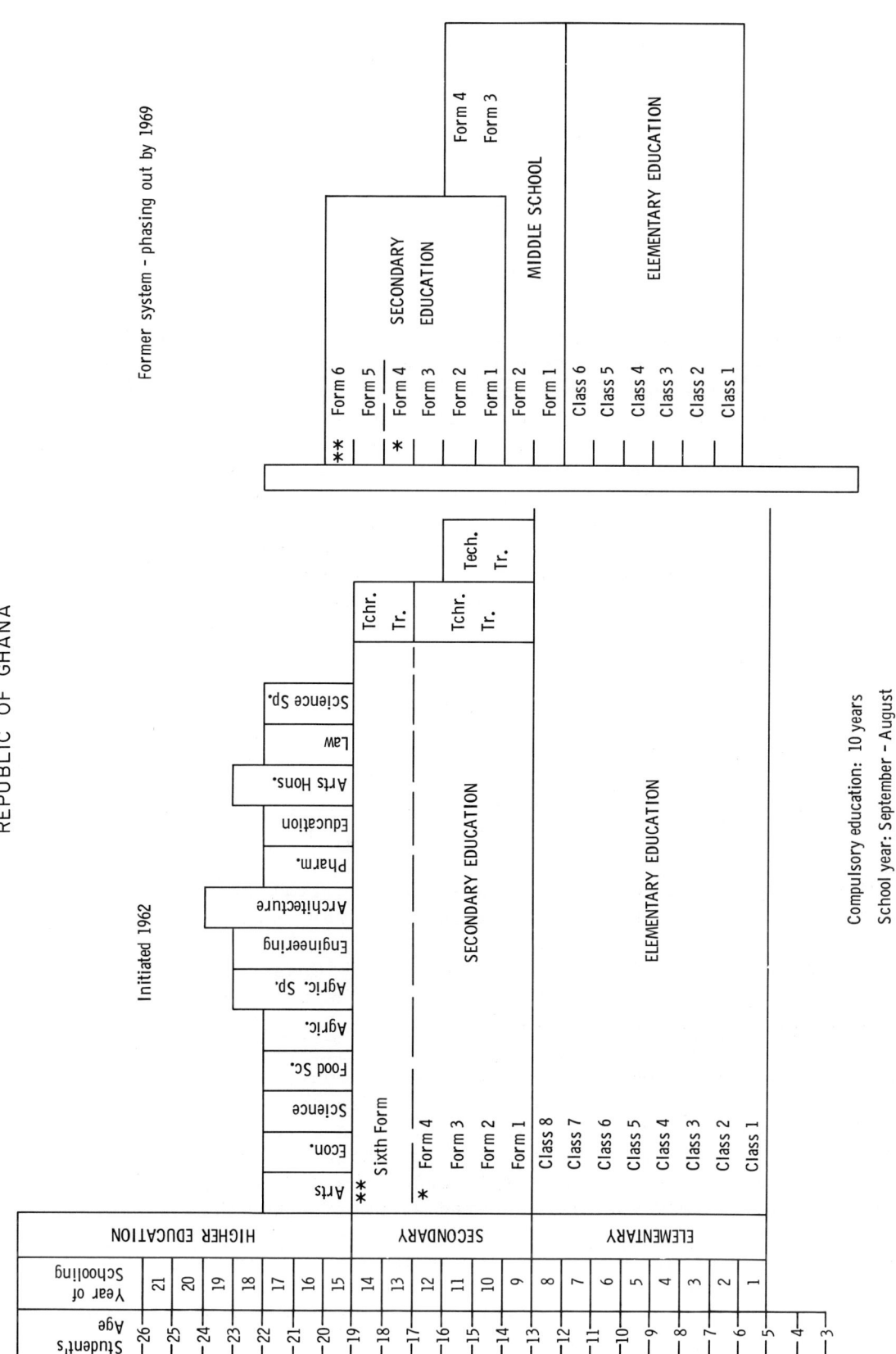

Initiated 1962

Former system – phasing out by 1969

Compulsory education: 10 years
School year: September – August
Secondary grading: 100%
        40% – 50% passing
        (For Secondary Certificates, see
        SECONDARY EDUCATION)

REPUBLIC OF GHANA

Independence:  March 6, 1957.


## BACKGROUND

Previous to independence, Ghana was known as the Gold Coast.  At independence, the name Ghana was chosen in the belief that the people were
the descendants of the early inhabitants of the empire of Ghana, which
flourished in western Sudan from about 300 A.D. to the 12th century.

Indigenous inhabitants are of Negroid stock.  Those in the northern
region belong to the Moshi-Dagomba group of Voltaic peoples or to the
Gonja.  In the South and in Ashanti, they belong to the Akan family
divided into the Twi, living in Ashanti and central Ghana, and the
Fanti, living in the coastal areas.  In the Southwest, there are the
Nzima, Ahanta, Evalue, and other tribes; on the Accra plains, the Ga;
east of the Volta River, the Ewe, living in what used to be British-
mandated Togoland.

There are 50 indigenous languages and dialects in Ghana, 31 mainly in
the northern part.  Languages follow tribal divisions; Twi and Fanti
are the most prominent.  In 1962, the government selected 9 Ghanian
languages besides English and French for development and use in educational institutions:  Asante-Twi, Dagbani, Ewe, Fanti, Ga, Kasem, and
Nzima.

Akan tribes came to the territory of Ghana in the 12th and 15th centuries;
Ga, in the 16th century; Ewe, in the 17th century.

1471, Portuguese traders in gold dust came to the Coast.  Later came
Dutch, Danes, Swedes, Germans, British.  After the gold trade there was
slave trade until it was declared illegal by the British in 1807.

1886, the coastal areas became the Gold Coast Colony under the British
Crown.  1897, the Northern Territories were declared a British Protector-
ate.  1900, Ashanti was annexed.  1922, a portion of the former German
colony of Togoland was placed under British mandate by the League of
Nations, passing to British Trusteeship under the U.N. after World War
II.  From 1922, Togoland was administered as part of the Gold Coast.

The country made demands for self-government in 1949.  By 1951, the
African majority assumed a large measure of responsibility for government.
1954, the Gold Coast became self-governing.  A resolution for independence
was formulated in August, 1956.

March 6, 1957, the Gold Coast, including Ashanti, the Northern Territories
Protectorate, and the Trust Territory of British Togoland attained full
independent membership in the British Commonwealth under the name  Ghana.

The country became a republic, July 1, 1960.

1946, a ten-year plan for educational development was initiated.  Primary
and middle school emphasized.  1951, an Accelerated Development Plan with
emphasis on secondary education.  1956, all government primary and middle
schools were transferred to local authorities.  A large number of such
schools are run under contract with local authorities by missionary organizations (mainly Roman Catholic, Methodist, Presbyterian, Anglican).

Ghana's Medical School opened October, 1964 at Korle Bu Hospital, Accra.
First class to be graduated, 1968.

## FORMER SYSTEM

### PRIMARY EDUCATION

Entry age:      6 years.

6-year course.

### POST-PRIMARY EDUCATION

Entry age:      12 years.

4-year course.

Curriculum:      For students taking housecraft or woodwork.

### TIMETABLE
(Approximate hours per week)

| Subjects | I | II | III | IV |
|---|---|---|---|---|
| Religious Instruction | 2½ | 2½ | 2½ | 2½ |
| Mathematics | 3 | 3 | 3 | 3 |
| English | 6 | 6 | 7 | 7 |
| History and Civics | 1 | 1 | 1 | 1 |
| Geography | 1½ | 1½ | 1½ | 1 |
| Nature Study | 1 | 1 | 1 | 1 |
| Hygiene | 1 | 1 | 1 | 1 |
| Ghana Language | 1½ | 1 | ½ | ½ |
| Music | 1 | 1 | 1 | 1 |

| | | | | |
|---|---|---|---|---|
| Art | 1 | 1 | 1 | 1 |
| Housecraft/Woodwork | 2 | 2 | 2 | 2 |
| Needlework/Crafts | 1½ | 1½ | 1½ | 1½ |
| Physical Education | 1 | 1 | 1 | 1 |
| Games | 1 | 1 | 1 | 1 |
| Gardening | 1 | 1 | 1 | 1 |

Curriculum:    For students not taking housecraft or woodwork.

| | | | | |
|---|---|---|---|---|
| Religious Instruction | 2½ | 2½ | 2½ | 2½ |
| Mathematics | 3 | 3 | 3 | 3 |
| English | 7 | 7½ | 8 | 8 |
| History and Civics | 1 | 1 | 1 | 1 |
| Geography | 1½ | 1½ | 1½ | 1½ |
| Nature Study | 1 | 1 | 1 | 1 |
| Hygiene | 1 | 1 | 1 | 1 |
| Ghana Language | 1½ | 1 | ½ | ½ |
| Music | 1 | 1 | 1 | 1 |
| Art | 2 | 2 | 2 | 2 |
| Needlework/Crafts | 1½ | 1½ | 1½ | 1½ |
| Physical Education | 1 | 1 | 1 | 1 |
| Games | 1 | 1 | 1 | 1 |
| Gardening | 1 | 1 | 1 | 1 |

## SECONDARY EDUCATION

Student entered after 2 years of middle school.

6-year course.

## CHANGE IN PRIMARY-SECONDARY PROGRAMMING

System changed from 6-year primary and 6-year secondary program to an 8-year elementary and 4-year secondary program.

1962-63 change-over began with 1st 3 classes of primary.
By 1966-67, Form I becomes Class 7 or Continuation School Class I.
By 1967-68, Form II becomes Class 8 or Continuation School Class II.
("Continuation School" tentatively suggested as the name for the 2-year period following the former basic 6-year primary course in the 8-year elementary school.)
By 1968-69, change-over complete with 8-year elementary program and new secondary 4-year program.

*   *   *

## PRESENT SYSTEM

### ELEMENTARY EDUCATION

Entry age:                 5 years.

8-year program.

Language of instruction:  English.

#### TIMETABLE
(Approximate hours per week)

| Subjects | 1 | 2 | 3 | 4 | 5 | 6 |
|----------|-----|-----|-----|-----|-----|-----|
| Physical Education | 2 | 2 | 2 | 2 | 2 | 2 |
| Religious Instruction | 2½ | 2½ | 2½ | 2½ | 2½ | 2½ |
| Ghana Languages | 2 | 2 | 2½ | 2½ | 2½ | 2½ |
| English | 5 | 5 | 5 | 6 | 6 | 6 |
| Writing | 1 | 1 | 1 | 1 | 1 | 1 |
| Arithmetic | 2½ | 2½ | 2½ | 2½ | 2½ | 2½ |
| Nature Study | ½ | ½ | ½ | 1 | 1 | 1 |
| Health Education | ½ | ½ | ½ | ½ | ½ | ½ |
| Centre of Interest | 1 | 1 | 1 | 1 | 1 | 1 |
| History | - | - | - | ½ | ½ | ½ |
| Geography | - | - | - | ½ | ½ | ½ |
| Music | 1½ | 1½ | 1 | ½ | ½ | ½ |
| Art and Handwork | 2 | 2 | 1 | 1 | 1 | 1 |

At close of program students take the Common Entrance Examination (West African Examinations Council).

### SECONDARY EDUCATION

Entrance requirements:    Common Entrance Examination organized by the West African Examinations Council.

Language of instruction: English.

4-year course.

Curriculum:               Mathematics, Science, English, French, Latin, Greek, Ghana Languages, History, Geography, Religious Knowledge, Music, Art and Crafts, Woodwork, Metal Work, Housecraft, and Technical Drawing.

Courses in Physics and Chemistry include laboratory work.

## COEDUCATIONAL SECONDARY SCHOOL
### (40-minute periods per week)

| Subjects | 1 | 2 | 3 | 4 |
|---|---|---|---|---|
| English | 6 | 6 | 6 | 6 |
| French | 5 | 5 | 4 | 4 |
| Ghana Language | 2 | 2 | 2 | 4 |
| Ghanaian Language | (2) | (2) | (2) | (4) |
| Latin | 3 | 3 | 3 | (4) |
| English Literature | 2 | 2 | 2 | 3 |
| Bible Knowledge | 2 | 2 | 2 | 3 |
| History | 2 | 2 | 2 | (3) |
| Mathematics | 6 | 6 | 6 | 6 |
| Additional Mathematics | - | - | - | 4 |
| General Science | 4 | 4 | 4 | 4 |
| Physics | - | - | - | 4 |
| Chemistry | - | - | - | 4 |
| Biology | - | - | - | 3 |
| Art | 2 | 2 | 2 | (4) |
| Music | 2 | 2 | 2 | (4) |
| Domestic Science | (3) | (3) | (3) | (4) |
| Physical Education | | | | |

## SIXTH FORM

Student enters at age 17.

Entrance requirements:   Grade I or Grade II of the West African School
Certificate Examination.

Language of instruction: English.

Duration of course:      2 years.

Curriculum:              Science: Physics, Chemistry, Zoology, Botany,
   Biology, Pure Mathematics, Applied Mathematics
Arts: English, French, Geography, History,
   Economics, Bible Knowledge, Art, Latin

### TIMETABLE
### (Periods per week)

| Subjects | 5th year | 6th year Arts | 6th year Science |
|---|---|---|---|
| English | 6 | - | - |
| French | 5 | 6 | - |
| Latin | 5 | 8 | - |
| Ghana Language | (4) | - | - |

| | | | |
|---|---|---|---|
| Ghanaian Language | (4) | - | - |
| English Literature | 3 | 6 | - |
| Bible Knowledge | 3 | 6 | - |
| History | (3) | 6 | - |
| Mathematics | 6 | - | - |
| Pure Mathematics | - | - | 6 |
| Additional Mathematics | 4 | - | - |
| Applied Mathematics | - | - | 6 |
| General Science | 4 | - | - |
| Physics | 4 | - | 8 |
| Chemistry | 4 | - | 8 |
| Biology | 3 | - | - |
| Botany | - | - | 8 |
| Art | (4) | - | - |
| Music | (4) | - | - |
| Domestic Science | (4) | - | - |
| Zoology | - | - | 8 |

Mathematics curriculum:

Numbers:
The ordinary processes of Arithmetic. The British and metric systems of weights, measures and money, including the monetary systems of the respective Commonwealth countries of West Africa; densities; temperature scales (Centigrade and Farenheit); speeds. Fractions, decimals; proportion and proportional parts; calculation of averages, percentage and simple interest. Use of common logarithms and square-root tables.

Mensuration:
The rectangle, triangle and figures derived from them, including easy extensions to 3 dimensions. The circle (including the length of an arc in terms of the angle at the center), cylinder, cone and sphere.

Algebraic Symbols, Expressions, and Equations:
Statement of rules and generalizations of arithmetical relations in symbols; interpretation of statements given in symbolic form. Evaluation of algebraic expressions; change of subject in a formula. The use of indices. Common factors, factors of such extensions as occur in mensuration. Factors of trinominal expressions. Simple fractions. Simple equations, quadratic equations and simultaneous linear equations in two variables.

Graphs, Variation, Functionality:
Graphs from numerical and statistical data. Translation into symbols of relations such as 'y is inversely proportional to x,' 'V varies as $X^3$,' and their illustration by sketch-graphs. The idea of a function of a variable and its graphical representation.

Plane Geometry and Trigonometry:
> Angles and parallel lines, triangles and parallelograms, similarity, Pythagoras's theorem, the circle.

Three-dimensional geometry:
> Parallel lines, parallel planes, normal to a plane, angle between a line and a plane, angle between two planes.

Applied Geometry:
> Solution of triangles by the use of the sine and cosine rules and trigonometrical tables.  Scale drawing.

Secondary Examinations:

Prior to 1965, students took the Joint Examination for the School Certificate and General Certificate of Education in Gambia, Ghana and Sierra Leone.+  After 1965, only General Certificate of Education Examination.+

Prior to 1965, 2 types of certificate awarded:

(1)  The School Certificate of the West African Examinations Council awarded to candidates who satisfied conditions for the award of a full Certificate.

(2)  The General Certificate of Education of the West African Examinations Council awarded to condidates who entered for the full Certificate and who gained at least 1 credit but did not qualify for the award of a School Certificate.

School Certificate eliminated, 1965.  Thereafter, only G.C.E. awarded, without any restrictions regarding minimum entry or subject grouping.

Grading scale:   1-9.
> 1     Excellent
> 2     Very Good
> 1-6   Pass with credit
> 7-8   Pass
> 9     Failure

Regulations prior to 1965:

> Candidates for the Joint Examination for the School Certificate and General Certificate of Education of the West African Examinations Council must sit for not less than 6 or not more than 9 subjects. These must include subjects chosen from at least 3 of the following Groups I, II, III, IV, V, and VI.  All requirements must be satisfied at one and the same examination.

+For booklet with detailed syllabuses for examination, send for REGULATIONS AND SYLLABUSES (University Press, Oxford; price, 5 shillings).  (See Appendix D for basic information.)

I.   Languages:
         English Language, Latin, Greek, French, German, Italian,
         Ewe, Fanti, Ga, Twi, Arabic.
II.  General Subjects:
         English Literature, Bible Knowledge, Islamic Religious
         Knowledge, History, Geography.
III. Mathematical Subjects:
         Mathematics, Additional Mathematics.
IV.  Science Subjects:
         General Science, Additional General Science, Physics,
         Chemistry, Biology, Agricultural Science.
V.   Arts and Crafts:
         Art, Music, Woodwork, Metalwork, Needlework and Dress-
         making, Cookery, General Housecraft.
VI.  Technical and Commercial Subjects:
         Technical Drawing, Commercial Subjects, Health Science.

To qualify for the School Certificate, candidates must:

(a)   Reach a satisfactory general standard as judged by their
      aggregate performance in their best 6 subjects, and either
(b)   Pass in at least 6 subjects, with credit in at least 1 of
      them or
(c)   Pass in 5 subjects, with credit in at least 2 of them.

First Division Certificates awarded for:
(i)    Pass in 6 or more subjects, drawn from not less
       than 3 of the Groups I through VI;
(ii)   Pass with credit in at least 5 of these subjects,
       which must include credits in subjects drawn from
       at least 2 of the Groups I through IV; and
(iii)  Reach a high general standard as judged by their
       performance in their best 6 subjects.

Second Division Certificates awarded for:
(i)    Pass in 6 more subjects drawn from not less
       than 3 of the Groups I through VI;
(ii)   Pass with credit in at least 4 subjects; and
(iii)  Reach a certain general standard as judged by
       their performance in their best 6 subjects.

A General Certificate of Education is awarded to candidates who:

(a)   Enter for a full School Certificate; and
(b)   Pass with credit in at least 1 of the subjects offered.

Certificates awarded to successful candidates will show the standards
attained - Excellent, Very Good, Credit, Pass - in all the subjects in
which the holder has passed. "Credit" in a subject of the Joint Examination for the School Certificate and General Certificate of Education

of the West African Examinations Council is equivalent to "Pass" at
ordinary level in the corresponding subject of the General Certificate
of Education Examination (it is the lowest standard generally recognized
for exemption from other examinations).

New standards from 1965:

>   Candidates will receive General Certificates of Education in respect
>   of such subjects as they can pass.  (Performance at the old School
>   Certificate level will be recorded on their Certificates.)

## HIGHER EDUCATION

### UNIVERSITY OF GHANA, Legon

Founded as University College of the Gold Coast in special relationship
with University of London in 1948; became University College of Ghana in
1957.  Became University of Ghana in 1963, and severed special relationship with the University of London.  Now awards its own degrees and
diplomas.

Entrance requirements:  Passes in at least 5 subjects, including English
                        Language, at G.C.E. or equivalent, of which at
                        least 2 must be at advanced level.

Faculties:

>   Arts
>   Law
>   Social Studies
>   Science
>   Agriculture
>   Institute of African Studies

### Bachelor's degrees

>   Usually, 3 years.

### Higher degrees

>   M.A. African Studies for graduates in Arts or Social Studies   - 2
>     years.
>
>   M.A. in all subjects in which B.A. (Honours) may be taken.
>
>   M.Sc. in all subjects in which B.Sc. (Special) may be taken - 2
>     years for B.Sc. (General) graduates, 1 year for B.Sc. (Special)
>     graduates.

<u>M.Sc. (Agriculture)</u>

<u>M.Ed.</u> for graduates with at least 2 years post-diploma in education or approved teaching experience.

## Certificates

Postgraduate Certificate in Education - 1 year.

Associate Certificate in Education for experienced non-graduate teachers.

Certificate in Social Administration for experienced social workers - 2 years.

## Faculty of Arts

## B.A. (General)

## 1st year

African Studies.

3 of the following:

Ancient History            Mathematics
Economics                  Modern History
English                    Philosophy
French                     Political Science
Geography                  Sociology
Greek (Classical)          Study of Religions
Latin

## 2nd and 3rd years

3 of the following each year:

Ancient History
Economics
English
Ethics and Political Philosophy <u>or</u> History of Philosophy
Political Science <u>or</u> Ethics and Political Philosophy
French
Geography
Mathematics
Modern History
Sociology
Study of Religions
Greek (Classical)
Latin
Logic

B.A. (Honours)
=====

Courses are available in the following subjects:

| | |
|---|---|
| English | Philosophy |
| French | Political Science |
| Geography | Sociology |
| Classics | Study of Religions |
| History | |

The selection of candidates for B.A. (Honours) courses after the First
University Examination in Arts is based on the results of that examination, and if required by the Department, includes an interview.


Faculty of Law
=====

Candidates wishing to take the B.A. Honours degree in Law are required
in their 1st year to pursue a course leading to the First University
Examination in Law in the following subjects:

> African Studies
> Introductory Political Theory and Practice
> Constitutional History of Ghana
> English or French Language and Literature
>
> 1 of the following:  Logic; Methodology of Social Science.

The B.A. Honours degree in Law comprises Parts I and II, each part being
of 1 year's duration.

Part I Examination:
=====

> Constitutional Law
> Criminal Law and Procedure
> Law of Tort
> Law of Immovable Property

Part II Examination:
=====

> Jurisprudence
> Administrative Law and Practice
> Comparative Law including Customary African Institutions
> Public International Law

Faculty of Social Studies

B.Sc. (Economics)

The selection of candidates for the B.Sc. (Economics) degree course is based on the results of the First University Examination in Arts. Candidates must have been examined in the following subjects:

African Studies
Economics

2 of the following:

Mathematics                      Geography
Political Science                Modern History
Sociology

The B.Sc. (Economics) degree course comprises Parts I and II, each part being of 1 year's duration.

Part I Examination:

Principles of Economics
Applied Economics
Economic History
Statistics

1 of the following:

Mathematics for Economists       Geography
Political Science                Mathematics Special Course
Sociology

Part II Examination:

Candidates have a choice of 2 optional fields:  (A) Economics and National Economic Planning, and (B) Statistics.

(A)  Economics and National Economic Planning

Economic Theory
Principles of Economic Planning
History of Economic Thought

2 of the following:
Econometrics                     International Economics
Money and Banking                Elements of Business
Public Finance                       Management

(B)  Statistics

Elements of Mathematical Economics and Economic Planning
Economic Statistics and National Accounting
Mathematical Statistics
Elements of Mathematical Programming

1 of the following:
   Demography
   Theory of Sampling
   Data Processing and Computer Programming
   Market Analysis

## Faculty of Science

### B.Sc. (General)

#### 1st year

African Studies

3 of the following:

| | |
|---|---|
| Botany | Mathematics |
| Chemistry | Physics |
| Geology | Zoology |

Candidates are required to satisfy the examiners at the First University
Examination in Science at the end of their 1st year in the subjects studied.

#### 2nd and 3rd years

2 of the following each year:

| | |
|---|---|
| Biochemistry and Nutrition | Geology |
| Botany | Mathematics |
| Chemistry | Physics |
| Food Science and Technology | Zoology |
| Geography | |

### B.Sc. (Special)

The B.Sc. (Special degree course is available in the following subjects:

| | |
|---|---|
| Botany | Physics |
| Chemistry | Zoology |
| Geology | Biochemistry and Nutrition |
| Geography | Food Science and Technology |
| Mathematics | |

#### Direct Entry requirements:

Botany:

Advanced level passes in Botany and 2 of the following:

Pure Mathematics or Mathematics (Pure and Applied), Biology, Chemistry, Geology, Physics, Zoology, Geography, Applied Mathematics or Mathematics.

Chemistry:

Advanced level Chemistry and advanced level in Pure Mathematics, or Mathematics (Pure and Applied), or Physics.

Geography:

Advanced level Geography.

Geology:

3 advanced level passes in the following:

Botany or Biology, Chemistry, Geology, Physics, Zoology or Biology, Geography, Pure Mathematics, or Mathematics (Pure and Applied) or
Advanced level passes in Geology and 1 other subject.

Mathematics:

Advanced level passes in Pure Mathematics and Applied Mathematics or Physics.

Physics:

Advanced level Physics.

Zoology:

Advanced level passes in Zoology and 2 of the following:

Botany or Biology, Chemistry, Geology, Physics, Geography, Pure Mathematics, or Mathematics (Pure and Applied), Applied Mathematics, or Mathematics, or Mathematics (Pure and Applied).

Biochemistry and Nutrition:

Advanced level pass in Chemistry and 2 of the following:

Botany or Biology, Geology; Physics, Geography, Pure Mathematics, or Mathematics (Pure and Applied), Applied Mathematics, or Mathematics, or Mathematics (Pure and Applied).

## Faculty of Agriculture

## B.Sc. (Food Science) General

On passing the First University Examination in Agriculture or its equivalent at the end of his 1st year in the University, a candidate may be admitted to the B.Sc. (Food Science) General degree course.

Duration of course:  2 years.

## B.Sc. (Food Science) Special

On passing the B.Sc. (Food Science) General Part I Examination at the end of his 2nd year in the University, a candidate may be admitted to the B.Sc. (Food Science) Special degree course.

Duration of course:  2 years.

## B.Sc. (Agriculture) General

Candidates for admission to the B.Sc. (Agriculture)General degree course must have obtained passes in at least 5 subjects including English Language at the London General Certificate of Education Examination (or its approved equivalent) of which at least 2 must be at advanced level.

The passes must have been obtained in:

(a)  Either Pure Mathematics (OL or AL)  or  Mathematics (Pure and Applied (AL).

(b)  At least 2 of the following subjects:

Botany or Biology                      Physics
Chemistry                              Zoology or Biology
Geology                                Geography
Pure Mathematics, or Mathematics (Pure and Applied)
Applied Mathematics, or Mathematics (Pure and Applied)

The B.Sc. (Agriculture) General degree is taken in 2 parts after the First University Examination in Agriculture.  Each part:  1 year.

Candidates for the First University Examination in Agriculture are examined in African Studies and the following subjects studied in the 1st year:

Agriculture                            Physics
Botany                                 Zoology
Chemistry

Candidates are required to satisfy the examiners at the Part I of the B.Sc. (Agriculture) General Degree Examination in the following subjects:

Animal Science
Crop Science and Soil Science
Agricultural Engineering and Agricultural Economics
Introductory Genetics
Introductory Microbiology

In addition, candidates are required to submit reports on practical work done in the long vacation.

Candidates are required to satisfy the examiners in the following subjects at the Part II of the B.Sc. (Agriculture) General Degree Examination:

>  Introductory Statistics
>  Animal Science
>  Crop Science and Soil Science
>  Agricultural Engineering and Agricultural Economics

Candidates may also be examined in Extension Methods. In addition, candidates are assessed on seminar work and reports on a vacation project.

Appropriate field training and vacation trips to agricultural regions of the country are an essential part of the course, and each candidate submits reports on this aspect of the course.

No candidate is passed unless he satisfies the examiners in both written and practical parts of the examination.

## B.Sc. (Agriculture) Special

On passing the B.Sc. (Agriculture) General Part I Examination at the end of his 2nd year in the University, a candidate may be admitted to the B.Sc. (Agriculture) Special degree course in 1 of the following:

>  Animal Science              Agricultural Economics
>  Crop Science                Agricultural Engineering
>  Soil Science

Duration of course: 2 years.

## Institute of African Studies

Entrance requirements: Good 1st degree from an approved university.
A reading knowledge of French is required.

2-year course leading to an M.A. in African Studies.

Courses:

(A) African Languages

>  Arabic                      Ga-Adangme
>  Hausa                       Twi-Fante
>  Mandinka                    Ewe
>  Dagbani
>  Introduction to African Linguistics

(B)  African History

History of the Western Sudan, to 1900 A.D.
History of Ghana
History of Archaeology of the Nile Valley before the coming
    of Islam
The Evolution of French-speaking West Africa, from 1900 A.D.
African Archaeology
The Geographical Background to West African History

(C)  African Social, Political and Economic Institutions

The Structure of West African Societies
African Political Systems (Pre-colonial and Modern Periods)
An Introduction to African Ethical, Political and Metaphysical
    Ideas
African National Movements - a Comparative Approach
Industrialization and Social Change in Modern Africa
Problems of Economic Development in West Africa

(D)  African Music and Related Arts

Music in African Culture
Vocal and Instrumental Forms
African Music and Oral Literature, Art and Dance

Every student takes at least 4 courses, of which 1 must be from section
A, 1 from section B, and 1 from section C.

A student specializing in African Languages is required to take 3 courses
from section A, 1 of which must be Introduction to African Linguistics.

A student specializing in African History takes not less than 2 courses
from section B.

A student specializing in African Social, Political and Economic Institutions takes not less than 2 courses from section C.

A student studying African Music and Related Arts takes a course in section D.

All students in addition are required to submit a thesis of not more than
25,000 words involving original research.


## KWAME NKRUMAH UNIVERSITY OF SCIENCE AND TECHNOLOGY, Kumasi

Founded as Kumasi College of Technology in 1951 in special relationship
with University of London.  Became Kwame Nkrumah University of Science
and Technology in 1963 offering its own degrees and diplomas.

Entrance requirements: Applicants must satisfy the minimum entrance requirements for matriculation (see section 3 below) before being considered for admission to degree courses or to the Preliminary Degree Courses, unless otherwise stated in the faculty requirements. In addition, candidates for direct admission to degree courses are required to have obtained qualifications in certain specific subjects at specific levels. (See under Faculty requirements.)

(1) Admission to Degree Courses:

    (a) Persons who have passed all examinations for a degree of any university recognized by the University for this purpose.

    (b) Holders of General Certificate of Education, or the approved equivalents (see section 2), satisfying Faculty requirements.

    (c) Holders of certificates or diplomas from technical institutions recognized by the University for this purpose.

(2) Equivalence of Examinations:

    (a) General Certificates of Education awarded with passes at advanced level or ordinary level by:

        The University of London
        West African Examinations Council
        Other Examining bodies approved by the University.

    (b) A credit gained in an approved School Certificate Examination or a pass at subsidiary level in an approved Higher School Certificate Examination will be counted as equivalent to a pass at ordinary level in the corresponding subject.

    (c) A pass in a principal or main subject in an approved Higher School Certificate Examination will be counted as equivalent to a pass at advanced level in the corresponding subject.

(3) Minimum Entrance Requirements for Entry into the Preliminary Courses:

4 credits in the School Certificate of the West African Examinations Council or 4 passes in the General Certificate of Education Ordinary Level Examination, and a School Certificate of the West African Examinations Council pass or a General Certificate of Education ordinary level pass in English Language.

Faculties:

Agriculture                          Engineering
Architecture                         Science
Art                                  Pharmacy

## Faculty of Agriculture

## B.Sc Agriculture

Duration of course:        3 years.

General entrance requirements:

(1)  For Degree Course in Agriculture

General Certificate of Education with passes at advanced level
in (a) Chemistry and (b) Biology or Botany/Zoology and (c)
ordinary level pass in either Pure Mathematics or Physics

or   The Cambridge Higher School Certificate with passes at principal
level in (a) Chemistry and (b) Biology or Botany/Zoology and (c)
credit pass at School Certificate level in either Elementary
Mathematics or Physics.

(2)  For Degree Course in Agricultural Engineering

General Certificate of Education with passes at advanced level
in (a) Pure Mathematics and (b) Physics and (c) ordinary level
pass in Chemistry or Biology or Botany/Zoology

or   The Cambridge Higher School Certificate with passes at principal
level in (a) Mathematics and (b) Physics and (c) credit pass in
Chemistry or Biology or Botany/Zoology.

Structure of course:

1st year or Part I or Pre-professional Year:

Statistics and Field Experimentation
Agricultural Botany I
Agricultural Zoology
Agricultural Chemistry I
Agricultural Engineering I
Soil Science I
Economics and Farm Accounting
Meteorology and Climatology
Introduction to Forestry, Agriculture and Horticulture

All subjects are examinable.

2nd year or Part II or 1st Professional Year:

       Crop Production I
       Horticulture I
       Animal Production I
       Agricultural Economics and Farm Management I
       Agricultural Chemistry II
       Agricultural Botany
       Agricultural Zoology II
       Soil Science II
       Agricultural Engineering II
       Crop and Animal Protection I

All subjects are examinable.

3rd year or Part III or Final or Second Professional Year:

    There are 3 main emphases; students choose the 1 in which they are interested.

| Subjects | Animal Production | Horticulture | Crop Production |
|---|---|---|---|
| Agricultural Engineering II | X | X | X |
| Agricultural Economics and Farm Management | X | X | X |
| Crop Production II | X | X | X |
| Crop Production III | | | X |
| Horticulture II | X | X | X |
| Horticulture III | | X | |
| Animal Production II | X | X | X |
| Animal Production III | X | | |
| Plant Protection II | | X | X |
| Animal Protection II | X | | |
| Agricultural Extension | X | X | X |

Degree awarded:

    1st Class Honours
    2nd Class Honours
    Pass

## Post-Graduate Degrees

A 2-year post-graduate course leading to the Master of Science degree (M.Sc.) for graduates who pass in Class I and those who pass at a certain grade in Class II is in preparation.

GHANA

## Diploma in Tropical Horticulture

Entrance requirements:    West African School Certificate and at least 2 years practical experience in the employ of a recognized horticultural organization.

Duration of course:    2 years.

Structure of course:

| Year | Term | Subjects |
|------|------|----------|
| 1 | 1 | Elements of Chemistry, Botany, Soils, Plant Nutrition and Surveying, Propagation, Plant Identification |
|  | 2 | Elements of Chemistry, Botany, Soils, Plant Nutrition and Surveying, Propagation, Plant Identification, Horticultural Machinery, Management |
|  | 3 | Crop Protection, Fruit, Vegetables, Ornamentals |
| 2 | 1 | Fruit, Vegetables, Ornamentals, Landscape Design. |
|  | 2 | Ornamentals, Landscape Design |
|  | 3 | Ornamentals, Landscape Design |

## Training of Agricultural Officers Courses (Mechanization)

The course which is of 6 months' duration trains graduates to be ready in time for the next major agricultural season.

Subjects:

    Workshop
    Tractor
    Implements and Equipment
    Soil Conservation and Reclamation
    Irrigation and Drainage
    Farm Records and Accounting
    Mechanization and Management

## Faculty of Architecture

## Diploma Course in Community Planning

Entrance requirements:     5 passes in the School Certificate of West
                           African Examinations Council including a pass
                           in English Language.  Preference is given to
                           candidates who have passes in Mathematics and
                           Geography.

A 2-year diploma course in the basic Theory of Settlement Planning and
Planning Analysis Techniques, instruction in analysis and presentation
of data and training in elementary design problems relating to Planning.

Diplomas in Community Planning awarded to successful candidates in the
final examination at the end of the course.

## Preliminary Course

Entrance requirements:     4 credits in the School Certificate of West
                           African Examinations Council or equivalent:
                             (i) 1 credit in Mathematics or Additional
                                 Mathematics and
                            (ii) 1 credit in General Science or Physics or
                                 Chemistry or Physics with Chemistry

                   or      The Ordinary Certificate (Overseas) of the City
                           and Guilds of London Institute plus 2 credits
                           in the School Certificate of West African Exam-
                           inations Council.

## Degree Courses in Architecture, Building Technology and Planning

Entrance requirements:     Same as for Preliminary Course with addition of
                           2 advanced level passes.

Structure of courses:

Year I is a common course for all degree courses in the Faculty and leads
to the Part I Examination at the end of the 1st year.  Students then
choose between a course in Building Technology or a general course in
Architecture/Planning.  Part II Examination which qualifies for a B.Sc.
is at the end of the 4th year.

To enter Part III of the course it is necessary to hold a bachelor's
degree or equivalent qualification (R.I.B.A. Intermediate).  This is
a 2-year post-graduate course in specialized fields.  5 alternative
courses are offered:
          Quantity Surveying, Management, Architecture, Urban Planning,
          Regional Planning.
The courses lead to Part III Examination at the end of the 6th year and
qualify for an M.Sc.

Subjects:

(a)  The Common First Year Course gives a comprehensive introduction
     to all fields of activities of the professions being trained
     within the Faculty, their inter-relationship and their position
     within the whole Building Industry.  Instruction is given in
     Design Methodology, verbal, written and graphic presentation,
     general cultural orientation, an introduction to Building Engin-
     eering and to Architecture Science.

(b)  Part II Architecture/Planning:  Basic course, years 2, 3 and 4.
     Training is continued by means of studio work in problem-solving
     ability in the whole field of Architecture and Planning in an
     ascending scale of complexity.  Theoretical subjects covered are:
     Architectural Science, Engineering, Planning Theory, Administra-
     tion and special subjects.

(c)  Building Technology:  Basic courses, years 2, 3 and 4.  A general
     course in Technology including Surveying, Quantities, Cost Control,
     Administration, Architectural Science, Structures and Construction.
     Special subjects are shared with the Architecture/Planning course
     and studio work is linked to the problems set for the Architecture/
     Planning course.

Examinations:

During year 1 and year 4 there are terminal examinations of the student's
portfolio; in years 2, 3, 5 and 6 there is an annual inspection of the
student's portfolio.  This must reach satisfactory level if the student
is to be allowed to sit the written papers or to advance in the course.

Part I

6 papers:  Administration, Cultural History, Theory of Projection,
           Mathematics, Building Engineering and Architectural
           Science

Part II

7 papers:  Administration, Planning Theory, Cultural History, Archi-
           tectural Science 1 and 2, and Building Engineering 1 and 2.

Building Technology - 7 papers:

Building Administration 1 and 2, Cultural History, Architectural
Science 1 and 2, Building Engineering 1 and 2.

Part III

    Management - 5 papers:

    Building Engineering 1 and 2, Quantities, Building Administration 1 and 2.  In addition candidates are required to submit a thesis based on the study of a selected building, or building type or techniques.

    Quantity Surveying - 5 papers:

    Building Engineering 1 and 2, Quantities 1 and 2, and Building Administration.  In addition the students are required to submit a History thesis and a final Design thesis.  The students must obtain a pass in the Design thesis in order to sit the written papers.

    Architecture - 5 papers:

    Professional Practice, Building Engineering 1 and 2, Building Science 1 and 2.  In addition students are required to submit a History thesis and a final Design thesis.  The students must obtain a pass in the Design thesis in order to sit the written papers.

    Urban Planning - 5 papers:

    Professional Practice, Planning Theory 1 and 2, Physical Geography, Sociology/Economics.  In addition the students are required to submit a History thesis and Design thesis.  Students must obtain a pass in the Design thesis in order to sit the written papers.

    Regional Planning - 5 papers:

    Professional Practice, Planning Theory, Demography, Economics, Physical Geography.  In addition the students are required to submit a Design thesis.  Students must obtain a pass in Design thesis in order to sit the written papers.

## 1st Degree to be Awarded:

    (a)   1st and 2nd Class Honours and Pass degree:  B.Sc. (Arch.) for students in Architecture/Planning Course.

    (b)   1st and 2nd Class Honours and Pass degree:  B.Sc. (Tech.) for students in Building Technology Course.

## Post-Graduate Courses

    (a)   Quantity Surveying:
               Major emphasis on the study of Specification, Quantities, Cost Control and Cost Planning Techniques.  The course includes periods spent in a Quantity Surveying office.

(b)  Management:

        Major emphasis on Management and Administration Techniques.
        Control Programming and Contract Procedure.  Both Courses
        (a) and (b) include studies of Advanced Building Technology,
        Prefabrication and Building Industrialization.

(c)  Architecture:

        Study of complex building types, Industrialized Building,
        Industrial Design, Advanced Building Technology and Pro-
        fessional Practice.  A History thesis and a final Design
        thesis must be submitted.

(d)  Urban Planning:

        Specialized study of the design techniques applicable to
        conurbations and resettlement problems.

(e)  Regional Planning:

        A specialized study of the design techniques applicable to
        Regional and National Planning.  Many of the theoretical
        subjects studied in this course are common Demography,
        Economics, Physical Geography and Planning Law.

## Faculty of Art

Entrance requirements:    Minimum university entrance requirements, including
                        a credit in Art.  Teachers' Certificate Grade "A"
                        (Post School Certificate) is considered equivalent
                        to 2 credits of the School Certificate of the West
                        African Examinations Council.

## B.A. (Art)

Duration of course:    3 years, preceded in most cases by a 2-year pre-
                    liminary course.  Part I of the degree course takes
                    2 years; Part II takes 1 year.

Preliminary Course:

Drawing and Painting          Museum and Library Studies
Modelling and Carving         English
Basic Design                  Wood and Metal Work
General History of Art        Pottery and Ceramics
   and Architecture           Textiles
Art Appreciation

1st Year Degree Course:

    Drawing and Painting
    Modelling and Carving
    Basic Design
    History of Art and Architecture
    Art Appreciation
    2 of (i) Woodwork
       (ii) Gold and Silversmithing
     (iii) Textiles
     (iv) Ceramics
    English
    Museum and Library Studies

2nd Year Degree Course:

    Drawing
    Specialization in any 2 of the following, 1 at main level and 1
      at additional level:

| | |
|---|---|
| Painting | Gold- and Silversmithing |
| Sculpture | Printing and Typography |
| Pottery and Ceramics | History of Art |
| Commercial Design | English |
| Graphic Design | Library and Museum Studies |
| Textile (woven and printed) | |

3rd Year Degree Course:

    Specialization in 1 of the following (both practical and theoretical)
    which must be 1 of the 2 chosen for the 2nd Year Degree Course:

| | |
|---|---|
| Painting | Textiles (woven and printed) |
| Sculpture | Gold- and Silversmithing |
| Pottery and Ceramics | Printing and Typography |
| Commercial Design | History of Art |
| Graphic Design | English |

Degree awarded:

    1st Class Honours
    2nd Class Upper Honours
    2nd Class Lower Honours
    Pass

## Post-Graduate Diploma in Art Education

For intending teachers of Art and Crafts, the Degree course may be followed
by the Post-Graduate Course in Art Education of 1 years' duration towards
the award of the Diploma in Art Education.

Subjects:

> The Study of the Principles of Art Education
> Practical Teaching
> Seminars and the Preparation of the Log of the Course
> Practical Work in Art and Craft

## Faculty of Engineering

### B.Sc. Engineering

Duration of course:        4 years.

Entrance requirements:     General Certificate of Education with "A" level
                           passes in Pure Mathematics, Applied Mathematics,
                           Physics, and "O" level Chemistry.

                           There are diploma courses of 3 years duration
                           leading to diplomas in Civil, Mechanical, and
                           Electrical Engineering open to School Certificate
                           holders.

Structure of Courses:

The courses in Civil, Electrical and Mechanical Engineering and Land
Surveying are divided into 3 parts - Part I takes 2 years, Part II
takes 1 year and Part III takes 1 year.

Subjects:

### Part I

> Mathematics, Mechanics of Fluids, Materials and Structures, Theory
> of Machines, Applied Heat, Engineering Drawing and Applied Electricity.

### Part II

> Mathematics (C,M,E), Mechanics of Fluids (C,M), Structures (C), Sur-
> veying (C), Geology (C), Civil Engineering Materials, Theory of
> Machines (M), Applied Thermodynamics (M,E), Strength    Materials,
> Electrical Engineering (C,M), Electrical Theory and Measurement (E),
> Electrical Power and Machines (E), Electronics and Telecommunication
> (E).

### Part III

> Mathematics, Mechanics of Fluids, Structures, Surveying, Geology, Soil
> Mechanics, Civil Engineering Materials, Mechanics of Machines, Applied
> Thermodynamics, Strength of Materials, Machine Design, Utilization of
> Electric Current, Power Generation and Supply, Electrical Theory and
> Measurements, Electronics and Telecommunication.

Examinations:

## Part I

7 papers

Mathematics, Mechanics of Fluids, Materials and Structures, Theory of Machines, Applied Heat, Engineering Drawing and Applied Electricity.

## Part II

Civil - 6 papers:

Mathematics, Mechanics of Fluids, Structures, Surveying, Strength of Materials  and Electrical Engineering.

Mechanical - 6 papers:

Mathematics, Mechanics of Fluids, Theory of Machines, Applied Thermodynamics, Strength of Materials and Electrical Engineering.

Electrical - 6 papers:

Mathematics, Applied Thermodynamics, Strength of Materials, Theory and Measurements, Power and Machines, and Electronics and Telecommunications.

## Part III

Civil - 6 papers:

Mathematics, Mechanics of Fluids, Structures, Surveying, Geology and Soil Mechanics and Civil Engineering Materials.

Mechanical - 6 papers:

Mathematics, Mechanics of Fluids, Mechanics of Machines, Applied Thermodynamics, Strength of Materials and Machine Design.

Electrical (Light) - 5 papers:

Mathematics, Theory and Measurement, Utilization of Electrical Current, Electronics and Telecommunications.

Electrical (Heavy) - 5 papers:

Mathematics, Theory and Measurement, Electronics, Utilization of Electrical Current, Power Generation and Supply.

## Degree awarded:

1st Class Honours
2nd Class Honours
Pass

## Diploma Courses

The duration of the course is 3 years leading to the Diploma Certificate in Civil, Mechanical and Electrical Engineering.

Entrance requirements:    Ordinary National Certificates awarded by Technical Institutes in Ghana or their equivalent.

These courses are intended to give the necessary basic training in Engineering Science and practical work for the technician grade leading to the award of a University Diploma in Engineering in the 3 branches of Civil, Mechanical, and Electrical. The level of the award is equivalent to the British Higher National Certificate or to the Continental "Ingenieur."

Students are required to spend their vacation in industry or in the field and the University will assist in making such arrangements. After the completion of 2 years course in the University, the students spend 12 months on industrial or field training, returning to the University for another year to complete their studies.

## Subjects:  Diploma III

Civil Engineering:

    Mathematics, Strength of Materials, Electrical Engineering, Mechanics of Fluids, Surveying and Structure.

Mechanical Engineering:

    Mathematics, Strength of Materials, Electrical Engineering, Mechanics of Fluids, Thermodynamics and Mechanics of Machines.

Electrical (Light) Engineering:

    Mathematics, Strength of Materials, Electrical Machines, Circuit Theory and Measurements, Electronics, Telecommunication and Radio.

Electrical (Heavy) Engineering:

    Mathematics, Strength of Materials, Thermodynamics, Electrical Technology, Electrical Machines, Circuit Theory and Measurements.

## Subjects:  Diploma IV

Civil Engineering:

    Mathematics, Civil Engineering Material and Construction, Mechanics of Fluids, Geology, Theory of Structures and Surveying.

Mechanical Engineering:

   Mathematics, Mechanics of Fluids, Strength of Materials and Metallurgy,
   Thermodynamics, Mechanics of Machines, Machine Design.

Electrical (Light) Engineering:

   Mathematics, Advanced Electrical Engineering, Electronics, Telecommunication and Physics.

Electrical (Heavy) Engineering:

   Mathematics, Advanced Electrical Engineering, Thermodynamics, Electrical Machines, Power Supply.


Faculty of Science

Entrance requirements:     (a)  For a degree in Mathematics and/or Physics:
                                "A" level passes in Physics and 1 of the
                                following:  Pure Mathematics, Applied Math-
                                ematics, Mathematics and Further Mathematics.

                           (b)  For a degree course which includes Chemistry:
                                "A" level passes in Chemistry, Physics and 1
                                of the following:  Pure Mathematics, Math-
                                ematics and Further Mathematics.

                           (c)  For a degree course which includes Biology,
                                Botany, Zoology or Biochemistry, either
                                "A" level passes in (i) Chemistry and (ii)
                                Botany or Zoology or Biology, and (iii) an
                                ordinary level pass in Additional Mathematics.

Structure of course:

(a)  Preliminary - 2 years.
(b)  Degree Course - Part I,  1 year
                     Part II, 2 years

Preliminary Course Subjects:

(a)  Pure Mathematics, Applied Mathematics, Physics
(b)  Biology, Chemistry, Physics
(c)  Pure Mathematics, Chemistry, Physics

Degree Course Subjects:

(a)  Pure Mathematics, Applied Mathematics and Physics in Part I, leading
     to Mathematics and Physics in Part II.

(b)  Mathematics, Physics and Chemistry in Part I, leading to Physics
     and Chemistry in Part II.

(c)  Botany, Zoology and Chemistry or Botany/Zoology, Physics and Chemistry
     in Part I, leading to Biochemistry and Botany/Zoology in Part II.

(d)  Botany, Zoology and Biochemistry in Part I, leading to Botany and
     Zoology in Part II.

Examinations:

(a)  Preliminary:

     General Certificate of Education (advanced level) internal examination
     in 1st year, Subsidiary Mathematics and 2nd year Subsidiary Physics.

(b)  B.Sc. Part I

     In each subject there are 2 theory papers and in practical subjects
     there are practical examinations.

(c)  B.Sc. Part II

     In each subject there are 3 theory papers except in Mathematics, where
     there are 4 theory papers.  In practical subjects there are practical
     examinations.

Degrees awarded:

     1st Class Honours
     2nd Class Honours
     Pass

Faculty of Pharmacy

B. Pharm.

Entrance requirements:            Passes at advanced level in (a) Chemis-
                                  try and (b) Biology or Zoology together
                                  with (c) credits in Physics and Elemen-
                                  tary Mathematics in the School Certificate
                                  of West African Examinations Council.

Duration of course:       3 years.

Structure of Course:

Part I covers 1 year and Part II, 2 years.

Subjects:

## Part I

    Chemistry                    Pharmacognosy
    Pharmaceutics             Physiology

## Examination: B.Pharm., Part I

Students are examined at the end of the 1st year in Physiology and Pharmacognosy. Successful candidates then proceed to Part II of the course.

## Part II

    Pharmaceutical Chemistry    Pharmacology
    Pharmaceutics

## Examination: B.Pharm., Part II (Final)

The examination in Bachelor of Pharmacy Part II of the B.Pharm. degree consists of both written and practical papers and oral tests in:

    Pharmaceutical Chemistry
    Pharmaceutics
    Pharmacology

## Degrees awarded:

    1st Class Honours
    2nd Class Honours
    Pass

## UNIVERSITY COLLEGE OF SCIENCE EDUCATION, Cape Coast

Founded as University College of Cape Coast in 1962 for the training of graduate teachers for secondary schools, granting external degrees of the University of Ghana. Became University College of Science Education in 1964 with the sole task of training graduate science teachers.

Entrance requirements:          Direct Entry into B.A. degree: 5 G.C.E. passes at "O" level including English Language of which at least 2 of the following must be at "A" level:

                            English Literature
                            History or British Constitution or
                                Economic History
                            Geography
                            French
                            Latin
                            Mathematics plus Greek and Economic
                              History

Direct Entry to B.Sc. degree:  5 G.C.E. passes
including English Language at "A" level and the
others chosen from the following:

Chemistry
Physics
Mathematics
Zoology
Botany or Biology

Faculties:

      Science                Education
      Arts

## Faculty of Science

Departments of Mathematics, Physics, Chemistry, Botany, and Zoology.

Duration of course:        3 years.

## Faculty of Arts

Departments of Economics, Geography, English, and Classical Studies.

Duration of course:        3 years.

Department of French

Duration of course:        3 years.

## Faculty of Education

Duration of course:        3 years.

## VOCATIONAL AND TECHNICAL EDUCATION

## CRAFT (TRADES) COURSES

Duration of courses:       3 years.  (1 year pre-technical and 2 years trade
                           courses.)

Pre-technical (1 year)

    English
    Mathematics
    Science
    Technical Drawing
    Wood/Metal Work

Craft Courses - Intermediate, 1st and 2nd years

Carpentry and Joinery:

| Subjects | 1st year | 2nd year |
|---|---|---|
| | (33 weeks, 10 hours a week) | |
| Technology and Science | 140 | 140 |
| Practical | 560 | 560 |
| Drawing | 140 | 140 |
| English and Social Studies | 140 | 140 |
| Calculation | 70 | 70 |

(1 year industrial experience or training)

Final Craft Courses

| Subjects | 3rd year |
|---|---|
| | (33 weeks, 10 hours a week) |
| Technology and Science | 140 |
| Practical | 560 |
| Drawing | 140 |
| English and Social Studies | 140 |
| Calculation | 70 |

Mechanical Engineering Technicians' Certificate

1-year Junior Technical Course (33 weeks).

| Subjects | Hours per week |
|---|---|
| Workshop Practice | 9 |
| Workshop Technology | 2 |
| Mathematics | 5 |
| Mechanical Engineering Science | 4 |
| Electrical Engineering Science | 2 |
| Engineering Drawing | 6 |
| English | 5 |

Followed by 1-year course in:

| | |
|---|---|
| Drawing of Materials | 5 |
| Engineering Science | 4 |
| Mathematics | 5 |
| Processes of Practice | 12 |
| General Studies | 4 |

## Ordinary Technician Diploma in Mechanical/Electrical Engineering

1-year Junior Technician Course (33 weeks).

| Subjects | Hours per week |
|---|---|
| Workshop Practice | 9 |
| Workshop Technology | 2 |
| Mathematics | 5 |
| Mechanical Engineering Science | 4 |
| Electrical Engineering Science | 2 |
| Engineering Drawing | 6 |
| English | 5 |

Followed by 1-year course in (a) Mechanical or (b) Electrical:

| Subjects | Hours |
|---|---|
| (a) Mechanical Course | |
| Power Production | 140 |
| Mathematics | 140 |
| Electrical Engineering | 105 |
| Mechanical Engineering | 70 |
| Workshop Practice | 210 |
| Drawing | 105 |
| Plant Maintenance | 140 |
| Social Studies | 105 |
| Industrial Orientation | 105 |
| (b) Electrical Course | |
| Physics and Chemistry | 105 |
| Mathematics | 175 |
| Electrical Science | 105 |
| Mechanical Science | 70 |
| Technology | 175 |
| Drawing | 105 |
| Workshop Practice | 210 |
| English | 140 |
| Industrial Orientation | 70 |

Diploma in Building Construction Technicians' Certificate and Civil
Engineering (1 year)

| Subjects | Periods per week | Hours per period |
|---|---|---|
| Building Construction | 2 | 2 |
| Workshop Practice/Technology | 2 | 3 |
| Properties of Materials | 1 | 2 |
| Surveying | 1 | 2 |
| Physics and Chemistry | 1 | 1 |
| Mathematics | 2 | $1\frac{1}{2}$ |
| Industrial Orientation | 1 | 1 |
| Geometry | 1 | 2 |
| Mechanics | 1 | 2 |
| English | 1 | 2 |

## HOME ECONOMICS EDUCATION

### Home Science Diploma Course

Entrance requirement:     West African School Certificate or equivalent.

Duration of course:       4 years.

Diploma in Home Science awarded at end of course.

TIMETABLE

1st Year
(45-minute periods per week)

| Subjects | Term 1 | Term 2 | Term 3 |
|---|---|---|---|
| Chemistry | 5 | 5 | 5 |
| Biology | 5 | 5 | 5 |
| English | 5 | 3 | 3 |
| Textiles | 4 | - | - |
| Clothing | 7 | - | 5 |
| Related Art | 3 | - | 3 |
| P. Study | 6 | 2 | 2 |
| Education Orientation | - | 2 | - |
| Laundrywork | - | 4 | - |
| Home Management | - | 4 | 4 |
| Foods | - | - | 4 |
| Psychology | - | - | 4 |

## 2nd Year
### (45-minute period per week)

| Subjects | Term 1 | Term 2 | Term 3 |
| --- | --- | --- | --- |
| Chemistry | 4 | 4 | 4 |
| Biology | 5 | 5 | 5 |
| Physics | 3 | 3 | 3 |
| Mathematics | 2 | 1 | 2 |
| English | 3 | 3 | 3 |
| Education | 3 | - | 3 |
| Human Development | - | 4 | 4 |
| Home Management | 2 | 2 | - |
| Foods | 5 | 5 | 5 |
| Clothing | 4 | 4 | 4 |
| Sociology | 4 | - | - |
| P. Study | | 1 | 2 |
| Related Art | - | 3 | - |

## 3rd Year
### (45-minute period per week)

| Subjects | Term 1 | Term 2 | Term 3 |
| --- | --- | --- | --- |
| Chemistry | 4 | 4 | 4 |
| Biology | 2 | 2 | 2 |
| Physics | 3 | 3 | - |
| Mathematics | 2 | 2 | - |
| English | 3 | 3 | 3 |
| Education | 3 | 3 | 4 |
| Research Prin./Methods | 4 | - | - |
| Research Practicum | - | 4 | - |
| Home Management | 4 | 4 | 4 |
| Foods | 3 | 3 | 2 |
| Clothing | 4 | 2 | 4 |
| P. Study | 3 | 1 | 4 |
| Study of Family | - | 4 | - |

## 4th Year
### (45-minute period per week)

| Subjects | Term 1 | Term 2 | Term 3 |
| --- | --- | --- | --- |
| Biochemistry | 3 | - | 3 |
| Education | - | - | 4 |
| Social Psychology | | | |
| Adult Education | 3 | - | - |
| English | 3 | - | 3 |
| Nutrition | 6 | - | 6 |

| | | | |
|---|---|---|---|
| Home Management | - | - | 7 |
| Psych. Personality | - | - | 4 |
| P. Study | 5 | - | 8 |
| Practice in Secondary Schools | - | 35 | - |

## 2-Year Housecraft Course

Entrance requirement:    Teachers' Certificate "A".

Duration of course:       2 years.

### TIMETABLE

#### 1st Year
(45-minute periods per week)

| Subject | Term 1 | Term 2 | Term 3 |
|---|---|---|---|
| Applied Science | 4 | 4 | 4 |
| Health Science | 4 | 4 | 4 |
| English | 4 | 4 | 4 |
| Education/Method | 2 | 2 | 2 |
| Home Management (including Laundry) | 4 | 6 | 6 |
| Food/Nutrition | 4 | 4 | 4 |
| Clothing | 4 | 4 | 4 |
| Textiles | 4 | - | - |
| Related Art | 3 | 3 | 3 |
| Gardening | 2 | 2 | 2 |

#### 2nd Year
(45-minute periods per week)

| Subject | Term 1 | Term 2 | Term 3 |
|---|---|---|---|
| Applied Science | 3 | 3 | 3 |
| Health Science | 4 | 4 | 4 |
| English | 4 | 4 | 4 |
| Education/Method | 4 | 3 | 2 |
| Mothercraft | (2) | (2) | - |
| Home Management | 4 | (3) | (6) |
| Foods/Nutrition | 4 | 5 | 5 |
| Nutrition | 2 | 2 | 2 |
| Clothing | 4 | 5 | 5 |
| Related Art | 3 | 3 | 3 |
| P. Study | | 1 | 1 |
| Teaching Practice | 3 weeks | 2 weeks | - |

TEACHER EDUCATION
=================

CERTIFICATE "A" COLLEGES
------------------------

Entrance requirements:    Common Entrance Examination organized by the West
                          African Examinations Council.

Duration of course:       4 years.

### TIMETABLE
### (40-minute periods per week)

| Subjects | 1st Year | 2nd Year | 3rd Year | 4th Year |
|---|---|---|---|---|
| English Language | 2 | 2 | 2 | 2 |
| English Composition | 2 | 2 | 2 | 2 |
| English Reading | 2 | 2 | 2 | 3 |
| English Speech | 1 | 1 | 1 | 1 |
| Ghana Language | 2 | 2 | 1 | - |
| Arithmetic | 3 | 2 | 2 | 2 |
| Algebra | 2 | 2 | 2 | 2 |
| Geometry | 1 | 1 | 1 | 2 |
| Science | 3 | 3 | 2 | 3 |
| Physical Education | 3 | 2 | 1 | 2 |
| History | 3 | 3 | 2 | 2 |
| Geography | 3 | 3 | 3 | 4 |
| Religious Knowledge | 2 | 2 | 2 | - |
| Arts and Crafts | 4 | 4 | 3 | 2 |
| Music | 2 | 2 | 2 | - |
| Singing | 4 | 4 | 4 | 4 |
| Demonstration Lesson | - | - | 3 | 3 |
| Education | - | - | 3 | 3 |
| Visual Aid | - | - | 2 | 2 |
| Radio Broadcasts (English) | 1 | 1 | - | - |
| Total | 40 | 40 | 40 | 40 |
| Agriculture | 2 | 2 | 2 | - |
| Physical Education | 2 | 2 | 2 | 2 |

CERTIFICATE "A" POST SECONDARY COLLEGES
---------------------------------------

Entrance requirements:    Common Entrance Examination organized by the
                          West African Examinations Council.

Duration of course:       2 years.

### TIMETABLE
(40 minute periods per week)

| Subjects | 1st Year | 2nd Year |
|---|---|---|
| English | 5 | 5 |
| Mathematics | 4 | 4 |
| General Science | 2 | 2 |
| Health Science | 2 | 2 |
| History | 2 | 2 |
| Geography | 2 | 3 |
| Physical Education | 1 | 1 |
| Music | 2 | 2 |
| Religious Knowledge | 1 | 1 |
| Art | 2 | 2 |
| Education | 4 | 4 |
| Education Handwork | 1 | 1 |
| Mathematics Method | 1 | 1 |
| English Method | 1 | 1 |
| Current Affairs | 1 | 1 |
| Library | 1 | 1 |
| Needlework | 2 | 2 |
| Education Broadcast | 1 | 1 |

For the internal examination conducted by the colleges for promotions, aggregate mark of 40% to 50% is required.


## Art and Craft Course

Entrance requirements:    West African School Certificate or equivalent and a Teachers' Certificate "A".

Duration of course:    3 years.

The National Teacher Training Council Examination in Art and Crafts is required for the award of the Art and Craft Certificate.

### TIMETABLE
(45 minute periods per week)

| Subject | 1st Year | 2nd Year | 3rd Year |
|---|---|---|---|
| Art History and Art Appreciation | 1 | 2 | 2 |
| General Drawing and Life Drawing | 4 | 5 | 5 |
| Art Education | 2 | 2 | 2 |
| Graphic Art | - | 4 | - |
| Lettering | 3 | - | - |
| English | 2 | 2 | 2 |

| | | | |
|---|---|---|---|
| Anatomy | 1 | 1 | - |
| Pictorial Composition | 5 | 5 | 5 |
| Modelling | 4 | 4 | 4 |
| Thesis | - | - | 2 |
| Design and Fabric Printing | 4 | - | - |
| Basketry | - | 3 | - |
| Pottery | 3 | - | - |
| Weaving (Traditional and Broad Loom) | 3 | 3 | - |
| Sculpture | - | - | - |
| Carving | - | 3 | - |
| Bookcraft | 3 | - | - |
| Special Craft | - | - | 7 |
| Subsidiary Craft | - | - | 5 |

## Diploma in Physical Education

Entrance requirement:      West African School Certificate or equivalent.

Duration of course:        4 years.

Lowest passing grade - 40%.

Distinction - 85% or above.

### TIMETABLE
#### (45-minute periods per week)

| Subjects | 1st Year | 2nd Year | 3rd Year | 4th Year |
|---|---|---|---|---|
| Theory P.E. | 2 | 2 | 1 | 2 |
| Health Education | 2 | 1 | 1 | 1 |
| Physiology | 1 | 1 | 1 | 1 |
| Anatomy | 1 | 1 | 1 | 1 |
| Games-Theory | 1 | 1 | 1 | 1 |
| Games Practical | 6 | 6 | 6 | 4 |
| Athletics Theory | 1 | 1 | 1 | 1 |
| Athletics Practical | 2 | 2 | 2 | 4 |
| Personal Gym | 6 | 6 | 6 | 4 |
| Primary School Gym | 1 | 1 | 1 | - |
| Middle School Gym | 1 | 1 | 1 | 1 |
| Sec. Trg. College Gym | - | 1 | - | 1 |
| Improvization | 1 | 1 | 1 | - |
| Apparatus Making | 1 | 1 | 1 | - |
| Art and Crafts | 1 | 1 | - | - |
| Education/Psychology | 1 | 1 | 1 | - |
| English | 2 | 2 | 4 | 1 |
| Teaching Practice | 3 | 3 | 2 | 3 |
| Kinesiology | - | - | - | 1 |

| | | | | |
|---|---|---|---|---|
| Minor and African Games | 1 | 1 | 1 | 1 |
| Swimming-Theory | 1 | 1 | 1 | 1 |
| Swimming-Practical | 2 | 2 | 2 | 2 |
| Circuit Training | 1 | 1 | 1 | 1 |
| First Aid | 1 | 1 | 1 | - |

## 2-Year Physical Education Course

Entrance requirements:    Teachers' Certificate "A" with at least 2 years teaching experience for men and 1 year for women.

Duration of course:    2 years.

Lowest passing grade - 40%.

Distinction - 85% or above.

Curriculum:    See above, columns 1 and 2.

## Specialist Music Course

Duration of course:    2 years.

### TIMETABLE
### (45-minute periods per week)

| Subjects | 1st Year | 2nd Year | 3rd Year | 4th Year |
|---|---|---|---|---|
| Music History | 1 | 1 | 1 | - |
| Male Voices | 2 | 2 | 2 | 2 |
| African Music | 1 | 1 | - | - |
| Piano Tuning | 1 | 1 | - | - |
| Form and Analysis | 1 | 1 | 1 | 1 |
| English | 1 | 1 | 1 | - |
| Rudiments | 2 | 2 | - | - |
| Keyboard Harmony | 1 | 1 | 1 | - |
| Harmony | - | - | 2 | 1 |
| Counterpoint | - | - | 2 | 1 |
| Singing Class | 1 | 1 | - | - |
| Singing Theory | - | - | 1 | 1 |
| School Music | 1 | 1 | - | - |
| Violin Class | 1 | 1 | - | - |
| Aural | 1 | 1 | 1 | 1 |
| Music Teaching Tutorial | 1 | 1 | - | - |
| Wind Ensemble | 1 | 1 | 1 | 1 |
| Orchestra | 2 | 2 | 2 | 1 |
| Orchestra Tuition | - | - | 1 | - |
| Mixed Voices | 1 | 1 | 1 | 1 |

| | | | | |
|---|---|---|---|---|
| Orchestration | - | - | 2 | 1 |
| Music Appreciation | 1 | 1 | 1 | 1 |
| (Individual Violin) | 1 | - | - | 3 |
| (Individual Piano) | 7 | 15 | 10 | 8 |
| (Individual Singing) | - | 14 | 8 | 5 |

The examination leading to the award of the <u>Licenciate of the Royal School of Music (London)</u> is given at the completion of  the course.

429

REPUBLIC OF LIBERIA

High School

Vocational and Technical Training

Teacher Training

SECONDARY EDUCATION

PRIMARY EDUCATION

Divinity | Arts

Com. & Bus. Ad.

Forestry

Agriculture

Education

Law

Science

Arts **

(Senior High)

(Junior High)

Grade

Kindergarten

| Student's Age | Year of Schooling | | |
|---|---|---|---|
| 26 | 20 | | HIGHER EDUCATION |
| 25 | 19 | | |
| 24 | 18 | | |
| 23 | 17 | | |
| 22 | 16 | | |
| 21 | 15 | | |
| 20 | 14 | | |
| 19 | 13 | | |
| 18 | 12 | | |
| 17 | 11 | | |
| 16 | 10 | | |
| 15 | 9 | | SECONDARY |
| 14 | 8 | | |
| 13 | 7 | | |
| 12 | 6 | | ELEMENTARY |
| 11 | 5 | | |
| 10 | 4 | | |
| 9 | 3 | | |
| 8 | 2 | | |
| 7 | 1 | | |
| 6 | | | |
| 5 | | | |
| 4 | | | |
| 3 | | | |

Compulsory education: 6–16 years of age
School year: March 1 – December 20

Secondary grading: Excellent 100–90
Good 89–80
Fair 79–70
Poor Below 70

REPUBLIC OF LIBERIA

Independence:   July 26, 1847.

## BACKGROUND

Liberia was established in 1822 by the American Colonization Society, a private, philanthropic organization, "to promote and execute a plan for colonizing in Africa, with their own consent, the free people of color residing in the U.S." Negro immigration to Liberia continued until close of U.S. Civil War.  Capital, Monrovia, named for U.S. President, James Monroe.

Population now composed of indigenous Africans and descendants of American negro  settlers, in ratio of 20-1.  The indigenous Africans constitute 20 negro tribes, each with its own language, which came several centuries ago from the North and the East, bringing the cultures of Arabia and Egypt.

Linguistically, the tribes are divided into four groups:
    Vai people in Southwest
    Kru tribes in coastal areas
    Golas in West Central area
    Kpelle in center and Northwest

2 tribes are not strictly Liberian:  Mandingo, itinerant Muslim traders, and Fanti, fishermen, who come from Ghana and stay a few years at a time.

6% of the population are non-Liberian:  Ghanian, Lebanese, American, Dutch, Italian.  Only the black man may hold citizenship and own property in Liberia.

English is the official language, but only 20% speak it.  Of the more than 20 tribal languages, only Vai, Bassa and Lorma can be written.

In 1847, the Republic of Liberia was established under a democratic constitution like that of the United States.  Boundary agreements with British and French were reached by turn of the century.  The Republic is comprised of 5 counties, 3 provinces, and 4 territories administratively. Liberia has been a Christian nation since its founding.

Firestone (U.S. rubber company) plantations established in 1920.

During 19th century, education was largely offered by missionary organizations.  Government established Department of Public Instruction in
1900.  Compulsory education law in 1912.  General Education Code in 1937;
amended in 1942 and 1944.

Up to 1944, the mission and private groups provided about 78% of education.
By 1958, 61% of 49,000 pupils in elementary and secondary schools were in
government schools, 29% in mission schools, and 10% in private schools.

By 1961, the religious bodies operating schools in Liberia (schools
inspected by the Bureau of Non-Governmental Schools of the Department of
Public Instruction) were:
- The Catholic Church and Convents
- The Protestant Episcopal Church (Foreign Board)
- The Holy Cross Mission (operated by the P.E. Foreign Board)
- The Presbytery of Western Africa (Liberian)
- The Methodist Church (Foreign Board)
- The African Methodist Episcopal Church (Foreign Episcopacy)
- The African Methodist Episcopal Zion Church (Liberian)
- The United Lutheran Church (Foreign and National)
- The National Baptist Convention (Foreign)
- The Liberian Baptist Missionary and Educational Convention (Liberian)
- The Swedish Free Mission (Foreign)
- The Ecumenical Church Foundation (Foreign)
- The Seventh-Day Adventist Mission (Foreign Board)
- The Church of the Lord (Foreign Board)
- The Assembly of God Mission (Foreign Board)
- The Liberian Inland Mission (Foreign Board)
- The Lighthouse Tabernacle Church (Foreign)
- The Pentacostal Assemblies of the World (Foreign)
- The Church of God in Christ (Foreign)
- The United Holiness Church (Foreign)
- The Refuge Church of Jesus Christ (Foreign)
- The Zoradee Pentecostal Mission
- The Lighthouse Full Gospel Church (Liberian)
- The Liberia Soul Clinic Mission (Foreign)
- The Carver Foreign Mission (Foreign Board)
- The Open Bible Standard Mission (Foreign)
- The Nyforquellie Gospel Mission (Foreign)
- The Refuge Mission of the Apostolic Faith (Foreign)
- Youth Mission for Christ (Foreign)
- Christ Mercy Mission (Foreign)
- The Bible Way Mission (Foreign)
- The Moslem Mission (Liberian)
    - (a) The Ahmadiyya Foreign Mission
    - (b) The Moslem Community School

By 1962, there were almost 900 schools in Liberia, including 29 secondary
schools and 3 institutions of higher education. Of these, 159 elementary
schools, 11 high schools and 2 colleges were operated by foreign mission
boards.

Educational system is patterned on that of the United States. Originally
8 years of primary and 4 years of secondary education, it has been reorganized on the 6-3-3 system (6 years, primary; 3 years, junior high school;
3 years, senior high school). It is a centralized system of education
with levels from kindergarten to university. 80,000 Liberians are now
in an educational program shared by the government, church and industry.
The Department of Education has classified the 29 High Schools according
to their standards relative to schools in Liberia. There are 3 that have
an "A" rating: Lutheran Training Institute, College of West Africa (a
Methodist Mission school), and the Protestant Episcopal High School, Cape
Mount. These are mission schools.

4-year accelerated program, 1960-63, initiated plans for the establishment
of 2 Rural Teacher Training Institutes (in Webbo, Eastern Province, and
Kakata, Central Province), 20 rural schools in each of the 3 provinces,
and 8 schools in each of the 5 counties.

1961, national examinations planned to be given at close of 6th and 9th
grades. By 1961, national school-leaving examinations for 12th grade
students.

In 1964, building started for Monrovia Torino School of Medicine and
Hospital, Congo Town, project aided by the Italian Government and the
Catholic Church.


## PRESENT SYSTEM


## PRE-ELEMENTARY EDUCATION

Entry age: 5 years.

40 government kindergartens in 5 counties and 2 provinces.
Kindergartens also connected with many mission and private schools.


## ELEMENTARY EDUCATION

Entry age: 6 years.

6-year program. Grades 1 through 6. (Some schools still on 8-4 system.)

Curriculum:          Language Arts (Oral Communication, Written Communi-
                     cation, Reading and Literature), Social Studies,
                     Mathematics, Science/Health, Health Education,
                     Music, Arts and Crafts.

Elementary School Certificate awarded at close of program.


## FIRESTONE PLANTATIONS SCHOOLS

Semi-public schools from pre-elementary through 8th grade.

School examinations given by teachers and Metropolitan Achievement Tests
given by Firestone Education Office. Along with these are the National
Examination on the 6th grade level. Report card indicating promotion
from the 8th grade to the 9th grade is given to student successfully
completing the 8th grade. Mark for promotion is 70.


## SECONDARY EDUCATION

6-year program.

**JUNIOR HIGH SCHOOL** - Grades 7 through 9.

**SENIOR HIGH SCHOOL** - Grades 10 through 12.

Major senior high schools:

| School | Type | Location |
|---|---|---|
| Laboratory High (U.L.) | Public | Monrovia |
| Peoples' College (U.L.) | Public | Monrovia |
| B.W. Harris | Public | Monrovia |
| College of West Africa | Mission | Monrovia |
| St. Patrick's | Mission | Monrovia |
| St. Teresa's | Mission | Monrovia |
| Monrovia College | Mission | Monrovia |
| Zion Academy | Mission | Monrovia |
| Lott Carey | Mission | Brewerville |
| Martha Tubman Academy | Private | Monrovia |
| Adult Jr. and Sr. High | Public | Harper City |
| Cape Palmas High | Public | Harper City |
| Our Lady of Fatima | Mission | Harper City |
| Bishop Fergusson | Mission | Harper City |
| Sinoe High School | Public | Sinoe |
| Bassa High School | Public | Bassa |
| Cape Mount High School | Public | Robertsport |
| Episcopal High School | Mission | Robertsport |
| Suehn High School | Mission | Suehn |
| Ricks Institute | Mission | Virginia |

| Sanniquellie High School | Public | Sanniquellie |
| W.D. Coleman | Public | Clayashland |
| Booker Washington Institute | Public | Kakata |
| Voinjama High School | Public | Voinjama |
| St. Augustine | Mission | Western Province |
| Lutheran Training Institute | Mission | Monrovia |

## Public school curriculum:

Junior High School courses

   Language Arts
      (Oral Communication, Written Communication, Reading, Literature)
   Mathematics
      7th grade:  arithmetical concepts and processes
                  geometric concepts
                  mathematics in home and community
      8th grade:  extension of arithmetical process and geometric and
                     algebraic concepts
                  arithmetic in home and community
                  geometry of mensuration
      9th grade:  further extension of arithmetic processes and algebraic
                     concepts
                  mathematics in home and community
   Science
      7th grade:  concepts of biology, chemistry, physics
      8th grade:  extension of biology, chemistry, physics
      9th grade:  extension of biology, chemistry, physics, and study of
                     atomic world
   Health Education
   Music
   Art
   Foreign Language (French)

Junior High School Certificate awarded on successful completion of 9th
grade work.


Senior High School courses:

   Language Arts (3 years required)
      Oral Communication, Written Communication, Reading and Literature
      (English Literature in 10th and 11th grades, American Literature,
       12th grade)
   Mathematics (1 year required)
      10th grade:  general mathematics and practical applications
                   1st year algebra (required of all academic students)
      11th grade:  intermediate algebra (required of all academic
                      students)
      12th grade:  geometry (required of all academic students)
                   electives:  trigonometry, advanced algebra, plane
                      and solid geometry

Science
  10th grade:  biology (required of all students)
  11th grade:  chemistry (required of all academic students)
  12th grade:  physics (required of all academic students)
               electives:  additional courses in chemistry, physics,
                 biology
Health Education (3 years required)
Music (elective)
Art (elective)
Foreign Language (French)

**Senior High School Certificate awarded on successful completion of 12th
grade work.


## COLLEGE OF WEST AFRICA, Monrovia

Methodist mission secondary school, founded in 1839.

(Its teacher training program has been incorporated into the University
of Liberia as the William V.S. Tubman School of Teacher Training.  See
HIGHER EDUCATION.)

Entry age:                  12 years (7th grade)

Entrance requirements:      Elementary School Certificate and achievement
                            test examination

Language of instruction:  English

6-year program, college preparatory

Curriculum:                 English, Social Studies, Mathematics, Science,
                            French, Electives (Business, Home Economics,
                            Industrial Arts)

Grading for promotion and lowest passing grade:  70.

**Diploma awarded on successful completion of program.


## LUTHERAN TRAINING INSTITUTE, Monrovia

Lutheran mission secondary school.  American textbooks used as prescribed
for respective grades in the U.S.  Materials adapted to local situations.

## TIMETABLE
### (45-minute periods per week)

| Subjects | 9th grade | 10th grade | 11th grade | 12th grade |
|---|---|---|---|---|
| English | 7 | 7 | 7 | 7 |
| Social Studies | | | | |
|   Civics, Geography | 4 | | | |
|   World History | | 4 | 4 | |
|   African History | | | | 4 |
| Mathematics | | | | |
|   Arithmetic/Algebra | 5 | | | |
|   Algebra/Geometry | | 5 | 5 | 5 |
| Sciences | | | | |
|   General Science | 5 | | | |
|   Biology | | 6 | | |
|   Chemistry | | | 5 | |
|    (and Lab.) | | | 2 | |
|   Physics | | | | 5 |
|    (and Lab.) | | | | 2 |
| French | 4 | 4 | 4 | 4 |
| Religious Education | | | | |
|   I and II | 5 (1 sem.) | 5 (1 sem.) | 5 (1 sem.) | 5 (1 sem.) |
| Physical Education | 2 | 2 | 2 | 2 |
| Other Subjects | | | | |
|   Art (elective) | 2 | | | |
|   Typing (elective) | | | 2 | 2 |
|   Teaching Methods (elective) | | | | 3 |

Grading:      E - Excellent
              A - Excellent
              S - Satisfactory
              B - Good
              C - Fair
              U - Unsatisfactory
              F - Failing

The high school completion diploma is granted by the Department of Education of Liberia on the basis of students passing the basic studies in English, Social Studies, Mathematics and Science at the Institute and passing a National Examination in these 4 subjects.

## THE LABORATORY HIGH SCHOOL

The Laboratory High School is operated in connection with the University of Liberia and controlled by the Board of Trustees of the University, but courses are set by the Department of Education.

Students from this School form the core of the University Freshman class.

4-year program

Requirements for graduation:

    21 units distributed to include:

| English | 4 units | Language | 3 units |
| Mathematics | 4 units | Elective | 1 unit |
| Social Science | 4 units | Physical Education | 1 unit |
| Natural Science | 4 units | | |

    (Mathematics includes Algebra and Plane Geometry)

| Grading: | Excellent | 100 - 90 |
| | Good | 89 - 80 |
| | Fair | 79 - 70 |
| | Poor | Below 70 |

Promotion from one class to another is based upon a pass in each course.

**Diploma awarded on successful completion of program.

## HIGHER EDUCATION

### UNIVERSITY OF LIBERIA, Monrovia

Founded in 1862 as Liberia College of Liberal and Fine Arts, and Science. Obtained University status, February 15, 1951, when Liberia College was merged with 5 other schools.

Academic year:        March-November

Entrance requirements:  Graduation, or the equivalent, from an accredited high school or preparatory school with no fewer than 16 units in the following fields: English (4), Mathematics (3 - 2 yrs. of Algebra and 1 yr. of Plane Geometry), Foreign Language (2), Science (3), Social Science (3), elective (1).
All candidates must take an Entrance Examination given yearly in February.

The University is composed of:

    (1)  Degree Schools

          The College of Liberal and Fine Arts
          Science Division of the College of Liberal and Fine Arts

The Thomas J. R. Faulkner College of Engineering and Applied
   Science
The Louis Arthur Grimes College of Law
The William V. S. Tubman College of Teacher Training
The College of Forestry
The College of Agriculture

(2)  Non-Degree Schools

The Laboratory High School (see SECONDARY EDUCATION)
The Extension School
The Benjamin J. K. Anderson School of Commerce and Business
   Administration

General Regulations:

Progress toward a degree is measured by "credits" per semester (2 semesters
to an academic year).  The unit in which courses are measured, a semester
hour, is defined as 50 minutes of lecture-recitation and approximately 2
hours of preparation.  Laboratory courses require not less than 2 hours per
week of laboratory work throughout a semester.

Quality of work is gauged by a system of credit ratio - the number of
credits received to the number of points elected:

| | |
|---|---|
| 90 - 100 | A, Excellent |
| 80 - 89 | B, Good |
| 70 - 79 | C, Fair |
| 60 - 69 | D, Poor |
| | F, Failure |

Grade points are assigned to course grades as follows:

Each credit with a grade of A = 3 grade points
Each credit with a grade of B = 2 grade points
Each credit with a grade of C = 1 grade point
        D and F grades = no grade points

Grade Point Average:
   (1)  To compute the grade point average for a semester, divide the
        total number of points earned by the total number of credits
        earned.  (Credits carried include those earned, failed, and
        conditioned.)

   (2)  To figure the cumulative grade point average, divide the total
        points earned by the total credits earned in all semesters.
        (If a course has been repeated, only count the credit and points
        of the last grade earned.)

A grade point average of 1.00 is required for graduation.

Those who obtain a cumulative grade point average of:
        from 2.25 - 2.49 are graduated cum laude;
        from 2.5  - 2.75 are graduated magna cum laude;
        from 2.75 - 3.00 are graduated summa cum laude.

Degrees awarded:

| | |
|---|---|
| Bachelor of Arts (B.A.) | 4 years |
| Bachelor of Science (B.Sc.) | 4 years |
| Bachelor of Law (LL.B.) | 4 years |
| Bachelor of Science in Education (B.Sc. - Ed.) | 4 years |
| Bachelor of Science in Forestry (B.Sc. - Forestry) | 4 years |
| Bachelor of Science in Agriculture (B.Sc. - Agric.) | 4 years |

## The College of Liberal and Fine Arts

General education requirements:  All students are required to follow a freshman and sophomore program of general education.

### COURSES OF STUDY (GENERAL PROGRAM)

| FRESHMAN YEAR | | SOPHOMORE YEAR | |
|---|---|---|---|
| 1st & 2nd Semester Courses | Hours | 1st & 2nd Semester Courses | Hours |
| English | 3 | English | 3 |
| Mathematics | 3 | Chemistry, Physics or Biology | 3 |
| Chemistry, Physics or Biology | 3 | Contemporary Civilization | 3 |
| World Geography | 3 | Electives+ | 6 |
| Elective+ | 3 | ROTC | ½ |
| Physical Education | 1 | | |
| ROTC | ½ | | |
| | 16½ | | 15½ |

+Electives in the various areas determined by the departments concerned.

### Bachelor of Arts

Degree requirements:  A minimum of 124 semester hours with a grade point average of at least 1.00.

Courses must include:

  (a)  completion of general education requirements;
  (b)  completion of 2 years of a foreign language during the 1st 2 years of college;
  (c)  completion of 2 additional years of English;
  (d)  completion of a major, taught in 1 of the academic departments (not less than 34 semester hours in the major subject and not less than 12 semester hours in the related subjects).

## The Division of Natural Sciences and Mathematics

Degree courses in:  Mathematics, Physics, Chemistry, Botany, Zoology.

It also provides basic science courses for students of the College of Liberal and Fine Arts (2 years of compulsory science courses, and 1 year compulsory mathematics course).

It offers service courses to students in College of Forestry, College of Agriculture, the Pre-Engineering Program and the Teachers College.

Students in the fields of Mathematics, Physics, Chemistry, Botany, Zoology, Pre-Engineering or High School Science Teaching are specially catered for in the science program.

Science students of the College of Liberal and Fine Arts are required to follow courses with the following semester hour ratings:

### CURRICULUM GUIDE

| SUBJECTS | FRESHMAN | SOPHOMORE | JUNIOR | SENIOR | TOTAL |
|---|---|---|---|---|---|
| Foreign Language Elective | - | 6 | 6 | - | 12 |
| Major Science | 6 | 6 | 12 | 18 | 42 |
| Minor Science | 6 | 6 | 12 | 12 | 36 |
| Supporting Science | 6 | 6 | - | - | 12 |
| Social Science | 6 | 6 | - | - | 12 |
| English | 6 | 6 | - | - | 12 |
| Political Science | - | - | 3 | - | 3 |
| Philosophy | - | - | - | 3 | 3 |
| Physical Education | 2 | - | - | - | 2 |
| ROTC | 1 | 1 | - | - | 2 |
| | 33 | 37 | 33 | 33 | 136 |

## Bachelor of Science

Degree requirements: For Bachelor of Science in Mathematics, Physics, Chemistry, Botany and Zoology, students must have taken 90 hours of natural science (including Mathematics) and have obtained 42 credits in the major area and 36 in the minor area with appropriate grade point average

Students in science of the College of Liberal and Fine Arts must offer 6 semester hours in Social Science beyond lower division requirements and 12 semester hours in a foreign language fulfillment of the requirement for a Bachelor of Science degree. These offerings are in addition to the lower division requirements.

The Pre-Engineering Program - The Thomas J. R. Faulkner College of
Engineering and Applied Science

Prospective students for the Pre-Engineering Program register in the
Division of Science in the College of Liberal and Fine Arts and must
successfully complete all Freshman and Sophomore work as science students
before being qualified for admission to the Pre-Engineering Program.

### CURRICULUM GUIDE

| SUBJECTS | FRESHMAN | SOPHOMORE | JUNIOR | SENIOR | TOTAL |
|---|---|---|---|---|---|
| English | 6 | 6 | - | - | 12 |
| Social Science | 6 | 6 | - | - | 12 |
| Foreign Language | 6 | 6 | - | - | 12 |
| Political Science | - | - | 3 | - | 3 |
| Philosophy | - | - | - | 3 | 3 |
| Mathematics | 6 | 6 | 12 | 6 | 30 |
| Physics | 6 | 6 | 6 | 6 | 24 |
| Applied Mechanics | - | - | 6 | 6 | 12 |
| Other Engineering Subjects | - | - | 12 | 18 | 30 |
| Physical Education | 2 | - | - | - | 2 |
| ROTC | 1 | 1 | - | - | 2 |
| | 33 | 31 | 39 | 39 | 142 |

Program trains junior engineers and technicians for technical positions,
and graduates are expected to be eligible for scholarships leading to a
professional degree in some field of engineering.

Louis Arthur Grimes School of Law

School of Law established in 1954.

Entrance requirements:     Applicant must have successfully completed
                           two years of college training or its equivalent.
                           Entrance examination given.

(LL.B. degree recommended only for those who during their course of study
have maintained a general average of 70 and a cumulative grade point average of 1.00 and who have not failed in more than 2 courses.)

4-year program.

CURRICULUM GUIDE

## 1st Year

| 1st Semester Course | Hours | 2nd Semester Course | Hours |
|---|---|---|---|
| Contracts | 3 | Contracts | 3 |
| Personal Property | 3 | Real Property I | 3 |
| Torts | 3 | Torts | 3 |
| Civil Procedure | 3 | Civil Procedure | 3 |
| Legal History and Method | 1 | Problems in Legal Research | 1 |
| Total | 13 | Total | 13 |

## 2nd Year

| 1st Semester Course | Hours | 2nd Semester Course | Hours |
|---|---|---|---|
| Real Property II | 3 | Accounting/Elective[+] | 3 |
| Negotiable Instruments | 3 | Sales | 3 |
| Equity | 3 | Equity | 3 |
| Criminal Law | 3 | Criminal Law | 3 |
| Moot Court | 1 | Moot Court | 1 |
| Total | 13 | Total | 13 |

## 3rd Year

| 1st Semester Course | Hours | 2nd Semester Course | Hours |
|---|---|---|---|
| Constitutional Law | 3 | Constitutional Law | 3 |
| Corporations | 3 | Corporations | 3 |
| Domestic Relations | 3 | Agency and Partnership | 3 |
| Trusts | 3 | Wills and Estates | 3 |
| Legal Ethics | 1 | Legal Drafting | 1 |
| Total | 13 | Total | 13 |

## 4th Year

| 1st Semester Course | Hours | 2nd Semester Course | Hours |
|---|---|---|---|
| International Law | 3 | International Law | 3 |
| Evidence | 3 | Evidence | 3 |
| Taxation | 3 | Conflict of Laws | 3 |
| Elective[+] | 3 | Elective[+] | 3 |
| Practice Court | 1 | Practice Court | 1 |
| Total | 13 | Total | 13 |

[+]Electives: Administrative Law, Admiralty, Civil Law, Creditors Rights, Customary Law, Damages and Restitution, Future Interests, Jurisprudence, Labor Law, Legislation, Trade Regulation and Economic Organization.

## Bachelor of Laws

Degree requirements:      Completion of a minimum of 100 semester hours
or 4 academic years.

## William V. S. Tubman Teachers College

Founded in 1947 as a division of the College of West Africa - a cooperative
enterprise of the Government of Liberia, the Methodist Church Mission in
Liberia and the Episcopal Church in Liberia.

1948, first certificate awarded for 2-year program.

1950, Division separated from the College; a 4-year program was launched
with Government assuming responsibility.

1951, merged with Liberia College and 5 other schools to form the University.

2 collegiate-level courses:    4-year baccalaureate program
2-year Junior Teaching Training program,
qualifying student for a Grade B Teaching
Certificate issued by the Department of
Education

Entrance requirements:    For both programs, general admission requirements for the University.

Program:    Broad general education in the 1st 2 years; specialized training in the last 2 years.

## Bachelor of Science in Education

Degree requirements:    Bachelor of Science in Elementary Education -
128 semester hours minimum
Bachelor of Science in Secondary Education -
128 semester hours minimum

In addition to meeting the minimum semester hour requirements as listed
above, all students must meet the appropriate specific minimum requirements as shown below:

Hours

(1)    General education requirement
(English, 12; Mathematics, 6; Natural Science, 12;
Social Science, 12; Physical Education, 2; Health
Education, 2)    46

(2)    Professional education requirement
(General Psychology, 3; Educational Psychology, 3;
History and Philosophy of Education, 3; Principles
of Education, 3; School Administration, 3; Student
Teaching, 3)    18

|                                                                          | Hours |
|--------------------------------------------------------------------------|-------|
| (3) Upper division English requirement (except for those in Mathematics and Science) | 12 |
| (4) ROTC for male students | 2 |
| (5) Professional education requirement for elementary education (Science in the Elementary School, 3; Mathematics, 3; Language Arts, 3; Social Studies, 3; Music, 3; Arts and Crafts, 3) | 18 |
| (6) Subject matter requirement in Art, Crafts, and Music for elementary education | 12 |
| (7) Professional education requirement for secondary education (Methods of teaching major subject) | 3 |
| (8) Subject matter requirement for secondary education (except for those in Mathematics and Science)<br>(a) Major field (excluding lower division required work) | 30 |
| (b) Minor field (excluding lower division required work) | 15 |

## Grade B Teaching Certificate (Junior Teacher Training Program)

Degree requirements:

|                                                                          | Hours |
|--------------------------------------------------------------------------|-------|
| (1) General education requirement (English, 12; Social Science, 6; Mathematics, 6; Natural Science, 9; Physical Education, 2; Health Education, 2) | 37 |
| (2) Professional education requirement (General methods, 3; Educational Psychology, 3; History of Education, 3; Teaching Language Arts and Social Studies, 4; Teaching Arithmetic and Science, 4; Student Teaching, 5) | 22 |
| (3) Subject matter requirement in Art, Crafts, and Music | 6 |
| (4) ROTC for male students | 2 |

## College of Forestry

Established in 1955 with the cooperation of the Department of Agriculture and Commerce.

4-year program.

## CURRICULUM GUIDE

### Freshman

| 1st Semester Course | Hours | 2nd Semester Course | Hours |
|---|---|---|---|
| English | 3 | English | 3 |
| World Geography | 3 | World Geography | 3 |
| Mathematics | 3 | Mathematics | 3 |
| Chemistry | 3 | Chemistry | 3 |
| Biology | 3 | Biology | 3 |
| Intro. to Forestry | 1 | Elements of Forestry | 1 |
| Physical Education | 1 | Physical Education | 1 |
| ROTC | ½ | ROTC | ½ |
| Total | 17¼ | Total | 17½ |

CAMP

### Sophomore

| 1st Semester Course | Hours | 2nd Semester Course | Hours |
|---|---|---|---|
| English | 3 | English | 3 |
| Cont. Civilization | 3 | Cont. Civilization | 3 |
| French | 3 | Soils | 3 |
| Physics | 3 | French | 3 |
| Forest Botany | 3 | Dendrology | 3 |
| Survey | 3 | Mapping | 3 |
| ROTC | ½ | ROTC | ½ |
| Total | 18½ | Total | 18½ |

CAMP

### Junior

| 1st Semester Course | Hours | 2nd Semester Course | Hours |
|---|---|---|---|
| Mensuration | 3 | Forest Inventory | 3 |
| Forest Ecology | 3 | Management | 3 |
| Wood Structure | 3 | Wood Technology | 3 |
| Forest Engineering | 3 | Logging | 3 |
| Silviculture | 3 | Silviculture | 3 |
| French | 3 | French | 3 |
| Total | 18 | Total | 18 |

## TOUR AND CAMP

### Senior

| 1st Semester Course | Hours | 2nd Semester Course | Hours |
|---|---|---|---|
| Management | 3 | Working Plans | 3 |
| Forest Economics | 3 | Forest Economics | 3 |
| Utilization | 3 | Utilization | 3 |
| Silviculture | 3 | Silviculture | 3 |
| Forest Policy | 3 | Law and Administration | 3 |
| Photo Interpretation | 3 | Resource Conservation and Productive Land Use | 3 |
| Total | 18 | Total | 18 |

Camps and Tours are requisites of the course which must be completed.
Rubber Culture, offered every 2 years to Senior and Junior classes.

## Bachelor of Science in Forestry

Degree requirements:  Successful completion of 144 semester hours.

## College of Agriculture

4-year program, training farm operators or supervisors, leaders in
business and industry, teachers in vocational agriculture, agricultural
extension agents, agricultural research workers and college professors,
civil servants, workers in public and private service.

### CURRICULUM GUIDE

### Freshman

| 1st Semester Course | Hours | 2nd Semester Course | Hours |
|---|---|---|---|
| English | 3 | English | 3 |
| Mathematics | 3 | Mathematics | 3 |
| General Botany | 3 | General Botany | 3 |
| General Chemistry | 3 | General Chemistry | 3 |
| World Geography | 3 | World Geography | 3 |
| Introduction to Agriculture | 1 | Introduction to Agriculture | 1 |
| Physical Education | 1 | Physical Education | 1 |
| ROTC | ½ | ROTC | ½ |
| Total | 17½ | Total | 17½ |

Vacation Period (University Farm)

Freshman Farm Practice:  6-8 weeks of Crop and Animal Production Farm
Practices.

### Sophomore

| 1st Semester Course | Hours | 2nd Semester Course | Hours |
|---|---|---|---|
| English | 3 | English | 3 |
| General Zoology | 3 | General Zoology | 3 |
| Physics | 3 | Physics | 3 |
| Organic Chemistry | 3 | Crop Production | 4 |
| General Animal Husbandry | 3 | Contemporary Civilization | 3 |
| Contemporary Civilization | 3 | ROTC | ½ |
| ROTC | ½ | | |
| Total | 18½ | Total | 16½ |

Vacation Period (University Farm)

Sophomore Farm Practice:  6-8 weeks of Farm Shop Work.

### Junior

| 1st Semester Course | Hours | 2nd Semester Course | Hours |
|---|---|---|---|
| Agricultural Engineering | 3 | Agricultural Engineering | 3 |
| Introduction to Agricultural Economics | 3 | Principles of Farm Management | 3 |
| Introduction to Agric. and Extension Education | 3 | Methods and Program Development in Agric. and Extension Education | 3 |
| Nature and Properites of Soils | 3 | Nature and Properties of Soils | 3 |
| Basic Horticulture | 3 | Botany of Crop Plants | 3 |
| Animal Nutrition and Feeding | 3 | Poultry Husbandry | 2 |
| Total | 18 | Total | 17 |

Vacation Period

Junior Farm Practice:  6-8 weeks of farm practice to be taken on either
the University Farm or some other farms to be
designated.

## Senior

| 1st Semester Course | Hours | 2nd Semester Course | Hours |
|---|---|---|---|
| Principles of Agric. Marketing | 3 | Farmer's Cooperative and Farm Finance | 2 |
| Soil Fertility and Conservation | 3 | Soil Classification and Survey | 3 |
| Plant Pathology | 3 | General Entomology | 3 |
| Genetics and Plant Breeding | 3 | Rural Sociology | 3 |
| Animal Reproduction and Breeding | 3 | Diseases and Health of Farm Animals | 2 |
| Apprentice Teaching in Agric. and Extension Education (for those in teaching career)[+] | 3 | Principles and Practices of Irrigation and Drainage | 3 |
| Business Management (for those in Agric. Business)[+] | 3 | Elementary Statistics (for those in Agric. Business - taken in Liberal and Fine Arts)[+] | 3 |
| Crop Physiology (for those in Agric. Research)[+] | 3 | Methods of Field Experimentation (for those in Agric. Research)[+] | 3 |
| Total | 18 | | 19 |

[+]Elective:  1 out of 2 in the semester.

## Bachelor of Science in Agriculture

Degree requirements:   Successful completion of 142 semester hours and farm practice works during the 3 consecutive vacation periods in the Freshman, Sophomore and Junior years.

## Benjamin J. K. Anderson School of Commerce and Business Administration

2-year program:

> For those employed - in-service training
> For students training for Stenographers - English, Shorthand and Typing
> For students training as Secretaries - English, Shorthand, Typing, Office Management and Procedure, Secretarial Practice
> For students training as Bookkeepers  and Accountants - Bookkeeping, Business Arithmetic, English, Office Management, Elementary and Advanced Accountancy.

Certificate of Proficiency awarded upon successful completion of program.

## Program of African Studies

Organized in 1957.

Main function:   to collect data and artifacts and to furnish information
                 relative to all phases of African life and culture.

Program:         8 seminars per year.


## CUTTINGTON COLLEGE AND DIVINITY SCHOOL, Suacoco

Founded as Cuttington Collegiate and Divinity School on February 22, 1889.
at Cape Palmas as high school and school of theology.  Closed in 1929.
Reopened in Suacoco in 1949 under the Protestant Episcopal Church.

In 1962, a cooperative relationship established with the Associated Colleges
of the Midwest (ten "small" liberal arts colleges of the Midwest, U.S.A.):
Beloit, Carleton, Coe, Cornell, Grinnell, Knox, Lawrence, Monmouth, Ripon
and St. Olaf.

Entrance requirements:

> For Liberian students - an official transcript of high school
> work, with at least 16 units of entrance credit and
> national examination.

> For foreign students - the Cambridge Overseas School Certificate,
> Division I or II, G.C.E. Advanced Level, West African School
> Certificate Advanced Level, or equivalent.

## Faculties:

> Liberal Arts
> Science
> Education
> Agriculture
> Divinity

Language of instruction:  English

4-year programs.

## Degrees awarded:

> Bachelor of Arts
> Bachelor of Science
> Bachelor of Science in Education
> Bachelor of Science in Agriculture
> Bachelor of Divinity

Course credit hours:   Based on 55-minute class sessions of 18 meetings
                       per credit hour.

Grade scale:

    3 honor points for each credit hour for work of unusual academic
      quality
    2 honor points for each credit hour for work of good quality
    1 honor point for each credit hour for work adequate for graduation
    0 no honor points for each credit hour for work of poor quality
  -1 minus one point for each credit hour of failure.

Graduation:

    A student must have at least 128 credit hours and 128 honor points
    to graduate.  30 hours must be taken during the Junior and Senior
    years in the major field.  He must have an average of 1 or better
    and must pass required courses.

## LIBERAL ARTS MAJORS

| 1st Year | Hours | 2nd Year | Hours |
|---|---|---|---|
| English | 6 | English | 6 |
| Religion | 6 | Religion | 4 |
| Mathematics | 6 | Foreign Language | 6 |
| Foreign Language | 6 | History | 6 |
| Physical Education | 2 | Science, Biology | 6 |
| History | 6 | Electives | 4 |
|  | 32 |  | 32 |

| 3rd Year | | 4th Year | |
|---|---|---|---|
| Electives | 32 | Electives | 32 |
|  | 32 |  | 32 |

(A total of 32 hours for the year, 16 hours per semester)

## SCIENCE MAJORS

| 1st Year | Hours | 2nd Year | Hours |
|---|---|---|---|
| English | 6 | History | 6 |
| Chemistry | 8 | English | 6 |
| Mathematics | 10 | Biology | 6 |
| Biology | 6 | Chemistry | 7 |
| Physical Education | 2 | Mathematics | 6 |
|  |  | Religion | 6 |
|  | 32 |  | 37 |

| 3rd Year | Hours | 4th Year | Hours |
|----------|-------|----------|-------|
| Religion | 4 | Physics | 6 |
| History | 6 | Electives | 26 |
| Physics | 8 | | 32 |
| Mathematics | 6 | | |
| Electives | 8 | | |
| | 32 | | |

(A total of 37 hours for the year, 19 hours first semester and 18 hours second semester.)

In the field of Liberal Arts, electives should include a full year course in each of the following fields: Literature, Fine Arts, Psychology or Anthropology, and Political Science.

In Science, electives should include a full course in each of the following fields: Physics, Biology, and Chemistry.

Education majors have a choice whether they wish to take Liberal Arts or Science courses for the first 2 years. A student may enter the field of Education after completing the Science or the Liberal Arts basic requirements.

Education courses and credits:

    History and Philosophy of Education (3)
    Educational Measurements and Evaluation (2)
    Principles and Methods of Elementary Education (5)
    Art in Elementary School (2)
    Teaching of Science (2)
    Teaching Arithmetic in the Elementary School (2)
    Teaching the Language Arts (2)
    Principles and Methods of Secondary Education (5)
    Teaching of Mathematics in the Elementary and Secondary School (3)
    Teaching of Social Studies (3)
    Teaching English as a Second Language (2)
    School Administration (2)
    Guidance (2)
    Supervision of Instruction (3)
    Comparative Education (2)
    Democratic Discussion Techniques (2)
    Independent Study in Education (1-3)
    Supervised Teaching (Elementary or Secondary) (12)
    Psychology of Human Development (3)

Agriculture majors must take the basic Science curriculum for the first 2 years.

Agriculture courses and credits:

> Agriculture Survey (2)
> Agronomy (3)
> Horticulture (3)
> General Animal Husbandry (3)
> Poultry Husbandry (3)
> Swine Production (3)
> Inland Fisheries (2)
> Plant Physiology (3)
> Introduction to Genetics (3)
> Agricultural Economics (3)
> Agricultural Extension (3)
> Plant Pathology (3)
> Entomology (3)
> General Agricultural Engineering (3)

## Nursing Program Leading to R.N. Certification

In cooperation with the School of Nursing of the Phoebe Lutheran Hospital, the College provides certain courses of instruction requisite for qualification in the nursing program. Courses offered at Cuttington are:

|  | 1st Year | | 2nd Year |
| --- | --- | --- | --- |
| Subject | 1st Semester (credits) | 2nd Semester (credits) | 1st Semester (credits) |
| English | 3 | 3 | 0 |
| Chemistry | 4 | 4 | 0 |
| Biology | 4 | 0 | 0 |
| Microbiology | 0 | 3 | 3 |
| Psychology | 0 | 0 | 3 |
| Religion | 3 | 3 | 0 |
| Anthropology | 0 | 0 | 3 |
| General Mathematics | 1 | 0 | 0 |
| Introd. Nursing | 1 | 1 | 0 |
| Physical Education | 1 | 0 | 0 |
| Nutrition | 0 | 2 | 0 |
|  | 17 | 16 | 9 |

Upon completion of the above program and 2½ years of study at Phoebe Station, student is qualified as registered nurse.

## The Divinity School

A joint endeavor of the Protestant Episcopal Church and the Methodist
Church.

Entrance requirement:     B.A. or equivalent

3-year program.

### SEMINARY CURRICULUM

#### 1st Year (Junior)

| 1st Semester | Hours | 2nd Semester | Hours |
|---|---|---|---|
| Old Testament Survey | 3 | Old Testament Survey | 3 |
| New Testament Survey | 3 | New Testament Survey | 3 |
| History Survey | 3 | History Survey | 3 |
| Theology Survey | 3 | Theology Survey | 3 |
| Basic Homiletics | 2 | Tutorial | 3 |
| Church Law | 1 | | 15 |
| | 15 | | |

#### 2nd Year (Middler)

| 1st Semester | Hours | 2nd Semester | Hours |
|---|---|---|---|
| Old Testament Survey | 2 | Johannine Corpus | 2 |
| Pauline Corpus, Romans | 2 | Work of Younger Church | 2 |
| African Church History | 2 | African Church History | 2 |
| Christian Ethics | 2 | Moral Theology | 2 |
| Deonominational History | 2 | Advanced Homiletics | 2 |
| Early Christian Fathers | 2 | Medieval Thinkers | 2 |
| Tutorial | 3 | Tutorial | 3 |
| | 15 | | 15 |

#### 3rd Year (Senior)

| 1st Semester | Hours | 2nd Semester | Hours |
|---|---|---|---|
| Apologetics | 2 | Advanced Apologetics | 2 |
| Worship | 2 | Senior Homiletics | 2 |
| Christian Education | 2 | Christian Education | 2 |
| Parish Administration | 2 | Elective | 2 |
| Elective | 2 | Elective | 2 |
| Elective | 2 | Thesis or Tutorial | 5 |
| Tutorial | 3 | | 15 |
| | 15 | | |

Total Hours:  90

At the end of 1st semester in Middle Year, student decides on his field
of concentration:  Biblical, Historical, Doctrinal, or Practical; Senior
electives are chosen accordingly.


## Bachelor of Divinity

Degree requirements:    Completion of 90 hours of course and tutorial work
                        with a grade of not less than C (1).

                        Presentation of a thesis (in the senior semester)
                        with a grade of not less than C (1)


## VOCATIONAL AND TECHNICAL EDUCATION

Major vocational and technical training at secondary level is given at
Booker Washington Institute.  Episcopal Missionary School (Cape Mount)
offers trade and technical training with primary and secondary programs.

Cuttington College offers an agricultural program at the higher educational level, and a nurse's training program.  (See HIGHER EDUCATION.)

Secretarial courses were started in 1963-64 in Cape Palmas, Bassa and
Voinjama High Schools and in Kolahun Junior High School.

In 1964, a new vocational school was established at Nimba, under a
bilateral agreement between the Royal Swedish government and the Liberian
government.  Courses are provided in Auto Mechanics, Carpentry and Joinery,
Cabinet Making, Welding and Forging, Electrical Installation.  In 1965,
4 new trade areas were added:  Masonry, Plumbing, Building Construction,
Machine Shop.

In 1964, Industrial Arts and Home Economics programs were begun in 6-weeks
vacation schools.


## BOOKER WASHINGTON AGRICULTURAL AND INDUSTRIAL INSTITUTE, Kakata

Vocational and technical high school.

Founded March 17, 1929.  Contributing agencies:  Phelps-Stokes Fund,
American Colonization Society, New York Colonization Society, Foreign
Board of the Methodist Church, Lutheran Board of Foreign Missions,
Episcopal Board of Foreign Missions, Harvey S. Firestone, Jr.

An Act passed February 15, 1951 incorporating the University of Liberia
was amended to incorporate Booker Washington Institute into the charter
of the University and to be known and styled as the Booker Washington
Agricultural and Industrial College; on July 1, 1953, the Institute passed
into the hands of the government.

In 1954, as a result of a contractual agreement between the Government
of Liberia and the United States, Prairie View Agricultural and Mechanical
College of Texas extended its services to supply technicians for the
Institute's vocational program.

Prior to 1958, the Institute was a college preparatory school offering a
minimum number of technical courses.  Under the director ICA-Prairie View
Contract personnel, a vocational high school curriculum was instituted in
1958, with training in Building Trades and Drafting, Metal Trades and
Auto Mechanics, Arts and Crafts, Home Sciences, Secretarial Science and
Bookkeeping, Vocational Agriculture.  Trade Shops, constructed in 1956-58,
were equipped for courses in Auto Mechanics, Machine Shop, Carpentry,
Plumbing, Cabinet-making, Electricity, Arts and Crafts, Radio and Communi-
cations, Air Conditioning and Refrigeration, and Drafting.

A cooperative industry-training program was initiated in 1959, giving
junior students an opportunity to test their newly-acquired skills in
actual jobs in business and industry.

The Institute is organized in 2 departments and 9 areas:

    (A)  Academic Department
           English
           Applied Mathematics
           Applied Science
           Social Science
           Military Science and Physical Education

    (B)  Vocational Department
           Agriculture
           Business
           Home Economics
           Industrial Education

School year:  February-November 30.  2 semesters, 18 weeks in length.

Entrance requirements:  Official transcript of elementary school records
                        showing credits earned through the 8th grade.

4-year program.

A vocational exploratory program is offered in the 1st year of the program
(9th grade) for all students as a basis for selection of a vocation at the
beginning of 10th year.

Exploratory courses:

    General Agriculture, General Arts and Crafts, General Building
    Construction, General Business, General Drafting, General Electricity,
    General Home Economics, General Mechanics, General Metals, General
    Refrigeration, and General Woodworking.

Specialization in one of the following courses during 10th, 11th and 12th
grades:

> Agriculture, Arts and Crafts, Auto Mechanics, Bookkeeping, Cabinet-
> making, Carpentry, Drafting, Electricity  Home Economics, Machine
> Shop, Masonry, Plumbing, Radio-Communications, Stenography.

Credit at the Institute is evaluated in terms of the unit.

> 1 unit in a lecture course is the equivalent of 1 high school study
> pursued for 36 weeks in five 45-minute recitation periods a week
> (with a minimum grade of 70).

> In science laboratory courses, 1 unit equals 3 recitation periods
> of 45-minutes each and 2 double periods of 90 minutes per week for
> 36 weeks.

> In vocational courses, 1 unit equals 5 double periods of 90 minutes
> each per week during 36 weeks.

## CURRICULA

### AGRICULTURE
(For majors in Agriculture)

#### Freshman

| Courses | 1st Sem. Units | 2nd Sem. Units |
|---|---|---|
| English | ½ | ½ |
| Applied Math. | ½ | ½ |
| Applied Science | ½ | ½ |
| Agriculture | ½ | |
| Exploratory Electives | ½ | 1 |
| Military Science or Physical Ed. | ¼ | ½ |
| | 2 3/4 | 2 3/4 |

#### Sophomore

| Courses | 1st Sem. Units | 2nd Sem. Units |
|---|---|---|
| English | ½ | ½ |
| Applied Math. | ½ | ½ |
| Social Science | ½ | ½ |
| Agriculture | 1 | 1 |
| Military Science or Physical Ed. | ¼ | ¼ |
| | 2 3/4 | 2 3/4 |

#### Junior

| Courses | | |
|---|---|---|
| English | ½ | ½ |
| Applied Science | ½ | ½ |
| Social Science | ½ | ½ |
| Agriculture | 1 | 1 |
| Military Science or Physical Ed. | ¼ | ¼ |
| | 2 3/4 | 2 3/4 |

#### Senior

| Courses | | |
|---|---|---|
| English | ½ | ½ |
| Applied Science | ½ | ½ |
| Electives | ½ | ½ |
| Agriculture | 1 | 1 |
| Military Science or Physical Ed. | ¼ | ¼ |
| | 2 3/4 | 2 3/4 |

## BUSINESS
### (For majors in Bookkeeping and Stenography)

#### Freshman

| Courses | 1st Sem. Units | 2nd Sem. Units |
|---|---|---|
| English | ½ | ½ |
| Applied Math. | ½ | ½ |
| Applied Science | ½ | ½ |
| Business | 3/4 | ¼ |
| Exploratory Electives | ½ | ½ |
| Military Science or Physical Ed. | ¼ | ¼ |
| | 3 | 2½ |

#### Sophomore

| Courses | 1st Sem. Units | 2nd Sem. Units |
|---|---|---|
| English | ½ | ½ |
| Applied Math. | ½ | ½ |
| Social Science | ½ | ½ |
| Vocational Business | 1 | 1 |
| Military Science or Physical Ed. | ¼ | ¼ |
| | 2 3/4 | 2 3/4 |

#### Junior

| Courses | 1st Sem. Units | 2nd Sem. Units |
|---|---|---|
| English | ½ | ½ |
| Social Science | ½ | ½ |
| Vocational Business | 1½ | 1½ |
| Military Science or Physical Ed. | ¼ | ¼ |
| | 2 3/4 | 2 3/4 |

#### Senior

| Courses | 1st Sem. Units | 2nd Sem. Units |
|---|---|---|
| English | ½ | ½ |
| Applied Science | ½ | ½ |
| Electives | ½ | ½ |
| Vocational Business | 1 | 1 |
| Military Science or Physical Ed. | ¼ | ¼ |
| | 2 3/4 | 2 3/4 |

## HOME ECONOMICS
### (For majors in Home Economics)

#### Freshman

| Courses | 1st Sem. Units | 2nd Sem. Units |
|---|---|---|
| English | ½ | ½ |
| Applied Math. | ½ | ½ |
| Applied Science | ½ | ½ |
| Home Economics | ½ | |
| Exploratory Electives | ½ | 1 |
| Physical Ed. | ¼ | ¼ |
| | 2 3/4 | 2 3/4 |

#### Sophomore

| Courses | 1st Sem. Units | 2nd Sem. Units |
|---|---|---|
| English | ½ | ½ |
| Applied Math. | ½ | ½ |
| Social Science | ½ | ½ |
| Home Economics | 1 | 1 |
| Physical Ed. | ¼ | ¼ |
| | 2 3/4 | 2 3/4 |

|  | Junior | |  | Senior | |
|---|---|---|---|---|---|
| Courses | 1st Sem. Units | 2nd Sem. Units | Courses | 1st Sem. Units | 2nd Sem. Units |
| English | ½ | ½ | English | ½ | ½ |
| Applied Science | ½ | ½ | Applied Science | ½ | ½ |
| Social Science | ½ | ½ | Electives | ½ | ½ |
| Home Economics | 1 | 1 | Home Economics | 1 | 1 |
| Physical Ed. | ¼ | ¼ | Physical Ed. | ¼ | ¼ |
|  | 2 3/4 | 2 3/4 |  | 2 3/4 | 2 3/4 |

## INDUSTRIAL EDUCATION

(For majors in Arts and Crafts, Auto Mechanics, Cabinet
Making, Carpentry, Drafting, Electricity, Machine Shop,
Masonry, Plumbing, and Radio Communications)

|  | Freshman | |  | Sophomore | |
|---|---|---|---|---|---|
| Courses | 1st Sem. Units | 2nd Sem. Units | Courses | 1st Sem. Units | 2nd Sem. Units |
| English | ½ | ½ | English | ½ | ½ |
| Applied Math. | ½ | ½ | Applied Math. | ½ | ½ |
| Applied Science | ½ | ½ | Social Science | ½ | ½ |
| Drafting | ½ | ½ | Shop Major | 1 | 1 |
| Exploratory (major) | ½ |  | Physical Ed. | ¼ | ¼ |
| Exploratory (elect.) |  | ½ |  | 2 3/4 | 2 3/4 |
| Physical Ed. | ¼ | ¼ |  | | |
|  | 2 3/4 | 2 3/4 |  | | |

Examinations in all subjects given at end of 1st and 2nd semesters.
Tests in all subjects given at end of each 6-week period of each semester.
Any grade below 70 is failing. Credit for a course in which a grade below
70 is given can be secured only by repeating the course.

Requirements for graduation in each vocation: 22 units.

Diploma (vocational high school) awarded which qualifies for college work
in the areas of Agriculture, Business, Home Economics, and Industrial
Education.

## TEACHER EDUCATION

2 Rural Teacher Training Institutes for elementary teachers at Kakata
and Zorzor. Another developing at Webbo. Maryland College of Our Lady
of Fatima (private) trains elementary teachers. Secondary school teachers
trained at university level. (See HIGHER EDUCATION.)

5-Year Plan (1964-68) for Teacher Training:

    (1) Produce 1,152 new elementary school teachers.
    (2) Enlarge Kakata Rural Training Institute to a capacity of 250 students by 1966.
    (3) Complete the construction of the Webbo Rural Training Institute to 250 students capacity.
    (4) Continue upgrading of all teachers through in-service training program.

## ZORZOR RURAL TEACHER TRAINING INSTITUTE

Established in 1961 for training elementary teachers, a project of the Tuskegee Institute (U.S.A.) and the U.S. Agency for International Development. Project designed to offer both pre-service and in-service training for elementary teachers, to develop instructional materials for use in schools, and to create a type of teacher education based on needs of students and communities. Tuskegee-Liberia contract extends through 1967.

Admission-placement examination for 8th and 9th grade graduates from government and mission schools.

Present program: 2 years (4 semesters).

## VACATION SCHOOL

First "vacation schools" organized in 1952 under a joint U.S.-Liberian cooperative program with courses in Arts, Social Studies, Languages, Elementary Arithmetic, Science, Nature Study, Physical Education, School Administration and Supervision.

Now, all Liberian public school teachers are required to attend vacation schools each year, offered at 12 centers for teachers below high school graduation, and at 2 centers for those on college level.

1963-64, Department of Education contracted with the University of Liberia and Cuttington College to offer credit courses for teachers who had not finished high school.

## EXTENSION SCHOOL

For the rapid upgrading of many teachers who cannot afford to attend training programs away from home.

2 centers: Monrovia and Lower Buchanan.

MARYLAND COLLEGE OF OUR LADY OF FATIMA, Cape Palmas

Private college, founded in 1952 for teacher training.  The College is
staffed by Missionary Fathers, Franciscan Sisters, and U.S. Peace Corps
volunteers.  (Its secondary school, Our Lady of Fatima High School, offers
junior (7th-9th grade) and senior (10th-12th grade) high school programs.)

Entrance requirements:   High School diploma approved by the Department of
                         Education, and an entrance examination.

Language of instruction: English.

4-year program.

### CURRICULUM

| 1st Semester | Credit Hours | 2nd Semester | Credit Hours |
|---|---|---|---|
| **FRESHMAN** | | | |
| English Composition I | 3 | English Composition II | 3 |
| World History (Ancient and Medieval) | 3 | World History (Modern) | 3 |
| Biology (Botany) | 4 | Biology (Zoology) | 4 |
| Introduction to Education | 3 | Introduction to Philosophy | 3 |
| General Mathematics | 3 | General Psychology | 3 |
| **SOPHOMORE** | | | |
| English Literature I | 3 | English Literature II | 3 |
| Educational Psychology I | 3 | Educational Psychology II | 3 |
| Contemporary Civilizations | 3 | Contemporary African History | 3 |
| Principles of Education | 3 | Personal and Community Health | 3 |
| Introduction to Sociology | 3 | Introduction to Anthropology | 3 |
| Algebra I | 3 | Algebra II | 3 |
| **JUNIOR** | | | |
| American Literature I | 3 | American Literature II | 3 |
| Child Psychology | 2 | Reading in the Elementary School | 3 |
| Plans and Procedures | 3 | Philosophy of Education | 3 |
| History of Education | 3 | Teaching of Language Arts | 2 |
| Basic Physics | 4 | Teaching of Arithmetic | 2 |
| Doctrine | 2 | Teaching of Social Science | 2 |

## SENIOR

| | | | |
|---|---|---|---|
| Children's Literature | 3 | World Literature | 3 |
| Tests and Measurements | 3 | Elementary Statistics | 3 |
| Logic | 2 | Ethics | 3 |
| Principles of Guidance | 3 | Principles of Economics | 3 |
| Principles of Administration | 3 | Student Teaching | 5 |
| Basic Principles of Curriculum Building | 3 | | |

Program extended from 4-5 years for students who are active teachers and unable to devote full time to study.

B.S. in Elementary Education awarded on successful completion of program.

FEDERATION OF NIGERIA

Independence:   October 1, 1960.

## BACKGROUND

Nigeria is composed of four regions--Eastern, Northern, Western, and Mid-Western--and the Federal Territory of Lagos.

The predominant racial group is negroid.   Other racial types include the Fulani, of Mediterranean extraction (throughout north but largely assimilated), and the Semitic Shuwa Arabs (confined to Lake Chad area of Bornu Province).   More than half of the population lives in predominantly Moslem Northern Region.

3 dominant ethnic groups:   Yoruba (over 5 million) in West, Ibo (5.5 million), in East, Hausa (5.5 million), largest single group in North. Other important groups:   Edo (462,000), in West, Ibibio (775,000)  and Ijaw (300,000), in East; Fulani (over 3 million), Kanuri (1.3 million), Nupe (360,000), and Tiv (780,000), in North.

English is the official language.   There are nearly 250 linguistic groups, all but 14 are in the North.   Hausa is most widely spoken.   In Northern Region, Hausa is spoken by 40% of population.

During the medieval times, Northern Nigeria had contact with the large kingdoms of western Sudan (Ghana, Melle and Songhai), and with the countries of the Mediterranean across the Sahara.   Islamic influence was firmly established by the end of the 15th century.   19th century, a "holy war" established a Fulani empire over the Hausa kingdoms until the British conquest at the end of the century.

1861, Britain annexed island of Lagos, center of palm oil trade, and extended her influence over Yorubaland mainland.   1885, British influence over eastern coast extended inland and became the Niger Coast Protectorate by 1893.   The various parts of Nigeria came under the rule of the British government in 1900 as 3 administrative separate units:   the Colony of Lagos, the Southern Nigeria Protectorate and the Northern Nigeria Protectorate.   The Colony and Protectorate of Southern Nigeria were merged into one administrative unit in 1906.   Systems of local administration were introduced.

Constitution of 1954 established federal form of government, extending functions of regional governments.

Constitutional conference of May-June 1957 laid plans for immediate self-
government for Eastern and Western regions, the Northern to follow in 1959.

October 1, 1960, Nigeria became a fully independent member of the British
Commonwealth.

Northern Cameroons became part of Nigeria on July 11, 1961.

Nigeria became a republic October 1, 1963.

Education was brought to Southern Nigeria through missions by 1900.
Education for children in the Muslim north was largely in Koranic schools.
First Education Ordinance for Lagos was passed in 1887 when Colony of
Lagos was separated from Gold Coast Colony (now Ghana).  By this Ordinance
Lagos had its own Board of Education and Inspectorate.  Infant, primary
and secondary schools were established.

The Education Ordinance of 1903 established an Education Department under
a Director of Education for the Colony and Protectorate of Southern
Nigeria where western education was already well established.  Education
Department for the Northern Provinces created in 1910.

Education Code of 1926 (for the Colony and Southern Provinces) set school
standards, required registry of teachers, inspection of mission schools,
raised the standard of education by adding a year to elementary education,
and initiated the Government Standard VI examination.  Examination
abolished in 1938.  (Primary School Leaving Certificate examination re-
introduced by Regional Governments as of 1952).  Education Departments of
Northern and Southern Nigeria unified in 1929.

Education Ordinance of 1948 became the only all-Nigeria ordinance because
soon thereafter the country became a Federation, with each region and the
Federal Territory making its own educational laws.  Ordinance of 1952 gave
the regions greater autonomy.  Federation, 1954; educational legislation
and functions became responsibility of the separate regions.

In all regions, schools are now regulated and inspected by the Regional
Government, but are managed by:  Region, local education authority, the
missions, other non-government bodies (called voluntary agencies), or by
private individuals.  The majority of schools are managed by either
voluntary agency or local authority.

Primary education has varied in length from region to region over the
years, but other areas of education have been more or less similar because
they have led to the external examinations.  Each regional government provides an approved syllabus to be followed by primary schools.  The syllabus
is keyed to a Nigerian background; textbooks are especially written.

Education during the colonial period was directed toward formal British
examinations:  Standard VI examination at close of primary school program,

leading to a Certificate. The grammar school external examination was the Cantab, at the close of the secondary program. Secondary schools examinations have now been taken over by the West African Examinations Council; successful candidates are awarded a West African School Certificate (grades 1, 2 or 3).

Technical training is now offered in all regions through Departments of the Federal Government, in addition to that of the regional Ministries of Education, such as Veterinary, Federal Posts and Telegraphs, Nigerianization Office, Civil Aviation, Railways, Broadcasting, Police, Army, Air Force, Forestry, Co-operatives. Private firms and business corporations are also concerned with the training of personnel, for example: oil companies, all large banks, United Africa Company, and other commercial organizations.

The educational systems of the <u>autonomous regions</u> are set forth in <u>3 separate sections</u> in the following pages:

    (1)   Eastern
    (2)   Northern
    (3)   Western, Mid-Western and Lagos

Where changes in the system have somewhat altered the educational structure, two charts are supplied.

465

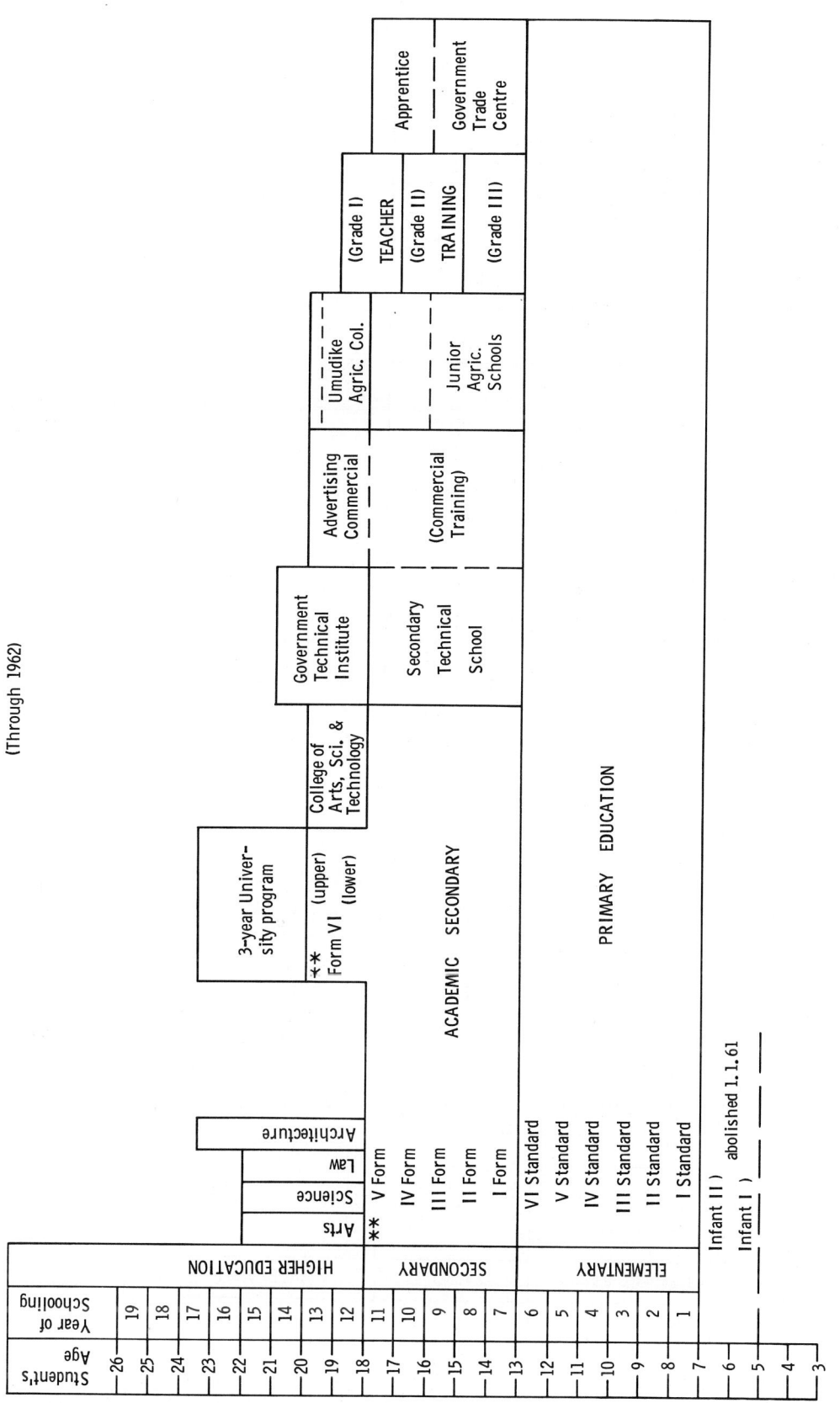

FEDERATION OF NIGERIA – EASTERN REGION
(Through 1962)

Student's Age: 26, 25, 24, 23, 22, 21, 20, 19, 18, 17, 16, 15, 14, 13, 12, 11, 10, 9, 8, 7, 6, 5, 4, 3

Year of Schooling: 19, 18, 17, 16, 15, 14, 13, 12, 11, 10, 9, 8, 7, 6, 5, 4, 3, 2, 1

HIGHER EDUCATION

SECONDARY

ELEMENTARY

3-year University program

** Form VI (upper) (lower)

College of Arts, Sci. & Technology

Government Technical Institute

Advertising Commercial

Umudike Agric. Col.

(Grade I) TEACHER (Grade II) TRAINING (Grade III)

Apprentice

Government Trade Centre

ACADEMIC SECONDARY

Secondary Technical School

(Commercial Training)

Junior Agric. Schools

PRIMARY EDUCATION

Architecture
Law
Science
Arts
**

V Form
IV Form
III Form
II Form
I Form

VI Standard
V Standard
IV Standard
III Standard
II Standard
I Standard

Infant II ) abolished 1.1.61
Infant I )

Compulsory education: None

School year: January – early December

Primary: 8 years to and through 1962
7 years through 1963
6 years starting 1964
(see other chart)

Secondary school grading: West African School Certificate 1 - 9

Cambridge Higher School Certificate 1 - 9

(See SECONDARY EDUCATION)

466

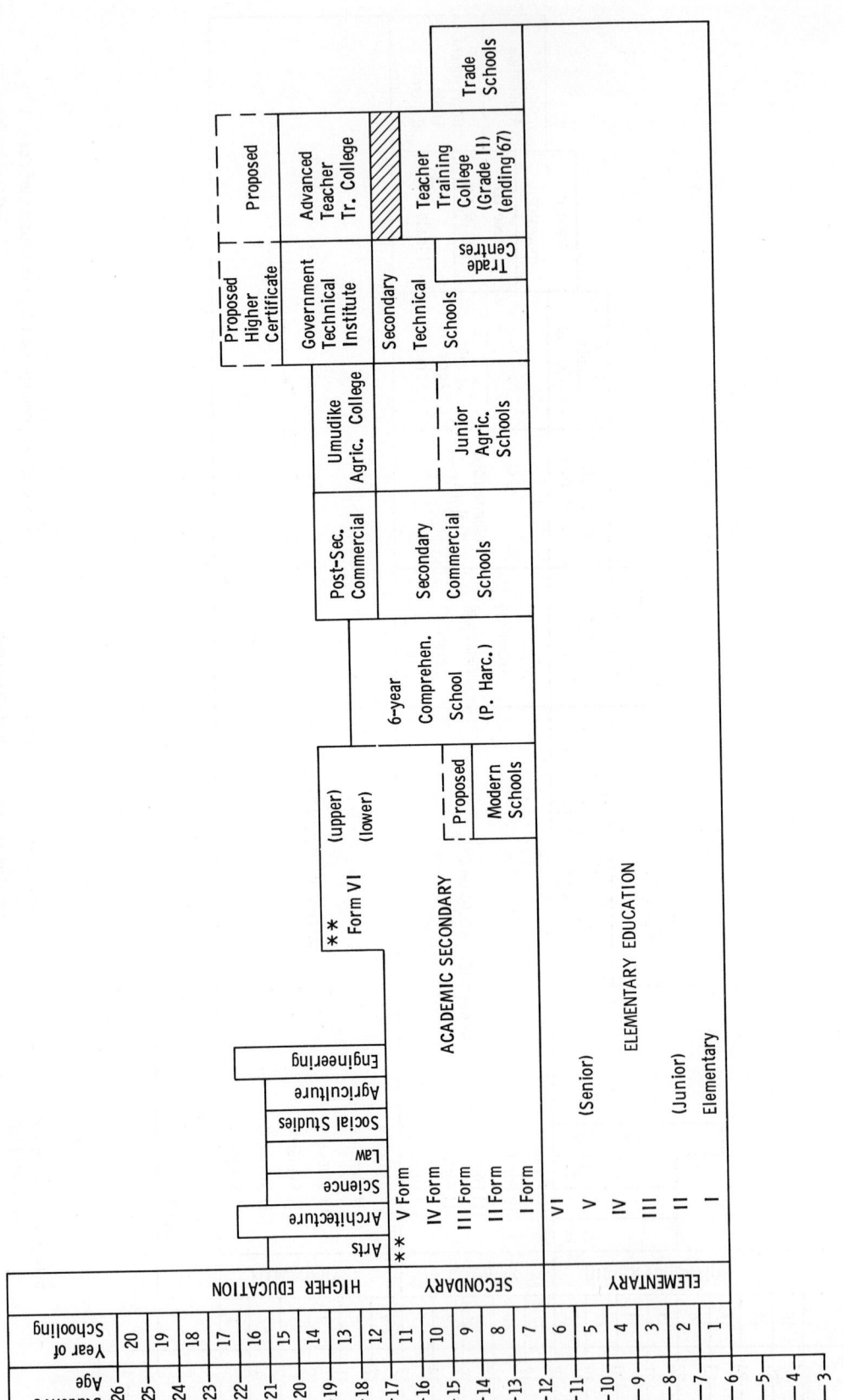

FEDERATION OF NIGERIA – EASTERN REGION

(1962 – with proposals for 1967 indicated)

Compulsory education:  None
School year:  January – Early December

Secondary school grading: West African School Certificate  1 - 9

Cambridge Higher School Certificate  1 - 9

(See SECONDARY EDUCATION)

E A S T E R N   R E G I O N

## ELEMENTARY EDUCATION

Entry age:       6 years.

Language of instruction:       I through III - Vernacular
                               IV through VI  - English

Length of program:   8 years through 1962 (Infant Schools I and II, ages
                        5-7, abolished January 1, 1961)
                     7 years, 1963
                     6 years, 1964 (Not fully effective until 1966)

Through 1961, primary classes called "Standards".  As of 1962, changed
to "Elementary".

Classes:       Elementary I through VI (Class VII through 1965)

Curriculum:    English (stress on both written and spoken English), Arith-
               metic, History, Geography, Handwriting, Health, Religious
               Knowledge, Physical Education, Nature Study, Gardening,
               Singing, Handwork.

               In some areas Civics, Domestic Science and simple General
               Science offered.

               A Nigerian language, Science and Agriculture recently made
               required subjects.

First School Leaving Certificate awarded at close of program.

## SECONDARY EDUCATION

Language of instruction:       English

| Types of Secondary Schools | Length of Course (in years) |
| --- | --- |
| Grammar Schools | 5 |
| Commercial Secondary Schools | 5 |
| Modern Schools (Girls) | 2 |
| Trade Centres | 3 |
| Junior Agriculture Schools | 2-5 |
| Technical Institutions | 3 |
| Comprehensive Secondary Schools | 6 |
| Teacher Training Colleges | 2-4 |

Entrance requirements for all secondary schools:

> First School Leaving Certificate or completion
> of elementary education, and competitive
> entrance examinations in English and Arith-
> metic.

Secondary grammar school curriculum:

> English, Mathematics, History, Geography,
> Religious Knowledge, Vernacular Language,
> Latin, French.
>
> Many schools provide General Science; some
> offer separate courses in Chemistry, Physics
> and Biology in last 2 or 3 years.
>
> Agriculture compulsory 1st 3 years (1964).
>
> Certain secondary girls' schools take Domestic
> Science and Art up to West African School
> Certificate standards.

Promotion more or less automatic in some schools up until 2 years before
West African School Certificate examination when weeding out of unqualified
pupils takes place.

### Government Secondary School, Owerri

### FIVE-YEAR SECONDARY GRAMMAR SCHOOL CURRICULUM
#### (40-minute periods per week)

| Subjects | I A | I B | II A | II B | III A | III B | IV | V |
|---|---|---|---|---|---|---|---|---|
| English[+] | 7 | 7 | 7 | 7 | 7 | 7 | 7 | 7 |
| Mathematics | 6 | 6 | 6 | 6 | 6 | 6 | 6 | 6 |
| Physics | - | - | - | - | 3 | 3 | 3 | 4 |
| Chemistry | - | - | - | - | 4 | 4 | 4 | 4 |
| Biology | 3 | 3 | 3 | 3 | 3 | 3 | 3 | 3 |
| Geography | 3 | 3 | 3 | 3 | 3 | 3 | 3 | 3 |
| History | 3 | 3 | 3 | 3 | 3 | 3 | 3 | 3 |
| Latin | 3 | 3 | 3 | 3 | 3 | 3 | 3 | 4 |
| French[++] | 4 | 4 | 4 | 4 | 4 | 4 | - | - |
| Religious Instruction | 1 | 1 | 1 | 1 | 1 | 1 | 1 | 1 |
| General Science | 3 | 3 | 3 | 3 | 3 | 3 | - | - |
| Singing | 1 | 1 | 1 | 1 | 1 | 1 | 1 | 1 |
| Rural Science | 2 | 2 | 2 | 2 | - | - | - | - |
| Additional Mathematics[+++] | - | - | - | - | - | - | - | 5 |

[+]English normally taught as a whole subject but if split because of
staffing difficulties:  English Language - 4
                         English Literature - 3

[++]Only taught to class 3 at present because introduced 3 years ago.

[+++]Taken as an alternative to Latin in class 5.

At close of the 5-year program students take the Joint Examination for the West African School Certificate and General Certificate of Education. (Under the control of the West African Examinations Council in collaboration with the University of Cambridge Local Examinations Syndicate.[+])

## Subjects of the Examination (1964 and previously)

Subjects grouped as follows:

I.   Compulsory subject:  English language.
     Optional subject:  Oral English.

II.  General subjects:  English Literature, Bible Knowledge, Islamic Religious Knowledge (available only if application is made), History, Geography.

III. Languages:  Latin, Greek, French, German, Efik, Hausa, Igbo, Yoruba, Arabic (papers may be set in Arabic by arrangement).

IV.  Mathematical subjects:  Mathematics, Additional Mathematics.

V.   Science subjects:  General Science, Additional General Science, Physics, Chemistry, Biology, Agricultural Science.

VI.  Arts and Crafts:  Art, Music, Woodwork, Metalwork, Needlework and Dressmaking, Cookery, General Housecraft.

VII. Technical and commercial subjects:  Geometrical and Mechanical Drawing, Geometrical and Building Drawing, Commercial Studies, Principles of Accounts (all previous subjects in this grouping included provisionally, papers may be set by arrangement), Health Science.

## Choice of Subjects (1964 and previously)

Normally candidates for the School Certificate sit for 6, 7, or 8 subjects. These must include English Language and subjects chosen from at least 3 of the Groups II, III, IV, V, VI, and VII. Candidates offering Additional Mathematics or Additional General Science may offer a total of 9 subjects. The optional oral test in English is not regarded as a subject for the purpose of this regulation and may be taken in addition to the 8 or 9 subjects chosen. Performance in the oral test is assessed separately from that in the written papers and a poor performance in the oral test does not affect candidates' result in English Language as a subject. Similarly, performance in the oral test is not taken into account at final Certificate award. Results recorded on Certificate.

[+]For REGULATIONS AND SYLLABUSES for the Joint Examination of the West African School Certificate and General Certificate of Education (taken in Nigeria only), write the Senior Deputy Registrar, The West African Examinations Council, Private Mail Bag 1022, Yaba, Nigeria. (See Appendix D for basic information.)

Conditions for the Award of a School Certificate (1964 and previously)

All requirements for the Certificate must be satisfied at one and the same examination.  To qualify for the Certificate candidates must:

> (a)  Reach a satisfactory general standard as judged by their aggregate performance in their best 6 subjects, and

either  (b)  Pass in at least 6 subjects (including English Language) with credit in at least 1 of them,

or      (c)  Pass in 5 subjects (including English Language) with credits in at least 2 of them.

A slightly more lenient aggregate accepted for candidates passing in English Language and in subjects chosen from more than 3 of the Groups II-VII, as compared to those passing in English Language and in subjects from 3 or less than 3 of these groups.

The Awarding Committee has certain discretion in the award of Certificates and in particular may award a Certificate to a candidate who fails by a narrow margin in English Language while satisfying the other conditions.

Classification of Successful Candidates (1964 and previously)

Successful candidates placed in three Divisions; Division indicated on the Certificate.

### First Division Certificate

Pass in 6 or more subjects, which must include subjects drawn from at least 3 of the Groups II, III, IV, V, VI, and VII.

Pass with credit in at least 5 of these subjects, including English Language.

Reach a high general standard as judged by their performance in their best 6 subjects.

### Second Division Certificates

Pass in 6 or more subjects, which must include English Language and subjects drawn from 3 of the Groups II, III, IV, V, VI, and VII.

Pass with credit in at least 4 of these subjects.

Reach a certain general standard as judged by their performance in their best 6 subjects.

### Third Division Certificates

The remaining successful candidates

N.B.  In 1964, English Language  was removed as a compulsory subject, thus the 1965 amendments to the regulations changed the subject groupings

and the conditions for the award of a School Certificate.  New
regulations are set forth in the following 3 sections.


## Subjects of the Examination (1965 on)

Subjects grouped as follows:

I.   Languages:  English Language, Latin, Greek, French, German,
     Efik, Hausa, Igbo, Yoruba, Arabic.  (Papers may be set in
     Arabic by arrangement.)

II.  General subjects:  English Literature, Bible Knowledge, Islamic
     Religious Knowledge (available only if application is made),
     History, Geography.

III. Mathematical subjects:  Mathematics, Additional Mathematics.

IV.  Science subjects:  General Science, Additional General Science,
     Physics, Chemistry, Biology, Agricultural Science.

V.   Arts and Crafts:  Art, Music, Woodwork, Metalwork, Needlework
     and Dressmaking, Cookery, General Housecraft.

VI.  Technical and commercial subjects:  Geometrical and Mechanical
     Drawing, Geometrical and Building Drawing, Commercial Studies,
     Principles of Accounts (all previous subjects in this grouping
     included provisionally, papers may be set by arrangement),
     Health Science.


## Choice of Subjects (1965 on)

Normally candidates for the School Certificate sit for 6, 7, or 8 subjects.
These must include subjects chosen from at least 3 of the Groups I-VI.
Candidates offering Additional Mathematics or Additional General Science
may offer a total of 9 subjects.


## Conditions for the Award of a School Certificate (1965 on)

All requirements for the Certificate must be satisfied at one and the same
examination.  To qualify for the Certificate, candidates must:

(a)  Reach a satisfactory general standard as judged by their
     aggregate performance in their best 6 subjects, and

either  (b)  Pass in at least 6 subjects with credit in at least 1 of
        them,

or      (c)  Pass in 5 subjects with credits in at least 2 of them.

## Classification of Successful Candidates (1965 on)

Successful candidates placed in three Divisions; Division indicated on the Certificate.

### First Division Certificate

Pass in 6 or more subjects, which must include subjects drawn from at least 3 of the Groups I-VI.

Pass with credit in at least 5 of these subjects.

Reach a certain general standard as judged by their performance in their best 6 subjects.

### Second Division Certificate

Pass in 6 or more subjects, which must include subjects drawn from 3 of the Groups I-VI.

Pass with credit in at least 4 of these subjects.

Reach a certain general standard as judged by their performance in their best 6 subjects.

### Third Division Certificate

The remaining successful candidates.

## Conditions for the Award of West African General Certificate of Education (before and after 1965)

Candidates who enter for a full Certificate, but who fail to qualify for the award of a School Certificate, will be awarded a West African General Certificate of Education if they pass with credit in 3 or more subjects.

From 1963, candidates who receive 3 or more credits are being given a G.C.E. showing the subjects in which they attain the G.C.E. pass standards (equivalent to the School Certificate credit standard) and showing also those subjects in which they reach the School Certificate pass standard.

## Grading System in the Joint Examination for the West African School Certificate and General Certificate of Education

The following table shows the equivalences of grades used before and after 1960.

| 1959 | 1960 onwards |
|------|--------------|
| 1    | 1            |
| 2    | 2            |

| 1959 | 1960 onwards |
|------|--------------|
| 3 | 3 |
| 4 | ( 4 |
|   | ( 5 |
| 5 | 6 |
| 6 | 7 |
| 7 ) | 8 |
| 8 ) |   |
| 9 | 9 |

Results of the examination indicate the standard reached in each subject
taken by the grading from 1 to 9.

1-6 pass with Credit

( 1 - Very Good
( 2 - Very Good
( 3 - Credit
( 4 - Credit
( 5 - Credit
( 6 - Credit

7 - Pass
8 - Pass
9 - Failure

*West African School Certificate awarded only to those who have satisfied
the conditions for the award of a full Certificate.

*West African General Certificate of Education awarded to those who
entered for a full Certificate but, while gaining at least 3 credits in
the examination, failed to qualify for the full Certificate.

N.B.  In both categories above, there are 2 kinds of certificates:

(a)  Forms of certificates which record the name of the school(s)
attended are issued only to those successful candidates who have
been in attendance for at least 3 years continuously at one or
more schools recognized by the Council for the award of the West
African School Certificate.

(b)  Other candidates if successful, receive a modified form of these
certificates.  (The question papers and pass standards are the
same for both kinds of certificates.)

HIGHER SCHOOL COURSE

Forms Lower VI and Upper VI.

As of 1965, the Higher School Course run at 28 secondary schools, offering
a 2-year training for the Higher School Certificate Examination.

Government Secondary School, Owerri

SAMPLE 2-YEAR SIXTH FORM COURSE, CONFINED TO SCIENCE ALONE
(40-minute periods per week)

| Subjects | Lower VI B[+] | Lower VI P[++] | Upper VI B | Upper VI P |
|---|---|---|---|---|
| General Paper | 3 | 3 | 3 | 3 |
| Physics | - | 7 | - | 8 |
| Chemistry | 7 | 7 | 8 | 8 |
| Zoology | 7 | 7 | 8 | 8 |
| Botany | 7 | 7 | 8 | 8 |
| Mathematics | - | 10 | - | 10 |
| Geography | - | 7 | - | 7 |
| Religious Instruction | 1 | 1 | 1 | 1 |
| Singing | 1 | 1 | 1 | 1 |

[+]The B class studies Botany, Chemistry, Zoology and General Paper.

[++]The P class studies:

either    (a)   Chemistry, Zoology, Physics

or        (b)   Chemistry, Physics, Mathematics

or        (c)   Geography, Botany, Zoology together with General
                Paper

Note:  In the Lower Sixths Practicals consist of 3 period Sessions.
       In the Upper Sixth, of 4 period Sessions.

[**]University of Cambridge Joint Examination for the Higher School Certificate
and General Certificate of Education at close of the 2-year program.  (For
details of the examination, see Appendix B.)

HIGHER EDUCATION

UNIVERSITY OF NIGERIA, Nsukka

Established in 1955.  Preliminary recommendations were made under joint
auspices of the Inter-University Council of the United Kingdom and the
Agency for International Development of the United States.  A Provisional
Council was authorized and entrusted by the Eastern Nigeria Legislature
1959, to establish the University.  Formal opening, 7 October, 1960.

Former Nigerian College of Arts, Science and Technology, Enugu, was incorporated into new institution in 1961.  The 1963 June graduates received
the first degrees granted by an autonomous Nigerian university.

Entrance requirements:          Candidates for degree courses in any college
                                or department must possess 1 or more of the
                                following requirements:

                        (a)     Passes in 2 relevant subjects at principal
                                standard in the Higher School Certificate
                                or advanced level in the General Certificate
                                of Education, provided the candidate has in
                                addition 3 other subjects at subsidiary
                                standard or ordinary level.  A candidate with
                                passes in 3 relevant subjects at principal
                                standard or advanced level would require only
                                1 other subject at subsidiary standard or
                                ordinary level; a candidate with passes in 4
                                or more subjects at principal standard or
                                advanced level would need no additional passes
                                at subsidiary standard or ordinary level.
                                The subjects need not be passed on one and
                                the same occasion.  A credit in the West
                                African School Certificate is regarded as
                                equivalent to a pass at subsidiary standard
                                or ordinary level.

                        (b)     West African School Certificate, with passes
                                at credit level in at least 5 subjects; or
                                West African School Certificate plus Nigerian
                                Teachers' Grade II Certificate; or General
                                Certificate of Education at ordinary level in
                                6 subjects passed at one and the same exami-
                                nation, including (i) English Language and
                                (ii) either Mathematics or an approved science
                                subject.

                        (c)     Post-secondary qualifications beyond the
                                levels of (a) and (b) above.  These include
                                degrees of universities approved by the Uni-
                                versity of Nigeria.

                        (d)     Qualifications obtained from other countries
                                and recognized by the University to be equi-
                                valent to (a), (b), or (c) above.

                                Candidates under (a) and (c) and in certain
                                cases (d), may, on the basis of outstanding
                                records, be admitted without an examination
                                (Direct Entry).  All other applicants are
                                required to take the University of Nigeria
                                Entrance Examination.


Entry requirements listed above may be modified for students admitted to
non-degree courses.

Additional requirements for entry to certain degree programs are indicated under individual departments below.

Degrees and Diplomas:

| Degree | Duration of course |
|---|---|
| Bachelor of Architecture  B. (Arch.) | 5 yrs. |
| Bachelor of Arts (B.A.) in: | |
| Education | 4 yrs. |
| English | 4 yrs. |
| Fine Arts | 4 yrs. |
| History | 4 yrs. |
| Journalism | 4 yrs. |
| Languages | 4 yrs. |
| Music | 4 yrs. |
| Philosophy | 4 yrs. |
| Religion | 4 yrs. |
| Sociology and Anthropology | 4 yrs. |
| Combined Subjects | 4 yrs. |
| Bachelor of Laws (Ll.B.) | 4 yrs. |
| Bachelor of Science (B.Sc.) in: | |
| Accountancy | 4 yrs. |
| Agricultural Economics | 4 yrs. |
| Agricultural Engineering | 5 yrs. |
| Agricultural Mechanics | 4 yrs. |
| Animal Science | 4 yrs. |
| Botany | 4 yrs. |
| Business Administration | 4 yrs. |
| Chemistry | 4 yrs. |
| Economics | 4 yrs. |
| Education | 4 yrs. |
| Civil Engineering | 5 yrs. |
| Electrical Engineering | 5 yrs. |
| Mechanical Engineering | 5 yrs. |
| Geography | 4 yrs. |
| Geology | 4 yrs. |
| Home Economics | 4 yrs. |
| Land Economics | 5 yrs. |
| Mathematics | 4 yrs. |
| Physical Education | 4 yrs. |
| Physics | 4 yrs. |
| Plant-Soil Science | 4 yrs. |
| Political Science | 4 yrs. |
| Psychology | 4 yrs. |
| Secretaryship and Company Administration | 4 yrs. |
| Surveying | 5 yrs. |
| Vocational Education | 4 yrs. |
| Zoology | 4 yrs. |
| Combined Subjects | 4 yrs. |

The following diplomas may be awarded by the University:

| | |
|---|---|
| Diploma in Animal Health and Husbandry | 3 yrs. |
| Diploma in Music Education | 3 yrs. |
| Diploma in Religion | 1 yr. |
| Diploma in Secretarial Studies | 2 yrs. |

General degree requirements:   Credit hours

Candidates for any Bachelor's degree must complete successfully a number of selected courses, a minimum aggregate of 192 credit hours for graduation. (The programs of particular departments may demand a higher aggregate than this.)

Credit hours for any courses from which a student may be exempted by qualifications obtained before admission to the University may be included in the aggregate.

Degree programs vary in number of credit hours required although they are never under 192, nor (except for Architecture, Engineering, Land Economics and Land Surveying) more than 220. Most programs allow, and many require elective courses from other departments; all allow 48 credit hours in General Studies (except for advanced entry students required to take only 2 courses in General Studies).

A class meeting 3 times per week ordinarily carries 3 credit hours per term (3 terms per year) and 9 per session. Laboratory and studio classes not requiring outside preparation receive 1 credit hour for each 2 hours in class. The average student carries 16 credit hours each term.

Duration of degree programs and exemption from courses:

Most degree programs (allowing for General Studies, subsidiary subjects and electives) are planned to cover 4 years for students admitted with the West African School Certificate or its equivalent.

For direct entry students who hold advanced level passes in 2 subjects relevant to their proposed program degree programs cover 3 years.

Degree requirements for B.A. and B.Sc. degrees in combined subjects:

The University makes provision for students who desire or are required to pursue a program leading to the B.A. or B.Sc. degree in 2 subjects.

Not more than 72 and not less than 60 credit hours may be completed in each of 2 of the advertised degree programs, with the consent in each case of the Heads of the Departments concerned.


Division of General Studies

All students are enrolled in the Division of General Studies as well as in 1 of the more specialized departments.

During his first academic year, class work for the student admitted by entrance examination will normally consist of 3 courses offered through the Division of General Studies, plus 1 course designated by his major department.  In the following year he will take Humanities in the Division of General Studies, and his other courses will be designated by his major department.

Students with advanced entry qualifications are required to take 2 General Studies courses only, and in their first year.  The 4 separate courses are:  The Use of English, Social Science, Natural Science, and Humanities.

In order to receive a degree all students are required to obtain the stated credits in each of the following courses.  Direct Entry students may, with the consent of the Division and their major department, be exempted from 2 of the courses:  The Use of English, Social Science, Natural Science, Humanities.


Grade Point Average

In addition to acquiring the stipulated credit hour aggregate of 192, students will be required to maintain a cumulative grade point average of 2.00 to qualify for graduation.

Grade points are determined on the basis of grades given in courses, thus:

              A      - Excellent:   4 grade points
              B      - Good:        3 grade points
              C      - Pass:        2 grade points
              D      - Poor:        1 grade point
              F      - Failure:     0 grade point

Any student whose cumulative average falls below the following levels will be required to withdraw from the University:

              1st year   - 1.50
              2nd year   - 1.75
              3rd year   - 2.00

Final Examinations

These examinations consist of 5 3-hour papers in areas specified by the respective departments.  One of these will take form of a General Paper.

When oral or practical examination is considered necessary, this will be additional to the 5 papers.

(1)  Final examination in 4-year degree programs carries 50% in final assessment.

Cumulative grade point average to end of penultimate year:  50% in final assessment.

(2)  Final examination in 5-year degree programs carries 40% in final assessment.

Cumulative grade point average to end of penultimate year:  60% in final assessment.

Honours Classificiations

There are no separate honours programs.  Honours awarded solely on basis of student's academic performance, as follows:

| | |
|---|---|
| Bachelor's degree with 1st Class Honours: | 3.50 - 4.00 |
| Bachelor's degree with 2nd Class Honours: | |
|     Upper Division | 3.25 - 3.49 |
|     Lower Division | 2.75 - 3.24 |
| Bachelor's degree with Pass: | 2.00 - 2.74 |

Final grade point average in all courses (major, subsidiary, elective, General Studies) and final examinations determine class of degree received.

Faculty of Agriculture

Department of Agricultural Economics

B.Sc. (4 years)

Entrance requirements:      Mathematics and Science subject in W.A.S.C.

Exemptions:  Holders of H.S.C. or G.C.E. at advanced level with qualifications in Chemistry, Biology, Mathematics or Economics exempted from equivalent introductory courses.

Two long vacations spent working on agricultural surveys or on agricultural extension projects.

## Department of Agricultural Engineering

Alternative programs offered in close cooperation with Faculty of
Engineering:

    (a)   Agricultural Mechanics:  B.Sc. (4 years)

    (b)   Agricultural Engineering:  B.Sc. (5 years)

Entrance requirements:

> Exemptions:  Holders of H.S.C., principal
> level, or G.C.E., advanced level, are
> exempted from introductory courses in
> Biology, Chemistry, Mathematics or Physics.

Two long vacation periods spent working with recognized organization or
industry in some aspect of Agriculture or Engineering.

## Department of Animal Science

B.Sc. (4 years)

Entrance requirements:

> Exemptions:  Holders of H.S.C., principal
> level, or G.C.E., advanced level, exempted
> from introductory courses in Chemistry,
> Biology, Mathematics, Physics or Economics.

Two long vacation periods spent working with a recognized agricultural
field organization.

Department offers courses for Diploma in Animal Health and Husbandry.

## Department of Home Economics

B.Sc. (4 years)

Degree requirements:

> All students required to complete, in
> addition to 48 credit hours in General
> Studies, certain courses in Natural Sciences,
> Sociology and Education.
>
> After completion of 2nd year students choose
> between:  Food and Nutrition, Home Economics
> Teaching, Textiles and Clothing.

## Department of Plant-Soil Science

B.Sc. (4 years)

Entrance requirements:

Holders of W.A.S.C. must have passes in
Mathematics, Chemistry and Biology.  Holders
of H.S.C. or G.C.E. advanced level, exempted
from introductory courses in Chemistry,
Chemistry with Physics, Botany or Biology.

Two long vacations spent working with a recognized agricultural field
organization.

## Department of Veterinary Science

Diploma in Animal Health and Husbandry (3 years)

Entrance requirements:

W.A.S.C. with qualifications in Science.
Recommendation for admission made by
Advisory Board.

Diploma requirements:

Ancillary personnel for Ministry of Agriculture Veterinary Division work under
direction of Veterinary Surgeons.  Students
required to complete 168 credit hours.

## Faculty of Arts

## Department of English

B.A. (4 years)

Degree requirements:

The program for the degree in English
provides the alternative of a Linguistics
stress or a Literature stress.  The choice
must be made before the end of a student's
second year.

All students are required to complete 48
credit hours in General Studies in addition
to certain courses in English, British History and Foreign Language.

Students electing the Linguistics stress are
also required to take certain courses in
English.

All students must in addition elect courses
from those offered by the Department of
English to bring their total of credits to
at least 192 (this will be 36 for the program
with Linguistics stress and 72 for the one
with Literature stress).

"Literature stress" students must complete a
minimum of 99 credit hours in literature

courses to graduate in English, including
the required literature courses. For
"Linguistics stress" students the minimum
of 99 credits must include both the literature and linguistics requirements.

## Department of Fine Arts

B.A. (4 years)

Entrance requirements:          A portfolio of work must be submitted or
                                an examination in Fine Arts taken.

A basic program is provided in the first 2 years. The choice of the area
of specialization is made by the end of the second year.

## Department of History and Archaeology

B.A. History (4 years)

Degree requirements:            The program for the B.A. in History
                                requires that every student complete the
                                7 main courses covering Archaeology, African
                                History (2 courses), the History of Nigeria,
                                Mediaeval and Modern European History, and
                                World History since 1815. In the final year
                                students choose two optional courses from
                                subjects which specialize in the history of
                                an area or topic, and one special subject,
                                of a detailed and documented nature. All
                                students must acquire reading knowledge of
                                a selected language through 2 years of study.
                                Students are advised as to their choice of
                                electives from other departments. Certain
                                courses from other departments (e.g. Economic
                                History, Religious History) may rank as
                                optional or special subjects in the Depart-
                                ment of History. All History students attend
                                tutorials where written work will be criticized
                                and discussed.

## Department of Journalism

B.A. (4 years)

Exemptions:     Direct entry students, although completing identical
                program in Journalism, carry fewer hours in General Studies
                and in subsidiary field, and are exempted from elective
                courses.

Degree requirements: Students required to complete between 71 and 90 credit hours in courses in Journalism, 3 credit hours in Typing, 18 in French, and at least 40 in subsidiary field, chosen from Agriculture, Business Administration, Economics, Languages, Law, Political Science, Religion, Sociology, or approved courses in Science. The degree program also allows for 12-30 credits in elective courses which may be taken outside their major and subsidiary fields.

## Department of Languages

B.A. (4 years)

Entrance requirements: G.C.E. ordinary level in Latin or English Literature.

Exemption: Holders of H.S.C. or G.C.E. advanced level in any modern language may be exempted from Grammar and Translation, Course I, in that language.

Degree requirements: Candidates must take the full course as prescribed in the syllabus for their major language. Students with no previous knowledge of the foreign languages offered may be required to take a longer time for their degree.

## Department of Music

B.A. (Music) (4 years)
Diploma in Music Education (3 years)

For Degree:

Entrance requirements: Tests and auditions given for voice or for an instrument.

Degree requirements: The program for the degree of B.A. in Music provides for specialization in Musical Theory, Applied Music, Ethnomusicology or Music Education.

All students are required to follow a 2-year basic course program in Musical Theory, Applied Music, History of Music, African Music and Conducting.

Candidates desiring certification as teachers will be required to complete certain additional courses in Education.

For Diploma:

Entrance requirements:    Entrants must hold at least the W.A.S.C. or its equivalent or the Teachers' Grade II Certificate plus at least 4 papers, including English Language, at ordinary level, or 2 papers at advanced level, in G.C.E., and in addition have passed the grade 7 examination of the Trinity College of Music or pass a comparable examination in Music set by the department.

Diploma requirements:    Candidates are required to take courses in subsidiary teaching subject.

Department of Philosophy

B.A. (4 years)

Degree requirements:    Candidates required to complete at least 108 credit hours in Philosophy, 48 credit hours in General Studies; 18 in a foreign language (French, German or Greek) and 18 in other courses outside the department.

Faculty of Education

Department of Education

B.A. and B.Sc. (4 years)

The title of the degree is determined by the choice of teaching subjects.

Degree requirements:    Candidates are required to complete a minimum of 51 credit hours in Education courses, in addition to a minimum of 57 credit hours in a major teaching subject and a minimum of 45 credit hours in a subsidiary reading field.

One long vacation period of Practical Teaching.

## Department of Physical Education

B.Sc. (4 years)

Program is designed for teachers in Physical Education, Health Education, Sports Organization, Coaching, and related fields.

Degree requirements:         Total of 219 credits required. All
                             students are expected to spend part of one
                             long vacation in teaching practice in
                             Nigerian schools.

## Department of Vocational Education

B.Sc. (4 years) in:

    Agricultural Education
    Business (Commercial) Education
    Home Economics (Dom. Sc.) Education
    Trade and Industrial (Technical) Education

Program is designed for teachers in specific fields in secondary schools and professional education for teachers in technical colleges, agricultural and home economics agencies.

Degree requirements:         Courses offered and credits required
                             published at beginning of each session.
                             Each student is required to spend a
                             designated period in a particular type of
                             school, with responsibility for teaching
                             and involvement in community activities and
                             after-school work.

## Faculty of Engineering

## Department of Architecture

B. (Arch.) (5 years)

Degree requirements:         Sequences of courses in Art and Drawing,
                             Architecture, Design, Building Techniques,
                             Physical and Social Sciences, and the
                             Humanities. 270 credits required.

                             Students are required to complete a 16-week
                             period of employment with a professional
                             architectural organization before graduation.

## Department of Civil Engineering

B.Sc. (Civil Eng.) (5 years)

Students with advanced entry qualifications may be able to complete the program in 4 years.

Degree requirements:

Candidates are required to complete not less than 254 credits, including 48 credits in General Studies and certain courses in Mathematics and Physics.  Attendance at a practical course in Surveying is required in the vacation following the second term of the second and third years.

A total of not less than 6 weeks' practical work, approved by the Head of Department, is required of all students in each of two long vacations.

## Department of Electrical Engineering

B.Sc. (Elect. Eng.) (5 years)

Students with advanced entry qualifications may be able to complete the program in 4 years.

Degree requirements:

Candidates are required to complete not less than 262 credits, including 48 credits in General Studies and certain courses in Mathematics and Physics.

A total of 6 weeks' practical work, approved by the Head of Department, is required of all students in each of two long vacations.

## Department of Land Economics

B.Sc. (Estate Management) (5 years)

Program in land management, valuation, land use control and town planning, land reform, land settlement, land development.

Degree requirements:          Total credits, 264, and research.

## Department of Mechanical Engineering

B.Sc. (Mech. Eng.) (5 years)

Students with advanced entry qualifications may be able to complete the program in 4 years.

Degree requirements:            Candidates are required to complete not less than 253 credits including 48 credits in General Studies and certain courses in Mathematics and Physics.

                                 A total of 6 weeks' practical work, approved by the Head of Department, is required of all students in each of two long vacations.

## Department of Surveying

B.Sc. (Surveying) (5 years)

Good entrance qualifications in Mathematics and Physics are desirable; approved training in a survey department is an advantage.

Degree requirements:            270 credits.

## Faculty of Law

## Department of Law

Ll.B. (4 years)

Entrance requirements:       A thorough knowledge of the English language.

Degree requirements:          Candidates must complete at least 109 credit hours in at least 13 courses offered in the department, in addition to 48 credit hours in General Studies. The remaining 38 credit hours required for graduation may be completed in courses offered by any department. At least 1 year of a foreign language recommended.

## Faculty of Science

## Department of Botany

B.Sc. (Botany) (4 years)

Candidates with appropriate qualifications in H.S.C. (principal level) or its equivalent may be granted exemption from the 1st year course in General Botany.

Degree requirements:          Students are required to complete 105 credits in courses offered by the department and supporting courses in Agriculture, Chemistry, Physics or Mathematics, and Zoology.

## Department of Chemistry

B.Sc. (Chemistry) (4 years)

Exemptions:          Students with principal level qualifications in
                     Chemistry, Physics and Mathematics in H.S.C. or with
                     equivalent qualifications, will be considered for
                     appropriate exemptions.

Degree requirements:          Students are required to visit centers of
                              chemical industry and write reports.

                              Sufficient knowledge of either German or
                              Russian is recommended for reading scien-
                              tific papers in one of these languages.


## Department of Geology

B.Sc. (Geology) (4 years)

Direct entry students may complete the program in 3 years if they possess
H.S.C. (principal standard) or G.C.E. (advanced level) in any 2 of the
following:  Chemistry, Mathematics, Physics or Zoology.

Degree requirements:          Candidates are required to complete 120
                              credit hours in courses offered by the
                              department, and certain other courses in
                              ancillary Sciences, a Modern Language, and
                              General Studies.

                              Fieldwork is required of all students, and
                              is normally arranged as follows:

                              1st year:     10 individual field trips
                              2nd year:     15 individual field trips
                              3rd year:     15 full working days
                              4th year:     21 full working days

                              Each student is required in his final year
                              to submit a report based on his field studies
                              carried out during the year.

                              In no case will a candidate be allowed to
                              take courses in Geology otherwise than in
                              strict sequence.


## Department of Mathematics

B.Sc. (Mathematics) (4 years)

Courses in Statistics and Astronomy are also available.

All students requiring basic courses in Mathematics will be enrolled in
1st year course in Pure Mathematics unless exempted on showing evidence
of equivalent attainment.

Degree requirements:          192 credits.


## Department of Microbiology

The department does not as yet offer a degree program.  Courses in
Microbiology and Entomology are offered primarily to serve students in
other fields such as Agriculture, Biological Sciences (Human and Veterinary),
Engineering, Home Economics and Institutional Food Services.


## Department of Physics

B.Sc. (Physics) (4 years)

Entrants are required to have a knowledge of Mathematics, and candidates
are required to complete 9 credit hours in a foreign language.

Degree requirements:          194 credits.


Department of Zoology

B.Sc. (Zoology) (4 years)

Degree requirements:          Candidates are required to complete 105
                              credit hours in Zoology, 48 credits in
                              General Studies, 24 in Chemistry, 12 in
                              Botany and 12 in either Physics or Mathematics.

                              The program includes fieldwork.


## Faculty of Social Studies

## Department of Business Administration

B.Sc. (Bus. Adm.) (4 years)

Entrance requirements:        Direct entry students should preferably have
                              G.C.E. advanced level passes (or their equi-
                              valent) in Principles of Economics, Economic
                              History, British Constitution or Geography,
                              and an ordinary level pass in Mathematics.

(1)  Sub-Department of Finance

B.Sc. (Accountancy) (4 years)

Degree requirements:            Minimum standard for graduation is geared
to final level required of candidates for
membership in various recognized professional
bodies of accountants.  Students must complete
at least 169 credit hours within the department's program.  A total of 1 year of practical training in professional accounting firms,
or in accounts departments of government,
banking, insurance, or other approved institutions is a prerequisite for graduation.

Practical training is arranged during each
of the long vacations.

(2)  Sub-Department of Secretarial Studies

(a)  B.Sc. in Secretaryship and Company Administration (4 years)

Degree requirements:  199-208 credits.

Candidates are required to do practical work
in offices during long vacations and research
into problems of administration.

(b)  Diploma in Secretarial Studies (2 years)

Diploma requirements:  108-144 credits.

High speed in Shorthand, Typewriting, and
Transcription are required.  Practical
office work.

Department of Economics

B.Sc. (Economics) (4 years)

Entrance requirements:          Sufficient background in Mathematics to
complete the course in Pure Mathematics
satisfactorily during first 2 years.

Degree requirements:            Candidates are required to complete at least
120 credit hours in courses within the depart-
ment, in addition to 48 credit hours in
General Studies.  Strong foundation in Statistics is recommended for students preparing
for post-graduate study.

## Department of Geography

B.Sc. (Geography) (4 years)

Degree requirements:

Candidates are required to complete 111 credit hours in courses offered by the department and 36 in a subsidiary field recommended by the department.

Fieldwork, normally during week-end and vacations, is required.

## Department of Political Science

B.Sc. (Pol. Sc.) (4 years)

Degree requirements:

Candidates are required to complete at least 96 credit hours in courses offered in the department; 48 and 24 credit hours in General studies for entrance examination and direct entry students respectively, and at least 27 credit hours in a subsidiary subject selected from Economics, History, Law or Sociology, and 9 in a foreign language.

The final year comprehensive examination covers the following subject areas: Political Theory, Comparative Government, Nigerian Government, Public Administration, International Relations.

## Department of Psychology

B.Sc. (Psych.) (4 years)

Degree requirements:

Candidates are required to complete 117 credit hours in courses offered by the department, 48 credit hours in General Studies, 18 in a foreign language, and 9 in Philosophy.

## Department of Religion

B.A. (Religion) (4 years)

Diploma (1 year)

Holders of an approved diploma in Theology may be able to graduate in 3 years (with specialization in Christian Scriptures only).

The department offers a 1-year program in the Forms and History of
Christianity, Islam and Traditional Religion in West Africa for a Diploma
in the Study of the Religions of West Africa.

Entrance requirements:       Candidates should possess a university
                             degree in Theology (Christian or Islamic)
                             or Religious Studies or with Theology or
                             Religious Studies as a major subject;

                    or       an approved diploma in Theology or a theo-
                             logical course approved by the department;

                    or       a degree of the University of Nigeria for
                             which a total of 36 or more credit hours in
                             courses in Religion (not being courses
                             available in the Diploma program) has been
                             completed;

                    or       such other qualifications as may be deter-
                             mined to be equivalent.

Degree requirements:         According to their choice, students may
                             specialize in Christian Scriptures or Islamic
                             Scriptures.

                             Candidates must complete at least 114 credits
                             within the department's program. They will
                             be expected to gain proficiency in either
                             Hebrew and Biblical Greek or Arabic.

                             Candidates must complete at least 6 credits
                             in Arabic or in an approved course offered by
                             the Departments of History, Languages, Philo-
                             sophy, or Sociology.

## Department of Sociology and Anthropology

B.A. (Soc. and Anth.) (4 years)

Degree requirements:         Candidates must complete 81 credit hours in
                             courses offered in the department, 48 in
                             General Studies, at least 27 in approved
                             courses selected from those offered by the
                             Departments of Economics, History, Political
                             Science, Psychology and Religion, and 18 in
                             a foreign language.

## VOCATIONAL AND TECHNICAL EDUCATION

### GOVERNMENT HANDICRAFT CENTRES

Located in 9 large urban towns.  12 handicraft rooms being established in government and county council elementary schools.

Length of course:    2-year vocational courses.

Entrance requirements:        Primary school training.

Curriculum:        Woodwork, Metalwork, Photography, Commerce, Retail Trade, Music, Art, Agriculture and Animal Husbandry, Shoemaking, Textile Weaving and Dyeing, Designing, Tailoring, Embroidery, Ceramics, Domestic Subjects and Hairdressing.

In addition, evening classes in Woodwork, Metalwork, Calculation and Drawing for elementary school leavers who wish to learn the use of simple hand tools.

### TRADE SCHOOLS

5 new schools opened in addition to Government Trade School for Girls, Aba (former Women's Occupational Training Centre).

Length of course:    3 years (catering largely to  day students).

Entrance requirements:        Primary school training.

Curriculum:        Machine Shop, Engineering Practice, Cabinet-making, Carpentry and Joinery, Motor Mechanics, Blacksmithery and Welding, Sheetmetal Work, Electricity, Bricklaying, Radio Repairing, Painting and Decorating, Tailoring, Photography, etc.

These courses train boys for either independent self-employment or further apprenticeship with approved institutions or firms.

Girls' Trade School Courses:

Dressmaking, Needlework, Hairdressing, Photography, Housecraft.

Best qualified students may after 2 years transfer to secondary grammar, technical or commercial school.  (Admission into secondary class 2 or 3 according to ability of student and policy of admitting school.)

### AGRICULTURAL SCHOOLS (Junior)

Counterpart to trade schools.

Entry age:  12-13 years.

Entrance requirements:          <u>Primary School Leaving Certificate</u>.

Length of course:        3-5 years.

Proposed curriculum:     English Language, Practical Mathematics (Geometry,
                         Mensuration Arithmetic, etc.), Practical Science
                         (Climatology, Chemistry, Biology, Physics,
                         Mechanics, etc.), Civics, Citizenship (Economics,
                         Local Government, etc.), Crop Production, Feeding
                         and Nutrition, Diseases and Pests, Farm Mechanics
                         (Machinery, Building, Plans and Drawing), Farm
                         Management (Farm Economics, Marketing, Records,
                         Surveying and Layout of Farms, Co-operatives and
                         Community Development).

                         Domestic Science or Home Economics (when co-
                         education introduced).


## GOVERNMENT TRADE CENTRE (Enugu)

Enugu Trade Centre, formerly operated for refresher trade training of ex-
service men between 1947-1949, was re-opened for apprentice training in
1950.

Entrance requirements:          Elementary VI pass (<u>School Leaving Certifi-
                                cate</u>); adaptability tests; competitive
                                entrance examination in English and Arith-
                                metic (written and oral).

Length of course:        3 years' preparation for trades and as artisans.
                         Full-time residential courses divided between
                         workshops and classrooms.

                         Where trainee is sponsored for further 2 years in
                         either government departments or approved
                         industrial firms, this would complete a full
                         5-year apprenticeship.


### 3-YEAR TRADE COURSE

| Subjects taught | | 1st yr. | 2nd yr. | 3rd yr. |
|---|---|---|---|---|
| (1) English ) | compulsory | 2 hours | 2 hours | 2 hours |
| (2) Mathematics ) | | 2 hours | 2 hours | 2 hours |
| (3) Workshop Practice | | | | |
| (4) Technology | | | | |
| (5) Trade Science | | | | |
| (6) Trade Calculations | | | | |
| (7) Drawing (Technical) | | | | |
| (8) Geometry | | | | |

| Trades | | 1st Year | | | | |
| --- | --- | --- | --- | --- | --- | --- |
| | W.P. | Tec. | T.S. | T.C. | Dr. | Geom. |
| Brickwork | 23 | 1½ | 1½ | 1½ | 2 | 1½ |
| Carpentry and Joinery | 23 | 1½ | 1½ | 1½ | 2 | 1½ |
| Cabinet-Making | 24 | 3 | 1 | 1 | (4 with ... ) | |
| Painting and Decorating | 22 | 3 | 1 | 1 | (4 with ... ) | |
| Sheet Metalwork | (22 3/4) | 2 | (2¼ | ... ) | (3 with ... ) | |
| Blacksmithing and Welding | 23 | 4 | (2 with ... ) | | (2 with ... ) | |
| Fitter Machinists | 19 | 4 | (4 with ... ) | | (4 with ... ) | |
| Electrical Installations | 21 | 4 | 2 | 1½ | (2½ with ...) | |
| Automobile Engineering | 17 | 4½ | 4 | 2 | (3½ with ...) | |

| | | 2nd Year | | | | |
| --- | --- | --- | --- | --- | --- | --- |
| Brickwork | 23 | 1½ | 1½ | 1½ | 2 | 1½ |
| Carpentry and Joinery | 23 | 1½ | 1½ | 1½ | 2 | 1½ |
| Cabinet-Making | - | 3 | 1 | 1 | (4 with ... ) | |
| Painting and Decorating | 22 | 3 | 1 | 1 | (4 with ... ) | |
| Sheet Metalwork | (22 3/4) | 2 | (2¼ | ... ) | (3 with ... ) | |
| Blacksmithing and Welding | 23 | 4 | (2 with ... ) | | (2 with ... ) | |
| Fitter Machinists | 19 | 4 | (4 with)... ) | | (4 with ... ) | |
| Electrical Installations | 21 | 4 | 2 | 1½ | (2½ with ...) | |
| Automobile Engineering | 17 | 4½ | 4 | 2 | (3½ with ...) | |

| | | 3rd Year | | | | |
| --- | --- | --- | --- | --- | --- | --- |
| Brickwork | 23 | 1½ | 1½ | 1½ | 2 | 1½ |
| Carpentry and Joinery | 23½ | 1½ | - | 1½ | 3 | 1½ |
| Cabinet-Making | - | 3 | 1 | 1 | (4 with ... ) | |
| Painting and Decorating | 22 | 3 | 1 | 1 | (4 with ... ) | |
| Sheet Metalwork | 22 3/4 | 2 | (2¼ | ... ) | (3 with ... ) | |
| Blacksmithing and Welding | 23 | 4 | (2 with ... ) | | (2 with ... ) | |
| Fitter Machinists | 19 | 4 | (4 with ... ) | | (4 with ... ) | |
| Electrical Installations | 21 | 4 | 2 | 1½ | (2½ with ...) | |
| Automobile Engineering | 17 | 4½ | 4 | 2 | (3½ with ...) | |

## COMMERCIAL SCHOOLS

Secondary commercial schools exist throughout the region; many are un-recognized, most are private concerns.

Courses include:    General subjects, Shorthand and Typing.

Students enter for the R.S.A. examinations in the United Kingfom.

The Etukokwu Secondary Commercial School, Onitsha typifies those institutions which are government approved.  The syllabus provides a basic program of strong academic courses as well as commercial subjects.

Students prepare for both W.A.S.C. and R.S.A. examinations.

Post-secondary pupils who enter 2-year senior commercial courses at the Government Technical Institute sit for advanced R.S.A. examinations.


### ETUKOKWU SECONDARY COMMERCIAL SCHOOL, Onitsha
### (Private but government-approved)[+]

(30-40 minute periods per week)

Strong academic program offered in addition to commercial-bias subjects.

Courses prepare for W.A.S.C. and Royal Society of Arts examinations.

| Subjects | I A | I B | II A | II B | III A | III B | IV A | IV B | V A | V B |
|---|---|---|---|---|---|---|---|---|---|---|
| English Language | 6 | 6 | 6 | 6 | 5 | 5 | 5 | 5 | 5 | 5 |
| English Literature | - | - | - | - | 3 | 3 | 3 | 3 | 3 | 3 |
| Practical English | 6 | 6 | - | - | - | - | - | - | - | - |
| Mathematics | 5 | 5 | 5 | 5 | 5 | 5 | 5 | 5 | 5 | 5 |
| Geography | 3 | 3 | 3 | 3 | 3 | 3 | 3 | 3 | 3 | 3 |
| Arithmetic | 3 | 3 | 3 | 3 | 3 | 3 | 3 | 3 | 3 | 3 |
| Accounts | 3 | 3 | 3 | 3 | 3 | 3 | 3 | 3 | 3 | 3 |
| History | 3 | 3 | 3 | 3 | 3 | 3 | 3 | 3 | 3 | 3 |
| Commerce | 3 | 3 | 3 | 3 | 3 | 3 | 3 | 3 | 3 | 3 |
| Shorthand | 2 |  | 3 | 3 | 3 | 3 | 3 | 3 | 3 | 3 |
| Ibo (Vernacular) | - | - | - | - | - | - | 3 | 3 | 3 | 3 |
| Office Practice | 2 | 2 | 2 | 2 | 2 | 2 | - | - | - | - |
| Typewriting | - | - | 2 | 2 | 2 | 2 | 2 | 2 | - | - |

Not less than 60 minutes per week for these hobbies:

Tailoring . . . . . . . . . . . . . Class IV
Photography . . . . . . . . . . . Class III
Typewriting Repair . . . . . . . Class II
Book-binding and Printing . . . . Class I
Domestic Science . . . . . . . . Girls
Native Dance . . . . . . . . . . Boys and Girls

[+]Some unapproved commercial schools provide more limited curriculum.


### THE PORT HARCOURT COMPREHENSIVE SCHOOL

Established in 1962 by the Eastern Region in cooperation with the United States Agency for International Development. This new secondary school is based on the best educational practices of the U.S. and Great Britain. Only boys are enrolled at present. When facilities are available, girls will be admitted.

During its first years of operation the school has established its objectives along comprehensive technical school lines.  Broad subject matter provided for academically as well as technically inclined.  Training for craftsmen, technicians and technologists in:  Manufacturing, agriculture and in retail trade and commerce.  Strong academic preparation for W.A.S.C.

Plans are to extend the 5-year program (1965) to a 6-year senior secondary institution preparing students for W.A.S.C. and for entry to the University.

General education runs through the entire program as preparation for specialized courses in the senior secondary section.

Junior Secondary:  Forms I, II, III

Forms I and II, all students take following courses:

> Mathematics, Science, Health Science, English, History, Geography, Civics, Arts and Crafts, Workshop, Physical Education.  (All subjects taught with strong Nigerian content.)  A Nigerian language included.

Form I:         Special emphasis on English; no electives.

Form II:        Same subjects continue; 1 elective.

Form III:       Offers choice and diversification (Biology added to above).

> (a)  Terminal courses (when facilities are available) in Agriculture, Commerce, Industrial Arts.

> (b)  General studies for W.A.S.C., Royal Society of Arts (III) examination, or other educational attainment.

Senior Secondary:  Forms IV,V (later VI)

General education requirements reduced as specialization increases:

(a)  Science and Mathematics bias preparatory for University.

(b)  Commercial preparation for R.S.A. (III) examination.

(c)  Trade and industry bias leading to:

(i)   University technical studies
(ii)  Technical institutes
(iii) General employment

General syllabus of school in preparation.


THE NIGERIAN COLLEGE OF ARTS, SCIENCE AND TECHNOLOGY

Discontinued in 1962.

Branches:   Ibadan (opened in 1954, followed by the other 2 branches)
            Zaria
            Enugu

The College was established along lines of the United Kingdom's Polytechnic Institutes.  1957-58 through special relationship with the University of London the College Engineering Course at Zaria became the
Faculty of Engineering of University College, Ibadan.  Through this
arrangement, students of the College (Arts, Science and Technology) and of
University College, Ibadan proceeded to a London B.Sc. (Engineering) degree
by way of the College Engineering Courses at Zaria.  External students
accepted, no age limit for candidates entering College.  Courses offered
both academic and professional.

2 types of courses offered:

(1)  Intermediate:  Leading to <u>General Certificate of Education</u>, advanced
                    level.

(2)  Professional:  Leading to <u>College Diploma</u> or <u>Certificate</u>, or for
                    qualifications of United Kingdom professional bodies.

## Intermediate (Preliminary) Courses

Conducted at all 3 branches.

Entrance requirements:          <u>Cambridge School Certificate</u> (<u>West African</u>
                                <u>School Certificate</u>) Division II with credits
                                in English, Mathematics and 3 other subjects.

Courses:        Arts or Science group of subjects at advanced level leading
                to the <u>General Certificate of Education</u> 'A' level.

                These 2-year residential courses were a necessary prelimi-
                nary to certain of the professional courses in the College.

## Professional Courses

Held at branches as indicated.

## Enugu Branch

## Estate Management

2-year course leading to 1st examination of Royal Institution of Chartered
Surveyors.

Entrance requirements:          <u>School Certificate</u> or <u>G.C.E.</u> 'O'.

## Land Surveying

3½-year course leading to 1st and intermediate examination of Royal Institution of Chartered Surveyors.

Entrance requirements:          School Certificate or G.C.E. 'O'.

## Ibadan Branch

### Accountancy

9 years (4-year resident attendance, 5-year practical training) leading to examinations of Association of Certified and Corporate Accountants.

Entrance requirements:          School Certificate or G.C.E. 'O'.

### Chartered Secretaryship

3-year course leading to intermediate examination of Chartered Institute of Secretaries.

5-year course leading to final examination of Chartered Institute of Secretaries.

Entrance requirements:          School Certificate, Division I or II or corresponding level in G.C.E. 'O'.

### Government and Administration

2-year course leading to Diploma in Government and Administration.

Entrance requirements:          G.C.E. 'A' level or Higher School Certificate.

### Pharmacy

4-year course leading to College Diploma in Pharmacy (equivalent to Part I of a British university degree in Pharmacy).

Entrance requirements:          School Certificate.

### In-Service Courses

   Accountancy:

   1-year course for students nominated by Nigerian government departments.

Local Government:

1-year course conducted in association with governments of Eastern and Western regions.


Zaria Branch

Architecture

3-year course leading to intermediate examination of Royal Institute of British Architects.

2-year course leading to (for those passing the intermediate course) College Diploma in Architecture (equivalent to final examination of Royal Institute of British Architects).

Entrance requirements:     School Certificate, Divisions I or II. or G.C.E. at corresponding level.


Education

(a)   Teacher's Certificate:

1 year leading to teaching in secondary schools.

Entrance requirements:     2 subjects at standard equivalent to G.C.E. 'A' level.

(2)   Teacher's Certificate:

1 year leading to teacher training and supervision.

Entrance requirements:     G.C.E. 'A' level and 5-year satisfactory teaching experience.

(c)   Teacher's Certificate:

3 years leading to teachers of Physical Education in secondary schools and training colleges.

Entrance requirements:     School Certificate or Grade II Teacher Certificate.


Engineering (Civil, Mechanical, Electrical)

(a)   Preliminary Engineering Course:

2-year course leading to G.C.E. 'A' level in Pure Mathematics, Applied Mathematics and Physics.

Entrance requirements:   School Certificate, Division I or II; or
                         G.C.E. 'O'.

(b)  Professional Engineering Course:

4-year course leading to B.Sc. (Eng.) Bachelor of Science in
Engineering degree of University of London in "Special Relationship."

Entrance requirements:   Students having taken the preliminary course
                         of the College.

                    or   G.C.E. 'A' level in appropriate subjects.

                    or   Equivalent qualifications in Higher School
                         Certificate.

Fine Art

(a)  Intermediate Certificate and Diploma in Fine Art:

4-year course leading to Diploma in Fine Art or Commercial Design.

(b)  Art Teacher's Diploma:

1-year (additional) course leading to post-graduate professional
teacher's diploma (Art Teacher's Diploma in Department of Education).

(c)  Teacher's Certificate Course:

3-year course leading to College Certificate as Teacher of Fine Art.

Entrance requirements:   School Certificate (Diploma courses);
                         Grade II Teacher's Certificate (Certificate
                         course).

GOVERNMENT TECHNICAL INSTITUTE, Enugu

Offers full and part-time courses.

Institute composed of following sections:

    I.    Secondary Technical School (junior courses)

   II.    Senior Courses (senior technicians)

  III.    Evening Classes

I.    Secondary Technical School

    Entry age:   12-13 years of age.

    Entrance requirements:      Elementary School Leaving Certificate or
                                        completed elementary education and
                                        competitive examination.

    Length of course:           4-year program training 1st grade craftsmen.

    Curriculum:                 Syllabus that of West African School Certi-
                                          ficate with bias towards Engineering and
                                        Commerce:  English, History, Geography,
                                        Mathematics, Physics, Practical Physics,
                                        Chemistry, Practical Chemistry.

                                        And in addition:

| Engineering Stream | Commercial Stream |
|---|---|
| Technical Drawing | Commerce |
| Metal Work | Accounts |
| Additional Mathematics | Shorthand/Typing[+] |

[+]To Royal Society of Arts standards up to 80/100.

No differentiation is made in the common subjects so that all
students may enter the senior course in any of the Engineering subjects or Commerce, depending on their success in West African School
Certificate and their aptitudes.

Successful students from the junior school accepted into the senior
courses.  For Mechanical, Electrical and Building they are normally
accepted into the 2nd year.

N.B. Secondary Technical School course to be discontinued December 1965.

II.   Senior Courses

    Entrance requirements:      See below.

    Length of course:           2 to 3-year programs.

Training offered in Mechanical Engineering, Electrical Engineering,
Building, Telecommunications, Commerce.

All senior courses offered are at  technician level or its equivalent
in Commerce, and all courses lead to external examinations and certification.

The certificates offered do not qualify the holder for university or
other technological training.  Exceptional students might be recommended

for such courses but the intention of the Institute course is to
build up the requirements of Nigerian industry and commerce for
technicians.

No craft training is carried out in the Institute, but minimum
practical bias is given to the syllabus.


(1)  Mechanical Engineering

Length of course:          2 or 3 years.

Entrance requirements:

(i)   From secondary schools with credits in the
West African School Certificate in 2 sub-
jects from Mathematics, English, Physics,
Chemistry.  3-year course.

(ii)  From secondary technical schools with
similar qualification.  2-year course.

(iii) From junior technical courses.  3-year
course.


CURRICULUM
(Periods per week)

| Subjects | 1st Yr. | 2nd Yr. | 3rd Yr. |
|---|---|---|---|
| Mathematics | 5 | 6 | 6 |
| Engineering Drawing | 5 | 6 | - |
| Mechanical Engineering Science | 4 | 6 | - |
| Applied Mechanics | - | - | 6 |
| Heat Engines of W/Shop Technology | - | - | 6 |
| Electrical Engineering Science | 4 | 6 | 6 |
| Basic Fitting and Allied Trades | 14 | - | - |
| Machine Shop | - | 7 | - |
| Engine Fitting Shop or Advanced Machine Shop | - | - | 5 |
| English | 3 | 2 | 2 |
| Liberal Studies | - | 2 | 2 |
| Management | - | - | 2 |


Certification:

The certificate offered is the Ordinary Certificate for Overseas
Students issued by the City and Guilds of London Institute.  Successful students must produce evidence of 1 year of employment in
industry before being granted the External Certificate and before
being admitted to the higher course.

An Institute Certificate of satisfactory completion of the course is
also issued.


(2)  Electrical Engineering

Length of course:          2 or 3 years.

Entrance requirements:   As for Mechanical Engineers.


CURRICULUM
(Periods per week)

| Subjects | 1st Yr. | 2nd Yr. | 3rd Yr. |
|---|---|---|---|
| Mathematics | 5 | 6 | 6 |
| Engineering Drawing | 5 | 6 | - |
| Mechanical Engineering Science | 4 | 6 | 6 |
| Electrical Science | 4 | 6 | - |
| Electrical Engineering Part 1 | - | - | 6 |
| Electrical Engineering Part 2 | - | - | 6 |
| Basic Fitting and Allied Trades | 14 | - | - |
| Electrical Workshops | - | 7 | - |
| Electrical Machines | - | - | 5 |
| English | 3 | 2 | 2 |
| Management | - | - | 2 |
| | Internal Quali-<br>fying Examination | S1 | S2 and<br>Internal for<br>Certification |


Certification:

The certificate offered is the Ordinary Certificate for Overseas
Students issued by the City and Guilds of London Institute.  Successful students must produce evidence of 1 year of employment in
industry before being granted the External Certificate and before
being admitted to the higher certificate course.

An Institute Certificate of completion of the course to a satisfactory
level is also issued.


(3)  Building

Length of course:          2 or 3 years.

Entrance requirements:   As for Mechanical Engineers.

## CURRICULUM
(Periods per week)

| Subjects | 1st Yr. | 2nd Yr. | 3rd Yr. |
|---|---|---|---|
| Mathematics | 5 | 6 | 6 |
| Building Science | 4 | 6 | 6 |
| Mechanics | 3 | 6 | 6 |
| Construction and Drawing | 8 | 6 | 6 |
| Carpentry and Joinery | 12 | - | - |
| Plumbing/Brick-work | - | 7 | - |
| Survey | - | - | 5 |
| English | 3 | 2 | 2 |
| Liberal Studies | - | 2 | 2 |
| Management | - | - | 2 |
| | Internal examination. Qualifying examination | S1 | S2 and Internal examination for qualification |

Certification:

The certificate offered is the Ordinary Certificate for Overseas Students issued by the City and Guilds of London Institute. Successful students must produce evidence of 1 year of employment in industry before being granted the External Certificate and before being admitted to the higher certificate course.

An Institute Certificate of satisfactory completion of the course is also issued.

(4) Telecommunications

Length of course:        3 years.

Entrance requirements:   West African School Certificate with credits in 2 of the subjects: Mathematics, English, Physics.

                    or   Completion of S1 Mechanical or Electrical Engineering in which case the 1st year of the course is omitted.

## CURRICULUM
(Periods per week)

| Subjects | 1st Yr. | 2nd Yr. | 3rd Yr. |
|---|---|---|---|
| Mathematics | 5 | 6 | 6 |
| Engineering Science | 6 | - | - |

| | Intermediate to C and G | External C and G | Final C and G and Internal Certificate |
|---|---|---|---|
| Engineering Drawing | 5 | - | - |
| Elementary Telecommunications Practice | 6 | - | - |
| Telecommunications Principles | 5 | 6 | 5 |
| Radio and Line Transmission | 5 | - | - |
| Radio | - | 6 | 6 |
| Line Transmission | - | 6 | 6 |
| Special Subjects | - | - | 6 |
| Practical Work | - | 7 | - |
| English | 3 | 2 | 2 |
| Liberal Studies | - | 2 | 2 |
| Management | - | - | 2 |

Certification:

The certificate offered is the <u>Final Certificate of the City and Guilds of London Institute for Telecommunication Technicians.</u>

The final examination must be passed at one sitting. The Full Technological Certificate will be awarded to those who pass 2 of the special subjects.

(5)  <u>Senior Commercial Course</u>

Length of course:        2 years.

Entrance requirements:   <u>West African School Certificate</u> with credits in 2 of the subjects: English, History, Geography, English Literature. (Those who have taken additional subjects of Commerce, Accounts or Shorthand/Typing have an advantage.)

CURRICULUM<br>(Periods per week)

| Subjects | 1st Yr. | 2nd Yr. |
|---|---|---|
| English | 5 | 6 |
| Principles of Law | 3 | 6 |
| Economic Geography | 5 | - |
| Elements of Statistics | 6 | - |
| Structure of Commerce | 6 | - |
| Accounting I | 6 | - |
| Accounting II | - | 6 |
| Economics | - | 6 |

| | | |
|---|---|---|
| Shorthand/Typing | 4 | 6 |
| Business Organization | - | 5 |
| | External Examination | Internal Examination and External Examination |

Certification:

The certificate offered is that of the Ordinary Certificate for Over-seas Students in Business Studies issued by the London Chamber of Commerce.

An Institute Certificate is also awarded for satisfactory completion of the course.

(6)    The Higher Certificate

This certificate will be offered when staff and equipment are available.  Entry to these courses will be offered only to holders of the Ordinary Certificate.  Subjects will be as follows:

Mechanical Engineering:

        Mathematics
        Mechanics and Machines
        Strength and Property of Materials
        Electro-technology

and    1 subject from:

        Power Plant
        Refrigeration and Air Conditioning
        Structures

Electrical Engineering:

        Circuit Theory and Measurement
        Machines
        Electronics
        Mathematics
        Mechanical Technology

Building/Civil Engineering:

        Construction and Materials
        Structures
        Surveying
        Measurement and Estimating

AND

| Building | C/E Roads/Water | C/E Structures |
|----------|-----------------|----------------|
| Site Organizations | Soil Mechanics | Soil Mechanics |
| Concrete or Timber | Road and Airfield | Stratification |
| | or | and Detailing |
| | Water Supply and Drainage | |

## III. Evening Classes

Evening classes at present offered in following subjects:

| | Courses | Examination | Qualification | Yrs. |
|---|---------|-------------|---------------|------|
| (a) | Mech. Engineering | Ordinary Cert. | As for day classes | 3 |
| (b) | Elec. Engineering | -do- | -do- | 3 |
| (c) | Building | -do- | -do- | 3 |
| (d) | Telecommunications (as required) | C. and G. Certif. separate subjects | Employment in Telecommunications | 4 |
| (e) | Commerce | R.S.A. subjects Single Certif. | Suitable standard by examination | 3 |
| (f) | Shorthand/Typing | R.S.A. | Suitable standard | Yearly |
| (g) | Introductory Technical | Internal | Standard VI | 3 |

All classes consist of 3 evenings per week from 6 to 8 p.m.
September to May annually.

## Institute Certification

All students are required to complete 75% of the possible attendances in
each subject.  Failure to do so bars entry to examination.

Failure in any examination, internal or external, necessitates repeating
that year or leaving the course.  In exceptional circumstances students
failing in 1 subject by narrow margin are permitted by the examining body
on the recommendation of the Principal to continue with the work of the
following year and to retake the failed subject with the next examination.
In no case are  students "referred" for a failure in the final year.

Students must obtain a minimum of 40% of the possible marks for class-work
and 40% for home-work.  These marks are added to the written examination
results and 40% of the total marks must be obtained for a pass in the
examination.

The Institute Certificate is awarded for completion of the course to a
satisfactory level.  The definition of "a satisfactory level" is 40% of the

total marks obtained in the final examination of the Institute, and a minimum of 75% attendances.

The Ordinary Certificate for Overseas Students is awarded by the City and Guilds of London Institute to all students who pass their examination and show evidence of the completion of one year of industrial experience. Such evidence must be submitted to the Principal for submission to the examining body.


New Technical Institute planned at Port Harcourt.


AGRICULTURAL TRAINING (under the Ministry of Agriculture)

SCHOOL OF AGRICULTURE, Umudike, Umuahia

Founded October, 1955.

Entrance requirements:

> For Agricultural Assistants Course:   Graduation from secondary grammar schools with West African School Certificate, or G.C.E. at ordinary or advanced level, with credits in English Language and at least 2 science subjects.

> For Assistant Agricultural Superintendent Diploma Course:   Graduation from the Agricultural Assistants course, plus 2-3 years experience in the field.

Assistant Agricultural Superintendent Diploma course:

> 2 years (6 terms, 12 weeks per term).

Agricultural Assistants course:

> 1 year (before 1962, 18 months.   18-month course projected after Development Plan period over).


### PROGRAM FOR ASSISTANT AGRICULTURAL SUPERINTENDENT COURSE
(Total periods for 6 terms)

| Subjects | Periods |
|---|---|
| Botany and related Subjects | 216 |
|   Foundation of Botany | |
|   The Plant Kingdom | |
|   Plant Physiology and Ecology | |
|   Systematic Botany and Plant Identification | |
|   Plant Pathology | |

Zoology, Entomology and Animal Physiology              252
   Zoology
   Entomology
   Animal Physiology

Chemistry and Soil Science                            216
   Inorganic Chemistry
   Organic Chemistry
   The Chemistry of Nutrition and Crop Products
   Soil Science

Agricultural Research                                 132

Agricultural Extension                                 84

Agricultural Mechanics                                120

Crop Production and Allied Subjects                   168
   Genetics and Plant Breeding
   Horticulture
   Crop Production

Livestock Production and Allied Subjects              288

Breeding and Improvement of Farm Livestock           288
   Animal Health and Veterinary Science
   Feeds and Feeding
   Poultry Production
   Pig Production
   Cattle Production
   Sheet, Goat and Rabbit Production
   General Livestock Management

Agricultural Economics                                144
   Theory of Economics
   Farm Management

Agricultural Statistics                                36

Surveying and Mapping                                  36


### PROGRAM FOR AGRICULTURAL ASSISTANTS COURSE
(Periods for year's program)

| Subjects | Periods |
| --- | --- |
| General Agriculture | 56 |
|    Introduction to Agriculture | |
|    Organization of the Ministry of Agriculture | |
|    Principles and Practices in Agriculture | |
|    Field Operations | |
|    Agricultural Terms or Cropping Systems | |
|    Types of Agriculture | |
|    Soils | |
|    Loss of Soil Fertility | |
|    Maintenance of Soil Fertility | |

Plant Nutrient Requirements
Agricultural Economics
Farm Management

Surveying                                                           42

General Farm Engineering                                            39
  Materials
  Simple Building Construction
  Fences
  Jointing of Metals
  Road Construction
  Workshop Practice
  Machinery
  Tractor and Implement Mechanization

Farm Practice                                                      46

Crop Husbandry                                                     42
  Cacao, Citrus, Rubber, Oil Palms, Coffee,
  Kola, Bananas and Plantains, Coconut,
  Cashew, Fuel (Gmelina and Teak)

Annual Crops                                                       14

Crop Protection                                                    28
  Insect Pests and their Control
  Plant Diseases and their Control
  Weeds and their Control

Agricultural Extension                                            42

Animal Husbandry                                                  58
  Poultry
  Pigs
  Cattle
  Small Stock
  General

Examinations are given on all subjects taught in the school and grades are
as follows:

                    40% pass mark for each subject
                    60% - 74% is credit for each subject
                    75% and over is distinction for each subject

For the entire examination 50% average is required for a pass.  Student who
scores the 50% but gèts below 40% in individual subjects is referred in a
maximum of 2 subjects.  If he scores below 40% in more than 2 papers, he has
failed the entire examination even if he scores the 50% overall average.

Diploma awarded:

    School of Agriculture Diploma

    (Graduates must satisfy the examiners in the final examination at the
    end of the 2-year course.)

Refresher courses are offered for some of junior technical staff.


## TEACHER EDUCATION

## TEACHER TRAINING COLLEGES

(1)   Primary Teachers (Elementary Grade III) Certificate

      Qualifying for:          Teaching elementary classes 1-4.

      Course:               2-year program for Primary School Leavers.

      All Grade III teachers to be trained as Grade II teachers by the end of 1966.


(2)   Primary Teachers (Higher Elementary Grade II) Certificate

      Qualifying for:          Teaching upper elementary classes and lower forms of secondary schools.

| Entrance qualifications | Length of Course |
|---|---|
| (a)  Grade III teachers | 2 years |
| (b)  West African School Certificate holders | 2 years |
| (c)  Exceptional Primary School leavers | 4 years (to end 1967) |

      Syllabus for centrally examined subjects:  English Language, Arithmetical Processes, Principles of Education, Practice of Education. (Taught as Theory and also Practical Teaching).


(3)   Teachers' (Grade I) Certificate

      Qualifying for:          Teaching in secondary schools.

Grade I Certificate awarded to teachers on the following conditions:

(a)  Possession of Teachers' Grade II Certificate.

(b)  At least 3 years of post Grade II Certificate teaching.

(c)  Pass in General Certificate of Education English or credit in the Teacher's Grade II Certificate English.

(d)  (i)  Pass in 2 school subjects at advanced level in General Certificate of Education

or  (ii)  First or second class pass at the Rural Education Centre course which is a 1-year course.

(e) Pass in practical teaching tests in subjects of specialization in the case of (d)(i).

or In the case of (d)(ii). Satisfactory practical work on school farm over a period of 2 years. Work is inspected by the Inspector (Rural Education).

Grade I teachers qualify for direct entry to universities.


## ADVANCED TEACHER TRAINING COLLEGES

Residential institutions established to train non-graduates for teaching in secondary schools and teacher training colleges.

Entry age:  18-20 years.

Length of course:          3 years.

Entrance qualifications:      Grade II teachers with G.C.E. '0' level.

West African School Certificate holders or equivalent qualifications.

## Academic Syllabuses

| | |
|---|---|
| Education | Foundation of Education, Educational Psychology, General Methods of Teaching, History of Education, Comparative Education, Measurement and Evaluation of Learning Outcomes, Subject Method Teaching, Educational Administration, Seminars and Teaching Practice. |
| English | (Language and Literature) Philology, Semantic Approach, Phonetics of English, Use of English, Media of Expression and Communication, Teaching Methods, Allied Activities. |
| Communicative English | Phonetics, Words, Written Expression, Reading. |
| French | Linguistics and Phonetics, Spoken Language, Principles of Grammar, Written Language, Literature and Culture in French, Bibliography. |
| History | Use of History, Ancient and Medieval History, British and European History, circ. 1500/1960, Europe Overseas, circ. 1450/1960, History of Music, circ. 1883-1960, History of Africa, Teaching Methods. |
| Geography | Physical Geography, Regional Geography, Economic Geography of the World, Methods of Teaching Geography (Pedagogy), Practical Work. |

| | |
|---|---|
| Mathematics | <u>Pure Mathematics</u>:  Algebra, Trigonometry, Calculus, Co-ordinate Geometry, Algebraic Solid Geometry. |
| | <u>Applied Mathematics</u>:  Statics, Dynamics, Hydrostatics, Statistics, Special Topics, History of Mathematics, Teaching Methods in Mathematics. |
| Library Science | (1-term course)  The Library in the School, Library Organization and Administration, Classification and Cataloguing. |
| Physical Education | Anatomy and Physiology, Health Education, Theory of Physical Activities.  Seminar, Practical Work (Calisthenics and Skill Training). |

Certificate awarded:   <u>Nigerian Certificate in Education</u> (<u>N.C.E.</u>) awarded at conclusion of 3-year program.

# FEDERATION OF NIGERIA - NORTHERN REGION

Com. Training

Gov't Technical Institute

Technical

Training Schools

Trade/Craft Schools

School for Arabic Studies

Advanced Teacher Training

(Grade II) TEACHER

(Grade III) TRAINING

Rural Ed. Col.

Higher School

ACADEMIC SECONDARY EDUCATION

PRIMARY EDUCATION

Art Tchr's Cert.
Ll. B. (Hon.)
B. Sc. (Hon.) Eng.
B. Sc. (Hon.) Vet.
B. Sc. (Hon.) Agric.
B. Sc. (C. Hon.)
B. Arch. (Hon.)
Dip. Pub. Ad.
B. A. (Hon.) Pub. Ad.
B. A. (C. Hon.) Arab.
B. A. (C. Hon.)
B. A. (Hon.) F. Art.

VI Form (Upper)
VI Form (Lower)

V Form
IV Form
III Form
II Form
I Form

VII Standard
VI Standard
V Standard
IV Standard
III Standard
II Standard
I Standard

**

*

| Student's Age | Year of Schooling | | |
|---|---|---|---|
| 26 | 20 | HIGHER EDUCATION | |
| 25 | 19 | | |
| 24 | 18 | | |
| 23 | 17 | | |
| 22 | 16 | | |
| 21 | 15 | | |
| 20 | 14 | | |
| 19 | 13 | | |
| 18 | 12 | SECONDARY | |
| 17 | 11 | | |
| 16 | 10 | | |
| 15 | 9 | | |
| 14 | 8 | | |
| 13 | 7 | ELEMENTARY | |
| 12 | 6 | | |
| 11 | 5 | | |
| 10 | 4 | | |
| 9 | 3 | | |
| 8 | 2 | | |
| 7 | 1 | | |
| 6 | | | |
| 5 | | | |
| 4 | | | |
| 3 | | | |

Compulsory education: None

School year: Mid-January – Mid-December

Secondary school grading: West African School Certificate 1 - 9

Cambridge Higher School Certificate 1 - 9
(See SECONDARY EDUCATION)

# N O R T H E R N   R E G I O N

## BACKGROUND

Early education for children in the North largely Koranic schooling
taught in Arabic.  Christian missions bringing Western education were not
admitted as soon as in southern regions.

Education Department of Northern Region established by British in 1910.

By 1929, 116 government schools (95 elementary, 8 craft, 12 middle, 1
secondary);152 mission schools (5 assisted);20,000 Koranic schools.  By
1964, 2684 primary schools (1372 Native Authority, 1311 Voluntary Agency,
1 government); 140 post-primary schools (12 craft, 5 commercial, 4 technical, 65 grammar, 54 teacher training).

Prior to 1954 primary school program was 8 years.

From 1955:      Primary school:      7-year program initiated.

                    4-year Junior Primary
                    3-year Senior Primary

                Middle school (Native Authority):   2-year program.

                    Forms I and II (Secondary)
                    Middle School renamed Junior Secondary, then changed
                    to Provincial Secondary.

                Secondary school:   5 years.

                    Forms I through V
                    Forms VI (Upper and Lower) (Higher School)

Schools and colleges controlled in one of 3 ways:
    (1)   Government
    (2)   Native Administration (N.A.) (Local Government)
    (3)   Voluntary Agency (V.A.).  Usually missionary societies, e.g.
          Sudan United Mission, Sudan Interior Mission (SIM), Roman
          Catholic Mission, Church Missionary Society (CMS), Church of
          the Brethren Mission.

          In addition a community may establish, with agreement of
          Ministry of Education, a school to serve its needs.

Recognized schools (Education Law does not permit the existence of any
others) whether N.A. or V.A. or Community almost universally grant-aided
by government.  Usually separate schools for boys and girls.

## PRIMARY EDUCATION

Entry age:     6 years.

Length of program:  7 years.

Language of instruction:     English, Hausa or Yoruba.
(If Hausa or Yoruba is initial language of instruction, a change may be
made to English at year 3 or later.  Alternatively, Hausa or Yoruba may
continue as language of instruction throughout the school.)

Curriculum:     English and Vernacular Studies, Writing, Arithmetic,
                History, Geography, Rural Science or Domestic Science,
                Handwork (including Art), Physical Education, Religion.

Certificate of Primary Education granted at end of 7 years.

Students then compete in common entrance examination for various branches
of post-primary education.


## SECONDARY EDUCATION

Entrance requirements:          Common entrance examination at end of
                                Primary VII.  Institutions may also use
                                examination of their own.  From these
                                results candidates are selected for
                                entrance to secondary schools, teachers'
                                colleges, craft schools and certain courses
                                at the Technical Institute.

Language of instruction:        English.

The 72 (1965) secondary schools in the Region all follow approximately
the same curriculum.  There are some variations according to locality
(e.g. a school in the north might offer Hausa, Arabic and Islamic
Religious Knowledge while one farther south might offer instead Yoruba
and Christian Religious Knowledge);and if facilities are available, some
schools offer technical subjects.

A balanced curriculum is imposed by the group system of the West African
School Certificate examination.

"Comprehensive schools" (academic, technical and commercial courses
offered in the same school) are expected to increase.

## SECONDARY SCHOOL TIMETABLE (including VIth Form)
### (Year of 37 weeks)

| Major Subjects | West African School Certificate | | | | | VIth Form Higher School Cert. | |
|---|---|---|---|---|---|---|---|
| | Year 1 | 2 | 3 | 4 | 5 | Lower | Upper |
| English Language ) | 10 | 10 | 8 | 5 | 5 | | |
| English Literature ) | | | | 3 | 3 | 8 | 8 |
| Islamic or Bible Religions Knowledge | 2 | 2 | 4 | 4 | 4 | | |
| Arabic | 3 | 3 | 4 | 4 | 4 | | |
| History | 3 | 3 | 3 | 3 | 3 | 8 | 8 |
| Geography | 3 | 3 | 3 | 3 | 3 | 8 | 8 |
| Mathematics | 8 | 8 | 6 | 6 | 6 | 8 | 8 |
| Additional Mathematics | | | | 4 | 4 | | |
| General Science | 4 | 4 | | | | | |
| Physics | | | 4 | 4 | 4 | 8 | 8 |
| Chemistry | | | 4 | 4 | 4 | 8 | 8 |
| Biology | | | 4 | 4 | 4 | | |
| Woodwork | 3 | 3 | 6 | 6 | 6 | | |
| Physical Training | 2 | 2 | | | | | |
| General Paper | | | | | | 2 | 2 |

In addition, a school may offer several of the following: Latin, French, Hausa, Yoruba, Additional Mathematics, Agricultural Science, Metalwork, Needlework, Cookery, Domestic Science.

In the final 2 years of the 5-year West African School Certificate course 8 subjects normally taken. The student's choice is limited by the W.A.S.C. "groups" and by the school's estimation of his abilities in particular subjects.

The content of the mathematics course is defined by the W.A.S.C. syllabus. Alternative 'B' is the preferred one. All science subjects include laboratory work.

Promotion from one class to the one above is normally automatic at the end of each year.

*At the close of the 5-year program students take the Joint Examination for the West African School Certificate and General Certificate of Education. (For details, see NIGERIA: Eastern Region, and Appendix D.)

## HIGHER SCHOOL CERTIFICATE COURSE

Certain schools offer, in addition to the 5-year West African School Certificate, an additional 2 years of training for the Higher School Certificate examination.

Schools offering Forms Lower VI and Upper VI (Higher school):

By 1963:

      Government College, Keffi
      Profincial Secondary School, Okene
      Sudan Interior Mission (S.I.M.) Titcombe College, Egbe
      Provincial Secondary School, Kano
      Boys' Secondary School, Gindiri
      Government College, Zaria
      St. Paul's College, Wusasa
      St. John's College, Kaduna
      Queen Elizabeth School (Girls), Ilorin

By 1965:

      Provincial Secondary School, Yola
      Provincial Secondary School, Ilorin
      St. Michael's Secondary School, Aliade

Curriculum:    General Paper compulsory for both sections.
                3 subjects, in addition to General Paper, are taken from
                following list.

| Arts | Science |
|------|---------|
| English Literature | Mathematics (Pure and Applied) |
| History | Mathematics (Pure) |
| Geography | Mathematics (Applied) |
| Mathematics | Physics |
| Bible Knowledge | Chemistry |
| | Zoology |
| | Botany |
| | Biology |

## HIGHER SCHOOL CERTIFICATE COURSES

| Course | | H.S.C. Subjects Available | W.A.S.C. Qualifying Subjects |
|--------|---|---------------------------|------------------------------|
| Arts | 1. | English, History, Geography | English Literature, History, Geography |
| | 2. | English, History, Math. | English Literature, History, Math. |
| | 3. | English, Geography, Math. | English Literature, Geography, Math. |
| | 4. | History, Geography, Math. | History, Geography, Math. |
| | 5. | History, Geography, French | History, Geography, French |
| | 6. | English, French, History  ) | English Literature, |
| | 7. | English, French, Geography ) | French, History/Geography |

| Science | 8. | Math., Geography, Chemistry | Math.,Geography, Chemistry |
|---|---|---|---|
| | 9. | Geography, Chemistry, Physics ) | Geography, Chemistry, |
| | 10. | Geography, Botany, Zoology   ) | Biology |
| | 11. | Math., Geography, Physics | Additional Math. |
| | 12. | Pure Math., Applied Math., Physics | Math., Physics, Chemistry |
| | 13. | Math., Physics, Chemistry | Math., Physics, Chemistry |
| | 14. | Chemistry, Physics, Zoology | Chemistry, Physics, Biology |
| | 15. | Chemistry, Physics, Botany | Chemistry, Physics, Biology |
| | 16. | Chemistry, Botany, Zoology | Chemistry, Physics, Biology |

** University of Cambridge Joint Examination for the Higher School Certificate and General Certificate of Education at close of 2-year program. (For details, see Appendix B.)


# HIGHER EDUCATION

## AHMADU BELLO UNIVERSITY, Zaria

Located at former site of the Nigerian College of Arts, Science and Technology.

Founded October, 1962.

Standards of the institution are expected to equate with those of London University.  External examiners are obtained from British universities and from Nigerian universities.

The Engineering Course (1964) is for external degree of London University. As of 1965 students will study for the University's own degree.


Faculties:

|  |  |
|---|---|
| Arts | Architecture |
| Science | Engineering |
| Law | Arabic and Islamic Studies |
| Agriculture | |

Language of instruction:        English

Degrees awarded:                                          Years

    B.A. (combined Honours) Degree                   3
    B.A. (Honours) Degree in Fine Arts               4
    B.A. (combined Honours) Degree in Arabic and
      Islamic Studies                               3
    B.A. (Honours) Degree in Public Administration   3
    Diploma in Public Administration                 2
    Bachelor of Architecture (Honours) Degree        5
    B.Sc. (combined Honours) Degree                  3
    B.Sc. (Honours) (Agriculture)                    3
    B.Sc. (Honours) (Veterinary) (B.Vet. Med.)     4-5
    B.Sc. (Honours) Degree in Civil, Mechanical
      or Electrical Engineering                     3
      (External Degree of University of London
      through 1963)
    LL.B. (Honours) Degree                           3
    Art Teacher's Certificate                        1

## Faculty of Arts

### B.A. (combined Honours) Degree - 3 years

Entrance requirements:    Examination and interview.

                           Candidates must have G.C.E. passes in 5
                           subjects, at least 2 at advanced level,

        or    G.C.E. passes in 4 subjects, at least 3
                           of which must be at advanced level; provided
                           in either case, a credit in English Language
                           in W.A.S.C. or pass in G.C.E. 'O' English
                           Literature or H.S.C. General Paper is
                           included.

### B.A. (Honours) Degree in Fine Arts - 4 years

Specializing in one of the following:

Sculpture, Painting, Illustration and Graphic Design, Textile
Design or Ceramics.

Entrance requirements:    Examination and interview.

                           To qualify for entrance examination and
                           interview, candidates must have passes in
                           G.C.E. ordinary level in 3 subjects other
                           than Art, or equivalent qualification.

## Art Teacher's Certificate - 1 year

Entrance requirements:    B.A. degree in Fine Art, or the Nigerian
College Diploma in Fine Art, or equivalent
qualification.

## B.A. (combined Honours) Degree in Arabic and Islamic Studies - 3 years

Entrance requirements:    Passes in 5 subjects in the G.C.E. with
Arabic and at least 1 of the following sub-
jects at advanced level:

English Literature, Hausa, History, Geography, Mathematics, Islamic History,

or    Passes in 4 subjects in the G.C.E. with
Arabic and 2 of the subjects listed above
at the advanced level or equivalent qualification;

Provided that in either case a credit in
English in W.A.S.C. or a pass in G.C.E. 'O'

or    G.C.E. 'A' English Literature

or    H.S.C. General Paper is included.

## B.A. (Honours) Degree in Public Administration - 3 years

Entrance requirements:    Aptitude test and interview.

Candidates must have 5 passes in G.C.E. of
which at least 2 must be at advanced level,

or    Passes in 4 subjects in the G.C.E. of which
at least 3 must be at advanced level or
equivalent qualification.

Provided that 1 of the following qualifications is included:

G.C.E. 'O' English Language

or    Credit in English Language in W.A.S.C.

or    G.C.E. 'A' English Literature

or    H.S.C. pass in General Paper

## Diploma in Public Administration - 2 years

Entrance requirements:    Aptitude test and interview.

Candidates must have
either (a) 2 years' service in a responsible post in

government or a Native Authority or equivalent administrative experience in a
commercial house, bank or corporation, and
have passed in English '0' level or English
Literature 'A' level, and 4 other subjects
in G.C.E., including 1 at the advanced level,

or   (b)   School Certificate including credit in English
English Language, have completed an H.S.C.
course and obtained a pass in 1 principal
subject.

## Faculty of Architecture

### B. Architecture (Honours) Degree - 5 years

Entrance requirements:   Examination and interview.

Candidates must have passes in 5 subjects
in the G.C.E. ordinary level including
English Language and Mathematics or a
Science subject; or equivalent qualification.

Students admitted with above qualifications
must obtain G.C.E. advanced level passes in
2 subjects within the first 2 years of the
course.

## Faculty of Science

### B.Sc. (combined Honours) Degree - 3 years

Entrance requirements:   Passes in 5 subjects in the G.C.E. of which
at least 2 must be passes at 'A' level,

or   Passes in 4 subjects in the G.C.E. of which
3 must be at 'A' level, or equivalent
qualification.

Provided that a credit in English Language
in the W.A.S.C. or a pass in G.C.E. '0'
English Language or G.C.E. 'A' English
Literature or H.S.C. General Paper is
included.

At least 1 of the advanced level subjects
must be from the following:  Biology,
Botany, Chemistry, Physics, Zoology.

### B.Sc. (Honours) Agriculture - 3 years

Entrance requirements:    As for B.Sc. degree, provided 1 of the advanced level passes is Chemistry.

### B.Sc. (Honours) Veterinary (B.Vet. Med.) - 4-5 years

Entrance requirements:    G.C.E. advanced level passes in Chemistry, Biology or Botany and G.C.E. ordinary level passes in English Language, and Physics or Physics-with-Chemistry; or equivalent qualification.

### B.Sc. (Honours) Degree in Civil, Mechanical or Electrical Engineering - 3 years

(External degree of University of London through 1964.)

Entrance requirements:    A pass with credit in the W.A.S.C. or a pass in G.C.E. 'O' English Language or a pass in G.C.E. 'A' English Literature or H.S.C. General Paper.

A pass in Chemistry at 'O' or 'a' level in the G.C.E.

Passes at the 'A' level in the G.C.E. or principal standard in the H.S.C. in either of the following 2 combinations of subjects:

(a)   Pure Mathematics, Applied Mathematics and Physics
(b)   Mathematics (Pure and Applied) and Physics

In special cases, candidates who have not obtained required qualification in Chemistry may, at discretion of Faculty Board, be considered.

## Faculty of Law

### LL.B. (Honours) Degree - 3 years

Entrance requirements:    Aptitude Test and interview.

Candidates  must have passes in 5 subjects in the G.C.E. with at least 2 at advanced level or equivalent qualification, provided that a pass in English Language in the G.C.E. 'O' level or equivalent qualification is included.

VOCATIONAL AND TECHNICAL EDUCATION

CRAFT SCHOOLS

Government craft schools:  12 schools established 1957-1961.

Each school located in a different Province (except Sardauna for which one is planned).

Entrance requirements:        Primary 7 years and common entrance exami-
                              nation (as for full secondary and teacher
                              training colleges).

3-YEAR PROGRAM[+]

(40-minute periods per week)

| Subjects | Periods |
|---|---|
| English | 8 |
| Mathematics | 6 |
| History | 2 |
| Geography | 2 |
| Science | 4 |
| Religious Study | 2 |
| Physical Education | 2 |
| Workshop | 10 |
| Technical Drawing | 2 |

[+]Much fluidity exists.  Bias to more practical work in 3rd year.

(Whole craft school curriculum structure under review.)

At end of course students sit for entrance examination to one of technical training schools or the Technical Institute (Commerce section).

GOVERNMENT TECHNICAL TRAINING SCHOOLS

3 schools:      Technical Training School, Bukuru  1962 (Craft courses begun)
                Technical Training School, Kano    1963    "       "        "
                Technical Training School, Ilorin  1964    "       "        "

Entrance requirements:        Examination taken by Craft School leavers.
                              Examination may also be taken by 3rd year
                              students of secondary schools.

3-year program (under review):

   General Education:  Being revised to raise standard in English,
                       Mathematics and Science.

Craft Courses:     Fitter/Machinists, Cabinet Makers, Carpenters
                   and Joiners, Motor Mechanics, Blacksmiths and
                   Welders, Sheet Metal Workers, Plumbers, Motor-
                   body Builders, Electricians, Bricklayers,
                   Painters and Decorators, Instrument Mechanics,
                   Leather Workers, Shipwrights, Diesel Mechanics,
                   Wood Machinists; (Motor Vehicle Electricians may
                   be introduced).

## TYPICAL TIMETABLE
(School year - 37 weeks)

| Subjects | Hours per week (35-minute periods) |
|---|---|
| Practical (Workshop) | 18 |
| Mathematics | 4 |
| English and Liberal Studies | 3 |
| Trade Theory (including Science) | 2 |
| General Science (mainly Physics) | 2 |
| Trade Drawing (and Calculations) | 3 |
| | 32 |

The trade course for the Federal Craft Training Certificate follows the
syllabus of the City and Guilds of London Institute at 1st Craft or
Intermediate Level.  The Federal Craft Training Certificate awarded upon
successful examinations.

Students also encouraged to enter for external examinations of the City
and Guilds Institute.


## GOVERNMENT TECHNICAL INSTITUTE, Kaduna

Former specially designed courses (internally examined) for Assistant
Technical Officers and Technical Assistants replaced, 1963.

As of 1961, Technician Courses offered, leading to City and Guilds of
London (Ordinary Certificate) in Mechanical or Electrical Engineering,
or Building and Civil Engineering.

Entrance requirements:    (i)   Training up to West African School Certi-
                                cate level.

                          (ii)  Former students of technical training
                                schools with City and Guilds (Intermediate
                                level) and some industrial experience also
                                accepted.

Program (under review):    2-year full time course, preceded by in case of
                           (i) 5-month Junior Engineering Course, (ii) 9-
                           month Junior Engineering Course.

Program leads to City and Guilds examination in above fields.

Students sponsored by government departments or commercial and industrial
firms.

General and technical education for the future will be coordinated more
closely.  This is intended in order that Government Craft School leavers
may enter comprehensive secondary schools (offering academic, technical
and commercial courses).

Under the auspices of West African Examinations Council and with the cooperation of the City and Guilds, "Nigerian Institute Examinations" may
eventually replace City and Guilds examinations.  These changes would
affect technical training schools also.

Designs for the new Kaduna Polytechnic have been completed.  Erection of
the workshop block is due for completion January 1966, and that of the
main building by September 1967.


## NIGERIAN COLLEGE OF ARTS, SCIENCE AND TECHNOLOGY, Zaria

Terminated 1963.

Entrance requirements:          West African School Certificate.

Length of course:    2 years.

Curriculum:          Arts subjects, Pure and Applied Mathematics, Physics,
                     Chemistry, Botany, Zoology, Biology.

Courses prepared students for Nigerian university entrance.
(For program details, see Eastern Region.)

(See 1962 Chart for Eastern Nigeria for educational level.)


## City and Guilds, London - I Technician Diploma

### Mechanical and Electrical Engineering

Entrance requirements:    West African School Certificate

              or    At least Intermediate Level Certificate of
                    City and Guilds in a particular trade.

Program:  Minimum of 1000 hours of study in each of 2 years for
          full-time students.


## TIMETABLE

### 1st Year

| Subjects | Hours per week |
|---|---|
| Mathematics | 5 |
| Mechanical Engineering Science | 3 |
| Electrical Engineering Science | 3 |
| Physics and Chemistry | 3 |
| Engineering Drawing | 5 |
| Workshop Technology | 2 |
| Workshop Practice | 7 |
| Industrial Orientation | 1 |
| English and Liberal Studies | 3 |
|  | 32 |

### 2nd Year

| | |
|---|---|
| Engineering Drawing | 3 |
| Mechanical Engineering | 3 |
| Mathematics | 5 |
| Electrical Engineering | 3 |
| Power Production | 3 |
| Workshop Practice | 6 |
| Industrial Orientation | 2 |
| Optional Technical Subject | 3 |
| English and Liberal Studies | 3 |
| Tutorial | 1 |
|  | 32 |


## City and Guilds, London - I Technician Diploma

### Building and Civil Engineering

Entrance requirements:     West African School Certificate

                     or    At least Intermediate Level Certificate
                           of City and Guilds in a particular trade.

Program:  Minimum of 1000 hours of study in each of 2 years for
          full-time students.

## TIMETABLE

### 1st Year

| Subjects | Hours per week |
|---|---|
| Building Construction and Drawing | 7 |
| Properties of Materials | 3 |
| Mathematics | 5 |
| Physics and Chemistry | 3 |
| Elementary Surveying (with 2-week camp) | 1 |
| Workshop Technology and Practice | 9 |
| Industrial Orientation | 1 |
| English and Liberal Studies | 3 |
| | 32 |

### 2nd Year

| Subjects | Hours per week |
|---|---|
| Geometry (Building students) | |
| or  Additional Mathematics (Civil Engin.) | 2 |
| Building Construction and Drawing | 5 |
| Mathematics | 3 |
| Properties of Materials | 3 |
| Structures | 4 |
| Surveying (with 2-week camp) | 1 |
| Quantity Surveying (Building students) | 3 |
| Quantity Surveying (Civil Engin. students) | 2 |
| Industrial Orientation | 2 |
| Workshop Technology and Practice | 6 |
| English and Liberal Studies | 3 |
| Tutorial | 1 |
| | 32 |

## COMMERCIAL TRAINING

Entrance requirements:    Previous to 1965:

Through common entrance examination from primary schools.

From 1965:

Recruitment from Craft School leavers and those having had 3 years of secondary training.

Program:    Previous to 1965:

2-year Junior Course (for those showing ability) leading to 1-year Senior Course.

From 1965:

Basically a 2-year course.  Possibly 1 extra year for those showing ability, leading to the Royal Society of Arts Examination and the General Certificate of Education.

Subjects: English, Mathematics, Geography, History, Bookkeeping, Typing and Shorthand.


AGRICULTURAL TRAINING:

Under Training and Education Division of the Ministry of Agriculture.

> Schools of Agriculture
> Provincial Farm Training Centres
> Farm Institutes


## SCHOOL OF AGRICULTURE, Samaru

Classes started 1923; school established 1928.  Capacity:  280 students.

### Agricultural Assistant Course (Middle/upper middle grade staff)

| | |
|---|---|
| Entrance requirements: | Secondary VI or West African School Certificate. |
| | Entrance examination for Agricultural Instructors (lower grade technical staff) with field experience and meritorious service. |
| 2-year program: | Fields of Study (major): |
| | Agronomy, Science, Horticulture, Livestock, Extension, Workshops. |
| | Fields of Study (minor): |
| | Economics, Government Procedure, Field Experimentation. |
| Examinations: | Terminal examination and final examination at end of 1st and 2nd year. |
| Certificate awarded: | Certificate in General Agriculture.  Must satisfy examiners in both theoretical subjects and practical work. |

### Assistant Agricultural Superintendent Course (1956)

| | |
|---|---|
| Entrance requirements: | At least 1 year's satisfactory experience in the field after Agricultural Assistants course.  Leading to promotion to upper middle staff grades. |

1-year program.

## Assistant Agricultural Superintendents (Mechanical)

Classes started 1962.

Entrance requirements:      As for 2 above, or a full-time apprenticeship in one of these trades, Motor Mechanics,
Blacksmithing and Welding, or Fitting.
Candidates must have not less than 3 years of
experience at their trade subsequent to
completing their apprenticeship.

2-year program.

Examinations:      Terminal examination and final examination at the end
of 1st year and final year.

## Training in Home Economics

Classes started in 1964.

Entrance requirements:      Completion of secondary school.

2-year program:

| 1st Year | 2nd Year |
|---|---|
| Clothing (Sewing) | Clothing (Repairs and Bying) |
| Food and Nutrition | Food and Nutrition |
| Cereal Crops | Child Care |
| Health and Sanitation | Home Improvement |
| Gardening Horticulture | Home Management |
| Chemistry Science | Arts and Crafts |
| Poultry | Beekeeping |
| Home Mechanics | Livestock |
| Family Relations | Government Procedures |
| Physical Education | Extension (Teaching) |

Certificate awarded:      Certificate in Home Economics. Examined in
theoretical and practical work as Home Agents.

## SCHOOL OF AGRICULTURE, Kabba

Established in 1964.

### Agricultural Assistant Course

Entrance requirements:      Same as School of Agriculture, Samaru.

| 2-year program: | Science, Crop Production, Livestock Production, Extension, Workshops, Surveying, Miscellaneous Special Subjects. |
|---|---|
| Certificate awarded: | Same as School of Agriculture, Samaru. |

## FARM TRAINING CENTRES

For lower grades of Agricultural Technical Officers.

Established in 1959, 15 soon in operation.

| Entrance requirements: | Middle II (Primary VII) plus experience in field. |
|---|---|
| 1-year program: | Crops, Cattle, Poultry, Extension, Horticulture, Arithmetic, Surveying, Soil and Soil Conservation, Mixed Farm Management, Government Procedure, Botany, Meteorology and General Science, Farm Crafts, Village Hygiene, Tutorials and Excursions, Special Assignments. |
| Certificate awarded: | Certificate on passing theoretical subjects and practical work. |

## FARM INSTITUTES

For training farmers.  Established in 1964; by 1968, 54 institutes planned.

| Entrance requirements: | Middle II (Primary Seven), but junior primary leavers (Class IV), accepted. |
|---|---|
| 1-year program: | Crops, Livestock and Poultry, Soil Conservation, Village Sanitation, Arithmetic and Accounting, Farm Crafts. |

Teaching direct from farm with explanations in classroom.

| Examinations: | None. |
|---|---|

## VETERINARY SCHOOL, Kaduna

Established in 1962.

## Livestock Assistants Course

Entrance requirements:      West African School Certificate or equivalent.

                                 (Students having completed secondary education, but failing the Certificate examination will not be accepted when fully qualified candidates increase.)

2-year program:      Revision course in General Science (1st 12 weeks of 1st year):

| General Chemistry | Zoology |
|---|---|
| Physical Chemistry | Physics |
| Organic Chemistry | |

1st year:

| Animal Management | (1st 24 weeks) |
|---|---|
| Anatomy and Physiology | (24 weeks) |
| Parasitology | (12 weeks) |
| Nutrition | (12 weeks) |
| Range Management | (12 weeks) |
| Animal Husbandry | (12 weeks) |

2nd year:

| Pathology and Bacteriology | (12 weeks) |
|---|---|
| Surgery | (12 weeks) |
| Pharmacology | (12 weeks) |
| Medicine | (20 weeks) |
| Jurisprudence | (8 weeks) |
| Animal Industries | (8 weeks) |

Conclusion of course:

(a) Livestock Assistants who possess full West African School Certificate (or equivalent) pass, and have passed the Livestock Assistants final examination may be selected for diploma training at Vom or elsewhere. Diploma holders eligible for promotion to Livestock Officer.

(b) Livestock Assistants not qualified for diploma training may be selected for promotion to Assistant Technical Officer-in-training and so to Technical Officer grades any time after completing 1-year field service after passing the Livestock Assistants final examination. (Short training course sometimes given not up to diploma level.)

## IRRIGATION SCHOOL, Sokoto

For training Technical Assistants in the Irrigation Division of the Ministry of Agriculture.

Entrance requirements:          Secondary VI or W.A.S.C.

2-year program.

Certificate for Technical Assistant Irrigation Division awarded.


FOREST SCHOOL, Naraguta

Established in 1965.

Courses offered:

Government Silvicultural Assistants

Entrance requirements:          Senior Primary VII and employed as Silvi-
                                cultural Assistant.

Program:        6 weeks (39 periods of 45 minutes each).

                Survey, Soil Survey, Simple Geology, Mensuration, Botany.

Certificate and conditions of award:    Silvicultural Assistants
                                        (Pass 50%)


Government Forest Guards

Entrance requirements:          Senior Primary VII and employed as govern-
                                ment Forest Guard.

Program:        6 months (39 periods per week of 45 minutes each).

                Forest Policy, Forest Protection, Forest Law, Court
                Procedure, Forest Mensuration, Forest Exploitation,
                Technical Terms, Nursery and Plantation Techniques,
                Seed Collection and Storage, Forest Surveying, Soil
                Surveying, Simple Geology, Botany and Identification
                of Trees.

Certificate and conditions of award:    Government Forest Guards
                                        (Pass 50%)


N.A. (Native Authority) Forest Supervisors

Entrance requirements:          Employed as Head of N.A. Forest Department.

Program:        6 weeks (39 periods per week of 45 minutes each).

                Supervisory Techniques, Forest Policy, Forest Protection,
                Forest Law, Forest Exploitation, Nursery and Plantation
                Techniques, Procedure in the Constitution of N.A. Forest
                Estate.

Certificate and conditions of award:     Satisfactory confidential report
                                          on performance.


## N.A. Foresters

Entrance requirements:        Employed as N.A. Forester.  Sernior Primary
                              VII, preferably Secondary II.

Program:        9 months (39 periods per week of 45 minutes each).

                Forest Policy, Forest Protection, Forest Law, Court
                Procedure, Forest Management, Forest Utilization, Silvi-
                culture, Mensuration, Nursery and Plantation Techniques,
                Survey, Soil Survey, Geology, Botany, Vegetation, Tech-
                nical Terms, Seed Collection and Storage.

Certificate and conditions of award:     N.A. Foresters
                                          (Pass 50%)


## N.A. Forest Guards

Entrance requirements:        Employed as N.A. Forest Guards.  Primary
                              VII.

Program:        6 months (39 periods, 45 minutes each).

                Syllabus same as for Government Forest Guards above.

Certificate and conditions of award:     N.A. Forest Guard
                                          (Pass 50%)


## TEACHER EDUCATION

By 1964:    51 training colleges for teachers in primary schools.
            (Grade II and III Teacher's Certificates)

            2 rural education colleges (Bauchi and Minna).  Primary school
            teachers and rural school tutors for training colleges.

            35 men's training colleges offering Rural Science courses.

            4 men's training colleges offering Nature Study courses.

            1 training college preparing secondary teachers:  Northern
            Secondary Teacher's College, Zaria.

TEACHER'S COLLEGES

Entrance requirements:          Primary School Leaving Certificate and
                                common entrance examination.

Program:          3-year post-primary course (leading to Grade III certifi-
                  cate).

Teacher's Elementary Certificate awarded at close of 3-year program.
Holder entitled to teach in first 4 primary grades.

N.B.    This program being phased out in favor of a 5-year post-primary
        course.

Program:          5-year post-primary course (leading to Grade II certifi-
                  cate).

Teacher's Higher Elementary Certificate (Grade II) awarded at close of
5-year program.  Holder entitled to teach all classes of primary school.

This certificate may also be achieved in a 2-year course subsequent to a
5-year course in secondary school.


(There have been available 2-year conversion courses for those holding
the Elementary Certificate enabling them to obtain Higher Elementary
Certificate.  These conversion courses being replaced by correspondence
courses supplemented by vacation courses.)


### 5-YEAR HIGHER ELEMENTARY CERTIFICATE

#### TIMETABLE (Sample only)
(40-min. periods per week)

| Subjects | Years 1 | 2 | 3 | 4 | 5 |
|---|---|---|---|---|---|
| English | 10 | 10 | 10 | 7 | 6 |
| Bible Knowledge or Islamic Religious Knowledge | 2 | 2 | 2 | 2 | 2 |
| History | 4 | 4 | 4 | 4 | 3 |
| Geography | 4 | 4 | 4 | 4 | 3 |
| Mathematics | 6 | 6 | 5 | 5 | 5 |
| Art | 4 | 4 | 4 | 4 | 4 |
| Principles of Education | - | - | 2 | 5 | 8 |
| Rural Science and Health | 4 | 4 | 4 | 4 | 4 |
| Physical Education | 3 | 3 | 3 | 3 | 3 |
| Library | 1 | 1 | - | - | - |
|  | 38 | 38 | 38 | 38 | 38 |

(In years 4 and 5, 2 and 8 weeks respectively are given to Teaching
   Practice.)

<u>3-YEAR ELEMENTARY CERTIFICATE</u>
and
<u>5-YEAR HIGHER ELEMENTARY CERTIFICATE</u>

<u>TIMETABLE FOR GRADE III/GRADE II</u>[+]
(40-minute periods per week)

('3' for those continuing 5-year program.  '3A' for those terminating
3-year program.)

| Subjects                          Years | 1 | 2 | 3 | 3A | 4 | 5 |
|------------------------------------------|----|----|----|----|----|----|
| English                                  | 10 | 10 | 8 | 8 | 7 | 5 |
| Mathematics                              | 6 | 6 | 4 | 5 | 4 | 5 |
| Physical and Health Education            | 2 | 2 | 3 | 2 | 3 | 2 |
| History                                  | (5 | 5) | 4 | 2 | 3 | - |
| Geography                                | ( | ) | 4 | 2 | 3 | - |
| Religious Instruction                    | 2 | 2 | 1 | 1 | 1 | 1 |
| Principles of Education                  | - | - | 2 | 6 | 5 | 8 |
| Practical Subjects and Electives[++]     | 10 | 10 | 9 | - | 7 | 1 |
| Holidays and Examinations                | 2 | 2 | 2 | 3 | 2 | 7 |
| Teaching Practice                        | - | 1 | - | 8 | 2 | 8 |
|                                          | 37 | 37 | 37 | 37 | 37 | 37 |

[+]Timetable recommended by conference of principals of Teacher
Colleges.  Each college will show some variation.

[++]Several of the following subjects are normally available as
practical subjects and electives:

| | |
|---|---|
| Music | Arabic Studies |
| Metalworking | General Science |
| Arts and Crafts | Vernacular Studies |
| Library Organization | Domestic Science |
| Woodworking | Rural Science |

For Grade III candidates a final examination arranged by the Ministry
of Education in the following subjects:

| | |
|---|---|
| English | History |
| Mathematics | Geography |
| Principles of Education and School Organization | Matter and Method of such other subjects in the |
| Physical and Health Educ. | Primary School curriculum |
| Method I (English and Arithmetic) | as Ministry of Education may require. |

<u>N.B.</u>  A pass in any of the optional subjects:  Religion, Arabic and
Vernacular is not essential to the award of the Certificate but
it will be shown on the Certificate.

Grade II candidates must fulfill following requirements for the Higher
Elementary Certificate:

A.   Satisfy the Inspectorate of the Ministry of Education (in consultation
     with the Principal) during the last year of the course in Practical
     Tests in class teaching (including Spoken English and the teaching of
     Physical Education).  Account will be taken of the records of the
     candidate's progress during the training.

B.   Pass an examination set by the West African Examinations Council in
     the last year of the course in:

     (1)  Principles and Practice of Education
     (2)  English Language
     (3)  Arithmetical Processes

C.   Pass an examination set as prescribed by the Ministry of Education,
     in Physical and Health Education, History and Geography.

D.   Pass an examination set during the penultimate year or the last year
     of the course, either by the Ministry or by Principal of the training
     institution in consultation with the Inspectorate of the Ministry,
     in 2 of the following subjects, provided that 1 subject taken at a
     more advanced level, which shall be known as "Special" level, shall
     be equal to 2 at "Normal" level (candidates may take a number of
     additional subjects as prescribed by the Ministry of Education):

     Normal Level Subjects

     English Literature                Nature Study
     Islamic History                   Approved African Language
     Mathematics                       Arabic
     Religious Knowledge               Crafts
     Rural Science (Theory and         Art
        Practice)                      Music
     Domestic Science (Theory          Needlework and Dressmaking
        and Practice)

     Special Level Subjects

     Physical and Health Education     Approved African Language
     English (including Literature)    Arabic
     Geography                         Crafts
     History or Islamic History        Art
     Religious Knowledge               Music
     Rural Science                     Needlework and Dressmaking
     Domestic Science

     Or other subjects as may be prescribed by the Ministry of Education.

E.   In a course of over 2 years' duration candidates must show evidence
     of having completed satisfactory work in at least 1 of the prescribed
     practical subjects.

Note:       A candidate may not offer the same subject at both levels.

All subjects in which a candidate passes are endorsed on his certificate together with the grade at which he passes.

A candidate offering a subject at special level who fails to reach the required standard but obtains a sufficient level of marks may be given a pass at the normal level in that subject.

Candidates who are referred in the examination are not required to take again the subject which they have already passed.

The examination may be taken <u>externally</u> by candidates who are presently engaged in whole time teaching in Northern Nigeria, and

(a)   if untrained have had not less than 9 years of teaching experience;

(b)   if in possession of a Grade III Certificate (not C.T.R.) have had at least 4 years of teaching experience, not less than 3 of which must have been served after certification.

The examination for external candidates is taken in 3 stages; candidates must pass in each stage before entering for the next.   Only 1 stage may be taken in any one year, in the following order:

Stage 1:   English (set by West African Examinations Council) Arithmetical Processes (set by West African Examinations Council).

Stage 2:   Internal papers set by training colleges. Candidates for Stage 2 may take the internal papers of any college of their choice, which they will be required to attend for this stage of the examination.

Stage 3:   Principles of Education (set by the West African Examinations Council).   Practical Tests conducted by the Inspectorate Division of the Ministry.


<u>Teacher's Senior Certificate</u> is awarded to holders of the <u>Higher Elementary Certificate</u> who have subsequently had not less than 3 years of satisfactory teaching experience and who in addition satisfy the following conditions:

A.   Either

(1)   have passed 1 of the following examinations:

(a)   Intermediate Examination of London University
(b)   Cambridge Overseas Higher School Certificate
(c)   London University General Certificate of Education
(d)   any other examination deemed equivalent by the Ministry of Education,

provided they have passed in at least 2 of the subjects listed below, which must be as principal subjects in the case of (b) and at advanced level in the case of (c).

The subjects, to which may be added from time to time other subjects approved by the Ministry of Education, are:

> English Literature
> Geography
> History (Branch to be approved by the Ministry of Education)
>    Economic History and British Constitution are not approved
>    subjects
> Religious Knowledge
> Mathematics
> Physics
> Chemistry
> Biology
> French
> Latin
> Art
> Arabic

A candidate must pass a practical examination in teaching in each of the subjects in which he has qualified before the certificate can be issued.


Or

(2)  have completed the course and reached the required standard in a special subject training course, e.g. Rural Science, as prescribed by the Ministry of Education.  They will not have completed the course satisfactorily until they have passed a practical teaching test and they must obtain 2 consecutive good annual reports by Inspectors of the Ministry.


B.   Have been awarded 1 of the following:

(1)  A merit in English in the Higher Elementary (Grade II) Teacher's Certificate examination.

(2)  A credit in English Language in the West African School Certificate examination.

(3)  A pass in English Language at 'O' level in the General Certificate of Education.


## RURAL EDUCATION COLLEGES

In 1964, at the Rural Education College, Minna, a 2-year course was introduced, leading to the Senior (Grade I) Certificate.

In 1966, a similar course to start at Bauchi Rural Education College.

Entrance requirements:          <u>Higher Elementary Certificate</u>.

In the second year of the course, students may take an examination for entry to the Northern Secondary Teacher's College.  If successful, they will proceed there to take a 2-year course including Agricultural Science, Biology and Chemistry leading to the <u>Nigerian Certificate of Education</u>.


## <u>NORTHERN SECONDARY TEACHERS' COLLEGE</u>, Zaria

Established in 1962.  1964, college admitted girls for the first time, becoming the first co-educational government institution.

Entrance requirements:          <u>West African School Certificate</u> or equi-
                                 valent.  <u>Higher Elementary Teachers' Certi-</u>
                                 <u>ficate</u>.  Royal Society of Arts or equivalent.

Program:        3 years.

This course has taken the place of the one formerly given at the Nigerian College of Arts, Science and Technology at Zaria.

<u>Nigerian Certificate of Education</u> awarded on successful completion.

First output from the college, June 1965.


## <u>ARABIC EDUCATION</u>

In 1962, Islamiyya schools owned by individuals and organizations received first financial grants from government in order to raise standard of Islamic education.

New training college opened at Sokoto to train teachers of Arabic and Islamic subjects.

Katsina, Kano and Bornu Native Authority have started to run 3-year courses for training Grade III Arabic teachers, with Government aid.


## <u>SCHOOL FOR ARABIC STUDIES</u>

Last of post-secondary classes transferred to the Ahmadu Bello University, 1964.  Grade II Teachers' Course and H.M.S. Course still exist.

542

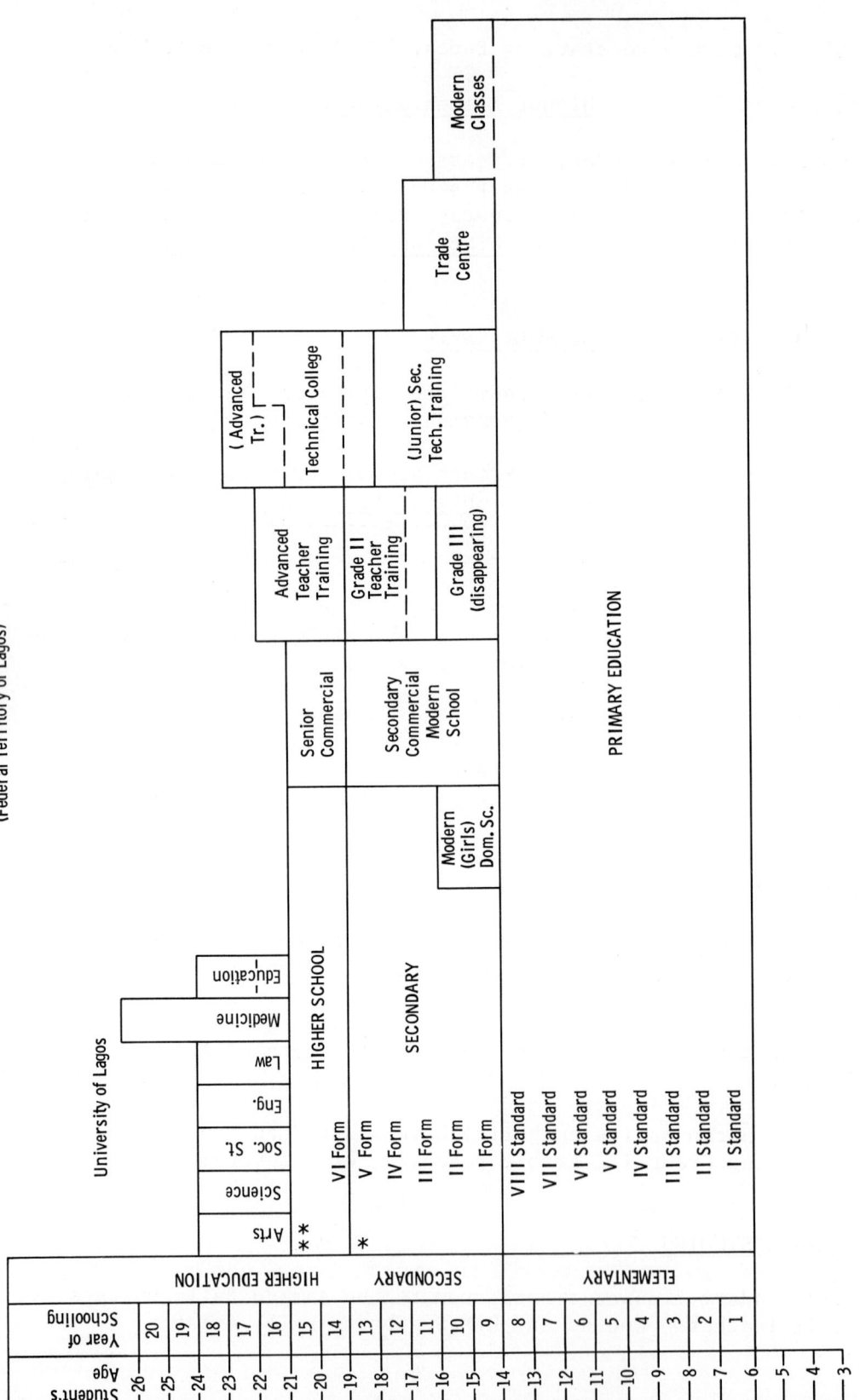

FEDERATION OF NIGERIA
(Federal Territory of Lagos)

University of Lagos

HIGHER SCHOOL

SECONDARY

PRIMARY EDUCATION

| | | | | | |
|---|---|---|---|---|---|
| Arts ** | Science | Soc. St. | Eng. | Law | Medicine | Education |
| | | | VI Form * | | |

Senior Commercial

Advanced Teacher Training

(Advanced Tr.)   Technical College

Trade Centre

Modern Classes

Secondary Commercial Modern School

Grade II Teacher Training

(Junior) Sec. Tech. Training

Modern (Girls) Dom. Sc.

Grade III (disappearing)

| Student's Age | Year of Schooling | | |
|---|---|---|---|
| 26 | 20 | HIGHER EDUCATION | |
| 25 | 19 | | |
| 24 | 18 | | Arts ** |
| 23 | 17 | | Science |
| 22 | 16 | | Soc. St. |
| 21 | 15 | | Eng. |
| 20 | 14 | | Law |
| 19 | 13 | SECONDARY | VI Form |
| 18 | 12 | | V Form |
| 17 | 11 | | IV Form |
| 16 | 10 | | III Form |
| 15 | 9 | | II Form |
| 14 | 8 | ELEMENTARY | I Form |
| 13 | 7 | | VIII Standard |
| 12 | 6 | | VII Standard |
| 11 | 5 | | VI Standard |
| 10 | 4 | | V Standard |
| 9 | 3 | | IV Standard |
| 8 | 2 | | III Standard |
| 7 | 1 | | II Standard |
| 6 | | | I Standard |
| 5 | | | |
| 4 | | | |
| 3 | | | |

Compulsory education: None
School year: Late January–Mid-December
Secondary school grading:
No grading for internal examinations
West African School Certificate 1 – 9
Cambridge Higher School Certificate 1 – 9
(See SECONDARY EDUCATION)

543

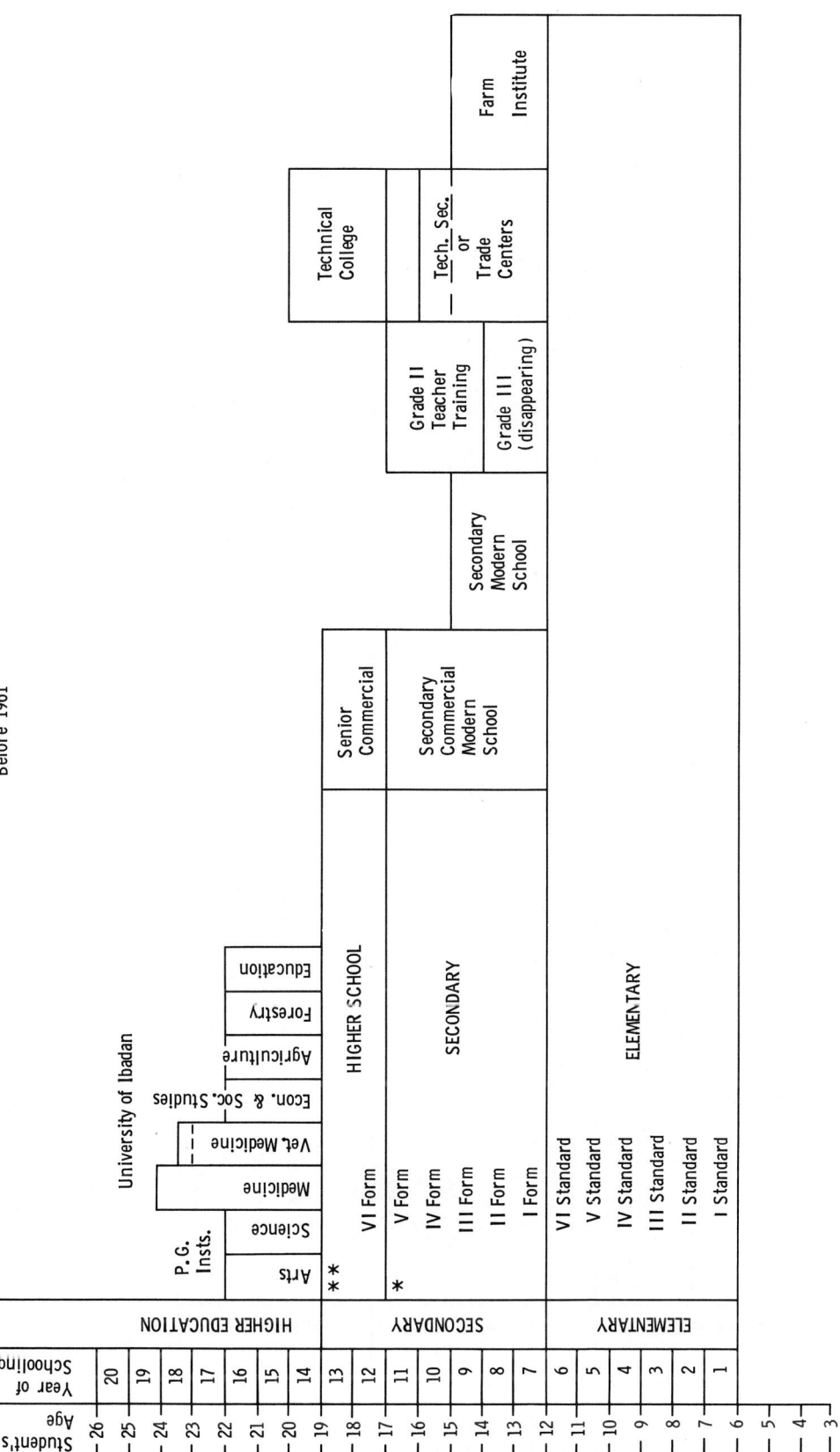

FEDERATION OF NIGERIA
(Western and Mid-western)
Before 1961

Compulsory education: None
School year: Late January – Mid-December
Secondary school grading: No grading for internal examinations
West African School Certificate 1 – 9
Cambridge Higher School Certificate 1 – 9
(See SECONDARY EDUCATION)

544

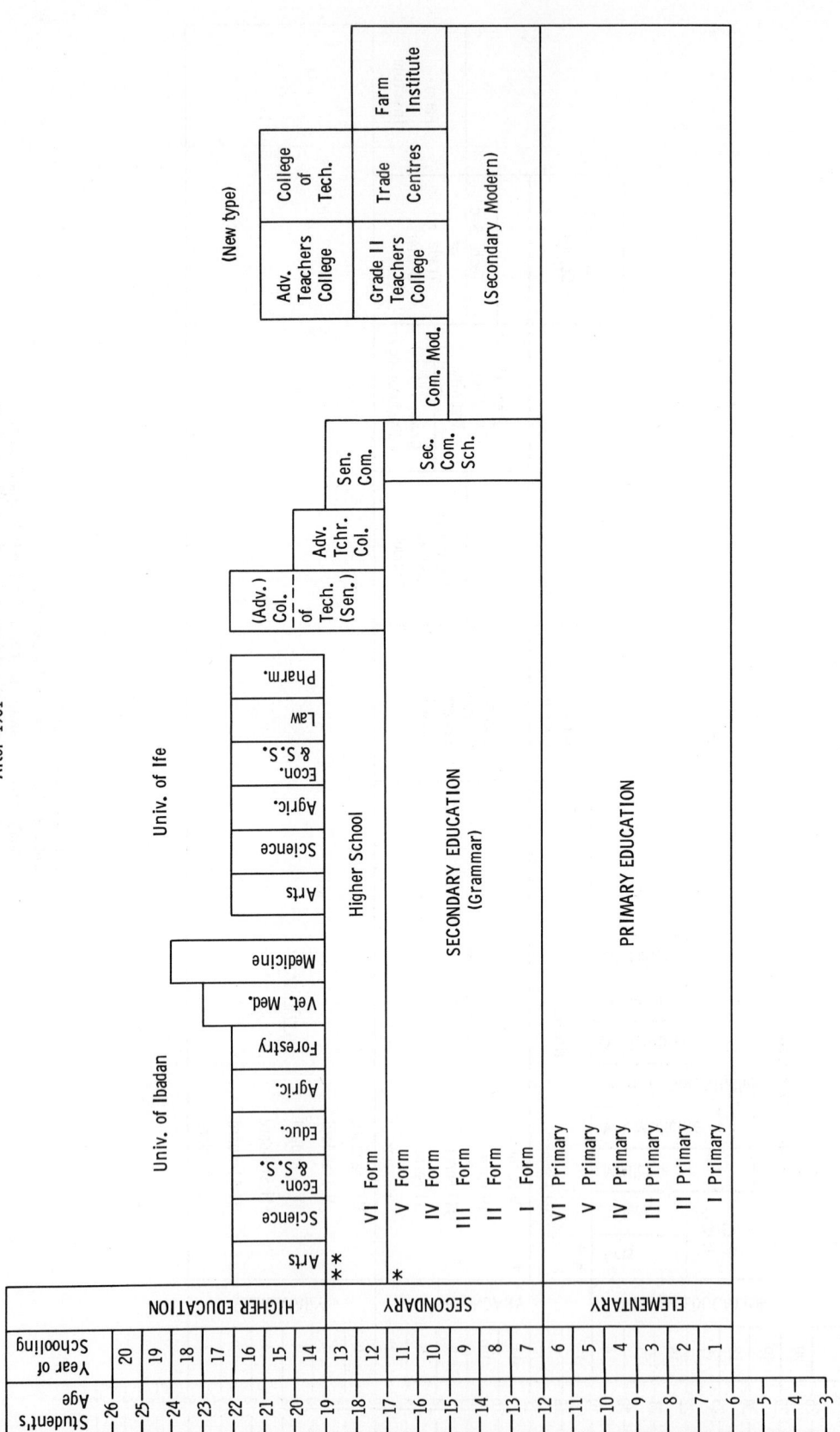

FEDERATION OF NIGERIA
(Western and Mid-Western)
After 1961

Univ. of Ife

Univ. of Ibadan

Higher School

SECONDARY EDUCATION
(Grammar)

PRIMARY EDUCATION

(New type)

| | | Farm Institute |
| Adv. Teachers College | College of Tech. | |
| | Grade II Teachers College | Trade Centres |
| | Com. Mod. | |
| | (Secondary Modern) | |

(Adv.) Col. of Tech. (Sen.)

Adv. Tchr. Col.

Sen. Com.

Sec. Com. Sch.

Arts
Science
Agric.
Econ. & S.S.
Law
Pharm.

Medicine
Vet. Med.
Forestry
Agric.
Educ.
Econ. & S.S.
Science
Arts

HIGHER EDUCATION

SECONDARY

ELEMENTARY

| Year of Schooling | | | Student's Age | |
|---|---|---|---|---|
| 20 | | | 26 | |
| 19 | | | 25 | |
| 18 | | | 24 | |
| 17 | | | 23 | |
| 16 | | | 22 | |
| 15 | | | 21 | |
| 14 | | | 20 | |
| 13 | | | 19 | |
| 12 | VI Form | | 18 | |
| 11 | V Form | * | 17 | |
| 10 | IV Form | | 16 | |
| 9 | III Form | | 15 | |
| 8 | II Form | | 14 | |
| 7 | I Form | | 13 | |
| 6 | VI Primary | | 12 | |
| 5 | V Primary | | 11 | |
| 4 | IV Primary | | 10 | |
| 3 | III Primary | | 9 | |
| 2 | II Primary | | 8 | |
| 1 | I Primary | | 7 | |
| | | | 6 | |
| | | | 5 | |
| | | | 4 | |
| | | | 3 | |

**

Compulsory education: None
School year: Late January–Mid-December
Secondary school grading: No grading for internal exams
(numerical marks usually given)
West African School Certificate 1 - 9
Cambridge Higher School Certificate 1 - 9
(See SECONDARY EDUCATION)

<u>F E D E R A L   T E R R I T O R Y   O F   L A G O S</u>
and
<u>W E S T E R N   A N D   M I D - W E S T E R N   R E G I O N S</u>

There are no differences between the educational systems in the Western
Region and the Mid-Western Region.  Both were one region until the fall
of 1963 when the latter region was created.

The system in the Federal Territory of Lagos is virtually the same as in
the West.

No differences exist between government and private schools in either
years or curriculum.

## PRIMARY EDUCATION

Entry age:      6 years.

Language(s) of instruction:

### Lagos:

(1)  Yoruba schools:  Classes 1-4    Yoruba
                      Classes 3-6    English, with Yoruba as
                                     supplementary language

(2)  International private schools:  Classes 1-6   English

In Lagos the mixture of people of various ethnic groups makes it
impracticable to adopt one vernacular as language of instruction
in the lower classes in primary school as in the West and Mid-West.
English is therefore the medium and vernacular is used, in the
main, as supplementary.

### Western Region:

        Classes 1-2    Yoruba
        Classes 3-6    English

### Mid-Western Region:

        Classes 1-2    Vernacular
        Classes 3-6    English

There are several ethnic groups in the Mid-West and the vernacular
used depends on the area.

Length of course:    <u>Western and Mid-Western</u>

6 years.  January 1966, Western Region will raise primary education to 8 years.

<u>Lagos</u>

8 years.  Lagos intends eventually to reduce to 6 years.

Curriculum (Rural and Urban):

Religious Knowledge (Protestant or Catholic), Hand-writing, Vernacular of area, English, Arithmetic, Physical Education, Civics, Nature Study, Domestic Science, Needlework, Music and Singing, Art, Handwork.

History and Geography in Forms V and VI only.

<u>Primary School Leaving Certificate</u> awarded at conclusion of the program.


## SECONDARY EDUCATION

4 types of secondary:     Secondary Modern School
                          Secondary Modern (Commercial) School
                          Secondary Grammar School
                          Secondary Grammar (Commercial) School

## SECONDARY MODERN SCHOOL

Entry age:      12-13 years.

Entrance requirements:       Primary School Leaving Certificate and competitive entrance examination.

Language of instruction:       English.

Length of course:    3 years (regular program)
                     4 years (commercial bias program)
                     2 years (Lagos).  May soon be raised to 3 or 4 years

Curriculum (Regular):

Mathematics, English, History, Geography, Home Economics, Rural Science, Art and Craft, Music and Singing, Religious Knowledge.

Curriculum (Commercial):

Mathematics, English, History, Geography, Home Economics, Rural Science, Art and Craft, Music and Singing, Religious Knowledge, Commerce, Bookkeeping, Accounting, Shorthand and Typing.

## SECONDARY GRAMMAR SCHOOL

Entrance requirements:    Being in Standard V or VI in Lagos, or
Primary VI in Western and Mid-Western, being
under 14 on January 1 of the year of commencement in secondary school, and common entrance
examination.

Length of course:    5-year program
2-year Sixth Form

Curriculum:    English, History, Geography, Mathematics (Arithmetic,
Algebra, Geometry, Trigonometry), General Science
(including laboratory work), Health Science, Biology
(including laboratory work), Chemistry (including
laboratory work), Physics (including laboratory),
Additional Mathematics, English Literature, French,
Latin, Art, and Religious Studies.

### TIMETABLE
for
### West African School Certificate
(Government College, Ibadan)

| Subjects | Hours per week (40-minute periods) | | | | |
|---|---|---|---|---|---|
| | Year I | II | III | IV | V |
| English | 6 | 7 | 6 | 4 | 4 |
| History | 2 | 2 | 2 | 3 | 3 |
| Geography | 3 | 3 | 3 | 3 | 3 |
| Mathematics | 5 | 6 | 4 | 4 | 5 |
| (Arithmetic, Algebra, Geometry, Trigonometry) | | | | | |
| General Science | 3 | 4 | 9 | 9 | 9 |
| (including laboratory work) | | | | | |
| Health Science | 3 | 4 | - | - | - |
| Biology | - | - | 3 | 3 | 3 |
| (including laboratory work) | | | | | |
| Chemistry | - | - | 3 | 3 | 3 |
| (including laboratory work) | | | | | |
| Physics | - | - | 3 | 3 | 3 |
| (including laboratory work) | | | | | |
| Additional Mathematics | - | - | - | - | 2 |
| English Literature | - | - | - | 3 | 3 |
| French | 4 | 4 | 4 | 5 | 4 |
| Latin | 2 | 2 | 2 | - | - |
| Art | 2 | 2 | 2 | | |

Most schools enter students for a minimum of 6 and a maximum of 8 subjects in the School Certificate examination.  In Lagos, a student may drop a few of his subjects at the end of the 3rd year.

In the West a student may not drop a core subject (English, Mathematics, History, Geography, 1 Science subject and as from 1967, Yoruba) until he has studied it for 4 years.

In the Mid-West a student may drop any of the subjects other than English Language after a year's study.  For this reason, schools usually start with a larger number of subjects than 6 to ensure that a student will eventually be able to offer at least 6 subjects which is the minimum for the School Certificate examination.  The Mid-West Regional Government now wants the school to adopt the system requiring each student to study any subject he starts for a minimum of 4 years.

*At the close of the 5-year program students take the Joint Examination for the West African School Certificate and General Certificate of Education. (For details, See NIGERIA, Eastern Region.)

## HIGHER SCHOOL CERTIFICATE COURSE (Sixth Form)

Entrance requirements:          West African School Certificate (Grade I or II).

Length of course:    2 years preparatory for university entrance.

Curriculum:          General Paper (English Language)

          and    3 of the following subjects:
                 English Literature, French, Latin, Greek, Religious
                 Studies, Geography, History, Mathematics (including
                 Algebra, Geometry, Calculus, Trigonometry), Biology,
                 Botany, Art, Music, etc.

**University of Cambridge Joint Examination for the Higher School Certificate and General Certificate of Education at close of 2-year program.   (For details, see Appendix B.)

## HIGHER EDUCATION

## UNIVERSITY OF LAGOS (Federal Territory)

Lagos and its university are in the Western part of Nigeria but are not in Western Nigeria politically.

The University of Lagos was established by an Act of the Federal Government in 1962 as a result of recommendations from the 1960 Ashby Report and those of an Advisory Commission of UNESCO 1961 requested by the Federal Government.

With the beginning of the first semester October 1962 at temporary premises in Suru-Lere, students were accepted by the Faculties of Business and Social Studies, Law and Medicine (the Medical School is an autonomous unit with the university).

The third academic year 1964 opened with the establishing of four new faculties: Arts, Education, Engineering, and Science. The university moved to its permanent site in North East Yaba (Lagos), 1965.

General entrance requirements:

The following are eligible to be considered for admission:

(1) Graduates of universities recognized by the Senate for this purpose.

(2) Candidates holding the <u>General Certificate of Education</u> including 5 subjects of which not less than 2 have been passed at advanced level,

<u>or</u> including 4 subjects of which not less than 3 have been passed at advanced level. Provided that

(a) no subject may be counted at both ordinary and advanced level;

(b) the subjects passed include English Language; except that candidates who show special ability in Science subjects but have not passed in English Language may be given special consideration for admission to the Faculty of Science by the Senate.

Credits gained in the 1st School Certificate and passes gained in subsidiary subjects in Higher School Certificate will be accepted as the equivalent of passes at ordinary level in the General Certificate of Education; passes in principal subjects in the Higher School Certificate will be accepted as the equivalent of passes at advanced level in the General Certificate of Education; and

(c) candidates for admission to the Faculty of Engineering should have Higher School Certificate or General Certificate of Education 'A' level passes in Physics, Pure Mathematics and Applied Mathematics, and a School Certificate or General Certificate of Education 'O' level pass in Chemistry.

Faculties:

    Arts (School of Humanities)
    Business and Social Studies
    Education
    Engineering
    Law
    Medicine
    Science
    Institute of Petroleum Studies

First degrees awarded:

| Faculty | Degree | Duration of Course (years) |
|---|---|---|
| Arts (School of Humanities) | B.A. | 3 (day) 5 (night) |
| Business and Social Studies | B.Sc. (Bus.) B.Sc. (Pol.) B.Sc. (Econ.) B.Sc. (Acc.) | 3 (day) 5 (night) |
| Education (Combined Degree and Diploma Course) | Dip. in Educ. B.A./B.Sc. and Dip. | 1 3 |
| Engineering | B.Sc. (Eng.) | 3 |
| Law | LL.B. | 3 (day) 5 (night) |
| Medicine | M.B., B.Sc. | 5 |
| Science (Schools of Physical and Biological Sciences) | B.Sc. | 3 |

Faculty of Arts (School of Humanities)

Examination required for B.A. degrees:

Part I examination taken at end of 1st academic year, in the following subjects:

(a)  3 subjects of which at least 2 must be chosen from Group A:

| Group A | Group B |
|---|---|
| English Geography History Mathematics (Pure and Applied) | Economics French Hausa (only for non-Hausas; available after 1964) |

Group B (cont'd)

Ibo (only for non-Ibos; available
   after 1964)
Pure Mathematics (only if Mathema-
   tics not taken in Group A)
Applied Mathematics
Political Science
Sociology (not in 1964-65)
Yoruba (only for non-Yorubas;
   available after 1964)
Education (compulsory for candi-
   dates for Diploma in Education)

<u>and</u>  (b)  African History and Culture.

Part II examination taken at end of 2nd year, in the following
subjects:

(a)  English
    Geography
    Mathematics (Pure and Applied)

<u>and</u>  (b)  Introduction to Science and Technology.  (Candidates for the
    Diploma in Education may be permitted to substitute Education.)

Part III examination at end of 3rd year in:

(a)  2 subjects studied for the Part II examination under Part II (a);

<u>or exceptionally</u>

(b)  1 of those subjects.  (Candidates taking 1 subject required to
    have attained proficiency in 1 of the foreign languages:  French,
    German or Russian.)

<u>Degrees awarded</u>:

Bachelor of Arts (B.A.) - 3 years

Degree awarded in first, second (Upper and Lower) and third class
Honours.  Classification determined by performance in both the Part
II and Part III examinations.

Above regulations apply only to <u>day</u> courses.

<u>Certificate of Proficiency in Modern Languages</u>

French (initiated 1964-65)

Hausa    )
Ibo      )     available 1965-66
Yoruba   )

Length of course to be prescribed at a later date.

## Faculty of Business and Social Studies

Examinations required for B.Sc. degrees in Business, Political Science, Economics, and Accounting:

Part I examination end of 1st academic year (evening students - 2nd year) taken in following subjects:

Accounting I
Economics
Introduction to Business
Fundamentals of Government
African History and Culture
French

Part II examination end of 2nd year (evening students, end of 4th year) taken in following subjects:

Sociology-Psychology
Money and Banking
Statistics
Introduction to Science and Technology
Legal Environment of Business
Constitutional Law (taken by Political Science major students)

and  1 subject in major area as follows:

| Major Area | Subjects |
|---|---|
| Business Administration | Marketing |
| Accounting | Accounting II |
| Economics | Economic Theory |
| Political Science | History of Political Thought |

Part III examination end of 3rd year (evening students, end of 5th year) taken in following:

Financial Management (including Public Finance)
Economic Growth and Development

and  3 subjects in major area as follows:

| Major Area | Subjects |
|---|---|
| Business Administration | International Trade<br>Human Resources<br>Business Policies and Decision-Making |
| Accounting | Accounting III<br>Business Policies and Decision-Making<br>Law for Accountants |
| Economics | History of Economic Thought<br>Business Policies and Decision-Making<br>International Trade or Human Resources |

| Political Science | International Relations |
| | International Trade |
| | Public Administration and |
| |     Social Services |

**Degrees awarded:**

| Bachelor of Science | B.Sc. (Bus.) | 3 years (5 years |
| | B.Sc. (Pol.) | 3 years (in case of |
| | B.Sc. (Econ.) | 3 years (evening |
| | B.Sc. (Acc.) | 3 years (students |

Degree awarded in first, second (Upper and Lower) and third class Honours. Classification determined by performance in both Part II and Part III examinations.

## Faculty of Education

The Diploma course in Education is given either after the 1st degree or concurrently with the 1st degree courses in the Faculties of Arts and Science.

Students wishing to follow the Combined Degree and Diploma course are expected to fulfill the following conditions:

(1)  Complete the normal requirements for a 1st degree in the Faculty of Arts or Science.

(2)  Take a course in the Theory and Practice of Education.

(3)  Undertake practical teaching during the vacations as may be prescribed.

(4)  Pass the prescribed examinations for the Diploma in Education.

**Diploma awarded:**

Diploma in Education - 1 year
B.A./B.Sc. and Diploma - 3 years

## Faculty of Engineering

Examinations required for B.Sc. (Eng.) degree :

Part I examination at end of 1st academic year in the following subjects:

Engineering subjects (to be prescribed)
and  African History and Culture

Part II examination at end of 2nd academic year in the following subjects:

       Engineering subjects (to be prescribed)

and  Introduction to Modern Thought

Part III examination at end of 3rd academic year in the following subjects:

       Engineering subjects (to be prescribed)

## Degree awarded:

Bachelor of Science in Engineering  B.Sc.(Eng.) - 3 years

Degree awarded in first, second (Upper and Lower) and third class Honours. Classification determined by performance in both the Part II and Part III examinations.

## Faculty of Law

Examinations required for LL.B. degree:

Part I examination at end of 1st year (evening students, end of 2nd year).  Subject to Regulation+ below, candidates for this 1st examination examined in the following 5 subjects:

      The Nigerian Legal System
      Nigerian Constitutional Law
      Criminal Law
      African History and Culture
      French I

Part II examination at end of 2nd year (evening students, end of 4th year).  Subject to Regulation+ below, candidates for 2nd examination examined in the following 5 subjects:

      Law of Contract
      Law of Tort
      Equity
      Land Law
      Introduction to Science and Technology

Part III examination at end of 3rd year (evening students, end of 5th year).  Subject to Regulation+ below, candidates for 3rd examination examined in the following 5 subjects:

      Jurisprudence and Legal Theory
      Family Law and Succession
      Conflict of Laws
      Public International Law

or    Company Law
Economic Institutions of West Africa or French II (available
    only to those students who are selected by the French teachers
    on the basis of their performance in French I).

+Regulation:    The following modifications apply in the case of students
    admitted to the University in the session 1962-63:

    (a)   French or Introduction to Science and Technology taken
    as an additional subject in the Part I examination.

    (b)   Economic Institutions of West Africa  taken instead of
    French or Introduction to Science and Technology in the
    Part II examination, and not in the Part III examination.

    (c)   Both Public International Law and Company Law will be
    required subjects in the Part III examination.


## Degree awarded:

Bachelor of Laws  LL.B. - 3 years   (5 years in case of evening students)

Degree awarded in first, second (Upper and Lower) and third class Honours.
Classification determined by performance in both Part II and Part III examinations.


## Medical School

Examinations required for M.B., B.S. degrees:

1st professional examination at end of 2nd year in following subjects:

    Anatomy
    Physiology
    Physiological Chemistry

2nd professional examination at end of 3rd year or not less than 9
months after passing 1st professional examination in following
subjects:

    Pharmacology
    Pathology
    Microbiology

3rd and final professional examination at end of 5th year or not less
than 21 months after passing the 2nd professional examination, at one
sitting, in following subjects:

    Medicine                              Surgery
    Paediatrics                           Obstetrics and Gynaecology
    Social Medicine and Psychiatry

The examination consists of papers, clinical and oral, in each subject. Questions in Anaesthesia may be asked in the papers of Surgery and Obstetrics and Gynaecology, and all the papers above may include questions in Applied Anatomy, Applied Physiology, Clinical Pathology, Microbiology and Therapeutics.

Candidates required to complete periods of practical course work in a teaching hospital, in addition to passing written, practical and oral tests specified for the various professional examinations.

## Degree awarded:

Bachelor of Medicine and Bachelor of Surgery (M.B., B.S.) - 5 years

Degrees awarded with Honours or as pass degree. A mark of distinction may be awarded to candidates in the individual subjects of the various professional examinations.

## Faculty of Science (Schools of Physical and Biological Sciences)

Examinations required for B.Sc. degree:

Part I examination at end of 1st academic year in following subjects:

(a)   3 of the following:

| | |
|---|---|
| Biology | Applied Mathematics |
| Chemistry | Mathematics (Pure and Applied) |
| Geography | Physics |
| Pure Mathematics | |

> N.B.   Mathematics (Pure and Applied) cannot be taken with Pure Mathematics or Applied Mathematics. Candidates for the Diploma in Education may be permitted to substitute Education for 1 of the 3 subjects.

and   (b)   African History and Culture

Part II examination at end of 2nd academic year in following subjects:

(a)   2 of the subjects in the Part I examination under (a) above (excluding Education)

and   (b)   Introduction to Modern Thought

> N.B.   Candidate for the Diploma in Education may be permitted to substitute Education for the subject in (b).

Part III examination at end of 3rd academic year in:

(a)  The 2 subjects taken for the Part II examination under (a)
     Part II

<u>or exceptionally</u>

(b)  1 of those subjects.

Candidates permitted to take 1 subject in the Part III examination
are required to satisfy the examiners that they have attained
proficiency in 1 of the foreign languages:  French, German or Russian.

<u>Degree awarded</u>:

Bachelor of Science (B.Sc.) - 3 years

Degree awarded in first, second (Upper and Lower) and third class Honours.
Classification determined by performance in both the Part II and Part III
examinations.

The above regulations apply only to <u>day</u> courses.

<u>Institute of Petroleum Studies</u>

Initiated with a 5-year financial grant from the Nigeria Gulf Oil Company
to the Federal Ministry of Mines and Power.

The objective is to provide scholarships for scientific and geological
training in Petroleum Studies.

<u>UNIVERSITY OF IBADAN (Western Region)</u>

Established by a 1948 ordinance as the University College of Ibadan.
Through the scheme of Special Relation, degrees were awarded by the University of London.

1962-63 the University College became the University of Ibadan, awarding
its own degrees.

General entrance requirements:

The following are eligible to be considered for admission:

(1)  Graduates of universities recognized by
     Senate for this purpose.

(2)  Candidates holding <u>General Certificates of
     Education</u> including 5 subjects of which not
     less than 2 have been passed at advanced
     level,

<u>or</u>    including 4 subjects of which not less than
           3 have been passed at advanced level.

The following subjects are approved for inclusion in <u>General Certifi-</u>
<u>cate of Education</u> or <u>School Certificate</u> qualifying for Matriculation:

| | |
|---|---|
| English Language | Geology |
| English Literature | General Science |
| Geography | Additional General Science |
| History | Botany |
| Indian History | Zoology |
| Ancient History | Biology or General Biology |
| English Economic History | Rural Biology |
| British Constitution | Human Anatomy |
| Economics | Hygiene and Physiology |
| Logic | Greek |
| Religious Knowledge | Classical Hebrew |
| Greek Literature in Translation | Modern Hebrew |
| Music | French |
| Art | German |
| Latin | Spanish |
| Pure Mathematics | Italian |
| Additional Pure Mathematics | Russian |
| Applied Mathematics | Classical Arabic |
| Mathematics (Pure and Applied) | Hausa |
| Physics | Ibo (Igbo) |
| Chemistry | Yoruba |
| Physics-with-Chemistry | |

## Concessional Entry

A candidate may qualify for concessional entry to the University for a
preliminary course by taking an entrance examination.  The entrance
examination is normally open only to candidates who have obtained, from
a school within 1 year of the proposed date of entry to this examination,
the following qualifications:

either    a <u>West African School Certificate</u> with passes at credit
          standard,

or        a <u>General Certificate of Education</u> with passes at ordinary
          level obtained at one and the same occasion in 5 subjects which
          shall include:

   (i)    English Language

   (ii)   <u>Either</u> Mathematics <u>or</u> 1 of the following approved Science
          subjects:

| | |
|---|---|
| Physics | Botany |
| Chemistry | Zoology |
| Physics-with-Chemistry | Biology |
| Geology | Rural Biology |
| General Science | General Biology |
| Additional General Science | Human Anatomy |
| | Hygiene and Physiology |

(iii)   3 other subjects selected as follows:

Candidates offering the General Certificate of Education as a qualification for admission to the entrance examination select the 3 subjects from the approved list above.

Candidates offering the West African School Certificate as a qualification for admission to the entrance examination select 3 subjects from the following list:

| | |
|---|---|
| Latin | Geography |
| Greek | English Literature |
| French | Religious Knowledge |
| German | Economics |
| Spanish | Art or Music |
| Italian | Elementary Mathematics |
| Bemba | Additional Mathematics |
| Ewe | Mechanics |
| Fante | Chemistry |
| Ga | Physics |
| Ganda | Botany or Biology |
| Ibo (Igbo) | General Science |
| Hausa | General Science (2nd subject) |
| Nyanja | Physics-with-Chemistry |
| Twi | Agricultural Science |
| Yoruba | Technical Drawing |
| any other approved language | Housecraft or Handicraft |
| History or History of the | Hygiene |
| British Empire | Physiology |

The entrance examination consists of:

(i)   A General Paper divided into the following sections:

| Section A | Section B | Section C |
|---|---|---|
| English | Pure Mathematics | Physics |
| History | Applied | Chemistry |
| Latin | Mathematics | Botany |
| Greek | Geography | Zoology |
| Religious Studies | | |

(ii)   An English Language paper.

The preliminary course is an additional year of study in the University before entry to a degree course.  Preliminary work includes the completion of any Faculty requirements that may be needed for admission to the selected course.

Faculties:

    Agriculture, Forestry and Veterinary Science
    Arts
    Economics and Social Studies
    Medicine
    Science
    Education and Extra-Mural Studies

Institutes:

    Institute of African Studies
    Institute of Librarianship
    Institute of Child Health
    Nigerian Institute of Social and Economic Research

First degrees awarded:

| Faculty | Degree | Duration (years) |
|---|---|---|
| Agriculture, Forestry and Veterinary Science | B.Sc.(Agric.) <br> B.Vet.Med. | 3 <br> 4 (and 1 term) |
| Arts | B.A. | 3 |
| Economics and Social Studies | B.Sc.(Econ.) <br> B.Sc.(Pol.) <br> B.Sc.(Soc.) | 3 <br> 3 <br> 3 |
| Medicine | M.B. | 5 |
| Science | B.Sc. | 3 |
| Education and Extra-Mural Studies | B.Ed. | 3 |

Faculty of Agriculture, Forestry and Veterinary Science

Entrance requirements:    Candidates must have passed at General Certificate of Education advanced level in Chemistry and Biology or in Chemistry, Botany and Zoology, and at ordinary level in Physics or Mathematics or Physics-with-Mathematics or have obtained equivalent qualifications.

To be admitted to the course leading to the Bachelor of Veterinary Medicine degree a candidate must have satisfied the minimum conditions for admission with passes in:

| Chemistry | Advanced level |
| Biology or Botany and Zoology | Advanced level |
| Physics or Physics-with-Chemistry | Advanced or ordinary level |

Examinations required for B.Sc.(Agric.) degree:

Candidates for Part I, Part II and the final examinations are examined in in following subjects:

Part I:   Agriculture, Agricultural Botany, Agricultural Zoology, Organic and Physical Chemistry, Physics-with-Mathematics.

Part II:  Agricultural Biochemistry, Geology and Introductory Soil Science, Statistics and Field Experimentation, Economics.

Final (including oral examination):

Animal Production, Crop Production, Agricultural Organization.

## Degree awarded:

Bachelor of Science in Agriculture, B.Sc.(Agric.) - 3 years

Degree awarded with Honours or as a pass degree.


Examinations required for B.Vet.Med. degree:

Curriculum divided into 5 parts, each of which is completed by an examination in the subjects specified.  All candidates take:

Part I of the pre-clinical examination at end of 1st year,

and  Examination in Animal Husbandry II during 5th term,

and  Part II of the pre-clinical examination end of 2nd year.

Candidates for Part I of the pre-clinical examination examined in:

Organic Chemistry at end of the 1st term
Physics-with-Mathematics at the end of the 2nd term, and
Animal Husbandry I and Veterinary Parasitology I at the
end of the 1st year.

Candidates for Part II of the pre-clinical examination examined in:

Animal Husbandry II at end of 5th term, and in
Anatomy, Physiology and Biochemistry, Pharmacology at end
of 2nd year.

Degree awarded:

    Bachelor of Veterinary Medicine, B.Vet.Med. - 4 years and 1 term.

Degree awarded with Honours or as a pass degree.


## Faculty of Arts

Entrance requirements:        Candidates who read Mathematics or a language
                                (including English but excluding Greek and
                                French) as their main subject normally re-
                                quired to have passed the General Certificate
                                of Education at advanced level, or its equi-
                                valent, in that subject.


## Courses leading to B.A. degree:

Based on a single principal subject or 2 combined subjects. All candidates
take the Part I of the B.A. degree examination at end of the 1st year in 3
subjects. This is followed by a course of study extending over 2 years
leading to the final examination in 1 of the prescribed schools.

Candidates examined in 3 subjects selected from the following:

| | |
|---|---|
| Arabic and Islamic Studies | English |
| Economics | History |
| Greek and Roman Culture | Latin |
| French | Pure Mathematics |
| Geography | Applied Mathematics |
| Sociology | Mathematics (Pure and Applied) |
| Geology | Political Science |
| Greek | Religious Studies |

The course is completed by satisfying the examiners in:

either    (a)    A single subject school selected from the following:

| | |
|---|---|
| Arabic and Islamic Studies | Religious Studies |
| Classics | Geography |
| English | History |
| French | Latin |
| | Mathematics |

or      (b)    1 of the following schools of combined subjects:

| | |
|---|---|
| Biblical and English Literature | French and Latin |
| English and French | Greek and Religious Studies |
| English and Latin | Latin and Religious Studies |

Degree awarded:

    Bachelor of Arts, B.A. - 3 years

Degree awarded with Honours or as a pass degree.


## School of Drama

School concerned with:    Development of the theatre in Nigeria

                          Educational uses of the drama

                          Training of students interested in pursuing work
                          in theatre, films, radio and television.

School provides courses in Literature and Practice of Theatre for students
in degree courses in Faculty of Arts and offers 2 Diploma courses:

    (a) Non-graduates--training teachers for educational drama for use
        in the schools.

    (b) Graduates (in any subject)--pursuing theoretical and practical
        training in Drama as a literary and performing art.


## Faculty of Economics and Social Studies

Entrance requirements:    (i)   Preference given to those who have passed
                                in Pure or Applied Mathematics as a subject
                                or obtained an equivalent qualification.

                          (ii)  Economics, Economic History and British
                                Constitution cannot be combined for entry
                                qualification.

                          (iii) A pass in Pure Mathematics or Applied
                                Mathematics at ordinary level in the General
                                Certificate of Education, or an equivalent
                                qualification, will be required in and after
                                1965 of those proposing to read Economics as
                                a main subject.


Examinations required for degree:

All candidates take the Part I examination at end of the 1st year in 3
subjects.  This is followed by a course extending over 2 years leading to
the final examination in 1 main subject and 2 subsidiary subjects.

    Part I (at end of 1st year).
    Candidates examined in 3 subjects selected from the following of

which at least 2 must be chosen from Group A:

| Group A | Group B |
|---------|---------|
| Economics | Geography |
| Political Science | History |
| Sociology | Pure Mathematics |
| | Mathematics-with-Statistics |
| | An approved Modern Language |

Final examination (at end of 3rd year).
Candidate is examined in 1 of the subjects offered in the Part I examination and selected from Group A above; and in subsidiary examinations in the 2 remaining subjects offered in the Part I examination.

## Degrees awarded:

Bachelor of Science, B.Sc. (Econ.) - 3 years
B.Sc. (Pol.) - 3 years
B.Sc. (Soc.) - 3 years

Degree awarded with Honours or as a pass degree.

## Faculty of Medicine

Entrance requirements:            Candidates must have satisfied the minimum conditions for admission with passes in Chemistry, Physics, and Zoology or Biology at principal level in the Higher School Certificate examination or at advanced level in the General Certificate of Education or the approved equivalent.

Examinations required for degree:

All candidates take a 1st professional examination in basic medical sciences at the end of the 5th term.

A 2nd professional examination is given not less than 12 months study after the 1st professional examination, followed by a 3rd professional examination not less than 30 months study after the 1st professional examination.

The final professional examination is given not less than 36 months after the 1st professional examination.

1st professional examination given in Anatomy, Physiology and Biochemistry.

2nd professional examination given in Pharmacology and Pathology.

3rd professional examination given in Obstetrics and Gynaecology and Paediatrics.

Final professional examination given in Medicine, Surgery and Preventive and Social Medicine.

## Degree awarded:

Bachelor of Medicine (M.B.) - 5 years

Degree awarded either with Honours or as a pass degree. Distinctions may be awarded in individual subjects, e.g. Surgery, Pathology, etc.

## Specialized Fellowship Courses:

With World Health Organization (W.H.O.) Fellowship Course in Nutrition. Post-graduate medical students.

## Faculty of Science

Entrance requirements:          Candidates must have satisfied the minimum conditions for admission with passes in 3 subjects chosen from the following list, of which 2 must be at General Certificate of Education advanced level or the approved equivalent:

| | |
|---|---|
| Biology | Zoology |
| Botany | Geography |
| Chemistry | Pure Mathematics |
| Geology | Applied Mathematics |
| Physics | Mathematics (Pure and Applied) |

Examinations required for B.Sc. degree:

All candidates take the Part I of the B.Sc. degree examination at the end of the 1st year in 3 subjects, the Part II at end of 2nd year in 2 subjects, and finals at end of the 3rd year in either 1 or 2 subjects.

Part I examination candidates examined in 3 subjects from the following list:

| | |
|---|---|
| Biology | Pure Mathematics |
| Botany | Applied Mathematics |
| Chemistry | Mathematics (Pure and Applied) |
| Geography | Physics |
| Geology | Zoology |

Part II examination candidates examined in 2 of the following:

| | |
|---|---|
| Biochemistry | Pharmacology |
| Biology | Physics |
| Botany | Pure Mathematics |
| Chemistry | Mathematics (Pure and Applied) |
| Geography | Pure Mathematics-with- |
| Physiology |    Statistics |
| Geology | Statistics |
| Zoology | Applied Mathematics |

Final examination candidates select 1 subject from the following:

| | |
|---|---|
| Biochemistry | Mathematics (Pure and Applied) |
| Botany | Pharmacology |
| Chemistry | Physics |
| Geology | Physiology |
| Geography | Zoology |

Candidates also required to show proficiency in 1 of the following foreign languages: French, German, Russian.

## Degree awarded:

Bachelor of Science (B.Sc.) - 3 years

Degree awarded with Honours or as a pass degree.

## Intermediate Special Laboratory Technicians' Course

Run by Department of Chemistry.

## Faculty of Education and Extra-Mural Studies

## Courses of study:

(1)  Degree course.

A 3-year course of Arts/Science subjects, Education and Practical Teaching leading to the Bachelor of Arts and Bachelor of Science in Education (B.Ed.).

(2)  Certificate in Education (post-graduate).

Entrance requirements:    Graduate of approved university.

Length of course:         1 year.

Course leads to Post-Graduate Certificate in Education.

(3) Associate Diploma (non-graduate).

Entrance requirements: Competitive examination for non-graduate teachers.

Length of course: 1 year.

Course leads to Associate Diploma of Education.

The Bachelor of Education degree is a modified Joint Honours and ranks as a Joint Honours degree.

Candidates for this degree take the same or parallel papers in their teaching subjects as Joint Honours candidates.

### Structure of the Bachelor of Education Degree

| | | | | |
|---|---|---|---|---|
| 1st yr: | Arts or Science Subject | Arts or Science Subject | Education | Practical Teaching during vacation |
| 2nd yr: | Arts or Science Subject | | Arts or Science Subject | Practical Teaching during vacation |
| 3rd yr: | Arts or Science Subject | | Education | Practical Teaching during vacation |

1st yr: Student carries 2 teaching subjects and Education. Does 1 month teaching practice during long vacation.

2nd yr: Student drops Education and carries on with the 2 teaching subjects of the 1st year. Again student has teaching practice of 1 month during long vacation.

3rd yr: Student carries 1 teaching subject and Education (in place of the 2nd teaching subject). The teaching subject must be 1 of the 2 studied in the 2nd year. Teaching practice of 1 month during long vacation.

Higher degrees:

Master's degree, normally 2 years (6 terms)
Degree of Doctor of Philosophy, normally 3 years (9 terms)

Master's degree:

    Candidates for the degree of Master must be graduates of the University with the degree of Bachelor with at least a 2nd class (upper division) Honours; or graduates of other approved universities with equivalent qualifications.

    Candidates for the degree of Master follow an approved course of study and/or research for a period of not less than 2 years (6 terms).

Degree of Doctor of Philosophy:

    Candidates for the degree of Doctor of Philosophy must be graduates of the University with at least a 2nd class (upper division) Honours; graduates of other approved universities with equivalent qualifications; or graduates of the University or other approved universities, who possess the degree of Master appropriate to the intended course.

    Candidates for the degree of Doctor of Philosophy follow an approved course of research for a period of not less than 3 years (9 terms).

    The examination for the degree of Doctor of Philosophy is by submission of a thesis and by an oral examination.

Higher degrees awarded:

| Faculty | Degree | |
| --- | --- | --- |
| Arts | Master of Arts | M.A. |
| | Doctor of Philosophy | Ph.D. |
| | Doctor of Letters | D.Litt. |
| Science | Master of Science | M.Sc. |
| | Doctor of Philosophy | Ph.D. |
| | Doctor of Science | D.Sc. |
| Medicine | Doctor of Philosophy | Ph.D. |
| | Doctor of Medicine | M.D. |
| Agriculture, Forestry and Veterinary Science | Master of Science (in Agriculture or in | M.Sc. |
| | (Veterinary Science | M.Sc. |
| | Doctor of Philosophy | Ph.D. |
| | Doctor of Science | D.Sc. |
| Economic and Social Studies | Master of Arts | M.A. |
| | Doctor of Philosophy | Ph.D. |
| | Doctor of Letters | D.Litt. |
| Education and Extra-Mural Studies | Master of Education | M.Ed. |
| | Doctor of Philosophy | Ph.D. |
| | Doctor of Letters | D.Litt. |

## Institute of African Studies

Founded in 1962, the Institute is an interdisciplinary organ providing a common meeting ground for all disciplines of the University concerned with African studies.

Three research chairs have been established in Archeology, Linguistics and Sociology.

Activities include:

    Research projects.
    Conferences and seminars.
    Responsibility for University collection of African art.
    Twice-yearly course: "Nigerian History and Culture". Organized for the Ministry of Foreign Affairs and Commonwealth Relations (by Institute of African Studies in conjunction with the Extra-Mural Department).

## Institute of Librarianship

Established to provide training for librarians at all levels of the profession.

Syllabus offers general training appropriate for all types of libraries: public, university, scientific institutions and governmental departments.

The Institute is intended primarily for graduates although non-graduates with professional experience also admitted.

Entrance requirements:     1st degree of an approved university.

    or At least 2 years full-time experience in a recognized library, together with at least 1 part of the Registration Examination of the Library Association, London.

    or In exceptional cases some other appropriate educational background.

Length of course:     1 year.

Certificate awarded:     Diploma of the University of Ibadan (based on written examination at end of session).

## Institute of Child Health

Program:     Research, Growth and Development, Virus Research.

Research Fellows appointed to work in Labos branch of Institute of Child Health.

Seminars.


Nigerian Institute of Social and Economic Research

Sponsored by Nigerian Federal Government and University of Ibadan.

Institute is center for independent research workers in various fields of economic and social study.


UNIVERSITY OF IFE

Established in 1961 as a new institution of higher learning in the Western Region.  Temporary location of the University at site of the Ibadan branch of former Nigerian College of Arts, Science and Technology.

When buildings have been completed, the University will move to its permanent 16,000 acre campus at Ile-Ife, famous as a center of early African culture.  Some departments, such as Pharmacy, are to remain at Ibadan.

October 1962, teaching first started in 5 Faculties:  Agriculture, Arts, Economics and Social Studies, Law and Science.  Research activities in the Institute of African Studies initiated in temporary buildings at Eleiyele.

Entrance requirements:     Admission to University by direct entry in all faculties.  In addition, a few students may be taken as a special or temporary concession into the Faculties of Science and Agriculture for a preliminary year.

either     General Certificate of Education with a minimum of 2 passes at advanced level and at least 3 other passes at ordinary level.

or     Higher School Certificate with a minimum of 2 passes at principal level and at least 3 other passes at the subsidiary level.

or     2 G.C.E. advanced level passes or 2 Higher School principal level passes plus credits in at least 3 other subjects in West African School Certificate.

The above passes must include either a credit in English Language in the West African School Certificate or an ordinary level pass in

English Language in the <u>General Certificate of Education</u>, or a pass in the General Paper of the <u>Higher School Certificate</u>.

<u>Faculties</u>:

    Agriculture
    Arts
    Economics and Social Studies
    Law
    Science

Institute of African Studies
Institute of Administration

Language of instruction:      English

<u>Degrees awarded</u>:

| Faculty | Degree | Duration of Course (years) |
|---|---|---|
| Agriculture | B.Sc. (Agric.) | 3 |
| Arts | B.A. (Arts) | 3 |
| Economic and Social Studies | B.Sc. (Econ.) | 3 |
| Law | LL.B. | 3 |
| Science | B.Sc. | 3 |
|  | B.Pharm | 3 |

<u>Advanced degrees</u>:

The University also offers facilities for study for advanced degrees in all faculties.

<u>Faculty of Agriculture</u>

Entrance requirements:    Direct entry candidates must have passes in Chemistry, Botany and Zoology at the principal standard in the <u>Higher School Certificate</u> or at the advanced level in the <u>General Certificate of Education</u>. Under the present circumstances, passes in Chemistry and Biology and either Botany or Zoology are admitted but are required to pass in addition an appropriate University examination in Zoology or Botany at the end of their 1st year. Passes at

credit or ordinary level in English Language,
Elementary Mathematics and Physics or
Physics-with-Chemistry are also obligatory.
A candidate without a credit or ordinary level
pass in English Language or in Physics is
required to pass an examination in these subjects.

Preliminary course:

In special cases those candidates admitted by the University for a 1-year
preliminary course should have at least 1 subject at advanced level in the
General Certificate of Education or at principal level in the Higher School
Certificate and satisfy other conditions.

Examinations required for B.Sc.(Agric.) degree:

Part I examination taken at end of 1st academic year.  Examination
consists of 6 papers and 5 practical examinations as follows:

| | |
|---|---|
| Chemistry | 2 3-hour written papers and 2 3-hour practical examinations. |
| Physics-with-Mathematics | 1 3-hour paper and 1 3-hour practical examination. |
| Botany | 1 3-hour paper and 1 3-hour practical examination. |
| Zoology | 1 3-hour paper and 1 3-hour practical examination. |
| History and Theory of Agriculture | 1 3-hour paper. |

Part II examination taken 1 academic year after completing Part I
examination.  Examination consists of 7 papers of 3 hours each and
4 practical examinations.  There will also be an oral examination.

| | |
|---|---|
| Geology and Pedology | 1 3-hour paper and 1 3-hour practical examination. |
| Agricultural Biochemistry | 1 3-hour paper and 1 3-hour practical examination. |
| Crop Production I) Animal Production I) | 1 3-hour paper ) 1 3-hour paper ) plus oral examination. |
| Agricultural Economics I | 1 3-hour paper. |
| Agricultural Biology | 2 3-hour papers, and 2 3-hour practical examinations. |

Part III examination must be taken 1 academic year after completing Part II examination.  Examination consists of 7 3-hour papers and 2 practical examinations.  In addition there are oral examinations.

| | |
|---|---|
| Soil Science | 1 3-hour paper and 1 3-hour practical examination. |
| Animal Nutrition and Biochemistry | 1 3-hour paper and 1 6-hour practical examination. |
| Agricultural Economics II | 1 3-hour paper. |
| Farm Management | 1 3-hour paper. |
| Animal Production II) Crop Production II) | 1 3-hour paper ) 1 3-hour paper ) plus oral examination. |
| Farm Mechanization | 1 3-hour paper plus oral examination. |

## Degree awarded:

Bachelor of Science in Agriculture, B.Sc.(Agric.) - 3 years

Degree awarded as first, second (Upper and Lower) or third class Honours, or as pass, in accordance with the performance of candidate.

## Faculty of Arts

| | |
|---|---|
| Entrance requirements: | Same as those required for admission by direct entry.  In addition, departments within the Faculty may ask for special departmental entry requirements.  No concessional entry, consequently no preliminary course. |

Structure of subjects for degree:

Part I (1st year):  All students required to choose 3 subjects from:

| | |
|---|---|
| Comparative Religion | German |
| Economics | History |
| English | Mathematics |
| French | Philosophy |

Part II (2nd and 3rd years):  Students choose final Honours subjects on basis of their performance in University examination at end of 1st year.  They may take either a Special Honours degree (1 subject) or a Combined Honours degree (2 subjects).

Instruction offered in the Faculty in following single subjects or groups:

Comparative Religion                 History/Government
English Literature and Language      History/Economics
Geography                            Geography/Economics
History                              Geography/Government
Mathematics                          Mathematics/with any of the
English/Comparative Religion            other 7 subjects
English/History                      History/Comparative Religion
History/Geography

Departmental entrance requirement for Geography only:  Advanced level
pass in G.C.E. or a principal level Higher School Certificate in
Geography.

Examinations required for B.A. degree:

Part I examination covers the 3 subjects studied in 1st year.  Number
of 3-hour papers in each subject not less than 2 and not more than 3.

Part II examination in Special Honours degree consists of not less
than 6 and not more than 10 3-hour papers.

Examination in Combined Honours degree not less than 3 and not more
than 5 3-hour papers in each subject.

## Degree awarded:

Bachelor of Arts (B.A.) - 3 years

Degree awarded first, second (Upper and Lower) or third class Honours.
Candidates failing to reach necessary standard for Honours degree awarded
a pass degree if sufficiently high standard achieved.

## Faculty of Economic and Social Studies

Entrance requirements:          Same as those for entry to the University,
                                but must include ordinary level pass in
                                Mathematics.

Structure of subjects for B.Sc.(Econ.) degree:

Part I (1st and 2nd years):  Following 5 subjects compulsory in 1st
year:

Economics, Principles            Political Theory
   and Applied                   Constitutions
Economic History                 French

2nd year students take 6 compulsory subjects and 2 alternative subjects in their speciality (either Economics or Government) and are
examined at end of that year in the Part I examination.

Part II (3rd year):  On basis of performance in the Part I examination students choose their final Honours subjects.  They take either 5 papers or 4 papers (3 hours each) and an essay paper (3 hours) in their special subject.

## Degree awarded:

Bachelor of Science in Economics, B.Sc.(Econ.) - 3 years

Degree awarded with first, second (Upper and Lower) or third class Honours. Students failing to reach necessary standard for Honours degree awarded pass degree if sufficiently high standard achieved.

## Faculty of Law

Entrance requirements:        Same as those required for admission to the University by direct entry.

Examinations required for LL.B. degree:

Examination for the degree consists of Parts I, II and III.  There is a 3-hour paper in each of the subjects of the examination as follows:

Part I (1st year):

| | |
|---|---|
| Introduction to Law | Nigerian Legal System |
| Law of Contract | Introduction to Constitutional Law |

Part II (2nd year):

| | |
|---|---|
| Nigerian Land Law | Equity |
| Law of Tort | Criminal Law |

Part III (3rd year):

Jurisprudence, and Application of Nigerian Customary Law
Law of Evidence
Nigerian Constitutional Law

1 of the following:

| | |
|---|---|
| Islamic Law | Conflict of Laws |
| Domestic Relations and Succession | Public International Law |

## Degree awarded.

Bachelor of Laws (LL.B.) - 3 years

Degree awarded first, second (Upper and Lower) and a pass.

## Faculty of Science

Entrance requirements:

Qualifying subjects must include a pass in Mathematics at ordinary level in the G.C.E. or a credit in the W.A.S.C. and 2 Science subjects at advanced level in the G.C.E. or principal level in the H.S.C.

In addition the advanced level or principal level pass must include the subjects specified below in order to qualify for entry into the following departments:

| | |
|---|---|
| Chemistry: | that subject |
| Geography: | that subject |
| Physics: | that subject and either Pure Mathematics or Mathematics (Pure and Applied) |
| Zoology: | that subject or Biology |
| Pharmacy: | (see below) |

Examination of subjects required for B.Sc. degree:

Part I (1st year):  3 subjects normally required from:

Botany
Chemistry
Geography
Pure Mathematics

Applied Mathematics (in combination with Pure Mathematics)
Physics
Zoology
Geology

Part II (2nd year):  1 or 2 subjects selected from those taken in 1st year.

Part III (3rd year):  1 or both subjects studied in 2nd year.

Entrance requirements for B.Pharm. degree:

G.C.E. at ordinary level or W.A.S.C. at credit level, in English Language and Mathematics.

In addition, G.C.E. at advanced level or H.S.C. at principal level in 3 subjects, namely:

Chemistry
Physics

either Biology or Botany or Zoology
or Mathematics at advanced or principal level with a biological subject at G.C.E. ordinary level or W.A.S.C. credit level.

Examinations required for B.Pharm. degree:

| Part I: | Written | Practical |
|---|---|---|
| Pharmaceutics | 2 3-hour | 1 3-hour |
| Pharmaceutical Chemistry | 1 3-hour | |
| Pharmacognosy | 1 3-hour | 1 3-hour |
| Physiology | 1 3-hour | 1 3-hour |

| Part II: | | |
|---|---|---|
| Pharmaceutics | 1 3-hour | 1 3-hour |
| Pharmaceutical Chemistry | 1 3-hour | 1 3-hour |
| Pharmacognosy | 1 3-hour | 1 6-hour |
| Pharmacology | 1 3-hour | 1 3-hour |

| Part III: | | |
|---|---|---|
| Pharmaceutics | 2 3-hour | Course work |
| Pharmaceutical Chemistry | 2 3-hour | Course work |
| Pharmacognosy | 1 3-hour | Course work |
| or  Pharmacology | 1 3-hour | Course work |

## Degrees awarded:

Bachelor of Science (B.Sc.) - 3 years
Bachelor of Pharmacy (B.Pharm.) - 3 years

Degree awarded with first, second or third class Honours.  A candidate whose performance does not merit the award of Honours may receive a pass degree.

## Institute of African Studies

Institute began its work 1962-63.  Proposed plans are to attract research scholars interested in African Studies from all over the world.

Work of the Institute is organized in the following divisions:

Anthropology and Sociology
Archaeology
Ethno-history Art and Folk Culture
Languages and Linguistics
The Maghreb and Arabic Influences
Africa-in-Transition

2 levels:

### Post-Graduate Level (Research Center)

Seminars
Open Lectures

Conferences
Exhibitions
Excavations
Journal

Under-Graduate Level

Open Lectures
Lectures on West African Life and Thought
Collaboration with other departments in providing courses as required


Institute of Administration

Institute created July 1963 with the objective of professionalizing all
elements of the Western Nigeria Government.

Instructional program consists of the following:

Diploma course:  Post-graduate residential, 37-week course.

'Bootstrap' Tutorials
2-week Seminar Workshops
2 to 3 Months Local Government Study Conference
Research and Consultancy Program


VOCATIONAL AND TECHNICAL EDUCATION

TRADE CENTRES:

Lagos:  Government Trade Centre
Western Nigeria:  Centres at Abeokuta, Oshogbo, Oyo, and Ijebu-Ode
Mid-Western Nigeria:  Sapele Trade Centre

Entrance requirements:          Variable age.  Primary education or more.

Length of course:  3 years.

Curriculum:          Cabinet Making, Fitting and Machinery, Blacksmithing
                     and Welding, Painting and Decorating.


COMMERCIAL SCHOOLS:

Training given in 3 types of schools:

## SECONDARY MODERN SCHOOLS (with commercial bias)

Entrance requirements:       Primary School Leaving Certificate.

Length of course:   3 years secondary modern and 1 year commercial bias.

Curriculum:         Shorthand, Typing and Elementary Accounting, English Language, Arithmetic, Civics, History and Geography.

## SECONDARY COMMERCIAL SCHOOLS

Entrance requirements:       Primary School Leaving Certificate.

Length of course:   5 years.

Curriculum (leading to Royal Society of Arts Certificate):

Shorthand, Shorthand Typing, Accounting, English Language, Mathematics, History, Geography, Health Science.

## SENIOR COMMERCIAL COLLEGES (part of Technical Institutes)

Entrance requirements:       5 years of secondary school.

Length of course:   2 years.

## TECHNICAL COLLEGES:

## FEDERAL SCHOOL OF SCIENCE, Lagos

Formerly known as Emergency Science School.  Established 1958.  Academic courses.

Entrance requirements:       West African School Certificate.

Length of course:   2 years.

Curriculum:         Pure and Applied Mathematics, Physics, Chemistry Botany, Zoology, Biology, Engineering, Drawing; Liberal Arts (1963).

Certificate awarded:    General Certificate of Education advanced level (University of London).

Students may enter Nigerian university.

## NIGERIAN COLLEGE OF ARTS, SCIENCE AND TECHNOLOGY

Discontinued in 1962.  Preparation for university entrance.

See EASTERN NIGERIA section for the program offered.


## TECHNICAL COLLEGE, Ibadan (Western Region)

Curriculum similar to that offered at College of Technology, Yaba.  See below.


## THE COLLEGE OF TECHNOLOGY, Yaba (Lagos)

This is the largest and most developed of the technical institutes.

Full-time day classes for Secondary School, Senior, and Advanced candidates.

Part-time day release classes.

Part-time evening classes for Preliminary and Senior candidates.

COLLEGE OF TECHNOLOGY, Yaba

SUMMARY OF COURSES OFFERED

1965

FULL-TIME DAY CLASSES

| | Course | Length of Course | Description | Minimum Qualification |
|---|---|---|---|---|
| A D V A N C E D | Higher Certificate in Building<br>Civil<br>Electrical<br>Mechanical | 2 academic sessions | Vocational training leading to Higher Certificate of City and Guilds and the Yaba Higher Diploma. | Pass in appropriate ordinary certificate of City and Guilds examination or Yaba Diploma in Engineering. |
| | Secretaryship<br>Accountancy | 2 academic sessions | Vocational training leading to the Intermediate examinations of A.C.C.A., C.C.S., and C.I.S. | Exemption from appropriate preliminary examination, or G.C.E. 'O' level in appropriate subjects, or W.A.S.C. with 4 credits in appropriate subjects or the Yaba Secondary Commercial Certificate. |
| S E N I O R | Building and Architecture<br>Civil Engineering<br>Electrical Engineering<br>Mechanical Engineering | Sandwich course of 1 full-time session at the College followed by 15 months in industry and a second full-time session at the College. | Vocational training leading to Yaba Diploma and the ordinary certificate of City and Guilds of London Institute. | (1) Yaba, Secondary Technical Certificate<br>or<br>(2) School Certificate with 4 credits (English, Math., Science and one other) or the equivalent in G.C.E. |

**SENIOR**

| Course | Length of Course | Description | Minimum Qualification |
|---|---|---|---|
| Art:<br>(a) Sculpture<br>(b) Printing<br>(c) Commercial Art<br>(d) Pottery | 2 years | Vocational training | School Certificate or G.C.E. with good artistic ability. Lower qualifications may be considered in special circumstances. |
| Laboratory Technician | 1 or 2 academic sessions | Leading to Science Laboratory Technicians' Certificate of City and Guilds, issued in conjunction with Institute of Science Technology | School Certificate with credits in 2 science subjects or the equivalent in G.C.E. |
| Printing:<br>(a) Compositor's Work<br>(b) Letterpress Machine Printing | 3 years | Vocational training leading to City and Guilds of London Institute Intermediate examination. | Secondary IV Certificate and pass in entrance examination. |

**JUNIOR SCHOOL**

| Course | Length of Course | Description | Minimum Qualification |
|---|---|---|---|
| Technical | 4 years | General education to G.C.E. 'O' level or West African School Certificate and a bias towards Applied Science. | Candidates must be over 13 and not more than 15 years on September 1st, and preferably possess a Standard IV, or the equivalent, or must be in Standard VI. Entry is through the Common Entrance Examination each year, of the West African Examination Council. |
| Commercial | | General education to G.C.E. 'O' level or West African School Certificate and a bias towards Commerce. | |

## PART-TIME DAY RELEASE

| Course | Length of Course | Description | Minimum Qualification |
|---|---|---|---|
| Art | 4 years (8 hours per week) | Vocational training for practicing artists and craftsmen. | By artistic ability. |
| Printing: (a) Compositor's Work (b) Letterpress Machine Work | 3 years (8 hours per week) | Vocational training leading to City and Guilds of London Institute, Inter-mediate Certificate. | Government employees admitted on nomination by their department. Private candidates employed in the printing industry are admitted by selection. |
| Secretaryship Accountancy | 2 years (10 hours per week) | Vocational training leading to inter-mediate examinations of professional bodies. | G.C.E., W.A.S.C. or exemp-tion from preliminary examination of professional bodies. |
| Stenography | 2 years (10 hours per week) | Vocational training leading to Royal Society of Arts examinations. | Typing 25 w.p.m., Shorthand 60 w.p.m. Sponsored by employer and subject to passing entrance test in Shorthand and Typewriting. |
| Structural Detailing | 2 years (10 hours per week) | Vocational training leading to City and Guilds Certificate. | Sponsored students with minimum Class IV. |
| Mechanical and Electrical Engineering | Up to 5 years (10 hours per week) | Vocational training leading to ordinary certificate of City and Guilds of London Institute. | Standard VI sponsored students only. |

| Course | Length of Course | Description | Minimum Qualification |
|---|---|---|---|
| Radio Service Work | 2 years | Leading to the Inter-mediate Certificate of the City and Guilds of London Institute. | Secondary IV sponsored students only. |
| Laboratory Technicians | 3 years (12 hours per week) | Leading to Science Laboratory Technicians' Certificate of City and Guilds. | Sponsored students with 2 years of secondary education or higher. |

P A R T - T I M E   E V E N I N G   C L A S S E S

| Course | Length of Course | Description | Minimum Qualification |
|---|---|---|---|
| Mechanical Eng. Electrical Eng. Building Construction | 2 to 3 years | Training in preparation for entry to the senior course. | Standard VI and by passing the entrance examination. |
| Refrigeration Practice | 2 years | Vocational training leading to City and Guilds Technicians' Certificate. | Sponsored students. |
| Commercial Shorthand and Typewriting | 1 year | Training in preparation for entry to the senior course. | Standard VI and by passing the entrance examination. |
| Monotype Keyboard | 3 years | Vocational training. | Sponsored students. |
| Linotype Keyboard | 1 year | Vocational training. | Sponsored students. |

PRELIMINARY

| Course | Length of Course | Description | Minimum Qualification |
|--------|------------------|-------------|------------------------|
| **SENIOR** | | | |
| Mechanical Eng. Building Construction Electrical Eng. | 3 years | Vocational training leading to ordinary certificate of City and Guilds of London Institute. | By promotion from the preliminary courses or by selection from holders of Secondary IV~. |
| Commercial Shorthand and Typewriting | | Training and preparation for the Royal Society of Arts examinations. | By promotion from preliminary courses or by selection from holders of Secondary IV or Stage I or II of the Royal Society of Arts certificates in the subjects of instruction. |
| Art | 4 years | Vocational training. | Good general education and artistic ability. |
| Institute of Transport | 2 years | Leading to Graduateship of the Institute of Transport. | Open to registered students of the Institute of Transport. |

Civil Engineering, Building Architecture and Quantity Surveying

### ORDINARY CERTIFICATE AND YABA DIPLOMA COURSES

Civil Engineering                                              Hours per week

1st yr:   CE. 1

|                                         |     |
| --------------------------------------- | --- |
| Mathematics                             | 6   |
| Science                                 | 4   |
| Surveying                               | 4   |
| Mechanics                               | 5   |
| Building Construction                   | 4   |
| Quantities and Specifications           | 2   |
| Engineering Drawing                     | 4   |
| Liberal Studies                         | 1   |

2nd yr:   CE. 2

|                                         |     |
| --------------------------------------- | --- |
| Mathematics                             | 4   |
| Science                                 | 4   |
| Surveying and Soil Mechanics            | 5   |
| Materials and Structures                | 3   |
| Hydraulics and Applied Mechanics        | 3   |
| Building Construction                   | 3   |
| Quantities and Specification            | 3   |
| Engineering Drawing                     | 4   |
| Liberal Studies                         | 1   |

Building Architecture

1st yr:   AA. 1

|                                         |     |
| --------------------------------------- | --- |
| Mathematics                             | 4   |
| Science                                 | 4   |
| Surveying                               | 4   |
| Mechanics                               | 4   |
| Building Construction                   | 6   |
| Building Drawing and Design             | 4   |
| History of Architecture                 | 3   |
| Liberal Studies                         | 1   |

2nd yr:   AA. 2

|                                            |     |
| ------------------------------------------ | --- |
| Mathematics                                | 4   |
| Science                                    | 4   |
| Mechanics                                  | 4   |
| Building Construction                      | 6   |
| Building Drawing and Design                | 4   |
| Building Technology                        | 3   |
| Town Planning and Building Management      | 4   |
| Liberal Studies                            | 1   |

## Quantity Surveying

1st yr:   <u>QS. 1</u>

| | |
|---|---|
| Mathematics | 4 |
| Surveying | 4 |
| Building Construction and Draftsmanship | 6 |
| Principles of Structural Design | 4 |
| Quantities | 4 |
| Building Services | 3 |
| Principles of Law | 2 |
| Economics | 2 |
| Liberal Studies | 1 |

2nd yr:   <u>QS. 2</u>

| | |
|---|---|
| Surveying | 4 |
| Building Construction and Draftsmanship | 3 |
| Principles of Structural Design | 4 |
| Quantities | 4 |
| Building Services | 4 |
| Specifications | 2 |
| Principles of Law | 2 |
| Economics | 2 |
| Practice and Procedure | 1 |
| Liberal Studies | 1 |

## HIGHER CERTIFICATE AND YABA HIGHER DIPLOMA COURSES

### Civil Engineering and Building

1st yr:   <u>HCE. 1, HAA. 1 common course</u>

| | |
|---|---|
| Mathematics | 4 |
| Surveying | 8 |
| Structures | 7 |
| Construction and Materials (general) | 8 |
| Liberal Studies | 3 |

2nd yr:   <u>HCE. 2, Sections A and B</u>

| | |
|---|---|
| Surveying | 6 |
| Measurement and Estimating | 4 |
| Soil Mechanics | 6 |
| Public Works (Roads and Airfields) | 6[+] |
| Public Works (Water Supply and Drainage) | 6[+] |
| Public Works (Structures) | 4[+] |
| Liberal Studies | 3 |

[+]Alternatives

1st yr:  <u>HCE. 2, Section C</u>

        Surveying (Building)                      6
        Public Works (Structures)             4
        Measurement and Estimating         4
        Soil Mechanics                         4
        Specification and Detailing        4
        Construction and Materials (Concrete)  5
        Liberal Studies                    3

2nd yr:  <u>HAA. 2</u>

        Surveying (Building Work)            6
        Construction and Materials (General)   4
        Construction and Materials (Timber)    $5^+$
        Construction and Materials (Concrete)  $5^+$
        Measurement and Estimating (Building)  5
        Specification and Detailing        4
        Site Organization and Administration   3
        Liberal Studies                    3

$^+$Alternatives

## Mechanical Engineering

1st yr:  <u>HM. 1</u>

        Mathematics                         4
        Mechanics and Machines            9
        Strength and Prop. of Materials     9
        Powerplant                        5
        Liberal Studies                    3

2nd yr:  <u>HM. 2</u>

        Electro. Tech.                     5
        Structures                        5
        Refrigeration and Air-Conditioning   5
        Fluids                          5
        Mechanical Engineering Design     4
        Management                     3
        Liberal Studies                    3

## Electrical Engineering

1st yr:  <u>HE. 1</u>

        Mathematics                         4
        Applied Mechanics                5
        Circuit Theory and Measurement     7
        Electrical Machines and Electronics  11
        Liberal Studies                    3

2nd yr:    <u>HE.2</u>

|  |  |
|---|---|
| Mech. Eng. Tech. | 4 |
| Circuit Theory and Measurement | 5 |
| Elect. Machines | 5 |
| Industrial Electronics | 5+ |
| Radio Communications | 5+ |
| Supply and Distribution | 5 |
| Management | 3 |
| Liberal Studies | 3 |

+Alternatives

## Mechanical and Electrical Engineering

### ORDINARY CERTIFICATE AND YABA DIPLOMA COURSES

## Mechanical Engineering

1st yr:    <u>ME. 1</u>

|  |  |
|---|---|
| Mathematics | 6 |
| Science | 3 |
| Engineering Drawing | 6 |
| Mechanical Engineering Science | 5 |
| Workshop Technology and Practice | 4 |
| Electrical Engineering Science | 5 |
| Liberal Studies | 1 |

2nd yr:    <u>ME. 2</u>

|  |  |
|---|---|
| Mathematics | 4 |
| Science | 4 |
| Engineering Drawing | 4 |
| Applied Mechanics | 5 |
| Heat Engines | 5 |
| Workshop Technology and Practice | 4 |
| Electrical Engineering Science | 4 |
| Liberal Studies | 1 |

## Electrical Engineering

1st yr:    <u>EE. 1</u>

|  |  |
|---|---|
| Mathematics | 6 |
| Science | 3 |
| Engineering Drawing | 6 |
| Mechanical Engineering Science | 5 |
| Electrical Engineering Science | 5 |
| Installation Theory and Practice | 4 |
| Liberal Studies | 1 |

2nd yr:    <u>EE. 2</u>

                Mathematics                                    4
                Science                                        3
                Engineering Drawing                            4
                Mechanical Engineering Science                 4
                Applied Electricity                            5
                Electrical Machines                            5
                Radio and Electronics Theory and Practice      4
                Liberal Studies                                1

## Commerce

### Secretaryship

1st yr:    <u>CS. 1</u>

                Accountancy                                    8
                Economics--Theory                              6
                Secretarial Practice (General)                 2
                General Principles of English Law              6
                English Language                               6
                Liberal Studies                                2

2nd yr:    <u>CS. 2</u>

                Accountancy                                    8
                Economics--Theory                              6
                Secretarial Practice                           2
                General Principles of English Law              6
                English Language                               6
                Liberal Studies                                2

### Accountancy

1st yr:    <u>CA. 1</u>

                Bookkeeping and Accounts                      10
                Costing                                        6
                Mercantile Law                                 4
                Auditing                                       4
                Economics and Business Statistics              4
                Liberal Studies                                2

2nd yr:    <u>CA. 2</u>

                Bookkeeping and Accounts                      10
                Costing                                        6
                Mercantile Law                                 4
                Auditing                                       4
                Economics and Business Statistics              4
                Liberal Studies                                2

Certificates and diplomas awarded are described in the summaries of courses. For general education (secondary) programs a <u>Secondary School Certificate</u> is awarded by the Ministry of Education of the Federal Government of Nigeria in addition to the <u>Yaba College of Technology School Leaving Certificate and Testimonial</u>.

TEACHER EDUCATION

TEACHER TRAINING COLLEGES:

PRIMARY TEACHERS COLLEGE (Elementary Grade III)

Phasing out.

Entrance requirements:          Primary school training.

2-year course preparing for teaching elementary classes I through IV.


PRIMARY TEACHERS COLLEGE (Grade II)

1965 - 3 different courses:

(1)  2-year "returned course" for Grade III teachers (with several years
     experience).  This 2-year "returned course" is disappearing as the
     Grade III teacher training colleges (2-year post-primary program)
     are being discontinued.

(2)  2-year course.

     Entrance requirements:     West African School Certificate or General
                                Certificate of Education 'O' level.

(3)  3-year pilot scheme.

     Entrance requirements:     Modern School Leaving Certificate, or 3
                                years of training in secondary grammar
                                school.

     The 3-year pilot scheme course, following upon either successful
     completion of the secondary modern school course or 3-year study
     in a secondary grammar school is still in the experimental stage
     and may become the future course for primary school teachers.

Curriculum:     Compulsory subjects for the Federation (Lagos):

                English Language, Arithmetic, Principles and Practice of
                Education.

                Regional subjects:

                Religious Knowledge, Music, Art, Domestic Science, Agri-
                culture, Needlework, English Literature, Elementary
                Mathematics, Geography, History.

Those pursuing the 2-year regular course indicated above also take any
2   subjects at an advanced level.

Examinations required:         Theory and Practical Teaching (see pp.597-601).

Grading scale:          In final examination for Teachers' Grade II Certifi-
                        cate, grading in individual subjects is designated
                        as:  Credit, Merit, Pass.

                        Candidate must be successful in at least 8 subjects,
                        including compulsory subjects, in order to qualify
                        for Certificate.  He must also pass the Practical
                        Teaching examination.  Lowest passing mark is 40%.

Certificate awarded:           Teachers' Grade II Certificate.


## TEACHERS' (Grade I) CERTIFICATE TRAINING

Qualifying for teaching in secondary schools.

Entrance requirements:         Grade II Teachers' Certificate only.

Training:          (a)  Usually 2 years in a rural science college or other
                        colleges approved for Grade I course.

                   (b)  Grade II teachers, who on their own pass 2 teaching
                        subjects at the advanced level in the G.C.E. exami-
                        nation, may apply for practical teaching test
                        (provided they have taught at least for 3 years as
                        Grade II teachers) and if successful are qualified
                        to receive Teachers' Grade I Certificate.


## FEDERAL ADVANCED TEACHERS' TRAINING COLLEGE, Yaba (Lagos) (as of 1961)

Preparation for teaching in junior forms of secondary schools and in
Grade II teacher training colleges.

Entry age:     18-20 years.

Length of course:     3 years.

Entrance requirements:         Competitive entrance examination

                        and  West African School Certificate, i.e.
                             successful completion of secondary school
                             course.

                        or   General Certificate of Education (G.C.E.)
                             'O' level.

                        or   Teachers' Grade II Certificate, i.e.
                             successful completion of first 3 years
                             teacher training course.

Curriculum:               Education, including Teaching Practice.

                          2 teaching subjects, e.g. Mathematics and Physics,
                          or History and Geography, English Language.

                          1 or 2 minor or ancillary subjects, e.g. Art, Music,
                          Home Economics, etc.

Grading scale:            In final examination only.  Distinction or Pass may
                          be awarded for individual subjects and Practical
                          Teaching.

                          Pass = 40%
                          Distinction = 70% and above.

Certificate awarded:      Nigerian Certificate in Education (N.C.E.)
                          (Awarded by the University of Ibadan.

## ADVANCED TEACHERS' TRAINING COLLEGE, Ibadan (West)

For requirements and conditions see Yaba College above.

## ADULT EDUCATION

The Federal Ministry of Education (Lagos) has now embarked upon an
Adult Education Project.  Its purpose is providing  remedial, professional,
technical and commercial education to people over 14 years of age.  The
remedial aspect deals with literacy and also both primary and secondary
education up to the G.C.E. 'A' level in Arts and Science.  The vocational
aspect includes the training of uncertified teachers for the Teachers'
Grade II Certificate.

N I G E R I A N   A P P E N D I X

UNIVERSITY OF LONDON GENERAL CERTIFICATE OF EDUCATION EXAMINATION HELD

OVERSEAS (for Nigeria and Sierra Leone) - June 1964 and January 1965

This examination is held for private candidates.  Those who pass in 3 or 4 subjects at advanced level may gain direct entry into the university, provided they have passed in English Language at the ordinary level.

A pass in 5 subjects at one sitting at the ordinary level is regarded as equivalent to a pass in the West African School Certificate.

SPECIAL PROVISIONS FOR PRIVATE CANDIDATES

The examination is held for private candidates in Nigeria and Sierra Leone subject to the following supplementary conditions:

(1)  A candidate who has neither passed nor gained exemption from the Qualifying Test of the West African Examinations Council must enter for the General Certificate of Education examination in English Language and either pass in it or attain Grade 7 or 8 before he may take the General Certificate of Education examination in any other subject(s).

(2)  A candidate who passes in English Language in the General Certificate of Education examination is awarded a certificate in that subject.

(3)  A candidate who gains a General Certificate of Education in English Language, or who attains Grade 7 or Grade 8 in English Language, or who has passed previously the Qualifying Test of the West African Examinations Council or who is in a category previously exempted from the Qualifying Test may take the General Certificate of Education examination in any subjects at the ordinary level chosen from the list in paragraph 8 below subject to a maximum of 10 subjects, and will receive a certificate for the subjects in which he passes.

(4)  A candidate who holds one of the following qualifications may enter in 1 or more subjects up to a maximum of 4 subjects at the advanced level and 10 subjects in all:

        a statement of eligibility.

    or  a General Certificate of Education gained not later than 1962.

    or  a Matriculation Certificate of the University of London.

or    a Cambridge Oversea School Certificate.

or    a West African School Certificate.

or    a School Certificate of the West African Examinations Council.

or    a certificate (recording passes in 3 subjects recognized by the University of London as equivalent to the ordinary level of the General Certificate of Education).

(The General Certificate of Education awarded by the Local Examinations Syndicate of the University of Cambridge as a result of a performance in the Oversea School Certificate Examination will only be accepted if it records passes in at least 3 subjects including English Language gained at one and the same examination, or if it records passes in 3 subjects at the ordinary level together with a full pass in English Language at the Oversea School Certificate Examination, all 4 subjects having been taken at one and the same examination.)

or    a statement of result in the Oversea or West African School Certificate or a School Certificate of the West African Examinations Council recording credits in 3 subjects, including English Language, or in 3 subjects and a pass in English Language.

or    a General Certificate of Education (see above note in parenthesis) irrespective of when gained, in 3 or more subjects.

or    a Nigerian Teachers' Grade I Certificate.

(5) A candidate in Sierra Leone who supplies a certificate from the Principal of a recognized secondary school in Sierra Leone certifying that he has completed his studies in Form IV may be admitted to the examination on the same terms as candidates in the category listed in paragraph 4 above.

(6) Candidates in Nigeria who hold the Teacher's Higher Elementary (Grade II) Certificate and who are seeking to satisfy the academic requirements for the award of a Teacher's Grade I Certificate may enter at the advanced level in 1 or 2 subjects chosen from the following list which has been approved by the Education Department for that purpose:

| | |
|---|---|
| English Literature | Pure Mathematics |
| Geography | Physics |
| History | Chemistry |
| Religious Knowledge | Biology |

(7) A candidate who has passed at the ordinary level in any subject may sit at the advanced level in that subject even though he does not satisfy any of the conditions in (4), (5), and (6) above.

(8)   Subjects offered must be chosen from the following lists:

    (a)   <u>Ordinary Level</u>

| | |
|---|---|
| Art, Syllabus A | Hausa |
| Biology | History |
| Botany | History, Ancient |
| British Constitution | History of the British Common- |
| Chemistry |    wealth and Empire |
| Economics | History, British Economic |
| English Language | Igbo (Ibo) |
| English Literature | Latin, Syllabus A |
| Ewe | Mathematics, Pure |
| Fante | Mathematics, Additional |
| French | Music |
| Ga | Physics |
| General Science | Religious Knowledge |
| Geography | Spanish |
| Geology | Technical Drawing |
| German | Twi |
| Greek | Yoruba |

    (b)   <u>Advanced Level</u>

| | |
|---|---|
| Art, Syllabus A | History, Ancient |
| Biology | History, British Economic |
| Botany | Latin |
| British Constitution | Mathematics, Pure |
| Chemistry | Mathematics, Applied |
| Economics | Mathematics |
| English Literature | Music |
| French | Physics |
| Geography | Religious Knowledge |
| Geology | Spanish |
| German | Technical Drawing |
| Greek | Zoology |
| History | |

<u>Marks awarded - Grade system:</u>

| Advanced Level | Ordinary Level |
|---|---|
| Grades 1 | Grades 1 |
| 2 | 2 |
| 3 (All) Pass | 3 (All) Pass |
| 4 | 4 |
| 5 | 5 |
| 6 - Ordinary Level Pass | 6 |
| 7 - Failure | 7 |
| | 8   Failure |
| | 9 |

TEACHER TRAINING EXAMINATIONS

THE WEST AFRICAN EXAMINATIONS COUNCIL EXAMINATION FOR TEACHERS' HIGHER
  ELEMENTARY (Grade II) CERTIFICATE EXAMINATION (in use from 1962)

This examination is taken by the following categories of teachers:

(a)   Those who have had a previous 2-year training at an elementary
      college plus 2-year training at a higher elementary college.

(b)   Those who have had a straight 4-year course at a higher elementary
      college.

(c)   Those who have had a 2-year course after obtaining the West African
      School Certificate.

N.B.   All elementary training colleges closed at end of 1964.  Sub-
       sequently, teachers trained only at the Higher Elementary (Grade
       II) College and at the Advanced Teachers' College

SYLLABUSES FOR THE CENTRALLY EXAMINED SUBJECTS:

A.   English Language Syllabus

     (1)   General aims

           (a)   The understanding of ordinary spoken and written English.

           (b)   Accurate and effective expression in oral and written
                 forms.

     (2)   Language study.

           (a)   It is recommended that training colleges include in their
                 English Language courses the linguistic study of texts of
                 the level of Oxford Tales Retold, Second Series, and
                 Longman's Simplified English Series and that particular
                 attention should be paid to the forms of modern spoken
                 English exemplified in the texts selected.

           (b)   Students should through oral drills and written exercises
                 achieve mastery of:

                 (i)   Structural words, such as the personal and possessive
                       pronouns.
                       The reflexive and emphatic pronouns.
                       The demonstrative adjectives and pronouns.
                       The definite and indefinite articles.
                       Other adjectives and pronouns of number and quantity.

Adverb and adverb phrases.
Interrogative words and phrases.
Conjunctions.
Relatives.
Propositions.

(ii) Constructions dependent on common nouns, verbs and adjectives.

(iii) Verb forms and their uses: tenses in active and passive voice; participles; gerunds; infinitives.

(iv) The use of phrases and the use and construction of subordinate clauses.

(v) Word order.

(c)  Also to be studied:

(i) The formation of negatives (with special attention to verbs in simple past tense).

(ii) Questions and answers including questions containing an alternative, negative questions.

(iii) The use and omission of relatives including the distinction between defining and non-defining clauses.

(iv) Reported speech.

Much of this work will necessarily be remedial.

(3)  Comprehension of spoken and written English.

In comprehension work a distinction is made between those aspects of the understanding of any piece of language which depend upon the learner's previous experience or general knowledge and those which depend upon his interpretation of the actual language used (words, structures, patterns, common idioms, figure of speech, punctuation).

(4)  Oral English.

Special attention is paid to students' oral mastery of vocabulary and sentence forms, particularly the vocabulary and sentence forms presented in the text-books commonly used for the teaching of English in the primary schools. This necessarily includes some attention to speech training.

(5)  Written English.

Students are trained to write well-constructed sentences arranged in paragraphs. Practice is given in the writing of English for narrative, descriptive, explanatory or imaginative purposes and for the expression of opinions (but not reflective or emotive purposes) and in the use of English in writing of formal and informal letters.

B.   <u>Arithmetical Processes Syllabus</u>

   (1)  (a)  The first four rules applied to number, money, length, weight, time and capacity.

       (b)  Processes connected with the above, including reduction, simple and compound practice, short methods of money calculation.

   (2)  Prime factors, rules of divisibility.  Index notation square root of whole numbers and decimals.  Simple examples of H.C.F. and L.C.M.

   (3)  Fractions and decimals.  Fractions of numbers and concrete quantities, including simple decimalization of money and some knowledge of significant figures and approximation.

   (4)  Unitary method.  Ratio and proportion.  Averages.  Percentages. Simple interest.  Easy examples of compound interest.  Profit and loss.  Discount for cash.  Rate of working.  Speed: relation between distance, time and speed.  Average speed.  Very elementary examples of relative speed.

   (5)  Rectangular area and volume.  Area of a triangle as half base times height.  Area of trapezium and parallelogram.  Volumes of solids of uniform cross section.  The circle:  diameter, radium, circumference, area.  The cylinder:  area of curved surface and total surface area; volume.

   (6)  Simple foreign exchange; French and American coinage.

   (7)  Simple metric system.  Comparison of litres, kilometres, kilograms, etc., with corresponding British units.

   (8)  Graphical representation of rainfall, temperature and easy statistics, e.g., market prices, exports and imports.  Straight line graphs, e.g., time and distance, conversion from metric units to British units.  Interpretation.  Interpolation.

   (9)  Simple cash account:  personal and school.

  (10)  Elementary scale drawing:  use of geometrical instruments, choice of scale, drawing to scale simple shapes met with in everyday life, e.g., classroom, football field with marking, tennis court, running track, etc.

C.    Principles and Practice of Education Syllabus

I.    Principles of Education

(1)   The meaning and aims of education from the point of view of
      the individual, the family and the community, taking into
      account the geographical and historical setting.

(2)   A study, through direct observation and enquiry in the home and
      in the school, of the growth and development of normal children
      from birth to maturity, with emphasis on the school years.
      (The study takes into account the landmarks of development; the
      physical, mental, social and emotional aspects of the development;
      individual and sex differences between children.  It also deals
      with the social and environmental influences, i.e., of the home,
      the school, religion, society and its organizations, upon them.)

(3)   The needs of children and the stresses operating upon and within
      them, physically, mentally, socially and emotionally.  The
      innate tendencies associated with those needs and stresses, and
      the attitudes and roles adopted by the children to deal with
      them.  The emotions of fear, anger and love; their causes and
      forms of expression; means of controlling them.

(4)   The growth of standards of judgment (moral, social, aesthetic
      and economic) and the influence upon them of the parents, the
      teacher and the school.

(5)   The study of how children learn; the mental processes involved;
      the situations leading to learning and their results.

II.    Practice of Education

(6)   Preparing to Teach.
      (a)   Making the best use of existing school facilities (build-
            ings, furniture, wall-space, books, pictures, etc.)
            How a teacher can improve his classroom.

      (b)   Considering what to teach and why.  The curriculum and
            syllabuses to be taught.  The place and value in the
            curriculum of the various school subjects.

      (c)   Preparing lessons; lesson notes.  Planning a series of
            lessons; making schemes of work.  Making provision for
            backward and very bright children.

      (d)   Learning to use teaching aids:  the blackboard, text-
            books, other books, visual aids, e.g., pictures, diagrams,
            posters, models.  Modern aids to teaching, e.g., film-
            strips, films, radio, television, where these are within
            reach.  Treatment of a variety of materials and the making
            of suitable apparatus.  Display and storage.

(7)  The Teacher in the Classroom.

(a)  Varied lesson patterns; class teaching; activity methods
     in the classroom; individual work; group work; projects
     and assignments.  School visits and expeditions; special
     exhibits.

(b)  The art of questioning; the treatment of children's
     questions and answers.

(c)  The setting, supervision and correction of classwork.

(d)  The problems of classroom discipline.

(8)  Assessing and Recording the Results of Classroom Teaching.

(a)  Tests and examinations.
     Examinations as a means of assessing progress and
     diagnosing weaknesses.

(b)  Keeping records:  school events, work done, children's
     progress, and other matters required by regulations.

(9)  Planning for the Future.

Ordering supplies; making the timetable; organizing repairs.

602

SIERRA LEONE

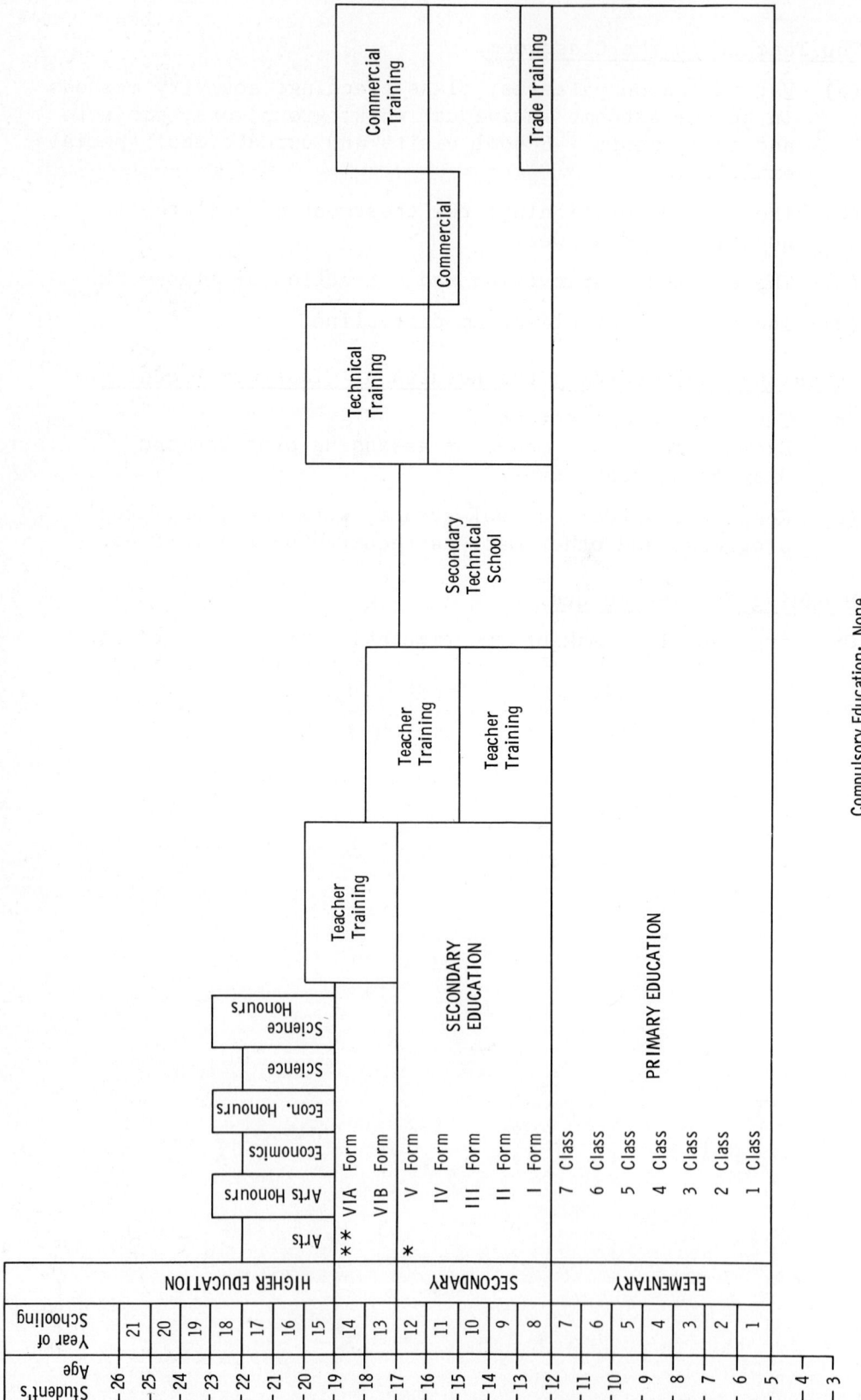

Compulsory Education: None       Academic Session: October–June
School year: September–July
Secondary Grading: 1–9 (Secondary Certificates)
1–Excellent
2–Very Good
3–6–Pass with Credit
7–8–Pass
9–Failure

SIERRA LEONE


Independence:  April 27, 1961.



BACKGROUND


Sierra Leone is composed of Northern Province (13,925 sq. mi.) with
Western Area (256 sq. mi.), Southern Province (7,868 sq. mi.), and Eastern
Province (5,876 sq. mi.).

Largest tribes are Mende and Temne, which make up 60% of African popu-
lation.  Smaller groups are:  Limba, Loko, Kono, Sherbro (Bulom), Susu
(Soso), Yalunka, Koranko, Kissi (Gisi), Krim, Vai, Mandingo, Fulani, and
Krios.  Europeans number approximately 3000; Asians, 5000.

English is the official language.  Mende is spoken widely in south, Temne
in north.  The lingua franca is Krio, a combination of English and words
from various West African and European languages.

1460, Portuguese explorer visited the coast of present Sierra Leone, and
called it "the land of the lion mountains."

Colony of Sierra Leone established by British philanthropists as home for
African slaves freed in England.  1787, first settlers sent to "Province
of Freedom."  In following years, other African settlers came from
England, West Indies, Nova Scotia, and elsewhere.

Sierra Leone Company formed, 1791, to administer the settlement.  1799,
the Company was given a Royal Charter, and Freetown given a corporation,
mayor, and alderman.  Up to 1861, additional land added through treaties
with local chiefs.  1807, when U.K. Parliament made slave trade illegal,
Colony was a base for enforcement.

Liberian frontier was established 1885 (changed in 1911); French frontier
was defined in 1895.  1896, British Protectorate was declared over the
hinterland of Sierra Leone, judicially and administratively separate from
the Colony.

During 19th and early 20th centuries, descendants of original Freetown
settlers--known as Creoles--became aristocracy with political influence.

1924, Constitution revised; 1951, an elected unofficial African majority
and party rule were provided; 1956, the Legislative Council was replaced
by a House of Representatives.  1958, conditions were set up for full
independence.

Became independent country, April 27, 1961, within Commonwealth of
Nations.

Western education was provided in Sierra Leone by 1787.  Christian
missions established elementary schools for girls and boys; later they
created separate secondary schools, designed for training Sunday School
teachers, mission workers, teachers, and clergy.

By 1910, a few schools came under government control, and grants were
made to primary and secondary schools conforming to uniform standards set
by Department of Education.


Colonial education:

> Primary education - 6 years:  Class 1 and Class 2, entrance 5-7
> years.  Standards 1-4.  Standards 5-7,
> in a few schools.

> From Standard 4, entry into secondary school after Common Entrance
> Examination; but 1-2 years additional training necessary.  Some
> entered secondary school from Standards 5, 6, 7, into Forms 1 or 2.

> Secondary education - 7 years:  Forms 1-6.  Form 6, 2 years (Parts
> B and A).

Primary teacher training schools admitted students from Standards 6 and
7 (primary) or Forms 1-2 (secondary).  Teachers' Elementary Certificate
(TEC) awarded.  Students from Forms 4-5, trained for Teachers' Certificate
(TC) and Teachers' Advanced Certificate (TAC) for secondary teaching.

1957, educational system revised, "Standards" in primary education renamed "Classes."  7-year primary course replaced 8-year course.

By 1959, 550 primary schools, 28 secondary schools (11 with Forms 1-6).


## PRESENT SYSTEM


## PRIMARY EDUCATION

Entry age:  5 years or older.

7-year course.

The language of instruction is generally English, although the vernacular
language is used in the early years.

CURRICULUM - GRADES III-VI
(Hours per week)

Subjects

| | |
|---|---|
| Arithmetic | 3 1/3 |
| Religion | 1 |
| Health | 1 |
| Reading | 5 |
| Social Studies | 1½ |
| English | 2 |
| Current Affairs | ½ |
| Art | 1 |
| Oral Composition | 1 |
| Written Composition | ½ |
| Music | 1 |
| Story and Drama | 1 |
| Physical Education | 1 |
| Science and Gardening | ½ |
| Spelling | ½ |
| Poetry | ½ |
| Handwork | ½ |
| Needlework | 1 |

## SECONDARY EDUCATION

There are 8 government secondary schools.  Other schools are private,
though government assisted.  The curriculum in each school leads to the
General Certificate of Education, the unifying factor for all schools.

Complete List of Secondary Schools

Government Schools:

| | |
|---|---|
| Prince of Wales | Koyeima |
| Bo Secondary | Jimmi |
| Magburaka Boys School | Freetown Secondary Technical |
| Kenema Girls School | Magburaka Girls School |

Sierra Leone Church:

| | |
|---|---|
| Annie Walsh | Schlenker |
| Sierra Leone Grammar School | Bishop Johnson |

**Methodist Church:**

Methodist Boys High School        Methodist Secondary
Methodist Girls High School       Wesley Boys Secondary
Njaluahun Girls School

**Evangelical United Brethren:**

Harford                           Jaiama Secondary
Albert Academy                    Yonibana
Taiama Secondary

**United Brethren in Christ:**

Centennial Secondary              Bumpe Secondary

**Roman Catholic Mission:**

St. Francis                       Holy Ghost
St. Joseph's Girls                Pujehum Girls
St. Joseph's Boys                 St. Joseph's
Queen of the Rosary               Yengema
St. Paul's Secondary

**West African Methodist Church:**

Collegiate

**United Christian Council:**

St. Andrews

**American Methodist Episcopal:**

AME High School

**American Wesley Mission**

Kamakwie                          Kamabai

**Ahmadiyya Mission:**

The Ahmadiyya, Bo                 The Ahmadiyya, Kissy

**Other:**

Freetown Secondary for Girls      Roosevelt Memorial
Secondary School                  Independence
Kalenten                          YWCA Vocational Institute
Kabala Secondary School           Huntingdon
Military School


Entry age:   12 years or older.

Entrance requirements:          Selective Entrance Examination.  Pupils
                                have to satisfy the requirements of the
                                Examination before proceeding to Form I.

Students failing Selective Entrance Examination may, if space permits,
enter Preparatory Form where they may again re-qualify for entrance
examination to Form I.

5-year course.

Curriculum:      Bible Knowledge, Biology, Chemistry, English, General
                 Science, Geography, Health Science, History, Mathematics,
                 Physics, Art, Domestic Science, French, Latin, Music, and
                 Physical Education.

## Mathematics Curriculum:

### Numbers

The ordinary processes of arithmetic.  The British and metric
systems of weights, measures, and money, including the monetary
systems of the respective Commonwealth countries of West Africa;
densities; temperature scales (centigrade and Farenheit); speeds.
Fractions, decimals; proportion and proportional parts; calculation
of averages, percentage and simple interest.  Use of common logarithms and square-root tables.

### Mensuration

The rectangle, triangle and figures derived from them, including
easy extensions to three dimensions.  The circle (including the
length of an arc in terms of the angle at the centre), cylinder,
cone, and sphere.

### Algebraic Symbols, Expressions, and Equations

Statement of rules and generalizations of arithmetical relations
in symbols; interpretation of statements given in symbolic form.
Evaluation of algebraic expressions; change of subject in a formula.
The use of indices.  Common factors, factors of such extensions as
occur in mensuration.  Factors of trinomial expressions.  Simple
fractions.  Simple equations, quadratic equations and simultaneous
linear equations in two variables.

### Graphs, Variation, Functionality

Graphs from numerical and statistical data.  Translation into
symbols of relations such as 'y is inversely proportional to x,'
'V varies as $X^3$,' and their illustration by sketch-graphs.  The
idea of a function of a variable and its graphical representation.

### Plane Geometry and Trigonometry

Angles and parallel lines, triangles and parallelograms, similarity,
Pythagoras's theorem, the circle.

## Three-dimensional Geometry

Parallel lines, parallel planes, normal to a plane, angle between a line and a plane, angle between two planes.

## Applied Geometry

Solution of triangles by the use of the sine and cosine rules and trigonometrical tables.  Scale drawing.

## Secondary Examinations

*At the end of the 5-year program, boys and girls sit for the General Certificate of Education of the West African Examinations Council, the members of which are Nigeria, Gambia, Ghana, and Sierra Leone.[+]

Subjects:

| | |
|---|---|
| Languages: | English Language, Latin, Greek, French, German, Italian, Ewe, Fante, Ga, Twi, Arabic. |
| General Subjects: | English Literature, Bible Knowledge, Islamic Religious Knowledge, History, Geography. |
| Mathematical Subjects: | Mathematics, Additional Mathematics. |
| Science Subjects: | General Science, Additional General Science, Physics, Chemistry, Biology, Agricultural Science. |
| Arts and Crafts: | Art, Music, Woodwork, Metalwork, Needlework and Dressmaking, Cookery, General House-craft. |
| Technical and Commercial Subjects: | Technical Drawing, Commercial Subjects, Health Science. |

Grading Scale:     1-9
                   1     Excellent
                   2     Very Good
                   3-6   Pass with credit
                   7-8   Pass
                   9     Failure

Previous to June 1965, students took the Joint Examination for the School Certificate and General Certificate of Education of the West African Examinations Council.  June 1965, West African School Certificate discontinued in Sierra Leone. (For Regulations prior to '65, see Gambia.)

[+]For booklet with detailed syllabuses for examination, send for REGULATIONS AND SYLLABUSES (University Press, Oxford; price 5 shillings).

Sixth Form
===========

2-year course.   Students take 1 to 4 subjects.

**Leads to <u>General Certificate of Education Advanced Level Examination of London University</u>.   (See Nigerian Appendix C.)

HIGHER EDUCATION
================

FOURAH BAY COLLEGE, THE UNIVERSITY COLLEGE OF SIERRA LEONE, Freetown
--------------------------------------------------------------------

Founded in 1827.   For a hundred years it was only institution of higher learning in West Africa.   Affiliated with Durham University in England in 1876, functioning thereafter as one of Durham University's Colleges. Academic programs, examinations and degrees all under supervision of Durham.   Plans to join Njala University College in the future, in establishing together an independent University of Sierra Leone.

| | |
|---|---|
| Entrance requirements: | <u>G.C.E.</u> with passes in English Language and either 4 or 5 other subjects including <u>either</u> Mathematics <u>or</u> 1 of the following: Biology, Botany, Chemistry, Chemistry-with-Physics, General Science, Geology, Physics, Zoology. At least 2 of the subjects must have been passed at advanced level. |

Faculty of Arts
----------------

| | |
|---|---|
| Entrance requirements: | 3-year course, see above. 4-year course:  <u>School Certificate</u>, <u>London Matriculation</u> or <u>G.C.E.</u> with at least 5 subjects at credit level including English Literature or a language other than English. |

Courses are offered for the degree of <u>B.A.</u> (General) in the following subjects:

   English, Latin, Greek, Greek and Roman Culture, Modern History, Religious Knowledge, Philosophy, French, Economics, Politics, Public Administration, Mathematics, Geography, and Geology.

There are Honours Schools in the following subjects:

   Mathematics, English, Geography, Theology, and History.

For admission to the Honours School in Mathematics a student must satisfy the examiners in Pure Mathematics and Applied Mathematics as set for the First Examination in General Studies or the equivalent.

At the end of the first year of Honours study, candidates pass a Preliminary Honours Examination in Mathematics and 1 of the following:

Philosophy, Geography, Physics, Economics, and Honours in English.

Candidates for Honours in English Language and Literature must pass Latin at the First Examination for the B.A. in General Studies or obtain the G.C.E. with Latin at advanced level.

Candidates pass at the end of their first year in the Honours School a Preliminary Honours Examination in English.

Candidates choose one of the following subsidiary subjects and pass the Second General Examination in it at the end of the first year of Honours Study, and the Final General Examination in it at the end of the second year of Honours Study:

French, Greek, Latin, History, Philosophy.

The Final Honours Examination consists of 9 papers.

Candidates for Honours in Geography must pass the Preliminary Honours Examination in Geography at the end of the first year in the Honours School.  This consists of:

(i)    Papers on Human, Physical and Regional Geography and an assessment in Practical Work.

(ii)   Papers to the level of the First or Second General Arts Examination in a modern language.

(iii)  Papers in one additional subject.

Candidates admitted to the Honours School from the first year of the General Arts Course have included 2 of the following in their university studies by the end of their Preliminary Honours year:

Economics, History, French, Geology, Statistics.

Candidates in the Honours School pass an examination at the end of the Honours I year in translation.

The Final Honours Examination consists of 8 papers of which 2 are taken at the end of the Honours I year.

For admission to the Honours School in Modern History a candidate must either have 2 advanced level subjects in the G.C.E. including History or a related subject, or have attained a satisfactory standard in the First Year General Arts Examination in Modern History.  At the end of the first year, there is a Preliminary Honours Examination.  The Final Honours Examination at the end of the third year shall consist of 9 papers.

## Education

### Diploma in Education

Entrance requirements:       Degree from an approved university.

1-year program.

### Master of Education

Admission is for graduates who already have a post-graduate qualification in Education and post-graduate teaching experience of at least one year. The course is in two parts:

  (a)  Preliminary Course which leads to examination in:

     (i)  A general paper and one paper in each of 2 of the following:
    (ii)  Theory of Education
   (iii)  History of Education
    (iv)  Comparative Education
     (v)  Educational Psychology

  (b)  On satisfactory completion of (a) candidates proceed by 2 years of further study to the Final Examination either by examination and dissertation or by thesis.

## Theology

Entrance requirements:      A degree from an approved university.

Religious Knowledge is offered for the B.A. in General Studies.

<table>
<tr><td><u>Licence in Divinity</u>:</td><td>3 year diploma course. Matriculation is not required for entrance, but candidates must hold the <u>West African School Certificate</u> or the <u>G.C.E.</u></td></tr>
<tr><td><u>Diploma in Biblical Studies</u>:</td><td>1-year course.</td></tr>
<tr><td><u>Diploma in Theology</u>:</td><td>2-year post-graduate course.</td></tr>
</table>

## Faculty of Economic Studies

### Bachelor of Arts in Economic Studies

Entrance requirements:      4-year course: <u>School Certificate</u>, <u>London Matriculation</u>, or <u>G.C.E.</u> with at least 5 subjects at credit level.
3-year course: general entrance requirements.

Courses are offered in the following subjects:

> Economics, Economic History, Law, Accounting, Public Administration, Public Finance, Statistics, Economic Geography, Comparative Government, Principles of Economic Development, International Relations, and French.

## Diploma in Public Administration

2-year course. Matriculation is not required.

Curriculum: Economics I, Economic History, Public Finance, Public Administration, Statistics, Comparative Government.

## B.A. with Honours in Economic Studies

Entrance requirements:    Bachelor of Commerce or Bachelor of Arts in Economic Studies or G.C.E. with passes in Economics and a modern foreign language at advanced level,

> or Residence for at least 3 terms and passes in 4 subjects including a foreign language in an examination for the degree of B.A. in General Studies or the degree of B.A. in Economic Studies,

> or Students who are qualified to matriculate and who present to the head of the Department of Economics evidence that they have pursued a systematic course of study which has prepared them to enter the Honours School.

The Preliminary Honours Examination consists of examinations in Economics, Economic History, and Statistics.

## Diploma in Economic Studies

2-year course. Matriculation not required.

The subjects of examination are similar to those for the degree of B.A. in Economic Studies. Candidates offer 4 subjects at the end of the first year and 4 at the end of the second year.

## Faculty of Pure and Applied Science

## Bachelor of Science, General Degree

Entrance requirements:    4-year course: School Certificate credit in 5 subjects including English Language,

Mathematics, and an approved science.

3-year course:  General requirements.

Departmental entrance requirements:

Botany:  Advanced level pass in Biology or Botany.
Chemistry:  Ordinary level pass in Chemistry.
Geography:  Ordinary level pass in Geography.
Pure Mathematics:  Ordinary level pass in Mathematics.
Physics:  Advanced level pass in Physics.
Zoology:  Ordinary level pass in either Biology or Zoology.

The University Examination consists of two parts:  the Qualifying Examination and the Final Examination for the General Degree.

The Qualifying Examination is conducted at two levels (Level I lower and Level II higher) and is taken in two stages.  The first is taken at the end of the first year of the 3-year degree course and consists of:

3 or 4 subjects at Level I.

The second stage taken one year later consists of:

2 or 3 subjects at Level II.

The Final General Degree Examination is taken in two subjects from Botany, Chemistry, Geography, Geology, Mathematics, Physics, Zoology.

## Bachelor of Science - Special Honours in One Subject

Candidates are selected for this degree after their Second Qualifying Examination.  The course covers a further 2 years in which one subject is studied intensively.

Special Honours Schools are available in Botany, Chemistry, Geography, Geology, Mathematics, Zoology, and Physics.

## Diploma in Engineering

3-year program including 6 months in industry.

Entrance requirements:      School Certificate or G.C.E. with at least
                            4 credits or "O" level passes including
                            English and Mathematics.  Physics and
                            Chemistry must have been offered with at
                            least a credit in one and pass in the other.
                            For direct entry into the 2nd year, candi-
                            dates must have at least 2 subjects at
                            advanced level including Mathematics or
                            Physics.

The Diploma may be taken in Civil Engineering, Mechanical Engineering, Electrical Engineering.

The Final Year Examination is taken in two parts.  Part I consists of written papers in all subjects in the branch of Engineering of specialization.  Part II consists of a written paper in one of the Final Year subjects in which advanced courses are given and submission of a short dissertation or an approved topic or design project.

## Bachelor of Science in Applied Science

Students who pass the Second Diploma Examination with sufficient distinction may transfer to the University of Newcastle to take the degree course with certain exemptions.

Students who complete the Diploma course and gain sufficient merit in the Final Examination may also be recommended for transfer to the University of Newcastle.

## Faculty of Law

To be established in October, 1965.

## NJALA UNIVERSITY COLLEGE, Njalo via Mano

Founded in 1964 with assistance of U.S. Agency for International Development to train agriculturists and teachers to degree level and for responsibility for all agricultural research and extensions.

Entrance requirements:     West African School Certificate with credits in English, Mathematics, or a science subject, and 3 additional subjects.

or     G.C.E. (University of London) at ordinary level in 5 subjects, including English and either Mathematics or a science subject.

or     G.C.E. (University of London) at advanced level in 2 subjects and at ordinary level in 2 subjects.

Faculties:

    Agriculture
    Education
    Basic Sciences

A Faculty of Arts is planned.

Language of instruction:        English.

Degree course:  4 years in all faculties.

Curricula are offered in Agriculture, Home Economics, and Teacher
Education.

<u>Degrees awarded</u>:

      Bachelor of Science in Agriculture
      Bachelor of Science in Home Economics
      Bachelor of Science or Bachelor of Arts in Education

There are also 2-year Certificate courses in Agriculture and Home
Economics with entrance requirements of at least 3 years of secondary
education.


## VOCATIONAL AND TECHNICAL EDUCATION

### TECHNICAL INSTITUTE, Freetown

Government secondary school, technical co-educational.

Entrance requirements:          Selective Entrance Examination.

Syllabus followed of <u>School Certificate</u> of the West African Examination
Council.

Subjects offered:

| | |
|---|---|
| English Language (Compulsory) | Technical Drawing |
| English Literature | Woodwork |
| Mathematics (alternative B) | Metalwork |
| Additional Mathematics | Housecraft |
| Physics | Needlework and Dressmaking |
| Chemistry | Biology |
| Commercial Subjects | |

Transfers from other recognized secondary schools are accepted in Form I,
II, or III.


### Certificate Course - Full Time

This course is designed to lead to the <u>Ordinary Certificate in Building</u>
or <u>Mechanical Engineering</u> of the City and Guilds of London Institute.

4-year program, but may be completed in 3 years by students with approved
qualifications.

<u>TIMETABLE</u>
(Hours per week)

<u>Subjects</u>

| | |
|---|---|
| English | 5 |
| Mathematics | 5 |
| Science | 4 |
| Technical Drawing | 6 |
| Woodwork | 3 |
| Metalwork | 3 |
| Projects | 4 |
| Total | 30 |

## Syllabus of Preliminary Year (PS1) in Mathematics and Science

### Arithmetic:

General method of finding square roots. Graphs based on formulas. Logarithms--powers, indices, use of tables, multiplication, division, powers and roots by logs.

### Mensuration:

Problems on areas. Surface areas of cone and pyramid. Volume of cone, pyramid and sphere. Volumes and weight per unit volume. Problems involving depth of liquid in cylinders.

### Algebra:

Simultaneous equations. Algebra fractions with easy denominators. Factors and simple factorization. $(a+b)(a-b)$; $(a+b)^2$; $(a-b)^2$ with geometric proofs.

### Trigonometry:

Ratios of sine, cosine and tangent of acute angles. Use of tables. Simple problems involving use of these rations.

### Mechanics:

Density. Archimedes' principle and flotation. Further work on moments. Graphical composition and resolution of forces. Triangle of forces. Work and efficiency. Horsepower. Introduction to friction and work lost due to friction.

### Heat:

Conversion of temperature scales. Quantity of heat, calorie, B.T.U., and therm. Specific heat. Latent heat and its application.

Electricity:

Induction. Principles of the electric motor and dynamo. Chemical
effects of an electric current. Simple cells. Electrical units.
Ohm's Law. Use of ammeters, voltmeters and galvanometers.

General:

Humidity of air. Hygrometers. Composition of water. Porosity.
Capillarity and methods of preventing it. Siphons and pumps. Acids,
bases and salts. Neutralization. Reduction and its use in metal
extraction. Simple introduction to atomic structure and the use of
symbols and formulae.

## Telecommunications Course - Full-Time

This course is for the Intermediate Certificate of the City and Guilds of
London Institute Telecommunications Technicians' Course.

1-year course.

Curriculum:    English, Mathematics, Engineering Science, Telecommunications
               Principles and Practice, Radio and Line Transmission, Labo-
               ratory Work.

Successful candidates from this course are eligible to attend a further
full-time course in preparation for the Final Telecommunications Technicians'
Certificate.

## Short Commercial Course

A course leading to the Clerk Typist's Certificate of the Royal Society
of Arts.

Entrance requirements:        Completion of Form III.

Duration of course:  3 terms.

Curriculum:    English, Bookkeeping, Typewriting.

## Long Commercial Course

A course leading to the Group Certificate in Secretarial Subjects of the
Royal Society of Arts.

Entrance requirements:        Completion of Form IV.

3-year program.

## CURRICULUM
### (Hours per week)

Subjects

1st year:

| | | |
|---|---|---|
| English Language and Literature | | 10 |
| Shorthand | | 10 |
| Typewriting | | 5 |
| Tutorial | | 5 |
| | Total | 30 |

2nd year:

| | | |
|---|---|---|
| English Language | | 7 |
| Shorthand | | 9 |
| Typewriting | | 7 |
| Secretarial Duties | | 7 |
| | Total | 30 |

3rd year:

| | | |
|---|---|---|
| English with Literature | | 5 |
| Shorthand | | 10 |
| Typewriting | | 5 |
| Office Practice | | 4 |
| Commerce and Accounts | | 3 |
| Tutorial | | 3 |
| | Total | 30 |

## Day Release Courses

It is a condition of articled apprenticeship that the apprentice is to be released for one day a week to attend formal instruction.

The Institute provides a class on one day a week for the following City and Guilds of London Institute courses:

Telecommunications Technicians' Course
Motor Vehicle Technicians' Work
Mechanical Engineering Craft Practice
Blacksmith's and Welders' Work
Ordinary Certificate in Building

Day Release students must attend compulsorily one evening a week, to advance their general education, particularly in written and spoken English.

## Evening Classes

Courses are offered leading to the G.C.E., Royal Society of Arts Certificates, and classes in General Engineering and General Building.

OTHER GOVERNMENT AIDED TECHNICAL INSTITUTIONS:

The Trade Centre, Magburaka

Freetown Trade Centre, Kissy

The Technical Institute, Kenema

The Vocational School for Girls, Bo

Young Women's Christian Association Vocational Institute, Freetown

PRIVATE TECHNICAL TRAINING:

The Trade Center, Lunsar

The Sierra Leone Selection Trust Institution, Yengema

The Delco Institution, Marampa

## TEACHER EDUCATION

## TEACHER'S ELEMENTARY CERTIFICATE

Discontinued in September, 1964, but students with work in progress issued the certificate until 1966.

Entrance requirements:        7 years of primary education.

3-year program.

The Examination is in 3 parts:

Part I:    Academic subjects
Part II:   Professional subjects
Part III: Practice teaching

Part I:    English Language, English Literature, Arithmetic, Geography, History, General Science, and 2 of the following:

Handicrafts/Needlework, Religious Knowledge, Music, Art, Physical and Health Education.

Part II:   Principles of Education, Methods of Teaching.

Part III:   Practical Teaching.

To obtain the certificate a candidate must obtain 45% in every subject offered in the examination.


TEACHER'S CERTIFICATE

Entrance requirements:          One of the following:

> (i)   Holder of Teacher's Elementary Certificate awarded at least 2 years earlier.
>
> (ii)  Persons who have completed Form III of a secondary school.
>
> (iii) Unqualified teachers with at least 4 years teaching experience.
>
> (iv)  Candidates who have passed the West African Examinations Council Form III Examination with English and Arithmetic.
>
> (v)   Candidates who have passed the School Certificate or G.C.E.   'O' level in English Language and one other subject of the T.C. course (Science, Mathematics, History, Geography, Religious Knowledge, Art, Music, or Domestic Science).

Duration of the course:   2 years for holders of the Teacher's Elementary Certificate; 3 years for others.

The Examination is in 3 parts:
    Part I:     Academic subjects
    Part II:    Professional subjects
    Part III:   Practical teaching

Part I:

A.  Compulsory subjects:   English Language, English Literature, Elementary Mathematics, History and Civics, Geography, General Science, Physical Education.

B.  Optional subjects:   Religious Knowledge, Domestic Science, Music, Art, Craft.

Part II:  Principles of Education, Methods of Education.

Part III: Practical Teaching.

To obtain a certificate a candidate must obtain 40% in every subject of the examination.  Candidates who obtain 60-69% are awarded a credit in

that subject.  Candidates who obtain 70% or over are awarded a distinction
in that subject.  Candidates who obtain at least 75% in 2 subjects are
awarded a certificate with distinction provided that they obtain not less
than 50% in Practical Teaching.


TEACHER'S ADVANCED CERTIFICATE

Entrance requirements:          School Certificate or 4 credits at School
                                Certificate or 4 passes at G.C.E. ('O'
                                level).

3-year program.

The Examination is conducted in 3 parts:

        Part I:    Academic subjects
        Part II:   Professional subjects
        Part III:  Practical teaching

Part I:    English Language and Literature, Mathematics, Geography, History,
           Religious Knowledge, Science, Domestic Science, Music, Art,
           Physical and Health Education, a modern language, Agriculture,
           Crafts, Commercial Subjects.

           A candidate must follow a course in English and 2 of the above.
           All students attend courses in Art, Physical Education, and
           Music in the first year.

Part II:   Principles of Education, Methods of Teaching.

Part III:  Practical Teaching.

To obtain a certificate a candidate must obtain 40% in every subject of
the examination.  Candidates who obtain 60% are awarded a credit in that
subject.  Candidates who obtain 70% or over are awarded a distinction in
that subject.  Candidates who obtain at least 75% in 2 subjects are
awarded a certificate with distinction provided that they obtain not less
than 50% in Practical Teaching and pass the whole examination at the
first sitting.

The training of non-graduate teachers is undertaken in the Freetown
Teachers' College and the Milton Margai Training College near Freetown
and at 6 institutions in the provinces:  a government college at Magburaka,
and Roman Catholic and Protestant institutions.


A.I.D.-SIERRA PROJECTS

Under a contract with the U.S. Agency for International Development (A.I.D.)
Hampton Institute in Virginia established the Rural Training Institute in
Kenema, October 1962.  The Institute serves as a demonstration training

center for improved methods of vocational education, including agriculture and related academic areas for out-of-school youths and adults for
the purpose of improving the economic and social living standards in
rural communities.  Hampton Institute has supplied a community development team, including personnel in agriculture, nutrition and child care,
electrical trades, masonry, carpentry, and allied crafts.

The first group of students graduated in June 1964.  Certificates were
provided for the graduates by A.I.D.

Since January 1965 the Institute has also held short courses for adult
students, primarily in the building trades.  These students include adults
from the A.I.D. "self-help projects" under the sponsorship of Earl
Diffenderfer, Rural Development Advisor.  The object of these courses is
to prepare workers for the construction of primary schools, health centers
and community buildings throughout the country.

A second Rural Training Institute opened in Batkanu, in the Northern Province, in September 1965.

# FRENCH-SPEAKING WEST AFRICA

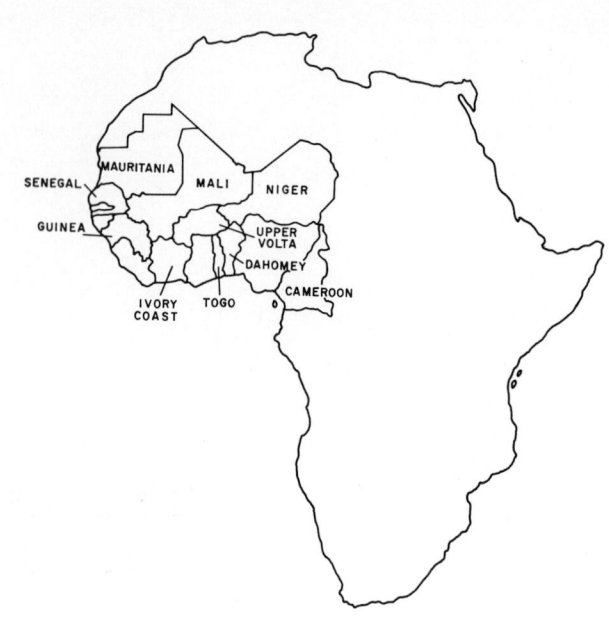

# FRENCH - SPEAKING

# WEST AFRICA

| Country and Capital | Area (sq. miles) | Est. Population | Independence Dates or Political Status | Official Language |
|---|---|---|---|---|
| FEDERAL REPUBLIC OF CAMEROUN<br>Yaoundé | 193,681 | 4,800,000 | 1 January 1960 (Remained within the French Community) | French |
| REPUBLIC OF DAHOMEY<br>Porto Novo | 44,685 | 2,050,000 | 1 August 1960 (Entente country) | French |
| REPUBLIC OF GUINEA<br>Conakry | 98,865 | 3,000,000 | 2 October 1958 | French |
| REPUBLIC OF IVORY COAST<br>Abidjan | 127,520 | 3,400,000 | 7 August 1960 (Entente country) | French |
| REPUBLIC OF MALI<br>Bamako | 465,050 | 4,900,000 | 22 September 1960 | French |
| ISLAMIC REPUBLIC OF MAURITANIA<br>Nouakchott | 491,300 | 1,000,000 | 28 November 1960 (Remained within the French Community) | French |
| REPUBLIC OF NIGER<br>Niamey | 459,180 | 2,900,000 | 3 August 1960 (Entente country) | French |
| REPUBLIC OF SENEGAL<br>Dakar | 76,084 | 3,100,000 | 20 August 1960 | French |
| REPUBLIC OF TOGO<br>Lomé | 22,002 | 1,000,000 | 28 November 1960 | French |
| REPUBLIC OF UPPER VOLTA<br>Ouagadougou | 113,100 | 4,400,000 | 5 August 1960 (Entente country) | French |

FEDERAL REPUBLIC OF CAMEROUN

| Student's Age | Year of Schooling | | | | |
|---|---|---|---|---|---|
| 26 | 20 | HIGHER EDUCATION | Law and Econ. Science ** * | Arts and Human Science | Science |
| 25 | 19 | | | | |
| 24 | 18 | | | | |
| 23 | 17 | | | | |
| 22 | 16 | | | | |
| 21 | 15 | | Higher Federal School of Agriculture | National Sports Institute | School of Admin. | Milit. Sch. |
| 20 | 14 | | | | |
| 19 | 13 | SECONDARY | Terminale | | |
| 18 | 12 | | I Première | | |
| 17 | 11 | | II Seconde | Short Cycle (cycle d'enseignement général moyen) | |
| 16 | 10 | | III Troisième | | Technical Education |
| 15 | 9 | | IV Quatrième | | |
| 14 | 8 | | V Cinquième | Observation (cycle d'observation) | Artisan/rural/ homemaking section |
| 13 | 7 | | VI Sixième | | |
| 12 | 6 | ELEMENTARY | Middle (Cours Moyen) | | |
| 11 | 5 | | | | |
| 10 | 4 | | Elementary (Cours élémentaire) | ELEMENTARY EDUCATION | |
| 9 | 3 | | Preparatory (Cours préparatoire) | | |
| 8 | 2 | | Initiation (Section d'initiation) | | |
| 7 | 1 | | | | |
| 6 | | | Nursery School | | |
| 5 | | | | | |
| 4 | | | | | |
| 3 | | | | | |

SECONDARY EDUCATION

TEACHER TRAINING

Practical agriculture

Compulsory education: none

School year: 9 months. North Cameroun: July–March
South Cameroun: Mid-September–June

Secondary grading: 20 Perfect
10/20 pass mark

FEDERAL REPUBLIC OF CAMEROUN
(République Fédérale du Cameroun)


Independence:  January 1, 1960.


BACKGROUND


The Federal Republic of Cameroun has a heterogenous population with
approximately 80 different tribes.  Main ethnic groups:  in south, Tiv
and Beti (the latter concentrated in Yaoundé area); in north, Bamileke,
Fang, and Fulani predominate.

French and English are official languages.  There are a large number of
tribal languages and dialects, most belonging to Bantu and semi-Bantu
language families.

Portuguese explorers, merchants, and missionaries came throughout the
15th century, but no permanent settlements.  1845, British missionaries.

In 1884, the territory came under German rule; United Kingdom recognized
German Protectorate.  During German occupation, 1884-1914, the areas
later to become British Cameroons and the Cameroun Republic were undiffer-
entiated parts of the German Protectorate of Kamerun.  British and French
military forces took possession and partitioned the Protectorate, 1916:
one-fifth of ex-German Cameroons, contiguous to Eastern Nigeria, claimed
by British; four-fifths of area ceded to France.  Versailles Treaty
ratified division of territory; under League of Nations, both territories
administered as Class B mandates.  In 1946, converted into trust territories under United Nations.  In 1957, French Cameroons became internally
self-governing.  January 1, 1960, acquired full independence, assuming
the name Cameroun Republic.

Former Southern Cameroons under British trusteeship and the Cameroun
Republic merged to become Federal Republic of Cameroun, October 1, 1961.
(Northern Cameroons became part of Nigeria, July 11, 1961.)  Following
unification, the territories renamed West Cameroun and East Cameroun.


East Cameroun - Pre-Federation

First western schools introduced by Baptist missionaries, 1843.  Until
German Protectorate, missions of various denominations set up schools.
By 1913, only 4 public schools, at Victoria, Douala, Yaoundé, Garoua.

July 25, 1921, the French educational system was introduced, with French the language of instruction, and cycles of study and final certificates patterned after metropolitan France.  By 1960, 63% of school-age population in school; 96% of this number in primary schools.

Ten-Year Development Program, 1960-1970, to emphasize adaptation of school system to national needs.

## West Cameroun - Pre-Federation

Formerly the southern section of the trust territory of the British Cameroons, West Cameroun was faced at the time of federation with the problem of integrating their former British system of education with the French system of education in East Cameroun.

Before October 1960, Nigeria (which became independent at that time) administered the trust territory under British supervision, with responsibility for the Southern Cameroons assigned to Lagos, for the Northern Cameroons, to Kano.  Nigeria also offered access to its secondary and technical schools, and to the University College of Ibadan.  At Nigeria's independence, Great Britain took direct administration.

The first schools were initiated by mission groups.  Among the earliest were the English Baptists, Catholic Pallotine Fathers, Basel Mission, and American Presbyterian mission.  By 1910, 410 mission schools:  more than half maintained by the Roman Catholic Mill Hill Fathers.

Education modeled on British system.  Those completing 8-year primary course and passing the government Standard 6 examination received a First School Leaving Certificate.

3 secondary schools:  2 for boys, St. Joseph's College, Sasse, conducted by Roman Catholic mission, with a 6-year course leading to West African School Certificate, and Southern Cameroons Protestant College, Bamenda area, conducted by Basel and Baptist missions, with a 5-year course leading to W.A.S.C.

Technical and vocational training in 3 schools.  Teacher training in 2 government and 11 voluntary-agency schools.  No higher education.  Students given overseas scholarships.

## PRESENT SYSTEM

### PRE-SCHOOL EDUCATION

Entry age:  3-5 years.

Nursery education concerned with the physical, intellectual, and moral development of young children.

## PRIMARY EDUCATION

Entry age:  6 years.

6-year program.  Instruction in French.

Curriculum:      Morals, Reading, Writing, French, Arithmetic, History and Geography, Observational Exercises, Manual Work and Art, Singing, Physical Education, Agricultural Work.

Certificat d'études primaires élémentaires (C.E.P.E.) awarded after final examination.

Sections pratiques de fin d'études:  special sections for those who have not been able to enter secondary or technical schools.  2-year course concentrating on agriculture and village life, after completion of primary education.

## SECONDARY EDUCATION

Entry age:  11-13 years.  Special age dispensations granted by government.

Entrance requirements:         C.E.P.E. and successful passing of the examination, concours d'entrée en sixième. C.E.P.E. may be waived according to age and placement of the concours.

Instruction in French.

2 types of secondary school:

    (1)  Lycée:  offers 7-year program leading to Baccalauréat.

    (2)  Collège d'enseignement général:  offers 2 types of courses: enseignement long, which enables student to continue after the Brevet (4 years) in another school towards a Baccalauréat; and enseignement court, leading only to the Brevet.

### LYCEE PROGRAM - SERIE MODERNE
#### (Hours per week)

| Subjects | Class: | 6 | 5 | 4 | 3 | 2 | 1 | Terminales Phil. | Sc.Exp. | Math. |
|---|---|---|---|---|---|---|---|---|---|---|
| French | | 7 | 6 | 5 | 5 | 4 | 4 | 2 | | |
| English | | 5 | 5 | 3 | 3 | 3 | 3 | 2 | 2 | 2 |
| 2nd Language | | - | - | 3 | 4 | 4(M) | 4(M) | - | - | - |

| Subject | | | | | | | | |
|---|---|---|---|---|---|---|---|---|
| Mathematics | 4 | 4 | 3 | 4 | 5 | 5 | 2 | 4 | 9 |
| History and Geography | 3 | 3 | 3 | 4 | 4 | 4 | 4 | 4 | 4 |
| Natural Sciences | 2 | 2 | 1 | 1 | 3(M') | 3(M') | 2 | 5 | 2 |
| Physical Sciences | - | - | - | - | 5 | 5 | 2 | 5 | 2 |
| Art | 1 | 1 | 1 | 1 | - | - | - | - | - |
| Music | 1 | 1 | 1 | 1 | 1 | - | - | - | - |
| Physical Education | 2 | 2 | 2 | 2 | 2 | 2 | 2 | 2 | 2 |
| National Youth | 3 | 2 | 2 | 2 | - | - | - | - | - |
| Philosophy | - | - | - | - | - | - | 9 | 5 | 3 |

## SERIE CLASSIQUE

| Subjects Class: | 6 | 5 | 4 | 3 | 2 | | 1 | |
|---|---|---|---|---|---|---|---|---|
| | | | | | AB | C | AB | C |
| French | 5 | 4 | 4 | 4 | 4 | 4 | 4 | 4 |
| English | 4 | 3 | 3 | 3 | 3 | 3 | 3 | 3 |
| Latin | 4 | 5 | 3 | 3 | 3 | 3 | 3 | 3 |
| 2nd Language | - | - | 3 | 3 | 4 | - | 4 | - |
| Mathematics | 4 | 4 | 3 | 4 | 3 | 5 | 3 | 5 |
| History and Geography | 3 | 3 | 3 | 3 | 4 | 4 | 4 | 4 |
| Natural Sciences | 2 | 1 | 2 | 1 | - | - | - | - |
| Physical Sciences | - | - | - | - | 3 | 4 | 3 | 5 |
| Art | 1 | 1 | 1 | 1 | - | - | - | - |
| Music | 1 | 1 | 1 | 1 | - | - | - | - |
| Physical Education | 2 | 2 | 2 | 2 | 2 | 2 | 2 | 2 |
| National Youth | 2 | 2 | 2 | 2 | - | - | - | - |

(Terminal year in série classique concentrates on French, Greek, and Latin, with the accent on classical languages.)

## ENSEIGNEMENT LONG - Collège d'enseignement général (C.E.G.)

| Subjects Class: | 6 | 5 | 4 | 3 |
|---|---|---|---|---|
| Geography | 1 | 1 | 1 | 1 |
| History | 1½ | 1½ | 1½ | 2 |
| French | 7 | 7 | 6 | 6 |
| Art | 1 | 1 | 1½ | 1½ |
| English | 5 | 5 | 4 | 4 |
| Science | 1½ | 1½ | 1 | 3 |
| Mathematics | 3 | 3 | 4 | 4 |
| Civics | ½ | ½ | - | - |
| Morals | - | - | ½ | 1 |
| German | - | - | 4 | 4 |
| Bible | 3 | 3 | 3 | 2 |
| Physical Education | 4 | 4 | 4 | - |
| Music | 1 | 1 | 1 | 1 |

ENSEIGNEMENT COURT

| Subjects               Class: | 6 | 5 | 4 | 3 |
|-------------------------------|---|---|---|---|
| French                        | 7 | 7 | 6 | 6 |
| Civics                        | 1 | 1 | - | - |
| History                       | 2 | 2 | 2 | 2 |
| Geography                     | 1 | 1 | 1 | 1 |
| Science                       | 2 | 2 | 5 | 5 |
| Music                         | 1 | 1 | 1 | 1 |
| English                       | 5 | 5 | 5 | 5 |
| Mathematics                   | 5 | 5 | 5 | 5 |
| Bible                         | 2 | 2 | 2 | 2 |
| Physical Education            | 1 | 1 | 1 | 1 |
| Girls:  Sewing                | 2 | 2 | 3 | 3 |
|         Home Economics        | 1 | 1 | - | - |
|         Art                   | 2 | 2 |   |   |
|         Cooking               | - | - | 3 | 3 |
|         Domestic Science      | - | - | - | 1 |

Programs[+] and working conditions are similar to corresponding ones in the French system. French, Geography, and History are now adapted to the Cameroun.

Grading:  from 0 to 20.  10/20 = average pass.

If total average of year is passing, but if total average for major subjects (French, Mathematics, English) is below 8/20, the student is not promoted.

Examinations prepared for:     Brevet élémentaire (in écoles normales sections), end of 4th year.

Brevet d'études du premier cycle (in lycées and C.E.G.). This is a Cameroun diploma countersigned by the Inspecteur d'Académie which the Académie of Bordeaux has in Yaoundé, working with the Cameroun Ministry of Education. Same value in French-speaking world as the French B.E.P.C. Examination and syllabi from Cameroun Ministry of Education.
Grade:  maximum 220 points, pass with 110/220. Mathematics, maximum 60 pts. French, 80 pts. English, 40 pts. Science, 20 pts. History-Geography, 20 pts. End of 4th year.

[+]May be obtained by writing for "Horaires Programmes Examens Instructions Officielles," from Editions S.U.D.E.L., 5 rue Palatine, Paris VI, France.

\*Probation (examen probatoire) - formerly the
first part of the Baccalauréat.  Examinations
direct from Bordeaux.  End of 6th year.

\*\*Baccalauréat - examinations direct from
Bordeaux.  End of 7th year.

## PRIVATE SECONDARY SCHOOLS

Curriculum identical to that of official institutions.  Only the government is able to grant diplomas.  Private schools may only grant a certificate showing enrollment, date, class and grade average.  This certificate
has no value except in transfer to another school.

When private schools are recognized, financial aid is given by government.

Some private schools admit pupils after 13 years of age.

## HIGHER EDUCATION

### THE FEDERAL UNIVERSITY OF THE CAMEROUN, Yaoundé

Created by decree of July 26, 1962.

Entrance requirements:          Hold a diploma of completion of secondary
                                studies (Baccalauréat, General Certificate
                                of Education, Advanced Level, Higher School
                                Certificate, or equivalent qualification).

                          or    Pass a probation examination for entry to
                                the university.

                          or    Hold the Brevet d'études du premier cycle,
                                or an equivalent diploma, for students
                                preparing for the Capacité en droit (Certifi-
                                cate of Legal Competency).

Faculties:

    Law anc Economic Sciences
    Art and Human Sciences
    Science

Instruction in French.

Diplomas awarded:

    Baccalauréat

    Licence en droit et ès sciences économiques

Capacité en droit

Licence ès lettres et ès sciences humaines

Licence ès sciences

Length of normal scholastic course:  3 years
                                 (2 years, Capacité en Droit)


Faculty of Law and Economic Sciences

Licence en droit (Bachelor of Laws)

| | |
|---|---|
| 1st year: | Civil Law, Constitutional and General Public Law, General Economics, History of Cameroun Institutions, History of Political Ideas, History of Economic Facts, Ideas of Sociology. |
| 2nd year: | Private Law, Administrative and General Economic Law, General Penal Law and Penal Proceedings. |
| 3rd year: | Licence in Private Law:  Business Law, Civil Proceedings, International Private Law. |
| | Licence in Public Law:  Business Law, Financial Institutions, Financial Economics, International Public Law and International Institutions, Public Liberty. |
| | Licence in Economic Sciences:  Business Law, Financial Economics, International and Inter-African Economic Relations, Systems and Structures. |

Capacité en droit

| | |
|---|---|
| 1st year: | Civil Law, Commercial and Business Law, Constitutional Law and Public Liberty. |
| 2nd year: | General Penal Law and Penal Proceedings, Civil Proceedings and Channels of Execution, General Economics, Management of Businesses and Accountancy, Fiscal Law. |

Baccalauréat en droit

2-year program.  May be taken with or without regular Baccalauréat of secondary studies.

## Faculty of Arts and Human Sciences

### Certificat d'études supérieures de littérature générale

Literary History, Linguistics, Modern Languages (optional Modern Letters), Classical Languages (optional Classical Letters), History of Civilizations, Geography, Philosophy.

### Certificat d'études supérieures d'histoire des civilisations

History and Geography Section: Literary History, History of Civilizations, Geography.

Human Sciences Section: Literary History, History of Civilizations, Philosophy.

## Faculty of Science

### Certificat d'études supérieures de sciences physiques, chimiques et naturelles

Animal Biology, Plant Biology, Geology, Physics, Chemistry, Mathematics.

OTHER HIGHER INSTITUTIONS:

## HIGHER FEDERAL SCHOOL OF AGRICULTURE (Ecole Fédérale Supérieure d'Agriculture

Created by decrees of May 8, 1960 and July 9, 1962.

Located at Nkolbisson-Yaoundé.

Entrance requirements:      Baccalauréat for the preparatory year.

Certificat d'études supérieures de sciences physiques, chimiques et naturelles, awarded for the 1st regular year of higher training after preparatory year.

Instruction in French.

Length of course:  4 years, including 1 preparatory year.

Preparation for Diplôme d'ingénieur agronome (diploma in Agricultural Engineering).

INSTITUT NATIONAL DES SPORTS (National Sports Institute), Yaoundé

Created by decree of December 31, 1960.

Entrance requirements:          Age 18-26 years.

                                B.E.P.C. for masters in Physical Education
                                (maîtres).

                                Baccalauréat for professeurs of Physical
                                Education.

                                Pass entry examination.

Length of course:    3 years for maîtres of Physical Education.
                     4 years for professeurs of Physical Education.

Diplomas awarded:

       Diplôme de maître  d'éducation physique
       Certificat de professeur d'éducation physique

ECOLE CAMEROUNAISE D'ADMINISTRATION (Cameroun School of Administration),
    Yaoundé

Created by decree of July 27, 1959.

Entrance requirements:          Age 18-30 years.

                                Baccalauréat for students.

                                B.E. or B.E.P.C. for civil servants and
                                4 years' seniority in category C of the
                                public service.

                                Pass entry examination.

Instruction in French.

Length of course:   2 to 3 years, according to the case.

Diploma awarded:

       Diplôme de l'école Camerounaise d'administration

ECOLE MILITAIRE INTERARMES, Yaoundé

Created by decree of May 31, 1962.

Entrance requirements:          Age 18-25 years.

Pass entrance examination (allowance is given
to holders of the Baccalauréat, B.E.P.C.,
B.E.C., or the B.E.I.).

Instruction in French.

Length of course:  2 scholastic years.

Students are subject to an examination on completion of the course.


## VOCATIONAL AND TECHNICAL EDUCATION

Professional and technical training given in:

Technical lycées:  7 years study

Technical collèges (collèges techniques):  5 years study

Colleges of technical instruction (collèges d'enseignement technique):  4 years study

Artisan, rural, and homemaking sections:  2 years study


Entrance requirements:        Pass entrance examination.

Entry age:      11-15 years for technical collèges and lycées
                13-17 years for the colleges of technical instruction

Examinations prepared for:    Baccalauréat technique

                              Brevet d'enseignement commercial et
                              industriel (B.E.C. and B.E.I.)

                              Certificat d'aptitude industrielle et
                              commerciale (C.A.P.I. and C.A.P.C.)


## TEACHER EDUCATION

No training.  Formerly the lowest grade of primary teachers (maîtres
certifiés) could teach with only the C.E.P.E.  After 5 years' service they
could sit for examination Diplôme de moniteur de l'enseignement général
(D.M.E.G.) to become maîtres diplômés in a higher salary range.  Now, no
longer possible to find teaching position with only the C.E.P.E.

Teacher training given in government and mission écoles normales.  Some
écoles normales give a full 4-year program leading to the Brevet élémentaire with special emphasis on Pedagogy.  Others offer a year's professional training to those with the B.E.P.C. or Probation.  At this level
can teach in primary schools as maîtres brevetés.  Known as instituteurs-
adjoints.

ECOLE NORMALE D'INSTITUTEURS, Nkongsamba

Entry age:        20 years or more for the cycle long.
                  25 years or more for the cycle court.

Entrance requirements:        Brevet élémentaire, B.E.P.C. or Probation
                              and pass appropriate entrance examination.

Instruction in French.

Length of programs:

    Cycle long:    4 years, 3 years for preparation for the Baccalauréat
                   and 1 year's professional training to become maîtres
                   bacheliers or instituteurs. These are the highest
                   grade of primary school teachers, usually in charge as
                   directeurs des écoles.

    Cycle court:   1 year's professional training to become instituteurs-
                   adjoints.

Program: Lycée subjects and teacher training.

Grading: 0-20, pass mark 10/20.

Examinations prepared for:      Baccalauréat and C.F.E.N. (cycle long)

                                C.E.F.E.N. (cycle court)


ECOLE NORMALE SUPERIEURE

Entry age:   18-20 for the preparatory year (cycle préparatoire)
             18-30 for the 1st regular year (première année normale).

Entrance requirements:        Into the cycle préparatoire, 1 year in
                              classe de première.

                              Into the première année normale, 1 year in
                              classe terminale or completion of cycle
                              préparatoire.

                              For all students: pass the appropriate
                              entrance examination.

Students in the normal pedagogical program are called élèves-professeurs.

There is also a program preparing school inspectors. Students called
élèves-inspecteurs. Entry by examination and 10 years of teaching
experience or as an assistant inspector.

Instruction in French.

Length of programs:        2 or 3 years.

Programs:

    Elèves-professeurs:    preparation for the exams for the <u>licence</u> in
                               specialty chosen, plus pedagogical training.

    Elèves-inspecteurs:    preparation for the <u>C.A.I.P.</u>

Grading:    from 0 to 20.

Examinations prepared for:    <u>Certificat d'aptitude à l'enseignement dans
les collèges d'enseignement général</u> (<u>C.A.P.
C.E.G.</u>)

<u>Certificat d'aptitude à l'enseignement du
second degré</u> (<u>C.A.P.E.S.</u>)

<u>Certificat d'aptitude à l'inspection des
écoles primaires et à la direction des écoles
normales d'instituteurs</u> (<u>C.A.I.P.</u>)

<u>Certificats de licence</u>, from the various
faculties, for the <u>élèves-professeurs</u>.

638

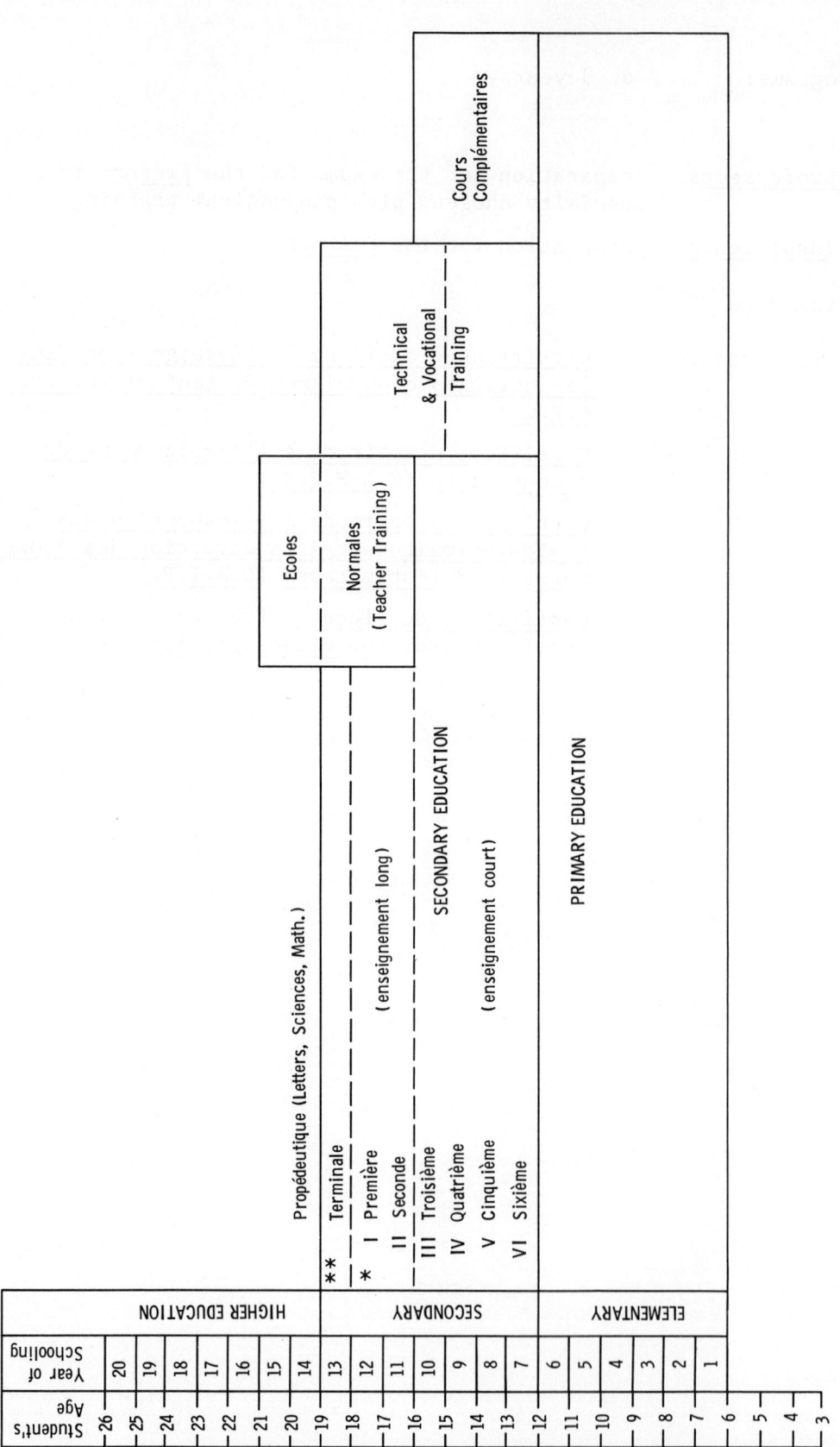

REPUBLIC OF DAHOMEY

Compulsory education: 6–14 years of age

School year: Mid-September – June

Secondary grading: 20 Perfect

10/20 pass mark (examination)

9/20 lowest passing to higher class

REPUBLIC OF DAHOMEY

(République du Dahomey)


Independence:   August 1, 1960.


## BACKGROUND


Most densely populated state of West Africa.

Not ethnically or linguistically homogeneous; marked division between
peoples of south and north.

Largest ethnic group, the Fon (or Dahomeyans) (over 700,000), the closely
related Adja (over 220,000), and Aizo (92,000), who live in south, are
mostly farmers.   The Bariba (175,000) are a Bargu group in the northwest.
The Yoruba, from Nigeria (over 160,000), living along eastern border, are
farmers.   The related Holli (15,000) live in the Pobe region.   The Somba
(about 90,000) in the northeast are subdivided into several distinct
groups; also in the northeast are Dendi and Pilapila (or Yowa).   The
Fulani (70,000), traditionally nomadic herders, are becoming sedentary.

In northern Dahomey, peoples have greater affinity with those in southern
Sudan than with those in south.   Unity of south due to several kingdoms,
dating from the 16th century, composed of immigrants of Adja stock (related to Ewe of south Togo and southeast Ghana); kingdoms of Allada, Abomey, Porto-Novo , and Juda.   Other smaller kingdoms of Popo and Mina.

Portuguese established first trading post in Benin Gulf, naming it Porto-
Novo, in early 17th century.   British, French, Dutch, Spanish traders
followed.   1851, French made treaty with King of Abomey to establish trading post at Cotonou; obtained rights to Porto-Novo, 1869.   Dahomey became
French Protectorate, 1892.   1892-1900, territory took modern shape.   Decree
of 1895 placed country under authority of the Governor-General of Sénégal.

1902, became component colony of the Federation of French West Africa.
1946, under new French Constitution, it was given a deputy and two senators
in the French Parliament and an elected Territorial Assembly with sub
stantial control of budget.

Reforms of 1956-57, powers of Territorial Assembly extended; universal
adult suffrage.

September 1958, Territory accepted new French Constitution and opted for
an autonomous representation within the French Community.

December 4, the Territorial Assembly was transformed into a National
Constituent Assembly and proclaimed the Republic of Dahomey  a member
state of French Community.

February 14, 1959, a new Constitution adopted.  August 1, 1960, independence;
November 25, new Constitution.

Private schools, largely in hands of Catholic missionaries, educate almost
50% of children.  Sulpicians run the Great Seminary in Ouidah and the Bro-
thers of the Christian Schools direct the secondary school in Bohicon.
Methodist teachers have more then 3500 pupils in continuation classes in
Porto-Novo and northern Dahomey, and the Assembly of God also have schools.
Complete Moslem school in Cotonou.

By 1960, these private organizations operated a total of 200 elementary
schools (out of 558), with 817 classes.  On the secondary level they provided 7 (out of 15) classical and modern secondary schools, 1 Catholic
teacher training school, 1 Methodist supplementary course, 1 Catholic home
economics school.


Public education:

Ecole Primaire Supérieure de Victor Ballot, Porto-Novo, established 1911
with cours supérieur and cours normal; vocational section added 1918; later
became Cours Secondaire de Porto-Novo; 1947 became Collège; 1956 became
Lycée Victor Ballot with classical and modern courses.

Vocational section transferred 1924 to Cotonou, becoming Ecole Professionnelle Reste; converted in 1947 into Collège Technique which provided
training course for apprentices.

Collège Moderne de Jeunes Filles, Porto-Novo, 1943, offered upper primary;
became Collège Moderne (short course, 4 years); in 1957 expanded to full
7-year course (enseignement long).

All other secondary and teacher training schools founded After World War II.
Agricultural Apprentice Center, Porto-Novo, 1952.
Apprenticeship Center at Ina, 1959.
Private technical education attached to a general secondary school  also for
Home Economics and Crafts.

French, official language of instruction.

Vernacular:  Fon, Yoruba, Nagot, Bariba, Somba--used in adult education
programs.

## PRESENT SYSTEM

### PRIMARY EDUCATION

Entry age:  6 years - 9 years.

6-year program.  Similar to that of France, except in History and Geography, where the progression goes from the local to the Republic, to the O.U.A. (Organization of African Unity), to France, and Europe.

Diploma at end of 6 years:  Certificat d'études primaires élémentaires.

### POST-PRIMARY EDUCATION

4-year post-primary program in cours complémentaires; for students not continuing into academic secondary schools.  Training similar to short ievel secondary education.

Brevet élémentaire (B.E.) or Brevet d'études du premier cycle (B.E.P.C.) awarded at end of classe de troisième.

### SECONDARY EDUCATION

Entrance requirements:     Certificat d'études primaires élémentaires, and selective entrance examination into classe de sixième.

Length of course:          7 years for enseignement long.
                           4 years for enseignement court.

Subjects taught same as in French secondary schools.  Physics and Chemistry include laboratory work.

Diplomas:

    Brevet d'études du premier cycle du second degré (B.E.P.C.) ) awarded at
                                                   ) close of
    Brevet élémentaire (B.E.)                                    ) 4 years
    *Baccalauréat première partie, called examen probatoire de fin de première taken at end of 6th year.
    **Baccalauréat (deuxième partie) taken at end of 7th year (terminale).

Examen probatoire de fin de première.  Choice of one program from 8 series.

    (1)  Série classique A
    (2)  Série classique A'

(3)  Série classique B
(4)  Série classique C
(5)  Série moderne
(6)  Série moderne-prime
(7)  Série technique
(8)  Série technique'

Baccalauréat de l'enseignement du second degré:    Choice of one of 5 series.

(1)  Série philosophie
(2)  Série sciences
(3)  Série mathématiques
(4)  Série mathématiques et technique
(5)  Série technique et économie

There are no special examinations for passing into the next class.  Student
is judged by general average of his year's grading in classes and in written
work.

Grading:        20 -    Perfect (rarely given)
                16 -    Average mark
                10/20 - Pass mark (examination)
                9/20 -  Lowest passing mark for entrance into next class


PRIVATE SECONDARY EDUCATION

Many private schools preparing students for B.E.P.C. or B.E.

Most well-known schools offering secondary courses (all established less
than 10 years):

At Porto-Novo:          Léon Bourgine
                        St. Joseph
                        Mehouda
                        Pera
                        St. Athanase
                        Zevounnou

At Cotonou:             Notre Dame des Apôtres
                        Aupiais (full Baccalauréat)
                        Lamartine
                        Houessinou
                        Tecou

At Abomey:              Gérard d'Alexis (est. 1962)

Entrance requirements, length of programs, and diplomas, same as those in
the official secondary schools outlined above.

## HIGHER EDUCATION

### CENTRE D'ENSEIGNEMENT SUPERIEUR, Porto-Novo

At the Center of Higher Education there is a propédeutique class,
created in 1962.

> Lettres modernes (Modern Letters)
> Sciences physiques, chimiques et naturelles (Physical, Chemical and
>    Natural Sciences)
> Mathématiques générales-physique (General Mathematics-Physics)

As well as being a higher education introductory course, it also provides
local training for teachers for the first cycle of academic secondary
education and other lower level secondary courses.

## VOCATIONAL AND TECHNICAL EDUCATION

Technical secondary programs, same as French pattern.

> In quatrième (class IV), students are divided into 2 sections:
> industrial and commercial.  To the close of the troisième (class III)
> they receive within each section comprehensive general training;
> specialization being given only in the seconde (class II) and pre-
> mière (class I):  Mechanics and Electricity for the industrial section,
> Office Work, Typing and Bookkeeping for the commercial section.

> Before 1964, students from these industrial and commercial sections
> from the troisième and seconde continued their studies in a foreign
> technical training program (Dakar, Bamako).
> From 1964, the Baccalauréat technique offered at Lycée Technique
> in Cotonou.

Private secondary school of Notre Dame des Apôtres at Cotonou prepares for
a Vocational Proficiency Certificate (Certificat d'aptitude professionnelle) (C.A.P.) in Shorthand, Typing and Office Work; also a 3-year course
in Domestic Science and Dressmaking.

Vocational training also given at the model farm at Ina, and by the O.C.D.N.
(Organisation Commune Dahomey-Niger de chemins de fer et de transport).

### LYCEE TECHNIQUE COULIBALY, Cotonou

Formerly called Collège Technique de Cotonou.

Secondary technical program.  It has also a Centre d'apprentissage with
5 sections:

|                      |                      |
|----------------------|----------------------|
| General Engineering  | Automotice Engineering |
| Carpentry            | Masonry              |
| Electricity          |                      |

Centre d'apprentissage admits pupils 14-17 years of age from primary education of classe de sixième.

Teacher personnel for the Centre same as for the Lycée Technique.

Students prepare for the industrial C.A.P.

CENTRE D'APPRENTISSAGE D'ARTISANAT RURAL, Ina

Established 1960, to train skilled workers for village cooperatives.

Recruitment from primary school graduates, from those at the 6th-year primary level, and from those with aptitudes for the building trades.

2 sections: Mechanics and Masonry.

2-3 year program. Curriculum, 42 hours a week: 8 hours, general subjects, Mathematics, French, Science. 3 hours, Drafting. 3 hours, Technology. 28 hours, Practical Work.

Technical training, theoretical and practical:

    For Mechanics:     Forge, Fitting, Soldering, Auto-mechanics.
    For Masonry:       Bricklaying, and also Carpentry/Joinery.

During the vacations, students take a month in agricultural training at a farm at Ina.

INSTITUT D'ETUDES JURIDIQUES

Courses initiated 1964-65 at the Palais de Justice, Cotonou, preparing students for the Capacité en droit. 2-year program.

ECOLE NATIONALE D'ADMINISTRATION, Cotonou

Projected for 1966 when students with the Capacité en droit from the Institut d'Etudes Juridiques will be eligible for entrance.

TEACHER EDUCATION

ECOLE NORMALE FELICIEN NADJO, Porto-Novo

Beginning October, 1965.

Entrance requirements:    Competitive examination (concours) at level of classe de seconde.

Language of instruction:  French and English.

Length of programs:  4-5 years.

Grading similar to secondary education.

Examinations:  <u>Examen probatoire</u> and <u>Baccalauréat</u>, and <u>Certificat de fin
                    d'études normales</u> (C.F.E.N.).

Students completing the <u>Baccalauréat</u> or the <u>C.F.E.N.</u> may continue in the
<u>propédeutique</u> program at the Center of Higher Education (see under HIGHER
EDUCATION).

646

REPUBLIC OF GUINEA

Compulsory schooling: 7 - 15 years
School year: October - July
Secondary Grading: 20 Perfect
10/20 passmark

Institut Polytechnique

Nat. Admin. School

Teacher training

Technical &
Vocational trg.

(Specialization)

SECONDARY

EDUCATION

(Orientation)

PRIMARY EDUCATION

3rd cycle

(cours moyen)
2nd cycle

1st cycle

** 12
11
10
9
8
7
6
5
4
3
2
1

| Student's Age | Year of Schooling | |
|---|---|---|
| 26 | 20 | HIGHER EDUCATION |
| 25 | 19 | |
| 24 | 18 | |
| 23 | 17 | |
| 22 | 16 | |
| 21 | 15 | |
| 20 | 14 | |
| 19 | 13 | |
| 18 | 12 | SECONDARY |
| 17 | 11 | |
| 16 | 10 | |
| 15 | 9 | |
| 14 | 8 | |
| 13 | 7 | |
| 12 | 6 | ELEMENTARY |
| 11 | 5 | |
| 10 | 4 | |
| 9 | 3 | |
| 8 | 2 | |
| 7 | 1 | |
| 6 | | |
| 5 | | |
| 4 | | |
| 3 | | |

REPUBLIC OF GUINEA
(République de Guinée)


Independence:   October 2, 1958.


BACKGROUND

The major ethnic groups composing the Republic of Guinea are the Fulani
(1,02 million) living in the Futa Zallon (Fouta Djallon) and occupying
most of northeastern Guinea; the Malinké (525,000), often referred to in
other parts of West Africa as the Mandingos, concentrated around Kankan,
Beyla and Kouroussa; the Soussou (250,000), centering around Conakry,
Forecariah and Kindia; and the Kissi (160,000), living around Guékédou.
There are 14 vernacular languages; Fulani, Malinké and Susu are the major
ones.

The territory of Upper Guinea fell within the ancient empire of Ghana
which flourished from the 5th to the 9th century, and was part of the
subsequent Mail empire which became dominant during the 13th and 14th
centuries and declined in the 17th century.

Portuguese explorers came to the Guinea coast in the middle of the 15th
century.  By the 17th century French, British and Portuguese traders were
in competition.  French rights along the coast were established by 1814,
and France assumed a Protectorate over Boké and surrounding areas in 1849.
Fulani chiefs of the Futa Zallon recognized the French Protectorate, 1861.
By 1898, Upper Guinea was occupied by France.

Boundaries were defined between Guinea and Portuguese Guinea, 1886;
Sierra Leone, 1889; Liberia, 1911.  Boundaries set during colonial rule
are not in keeping either with ethnic or national geographic borders.

In 1891 Guinea was constituted a French territory separate from Sénégal
of which it had been a part.  1893, its name was changed from Rivières
du Sud to Guinée Française (French Guinea).  1895, Guinea became one of
several French territories in Federation of West Africa.  An elected
Territorial Assembly was established in 1946.  By 1951 all Africans in
Guinea were given French citizenship; replaced by universal adult
suffrage, 1957.

In the September 1958 referendum on the new French Constitution, Guinea
rejected the offer to stay within the French Community, and thus became
an independent state October 2, 1958.

Mid-1961 Guinea formed with Ghana and Mali the Union of African States.
A committee was created to study effective ways of merging currency,
military commands, cultural programs, and of coordinating foreign
policies.  Cooperation with France in economic and cultural matters
established by convention, May 22, 1963.

Previous to independence, the educational system was patterned on that of
France.  Local adaptations are now being made.  French remains the
language of instruction; English is the second language, but the three
major vernaculars are taught.  Political instruction has been added to
primary and secondary education.  In August 1961 all denominational schools
were nationalized.


## BEFORE 1960-61 REFORM

Education patterned on French system, similar to other territories
composing the federation.

Structure:       6 years elementary
                 4 years 1st cycle secondary
                 3 years 2nd cycle secondary

        Total of 13 years education


## PRESENT SYSTEM

12 years of schooling organized into 3 cycles:

                1st cycle - 4 years
                2nd cycle - 5 years (cours moyen)
                3rd cycle - 3 years (lycée)


## PRE-PRIMARY EDUCATION

Short period of pre-primary education given in kindergartens, nursery
schools and infant classes attached to primary schools.


## PRIMARY EDUCATION

Entry age:      7 years.

Language of instruction:        French as far as possible.  Tribal
                                languages still widely spoken.

Primary education characterized by rapid enrollment and expansion, and Africanization of programs and teaching staff.  French teachers eliminated at primary level.

Examen d'orientation taken at end of primary school or at CM2 level (cours moyen 2).  This is a preliminary test of aptitude for entry into secondary school.


## SECONDARY EDUCATION

Entry age:       13 years.

Language of instruction:        French.  English always 1st modern
                                language.

Length of course:       Orientation cycle - 3 years (last 3 years of
                                                        cours moyen)
                        Specialization cycle - 3 years

Programs:

    Orientation:        Standard basic education including practical work
                        varying slightly according to individual bent.
                        Heavy stress on French grammar and composition.
                        Mathematics generally follows French pattern.

                        Curriculum:  Negro-African Literature and General
                        Literature, Mathematics, Science, Physical
                        Culture, Civics, Moral Instruction, Artistic
                        Training, Introduction to World of Production,
                        Social Work, French.

    Specialization:  Theoretical or vocational and apprenticeship.
        Theoretical (a)  General secondary
                            (1)  Humanities, Modern Languages
                            (2)  Mathematics, Experimental Sciences

                        (b)  Technical secondary
                            (1)  Mechanics, including Physical Sciences
                                 and Mechanics
                            (2)  Chemistry and Biology
                            (3)  Economics and Social Sciences

    Vocational and apprenticeship:
                        2-year course of general education and manual and
                        technical work, leading to C.A.P.  Best pupils
                        continue with 1 preparatory year for higher
                        vocational school.  (See Vocational and Technical
                        Education.)

Certificates awarded:   <u>Brevet d'études du premier cycle</u> (<u>B.E.P.C.</u>) at end of orientation cycle.

                                <u>Certificat d'aptitude professionnelle</u> (<u>C.A.P.</u>) at end of 2-year vocational course (5 years' secondary).

                            **<u>Baccalauréat</u> at end of specialization cycle (6 years' secondary).

Secondary institutions:   <u>Ecole secondaires incomplètes</u> (junior secondary schools) providing 3-year orientation cycle to <u>B.E.P.C.</u> level.

                                  <u>Lycées</u> and <u>lycées techniques</u> provide full 6-year secondary education in general and technical sections.

                                  Vocational schools (see Vocational and Technical Education).

                                  Evening schools and secondary correspondence school, providing continuation courses for those leaving school at 15.

                                  Teacher training schools at secondary level (see Teacher Education section).

## HIGHER EDUCATION

None.  Nucleus of higher education in Institut Polytechnique and Ecole Nationale d'Administration, both in Conakry (see under Vocational and Technical Education).  Students have government scholarships to study abroad, in Sénégal and France predominantly.

## VOCATIONAL AND TECHNICAL EDUCATION

### VOCATIONAL SCHOOLS

2 levels: (1)   2-year vocational and apprenticeship courses, providing general subjects and manual and technical training, nursing, midwifery, social work, mining, agriculture.

                  Entrance requirements:      Completion of primary school.

                  Certificate awarded:   <u>Certificat d'aptitude professionnelle</u> (<u>C.A.P.</u>).

                  Best pupils continue with 1 preparatory year for higher vocational school.

(2)  2 and 3-year courses in higher vocational schools to train
     specialized technicians and supervisors.  Best pupils go
     on to higher education.

     Certificate awarded:  <u>Brevet</u> in chosen specialty.


## INSTITUT POLYTECHNIQUE, Conakry

Newly established institute training highly qualified engineers and
technical teachers for both Guinea and other African states.

Director of Studies controls pedagogic aspects; military type organization.

<u>Faculties:</u>

        Sciences                        Agriculture
        Civil Engineering               Letters
        Geology and Mines

Projected faculties:  Medicine and Pharmacy, Chemistry, Electricity.

Entrance requirements:         <u>Baccalauréat</u> and pass entrance examination.

Length of course:      4 years - 1 preparatory year (<u>année propédeutique</u>),
                       at present divided into 2 sections:  1
                       common to Sciences, Civil Engineering,
                       Geology-Mines and Agriculture, and 1 for
                       Letters.

                       3 years of specialization, with 1
                       additional semester for preparation of
                       the project or <u>certificat d'études
                       supérieures</u>.

Academic year:         2 semesters, each of 17 weeks.  6-hour day, 2-hour
                       sessions.

Program:  Mathematics, Physics, Chemistry, Specialized Engineering sub-
          jects, Human and Economic Sciences.

          Conferences, seminars and practical work.

Certificate awarded:  <u>Diplôme</u> in specialty.


## ECOLE NATIONALE D'ADMINISTRATION, Conakry

Newly established school for training government officials.  Professional
training at university level.

Entrance requirements:         <u>Baccalauréat</u> or equivalent.

Duration of course:    Approximately 2 years.


## TEACHER EDUCATION

### ECOLES NORMALES PRIMAIRES

Located at Conakry, Kankan and Macenta.  Attached to the Ecole Normale
Primaire at Conakry-Bellevue, is an Institut de Langue (English, German)
and an Ecole des Beaux Arts.

Entrance requirements:           Students in 9th year.

Length of course:      9 months, 29 weeks tuition.

Certificate awarded:   Certificat élémentaire d'aptitude pédagogique
                       (C.E.A.P.) to become instituteurs-adjoints for
                       teaching 1st cycle and 5th and 6th classes of 2nd
                       cycle, i.e. primary school.


### ECOLE NORMALE SECONDAIRE, Kankan

Entrance requirements:           Completion of cours moyen, 4 years 1st
                                 cycle, 2 years 2nd cycle, B.E.P.C. level.

Length of course:      23 months' course of 67 weeks plus 4 weeks of
                       practice teaching.

Certificate awarded:   Certificat d'aptitude pédagogique (C.A.P.) to
                       become instituteurs for teaching 7, 8, 9th year
                       classes, i.e. 1st cycle of secondary education.


### ECOLE NORMALE SUPERIEURE

Entrance requirements:       Baccalauréat.

Trains secondary school teachers for 3rd cycle, 10, 11, 12th classes.

Length of course:      1 year.


### ECOLE NORMALE D'ENSEIGNEMENT TECHNIQUE

Entrance requirements:       C.A.P.

Length of course:      23 months' course of 67 weeks plus 4 weeks of
                       professional training in industry or other
                       appropriate situations.

Trains teachers for technical schools in practical work and technical drawing.

## IN-SERVICE TRAINING

Short courses are held each year for _moniteurs_ who were recruited straight from primary school without any professional training.  Opportunities to pass professional examinations for promotion.

At present majority of secondary teaching personnel is European, while teaching staff at primary level has been completely Africanized.

REPUBLIC OF IVORY COAST

| Student's Age | Year of Schooling | | | |
|---|---|---|---|---|
| 26 | 20 | HIGHER EDUCATION | | |
| 25 | 19 | | | |
| 24 | 18 | | | |
| 23 | 17 | | | |
| 22 | 16 | | | |
| 21 | 15 | | | |
| 20 | 14 | | | |
| 19 | 13 | | Law ** | Classe terminale |
| 18 | 12 | SECONDARY | Letters * | 1e (première) |
| 17 | 11 | | Sciences | 2e (seconde) |
| 16 | 10 | | Med. | 3e (troisième) |
| 15 | 9 | | Bus. | 4e (quatrième) |
| 14 | 8 | | | 5e (cinquième) |
| 13 | 7 | | | 6e (sixième) |
| 12 | 6 | ELEMENTARY | | CM 2 ) |
| 11 | 5 | | | CM 1 ) |
| 10 | 4 | | | CE 2 ) |
| 9 | 3 | | | CE 1 ) |
| 8 | 2 | | | CP 2 ) |
| 7 | 1 | | | CP 1 ) |
| 6 | | | | Pre-primary |
| 5 | | | | |
| 4 | | | | |
| 3 | | | | |

Deuxième cycle (2nd cycle)

Premier cycle (1st cycle)

Cours moyen

Cours élémentaire

Cours préparatoire

LYCEES, COLLEGES

LYCEE TECHNIQUE

ECOLE NORMALE

ECOLES NORMALES d'APPRENTISSAGE

C.N.E.P.C.

COURS NORMAUX

CENTRES d'APPRENTIS-SAGE

COURS COMPLEMENTAIRES

Compulsory education : to 15 years of age
School Year : October – June
Secondary Grading : 20 – rarely given
      20 - 17  Très Bien
      16 - 14  Bien
      13 - 12  Assez Bien
      11 - 10  Passable
      10 - lowest passing grade
      Below 10 - Mal

REPUBLIC OF IVORY COAST
(République de Côte d'Ivoire)


Independence:  August 7, 1960.


## BACKGROUND

5 major ethnic groups:  The Agni-Ashanti (Baoulé, Attié, Abouré ...), in eastern forest region, related to Ghanian groups; the Lagoon-dwellers (Adjoukrou, Alladian, Apollo, Ebrié ...); the Krou in the West, related to Liberian Krou; the Mande (Dioula, Malinké, with cultural center in Guinea and Mali); and the Senufos in the North, Voltaic people.

Europeans, 20,000.

One of the most heterogeneous countries in Africa.  Density of population in West and South-East.  Republic administratively divided into 4 departments:  North, West, Central, and South-East.

1365, first Dieppese navigators landed on the West to trade with natives.

1687, French missionaries established themselves at Assinie.  French military forces withdrawn, 1870.

March 10, 1893, Ivory Coast decreed a French colony, and placed under the authority of a governor, responsible to the Colonial Minister.

Up to this time, Ivory Coast had been known by a variety of names:  The Coast of the Good People, Coast of Seeds (oil-palm seeds), Coast of the Malinguette, Coast of Teeth, Coast of the Morphyl, Coast of the Bad People, and Gold Coast.

Until middle of 19th century only southeast corner of country had European contact; western coast, known as Côte des Malgens, none.

Organization and pacification of the new French colony continued until 1912.  1916-1938, development of the country's economy.

January 1, 1933, portion of Upper Volta was added to Ivory Coast but on January 1, 1948, the districts of Bobo-Dioulasso, Gaoua, Koudougou, Ouaga-dougou, Kaya, Tenkodogo, and Dedougou were transferred to the reconstituted Upper Volta.

In World War II, remained under Vichy government of France between 1940-43.

1946, the Ivory Coast became an Overseas Territory within the French Union, according to the Fourth French Republic.

1956, Ivory Coast in accordance with the "loi-cadre" formed its own Government Council, whose members were appointed by the Territorial Assembly.

December 4, 1958, Republic of Ivory Coast proclaimed member state of the Community.  March 26, 1959, adopted first constitution.

August 7, 1960, new republic left the jurisdiction of the Community and proclaimed its independence.

October 31, 1960, the National Assembly unanimously adopted a new constitution of the Republic of Ivory Coast.

First government schools, 1887.  1895, Catholic mission.  1903, French West African education unified.

Village schools taught basic skills.  Best students continued into regional schools for 3-year course leading to certificate of agricultural or manual proficiency.

After 1908, some Africans permitted to attend French-type schools.  A few went on to higher primary school, St. Louis, Sénégal, or from 1910 to the Ecole Primaire Supérieure, Bingerville (then capital of the Ivory Coast) for 2 years of general education.

From World War II, 6-year elementary education (conducted in French) was more practical than usual French pattern, emphasizing manual skills and agricultural training.  Those completing primary course went to Sénégal: Ecole William Ponty or Lycée Faidherbe.

Creation of the French Union in 1946 began a new era.  Between 1947-57 educational system took on French content and standards.  Colonial features of pre-war system, such as agricultural training, considered degrading and were eliminated.  Secondary education developed with expenditure of millions. Students offered ready access to French universities.

From 1957, secondary education formed a coherent ensemble:

(1)  lycées and collèges for enseignement long for training for baccalauréat and higher education.

(2)  école normale and cours normaux for teacher training.

(3)  cours complémentaires for formation of lesser cadres for public and private sectors.

Cours complémentaires first established 1957, post-primary training.

Creation of Ministry of Technical Education, 1957.

By 1959, 5 vocational schools (centres d'apprentissage), including 1 for girls.  Short course (2 years) ending in qualifying certificates.  Long course (usually 4 years) ending in brevet industriel or commercial.

By 1961, 30 cours complémentaires; entrance on C.E.P.E. (primary school certificate).  Manual and agricultural training.  Students in this program usually those who had failed entrance to secondary school (examen d'entrée en sixième).

By 1961, 11 collèges (6 public, 5 private).  Abidjan lycée.  Collège technique advanced to rank of lycée, with 3 sections:  industrial, mathematical, economic.

1958, Institut des Hautes Etudes established in Abidjan under University of Paris.  Institute to become a university in 1962, with French standards, granting licenses in Law, the Natural Sciences, Physics, Modern Letters. This institute was to serve needs of other Entente countries:  Upper Volta, Dahomey, Niger.

Institut Français d'Afrique Noire set up local branch in 1944; transferred to local government, 1958.  Later split into 2 centers:  (1) for the study of the Social Sciences (mostly Ethnology), and (2) the Arts, Religion, and Natural Sciences (mostly Oceanography).

1959, Centre de Perfectionnement de la Fonction Publique, a temporary center for rapid training of civil servants.

Plans for an Ecole Nationale d'Administration, modeled on French grande école of same name, admitting holders of baccalauréat, to train for high-ranking posts.

Plans for Ecole Normale Supérieure to be created by UNESCO for training secondary teachers for Entente countries.

Institut d'Enseignement et de Recherches Tropicales, local branch under French control, largely devoted to experimental agricultural research.

May 1963, a Commission created to select from all the students in the 3ème classe of all the collèges, lycées and cours complémentaires those students capable of pursuing secondary studies for the baccalauréat.


PRESENT SYSTEM

G O V E R N M E N T    S C H O O L S

PRE-PRIMARY EDUCATION

Entry age:      4-5 years of age.

Program:  1-2 years.  Songs, drawing, games.


## PRIMARY EDUCATION

Free primary education (enseignement du premier degré).

1964, public schools:  Abidjan, 625; Douake, 436; Daloa, 232.  Private schools:  Catholic, 544; Protestant, 25; non-confessional, 15.

Entry age:      Approximately 6 years.  Children not permitted to stay in school after 14 years of age.

6-year program, similar to French schools.

    Class 1 and 2:   cours préparatoire
    Class 2 and 3:   cours élémentaire
    Class 5 and 6:   cours moyen

Program:  Reading, Writing, Arithmetic, History, Geography, Morals.

Language of instruction:      French.

Successful completion of final examination entitles student to certificat d'études primaires élémentaires (primary school leaving certificate).

Student wishing to continue into secondary education must pass examen d'entrée en sixième (examination for entrance into 6th class - first year of secondary program).


## SECONDARY EDUCATION

Entrance by examination, see above.

2 types of general secondary education (enseignement secondaire):

    collèges          )
    cours complémentaires )   short course (4-year course)

    lycée                        long course (7-year course)

1964, public secondary:  1 lycée, 9 collèges, 27 cours complémentaires.
       private:      15 collèges, cours secondaires; 4 cours complé-mentaires.

Premier cycle (1st cycle):   lower 4 years
                       Classical or modern academic courses at the lycée, collèges, or in the cours secondaires.

Classes:  6 (sixième), 5 (cinquième), 4 (quatrième), 3 (troisième).

At end of 4th year (class 3), an examination for the brevet d'études du premier cycle (B.E.P.C.) (lower cycle  secondary certificate).

Deuxième cycle (2nd cycle):     upper 3 years
                                Courses at lycée or collèges, preparing for
                                baccalauréat examination.

Classes:   2 (seconde), 1 (première).

*At close of classe première, first part of baccalauréat examination, examen probatoire.

Classes:   Terminales (final year).

In the final year, specialization in Liberal Arts, Science, or Mathematics: Philosophie, Mathématiques élémentaires, Sciences experimentales.

At close of classe terminale, second part of baccalauréat examination.

**Baccalauréat awarded upon successful examination.


Private secondary schools recognized by government (religious and non-denominational):  20.  Main schools:  Collège Jean-Mermoz (Abidjan), Collège Voltaire, Collège Notre-Dame, Ecole Ajavon.

Same programs and final examinations as public schools.


## HIGHER EDUCATION

### UNIVERSITY OF ABIDJAN

First higher education courses given 1958-59 under auspices of University of Dakar and the Education Department of the Ivory Coast.  Students studied for the propédeutique (preliminary certificate) in Letters and Sciences, the first year of the capacité en droit.

Centre d'Enseignement Supérieur d'Abidjan established in 1959 with the first courses being given in 1960 after the proclamation of independence.  Achieved university status in 1963.

The structure of studies, grades, diplomas, etc. is the same as in French universities.  Teaching personnel chosen following the same criteria as in France, whose government also supplied the teachers and contributes to university expenses.

Centre d'Enseignement Supérieur began with Schools of Law, Sciences and Letters.  School of Medicine opened in 1962.

3 examination sessions:  February, June/July, October.

General entrance requirements:  <u>Baccalauréat</u> or equivalent, or entrance
                                  examination.


## Ecole de Droit (School of Law)

Programs offered:        <u>Capacité en droit</u> - 2 years
                         <u>Licence en droit</u> (Public Law elective) - 4 years
                         <u>Licence ès sciences économiques</u> (1st 2 years)
                         <u>Doctorat de droit public</u>
                         <u>Doctorat de sciences économiques</u>

Entrance requirements:           <u>Baccalauréat</u>, <u>brevet supérieur</u>, or <u>diplôme
                                 de fin d'études secondaires de l'enseignement
                                 public</u>, or other equivalent certificate.
                          or     Holders of the <u>capacité en droit</u>.
                          or     Successful passing of special entrance exami-
                                 nation conducted by the School.


## Capacité en droit

1st yr:  Private Law (120 hrs.), Public Law (60 hrs.).

2nd yr:  Civil Procedure and Channels of Execution (30 hrs.), Penal Law
         and Procedure (30 hrs.), Political Economics (30 hrs.), Special
         Administration Law (30 hrs.).
         Optional attendance at practical sessions.


## Licence en droit

4 years with examination at the end of each year.

<u>Diplôme d'études juridiques générales</u> awarded after 2nd year.

1st year common to both <u>licence en droit</u> and <u>licence ès sciences écono-
miques</u>.  4th year, choice of examination for <u>certificat de droit privé</u>
(Private Law), or <u>certificat de droit public et science politique</u> (Public
Law and Political Science).

Compulsory attendance at two weekly practical sessions.


## Licence ès sciences économiques

At present only first 2 years offered.

4 years with examination at the end of each year.  Compulsory attendance
at two weekly practical sessions.

Doctorat

Awarded a <u>diplôme d'études supérieures</u> in:  Private Law, Criminal Sciences, Public Law, Political Science, Economic Sciences, History of Law, and Social Facts.

1 hour of course work per week.  Written and oral examinations and defense of a thesis in the chosen field.


Doctorat de spécialité (3rd cycle)

Minimum of 2 years' preparation.  Higher research degree.

Defense of thesis.


Institut de Perfectionnement des Cadres Supérieurs

2-year program of training in Business Administration.

Admission on permission of the Admissions Committee, after study of applicant's dossier and interview.

Diploma awarded.


Ecole de Médecine (School of Medicine)

Doctorat en médecine

At present only the first 2 years.  6-year course with 12-month practical experience in the final year.  Practical and clinical experience throughout the course.

Subjects taught at present in 1st 2 years of <u>doctorat</u>:  Anatomy, Histology and Embryology, Physiology, Metabolic Biochemistry, Biophysics, Psychology, Semiology, Microbiology.


Ecole des Sciences (School of Sciences)

Licence ès sciences

2 cycles:        1st cycle - choice of 1 of the following <u>certificats d'études</u>:

<u>supérieures préparatoires</u>:    General Mathematics and
                                       Physics (M.G.P.)
                                    Mathematics, Physics and
                                       Chemistry (M.P.C.)
                                    Physical, Chemical and
                                       Natural Sciences (S.P.C.N.)

2nd cycle, 5 <u>certificats d'études supérieures</u> chosen from the following:

Mathematical Techniques of Physics
Optics
Thermodynamics and Physical Mechanics
General Chemistry I
Organic Chemistry
Botany
Zoology
Biochemistry, Microbiology, Plant Physiology (B.M.P.P.)
General Biology
Animal Physiology
General Geology

Not more than 3 certificates may be taken at the same examination session.

## WEEKLY TIMETABLES FOR
### CERTIFICATS D'ETUDES SUPERIEURES PREPARATOIRES

|  | Theory | Practical | Total |
|---|---|---|---|
| **General Mathematics and Physics (M.G.P.)** |  |  |  |
| Mathematics | 5½ | 6 |  |
| Physics | 2½ | 3 | 17 hrs. |
| **Mathematics, Physics and Chemistry (M.P.C.)** |  |  |  |
| Mathematics | 3½ | 3½ |  |
| Physics | 3½ | 5 |  |
| Chemistry | 2½ | 4 | 22 hrs. |
| **Physical, Chemical and Natural Sciences (S.P.C.N.)** |  |  |  |
| Animal Biology | 1½ | 3 |  |
| Plant Biology | 1½ | 3 |  |
| Geology | 1½ | 2½ |  |
| Physics | 1½ | 3 |  |
| Chemistry | 2 | 3 |  |
| Mathematics | 1 | 1 | 24½ hrs. |

## Diplôme d'études supérieures de sciences physiques and Diplôme d'études supérieures de sciences naturelles

Candidates must spend at least 2 semesters in a university laboratory, present the results of their work for interrogation and answer questions in related fields. Research may be original or in verification of other work.

## Diplôme de docteur-ingénieur

2 years of study and research in a scientific laboratory with 2 theses,

one of original study, and the other on more general lines, the subject being chosen by the professor; both theses to be defended orally.


## Doctorat ès sciences

Must have licence with certain combinations of certificates.


## Higher Technical Studies

It is proposed eventually to offer certificates and diplomas corresponding to the scientific ones in more technical fields such as Metallurgy, Mineralogy, Electronics, Astronomy, etc.


## Ecoles des Lettres (School of Letters)

### Licence ès lettres

2 cycles:

> 1st cycle, certificat d'études littéraires générales (classical and modern).

> 2nd cycle, 4 certificats d'études supérieures from the following:
>> French Literature
>> Foreign Letters - English
>> French Grammar and Philology
>> Modern and Contemporary History
>> English Literature
>> English Philology
>> Practical Studies in English
>> General Geography

2 types of licence:  the licence libre and the licence d'enseignement, the latter for those wishing to become teachers of the 2nd degree.

The above certificates make up the complete licence de lettres modernes, licence d'enseignement de l'anglais, and the 1st year of the licence d'histoire et géographie.


## Future Plans for Extension of University Instruction:

> Plans for creating courses that are more typically African as well as completing all existing cycles.

Ecole de Droit:

African Law and Juridical Customs.  Diploma of Private Law (4th year elective).  2 final years of licence ès sciences économiques.

Ecole de Médecine:

Creation of 3rd and 4th year instruction for the doctorat, as well as more subjects for 1st and 2nd years.

Ecoles des Sciences:

Africanization of programs in existing certificates; creation of certificat d'écologie tropicale; more choice in the M.G.P. certificate in 1st cycle; in the 2nd cycle 3 additional Chemistry certificates and a certificat de géologie historique.

Ecole des Lettres:

Particular stress on Africanization; completion of licence d'histoire et géographie with certificates in African History and Tropical Geography; 2 research centers:  Ethno-Sociology, and Educational and Social Psychology.

3 new schools already begun:  Agriculture, Public Works, PTT.

VOCATIONAL AND TECHNICAL EDUCATION

4 branches:  Industrial, commercial, feminine, adult.

Industrial education offered in:  1 lycée technique, 2 centres d'apprentissage, and 3 centres techniques ruraux.

LYCEE TECHNIQUE, Abidjan

3-year, basic programs:

> Classe préparatoire - 5e moderne
>
> Classe de 4e )
> Classe de 3e ) moderne technique, industrielle, commerciale

Subsequent 3-year programs leading to technical baccalauréats; 2-year programs leading to technical brevets.

| Diplomas awarded | Classes |
|---|---|
| Brevet de géomètre | T.G. |
| | 1e T.G. |
| | 2e T.G. |
| | |
| Baccalauréat technique et mathématiques | T.M. |
| Probatoire | 1e T.M. |
| | 2e T.M. |
| | |
| Baccalauréat technique et économique | T.E. |
| Probatoire | 1e T.E. |
| | 2e T.E. |
| | |
| Brevet d'enseignement industriel | 1e T.I. |
| | 1e Electricité |
| | 2e Spec. I. |
| | 2e T.I. |
| | 2e Electricité |
| | 3e T.I. |
| | 4e M.T. |
| | |
| Brevet de technicien comptable | 2e Technic. Compt. |
| Brevet supérieur d'enseignement commercial | 1e B.S.E.C. |
| Brevet d'enseignement commercial | 1e T.C. |
| | 2e Spec. Compt. |
| | 2e Spec. Secr. |
| | 2e T.C. |
| | 3e T.C. |
| | Prépar. Commerc. |
| | |
| C.A.P. géomètre | 2e C.A. Géomètre |

Baccalauréat technique et mathématiques admits to grandes écoles.
Baccalauréat technique et économique admits to enseignement supérieur
(university).

Lycée technique being transformed into 2nd cycle training. From October
1964, recruitment from classe seconde. Students can continue for baccalauréat or diplôme de technicien in 3 years. 32 hours weekly.

Lycée opened October 1963 the 4e moderne technique to experiment with an
economic and technical program that could be introduced into the classes
de 4e and 3e of the cours complémentaires.


CENTRES D'APPRENTISSAGE

Prepare for various certificats d'aptitude professionnelle.

1 to 4-year programs, admitting from cours moyen, 2nd year. Plans to cut
the course to 3 years and recruit from the end of classe 5e.

Classes (at Centre d'Apprentissage, Treichville)          Diploma

| | | | |
|---|---|---|---|
| 1st yr: | Mécanique générale | (General Mechanics) | C.A.P. |
| | Chaudronnerie | (Metal Work) | |
| | Electricité | (Electricity) | |
| | Arts graphiques | (Graphic Arts) | |
| | | | |
| 2nd yr: | Ajustage | (Fitting) | C.A.P. |
| | Mécanique auto | (Auto Mechanics) | |
| | Tourneur | (Turning) | |
| | Chaudronnerie | (Metal Work) | |
| | Monteur électricien | (Electrical Fittings) | |
| | Electro-mécanique | (Electro-Mechanics) | |
| | Maçon | (Masonry) | |
| | Menuisier | (Carpentry) | |
| | Arts graphiques | (Graphic Arts) | |
| | | | |
| 3rd yr: | Ajusteur | (Fitting) | C.A.P. |
| | Mécanique auto | (Auto Mechanics) | |
| | Tourneur | (Turning) | |
| | Chaudronnerie | (Metal Work) | |
| | Monteur électricien | (Electrical Fitting) | |
| | Electro-mécanique | (Electro-Mechanics) | |
| | Arts graphiques | (Graphic Arts) | |
| | | | |
| 4th yr: | Frigoriste | (Refrigeration) | C.A.P. |

CENTRES TECHNIQUES RURAUX

18 rural technical centers planned for construction within the next few years.

3 characteristics which distinguish this training from traditional technical industrial training:

(1) Schools situated outside of villages, preparing students for their own milieu.

(2) Most of the work outside the schools in practical training.

(3) Students have the opportunity to participate under direction in the economic market of which they will be a part.

COMMERCIAL TRAINING (Enseignement Commercial)

1 lycée technique, Abidjan:  preparation to brevet de technicien.

2 centres d'apprentissage: preparation for the certificats d'aptitude professionnelle in 3 years.

## WOMEN'S TRAINING (Enseignement Féminin)

1 école normale ménagère.   2 centres d'enseignement des métiers féminins.

October 1964, école normale transformed into a lycée technique féminin. Recruitment from classe 2e; training for brevet de technicien. 40-hour program.

2 centres d'enseignement des métiers féminins offer 4-year preparation for certificat professionnel. Recruitment from cours moyen, 2nd year. 40 hours weekly. Plans to cut this preparation to 3 years and recruit from end of classe 5e. Dressmaking, Mother-Craft, Domestic Science.


## ADULT EDUCATION (Formation Professionnelle des Adultes)

Industrial and commercial courses. Full-time, part-time, evening courses. Varied levels of courses for preparation for brevets professionnels.

Instruction in the centres techniques ruraux and in:

| | |
|---|---|
| 1 Centre de Formation et de Perfectionnement du Personnel d'Encadrement | ) |
| 1 Centre de Formation Professionnelle Commerciale | )  All |
| 1 Centre de Formation Professionnelle Industrielle | )  in |
| 1 Centre Technique de la Mécanique | )  Abidjan |
| 1 Centre Technique de l'Electricité et de Radio Electronique | ) |
| 1 Centre de Perfectionnement des Métiers du Bois | ) |
| 1 Ecole de Céramique et de Poterie, in Katiola | |


## TEACHER EDUCATION

Teacher designations:   Instituteurs, instituteurs-adjoints, moniteurs, moniteurs-adjoints.


## COURS NORMAUX

8 public, 3 private

Entrance requirements:          Primary school leaving certificate

Lower 4-year teacher training program.  Classes: 6ème, 5ème, 4ème, 3ème.

At close of program, examination for brevet élémentaire (B.E.), the elementary certificate.

With an additional year of professional training, student qualified as moniteur.

ECOLE NORMALE, Dabou

Upper 3-year teacher training program.  Classes:  2, 1, terminale.

Prepares students from the baccalauréat de l'enseignement.

After an additional year of professional training and pedagogical examination, student qualified for rank of instituteur ordinaire.


ECOLE NORMALE D'ENSEIGNEMENT TECHNIQUE

Prepares professeurs d'enseignement pratique for the centres d'apprentissage.

40 hours weekly.

Plans to develop 3 branches of training:

  (1)  Industrial branch for the training of personnel for the centres
       techniques ruraux.
  (2)  Commercial branch for the training of personnel for commercial
       education in the centres d'apprentissage and the courses in
       adult education.
  (3)  Woman's branch for the training of personnel for the women's
       sections of the centres d'apprentissage.


ECOLES NORMALES D'APPRENTISSAGE:

ECOLE NORMALE INDUSTRIELLE

Entrance requirements:              C.A.P.

2-year industrial training.

Competitive examination.  Title of maître-adjoint des travaux manuels
awarded.


ECOLE NORMALE MENAGERE

Entrance requirements:              B.E., B.E.P.C., C.A.P.

3-year program.

Diplôme de technicienne de l'enseignement ménager.

                         *   *   *

ECOLE NORMALE SUPERIEURE, Abidjan

Established in 1962.  Liaison with University of Abidjan for certain studies.
Co-educational.  All students on government grant with 10-year contract to
teach in government service on completion.

3 sections:

1st section:        Trains teachers for the 1st cycle of secondary
                    education and short secondary education (cours
                    complémentaires, cours normaux, collèges d'enseigne-
                    ment général, and enseignement général in technical
                    collèges and centres d'apprentissage).

2nd section:        Trains inspectors of primary education and eventually
                    conseillers pédagogiques (educational counsellors)
                    and directors of the regional centres pédagogiques.

3rd section:        Professional training to prepare teachers with a
                    licence or certificate to teach in the 2nd cycle of
                    a lycée, also the general education section of
                    secondary technical establishments; the students
                    follow their licence studies at the university.

Entrance requirements:

1st section - preparatory year:  Competitive examination open to
                    students from terminal class or with at least the
                    level of the examen probatoire; or instituteurs
                    actually employed, holding the C.A.P., but not the
                    baccalauréat.
              1st year:  Competitive examination open to holders of
                    the baccalauréat, or to instituteurs with the
                    baccalauréat or equivalent diploma.
              2nd year:  Successful passing of 1st-year examination;
                    or holders of a preliminary licence certificate
                    (certificat d'études littéraires générales) or one
                    or more certificats d'études supérieures.  Pupils
                    who have failed the preliminary licence certificate
                    and cannot repeat it, may be allowed to enter this
                    2nd year on advice from the conseil pédagogique of
                    E.N.S.

2nd section - preparatory year:  Competitive examination open to
                    instituteurs not holding the baccalauréat, but with
                    the C.A.P. of at least 5 years' standing and 10
                    years' teaching experience.
              1st year:  Competitive examination open to instituteurs
                    with the baccalauréat or equivalent, if they have
                    the C.A.P. and a total of 5 years' teaching experience.
              2nd year:  Teachers with a licence, or teachers of cours
                    complémentaires holding a preliminary certificate,

who are individually selected; <u>instituteurs</u> having
passed the final examination of 1st year in
General Culture.  <u>Instituteurs</u> without the above
qualifications may be admitted into this section to
train as an educational counsellor for primary
education.

3rd section:  Holders of a preliminary university certificate
leading to a teaching career.  Holders of the first
part of <u>C.A.P.E.S.</u>

Programs:

1st section:  2 years plus 1 preparatory year.  This preparatory
year is for the beginning transition period only
and may or may not be continued.  These preparatory
studies permit entry to 1st year in the specialty
chosen.

1st year:  General instruction at a level higher than
the <u>baccalauréat</u> with 4 fields of specialization:
(1)  French, History and Geography, Civics.
(2)  French, English.
(3)  Mathematics, Physical Sciences.
(4)  Physical Sciences, Natural Sciences.
Examination at the end of the year comprising the
theoretical part of the <u>certificat d'aptitude
pédagogique</u> (<u>C.A.P.</u>).

2nd year:  Pedagogical and practical instruction with
general sections in Psychology, Sociology, Pedagogy,
and special sections in the specialty chosen.  11
weeks of practical teaching experience.  At the end
of the year pedagogical and practical examination
sections of <u>C.A.P.</u>

2nd section:  2 years plus 1 preparatory year in the preliminary
transition period.  This preparatory year may or
may not be continued.
The 2 years are devoted to cultural, pedagogical and
administrative studies, including a course in typewriting.

Diplomas awarded:

1st section:  <u>Certificat d'aptitude pédagogique</u> (<u>C.A.P.</u>) for <u>cours
complémentaires</u>, <u>cours normaux</u>, <u>collèges d'enseignement général</u> and all establishments with the 1st
cycle of secondary education.

2nd section:  <u>Certificat d'aptitude à l'inspection primaire</u>
(<u>C.A.I.P.</u>).  If results of final examination are not
good enough for this certificate, a diploma is
awarded qualifying the student as an educational
counsellor.

3rd section:     Certificat d'aptitude du professorat de l'enseignement secondaire (C.A.P.E.S.).

## OTHER EDUCATION

### CENTRE NATIONAL D'ENSEIGNEMENT PAR CORRESPONDANCE ET INTERNAT DE JEUNES FILLES

4-year correspondence program (classes 6e-3e) leading to B.E.P.C.

2 additional years of training.

### SCHOOL OF CIVIL SERVICE

August 1961, armed forces created for the first time. Although the army's main purpose is national defense, it has been assigned an economic mission. The mission is to combine tactical exercises with a program for agricultural development in the most impoverished areas.

With technical cooperation, a fully equipped School of Civil Service was built. In farming and breeding, all the most efficient and modern methods initiated.

Program:

1st yr:  Basic training, specialization, elementary farming and stock-breeding.

2nd yr:  Transfer to one of 6 farms, where stress is on productivity, but military instruction is included.
1 farm specializes in dairy-farming; others in agriculture.

Armed Forces School, agricultural section, being developed.

REPUBLIC OF MALI

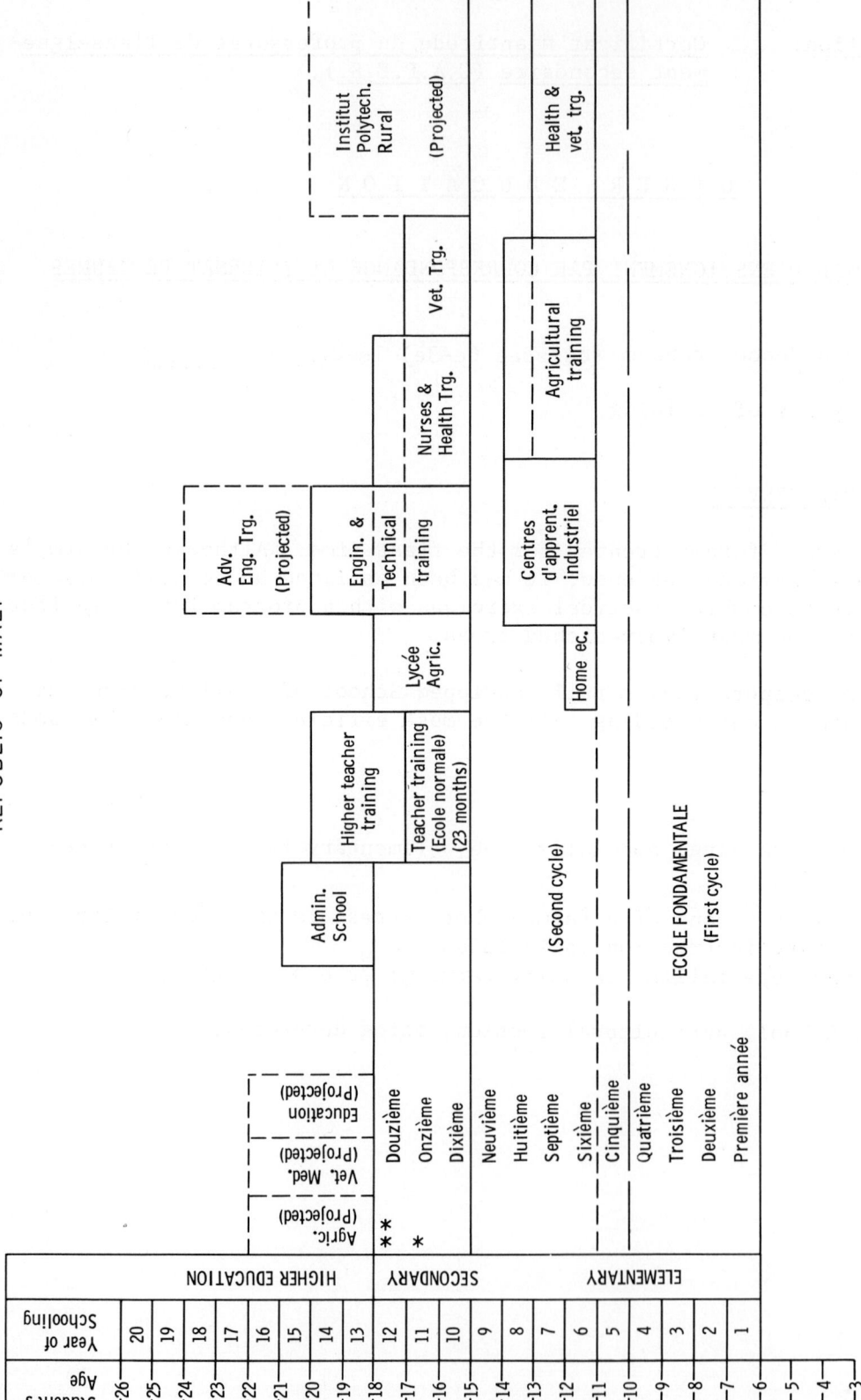

Compulsory education: Fundamental school compulsory, but not
enforced until facilities available.

School year: October 15 - July 15

Secondary grading:
20 - 17  -Très Bien
16 - 14  -Bien
13 - 12  -Assez Bien
11 - 10  -Passable
Below 10  -Mal

REPUBLIC OF MALI
(République du Mali)


Independence:  September 22, 1960



BACKGROUND


The Republic of Mali is a large land-locked country.  The word "Mali"
means "hippopotamus" in the Bambara language, signifying strength.  90% of
population Muslim.

Ethnic groups:  Bambara (mostly farmers), Fulani (semi-sedentary herdsmen),
Marka (believed to have founded the Empire of Ghana), Songhai (farmers and
fishermen), Malinke, Tuareg (mainly nomadic), Minianka (largely farmers),
Senufo (farmers), and Dogon (regarded as first inhabitants of Mali).

French, official language.  Other languages almost as numerous as ethnic
groups.

Between the 4th and the 19th centuries, a series of extensive "empires"
existed, founded by whites from Morocco and Algeria, but later maintained
by negroid peoples.  Best known empires:  Ghana, Mali, and Gao.

Ghana developed in the 8th century; declined after 1076 (see background
data in the study on Ghana).  The richest and most powerful empire, Mali,
after which the present republic is named, was established about the
middle of the 11th century;  it reached its peak by the 13th century and
declined after the death of Emperor Mansa Musa (1307-1332).  Then Tuaregs
took Tombouctou and northern area, and various peoples took other parts of
the empire.  The Empire of Gao, developed around the 9th century; ruled by
Mali, 1325-1335; thereafter broke away, subsequently having a series of
rulers.

By 1585, the Mali empire so loosely held together that an army of the
Sultan of Morocco captured the area and for 23 years attempted, unsuccessfully, to maintain control.  By 1780, the area fragmented into many small
states.  The 4 states of Kaarta, Segou, Futa, and Massina made up approximately the western "Soudan" (name of Mali up to 1959).  From 1857 to 1898,
there were frequent battles between Africans and French forces.  The French
were finally successful in gaining control of the area.

1946, the French Union replaced the Colonial Empire.  Territorial Assembly
established in Soudan; representatives in French Parliament.  Universal

suffrage, 1957.  Council of Ministers elected for administration of
internal affairs.

1958, a new French constitution was accepted and Soudan became an autonomous republic within the French Community.

January 17, 1959, in Dakar, representatives of Soudan, Dahomey, Sénégal,
and Upper Volta drafted a Constitution of the Federation of Mali (named
after the medieval empire); only the Assemblies of Soudan and Sénégal
ratified it and became members of the Federation.

Early in 1960, the French Community revised its charter so that the Mali
Federation might have complete sovereignty while remaining a member of
the Community.  Mali Federation became a sovereign state, June 1960.
August 20, 1960, Federation dissolved.  Break with Sénégal, followed by
decision to leave the French Community.

Soudan retained name of the Federation and became known as the Republic of
Mali.  All bonds between Mali and Sénégal were severed; relations resumed
in 1963.

Education began in the 19th century when the military were put in charge
of schools to train interpreters for the administration; taught by non-
commissioned French officers and soldiers.  Some Catholic mission schools
and Koranic schools.

By 1903, the educational system was similar to that found in the rest of
A.O.F. (Federation of French West Africa).  Village schools of 6 years,
followed by regional schools of 3 years for best students.  After 1913,
the best students went to Ecole William Ponty in Sénégal.  Eventually,
some graduates of the regional schools could also go to the Ecole de Katibougou to train as foresters, the Ecole Normale de Dabou (Ivory Coast), or
the Ecole des Vétérinaires in Bamako.  From 1903 to 1947, 836 students
from French Soudan had gone through upper primary, vocational, or secondary
schools in French West Africa.

1945, the first systematic educational structure was created, modelled on
French.  With independence (1960), Mali had 383 public and 42 private
primary schools, 1 public lycée, 1 public normal school, 1 public and 1
private collège, 11 public and 4 private cours complémentaires, 1 technical
collège, 1 centre d'apprentissage.

Consultative Council on Education, June 1960, initiated expansion program.
Two parallel systems of education proposed:  (1) classical education of
6-year primary cycle, leading to 6th year examination and certificate, and
(2) rural level, 4-year system to extend literacy; eventual integration of
these schools into regular classical cycle.

Until 1962, the basically French system was retained.  Certificates and
diplomas included the C.E.P.E. (Primary School certificate), B.E.P.C.
(Brevet for first cycle of secondary school), and Baccalauréat.  In

addition, a number of special diplomas were awarded upon completion of
cours complémentaires (continuation courses), and normal courses.

The educational system was reorganized in 1962, under a Five-Year Plan.
There was a revision of subject matter, hours, length of school year, and
diplomas, to speed the education of both the masses and the élite, while
maintaining the same standards and enlarging the subject range so that
emphasis would be placed on a universal basis.  For the students who had
been under the former system, a period of time was allotted so that they
might finish and receive the same diplomas as before.  All new students,
and all students at the 6th year level were to work into the reformed
program.


## PREVIOUS SYSTEM


### PRIMARY EDUCATION

6 years leading to Certificat d'études primaires élémentaires (C.E.P.E.).

1960, 383 public primary schools, 42 private.


### SECONDARY EDUCATION

Short course:   4 years in collèges and cours complémentaires, leading to
                Brevet élémentaire or Brevet d'études du premier cycle
                (B.E. or B.E.P.C.).

Long course:    1st cycle leading to B.E.P.C. given in collèges and lycées,
                4 years.
                2nd cycle leading to Baccalauréat only in lycées, 3 years.

Complete secondary education of 7 years given only in lycées.

1960, 1 public lycée.
      1 public collège, 1 private.
      11 public cours complémentaires, 4 private.
      1 public normal school.
      1 public centre d'apprentissage.

No higher education.


### 1962 Reform

Revision of subject matter, hours, length of school year, diplomas, to
speed the education of both the masses and the élite, while maintaining

the same standards, and enlarging the viewpoint of subject, so that emphasis placed on a universal base rather than a narrow African one.


PRESENT SYSTEM
(After 1962 Reform)

## PRE-SCHOOL EDUCATION

Not compulsory.

Only 6 nursery schools (jardins d'enfants), mainly in Bamako, organized by Catholic Education, Croix Rouge, and Service Social.  Small fee charged in most.

Entry age:  2½ to 5.

Program:  Songs, drawing, games, French, writing, arithmetic.


## PRIMARY EDUCATION (Enseignement Fondamental)

Free primary education for all children as space becomes available. Priority given to older children.  Co-educational first cycle.

Entry age:  6 to 10 years.

Length of course:    1st cycle - 4 years.

2nd cycle - 5 years.


### First Cycle

Language of instruction:  French.

Program:  32½ hours per week.  18½ hours for French Language, Reading, and Writing.  ½ hour of History.  General subjects plus Home Economics, Shop, or, in rural areas, Farming, Fishery.

Selection at end of first cycle.  Best students go on to fifth year (beginning of second cycle).  Others oriented toward écoles saisonnières.

Ecoles saisonnières:  training in Fishing, Animal Husbandry, Agriculture. Length of course:  1 growing season (a few months).

1961, 4 écoles saisonnières, with 15 to 20 young  farmers or fishermen in each.

<u>Medersas</u>:   these are <u>écoles fondamentales</u>, with the same curriculum as government schools, but mainly in Arabic.  1st year, 20% in Arabic, gradually increasing to 80% in Arabic by 6th or 9th year.  The remainder is taught in French.  Future plans to expand the <u>Medersa</u> of Timbuktu to the secondary level.

<u>Medersas</u> are different from Koranic schools, which give Moslem religious education to boys, with traditional curriculum.


## Second Cycle

1st year of second cycle (<u>cinquième année</u>) is second period of fundamental education.  Best students go on to third period or rest of second cycle.  Others (including those too old) directed to 2 or 3-year courses in <u>centres d'apprentissage</u> for training as home economics teachers for fundamental schools, health assistants, or agricultural assistants.  3-year course leads to <u>Certificat d'aptitude professionnelle</u> in specialty (<u>C.A.P.</u>).

Third period or remainder of second cycle:  4 years (<u>sixième</u> to <u>neuvième</u>).

1st Modern Language (usually English) begun in 6th year.

Program:   French, Mathematics, Physics, Chemistry, Natural Sciences, History, Geography, Modern Language, Morals, Civics, Political Education, Physical Education, Drawing, Manual Work.

Certificate awarded:       <u>Diplôme d'études fondamentales</u> (<u>D.E.F.</u>) at end of 9 years of fundamental education, after passing examination.
This <u>diplôme</u> necessary to enter general secondary education.  May be waived for entrance examination to special schools.


### D.E.F. EXAMINATION COEFFICIENTS

| Subjects | | | Written | Oral |
|---|---|---|---|---|
| French: | a) | Dictation and Text Explanation | 2 | - |
| | b) | Composition | 2 | - |
| | c) | Reading and Text Explanation | - | 1 |
| Mathematics: | | Geometry, Arithmetic, Algebra | 3 | 1 |
| Sciences: | | Physics, Chemistry, Natural Sciences | 2 | 1 |

(oral on Science not chosen for written paper)

| | | |
|---|---|---|
| History or Geography<br>   (oral on subject not chosen<br>    for written paper) | 2 | 1 |
| Modern Language 1 | 2 | 1 |
| Morals, Civics, Political Education | - | 1 |

Practical

| | |
|---|---|
| Physical Education | 1 |
| Drawing | 1 |
| Manual Work | 1 |

Admission to oral based on average score of 10/20 on written.

## Mathematics program for fifth year of fundamental education:

A.  Arithmetic:  Whole and decimal numbers, multiplication and division, change of units, everyday problems, mental arithmetic, rule of three, using divisibility symbol for simplification of a quotient, percentage, decimal fractions, ordinary fractions, operations on fractions, mixed numbers, problems.

B.  Metric System: Units of length, multiples and submultiples of the meter, ordinary measuring instruments, measure of weight, scale balance, weights, multiples and submultiples of the gram, measure of volume, multiples and submultiples of the liter, measures of area, measure of volume, relations between the measures of volume and the weight, scales, plans, tables, problems of scales, specific weight.

Practical problems, family economics, national economics, price of buying, of selling, profit, loss, debts, expenses, invoices, equal shares, unequal shares, averages, postal operations.

C.  Geometry:  Lines, angles, measure of angles, square, rectangle, parallelogram, rhombus, trapezoid, triangle, circle and its circumference, regular polygons, perimeters and areas, cubes, rectangular parallelepiped, cylinder, right prisms, volumes, and developed solids.

## SECONDARY EDUCATION

General secondary institutions: Lycée Askia Mohammed, Bamako (formerly Terrason de Fougères), Lycée des Jeunes Filles, Bamako, and Lycée Notre-Dame du Niger, Bamako.

Existing collèges will gradually be made into lycées as more classes and professors are provided.

Length of secondary education: 3 years beyond the D.E.F. (dixième to douzième).

Language of instruction: French.

Grading: 0-20 multiplied by coefficient for each test.

        Average of less than 12: Passable
                   12-14: Assez bien
                   14-16: Bien
          16 or better: Très bien

Passable only given after special oral to check level of student.

Examinations prepared for:

  * Baccalauréat première partie at end of onzième (11th class).

  ** Baccalauréat deuxième partie at end of douzième (12th class).

    Students must be at least 17 to take première partie.

    Choice of Baccalauréat option malienne or option étrangère, both recognized by French Ministry of Education.


### BACCALAUREAT PREMIERE PARTIE COEFFICIENTS

Option malienne, 4 séries:      LC, lettres classiques

                                 LM, lettres modernes

                                 SE, sciences exactes

                                 SB, sciences biologiques

Option étrangère, 6 séries:  A, A', B, C, M, M'.

Série T: common to both options.

## Option malienne

| Subjects                    Série: | LC  | LM  | SE  | SB  | T   |
|-------------------------------------|-----|-----|-----|-----|-----|
| **Written**                         |     |     |     |     |     |
| French Composition                  | 5   | 5   | 3   | 3   | 3   |
| Latin Translation                   | 4   | -   | -   | -   | -   |
| Greek Translation                   | 4   | -   | -   | -   | -   |
| Modern Language I                   | 2   | 3   | 1   | 1   | 1   |
| Modern Language II                  | -   | 3   | 1   | 1   | -   |
| Mathematics                         | 2+  | 2   | 5   | 3   | 4   |
| Physics                             | 2+  | 2   | 5   | 3   | -   |
| Natural Sciences                    | -   | -   | 1   | 5   | -   |
| Physical Sciences                   | -   | -   | -   | -   | 4   |
| History or Geography                | 3   | 3   | 2   | 2   | 2   |
| Mechanical Construction             | -   | -   | -   | -   | 5   |
| **Oral and practical**              |     |     |     |     |     |
| Political and Civic Education        | 2   | 2   | 2   | 2   | 2   |
| French                              | 1   | 2   | -   | -   | -   |
| Greek or Latin                      | 1   | -   | -   | -   | -   |
| Modern Language I                   | 1   | 2   | 1   | 1   | 1   |
| Modern Language II                  | -   | 2   | -   | -   | -   |
| Mathematics                         | -   | -   | 1   | -   | -   |
| Natural Sciences                    | -   | -   | -   | 2   | -   |
| Physical Education                  | 1   | 1   | 1   | 1   | 1   |
| Manual Work                         | 1   | 1   | 1   | 1   | 1   |

+In série LC either Mathematics or Physics is chosen.

## Option étrangère

| Subjects              Série: | A   | A'  | B   | C   | M   | M'  | T   |
|------------------------------|-----|-----|-----|-----|-----|-----|-----|
| **Written**                  |     |     |     |     |     |     |     |
| French Composition           | 4   | 3   | 4   | 3   | 4   | 4   | 3   |
| Latin Translation            | 4   | 3   | 4   | 3   | -   | -   | -   |
| Greek Translation            | 4   | 3   | -   | -   | -   | -   | -   |
| Modern Language I            | 2   | 2   | 2   | 2   | 2   | 2   | 1   |
| Modern Language II           | -   | -   | 2   | -   | 2   | -   | -   |
| Mathematics                  | 2+  | 4   | 2+  | 5   | 4   | 4   | 4   |
| Physics                      | 2+  | 2   | 2+  | 4   | -   | -   | -   |
| Natural Sciences             | -   | -   | -   | -   | -   | 3   | -   |
| Physical Sciences            | -   | -   | -   | -   | 4   | 3   | 4   |
| History or Geography         | 3   | 2   | 3   | 2   | 2   | 2   | 2   |
| Mechanical Construction      | -   | -   | -   | -   | -   | -   | 5   |

Oral and practical

| | | | | | | | |
|---|---|---|---|---|---|---|---|
| Political and Civic Education | 2 | 2 | 2 | 2 | 2 | 2 | 2 |
| Modern Language I | 1 | 1 | 2 | 1 | 1 | 1 | 1 |
| Physical Education | 1 | 1 | 1 | 1 | 1 | 1 | 1 |
| Manual Work | 1 | 1 | 1 | 1 | 1 | 1 | 1 |

+In séries A and B either Mathematics or Physics is chosen.

Modern languages chosen from the following: German, English, Literary Arabic, Arab dialect of Maghreb, Spanish, Italian, Russian, Vietnamese. No dictionary may be used except for written test in Arabic. For Latin or Greek a dictionary may be used for the translation.

Political and Civic Education examinations compulsory for Malian students, whether taking Malian or foreign option. Include questions on Malian government and international affairs.

Optional examinations in Music, Domestic Science, Drawing.

## BACCALAUREAT DEUXIEME PARTIE COEFFICIENTS

Option malienne, 4 séries:   Philo-lettres

Philo-langues

Sciences exactes terminales

Sciences biologiques terminales

Option étrangère, 5 séries:   Philosophie

Sciences expérimentales

Mathématiques élémentaires

Mathématiques et technique

Technique et économie

| Option malienne<br>Subjects | Philo-<br>lettres | Philo-<br>langues | Sc.ex.<br>term. | Sc.biol.<br>term. |
|---|---|---|---|---|
| **Written** | | | | |
| Philosophical Dissertation | 8 | 8 | 3 | 3 |
| Latin Translation | 3 | - | - | - |
| Greek Translation | 3 | - | - | - |
| Modern Language I | 1 | 3 | 2 | 2 |
| Modern Language II | - | 3 | - | - |
| Mathematics | 2+ | 2+ | 7 | 4 |

| | | | | |
|---|---|---|---|---|
| Physical Sciences | 2[+] | 2[+] | 6 | 4 |
| Natural Sciences | 2 | 2 | 1 | 5 |
| History or Geography | 2 | 3 | 2 | 2 |

**Oral and practical**

| | | | | |
|---|---|---|---|---|
| Political and Civic Education | 2 | 2 | 2 | 2 |
| Philosophy | 2 | 2 | - | - |
| Modern Language I | 1 | 1 | - | - |
| Modern Language II | - | 1 | 1 | 1 |
| Mathematics | - | - | 1 | - |
| Physical Sciences | - | - | 1 | - |
| Natural Sciences | - | - | - | 2 |
| Physical Education | 1 | 1 | 1 | 1 |
| Manual Work | 1 | 1 | 1 | 1 |

[+]Either Mathematics or Physical Sciences chosen.

**Option étrangère**

| Subjects | Philo. | Sc. exp. | Math. elem. | Math. et tech. | Tech. et ec. |
|---|---|---|---|---|---|
| **Written** | | | | | |
| Philosophy | 8 | 6 | 2 | 3[++] | 3 |
| Mathematics | 2 | 3 | 7 | 5 | 4 |
| Physical Sciences | 2 | 4 | 6 | 4 | - |
| Natural Sciences | 2 | 3 | 1 | - | - |
| Modern Language I | 3 | 2 | 2 | 2 | 3 |
| History or Geography | 3 | 2 | 2 | 3[++] | 3 |
| Mechanical Construction | - | - | - | 4 | - |
| Economics | - | - | - | - | 5 |
| **Oral and practical** | | | | | |
| Political and Civic Education | 2 | 2 | 2 | 2 | 2 |
| Modern Language I | 1 | 1 | 1 | - | - |
| Modern Language II | - | - | - | - | 1 |
| Practical Techniques | - | - | - | 2 | - |
| Physical Education | 1 | 1 | 1 | 1 | 1 |
| Manual Work | 1 | 1 | 1 | 1 | 1 |

[++]Either Philosophy or History or Geography chosen.

Laboratory work in science courses almost nonexistent outside of Bamako. In Bamako a _bloc scientifique_ built by AID and ORT for use of the Lycée Technique and the Lycée Askia. Completely equipped with laboratories, draughtsman's tables, typewriters, etc.

Students also make science kits, boxes of simple versatile laboratory equipment to be used by _écoles fondamentales_ in science classes.

## HIGHER EDUCATION

No higher education.  Scholarships to Dakar or Paris.

The Mali government considers the Ecole Nationale d'Administration and the Ecole Normale Supérieure as the nucleus of higher education.

## VOCATIONAL AND TECHNICAL EDUCATION

ELEMENTARY LEVEL INSTITUTIONS:

    Centres d'apprentissage in industrial and agricultural subjects

    Ecole des Maîtresses d'Enseignement Ménagèr , Ségou

    Ecole des Infirmiers du premier degré, Bamako

    Ecole des Aides Sociales, Bamako

    Ecole des Infirmiers Vétérinaires, Bamako

Entrance requirements for elementary level technical training:  Completion of fifth year fundamental school.

Certificate awarded:    Certificat d'aptitude professionnelle (C.A.P.) in chosen specialty.

Length of course:    2 years for C.A.P. of first degree.

                     3 years for C.A.P. of second degree.

## CENTRES D'APPRENTISSAGE INDUSTRIEL

2 or 3-year course depending on specialty.

Program:

    General subjects:    French, History, Geography, Morals, Mathematics, Physics, Physical Education.

    Technical specialties:  Welding, Reinforced Concrete Work, Metal Construction, Electricity, Carpentry and Joinery, Auto Mechanics, Office Work.

## CENTRES D'APPRENTISSAGE AGRICOLE

1-year course with 1 year on-the-job training.

Entry age:  15-20 years.

Program:   General subjects plus General and Specialized Agriculture, Plant
           Husbandry, Surveying, Agricultural Technology, Zootechnics,
           Banking, Mutual Insurance, Agricultural Cooperatives.
           Practical instruction on farms using implements and machinery.

Trains agricultural assistants and instructors.   Top 5 graduates can take
competitive examination for the Lycée Agricole.

1963-64, 2 centres d'apprentissage, 90 students.   Controlled by Ministry
of Development.

## CENTRE D'APPRENTISSAGE RURAL, Ntonimba

3-year course.

Private school.   Agricultural training.

## ECOLE DES MAITRESSES D'ENSEIGNEMENT MENAGER , Ségou

Entrance requirements:            Competitive examination after 5th year
                                  fundamental.

1-year course for teachers of Home Economics at fundamental level.

## ECOLE DES INFIRMIERS DU PREMIER DEGRE, Bamako

2-year course, for elementary level health assistants.

Entry age:   17 years minimum.

Program:   Obstetrics, Childcare, and training for nurses in laboratories,
           hospitals or pharmacies.

## ECOLE DES AIDES SOCIALES

2-year course, followed by practical training for health assistants at
Centre de Formation Ménagère.

Entry age:   16-25 years.

## ECOLE DES INFIRMIERS VETERINAIRES, Bamako

15-18 month course for veterinary assistants.

MIDDLE LEVEL INSTITUTIONS:

    Lycée Technique, Bamako

    Ecole des Travaux Publics, Bamako

    Lycée Agricole, Katibougou

    Ecole Secondaire de Santé, Bamako

    Ecole des Assistants d'Elevage, Bamako

Entrance requirements for middle level technical training:  Must hold the D.E.F. or pass entrance examination.

Certificates awarded:    Brevet for technical and professional education of first degree (2 years) or second degree (3 years) and Baccalauréat in Elementary Mathematics (5 years).


LYCEE TECHNIQUE, Bamako

Length of course:    2 years for technicien du 1er degré.

    3 years for technicien du 2ème degré.

    5 years for ingénieur du 1er degré.

Program:

    General subjects:    French, History, Geography, English, Morals, Mathematics, Physics, Hygiene, Physical Education.

    Specialized sections for technicians in Meteorology, Construction, Mechanics, Electricity, Public Works.

    Specialized sections for engineers in Projection or Calculation, Direction of Industrial Complexes, Agricultural Enterprises, Public Works.

Engineers with the Baccalauréat in Elementary Mathematics may go on to engineering school in France.  Projected higher level engineering training, but does not yet exist in Mali.


ECOLE DES TRAVAUX PUBLICS, Bamako

Controlled by Ministry of Public Works.

Length of course:    5 years for ingénieur d'exécution, in one specialty.

    Formerly 3 and 4-year courses for technical assistants, but this training is now given in the Lycée Technique.

Program:

General subjects:    French, History, Geography, Mathematics,
                     Physics, Natural Science, Physical Education.

Technical subjects: (1)  Public Works section
                    (2)  Topography section
                    (3)  Cartography section
                    (4)  Geology section

LYCEE AGRICOLE, Katibougou

Highest level of agricultural education.

   (1)  Ecoles saisonnières
   (2)  Centres d'apprentissage agricole
   (3)  Lycée Agricole

Controlled by Ministry of Development.  Formerly the Agricultural
Technical School.  Boarding school.

Entrance requirements:       Competitive examination after D.E.F.

Length of course:       3 years:  2 years' coursework, 1 year on-the-job
                        training.

Program:

General subjects:    French, Geography, History, Arithmetic, Algebra,
                     Geometry, Physics, Chemistry, Natural Sciences.

Specialized subjects: Agricultural Technology, Technology of Agri-
                     cultural Industries, Geology, Botany, Systematic
                     Zoology and Physiology, Human and Animal Anatomy,
                     General and Specialized Agriculture, Comparative
                     Agriculture, Agricultural Implements, Horti-
                     culture, Arboriculture, Zootechnics, Veterinary
                     Science, Rural Economy.

Practical training periods in agricultural centers and departments.

ECOLE SECONDAIRE DE SANTE, Bamako

Entrance requirements:        D.E.F. or B.E.P.C., or competitive exami-
                              nation for nurses from Ecole des Infirmiers
                              du Premier Degré or Ecole des Aides Sociales
                              with 3 years' experience.

Entry age:  18-25 years.  May be stretched at upper limit for those taking
            competitive examination.

Length of course:        (1)  Nurses:  2 years.

                         (2)  Midwives:  3 years.

                         (3)  Social assistants:  3 years.

                         (4)  Medical secretaries:  3 years.

Certificate awarded:     Diplôme d'Infirmier

Controlled by Ministry of Health.


ECOLE DES ASSISTANTS D'ELEVAGE, Bamako

2-year course in veterinary education.


OTHER VOCATIONAL AND TECHNICAL INSTITUTIONS:

ECOLE NATIONALE D'ADMINISTRATION, Bamako

Controlled by Ministry of Civil Service.

Trains Baccalauréat holders for higher administrative posts.  Also provides
advanced training for promotion.

Entrance requirements:   (a)  Competitive examination for holders of
                              Baccalauréat under 30.  Also, for civil
                              servants of B hierarchy with 3 years
                              seniority.

                         (b)  Recruitment of holders of D.E.F. under 30.
                              Also civil servants of C  hierarchy with 3
                              years seniority and under 35.

Length of course:        3 years:  2 years' coursework, 1 year on-the-job
                         training, now spent in foreign countries.

Program:

    Specialty sections: (1)  General administration
                        (2)  Magistracy and juridical services
                        (3)  Economic and financial services
                        (4)  Diplomatic careers
                        (5)  Social services

Certificate awarded:     Brevet de l'Ecole Nationale d'Administration,
                         after presentation of a thesis.
                         Students are then placed as civil servants,
                         depending on level achieved.

## MAISON DES ARTS (Formerly Sudanese Crafts Center), Bamako

To be enlarged to serve as the nucleus of a Fine Arts Institute, while retaining and improving techniques of local artisans.

Open to adult craftsmen.

Program:

  General subjects:   French, Mathematics, Drawing.

  Technical subjects: Jewelry, Weaving and Upholstery, Ironwork, Leatherwork, Woodwork, Cabinet Making, Carving, Sculpture.

  Emphasis on workshop practical sessions.

## INSTITUT DES SCIENCES HUMAINES, Bamako

Formerly the Institut Français de l'Afrique Noire. Essentially a research organization. Has library and museum.

## TEACHER EDUCATION

## ECOLES NORMALES

Entrance requirements:    D.E.F. and 16 years old, or less, or pass entrance examination,

                          or  first part of Baccalauréat and up to 17 years old.

Length of course:    23 months: two 11-month periods with 1 month vacation.

Program:

  (1)  Section lettres:    Literature, History, Geography.

  (2)  Section langues:    Modern Languages and Literature (French and one other).

  (3)  Section Math-Science: Mathematics, Physical and Natural Sciences.

  4 weeks of practice teaching in second year.

Certificate awarded:    Diplôme des écoles normales (D.E.N.) after successful completion of chosen section with final examination of 10-15 hours written, 6 hours oral.

                        Level of Diplôme approximately equivalent to Baccalauréat.

Holders of the Diplôme may teach in second
cycle fundamental school.

Grading:  Average of less than 12:   Passable
                          12-14:   Assez bien
                          14-16:   Bien
                    16 or better:   Très bien

## CENTRES PEDAGOGIQUES REGIONAUX

Formerly cours normaux.

Entrance requirements:        D.E.F. or pass entrance examination.

Length of course:        1 year of pedagogical training.

Certificate awarded:        Diplôme des centres pédagogiques régionaux
                            (replacing old Certificat de fin d'études des
                            cours normaux).

                            Holders of this Diplôme may teach in first cycle
                            of fundamental school.

## ECOLE NORMALE SUPERIEURE

Under construction by AID.  1963-64, 15 classes.

Entrance requirements:        Baccalauréat.

Length of course:        3 years, to form secondary level teachers.

## ADULT EDUCATION

Cours du soir (evening classes) taught at Collège Moderne du Soir, Bamako,
by lycée teachers.  Equal to last 4 years of fundamental education.  Women
also learn Hygiene and First Aid.

Entrance requirements:        Proof of having completed 5th year funda-
                              mental.

Entry age:  17-30.

1965, 7 cours, meeting from 6 to 9 o'clock every evening.

ISLAMIC REPUBLIC OF MAURITANIA

| Student's Age | Year of Schooling | | | |
|---|---|---|---|---|
| 26 | 20 | HIGHER EDUCATION | | |
| 25 | 19 | | | |
| 24 | 18 | | | |
| 23 | 17 | | | |
| 22 | 16 | | | |
| 21 | 15 | | | |
| 20 | 14 | | | |
| 19 | 13 | ** | Terminale | |
| 18 | 12 | * | I Première | SECONDARY |
| 17 | 11 | | II Seconde | |
| 16 | 10 | | III Troisième | |
| 15 | 9 | | IV Quatrième | |
| 14 | 8 | | V Cinquième | |
| 13 | 7 | | VI Sixième | |
| 12 | 6 | | | ELEMENTARY |
| 11 | 5 | | | |
| 10 | 4 | | | |
| 9 | 3 | | | |
| 8 | 2 | | | |
| 7 | 1 | | | |
| 6 | | | | |
| 5 | | | | |
| 4 | | | | |
| 3 | | | | |

None

SECONDARY EDUCATION (enseignement long)

SECONDARY EDUCATION (enseignement court)

Cours complémentaires

ELEMENTARY EDUCATION

Institut des Hautes Etudes Islamiques

(Ecole normale) Teacher Training

Centre de Formation Mamadou Touré

Compulsory education: Primary school only (6 years)

School year: October 15 – July 15. 3 terms.

Secondary grading: 20 Perfect

10/20 pass mark

ISLAMIC REPUBLIC OF MAURITANIA

(République Islamique de Mauritanie)


Independence:  November 28, 1960


## BACKGROUND

Mostly desert and semi-desert country.  90% of population live on agriculture.  Very little modernizing with French colonial rule compared with
other parts of French Africa.  Forms a geographic and cultural bridge
between black Africa and the Maghreb.

Two-thirds of the population are Moors, mixture of Arab and Berber stock,
related to the Tuareg of Central Sahara.  Moors divided into warrior and
marabout tribes; latter more numerous, embodying Islamic culture and
learning.  (In Africa the Moorish marabouts, hermits or priests, have been
the propagators of an authentic Arab culture which extended to Morocco in
the north to the Black African lands in the south.  In the families of the
marabouts, Islamic law, history and theology taught.)

Remainder of population live principally in Senegal River valley, and the
plains of Brakna and Gorgol.  They are the Sarakolle, Wolof, Bembera,
Fulani, and Toucouleurs.  More than 95% are practicing Moslems, the
conservative Qadiriyya order being dominant.

Before arrival of Europeans in 15th century, Arabs and Berbers were
invaders.  14th-15th centuries Arab tribes from Egypt gained control,
establishing Islamic religion for all; 17th century, complete dominance
over Berbers.

After the Portuguese arrived in the 15th century, they were followed by
Dutch, French, and English traders for the gum trade.

French explorers came in the 19th century.  By 1903, Territory of Mauritania was established as an administrative unit of France and its capital
was founded at Saint-Louis in Sénégal.  1920, Mauritanie became a colony
attached to French West Africa (a federation of 8 French territories in
West Africa).

1946, a Mauritanian Territorial Assembly was established and elected representatives to French Parliament and the Assembly of French Union.  1946-
56, more power to local political leaders.

Became self-governing member of French Community, from referendum of September 28, 1958. Islamic Republic of Mauritania established by a constituent Assembly March 1959; independence in 1960; remained within the French Community.

Arabic, the national language. French proclaimed the official language, 1959. Dialects spoken, Hassania, Wolof, Sarakole, and Fulah, but not taught in schools.

Public education not emphasized until recent years. Christian missions provided some schooling for Africans for Sénégal River valley, but not for Moors because of objections of Islamic leaders and nomadic life of people.

According to Islamic tradition, upper class children studied at home simple Arithmetic, Arabic, and the Koran. At 8 years of age, both boys and girls sent to local Koranic schools (which generally had higher standards than those farther south). Girls remained 2 years, boys until age 15.

3 principal marabout schools (<u>grandes Medersas</u>) at Boutilimit, Kiffa, and Kerna. Courses in Grammar, Logic, Theory, Methods, Mystique, and traditional subjects. Except for Koranic schools giving religious instruction, there are no private schools. All educational establishments under government control and all subsidized by government.

At the request of the Territorial Assembly, Franco-Arabic curriculum introduced into state primary schools, 1947. French system of education gradually introduced; by 1960, first cycle complete in all primary schools. Government is experimenting with nomad schools traveling with the tribes.

<u>PRESENT SYSTEM</u>

<u>PRIMARY EDUCATION</u>

Entry age: 6 years.

Language of instruction: Arabic and French.

Length of course: 6 years.

Subjects taught in primary schools are exactly the same as in French primary schools, except that Mauritanian history and geography are taught and Arabic is the national language, according to the Mauritanian Constitution.

Subjects: Arabic, French, Grammar, Orthography, Arithmetic, Nature Study, History, Geography, Drawing, Music, Physical Education and Sports.

Diploma at end of 6 years:  Certificat d'études primaires élémentaires.


## SECONDARY EDUCATION

Entrance requirements:    Necessary to pass an examination for entrance
                          into classe de sixième.  This examination is on
                          subjects taught in primary schools, designed to
                          test aptitude of candidates to follow a course
                          of secondary education.  It is a selective
                          examination.

Languages of instruction:  1) French, 2) Arabic, 3) English.

English was taught as an optional language, but since independence, it has
become more and more important, because of greater contact with the rest
of the world and because there are so many English-speaking African countries.

Length of course:  7 years for enseignement long.

                    4 years for enseignement court.

Subjects taught same as in French secondary schools, except that Arabic is
compulsory as the first foreign language, and English compulsory as the
second foreign language.  In Physics and Chemistry, practical work and
experience, as well as laboratory work, is compulsory.  Each secondary
school has a laboratory.


## Secondary Institutions in Mauritania:

        Lycée Nouakchott
        Collège Rosso
        Cours complémentaires at Atar, Aioun-el-Atrouss, and Kaédi.  Courses
                        of 4 years leading to B.E.P.C. or Brevet élémen-
                        taire (B.E.)
        Institut des Hautes Etudes Islamiques, Boutilimit.  Gives religious
                        instruction and general bilingual (Arabic-French)
                        instruction.  Entry by competitive examination,
                        similar to entry examination for sixième, except
                        that all subjects are in Arabic.  Diplomas
                        awarded are the Brevet and the Baccalauréat Arabe.

## Diplomas:

        Brevet d'études du premier cycle du second degré (B.E.P.C.) awarded
        by Ministry of Youth and Education of Mauritania at the end of 4th
        secondary year.  Contains an obligatory examination in Arabic.

        *Baccalauréat première partie called examen probatoire de fin de
        première taken at end of 6th year.

**Baccalauréat (deuxième partie) taken at end of 7th year.
Both <u>Baccalauréats</u> set and awarded by the University of Dakar, Sénégal.

<u>Examen probatoire de fin de première</u>:  Choice of one program from 8 series.

(1)  Série classique A:      French, Greek, Latin, Language, History
                             or Geography, Mathematics or Physical
                             Sciences.

(2)  Série classique A':     French, Latin, Mathematics, Language,
                             Physical Sciences, History or Geography,
                             Greek.

(3)  Série classique B:      French, Language II, Latin, Language I,
                             History or Geography .

(4)  Série classique C:      French, Physical Sciences, Mathematics,
                             Language, History or Geography, Latin.

(5)  Série moderne:          French, Physical Sciences, Mathematics,
                             Language I, Language II, History or
                             Geography.

(6)  Série moderne-prime:    French, Physical Sciences, Mathematics,
                             Language, History or Geography, Natural
                             Sciences.

(7)  Série technique:        French, Mechanical Construction,
                             Mathematics, Language, History or
                             Geography, Physical Sciences.

(8)  Série technique':       French, Language I, Language II,
                             Mathematics and Mathematical Statistics,
                             or Problems of Economic Order, History
                             or Geography, Physical Sciences or
                             Technology of Saleable Products.

     Optional subjects:  Art, Music, Homemaking, German, English, Arab
                         Literature, Arab Dialects, Spanish, Italian,
                         Portuguese, Russian, Modern Hebrew.

<u>Baccalauréat de l'enseignement du second degré</u>:  Choice of one of 5 series.

(1)  Série philosophie:      Philosophy, History and Geography,
                             Mathematics and Philosophical Sciences,
                             Modern Language, Natural Sciences.

(2)  Série sciences expérimentales:  Philosophy, Physical Sciences,
                             Mathematics, Modern Language, History or
                             Geography, Natural Sciences.

(3)  Série mathématiques élémentaires:  Philosophy, Physical Sciences,
                             Mathematics, Modern Language, History or
                             Geography, Natural Sciences.

(4)  Série mathématiques et technique:  Philosophy or History or
Geography, Physical Sciences, Mathe-
matics, Modern Language, Mechanical
Construction.

(5)  Série technique et économie:  Philosophy, Economics, Mathematics,
Modern Language, History or Geography.

Optional subjects:  Art, Music, Homemaking, German, English, Arab
Literature, Arab Dialects, Spanish, Italian,
Portuguese, Russian, Modern Hebrew, Greek-Latin.

For both the Examen probatoire and the Baccalauréat, not more than two
optional subjects may be taken.  Also, no need to take any optionals at all.

## SECONDARY CURRICULUM
(Hours per week)

| Subjects | 6M | 6A | 5M | 5A | 4M | 4B | 3M | 3B |
|---|---|---|---|---|---|---|---|---|
| French | 6 | 5 | 6 | 5 | 5 | 4 | 5 | 4 |
| Mathematics | 4 | 4 | 3 | 3 | 3 | 3 | 3 | 3 |
| Arabic | 5 | 5 | 4 | 4 | 4 | 4 | 4 | 4 |
| English | 4 | 4 | 4 | 4 | 3 | 3 | 3 | 3 |
| Natural Sciences | 1½ | 1½ | 1½ | 1½ | 1½ | 1½ | 1½ | 1½ |
| History-Geography | 2½ | 2½ | 2½ | 2½ | 2½ | 2½ | 2½ | 2½ |
| Spanish | - | - | - | 4 | 4 | 4 | 3 | 3 |
| Civics | ½ | ½ | ½ | ½ | ½ | ½ | ½ | ½ |
| Physical Education | 2 | 2 | 2 | 2 | 2 | 2 | 2 | 2 |
| Art | 2 | 2 | 2 | 2 | 2 | 2 | 2 | 2 |
| Sewing (girls) | 2 | 2 | 2 | 2 | 2 | 2 | 2 | 2 |

| Subjects | 2M | 2M' | 1M | 1M' | Terminale Phil. | Terminale Math. | Terminale Exp.Sc. |
|---|---|---|---|---|---|---|---|
| French | 4 | 4 | 4 | 4 | - | - | - |
| Philosophy | - | - | - | - | 9 | 4 | 5 |
| Mathematics | 5 | 5 | 5 | 5 | 1⅓ | 9 | 4 |
| Physics and Chemistry | 4½ | 4½ | 4½ | 4½ | 4 | 6 | 5 |
| English | 3 | 3 | 3 | 3 | 1½ | 1½ | 1½ |
| Arabic | 4 | 4 | 4 | 4 | 1½ | 1½ | 1½ |
| Spanish | 3 | 3 | 3 | 3 | 1½ | 1½ | 1½ |
| History-Geography | 3 | 3 | 3 | 4 | 4 | 6 | 4 |
| Natural Sciences | 3 | 3 | 3 | 1½ | 1½ | 1½ | 4 |
| Physical Education | 2 | 2 | 2 | 2 | 2 | 2 | 2 |
| Art | 1 | 1 | 1opt. | 1opt. | 1opt. | 1opt. | 1opt. |
| Latin | 3 | 3 | 3 | 1½ | 1½ | 1½ | 1½ |

Grading:  20 - Perfect.
          Lowest Pass mark:  10/20.  This is the minimum to pass on to the
          next class, and to pass an examination.  The Council of teachers
          can pass a pupil with a mark of 9.75, when it is considered that
          he could have been better marked, or when it is wished to give
          him a chance.

          Best marks:  17, 18, and 19/20 rarely given; only for excellent
          pupils.

## HIGHER EDUCATION

Students study abroad (France, Sénégal, Tunisia, U.A.R., etc.)  Higher
education therefore essentially analogous to French higher education.

## VOCATIONAL AND TECHNICAL EDUCATION

### CENTRE DE FORMATION MAMADOU TOURE

Attached to the Ministry of Works.  Forms specialized tradesmen.

Includes following sections:

        Masonry and Tiling
        Reinforced Concrete Masonry
        Ocean Fishing
        Mechanics I and II
        Manual Trades
        Carpentry
        Plumbing and Electricity
        Typing
        Business Administration

Length of program:  8 months.

At close of program, final examination (examen de fin de stage) and 6 months
practical experience.

Student then receives a diploma (diplôme) in one of the 9 specialties.

## TEACHER EDUCATION

First teacher training school in Mauritania opened October 1964, Ecole
Normale de Nouakchott.  Formerly the Institut Pédagogique National,
founded in 1960.

Entry age:  Not yet firmly determined, because of need to create more
            teaching personnel.

Entry conditions:      At present, with required level or diploma only.
                       No competitive examination yet, but an entrance
                       examination is projected for the future.

Length of courses:     Admittance in <u>classe de sixième</u>, (must be 12 years
                       of age), for study to the <u>Baccalauréat</u>.  Programs
                       based on general instruction and teacher training.
                       Forms <u>instituteurs</u>.

                       Admittance to cinquième.   3 years of study to become
                       <u>instituteur adjoint</u>.

                       Admittance after <u>troisième</u> with <u>B.E.P.C.</u>  3 years of
                       study to become <u>professeurs</u> of the <u>cours complémen-
                       taires</u>.

<u>Diplomas</u>:

    <u>Certificat élémentaire d'aptitude pédagogique</u> (<u>C.E.A.P.</u>)

    <u>Certificat d'aptitude pédagogique</u> (<u>C.A.P.</u>)

Teacher training in Arabic is also given under the guidance of teaching
advisers and inspectors of Arabic instruction.  Diplomas awarded: <u>Diplôme
pédagogique arabe de première  sélection</u> (equivalent to <u>C.E.A.P.</u>) and
<u>Diplôme pédagogique arabe de deuxième sélection</u> (equivalent to <u>C.A.P.</u>).

698

REPUBLIC OF NIGER

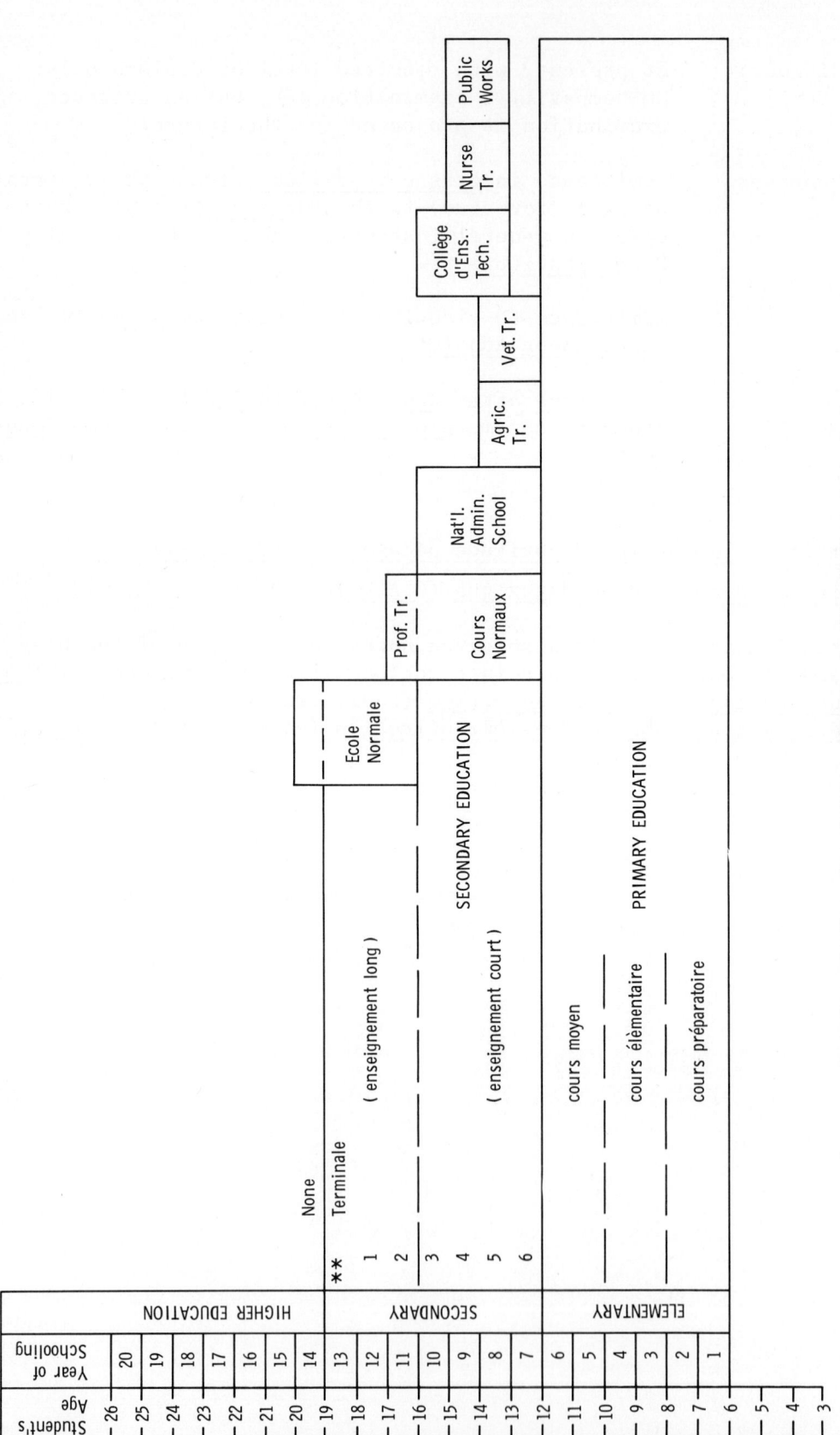

Compulsory education: through Primary Education for all pupils in reach of school

School year: October 1 - June 30.   3 terms.

Secondary Grading: 20 Perfect
                   10 / 20 pass mark ( examinations )

REPUBLIC OF NIGER
(République du Niger)


Independence:  August 3, 1960.


## BACKGROUND


The country's geographical position (vast plateau in center of continent, largely barren desert) and the economic situation has made Niger's entry to the modern world slow.

There are 2 major categories of population:  3/4 of population are Hausa farmers and fishermen along the Niger River in the South, the Djerma and the Songhai; remaining 25% are Caucasian Hamites, nomadic and semi-nomadic people of the central and northern areas, comprising the Taureg, the Toubou, the Peuls.  Approximately 80% of the population are Moslem.

In 11th and 12th centuries, Arabs of North Africa pushed southward, establishing "empires"; later empires created by African leaders converted to Islam.  These empires included Mali, Ghana and Gao in the West, and Hausaland and Bornu in the area that is now the Niger Republic.

17th century, Djerma and other nomad tribes entered from North.  1804-1810, a Fulani Muslim subjugated the Hausa states and the Bornu empire.

1882, British explorers arrived.  First French military expeditions, 1890. There were major uprisings after World War I.  In 1921, a civil administration established, following the French colonial pattern.  After World War II, party politics developed.

September 18, 1958, voters in the Niger Republic approved the constitution of the French Fifth Republic, and on December 19, 1958, Republic of Niger became an autonomous state within the French Community.

1959, Niger joined the Conseil de l'Entente with Dahomey, Ivory Coast, and Upper Volta.

French, official language; Hausa, the language of trade.

From 1921-1961, French pattern of primary, secondary and technical studies. Higher education in France and Dakar.

Since mission schools were not encouraged by the religion of Islam, education has played a minor role.  By 1957, only 4% of school-age children

were in school;  by 1964, 8.9%.  Most education is at the primary level;
only half complete the 6-year primary course.

There are some nomadic schools.  Koranic schools offering oral religious
education.


## PRESENT SYSTEM


## PRIMARY EDUCATION

Entry age:      6 years minimum, 8 years maximum.

Language of instruction:      French.

Length of course:   6 years - Cours préparatoire, including classe
                                  d'initiation, 2 years
                             - Cours élémentaire, 2 years
                             - Cours moyen, 2 years

### TIMETABLE
(Hours per week)

| Subjects | Cours prép. | Cours élém. | Cours moyen |
|---|---|---|---|
| Morals and Civics | 3/4 | 1 | 1 |
| French | 7 | 6 | 6 |
| Reading | 9 | 7 | 4 |
| Writing | 2½ | 2 | 1 |
| Nature Study | - | 1 | 3 |
|  |  |  | (incl. 1h. practical) |
| Arithmetic | 3 3/4 | 4 | 5 |
| History | - | ½ | 1 |
| Geography | - | 1 | 1 |
| Art and Handicrafts | 1½ | 1 | 1 |
| Singing | 1 | 1 | 1 |
| Physical Education | 2 | 2½ | 2½ |
| Directed Activities, or Practical Work | - | ½ | 1 |
| Recreation | 2½ | 2½ | 2½ |

Total hours per week:   30

N.B.  Nature study, practical scientific work and directed activities
      may be replaced in the cours moyen by preliminary agricultural
      work.

Diploma awarded after 6 years:  Certificat d'études primaires élémentaires
                                  (C.E.P.E.)

Primary school administration is becoming more and more decentralized.
1959, 3 administrative districts; 1964, 8 administrative districts.  Some
nomadic primary schools.

1964, 493 primary schools:  481 public and 12 private, comprising 10
Catholic mission schools at Doutchi, Niamey, Niamey-Canada, Dolbel,
Maradi, Zinder, Tchirozerine; 1 Protestant mission school at Goudel; and
1 non-denominational, Cours La Fontaine.


## SECONDARY EDUCATION

Entry age:        12 years average.  At least 11, no more than 15 years.

Entrance requirements:        Competitive examination, concours d'entrée
                              en sixième.

Length of course:    4 years enseignement court
                     7 years enseignement long

Language of instruction:        French.

Programs:        The same as for French secondary schools, with African
                 adaptations in Geography and History.
                 The tests are sent direct from the University of Bordeaux.

Diplomas awarded:        Brevet d'études du premier cycle (B.E.P.C.) after
                         4-year enseignement court, given in the collèges
                         d'enseignement général.

                         Brevet élémentaire (B.E.) after 4-year enseignement
                         court, given in the cours normaux.

                         Examen probatoire de fin de première (formerly the
                         first part of the baccalauréat), awarded in the
                         lycée at end of 1st class, after 6 years.

                         Baccalauréat awarded in Philosophy, Experimental
                         Sciences, or Elementary Mathematics, in the lycée at
                         end of terminal class, after 7 years.

15 public secondary schools:

   10 collèges d'enseignement général (formerly cours complémentaires) at
      Niamey, Zinder, Tahoua, Maradi, Agades, Dosso, Maine-Soroa, Doutchi,
      Tessaoua, Magaria.  Offer enseignement court and award the B.E.P.C.
      after 4 years.  Pupils may then go on to 2nd class of the lycée or
      into the professional training class of the cours normaux to become
      teachers.  Some pupils lodged close to C.E.G. under government grants.

   3 cours normaux at Zinder, Tahoua, Tillabéri.  Offer enseignement court,
     leading to B.E., followed by a year of professional training to become
     instituteurs adjoints.

1  école normale at Zinder.  Offers 4-year course from 4th class to
       terminal, with additional year of professional training to become
       instituteur.  Baccalauréat in Experimental Sciences at end of terminal.

1  lycée national at Niamey.  Offers full secondary cycle of 7 years
       from 6th class to terminal.  Probatoire after 1st class, 6 years, and
       baccalauréat in Philosophy, Experimental Sciences or Elementary
       Mathematics after terminal, 7 years.

1 private girls' school, Collège Mariana, the Catholic Mission, Niamey,
       offers 2 years (6th and 5th classes) of secondary instruction.


## HIGHER EDUCATION

None.


## VOCATIONAL AND TECHNICAL EDUCATION

7 technical schools, all at lower secondary level, each operating under
direction of Ministry concerned.  The first 6 train only candidates for
government service.  Pupils selected on basis of psychological and technical
tests.


## CENTRE D'APPRENTISSAGE AGRICOLE, Kolo

Attached to Ministry of Rural Economy. 2-year course (6th and 5th classes),
training agricultural extension agents.  2nd year course for forestry
agents.


## VETERINARY SCHOOL, Maradi

Attached to Ministry of Rural Economy.  2-year course (6th and 5th classes),
training veterinary agents.


## NATIONAL ADMINISTRATION SCHOOL, Niamey

Attached to Ministry of Public Service.  9-month courses in Public Administration, Finance and Law, at the levels of 6th to 2nd classes.


## NURSES TRAINING SCHOOL, Niamey

Attached to Ministry of Health.  2-year course for hospital nurses (male
and female), level 5th to 3rd classes.

## PUBLIC WORKS SCHOOL, Niamey

Attached to Ministry of Public Works.  6-month course for supervisory personnel, at levels of 5th and 4th classes.  Founded 1962.

## COLLEGE D'ENSEIGNEMENT TECHNIQUE, Maradi

Attached to Ministry of Education.  3-year courses in Auto Mechanics, Masonry, Metalworking.  Level 5th to 3rd classes.

Certificates awarded:       Certificat d'aptitude professionnelle (C.A.P.)
                            Concours Berliet

## VOCATIONAL SCHOOL (C.F.P.R.), Niamey

Attached to Ministry of Labor.  9-month courses in Auto-Mechanics, Electricity, Masonry, Stenography.

## TEACHER EDUCATION

### ECOLE NORMALE DE ZINDER

Founded in 1960.

Entrance requirements:      Competitive examination for holders of
                            B.E.P.C. or B.E.

Length of course:       3 years of secondary training specializing in
                        Experimental Sciences, plus 1 year of professional
                        training.

Language of instruction:       French.

Diplomas awarded:       Baccalauréat in Experimental Sciences, after 3 years.
                        Certificat de fin d'études des cours normaux, after
                            4 years, to become an instituteur.

Program:       The same as in French écoles normales.

### COURS NORMAUX

At Zinder, Tahoua, Tillabéri.

Entrance requirements:      Completion of primary education and concours
                            d'entrée en sixième.  Maximum entry age, 16.

Length of course:    4 years of first cycle secondary training (<u>enseigne-</u> <u>ment court</u>), plus 1 year of professional training.

Diploma awarded:    <u>Brevet élémentaire</u> (<u>B.E.</u>), after 4 years.
<u>Certificat de fin d'études des cours normaux</u>, after 5 years, to become an <u>instituteur-adjoint</u>.

Professional examinations for upgrading teachers:

<u>Certificat d'aptitude du monitorat</u> (<u>C.A.M.</u>)
<u>Certificat élémentaire d'aptitude pédagogique</u> (<u>C.E.A.P.</u>)
<u>Certificat d'aptitude pédagogique</u> (<u>C.A.P.</u>)
<u>Brevet supérieur de capacité pédagogique</u> (<u>B.S.</u>)

## ADULT EDUCATION

1962-63, literacy campaign for adults in rural areas:  how to read and write tribal language, do special arithmetic, speak French, and general knowledge of agriculture, child-rearing, and home-making.

REPUBLIC OF SENEGAL

Student's Age / Year of Schooling table:

| Student's Age | Year of Schooling | |
|---|---|---|
| 26 | 20 | HIGHER EDUCATION |
| 25 | 19 | |
| 24 | 18 | |
| 23 | 17 | |
| 22 | 16 | |
| 21 | 15 | |
| 20 | 14 | |
| 19 | 13 | |
| 18 | 12 | SECONDARY |
| 17 | 11 | |
| 16 | 10 | |
| 15 | 9 | |
| 14 | 8 | |
| 13 | 7 | |
| 12 | 6 | ELEMENTARY |
| 11 | 5 | |
| 10 | 4 | |
| 9 | 3 | |
| 8 | 2 | |
| 7 | 1 | |
| 6 | | |
| 5 | | |
| 4 | | |
| 3 | | |

Law & Pol. Sc. **
Medicine/Pharmacy
Letters & Soc. Sc.
Science

Terminale
1 Première
2 Seconde
3 Troisième
4 Quatrième
5 Cinquième
6 Sixième

Middle (cours moyens)
Elementary (cours élémentaires)
Preparatory (cours préparatoire)
Initiation (cours d'initiation)

Nursery School

HIGHER EDUCATION

SECONDARY EDUCATION

(Enseignement long)

(Enseignement court )

ELEMENTARY EDUCATION

Teacher Training

Technical Education

Compulsory Education: 6 years primary education (not enforced)

School Year: Oct. 13 to July 13 (primary and secondary)

Secondary grading: 0 - 20 10/20 passing

REPUBLIC OF SENEGAL
(République du Sénégal)


Independence:   August 25, 1960.



## BACKGROUND


Largest ethnic groups:  The Wolof, Serer (skilled peanut cultivators), and
Lebu (fishermen and farmers, concentrated in Dakar area).   Others are
Tucular, Fulani (living in Sénégal Valley), and Mandingos (in southeast
and northern Casamance), and Diola (in southern Casamance).

French is the official language.  Wolof is spoken by Wolof and Lebu.  Serer
related to Fulani, which is language of Fulani and Tukular in northeast.
In Casamance, languages of the Mande group are spoken.

In 14th century, Wolof and Serer tribes from northeast entered the territory.
Parts of Sénégal were at various times in medieval empires of Tekrur, Ghana,
and Mali.   From 14th to 17th centuries, Jolof empire controlled the six Wolof
states of Kayor, Baol, Walo, Sine, Salum, and Jolof.

Portuguese explorers arrived in the middle of 15th century; Dutch, later.
17th century, Jolof power declined.   18th century marked by struggles among
northern Wolof states and attacks from Mauritania.

Saint-Louis, established as trading post by French, 1659, and Gorée, small
island near modern Dakar, were centers of activity until mid-19th century.
Both captured by English during Napoleonic wars; restored to France, 1815.
Through 17th and 18th centuries, main trading in slaves and gum arabic.
Slave trade abolished in 1815.   Peanut cultivation, begun by Africans mid-
19th century, the foundation of Sénégal's economy.

French expansion during governorship of General Faidherbe (1854-65),
extended in Third Republic, last 30 years of 19th century.   Municipalities
on French model established in Saint-Louis, Gorée, Dakar, and Rufisque;
other areas regarded as a Protectorate and under separate administration.

1902, all other territories in West Africa separated from the government of
Sénégal and formed into a Government General.

1914, first African deputy elected to French Parliament.  All elected bodies
suppressed, 1940; restored at end of World War II.   1946, Sénégal given 2

deputies.  Under Constitution of 1946, Territorial Assembly established.
Universal suffrage, 1957.  Territorial Assembly given right to elect a
Council of Ministers responsible for administration of  internal affairs.

1958, Sénégal accepted new French Constitution and became an autonomous
republic within the French Community.

January 17, 1959, in Dakar, representatives of Sénégal, Soudan (present
Mali), Dahomey and Upper Volta drafted a Constitution of the Federation of
Mali.  Only the Assemblies of Sénégal and Soudan ratified and became
members of the Federation.  Mali Federation became a sovereign state, June
20, 1960.  Break-up of Federation, August 20, 1960.

Legislative Assembly of Sénégal proclaimed Sénégal's national independence
and announced its withdrawal from Federation.

New Constitution adopted August 25, 1960.  After several government re-
shuffles, new draft Constitution, February 6, 1962.

Under the Third Republic, French educational system initiated in Saint-
Louis, Gorée, Dakar, Rufisque.  Catholic missions have been active in
education since the founding of the first schools.  By 1961, there were
567 primary schools, 38 secondary schools, 19 technical schools.  Present
attempts to adapt French system to local traditions and needs.

## PRESENT SYSTEM

## PRE-SCHOOL EDUCATION

All private, whether denominational or non-denominational.

Entry age:  4-5 years.

Majority of nursery schools use the Montessori method.

## PRIMARY EDUCATION

## GOVERNMENT AND NON-GOVERNMENT SCHOOLS

Entry age:  6-8 years.

Language of instruction:  French

Length of primary education:  6 years.  4 years minimum, 8 years maximum.

|  |  |
|---|---|
| Cours d'initiation | 1 year |
| Cours préparatoire | 1 year |

SENEGAL

|  | Cours élémentaires | 2 years |
|--|--|--|
|  | Cours moyens | 2 years |

Fixed timetables and programs for both government and private primary schools.

## PRIMARY PROGRAM
(Hours per week)

| Subjects | Initiation/Preparatory | Elementary | Intermediate |
|---|---|---|---|
| Morals, Civics, Health | 1¼ | 1¼ | 1 3/4 |
| French | 8 | 7 3/4 | 7 3/4 |
| Reading | 9½ | 7½ | 4½ |
| Writing | 2½ | 1½ | ½ |
| Observation and Hygiene | - | 1½ | 3 |
| Arithmetic | 3 3/4 | 4 | 5 |
| History | - | ½ | 1 |
| Geography | - | 1 | 1 |
| Art and Manual Arts | 1 | 1 | 1 |
| Singing | ½ | ½ | ½ |
| Physical Education | 1 | 1 | 1½ |
| Recreation | 2½ | 2½ | 2½ |
| Total | 30 | 30 | 30 |

Certificate awarded on completion of 6 years:  Certificat d'études primaires élémentaires (C.E.P.E.)

After 6 years eligible for the entrance examination into 6th class of the classical, modern, or technical secondary schools:  Concours d'entrée en sixième.


## SECONDARY EDUCATION

### GOVERNMENT AND NON-GOVERNMENT SCHOOLS

Entry age:  11-14 years.

Entrance requirements:  Pass entry examination consisting of:

Short dictation of 80 words (coefficient 2).
Study of a text with expressive reading and grammatical questions (coefficient 8).
Arithmetic (coefficient 4).

Total points in examination:  170; minimum for admittance:  85.

Through this examination student directed towards lycée education (leading to Baccalauréat in 7 years - enseignement long), or towards 4-year short cycle (enseignement court, leading to Brevet d'études du premier cycle, B.E.P.C.).

Language of instruction:  French.

Compulsory modern language I:   English.
Choice of modern language II:   Spanish, Arabic, Portuguese, Russian.
Classical languages:            Greek, Latin.

### SECONDARY PROGRAM
(Hours per week)

Classes 6 and 5

|  |  | 2nd, 3rd terms 6th class and 5th class | |
|---|---|---|---|
| Subjects | 1st term 6th class | Classique | Moderne and Tech. |
| Mathematics | 3 | 3 | 3 |
| Observational Sciences | 1½ | 1½ | 1½ |
| History and Geography | 2½ | 2½ | 2½ |
| Experimental Scientific Work | 1 | - | 1 |
| Civics | ½ | ½ | ½ |
| French | 7 | 4 | 6 |
| Latin | - | 5 | - |
| Modern Language | 4 | 3 | 5 |
| Art | 1 | 1 | 1 |
| Musical Education | 1 | 1 | 1 |
| Manual Arts | 1 | 1 | 1 |
| Physical Education | 2 | 2 | 2 |
| Total | 24½ | 24½ | 24½ |

Class 4

| Subjects | Classique A | Classique B | Moderne |
|---|---|---|---|
| French | 3½ | 3½ | 5½ |
| Latin | 3½ | 3½ | - |
| Greek | 3 | - | - |
| Civics | ½ | ½ | ½ |
| Modern Language I | 3 | 3 | 3 |
| Modern Language II | - | 3 | 4 |
| History and Geography | 2½ | 2½ | 2½ |
| Mathematics | 3 | 3 | 3 |
| Observational Sciences | 1½ | 1½ | 1½ |
| Physical Education | 2 | 2 | 2 |
| Art | 1 | 1 | 1 |
| Musical Education | 1 | 1 | 1 |
| Manual Arts | 1 | 1 | 1 |
| Total | 25½ | 25½ | 25½ |

## Class 3

| Subjects | Classique A | Classique B | Moderne |
|---|---|---|---|
| French | 3½ | 3½ | 3½ |
| Latin | 3½ | 3½ | - |
| Greek | 3 | - | - |
| Civics | ½ | ½ | ½ |
| Modern Language I | 3 | 3 | 3 |
| Modern Language II | - | 3 | 4 |
| History and Geography | 3 | 3 | 3 |
| Mathematics | 3 | 3 | 3 |
| Observational Sciences | 1 | 1 | 1 |
| Physical Education | 2 | 2 | 2 |
| Art | 1 | 1 | 1 |
| Manual Arts | 1 | 1 | 1 |
| Total | 25½ | 25½ | 25½ |

## Class 2

| Subjects | A | A' | B | C | M | M' |
|---|---|---|---|---|---|---|
| French | 4 | 4 | 4 | 4 | 4 | 4 |
| Latin | 3 | 3 | 3 | 3 | - | - |
| Greek | 4 | 3 | - | - | - | - |
| Civics | ½ | ½ | ½ | ½ | ½ | ½ |
| Modern Language I | 3 | 3 | 3 | 3 | 3 | 3 |
| Modern Language II | - | - | 4 | 2 opt. | 4 | 2 opt. |
| History | 2 | 2 | 2 | 2 | 2 | 2 |
| Geography | 1½ | 1½ | 1½ | 1½ | 1½ | 1½ |
| Mathematics | 2+1 opt. | 5 | 2+1 opt. | 5 | 5 | 5 |
| Physical Sciences | 2 3/4 | 3 3/4 | 2 3/4 | 4½ | 4½ | 4½ |
| Natural Sciences | - | - | - | - | - | 3 |
| Physical Education | 2 | 2 | 2 | 2 | 2 | 2 |
| Art | 1 | 1 | 1 | 1 | 1 | 1 |
| Music (optional) | 1 | 1 | 1 | 1 | 1 | 1 |
| Manual Arts (optional) | 1 | 1 | 1 | 1 | 1 | 1 |
| Total (compulsory hours) | 25 3/4 | 28 3/4 | 25 3/4 | 26 3/4 | 27½ | 26½ |

## Class 1

| Subjects | A | A' | B | C | M | M' |
|---|---|---|---|---|---|---|
| French | 4 | 4 | 4 | 4 | 4 | 4 |
| Latin | 3 | 3 | 3 | 3 | - | - |
| Greek | 4 | 3 | - | - | - | - |
| Civics | ½ | ½ | ½ | ½ | ½ | ½ |
| Modern Language I | 3 | 3 | 3 | 3 | 3 | 3 |
| Modern Language II | - | - | 4 | 2 opt. | 4 | 2 opt. |
| History | 2 | 2 | 2 | 2 | 2 | 2 |
| Geography | 2 | 2 | 2 | 2 | 2 | 2 |

| Mathematics | 2+1 opt. | 5 | 2+1 opt. | 5 | 5 | 5 |
|---|---|---|---|---|---|---|
| Physical Sciences | 2¼ | 3¼ | 2¼ | 4½ | 4½ | 4½ |
| Natural Sciences | - | - | - | - | - | 3 |
| Physical Education | 2 | 2 | 2 | 2 | 2 | 2 |
| Art (optional) | 2 | 2 | 2 | 2 | 2 | 2 |
| Music (optional) | 1 | 1 | 1 | 1 | 1 | 1 |
| Manual Arts | 1 | 1 | 1 | 1 | 1 | 1 |
| Total (compulsory hours) | 24 3/4 | 27 3/4 | 24 3/4 | 26 | 27 | 26 |

## Terminal Class

| Subjects | Philosophy | Experimental Sciences | Elementary Mathematics |
|---|---|---|---|
| Philosophy | 9 | 5 | 3 |
| Letters | 1 | 1 (opt.) | - |
| Modern Language I | 2 | 2 | 2 |
| Classical Language or Modern Language II (opt.) | 1½ | 1½ | 1½ |
| History | 2 | 2 | 2 |
| Ccography | 2 | 2 | 2 |
| Mathematics and Cosmography | 1½ | 4 | 9 |
| Physical Sciences | 2 | 5 | 6 |
| Natural Sciences | 2 | 4 | 2 |
| Physical Education | 2 | 2 | 2 |
| Art (optional) | 2 | 2 | 2 |
| Music (optional) | 1 | 1 | 1 |
| Manual Arts for Girls (opt.) | 1 | 1 | 1 |
| Total (compulsory hours) | 24 | 26½ | 28½ |

Mathematics program in final 2 years of secondary education:

### Class 1

Classique A, B:  2 hours compulsory, 1 hour optional per week. Algebra, trigonometry, notions of analysis (2nd degree multinomials, derivations, circular functions); plane geometry and notions of analytical plane geometry.

Classique A', C, M and M':  5 hours compulsory per week. Algebra, trigonometry, notions of analysis (2nd degree multinomials and homographic functions, derivations, circular functions, applications); plane and solid geometry and notions of analytical plane geometry (scalene products, plane geometry, analytical plane geometry, solid geometry).

## Terminal classes

Philosophy:  1½ hours compulsory per week.
Trigonometry, algebra, cosmography.

Experimental Sciences:  4 hours compulsory per week.
Arithmetic (decimal numerations, fractions, decimal values, combinations); algebra and trigonometry (definition of algebraic numbers, 1st and 2nd degree equations); mechanics (relativity of movement of a point, trajectory, uniform rectilinear movement, vector-speed); cosmography.

Elementary Mathematics:  9 hours compulsory per week.
Arithmetic, algebra and notions of analysis (numbers-natural entities, relative entities, rational numbers, real numbers, complex numbers; analytical combinations, division, first numbers, fractions, numerations, decimals, arithmetical and geometrical progressions, approximate calculus); first definitions of functions; multinomial functions and rational fractions; generalities on the functions of a real variable; study of several functions of a real variable; equations and inequations; geometry and kinematics (descriptive, solid, plane geometry, solid Cartesian coordinates, punctual transformations, conics, trajectories, vector-speed, vector-acceleration, movement); astronomy.

Laboratory work in Physics and Chemistry:
  (a)  Class 2:    A, B:    1½ hours per fortnight.
                   A', C, M, M':  1½ hours per fortnight.

  (b)  Class 1:    A', C, M, M':  1½ hours per fortnight.

  (c)  Terminal class:

      Philosophy:  1 hour per fortnight.
      Elementary Mathematics:  1½ hours per fortnight.
      Experimental Sciences:  1 hour Physics, 1 hour Chemistry per week

Grading:  10/20 to pass into next class.  On advice from Professorial Council, this may be lowered to 8½/20.

Diplomas awarded:

    1st cycle:      At the end of 3rd class (4 years), Brevet d'études du premier cycle (B.E.P.C.).

    2nd cycle:      *At the end of 1st class, examen probatoire de fin de première (formerly first part of Baccalauréat). This is being maintained in Sénégal, even though it is to be abolished in France from 1965.

                **At the end of terminal class, Baccalauréat.

## Cours complémentaires

For primary school candidates who have failed examination to lycées or collèges, and those with some secondary education lacking the B.E. or B.E.P.C.

## Government lycées

At St. Louis (Lycée Faidherbe), Thiès, Zinguinchor, Rufisque, and lycée for girls at Dakar.

## Catholic secondary schools

2 colleges of St. Mary (Dakar and Zinguinchor), girls' school of Joan of Arc, boarding school of Notre Dame (Dakar), and 3 teacher training schools at Thiès, Zinguinchor, Rufisque.

Private schools must follow same programs as public schools. State has inspectors, provides examinations, and awards the certificates.


## HIGHER EDUCATION

## UNIVERSITY OF DAKAR

State university, open to all French-speaking Africans, Europeans, Americans.

Council of the university consists of President, Vice-President (elected each year by the Council, from among the deans), elected members, members appointed by the Council (close liaison with government).

Established as Medical School before World War II to train African "physicians" - degree lower than that of fully trained French doctors.

Renamed as Medical and Pharmaceutical School, 1947-48.

Became university in 1957, with following faculties:

    Faculty of Law and Economic Sciences
    Faculty of Letters and Social Sciences
    Faculty of Medicine and Pharmacy
    Faculty of Sciences
    French Institute of Black Africa
    Tropical African Institute of Applied Economic and Commercial Sciences
    Cancer Research Institute
    Institute of Social Pediatrics
    Institute of Pedagogical Studies
    Institute of Tropical Medicine
    Institute of Islamic Studies
    Institute of African Administrative Studies
    Institute of Meteorological Physics


General entrance requirements:    Baccalauréat or equivalent recognized
                                  diploma.
                                  Entrance examination for those without
                                  Baccalauréat.

Examinations at the end of each year.

Compulsory attendance at practical sessions.

Grading:  Average grades:  10-12    Passable
                           13-14    Assez bien
                           15-16    Bien
                              17    Très bien


Faculty of Law and Economic Sciences

Length of courses:

    Capacité en droit:          2 years.  Baccalauréat not needed for this
                                course.

    Licence en droit:           4 years.

    Licence ès sciences
    économiques:                4 years.

    Diplôme d'études
    juridiques générales:       awarded after successful completion of 2nd
                                examination of the Licence en droit.

    Doctorat en droit:          awarded in the following fields:

                                History of Law and Social Situations
                                Private Law
                                Criminal Science
                                Public Law

Political Science
Economic Sciences

Candidates for the doctorate must have a
<u>Diplôme d'études supérieures</u> in the corre-
sponding field.  This is gained by coursework and written and oral examinations after
the <u>Licence</u>.  The doctorate is obtained by
presentation and defense of a thesis in the
chosen field.

## Capacité en droit

| | |
|---|---|
| 1st year: | Private Law (2 semesters), Public Law (1½ semesters) includes Constitutional, Administrative, Financial Law. |
| 2nd year: | Civil Procedure and Channels of Execution (30 hrs.), Penal Law and Penal Procedure (30 hrs.), Political Economics (30 hrs.), Special Administrative Law (30 hrs.), Social Law (30 hrs.), Financial Law (30 hrs.), Further Commercial Law (30 hrs.). |

## Licence en droit

1st year:

<u>Theory</u>
Introduction to Study of Law and Civil Law (2 sem.),
Constitutional Law and Political Institutions (2 sem.),
General Political Economics (2 sem.), History of Public
Institutions and Social Facts to the Revolution (2
sem.), Introduction to Political Sociology (1 sem.),
International Institutions (1 sem.).

<u>Practical</u>
2 of the following:  Introduction to Study of Law and
Civil Law, Constitutional Law and Political Insti-
tutions, General Political Economics, History of Public
Institutions and Social Facts to the Revolution,
Statistics and Mathematics preparatory for Economics.

2nd year:

<u>Theory</u>
Civil Law (2 sem.), Administrative Law (2 sem.),
Political Economics (2 sem.), Public Finances (2 sem.),
Penal Law and Penal Procedures (2 sem.), Ancient Poli-
tical and Social Institutions (1 sem.).

<u>Practical</u>
2 of the following:  Civil Law, Administrative Law,
General Penal Law and Penal Procedure, Public Finances.

3rd year:

<u>Theory</u>
Commercial Law (2 sem.), Industrial Law and Social
Security (2 sem.), Public Liberties (1 sem.), History
of Private Law or History of Public Institutions since

the French Revolution (1 sem.).  Choice of 5 semesters
total in the fields of Civil and Private Judiciary Law
or Public International and Administrative Law; Public
International Law (2 sem.), Civil Law (2 sem.),
Administrative Law (1 sem.), Social Science Methods (1
sem.), Private Judiciary Law (1 sem.), Criminology and
Penitentiary Science (1 sem.), History of Private
Institutions (property) (1 sem.).

Practical
2 of the following:  Civil Law, Commercial Law,
Industrial Law and Social Security, Public International Law.

4th year:
Certificat de droit privé
Civil Law (2 sem.), Commercial Law and Fiscal Business
Law (2 sem.), International Private Law (1 sem.),
History of Private Law or Comparative Private Law (1
sem.).

Certificat de droit public et sciences politiques
Large Public Services and National Enterprises (2 sem.),
History of Political Ideas to the End of the XVIII
Century (1 sem.), History of Political Ideas from the
XIX century (1 sem.), European Organizations (1 sem.),
Overseas Law and Cooperation or Important Contemporary
Political Problems (1 sem.).

Choice of 5 semesters total in History of African
Political and Social Structures (1 sem.), Maritime Law
(1 sem.), Private Institutions of African Countries
(1 sem.), African Unwritten Law (1 sem.), Juridical
Ethnology (1 sem.), African Constitutional Systems
(1 sem.).

Candidate has choice of any 2 of the above 3 groups.

Licence ès sciences économiques

1st year:
Theory
Introduction to Study of Law and Civil Law (2 sem.),
Constitutional Law and Political Institutions (2 sem.),
General Political Economics (2 sem.), History of
Public Institutions and Social Facts to the Revolution
(2 sem.), Statistics (1 sem.), Mathematics Preparatory
for Economics (1 sem.).

Practical
As for 1st year of Licence en droit.

2nd year:
Theory
General Political Economics (2 sem.), Theory of
Obligations (1 sem.), Administrative Institutions (1
sem.),  History of Contemporary Economics Facts (1 sem.),

Demography (1 sem.), International Institutions (1 sem.), Public Finances (1 sem.), Mathematics (1 sem.), Statistics (1 sem.), Principles of Private Accountancy (20 hrs.).

Practical
2 weekly sessions each of 1½ hours in General Political Economics (2 sem.), Mathematics and Statistics (1 sem.), 1 other subject chosen by the faculty (1 sem.).

3rd year:   Theory
Political Economics (2 sem.), International Economics (2 sem.), History of Economic Thought (2 sem.), Commercial Law (2 sem.), Industrial Law (1 sem.), Statistics (1 sem.), Mathematics (1 sem.).

Practical
2 weekly sessions in Political Economics (2 sem.), Mathematics and Statistics (1 sem.), 1 other subject chosen by the faculty (1 sem.).

4th year:   Political Economics (2 sem.), Financial Economics and Institutions (2 sem.), National Accountancy (1 sem.).

Choice of 1st group:   Fiscal Law and Commercial Business Law (2 sem.), Integration of the African Economy (1 sem.), Economic Geography (1 sem.).

2nd group:   Fiscal Law and Commercial Business Law (2 sem.), Integration of the African Economy (1 sem.), Business Management (1 sem.).

Practical
2 weekly sessions each of 1½ hours in Political Economics (1 sem.), Financial Economics (2 sem.), National Accountancy (1 sem.).

Other certificates and diplomas awarded by the faculty:

Certificate of Political and Social Economics.  1 year, open to students with Baccalauréat or equivalent.

Certificate in Overseas Laws and Customs.  This is the first certificate for the Licence d'études des populations d'outre-mer, which is completed and awarded in the Faculty of Letters and Social Sciences.

Diplomas awarded by the Institute of African Administrative Studies for the cycle du premier degré and the cycle du second degré.

Faculty of Medicine and Pharmacy

Length of courses:

Diplôme de pharmacien:     5 years comprising 1 preparatory year, 3
                           years of general study and 1 year of
                           specialization.

Diplôme de docteur en
médecine:                  6 years including 1 preparatory year for the
                           Certificat préparatoire aux études médicales.
                           Final year is compulsory internship. Exami-
                           nation at the end of each year. Instruction
                           consists of theory, practical, directed work,
                           and clinical.

Diplôme de chirugien-
dentiste:                  not awarded by the Faculty, but the 3 years'
                           general study after preparatory year also
                           count towards this diploma.

The Faculty also awards the Diplôme d'Etat de docteur en pharmacie:  1 year
specialized research and presentation and defense of a thesis.


Diplôme de docteur en médecine

1st year:     Mathematics (25 hrs.), Chemistry (90 hrs.), Physics
              (90 hrs.), Biology (170 hrs.), Introduction to Medical
              Studies (5 hrs.), Biophysics (40 hrs.), Biochemistry
              (60 hrs.), Anatomy (85 hrs.), Physiology (60 hrs.),
              Histology and Embryology (70 hrs.).

2nd year:     Anatomy (140 hrs.), Physiology (150 hrs.), Histology
              and Embryology (70 hrs.), Biochemistry (85 hrs.), Bio-
              physics (95 hrs.), Clinical Semiology (350 hrs.).

3rd year:     Clinical Semiology (420 hrs.), Microbiology, Bacterio-
              logy, Virology, Hematology, Immunology, Parasitology
              (120 hrs.), Semiology, Pathology, Applied Physics,
              Radiology, Anatomy, Histology, Cytology (250 hrs.),
              Clinical Work (480 hrs.), Anatomical Pathology (60 hrs.),
              Semiology and Pathology (250 hrs.).

4th year:     Clinical Work, Social Medicine, Anatomical Pathology,
              Medical, Surgical or Obstetrical Pathology.

5th year:     Clinical Work, Pharmacology and Pharmacodynamics,
              Therapeutics, Social Medicine, Psychology.

6th year:     Clinical and Hospital Work.

Diplôme de pharmacien

Courses in Mathematics, Physics, Organic Chemistry, General and Mineral Chemistry, General Botany, Zoology and Animal Biology, Galenic Pharmacy, Pharmaceutical Legislation, Professional Conduct, Plant Biology, Anatomy and Physiology, Analytical Chemistry, Cryptogamy, General Pharmacodynamics, Elements of Semiology and General Pathology, Hematology, Microbiology, Parasitology, Hygiene, Toxicology, Hydrology, Parasitology.

5th year specialization in Biological Technology, Industrial Pharmaceutical Technology, Health and Social Education, Applied Analytical Chemistry, Physico-chemical Technology.

Faculty of Sciences

Diplomas and titles prepared for in the Faculty:

Certificat préparatoire aux études médicales

Certificat d'études préparatoires à la licence ès sciences:

General Mathematics and Physics
Mathematics, Physics, Chemistry
Physical, Chemical and Natural Sciences

Certificat d'études supérieures de licence:

Mathematics I
Mathematics II
General Mechanics
Calculus of Probabilities
Analytical Mechanics
Vibratory Dynamics
Mathematical Techniques in Physics
Mathematical Methods in Physics
Electricity
Optics
Thermodynamics and Physical Mechanics
Experimental Physics
General Chemistry I
General Chemistry II
Mineral Chemistry
Organic Chemistry
Botany
Advanced Botany
Biochemistry, Microbiology and Plant Physiology
Geology
General Biology
Animal Physiology
General Psychophysiology
General Geology

Historical Geology
Mineralogy
Electronics

Diplôme d'études supérieures techniques:

Mechanics
Electrotechnology

Diplôme d'études scientifiques générales

Licence ès sciences, mathématiques, physiques et naturelles

Diplôme d'études supérieures:

Mathematics
Physical Sciences
Natural Sciences

Diplôme de docteur-ingénieur

Doctorat de l'Université de Dakar (in Science)

Doctorat d'Etat ès sciences

Length of course:    Licence ès sciences consists of 1st preparatory cycle of 1 year ending in one Certificat d'études préparatoires à la licence ès sciences; and 5 Certificats d'études supérieures, each of which has 2 examinations per year.

## TIMETABLES FOR THE
## CERTIFICATS D'ETUDES PREPARATOIRES
(hours per week)

1.  General Mathematics and Physics (M.G.P.)

|  | Theory | Practical |
|---|---|---|
| Mathematics | 5½ | 6 |
| Physics | 2½ | 3 |
|  | 8 | 9 |

2.  Mathematics, Physics, Chemistry (M.P.C.)

|  | Theory | Practical |
|---|---|---|
| Mathematics | 3½ | 3½ |
| Physics | 3½ | 5 |
| Chemistry | 2½ | 4 |
|  | 9½ | 12½ |

3.   Physical, Chemical and Natural Sciences (S.P.C.N.)

|                 | Theory          | Practical        |
|-----------------|-----------------|------------------|
| Animal Biology  | 1½              | 3                |
| Plant Biology   | 1½              | 3                |
| Geology         | 1½              | 2½               |
| Physics         | 1½              | 3                |
| Chemistry       | 2               | 3                |
| Mathematics     | 1               | 1                |
|                 | 9               | 15½              |

## Faculty of Letters and Social Sciences

Length of course:   Licence ès lettres, 1 preparatory (propédeutique) year
for the Certificat d'études littéraires générales classiques ou modernes (C.E.L.G.) plus 3 or 4 years to gain
4 Certificats d'études supérieures.  In the 1st year
after the C.E.L.G. the candidate may not take more than
2 Certificats.  Before the third Certificat, compulsory
oral examination on a modern language, consisting of
translation from a work bearing on the student's field
of specialization.  Graded from 0 to 20, failing all
those below 10/20.

2 types of Licence:   Licence libre and Licence d'enseignement, the last for
those wishing to become teachers of the 2nd degree.

Licence libre:   4 Certificats chosen from the following fields:

Philosophy
Sociology
Classical Letters (French, Latin, Greek)
History and Geography
Modern Languages (English, Spanish, Arabic)
Modern Letters
African Linguistics

Licence d'enseignement:   4 Certificats chosen from the following fields:

Classical Letters (French, Latin, Greek)
History and Geography
Modern Languages (English, Spanish)
Modern Letters

Candidates studying for the Licence d'enseignement may
do so within the Institut de préparation aux enseignements du second degré and after the Licence go on to
Centre pédagogique régional for 1 year's professional
training.

The Faculty also awards:

Diplôme d'études supérieures:

Philosophy, Sociology, Classical Letters, History, Geography, English Language and Literature, Spanish Language and Literature, Modern Letters, African Linguistics.

Awarded on thesis.

Doctorat ès lettres: awarded on thesis.

Doctorat du troisième cycle:

Awarded on thesis in following fields:

French Literature, History of the French Language, Philosophy, Geography, History, Latin Studies, English Studies, North-American Studies, Iberian Studies, Latin-American Studies, African Studies.

Agrégation:

The highest diploma awarded by the university on results of competitive examination. Holders may teach in terminal classes of the lycée or as assistants in the university. Candidates for the Concours de l'agrégation must hold a Diplôme d'études supérieures in Mathematics, Physical Sciences, Natural Sciences, Philosophy, Sociology, Classical Letters, History, Geography, English Language and Literature, Spanish Language and Literature, Modern Letters, African Linguistics. Age limit: 35. Limited number of places available each year.

## TECHNICAL AND VOCATIONAL EDUCATION

### LYCEE TECHNIQUE MAURICE DELAFOSSE, Dakar

Entrance requirements:     Concours d'entrée en sixième equal to entry into lycée 1st cycle.

Length of course:     6 years leading to Brevet d'enseignement industriel (B.E.I.) or to Brevet d'enseignement commercial (B.E.C.). This course comprises 2 sections: 2 years of general studies (classes 6 and 5), and 4 years of general, technical, theoretical and practical studies (classes 4, 3, 2, 1).

7 years leading to Baccalauréat in technical mathematics or technical economics. Division for this section made from class 2 onwards.

Cycle d'observation:     First 2 years of both the 6-year and 7-year courses. General education.

Industrial section:       Brevet d'enseignement industriel awarded after 4
                          further years in following specialties:  Chemistry,
                          Metal Manufactures, Electricity, General Mechanics,
                          Automotive Mechanics.

Commercial section:       Brevet d'enseignement commercial awarded after 4
                          further years in following specialties:  Account-
                          ancy, Secretarial, Commerce.

                          B.E.C. may be followed by 1-year class leading to
                          Brevet supérieur d'études commerciales (B.S.E.C.).

                          There is also a 1-year class for Shorthand-Typing,
                          and a practical 3-year course after class 5, lead-
                          ing to Certificat d'aptitude professionnelle du
                          commerce.

                          Also a special class 3 with intensive instruction
                          in Accountancy, to enable pupils from normal
                          lycées to continue studies towards B.E.C.

Baccalauréat techniques mathématiques, or Baccalauréat techniques économiques:                   2 years of general education after cycle d'obser-
                          vation plus 3 years of further theoretical
                          technical studies leading to Baccalauréat.

Centre d'apprentissage (C.A.):  3 years leading to Certificat d'aptitude
                          professionnelle (C.A.P.).  Predominance of
                          practical studies supplemented by technical theory
                          and general education.

                          Also has a 4th year either for obtaining a second
                          C.A.P. or a year of specialization in Radio-
                          electricity, Refrigeration, Diesel engines.

## LYCEE TECHNIQUE DE SAINT-LOUIS

Same type as Lycée Delafosse, Dakar.

Also has une section féminine, teaching Housecraft, and a horticultural
section.

## ECOLE NATIONALE DES TRAVAUX PUBLICS ET DU BATIMENT (E.N.T.P.B.), Dakar

Entrance requirements:    Completion of class 3 (1st cycle) in
                          secondary or technical school.

Length of course:   4 years.  Final examination after which students may
                    work for the Minister of Public Works.  Some students
                    continue on with higher technical studies.  Courses in
                    Civil Engineering and Surveying.

ECOLE NATIONALE DES CADRES RURAUX, Dakar

Entrance requirements:        Completion of class 3 (1st cycle) in secondary
                              or technical school.

Length of course:   4 years.  General 1st year.  Following 3 years in
                    specialties:  Agriculture, Water and Forests, Rural
                    Character, Breeding, Fishing.


CENTRE D'ENSEIGNEMENT TECHNIQUE ET PROFESSIONNEL FEMININ, Dakar

Entrance requirements:        Completion of primary education.

Courses:

  (1)   Preparatory cycle of 1 or 2 years.

  (2)   Home instruction (maîtresse de maison) after 1st preparatory year.

  (3)   Professional cycle of 3 years leading to Certificat d'aptitude
        professionnelle in Mother's Help, Office Work, or Shorthand-
        Typing.


CENTRE PEDAGOGIQUE FEMININ

Entrance requirements:        Hold the B.E.P.C.

Length of course:   2 or 3 years; prepares schoolmistresses of practical
                    teaching.


ECOLE DES AGENTS TECHNIQUES DE L'AGRICULTURE, Longa

Entrance requirements:        Completion of primary education.

Length of course:   4 years, including compulsory professional probationary
                    periods, leading to Diplôme d'agent technique d'agri-
                    culture.


CENTRE DE FORMATION HOTELIERE, Dakar


CENTRE DE FORMATION ARTISANALE, Dakar


CENTRE DE FORMATION PROFESSIONNELE D'HORTICULTURE ET D'ENSEIGNEMENT
    MENAGER RURAL DE LA REGION DE THIES

There are also several private technical schools offering courses leading to <u>Certificats d'aptitude professionnelle</u> in Accountancy, Shorthand-Typing, Office Work, Tailoring, Housecrafts, Metalworking, Printing.


## TEACHER EDUCATION

## COURS NORMAUX

Teacher training courses either within <u>lycées</u> or corresponding to 1st cycle of <u>lycée</u>.

<u>Government</u>:

Le cours normal de M'bour (male)
Le cours normal de Zinguinchor (male)
Le cours normal de jeunes filles de Rufisque (female)

<u>Catholic</u>:

Le cours normal de St. Gabriel de Thiès (male)
Le cours normal du Sacré-Coeur de Zinguinchor (male)
Le cours normal de Sainte-Agnès de Rufisque (female)

Entrance examination to <u>cours normaux</u> same as for <u>lycées</u>. Apart from the successful candidates, students who gain entrance to <u>lycées</u> but are disqualified because of age gain entrance to <u>cours normaux</u>.

Length of course:    4 years general training, with 5th year of professional training to qualify as <u>instituteur-adjoint</u>.

<u>Diploma</u>:

<u>B.E.P.C.</u> or <u>Brevet élémentaire</u> (<u>B.E.</u>).  The <u>B.E.P.C.</u> is gradually replacing the <u>B.E.</u> on a slightly higher mathematical level, but without the foreign language (English).

Students who hold <u>B.E.P.C.</u> are called <u>instituteurs-adjoints</u>.  Those with less than 10/20 but not less than 8/20 may become <u>moniteurs</u> (according to availability of <u>moniteur</u> positions), but must obtain the <u>Certificat d'aptitude au monitariat</u> (<u>C.A.M.</u>).  Students of classes 4 and 3 with less than 8/20 may become <u>moniteurs auxiliaires</u> (this title may be revoked). Teach in primary schools.


## ECOLES NORMALES REGIONALES

These are being opened from October 1964.

Entrance requirements:        15-18 years for boys, 15-19 years for girls.
                              Must be of Senegalese nationality.

                                Undertake to teach in state teaching system
                                for at least 10 years.
                                Hold the B.E. or B.E.P.C. or other recognized
                                diploma.

Length of course:    3 years.

General and professional education given, with practical training over the
3 years in application classes and in schools compulsorily annexed to the
E.N.R.

Grading:   10/20 to pass into next class.

Diploma:

        Brevet supérieur d'études normales.  Students with this Brevet are
        called instituteurs ordinaires, the same as those in the Ecole Normale
        de William Ponty.  However, they cannot go on to the university with-
        out the Baccalauréat.

Best students from E.N.R. may go on to Ecole Normale Supérieure to become
professeurs in the collèges d'enseignement général (C.E.G.).

All levels, timetables, and programs in the E.N.R. controlled by government.


ECOLE NORMALE DE WILLIAM PONTY

Now known as l'Ecole Normale d'Instituteurs et d'Institutrices de Sebikotane.
Has provided French-speaking Africa in general with many leaders of thought
and action and the Sénégal in particular with much of the leadership which
has made it one of the most advanced states in Africa.

Provides training for 2 groups:

    (1)   Holders of B.E. or B.E.P.C. from cours normaux admitted to 4-year
          general education course leading to Baccalauréat in Philosophy,
          Elementary Mathematics, or Experimental Sciences (same as lycée).
          Then 1 year's professional training to gain the Certificat de fin
          d'études normales (C.F.E.N.).

    (2)   Holders of Baccalauréat from lycées or collèges, or the school
          itself, may take 1 year's professional training (année de
          formation pédagogique - A.F.P.) for the C.F.E.N.

Professional training program:

        Child Psychology, Pedagogy, Professional Ethics, Practical
        classwork in primary school annexed to the school.

Students become instituteurs, teach in primary schools.

## ECOLE NORMALE SUPERIEURE

Formerly the Centre Pédagogique Supérieur.  Created in 1963 with UNESCO
funds.  The government has projected a reform of the E.N.S. which would
then gradually take over the functions of the I.P.S. and C.P.R. attached
to the university (see below).  The reform allows for 4 distinct sections:
a) for inspecteurs, b) for inspecteurs-adjoints, c) for professeurs of the
C.E.G. (1st cycle secondary), and d) for professeurs of the 2nd cycle
secondary who would be recruited from those finishing section c).  After
completing the C.A.P.E.S., they would be able to prepare for the agrégation.

Present facilities in the E.N.S.:

Section 1:      Trains professeurs for collèges d'enseignement général,
                (C.E.G.).  2-year program.

      Entrance requirements:    Baccalauréat or competitive entrance
                                examination for instituteurs without the
                                Baccalauréat.

      Program:  Choice of (a)  Letters, History and Geography
                         (b)  Letters, Modern Languages
                         (c)  Mathematics, Sciences

      Certificate awarded:    Certificat d'aptitude à l'enseignement dans
                              les C.E.G.(C.A.E.C.E.G.), 1st part taken end
                              of 1st year, 2nd part at end of final year.

Section 2:      Trains inspecteurs primaires and inspecteurs primaires
                adjoints conseillers pédagogiques.

      Entrance requirements:    Pass competitive examination, examen proba-
                                toire du C.A.I.P., in Science or Letters.
                                Candidates must be at least 29, hold
                                Baccalauréat, C.F.E.N. or Brevet supérieur,
                                and have at least 5 years' teaching
                                experience.
                                Holders of Licence d'enseignement or C.A.E.
                                C.E.G. (2 years' experience in C.E.G.) are
                                exempt from examination.

      Length of course:   1 year (formerly 2 years).

      Certificate awarded:    Certificat d'aptitude à l'inspection des
                              écoles primaires (C.A.I.P.), after written,
                              oral, and practical examinations.

Students failing the examinations for C.A.I.P., but having gained the
average pass mark over the year, may become inspecteurs primaires
adjoints conseillers pédagogiques.

INSTITUT DE PREPARATION AUX ENSEIGNEMENTS DU SECOND DEGRE, University of
  Dakar

Students may take a Licence d'enseignement within the Institute, after the
propédeutique year, in order to teach in the 2nd cycle secondary.

The oral tests of the theoretical section of Certificat d'aptitude pédagogique à l'enseignement secondaire (C.A.P.E.S.) taken on completion of
Licence.   1 year's professional training (includes teaching methods and
techniques, audio-visual aids, etc.) in Centre Pédagogique Régional with
practical tests of C.A.P.E.S. on completion.


Professional examinations give access to higher grades.  Teacher passing
the Brevet supérieur de capacité can be placed in the instituteur bachelier
grade without having the Baccalauréat.

729

REPUBLIC OF TOGO

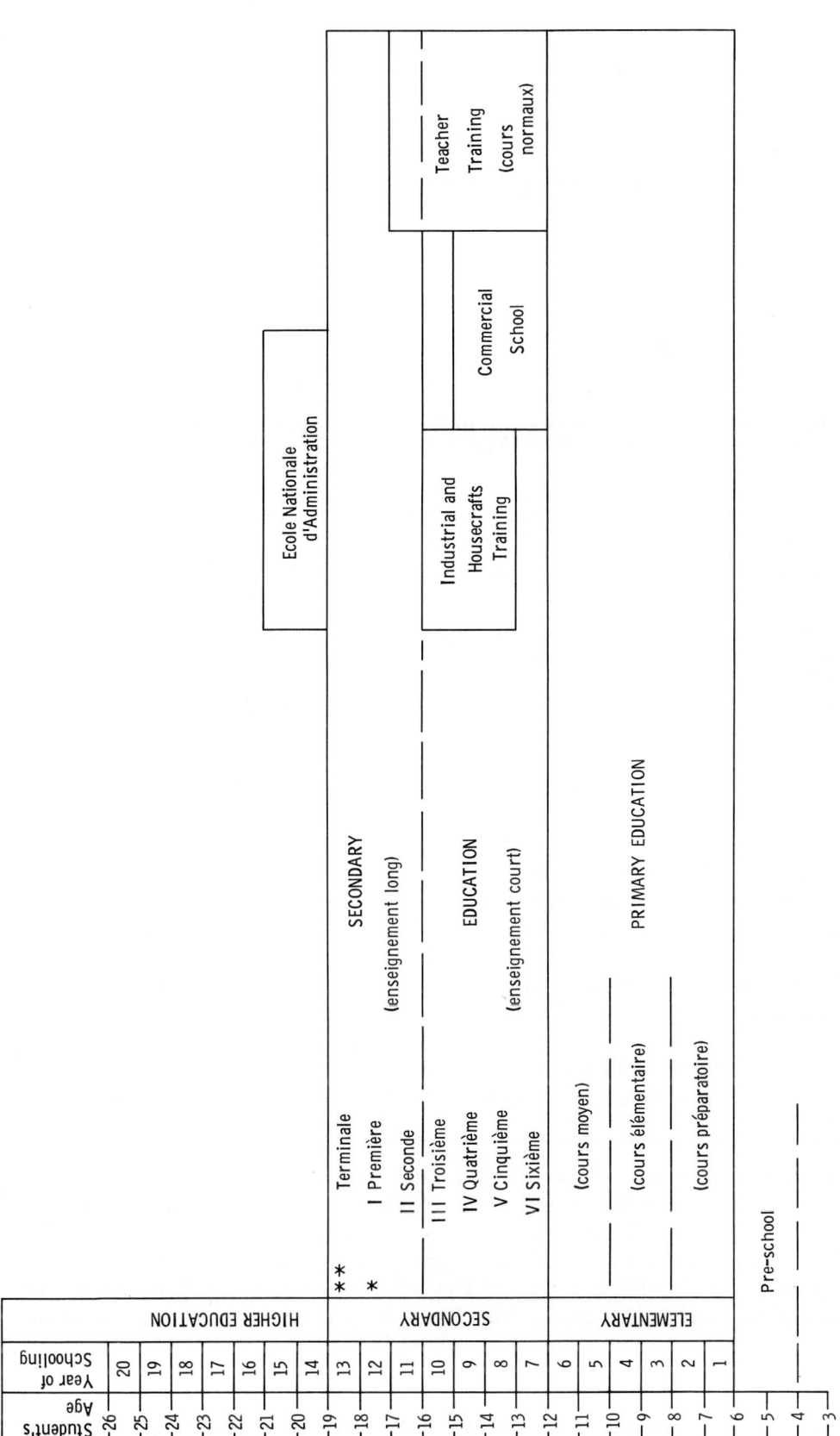

Compulsory education: 6 years of primary school

School year: October–July. 3 terms

Secondary grading: 20 Perfect

10/20 Pass mark

REPUBLIC OF TOGO

(République Togolaise)

Independence:   April 27, 1960

## BACKGROUND

Essentially an agricultural country.  It has a complex ethnic population.
Tribal groups have neither common language nor history.  Three main ethnic
groups, speaking 44 different dialects:  Ewé and Adja-Watyi, of Bantu
origin, speaking Ewé and Mina, living in south; Kabrai-Losso, of Sudanic
origin, speaking many languages (most important, Dagomba, Tim, and Cabrais),
living in north.

French, official language.  In the north, Haoussa (foreign language of
Niger origin) is spoken everywhere.

In the 12th and 14th centuries, Ewé people (now a majority of population
of Southern Togo and neighboring Ghana) came from the Niger River Valley.

Portuguese sailors visited coast 15th and 16th centuries, began shipping
slaves from Grand Popo, Petit Popo (Anecho) and other villages on the
coast.  German traders came to Grand Popo 1856, arrived in large numbers
by 1880.  July 5, 1885, by treaty with a Togo chief, German Protectorate
established over small coastal area.  Capital at Baguida; then at Zebe,
and in 1897, at Lomé.

Boundaries defined with French and British 1897, 1899, which resulted in
splitting the Ewé, Adja-Watyi, Fon, and other tribes between Gold Coast,
Togo, and Dahomey.

During World War I, August 1914, British and French troops in adjoining
countries took control of Togo; British provisionally took coastal region
and railroads, French took interior.  June 28, 1919, Treaty of Versailles
gave administration mandates to France (three-quarters) and England (one-
quarter).  October 1920, formal partition of former German Togo into two
ethnic groups also divided.  1947, the Ewés began to demand unification.
After World War II, U.K. and French territories in Togoland placed under
international trusteeship of U.N.

For 9 years from 1947, Ewé leaders petitioned U.N. for unification of their
people and of Togoland (Ewé then under 3 different administrations:  Gold
Coast, British Togoland, French Togoland).

Plebiscite in British Togoland May 9, 1956, under U.N. supervision. The Ewés of South British Togoland decided to join with French Togoland, and the Dagombas of the North wished to join the Gold Coast. However, the U.N. decided on the basis of the overall results to join all British Togoland to the Gold Coast. Thus, when Gold Coast became independent state of Ghana, British Togoland ceased to exist.

October 28, 1956, referendum in French Togoland, in which 72% voted to end French trusteeship and accept status of internal autonomy. Attempt to end trusteeship not accepted by U.N. April 1958, new elections, under U.N. supervision. National Unity Party won control of Togo Assembly. October 13, 1958, France announced plans for full independence. Independence granted, April 27, 1960.

## PRESENT SYSTEM

### PRE-SCHOOL EDUCATION

Entry age: 4 to 6 years.

Program: Singing, recitations, games, free artistic activities, stories.

1 full nursery school, run by Catholic mission at Tokoin, mainly for orphans.

8 government kindergartens (Ministry of Social Affairs), and numerous private kindergartens. Total of 4 hours per day.

### PRIMARY EDUCATION

Primary education is, in principle, compulsory. Free and co-educational.

Entry age: 6 years.

Language of instruction: French, although many have no knowledge of French on entering school.

Length of course, 6 years: Cours préparatoire or cours d'initiation, 2 years; cours élémentaire, 2 years; cours moyen, 2 years.

Program: Cours préparatoire - Spoken French, Reading, Writing, Arithmetic.
Cours élémentaire - French, Reading, Writing, Arithmetic, History, Geography, Nature Study.
Cours moyen - Same as cours élémentaire in more detail.

Certificate awarded:    <u>Certificat d'études primaires élémentaires</u> (<u>C.E.P.E.</u>)

From 1962-63, a tentative plan has been put into effect for a special session of the <u>C.E.P.E.</u> for adults.

1962-63, 435 government schools, 319 private schools (Catholic, Protestant, and non-denominational).

## SECONDARY EDUCATION

Entrance requirements:    Pass <u>concours d'entrée en sixième</u>, competitive examination.

Length of course:    <u>Premier cycle</u>, 4 years of <u>enseignement long</u> in <u>lycées</u> and <u>collèges</u>, and <u>enseignement court</u> in <u>cours complémentaires</u>.

<u>Second cycle</u>, 3 years continuing <u>enseignement long</u> in <u>lycées</u> and <u>collèges</u>.

Language of instruction: French

### SECONDARY TIMETABLES
(Hours per week)

| Classes 6 and 5<br>Subjects | Class 6<br>1st term | Class 6-2nd and 3rd terms<br>Class 5-Classique | Class 5-Moderne |
|---|---|---|---|
| Mathematics | 3 | 3 | 3 |
| Natural Sciences | 1½ | 1½ | 1½ |
| History and Geography | 2½ | 2½ | 2½ |
| French | 7 | 4 | 6 |
| Latin | 5 | 5 | - |
| Modern Language I | 4 | 3 | 5 |
| Art | 1 | 1 | 1 |
| Music | 1 | 1 | 1 |
| Domestic Science | 1 | 1 | 1 |
| Physical Education | 2 | 2 | 2 |

<u>Class 4</u>

| Subjects | Classique | Moderne |
|---|---|---|
| French | 3½ | 5½ |
| Latin | 3½ | - |
| Modern Language I | 3 | 3 |
| Modern Language II | 3 | 4 |
| Mathematics | 3 | 3 |
| Natural Sciences | 1½ | 1½ |
| Art | 1 | 1 |
| History and Geography | 2½ | 2½ |
| Physical Education | 2 | 2 |
| Music | 1 | 1 |
| Domestic Science | 1 | 1 |

## Class 3

| Subjects | Classique | Moderne |
|---|---|---|
| French | 3½ | 5½ |
| Latin | 3½ | - |
| Modern Language I | 3 | 3 |
| Modern Language II | 3 | 4 |
| Mathematics | 3 | 3 |
| Natural Sciences | 1 | 1½ |
| Art | 1 | 1 |
| History and Geography | 3 | 3 |
| Physical Education | 2 | 2 |
| Music | 1 | 1 |
| Domestic Science | 1 | 1 |

## Class 2

| Subjects | Classique | Moderne | Moderne prime (m') |
|---|---|---|---|
| French | 4 | 4 | 4 |
| Latin | 3 | - | - |
| Modern Language I | 3 | 3 | 3 |
| Modern Language II | 4 | 4 | - |
| Mathematics | 3 | 5 | 5 |
| Physical Sciences | 3 | 4½ | 4½ |
| Art | 1 | 1 | 1 |
| History and Geography | 3½ | 3½ | 3½ |
| Physical Education | 2 | 2 | 2 |
| Music (optional) | 1 | 1 | 1 |
| Natural Sciences | - | - | 3 |

## Class 1

| Subjects | Classique | Moderne | Moderne prime (m') |
|---|---|---|---|
| French | 4 | 4 | 4 |
| Latin | 3 | - | - |
| Modern Language I | 3 | 3 | 3 |
| Modern Language II | 4 | 4 | - |
| Mathematics | 2 | 5 | 5 |
| Physical Sciences | 2½ | 4½ | 4½ |
| Natural Sciences | - | - | 3 |
| History and Geography | 4 | 4 | 4 |
| Physical Education | 2 | 2 | 2 |

## Terminal Class

| Subjects | Philosophy | Experimental Science | Elementary Mathematics |
|---|---|---|---|
| Philosophy | 9 | 6 | 3 |
| Modern Language I | 2 | 2 | 2 |
| Modern Language II (opt.) | 1½ | 1½ | 1½ |
| Mathematics | 2 | 4 | 9 |
| Physical Sciences | 2 | 6 | 6 |
| Natural Sciences | 2 | 4 | 2 |
| History and Geography | 4 | 4 | 4 |
| Physical Education | 2 | 2 | 2 |

Certificates awarded:     Brevet d'études du premier cycle (B.E.P.C.) or
                          Brevet élémentaire (B.E.) at close of premier
                          cycle. The B.E. will be eliminated in the near
                          future under the 1st 5-year education plan to
                          begin from January 1, 1966.

                      *   Examen probatoire end of classe de première, 6
                          years.

                     **   Baccalauréat end of terminal class, 7 years.

1963, cours complémentaires:

                          12 government (7 with complete cycle) at Atakpamé,
                          Bassari, Dapango, Hihéatro, Lama-Kara, Mango,
                          Sotouboua, Tabligbo, Palimé, Vogan, Woamé, Tsévié.

                          6 Catholic at Lomé, Anécho, Tsévié, Agou (Kiouto),
                          Atakpamé, Tomégbé (Akposso).

                          2 Protestant at Palimé, Anécho.

                          Several private, non-denominational cours complé-
                          mentaires have been opened with consent of the
                          Ministry of National Education, to help students
                          who, because of age, have not been able to take
                          the concours d'entrée en sixième.

1963, lycées and collèges with complete 7-year secondary cycle:

                          2 government: Lycée Bonnecarrère, Lomé and
                          Collège Moderne et Classique, Sokodé.

                          3 Catholic at Lomé (2 collèges) and Lama-Kara.

                          1 Protestant at Lomé.

Many Togolese go to Ghana to secondary school.


## HIGHER EDUCATION

No higher education.  Students receive overseas scholarships.

See Ecole Nationale d'Administration.


## VOCATIONAL AND TECHNICAL EDUCATION

Technical education supplied in:

                          Ecole Pratique de Commerce et d'Industrie, Sokodé

                          Ateliers-écoles (workshop schools) at Lomé and
                          Dapango (Catholic), and Pya and Bassari (Protes-
                          tant).

Many private commercial schools in Commerce and Shorthand-Typing for those past school age.

2 largest industrial groups in Togo (CFT and Phosphat, Kpémé) have their own professional training courses.

Most professional training is given by craftsmen who hire apprentices under contract, but it is only practical training with no theoretical teaching of general subjects.

## COLLEGE TECHNIQUE DE COMMERCE, Lomé

Catholic commercial school.

Entrance requirements:    C.E.P.E. or have reached this level.

Length of course:         3 years.

Program:  French, Grammar, Spelling, Arithmetic, Mental Arithmetic, Accountancy, Commercial Correspondence, Commerce, Commercial Law, Industrial Legislation, Geography, Reading.

Certificates awarded:     Certificat d'aptitude professionnelle (C.A.P.) in Assistant Bookkeeping, Banking, and Office Work.

Certificates equivalent to French, Togolese government examinations.

## ECOLE NATIONALE D'ADMINISTRATION, Lomé

Directed by the Public Service Ministry.  Prepares civil servants for the Togolese government.  Contract to work at least 10 years after graduation.

Entrance requirements:    Competitive examination to be open to holders of the Baccalauréat, 18-30 years.

1964, examination open to holders of B.E.P.C. 1965, examination open to holders of examen probatoire.

Also open to certain public servants with at least 4 years' service and education equivalent to above level.

Program:  2 different cycles (A and B) for different categories of the public service.  Both include:  General Administration, Economics and Finance, Judiciary Section.  And eventually diplomatic and social sections.

Length of course:         2 years.

1st year common to all above sections:  General

Culture, juridical and administrative training, Civics, special courses on Togo and Africa, practical exercises in administrative work, Physical Education.

2nd year specialization, both theory and practical exercises. Towards the end of the second year, 2-month in-service training.

Grading: Average grade of not less than 12/20 necessary to pass into 2nd year. 1st year repeat only granted exceptionally.

Certificate awarded:   Brevet de l'Ecole Nationale d'Administration.

Certificat de scolarité awarded to those with average grade of 10/20 or more, but less than 12/20.

Students may audit the courses and receive a certificate stating courses taken and grades obtained. Admitted only with qualifications as above.

## CENTRE DE PREPARATION ET DE PERFECTIONNEMENT ADMINISTRATIF

Attached to the School to prepare students for the entrance examination and for other public service examinations.

## ECOLE PRATIQUE DE COMMERCE ET D'INDUSTRIE, Sokodé

Entrance requirements:   Entrance examination at level of class 5 secondary.

Length of course:   3 years.

Programs:   2 branches: industrial and domestic science.

Branche industrielle:
Metalwork section (Fittings, Ironwork, Sheet-metal work, Auto-mechanics)
Carpentry section
Building section
Electricity section

Short orientation period before specialization.

General subjects: French, Mathematics, Sciences, Hygiene, Chemistry, Physics, History, Geography, Professional Legislation.

Technical subjects: Technology, Industrial Design, practical workshop classes.

Cours ménager:   Domestic Science for girls.

General subjects: Child Rearing, Domestic Economics, Hygiene, Technology, Sewing, Cooking, etc.

Certificate awarded:        Certificat d'aptitude professionnelle (C.A.P.)
                            in specialty.

Programs and examinations the same as for the collèges d'enseignement
technique in France.

Housecraft sections:        2 at Lomé and Sokodé government schools.

                            Several annexed to Catholic primary or secondary
                            schools.


## TEACHER EDUCATION

The only teacher training is given in cours normaux which prepare instituteurs-adjoints.

1963, 3 cours normaux:      1 government, Ecole Normale d'Atakpamé.
                            1 Catholic, at Togoville.
                            1 Protestant, at Lomé.

Length of course:           5 years.

                            4 general years of premier cycle given either in
                            the cours normal or a cours complémentaire (en-
                            seignement court), plus 1 year of professional
                            training given in all the cours normaux.

Certificates awarded:       B.E.P.C. or B.E. after premier cycle.

                            Certificat de fin d'études normales (C.F.E.N.)
                            after professional training year.

Instituteurs-adjoints are awarded a further diploma after further practical in-service training, Certificat élémentaire d'aptitude pédagogique
(C.E.A.P.).

738

REPUBLIC OF UPPER VOLTA

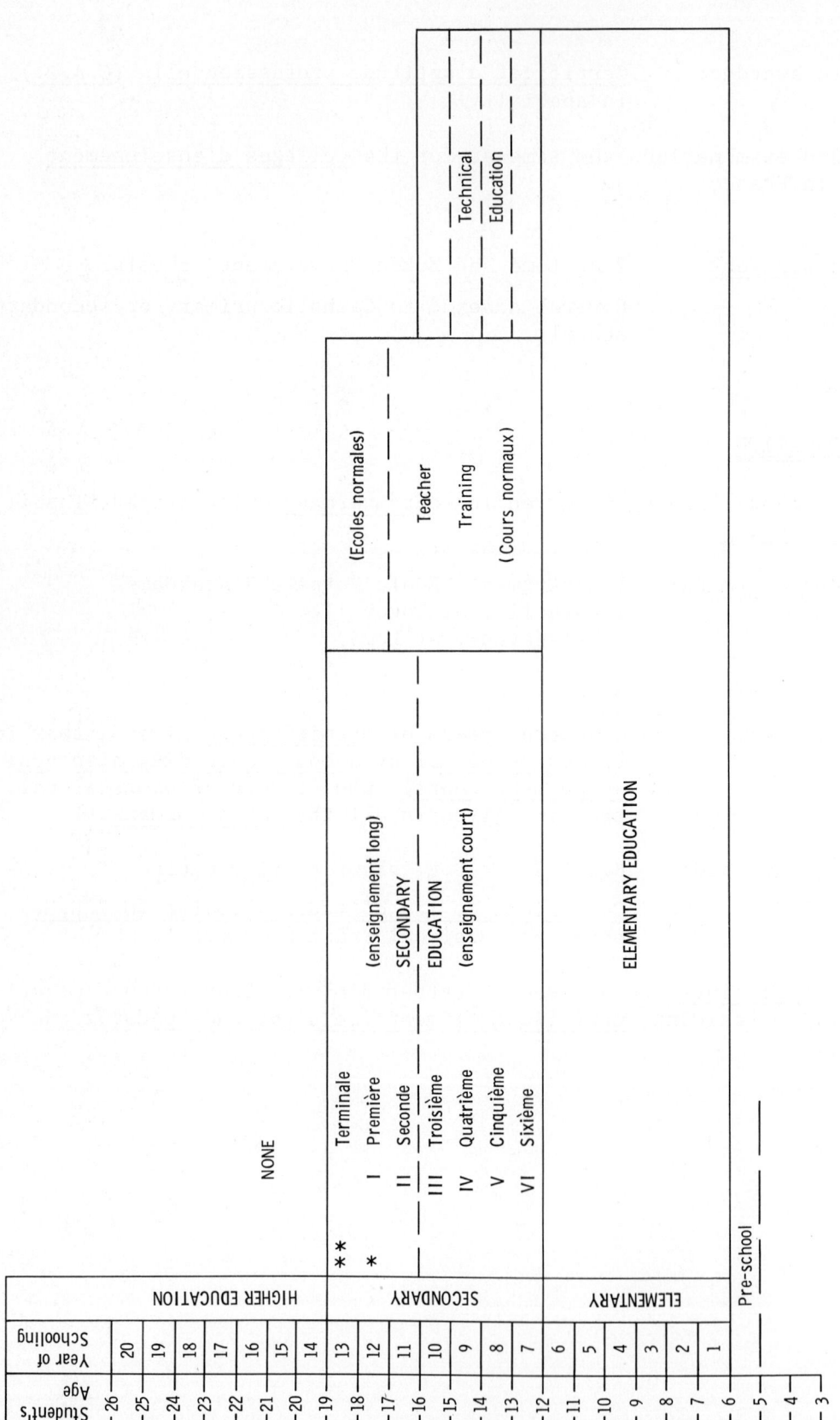

Compulsory education: 6 years primary education

School year:   October 1 – June 30

Secondary grading: 20 perfect.
7/20 lowest pass mark; 10/20 to pass into next class.

REPUBLIC OF UPPER VOLTA

(République de Haute Volta)


Independence:  August 5, 1960



BACKGROUND


Landlocked country with few natural resources.  The most heavily populated
of all 8 territories of former French West Africa, but varying from region
to region.

95% of population engaged in agricultural pursuits.  Principal ethnic
groups:  Voltaic people and Mandingos.  Of the Voltaic people, Mossi
(about 2.2 million) are most numerous; mainly farmers in central part of
country.  Other groups include approximately 250,000 semi-nomadic Fulani,
mainly merchants.

French, official language.  Language, though varying from tribe to tribe,
all belong to Niger-Congo family of languages.

Early history of Mossi tribes between 11th and 13th centuries centers
around regions at Bend of Niger.  Land called Mogho, "country of the Mossi,"
with the kingdoms of Ten Kodogo and Yatenga Ouagadougou, each ruled by
mogho or moro naba (ruler of the Mosse).  Through the centuries, Mossi
population was augmented by Hausa and Fulani (refugees from wars).  From
15th-16th centuries Mossi power declined.

French conquered most important Mossi centers, 1896.  1904, Mossi country
incorporated into new colony called Haut-Sénégal et Niger.  Replaced by the
colony of Upper Volta, 1919, covering present territory and included beside
the Mossi several neighboring Voltaic and Mandingo ethnic groups.  Administrative center, Ouagadougou.

1932, colony partitioned between surrounding colonies of Soudan, Niger, and
Ivory Coast.  1937, the Ouagadougou region was made part of an administrative
unit called the Upper Ivory Coast.

Restoration of Upper Volta as a territorial entity, 1947.  September 28,
1958, Upper Volta approved the new constitution of the Fifth French Republic; December 11, 1958, became an autonomous state, called the Voltaic
Republic, within the French Community.

Name changed back to Upper Volta, 1959.  Independent status, August 5, 1960; withdrew from the French Community.

By 1959, approximately 9% of children in school; 95% in primary education; 80% of schools providing only 2 years of elementary training.  3 public primary schools with full program:  at Koudougou and Ouahigouya for boys, at Ouagadougou for girls.  2 Catholic primary schools:  boys at Toussinna, girls at Tounouna.  1961, 2 public secondary schools, at Ouagadougou and Bobo Dioulasso, offering full program leading to <u>Baccalauréat</u>.  5 private secondary schools:  Catholic secondary school for boys, Ouagadougou; Protestant secondary college for boys and girls, Ouagadougou; Notre Dame Institute for girls, Ouagadougou.  Private Catholic education in 2 seminaries.

By 1961, plan for a new educational system geared to rural needs:  adult literacy, improvement of sanitary conditions, modernizing of agricultural techniques.  3-year primary instruction in reading, writing, and arithmetic, with practical work in agriculture.

Plans for a new university in Ouagadougou, according to French agreement with 4 Entente states.

## PRESENT SYSTEM

## PRE-SCHOOL EDUCATION

Entry age:        5-6 years.

Type of education:        Sensory education.  Introduction to reading, writing, and arithmetic.

Length of program:        1 year.

There are very few nursery schools in Upper Volta, and the majority of children enter directly into primary school.

## PRIMARY EDUCATION

Entry age:      7-9 years.

Language of instruction: French.

Length of course:        6 years.  Only 2 classes may be doubled, which would make 8 years.

Program:        French, Arithmetic, Morals and Introduction to Civics, History, Geography, Nature Study, Handicrafts.

Certificate awarded:    Certificat d'études primaires élémentaires
                        (C.E.P.E.).


SECONDARY EDUCATION

Entry age:      12-13 years.

Entrance requirements:  Pass the entrance examination, concours d'entrée
                        en sixième of the lycées, collèges d'enseignement
                        général (C.E.G.), collèges d'enseignement tech-
                        nique (C.E.T.), and the cours normaux (C.N.).

Language of instruction: French.

Length of course:       1st cycle (enseignement court) 4 years.

                        1st and 2nd cycle (enseignement long) 7 years.

Enseignement court given in lycées, C.E.G., and C.N. (teacher training
schools).

Enseignement long given only in lycées.

        N.B.    Modern Language I is always English.  German or Spanish is
                offered as Modern Language II.


## PROGRAM FOR ENSEIGNEMENT COURT
### (Hours per week)

| Classes 6 and 5 Subjects | 1st term 6th class | 2nd and 3rd terms 6th class and the 5th class | |
|---|---|---|---|
| | | Section classique | Section moderne et technique |
| Mathematics | 3 | 3 | 3 |
| Nature Study | 1½ | 1½ | 1½ |
| History and Geography | 2½ | 2½ | 2½ |
| Science | 1 | - | 1 |
| Civics | ½ | ½ | ½ |
| French | 7 | 4 | 6 |
| Latin | - | 5 | - |
| Modern Language | 4 | 3 | 5 |
| Art | 1 | 1 | 1 |
| Music | 1 | 1 | 1 |
| Handicrafts | 1 | 1 | 1 |
| Physical Education | 2 | 2 | 2 |
| Total | 24½ | 24½ | 24½ |

Class 4

| Subjects | Classique A | Classique B | Moderne |
|---|---|---|---|
| French | 3½ | 3½ | 5½ |
| Greek | 3 | - | - |
| Latin | 3½ | 3½ | - |
| Civics | ½ | ½ | ½ |
| Modern Language I | 3 | 3 | 3 |
| Modern Language II | - | 3 | 4 |
| History and Geography | 2½ | 2½ | 2½ |
| Mathematics | 3 | 3 | 3 |
| Nature Study | 1½ | 1½ | 1½ |
| Physical Education | 2 | 2 | 2 |
| Art | 1 | 1 | 1 |
| Music | 1 | 1 | 1 |
| Handicrafts | 1 | 1 | 1 |
| Total | 25½ | 25½ | 25½ |

Class 3

| Subjects | Classique A | Classique B | Moderne |
|---|---|---|---|
| French | 3½ | 3½ | 5½ |
| Latin | 3½ | 3½ | - |
| Greek | 3 | - | - |
| Civics | ½ | ½ | ½ |
| Modern Language I | 3 | 3 | 3 |
| Modern Language II | - | 3 | 4 |
| History and Geography | 3 | 3 | 3 |
| Mathematics | 3 | 3 | 3 |
| Nature Study | 1 | 1 | 1½ |
| Physical Education | 2 | 2 | 2 |
| Art | 1 | 1 | 1 |
| Music | 1 | 1 | 1 |
| Handicrafts | 1 | 1 | 1 |
| Total | 25½ | 25½ | 25½ |

## PROGRAM FOR ENSEIGNEMENT LONG
### (Hours per week)

Class 2

| Subjects | A | A' | B | C | M | M' |
|---|---|---|---|---|---|---|
| French | 4 | 4 | 4 | 4 | 4 | 4 |
| Latin | 3 | 3 | 3 | 3 | - | - |
| Civics | ½ | ½ | ½ | ½ | ½ | ½ |
| Greek | 4 | 3 | - | - | - | - |
| Modern Language I | 3 | 3 | 3 | 3 | 3 | 3 |
| Modern Language II | - | - | 4 | 2 opt. | 4 | 2 opt. |

| Subject | | | | | |
|---|---|---|---|---|---|
| History | 2 | 2 | 2 | 2 | 2 | 2 |
| Geography | 1½ | 1½ | 1½ | 1½ | 1½ | 1½ |
| Mathematics | 2+1 opt. | 5[+] | 2+1 opt. | 5[+] | 5[+] | 5[+] |
| Physical Sciences | 2 3/4 | 3 3/4 | 2 3/4 | 4½ | 4½ | 4½ |
| Natural Sciences | - | - | - | - | - | 3 |
| Physical Education | 2 | 2 | 2 | 2 | 2 | 2 |
| Art | 1 | 1 | 1 | 1 | 1 | 1 |
| Music (optional) | 1 | 1 | 1 | 1 | 1 | 1 |
| Handicrafts (optional) | 1 | 1 | 1 | 1 | 1 | 1 |
| Total hours | 28 3/4 | 30 3/4 | 28 3/4 | 30½ | 29½ | 30½ |
| Compulsory hours | 25 3/4 | 28 3/4 | 25 3/4 | 26 ½ | 27 ½ | 26 ½ |

[+]Includes 1 hour of practical work

## Class 1

| Subjects | A | A' | B | C | M | M' |
|---|---|---|---|---|---|---|
| French | 4 | 4 | 4 | 4 | 4 | 4 |
| Latin | 3 | 3 | 3 | 3 | - | - |
| Greek | 4 | 3 | - | - | - | - |
| Civics | ½ | ½ | ½ | ½ | ½ | ½ |
| Modern Language I | 3 | 3 | 3 | 3 | 3 | 3 |
| Modern Language II | - | - | 4 | 2 opt. | 4 | 2 opt. |
| History | 2 | 2 | 2 | 2 | 2 | 2 |
| Geography | 2 | 2 | 2 | 2 | 2 | 2 |
| Mathematics | 2+1 opt. | 5[+] | 2+1 opt. | 5[+] | 5[+] | 5[+] |
| Physical Sciences | 2¼ | 3¼ | 2¼ | 4½ | 4½ | 4½ |
| Natural Sciences | - | - | - | - | - | 3 |
| Physical Education | 2 | 2 | 2 | 2 | 2 | 2 |
| Art (optional) | 2 | 2 | 2 | 2 | 2 | 2 |
| Music (optional) | 1 | 1 | 1 | 1 | 1 | 1 |
| Handicrafts (optional) | 1 | 1 | 1 | 1 | 1 | 1 |
| Total hours | 29 3/4 | 31 3/4 | 29 3/4 | 32 | 31 | 32 |
| Compulsory hours | 24 3/4 | 27 3/4 | 24 3/4 | 26 | 27 | 26 |

[+]Includes 1 hour of practical work

## Terminal Class

| Subjects | Philosophy | Experimental Sciences | Elementary Mathematics |
|---|---|---|---|
| Philosophy | 9 | 5 | 4 |
| Letters | 1 | 1 opt. | - |
| Civics | ½ | ½ | ½ |
| Modern Language I | 2 | 2 | 2 |
| Classical Language or Modern Language II | 1½ | 1½ | 1½ |

| | | | |
|---|---|---|---|
| History | 2 | 2 | 2 |
| Geography | 2 | 2 | 2 |
| Mathematics and Cosmography | 1½ | 4 | 9 |
| Physical Sciences | 2 | 5 | 6 |
| Natural Sciences | 2 | 4 | 2 |
| Physical Education | 2 | 2 | 2 |
| Art (optional) | 2 | 2 | 2 |
| Music (optional) | 1 | 1 | 1 |
| Handicrafts-girls (opt.) | 1 | 1 | 1 |
| Total hours | 29½ | 33 | 34 |
| Compulsory hours | 24 | 26½ | 28½ |

In the last 4 years the mathematics program includes: Arithmetic, Algebra, Plane Geometry, Solid Geometry, Trigonometry, Cosmography.

In experimental sciences and elementary mathematics sections of terminal class the program makes provision for the study of Mechanics.

In principle Physics and Chemistry include practical laboratory work. Often, however, the scientific equipment available is insufficient.

Grading:   From 0 to 20.  7/20 the lowest acceptable Pass mark.  10/20 necessary to pass into the next class. 20/20 given infrequently.

Grading depends to a great extent on the school and the teachers concerned.

In general, a student who has obtained 10/20 in each term is automatically admitted to the next class. Without this average a student can take an examination in his weak subjects (Composition, Dictation, English, or Mathematics).

Diplomas:

Brevet d'études du premier cycle (B.E.P.C.), end of 4th year (class 3) in lycées and C.E.G.

Brevet élémentaire (B.E.), end of 4th year (class 3) in cours normaux.

* Examen probatoire (formerly first part of the Baccalauréat), end of 6th year (class 1).

** Baccalauréat in Philosophy, Experimental Sciences, or Elementary Mathematics, end of 7th year (terminal class).

PRIVATE SECONDARY SCHOOLS

Entry age, conditions of entry, language of instruction, programs, and diplomas awarded same as those in government schools. Only the government is able to grant diplomas.

Private secondary schools:

    to <u>Baccalauréat</u> level:    Collège La Salle (boys), Ouagadougou
                                  Institut Notre Dame de Kologh-Naba (girls),
                                      Ouagadougou

    to <u>B.E.P.C.</u> level:    Collège Joseph Moukassa, Koudougou
                                    Collège Moderne de Tounouma (boys)
                                    Cours Normal at Tounouma (girls), and
                                        Toussiona (boys)
                                    Collège Charles Lwanga, Nouna
                                    Collèges Modernes de Jeunes Filles, at Banfo-
                                    ra, Tenkodogo, Koudougou, Ouahigouya
                                    Collège Privé Protestant (coed.) at Ouagadou-
                                    gou (girls) at Loumbila

## HIGHER EDUCATION

There is no higher education at present.  Students study at Dakar, Abidjan, Europe or America.

Plans are being made for a university at Ouagadougou.

## VOCATIONAL AND TECHNICAL EDUCATION

Short professional training only offered in <u>collèges d'enseignement technique</u> and private <u>centres</u>.

Length of course:        3 years, plus in some cases 4th year of specialization.  Shorter courses given at some private institutions (1 or 2 years) in Housecrafts, Agriculture, and Rural Life.

Programs:      <u>C.E.T.</u> offer sections in Masonry, Carpentry, Metalwork, Auto Mechanics, Electricity.

                Various <u>centres</u> offer courses in Housecrafts, Masonry, Carpentry, Auto Mechanics and Welding, Lathework, Cycle and Motorcycle Mechanics, Industrial Design, Topographical Design.

<u>Diploma</u>:

    <u>Certificat d'aptitude professionnelle (C.A.P.)</u> in the candidate's specialty.

## TEACHER EDUCATION

<u>Cours normaux</u> offer general secondary education to <u>B.E.</u>, followed by 1 year of professional training.

<u>Diploma</u>:

    <u>Diplôme de fin d'études de cours normaux</u>.  Prepares <u>instituteurs-adjoints</u>.


<u>ECOLES NORMALES</u>

Entry age:     15 to 18 years.

Entrance requirements:  Competitive examination at level of <u>B.E.</u> or <u>B.E.P.C.</u>

Language of instruction: French.

Length of course:    4 years.

Program:    Preparation for <u>Baccalauréat</u> in first 3 years, as in <u>lycées</u>.  4th year consists of professional training: Theoretical and Practical Pedagogy, Psychology, School Administration, Professional Ethics.

Certificates awarded:    <u>Baccalauréat</u>
                         <u>Certificat de fin d'études des écoles normales</u>

Prepares <u>instituteurs</u>.

# FRENCH-SPEAKING

# EQUATORIAL AFRICA

# F R E N C H - S P E A K I N G
# E Q U A T O R I A L   A F R I C A

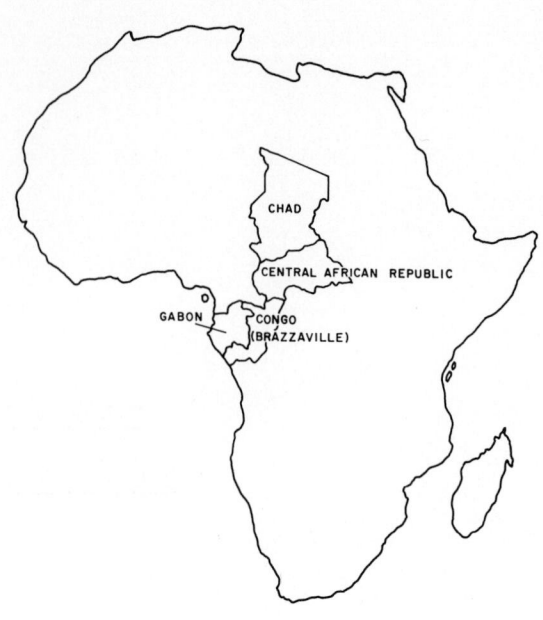

| Country and Capital | Area (sq. miles) | Est. Population | Independence Dates or Political Status | Official Language |
|---|---|---|---|---|
| CENTRAL AFRICAN REPUBLIC<br>Bangui<br>Formerly: Ubangi-Shari<br>(Bangui) | 238,220 | 1,229,000 | 13 August 1960 (Remained within the French Community) | French |
| REPUBLIC OF CHAD<br>Fort-Lamy | 495,370 | 2,800,000 | 8 August 1960 (Remained within the French Community) | French |
| THE CONGO REPUBLIC<br>Brazzaville | 132,046 | 900,000 | 15 August 1960 (Remained within the French Community) | French |
| REPUBLIC OF GABON<br>Libreville | 103,089 | 450,000 | 17 August 1960 (Remained within the French Community) | French |

CENTRAL AFRICAN REPUBLIC

Agricultural
Institute

Teacher

Training

Vocational
and
Technical
Training

C. E. G.

SECONDARY EDUCATION

PRIMARY EDUCATION

None
** Terminale
1 Première
2 Seconde
3 Troisième
4 Quatrième
5 Cinquième
6 Sixième

| | HIGHER EDUCATION | | | | | | | | | SECONDARY | | | | | | | ELEMENTARY | | | | | |
|---|---|---|---|---|---|---|---|---|---|---|---|---|---|---|---|---|---|---|---|---|---|---|
| Year of Schooling | 20 | 19 | 18 | 17 | 16 | 15 | 14 | 13 | 12 | 11 | 10 | 9 | 8 | 7 | 6 | 5 | 4 | 3 | 2 | 1 | | |
| Student's Age | 26 | 25 | 24 | 23 | 22 | 21 | 20 | 19 | 18 | 17 | 16 | 15 | 14 | 13 | 12 | 11 | 10 | 9 | 8 | 7 | 6 | 5 4 3 |

Compulsory education:

School year: October through June

Secondary grading: 0 - 20
10/20 usual pass grade

CENTRAL AFRICAN REPUBLIC
(République Centrafricaine)

Independence:  August 13, 1960.

## BACKGROUND

Central African Republic was known as Ubangi-Shari (Oubangui Chari)
until 1958.

The population is made up largely of agriculturalists.  The ethnic groups
are the Azandi, Banda, Banziri, Baya, Bunga, Mandja, Mbum, and Pambia,
having within them many subtribes.  There are numerous African languages
and dialects.  Sangho is the lingua franca, spoken in all territories.
French is the official language.

From 1890-1900, French explorers extending French control from Brazzaville to Lake Chad made treaties with the tribal chiefs in the area now
comprising Central African Republic.  The territory of Ubangi-Shari was
formally established in 1894.  In 1895, the eastern border was settled by
a treaty with Germany.  The southern border was determined after the
Ubangi River had been explored by the Rouvier-Bellay mission when the
French authorities and the government of the Congo Free State agreed upon
the border between the two countries.

In 1905 Ubangi-Shari and Chad were merged.  In 1910, Gabon, Middle Congo
and Ubangi-Shari (which included Chad) were constituted as French colonies,
forming French Equatorial Africa.

The territory was used as a French base during World War II.  September,
1940, it joined the Free French group and participated in World War II.
After the war, the country elected its own Representative Assembly and
sent representatives to the French Parliament in Paris.  On the referendum
of September 28, 1958, the territory voted to become an autonomous republic
within the French Community.  December 1, 1958, Ubangi-Shari was proclaimed
the Central African Republic, a member state of the French Community.

Educational system has been patterned on that of France, but adaptations
have been made to meet local needs. Not until the middle of the 20th
century were French and American Protestant mission schools established.
By 1960 there were 384 primary schools, 15 secondary schools (7 public, 8
private), and 22 technical and vocational schools (1 private).

As of 1962, all education under state control.  Only "private" schools
are those established by foreign countries, conducted according to the
educational system of the foreign country and using its language.

Mission schools continue as before, but are under government control.
Religious education in non-denominational schools is optional and
additional to the regular timetable.  In mission schools, it is given as
previously.

Administrative measures of April 28, 1962, December 14, 1962 and March 23,
1963 created educational reforms.  Major ones:  reduction of primary
school training to 5 years, and construction of 8 Collèges d'Enseignement
Général with 5 classes each.


## PRESENT SYSTEM


## PRIMARY EDUCATION

Entry age:      6 years.

Language of instruction:       French.

5-year program.  Prior to 1963, 6-year program.

Course of study:      Language, Reading, Writing, Arithmetic, Nature
Study, History, Geography, Hygiene, Manual Training.

Curriculum reform:    In year 1 (cours préparatoire), language instruction
increased from 6 hours 40 minutes per week to 8
hours 45 minutes, and lectures reduced from 10 hours
to 7 hours 55 minutes.

In years 2-3 (cours élémentaire), 1 hour of manual
training added.

In years 4-5 (cours moyen), practical work in grammar
included during the usual hour for French.

Certificat d'études primaires élémentaires (C.E.P.E.) awarded at close of
program.


## SECONDARY EDUCATION

Entrance requirements:       Pass entrance examination, concours d'entrée
en sixième.

Language of instruction:        French.

Duration of course:        Enseignement long (long course):
7-year program in lycées and collèges.
1953, Collège Emile Gentil offered first long
course.
Up to 1962, no terminal classes at 7th year level.

Enseignement court (short course):
4-year program in collèges d'enseignement général
(C.E.G.).

Programs:        Similar to French with local adaptations.

Certificat de fin d'études du premier cycle secondaire offered at close
of 4-year program (études secondaires moyennes), with the following
options:
Techniques, Industrielles, Commerciales, Agricoles,
Ménagères-sociales, Pédagogiques, Enseignement Général:
Brevet d'études du premier cycle (B.E.P.C.) and Brevet
Elementaire (B.E.).

Certificat de fin d'études secondaires offered at close of full 2/3 cycle
(études secondaires complètes) with above options, adding to Enseignement
Général, Lettres, Mathématiques and Sciences:  Baccalauréat.


## HIGHER EDUCATION

None.  Under the terms of a cooperative agreement concerning higher
education concluded between the Central African Republic, Congo Republic
(Brazzaville), Chad and Gabon, and the French Republic, students from
Central African Republic may pursue their studies at the Centre d'En-
seignement Supérieur de Brazzaville (see Higher Education, THE CONGO
REPUBLIC).   Since 1961, the Center for Higher Education in Brazzaville
has been under the jurisdiction of the Fondation de l'Enseignement
Supérieur en Afrique Centrale (Foundation for Higher Education in Central
Africa), whose authority now covers the Institut d'Etudes Agronomiques in
Wakambo (see section on Vocational and Technical Education), the Institut
d'Etudes Zootechniques in Fort-Lamy, Chad, the Institut Polytechnique in
Libreville, Gabon, and the Ecole Normale Supérieure in the Congo Republic.


## VOCATIONAL AND TECHNICAL EDUCATION

### TRADE SCHOOLS

Entrance requirements:        Pass entrance examination at C.E.P.E. level.

1-2 year programs.

Ecole Artisanale for boys offers courses in Basketweaving, Leatherwork, Carving, Bookbinding.

School for girls offers Sewing, Dressmaking, Embroidery and Social Work.

## COLLEGES D'ENSEIGNEMENT TECHNIQUE

Entrance requirements:        Pass entrance examination at C.E.P.E. level.

3-4 year program in Carpentry, Metal-Work, Motor Mechanics, clerical training and Bookkeeping, leading to Certificat d'aptitude professionnelle (C.A.P.).

## INSTITUT D'ETUDES AGRONOMIQUES D'AFRIQUE CENTRALE (de Wakombo), M'Baiki

First classes opened October, 1961. Trains medium and higher level agricultural officers with particular knowledge of Central African agricultural cultivation and research. Under the jurisdiction of the Fondation de l'Enseignement Supérieur en Afrique Centrale.

Entrance requirements:
>
> 1st cycle
> Competitive examination at level of French B.E.P.C. Preference given to students from Central African Republic, Tchad, Gabon, and Congo (Brazzaville).
>
> 2nd cycle (opened October, 1964) Competitive examination at level of baccalauréat, or examination after completion of 3rd year, 1st cycle, of Institut training.

1st cycle:

3 years, for training of agricultural technicians.

Specializations:        Dissemination of agricultural principles, co-operatives, rural engineering.

Diplôme de technicien d'agriculture tropicale awarded at close of 1st cycle for general average of 10 or more. Holder able to enter public service in charge of agricultural projects.

Students with higher than 12 average may take examination for 2nd year of Section A, 2nd cycle.

1st cycle program:

General subjects:    Mathematics, Physics, Chemistry, French,
                     History-Geography, English.

Technical subjects:

(1) Biological Sciences
    Vegetable Biology, Botany, Zoology, Animal Biology.

(2) Phytotechniques
    General Tropical Agriculture, Meteorology, Phytopathology,
    Sylviculture, Special Tropical Agriculture, Arboriculture,
    Fodder-Plants.

(3) Zootechniques
    General and Special Zootechniques, Veterinary Hygiene.

(4) Rural Engineering and Technology
    Land Management, Agricultural Mechanics, Rural Building, Topo-
    graphy, Technology of Agricultural Products, Conditioning and
    Control.

(5) Human and Economic Sciences
    Methodology of Dissemination of Agricultural Principles,
    Regional Adaptations, Rural Economy, Accountancy, Administration.

Practical training:   Farm, workshop, and outside work.


2nd cycle:

Section A:      2 years for students admitted by competitive examination
                (baccalauréat level).  First examination in May, 1965.

                1 year for students with a higher than 12 average from
                1st cycle, who may enter directly into 2nd year after
                special examination.

In addition to the above specializations in 1st cycle, it is planned
that a research section will be added in 2 years.

Diplôme d'ingénieur des travaux agricoles awarded at close of Section A.

Section B:      3 years for students admitted by competitive examination
                at the level of mathématiques supérieures (to open 1966-67).

Diplôme d'ingénieur d'agronomie tropicale awarded at close of Section B.

TEACHER EDUCATION

COURS NORMAUX

At Bania and Yaloké.

Entrance requirements:          Pass examination at C.E.P.E. level.

2-year program.

Cours normaux curriculum reform, 1963:

1st yr:   15 hrs. French, 15 hrs. Scientific Study, Mathematics, Science,
          Geography, Manual Training, 3 hrs. Drawing, Singing, Physical
          Education, 3 hrs. General Introduction to Pedagogy, Morals,
          Civics, History.

2nd yr:   14 hrs. Pedagogy, Theoretical, Practical, 6 hrs. French, 10 hrs.
          Education.


COLLEGE NORMAL DE BAMBARI

Entrance requirements:          B.E.P.C.

1 year professional training.

Certificat de fin d'études des collèges normaux (C.F.E.C.N.) awarded for
instituteurs-adjoints.


ECOLE NORMALE SUPERIEURE

Entrance requirements:          Pass examination at classe de seconde level.

3-year programs.

Section des Elèves-Inspecteurs opened in 1964.  Has ultimate end for
preparing instituteurs expérimentés and professeurs de C.E.G. not only
for their administrative and inspection tasks (inspecteurs and conseillers
pédagogiques, directeurs d'écoles normales et de collèges  normaux) but
also for teaching pedagogy.

Institut Pédagogique opened in 1964 as part of the Ecole Normale Supérieure,
ready for full use in 1967.

Purposes:      To enrich library, start a Centre de Documentation Pédago-
               gique for use of professors in C.E.G. and of 2nd cycle,
               cooperate with Ministry in program reform, create a
               laboratory of psychological, pedagogical research.

Programs:          en lettres - année préparatoire
                               1ère année normale
                               2ème année normale

                   en sciences- same as above

Examen de sortie de l'Ecole Normale Supérieure:  This examination
consists of the theoretical matter of C.A.P.

Examination:   Letters option - Dissertation        4 hrs.
                                 Psycho-Pedagogy     4 hrs.
                                 History             4 hrs.

               Science option - Mathematics         4 hrs.
                                 Natural Science     2 hrs.
                                 Physics             4 hrs.


Certificates awarded:     Certificat d'aptitude à l'inspection des écoles
                          et à la direction des écoles normales d'insti-
                          tuteurs (C.A.I.P.)

                          Certificat d'aptitude à l'enseignement du
                          second degré (C.A.P.E.S.)

REPUBLIC OF CHAD

| Student's Age | Year of Schooling | | | | | | | | | |
|---|---|---|---|---|---|---|---|---|---|---|
| 26 | 20 | | | | | | | | | |
| 25 | 19 | | | | | | | | | |
| 24 | 18 | HIGHER EDUCATION | | | | | | | | |
| 23 | 17 | | | | | | | | | |
| 22 | 16 | | | | | | | | | |
| 21 | 15 | | | | | | | | | |
| 20 | 14 | | | | | | | | | |
| 19 | 13 | ** | None | Zoo-Tech./Vet. | | | | | | |
| 18 | 12 | * | Terminale | Post. & Tele. | | | | | | |
| 17 | 11 | | Première | Agriculture | Vocational | | | | | |
| 16 | 10 | | Seconde 1 | Nat'l Admin. | and | | | | | |
| 15 | 9 | SECONDARY | Troisième 2 | Nurses' Tr. | Technical | Cours | | | | |
| 14 | 8 | | Quatrième 3 | Collège | Training | Normal | | | | |
| 13 | 7 | | Cinquième 4 | d'Enseignement | | and | | | | |
| 12 | 6 | | Sixième 5 | Général | | Centres | | | | |
| 11 | 5 | | 6 | SECONDARY EDUCATION | | Pédagogiques | | | | |
| 10 | 4 | ELEMENTARY | | | | | | | | |
| 9 | 3 | | | | | | | | | |
| 8 | 2 | | | PRIMARY EDUCATION | | | | | | |
| 7 | 1 | | | | | | | | | |
| 6 | | | | | | | | | | |
| 5 | | Ecole Maternelle | | | | | | | | |
| 4 | | | | | | | | | | |
| 3 | | | | | | | | | | |

Compulsory education: 6-12 years of age (where schools exist)

School year: October 1 - June 30

Secondary Grading: 20 - Perfect

9/20 - lowest passing mark

REPUBLIC OF CHAD (TCHAD)
(République du Tchad)


Independence:   August 11, 1960.



## BACKGROUND


Chad is one of the 4 countries included in French-speaking Equatorial
Africa (others:  the Congo Republic, Gabon, Central African Republic).
The cross-road between Sahara and Tropical Africa.

Chad is divided into 3 climatic zones:  Saharan (wide range of temperature),
Sahelian (semi-desert), and Sudanic (relatively moderate temperature ).

96% of population is rural, 4% urban.

Population is mixture of many tribal groups, divided between Caucasians
in the north who follow Islamic faith, and the Kirdi (animists), predominantly Negroid, in the south.   Arab invaders brought Islam to regions
of Baguirmi and Wadai; some indigenous tribes such as  Salamat and Tungur
were Arabized by inter-marriage.

Islamic population:

    The Arabs, cattle and camel breeders.
    The Peuls, traditional nomadic shepherds (do not intermarry, their
       population remains racially pure)
    The Ouaddaians, farmers who are in the east, near the Sudan border
    The Baguirmians, farmers
    The Kanembus, farmers and animal husbandrymen
    The Tubus (or Tedas), desert nomads, living in the Tibesti region
       (are believed to have originated centuries ago in Egypt)
    The smallest groups, including Kotokos, the Boudoumas and the Hadjarais

Non-Islamic population:

    The Saras, the dominant group, made up of a diversity of tribes;
       farmers
    The Massas
    The Moundangs


Various languages spoken by tribal groups; Arabic in common use; French,
official language.

Between 9th and 18th centuries the Kingdom of Kanem, the Bornu Empire, the Sultanate of Baguirmi and the Ouaddai Empire controlled at various times the major parts of the territory forming present Chad.

British explorers came in 1822, 1853 and 1870.  1890, French expedition brought French control over areas south and east of Lake Chad.  Full control of territory by 1913.

Borders of Chad secured by conventions between France and Germany in 1894, and France and the United Kingdom in 1898.

In 1910, Gabon, Middle Congo and Ubangi-Shari (present Central African Republic which included Chad) were constituted administratively as colonies; together they formed French Equatorial Africa (F.E.A.).

Slow development between World War I and II.  August 16, 1940, Chad was the first of the French territories to rally to the cause of Free France.

After 1945, Chad became one of the territories of French Equatorial Africa in the French Union, and in the referendum of September 28, 1958 the territory voted to become an autonomous republic within the French Community.

November 26, 1958, Territorial Assembly became a constituent Assembly and proclaimed the autonomous Republic of Chad.  August 11, 1960, full independence; remained within the French Community.

Chad had no missionaries until the 20th century; American Protestants went to southern areas and established first school in 1920.  Catholics followed. Missions were left free to organize education as they desired until after World War II, except that French was to be the language of instruction and vernacular used only for religious instruction.

Subsidies provided for both Catholic and Protestant missions.  1925 regulations required mission schools to follow same curriculum as state schools in order to qualify for recognition and subsidy.

1947, financial responsibility for primary education transferred from France to individual territories.

By 1964, 270 primary schools, largely public.

PRESENT SYSTEM

P U B L I C   E D U C A T I O N

PRE-PRIMARY EDUCATION

ECOLE MATERNELLE

Entry age:  5 years.

1-year program.


PRIMARY EDUCATION

Entry age:  6 years.

6-year program.

Language of instruction:  French.

Many schools in Moslem north provide only 2-3 years.

Certificat d'études primaires élémentaires tchadien awarded at close of 6-year program.


SECONDARY EDUCATION

COLLEGES D'ENSEIGNEMENT GENERAL (former Cours Complémentaires)

1959, Cours Complémentaires, 4-year post-primary education, established at Fort-Archambault and Moundu for students not continuing to academic secondary schools.  Program usually attached to primary schools; similar to short level secondary education.  Teacher training sections sometimes included.

Present Collèges d'Enseignement Général (C.E.G.) now considered part of secondary education, offering the first cycle: enseignement court.  There is a C.E.G. for boys, and one for girls in Fort-Lamy; others which are co-educational are located in Ati, Baibokoum, Doba, Kelo, Kourma, Faya-Largeau, Fianga, Lere, Moissala, Mongo, Moundu, Moussoro, Pala.

4-year program, leading to Brevet élémentaire (B.E.) and Brevet d'études du premier cycle (B.E.P.C.).

## LYCEES

Training similar to French system.  Examinations and diplomas same as those in France.

Entrance requirements:          C.E.P.E. and successful passing of the
                                competitive examination, concours d'entrée
                                en sixième.

7-year program.

At close of first 4 years (1st cycle), diploma awarded:  Brevet élémentaire du premier cycle.

At close of final 3 years (2nd cycle), diploma awarded:  Baccalauréat.


## LYCEE FELIX EBOUE, Fort-Lamy

Established in 1947.  Up to 1963, only institution offering full French secondary education with complete classical and modern courses.

Curriculum:     Natural Sciences, Mathematics, Classical and Modern
                Literature, English, Spanish, German.

1st cycle:      Leading to B.E.P.C.

*2nd cycle:     Leading to examen probatoire at close of 2 years.

**Terminal classes (established in 1960), final year:  Philosophy, Mathematics, Experimental Sciences.  Preparing for Baccalauréat.


## LYCEE FRANCO-ARABE, Abéché

Created in 1952 as Collège de Ouaddai with instruction in Arabic only. 1956, name changed to Collège Franco-Arabe, with regular French school courses introduced, and Arabic as leading foreign language.  In 1960, a mixed Arabic-French curriculum.  1 section for élèves-moniteurs instructed in French and Arabic.

1963, name changed to Lycée.  Presently offers full 7-year secondary program, ending in final Baccalauréat.


## LYCEE 'AHMED MANGUE'

Previous to 1964, this lycée called a collège,  offering regular secondary program through the classe de troisième (4 years).  From 1964, full 7-year secondary program, ending in final Baccalauréat.

LYCEE JACQUES MODEINA, Bongor

Established in 1942 as Collège Moderne de Bongor, offering a 4-year secondary program through classe de troisième, leading to the Brevet élémentaire du premier cycle (B.E.P.C.).

Teacher training program also offered until 1959, when Centre Pédagogique de Bongor was created to take over the normal school training (see TEACHER EDUCATION).

Presently, offers full 7-year secondary program, ending in final baccalauréat.


ARABIC SECONDARY EDUCATION

MOSLEM INSTITUTE, Fort-Lamy

Offers secondary program for some of its students.


MOSLEM CENTER, Fort-Lamy

Also provides some secondary level training.


HIGHER EDUCATION

None.  Under a cooperative agreement concerning higher education concluded between Chad, Congo Republic (Brazzaville), Central African Republic and Gabon, and the French Republic students from Chad may pursue their studies at the Centre d'Enseignement Supérieur de Brazzaville.  (See Higher Education, THE CONGO REPUBLIC.)  Since 1961, the Center for Higher Education in Brazzaville has been under the jurisdiction of the Fondation de l'Enseignement Supérieur en Afrique Centrale (Foundation for Higher Education in Central Africa), whose authority now covers the Institut d'Etudes Zootechniques in Fort-Lamy (see section on  Vocational and Technical Education), the Institut Polytechnique in Libreville, Gabon, the Institut d'Etudes Agronomiques in Wakambo, Central African Republic, and the Ecole Normale Supérieure in the Congo Republic.


VOCATIONAL AND TECHNICAL EDUCATION

LYCEE TECHNIQUE COMMERCIAL, Fort-Lamy

Entrance requirements:            11 years of age, not more than 18 years.
                                  Competitive entrance examination.

6-year program.

At the close of 4 years, candidate receives Certificat d'aptitude pro-fessionnelle (C.A.P.).

At the close of the final 2 years, Brevet industriel commercial awarded.


COLLEGE TECHNIQUE INDUSTRIEL, Fort-Archambault

Entrance requirements:          11 years of age, not more than 18 years.
                                Competitive entrance examination.

6-year program.

At the close of 4 years, candidates receive Certificat d'aptitude pro-fessionnelle (C.A.P.).

At the close of the final 2 years, Brevet industriel technique awarded.


COLLEGE D'ENSEIGNEMENT TECHNIQUE, Fort-Lamy

Entrance requirements:          11 years of age, not more than 18 years.
                                Competitive entrance examination.

4-year program, preparing for various C.A.P.:  Carpentry, Masonry,
Electricity, Auto-Mechanics.


INSTITUT D'ETUDES ZOOTECHNIQUES D'AFRIQUE CENTRALE, Fort-Lamy

Established in 1963.  Under jurisdiction of Fondation de l'Enseignement
Supérieur en Afrique Centrale.

Training of cattle raising teaching staff with knowledge of particular
conditions of cattle raising and zootechnical research in countries of
Central Africa.

Entrance requirements:          For 1st cycle:  Competitive examination
                                (B.E. and B.E.P.C. level).

                                For 2nd cycle:  Baccalauréat or equivalent.

2 cycles:     1st cycle -    3 years, training cattle raising super-
                             intendents (contrôleurs d'élevage).

              2nd cycle -    2 years, training engineers of cattle raising
                             works (ingénieurs des travaux d'élevage).

ECOLE DE POSTES ET TELECOMMUNICATIONS, Fort-Archambault

Established in 1963.

Entrance requirements:          16 years of age, not more than 18 years.
                                B.E.P.C. and competitive entrance exami-
                                nation.

4-year program.  (Name of final diploma not yet determined.)


ECOLE DES ADJOINTS-TECHNIQUES DES TRAVAUX PUBLICS

Established in 1964.

Entrance requirements:          16 years of age, not more than 18 years.
                                B.E.P.C. and competitive entrance exami-
                                nation.

4-year program.  (Name of final diploma not yet determined.)


ECOLE NATIONALE D'ADMINISTRATION, Fort-Lamy

Established in 1963.

Entrance requirements:          16 years of age, not more than 18 years.
                                B.E.P.C. and competitive entrance exami-
                                nation.

2-year program.  (Name of final diploma not yet determined.)


ECOLE DE BA-ILLI (Agriculture)

Entrance requirements:          15 years of age, and not more than 20 years.
                                B.E.P.C. and competitive entrance examination.

4-year program.  (Name of final diploma not yet determined.)


ECOLE NATIONALE DES INFIRMIERS ET DES INFIRMIERES, Fort-Lamy

Established in 1962.

Entrance requirements:          15 years of age, not more than 20 years.
                                B.E.P.C. and competitive entrance examination.

2-year program.

Upon successful completion of program, <u>Diplôme d'Etat de l'Ecole Nationale</u> <u>des Infirmiers, Infirmières, Aides Sociales et Infirmières Accoucheuses</u> awarded.


## <u>TEACHER EDUCATION</u>

### <u>CENTRES PEDAGOGIQUES</u>

2 Centres Pédagogiques: at Fort-Lamy and at Bongor. Centre Pédagogique de Bongor established in 1959 to take over the teacher training classes of the Collège Moderne de Bongor.

#### <u>Section des élèves moniteurs</u>

Entrance requirements: <u>Brevet élémentaire du premier cycle</u>, and competitive examination (<u>concours</u>).

2-year program.

<u>Diplôme de fin d'études de la section des moniteurs</u> awarded.

#### <u>Section des élèves instituteurs-adjoints</u>

Entrance requirements: <u>Brevet élémentaire du premier cycle</u>, and competitive examination (<u>concours</u>).

2-year program.

<u>Diplôme de fin d'études de la section normale</u> awarded.


### <u>COURS NORMAL, Fort-Archambault</u>

Entrance requirements: Competitive examination at the level of the <u>classe de sixième</u>.

6-year program:   4 years, <u>enseignement général</u>.
                  2 years, <u>formation professionnelle</u>.

<u>Certificat élémentaire d'aptitude pédagogique (C.E.A.P.)</u> awarded.


# P R I V A T E   E D U C A T I O N

## <u>COLLEGE PRIVE CATHOLIQUE CHARLES LWANGA, Fort-Archambault</u>

Parochial secondary school, established 1959. Outgrowth of the Catholic school for the training of monitors and teaching assistants for primary schools.  Training school still in operation.

Secondary program:  7 years.  Same examinations, grading, and diplomas as government schools.

# THE CONGO REPUBLIC
### (Brazzaville)

Ecole Normale Supérieure

Teacher Training

Technical

and

Vocational Training

Med./Soc. Sec. of the Center for Higher Studies

SECONDARY EDUCATION

PRIMARY EDUCATION

Science

Letters

Law

**

Terminale
1 Première
2 Seconde
3 Troisième
4 Quatrième
5 Qinquième
6 Sixième

| Student's Age | Year of Schooling | |
|---|---|---|
| 26 | 20 | HIGHER EDUCATION |
| 25 | 19 | |
| 24 | 18 | |
| 23 | 17 | |
| 22 | 16 | |
| 21 | 15 | |
| 20 | 14 | |
| 19 | 13 | SECONDARY |
| 18 | 12 | |
| 17 | 11 | |
| 16 | 10 | |
| 15 | 9 | |
| 14 | 8 | |
| 13 | 7 | |
| 12 | 6 | ELEMENTARY |
| 11 | 5 | |
| 10 | 4 | |
| 9 | 3 | |
| 8 | 2 | |
| 7 | 1 | |
| 6 | | |
| 5 | | |
| 4 | | |
| 3 | | |

Compulsory education: 6-16 years of age

School year: October through June

Secondary grading: 0-20

10/20 usual passmark

768

THE CONGO REPUBLIC (Brazzaville)
(République du Congo)


Independence:  August 15, 1960


## BACKGROUND


There are four major ethnic groups in the Congo Republic comprising
about 73 tribes.  The largest group, the Kongo (350,000) with about 15
tribes including the Bakongo and Balali, lives southeast of Brazzaville,
occupying 15% of the country's area and accounting for almost half of its
population.  The Bateke (150,000) live north of Brazzaville.  The Mboshi
(95,000) with about 10 tribes live "where the savanna and forest meet."
Of this group the Mboshi (53,000),Kuyu (15,000), and Makua (10,000) form
10% of the population of Brazzaville and represent the majority of its
skilled workers and civil servants.  The Sanga with about 15 tribes live
in the northern forest zone.  The foreign population numbers about 10,000:
Europeans (mostly French) and those from other African nations.

There are as many languages as tribes; Mouman Koutouba is a vernacular
generally understood.  French is the official language.

In medieval times a Congo Empire extending into the present Congo Republic
was at its height in the 16th century.  The Bateke people constituted the
Anzico kingdom which also flourished previous to the 17th century.

The coastal areas of the Congo Republic were explored by Portuguese
sailors in the 15th century.  In the 17th century French trading companies were active.  By 1766 Catholic missions were established.  Due to
the thick forests and swift rivers penetration into the interior was
difficult.  Early French explorers were followed by Pierre Savorgnan de
Brazza and Henry Morgan Stanley toward the close of the 19th century.
They explored the interior, and Brazza signed a treaty with the Bateke
ruler in October, 1880, which gave control of both banks of the Congo
River to France.

France's claim to the territory was given formal recognition by Congress
of Berlin, 1885.  In 1910, Gabon, Middle Congo (Moyen Congo) and Ubangi-
Shari were constituted administratively as colonies, forming French
Equatorial Africa.

August, 1940, Middle Congo supported Free French group and became a base
for troops during World War II.  September 28, 1958, colony voted to

become an autonomous republic within the French Community.  November 28, the Territorial Assembly proclaimed the Congo Republic and transformed itself into a legislative and constituent assembly.  February 20, 1959, the official government was established.  August 15, 1960, Republic became independent.

Educational system originally patterned on that of France, but since independence is being adapted to local needs.  Primary schools established by Catholic and Protestant missions at the end of the 19th century.  By 1882 French public education was free.  From 1883-1915 various laws were passed to prevent the Church from influencing education.  By 1911, public education consisted of elementary primary, higher primary, and vocational training.  Between 1937 and 1940 education was reorganized.  1944, collèges modernes established.  By 1945, 3 types of vocational training: apprenticeship sections, 4-year trade schools, 4-year vocational schools. A 1961 education law opened education to all children without discrimination, made education compulsory from 6-16 years of age, authorized both public and private education, the latter in 3 categories:

> (1)  Assimilated establishments:
>      (a)  Private primary schools.
>      (b)  Same instruction as public schools.
>      (c)  Teachers have all received training in private
>           institutions.
>
> (2)  Subsidized establishments:
>           Those receiving an annual state subsidy for adhering to
>           government study plans and programs as specified by
>           contract.
>
> (3)  Free establishments:
>           Those not receiving subsidies from the state or local
>           bodies.

By 1963, there were 600 primary schools, 15 secondary schools, and 2 technical and vocational schools, and 30 apprenticeship centers, home economics and technical courses and centers offering accelerated vocational training.

In 1959, Centre d'Etudes Administratives et Techniques Supérieures opened in Brazzaville offering higher educational training to students from Central African countries.  1960, renamed Centre d'Enseignement Supérieur de Brazzaville.  In 1961, the Fondation de l'Enseignement Supérieur en Afrique Centrale was created as a university agency carrying the French traditions, programs and examinations, but legally under the jurisdiction of the four republics of Congo, Central Africa, Gabon and Tchad, its authority to cover the various centers in the four countries offering higher educational programs.

PRESENT SYSTEM

PRIMARY EDUCATION

Almost 75% of children are enrolled in primary schools.  One-third of
these are girls, an unusually high percentage for Africa.  More than half
of the students are in private primary schools.

Entry age:      6 years.

Language of instruction:        French.

6-year program:    2 years, cours préparatoire
                   2 years, cours élémentaire
                   2 years, cours moyen

Certificat d'études primaires élémentaires, awarded on successful examination, and recommendation by principal, at close of program.


SECONDARY EDUCATION

3 out of 4 students attend public schools.

Secondary School Entrance Examination - Examen d'entrée en sixième:

Competitive examination held about one month before the Primary Certificate Examination.

If 13 years of age or less, the candidate is oriented toward the "long
course" in lycées and Catholic collèges.

If 14 years old, directed to the "short course" in Collèges d'Enseignement
Général and in the vocational sections of the Lycée Technique in Brazzaville.  (Exceptionally strong candidates from this group sent on to "long
course".)

If older than 14, students are directed to teacher training institutions
or to the Agricultural School in Sibbite.

Girls up to 20 are admitted to nearby vocational schools for secretarial
training.

Long course:    7-year academic course in lycées and in collèges classiques
                et modernes.  Curriculum identical to lycées in France.
                (Few Congolese take the classical program.)

                1st cycle - 4 years
                2nd cycle - 3 years

Collèges modernes established in 1944 to prepare candidates to Ecole des Cadres Supérieurs Indigènes Edouard-Renard. 4-year post-elementary course. First 3 years, general education (no classical language). 4th year included general and specialized courses and internships, 6 sections: teacher training, administrative and commercial, mining, public works, medical, veterinary.

Short course:   4-year general course, usually given in collèges d'enseignement général.

Examinations at end of short cycle:

At close of classes de troisième, 2 different examinations are given:

(1)   If students have not studied a foreign language, a particularly difficult examination is given in French, Mathematics, and Science.
Successful candidates receive the Brevet élémentaire (B.E.), normally a terminal certificate.

(2)   If students from either the lycées or collèges d'enseignement général have studied 1 or 2 modern foreign languages, the examination includes these subjects.
Successful candidates receive the Brevet d'études du premier cycle (B.E.P.C.). Does not automatically enable holder to pursue further general or specialized studies.

Competitive examinations, given by lycées, may be taken by students originally directed to the short course who wish to continue in the deuxième cycle of secondary school.

Examen probatoire given at close of classe de première.

Baccalauréat in Philosophy, Experimental Sciences or Elementary Mathematics at close of terminal class (terminale) - 7 years. University of Bordeaux prepares, supervises, and controls the baccalauréat examinations. Candidates scoring 10 out of 20 receive the baccalauréat. Candidates between 7 and 10 are given a second chance.

HIGHER EDUCATION

CENTRE D'ENSEIGNEMENT SUPERIEUR, Brazzaville

Established in 1959 as Centre d'Etudes Administratives et Techniques Supérieures. In October 1960, the section preparing for the Capacité en droit and the literary and scientific sections preparing for the Certificat d'études littéraires générales and Certificat d'études mathématiques générales detached themselves from the Center to form a Law School, a Higher School of Science, and a Higher School of Letters to compose the Centre d'Enseignement Supérieur de Brazzaville.

After the creation in December 1961 of the Fondation de l'Enseignement Supérieur en Afrique Centrale, the Centre d'Enseignement Supérieur came under its jurisdiction along with other higher educational institutions in the 4 Central African countries:  the Institut d'Enseignement Agronomique in Wakambo (Central African Republic) in 1961, the Institut d'Enseignement Zootechnique in Fort-Lamy (Chad) in 1963, and the Institut Polytechnique in Libreville (Gabon) in 1964.

> Entrance requirements:        Baccalauréat or equivalent, or the passing of examinations to particular faculty, or for particular program.

## Ecole Supérieure d'Administration (Higher School of Administration)

School was created from the former administrative and legal sections of the Centre d'Etudes Administratives et Techniques Supérieures which trained in 2 years with appropriate study covering the Capacité en droit, and a year's study in France, the administrators and magistrates.

Recruitment was on the level of B.E.P.C.  The last entrance examination was given in 1963.  In June 1964, the judiciary section was terminated. The administrative section continued through 1964-65.  School closed June 1965.  To be substituted will be Ecoles Nationales d'Administration in each of the 4 central African countries.

Program:

> General subjects:   French, English, History, Geography.
> Special subjects:   Economics, Administrative Sciences, 2nd year of Capacité en droit.

Final awards:  Certificat (with an average less than 12/20).
               Diplôme (with an average of at least 12/20).

## Ecole de Droit (Law School)

### Faculties of Law and Economic Sciences

### Capacité en droit

Courses for the capacité are also offered in Bangui, Fort-Lamy and Libreville.

> Entrance requirements:        No qualification required, however B.E. or B.E.P.C. or the level of classe de troisième is recommended.

2-year program.  Entrance into the 2nd year depends upon success in first year final examination.

Curriculum (hours):

1st yr:    Private Law (12), Public Law (60).

2nd yr:    Common Procedure and Executory Means (30), Penal Law and Penal Procedure (30), Economics (30), Special Administrative Law (30), Overseas Fiscal Law (30), Social Law (30).

Examinations:

1st yr:    Written (eliminatory):  Private Law, Public Law.
           Oral:  2 questions on Private Law, 1 question on Public Law.

2nd yr:    Written (eliminatory):  On 2 subjects chosen by the candidate among the 2nd year subjects.
           Oral:  4 questions, each one on a subject chosen by the candidate among the ones taught in 2nd year, and not included in the written examinations.

Certificat de capacité en droit awarded on successful examination at close of 2-year program.


Licence en droit and Licence ès sciences économiques

Entrance requirements:    Baccalauréat or equivalent, or the Certificat de capacité en droit obtained with an average of 12/20, or by special examinations.

The Licence en droit and the Licence ès sciences économiques require a 4-year program.  This Law School offers only the first 2 years.

First year of legal studies is common to both.

Students admitted to the 2nd year are permitted to prepare simultaneously for the Licence en droit and the Licence ès sciences économiques provided that they satisfy the required standards for each of the two licences.

1st yr:    Theoretical

           Subjects common to all candidates:  Introduction to the Study of Law and Common Law (2 sem.), Constitutional Law and Political Institutions (2 sem.), General Political Science (2 sem.), History of Public Institutions and Social Facts up to the Revolution (2 sem.).

           Special subjects for candidates to the licence in Law: Introduction to Sociological Politics (1 sem.), International Institutions (1 sem.).

Special subjects for candidates to the <u>licence</u> in
Economics:  Statistics (1 sem.), Preparatory Mathematics
for Economics (1 sem.).

Practical

2 subjects chosen from the theoretical subjects.  Student
participation in the practical work meetings is compulsory.
No one can take the examination if he has not attended
regularly.  However, there are corresponding courses (for
certain subjects) for students who are unable to attend
the regular meetings.

Examinations:

Written (eliminatory):  2 examinations (1 on theoretical, 1 on
practical studies), 3 hrs. each.
Oral:  1 question on each subject not covered in written tests.

2nd yr:    <u>Licence en droit</u>

Theoretical

Civil Law (2 sem.), Administrative Law (2 sem.), Political
Science (2 sem.), General Penal Law and Penal Procedure
(2 sem.), Political and Social Institutions from Antiquity
(1 sem.).

Practical

2 subjects chosen from the theoretical subjects.  Compulsory
attendance at practical work meetings.

Examinations:

Written (eliminatory):  2 examinations (1 on theoretical, 1 on
practical studies), 3 hrs. each.
Oral:  1 question on each subject not covered in written tests.

<u>Diplôme d'études juridiques générales</u> awarded on successful exami-
nation at close of 2nd year.

2nd yr:    <u>Licence ès sciences économiques</u>

Theoretical

General Political Economy (2 sem.), Theory of Obligations
(1 sem.), Public Finances (1 sem.), Administrative Institutions (1 sem.), History of Contemporary Economics Facts
(1 sem.), Vital and Social Statistics (1 sem.), International Institutions (1 sem.), Mathematics (1 sem.),
Statistics (1 sem.), Principles of Private Accounting
(20 hrs.).

Practical

General Political Economy, Mathematics and Statistics, a subject chosen by School (Theory of Obligations, 1964-65).

Examinations:

Written: General Political Economy, Mathematics or Statistics, Vital and Social Statistics or International Institutions or Public Finances.

Oral (8): General Political Economy, Mathematics (if the written examination has been Statistics) or Statistics (if the written examination has been Mathematics), 2 subjects not included for the 3rd written examination, Theory of Obligations, Administrative Institutions, History of Contemporary Economic Facts, Principles of Private Accounting. Optional, foreign language (German, English, Spanish).

Diplôme d'études économiques générales awarded on successful examination at close of 2nd year.

## Ecole Supérieure des Sciences (Higher School of Sciences)

Preparation for:

(1) Scientific studies

1st cycle:     Certificats préparatoires (preparatory certificates)
                - General Mathematics and Physics (M.G.P.)
                - Mathematics, Physics and Chemistry (M.P.C.)
                - Physical, Chemical and Natural Sciences (S.P.C.N.)

2nd cycle:     Certificats de licence (licence certificates)
                - Botany
                - Zoology
                - General Geology

(2) Medical studies

        - Certificat préparatoire aux études médicales
          (preparatory certificate for medical studies)

### S C I E N T I F I C   S T U D I E S - 1st C Y C L E

## Certificat d'études supérieures de mathématiques générales et physique (M.G.P.)

The certificate of M.G.P. is one of 3 preparatory certificates of the 1st cycle required for the Licence ès sciences.

Entrance requirements:        Baccalauréat or equivalent, or special
                              entrance examination.

### TIMETABLE
(Hours per week)

|             | Theoretical | Practical | Total |
|-------------|-------------|-----------|-------|
| Mathematics | $5\frac{1}{2}$ | 6 | |
| Physics     | $2\frac{1}{2}$ | 3 | |
|             | 8 | 9 | 17 |

Examinations:

Written (eliminatory: First test in Mathematics (4 h., coefficient
    2), second test in Mathematics (3h., coefficient 1), one test
    in Physics (3h., coefficient 1).
Practical and oral: Practical test in Physics (coefficient 1), one
    question on Mathematics (coefficient 2), one question on
    Physics (coefficient 1).

## Certificat d'études supérieures de mathématiques, physique et chimie (M.P.C.)

The certificate of M.P.C. is one of 3 preparatory certificates of the 1st
cycle required for the Licence ès sciences.

Entrance requirements:        Baccalauréat or equivalent, or special
                              entrance examination.

### TIMETABLE
(Hours per week)

|             | Theoretical | Practical | Total |
|-------------|-------------|-----------|-------|
| Mathematics | $3\frac{1}{2}$ | $3\frac{1}{2}$ | |
| Physics     | $3\frac{1}{2}$ | 5 | |
| Chemistry   | $2\frac{1}{2}$ | 4 | |
|             | $9\frac{1}{2}$ | $12\frac{1}{2}$ | 22 |

Examinations:

Written (eliminatory): Mathematics (3h., coefficient 2), Physics
    (3h., coefficient 2), Chemistry (2h., coefficient 2).
Practical (eliminatory): Mathematics (coefficient 1), Physics
    (coefficient 1), Chemistry (coefficient 1).
Oral: Question on Mathematics (coefficient 2), question on Physics
    (coefficient 2), question on Chemistry (coefficient 2).

## Certificat d'études supérieures de sciences physiques, chimiques et naturelles (S.P.C.N.)

The certificate of S.P.C.N. is one of 3 preparatory certificates of the 1st cycle required for the Licence ès sciences.

Entrance requirements:          Baccalauréat or equivalent, or special entrance examination.

### TIMETABLE
### (Hours per week)

|                | Theoretical | Practical | Total |
|----------------|-------------|-----------|-------|
| Animal Biology | 1½          | 3         |       |
| Vegetable Biol.| 1½          | 3         |       |
| Geology        | 1½          | 2½        |       |
| Physics        | 1½          | 3         |       |
| Chemistry      | 2           | 3         |       |
| Mathematics    | 1           | 1         |       |
|                | 9           | 15½       | 24½   |

Examinations:

> Written (eliminatory):  Physics (course question with numerical application, time:  2h., coefficient 2), Chemistry (2h., coefficient 2), Animal Biology (2h., coefficient 3), Vegetable Biology (2h., coefficient 3), Geology (2h., coefficient 3), Mathematics (2h., coefficient 2).
> Practical (eliminatory):  Physics (coefficient 2), Chemistry (coefficient 2), Animal Biology (coefficient 2), Vegetable Biology (coefficient 2), Geology (coefficient 2).
> Oral:  Questions on Physics (coefficient 2), Chemistry (coefficient 2), Animal Biology (coefficient 3), Vegetable Biology (coefficient 3), Geology (coefficient 3), Mathematics (coefficient 2).

## S C I E N T I F I C   S T U D I E S - 2nd   C Y C L E

The title of Licencié ès sciences is awarded after a candidate has obtained one preparatory certificate (M.G.P., M.P.C., S.P.C.N.) or equivalent, and the appropriate number of certificats de licence varying with the nature of the licence.

The Licences ès sciences are divided into 8 groups:

    I.    Sciences mathématiques (5 certificats)
   II.    Sciences mathématiques appliquées (6 certificats)
  III.    Sciences physiques (mention Physique I) (6 certificats)
   IV.    Sciences physiques (mention Physique II) (6 certificats)

V.   Sciences physiques (mention Chimie) (6 certificats)
VI.  Sciences naturelles (mention Sciences biologiques) (6 certificats)
     (1)  Botanique
     (2)  Zoologie
     (3)  Biochimie, microbiologie et physiologie végétale
     (4)  Biologie générale
     (5)  Physiologie animale
     (6)  Géologie générale

VII. Sciences naturelles (mention Sciences de la terre) (6 certificats)
     (1)  Botanique
     (2)  Zoologie
     (3)  Géologie générale
     (4)  Biologie générale
     (5)  Géologie historique
     (6)  Minéralogie, or Physiologie animale, or Chimie minérale, or
          Chimie systématique

## Certificat d'études supérieures de botanique

### TIMETABLE
(Hours per week)

| Theoretical | Practical | Total |
|---|---|---|
| 3 hrs. maximum | 6 hrs. maximum | 9 |

Examinations:

    Written (eliminatory):  4 hrs.
    Practical (eliminatory)
    Oral

## Certificat d'études supérieures de zoologie

### TIMETABLE
(Hours per week)

| Theoretical | Practical | Total |
|---|---|---|
| 4 hrs. maximum | 7 hrs. maximum | 11 |

Examinations:

    Written (eliminatory):  4 hrs.
    Practical (eliminatory)
    Oral

Certificat d'études supérieures de géologie générale

### TIMETABLE
#### (Hours per week)

| Theoretical | Practical | Total |
|---|---|---|
| 3 hrs. maximum | 5 hrs. maximum | 8 |

Examinations:

> Written (eliminatory):  3 hrs.
> Practical
> Oral

## M E D I C A L   S T U D I E S

### Certificat préparatoire aux études médicales (C.P.E.M.)

Required for entrance into first year of medicine.

### TIMETABLE

| Subjects | Faculty of Science | | | Faculty of Medicine | | |
|---|---|---|---|---|---|---|
| | theor. | pract. | total | theor. | pract. | total |
| Mathematics | | | 30h. | | | |
| Statistics | | | 10h. | | | |
| Physics | 70 | 70 | 140h. | | | |
| Chemistry | 45 | 45 | 90h. | 48 | 42 | 90h. |
| Biology | 82 | 78 | 160h. | 45 | 35 | 80h. |

> Total:  600 hours

Examinations:

> Written tests:  Mathematics and Statistics (1½h., coefficient 1),
> Physics (1½h., coefficient 2.5), Chemistry (1h., coefficient
> 1.5), Biochemistry (1h., coefficient 1.5), Biology (animal and
> cellular) (1½h., coefficient 2), Biology (histology and embry-
> ology) (1h., coefficient 1.5).
> Oral tests:  Mathematics and Statistics (coefficient 1), Physics
> (coefficient 2.5), Chemistry (coefficient 1.5), Biochemistry
> (coefficient 1.5), Biology (animal and cellular) (coefficient
> 2), Biology (histology and embryology) (coefficient 1.5).
> Practical tests:  Physics and Mathematics (coefficient 1), Chemistry
> (coefficient 1), Biology (animal and cellular) and Statistics
> (coefficient 2), Histology and Embryology (coefficient 1).

Ecole Supérieure des Lettres

1st cycle:       Propédeutique (preparatory certificate)
                 - Certificat d'études littéraires générales (C.E.L.G.)
2nd cycle:       Certificats de licence (licence certificates)
                 - Littérature française
                 - Etudes pratiques d'antlais
                 - Linguistique bantoue (en direction d'études
                 - Littérature anglaise
                 - Philologie anglaise
                 - Littérature et civilisation américaines
                 - Lettres étrangères (English-German, English-Spanish)
                 - Littérature espagnole
                 - Etudes pratiques d'allemand

## 1st CYCLE - PROPEDEUTIQUE

Certificat d'études littéraires générales (C.E.L.G.)

The C.E.L.G. is the first certificate of the licence ès lettres.

Entrance requirements:            Baccalauréat or equivalent, or special
                                  entrance examination.

### TIMETABLE
(Hrs. per week)

1. Compulsory Instruction

(a)  Preparatory general studies for the 1st examination:

     Theoretical:    French, Philosophy and History (together) (3).
     Practical:      French (2) or Philosophy (2) or History (2).

(b)  Preparatory studies for the 2nd examination:

     Theoretical:    Latin (2) or Greek (2) or Foreign living language (1).
     Practical:      Latin (2) or Greek (2) or Foreign living language (1).

(c)  Preparatory studies for the 3rd examination:

     Theoretical:    Greek (2) or History (2) or Geography (2) or Foreign
                     living language (1).
     Practical:      Greek (2) or History (2) or Geography (2) or Foreign
                     living language (1).

2. Optional Instruction

Initiation to a training chosen by the student:  3 hours per week.

History program:       The Roman World under the Antonins and the Sévères.
                       The Carolingian world.
                       The Revolution and the Empire (1789-1814).

                         The movement of social and religious ideas from 1815
                            to 1914.
                         Black Africa in the 19th and 20th centuries.

Geography program:    Geography:  definition and methods.
                         Types of agriculture and systems of agriculture.
                         Black French Africa.
                         The United States.
                         India.

Examinations:

Classical section

    (a)  French Composition:  Option Literature, Philosophy or History
        (4h., coefficient 2).
    (b)  Translation from Latin or Greek, according to candidate's choice
        (3h., coefficient 1).
    (c)  An essay in History or Geography, according to the candidate's
        choice (4h., coefficient 1).

Modern section

    (a)  French Composition:  Option Literature, Philosophy or History
        (4h., coefficient 2).
    (b)  Theme in English, or Spanish, or German, according to the
        candidate's choice (3h., coefficient 1).
        Or, translation from English, Spanish, German, or Italian,
        according to the candidate's choice, followed by a composition
        of applied grammar based on the translation (4h., coefficient
        for the theme 0.5, for the composition 0.5).
    (c)  Translation from a second living language (3½h., coefficient 1),
        or an essay in History or Geography (4h., coefficient 1).


## 2nd C Y C L E - L I C E N C E   C E R T I F I C A T E S

The title of Licencié ès lettres is awarded after a candidate has obtained
the Certificat d'études littéraires générales (section classique/section
moderne), and 4 certificats de licence.

Composition of the licence certificates is as follows:

Classical Lettres:  Greek Studies
                    Latin Studies
                    French Literature
                    Grammar and Philology (classical)

Modern Letters and Literature:
                    French Literature
                    French Grammar and Philology
                    Foreign Letters

Comparative Literature, or Phonetics, or Modern and
Contemporary History, or General Geography, or
Philology of the Foreign Living Language (chosen
principally for the Certificate of Foreign Letters),
or Latin Studies.

Living Languages:    Foreign Literature
                     Philology
                     Practical Studies
                     Greek Studies or Latin Studies, or French Literature
                     or French Philology, or Grammar and Philology
                     (classical) or Grammar and French Philology, or
                     Comparative Literature, or Literature, or Philosophy
                     of a 2nd living foreign language, or General
                     Linguistics, or Scandinavian Language and Literature,
                     or American Literature and Civilization, or Celtic
                     Grammar and Philology, or Historical Grammar and
                     Comparative Slavic Languages.


## Certificat de littérature française

### TIMETABLE
(Hours per week)

| Theoretical | Practical | Total |
|---|---|---|
| 4 | 4 | 8 |

Examinations:

Written:  French Composition.
Oral:     Interpretation of 2 texts, one by an author of the Middle
          Ages or the XVIth century, and one by a modern author;
          questions on the history of French Literature.


## Certificat d'études pratiques d'anglais

### TIMETABLE
(Hours per week)

| Theoretical | Practical | Total |
|---|---|---|
| 2 | 1 | 3 |

Examinations:

Written:  Translation.
Oral:     Conversation in the foreign language on the civilization
          of the country where the candidate has stayed (based on a
          list of books to be consulted, submitted in advance).
          Graded 0 to 20.
          Questions on a 2nd foreign living language.

## Certificat de linguistique bantoue

### TIMETABLE
(Hours per week)

| Theoretical | Practical | Total |
|:---:|:---:|:---:|
| 3 | 3 | 6 |

Examinations:

Written: Dissertation on a subject of general scope concerning the structure of the Bantu languages.
Practical test in Phonetics.

Oral: Question on special point of program studies; question on a work of Bantu Linguistics written in a language other than French (language chosen by candidate). Presentation from memory of Experimental Phonetics prepared by candidate during the year.

## Certificat de littérature étrangère (Anglais, Espagnol)

### TIMETABLE
(Hours per week)

|         | Theoretical | Practical | Total |
|---------|:---:|:---:|:---:|
| English | 2 | 2 | 4 |
| Spanish | 2 | 1 | 3 |

Examinations:

Written: Composition in the living foreign language chosen by the candidate, in a subject taken from the literature of that language.

Oral: Explication of a text of an author in the same living foreign language. Question on the history of foreign literature chosen by the candidate.

## Certificat de philologie anglaise

### TIMETABLE
(Hours per week)

| Theoretical | Practical | Total |
|:---:|:---:|:---:|
| 2 | 1 | 3 |

Examinations:

Written: Theme.

Oral: Question on the grammar of the language chosen by the candidate.
Question on the history of this language, following an author's text.

## Certificat de littérature et civilisation américaines

### TIMETABLE
(Hours per week)

| Theoretical | Practical | Total |
|:---:|:---:|:---:|
| 2 | 1 | 3 |

Examinations:

Written:  Composition in French or in English on a subject of
American literature or civilization.

Oral:  Questions on American literature and civilization; interpretation of an American author.

## Certificat de lettres étrangères (Anglais-Espagnol, Anglais-Allemand)

### TIMETABLE
(Hours per week)

| Theoretical | Practical | Total |
|:---:|:---:|:---:|
| 1 | 1 | 2 |

Examinations:

Written:  Composition in French or in the principal foreign living
language, according to the candidate's choice, on a subject
of foreign literature.  Translation from a text of the
principal foreign living language.

Oral:  Translation of a text from the principal foreign living
language, followed by a commentary, either in French or in
the foreign language, according to the candidate's choice.
Question on the 2nd foreign living language chosen from a
list (set by the School), consisting of a lecture and
translation of a literary text from the modern and
contemporary epoch.

## Certificat d'études pratiques d'allemand

### TIMETABLE
(Hours per week)

| Theoretical | Practical | Total |
|:---:|:---:|:---:|
| 1 | 1 | 2 |

Examinations:

Written:  Translation.

Oral:  Conversation in foreign language, on the civilization of the
country where the student has stayed (based on a list of
books to be consulted, submitted in advance).

Question on a 2nd foreign living language.

## Medico-Social Section

The Medico-Social Section was originally part of the Centres des Hautes Etudes Administratives et Techniques and is especially oriented toward the efficient technical training of a sanitary staff to fill the needs of Africa today.

Includes:
School for sanitary hygiene inspectors (Ecole d'Inspecteurs d'Hygiène sanitaire), for which the students are recruited among the registered nurses.
School of nurses (Ecole d'Infirmiers et d'Infirmières)
School for midwives (Ecole de Sages-Femmes)
School for social workers (Ecole d'Assistantes Sociales)

Nurses and midwives are granted a degree equivalent to the French state degree.

Prevention of diseases (infectious, parasitic and nutritional), emergency care, protection of mother and child, knowledge of the main economic, demographic, sociological African problems constitute the essential teaching objectives of the Section.

Compulsory terms in the brush complete the training acquired at the Centre d'Enseignement Supérieur and at the General Hospital in Brazzaville.

Entrance requirements:
Study level equivalent to classe de troisième of the lycée or collège. There is a competitive entrance examination appropriate to each school.

## School for Sanitary Hygiene Inspectors

Sanitary hygiene inspectors and medical technicians assume important responsibilities, mainly in the brush; they practice in different fields of hygiene, preventive medicine, emergency care, and sanitary education.

Entrance requirements:
Nurse's diploma of the state or the Fondation de l'Enseignement Supérieur en Afrique Centrale (F.E.S.A.C.).

Length of studies:
2 years and 1-year term as assistant to a physician.
6 months - medical post in the brush.
6 months - medical post in the Hygiene Services.

Program:

General Culture:
French, Economic Sociology, African Demography, African History and Literature, Psychology

Animal Biology
General and Organic Chemistry

Specialized training:  Embryology, Histology, Physiology, Bio-
                         chemistry
                       General and Tropical Nutrition
                       Bacteriology, Virology, Parasitology,
                         Hematology, Serology, Entomology, Malaco-
                         logy
                       Medical and Surgical Semiology
                       Epidemiology and Prophylaxis of Contagious
                         Diseases
                       Social Hygiene
                       Sanitary Education of the Public
                       Tropical Pathology
                       Tropical Pediatrics
                       Pathological Obstetrics
                       Emergency Surgery
                       Emergency Medicine
                       Minor Surgery

Term of probation:     Hospital, urban and rural; clinic, urban
                       and rural; urban, mobile and school hygiene.


                              TIMETABLE
                          (Hours per week)

|            | 1st yr. | 2nd yr. |
|------------|---------|---------|
| Courses    | 19      | 14      |
| Work term  | 16      | 24      |
| Total      | 35      | 38      |

Diploma of the F.E.S.A.C. awarded.

After 2 years of professional work, an inspecteur d'hygiène sanitaire F.E.S.A.C. may enter the 3rd year of the Faculty of Medicine
and prepare for the doctorat d'université, mention médecine.


School for Nurses

Entrance requirements:  Admission upon title:
                        Candidates having passed the examen proba-
                        toire, or holders of the following diplomas:
                        Brevet supérieur de capacité de l'enseigne-
                        ment primaire, Diplôme complémentaire
                        d'études secondaires de jeunes filles,

Capacité en droit, Brevet des écoles nationales professionnelles.

Competitive entrance examination (same
as the one required for the French State
nurses).  Candidates of both sexes should
be 17 years and 8 months old the 1st of
January following their entrance to the
school.  There is no maximum age limit.
Examination is at the level of B.E.P.C.

Duration of course:        2 years.

Program:   Same as for French State nurses plus the following:

Elements of Hygiene and Tropical Pathology and Laboratory
Techniques.

TIMETABLE
(Hours per week)

|            | 1st year | 2nd year |
|------------|----------|----------|
| Courses    | 18       | 18       |
| Work term  | 24       | 24       |
| TOTAL      | 42       | 42       |

Diploma of the F.E.S.A.C. awarded, equivalent of the French State
Diploma.

After the diploma has been obtained, a 3-month residence is
required in a rural hospital headed by a doctor and located in the
republic where the nurse is originally from.

School for Midwives

Entrance requirements:     Admission upon title:
Candidates having passed the examen probatoire, or holders of the Brevet supérieur
de capacité de l'enseignement primaire,
or the Diplôme complémentaire d'études
secondaires de jeunes filles, are exempted
from the competitive examination.

Competitive entrance examination:  Candidates should be 18 years old.  No maximum age limit.  Qualification for entry to examination:  studies at the B.E.P.C. or B.E. level, or a school certificate of 2nd or 1st year.  Examination at level of B.E.P.C.

Duration of course:        3 years.

## TIMETABLE
(Hours per week)

|             | 1st yr. | 2nd yr. | 3rd yr. |
|-------------|---------|---------|---------|
| Courses     | 18      | 18      | 18      |
| Work term   | 24      | 24      | 24      |
| Total       | 42      | 42      | 42      |

Diploma of the F.E.S.A.C. awarded, equivalent of the French State Diploma.

After the diploma has been obtained, a 3-month residence is required in a hospital headed by a doctor and located in the republic where the mid-wife is originally from.


## School for Social Workers

Entrance requirements:     At least 17 years of age.  B.E.P.C. or level of studies of classe de troisième.  Competitive entrance examination.

Duration of course:        3 years.

## TIMETABLE
(Hours per week)

|                  | 1st yr. | 2nd yr. | 3rd yr.          |
|------------------|---------|---------|------------------|
| Courses          | 10      | 17      | 33 (per month)   |
| Term of probation | 24     |         | 102 (per month)  |
| Practical work   |         | 17      |                  |
| Total            | 34      | 34      | 135 (per month)  |

1st yr:    Common with the 1st year nurse's training.

Medical divisions:  Pediatrics
                    Maternity

                              General Medicine
                              Surgery
                              Tuberculosis

        Courses:              Anatomy
                              Physiology
                              Obstetrics
                              Hygiene
                              Diseases

2nd yr:    General Culture and Social Work:

                              French
                              History   )
                              Geography )  General and of Africa
                              Psychology
                              American Sociology
                              Demography
                              Alimentary Hygiene
                              Domestic Science
                              Social Legislation

        Practical work:       Cutting, Dressmaking
                              Home Management
                              Typing
                              Group Work

Administrative term of 1½ months' probation in 1 of the
following:
                              Ministry of Youth and Sports
                              Ministry of Public Works
                              Ministry of Health
                              National Fund for Social Welfare
                              Palace of Justice

3rd yr:    Social Work.

        Courses (1 week per month):

                              Work Legislation
                              Psychology
                              Law
                              Economic Sociology
                              African Sociology
                              Medical Social Problems
                              Accounting
                              Methodology of Social Work
                              Ethics of Social Work

        Term of probation:    3 weeks a month in 1 of the following:

                              Social work for Prefecture
                              Social work for Police
                              Social work for Army

                    Social work in General Hospital (tuberculosis
                       section)
                    Inter-enterprises social work
                    Rural social work for the National Fund for
                       Social Welfare
                    Polio Centre
                    Centre for Alcoholism
                    School Hygiene Centre

         Practical work:       Group work


## Courses by Correspondence:  1964-1965

### Law and Economic Sciences

    1st and 2nd years of Capacité en droit
    1st year of Licence en droit et sciences économiques
    2nd year of Licence en droit
    2nd year of Licence ès sciences économiques


### Letters and Humane Sciences

    1st cycle (propédeutique littéraire):
    - Certificat d'études littéraires générales (C.E.L.G.)

    2nd cycle (licence):
    - Certificat de littérature française
    - Certificat de littérature anglaise
    - Certificat de philologie anglaise
    - Certificat d'études pratiques d'anglais
    - Certificat de littérature et civilisation américaines
    - Certificat de lettres étrangères (anglais, allemand, espagnol)
    - Certificat de littérature espagnole
    - Certificat d'études pratiques d'allemand


### Science

    1st cycle (propédeutique scientifique):
    - Mathématiques générales et physique (M.G.P.)
    - Mathématiques, physique et chimie (M.P.C.)
    - Sciences physiques, chimiques et naturelles (S.P.C.N.)

    2nd cycle (licence):
    - Certificat d'études supérieures de botanique
    - Certificat d'études supérieures de zoologie
    - Certificat d'études supérieures de géologie générale

    N.B.  In Brazzaville and in certain centers, practical laboratory work,
       obligatory, is organized for groups of students from the 1st and
       2nd cycles.

## Secondary Studies

    Seconde M et M'
    Première M et M'
    Philosophie
    Sciences expérimentales
    Mathématiques élémentaires

The Correspondence Service also prepares special entrance examinations into Faculties of Law, Letters, Science and Medicine.

## VOCATIONAL AND TECHNICAL EDUCATION

By 1945, vocational education was of 3 types:

    Apprenticeship sections
    Trade schools - 4-year courses
    Vocational schools - 4-year courses

Trade school graduates admitted to 3rd class.

## APPRENTICESHIP CENTERS

3-year courses.

## HANDCRAFT CENTERS

For developing the skill of local artisans.

## BRAZZAVILLE VOCATIONAL SCHOOL

Offering courses in:  Fitting and Machine Tools, Automobile Mechanics, Forging, Locksmithing and Soldering, Electricity, Cabinet-Making and Carpentry, Masonry, commercial subjects.

Also trains instructors for classes in manual skills and for elementary schools.

4-year programs.

## COLLEGE TECHNIQUE

Established by expansion of a vocational school.

POTO-POTO SCHOOL OF ART

Founded by Pierre Lods, for developing African style painting.


SCHOOL OF TECHNICAL ARTS

Offering classes ranging from pottery and ceramics to wood and ivory
carving.


TEACHER EDUCATION

MOUZOUNDZI NORMAL SCHOOL

Created 1947.

Entrance requirements:        Graduation from collège moderne.

Section A:  1-year program, preparing assistant teachers (instituteurs-
            adjoints).
Section B:  1-year program, preparing moniteurs supérieurs.

Normal School Certificate awarded to those from Section A.
Normal School Leaving Diploma awarded to those from Section B.


ECOLE NORMALE SUPERIEURE D'AFRIQUE CENTRALE, Brazzaville (Advanced Teachers'
    College)

Under jurisdiction of the Fondation de l'Enseignement Supérieur en Afrique
Centrale.

Trains candidates from Central African countries for secondary school
teachers, inspectors of primary schools, principals and teachers of
teacher-training schools.

                        1st  S E C T I O N

Training of teachers for collèges d'enseignement général.  This section
functioned in the framework of the Sections Pédagogiques of the Centre
d'Enseignement Administratives et Techniques Supérieures from October 1959
to June 1962.  Since October 1962, in Ecole Normale Supérieure.

Entrance requirements (1964):        For the candidates without baccalauréat:
                                     Must be at least 20 years old and not
                                     older than 30 by December 31 of the year
                                     in which examination will be taken.  Must

hold <u>B.E.</u> or <u>B.E.P.C.</u>  Competitive examination at level of classes of <u>troisième et
seconde modernes</u> of secondary schools.

Examinations:

  <u>Option letters</u> - 2 examinations

  French Composition on literature (3 hrs.)
  25 questions (2½ hrs.)
  - 10 literary questions
  -  5 History questions
  -  5 Geography questions
  -  5 English questions
  Each question is graded on 4; the whole is graded on 100.

  <u>Option science</u> - 3 examinations

  Problems or exercises on Geometry, Algebra and Arithmetic (3 hrs.)
  Graded on 40; coefficient 3.
  20 questions (2 hrs.)
  - 5 questions on Mathematics
  - 5 questions on Physics
  - 5 questions on Chemistry
  - 5 questions on Natural Science
  Each question is graded on 5; the whole is graded on 100.
  French Composition on a general subject (3 hrs.)
  Graded on 20; coefficient 5.

For the candidates with <u>probatoire</u> and <u>baccalauréat</u>:  No minimum age
required.  Must not be older than 25 on December 31 of the year in which
the examination will take place.  Placement examination.  Program and
level:  Probatory examination, <u>classes de 1ère</u>, <u>baccalauréat</u>, terminal
classes of 2nd degree.

The examinations include written tests or oral tests on the fundamental
training,

    Letters:  French - interpretation of text (literary or philosophical)
    Science:  Mathematics, Physics, Chemistry, Natural Science

and for the 2 options, an interview with the Jury.


Final admissions regulations anticipate the following recruitment:

    In preparatory year:      Upon competitive examination, at the <u>examen
                              probatoire</u> level, or the probatory examination
                              of secondary teaching.

    In 1st normal year:       Upon competitive examination, complete
                              <u>baccalauréat</u>.

In 2nd normal year:        Upon title, bearers of certificate propédeu-
                           tique littéraire (C.E.L.G.) or propédeutique
                           scientifique (M.G.P., M.P.C., S.P.C.N.).

Program:  3 years - Preparatory, 1st normal year, 2nd normal year.

Preparatory year to be abolished as soon as first-year recruitment will
be sufficient.

The preparatory year is essentially devoted to raise the general cultural
level of students.  When the normal recruitment will be reached, 1st-year
students with baccalauréat will be automatically registered in propédeutique.  Apart from the training received at the Ecole Normale Supérieure,
they will follow courses at the Ecoles Supérieures de Lettres et de
Sciences of the Centre d'Enseignement Supérieur.  The 2nd normal year is
essentially reserved for professional training.

The following subjects are taught by teachers of the Ecole Normale
Supérieure, Centre d'Enseignement Supérieur and the lycées:

| Letters | Science |
|---|---|
| French | Mathematics |
| Philosophy | Physics |
| English | Chemistry |
| History | Natural Science |
| Geography | French |
| Literary Teaching Pedagogy | Scientific Teaching Pedagogy |

### Common Teaching (subjects)

General Pedagogy
Child and Adolescent Psychology
School Administration
Economic and Social Problems
Drawing, Graphic Expression

2 options in the Letters series:    Letters - English
                                    Letters - History/Geography

2 options in the Science series:    Mathematics - Physics and Chemistry
                                    Physics - Chemistry - Natural
                                        Science

In addition to the courses, there are 5 or 6 hours per week during which
the students do their homework and exercises under the supervision and the
assistance of the teachers.  Also, student teaching in the collèges
d'enseignement général.

Certificat d'aptitude à l'enseignement dans les collèges d'enseignement
général awarded at close of program.

### 2nd  S E C T I O N

Training for inspectors of primary schools, principals and teachers of teachers' training schools.

Entrance requirements:      Competitive entrance examination for time in October 1964.  Consideration given to seniority in the teaching service, the title of licencié d'enseignement or professeur de C.E.G.  Examination includes 2 parts:  tests on general culture, and probatory tests (interview with Jury, analysis of a document, explanation of a question, etc.).

1-year program:    General culture, literary or scientific Professional training (Education, Psychology, School Administration, practical work of inspection).

Certificat d'aptitude à l'inspection de l'enseignement primaire (C.A.I.P.) awarded at close of program.

### 3rd  S E C T I O N

Training of secondary school certified teachers.

Entrance requirements:      Seniority in the teaching service, title of licencié d'enseignement or professeur de C.E.G.
Competitive examination given for the time in October 1964.  It included probatory tests (interview with the Jury , analysis of a document, interpretation of a question, etc.), test on general culture based on a limited program.

Candidates are granted the Licence d'enseignement and are submitted to all the tests of the Certificat d'aptitude  à l'enseignement secondaire (C.A.P.E.S.) of their specialization.

796

REPUBLIC OF GABON

Compulsory education:  6 - 16 years

School year:  Beginning October - end June

Grading:  0 - 20

10 / 20 usual pass grade

REPUBLIC OF GABON
(République Gabonaise)


Independence:  August 17, 1960.


## BACKGROUND


Gabon lies directly on the Equator.  It is largely covered by jungle.
Pygmies were the original inhabitants; about 3000 remain in small groups
in the forests.  There are now nearly 40 ethnic groups.  One of the
largest groups is the Merié, with approximately 120,000, which includes
the Eshira (or Echira), Bapounu, Balumbu, and Masango tribes.  The Fang
(Pahuin) group came from the north in the 19th century, settling in
Port-Gentil and Mekambo.  The Omiene group including the Mpongwe, Galoa,
Nkoni, Orungu, Adjumba, and Eneuga lives in the region along the lower
Ogowe River, from Lambaréné to Port-Gentil.  The Bakota live in the
northeast; some south.  Other major tribes are the Mbede, Seke, Okande,
Bakele.  There are approximately 8500 non-Africans in the country.  The
population is 91.8% rural.

French is the official language.  Fang is spoken in northern Gabon.  Bantu
languages in other parts of the country.

Portuguese explorers came to the coast in 1470, founding trading posts.
After them came the Dutch, English and French.  Missionaries followed,
and during the next three centuries Jesuit missionaries were particularly
active along the coast.

In 1839 and shortly after, treaties made by French explorers with African
rulers brought the northern and southern Gabon coasts under French protection.  After 1847, French explorers penetrated the interior.  1849,
Libreville was founded when freed slaves settled there.

1874-1883, Pierre Savorgnan de Brazza explored the length of the Ogowe
River and made treaties with chiefs.  1885, Congress of Berlin recognized
France's jurisdiction over right bank of Congo.  1890, Gabon formally
became a part of French Congo.  It was separated into a distinct adminis-
trative region, 1903, and organized as a colony, part of French Equatorial
Africa, 1910.

November 28, 1958, as a result of the referendum of September 28, 1958,
the territory became an autonomous republic within the French Community.
February 19, 1959, a constitution was adopted, and the Constituent

Assembly became the Legislative Assembly of the republic.   Independence
was proclaimed August 17, 1960.

Early education was conducted by the missionaries.  Government became
responsible for education, 1958.  Presently the state controls both public
and private education, pedagogically and financially.  Private schools get
100% subsidy.  Full cooperation between public and private,  no discrimination.  The educational system is modelled on the French pattern.
Approximately 85% of primary schools are Catholic.

There were no secondary schools before World War II, but secondary level
instruction was offered by a seminary at Libreville, dating back to 1845.
In 1944, a higher primary school established (école supérieure), became a
college, 1947, and a lycée in 1958.  In 1953, a private école supérieure
became the Collège Bessieux.  Technical education came into being during
World War II.  Owendo Vocational School established 1942, became Collège
Technique, 1960.  Law of 1959 made education compulsory for children
between 6 and 16 years of age.

## PRESENT SYSTEM

### PRE-PRIMARY EDUCATION

Nursery schools (écoles maternelles or jardins d'enfants) not very widespread.

Entry age:      4-5 years.

Program:  Lessons in manual dexterity, cleanliness, tidiness, elementary
             discipline, etc.

Length of course:     1 or 2 years, according to entry age.

### PRIMARY EDUCATION

Entry age:      6-9 years.

Language of instruction:      French.

Length of course:     6 years - cours préparatoire, 2 years
                                 cours élémentaire, 2 years
                                 cours moyen, 2 years

Program:  Reading, Writing, Arithmetic, Language, History, Geography,
             Nature Study.
             Program the same for both urban and rural areas.

Religious instruction is given in public schools on written request of parents.

Certificate awarded:    Certificat d'études primaires élémentaires (C.E.P.E.) awarded end of 6 years.

1964, 561 primary schools; approximately half the children in mission schools (majority Catholic, rest Protestant), half in government schools.
   191 primary schools with complete 6-year cycle.
   370 primary schools with incomplete cycle. About half leave school after 1st year, approximately one-fourth remain at end of 6 years.

## POST-PRIMARY EDUCATION

Called enseignement primaire supérieur or enseignement complémentaire. Collèges d'enseignement général provide short course (4 years) of secondary education. Formerly the cours complémentaires. Entrance requirements as for regular secondary education. Prepare for brevet d'études du premier cycle and entrance examination for the écoles normales. Rapid increase in collèges of this type.

1964, 21 C.E.G. approximately half government, half mission schools. Many do not offer 4 years, but only 1 or 2 years.

## SECONDARY EDUCATION

Entry age:        10-13 years. Some girls admitted if 14 years.

Entrance requirements:        Pass concours d'entrée en sixième, entrance examination for both technical and general secondary education. C.E.P.E. is not a requirement for admission.

Language of instruction:        French. English and/or German and/or Spanish taught as foreign languages. Latin and Greek compulsory in classique section of lycées, as in France.

Length of course:        1st cycle of 4 years - short modern course given in C.E.G.'s. 1st 4 years of long course (classique or moderne) given in lycées and collèges.

        2nd cycle of 3 years - completion of long course given only in lycées and collèges.

Programs: Same as French programs. Attempts to adapt these to local conditions are at present under way, particularly in History, Geography, Natural Sciences, Philosophy and English. Laboratory work where facilities available. Mathematics and Physics remain the same as the French program.

Grading:    10/20 usual pass grade.  9/10 sometimes allowed.  8/10 allows repeat of the year.  19/20 given only very rarely.

Certificates awarded:                Brevet élémentaire or brevet d'études du premier cycle at end of 1st cycle.

Examen probatoire de fin de première at end of 1st class (6 years), formerly first part of baccalauréat.

**Baccalauréat in Philosophy, Experimental Sciences or Elementary Mathematics at end of terminal class (7 years).

1964, 7 secondary schools providing long course.

Only 2 provide complete cycle of 7 years:

Lycée Classique et Moderne de Léon Mba, Libreville (public)
Collège Bessieux, Libreville (Catholic)

Incomplete cycle of long course given in:

Collège Moderne, Oyem (public)
Collège Moderne de Jeunes Filles, Libreville (Catholic)
Collège Michel Fanguinovény, Lambaréné (Protestant)
Collège Moderne, Port-Gentil (public)
Collège Moderne, N'Dendé (public)

## HIGHER EDUCATION

None.  Under a cooperative agreement concerning higher education concluded between Gabon, Central African Republic, Congo Republic (Brazzaville), and Chad, and the French Republic, students from Gabon may pursue their studies at the Centre d'Enseignement Supérieur de Brazzaville.  (See Higher Education, THE CONGO REPUBLIC.)  Since 1961, the Centre for Higher Education in Brazzaville has been under the jurisdiction of the Fondation de l'Enseignement Supérieur en Afrique Centrale (Foundation for Higher Education in Central Africa), whose authority now covers the Institut Polytechnique in Libreville (see section on "Vocational and Technical Education), the Institut d'Etudes Zootechniques in Fort-Lamy, Chad, the Institut d'Etudes Agronomiques in Wakambo, Central African Republic, and the Ecole Normale Supérieure in the Congo Republic.

VOCATIONAL AND TECHNICAL EDUCATION

CENTRES D'APPRENTISSAGE

Entry age:        14-16 years.

Entrance requirements:         Pass entrance examination at C.E.P.E. level.

Length of course:     1 or 2 years.

Program:  Similar to the French programs, concentrating on a practical
          professional training in industrial and other subjects.
          1-year courses in Carpentry, Electricity, Auto Mechanics,
          Metalwork.
          2-year courses in Carpentry, Commerce, Crafts, Building.

Certificate awarded:   Certificat élémentaire d'aptitude professionnelle
                       (C.E.A.P.)

1964, 10 centres d'apprentissage, only 2 with 2-year courses.

COLLEGES D'ENSEIGNEMENT TECHNIQUE

Entry age:        14-15 years.

Entrance requirements:         Pass entrance examination at C.E.P.E. level.
                               Students with C.E.A.P. may also sit for the
                               examination.

Length of course:     3 or 4 years.  Some collèges still only have 2 years
                      of instruction.

Program:  2-year courses at Oyem:   Diesel and Auto Mechanics
                          N'Dendé:  Diesel, Carpentry, Building
                           Moanda:  General Mechanics, Electricity, Auto
                                    Mechanics, Welding

          3- and 4-year courses at Collège Technique, Libreville, in
          industrial and commercial subjects.  Has section artisanale
          (crafts section) attached.

          Primarily French programs followed with Mathematics and Sciences
          predominating over letters among the general subjects.  These
          programs are being adapted where necessary according to the
          national plan for the economic and social development of the
          country.

          Section artisanale:      4-year course, 6 hrs. general, 24 hrs.
                                   vocational subjects per week in 1st
                                   year.

Certificate awarded:   <u>Certificat d'aptitude professionnelle</u> (<u>C.A.P.</u>) after
3 years, or 4 years in some cases, according to
specialty.

1964, 4 <u>collèges techniques</u> at Libreville, Oyem, N'Dendé, Moanda.


<u>LYCEE TECHNIQUE, Libreville</u>

Began as the Ecole des Métiers at Owendo.  1959, transferred to Libreville
and 1961, became the Lycée Technique.

Trains students for higher technical education and for middle-level
administrative and technical posts.

Entry age:        11-13 years.

Entrance requirements:          Pass entrance examination (<u>concours d'entrée
en sixième</u>).

Length of course:     6-7 years.

Program:   Similar to French programs in industrial and commercial subjects,
with local adaptations.  First 2 years common to both industrial
and commercial sections.  From 3rd class industrial section
divided into 2 specialties:  Carpentry and Machine-Tools.

Certificates awarded:            <u>C.A.P.</u> after 3 years.

<u>Brevet d'enseignement industriel ou d'agents
technique</u> (<u>B.E.I.</u>) or <u>brevet d'enseignement
commercial</u> (<u>B.E.C.</u>) after 6 years.

<u>Baccalauréat technique</u> after 7 years.


<u>ECOLE NATIONALE DES INFIRMIERS ET INFIRMIERES D'ETAT</u>

Training for hospital attendants.  Has a section for midwives (<u>sages-
femmes</u>).  2-year program.

Entrance requirements:          18-35 years of age.  <u>B.E.P.C.</u> or successful
competitive entrance examination.

<u>Diplôme d'infirmier d'état</u> (or <u>de sage-femme</u>) awarded.


<u>ECOLES MENAGERES</u>

Offer 2 or 3-year courses in Housecrafts for girls.  Mainly situated on
Catholic missions.

## COLLEGE NATIONAL D'AGRICULTURE, Oyem

Established in 1945 under the Ministry of Agriculture.

Entry age:     14 years minimum.

Entrance requirements:     Pass entrance examination at C.E.P.E. level, consisting of Dictation and Questions, Composition, Arithmetic, Agriculture.

Length of course:     4 years in 2 cycles.  3 terms in each year.

Program:

1st yr:   General Agriculture, General Zootechnology, Fish Breeding, Zoology, Vegetable Cultivation, Fruit Cultivation, Mathematics, Botany.

2nd yr:   Special Zootechnology, Special Agriculture, Meteorology, Fish Breeding, Botany, General Zootechnology, General Agriculture, Fruit Cultivation, Mathematics, Zoology.

3rd yr:   General Zootechnology, General Agriculture, Special Zootechnology, Fish Breeding, Entomology, Physics, French, Land-Surveying, Meteorology, Geology, Special Agriculture, Mathematics, Chemistry.

4th yr:   Topography, Agricultural Chemistry, Rural Economy, Mycology, Physics, French, Efforts towards Plant Health, Child Development, Mathematics, Chemistry, Natural Sciences.

Grading:

1st cycle:   Yearly grade is made up for each subject of 30% classwork grades plus 70% of the examination paper grade.

Coefficients applied in 1st and 2nd years:

| Practical work | coeff. | 3 |
|---|---|---|
| Theory | | 2 |
| General subjects | | 1 |
| Conduct | | 1 |

General average at end of 2nd year:

| 1st year | coeff. | 1 |
|---|---|---|
| 2nd year | | 2 |
| Final examination | | 1 |

Final examination consists of written, oral and practical tests, each with coefficient 1.

12/20 needed to pass into 2nd year and for diploma at end of 2nd year.  12.5/20 needed for automatic pass into 2nd cycle.

2nd cycle:          Coefficients applied in 3rd and 4th years:

                    Technical                    coeff. 2
                    Practical                           2
                    General subjects                    2
                    Conduct                             1

                    General average at end of 4th year:

                    3rd year                     coeff. 1
                    4th year                            2
                    Final examination                   1

                    Final examination coefficients:

                    Written                      coeff. 1
                    Oral                                1
                    Practical                           2

                    12/20 needed for pass into 4th year and for final diploma.

Certificates awarded:          Diplôme at end of 2nd and 4th years.

                               Certificat de scolarité awarded to those with
                               average grade below 12/20.


ECOLE GABONAISE D'ADMINISTRATION, Libreville

Controlled by Ministry of Public Service.  Trains middle and higher level
officials for the public service.

Entrance requirements:    (1)  Age 30 years maximum on January 1 of the
                               examination year and hold B.E.P.C., B.E.,
                               examen probatoire (or baccalauréat part 1),
                               1st certificate of the capacité en droit,
                               or equivalent recognized diploma.

                          (2)  Public service officials of C2, C1 and B2
                               levels, maximum age 35 years, with either 4
                               years' service, or one of the certificates
                               mentioned in (1).

                          (3)  Auxiliary or contracting agents of the public
                               service, with one of the above certificates
                               and 5 years' service, maximum age 35, except
                               under special cases when limit increased to
                               45 years.

                          Entrance examination in May of each year.

Length of course:         Short cycle - 2 years
                          Long cycle  - 3 years

Program (hours per week):

1st yr:    French (3), Mathematics and Statistics (1), attending conferences or visiting embassies (2), Economic Geography (2), Accountancy (2), History and Geography of Gabon and Africa (2), English (2), Practical Work (3), Contemporary History (2), General Economics (2), Organization and Administrative Practice (2), Physical Education (2).

2nd yr:    Contemporary History (2), attending conferences or visiting embassies (1), Administrative Law (2), International Economic Relations (2), Private Accountancy (2), Organization and Administrative Practice (1), History of Social and Labor Movements (1), English (2), Planning (2), Legal Organization (1), Economic Geography (2), Political Economics (2), Commercial, Maritime and Social Law (2), French (2), Industrial International Law and Industrial Economics (1), Public International Law (1), Private International Law (1), Physical Education (2).

    In-service training of 4 months in 2nd year and 2 months in 3rd year.

Grading:    General average of 10/20 in final examination for <u>brevet</u>.

            Students with average of 12/20 in long cycle may go on to the Institut des Hautes Etudes d'Outre-Mer (teacher training section) in France.

            Students with average of 12/20 in short cycle may enter 2nd year of the long cycle.

Certificate awarded:    <u>Brevet de l'Ecole Gabonaise d'Administration</u>.

The school also includes the Centre d'Etudes Juridiques in which courses and examinations are held for the <u>capacité en droit</u>, directed by the Ecole de Droit of the Fondation de l'Enseignement Supérieur en Afrique Centrale (F.E.S.A.C.), Brazzaville. For programs of the <u>capacité</u>, see the F.E.S.A.C. section under THE CONGO REPUBLIC (Brazzaville).


<u>ECOLE FORESTIERE</u>, Cape Esterias

Controlled by Forestry Department.

Entrance through competitive examination. Students include scholarship holders from other countries and those sponsored by private firms.

Practical courses periodically arranged by Forestry School for qualified workers for private firms.


<u>INSTITUT POLYTECHNIQUE D'AFRIQUE CENTRALE</u>, Libreville

Newly established. Part of the F.E.S.A.C., Brazzaville. Will train officials for the middle and higher levels of industry with knowledge of particular conditions of installation and development of industries and scientific research in countries of Central Africa.

Entrance requirements:     1st cycle:   Entrance examination at <u>B.E.</u> or <u>B.E.P.C.</u> level.

2nd cycle:   With <u>baccalauréat</u> or equivalent.

Length of courses:         1st cycle:   3 years to train technicians (<u>techniciens</u>).

2nd cycle:   3 years to train construction engineers (<u>ingénieurs de construction</u>).

Programs:  Not yet available.


## CENTRES DE FORMATION PROFESSIONNELLE RAPIDE DES OUVRIERS

Short courses, average 9 months, for workers without professional qualification.

Libreville:    Auto Mechanics, Bricklaying-Stonemasonry, Reinforced Concrete-Scaffolding, Carpentry-Cabinet Making.

Port-Gentil:   Auto Mechanics, Sheetmetal-Tin Manufacturing.

Entrance requirements:

<table>
<tr><td>Auto Mechanics<br>Sheetmetal Work</td><td>) Gabonese nationality, 17-35 years, with-<br>) out professional qualification, but with<br>  <u>C.E.P.E.</u>, or proof of having completed<br>  6th class of secondary school.</td></tr>
<tr><td>Bricklaying<br>Concrete-<br>  Scaffolding<br>Carpentry</td><td>) Already in paid employment, Gabonese<br>) nationality, 17-35 years, without<br>) professional qualification, but with<br>) <u>C.E.P.E.</u> or that level.</td></tr>
</table>


## TEACHER EDUCATION

## SECTION ELEVES MONITEURS

1964, 7 <u>sections</u> attached to <u>collèges</u> at Oyem, Libreville, Makokou, Mouila, Bongolo, Lambaréné (public, Catholic and Protestant).

Entrance requirements:                    Pass entrance examination at <u>C.E.P.E.</u> level.

Length of course:     2 years.

Certificate awarded:   Diplôme de moniteur.  Moniteurs teach in primary
                       schools.  Moniteurs auxiliaires hold the C.E.P.E.
                       and pass the concours d'élèves moniteurs but have
                       no pedagogical training.

                       Moniteurs principaux must teach for 2 years and pass
                       additional examination to be upgraded from moniteur.

## COLLEGE NORMAL

1964, 1 collège normal, the Protestant Collège Edzang Nkoulou at Bitam.

Entrance requirements:      B.E.P.C.

Length of course:      1 year's professional training.

Certificate awarded:   Certificat de fin d'études des collèges normaux
                       (C.F.E.C.N.) to become instituteur-adjoint.

                       Moniteurs principaux may become instituteurs-adjoints
                       with 2 years' service and obtaining the certificat
                       élémentaire d'aptitude pédagogique (C.E.A.P.).

## ECOLES NORMALES

Entrance requirements:      15-18 years and pass entrance examination at
                            B.E.P.C. or B.E. level.

Length of course:      3 years.  Prior to October 1964, special years of
                       pedagogical training.  Now included in final year of
                       3-year course.

Program:  Corresponds to 2nd, 1st and terminal classes of collèges modernes,
          with letters, Experimental Sciences, Pedagogy and Child Psychology
          in last year.

Certificate awarded:   Brevet supérieur de fin d'études normales or bacca-
                       lauréat.  Trains instituteurs.

                       Instituteurs-adjoints with 4 years' service may take
                       the certificat d'aptitude pédagogique for upgrading
                       to instituteur.

1964, 2 écoles normales:  Mitzic (public), and Mouila (Catholic).

## CENTRE DE FORMATION PEDAGOGIQUE DE MAITRES DE C.E.G., Libreville

Public school opened November 1962.

At present a 3-year program.  Pupils on completion may be sent to the
section pédagogique of the Ecole Normale Supérieure, Brazzaville.

Trains teachers for the collèges d'enseignement général.


## ADULT EDUCATION

Classes given by radio in many centers.

CENTRAL AFRICA

C E N T R A L   A F R I C A

| Country and Capital | Area (sq. miles) | Est. Population | Independence Dates or Political Status | Official Language(s) |
|---|---|---|---|---|
| KINGDOM OF BURUNDI<br>Usumbura | 10,747 | 2,750,000 | 1 July 1962 | French |
| DEMOCRATIC REPUBLIC OF THE CONGO<br>Léopoldville | 905,378 | 15,000,000 | 30 June 1960 | French |
| MALAWI<br>Zomba (Plan to move to Lilangwe)<br>Formerly: Nyasaland (Zomba) | 49,177 | 2,890,000 | 6 July 1964 | English |
| RHODESIA<br>Salisbury<br>Formerly: Southern Rhodesia (Salisbury) | 150,333 | 3,849,000 | 11 November 1965 | English |
| REPUBLIC OF RWANDA<br>Kigali | 10,169 | 2,694,749 | 1 July 1962 | French |
| ZAMBIA<br>Lusaka<br>Formerly: Northern Rhodesia (Lusaka) | 290,323 | 3,600,000 | 23 October 1964 | English |

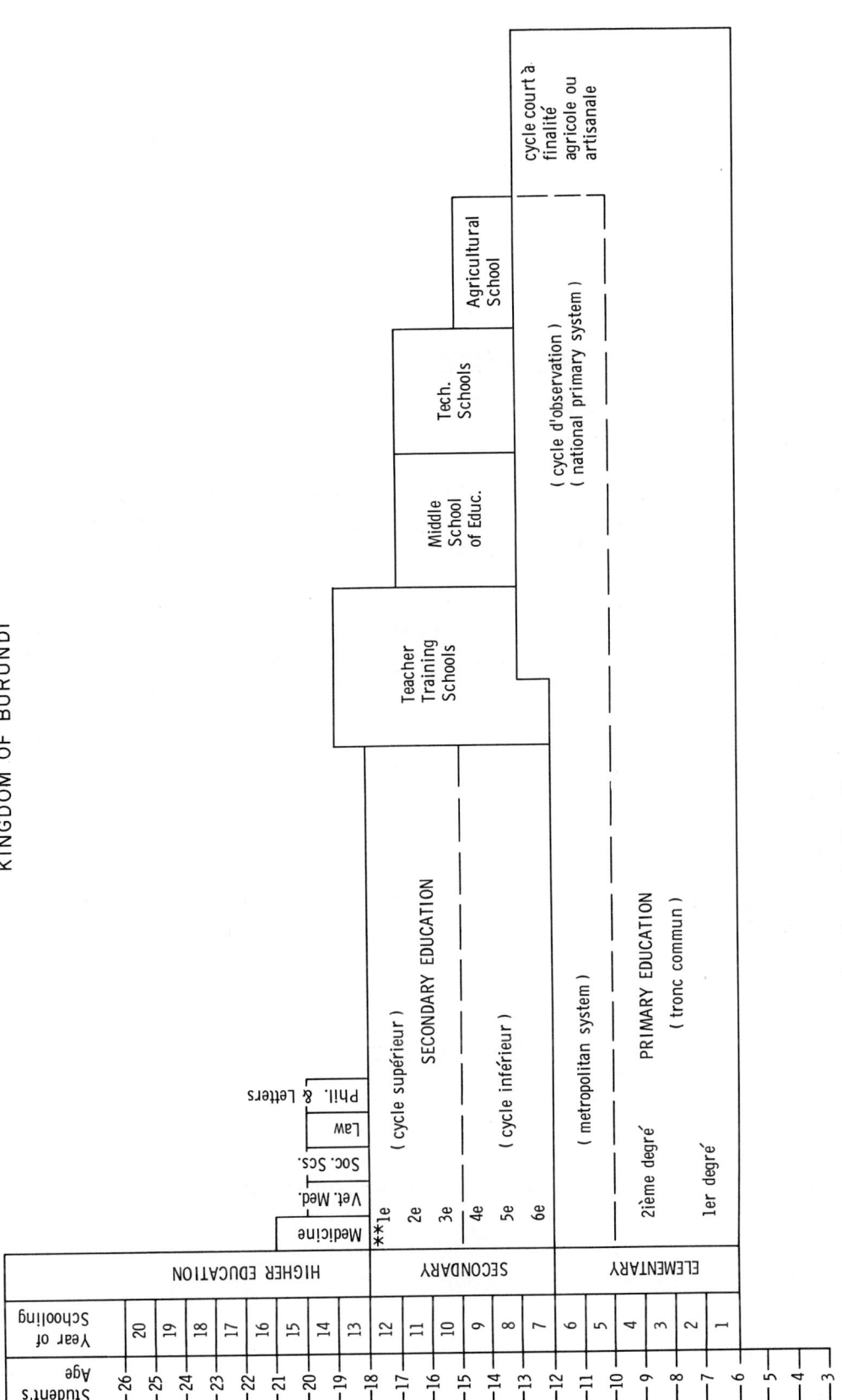

# KINGDOM OF BURUNDI

Compulsory education: None

School year: mid-September-June

Secondary grading: SECONDARY EDUCATION - 80% - le plus grand fruit
- 70% - grand fruit
- 60% - fruit
- 50% - satisfaction

KINGDOM OF BURUNDI

Independence: July 1, 1962.


## BACKGROUND

Burundi is a constitutional monarchy.

3 ethnic groups: Hutu (Bahutu), agricultural people, the great majority. Tutsi (Batutsi), Nilo-Hamitic people, 14% of the population. And Twa (Batwa), pygmoid, hunting people indigenous to the area, less than 1%.

1919, Burundi formed part of Ruanda-Urundi. Administered by Belgium first as League of Nations mandate from 1923. Status changed in 1946 to Belgium-administered U.N. Trust Territory. Elections supervised by U.N., September 1961. Internal self-government granted January 1, 1962, followed by independence, July 1.

(For more detailed description, see RWANDA.)

Languages: French, official. Local, Kirundi, a Bantu language. Kiswahili, spoken in commercial centers.

Education is largely the function of the Catholic Church in missions and state-supported mission schools.


## PRESENT SYSTEM

### KINDERGARTENS

Only mission schools. The government no longer subsidizes kindergartens or nursery schools.

### PRIMARY EDUCATION

Entry age: 6 years.

Language of instruction:   Kirundi in first 2 years; from 3rd year, French
                           used progressively.  French used in some urban
                           schools from 1st primary year.

Programs:        7 years in the national primary schools.
                 6 years in the 2 schools following the "metropolitan
                 system".

1st and 2nd years     = ler degré
3rd and 4th years     = 2ème degré
5th - 7th years       = cycle d'observation

Subjects:        Kirundi, French, Arithmetic, Natural Science (Elements of
                 Zoology, Botany, Anatomy, Physics), History, Geography,
                 Hygiene, Singing, Morals, Crafts.

                 For girls:  Home-Making.  For boys:  Agriculture, Manual
                 Training.

Cycle court à finalité agricole ou artisanale (short cycle in preparation
for agriculture and crafts - classes 5 through 7) is directed to the large
population which returns to agriculture and the crafts at the close of the
final 3 years of primary education.

In the training during the first 3 years in the tronc commun the agriculture and crafts work is "experimental"; in the cycle court emphasis is
on "productivity."  The first 2 years of the cycle court are devoted to
agricultural and crafts training suitable for all the students.  In the
3rd year, more definite orientation suited to the child's talents:  some
toward agriculture, others toward arboriculture, cattle raising, or arts
and crafts.

At close of the 7-year program, the principal of the school gives a general
examination for the Certificat d'études primaires (Certificate of Primary
Studies).  The Certificat is granted by the Ministry of National Education
and states that the student has successfully passed the tests in French,
Arithmetic, Civic Education, Geography, Natural Sciences listed among the
courses required by the national program.


SECONDARY EDUCATION

1950-56 secondary schools rose from 1 to 9.

Notable:   Athénée Royal, non-denominational state schools for boys and
           girls, Usumbura.  Lycée Stella Matutina, Catholic Girls School
           in Usumbura.  Others at Nyanza, Kibeta, Nyakinbanda, Birambo.

January 1960, Collège du Saint-Esprit, Usumbura, run by Jesuits:   European
           and Asian day students, African boarders.

GENERAL SECONDARY SCHOOLS

6-year program (two 3-year cycles).

Language of instruction:  French.

Entry age:      12-13 years; maximum, 16 years.

Entrance requirements:           Before 1963:
                                 Success in the examen d'entrée (entrance
                                 examination), prepared by the school.

                                 After September 1963:
                                 Success in the examen national d'accession
                                 à l'enseignement secondaire (national
                                 entrance examination to secondary school).

Program:  3 years - cycle inférieur  )
                                     )   Latin-Greek, Latin-Sciences,
          3 years - cycle supérieur  )   Latin-Math., Scientific Modern,
                                         Economic Modern

Prior to 1965, government schools (écoles officielles) offering the athénée
program.  Government-aided schools (écoles subventionnées) offering the
program of the Catholic Federation of Middle Education (Fédération de
l'Enseignement Moyen Catholique).

From 1965-66, only one program (programme unique).

During the 6-year program the following subjects are studied:

> French, Latin, Greek, English, German, History, Mathematics (includ-
> ing Algebra, Geometry, Trigonometry), Economics, Natural Science,
> Geography, Physical Education, Drawing, Music, Home Economics,
> Feminine activities, Physics (including laboratory), Chemistry
> (including laboratory), Biology, Introduction to Scientific
> Literature.

### ATHENEE CURRICULUM
### (Hours per week)

| Subjects | 6e Latin | 6e Modern | 5e Latin | 5e Modern | 4e Lat.Math. | 4e Modern | Greek-Lat. |
|---|---|---|---|---|---|---|---|
| Relig. and Ethics | 2 | 2 | 2 | 2 | 2 | 2 | 2 |
| Latin | 5 | | 5 | | 5 | | 5 |
| Greek | | | | | | | 6 |
| French | 5 | 7 | 5 | 6 | 5 | 7 | 5 |
| English | 4 | 4 | 4 | 4 | 4 | 4 | 4 |
| German | | | | 3 | 2 | 3 | 2 |
| History | 2 | 2 | 2 | 2 | 2 | 2 | 2 |
| Geography | 2 | 2 | 1 | 2 | 1 | 1 | 1 |

## Athénée Curriculum (cont'd)

| Subjects | 6e Latin | 6e Modern | 5e Latin | 5e Modern | 4e Lat.Math. | 4e Modern | 4e Greek-Lat. |
|---|---|---|---|---|---|---|---|
| Mathematics | 4 | 4 | 4 | 4 | 4 | 4 | 4 |
| Biology | 2 | 2 | 2 | 2 | | 1 | 1 |
| Physics | 2 | | 1 | 1 | 1 | 1 | 1 |
| Chemistry | | | | | 1 | 1 | 1 |
| Economics | | | | | | 3 | |
| Drawing | 2 | 2 | 2 | 2 | 2 | 2 | |
| Physical Education | 2 | 2 | 2 | 2 | 2 | 2 | 2 |
| | 32 | 27 | 30 | 30 | 31 | 33 | 36 |

| 3e | Greek-Latin | Latin-Math. | Sc. A | Econ. | Sc. B |
|---|---|---|---|---|---|
| Relig. and Ethics | 2 | 2 | 2 | 2 | 2 |
| Latin | 5 | 5 | | | |
| Greek | 5 | | | | |
| French | 5 | 5 | 5 | 5 | 6 |
| English | 4 | 4 | 4 | 4 | 4 |
| German | 2 | 2 | 3 | 3 | 2 |
| History | 2 | 2 | 2 | 2 | 2 |
| Geography | 1 | 1 | 1 | 2 | 1 |
| Mathematics | 3 | 7 | 7 | 3 | 4 |
| Biology | | | | | 2 |
| Physics | 1 | 2 | 2 | 1 | 3 |
| Chemistry | 1 | 1 | 1 | 1 | 2 |
| Economics | | | | 5 | |
| Drawing | | 2 | 2 | | 2 |
| Physical Education | 2 | 2 | 2 | 2 | 2 |
| | 33 | 35 | 31 | 30 | 32 |

| 2e | Greek-Latin | Latin-Math. | Sc. A | Econ. |
|---|---|---|---|---|
| Relig. and Ethics | 2 | 2 | 2 | 2 |
| Latin | 5 | 5 | | |
| Greek | 5 | | | |
| French | 5 | 5 | 5 | 5 |
| English | 4 | 4 | 4 | 4 |
| German | 2 | 2 | 3 | 3 |
| History | 2 | 2 | 2 | 2 |
| Geography | 1 | 1 | 1 | 2 |
| Mathematics | 3 | 7 | 7 | 3 |
| Biology | 1 | | | |
| Physics | 1 | 2 | 2 | 1 |
| Chemistry | 1 | 1 | 1 | 1 |
| Economics | | | | 5 |

## Athénée Curriculum (cont'd)

| Subjects | 2e Greek-Latin | 2e Latin-Math. | Sc. A | Econ. |
|---|---|---|---|---|
| Drawing | 2 | 2 | | |
| Physical Education | 2 | 2 | 2 | 2 |
| | 36 | 35 | 29 | 30 |

| Subjects | 1e Rhet. Gr.-Lat. | 1e Rhet. Lat.-Math. | Sc. A | Econ. |
|---|---|---|---|---|
| Relig. and Ethics | 2 | 2 | 2 | 2 |
| Latin | 5 | 5 | | |
| Greek | 5 | | | |
| French | 5 | 5 | 5 | 5 |
| English | 4 | 4 | 4 | 4 |
| German | 2 | 2 | 3 | 3 |
| History | 2 | 2 | 2 | 2 |
| Geography | 1 | 1 | 1 | 1 |
| Mathematics | 3 | 7 | 5 | 3 |
| Biology | 1 | 2 | 2 | 1 |
| Physics | 1 | 2 | 2 | 1 |
| Chemistry | 1 | 2 | 2 | 1 |
| Economics | | | | 5 |
| Drawing | | 2 | 1 | |
| Physical Education | 2 | 2 | 2 | 2 |
| | 34 | 38 | 31 | 30 |

## HUMANITIES CURRICULUM
(Fédération de l'Enseignement Catholique)
(Hours per week)

### CYCLE INFERIEUR

#### Humanités Anciennes

| Subjects | Latin-Grec 6e | Latin-Grec 5e | Latin-Grec 4e | Latin-Mathématiques 6e | Latin-Mathématiques 5e | Latin-Mathématiques 4e |
|---|---|---|---|---|---|---|
| Religion | 2 | 2 | 2 | 2 | 2 | 2 |
| French | 5 | 4 | 4 | 5 | 4 | 5 |
| Latin | 9 | 6 | 6 | 9 | 6 | 6 |
| Greek | | 4 | 4 | | | |
| 2nd Lang.(English) | 4 | 4 | 4 | 4 | 4 | 4 |
| History | 2 | 2 | 2 | 2 | 2 | 2 |
| Mathematics | 4 | 3 | 3 | 4 | 5 | 5 |
| Natural Sciences | | 1 | 1 | | 1 | 1 |
| Geography | 1 | 1 | 1 | 1 | 1 | 1 |

## Humanities Curriculum (cont'd)

### Humanités Anciennes

| Subjects | Latin-Grec 6e | 5e | 4e | Latin-Mathématiques 6e | 5e | 4e |
|---|---|---|---|---|---|---|
| Physical Education | 1 | 1 | 1 | 1 | 1 | 1 |
| Drawing | | | | | | 1 |
| Women's Activities | 1 | 1 | 1 | 1 | 1 | 1 |

| Subjects | Humanités Modernes Moyenne générale 6e | 5e | 4e | Familiale 1e | 2e | 3e |
|---|---|---|---|---|---|---|
| Religion | 2 | 2 | 2 | 2 | 2 | 2 |
| French | 8 | 6 | 4 | 6 | 5 | 5 |
| 2nd Lang.(English) | 6 | 5 | 4 | 4 | 4 | 4 |
| 3rd Lang.(German) | | 3 | 3 | | | |
| History | 2 | 2 | 2 | 2 | 2 | 2 |
| Mathematics | 6 | 5 | 5 | )3 | 3 | 3 |
| Economic Sciences | | | 4 | ) | | |
| Natural Sciences | 1 | 2 | 2 | 2 | 2 | 2 |
| Geography | 1 | 1 | 1 | 1 | 1 | 1 |
| Physical Education | 1 | 1 | 1 | 2 | 2 | 2 |
| Drawing | 1 | 1 | 1 | 2 | 2 | 2 |
| Music | | | | 1 | 1 | 1 |
| Domestic Science | | | | 2 | 4 | 4 |
| Women's Activities | 1 | 1 | 1 | 5 | 5 | 5 |

## CYCLE SUPERIEUR

### Humanités Anciennes

| Subjects | Latin-Grec 3e | 2e | 1e | Latin-Mathématiques 3e | 2e | 1e | Latin-Sciences 3e | 2e | 1e |
|---|---|---|---|---|---|---|---|---|---|
| Religion | 2 | 2 | 2 | 2 | 2 | 2 | 2 | 2 | 2 |
| French | 3 | 3 | 3 | 3 | 3 | 3 | 3 | 3 | 3 |
| Latin | 6 | 5 | 5 | 6 | 5 | 5 | 6 | 5 | 5 |
| Greek | 4 | 4 | 4 | | | | | | |
| Greek Culture, Intro. | | | | | | | | 1 | 1 |
| 2nd Lang.(English) | 4 | 4 | 4 | 4 | 4 | 4 | 4 | 4 | 4 |
| 3rd Lang.(German) | 1 | 1 | 1 | 1 | 1 | 1 | 1 | 1 | 1 |
| Mathematics | 3 | 3 | 3 | 7 | 8 | 9 | 4 | 4 | 4 |
| Physics | ) | | | ) | | | 2 | 2 | 3 |
| Chemistry | )1 | 2 | 2 | )1 | 2 | 2 | 1 | 1 | 1 |
| Biology | ) | | | ) | | | | | |
| Geography | 1 | 1 | 1 | 1 | 1 | 1 | 1 | 1 | 1 |
| Physical Education | 1 | 1 | 1 | 1 | 1 | 1 | 1 | 1 | 1 |
| Drawing | | | | 1 | 1 | 1 | | | |
| | 26 | 26 | 26 | 27 | 28 | 29 | 25 | 25 | 26 |

## Humanities Curriculum (cont'd)

| Subjects | Humanités Modernes Scientific A | | | Scientific B | | | Economics | | |
|---|---|---|---|---|---|---|---|---|---|
|  | 3e | 2e | 1e | 3e | 2e | 1e | 3e | 2e | 1e |
| Religion | 2 | 2 | 2 | 2 | 2 | 2 | 2 | 2 | 2 |
| French | 5 | 5 | 4 | 5 | 5 | 4 | 5 | 4 | 4 |
| Ancient Culture, Intro. |  |  |  |  | 1 | 1 |  |  |  |
| 2nd Lang.(English) | 4 | 4 | 4 | 4 | 4 | 4 | 4 | 4 | 4 |
| 3rd Lang.(German) | 3 | 2 | 2 | 3 | 3 | 2 | 3 | 2 | 2 |
| 4th Lang. |  |  |  |  |  |  | 3 | 3 | 2 |
| Mathematics | 7 | 8 | 9 | 5 | 5 | 5 | 3 | 3 | 4 |
| Economic Sciences |  |  |  |  |  |  | 4 | 5 | 6 |
| Physics | ) |  |  | 2 | 2 | 3 | ) | | |
| Chemistry | ) 2 | 2 | 2 | ) 3 | 3 | 3 | ) 2 | 2 | 2 |
| Biology | ) |  |  | ) |  |  | ) | | |
| Intro. to Sc. Lit. |  |  |  |  |  | 1 |  |  |  |
| Geography | 1 | 1 | 1 | 1 | 1 | 1 | 1 | 1 | 1 |
| Physical Education | 1 | 1 | 1 | 1 | 1 | 1 | 1 | 1 | 1 |
| Drawing | 1 | 1 | 1 | 1 | 1 | 1 |  |  |  |
|  | 26 | 26 | 26 | 27 | 28 | 28 | 28 | 27 | 28 |

Examination of lower cycle in Humanities for those desiring a diploma at the end of 3 years. On successful completion, Diplôme de fin du cycle inférieur (diploma of lower cycle) awarded.

Final examination at close of 6-year program (études moyennes). On successful completion, Diplôme homologue d'humanités (diploma in Humanities) awarded, entitling holder to university entrance without examination. Diploma lists faculties accessible to the holder. The Jury d'homologation des diplômes de fin d'humanités is very severe in the examinations.

Grading:  80% - le plus grand fruit
          70% - grand fruit
          60% - fruit

Students from the Petits Seminaires (these establishments are neither subsidized nor inspected by the government) have followed the program of the humanités anciennes de la Fédération de l'Enseignement Catholique and are permitted to take examinations for the diploma of fin d'humanités.

## HIGHER EDUCATION

UNIVERSITE OFFICIELLE DE BUJUMBURA (University of Usumbura)

By legislative ordinances of May 3, 1961 and June 30, 1962, the University was constituted by a union of the Faculty of Agronomy of the Official University of the Belgian Congo and Ruanda-Urundi (founded by the government at Astrida in 1958 and transferred to Bujumbura in 1960) and the Faculties of Philosophy and of Economic and Social Sciences (created by the Society of Jesus in October 1960).

Became official University of Bujumbura by royal decree, January 10, 1964. Called "official" because it is recognized and subsidized by the state.

Entrance requirements:          Secondary school diploma based on a 6-year course.

Language of instruction:        French.

Faculties:

        Philosophy and Letters
        Science
        Economic and Social Sciences

The diplomas awarded are already recognized by Congolese and Belgian universities.

The teaching staff usually comes out of 4 Belgian universities, several French universities, and one university from Switzerland.

| Degrees awarded | Years |
|---|---|
| B.A. (Law) | 2 |
| B.A. (History) | 2 |
| B.A. (Classics) | 2 |
| B.Sc. (Chemistry) | 2 |
| B.Sc. (Biology) | 2 |
| B.Sc. (Geography) | 2 |
| B.Sc. (Geology) | 2 |
| B.Sc. (Veterinary Medicine) | 2 |
| B.Sc. (Pharmacy) | |
| B.Sc. (Agronomy) | 2 |
| B.Sc. (Medicine) | 3 |
| B.S.Sc. (Political and Social Sciences) | 2 |
| B.S.Sc. (Economics) | 2 |
| B.S.Sc. (Business Administration) | 2 |

Faculty of Philosophy and Letters

Candidature en Philosophie et Lettres

(1)   Preparing for the doctorat en droit and the licence en notariat:

|  |  | (hours) |
|---|---|---|
| 1st yr: | Religious Science (Catholics only) | 30 |
|  | Intro. to Philosophy and Metaphysics | 45 |
|  | Logic+ | 45 |
|  | Psychology++ | 45 |
|  | Intro. to African Linguistics (incl. Phonetics, Phonology and Morphology) | 45 |
|  | African Literatures | 15 |
|  | History of French Literature+ | 45 |
|  | Interpretation of a Latin author | 30 |
|  | Historical Criticism | 30 |
|  | History of Ancient Greece and Rome | 45 |
|  | History of the Middle Ages++ | 45 |
|  | History of Modern Times+ | 45 |
|  | Intro. to the Study of Law | 45 |
| 2nd yr: | Ethics++ | 45 |
|  | Natural Law+ | 60 |
|  | Intro. to Modern Literatures++ | 30 |
|  | Intro. to African Structures++ | 30 |
|  | African History++ | 30 |
|  | Contemporary History+ | 45 |
|  | History of Civil Law | 30 |
|  | Intro. to Custom Law | 45 |
|  | Roman Law | 120 |
|  | Survey of Law | 45 |
|  | Political Economy | 60 |

(2)   Preparing for the licence:

A.  History

| 1st yr: | Religious Science (Catholics only) | 30 |
|---|---|---|
|  | Intro. to Philosophy | 45 |
|  | Logic+ | 45 |
|  | Latin Translation I | 30 |
|  | African Linguistics | 45 |
|  | African Literatures | 15 |
|  | French Literature | 45 |

+Given every other year to 1st and 2nd-year students simultaneously; will be offered in 1965-66.

++Given every other year; required in 1964-65 from all 1st and 2nd-year students.

|                                                         |    |
|---------------------------------------------------------|----|
| Latin Literature I                                      | 30 |
| Historical Criticism                                    | 30 |
| History of Ancient Greece and Rome                      | 45 |
| History of the Middle Ages++                            | 45 |
| History of Modern Times+                                | 45 |
| Pro-Seminar in History                                  | 90 |
| Greek Literature (elective)                             | 30 |
| Elementary German (elective)                            | 30 |

|          |                                                      |    |
|----------|------------------------------------------------------|----|
| 2nd yr:  | Ethics++                                             | 45 |
|          | Psychology++                                         | 45 |
|          | Latin Translation II                                 | 30 |
|          | Latin Literature II                                  | 30 |
|          | Intro. to History of Modern Literature               |    |
|          |   (incl. English and French African Lit.)++ | 30 |
|          | Art History and Archeology+                          | 30 |
|          | Intro. to African History++                          | 30 |
|          | African History (esp. Burundi, Rwanda                |    |
|          |   and Congo)++                             | 30 |
|          | Contemporary History++                               | 45 |
|          | Survey of World History                              | 60 |
|          | Pro-Seminar in History                               | 90 |
|          | Pro-Seminar in Human Geography                       | 60 |
|          | Political Economics                                  | 60 |
|          | Intro. to Methods of Teaching and                    |    |
|          |   Practice Teaching                        | 30 |
|          | Greek Literature (elective)                          | 30 |
|          | Elementary German (elective)                         | 30 |

## B. Classical Philology

|          |                                                   |    |
|----------|---------------------------------------------------|----|
| 1st yr:  | Religious Science (Catholics only)                | 30 |
|          | Intro. to Philosophy                              | 45 |
|          | Logic+                                            | 45 |
|          | African Linguistics and Literatures               | 45 |
|          | French Literature+                                | 45 |
|          | Historical Criticism                              | 30 |
|          | History of Ancient Greece and Rome                | 45 |
|          | History of the Middle Ages                        | 45 |
|          | History of Modern Times+                          | 45 |
|          | Latin Translation I                               | 30 |
|          | Latin Literature I                                | 30 |
|          | Latin Exercises I                                 | 30 |
|          | Greek Translation I                               | 30 |
|          | Greek Literature I                                | 30 |
|          | Greek Exercises I                                 | 30 |
|          | German I                                          | 30 |

+Given every other year to 1st and 2nd-year students simultaneously; will be offered in 1965-66.

++Given every other year; required in 1964-65 from all 1st and 2nd-year students.

| 2nd yr: | Ethics++ | 45 |
|---|---|---|
| | Psychology++ | 45 |
| | Intro. to Modern Literatures++ | 30 |
| | Intro. to History of Art+ | 30 |
| | Intro. to African Structures | 30 |
| | African History (esp. Burundi, Rwanda and Congo)++ | 30 |
| | Contemporary History+ | 45 |
| | Latin Translation II | 30 |
| | Latin Literature II | 30 |
| | Latin Exercises II | 30 |
| | Greek Translation II | 30 |
| | Greek Literature II | 30 |
| | Greek Exercises II | 30 |
| | Survey of Classical Philology | 60 |
| | Intro. to Methods of Teaching and Practical Teaching | 30 |
| | German II | 30 |

## C. Romance Philology

| 1st yr: | Religious Science (Catholics only) | 30 |
|---|---|---|
| | Intro. to Philosophy | 45 |
| | Logic+ | 45 |
| | African Linguistics and Literatures | 45 |
| | History of French Literature+ | 45 |
| | Interpretation of French Authors I | 45 |
| | Historical French Grammar:  Phonetics | 45 |
| | Philological Exercises on Romance Languages:  French | 45 |
| |                      Spanish | 30 |
| | Practical Exercises in French I | 30 |
| | Latin Translation I | 30 |
| | Latin Literature I | 30 |
| | Historical Criticism | 30 |
| | History of Ancient Greece and Rome | 45 |
| | History of the Middle Ages++ | 45 |
| | History of Modern Times+ | 45 |

| 2nd yr: | Psychology++ | 45 |
|---|---|---|
| | Ethics+ | 45 |
| | Interpretation of French Authors II | 45 |
| | Historical French Grammar:  Morphology | 30 |
| | Philological Exercises in Romance Languages:  French | 45 |
| |                      Italian | 30 |

+Given every other year to 1st and 2nd-year students simultaneously; will be offered in 1965-66.

++Given every other year;  required in 1964-65 from all 1st and 2nd-year students.

|                                                               |    |
|---------------------------------------------------------------|----|
| Practical French Exercises II                                 | 30 |
| Survey of Romance Philology                                   | 60 |
| Intro. to Modern Literatures (incl. English and French African Lit.) | 30 |
| Latin Translation II                                          | 30 |
| Latin Literature II                                           | 30 |
| Intro. to African Structures[++]                              | 30 |
| African History (esp. Burundi, Rwanda and Congo)[++]          | 30 |
| History of Modern Times[+]                                    | 45 |
| Intro. to the History of Art[+]                               | 30 |
| Intro. to Methods of Teaching and Practical Teaching          | 30 |

## Faculty of Economic and Social Sciences

### Candidature en Sciences Sociales

(1)  Preparing for the licence en sciences politiques et sociales and the licence en sciences politiques et administratives:

|         |                                                    |    |
|---------|----------------------------------------------------|----|
| 1st yr: | Religious Science (Catholics only)                 | 30 |
|         | Intro. to Philosophy                               | 45 |
|         | Logic[+]                                           | 45 |
|         | Psychology[++]                                     | 45 |
|         | Historical Criticism                               | 30 |
|         | Contemporary History[+]                            | 45 |
|         | Private Law:  Civil I                              | 30 |
|         | Public Law and Political Institutions I            | 45 |
|         | Private Law:  Commercial I                         | 30 |
|         | Scientific Methodology I                           | 15 |
|         | Political Economics I                              | 30 |
|         | Intro. to Statistics                               | 30 |
|         | Physical and Human Geography of Africa             | 45 |
|         |                                                    |    |
| 2nd yr: | Ethics[++]                                         | 45 |
|         | Natural Law[+]                                      | 60 |
|         | General Sociology[+]                                | 60 |
|         | Complementary General Sociology[++]                | 30 |
|         | History of French Literature[+]                    | 45 |
|         | Intro. to African Structures[++]                   | 30 |
|         | History of Africa (esp. Burundi, Rwanda and Congo)[++] | 30 |
|         | Intro. to Juridical Sciences                       | 45 |
|         | Private Law:  Civil II                             | 30 |

[+]Given every other year to 1st and 2nd-year students simultaneously; will be offered in 1965-66.

[++]Given every other year; required in 1964-65 from all 1st and 2nd-year students.

```
          Public Law and Political Institutions II  45
          Private Law:  Commercial II               30
          Scientific Methodology II                 30
          Political Economics II                    30
          General Statistics and Exercises          60
```

(2)  Preparing for the <u>licence en sciences économiques</u>:

```
   1st yr:  Religious Science (Catholics only)       30
            Intro. to Philosophy                     45
            Logic+                                    45
            Psychology++                              45
            English                                  90
            Historical Criticism                     30
            Contemporary History+                    45
            Private Law:  Civil I                    30
            Public Law and Political Institutions I  45
            Private Law:  Commercial I               30
            Scientific Methodology I                 15
            Political Economics I                    30
            General Accountancy and Exercises        90
            Higher Mathematics I                     30
            Mathematics Exercises                    45
            Intro. to Statistics                     30
            Physical and Human Geography of Africa+  45

   2nd yr:  Ethics++                                 45
            Natural Law+                             60
            General Sociology+                       60
            Advanced English                         60
            Intro. to African Structures++           30
            History of Africa (esp. Burundi, Rwanda
               and Congo)++                          30
            Private Law:  Civil II                   30
            Public Law and Political Institutions II 45
            Private Law:  Commercial II              30
            Scientific Methodology II                30
            Political Economics II                   30
            Commercial Economics                     30
            Survey of Economics                      15
            Higher Mathematics II                    30
            Mathematics Exercises                    30
            General Statistics and Exercises         60
            Economic Geography of Africa++           30
```

+Given every other year to 1st and 2nd-year students simultaneously; will be offered in 1965-66.

++Given every other year; required in 1964-65 from all 1st and 2nd-year students.

## Candidature en Sciences Commerciales

| | | |
|---|---|---:|
| 1st yr: | Religious Science (Catholics only) | 30 |
| | Intro. to Philosophy | 45 |
| | Psychology++ | 45 |
| | English | 90 |
| | Elementary German | 30 |
| | Business Dutch+++ | 60 |
| | Contemporary History+ | 45 |
| | Private Law:  Civil I | 30 |
| | Private Law:  Commercial I | 30 |
| | Scientific Methodology I | 15 |
| | Political Economics I | 30 |
| | Commercial Economics | 30 |
| | Intro. to Negotiable Products | 15 |
| | General Accountancy and Exercises | 90 |
| | Higher Mathematics I | 30 |
| | Mathematics Exercises | 45 |
| | Intro. to Statistics | 30 |
| | Physical and Human Geography of Africa+ | 45 |
| | | |
| 2nd yr: | Ethics++ | 45 |
| | Advanced English | 60 |
| | German | 30 |
| | Advanced Business Dutch+++ | 60 |
| | History of Africa (esp. Burundi, Rwanda and Congo)++ | 30 |
| | Private Law:  Civil II | 30 |
| | Private Law:  Commercial II | 30 |
| | Scientific Methodology II | 30 |
| | Political Economics II | 30 |
| | Negotiable Products | 45 |
| | Conducted visits to industrial, commercial and financial enterprises | |
| | Enterprise Economics | 45 |
| | Corporation Accounting | 15 |
| | Financial Algebra | 60 |
| | Survey of Economics | 15 |
| | Higher Mathematics II | 30 |
| | Mathematics Exercises | 30 |
| | General Statistics and Exercises | 60 |
| | Economic Geography of Africa | 30 |

+Given every other year to 1st and 2nd-year students simultaneously; will be offered in 1965-66.

++Given  every other year; required in 1964-65 from all 1st and 2nd-year students.

+++Elective, except for Belgian students.

Additional courses for the <u>licence en sciences politiques et sociales</u>
in conjunction with the <u>doctorat en droit</u>:

| | |
|---|---|
| General Sociology[+] | 60 |
| Scientific Methodology | 45 |
| Statistics and Exercises | 90 |
| Physical and Human Geography of Africa[+] | 45 |

Additional courses for the <u>licence en sciences économiques</u> in
conjunction with the <u>doctorat en droit</u>:

| | |
|---|---|
| English (1 test) "épreuve unique" | |
| Scientific Methodology | 45 |
| General Accountancy and Exercises | 90 |
| Survey of Economics | 15 |
| Higher Mathematics and Exercises | 135 |
| Statistics and Exercises | 90 |

Additional courses for the <u>licence en sciences économiques</u> in
conjunction with the <u>licence en sciences politiques et sociales</u>:

| | |
|---|---|
| English (1 test) | |
| Commercial Economics | 30 |
| Accountancy and Exercises | 90 |
| Survey of Economics | 15 |
| Higher Mathematics and Exercises | 135 |

[+]Given every other year to 1st and 2nd-year students simultaneously;
will be offered in 1965-66.

## Faculty of Science

### Candidature en Sciences

(1) Preparing for the <u>licence en sciences chimiques</u>:

| 1st yr: | | |
|---|---|---|
| | Religious Science (Catholics only) | 15 |
| | Intro. to Philosophy-Partim: Logic | 15 |
| | Intro. to Philosophy-Partim: Ethics | 15 |
| | General and Experimental Physics | 120 |
| | Practical Work in Physics | 90 |
| | General Chemistry | 90 |
| | Practical Work in Chemistry | 90 |
| | General Biology-Partim: Animal Biology incl. Comparative Anatomy | 60 |
| | Practical Work in Zoology | 60 |
| | Elements of Theoretical and Applied Mathematics | 30 |
| | Mathematics Exercises | 45 |

2nd yr:     Intro. to Philosophy-Partim:  Ethics[+]    15
              Intro. to Philosophy-Partim:  Psychology   30
              General Biology-Partim:  Vegetable
                Biology and Elements of Botany[++]   60
              Practical Work in Botany   60
              Elements of Mineralogy, Geology and
                Physical Geography   45
              Practical Exercises in Mineralogy and
                Geology   25
              Complements of Mathematics   45
              Mathematics Exercises   45
              Elements of Calculus of Probabilities,
                Mathematic Statistics and Biometric
                Laws   15
              Statistics Exercises   15
              General Chemistry   60
              Practical Work in Chemistry   90
              Elements of Physical Chemistry   30
              Practical Work in Physical Chemistry   30
              Crystallography   30
              Practical Work in Crystallography   30
              Analytical Mechanics and Theoretical
                Physics   30
              Exercises in Analytical Mechanics   30

(2)  Preparing for the <u>licence en sciences géologiques et minéralogiques</u>:

1st yr:     Religious Science (Catholics only)   15
              Intro. to Philosophy-Partim:  Logic   15
              Intro. to Philosophy-Partim:  Ethics   15
              General and Experimental Physics   120
              Practical Work in Physics   90
              General Chemistry   90
              Practical Work in Chemistry   90
              General Biology-Partim:  Animal Biology
                incl. Comparative Anatomy   60
              Practical Work in Zoology   60
               Physical Geography of Africa (elective)   30
              Elements of Theoretical and Applied
                Mathematics   30
              Mathematics Exercises   45

2nd yr:     Intro. to Philosophy-Partim:  Ethics[+]    15
              Intro. to Philosophy-Partim:  Psychology   30
               General Biology-Partim:  Vegetable Biology
                and Elements of Botany[++]   60

[+] Only in 1964-65.

[++] Students who have taken this course in 1st year are exempted.

|  |  |
|---|---|
| Practical Work in Botany | 60 |
| Elements of Mineralogy, Geology and Physical Geography | 45 |
| Practical Exercises in Mineralogy and Geology | 25 |
| Elements of Calculus of Probabilities, Mathematics1 Statistics and Biometric Laws | 45 |
| Statistics Exercises | 45 |
| General Chemistry | 60 |
| Practical Work in Chemistry | 90 |
| Elements of Physical Chemistry | 30 |
| Practical Work in Physical Chemistry | 30 |
| Crystallography | 30 |
| Practical Work in Crystallography | 30 |
| Analytical Mechanics and Theoretical Physics | 30 |
| Exercises in Analytical Mechanics | 30 |

(3)  Preparing for the <u>licence en sciences géographiques</u>:

| 1st yr: |  |  |
|---|---|---|
|  | Religious Science (Catholics only) | 15 |
|  | Intro. to Philosophy-Partim:  Logic | 15 |
|  | Intro. to Philosophy-Partim:  Ethics | 15 |
|  | General and Experimental Physics | 120 |
|  | Elements of General Chemistry | 90 |
|  | Practical Work in Chemistry | 90 |
|  | General Biology-Partim:  Animal Biology incl. Comparative Anatomy | 60 |
|  | Practical Work in Zoology | 60 |
|  | Elements of Theoretical and Applied Mathematics | 30 |
|  | Mathematics Exercises | 45 |

(4)  Preparing for the <u>licence en sciences biologiques</u>:

| 1st yr: |  |  |
|---|---|---|
|  | Religious Science (Catholics only) | 15 |
|  | Intro. to Philosophy-Partim:  Logic | 15 |
|  | Intro. to Philosophy-Partim:  Ethics | 15 |
|  | General and Experimental Physics | 120 |
|  | Practical Work in Physics | 90 |
|  | General Chemistry | 90 |
|  | Practical Work in Chemistry | 90 |
|  | General Biology-Partim:  Animal Biology incl. Comparative Anatomy | 60 |
|  | Practical Work in Zoology | 60 |
|  | Elements of Theoretical and Applied Mathematics | 30 |
|  | Mathematics Exercises | 45 |

| 2nd yr: | Intro. to Philosophy-Partim:  Ethics[+] | 15 |
| | Intro. to Philosophy-Partim:  Psychology | 30 |
| | General Biology-Partim:  Vegetable Biology and Elements of Botany[++] | 60 |
| | Practical Work in Botany | 60 |
| | Complements of Zoology | 60 |
| | Practical Work in Zoology | 60 |
| | Complements of Botany | 45 |
| | Practical Work in Botany | 60 |
| | Elements of Mineralogy, Geology and Physical Geography | 45 |
| | Practical Work in Mineralogy and Geology | 25 |
| | Elements of Calculus of Probabilities, Mathematical Statistics and Biometric Laws | 15 |
| | Statistics Exercises | 15 |
| | General Chemistry | 60 |
| | Practical Work in Chemistry | 90 |

(5)   Preparing for the <u>licence en pharmacie</u>:

| 1st yr: | Religious Science (Catholics only) | 15 |
| | Intro. to Philosophy-Partim:  Logic | 15 |
| | Intro. to Philosophy-Partim:  Ethics | 15 |
| | General and Experimental Physics | 120 |
| | Practical Work in Physics | 90 |
| | General Chemistry | 90 |
| | Practical Work in Chemistry | 90 |
| | General Biology-Partim:  Animal Biology incl. Comparative Anatomy | 60 |
| | Practical Work in Zoology | 60 |
| | Elements of Theoretical and Applied Mathematics | 30 |
| | Mathematics Exercises | 45 |

| 2nd yr: | Intro. to Philosophy-Partim:  Ethics[+] | 15 |
| | Intro. to Philosophy-Partim:  Psychology | 30 |
| | General Biology-Partim:  Vegetable Biology and Elements of Botany[++] | 60 |
| | Practical Work in Botany | 60 |
| | Complements of Zoology | 45 |
| | Practical Work in Zoology | 60 |
| | Complements of Botany | 45 |
| | Practical Work in Botany | 60 |
| | Elements of Mineralogy, Geology and Physical Geography | 45 |

[+]Only in 1964-65.

[++]Students who have taken the course in 1st year are exempted.

|                                                                              |     |
|------------------------------------------------------------------------------|-----|
| Practical Exercises in Mineralogy and Geology                                | 25  |
| Elements of Calculus of Probabilities, Mathematical Statistics and Biometric Laws | 15  |
| Statistics Exercises                                                         | 15  |
| General Chemistry                                                            | 60  |
| Practical Work in Chemistry                                                  | 90  |
| Elements of Physiology                                                       | 45  |
| Practical Work in Physiology                                                 | 30  |

(6)  Preparing for the <u>licence en médecine vétérinaire</u>:

1st yr:  Same program as <u>licence en pharmacie</u>.

2nd yr:  Same program as <u>licence en sciences biologiques</u>.

(7)  Preparing for the title of <u>Ingénieur Agronome</u>:

1st yr:

| Religious Science (Catholics only)                         | 15  |
|------------------------------------------------------------|-----|
| Intro. to Philosophy-Partim:  Logic                        | 15  |
| Intro. to Philosophy-Partim:  Ethics                       | 15  |
| General and Experimental Physics                           | 120 |
| Practical Work in Physics                                  | 90  |
| General Chemistry                                          | 90  |
| Practical Work in Chemistry                                | 90  |
| General Biology-Partim:  Animal Biology incl. Comparative Anatomy | 60  |
| Practical Work in Zoology                                  | 60  |
| Elements of Theoretical and Applied Mathematics            | 30  |
| Mathematics Exercises                                      | 45  |

2nd yr:

| Intro. to Philosophy-Partim:  Ethics[+]                    | 15  |
|------------------------------------------------------------|-----|
| Intro. to Philosophy-Partim:  Psychology                   | 30  |
| General Biology-Partim:  General Biology and Elements of Botany[++] | 60  |
| Practical Work in Botany                                   | 60  |
| Complements of Zoology                                     | 45  |
| Practical Work in Zoology                                  | 60  |
| Complements of Botany                                      | 45  |
| Practical Work in Botany                                   | 60  |
| Elements of Mineralogy, Geology and Physical Geography     | 45  |
| Practical Exercises in Mineralogy and Geology              | 25  |

[+]Only in 1964-65.

[++]Students who have taken the course in 1st year are exempted.

|                                                                |     |
|----------------------------------------------------------------|-----|
| Complements of Mathematics                                     | 45  |
| Mathematics Exercises                                          | 45  |
| Elements of Calculus of Probabilities, Mathematical Statistics and Biometric Laws | 15  |
| Statistics Exercises                                           | 15  |
| General Chemistry                                              | 60  |
| Practical Work in Chemistry                                    | 90  |
| Analytical Mechanics and Theoretical Physics                   | 30  |
| Exercises in Analytical Mechanics                              | 30  |

(8) Preparing for the <u>licence en sciences naturelles et médicales</u>:

1st yr:
| | |
|---|---|
| Religious Science (Catholics only) | 15 |
| Intro. to Philosophy-Partim: Logic | 15 |
| Intro. to Philosophy-Partim: Ethics | 15 |
| General and Experimental Physics | 120 |
| Practical Work in Physics | 90 |
| General Chemistry | 120 |
| Practical Work in Chemistry | 120 |
| General Biology-Partim: Animal Biology incl. Comparative Anatomy | 60 |
| Practical Work in Zoology | 60 |
| Elements of Mathematics applied to Biology | 30 |
| Mathematics Exercises | 45 |

2nd yr:
| | |
|---|---|
| Intro. to Philosophy-Partim: Ethics[+] | 15 |
| General Biology-Partim: Vegetable Biology incl. Elements of Botany[++] | 60 |
| Practical work in Botany | 60 |
| Physiological Chemistry-Partim: General Biochemistry | 60 |
| Practical Work in Physiological Chemistry | 60 |
| Elements of Embryology | 15 |
| Practical Work in Embryology | 15 |
| Systematic Human Anatomy, Topological and Comparative Anatomy I | 90 |
| Practical Work in Anatomy | 60 |
| Histology-Partim: General Histology | 30 |
| Practical Work in Histology | 30 |
| Physiology-Partim: General Physiology | 90 |
| Practical Work in Physiology | 60 |
| Elements of Calculus of Probabilities, Mathematical Statistics and Biometric Laws | 15 |

[+]Only in 1964-65.

[++]Students who have taken this course in 1st year are exempted.

|  |  |  |
|---|---|---|
| Statistics Exercises | 15 |
| Medical Entomology | 30 |
| Practical Work in Entomology | 30 |

3rd yr:
| | |
|---|---|
| Intro. to Philosophy-Partim: Psychology | 30 |
| Physiological Chemistry-Partim: Human Biochemistry | 60 |
| Practical Work in Physiological Chemistry | 60 |
| Complements of Physics | 15 |
| Elements of Embryology | 15 |
| Systematic Human Anatomy, Topological and Comparative Anatomy II | 120 |
| Practical Work in Anatomy | 90 |
| Histology-Partim: General Histology | 60 |
| Practical Work in Histology | 60 |
| Physiology-Partim: General Physiology | 90 |
| Practical Work in Physiology | 60 |
| Helminthology | 30 |
| Practical Work in Helminthology | 30 |

## Higher Scientific Course (1 year)

Preparing candidates for the special Schools of Engineering:

| | |
|---|---|
| Arithmetic and Complements | 105 |
| Algebra and Complements | 245 |
| Rectilinear and Spherical Trigonometry | 70 |
| Geometry and Complements | 175 |
| Analytical Geometry | 210 |
| Descriptive Geometry | 70 |
| Drafting and Free-hand Drawing | 105 |

## VOCATIONAL AND TECHNICAL EDUCATION

By 1956 vocational training at vocational schools in Usumbura, Kigali, for carpenters, masons, mechanics, tailors.

5 manual training shops at Usumbura.

Technical training at Astrida School and School for Auxiliary Administrative Staff, Nyanza. 9-month post-secondary program at School of Administration in Astrida.

Rubana Agricultural School.

By 1954, 3-year post-primary domestic science schools.

## PROFESSIONAL, COMMERCIAL AND TECHNICAL SCHOOLS

Entrance requirements:        Same as secondary school.

Language of instruction:      French.

Professional Technical School:    4 years.
Professional Agricultural School:  2 years.

Basic studies at Technical School (Ecole Technique), Usumbura (4 years, approximately 35 hours per week):

> Religion, Social and Civic Education, French, English, History, Geography, Arithmetic, Algebra, Geometry, Trigonometry, Natural Sciences, Physics, Chemistry, Physical Education, Technical Drawing, Knowledge of Materials, Technology, Mechanics, Electricity, Industrial Organization, Practical Work.

Basic studies at Professional Agricultural School (Ecole Professionnelle Agricole), Karuzi (2 years):

> General Agriculture, Special Cultures, Forestry, Bee-Keeping, Soil Conservation, Surveying, Arithmetic, French, Hygiene, Cattle-Raising.

Grading:  Same as secondary school.

Upon successful examinations, diplomas awarded, listing subjects studied, and grades received.


## TEACHER EDUCATION

### TEACHER TRAINING SCHOOLS (Ecoles Normales)

Entrance requirements:        Same as secondary school.

Language of instruction:      French.

Program:  7 years.

During the first 5 years, the same program as the Humanités modernes scientifiques B.  During the 6th and 7th years, the program of the 1ère scientifique B (last year of the Humanités scientifiques B) is combined with teacher training courses.

The Training School subsidized and inspected by the government follows the program of the Fédération de l'Enseignement Catholique - Humanités scientifiques B (see timetable).

The State Training School follows the program of the <u>Humanités scienti-fiques B</u> of the Athénées (see timetable).

Grading:  Same as secondary schools.

Upon successful examinations, <u>diplôme de fin d'études</u> (diploma of completion of studies) awarded.

The subsidized Training School granted first teachers' diplomas in June 1964.  The State Training School will soon grant diplomas.


## MIDDLE SCHOOLS OF EDUCATION (Ecoles Moyennes Pédagogiques)

Entrance requirements:          Same as secondary school.

Language of instruction:        French.

Program:  4 years.

Lower cycle of the <u>Humanités moyennes</u> de la Fédération de l'Enseignement Moyen Catholique plus 1 year of education (<u>année pédagogique</u>).

Some Middle Schools of Education for Girls follow the program of the <u>Humanités familiales</u> of the Fédération de l'Enseignement Catholique plus 1 year of education.

Grading:  Same as secondary school.

Upon successful examinations, <u>diploma of completion of studies</u> awarded.

835

DEMOCRATIC REPUBLIC OF THE CONGO (Leopoldville)

Compulsory education: None

School year: Mid-September to end of June
2 equal semesters

Secondary Grading: 100% – Perfect

50% – lowest passing grade

DEMOCRATIC REPUBLIC OF THE CONGO (LEOPOLDVILLE)
(République Démocratique du Congo)

Independence:  June 30, 1960.

## BACKGROUND

African inhabitants are mostly Bantu (9-10 million).  There are also
Sudanese (2-3 million), and a small number of Nilotic Pygmy and Hamitic
peoples.

Non-African population:  Belgian, Italian, Portuguese, Greek, French, and
British.

The Congolese languages are basically of the Bantu family.  Of many
languages and dialects spoken, most important are Swahili in East and
South, Tshiluba in Kasai, Kinkongo in the Lower Congo, and Lingala, along
most of the Congo River.

Under the Belgian administration, French and Dutch were the two official
languages.  French is the principal social and business language.

The Pygmy tribes, earliest inhabitants of the Congo, were taken over by
invading Bantu and Nilotic tribes.

1482, Portuguese made the first contact with region at mouth of Congo
River.

1877, Stanley's trip down the Congo brought interest in the wealth of the
Congo basin.  1878, King Leopold II of Belgium commissioned Stanley to
explore further and make treaties with tribal chiefs, and the monarchy
formed the International Association of the Congo, a development company.

The Berlin Conference, 1884-85, recognized the Independent State of the
Congo, ruled by Leopold II, and its boundaries were established by treaties
with other colonial powers.  Territory was transferred to Belgium as a
colony, called the Belgian Congo, 1908, and a colonial Charter set up its
basic structure of government.

The Congolese fought against Germany, 1916.  After World War I, the
territory of Ruanda-Urundi taken from Germany in 1916 was mandated to the
Belgian Congo administration.

1959, after Congolese riots for independence, the Belgian government outlined a program from self-rule.

June 30, 1960, independence was achieved, and Belgium assistance was pledged in the training of Congolese administrators.

Educational policies were developed by Belgians between 1892-1959.  In last years of Belgian administration, 3 types of schools:

> State schools
> State-aided independent mission schools meeting government
>     standards
> Unassisted mission or private schools

By 1957, state-aided independent schools (mainly Catholic) were educating more than 75% of all school children.  All elementary education free.

Up to 1957, separate schools for Europeans and for Africans.  System then changed:  former European schools became "schools of metropolitan type," accepting children of registered Congo citizens on same basis as European children.

2 higher educational institutions founded in last years of Belgian administration:  state-aided independent Catholic University of Lovanium (1954) near Léopoldville, and State University of the Belgian Congo and Ruanda-Urundi (1956) at Elizabethville (reorganized in 1960 as the State University of the Congo).

1958, Government set up a Plan d'Etudes to widen state education and reform the system.

1960, with independence, Government passed a law for large-scale reform to adapt education more to Congolese rather than European programs and methods, and to make education more widespread and more inclusive.

1960, U.N. commission founded a school of administration and law in Léopoldville for training Congolese senior administrators, magistrates, and judges.  1961, U.N. and UNESCO sent educational experts, recruited secondary and technical school teachers, and helped to establish the first institute for training secondary school teachers, the National Pedagogical Institute.

As of 1964, the largest number of primary and secondary school children receive their education in Catholic and Protestant government-subsidized schools.  The programs of these schools must conform exactly to government regulations.  Other private schools are Kimbanguiste government-subsidized schools and non-subsidized schools of any affiliation (diplomas of the latter are not recognized by the government).

PRESENT SYSTEM

PRE-PRIMARY EDUCATION

Kindergartens and nursery schools, privately owned.

Length of course:      from 1-3 years.  Mainly educational games.

PRIMARY EDUCATION

## B E F O R E   1 9 6 0   R E F O R M

Language of instruction:        Native idioms:  Lingala, Bapende, Kikongo,
                                Swahili, Tshiluba, or local dialects such
                                as Zande, Kirundi, Kinyaruanan.

3 divisions:

| | |
|---|---|
| 1st degree: | 1st and 2nd years. |
| 2nd degree: | 3rd and 4th years. |
| 3rd degree: | 5th year. |

5th year.
Students considered too old to enter secondary
education, ended their primary cycle and were
directed into trade schools for boys or home
economics schools for girls.

5th and 6th years (primaire ordinaire)
Students not too old after their 5th years completed
their 6 years of primary study.  In the urban schools,
training for trades or mechanical work; in rural
schools, training in agriculture, animal husbandry,
related subjects.  At the close of the 6 years,
students were directed into apprenticeship or professional schools.

5th and 6th years, and 6th year (primaire sélectionnée)
Students with academic aptitude who after 5th and 6th
years were not too old continued into the 6th year
(primaire sélectionnée), preparing for academic
secondary or technical courses.  The more gifted
students moved from the 5th year directly into the
6th year, sélectionnée.  Language of instruction:
French.

A F T E R   1 9 6 0   R E F O R M

GOVERNMENT AND GOVERNMENT-SUBSIDIZED SCHOOLS

Entry age:      At least 6 years, not older than 8 for boys and 9 for girls.

Language of instruction:      French.  The use of Congolese dialects in cases of necessity (i.e. on first entering school) is controlled by the government.

Length of primary education:      6 years divided into 3 sections of 2 years each:  degré élémentaire, degré moyen, degré terminal.

A single national program has replaced the former separate programs for Congolese, Metropolitan, Boys, Girls, Ordinary and Selected Schools, etc. Now, emphasis is laid on adapting the basic lessons to the milieu the child knows and understands.

Recommended hours per week to each subject:

| Subjects                         | Class | 1 | 2 | 3 | 4 | 5 | 6 |
|----------------------------------|-------|---|---|---|---|---|---|
| French                           |       | 9 | 9 | 8 | 8 | 7 | 7 |
| Arithmetic                       |       | 7 | 7 | 6 | 6 | 5½ | 5½ |
| Religious and Moral Institutions |       | 3 | 3 | 3 | 3 | 2½ | 2½ |
| History and Geography            |       | - | - | 2 | 2 | 3 | 3 |
| Civics                           |       | - | - | 1 | 1 | 1 | 1 |
| Study of Milieu and Observation  |       | 3 | 3 | 2 | 2 | - | - |
| Physical and Natural Sciences    |       | 3 | 3 | 2 | 2 | - | - |
| African Language and Traditions  |       | - | - | 1 | 1 | 1 | 1 |
| Manual Arts and Art              |       | 1 | 1 | 2 | 2 | 2 | 2 |
| Physical Education               |       | 1 | 1 | 1 | 1 | 1 | 1 |
| Singing                          |       | 1 | 1 | ½ | ½ | ½ | ½ |
| Recreation                       |       | 2½ | 2½ | 2½ | 2½ | 2½ | 2½ |
| Total                            |       | 30½ | 30½ | 31 | 31 | 26 | 26 |

Certificat d'études primaires  awarded at close of primary program.

Successful completion of examen sélectif (government selective examination given the same day in each province) required for entrance into secondary education.

SECONDARY EDUCATION

B E F O R E   1 9 6 0   R E F O R M

Separate schools offering régime congolais for Congolese and régime métropolitain for Europeans.  1958 reform raised Congolese standards to those
of the régime métropolitain.

Students completing primaire ordinaire access to:  post-primary schools
(teaching time shortened), école d'auxiliaires (school for clerical
assistants), école d'apprentissage pédagogique (student teachers' training
school), atelier d'apprentissage artisanal (trade apprenticeship school),
école ménagère post-primaire (post-primary home economics school).  Also
schools providing training for medical and veterinary assistants, agricultural instructors, etc.

Students completing primaire sélectionnée access to:  various branches of
general and special secondary education, schools for moniteurs, vocational
and technical schools for nurses and midwives, etc.


GENERAL SECONDARY SCHOOLS

From 1958 taught Classical and Modern Humanities at upper and lower levels.
Lower level the same for both sections.

Modern Humanities upper:

            (1)     Economics section
            (2)     Scientific section "A"
            (3)     Scientific section "B"

Classical Humanities upper:

            (1)     Latin-Greek section
            (2)     Latin-Science section
            (3)     Latin-Mathematics section.

Upon completion of Humanities upper and lower, Humanities Certificate
awarded, qualifying student for immediate admission to most university
faculties and schools, and other institutions at higher or post-secondary
level.

Entrance requirements:        Competitive examination on main subjects
                              taught during last year of primary studies.

Grading:  6, 5, or 4/10, according to importance of subject.  Also
          satisfactory average (5/10) for work as whole to be promoted.

Terminal examinations both written and oral.  Greater importance attached
to oral examinations in upper classes.

Examen de passage taken by students failing to pass particular subject,
before entering higher class.


SPECIAL SECONDARY SCHOOLS

On same level as general secondary schools.  Provide training for:
administrative assistants, clerks and typists, medical assistants, health
assistants, veterinary assistants, agricultural assistants, men and women
nurses, midwives, foresters, veterinary officials, health officials,
agricultural moniteurs (instructors), etc.

Language of instruction at all secondary levels:  French.


## A F T E R   1 9 6 0   R E F O R M

### GOVERNMENT AND GOVERNMENT-SUBSIDIZED SECONDARY SCHOOLS

Entrance requirements:      Competitive examination open to students
                            having passed the examination for the Certi-
                            ficat d'études primaires, and who are less
                            than 15 years of age on December 31 of
                            current year.  The examination consists
                            only of tests in French and Mathematics.

Language of instruction:    French.

Length of courses:    Cycle d'orientation - 2 years for all sections.

                      Enseignement professionnel (cycle court) - 2 or 3
                      years  (see under VOCATIONAL AND TECHNICAL EDUCATION).

                      Humanités (cycle long) - 4 years.

The unity of primary school education has been carried over into the 2
years of the cycle d'orientation of secondary education, with a program
common to all sections.  Furthermore, compulsory general subjects are
taught in addition to specialized subjects throughout secondary education.
These general subjects are:  Religion/Morals, French, History and Civics,
Geography, Mathematics, Sciences, Physical Education, African Sociology,
English (optional).


Cycle d'orientation - Curriculum:

School week:    Minimum of 31 hours, maximum of 34 hours.

Program divided into 3 groups:

     I.    French, Mathematics
    II.   History, Geography, Natural Sciences, Technology
   III.  Civics, English, Music, Art, Physical Education

To pass from 1st into 2nd year and to obtain the Brevet du cycle d'orientation, a minimum of 50% of the total marks in each group must be gained. For the brevet the total of both years is taken into account. Religion/Morals is non-examinable.

TIMETABLE
(Hours per week)

| Subjects | 1st year | 2nd year |
|---|---|---|
| Religion/Morals | 2 | 2 |
| Civics | 1 | 1 |
| French | 10 | 8 |
| English | - | 0+ |
| History | 2 | 3 |
| Geography | 2 | 2 |
| Mathematics | 7+ | 6 |
| Natural Sciences | 2 | 2 |
| Technology | 1 | 3+ |
| Physical Education | 2+ | 2+ |
| Music | 0+ | 0+ |
| Art | 2 | 2 |

+ An hour may be added weekly if required.

Classes progressives:     Students whose knowledge of French is not very good, or who are slower learners are regrouped in classes progressives, either after the secondary entrance examination, or during the first semester of the cycle d'orientation. 3-year program, instead of the 2-year program of the cycle d'orientation. At the end, Brevet du cycle d'orientation is taken.

Humanités (long cycle) - Curriculum:

4-year program. Student may pass on to a profession through the Institution Nationale de Préparation Professionnelle, or on to higher education.

Humanities diploma awarded in the special sections after 4 years.

## TIMETABLE
(Hours per week)

Science Section:   (a) Mathematics-Physics   (b)  Chemistry-Biology

| Subjects | Class | 3 | 4 | 5 | 6 |
|---|---|---|---|---|---|
| Religion/Morals | | 2 | 2 | 2 | 2 |
| French | | 5 | 5 | 5 | 5 |
| History | | 2 | 2 | 2 | 2 |
| Geography | | 2 | 2 | 2 | 2 |
| Physical Education | | 2 | 2 | 2 | 2 |
| Political Economics | | - | 2 | - | - |
| African Sociology | | 2 | - | - | - |
| Aesthetics | | - | - | 2 | - |
| Philosophy | | - | - | - | 2 |
| English | | 5 | 5 | 5 | 5 |
| Mathematics | | 6 | 6 | (a)7+ (b)4+ | (a)7+ (b)4+ |
| Art/Design | | 1 | 1 | 1 | 1 |
| Physics | | 3 | 2 | 3 | 3 |
| Chemistry | | 2 | 2 | 1½ | 1½ |
| Biology | | - | 1 | (a)1 (b)2½ | (a)1 (b)2½ |

Literary Section

| Subjects | Class | 3 | 4 | 5 | 6 |
|---|---|---|---|---|---|
| Religion/Morals | | 2 | 2 | 2 | 2 |
| French | | 5 | 5 | 5 | 5 |
| History | | 2 | 2 | 2 | 2 |
| Geography | | 2 | 2 | 2 | 2 |
| Physical Education | | 2 | 2 | 2 | 2 |
| Political Economics | | - | 2 | - | - |
| African Sociology | | 2 | - | - | - |
| Aesthetics | | - | - | 2 | - |
| Philosophy | | - | - | - | 2 |
| English | | 5 | 5 | 5 | 5 |
| Mathematics | | 4 | 4 | 2 | 2 |
| Latin | | 6 | 6 | 7 | 6 |
| Greek (optional) | | 4 | 4 | 4 | 4 |
| Physics | | 1 | 1 | 2 | 2 |
| Chemistry | | 1 | 1 | 1 | - |
| Biology | | - | - | 1 | 1 |

If the 4-hour optional Greek course is taken, the 2 hours of African
Sociology, Political Economics, Aesthetics or Philosophy, may be
omitted.

## Pedagogical Section

Short or long cycle.  Any student may finish after 4 years' secondary studies and do 1 additional year of purely pedagogical training.

Brevet d'instituteur awarded after 4 years, Diplôme d'instituteur awarded after 6 years.  Instituteurs then teach in primary schools.

| Subjects | Class | 3 | 4 | 5 | 6 |
|---|---|---|---|---|---|
| Religion/Morals | | 2 | 2 | 2 | 2 |
| French | | 6 | 6 | 6 | 6 |
| English | | 5 | 5 | 5 | 5 |
| History | | 2 | 2 | 2 | 2 |
| Geography | | 2 | 2 | 2 | 2 |
| African Sociology | | 2 | - | - | - |
| Political Economics | | - | 2 | - | - |
| Aesthetics | | - | - | 2 | - |
| Philosophy | | - | - | - | 2 |
| Mathematics | | 5 | 5 | 2 | 2 |
| Physics | | 3 | 2 | 2 | 2 |
| Chemistry | | 2 | 2 | - | - |
| Biology/Hygiene | | - | 1 | 1 | 1 |
| Physical Education | | 2 | 2 | 2 | 2 |
| Art/Manual Work/Writing | | 2 | 2 | 2 | 2 |
| Music/Singing/Choral/Theatre | | 1 | 1 | - | 1 |
| Pedagogical Training | | - | 1 | 7 | 7 |

## Commercial and Administrative Section

| Subjects | Class | 3 | 4 | 5 | 6 |
|---|---|---|---|---|---|
| Religion/Morals/Civics | | 2 | 2 | 2 | 2 |
| French | | 6 | 5 | 5 | 5 |
| English | | 4 | 4 | 4 | 4 |
| History | | 1 | 1 | 1 | 1 |
| Geography | | 2 | 2 | 2 | 2 |
| Political Economics | | - | 1 | 1 | 1 |
| African Sociology | | - | - | 1 | 1 |
| Mathematics | | 6 | 3 | 3 | 3 |
| Physics | | 1 | 2 | 1 | 1 |
| Chemistry | | 1 | 1 | 2 | 1 |
| Physical Education | | 1 | 1 | 1 | 1 |
| Commercial Techniques | | 2 | 2 | - | - |
| Accountancy | | 3 | 3 | 3 | 3 |
| Commercial Arithmetic | | 1 | 1 | 1 | - |
| French Correspondence | | - | 1 | 1 | 1 |
| English Correspondence | | - | - | 1 | 1 |
| Merchandising | | - | - | - | 1 |

| | | | | |
|---|---|---|---|---|
| Law | - | 1 | 1 | 1 |
| Complementary Activities | - | 1 | 1 | 1 |
| Business Organization | - | - | - | 2 |
| Shorthand-Typing | 4 | 2 | 2 | 2 |

Technical and Agricultural Sections:   See VOCATIONAL AND TECHNICAL
                                        EDUCATION


Diplôme d'humanités (modernes, scientifiques, greco-latines, etc.)
awarded by schools at close of secondary programs.

**Students judged most capable of continuing into higher studies receive a
   Certificat homologué d'humanités from the government.  To receive this
   diploma, the head of a school sends all of the student's academic documents, notebooks, and examinations to a jury d'homologation, composed of
   an equal number of professors in government schools (Enseignement Officiel)
   and Catholic and Protestant schools (Enseignement Libre).  From these
   records, the jury decides the student's capabilities.  A Certificat homologué, admitting to the university, indicates the faculties accessible to
   the student.

Students who have failed to receive a Certificat homologué, or who have
pursued secondary studies without going to school, may take "eliminatory"
examinations offered by the government on the same day in each province.
Those who are successful take an oral examination and receive from the
administration a titre de voyage.  This entitles them to present themselves in the capital (once a year, all expenses paid by the government)
to take an examination covering material of the full 6 years of secondary
training.  This examination, corrected by a government Central Jury (Jury
Central), successfully completed, admits to the university.


HIGHER EDUCATION

INSTITUTIONS:

| | |
|---|---|
| Université Lovanium, Léopoldville | (Catholic) |
| Université Officielle du Congo, Elisabethville | (State) |
| Université Libre du Congo, Léopoldville and Stanleyville | (Protestant) |
| Institut National d'Etudes Politiques, Léopoldville (Ecole Technique Supérieure) | (State) |
| Institut Supérieur de Commerce (Ecole Technique Supérieure) | (Graduate) |

Institut National du Bâtiment et des Travaux                   (State)
Publics, Léopoldville (Ecole Technique Supérieure)

Institut Supérieur des Mines, Bukavu                          (State)
(Ecole Technique Supérieure)

Institut Supérieur d'Architecture, Léopoldville              (State)
(Ecole Technique Supérieure)

Institut National de Navigation et de Pêche,                  (State)
Moanda (Ecole Technique Supérieure)

Institut Congolais d'Enseignement Social,                     (Catholic)
Léopoldville (Ecole Technique Supérieure)

Institut Pédagogique National, Léopoldville                   (State)

Ecole Supérieure Pédagogique, Boma                           (Catholic)
(Régence Scientifique de Boma)

Ecole Supérieure Pédagogique, Bukavu                         (Catholic)
(Régence de Bukavu)

Ecole Supérieure Pédagogique, Bukavu                         (Catholic)
(Régence Sacré-Coeur Littéraire)

Ecole Supérieure Pédagogique, Elisabethville                 (Catholic)
(Régence d'Elisabethville)

Four higher institutes function equally, without depending directly upon
the National Ministry of Education:

Institut d'Enseignement Médical, Léopoldville

Ecole Nationale des Télécommunications, Léopoldville

Institut d'Aviation Civile, Léopoldville

Ecole Nationale de Droit et d'Administration,                (State)
Léopoldville


## UNIVERSITY OF LOVANIUM, Léopoldville

Began as Medical Foundation and Agricultural Center in 1925, founded by
the University of Louvain in Belgium.  1949, created as Lovanium, the
Congolese University Center.  February 3, 1956, given the title of
University.

Academic year:   2 semesters, normally totalling 30 weeks of instruction.
                 Begins the last Tuesday of October and finishes the last
                 Saturday in June.
                 2 examination sessions.

Faculties:

|                          |                              |
|--------------------------|------------------------------|
| Theology                 | Political and Social Sciences |
| Law                      | and Economics                 |
| Medicine                 | Polytechnical                 |
| Philosophy and Letters   | Agriculture                   |
| Science                  |                               |

Sections - Propédeutique:

Institute of Psychology and Pedagogy
Institute of Economics and Social Research (IRES)
Centre for Studies on Comparative African Law (CEDCA)
Centre for Studies on Roman Literature of African Inspiration
School for Nurses

Entrance requirements:          See under each Faculty.


Section Propédeutique

Conducts the entrance examinations of the Central Jury for entry to the
candidature of Philosophy and Letters, of Agricultural Engineering, of
Commercial Sciences, etc., and to the Polytechnical Faculty.


Faculty of Theology

Entrance requirements:          Diploma of 6 years' secondary schooling,
                                plus certificate of completion of philo-
                                sophical studies and 3 years theological
                                studies in a seminary.


Baccalauréat en théologie

Duration of course:    2 years.

Premier baccalauréat:           General Dogmatic Theology, Specialized Dogmatic
    1st year                    Theology, General Moral Theology, Specialized
                                Moral Theology, Moral Theology - Apostolic Prob-
                                lems and Methods, Introduction to Ecclesiastical
                                History, Ecclesiastical History, Latin Christian
                                Literature of the IVth and Vth Centuries,
                                Biblical Psalter, New Testament, Biblical Greek,
                                Hebrew, Ascetic and Mystic Theology, Public
                                Church Law, Scholastic exercises, Criticism of
                                degree dissertations.

Deuxième baccalauréat:          Same subjects as for the 1st year.
    2nd year

## Licence en théologie

Duration of course:    2 years.

Première licence:       General courses:
   1st year             Dogmatic Theology, Moral Theology, Old Testament,
                        New Testament, Ecclesiastical History, Liturgy,
                        Pastoral Theology.

                        Special courses - Biblical:
                        Old Testament, History of the Chosen People, New
                        Testament, Biblical Theology of the Old Testament,
                        Biblical Theology of the New Testament, Greek,
                        Hebrew, Aramaic.

                        Special courses - Dogma:
                        Fundamental Dogmatic Theology, Specialized Dogmatic
                        Theology, Biblical Theology of the New Testament,
                        Temporal History of the New Testament, Patrology and
                        Dogmatic History, Religious Philosophy, Religious
                        History, History of Modern Philosophy.

                        Special courses - Moral and Canonical:
                        Fundamental Moral Theology, Specialized Moral Theo-
                        logy, Canonical Legal Institutions, Moral, Social
                        and Legal Institutions in the Congo and Africa,
                        Philosophical and Social Psychology, Liturgy.

Deuxième licence:       General and special courses as for the première
   2nd year             licence.  Also orals on these courses and on the
                        body of Theology, and a thesis on an approved subject.

## Doctorat en théologie

Duration of course:    1 year.

10 courses, each of 30 hours.

Final examination comprises:

   (1)   Orals on chosen courses.
   (2)   Presentation and formal defense of a typed thesis.
   (3)   Public defense of twenty additional theses.

Title of Doctor in Theology is not granted until at least a part of the
thesis has been published.

## Higher Institute of Religious Sciences

Presents several series of conferences given by the professors of the
Faculty of Theology.

## Faculty of Law

Entrance requirements:   (1)  Baccalauréat diploma in Philosophy and
Letters preparatory for Law.
(2)  Diploma of first candidature in Philosophy
and Letters.
(3)  Diploma of first candidature in Political,
Social and Economic Sciences, provided the
candidate has a recognized diploma showing
he is eligible for the examinations in
Philosophy and Letters.

(2) and (3) only applicable until January 1, 1962.

## Licence en droit

Duration of course:   2 years.

Première licence:
1st year

Introduction to the Study of Law (45h.), Fundamental
Principles of Private Law (30h.), Common Law and
Institutions (45h.), Civil Law (90h.), Public Law
and Political Institutions (90h.), Penal Law and
Ideas of Criminology (135h.), Judicial Law and
Judicial Institutions (30h.), Financial Law and
Financial Institutions (45h.), Elements of Accountan-
cy (15h.), Political Economics (60h.).

Deuxième licence:
2nd year

Civil Law (195h.), Administrative Law and Administrative Institutions (90h.), Fiscal Law and Fiscal
Techniques (90h.), Judicial Law and Judicial Institutions (45h.), Public International Law and International Institutions (45h.), Common Law and Institutions (45h.), Industrial Law and Social Security
(45h.), Introduction to the Principal Contemporary
Juridical Systems (45h.), Financial Law and
Financial Institutions (45h.), Elements of Accountancy (15h.), Logic (45h.).

## Doctorat en droit

Deuxième doctorat:

Civil Law (150h.), Administrative Law (90h.),
People's Law (45h.), Fiscal Law and Fiscal Tech-
niques (90h.), Social Law (45h.), Common Law (45h.),
Church and State (30h.), Ideas on the Principal
Contemporary Juridical Systems (45h.).

Troisième doctorat:

Questions on Religious Sciences and Moral Philosophy
(30h.), Commercial Law (105h.), Private International
Law (45h.), Fiscal Law and Fiscal Techniques (90h.),

Ideas on the Principal Contemporary Juridical
Systems (45h.), Social Law (45h.), Deontology
(15h.), Common Law (30h.).

Also 3 optional subjects to be chosen from:

Insurance (45h.), Industrial and Mining Legislation
(45h.), Maritime and Fluvial Law (45h.), History of
Law (45h.), Political and Administrative Structures
and Institutions (45h.), Public Finance (45h.),
General Theory of Public Administration (45h.),
Comparative and Extensive Penal Law (45h.), Notions
of Criminology (45h.), Social Psychology (45h.),
Business Financial Organization (45h.), Special
Questions on Common Law (45h.), Social Anthropology
(45h.), Special Questions on Social Anthropology
(45h.).

All these courses can be taken in either the
deuxième or the troisième doctorat.

Courses only to be taken in the troisième doctorat:

Comparative Civil Law (45h.), Comparative Commercial
Law (45h.), International Structures and Institutions (30h.).

Also presentation and public defense of a thesis on an approved subject.

## Faculty of Medicine

Entrance requirements:  (1)  Recognized Humanities diploma in Greek-Latin,
                              Latin-Mathematics, or Latin-Science.
                    or  (2)  Special certificate or diploma given by a
                              central jury who decides upon academic
                              standards.

## Candidature en sciences naturelles et médicales

Duration of course:    3 years.

Première candidature:   See program of the Faculty of Science.

Deuxième candidature:   Ideas of Philosophy (Psychology) - (45h.),
                        Experimental Physics (75h.), Elements of Embryo-
                        logy (15h.), Human Anatomy (90h.), Anatomy
                        Demonstrations (60h.), General and Special Histo-
                        logy (90h.), Practicals in Histology (75h.),
                        General Experimental Physiology (75h.), Practicals
                        in Physiology (60h.), Physiological Chemistry
                        (60h.), Practicals in Physiological Chemistry

| | |
|---|---|
| | (75h.), Medical Entomology (30h.), Practicals in Medical Entomology (45h.). |
| Troisième candidature: | Moral Philosophy (30h.), Human and Comparative Anatomy (105h.), Topographical Human Anatomy (15h.), Anatomy demonstrations (90h.), Special Experimental and Comparative Physiology (120h.), Practicals in Physiology (90h.), Elements of Embryology (30h.), Physiological Chemistry (60h.), Practicals in Phys. Chemistry (75h.), Helminthology (30h.), Practicals in Helminthology (30h.), Elements of Mineralogy, Geology, Physical Geography (45h.). |

## Doctorat en médecine

Duration of course:   4 years.

Admittance with <u>Candidature en sciences naturelles et médicales</u>.

| | |
|---|---|
| Premier doctorat: | Physiopathology and General Therapeutics (45h.), Pharmacology and Pharmacodynamics (45h.), Pathological Anatomy (90h.) and practicals (60h.), Pathology and Special Therapeutics of Internal Illnesses (75h.), Pathology and General Surgical Therapeutics (30h.), Pathology and Special Surgical Therapeutics (60h.), Basic Principles of Surgery and Radiodiagnostic of Surgical Affections (15h.), Bacteriology, Virology and Parasitology (60h.) and practicals (60h.), Protozoology (30h.) and practicals (30h.), Basic Medical Principles and Elements of Radiodiagnostic of Internal Affections (120h.) and practicals (30h.), Clinical Medicine (45h.), Clinical Surgery (90h.), Autopsies (60h.). |
| Deuxième doctorat: | Clinical Medicine (90h.), Clinical Surgery (90h.), Pathology and Special Therapeutics of Internal Illnesses (15h.), Tropical Pathology (60h.), Clinical Tropical Medicine (60h.), Pathology and Special Surgical Therapeutics (60h.), Theory of Obstetrics (60h.), Clinical Obstetrics (30h.), Elements of Neurology (30h.), Clinical Neurology (30h.), Pharmacodynamics (45h.) and practicals (30h.), Exercises in Basic Medical Principles (45h.), Exercises in Basic Surgical Principles (40h.). |
| Troisième doctorat: | Questions of Religious Sciences (15h.), Special Questions on Moral Philosophy (15h.), Clinical Medicine (90h.), Clinical Surgery (90h.), Clinical |

Obstetrics (30h.), Elements of Gynaecology (25h.), Clinical Gynaecology (30h.), Policlinical Gynaecology (-h.), Elements of Pediatrics (30h.), Clinical Pediatrics (45h.), Policlinical Pediatrics (-h.), Elements of Ophthalmology and Clinical Ophthalmology (45h.), Policlinical Ophthalmology (-h.), Elements of and Clinical Oto-Rhino-Laryngology (30h.), Policlinical Oto-Rhino-Laryngology (15h.), Elements of and Clinical Dermatology (30h.), Policlinical Dermatology (-h.), Elements of and Clinical Psychiatry (45h.), Exercises in Radio-diagnostics (-h.), Theory and practice of Surgical Operations (60h.), Elements of Stomatology (15h.), Clinical Stomatology (120h.), Exercises in medical laboratory work (15h.).

Quatrième doctorat:    Deontology (15h.), Hygiene (15h.), Legal Medicine (15h.), Physiotherapy (15h.), Instruction in the different clinics:  medical, surgical, gynaecological, obstetrical, pediatric (full time).

Before taking the quatrième doctorat it is necessary to spend at least 12 months working in the clinics.

Specialist diplomas:   Internal Medicine              - full time 4 yrs.
                       Surgery                        - full time 4 yrs.
                       Gynaecology and Obstetrics     - full time 4 yrs.

At least half the specialist work must be done at Lovanium.  Final examination comprises oral presentation of research contained in candidate's thesis, theoretical examination, and clinical cases.

No specialist diploma may be given less than 3 years after the doctorat.


Licence en science dentaire (Dental Science)

Duration of course:    2 years.

Admittance with Candidature en sciences naturelles et médicales.

Première licence:      Physiopathology and General Therapeutics (45h.), General Surgical Pathology (30h.), Pathological Anatomy (90h.) and practicals (60h.), Pharmacology and Pharmacodynamics (45h.), Bacteriology, Virology and Parasitology (60h.) and practicals (60h.), Comparative Morphology and Microscopic Anatomy of the Dental System (15h.), Practicals in Dental Anatomy (60h.), Operative Dentistry (15h.), Prosthetics (60h.), Practicals in Operative Dentistry and Prosthetics (60h.), Pathology and Dental Therapeutics (15h.), Clinical Stomatology (270h.).

<u>Deuxième licence:</u>      Questions of Religious Science, or special questions
                          on Moral Philosophy (15h.), Pharmacodynamics (45h.)
                          and practicals (60h.), Pathology and Dental Thera-
                          peutics and Ideas of Internal Pathology (45h.),
                          Orthodonty (30h.), Clinical Operative Dentistry
                          (270h.), Practical exercises in Prosthetics and
                          Orthodonty (120h.), Professional Deontology (15h.).


## Certificat de médecine tropicale

Duration of course:    1 year.

Admittance with <u>Doctorat en médecine</u>.

Program:   Medical Entomology (30h.) and practicals (30h.), Helminthology
           (30h.) and practicals (30h.), Further Bacteriology (15h.),
           Protozoology (30h.) and practicals (30h.), Tropical Pathology
           (30h.), Hematology (15h.) and practicals (15h.), Tropical
           Hygiene (30h.), Clinical Tropical Medicine (15h.).


## Graduat en pharmacie

Admittance with recognized secondary diploma, medical assistant diploma,
or by entrance examination.

Program:   Philosophy (30h.), Botany (60h.) and practicals (120h.),
           Physics (60h.) and practicals (60h.), General Chemistry (90h.)
           and laboratory work (40h.), Analytical Chemistry (60h.) and
           laboratory work (120h.), Human Organisms (60h.), Mathematics
           (67.5h.) and practicals (15h.), French (60h.) and practicals
           (30h.).


## School of Nursing

    Entrance requirements:   3 years secondary, or 4 years post-primary,
                             plus entrance examination.

    3-year course including at least 26 months' practical hospital work.
    Examination at the end of each year, with a final diploma.

    Courses include Tropical Medicine, Microbiology and Parasitology.
    Practical hospital and clinic work in contagious, mental and internal
    illnesses, Surgery, Obstetrics, Pediatrics, and specialist work in
    Oto-Rhino-Laryngology, Dermatology, study of Leprosy, Urology,
    Ophthalmology, Dental Hygiene, Radiography.

## Faculty of Philosophy and Letters

### Baccalauréat en philosophie et lettres

Preparatory for Licence en droit.

Admittance with recognized Humanities diploma in Greek-Latin, or with special certificate or diploma awarded by central jury.

Program:  Metaphysical Philosophy (45h.), Logic (45h.), Ethics (45h.),
1 yr.    Philosophy-Psychology (45h.), Great Streams of Thought (45h.),
         Sociology and Demography (30h.), Principles of Historical
         Criticism (30h.), View of Human History to the Present (90h.),
         Contemporary History (60h.), Grand Movements of Literature and
         Art (90h.), Political Economics (75h.), English Language
         (optional).

### Candidature en philosophie et lettres

Admittance with recognized Humanities diploma in Greek-Latin, or with special certificate or diploma awarded by central jury.

African Philology:

| | |
|---|---|
| Duration of course: | 2 years. |
| Première candidature: | Metaphysics (45h.), Moral Philosophy (45h.), Philosophy-Psychology (45h.), Great Works of Universal Literature (60h.), Commentaries on Great Works (optional 30h.), History of Civilization (60h.), History of Civilization II (15h.), History of Art and Archaeology (30h.), Phonetics and Phonology (15h.), Introduction to African Linguistics (30h.), First African language - Bantu (90h.). |
| Deuxième candidature: | Logic (45h.), History of Africa, particularly Congo, Rwanda, Burundi (15h.), History of Principal Modern Literatures (30h.), Contemporary History (60h.), Principles of Historical Criticism (30h.), African Literature (45h.), African Societies and Institutions (60h.), Problems and methods of Cultural Anthropology (30h.), Problems and methods of African Philology (15h.), General Linguistics and application to African Language (15h.), Second African Language - Bantu (90h.). |

Romance Philology:

    Duration of course:      2 years.

    <u>Première candidature</u>:    Metaphysics (45h.), Philosophy-Psychology (45h.), Societies and Institutions of Classical Antiquity (30h.), Societies and Institutions of the Middle Ages (30h.), Societies and Institutions of Modern Times (30h.), Explication and translation of a Latin author (30h.), History of Art and Archaeology (30h.), History of French Literature (45h.), History of Principal Modern Literatures (30h.), French Literature (15h.), Explication of French authors (60h.), French Historical Grammar (30h.), Contemporary French Grammar (30h.), Phonetics and Philology (15h.), Romance Philology (60h.), Philological exercises (90h.).

    <u>Deuxième candidature</u>:    Moral Philosophy (45h.), Logic (45h.), Psychology (30h.), History of Africa (15h.), Principles of Historical Criticism (30h.), Contemporary History (60h.), African Society (60h.), African Literature (15h.), History of French Literature (45h.), History of Principal Modern Literatures (30h.), Explication of French authors (60h.), Explication and translation of a Latin author (30h.), Historical French Grammar (30h.), Romance Philology (60h.), Philological exercises (90h.), Belgian History (optional).

Classical Philology:

    Duration of course:      1 year.

    <u>Première candidature</u>:    Metaphysics (45h.), Psychology (45h.), Society and Institutions of Classical Antiquity (45h.), Society and Institutions of the Middle Ages (30h.), Society and Institutions of Modern Times (30h.), Explication and translation of a Latin author (30h.), Translation of a Latin text (30h.), History of Art and Archaeology (30h.), History of French Literature (45h.), History of Principal Modern Literatures (30h.), Explication of a Greek author (30h.), Translation of a Greek author (30h.),

Classical Philology (15h.), Philological
exercises in Greek (30h.), Philological
exercises in Latin (30h.), Classical
Philology (15h.).

English Philology:

    Duration of course:    1 year.

    Première candidature:    Metaphysics (45h.), Psychology (45h.),
Society and Institutions of the Middle Ages
(30h.), Society and Institutions of Modern
Times (30h.), History of Art and Archaeology
(30h.), History of Principal Modern Literatures (30h.), African Literatures (15h.),
History of English Literature (60h.), Translation and explication of English authors
(60h.), English Phonetics and Phonology
(60h.), English Philological exercises (30h.).

## Licence en philologie africaine

Duration of course:    2 years.

Admittance with Candidature en philosophie et lettres.

    Première licence:    Compulsory subjects:
History of Modern Philosophy (30h.), General
Cultural Anthropology (60h.), Systems of Social
Relations in Africa (-h.), African Religions and
Philosophies (30h.), Dialectology applied to African
Languages (30h.), Grammar of Bantu Linguistic
Groups (60h.), African Historical Linguistics (15h.),
Practical exercises in Linguistic Research (15h.),
Third African Language (non-Bantu) - (90h.).

    Optional subjects (at least 2 of the following):
Social Psychology (30h.), Arts and Technology of
Africa (30h.), Cultural Dynamics (30h.), African
Common Law (45h.), Indo-European Grammar (30h.),
General Aesthetics (30h.), History of Music (15h.),
Applied Historical Criticism (30h.).

    One subject chosen either from this Faculty or
another approved by jury.

    Deuxième licence:    Compulsory subjects:
Religious Sciences or Moral Philosophy (15h.),
Study of 1 African Oral Literature (30h.), Sociology
of Language (15h.), Comparative Grammar of non-Bantu
African Linguistic Groups (30h.), General Linguistics

and Descriptive African Linguistics (30h.), Practical exercises in Linguistic Research (15h.), Third African Language (non-Bantu) - (90h.).

Optional subjects (at least 2 of the following): Social Psychology (30h.), Arts and Technology of Africa (-h.), Cultural Dynamics (30h.), African Common Law (45h.), Indo-European Grammar (30h.), General Aesthetics (30h.), History of Music (15h.), Applied Historical Criticism (30h.).

One subject chosen either from this Faculty or another approved by the jury and not already taken in examination.

Presentation and public defense of thesis on approved subject.

## Licence en philologie romane

Duration of course:     2 years.

Admittance with Candidature en philosophie et lettres.

**Première licence:**     One Latin author (15h.), Comparative Grammar of Indo-European and Romance Language (30h.), History of Modern Literatures (60h.), History of Romance Literatures - Middle Ages (45h.), Modern Times (45h.), Mediterranean (30h.), Historical French Grammar (60h.), Interpretation of French Texts of Classical and Middle Ages (30h.), Modern French authors (45h.), History of Modern Philosophy (30h.), History of Mediaeval Philosophy (15h.), Seminar work (2h. per month).

**Deuxième licence:**     Religious Sciences or Moral Philosophy (15h.), One Latin author (15h.), Comparative Grammar of Indo-European and Romance Languages (60h.), History of Modern Literatures (60h.), History of Romance Literatures - Middle Ages (45h.), Modern Times (45h.), Mediterranean (30h.), Historical French Grammar (60h.), Interpretation of French Texts of Classical and Middle Ages (30h.), Modern French authors (45h.), History of Modern Philosophy (30h.), Seminar work (2h. per month).

Also at least 2 subjects chosen from the following: Mediaeval and Vulgar Latin (30h.), Applied Historical Criticism (30h.), Methods of Modern Dialectology (30h.), General Aesthetics (30h.), French Phonetics and Orthography (-h.), General Linguistics (15h.).

One subject chosen from this Faculty or from another
Faculty and approved by the jury and not already
taken in examination.

A thesis.


## Faculty of Science

### Candidature en sciences

Duration of course:    2 years.

Entrance requirements:

Biology, Chemistry, Geology and Mineralogy,
Geography, Pharmacy:
Recognized Humanities diploma in Greek-Latin,
Latin-Math., or Latin-Sciences
or   Certificate or diploma from Central Jury.

Mathematics or Physics:
Recognized Humanities diploma in Latin-Math.,
or Modern Science
or   Diploma from Central Jury
or   Certificate from the University testifying
that the candidate has passed the examination
for entrance to the Polytechnical Faculty.

Agricultural Engineering:
Recognized Humanities diploma in Greek-Latin,
Latin-Math., Latin-Science, or Modern Science
or   Certificate or diploma from the Central Jury
or   Certificate from the University testifying
that the candidate has passed the examination
for entrance to the Polytechnical Faculty.
Candidates with an agricultural assistant
diploma or an agronomy technician diploma may
also apply to the Central Jury.

Civil Engineering:
Admission examination to the Polytechnical
Faculty.

Sciences naturelles et médicales. Sciences biologiques, chimiques, géologiques et minéralogiques, et géographiques.  Pharmacie.  Ingénieur
Agronome:

Première candidature:    Philosophy (Logic)-(30h.), Experimental
Physics (90h.) and exercises (45h.), General
Biology-Zoology (90h.) and exercises (45h.),
General Biology-Botany (90h.) and exercises
(45h.), General Chemistry (90h.) and exer-
cises (60h.).

For candidates in Biology, Chemistry, Geology and Mineralogy, Geography, and Agricultural Engineering:  Theoretical and
Applied Mathematics (60h.) and exercises
(45h.).

For candidates in Natural Sciences, Medicine,
and Pharmacy:  Math. applied to Biology
(60h.) and exercises (45h.).

Sciences biologiques:

    Deuxième candidature:    Philosophy-Psychology (45h.), Moral Philo-
sophy (30h.), Experimental Physics (45h.)
and exercises (45h.), Theoretical and Applied
Mathematics (37.5h.) and exercises (45h.),
Statistics (Theoretical and Applied Math.)
-(-h.), Mineralogy, Geology and Physical Geography (45h.) and exercises (45h.), General
Chemistry (60h.) and exercises (60h.), Zoology (30h.), Botany (45h.) and exercises
(30h.).

Sciences chimiques, géologiques et minéralogiques:

    Deuxième candidature:    Philosophy-Psychology (45h.), Moral Philo-
sophy (30h.), Experimental Physics (45h.),
and exercises (45h.), Theoretical and Applied
Mathematics (37.5h.) and exercises (45h.),
General Chemistry (60h.) and exercises (60h.),
Crystallography (30h.) and exercises (22.5h.),
Analytical Mechanics and Theoretical Physics
(30h.) and exercises (30h.), Physical Chemis-
try (30h.), Mineralogy, Geology and Physical
Geography (45h.) and exercises (45h.).

Pharmacie:

    Deuxième candidature:    Philosophy-Psychology (45h.), Moral Philo-
sophy (30h.), Experimental Physics (45h.)
and exercises (45h.), General Chemistry
(60h.) and exercises (60h.), Botany (45h.),
Zoology (30h.), Physiology (30h.).

Ingénieur agronome:

    Deuxième candidature:    Experimental Physics (45h.) and exercises
(45h.), Theoretical and Applied Mathematics
(37.5h.) and exercises (45h.), General
chemistry (60h.) and exercises (60h.),
Botany (45h.) and exercises (30h.), Mineralogy, Geology and Physical Geography (45h.)

and exercises (45h.), Zoology (30h.),
Mechanics (30h.).

Sciences mathématiques:

   Première candidature:          Philosophy (Logic)-(30h.), Infinitesimal
                                  Analysis (60h.) and exercises (60h.),
                                  Analytical Mechanics (30h.) and exercises
                                  (30h.), Principles of Projective Geometry
                                  (30h.), Principles of Descriptive Geometry
                                  (22.5h.), Algebraic Analysis (60h.) and
                                  exercises (45h.), General Physics (60h.),
                                  General Chemistry (45h.) and exercises
                                  (45h.), Numerical Analysis (30h.) and
                                  exercises (30h.).

   Deuxième candidature:          Infinitesimal Analysis (60h.) and exercises
                                  (15h.), Algebraic Analysis (15h.) and
                                  exercises (15h.), Analytical Mechanics
                                  (45h.) and exercises (37.5h.), Mathematical
                                  Physics (30h.) and exercises (15h.),General
                                  Physics (90h.) and exercises (90h.), Comple-
                                  ments of Infinitesimal Analysis (30h.) and
                                  exercises (15h.), Complements of Algebraic
                                  Analysis (30h.).

Sciences physiques:

   Première candidature:          Philosophy-Logic (30h.), Infinitesimal
                                  Analysis (60h.) and exercises (60h.),
                                  Algebraic Analysis (60h.) and exercises
                                  (45h.), Analytical Mechanics (30h.) and
                                  exercises (30h.), Principles of Descriptive
                                  Geometry (22.5h.), General Physics (60h.),
                                  General Chemistry (45h.) and exercises
                                  (45h.), Numerical Analysis (30h.) and
                                  exercises (30h.).

   Deuxième candidature:          Infinitesimal Analysis (60h.) and exercises
                                  (15h.), Analytical Mechanics (45h.) and
                                  exercises (37.5h.), Mathematical Physics
                                  (30h.) and exercises (15h.), General Physics
                                  (90h.) and exercises (90h.), Complements of
                                  Infinitesimal Analysis (30h.) and exercises
                                  (15h.), Algebraic Analysis (15h.) and exer-
                                  cises (15h.), Complements of Algebraic
                                  Analysis (30h.), General Chemistry (45h.)
                                  and exercises (45h.), Crystallography (30h.)
                                  and exercises (22.5h.), Physics seminar
                                  (30h.).

Ingénieur civil:

Première candidature:   Infinitesimal Analysis (60h.) and exercises
(60h.), Algebraic Analysis (60h.) and
exercises (45h.), Analytical Mechanics
(30h.) and exercises (30h.), Descriptive
Geometry (22.5h.), General Physics (60h.),
General Chemistry (45h.) and exercises
(45h.), Numerical Analysis and exercises
(30h.), Diagrams (45h.).

Deuxième candidature:   Infinitesimal Analysis (60h.) and exercises
(15h.), Algebraic Analysis (15h.) and
exercises (15h.), Analytical Mechanics
(45h.) and exercises (37.5h.), Mathematical
Physics (30h.) and exercises (15h.), General
Physics (90h.) and exercises (90h.), Graphstatistics (37.5h.), Complements of Mechanics
(15h.), General Chemistry (45h.) and exercises (45h.), Calculus of Probabilities and
Statistical Analysis (30h.) and exercises
(15h.), Diagrams (90h.).


Licence en sciences

Duration of course:   2 years with Candidature.

Sciences zoologiques:

Première licence:   Animal Morphology (60h.) and exercises (60h.),
Anatomy and Embryology (150h.) and exercises
(180h.), Animal Physiology (120h.) and exercises
(180h.), Animal Ecology (45h.), Systematic Zoology (90h.) and exercises (90h.), Zoopaleontology (30h.) and exercises (90h.), General
Genetics (15h.), Physiological Chemistry (60h.)
and exercises (90h.), Comparative Biochemistry
(90h.), Anthropology (15h.), Human Paleontology
(15h.), Statistics and exercises (60h.).

Deuxième licence:   Religious Sciences or Moral Philosophy (15h.),
Animal Morphology (30h.) and exercises (30h.),
Anatomy and Embryology (75h.) and exercises
(90h.), Animal Physiology (60h.) and exercises
(90h.), Animal Ecology (45h.), Animal Zoology
(45h.), Zoopaleontology (15h.) and exercises
(45h.), Comparative Biochemistry (45h.), Anthropology (15h.).

Also a test in 1 of the following groups:
Animal Morphology, Animal Physiology and Ecology,

or Systematic Zoology.

Also a thesis.

Sciences mathématiques:

Première licence: Infinitesimal Analysis (45h.), Mathematical
Methodology (30h.), Seminar on Mathematical
Methods of Physics (30h.), Differential Geometry
(30h.), Algebraic Analysis (45h.), Complements
of Mechanics (45h.), Theoretical Physics (60h.)
and exercises (30h.), Calculus of Probabilities,
Statistics and Theory of Errors (30h.) and
exercises (15h.).

Sciences physiques:

Première licence: General Physics (60h.), Theoretical Physics
(60h.), Physical Chemistry (Thermodynamics)-
(45h.), Calculus of Probabilities, Statistics
and Theory of Errors (30h.), Complements of
Mathematics (45h.), Complements of Mechanics
(45h.), Electronics (30h.), Electrometry (30h.),
Exercises in Mathematical Physics (30h.), Lab.
work in Physics (270h.), Seminar in Physics
(30h.), Seminar on Mathematical Methods in
Physics (optional)-(30h.).

## Docteur en sciences

Not less than 2 years after licence, these 2 years to be spent at the
University. Comprises a test on at least one foreign language, an oral
examination on the chosen science, and presentation and public defense of
a dissertation and thesis showing original research.

## Faculty of Political, Social and Economic Sciences

## Candidature en sciences politiques, sociales et économiques

Duration of course:   2 years.

Entrance requirements:          Recognized Humanities diploma in Greek-Latin,
Latin-Math., Latin-Science, Modern Science
or Economics.
or     Certificate from the Central Jury.
or     Certificate of at least 2 years' post-
secondary study.

<u>or</u>    Non-recognized diploma of 6 years'
          secondary study plus pass at a special
          admission examination.

<u>Première candidature</u>:    Metaphysics (45h.), Ethics (45h.), Logic (45h.),
General Psychology (45h.), History of Africa
(15h.), Traditional Structures and Institutions
of Africa (45h.), Private Law (60h.), Great
Works of Universal Literature (60h.) and
optional lectures (30h.), Scientific Methodology
(30h.) and exercises (15h.), General Statistics
(30h.) and exercises (37.5h.), Principles of
Historical Criticism (30h.), Contemporary
History (60h.).

<u>Deuxième candidature</u>:    Social Philosophy (45h.), Natural Law (60h.),
Constitutional Law and Political Institutions
(60h.), Constitutional Law and Political Insti-
tutions II (30h.), Political Economics (75h.),
General Sociology (90h.), Scientific Methodo-
logy (30h.) and exercises (30h.), General
Statistics (30h.) and exercises (37.5h.),
Higher Mathematics and exercises (60h.),
Traditional African Structures and Institutions
(45h.), Private Law (60h.), Principles of
Historical Criticism (30h.), Contemporary
History (60h.).

## Licence en sciences politiques et administratives

Duration of course:    2 years with <u>Candidature</u>.

<u>Première licence</u>:    Political, Social and Economic Theories and
Doctrines (60h.), Public International Law and
International Institutions (45h.), Social Structures
and Institutions (45h.), Social Legislation and
Politics (60h.), Political Sociology (30h.),
Comparative Political Regimes (45h.), General Theory
of Public Administration (60h.), Administrative Law
(90h.), Economic and Social Public Services (30h.),
Seminar and practical work on Political and
Administrative Sciences (90h.).

<u>Deuxième licence</u>:    Religious Sciences or Moral Philosophy (15h.),
Political, Social and Economic Theories and
Doctrines (60h.), Social Dynamics and Contacts of
Civilization (45h.), Economic Structures and Insti-
tutions (45h.), Administrative Structures and
Institutions (60h.), Public Finance (45h.), Inter-
national Organizations (30h.), Analysis of Contempo-
rary Political Problems (30h.), Seminar on

International Relations or on Administrative
Sciences (60h.).

## Licence en sciences sociales

Duration of course:   2 years with Candidature.

Première licence:     Political, Social and Economic Theories and
                      Doctrines (60h.), Public International Law and Inter-
                      national Institutions (45h.), Social Structures and
                      Institutions (45h.), Cultural Anthropology (60h.),
                      Social Legislation and Politics (60h.), Social Psy-
                      chology (45h.), Demography (45h.), Social Ecology
                      and Urban Sociology (30h.), Rural Sociology (30h.),
                      Industrial Sociology (30h.), Industrial Economics
                      (30h.), Seminar and practical work in Social
                      Science (90h.).
                      2 optional courses from the following:  Special
                      questions of Sociology (Political or Family),
                      Cultural Anthropology, Social Psychology, Social
                      Politica, Demography (each 30h.).

Deuxième licence:     Religious Science or Moral Philosophy (15h.), Poli-
                      tical, Social and Economic Theories and Doctrines
                      (60h.), Economic Structures and Institutions (45h.),
                      Social Dynamics and Contacts of Civilization (45h.),
                      Social Pathology (30h.), Analysis of Contemporary
                      Social Problems (30h.).
                      2 courses chosen from the following:  Special
                      questions of Sociology, Cultural Anthropology,
                      Social Psychology, Social Politica, Demography
                      (each 30h.).
                      1 seminar chosen from:  Sociology, Cultural Anthro-
                      pology, Social Psychology, Industrial Relations and
                      Problems (each 60h.).

## Licence en sciences économiques

Duration of course:   2 years with Candidature.

Première licence:     Political, Social and Economic Theories (60h.),
                      Social Structures and Institutions (45h.), Pure
                      Economics (60h.), Public International Law and Inter-
                      national Institutions (45h.), Social Legislation and
                      Politics (60h.), Analysis of Balance Sheets (30h.),
                      Demography (45h.), Conjuncture (30h.), Money and
                      Credit (30h.), International Economic Relations
                      (45h.), Higher Mathematics and exercises (60h.),
                      Economic readings in English (60h.), Seminar and
                      practical work in Economic Sciences (90h.).

Deuxième licence:     Religious Science or Moral Philosophy (15h.),
                      Political, Social and Economic Theories and

Doctrines (60h.), Economic Structures and Institutions (45h.), Economic History (45h.), Public Finance (45h.), Business Economics (30h.) and Economic Sociology (30h.), Industrial Economics (30h.), Analysis of Contemporary Economic Problems (30h.), Seminar in Pure Economics (60h.) and in Conjuncture (60h.).

## Candidature en anthropologie culturelle africaine

Duration of course:     2 years.

Entrance requirements:          As for Candidature en sciences politiques, sociales et économiques.

Première candidature:          Metaphysics (45h.), Ethics (45h.), Logic (45h.), General Psychology (45h.), Principles of Historical Criticism (30h.), Contemporary History (60h.), History of Africa (15h.), Traditional African Institutions and Society (60h.), Great Works of Universal Literature (60h.) and optional readings (30h.), General Linguistics (30h.), Introduction to African Linguistics (30h.), Scientific Methodology (30h.) and exercises (15h.), General Statistics (30h.) and exercises (37.5h.).

Deuxième candidature:          General Sociology (90h.), Political Economics (30h.), Modern Political and Administrative Structures and Institutions of Africa (45h.), History of Civilization (45h.), African Literature (15h.), 1 Bantu Language (45h.), African Philology (15h.), African Prehistory and Archaeology (15h.), Scientific Methodology (30h.) and exercises (22.5h.), General Statistics (30h.) and exercises (37.5h.).

## Licence en anthropologie culturelle africaine

Duration of course:     2 years with Candidature.

Première licence:          General Cultural Anthropology (60h.), African Systems of Social Relations (30h.), Cultural Anthropology (30h.), African Common Law (45h.), African Religions and Philosophies (30h.), Social Psychology (45h.), Social Structures and Institutions (45h.), Social Ecology and Urban Sociology (30h.), Rural Sociology (30h.), Demography (30h.), Seminar and practical work in Cultural Anthropology (90h.).

Deuxième licence:          Religious Science or Moral Philosophy (15h.),
                           Social Dynamics and Contacts of Civilization
                           (45h.), Cultural Anthropology (30h.), Culture and
                           Personality (30h.), Sociology of Language (15h.),
                           Study of an African oral Literature (30h.), African
                           Arts and Technology (15h.).

                           2 optional courses chosen from the courses for the
                           licence in African Philology or Social Sciences.
                           Seminar (60h.).


## Certificat d'anthropologie culturelle africaine

Duration of course:    1 year.

Entrance requirements:        Final university diploma.

Program:   Cultural Anthropology (60h.), Social Dynamics and contacts of
           Civilization (45h.), Traditional African Structures and Insti-
           tutions (60h.), African Systems of Social Relations (30h.),
           Seminar and practical work in Cultural Anthropology (90h.).


## Certificat de journalisme

Duration of course:    1 year.

Entrance requirements:        Licence diploma.

Program:   History of Law of the Press (30h.), Deontology of the Press
           (15h.), Journalistic Techniques (60h.), Exercises in French
           Language (60h.) and Edition (60h.).

           2 months on the staff of a newspaper.


## Candidature en sciences commerciales

Duration of course:    2 years.

Entrance requirements:        Recognized certificate of études moyennes.
                         or   Pass preparatory test.
                         or   Certificate of 6 years' études moyennes in
                              Modern Humanities or Economics.
                         or   Certificate awarded by Central Jury.

Première candidature:         General Psychology (45h.), Moral Philosophy
                              (30h.), Contemporary History (45h.), Civil Law
                              (60h.), General Mathematics (60h.), Political
                              Economics (30h.), Commercial Techniques (45h.)

and exercises (15h.), General Accountancy (75h.), General Statistics (30h.) and exercises (37.5h.), French (30h.), English (90h.), Choice of a Congolese language, German or Dutch (each 30h.), Guided visits.

Deuxième candidature: Philosophy-Logic (30h.), Commercial Psychology (15h.), Economic Geography (45h.), General Statistics (30h.) and exercises (37.5h.), Political Economics (75h.), Commercial Law (60h.), Saleable Products (30h.), Business Administration (45h.), Accountancy (30h.), French (30h.), English (60h.), Choice of a Congolese language, German or Dutch (each 30h.), 8 guided visits.

## Licence en sciences commerciales

Duration of course: 2 years with Candidature.

Première licence: Political Economics (30h.) and Conjuncture (30h.), Commercial, Financial and Economic Politics (30h.), Economic Geography (30h.), Public Law (15h.), Financial Economy (60h.), Financial Legislation (15h.), Banks (30h.), Control and Business Financing (60h.), Transport Economics (15h.), Assurance (30h.), Statistics (15h.), Personnel (30h.), Technical Direction of Industrial Businesses (30h.), Industrial Technology (45h.), Fiscal and Customs Legislation (30h.), Choice of language (30h.), English (30h.), Seminar and practical work in Commercial and Financial Science (90h.), 8 guided visits.

Optional courses: Accounting Multicopying (30h.) or Industrial Accountancy (30h.).

Deuxième licence: Religious Science or Moral Philosophy (15h.), Business Deontology (15h.), Political Economics (30h.), Transport Economics (15h.), Industrial Technology (45h.), Industrial Law (15h.), Commercial Law (15h.), Social Legislation (15h.), Distribution of Goods (45h.), Administrative Techniques (60h.), Operational Research (60h.), Insurance Legislation (15h.), Choice of language (30h.), English (30h.), Seminar (60h.).

2 months of business experience; options as above.

## Licence complémentaire

Open to any student enrolled in any licence program in the Faculty. May be taken simultaneously over 2 years. Must take 2 examinations in the compulsory and optional subjects making up at least 42 semester hours, also must attend seminars and present a thesis.

## Graduat en sciences économiques et sociales

Admittance with recognized diploma of secondary studies, or admission examination.

At present only first-year program. Subjects in French, Mathematics, Law, History, Economics, Demography, Logic, English.

## Graduat en sciences commerciales

Admission as above.

At present only first-year program. Subjects in French, Mathematics, Economics, Accountancy, Commercial Techniques, Statistics, Law, Logic, English.

## Certificat en administration des entreprises

Entrance requirements:     University diploma.
                    or  Higher technical teaching diploma.
                    or  Those aged at least 25, in business and with a diploma of études moyennes.
                    or  Those aged at least 30, in public or private business for 10 years.

Entrance examination on Political Economics, commercial techniques, Accountancy and Business Administration.

One examination on Statistics, Personnel Management, Business Administration, Accountancy, Business Control and Financing, Distribution of Goods. Several examinable and non-examinable courses.

## Polytechnical Faculty

## Candidature ingénieur civil

See Faculty of Science.

## Etudes d'ingénieur civil

Duration of course:   3 years.

1st yr:   General courses:
Cinematics and Machine Dynamics (45h.) and exercises (45h.),
Thermodynamics (60h.) and exercises (45h.), Technology (15h.)
and exercises (15h.), Elasticity and Resistance of Materials
(90h.) and exercises (90h.), General Electrotechniques (45h.)
and exercises (30h.), General Hydraulics (22.5h.) and exercises (22.5h.), General Constructional Procedures (15h.).

Special courses:
Electricity, Mechanics, Construction.

2nd yr:   General courses:
Description and Construction of Machines (45h.) and exercises
(45h.), Stability (60h.) and exercises (22.5h.), General
Electrotechniques (45h.) and exercises (30h.), General
Metallurgy and Metallography (60h.) and exercises (22.5h.),
Topography (15h.), Industrial Chemistry (30h.).

Special courses as in 1st year.

3rd yr:   General courses:
Religious Science or Moral Philosophy (15h.), Machine
Construction (60h.) and exercises (45h.), General Metallurgy
(30h.) and exercises (22.5h.), Topography (15h.), Industrial
Law (22.5h.), Industrial Chemistry (30h.), Philosophy (22.5h.).

Special courses as in 1st year.  Also a thesis.

## Etudes de conducteur civil

Duration of course:   2 years.

Entrance requirements:        Recognized Humanities diploma in Latin-
                              Math. or Modern Science.
                   or         Pass entry examination.
                   or         Certificate from Central Jury.

1st yr:   Theoretical and Applied Mathematics (60h.) and exercises
(67.5h.), Experimental Physics (45h.) and exercises (45h.),
Descriptive Geometry (22.5h.) and Graphic work (45h.),
Mechanics (30h.), Architecture (45h.) and exercises (30h.),
Graphstatistics (30h.) and exercises (67.5h.), Geology
(22.5h.), Architectural exercises (30h.).

2nd yr:   Theoretical and Applied Mathematics (37.5h.) and exercises
(45h.), Experimental Physics (30h.) and exercises (30h.),
Elasticity (60h.) and exercises (90h.), Machine Technology
(15h.), Construction Materials (15h.), Architecture (15h.),

Mechanics (15h.) and exercises (22.5h.), Topography (15h.)
and exercises (15h.), General Hydraulics (22.5h.) and exercises (22.5h.), Architectural exercises (30h.), Topographical
exercises (15h.).

## Faculty of Agriculture

### Candidature ingénieur agronome

See Faculty of Science.

### Etudes d'ingénieur agronome des régions tropicales

Duration of course:    3 years with Candidature.

1st yr:   Climatology, Soil, Geology and Physical Geography, Ecology,
          Plant Physiology, Phytosociology, Tropical Plants, Microbiology,
          Anatomy and Physiology of Domestic Animals, Zootechnology,
          Genetics, Agriculture, Soil Fertilization, Biochemistry,
          Analytical Chemistry, Electricity and Motors, Hydraulics,
          Topography, Political and Social Economics.

2nd yr:   Climatology, Soil, Ecology, Phytogeography, Phytosociology,
          Tropical Plants, Microbiology, Phytopathology, Zootechnology,
          Entomology, Animal Alimentation, Limnology and Pisciculture,
          Plant Improvement, Biometry, Special Tropical Culture, Soil
          Fertilization, Biochemistry, Electricity and Motors, Hydraulics,
          Topography, Agricultural Technology, General Legislation,
          Agricultural Economics.

3rd yr:   Religious Science or Moral Philosophy, Soil, Phytopathology,
          Zootechnology, Entomology, Animal Alimentation, Plant Improve-
          ment, Special Cultures, Forestry and Sylviculture, Electricity
          and Motors, Agricultural Machines, Irrigation, Agricultural
          Technology, General Legislation, Agricultural Economics and
          Sociology, Accountancy, Hygiene.

          Also, presentation and public defense of a thesis.

### Graduat en agronomie

Duration of course:    2 years.

Entrance requirements:            Recognized secondary studies diploma.
                          or      Pass entrance examination open to those
                                  with a 6-year post-primary certificate.
                                  or at least a 4-year post-primary certifi-
                                  cate obtained at least 2 years previously.

1st yr:     Philosophy-Logic, Mathematics, Inorganic Chemistry, Physics,
            Botany, Zoology, Geology and Physical Geography, Anatomy and
            Histology of Domestic Animals, General Agriculture.

2nd yr:     Climatology, Soil, Tropical Plants, Microbiology, Physiology
            of Domestic Animals, Zootechnique, Limnology and Pisciculture,
            Genetics, Tropical and Subtropical Cultures, Soil Fertilization,
            Plant Biochemistry, Electricity, Motors, Agricultural Machines,
            Irrigation, Topography, General Legislation, Agricultural
            Economics, Accountancy.

## Institute of Psychology and Pedagogy

## Candidature en sciences psychologiques

Duration of course:     2 years.

Entrance requirements:            Recognized Humanities diploma in Greek-
                                  Latin, Latin-Math., Latin-Science, Modern
                                  Science or Economics.
                            or    Certificate from Central Jury.
                            or    Certificate of at least 2 years' post-
                                  secondary study.
                            or    Certificate of 6 years' secondary study
                                  and pass an entrance examination.

Première candidature:       Metaphysics (45h.), Moral Philosophy (45h.),
                            Sociology (45h.), Physics and Chemistry (45h.),
                            Biology (30h.), Human Organism (60h.), General
                            Mathematics (60h.), Statistics (15h.), General
                            Psychology (45h.), History of Psychology (60h.),
                            Child and Adolescent Psychology (45h.), Physics
                            lab. and demonstrations (30h.), Experimental
                            Psychology Lab. and demonstrations (30h.),
                            Exercises in Statistics (30h.), Experimental
                            Physiology lab. and demonstrations (30h.),
                            Exercises in Child and Adolescent Psychology
                            (30h.).

Deuxième candidature:       Logic (45h.), African Linguistics (30h.),
                            Experimental Psychology (60h.), Individual
                            Psychology (45h.), Social Psychology (45h.),
                            Culture and Personality (30h.), Psychology
                            Methods and Techniques (30h.), Statistics (45h.),
                            Testing Methods (45h.), Experimental Pedagogy
                            (30h.), Physiology (60h.), Political Economics
                            (45h.), Statistics exercises (30h.), Experimental
                            Psychology demonstrations and lab. (30h.), Indi-
                            vidual Psychology exercises (30h.), Practical
                            Testing (30h.).

## Licence en sciences psychologiques

Duration of course:     2 years with Candidature.

Première licence:       History of Modern Philosophy (30h.), Philosophical
                        Psychology (22.5h.), Experimental Psychology (30h.),
                        Child and Adolescent Psychology (30h.), Social
                        Psychology (30h.), History of Psychology (30h.),
                        Exceptional and Abnormal Child Psychology and
                        Education (15h.), Delinquent Child Psychology and
                        Re-education (15h.), Religious Psychology (30h.),
                        Psychopathology (30h.), Comparative Psychology
                        (22.5h.), Clinical Psychology (-h.), Educational
                        and Professional Orientation (30h.), Industrial
                        Psychology (30h.), Study and Analysis of Pro-
                        fessions (15h.), Commercial Psychology (15h.),
                        Exercises in Education and Professional Orientation
                        (30h.), Testing Methods (30h.).

                        Choice of seminar, 2 optional courses, 1 month in
                        practice.

Deuxième licence:       Religious Sciences or Moral Philosophy (15h.),
                        Philosophical Psychology (22.5h.), Experimental
                        Psychology (30h.), Child and Adolescent Psychology
                        (30h.), Social Psychology (30h.), History of
                        Psychology (15h.), Exceptional and Abnormal Child
                        Psychology and Education (15h.), Delinquent Child
                        Psychology and Re-education (15h.), Religious
                        Psychology (30h.), Psychopathology (-h.), Compara-
                        tive Psychology (22.5h.), Clinical Psychology
                        (-h.), Educational and Professional Orientation
                        (30h.) and exercises (30h.), Industrial Psychology
                        (30h.), Professional Study and Analysis (15h.),
                        Psychological Consultation exercises (30h.).

                        Choice of seminar (30h.), 1 optional course,
                        presentation and public defense of a thesis.


## Candidature en sciences pédagogiques

Duration of course:     2 years.

Entrance requirements:          As for Candidature en sciences psycho-
                                logiques.

Première candidature:   Metaphysics (45h.), Moral Philosophy (45h.),
                        Philosophical and Religious Principles of
                        Education (15h.), Elements of Biology (30h.),
                        Anatomy, Physiology, Pathology and Hygiene of

the Human Organism (45h.), General Mathematics
(60h.), Statistics (15h.), General Psychology
(45h.), Encyclopaedia of Pedagogy (30h.),
Psychology of the Child and Adolescent (30h.),
History of Pedagogy (30h.), Modern Pedagogical
Methods (45h.), Statistical exercises (30h.),
Experimental Psychology Demonstrations and lab.
work (30h.), Exercises in Psychology of the
Child and Adolescent (30h.).

Deuxième candidature:    Logic (45h.), Introduction to African Linguistics
(30h.), Principles of Historical Criticism (30h.),
Experimental Psychology (60h.) and demonstrations
and lab.work (30h.), Individual Psychology (45h.),
and exercises (30h.), Social Psychology (45h.),
Philosophical and Religious Principles of Edu-
cation (15h.), General Methodology (30h.),
Statistics (15h.), Testing Methods (45h.),
Experimental Pedagogy (15h.), History of Pedagogy
(30h.), Organization of Teaching and School
Legislation (30h.), Statistical exercises (30h.),
Practical Testing (30h.).

## Agrégation de l'enseignement moyen du degré supérieur

Duration of course:  1 year.

Entrance requirements:  Hold the equivalent of a _licence_.

Program:    Experimental Pedagogy (30h.), History of Pedagogy (30h.),
General Methodology (30h.), Special Teaching Methodology in
a) Romance Philology, b) African Philology, c) Commercial
Sciences, d) Zoological Sciences, e) Biological Sciences,
f) Agricultural Sciences, g) Physical Sciences, h) Mathematical
Sciences (15h. each), Didactic exercises and lessons in the
above sections (15h. each).

## Licence en sciences pédagogiques

Duration of course:  2 years with _Candidature_.

Première licence:    History of Modern Philosophy (45h.), Philosophical
Psychology (15h.), General Experimental Psychology
(30h.), Psychology of the Child and Adolescent
(30h.), History of Pedagogy and Pedagogical Writings
(30h.), Psychology and Education of Exceptional and
Abnormal Children (15h.), Psychology and Re-education
of Delinquent Children (-h.), Psychopedagogy (30h.),

Psychopathology (-h.), Special Methodology (15h.), Experimental Didactics (30h.), Principles and Methods of Educational and Professional Orientation (30h.), Religious Psychology (30h.), Methods of Religious Teaching (30h.), Exercises in Didactics and School Inspection (30h.), Practical exercises in Education and Professional Orientation (-h.), Didactic lessons (15h.).

Deuxième licence:    Religious Science or Moral Philosophy (15h.), Philosophical Psychology (15h.), General Experimental Psychology (30h.), Psychology of Child and Adolescent (30h.), History of Pedagogy and Pedagogical Writings (30h.), Psychology and Education of Exceptional and Abnormal Children (15h.), Psychology and Re-education of abnormal children (-h.), Psychopathology (-h.), Special Methodology (15h.), Experimental Didactics (30h.), Education and Professional Orientation (30h.) and practical exercises (-h.), Exercises in Didactics and School Inspection (30h.), Didactic lessons (30h.).

Final examination also includes the giving of two public lessons and the presentation and public defense of a thesis.

## UNIVERSITE OFFICIELLE DU CONGO, Elisabethville

Originally the State University of the Belgian Congo and Ruanda-Urundi. Set up at Elisabethville by decree of October 1955, opened November 1956.

Faculties:

Philosophy and Arts
Science and Applied Science
Law
Medicine
Pedagogy

Inter-Faculty Centre of African Anthropology and Linguistics

Programs are the same as those at the University of Lovanium.

## UNIVERSITE LIBRE DU CONGO, Stanleyville

Established February, 1963 under sponsorship of the Agricultural and Technical Assistance Foundation (Los Angeles 28, California), a non-profit organization, in conjunction with UNESCO, and the Council of Protestant Churches in the Congo.

1964, the University became independent of the Foundation.

To be an all-African University, and bi-lingual (French and English).

Entrance requirements:          Recognized diploma of completion of
                                6 years' secondary education.

Pre-university year (année propédeutique) initiated October, 1963.
3 sections:  Literature, Science, Mathematics.

Pre-university training program of the Congo Polytechnic Institute (CPI)
begun in 1960, integrated in 1963 with the Université Libre du Congo
program.

Plans for 4 Faculties:    Theology
                          Philosophy and Letters
                          Natural Sciences
                          Human Sciences

1964-65 academic year held in Léopoldville, sharing the facilities of
the Université Lovanium.  Propédeutique classes in Faculty of Medicine
and Faculty of Law.  When the University is able to return to Stanleyville, it will continue to develop the same faculties as the University
of Lovanium as student demands require.  All programs are the same as
those of Lovanium.

First licences to be awarded in June, 1968.


## INSTITUT NATIONAL D'ETUDES POLITIQUES, Léopoldville

The Institute (I.N.E.P.), a public service institution, created an
evening school in 1964, the Ecole Supérieure du Développement.  Training
for administrative cadres, public and private.

Entrance requirements:          To cycle normal:
                                Diplôme agréé or homologué.

                                To preparatory year:
                                4-5 years of post-primary studies.

Duration of course:   3 years (450 hours of evening classes a year).

Preparatory year:     Mathematics (3h.)          English (2h.)
                        History (3h.)             Geography (2h.)
                        French (6h.)              Sciences (1h.)

First year:  Formation générale

A.   General Culture (120h.)
         French (30h.)
         Philosophy and Logic (30h.)
         Historic World Societies (30h.)
         History of Africa (30h.)

B.   Introduction to Social Sciences (120h.)
         Encyclopedia of Social Sciences (30h.)
         Methods and Techniques of Research in the Social Sciences (45h.)
         Mathematics:  Statistics (45h.)

C.   Economic Sciences (210h.)
         Fundamental Concepts of Political Economy (90h.)
         Economic Geography (30h.)
         Demography (30h.)
         Money and Credit (30h.)
         Doctrines and Economic Systems (30h.)

Practical work

Second year:   Analytical Description of Economic, Political, Administrative
                  and Social Problems

A.   Economic Sciences (150h.)
         Under-development and Political Economics of Development (75h.)
         Economic Structures of the Congo (30h.)
         International Economic Relations (45h.)

B.   Political Sciences (210h.)
         History of the Congo (30h.)
         Contemporary History (30h.)
         Political Institutions and Forces (60h.)
         Administrative Institutions (120h.)

C.   Sociology (90h.)
         Sociology of Traditional African Societies (30h.)
         Sociology of Industrial Societies (30h.)
         Social Changes (30h.)

Practical work

Third year:  Politics and Techniques of Economic and Social Development

A.   Political Economy (240h.)
         Political Economy of Development (120h.)
         Planning in Africa, a case study (30h.)
         Technical and Financial Assistance (30h.)

B.   Social Politics (120h.)
         Politics and Social Legislation (30h.)
         Syndicalism (30h.)
         Cooperation (30h.)

C.   Report

Diploma awarded at the level equivalent to 2 years of Candidature in a
Belgian university.


## INSTITUT SUPERIEUR DE COMMERCE, Léopoldville

Also called Ecole Supérieure de Commerce.  Under the direction of the
Scheut Missionaries.

Entrance requirements:          Certificat homologué d'humanités
                          or    Diploma from a secondary technical school
                                (long cycle)
                          or    Full cycle of secondary studies and success-
                                ful entrance examination.

Duration of course:    3 years.

### TIMETABLE
(Periods per week)

| Subjects | 1st year | 2nd year |
|---|---|---|
| Philosophy | 1 | 1 |
| Civic Education | 1 | 1 |
| French | 4 | 4 |
| English | 4 | 4 |
| Third Language | 3 | 3 |
| Economics | 2 | 4 |
| Economic History | 1 | 1 |
| Economic Geography | 1 | 1 |
| African Anthropology | 1 | 1 |
| Law | 2 | 2 |
| Mathematics applied to Economics | 3 | 0 |
| Statistics | 2 | 0 |
| Accounting | 1 | 1 |
| Negotiable Products | 1 | 1 |
| Business Organization | 1 | 1 |
| Physical Education and Sports | 1 | 1 |
| Seminar | 3 | 3 |
|  | 32 | 29 |

3rd year

Professional Practical Work
Preparation of a thesis
Preparation of a statement of account

General courses:
| | |
|---|---|
| Accounting | 180 h. |
| Administrative and Fiscal Law | 60 h. |
| Commercial Psychology | 15 h. |
| Economic Problems | 15 h. |
| | 270 h. |

Examinations:   Written and oral at close of each year.  Candidate must
obtain 50% of points assigned to each subject and 60% in
overall average.  At the end of the 3rd year, candidate
must take an examination, and in addition present and
defend a thesis and a final study report (which is public).

Diplôme awarded with the following mentions:   La plus grande distinction
Grande distinction
Distinction
Satisfaction

## INSTITUT NATIONAL DU BATIMENT ET DES TRAVAUX PUBLICS, Léopoldville

Founded November, 1961.  Government-controlled with Council of Administration.

Entry age:       Up to 27 years.

Entrance requirements:        Recognized secondary education certificate.
or    Completion of 6 years' secondary plus
entrance examination.

Language of instruction:        French.

Duration of course:   1 preparatory year (optional, if students wish to
revise or complete earlier scientific training).

3 years.

## Curriculum (hours per week):

Preparatory year:     Arithmetic (3h.), Algebra (3h.), Plane and Solid
Geometry (3h.), Trigonometry (2h.), Descriptive
Geometry (3h.), Geometric and Industrial Design
(4h.), General Physics including lab. work (5h.),
Practical Ethics (1h.), French (5h.), Practical
work (5h.).

1st yr:    Descriptive Geometry (2h.), Analytical Geometry (2h.), Infinite-
           simal Calculus (5h.), Materials (3h.), Civil Architecture (5h.),
           Mechanics (3h.), Accountancy (2h.), Organization and Workshop
           Equipment (2h.), Elements of Construction Design (6h.), Psycho-
           logy (1h.).

2nd yr:    Architecture (2h.), Industrial Constructions (5h.), Topography
           (2h.), Electricity (4h.), Accountancy (1h.), Factory Organi-
           zation (1h.), Material Resistance (4h.), Civil Engineering
           (5h.), Technical Writing (1h.), Industrial Construction
           Projects (4h.), Scientific Method (1h.)

3rd yr:    Industrial Physics (4h.), Civil Law (2h.), Reinforced Concrete
           (4h.), Accountancy Applications (2h.), General Philosophy (1h.),
           Reinforced Concrete project (8h.), Civil Engineering project
           (8h.), Architecture project (8h.).

           In the last year students choose the specialty of Public Works
           or Building.  In the last semester they undertake an "end of
           studies" project in Reinforced Concrete, Civil Engineering or
           Architecture.

Diplôme d'ingénieur-technicien awarded.


ACADEMIE DES BEAUX ARTS (including the INSTITUT SUPERIEUR D'ARCHITECTURE),
  Léopoldville

Founded in 1943.

Entry age:      Approximately 15 into the secondary cycle of the Académie.

Entrance requirements:        Completion of 2-year secondary cycle
                              d'orientation.

Language of instruction:      French.

Programs:       4-year secondary cycle with final Diplôme en humanités
                artistiques awarded in 3 sections:

                        Decorative and Plastic Arts
                        Architecture
                        Arts and Techniques of Communication - Radio,
                          Television, Cinema, Photography, etc.

                Normal government curriculum for general subjects followed.

Grading:        50% of total at end of year to pass.
                Highest mark usually given:  70%.

Post-secondary education:       4-year programs in the above 3 sections,
leading to Maître en art décoratif, Maître en architecture, or Maître
en art de diffusion.

INSTITUT DE L'AVIATION CIVILE, Léopoldville

Entrance requirements:          2 years after the cycle d'orientation or
                                 4th year of the secondary program,
                                 technical bias (humanités techniques).

Duration of course for contrôleurs de la circulation aérienne and chefs
d'aérodrome:  2 years of theoretical study and 2 years of practical work
in employed training.

Duration of course for opérateurs radioaéronautiques and radio techniciens:
2 years of theoretical study and 1 year of practical work in employed
training.

### TIMETABLE
(Hours per week)

| General courses | | Technical courses | |
|---|---|---|---|
| Mathematics | 4 | Air Circulation | ) |
| French | 3½ | Navigation/Radio Navigation | ) |
| Physics | 2 | Radio Electricity | ) |
| Chemistry | 2 | Meteorology | ) |
| History | 1 | Meteorological Plan | ) |
| Geography | 2 | Aerodynamics | ) |
| English | 4 | Procedures of Tele- communications | ) |
| | | Air Law/Management | ) |
| | | Engineering/Structure | ) |
| | | Operation | ) |
| | | Practical Work | ) |

19

Diplôme des humanités techniques awarded at close of 2-year theoretical
study.

Brevet de technicien aéronautique awarded at close of practical training.


ECOLE NATIONALE DE DROIT ET D'ADMINISTRATION, Léopoldville/Kalina

Government-controlled with Council of Administration and Director General
nominated by the Chief of State.

Founded in December, 1960.

Entry age:     18-30 years.

Entrance requirements:          Preparatory year:
                                4 years post-primary plus 2 years in

government service, or 5 years post-
primary plus 1 year in government service,
plus an entrance examination.

1st year:
With recognized secondary certificate, no
entrance examination required; or 6 years
post-primary education non-certificated,
plus an entrance examination.

Language of instruction:          French.

Duration of course:    1 preparatory year (optional).

4 years, with specialization in 3rd and 4th years
in 3 sections:
        Economic and Financial
        Administrative and Social
        Legal

## Curriculum (hours per semester):

Preparatory year:      French (180), History of Africa and the Congo (120),
Geography (120), Sciences (90), Mathematics (120),
Geometry (60).

1st yr:    African Anthropology (90), Political Economics (90, practical
30), Introduction to Law (60), Introduction to Political
Science (60, practical 45), The Contemporary World (90),
French (60, practical 45), Mathematics (60, practical 30),
English (practical 45).

2nd yr:    Constitutional Law (45), Administrative Law (90, practical 30),
Civil Law (90, practical 30), Public International Law (60),
Public Finance (45), International Economic Relations (90,
practical 30), French Language and Literature (30, practical
45), Fiscal Mathematics (30, practical 30), Accountancy (30),
English (practical 45).

3rd yr:    Economic and Financial:
Political Economics (60, practical 30), History of Economic
Doctrines (30), Advanced Public Finance (60, practical 30),
Business Law (90, practical 30), Statistics and Accountancy
(60), Public Administration (30, practical 30), Large Public
Services (75), Social Law (30), Demography (30), Civil Law
(30), English (practical 45).

Administrative/Social:
Social Law and Institutions (120, practical 30), Public
Administration (30, practical 45), Large Public Services (75),
Local Institutions (45), Penal Law (60), Civil Law (60),
Political Economics (60, practical 30), Public Accountancy
(45), English (practical 45).

        <u>Legal</u>:
        Civil Law (135, practical 45), Penal Law and Criminology (90,
        practical 30), Business Law (90, practical 30), Civil Pro-
        cedure (30), Penal Procedure (30), Social Law (30), Political
        Economics (30), Public Administration (30), English (practical
        45).

4th yr:   7 months' practical experience comprising 2 months in Congolese
        territories and 5 months in administrative or legal services
        abroad.

        Period of study: Theory (6h. per week), Seminars (2h. per week),
                     Practical work groups (4h. per week), Thesis.

<u>Diploma</u> awarded at end of 4th year in the above 3 special fields.


## VOCATIONAL AND TECHNICAL EDUCATION

All technical education is now being incorporated into the new national
program of secondary education.

### B E F O R E   1 9 6 0   R E F O R M

Vocational and technical education all at secondary level given in the
following schools, which are continuing to function as in the past, where
it has not been possible to adjust them to the new national program.
Where it has been possible, they are being changed into a <u>cycle d'orienta-
tion</u> program.  The <u>écoles artisanales</u> and the <u>fermes-écoles</u> still only
require 5 years' primary education for entry.


## ECOLES ARTISANALES (Trade Schools)

Entry with 5 years' primary education.  Trained artisans for rural areas.
Missionary organized and conducted.  Teaching almost entirely in vernacular.

6 hours general, 33½ hours workshop.  Carpentry, Rural Building, Sculpture,
Basketmaking, Forging, Clothes and Shoemaking.


## FERMES-ECOLES (Farm Schools)

Same level as <u>écoles artisanales</u>.  To encourage young people to remain in
villages.

Timetable comprised 6 hours' general training, 33½ hours' practical work on farm, nurseries, etc.

2-year course for both écoles artisanales and fermes-écoles.


ECOLES PROFESSIONNELLES (Vocational Training Schools)

Entry with 6 years' primary and good knowledge of French.  4-year course. Specialization intensified in last 2 years.

Practical and theoretical training:  Fitting, Turning and Machine Tools, Maintenance Mechanics, Motor Mechanics, Electric Assembling, Carpentry and Cabinetmaking, Building, Mining, Public Works, Weaving, Readymade Clothing, Sculpture, Painting, Ceramics, Cutting and Dressmaking (girls).


ECOLES PROFESSIONNELLES AGRICOLES (Agricultural Vocational Training Schools)

Entry by entrance examination (level of 6th class selective upper primary), open to older pupils.

3-year course for subordinate auxiliary staff of agricultural services. Trained agricultural instructors, market gardeners, foresters, fishery instructors, plantation workers, subordinate staff for veterinary service.


ECOLES D'APPRENTISSAGE (Apprenticeship Schools)

Entry with 6 years' primary and good knowledge of French.

Teach industrial and urban trades:  Motor Mechanics, Carpentry, Masonry, Mechanical Weaving, Electric Assembling, Maintenance Mechanics, Printing, Shoemaking, Bookbinding, Forging, Fitting, Soldering and Welding.

2 or 3-year program.


ECOLES TECHNIQUES (Technical Schools)

Entry on completion of lower stage of secondary school or trade vocational course, with entrance examination.  Two technical schools at Léopoldville and Jadotville.

Train technicians for industrial trades, fine arts and agriculture.  18 to 30 lessons a week given to general training.

ECOLES D'ASSISTANTS AGRICOLES (Agricultural Assistants' Schools)

Entry on completion of lower secondary course and entrance examination.

4-year course.  Train subordinate agricultural staff (assistant agrono-
mists), also agricultural assistants for private companies.


A F T E R   1 9 6 0   R E F O R M

All the courses listed below follow the complete primary cycle of 6
years.  There are no longer any courses which can be followed after only
5 years of primary except in the écoles artisanales and fermes-écoles not
yet adapted to the new national program.


LOWER SECONDARY TECHNICAL EDUCATION

Enseignement professionnel (professional training - short cycle):

Usually a 2-year program, sometimes 3.  May go on to the Institution
Nationale de Préparation Professionnelle and from there into the chosen
profession.

Maximum hours per week:  40.

Sections:        General Mechanics, Auto Diesel Mechanics, Electricity,
                 Carpentry, Construction, Social and Family, Cutting and
                 Dressmaking.


### THIRD-YEAR TIMETABLE
(hours per week)

| Subjects | General Mechanics | Auto Diesel | Electricity | Carpentry | Construction |
|---|---|---|---|---|---|
| Religion, Morals and Civics | 1 | 1 | 1 | 1 | 1 |
| French | 4 | 4 | 4 | 4 | 4 |
| Mathematics | 4 | 4 | 4 | 4 | 4 |
| Physics | 1 | 1 | 1 | 1 | 1 |
| Chemistry | 1 | 1 | 1 | 1 | 1 |
| Physical Ed. | 1 | 1 | 1 | 1 | 1 |
| Mechanics | 2 | 2 | 2 | 2 | - |
| Electricity | 2 | 1 | 3 | - | - |
| Metallurgy | 1 | - | - | - | - |
| Technology | 2 | 2 | 2 | 2 | 4 |
| Design | 4 | 4 | 4 | 4 | 8 |
| Materials | - | 1 | - | 1 | - |
| Building Constr. | - | - | - | - | 4 |
| Workshop and Prac. Work | 16 | 17 | 16 | 18 | 11 |

| Subjects | Social and Family | Subjects | Cutting and Dressmaking |
|---|---|---|---|
| Religion, Morals and Civics | 2 | Religion, Morals and Civics | 2 |
| French | 4 | French | 4 |
| Current Affairs | 2 | General Interest | 1 |
| Local Customs | 1 | Applied Sciences | 2 |
| Plastic/Musical Ed. | 2 | Physical Ed. | 1 |
| Physical/Rhythmic Ed. | 1 | Applied Arithmetic and Geometry | 3 |
| Anatomy, Physiology, Hygiene, First Aid, Child Rearing | 4 | Technology | 2 |
| Childhood/Adolescence | 2 | Tech. of Materials | 2 |
| Social Action Methods | 2 | Technical Design | 2 |
| Technology | 3 | Homemaking | 3 |
| Family Management | 1 | Mechanization | 2 |
| General Economics | 1 | Adaptation of Patterns | 3 |
| Tech. Applications | 11 | Workshop and Tech. Exercises | 13 |
| Home Art | 2 | | |
| Child Care | 2 | | |

Diplomas awarded:

    (1)  Old program:        3 years' study, followed by 1 or sometimes 2 years of further training in a specialty.
                                    Diplôme A 3.

    (2)  New national program:  2 years' orientation without specialization.
                                      Brevet du cycle d'orientation.

    (3)  New national program:  2 or 3 years after the cycle d'orientation in a chosen specialty (short cycle, equivalent to old Diplôme A 3).
                                      Brevet d'aptitude professionnelle.

## HIGHER SECONDARY TECHNICAL EDUCATION

Humanités (cycle long) - 4 years:

### TIMETABLE - TECHNICAL SECTION
(hours per week)

Electricity

| Subjects | Class 3 | 4 | 5 | 6 |
|---|---|---|---|---|
| Religion/Morals | 1 | 1 | 1 | 1 |
| French | 6 | 5 | 3 | 2 |
| English | 4 | 2 | 2 | 2 |

| Electricity (cont'd):          | Class 3 | 4 | 5 | 6 |
|--------------------------------|---------|---|---|---|
| History                        | 2 | 1 | 1 | 2 |
| Geography                      | 1 | 1 | 1 | 1 |
| Sociology                      | 1 | 1 | - | - |
| Mathematics                    | 6 | 6 | 7 | 7 |
| Physics                        | 1 | 2 | 1 | - |
| Chemistry                      | 1 | 1 | 1 | - |
| Physical Education             | 1 | 1 | 1 | 1 |
| Metallurgy                     | - | - | - | 1 |
| Mechanics                      | 2 | 2 | 2 | 2 |
| Electricity                    | 1 | 4 | 2 | - |
| Electrical Machines            | - | - | 3 | 6 |
| Electronics                    | - | - | 2 | 2 |
| Design                         | 4 | 4 | 3 | 3 |
| Technology                     | 3 | 2 | 2 | 1 |
| Lab. work - Electricity        | - | 2 | 2 | 2 |
| Lab. work - Electronics        | - | - | 2 | 2 |
| Workshop                       | 6 | 5 | 4 | 5 |

## Mechanics

| | Class 3 | 4 | 5 | 6 |
|--------------------------------|---------|---|---|---|
| Religion/Morals                | 1 | 1 | 1 | 1 |
| French                         | 6 | 5 | 3 | 2 |
| English                        | 4 | 2 | 2 | 2 |
| History                        | 2 | 1 | 1 | 2 |
| Geography                      | 1 | 1 | 1 | 1 |
| Sociology                      | 1 | 1 | - | - |
| Mathematics                    | 6 | 6 | 7 | 7 |
| Physics                        | 1 | 2 | 1 | - |
| Chemistry                      | 1 | 1 | 1 | - |
| Physical Education             | 1 | 1 | 1 | 1 |
| Industrial Physico-Chemistry   | - | 1 | - | - |
| Metallurgy                     | - | - | 1 | 1 |
| Mechanics                      | 2 | 2 | 2 | - |
| Mechanisms                     | - | 1 | - | 1 |
| Motorized and Receiving Machines | - | - | 3 | 4 |
| Electricity                    | 1 | 1 | 1 | 2 |
| Design                         | 4 | 4 | 4 | 4 |
| Technology                     | 3 | 3 | 1 | 1 |
| Resistance                     | - | - | 1 | 2 |
| Laboratory Work                | - | 2 | 4 | 4 |
| Workshop                       | 6 | 5 | 5 | 5 |

## Construction

| | Class 3 | 4 | 5 | 6 |
|--------------------------------|---------|---|---|---|
| Religion/Morals                | 1 | 1 | 1 | 1 |
| French                         | 6 | 5 | 3 | 2 |
| English                        | 4 | 2 | 2 | 2 |
| History                        | 2 | 1 | 1 | 2 |
| Geography                      | 1 | 1 | 1 | 1 |

Construction (cont'd):

| | Class 3 | 4 | 5 | 6 |
|---|---|---|---|---|
| Sociology | 2 | - | - | - |
| Mathematics | 6 | 6 | 7 | 7 |
| Physics | 2 | 2 | 1 | - |
| Chemistry | 2 | 2 | - | - |
| Physical Education | 1 | 1 | 1 | 1 |
| Mechanics | - | - | 2 | - |
| Statistics and Resistance | 1 | 1 | 2 | 2 |
| Electricity | - | - | 2 | 1 |
| Workyard Tools | - | - | - | 2 |
| Design | 4 | 4 | 4 | 4 |
| General Technology | 2 | 2 | 2 | 2 |
| Building Construction | - | 2 | 2 | 2 |
| Communication Channels | - | 2 | 2 | 2 |
| Topography | - | 2 | 2 | - |
| Hygiene and Cleanliness | - | - | - | 1 |
| Laboratory Work | - | - | 3 | 3 |
| Practical Work | 6 | 6 | 2 | 5 |

## TIMETABLE - AGRICULTURAL SECTION
### (hours per week)

(a)  Agriculture.  (b)  Forestry.  (c)  Economics.

| Subjects | Class 3 | 4 | 5 | 6 |
|---|---|---|---|---|
| Religion/Morals | 1 | 1 | 1 | 1 |
| French | 6 | 5 | 3 | 2 |
| English | 3 | 3 | 2 | 2 |
| History and Civics | 1 | 1 | 1 | 3 |
| Geography | 1 | 1 | 1 | 1 |
| Mathematics | 6 | 6 | 6 | 2 |
| Physics | 3 | 2 | 2 | 1 |
| Chemistry | 2 | 2 | 2 | 1 |
| Biology | 3 | 2 | 3 | 1 |
| Physical Education | 1 | 1 | 1 | 1 |
| Art/Design | 2 | 2 | - | - |
| Cultivated Plant Improvement | - | - | - | 1 |
| Topography | 2 | 2 | - | - |
| Rural Character | 1 | 1 | 1 | 2 |
| Technology | - | - | 1 | 2 |
| Agricultural Sociology | - | - | - | (a) 2 |
| | | | | (b) 2 |
| | | | | (c) 3 |
| Agricultural Economics | - | - | (a) 2 | (a) 1 |
| | | | (b) 2 | (b) 1 |
| | | | (c) 4 | (c) 3 |

Agricultural Section (cont'd):

| | Class 3 | 4 | 5 | 6 |
|---|---|---|---|---|
| Agriculture | 2 | 3 | (a) 4 | (a) 4 |
| | | | (b) 1 | (b) 1 |
| | | | (c) 3 | (c) 2 |
| Sylviculture | - | - | (a) 1 | (a) - |
| | | | (b) 5 | (b) 5 |
| | | | (c) 1 | (c) - |
| Zootechniques | 1 | 3 | (a) 3 | (a) 3 |
| | | | (b) 2 | (b) 2 |
| | | | (c) 2 | (c) 2 |
| Plant Pathology | - | - | (a) 1 | (a) 3 |
| | | | (b) 1 | (b) 2 |
| | | | (c) 1 | (c) 3 |
| Practical Work | 5 | 5 | 5 | 7 |

Diplomas awarded:

(1)  Old program:  3 years' study after lower technical, making a
     total of 6 years' study.
     Diplôme de technicien A 2.

(2)  Long cycle of the new national program:
     4 years after the cycle d'orientation, making a
     total of 6 years.  First diploma in this
     Diplôme d'humanités techniques.


AGRICULTURAL AND TECHNICAL ASSISTANCE FOUNDATION PROGRAMS:

Projects sponsored by the Agricultural and Technical Assistance Foundation
(6333 Yucca, Los Angeles 28, California) are Agricultural Schools, Home
and Family Life Centers, and a girls' high school.  Under this Foundation
the University of the Congo was created.


CONGO POLYTECHNIC INSTITUTE TECHNICAL AGRICULTURAL SCHOOLS

3 schools established at Gemena, Sandoa, Vanga.

Basic objective:  to train rural youth to become proficient in farming.

3-year program  (11 months each year):

1st yr:  Orientation and Guidance, Agriculture of the region, Supervised
         farm program, Animal Production, Agronomy, Farm Mechanics,
         Horticulture, Arithmetic, Agricultural Geography, General
         Science and Natural Sciences.

Ethics, Music, French, English.

2nd yr:   Supervised farm program, Animal Production, Agronomy, Farm
          Mechanics, Horticulture, General Science, Physics, Chemistry
          Agricultural Economics, Arithmetic.
          Ethics, Music, French, English, Geography.

3rd yr:   Animal Production, Agronomy, Farm Mechanics, Horticulture,
          Agricultural Economics, Business Agriculture, Supervised farm
          program, Arithmetic.
          Ethics, Music, French, English, Geography.

Short courses also given on such subjects as Poultry Raising.  Graduates
of these short courses encouraged to form cooperatives under advice and
help of the CPI Technical Agricultural Schools staff.

Local committees nominate prospective students from their region.

Entrance requirements:        Successful completion of the primary school
                              cycle (5th grade).  Age under 30, good
                              health certificate for self and family.
                              Letter of recommendation from local
                              authority or religious worker.

Students showing promise for higher level agricultural training program
to receive assistance.


## College of Home Economics

Establishment, 1964.  4-year course for B.S. degree.

1st yr:   Orientation in Home Economics, Nutrition, Personal Hygiene and
          Physical Education, Bacteriology, Language (French, English and
          1 African language), Mathematics (general), Arts and Crafts,
          General Economics.

2nd yr:   Food Study and Preparation, General Chemistry, Child Care and
          Feeding, Clothing and Textiles, Language, Anthropology, House-
          hold Management, General Psychology.

3rd yr:   World Literature, Public Speaking and Demonstration Methods,
          Home Management Residence, General Psychology, Art and Music
          Appreciation, Family Economics, Family Health, Nursery School
          and Child Development.

4th yr:   World History, Sociology, Methods of Teaching Home Economics,
          Home Economics Extension, Family Relationships and Cultural
          Patterns, Field Work.

HOME AND FAMILY LIFE CENTERS

5, at Léopoldville, Stanleyville, Vanga, Sandoa, Gemena.

Women learn family care, how to prepare foods and other household
matters as well as such subjects as French and Mathematics.


GIRLS' HIGH SCHOOL (Lycée), Léopoldville

In addition to a regular lycée program, there is a special Department of
Business and Secretarial Training.

* * *


INSTITUT CONGOLAIS D'ENSEIGNEMENT SOCIAL, Léopoldville

Entrance requirements:      6 years of primary education, and 2 years
                            of lower secondary studies.

Duration of programs:    4 years.


## TIMETABLE
(Hours per week)

| General Courses | Class 3 | 4 | 5 | 6 |
|---|---|---|---|---|
| Religion/Morals | 1 | 1 | 1 | 1 |
| History | 2 | 2 | 2 | 2 |
| Geography | 2 | 2 | 1 | 1 |
| French | 6 | 5 | 5 | 4 |
| English | 4 | 3 | 3 | 2 |
| Mathematics | 4 | 4 | 2 | 2 |
| Sciences: Chemistry, Physics, Biology | 2 | 3 | 2 | 1 |
| Civics | 1 | - | - | 1 |
| Physical Education | 1 | 1 | 1 | 1 |
|  | 23 | 21 | 17 | 15 |

| Technical Courses | | | | |
|---|---|---|---|---|
| Law | - | 2 | 3 | 4½ |
| Psychology/Pedagogy | - | 2 | 3 | 2 |
| Philosophy | - | - | - | 2 |
| Economics | 1½ | 1 | 2 | 2 |
| Hygiene | 5 | 1 | 1 | 1 |
| Methodology | 1½ | 1 | - | - |
| Social Institutions | 2 | 2½ | 2 | - |

| | 1 | 2½ | 3 | 3 |
|---|---|---|---|---|
| Sociology | 1 | 2½ | 3 | 3 |
| Methods of Social Action | 2 | 3 | 5 | 6½ |
| | 13 | 15 | 19 | 21 |
| TOTAL | 36 | 36 | 36 | 36 |

<u>Diplôme de technicien social</u> awarded at close of program.  Permits student to first-year candidacy in University Faculty of Political, Social and Economic Sciences.


## TEACHER EDUCATION

Teacher training at the secondary level is now being incorporated into the new national program of secondary education.


## B E F O R E   1 9 6 0   R E F O R M


## ECOLE D'APPRENTISSAGE PEDAGOGIQUE (Apprentice Teachers' Training School)

Entry with 5 years' primary.  Trained supplementary teachers for village school.

Course included revision of subjects taught at primary school and introduction to primary school teaching methods.


## ECOLE DE MONITEURS (Instructors' Training School)

Entry with 6 years' primary.  Trained lower primary school and ordinary upper primary school teachers.

4-year course.  General training comparable to lower stage of Modern Humanities, plus pedagogical training in last 2 years.

Certificate of Lower Humanities and Instructor's Diploma awarded.


## ECOLE NORMALE SECONDAIRE (Secondary Teacher Training School)

Entry after 6 years' primary.

6-year course in 2 stages:  1st stage (3 years) general training.  2nd stage (3 years) completion of general training plus pedagogical training. Trained teachers for selective upper primary schools.

SECTIONS NORMALES PRIMAIRES (Teacher Training Sections in Secondary
    Schools)

Awarded primary teachers' diploma and Humanities certificate.


A F T E R   1 9 6 0   R E F O R M


Timetables given in pedagogical section of new national program of
secondary education.

Short or long cycle.  Any student may finish after 4 years' secondary
studies and do 1 additional year of purely pedagogical training.

Brevet d'instituteur awarded after 4 years.  Diplôme d'instituteur
awarded after 6 years.

Instituteurs then teach in primary schools.


TEACHER TRAINING AT A HIGHER EDUCATION LEVEL (Non-University)

This is provided in the Institut Pédagogique National and in 5 Ecoles
Supérieures Pédagogiques in Boma, Elisabethville, Bukavu, and Kalina-
Léopoldville.  These 5 écoles supérieures pédagogiques are all Catholic
schools, but must conform to the program of the Institut Pédagogique
National.

These establishments form régents who teach the lower secondary cycle of
the 1st three years.


INSTITUT PEDAGOGIQUE NATIONAL, Léopoldville

Government-controlled through Council of Administration.  Works in close
collaboration with the Ministry of National Education and Fine Arts.

Founded October, 1961.

Entry age:      No age limit.

Entrance requirements:        Preparatory year:
                              4 years  secondary pedagogical plus 1 year
                              of teaching experience.
                    or        5 years secondary plus entrance examination.

                              1st year:
                              6 years secondary plus entrance examination.
                    or        Recognized Humanities diploma.

Language of instruction:        French.

Duration of course:     1 preparatory year (optional).
                        2 years plus 1 year practical teaching experience.

Diplomas awarded:

        2nd year:   Brevet de régent
        3rd year:   Diplôme de régent, after presentation and defense
                        and thesis.

Programs: 1st year:     Letters section, Science section.

        2nd year:   4 sections for specialization:  French, History,
                        Mathematics-Technology, Natural Sciences-Geography.

Curriculum (hours per week):

Preparatory year:       French (7), English (3), History (3), Geography
                        (3), Mathematics (5), Physics (2), Chemistry (1),
                        Natural Sciences (3), Art (2).

1st yr:   Letters:
          French (10), English (3), African Languages (3), History (4),
          Geography(2), Mathematics (1), Biology and Hygiene (1), Art
          (2), Pedagogical Psychology (3), General Methodology (2).

          Science:
          French (3), English (1), Geography (3), Mathematics (6),
          Natural Sciences (5), Physics (3), Chemistry (1), Technology
          (1), Practical Workshop in Wood, Metal (1), Art (2), Pedagogical
          Psychology (3), General Methodology (2).

2nd yr:   General:
          General Pedagogy (2), Pedagogical Psychology (2), Art (2),
          Cultural Activities (3), Special Methodology and Professional
          Practice of the Specialty and study of cycle d'orientation
          programs.

          French:
          French (16), African Culture (6), English (5).

          History:
          History (14), African Culture (6), English (5).

          Mathematics/Technology:
          Mathematics (11), Physics, Technology, Workshop (10), Chemistry
          (2), French (2), English (2).

          Natural Sciences/Geography:
          Natural Sciences (11), Geography (10), Chemistry (2), French
          (2), English (2).

Examination at end of 2nd year includes a practical test consisting of 2
public lessons.

Brevet d'aptitude à l'enseignement secondaire inférieur awarded.

3rd yr:    Practical Teaching Experience.

At the end of the year, Diplôme de régent awarded after presentation and defense of a thesis.


TEACHER TRAINING AT UNIVERSITY LEVEL

Licence holders may take a 1-year course for the Agrégation de l'enseignement moyen du degré supérieur in order to teach in the second cycle of secondary education in their specialty.

The course in the Institute of Psychology and Pedagogy of the University of Lovanium comprises:

>   Experimental Pedagogy, History of Pedagogy, General Methodology, Special Teaching Methodology in the specialty, and Didactic exercises and lessons in the specialty.

A candidature and licence in Pedagogy is awarded in the Institute of Psychology and Pedagogy of the University of Lovanium.

MALAWI
(Nyasaland)

Colonial and Federation Education

To 1963

From 1963
through 1964

Agric.
Training

Vocational
and
Technical
Training

Teacher
Training

Secondary

**VI ( Sixth Form )
V
*IV
III
II
I Form ( Standard VII )

( Higher School )

( Senior Secondary )

( Junior Secondary )

SECONDARY EDUCATION

*V
IV    Secondary
III
II
I

Primary

VI
V
IV
III
II
I Standard
Sub - Standard B
Sub - Standard A

( Senior Primary )

( Junior Primary )    PRIMARY EDUCATION

None

| Student's Age | Year of Schooling | | |
|---|---|---|---|
| 26 | 19 | | |
| 25 | 18 | | HIGHER EDUCATION |
| 24 | 17 | | |
| 23 | 16 | | |
| 22 | 15 | | |
| 21 | 14 | | |
| 20 | 13 | | SECONDARY |
| 19 | 12 | | |
| 18 | 11 | | |
| 17 | 10 | | |
| 16 | 9 | | |
| 15 | 8 | | |
| 14 | 7 | | ELEMENTARY |
| 13 | 6 | | |
| 12 | 5 | | |
| 11 | 4 | | |
| 10 | 3 | | |
| 9 | 2 | | |
| 8 | 1 | | |
| 7 | | | |
| 6 | | | |
| 5 | | | |
| 4 | | | |
| 3 | | | |

Compulsory education:  None

School year:  January - December

Secondary grading:  Distinction - 75% and over
Credit    - 60% and over
Pass      - 40% - 59% and above
Fail      - Below 40%

MALAWI
From 1966

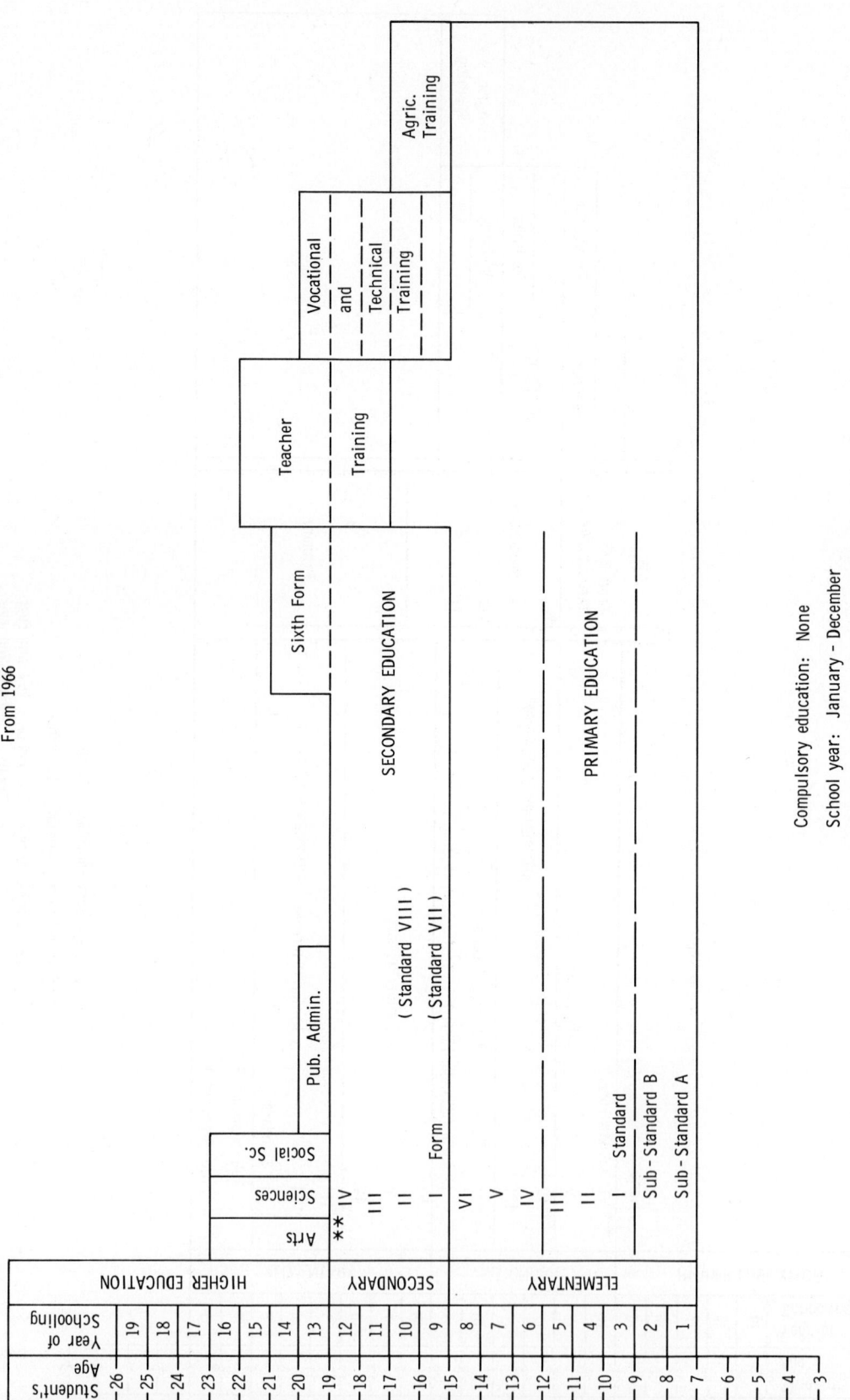

Compulsory education: None

School year: January - December

Secondary grading:  Distinction - 75% and over
                    Credit      - 60% and over
                    Pass        - 40% - 59% and above
                    Fail        - Below 40%

MALAWI
(Formerly Nyasaland)

Independence, July 6, 1964.


BACKGROUND

The African population is composed of Bantu tribes. Largest of these are
the Ngutu, Chewa, Nyanja, Yao, Ngoni, and Tumbuka. Europeans, mostly of
British origin and some Afrikaans-speaking peoples from Republic of South
Africa. Asians (mostly Indians), Portuguese and persons of mixed races.

English is the official language. Bantu tribes speak their own languages
and dialects. Nyanja (Chinyanja) is lingua franca and is taught in school.
Yao is spoken by Yao tribes; Tumbuka (Chitumbuka) is widely used in northern province.

Before the explorations of David Livingstone in last half of the 19th
century, Arab slave traders operated in Nyasaland. Livingstone's explorations, 1850-60, prompted the establishment of two mission stations in
Nyasaland, 1875-76. In 1878, Scottish business men formed the African
Lakes Company. As the company extended operations it met with resistance
from Arabs.

British annexed territory, 1891. Up to 1910, a small number of European
planters settled in Shire Highlands. Between World Wars I and II, United
Kingdom extended increasing responsibility to African peoples.

1953, by decision of the British government, Nyasaland was joined with
Northern Rhodesia and Southern Rhodesia in the Central African Federation
(Federation of Rhodesia and Nyasaland). African opposition to Federation
caused a state of emergency to be declared. Between 1953 and 1963,
Nyasaland was a British Protectorate within the Federation of Rhodesia
and Nyasaland.

After April 1960, Nyasaland granted increased right to conduct internal
affairs. At constitutional conference in London, November 1962, it was
agreed that Nyasaland would become fully self-governing early in 1963.
On December 12, 1962, British government accepted Nyasaland's proposal to
secede from the Federation; on February 1, 1963 the country became self-
governing. Nyasaland became independent on July 6, 1964 and name changed
to Malawi.

From the Scottish missions of the late 19th century, Christian missions
carried the burden of African education until 1953 when the federal government assumed responsibility for education of the Europeans, Asians and

Coloureds, and African education was made the responsibility of the territorial government. Thereafter, many mission schools grant-aided.

Under Educational Plan of 1957-61:
    (a)  Primary education expanded and 21 new schools built.
    (b)  Junior secondary schools were increased from 8 to 12.
    (c)  Secondary schools were expanded and new school built.
    (d)  New teacher training college opened; 2 existing ones rebuilt.
    (e)  Secondary schools for girls and coeducational schools enlarged.

A new Education Ordinance became law March 1962, establishing an Advisory Council and strengthening public control over education. The Ministry of Education, Social Development and Information (1963 became Ministry of Education and Local Government) was responsible for African education, controlling primary and secondary education, technical and trade schools, teacher training colleges, homecraft centers, a college of commerce and a junior college. Previously when the Department of Information and the Training Office were incorporated into the Ministry, training for higher civil service posts, scholarships and study overseas were also dealt with.

As of July 6, 1964, the Malawi educational system became multiracial.


### COLONIAL AND FEDERATION EDUCATION (THROUGH 1964)

In addition to providing the major portion of African education, some missions offered primary training to mixed classes. 1947, 1 government school started for Coloured children (Eurafricans). Private Indian schools were managed by Indian School committees.

As of 1953 there were 5 full range government primary schools for European children, but no vocational training nor secondary education available.

Training of Africans became increasingly the responsibility of local education authorities and voluntary agencies, administering large proportion of primary schools. Some are "unassisted" but most receive government grants. The majority of secondary schools are assisted.


### PRIMARY EDUCATION

8-year Program:     Infant School       Sub-Standards A and B
                    Junior Primary      Standards I through III
                    Senior Primary      Standards IV through VI

Language of instruction:   Nyanja and Tumbuka in Sub-Standards.

English introduced as subject in Standard I and
as language of instruction in Standard IV.

Entry age:      7 years.

Curriculum:    English, Nyanja, History, Arithmetic, Rural Science, Geography, Hygiene, Bible Studies.

Certificate awarded:      <u>Government Primary School-Leaving Certificate</u>.


## SECONDARY EDUCATION

First high school built 1941.  1958 Dedza Government Secondary School
added 2 years to prepare pupils for Higher School Certificate.

As of 1963 there were 34 secondary schools including junior colleges.  Of
these, 2 schools and 2 junior colleges offered post-certificate courses
preparing for university entrance.

7 day secondary schools built 1963 (government):

Port Herald
Chiradzulu
Zomba
Fort Johnston
Ncheu
Kasungu
Soche Hill (Demonstration Secondary School of the Teachers' College)

2 secondary schools administered by Boards of Governors:

Blantyre Secondary School
Zomba Secondary School

Other government secondary schools included:

Dedza Secondary School            Higher School
Mzuzu Secondary School
Lilongwe Secondary School
Livinstonia Junior College        Sixth Form program
                                  (Operating only between 1963 and 1964).

Other secondary schools:

English schools
Indian schools (administered by Indian School committees)

6-year Program (Forms I through VI)

Curriculum:     English Language, English Literature, General Science,
                Arithmetic, Algebra, Geometry, Trigonometry, Scripture,
                Nyanja, History and Geography.

Certificates awarded:     Conclusion of Form II (Junior Secondary)
                        +Junior Certificate of Education

                          Conclusion of Form IV (Senior Secondary)
                          Cambridge School Certificate

                          Conclusion of Sixth Form (Higher School)
                          Higher School Certificate

+Junior Certificate examination taken only by "External" (non-school)
pupils beginning 1963.


TECHNICAL AND VOCATIONAL EDUCATION


FURTHER EDUCATION CENTER, Blantyre.

This technical college was initiated 1961, planned through cooperation
between the U.S. Agency for International Development (A.I.D.) and the
Malawi Ministry of Education.  Plans provided for the Correspondence
College (a New Zealand project) and the College of Commerce to be incorporated at all levels of training.

Courses developed by Technical Education Officer and Principal to meet
immediate needs of commerce, industry and the workers themselves.  The
improvised technical training school established to be later absorbed
by the new Malawi Polytechnic School (see Technical and Vocational Education under Present System).

Between 1962 and 1963, size of attendance in following order:

        Evening classes
        Day-release classes (1/2 day, later extended to entire day per week)
        Full-time classes

Entrance requirements:              Primary School-Leaving Certificate.
                                    (Some students admitted without full
                                    primary.)

                                    Form II (secondary)

Courses offered:    Preliminary technical classes in:
                    Mechanical, Electrical Engineering, Woodwork, Tech-
                    nical Drawing and Mathematics, Printing and General
                    Subjects.

Following program provided, January through December 1964, under British and American cooperative teaching and administration.

Entrance requirements:       Much the same as above but qualifications raised.

Course offered:    1 year of preparatory and remedial work in academic and technical fields.

## Subjects

| Full-time: | Mechanical Craft I-II | Carpentry |
|---|---|---|
| | Metal Craft (Prelim.) | Brickwork (Prelim.) |
| | Motor Vehicles | Teacher Training |

| Day-release: | Motor Vehicle | Composition Printers |
|---|---|---|
| | Electric Technician | |

| Evening: | G.C.E. (British Constitution, Geography, English, Economics, Mathematics) | Junior Certificate of Nyasaland (J.C.N.) (English, General Science, Mathematics (A and B), Geography, Mathematics, History) |
|---|---|---|
| | Carpentry and Joinery II-III | Painters Trade Test II-III |
| | Painting | Electric Technicians Science (Mathematics, English, Technology) |
| | Electrical Technician | |

Certificates awarded:   City and Guilds of London Institute; Craft Certificates and Diplomas.

## PRESENT SYSTEM

As of 1965 all Malawi schools integrated, except 4 European schools (1 secondary and 4 primary).

## PRIMARY EDUCATION

1,129 primary schools - 1965.

7-year primary program (1963-65).

8-year primary program re-established as of January 1966:

| Infant (Village School) | Sub-Standards A and B |
|---|---|
| Junior Primary | Standards I through III |
| Senior Primary | Standards IV through VI |

Language of instruction:  Nyanja and Tumbuka in Sub-Standards A and B.

Entry age:      Government prefers 8 years.

Curriculum:     English, Nyanja, History, Arithmetic, Rural Science,
                Geography, Hygiene, Bible Studies.

Certificate awarded:     Primary School-Leaving Certificate.
                         (50% passing grade)


## SECONDARY EDUCATION

37 secondary schools - 1965.  Many 2-year "Junior" secondary schools
expanded to full secondary program.

5-year secondary program - Forms I through V (1963-1965 only)

4-year secondary program - Forms I through IV re-established as of January
1966.  No division of "Junior" and "Senior" secondary school as of January
1966.

Entrance requirements:          Internal Secondary School examination.


### DEDZA SECONDARY SCHOOL

#### TYPICAL WEEKLY TIMETABLE (As of October 1965)
#### (40-minute periods per week)

|                    |          |     | F O R M S |          |                                  |
| Subjects           | 1A, 1B, 1C | 2A, 2B | 3A, 3B | 4A, 4B | 5A, 5B, 5C (through 1965 only) |
|--------------------|----------|--------|--------|--------|--------------------------------|
| English            | 9        | 7      | 7      | 7      | 8                              |
| Mathematics        | 5        | 5      | 5      | 5      | 6                              |
| Additional Math.   | -        | -      | -      | 4      | 3                              |
| History            | 3        | 3      | 3      | 4      | 4                              |
| Geography          | 3        | 3      | 3      | 4      | 4                              |
| Chemistry          | -        | 3      | 3      | 4      | 4                              |
| Physics            | -        | 3      | 3      | 3      | 4                              |
| Biology            | -        | 3      | 3      | 3      | 4                              |
| General Science    | 6        | -      | -      | -      | -                              |
| Health Science     | -        | -      | -      | -      | 1                              |
| Art                | 3        | 3      | 3      | 4      | 4                              |
| French             | 3        | 3      | 3      | 4      | 7                              |
| Nyanja             | -        | -      | -      | -      | 2                              |
| Total              | 32       | 33     | 33     | 42     | 51                             |

Candidates may offer a minimum of 6 subjects and a maximum of 9 subjects.
Those passing in 6 subjects receive a full Cambridge certificate, and
G.C.E. "O" level if they pass in less than 6 subjects.

Certificate awarded:        Cambridge School Certificate or G.C.E. "O" level.

Adults (External students) enter for G.C.E.
(London University) and are prepared by correspondence colleges.


## SIXTH FORM

Curriculum:     Arts courses or Science courses.

Certificate awarded:     Cambridge Higher School Certificate.

As of 1965 government policy to develop Sixth Form studies only for those
students preparing for professional courses not offered by the new University.

Dedza Sixth Form transferred to Blantyre Secondary School which offers
Sixth Form as of 1966.


## HIGHER EDUCATION

### UNIVERSITY OF MALAWI, Zomba

Founded 1965.  Temporary headquarters, Blantyre.

The University of Malawi accepted its first students September 1965.  New
institution to act as integrating center for all higher and further education in the country.

Constituent professional colleges - Soche Hill Training College, Institute
of Public Administration and the higher technical and commercial components
of the Malawi Polytechnic are schools and faculties of the University.  The
new Bunda School of Agriculture is the nucleus for the University's Faculty
of Agriculture.

General entrance requirements        5 credits in the Cambridge School Cer-
        for degree courses:          tificate
                                  or 5 passes at "Ordinary" level in General
                                     Certificate of Education (G.C.E. "O").

A special Mature Entry planned in 1966
for those unable to obtain entrance
September 1965.

Duration of degree courses:  4 years.

| Main courses:<br>(from 1965-66) | Chemistry<br>Physics<br>Biology<br>French | Mathematics<br>English<br>Geography<br>History |
|---|---|---|
| Projected courses:<br>(from 1966) | Education<br>Agriculture<br>Economics | Philosophy<br>Psychology<br>Sociology |

N.B.: It is proposed to form a single degree subject (called PPS) out of
mutually reinforcing aspects of Philosophy, Psychology and Sociology.
This course is intended especially for prospective teachers and
administrators.

Degree awarded:     <u>Ordinary Degree</u>, arts, science, and social science
                    subjects at first.

Honours courses and graduate work will be offered at a later date.
Research in selected areas is already being planned.


<u>Institute of Public Administration</u>

Constituent body of University as of 1966.  Permanent location, Zomba;
temporary location, Mpemba (until 1968).

Previous to 1965, 3 schools, with training to bring about localization
of the Civil Service:  Administration, Law, Co-operative Training.

| Courses | Duration |
|---|---|
| Court Presidents | 3 months |
| Court Clerks | 3 months |
| Court Supervisors | 3 months |
| Magistrates | 6 months |
| Co-operative Trainees | 6 months |
| Co-operative Managers | 6 months |

1st Administrative and Executive Courses established 1963:

| Administrative Course No. 1 | 9 months |
|---|---|
| Executive Course No. 1 | 6 months |
| Co-operative Managers' Course No. 2 | 6 weeks |
| Law Course No. 2 | 12 months |

## TECHNICAL AND VOCATIONAL EDUCATION

### TRADE SCHOOLS

Artisan and junior trade training centers:

    Namitete Trade School
    Mzuzu Trade School
    Livingstonia Trade School

Entrance requirements:          Some primary training if not School-Leaving Certificate.

Duration of course: 1 year.

Curriculum:          Preliminary classes in Carpentry and Building Trades.

### GOVERNMENT TECHNICAL SCHOOLS

Entrance requirements:          Standard VIII
School-Leaving Certificate.

Duration of course: 1 year.

Curriculum:

    Soche Technical School:   Woodworking, Building, Engineering.
    Lilongwe Technical School: Woodworking, Building.
     (New, 1963)

Certificates awarded:    Grade III Trade Test
                     Grade II and I after in-service training
                     City and Guilds of London Institute Craft examinations in Carpentry of Bricklaying

### MALAWI POLYTECHNIC ANNEX

Further Education Center (see Technical and Vocational Education under Colonial and Federation Education) served for 1 year as a temporary base of operation for the preliminary stages of the new Polytechnic School from January through December 1964.

Beginning January through December 1965, name of temporary school changed to "Malawi Polytechnic Annex" from "Further Education Center." Physical location the same until January 1966.

| Full-time day courses | Subjects | Hours per week |
|---|---|---|
| I. Carpentry | Carpentry | 16 |
| | Mechanical Drawing | 3 |
| | Mathematics | 4 |
| | English | 3 |
| | Social Studies | 1 |
| | Science | 2 |
| | Library | 1 |
| II. Technical Teachers | Educational Theory | 4 |
| | Mechanical Drawing | 2 |
| | Mathematics | 4 |
| | English | 2 |
| | Engineering Science | 4 |
| | Engineering Tutorial | 2 |
| | Shop Theory and Practice | 14 |
| III. Mechanical Craft | Shop and Theory | 18 |
| | Mechanical Drawing | 2 |
| | Mathematics | 5 |
| | English | 2 |
| | Social Studies | 1 |
| | Tutorial | 1 |
| | Library | 1 |
| IV. Mechanical Craft | Shop and Theory | 19 |
| | Mechanical Drawing | 2 |
| | Mathematics | 3 |
| | English | 2 |
| | Social Studies | 1 |
| | Tutorial | 1 |
| | Library | 2 |
| V. Mechanical Craft | Shop and Theory | 19 |
| | Mechanical Drawing | 2 |
| | Mathematics | 4 |
| | English | 3 |
| | Social Studies | 1 |
| | Library | 1 |
| VI. Motor Vehicle Mechanics | Shop and Theory | 16 |
| | Mechanical Drawing | 2 |
| | Mathematics | 3 |
| | English | 3 |
| | Science | 2 |

|  |  | Auto Science | 2 |
|  |  | Social Studies | 1 |
|  |  | Library | 1 |
| VII. | Basic Technology | Metals | 10 |
|  |  | Electricity | 2 |
|  |  | Power Mechanics | 5 |
|  |  | Technical Drawing | 2 |
|  |  | Mathematics | 3 |
|  |  | English | 4 |
|  |  | Social Studies | 1 |
|  |  | Library | 1 |
| VIII. | Basic Technology | Metals | 10 |
|  |  | Electricity | 2 |
|  |  | Power Mechanics | 5 |
|  |  | Technical Drawing | 2 |
|  |  | Mathematics | 3 |
|  |  | English | 4 |
|  |  | Social Studies | 1 |
|  |  | Library | 1 |
| IX. | Basic Technology | Metals | 10 |
|  |  | Electricity | 5 |
|  |  | Power Mechanics | 5 |
|  |  | Mechanical Drawing | 3 |
|  |  | Mathematics | 3 |
|  |  | English | 2 |
|  |  | Social Studies | 1 |
|  |  | Library | 1 |

| Day-release courses | Subjects | Hours per week |
|---|---|---|
| I. Motor Mechanics | Theory | 2 |
|  | +Mathematics | 1 |
|  | +English | 1 |
| II. Electrical Technician | Electrical Science | 2 |
|  | +English | 1 |
|  | +Mathematics | 1 |
| III. Basic Electricity | Theory and Practice | 6 |
|  | +English | 2 |
|  | +Mathematics | 2 |

+These subjects also taken at part-time classes.

| Evening classes | Subjects | Hours per week |
|---|---|---|
| Offered 2 evenings each week: | G.C.E. (A) English | 2 |
| | G.C.E. (B) English | 2 |
| | G.C.E. (A) Mathematics | 2 |
| | G.C.E. (B) Mathematics | 2 |
| | Machine Shop Turning | 2 |
| | Painting III and II | 2 |
| | Machine Shop Fitting | 2 |
| | Carpentry and Joinery | 2 |
| | Basic Electricity | 2 |
| Offered 1 evening each week: | Basic Radio Mathematics | 2 |
| | Machine Shop Turning | 2 |
| | Motor Vehicle Mechanics | 2 |
| | Electrical Technicians Course | 5 |

Beginning September 1965 - 6 additional courses:  full-time.

    Building and Civil Engineering Technician
    Mechanical and Electrical Engineering Technician
    Land Surveying
    Laboratory Technicians (General)
    Business and Social Studies
    Textiles

Duration:  3 years.

Certificate awarded:  Diploma.

Evening classes also expanded.

MALAWI POLYTECHNIC, Blantyre

Opened January 1966.

The following institutions were phased out, incorporated or affiliated
with the new Polytechnic:

    Further Education Center
    College of Commerce
    Correspondence School

New school to be flexible, comprehensive institution offering both full
and part-time programs in industrial and commercial fields, providing
adult training in vocational and general subjects.

The Polytechnic will supply technical information for the entire country,
develop apprenticeship in industry and coordinate training for Malawi
Ministries - Post Office and Telecommunications, Police, Works and Housing,
Transport and Communications, etc.

As the Polytechnic opened the range of courses was equivalent to a Junior
College of technical students with program at secondary level including
continuation training to complete primary schooling. However the institution is to be staffed and equipped for higher level technical studies
in the future.

Entrance requirements:                 School-Leaving Certificate
                                       Standard VIII

                                       Junior Certificate

                                       Cambridge School Certificate

                                       Employer's recommendation

Duration of course:   Range from short duration to 3 years.

Courses offered:      Full-time, day-release and evening classes as listed
                      for MALAWI POLYTECHNIC ANNEX.

Diplomas and certificates awarded: City and Guilds of London Institute
                                   Craft and Intermediate Certificates

                                   City and Guilds of London Institute
                                   Technician Diploma (3-year course)
                                      Mechanical, Electrical, Building and
                                      Civil Engineering

Technical Secondary Teacher's Diploma Course:

    Beginning January 1966, 2 terms, 3 subjects with Mathematics, Physics
    and English.

GOVERNMENT COLLEGE OF COMMERCE

Became part of new Polytechnic.

Courses offered, full and part-time:

                      Business Studies, Shorthand, Typing and general
                      clerical subjects.

(1)  Bookkeeping and Commerce (Evening classes)

    Entrance requirements:        Standard VI

(a)  Course:   2 nights per week for 1 year.

     Award:   <u>Elementary Certificate</u> - Royal Society of Arts

(b)  Course:   2 nights per week for additional 1 year.

     Award:   <u>Intermediate Certificate</u> - R.S.A.

(2)  Commercial Training

Entrance requirements:          Standard VII

(a)  Course:   2 nights per week - 1 year.

     Award:   <u>Elementary Certificate</u> - R.S.A.

(b)  Course:   2 nights per week - additional 1 year.

     Award:   <u>Intermediate Certificate</u> - R.S.A.

(3)  Secretarial Training

Entrance requirements:          Standard X

Duration of course:  2 years (full-time)

Award:              <u>Elementary and Intermediate Certificates</u> - R.S.A.


<u>GOVERNMENT TRAINING PROGRAMS</u> (Other than Ministry of Education)


<u>Ministry of Works and Housing</u>

Training in special courses.


<u>Railway Training Programs</u>

Entrance requirements:          Standard VI

Duration of course:     5 years.

    18-month course followed by 18-month workshops preparing for:
       Railways Trade Test III
    Additional year - Test II
    End of 5th year - Test I

Ministry of Agriculture

See following section.


AGRICULTURAL TRAINING:


COLBY SCHOOL OF AGRICULTURE, Lilongwe

Course A:          Pre-Service Course

Entrance requirements:                    Primary School-Leaving Certificate
                                          (Formerly required)

                                          2 or more years of secondary work
                                          (As of 1966 entry qualifications)

Duration of course:  2 years full-time.

Certificate awarded: Certificate in Agriculture

                    Successful students appointed as Field Extension
                    Workers in the Department of Agriculture.

Course B:          In-Service Training Courses

Entrance requirements:                    Restricted to serving officers
                                          (No specific qualifications)

Duration of course:  Vary from 10 days to 11 months.  No regular program,
                     designed to suit specific training needs.

Certificate awarded: Certificate for 11-month courses (only).

Course C:          Special Courses for teachers of rural science and technical
                   demonstrators in Department of Agriculture.

Entrance requirements:                    Same as Course B.

Duration of Course:  Planned as requested by government.

Certificate awarded: No standardized award.


BUNDA COLLEGE OF AGRICULTURE, near Lilongwe

Proposed opening June 1966.  This institution planned as nucleus of the
Faculty of Agriculture in the new Malawi University.

Entrance requirements:          Cambridge School Certificate with
                                passes in 5 subjects including English,
                                Mathematics and Science.

Courses planned:        3 full-time courses.

Certificate awarded:    Diploma in Agriculture


VETERINARY TRAINING SCHOOL, Mikolongwe, near Limbe

Entrance requirements:          Standard VI and VII.


FORESTRY TRAINING SCHOOL, Chongone

Entrance requirements:          Standard VII

Duration of course:     2 years.

Certificate awarded:    Technical Assistant Grade I.


TEACHER EDUCATION

Government provides financial assistance to voluntary agencies, missions,
and local authorities who own majority of schools.

As of 1965, 11 training colleges in country, all residential.  9 operated
by voluntary agencies; 2 by government.

Government-operated colleges:

    Domasi Training College  (Primary teaching)
    Soche Hill Training College (Only school training for secondary
        teaching in Malawi)


## GRADES OF TEACHERS

| GRADE | ENTRANCE REQUIREMENTS | DURATION OF TRAINING | TEACHING AREA |
|-------|----------------------|---------------------|---------------|
| T 5 | Standard VI | (None as of 1965) (previously) 3 years | Lower Primary |
| T 4 | Standard VIII (Form II) | (new) 2 years | Lower Primary |

| +T 3 | Junior Certificate | (previously) 3 years | Upper Primary |
|---|---|---|---|
| | | (new) 2 years | |
| T 2 | Cambridge School Cer-tificate | (new) 3 years | Lower classes of Secondary |
| | ++Cambridge School Cer-tificate | (previously) 2 years | |
| +++T 1 | Higher School Certi-ficate | | Upper classes of Secondary |
| +++Graduate Teachers | University degree | | Upper Secondary and Sixth Form |

+Introduction of full secondary program at all secondary schools abolished entrance requirement of Junior Certificate for T 3 (this grade retained only for promotion of T 4 teachers passing external Junior Certificate examination).

++Former T 2 grading given after a 2-year course from School Certifi-cate level, obsolescent as of 1963 (replaced by Diploma of Education at Soche Hill College (see below).

T 2 qualifications retained for serving teachers able to reach this grade either by passing Cambridge School Certificate or 4 "O" level subjects, including English, in G.C.E. or by in-service course such as Upgrading Course at Soche Hill in 1963 (see below).

+++Training of T 1 and Graduate teachers done outside of Malawi:

    T 1 Grade at Chalimbana Training College - Zambia.
    Graduate Teachers at Institute of Education of the University
        College of Rhodesia and Nyasaland in Salisbury (Southern
        Rhodesia).
    A few teachers take U.K. Ministry of Education type course at
        University College of Rhodesia and Nyasaland.

In 1963 primary schools were decreased to 7 years; secondary programs were lengthened to 5 years and Grade T 3 training of teachers was discontinued. This necessitated an increase of from 2 to 3 years program for training T 4 teachers (main supply of Primary teachers). As of 1965 this additional year was reduced again to 2 years due to the expansion of Malawi's educa-tional facilities.

## SOCHE HILL GOVERNMENT COLLEGE (near Blantyre)

1st phase of new training college opened for students September 1962. T 3 and T 2 teacher trainees were transferred from Domasi Government Teachers College.

4-term course for serving T 3 teachers to upgrade them to T 2 grading was conducted as temporary measure.

January 1964, <u>Diploma of Education Course</u> initiated.

Entrance requirements:                    <u>Cambridge School Certificate</u>

Duration of course:          3 years.

Area of teaching:            Lower classes in Secondary School (qualified in 2 teaching subjects with emphasis on English and Science).

Curriculum:

General subjects:        English, Education, African History, Art and Craft, Library, Needlework (girls).

Option subjects:         English Literature, Mathematics, Geography, History, French, Biology, Chemistry, Physics.

Certificate awarded:         Students attempt 2 "A" level subjects in G.C.E. University of London examination.

<u>Diploma of Education</u>.

RHODESIA
European Education
( Including Asian & Coloured )
and for
Northern Rhodesia and Nyasaland ( Years of Federation )

| Student's Age | Year of Schooling | | | |
|---|---|---|---|---|
| 26 | 21 | HIGHER EDUCATION | | |
| 25 | 20 | | | |
| 24 | 19 | | | |
| 23 | 18 | | | |
| 22 | 17 | | | |
| 21 | 16 | | | |
| 20 | 15 | | | |
| 19 | 14 | | Arts | Education |
| 18 | 13 | ** VI (Upper) | Medicine | Science | Soc. St. |
| 17 | 12 | (Lower) | | |
| 16 | 11 | SECONDARY | * IV Form | Higher School (Form V – slower stream "O" level) |
| 15 | 10 | | III Form | |
| 14 | 9 | | II Form | SECONDARY EDUCATION |
| 13 | 8 | | I Form | |
| 12 | 7 | ELEMENTARY | 5 Standard | |
| 11 | 6 | | 4 Standard | |
| 10 | 5 | | 3 Standard | PRIMARY EDUCATION |
| 9 | 4 | | 2 Standard | |
| 8 | 3 | | 1 Standard | |
| 7 | 2 | | { Infant | |
| 6 | 1 | | | |
| 5 | | | | |
| 4 | | | | |
| 3 | | | | |

Technical Institutions

and Apprenticeship

Craft

(Tech.) High School

Agriculture

Commerce

Commercial Courses

Teacher Training

Compulsory education:  7 - 15 years of age

School year:  Late January - Early December

Secondary grading:  1 - 100
50 pass mark
( For secondary certificates, see SECONDARY EDUCATION )

RHODESIA
African Education

Compulsory education:  6 - 11 years of age ( urban )

School year:  Late January - Early December ( 3 terms )

Grading:   1 - 100
          50 pass mark
          ( For secondary certificates, see SECONDARY EDUCATION )

| Student's Age | Year of Schooling | | | | | |
|---|---|---|---|---|---|---|
| 26 | 20 | HIGHER EDUCATION | Arts | Education | Science | Medicine | Soc. St. |
| 25 | 19 | | | | | |
| 24 | 18 | | | | | |
| 23 | 17 | | | | | |
| 22 | 16 | | | | | |
| 21 | 15 | | | | | |
| 20 | 14 | SECONDARY | ** VI Form ( Higher School ) |
| 19 | 13 | | V Form |
| 18 | 12 | | * IV Form ( Senior Secondary ) |
| 17 | 11 | | III Form |
| 16 | 10 | | II Form ( Junior Secondary ) |
| 15 | 9 | | I Form |
| 14 | 8 | PRIMARY | 6 Standard ( Upper Primary ) |
| 13 | 7 | | 5 Standard |
| 12 | 6 | | 4 Standard |
| 11 | 5 | | 3 Standard ( Lower Primary ) |
| 10 | 4 | | 2 Standard |
| 9 | 3 | | 1 Standard |
| 8 | 2 | | Sub - Standard B |
| 7 | 1 | | Sub - Standard A |
| 6 | | | |
| 5 | | | |
| 4 | | | |
| 3 | | | |

Correspondence courses for all levels

Teacher Tech. Tr. / Teacher Training
( P.T.H. )
( P.T.L. )

Agricultural College
( Adv. Agric. )
( Spec. Tr. )
( Jr. Tech. Bias Agric. )

Technical Colleges
Technical Tr. ( Intermed. )
( second )
( Jr. Tech. )

( post - Camb. )
Commercial Training
( post - Jr. )
( Jr. Sec. )

PRIMARY EDUCATION

RHODESIA
(Formerly Southern Rhodesia)


Independence, November 11, 1965.


BACKGROUND

Africans inhabiting Rhodesia are mainly Bantu, with little difference in language and customs.  Two large main groups are the Mashona, who have been living in southeast area of territory for at least 400 years, and the Matabele, a branch of the Zulus, who immigrated to Southern Rhodesia from the Transvaal, South Africa, about 1836.

In Mashonaland, the Mashona include the tribes of:  the Makorekore, in the north; the Vazezuru, in the center; the Vakaranga, in the south.  The Barozwi are scattered throughout the area.  The Batonga occupy the Zambesi River valley.  The Manyika live in Umtali and Inyanga districts; the Babudja in Mtoko district and elsewhere.

In Matabeleland, the Matabele include the tribes of:  the Amatshangana and Amandabele, in the center, the Basuto and Bakaka elsewhere.  Remnants of the Batwa are on the western border.

Europeans are almost all of British origin, either from the United Kingdom or South Africa, the latter including a large number of South African Dutch descent.  Small groups also of Portuguese, Italians, and persons of mixed races.  Asiatics are chiefly Indians.

Africans speak mainly Bantu languages and dialects.  The Makorekore, Vazezuru and Vakaranga speak Chizezuru or Chikaranga (sometimes called Chitonga).  Chirozwi widely spoken in Mashonaland.  The Amatshangana and Amandabele speak a modified version of Neuni.  The Bakaka speak Sechuana; the Batwa speak their own language.

From 1514-1569, three Portuguese explorers touched on Rhodesian shores.  For the next 3 centuries, no other Europeans were known to have come.  Europeans arriving mid-19th century found small separate Bantu tribes in stockaded villages.  David Livingstone's explorations in 1850 led to an opening up of the whole area.  His reports brought two Scottish missions to Nyasaland, 1875-76.

British and Portuguese conflicts in the area centered in Nyasaland and Bechuanaland.  In 1888, chief of Matabele, Lobengula, made treaty with British to prevent Portuguese and Boer conquest.  Same year, an agent from Cecil Rhodes, who controlled diamond mining in South Africa, made treaty with Lobengula for exclusive mineral rights.  Gold had already been dis-covered in Mashonaland, and with the grant, Rhodes formed the British South

Africa Company; royal charter granted 1889. Salisbury founded 1890 by
settlers from Rhodes' company. From 1890 for 33 years the British South
Africa Company operated as government in Southern Rhodesia.

1911, settlers granted the right to elect a majority of Legislative Council for the territory. 1921, British agreed to self-government. Referendum 1922, separate government voted rather than a merger with Union of
South Africa. September 12, 1923, Southern Rhodesia, as self-governing
colony, was annexed to His Majesty's Dominions: African inhabitants became
British subjects.

1930, Land Apportionment Act gave 52 million acres (including all mining
and industrial areas and those regions with roads and railroads) to the
Europeans; the 42 million acres remaining were divided into native reserves,
native purchase areas, forest reserve and unassigned land.

1953, Southern Rhodesia joined with the Protectorates of Northern Rhodesia
and Nyasaland to form Federation of Rhodesia and Nyasaland, each of which
retained its constitutional status held previous to Federation. 1957,
Federation was given the right to conduct most of its internal affairs.

1962, Nyasaland's withdrawal from the Federation approved by the United
Kingdom. Federation dissolved December 31, 1963. Southern Rhodesia
reverted to the status of a self-governing member of the Commonwealth.
"Southern" dropped from name after Nyasaland became Malawi, July 6, 1964
and Northern Rhodesia became Zambia, October 23, 1964. Unilateral declaration of independence (U.D.I.), November 11, 1965.

First mission school for Africans in Southern Rhodesia founded by London
Missionary Society, 1859. Thirty other religious groups followed. By
1950, the main mission schools were run by Church of England, Roman Catholics, Dutch Reformed, Wesleyan Methodists, American Methodists, Salvation
Army. First Director of Native (African) Education appointed 1928 under
the Native Development Act which was the beginning of the present African
educational system. Since this time, mission schools which meet certain
requirements have been grant-aided. As of 1953, the federal government
became responsible for the education of Europeans, Asians, and Coloureds,
African education being administered by each territorial government.

Following World War II, a Ten-Year Plan for Education, 1947-56, was established. Considerable expansion of primary education resulted. Five-Year
Plan for 1956-61 was initiated to (a) provide 5 years of education for
children up to 14 years in rural areas; (b) add annually in rural areas
60 schools up to Standard 6 education; (c) provide 8 years of school in
urban areas for children, provided they were not over 14 years of age when
reaching Standard 4.

European and African systems of education are presented SEPARATELY in the
following pages.

ADMINISTRATION OF EDUCATIONAL SYSTEMS

for

SOUTHERN RHODESIA, NYASALAND, NORTHERN RHODESIA

(Rhodesia)        (Malawi)        (Zambia)

1923   through   1964

| EUROPEAN (Asian and Coloured) | DATES | A F R I C A N |
|---|---|---|

| So. Rhodesia | Nyasa-land | North Rhodesia | | So. Rhodesia | Nyasa-land | North Rhodesia |
|---|---|---|---|---|---|---|

| EDUCATION administered by: | | | 1923-1953 | EDUCATION administered by: | | |
|---|---|---|---|---|---|---|
| Self-govern-ing colony | British Colonial Administration | | | Rhodesian Ministry of Native Education | British Colonial Administration | |

FEDERATION OF RHODESIA AND NYASALAND

1953-1963

| EDUCATION administered by: | EDUCATION administered by: |
|---|---|
| Federal Ministry of Education | Rhodesian Territorial Ministry of African Education / British Colonial Administration |

Dissolution of FEDERATION

1963

| Rhodesia | Malawi | Zambia | 1964 – onward | Rhodesia | Malawi | Zambia |
|---|---|---|---|---|---|---|
| Self-govern-ing colony | Independent 1964 | | | Self-govern-ing colony | Independent 1964 | |

| EDUCATION administered by: | | EDUCATION administered by: | |
|---|---|---|---|
| Rhodesia Ministry of Education (Division of European, Asian & Coloured Education) | MULTIRACIAL EDUCATION SYSTEM | Rhodesia Ministry of Education (Division of African Education) | MULTIRACIAL EDUCATION SYSTEM |

## E U R O P E A N ,   A S I A N   A N D   C O L O U R E D

European education initiated by missions; 1st school opened in 1892 in Salisbury by Dominican Sisters, followed by other missionary schools.

Between 1923 and 1953, education for Europeans (and Asians and Coloureds) was administered by the self-governing colony of Southern Rhodesia. In the protectorates of Nyasaland and Northern Rhodesia, European education was under the administration of the British Colonial Office.

With the establishment of the Federation of Rhodesia and Nyasaland in 1953, the Federal government in Salisbury undertook the responsibility for all levels of European education, including higher education and university training for Europeans and Africans alike. During this period a new Education Act, 1957, provided for free education for children whose parents resided in the Federation, the registration of privately-run schools in order to standardize conditions, and compulsory education for all children between 7 and 15 years of age if living within 3 miles of a school.

With the dissolution of the Federation in 1963, Nyasaland as Malawi and Northern Rhodesia as Zambia became independent nations in 1964. Both countries established multi-racial educational systems. Southern Rhodesia became Rhodesia, 1 ministry administering 2 separate systems of education through the Division of European, Asian and Coloured Education and the Division of African Education.

(For current education in former Nyasaland and Northern Rhodesia, see MALAWI and ZAMBIA.)


## PRESENT SYSTEM

## PRIMARY EDUCATION

Co-educational with few exceptions. No government nursery schools.

First 2 - 2½ years spent in Infant Classes (Kindergarten) often in same building as primary school.

Entry Age:      5 years.

Program:        Infants 1 and 2.   Standards 1 through 5.

Curriculum:     Similar subjects offered in all primary schools.

School-Leaving Examination:  None. Students transfer at about 12+ years
                                    of age.

Also private schools for Europeans, Asians and Coloureds.
Private Indian schools maintained and managed by Indian school committees.
Private schools may apply for a government grant per capita.


## SECONDARY EDUCATION

All government institutions at secondary level are comprehensive, except
for Rhodesian technical schools.

Streams:  Academic, Slow Academic, General, Technical (or Commercial).


ACADEMIC:

| | |
|---|---|
| Forms I through IV | Most able pupils (similar to grammar schools in the United Kingdom) prepare for [+]General Certificate of Education G.C.E. "O" |
| Sixth Form (Lower VI) (2 years) | [+]G.C.E. "M" level (Matriculation) for entrance to South African universities (5-year course) |
| (Upper VI) | [+]G.C.E. "A" |


SLOW ACADEMIC

| | |
|---|---|
| Forms I through V | May take 5 years to prepare for external examinations.  From 1961 students take [++]College of Preceptors Examination as in intermediate step in 4th year (Form IV). |

[+]Associated Examining Board of London examines for G.C.E. "O", "A",
and "M".

[++]College of Preceptors (examining board in London).


| | |
|---|---|
| Slow Academic Curriculum: | Commerce, Housecraft, Woodwork, Metalwork, Technical Drawing. |
| | These subjects may be offered for both College of Preceptors and G.C.E. "O" examinations. |

If competent, "slow academic" stream free to take G.C.E. "A" course.

GENERAL:                          For students whose requirements will
                                  be met by a full or partial College
                                  of Preceptors Certificate.

                                  Choice of subjects permits variety of
                                  practical subjects in addition to Eng-
                                  lish, Mathematics, and Science.


TECHNICAL or COMMERCIAL:          offered at Gifford High, Bulawayo and
                                  Allan Welsen, Salisbury.


                                  Prepare for G.C.E. "O" (former Higher
                                  School Certificate), G.C.E."A" or
                                  South African National Technical exam-
                                  ination.  Progressively from 1961
                                  these latter to be replaced by College
                                  of Preceptors examination, Form IV.


In addition to courses determined by examination requirements, Religious
instruction, Music, and Physical Education included in all schools.  When
2nd language studied, choice is between French, Afrikaans or sometimes
German.

Pupils passing (Higher School Certificate) G.C.E. "A" are qualified for
admission to universities and institutions of engineering.

Those passing G.C.E. "M" (1-year post G.C.E. "O" level) are qualified for
admission to South African universities.


*At close of 4-year program students sit for the +Associated Examining
Board's G.C.E. "O" level Certificate.

**At close of 6-year program students sit for the +Associated Examining
Board's G.C.E. "A" level Certificate.


+For Regulations, write to:  Associated Examining Board, Hesketh House,
                             Portman Square, London, W.1.

## HIGHER EDUCATION

## UNIVERSITY COLLEGE OF RHODESIA AND NYASALAND, Salisbury

The University College of Rhodesia and Nyasaland is an autonomous institution established by Royal Charter in 1955.  First classes were held in 1957 at which time the University College was admitted to special relation with the University of London, teaching for London degrees of that university.

The institution is multiracial, coeducational and admits students from countries outside Rhodesia.

## Academic Year and Terms:

|           |                     |
|-----------|---------------------|
| 1st term: | March - May         |
| 2nd term: | June - August       |
| 3rd term: | September - November |

Minimum entrance requirements:     Minimum requirements may be satisfied under either Scheme A or Scheme B, which are as follows:

## SCHEME A

Passes in 5 subjects obtained at 1 or more of the following examinations, at the standard or level indicated, of which at least 2 must have been at the level specified under II.

I.  "O" - Ordinary

    (1)  Ordinary level of the London General Certificate of Education or approved equivalent.

    (2)  Credit standard of the Cambridge School Certificate.

    (3)  Subsidiary standard of the Cambridge Higher School Certificate.

    (4)  Not less than 40% in certain approved subjects recorded on the Matriculation Certificate of the South African Joint Matriculation Board or the approved equivalent.

II.  "A" - Advanced

    (1)  Advanced level of the London General Certificate of Education or approved equivalent.

    (2)  Principal subject standard of the Cambridge Higher School Certificate.

SCHEME B

Passes in 4 subjects obtained at 1 or more of the above examinations of which at least 3 must have been at the level specified under II.

The following provisions must be fulfilled in either Scheme A
or Scheme B

(a)  The subjects must have been chosen from the approved list
     (see below).
(b)  No subject can be counted at both the level specified in
     I and the level specified in II above.

There is no  requirement  that a certain number of subjects must
be passed at one and the same time.

Approved subjects for minimum entrance requirements:

The titles of subjects are in most cases given in the form used
in the General Certificate of Education examination of the University of London.  The symbols "O" and "A" indicate whether
subject can be offered at ordinary level or advanced level.

| Level | | Subjects | Level | | Subjects |
|---|---|---|---|---|---|
| O | | English Language | O | A | Physics |
| O | A | English Literature | O | A | Chemistry |
| O | A | Geography | O | | +Physics-with-Chemistry |
| | A | Indian History | O | A | Geology |
| O | A | History | O | | General Science |
| O | A | Ancient History | O | | Additional General |
| O | A | English Economic | | | Science |
| | | History | O | A | Botany |
| O | A | British Constitution | | A | Zoology |
| O | A | Economics | O | A | Biology or General |
| O | | Logic | | | Biology |
| O | | Greek Literature in | O | | Rural Biology |
| | | Translation | O | A | Music |
| O | | Additional Pure Math- | O | A | Art |
| | | ematics | | | |
| O | A | Pure Mathematics | O | | Human Anatomy, Hygiene |
| O | A | Religious Knowledge | | | and Physiology |
| | A | Mathematics (Pure and | | | Any approved language |
| | | Applied) | | | |

+It should be noted that the Cambridge Higher School Certificate
principal level subject Physics-with-Chemistry can not be counted
as an advanced level subject.

The following subjects in the <u>Cambridge Local Examinations Syndicate General Certificate of Education</u> and <u>School Certificate</u>, and in the <u>General Certificate of Education</u> of the Oxford and Cambridge Schools Examination Board, for which there is no similar syllabus in the London General Certificate of Education examination, are approved for acceptance under Scheme A or B at ordinary level:

## Cambridge Local Examinations Syndicate

| | | | |
|---|---|---|---|
| O | Human Biology | O | General Paper |
| O | French Literature, History and Institutions (not equivalent to a foreign language) | O | West Indian History |
| | | O | Health Science |
| | | O | Navigation and Astronomy |

## Oxford and Cambridge School Examination Board

A + 2 "O"    History with Foreign Texts (accepted as 3 separate subjects: (i) History at "A"; (ii) Latin at "O"; (iii) a modern foreign language at "O" - which are also subjects approved for entry to B.A. courses).

O    General Classics (accepted also as an approved subject for entry to B.A. courses, but not as equivalent to a foreign language).

A    Latin Translation and Roman History (accepted also as an approved subject for entry to B.A. courses at an advanced level.

O    Physical Geography and Elementary Geology (accepted also as an approved subject for entry to B.A. courses).

O    General Paper.

## Approved Languages

Languages approved for the purpose of entry to courses for the B.A. degree include:

| Level | | Subjects | Level | | Subjects |
|---|---|---|---|---|---|
| O | A | Afrikaans | O | A | Latin |
| O | A | Classical Arabic | O | A | Norwegian |
| O | | Bemba | O | | Nyanja |
| O | A | Danish | O | A | Polish |
| O | A | Dutch | O | A | Portuguese |
| O | A | French | O | A | Russian |
| O | A | German | O | A | Sanskrit |
| O | A | Classical Greek | O | | Shona |
| O | A | Modern Greek | O | | Sotho |
| O | A | Gujarati | O | A | Spanish |

|   |   |                  |   |   |        |
|---|---|------------------|---|---|--------|
| O | A | Classical Hebrew | O | A | Tamil  |
| O |   | Modern Hebrew    | O |   | Tswana |
| O | A | Hindi            | O | A | Urdu   |
| O | A | Italian          | O |   | Xosa   |
| O | A | Swedish          | O |   | Zulu   |

Certain other languages may be approved for purposes of entry
to B.A. degree courses, and a larger number for the purpose of
minimum entrance requirements.


## Restrictions

The selection of subjects under Scheme A or Scheme B is subject
to the following limitations:

> Greek Literature in Translation cannot be counted with
>   Greek.
> Modern Hebrew cannot be counted with Classical Hebrew.
> Not more than 1 of the approved African languages may be
>   counted.
> Not more than 1 of the approved Eastern languages may be
>   counted.
> Mathematics (Pure and Applied) cannot be counted with Pure
>   Mathematics or Applied Mathematics.
> Additional Pure Mathematics cannot be counted with Pure
>   Mathematics or Mathematics (Pure and Applied).
> Physics-with-Chemistry cannot be counted with Physics,
>   Chemistry, General Science, or Additional General Science.
> General Science or Additional General Science cannot be
>   counted with Physics, Chemistry, Physics-with-Chemistry,
>   Botany, Biology, General Biology, Rural Biology or Zoology.
> Botany cannot be counted with Biology, General Biology or
>   Rural Biology.
> Biology cannot be counted with General Biology or Rural
>   Biology.


## Faculties:

> Arts
> Education
> Medicine
> Science
> Social Studies

Degrees Awarded:

| Faculty | Degree | Duration of Course (years) |
|---|---|---|
| Arts | B.A. (General) - University of London | 3 |
| | B.A. (Honours) | 3 |
| Education | Postgraduate Certificate in Education - University of London | ( 1 (full time) ( 2 (part time) |
| | Diploma in Education - University of London | ( 1 (full time) ( 2 (part time) |
| | Associateship of the Institute of Education, University of Rhodesia and Nyasaland | 2 (part time) |
| | Certificate in Adult Education - University of Rhodesia and Nyasaland | 2 (part time) |
| Medicine | M.B., Ch.B. - University of Birmingham | 6 |
| Science | B.Sc. (General) - University of London | 3 |
| | B.Sc. (Special) in Geology University of London | 1 - after obtaining the B.Sc. (General) degree |
| | B.Sc. (Agric.) | 3 |
| Social Studies | B.Sc. (Economics) - University of London | 3 |
| | LL.B. - University of London | 3 |
| | Diploma in Applied Economics University of Rhodesia and Nyasaland | 3 (part time) |
| | Diploma in Public Administration - University of Rhodesia and Nyasaland | 1 |

Faculty of Arts

Entrance requirements:     A candidate must satisfy the minimum entrance requirements under Scheme A or Scheme B by means of subjects selected only from the approved list

below.  In satisfying the general minimum conditions for entry, candidates
must:

either   (i)   qualify in 2 languages of which 1 must
be English.

In order to qualify in English a candidate must have passed in either English
Language at ordinary level (or the
approved equivalent) or in English Literature at advanced level (or the
approved equivalent).

A candidate whose mother tongue is not
English may qualify by means of a pass
in English Literature at advanced level
(or the approved equivalent) and without
a pass in the 2nd language.

or    (ii)   Candidates entering the College in 1964
may qualify by means of 2 languages
other than English, of which 1 must be
Latin or Classical Greek or Classical
Hebrew or French or German.

Approved list of subjects for entry to B.A. Courses:

English Literature          Chemistry
Geography                   Physics-with-Chemistry
History                     Geology
Ancient History             General Science
Economics                   Additional General Science
Logic                       Botany
Religious Knowledge         Zoology
Pure Mathematics            Biology or General Biology
Mathematics (Pure and       Music
   Applied)                 Any language approved for
Physics                        entry B.A. (General)


Departments:

African Languages           Economics
Classics                    Government
English                     Mathematics
History                     Sociology
Modern Languages            Theology

## B.A. (General)

Duration of course: 3 years.

Before admission to Part I of the examination, a candidate must have pursued the approved course in 3 of the subjects listed below for not less than 1 academic year.

For admission to Part II of the examination, a candidate must have passed Part I of the B.A. (General) examination and subsequently pursued for not less than 2 academic years the approved courses in 2 of the subjects offered at Part I.

Subjects:
African Languages (Shona)　　Greek
Ancient History　　　　　　　Latin
English　　　　　　　　　　　Mathematics
French　　　　　　　　　　　Portuguese
Government　　　　　　　　　Social Anthropology and
Theology　　　　　　　　　　　　Sociology
　　　　　　　　　　　　　　　History

The 3 subjects are studied to the same level, no subsidiary subjects. Candidate must pass in both subjects of the Part II examination and all 3 subjects in the Part I examination on the same occasion.

B.A. (General) of the University of London is awarded in 1st, 2nd (upper and lower) and 3rd class.

## B.A. (Honours)

May be taken in English, French, History, Latin and African Studies.

Duration of course: 3 years.

Candidates must normally pursue the approved courses in 3 of the subjects for the B.A. (General) degree for 1 term. Those wishing to proceed to B.A. (Honours) in either English, French, History or Latin must include among the approved courses in 1st term the subject in which they wish to proceed to B.A. (Honours) course.

Candidates wishing to proceed to the B.A. (Honours) in African Studies should include African Languages, Social Anthropology and Sociology in 1st term.

B.A. (Honours) of the University of London is awarded in 1st, 2nd (upper and lower) and 3rd class.

Faculty of Education

Departments:

> Institute of Education
> Department of Education
> Institute of Adult Education

## Postgraduate Certificate in Education of the University of London

Eligibility:           Graduates of any approved university.

Duration of course:    1 year    (full time)
                       2 years   (part time)

Training:              Theoretical and practical courses including substantial
                       amount of teaching practice.

## Diploma in Education of the University of London

Eligibility:           Candidates must have obtained

> either    (a)   the Postgraduate Certificate in Education (for-
>                 merly called the Teacher's Diploma) or Teacher's
>                 Certificate of the University of London,
> or        (b)   undergone a course of training for the profession
>                 of teacher, approved by the University for this
>                 purpose and passed an approved professional exam-
>                 ination,
> or        (c)   possess qualifications accepted by the University
>                 as equivalent to 1 of the foregoing.

Duration of course:    1 year    (full time)
                       2 years   (part time)

## Associateship of the Institute of Education of the University College of Rhodesia and Nyasaland

Eligibility:           Candidates must normally have had at least 5 years'
                       experience in approved educational work and be qual-
                       ified by previous training and/or experience to under-
                       take advanced studies in Education.

Duration of course:    2 years (part time)

Certificate in Adult Education of the University College of Rhodesia and
Nyasaland

Eligibility:          Candidates must
          either     have graduated from any approved university
          or         have passed in at least 5 subjects including English
                     Language at ordinary level of the General Certificate
                     of Education or an approved equivalent, and have
                     experience in adult education approved by the Univer-
                     sity College of Rhodesia and Nyasaland.

Duration of course:  2 years (part time)

Course of study:  Supervised preparation by correspondence and practical
                  work.

                  Obligatory attendance at teaching sessions covering 5
                  weeks during the period of the course.

Scheme of Examination:

      All students examined in four 2-hour papers:

      (a)  Aims and principles of Adult Education
      (b)  Adult learning and teaching methods
      (c)  Adult Education in Central Africa
      (d)  A special study


Faculty of Medicine

In March 1963 the College introduced full-time courses leading to the
degrees of M.B., Ch.B. of the University of Birmingham.

Departments:

      (Previous to July 1965)

                  Botany              Physics
                  Chemistry           Zoology

      (After July 1965)

                  Anatomy             Medicine
                  Chemistry           Physics
                  Medical Biology     Physiology

<u>M.B., Ch.B.</u>

Eligibility:          Candidate must satisfy:

                 (1)   Requirements of the Joint Matriculation Board of
                      the University of Manchester, Liverpool, Leeds,
                      Sheffield and Birmingham.

                 (2)   Course requirements.

<u>Joint Matriculation Board requirements</u>:

The Board's present requirements applicable to students of the
University College are normally satisfied by 1 of the methods
A through D below.

(A)   By <u>General Certificates of Education</u> issued by approved
      examining bodies which show:

<u>either</u>   A pass in an English test together with passes in 5 subjects
      of the General Certificate of Education which include:

      (i)  <u>either</u> Mathematics <u>or</u> an approved science;
      (ii)  at least 2 subjects at the advanced level

      provided that

      (a)  A pass in the English test is not counted for this
           purpose unless the candidate passes also in at least
           1 of the required advanced subjects in the same calen-
           dar year.
      (b)  The required 5 subjects must be selected from the
           approved list (excluding English Language "0") except
           that 1 of the "technical" subjects listed in List II
           below may be included as a subject at "0" level,
           whether passed at "0" or "A" level.
      (c)  no subject may be counted both at the ordinary and at
           the advanced level.

<u>or</u>     Passes, all at advanced level and at one sitting of the
      Joint Matriculation Board's examination, in General Studies
      and in 2 advanced subjects from List I below.

      (A pass in English Language at "0" level is <u>not</u> acceptable
      as a "test in English" for this purpose. Candidates at
      overseas centers will not be required to pass in the "Use
      of English" paper but will be required to pass in "English
      Language" at the ordinary level of the <u>General Certificate
      of Education</u>.)

(B)   Candidates who have otherwise qualified by means of the
      <u>Cambridge School Certificate</u> and the <u>Cambridge Higher School
      Certificate</u> are regarded as having satisfied the Board's

university entrance requirements providing that instead of passing in a test in English they have obtained:

    (i)   a pass with credit in English Language in the School Certificate examination, and subsequently

   (ii)   a pass in the General Paper (Higher School Certificate subsidiary) in the same calendar year that they passed at least 1 of the required subjects to be passed at the principal standard in the Higher School Certificate.

(C)   Candidates who have otherwise qualified by means of the General Certificate of Education of the University of London gained wholly at overseas centers will be regarded as having satisfied the Board's university entrance requirements providing they have obtained General Certificates of Education which show:

either   passes in 6 subjects which include:

    (i)   English Language
   (ii)   either Mathematics or an approved science
  (iii)   at least 2 subjects at the advanced level.

provided that:

   (a)   the required 6 passes must be shown on not more than 3 General Certificates (though there is no limit placed by the Board on the number of times a candidate sits for the examination).

   (b)   the required subjects must be selected from the list given in List I below, except that 1 of the "technical" subjects in List II below may be included as a subject at "O" level whether passed at "O" or "A" level.

   (c)   No subject may be counted both at the ordinary level and at the advanced level.

or   Passes in 5 subjects which include:
    (i)   English Language
   (ii)   either Mathematics or an approved science
  (iii)   at least 2 subjects at the advanced level passed at the same sitting as at least 1 other of the 5 required subjects

provided that:

   (a)   the required subjects must be selected from list I below.

   (b)   no subject may be counted both at ordinary and at the advanced level.

(D)   Candidates who otherwise satisfy the entrance requirements of the Joint Matriculation Board by means of other certificates such as degree diplomas of an approved university are not required to pass the test in English providing that the certificates submitted were gained overseas.

List I

The following subjects of the Northern Universities Joint Matriculation
Board's General Certificate examination and the corresponding subjects
in examinations of other approved examining bodies will be accepted for
the purposes of satisfying the Board's requirements. (Numbers 28 to 39,
both inclusive, are recognized as "approved sciences" for the purposes
of the Joint Matriculation Board requirements, but not necessarily for
course requirements).

1.  General paper
2.  English Language
3.  English Literature
4.  History
5.  Ancient History and Literature
    (may not be counted with
    History)
6.  Outlines of British Government
7.  Geography
8.  Economics
9.  Scripture Knowledge
10. Art
11. History and Appreciation of
    Art (may not be counted
    with Art)
12. Music
13. Greek and Roman Literature in
    Translation (may not be
    counted with Greek and/or
    Latin)
14. Greek
15. Latin
16. French
17. German
18. Spanish
19. Italian
20. Russian
21. Welsh
22. Specially approved languages
23. Mathematics[+]
24. Further Mathematics[+]
25. Pure Mathematics with Statis-
    tics[+]
26. Pure Mathematics[+]
27. Mathematics and Theoretical
    Mechanics (counts as 2
    advanced subjects)

28. Physics
29. Chemistry
30. Physics-with-Chemistry (may
    not be counted with any of
    following: Physics, Chem-
    istry, General Science,
    Agricultural Science, Build-
    ing Science)
31. Botany
32. Zoology
33. Biology (may not be counted
    with Botany and/or Zoology)
34. Geology
35. General Science I (General
    Science I and/or II may not
    be counted with any of the
    following: Physics, Chemis-
    try, Physics-with-Chemistry,
    Botany, Zoology, Biology,
    Agricultural Science, Build-
    ing Science)
36. General Science II
37. Agricultural Science (may not
    be counted with Physics,
    Chemistry, Physics-with
    Chemistry, Biology, General
    Science)
38. Physiology and Hygiene (may
    not be counted with Zoology
    or Biology)
39. Building Science (may not be
    counted with any of the fol-
    lowing: Physics, Physics-
    with-Chemistry, General
    Science

[+]Certain combinations are not accepted.

## List II

One of the following "technical subjects" may be included among the 6
subjects required under A of the Northern Universities Joint Matriculation Board requirements. The subject will be counted as 1 ordinary subject whether it has been passed at ordinary or at advanced level.

1. Commerce (may not be counted with Economics)
2. Commercial Mathematics[+]
3. Woodwork
4. Metalwork
5. Mechanical Science
6. Geometrical and Engineering Drawing
7. Building Construction and Geometrical Drawing
8. Engineering Workshop Theory Practice
9. Surveying
10. Pottery
11. Domestic Science
12. Textiles
13. Spinning and Handloom Weaving
14. Bookkeeping and Accounting (advanced)
    N.B. Bookkeeping (ordinary) is not acceptable

[+]Commercial Mathematics may not be counted with any of the subjects
23-27 of List I, and will not be accepted as a pass in Mathematics
or an approved science.

Duration of course: 6 years.

In the 1st year students follow courses in existing science departments
of Botany, Chemistry, Physics and Zoology in the College. Subsequent
courses are provided by departments in the Faculty of Medicine as well
as departments in the Faculty of Science.

Course requirements: A candidate must satisfy the requirements of the
Joint Matriculation Board, normally by means of
subjects which include at least 3 subjects
selected from the following list, of which at
least 2 must be at the advanced level. At least
1 of the advanced level subjects must be selected
from the group numbered 1 - 6.

1. Biology
2. Botany
3. Chemistry
4. Geology
5. Zoology
7. Geography
8. Mathematics - Pure
9. Mathematics - Applied
10. Mathematics - Pure and Applied

N.B. 1 may not be counted with 2 or 6;
10 may not be counted with 8 or 9.

Previous knowledge of Mathematics at least up to the ordinary level will normally be required of candidates for Medicine.

A pass with credit in the Cambridge School Certificate or a pass at subsidiary standard in the Cambridge Higher School Certificate examination will be accepted as equivalent to a pass in the corresponding subject at ordinary level in the General Certificate of Education.


## Faculty of Science

Departments:

|  |  |
|---|---|
| Agriculture | Mathematics |
| Botany | Physics |
| Chemistry | Zoology |
| Geology | |


## B.Sc. (General) of the University of London

Eligibility:

Candidates must satisfy minimum entrance requirements under Scheme **A** or Scheme **B** by means of subjects which must include at least 3 subjects selected from following list, of which at least 2 must be at advanced level. At least 1 of the advanced level subjects must be selected from group 1 - 6.

| | |
|---|---|
| 1. Biology | 6. Zoology |
| 2. Botany | 7. Geography |
| 3. Chemistry | 8. Mathematics (Pure) |
| 4. Geology | 9. Mathematics (Applied) |
| 5. Physics | 10. Mathematics (Pure and Applied) |

A previous knowledge of Mathematics up to ordinary level is assumed in respect of all degree courses which include a study of Physics or Chemistry.

Some examples of the restrictions against the combination of overlapping subjects are: Biology may not be counted with Botany or Zoology, General Science may not be counted with a number of other subjects, Mathematics (Pure and Applied) may not be counted with Pure Mathematics or Applied Mathematics.

Duration of course: 3 years.

Courses and Examinations:

For admission to Part I of examination at end of 1st year, candidate must have pursued the approved courses in 3 of the following subjects for not less than 1 academic year:

| | |
|---|---|
| Botany | Mathematics |
| Chemistry | Physics |
| (Syllabus A or B) | Zoology |
| Geology | |

For admission to Part II of examination at end of 3rd year, candidate must have passed in all 3 subjects on same occasion in Part I of either the B.Sc. (General) or the B.Sc. (Agriculture) examination and subsequently pursued for not less than 2 academic years the approved courses in 2 of the subjects he has taken in Part I. Candidates taking Chemistry at Part II must have taken Chemistry (Syllabus A) in Part I.

The subject "Mathematics" comprises Pure and Applied Mathematics, as 1 subject, both in Part I and in Part II. An alternative subject option at Part II "Pure Mathematics and Statistics" cannot at present be offered.

Candidates must pass in both subjects at Part II on the same occasion.

B.Sc. (General) of the University of London is awarded in 1st, 2nd (upper and lower) and 3rd class Honours, or as a pass degree.

## B.Sc. (Special) in Geology of the University of London

Eligibility:               Candidate for entry to the course must have obtained a B.Sc. (General) degree of the University of London with Geology as 1 of the subjects taken in the Part II examinations.

Duration of course:  1 year after B.Sc. (General)

B.Sc. (Special) in Geology of the University of London is awarded in 1st, 2nd (upper and lower) and 3rd class Honours.

## B.Sc. (Agriculture) of the University of London

Eligibility:               Same requirements as for B.Sc. (General).

Duration of course:  3 years.

Courses and Examinations:

> For admission to Part I of the examination at end of 1st year, a candidate must have pursued the approved course in Botany, Chemistry (Syllabus B) and Zoology for not less than 1 academic year.

> For admission to Part II of the examination at end of 2nd year, a candidate must have passed in all 3 subjects on the same occasion in Part I B.Sc. (Agric.) or Part I B.Sc. (Gen.) examination in the subjects Botany, Chemistry (Syllabus B) and Zoology and subsequently pursued the approved courses in Economics, Pedology, Soil Science, Crop Science, and Animal Science for not less than 1 academic year.

> For admission to Part II of the examination at the end of the 3rd year, a candidate must have passed Part I and not less than 3 of the 4 subjects of Part II, and have pursued for not less than 2 academic years after passing Part I the approved courses in Agricultural Chemistry, Crop Husbandry, Animal Husbandry, Agricultural Engineering and Farm Mechanization, Farm Organization and Management, and Agricultural Economics.

> A candidate must pass in all subjects at Part III on the same occasion.

B.Sc. (Agriculture) of the University of London is awarded with 1st or 2nd class Honours (upper and lower), or as a pass degree.

## Faculty of Social Studies

Departments:

|            |           |
|------------|-----------|
| Economics  | Law       |
| History    | Sociology |
| Government  |           |

## B.Sc. (Economics) of the University of London

Eligibility:          Candidate must satisfy the minimum entrance requirements under either Scheme A or Scheme B.

Duration of course:  3 years.

Courses and Examinations:

> For examination Part I taken at end of 1st year candidate must have pursued approved courses in Economics, Government, History and 2 optional subjects for not less than 1 academic year.

For examination Part II taken at end of 3rd year, candidate must have pursued approved courses in 1 of the following special subjects for not less than 2 academic years after passing Part I of the examination:

| | |
|---|---|
| Economics (analytical and descriptive) | Social Anthropology |
| Government | Sociology |

B.Sc. (Economics) of the University of London is awarded with 1st, 2nd (upper and lower) and 3rd degree Honours, or as a pass degree.


## LL.B. of the University of London

LL.B. degree introduced March 1965.

Eligibility:          As for B.Sc. (Economics)

Duration of course: 3 years.


## Diploma in Applied Economics of the University College of Rhodesia and Nyasaland

Eligibility:          Candidate must satisfy the minimum entrance require-
                      ments under either Scheme A or Scheme B.

Duration of course: 3 years (part time)

Courses and Examinations:

For examination Part I taken at end of 2nd year a candidate must have pursued the approved part-time courses in Accountancy, Economics, and Law for not less than 2 academic years.

For examination Part II taken at end of 3rd year a candidate must have pursued the approved part-time courses in Accountancy, Economics, and Law for not less than 3 academic years.

Candidates must be successful in all subjects of Part I and Part II examinations.


## Diploma in Public Administration of the University College of Rhodesia and Nyasaland

Eligibility:          Candidates must be

either     (a)  Graduates of an approved university
or         (b)  Persons who have other qualifications and/or
                relevant experience sufficient in the opinion
                of the College to warrant acceptance as mature
                students.

Duration of course:  1 year.

Courses and Examinations:

    The examinations consist of five 3-hour papers.
    ALL candidates examined in:
        Economics
        British Government:  an Introduction to Politics.

    In addition, candidates shall be examined in 3 approved subjects
    chosen from the following:

        Principles and Methods of Social Anthropology
        Political History
        Legal Institutions of Former Federation
        Elementary Statistical Theory
        Methods of Social Investigation
        Ethnography of Central Africa
        Aspects of Constitutional Development in British African
           Territories
        Criminal Law
        Evidence and Procedure
        Agricultural Economics

## VOCATIONAL AND TECHNICAL EDUCATION

### GOVERNMENT TECHNICAL SECONDARY HIGH SCHOOLS

Boys only.

Entrance requirements:              Standard 5 and entrance examination.

4-year program:     Science subjects - Mathematics, Science, Technology
                    General subjects - English, History, Geography, etc.

Students failing to pass entrance examinations to a technical high school
may take a number of practical technical subjects at a regular secondary
school.

### SALISBURY POLYTECHNIC COLLEGE

Technical education in up-to-date form for classes of vocational students
from craft to professional levels in industry, and also the equivalent in
commerce.

Departments:

Civil Engineering
Mechanical Engineering
Electrical Engineering
Building
Adult Education

Printing
Mathematics and Science
Commerce
Hairdressing

Entrance requirements:     Southern Rhodesia Junior Certificate (S.R.J.C.) or its equivalent Form II standard.

Higher minimum for more advanced courses, such as those leading to technician and technologist levels.

## Civil Engineering

Full-time and part-time courses leading to the examinations of the Institution of Civil Engineers.

Full-time courses in Building Craft.

Part-time courses in Structural Engineering, Municipal Engineering, Concrete Practice, Surveying, Geology, Soil Mechanics, Theory of Structures. Advanced Technical Certificates of South Africa in Building, and technical officers courses for government departments.

## Mechanical Engineering

Full-time courses leading to the examinations of the Institution of Mechanical Engineers.

Part-time courses for the Ordinary and Higher Certificates of the City and Guilds of London Institute (block release).

Apprenticeship courses for the Mechanical Engineering Technicians' Certificates of the City and Guilds of London Institute (block release).

Part-time apprenticeship courses in Automobile Engineering Practice and Mechanical Craft Practice (block release).

Part-time preliminary craft courses for the following trades:
    Motor Mechanics, Fitters and Turners, Precision Machinists, Sheet-metal Worker and Panelbeaters.

## Electrical Engineering

Full-time courses leading to the examinations of the Institution of Electrical Engineers, London, Parts I, II, and III.

Part-time courses in Electrical Engineering Practice (block release).

Part-time courses for Telecommunications Technician (block release).

Part-time courses for Electrical Fitter (block release).

Part-time courses for Electrical Installation (block release).

## Aircraft Engineering

This branch has been transferred to Central African Airways where special staff and equipment are available.

## Building

Apprenticeship courses in carpentry and joinery.

Part-time courses for Advanced Building.

Part-time courses for Building Inspectors Certificate.

Part-time courses leading to the Diploma of Clerk of Works.

Part-time courses leading to the examinations of the Institution of Quantity Surveyors, and a course for the Royal Institution of Chartered Surveyors.

## Printing

Part-time courses leading to the examinations of the City and Guilds of London Institute in the following subjects:
>       Compositor's Work
>       Letterpress Machine Minder's work
>       Lithography
>       Stereotyping
>       Process Engineering
>       Binding and Warehouse Basic Craft

## Mathematics and Science

Part-time courses leading to the examinations of the City and Guilds of London Institute in the following subjects:
>       General Certificate of Education:  "O", "M", and "A" levels.
>       Laboratory Technician's Certificate
>       Laboratory Technician's Certificate (Advanced)
>       Radiographers

In addition, the Department acts as an auxiliary to the other Departments.

## Commerce

Full-time courses in preparation for secretarial and clerical posts.

Part-time courses for the Intermediate and Final examinations of the Chartered Institute of Secretaries, the Institute of Cost and Works Accountant, the Institute of Transport and the Institute of Bankers.

Part-time courses for the B.Com. degree and B. Admin. degree of the University of South Africa.

Part-time courses in Civil Service Law.

Part-time commercial courses in such subjects as Bookkeeping, Shorthand
and Typewriting and certain G.C.E. subjects.

## Hairdressing

Day-release classes preparing students for the National Hairdressing Certificate of the Department of Education of South Africa.

## Adult Education

Part-time women's classes in the following subjects:
    Cookery, Cake Icing, Floral Arrangements, Dressmaking and Millinery.

Part-time general classes in the following subjects:
    African Languages, Art, Motor Car Maintenance, English, Public Speak-
    ing, French, Photography, Copper and Pewter Work, Gardening, Brick
    and Concrete Work, Afrikaans, Portuguese, and Salesmanship.

These classes are subject to public demand. All language classes are
based on a twelve-month period. The others are usually of 1 term's duration.

## BULAWAYO TECHNICAL COLLEGE

This College has recently been equipped and the courses extended to train
students from craft to technological level, and the equivalent in commerce.

## Civil Engineering and Building

Sandwich technologist courses for pupil civil engineers.

Part-time courses for Graduateship of the Institute of Structural Engineering.

Part-time evening courses of the South African National Advanced Technical
Certificates in building subjects.

Block release (short full-time) and part-time courses of the City and
Guilds' building subjects for apprentices and craftsmen.

Mechanical Engineering.

Sandwich technological courses for pupil mechanical engineers.

Part-time evening courses for higher technicians, leading to the Engineering Diploma of South Africa.

Block release and part-time technicians' courses of the City and Guilds'
in Motor Vehicle Mechanics and Mechanical Engineering including Metallurgy.

Electrical Installation Course of the City and Guilds for apprentices on a
block release basis. Part-time courses in basic electricity, radio and
television servicing.

## Mining

Full-time and block release courses for Learner Officials (Production and Technical), qualifying as Junior Underground Officials.

## Commerce

Full-time preliminary courses in Business Administration.

Full-time Private Secretaries Diploma course.

Full-time Secretarial (Office Arts) Diploma course.

Full-time Shorthand-Typist Diploma course.

Full-time Bookkeeper/Costing Clerks Diploma course.

Full-time Clerk/Typist Diploma course.

Full-time course of office training for adults.

Full-time Teachers' Commercial Training course.

Part-time day course for Chartered and Incorporated Secretaries.

Part-time day course for Civil Service Lower Law.

Part-time evening course for degree in Commerce and Administration.

Part-time evening professional courses in the following:
  Accountancy, Banking, Company Secretaries, Transport, Work Study,
  Civil Service Law, Mining.

G.C.E. Courses: "O", "M", and "A" level.

Royal Society of Arts, Elementary, Intermediate and Advanced Commercial subjects.

Modern languages.

Laboratory Technicians' Course of the City and Guilds for Laboratory Assistants and Technicians.

Radiographers' course for student radiographers.

## Cooks and Waiters Courses

These are conducted on a full-time basis. Cooks and waiters (trainees) are sponsored by the Hotel Association and undergo extensive practical training in the Department of Catering. Cook trainees study for the City and Guilds' Basic Cookery Course which is of 2 years' duration. Waiter trainees are trained for a period of 1 year.

## Textile

Training for this industry is to be implemented shortly.

## Adult Education

Dressmaking, Cake Icing, Pewter Work, Art from the Model, Public Speaking, Floral Arrangements, Motor Car Maintenance, Millinery, Soft Furnishing, Cookery Around the World, Clay Modelling, Buffet Preparation.

AGRICULTURAL TRAINING:

## GWEBE COLLEGE OF AGRICULTURE

Established 1950.
Farm highly mechanized.  Mixed farming practiced.

Entrance requirements:                18 - 19 years of age.
                                      Good pass in G.C.E. "O".
                                      Important subjects:  English, Mathe-
                                      matics, General Science.

                                      Also considered, those having taken
                                      Modern and General Course or National
                                      Technical Certificates (South Africa).

2-year program:      Field Husbandry (including Crops and Pastures), Animal
                     Husbandry (including Veterinary Science), Agricultural
                     Engineering, Building Construction and Farm Management.

Certificate awarded:      Diploma in Agriculture.

## TEACHER EDUCATION

## TEACHERS' COLLEGE, Bulawayo

Trains European, Asian and Coloured teachers for London Certificates.

Entrance requirements:                General Certificate of Education "O"
                                      with 5 passes and 1 year in Sixth Form.

### Faculties

        Arts       - Divinity, English, History, Afrikaans
        Science    - Geography, Mathematics, Life Sciences, Physical Sciences
        Fine Arts  - Art, Crafts, Needlework, Music
        Education  - Infant Department, Junior Department, Senior Department,
                     Audio-Visual Aids Department

Programs:  3-year course (completion of 10 units).

All subjects are organized in course units of 1-year length or half-units
of 1 semester length.

Sections - All students must pass in each and all of the following 4
           sections:

    1. Practical Teaching
    2. Education
       Candidates must complete 3 units in Education.
    3. Main Subject Studies.
       Candidates require either 3 units in one subject or 2 units
       in each of two subjects in Main Subject Studies.
    4. General Courses
       Of the 10 units for a certificate, at least one must be ob-
       tained in subjects within each of the Faculties of Science,
       Arts and Fine Arts.

1-year Mature Teacher Course for teachers without above requirements.
Non-graduate teachers trained for work in lower forms of secondary
schools -- M - 2 Teachers.

(For further teacher training programs, see Faculty of Education, UNIVER-
SITY COLLEGE OF RHODESIA AND NYASALAND.)


# AFRICAN EDUCATION

In Rhodesia, the African educational system is a partnership between the
missions and the government. In 1961, out of a total of 3,082 schools,
80 were government.

Department of Native (African) Education divides government and non-government schools in following manner:

Government Schools - 4 Grades

Grade A1 - Teacher training schools: Courses preparatory for teaching in
           primary and secondary schools.

Grade A2 - Technical teacher training schools.

Grade B1 - Schools providing courses of instruction in secondary education
           only.

Grade B2 - Schools providing junior technical courses.

Non-Government Schools - 10 Grades

Grade A    (i) Teacher training lower
               2-year post-standard 6.

(ii) Teacher training higher
2-year post-Junior Certificate
(iii) Domestic Science

Grade B    Central Primary - Sub-Standard A to Standard 6,   including
boarders.

Grade C    (i) Lower Primary - Sub-Standard A to Standard 3.
(ii) Higher Primary - Standard 4 to Standard 6.

Grade D    Community Schools - Adult classes.

Grade E    Specialist, e.g. schools for blind, deaf and dumb.

Grade F    (i) Post primary industrial
(ii) Secondary

Grade G    Homecraft and Domestic Training.

Grade H    Correspondence Schools.

Grade I    Schools established in European areas for primary or community
classes.

Grade J    Unaided schools providing classes or courses to meet special
needs.

## School System

Sub-Standard:      A, B
Primary Standards: 1, 2, 3, 4, 5, 6
Secondary Forms:   I, II, III, IV - V, VI

## Examinations

The Ministry of African Education is responsible for setting the following
examinations:

Standard 6
Rhodesia Junior Certificate (Form II)
Lower Primary Teachers' Certificate
Higher Primary Teachers' Certificate
Elementary Industrial Certificate in:  Building, Carpentry, Leather-
work, Agriculture and Domestic Science Teachers' Certificate

The Ministry of African Education is also responsible for administering
the entry of pupils for:

Cambridge Examination
Higher School Examination
Technical Examinations of South Africa.

Private students are also entered by the Ministry for:

All National Examinations:  Standard 6 (plus above examinations)
Matriculation Exemption set by South Africa
General Certificate of Education, London
University

## PRIMARY EDUCATION

Entry age:          6 years.

8-year program:  Lower Primary - Sub-Standard A and B; Standards 1, 2 and 3.
                 Upper Primary - Standards 4, 5 and 6.

Immediate aim to  provide 5 years education for all children from Sub-
Standard A through Standard 3, and for as many as possible between Standard
4 and 6.

Aided primary schools comprise following types:

Mission schools:     Conducted and supervised by various religious
                     denominations.  In typical mission "district"
                     2 to 300 primary schools (most only to Standard
                     3).

Committee schools:   Joint mission endeavors; industrial and mine
                     companies; council schools (administered by local
                     native councils).

Undenominational schools:   In urban or industrial areas and on some
                            large mines.

Schools on European farms:  Mission or committee schools.

Curriculum:     English, Arithmetic, History, Geography, General Science,
                Vernacular,[+] Civics, Religious Science, Domestic Science,
                Hygiene, Manual Trades (Art, Craft, Agriculture for boys;
                Agriculture, Needlework for girls), Woodwork, Metalwork.

[+]Vernacular (either Sindebele  (Ndebele), or one of 3 main dialects
of Shona) chosen by administrator in specific area as language of
instruction through Standard 3.

Language of Instruction:  Shona and Sindebele through Standard 1.
                          English (gradually introduced at Standard 2)
                          becomes language of instruction at Standard 4.

Universal similarity of subjects and teaching methods for all subjects in
5 grades (lower primary) through Standard 3.  Detailed "Scheme Books"
drawn up by Ministry of Education used by teachers in all primary schools,
teaching same lesson with same procedure same day of each week.

Certificate Awarded:     Standard 6 School Certificate (Departmental exam-
                         ination).

For many years "Standard 6" was highest academic qualification awarded
within colony.  As of 1963, certificates stated overall standard of
attainment and grades awarded in English and Arithmetic.  External examination requires pass in English, Arithmetic, History and Geography.

Subject successes may be accumulated towards obtaining "full" certificate.

Standard 6 examination results published in 5 grades:  1, 2, 3, 4, and 5. Advance to post-primary academic courses normally limited to Grade 1 and better Grade 2 passes, and Grade 3 passes for girls.

1963 Proposals:      7-year primary training - Sub-Standards A  and B plus
                                                Standards 1 through 5.

                    Junior Secondary school - 3 years to Junior Certificate.


## SECONDARY EDUCATION

First African secondary school established 1947.

Types of secondary schools:

### Missions

> Largest group.  Only about one-half have attained level of Cambridge School Certificate.  Remaining half provide training for Rhodesia Junior Certificate examination after Forms I and II.  Preference given to members of denomination concerned.  Majority of these schools aided by government.

> | | |
> |---|---|
> | Old Umtali Mission | - Forms I - IV |
> | St. Augustine Secondary | - Forms I - IV |
> | Tegwane Secondary School | - Forms I - IV |
> | Empandeni Secondary School | - Forms I - IV |

### Government Day Schools

> All government secondary schools are academic except Chibero (agriculture) and Mzinwane (technical and agricultural bias)  About 150 pupils selected annually from urban primary schools, having passed Standard 6 and with genuine residential qualifications.  Day schools advancing beyond Form II as of 1963.  9 schools including recent establishment of new institutions in Salisbury, Bulawayo and Umtali.

### Government Boarding Schools

> 2 full high schools (presenting candidates for Higher School Certificate) Forms I through IV and Forms V and VI (Higher School)

>> Fletcher High School (boys only)
>> Goromonzi High School (coeducational)  (See Higher School Timetable)

> 1 Technical secondary school (developed from former industrial or trade schools)

>> 1st secondary school with technical bias - 1960.
>> 1st secondary school with agricultural bias - 1963.

## Community Schools

For students without adequate residential qualifications at other schools or for those outside the accepted age limit.  These schools attached to existing primary schools or at mission centers.

> Highfields Community School
> Bulawayo Community School

Study Groups
Mentored classes for Standard 6 school leavers.

## Independent Schools

Nyatsime College.  Established 1962, near Salisbury.  First school in Central Africa to be established and operated by Africans and for Africans.  Private institution, non-denominational, coeducational. Financed by Rhodesian Government aid, private contributions and U.S. Agency for International Development funds.

| | |
|---|---|
| Program: | Forms I - IV leading to G.C.E. "O" and Cambridge School Certificate. |
| Immediate aim: | Technical and commercial training for boys and girls after Cambridge School Certificate. |
| Long-term aim: | Forms V and VI (Sixth Form) leading to Higher School Certificate. |

## SECONDARY SYSTEM:

Junior Secondary - Forms I and II
                   Local education leading to Rhodesian Junior Certificate examination.

Senior Secondary - Forms III and IV
                   Preparing for Cambridge School Certificate examination.

Higher School    - Sixth Form (Higher School)
                   Preparing for Higher School Certificate examination (Provided in 2 government schools).

## JUNIOR SECONDARY SCHOOL

Entry Age:  14 years.

Language of Instruction: English.

Entrance requirements:            Pass Standard 6 School Certificate (Division 1 and 2)

Length of Program:  2 years, leading to Rhodesian Junior Certificate.

General Conditions for Rhodesia Junior Certificate:

(1)  Examination open only to pupils having attended an approved secondary school for at least 2 years immediately preceding the examination.
(2)  All candidates offer at least 8 subjects for the examination.
(3)  Subjects:

Group    I:   English, Arithmetic
Group   II:   History, Geography, Bible Knowledge
Group  III:   Latin, French, Shona, Zulu.
Group   IV:   Mathematics, Technical Drawing.
Group    V:   General Science, Biology, Physical Science.
Group   VI:   Health Science, Art, Bookkeeping, Needlework, Cookery, Housecraft, Woodwork, Metalwork, Brickwork.

Further subjects may be added from time to time on recommendation of the Secondary Schools Advisory Committee and acceptance by Secretary for African Education.

Restriction of subject entries:

(a)  Only 1 African language may be offered.
(b)  General Science may be offered together with any other subject in Group V.

(4)  The 8 subjects are selected as follows:
(a)  Both subjects from Group I.
(b)  Not fewer than 6  other subjects chosen from not fewer than 3 other groups.
(c)  Not more than 3 subjects may be offered from any one Group.

(5)  Condition for Award of Certificate:
(a)  Obtain a pass mark in
   (i)   English
  (ii)   Arithmetic or Mathematics
 (iii)   A total of 6 subjects.
(b)  Satisfy the requirements of (a) above at one and the same examination.

(6)  Marks:
(a)  All subjects carry the same number of marks, i.e., 200.
(b)  The pass  mark in all subjects is 50%.
(c)   (i)  A "Good" is awarded for a mark of 60% - 69%.
     (ii)  A "Very Good" is awarded for a mark of 70% and over.
(d)  For a pass in English, a pass in the composition paper as well as the whole subject is compulsory.


Rhodesia Junior Certificate qualifies for entry to:
   Forms III and IV preparing for Cambridge School Certificate
   Primary Teachers' Higher Training course
   State Registered Nursing Training
   Domestic Science course
   1-Year commercial course
   2-Year agriculture course
   Apprenticeship

## TYPICAL ACADEMIC SECONDARY TIMETABLE
### (40-minute periods per week)

|                              | F O R M |    |     |    |
| ---------------------------- | --- | --- | --- | --- |
| Subjects                     | I   | II  | III | IV  |
| English                      | 7   | 7   | 8   | 8   |
| Arithmetic                   | 4   | 4   | -   | -   |
| Mathematics                  | 5   | 5   | 8   | 8   |
| History                      | 3   | 3   | 4   | 4   |
| Geography                    | 3   | 3   | 4   | 4   |
| Bible                        | -   | 4   | -   | -   |
| Latin                        | 3   | 3   | 4   | 4   |
| French                       | 3   | 3   | -   | 4   |
| Shona/Zulu                   | 2   | 2   | 4   | 4   |
| Physical Science             | 4   | 4   | 4   | 4   |
| Health Science               | -   | -   | 3   | -   |
| Woodwork (boys) or Needlework (girls) | 3 | 3 | - | - |
| Art                          | 3   | 3   | -   | -   |
| Total                        | 40  | 44  | 39  | 40  |

## SENIOR SECONDARY SCHOOL

*In the last 2-year program (Forms III and IV) students prepare for the University of Cambridge Joint Examination for the School Certificate and General Certificate of Education. (For details, see Appendix, page

Those who pass the examination in the 1st Division usually enter the lower 6th Forms at either Goromonzi or Fletcher higher schools.

Of the rest, half usually proceed to teacher training or directly to primary teaching. The remainder go on to technical training, agriculture, clerical occupations with banks, railways, municipalities or commercial firms.

## HIGHER SCHOOL

2-year program: Form VI (lower and upper).

GOROMONZI SECONDARY SCHOOL
Higher School
(2-year Sixth Form Course)


TIMETABLE
(40-minute periods per week)

| Subjects | Lower VI | Upper VI |
|---|---|---|
| **Arts** | | |
| English | 7 | 5 |
| General Paper | 2 | 2 |
| English-Greek | - | 3 |
| Geography | 7 | 8 |
| History | 8 | 8 |
| Latin | 6 | 6 |
| | 30 | 32 |
| **Science** | | |
| Physics | 8 | 8 |
| General Paper | 2 | 2 |
| Mathematics | 7 | 7 |
| Biology | 8 | 8 |
| Chemistry | 7 | 8 |
| | 32 | 33 |

**University of Cambridge Joint Examination for the Higher School Certificate and General Certificate of Education at close of program. (For details, see Appendix B.)

CORRESPONDENCE COURSES

Central African Correspondence College: only correspondence courses registered in Rhodesia and grant-aided by the government. Courses: preparation for Standard IV examination through G.C.E. "A" level.

University of South Africa - correspondence courses. (For further information, see HIGHER EDUCATION, REPUBLIC OF SOUTH AFRICA.)

VOCATIONAL AND TECHNICAL EDUCATION

Some primary schools in Standards 4-5-6 offer students the choice of the following technical subjects (in addition to regular academic courses): Boys - Crafts, Agriculture and Art; Girls - Needlework, Art, Crafts,

Agriculture or Domestic Science.  Each of these subjects chosen is taken 2 hours per week.

Finishing courses in workshops for trade school trainees.

Until 1963, mission secondary schools offered a "handyman course" in building, carpentry and agriculture in addition to general academic subjects up to Junior Certificate.

## GOVERNMENT AND GOVERNMENT-AIDED SCHOOLS

Comprehensive courses with technical bias.

TECHNICAL TRAINING:

(1)  Secondary Schools

TEGWANI SECONDARY SCHOOL (near Plumtree)
Mission School

Primary:    8 years.
Secondary:  Forms I - II;  (1959) added Forms III - IV.
            Junior Certificate, School Certificate.
Teacher Training:  Primary Teacher Lower.

EMPANDENI SECONDARY SCHOOL (Near Plumtree)
Mission School

Primary classes:    8 years.
Secondary classes:  Forms I through IV.
                    Preparing for Cambridge Schools Certificate.

HOPE FOUNTAIN SCHOOL (near Bulawayo)
Mission School

Primary:       8 years.
Post-Primary:  3-year industrial and craft training leading to Education Department Elementary Industrial examination. Closed as of 1965.
Teacher Training:  Primary Teacher (Lower) Certificate.
                   P.T.L  replaced by Primary Teacher Higher Certificate as of 1965.

REGINA MUNDI SECONDARY SCHOOL
Mission School

(2)  Junior Technical Schools or Trade Schools (Government)

DOMBOSHAWA SCHOOL (near Salisbury)

Established 1921, offering building trades, carpentry and other 2-year vocational courses.

Entrance requirements:  Pass Standard 6 examination with good English, Arithmetic and primary Industrial Work.

Course preparing for apprenticeship when available and the National Certificate examination (South Africa).

As of 1965, Domboshawa converted into a Training Center for Community Development Officers.

MZINGWANE SCHOOL (near Essexville)

Offers engineering trades.

Entrance requirements:  Pass Standard 6 examination with good English, Arithmetic and primary Industrial Work.

2-year program.  Courses prepare for apprenticeship when available and the National Certificate examination (South Africa).

WADDILOVE TRADE SCHOOL

Closed as of 1965.

(3)  Senior Technical College (Government)

Open to all races.

LUVEVE TECHNICAL COLLEGE

Entrance requirements:  Cambridge School Certificate or G.C.E.

Established 1960.

Technical program closed 1963.  Teacher training program closed 1964.

4-year program:       Practical and technical courses - Bricklaying, Carpentry, Woodwork, Plastering, Painting and Decorating, Plumbing, Electrical Installation, Metalwork, Motor Mechanics.

Courses preparing for City and Guilds examinations, Ordinary, Intermediate and Final levels.

(4)  Institutes of Further Education (Government)

Open to all races.  Continuity courses for technical apprentices during off-block release periods.  Commercial and other courses are organized according to local requirements.

Entrance requirements:  Junior Certificate, or equivalent.

UMTALI TECHNICAL INSTITUTE

Subjects: Typing, Shorthand, Bookkeeping, Chi-Shona, Portuguese, Dressmaking, English for Foreign Students.

GWELO TECHNICAL CENTRE

Subjects: Typing, Shorthand, Bookkeeping.

QUE QUE TECHNICAL CENTRE

Subjects: Shorthand, Typing, Chi-Shona.

WANKIE TECHNICAL CENTRE

Subjects: Typing, Shorthand, Bookkeeping.

COMMERCIAL TRAINING:

FLETCHER SECONDARY SCHOOL, Gwelo

Established, 1960.

Entrance requirements:       Standard 6 School Certificate.

Courses:     (Commercial) Bookkeeping, Business Calculation, Shorthand, Typing, Commercial Practice, Commercial English. Closed as of 1965.

Fletcher School also offers full higher school program: Forms I through VI leading to Cambridge School Certificate and Higher School Certificate.

GOVERNMENT SCHOOLS IN HARARE AND LUVEVE

Entrance requirements:       Junior Certificate
Course:     1-year commercial program.

Entrance requirements:       Cambridge School Certificate
Course:     1-year commercial program.

VOLUNTARY TRAINING ESTABLISHMENTS

Kafunda College (A.C.A.C.)   )   Commercial training at Junior
Y.M.C.A.                     )   Certificate level

Jairus Jiri Center, Bulawayo  )
Mukwapasi Center, Rusape      )    Both for physically handicapped

Ranche House College for Adult Education

AGRICULTURAL TRAINING:

2-year academic Junior Certificate course (Forms I-II) with either a
Technical or Agricultural bias, replaced previous 3-year "handyman"
program.

Students qualified in this field may pursue following levels of instruction:

> Junior Certificate (bias Agriculture)
> 2-year training in Agricultural school.
>> Awarded Rhodesian Agricultural Certificate which qualifies for
>> employment as:  Agricultural Extension Assistant, Department of
>> Agriculture.

> 2-year further study for London G.C.E. prepares for entry to Chibero
> Agriculture College.
>> Awarded Diploma which qualifies for employment as:  Agriculture,
>> Forest, or Conservation Officers and Animal Health Inspectors.

> Possible entry to University College of Rhodesia and Nyasaland.
> Full professional degree.


AGRICULTURAL SCHOOLS

4-year courses.

Entrance requirements:             Standard 6 School Certificate

Mzingwane (Government)       - General academic, strong bias in agriculture
Mlezu  (Gue Gue) (Government)- Technical and Mechanical agricultural train-
                              ing
Gloag Ranch School (Mission)


CHIBERO AGRICULTURAL COLLEGE

Established, 1961.

Entrance requirements:             Cambridge School Certificate
                                   G.C.E. "O" level

OTHER GOVERNMENT DEPARTMENTAL TRAINING:

> British South Africa Police
> Army Corps of Signals
> Medical - Nurses' training (Impilo Hospital, Bulawayo)
> Survey
> Veterinary
> Rhodesia Railways
> Postal and Telegraph

Entrance requirements for above Departments:     Standard 6
                                                 School certificate

Award:    Junior certificate

The government also offers Adult Education and Literacy Training program.

## TEACHER EDUCATION

As of 1963, Primary Teachers' Lower and Primary Teachers' Higher Certificate training was offered at Government College, Umtali (133 students) and at 20 different mission centers (847 enrolled).  First government school at Umatali opened 1956; new Teacher Training Center at Gwelo assisted by U.S. Agency for International Development, 1963.

## TEACHER TRAINING SCHOOLS

| Entrance Requirements and Training | Certificate | Teaching Area |
|---|---|---|
| Post-Standard 6 plus 2 years training | Primary Teachers' Lower Certificate (P.T.L.) | Teach in Sub-Standards A-B and Standards 1-3 (T-4) |
| 2-Year Secondary School plus 2 years training (after Junior Certificate) | Primary Teachers' Higher Certificate | Teach in Standards 4-5-6  Primary school (T-3) |
| Post-Cambridge School Certificate plus 2 years training (Offered by Department of Native Education) | | Teach in Junior Secondary school (T-2) (Gwelo Training College) |

(Examinations for above courses administered by the Ministry of Education)

| Post-Cambridge School Certificate (5 credits, 1 in English) plus 3-year training <u>or</u> Higher School Certificate or G.C.E. "A" plus 2 years training | <u>University</u> <u>Diploma</u> | Teach in Secondary school (lower forms) (T-1) (Both of these trainees awarded Diploma by University College of Rhodesia and Nyasaland) |
|---|---|---|
| 5-year Post-School Certificate Course - Bulawayo Technical Teacher Training College City and Guilds examinations at end of 4th year. | | Teach in Technical schools |
| T-4 Certificate plus 1 year training <u>or</u> Post-Standard 6 plus 2-year training | | Teach Domestic Science in Standards 4-5-6. |
| Post-School Certificate plus 3-years training | <u>University</u> <u>Diploma</u> | Teach Domestic Science in secondary school |

## <u>PRIMARY TEACHERS' LOWER (P.T.L.) CERTIFICATE COURSE</u>

Entrance requirements: <u>Standard 6 School Certificate.</u>

Teaching area: Sub-Standards A-B and Standards 1-3.

Duration of course: 2 years.

### <u>Nyadiri Centre Schools</u>

#### TIMETABLE
(40-minute periods per week)

| Subjects | 1A | 1B | 2A | 2B |
|---|---|---|---|---|
| Education | 14 | 13 | 11 | 13 |
| English | 9 | 8 | 9 | 8 |
| Arithmetic | 2 | 2 | 2 | 2 |
| Shona | 2 | 2 | 3 | 2 |
| History | 2 | 2 | 2 | 2 |
| Physical Education | 4 | 4 | 3 | 3 |
| Geography | 1 | 1 | 2 | 2 |
| Music | 3 | 3 | 3 | 3 |
| Nature Study | 1 | 1 | 2 | 2 |
| Agriculture/Needlework | 3 | 3 | 3 | 3 |
| Arts and Crafts | 2 | 2 | 2 | 2 |
| | 43 | 41 | 42 | 42 |

PRIMARY TEACHERS' HIGHER CERTIFICATE (P.T.H.) COURSE (Division of Native
  Education)

Entrance requirements:            Rhodesia Junior Certificate or equiva-
                                  lent

Minimum entry age:  17 years.

Teaching area:      Standards 4-5-6.  Teachers must also be acquainted
                    with subjects taught in lower classes.

Duration of course: 2 years.

### Nyadiri Teacher Training Department

### TIMETABLE
(40-minute periods per week)

| Professional Subjects | | Periods |
|---|---|---|
| Principles of Education | | 2 |
| Methods of Teaching | | 3 |
| School Organization | | 1 |
| Blackboard Work | | 2 |
| Teaching Apparatus | | 2 |
| Criticism, Discussion and Demonstration Lessons | | 5 |
| | Total | 15 |

(Minimum of 6 weeks Practical Teaching per year)

| General Subjects | | |
|---|---|---|
| Religious Instruction | | 5 |
| English | | 8 |
| African Language | | 2 |
| Arithmetic | | 2 |
| History/Geography | | 3 |
| Physiology, Hygiene, First Aid and Nature Study | | 3 |
| Physical Education | | 3 |
| Music | | 2 |
| Arts and Crafts | | 5 |
| Agriculture/Needlework | | 4 |
| | Total | 37 |

In-service training through Correspondence College 1962.  Entrance requirement 3 years of teaching for vacation course extending over 2 years.  Students then sit for same examinations given in training colleges.

## PROPOSALS

(1)  To build Higher Training College at Gwelo (to be African counterpart of new college at Bulawayo, replacing Heany Training College.

1 year specialist courses for teachers of Art, Music and Physical Education.  Diploma to be awarded.

(2)  Secondary School Training College, Salisbury:
To be multi-racial institution in coordination with the Institute of Education at the University College.

(3)  New Training College:  United College of Education, Bulawayo.

New teacher education center planned to open 1967, under sponsorship of the Anglican, Congregational and Methodist Churches and the Church of Christ in the Bulawayo area.

Additional assistance given by Bulawayo City Council, British Department of Education's Building Unit, the "United College Appeal Fund."

(4)  In Salisbury, various denominations are still negotiating for a united approach towards a United College of Education on the Bulawayo pattern.

962

REPUBLIC OF RWANDA

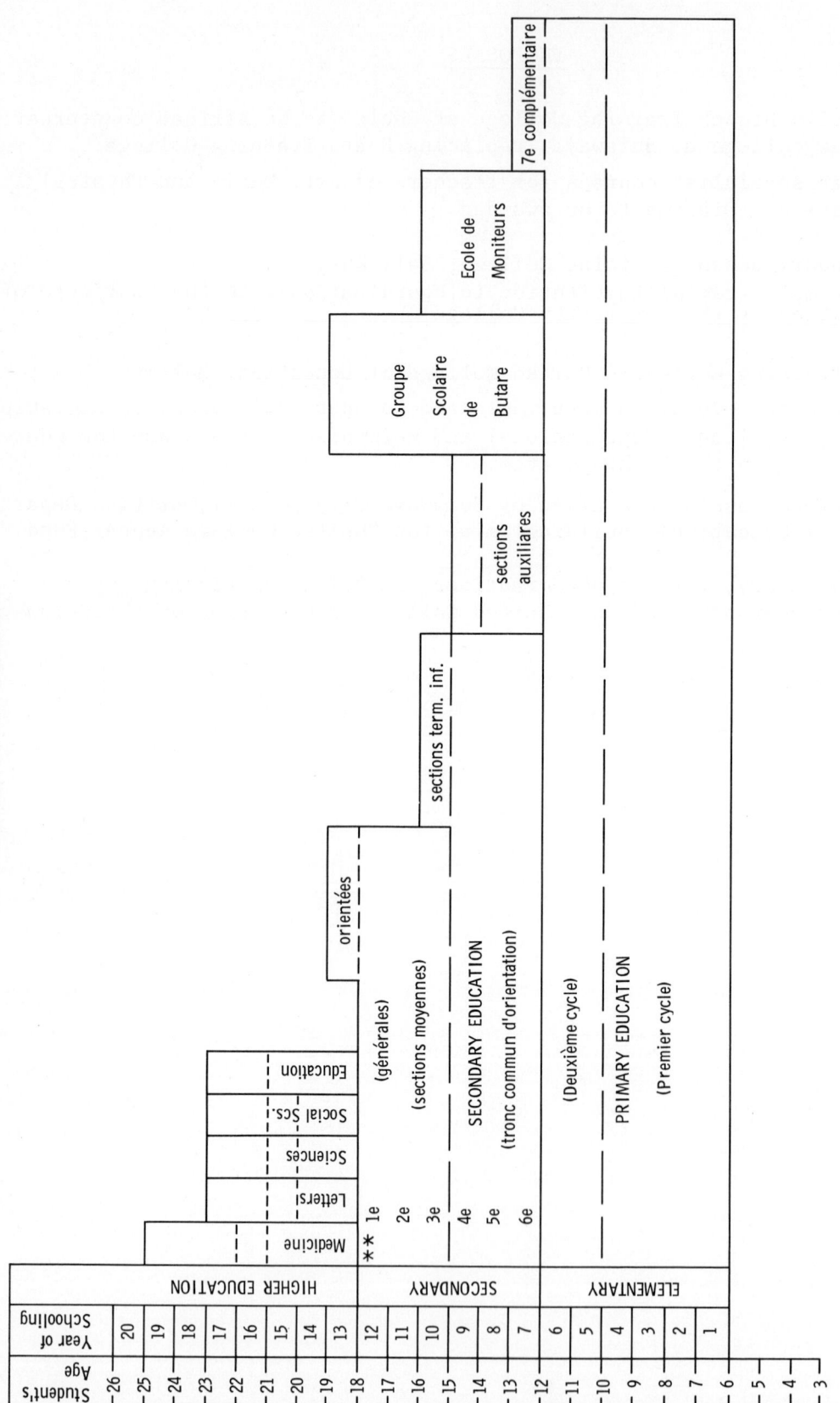

Compulsory education: Through 6-year primary cycle

School year: Mid-September – June

Secondary Grading: Secondary education – 100% – Perfect
50% – Passing
(for primary education, see under Primary Education)

REPUBLIC OF RWANDA
(République Rwandaise)


Independence:   July 1, 1962.



BACKGROUND


Population mostly Hutu (known also as Bahutu) and Tutsi (Watutsi, Watusi, or Batutsi), Bantu people (traditionally farmers; they comprise 90% of population.  Tutsi, 9% of population, probably came from Ethiopia to Rwanda before 15th century.  1% of population, Twa (Batwa), a Pygmy tribe of hunters related to pygmies of former Belgian Congo; they were earliest inhabitants.  Europeans, 3000; Asians, 2000.

Tutsi kingdom under successive Mwamis as early as 16th century.  From 16th century to 1959, Tutsi kingdom shared history of Burundi.

First Europeans came in 1858.  1871, Stanley and Livingstone landed at Usumbura and explored Ruzizi River region.  German explorers later.  White Fathers established Roman Catholic missions.

After Berlin Conference 1884-85, German zone of influence in East Africa was extended to include Rwanda and Burundi.  Single administrative authority.  1897, Rwanda detached from governor's authority at Usumbura and separate headquarters were established at Kigali.

Belgium occupied territory in 1916, during World War I (when Burundi formed part of Ruanda-Urundi).  Placed  under Belgian mandate by League of Nations, 1923.  1925, became integral part of Belgian Congo.

1946, Ruanda-Urundi became U.N. Trust Territory under Belgian administration.  Clashes between Hutu and Tutsi after World War II.  1959, uprising of Hutu destroyed the Tutsi feudal hierarchy and led to the departure of the Mwami Kigeri V.  1960, U.N. mission sent to Ruanda-Urundi.  Provisional government, composed mainly of Parmehutu Party established, October 1960. Republican regime, January 28, 1961.  New regime recognized by administering authority, but U.N. declared it unlawful.  September 25, 1961, legislative elections and referendum under supervision of the U.N. Commission for Ruanda-Urundi; 95% vote to abolish the monarchy.  U.N. recommended independence of a united Rwanda and Burundi but the elections were won by the party favoring separation and July 1, 1962 Rwanda became an independent country.

Languages:  French, official; Kinyarwanda, local; Kiswahili, spoken in commercial centers.

Education largely the function of the Catholic church in missions and state-supported mission schools.  Up to 1951, 75% of school children enrolled in écoles de simple lecture (rudimentary reading schools) operated by Catholic and Protestant missions.  1952, Ten-Year Plan for more secondary and vocational schools.  Until 1957, those going beyond elementary level were trained for the priesthood.

More than 80% of primary and almost all secondary schools are still Church schools, subsidized by the government.

With independence, Rwanda called on UNESCO to help with the reform of the educational system.  Their first suggestions put into operation from September, 1964.

# GOVERNMENT AND GOVERNMENT-SUBSIDIZED EDUCATION

## PRE-PRIMARY EDUCATION

None.

## PRIMARY EDUCATION

Entry age:          6-7 years.

Language of instruction:          Kinyarwanda first 4 years, then French introduced for the remainder of primary and secondary education.

Length of primary education:      6 years divided into 2 cycles.

Premier cycle of 4 years with a system of double vacation in 1st 3 years--pupils only go to school for half a day, so that two different groups may be taught in same day.

Deuxième cycle of 2 years.

At the end of the 6-year primary education, those not passing the examination well enough to begin secondary education may take 7ème complémentaire, 1-year post-primary course.

Also projected is a para-primary cycle for those not admitted to the 2nd cycle of primary school.

Program:            Flexible program includes Religion, Kinyarwanda, French
                    (in 2nd cycle), Arithmetic, Geography, History, Civics,
                    Art, Physical Education, observation lessons.

Certificates awarded:              Certificat d'études primaires élémentaires
                                   on completion of 1st cycle

                                   Diplôme de fin d'études primaires on
                                   completion of 2nd cycle

Grading:       1st cycle      50% of total points of year to pass into
                              higher class.

               2nd cycle      to pass 4th to 5th class 60% of total of
                              first 2 terms, plus exam results at end of
                              year;
                              to pass 5th to 6th class 50% of year's
                              total points.

               Not more than 1 class may be doubled in the course of
               the 6 years.


## SECONDARY EDUCATION

Secondary institutions:

   3 humanities collèges for boys, only 1 with complete cycle.

   1 technical secondary school for boys (Carpentry, Mechanics, Tailor-
      ing, etc.).

   16 écoles normales (teacher training schools) for boys and girls,
      most of them having only the lower cycle.

   1 collège  for girls, cycle not complete.

   4 lower technical and craft schools.

   2 schools for auxiliary nurses.

   1 school of nursing.

   1 school for auxiliary social assistants.

   The Groupe Scolaire de Butare, a unique institution, giving at the
   same time as a general training, a specialized training in many fields:
   Teaching, Medical, Veterinary, Agricultural, Business Administration,
   etc.

Entry age:     no more than 15 years.

Entrance requirements:             Diplôme de fin d'études primaires and
                                   success at competitive examination, concours,
                                   official government examination.

Length of courses:      According to results of <u>concours</u>, students directed

    <u>either</u> into the <u>tronc commun d'orientation</u> (general
       orientation section).  3-year course giving a
       general preparatory secondary education, adaptable
       to further study.

    <u>or</u>  into <u>sections auxiliaires</u>.  2 or 3-year terminal
       courses training auxiliaires in teaching, crafts,
       trades, etc.

       After the 3-year <u>tronc commun</u>, choice of terminal or
       continued secondary courses:

       <u>sections terminales inférieures</u>, for students not
       showing the aptitude for further study.  Preparation
       for teaching, nursing, midwifery, etc.  2 or 3 years
       according to specialty.

       <u>sections moyennes</u> leading to higher education of
       2 types:

       (a) <u>sections moyennes générales</u>.  3-year course
         (modern, classical) leading to university;

       (b) <u>sections moyennes orientées</u>, 4-year courses
         either leading to higher studies or forming
         technical assistants, e.g. teachers (<u>institu-
         teurs</u>), medical assistants, agricultural
         assistants, etc.

Certificates awarded:      <u>Diplôme</u> in chosen specialty at end of
       <u>sections auxiliaires</u> and <u>sections terminales
       inférieures</u>.

       The name of the diploma recognizing end of
       <u>tronc commun</u> has not yet been fixed.

      **<u>Diplôme de fin d'humanités secondaires</u>, or
       <u>homologation</u>, at end of <u>sections moyennes</u>.

Grading:        100% perfect, 50% pass.


    <u>TIMETABLE - SECTIONS MOYENNES GENERALES</u>
      (Hours per week)

<u>Latin-Greek Section</u>

| <u>Subjects</u> | Class | 6 | 5 | 4 | 3 | 2 | 1 |
|---|---|---|---|---|---|---|---|
| Religion | | 2 | 2 | 2 | 2 | 2 | 2 |
| Kinyarwanda | | 2 | 2 | 2 | 2 | 2 | 2 |
| French | | 5 | 5 | 5 | 4 | 4 | 4 |
| Latin | | 9 | 6 | 6 | 6 | 5 | 5 |
| Greek | | - | 4 | 4 | 4 | 4 | 4 |

| English     | 2 | 2 | 2 | 3 | 3 | 3 |
|-------------|---|---|---|---|---|---|
| Mathematics | 4 | 3 | 3 | 3 | 3 | 3 |
| History     | 2 | 2 | 2 | 2 | 2 | 2 |
| Geography   | 2 | 1 | 1 | 1 | 1 | 1 |
| Science     | - | 1 | 1 | 1 | 2 | 2 |
| Civics      | 1 | 1 | 1 | 1 | 1 | 1 |
| Aesthetics  | 1 | 1 | 1 | 1 | 1 | 1 |

### Latin-Sciences Section

| Subjects                     | Class | 6 | 5 | 4 | 3 | 2 | 1 |
|------------------------------|-------|---|---|---|---|---|---|
| Religion                     |       | 2 | 2 | 2 | 2 | 2 | 2 |
| Kinyarwanda                  |       | 2 | 2 | 2 | 1 | 1 | 1 |
| French                       |       | 5 | 5 | 6 | 4 | 4 | 4 |
| Latin                        |       | 9 | 6 | 6 | 6 | 5 | 5 |
| English                      |       | 2 | 2 | 2 | 2 | 2 | 2 |
| Mathematics                  |       | 4 | 5 | 5 | 4 | 4 | 4 |
| History                      |       | 2 | 2 | 2 | 2 | 2 | 2 |
| Geography                    |       | 2 | 1 | 1 | 1 | 1 | 1 |
| Natural Sciences             |       | - | 1 | 1 | - | - | - |
| Physics, Chemistry, Biology  |       | - | - | - | 4 | 4 | 5 |
| Civics                       |       | 1 | 1 | 1 | 1 | 1 | 1 |
| Greek Culture                |       | - | - | - | - | 1 | 1 |
| Scientific Literature        |       | - | - | - | - | - | 1 |
| Aesthetics                   |       | 1 | 1 | 1 | 1 | 1 | 1 |
| Art                          |       | - | 2 | 1 | - | - | - |

In the above programs, laboratory work is given in Physics and Chemistry where there is a laboratory.

N.B.    All secondary education programs, except those for technical schools, are from the Fédération Nationale de l'Enseignement Moyen Catholique of Belgium. This applied even to Protestant mission schools.

A start has been made on the Africanization of the programs with some amendments in History and Geography from the Ministry of National Education.

## HIGHER EDUCATION

## NATIONAL UNIVERSITY OF RWANDA

May 1963, agreement signed by government of Rwanda and the Dominican Order for the creation of a university. November 1963, opening of first academic session. May 1964, law for the official creation and organization of the National University of Rwanda, a public, autonomous institution.

Faculties:

    Medicine
    Social Science
    Science
    Letters

Institut de Normale Supérieure - pedagogical institute training students in Science and Letters.

University extension:  adult education center.

Entrance requirements:       Successful completion of <u>sections moyennes</u> with the <u>Diplôme</u> or <u>homologation</u>, or recognized equivalent.

## Faculty of Medicine

| Length of courses: | | |
|---|---|---|
| <u>Candidature</u> | | 3 years |
| <u>Baccalauréat spécialisé en médecine</u> | | 4 years |
| <u>Docteur en médecine</u> | | 7 years |

Program:

1st yr:    Physics, Chemistry, Zoology, Botany, Medical Physics, Introduction to Higher Mathematics.

2nd yr:    Medical Physics, Calculus, Psychology, Logic, Histology, Physiology, Biochemistry, Anatomy.

3rd yr:    Histology, Physiology, Biochemistry, Anatomy, Embryology.

4th yr:    Pathological Biochemistry, Pathology, Pharmacology, Bacteriology, Entomology, Hematology, Preliminary Medical and Surgical Ailments, Practical clinical work, Social Medicine.

5th yr:    Pathology, Obstetrics, Radiognostics, practical clinical work.

6th yr:    Practical clinical work only.

7th yr:    Practical clinical work, Social Medicine and optional courses in Physiotherapy, Radiotherapy, Radiognostics, Tuberculosis.

Practical experience in Internal Medicine, Surgery, Gynecology, Pediatrics, Social Medicine.

Practical and laboratory work throughout the course.

## Faculty of Science

Length of courses:    Candidature                              2 years

                      Baccalauréat spécialisé ès sciences      3 years

                      Licence or maître ès sciences            5 years

Courses offered in:   Mathematics, Physics, Chemistry, Biochemistry,
                      Biology, Physiology, Geography, Geology, Mineralogy,
                      Cartography, Climatology, Philosophy, French
                      Language and Literature, African Studies in History,
                      Ethnology, Geography, Arts.

## Faculty of Letters

Length of courses:    Candidature                              2 years

                      Baccalauréat spécialisé ès lettres       3 years

                      Licence or maître ès lettres             5 years

Courses offered in:   Philosophy, French Language and Literature, Latin,
                      History, African Studies in Linguistics, Literature,
                      History, Ethnology and Arts, Foreign Literature,
                      Art and Archeology, English Language and Literature.

## Faculty of Social Sciences

Length of courses:    Candidature                              2 years

                      Baccalauréat spécialisé ès sciences sociales  3 years

                      Licence or maître in Economics, Sociology,
                      or Political and Administrative Sciences   5 years

General courses to the Baccalauréat spécialisé:

                      Philosophy, Scientific Methodology and Instrumenta-
                      tion, History, Social Sciences, Law, African Studies
                      in History, Ethnology and Arts, Art and Archeology,
                      Social and Preventive Medicine.

Final 2 years of specialization for the licence or maître in:  Economics,
Sociology, or Political and Administrative Sciences.

## Institut de Normale Supérieure

Length of courses:    Agrégation de l'enseignement secondaire, cycle
                      inférieur: 3 years, with the Baccalauréat spécialisé.

Agrégation de l'enseignement secondaire, cycle
supérieur: 5 years, with the licence or maîtrise.

Courses given in conjunction with regular studies in Faculties of Letters
and Science:

> Philosophy of Education and History of Pedagogy
> General Methodology
> Methodology applied to Science or Letters
> Experimental Psychology
> Child and Adolescent Psychology
> Experimental Pedagogy
> Mental Hygiene
> Educational Legislation
> Educational Organization and Administration in
>     Central Africa
> Professional Orientation in Testing
> Didactic exercises in Science or Letters
> Special Methodology in Science (Mathematics,
>     Chemistry, Physics, Zoology, Botany)
> Special Methodology in Letters (Philosophy,
>     Literature, History)
> Comparative studies of different systems of
>     education, particularly those still in develop-
>     mental stage.

## TECHNICAL AND VOCATIONAL EDUCATION

### ECOLE DE METIERS OFFICIELLE DE KICUKIRO

Length of course:     4-6 years after 6 years of primary education.

Sections:     Carpentry, Cabinet Making
Mechanics and Automechanics
Electricity
Welding

### ECOLE D'INFIRMIERES DE KABGAYI

Trains nurses at the European level.

### ECOLE D'ASSISTANTES SOCIALES DE BUTARE

Trains auxiliary social assistants.

GROUPE SCOLAIRE DE BUTARE

Length of courses:    5-7 years.

General education and specialized training for:

> Instituteurs (Letters and Science)
> Scientific Humanities
> Mathematical Humanities
> Medical Assistants
> Veterinary Assistants
> Agricultural Assistants
> Business Administration
> etc.


TEACHER EDUCATION

Ecoles normales called écoles moniteurs.   Entry after completion of primary school.

In the future with the extension of the educational reform, pupils will be required to complete the tronc commun of 3 years before entering the écoles moniteurs to take 1 or 2 years of  edagogy and Methodology.

At present the écoles de moniteurs offer 4 years of general secondary education with intensive pedagogical training in the 3rd and 4th years. Moniteurs teach in primary school.


### TIMETABLE
(Hours per week)

| Subjects | Class | 1 | 2 | 3 | 4 |
|---|---|---|---|---|---|
| Religion | | 2 | 2 | 2 | 2 |
| Kinyarwanda | | 2 | 2 | 2 | 2 |
| French | | 7 | 6 | 3 | 3 |
| English | | 4 | 4 | 2 | 2 |
| Mathematics | | 6 | 6 | 3 | 3 |
| Sciences | | 1 | 2 | 2 | 1 |
| Economic Science | | - | - | 2 | 1 |
| History | | 2 | 2 | 2 | 1 |
| Geography | | 2 | 1 | 1 | 1 |
| Civics | | 1 | 1 | 1 | 1 |
| Art | | 2 | 2 | 2 | 2 |
| Music | | 1 | 1 | 1 | 1 |
| Pedagogy | | 1 | 1 | 10 | 13 |

Group Scolaire de Butare prepares <u>instituteurs</u>.  7-year secondary course
with pedagogical training.  Able to teach in 1st cycle of secondary
education, both the <u>tronc commun</u> and the <u>sections auxiliaires</u>.

Diploma awarded:       <u>Diplôme d'instituteur</u>


<u>INSTITUT DE NORMALE SUPERIEURE</u>

(See under HIGHER EDUCATION)

Part of the National University of Rwanda.  Gives pedagogical training to
students in the Faculty of Letters and the Faculty of Science simultaneously with <u>licence</u> studies.

Awards the <u>Agrégation de l'enseignement secondaire, cycle inférieur</u> with
the <u>Baccalauréat spécialisé</u>, and <u>cycle supérieur</u> with the <u>licence</u> or
<u>maîtrise</u>.  Provides teachers for the 2nd cycle of secondary education.

ZAMBIA
(NORTHERN RHODESIA)
Colonial and Federation

African Education

(Through 1964)

SECONDARY EDUCATION

PRIMARY EDUCATION

T2

Teacher
T3

Training
T4

Technical
College

Trade
School

(Higher School)

(Senior Secondary)

(Junior Secondary)

(Upper Primary)

(Middle Primary)

(Lower Primary)

** Form VI — Upper
— Lower

* 1/2+ or 1

Form IV
Form III
Form II
Form I
6
5
4
3
2
1 Standard
Sub-Standard B
Sub-Standard A

Compulsory education: None

School year: January – December

Secondary grading: Distinction – 75% and over

Credit – 60% and over

Pass – 40% – 59% and above

Fail – Below 40%

| Student's Age | Year of Schooling | HIGHER EDUCATION | SECONDARY | ELEMENTARY |
|---|---|---|---|---|
| 26 | 20 | | | |
| 25 | 19 | | | |
| 24 | 18 | | | |
| 23 | 17 | | | |
| 22 | 16 | | | |
| 21 | 15 | | | |
| 20 | 14 | | | |
| 19 | 13 | | | |
| 18 | 12 | | | |
| 17 | 11 | | | |
| 16 | 10 | | | |
| 15 | 9 | | | |
| 14 | 8 | | | |
| 13 | 7 | | | |
| 12 | 6 | | | |
| 11 | 5 | | | |
| 10 | 4 | | | |
| 9 | 3 | | | |
| 8 | 2 | | | |
| 7 | 1 | | | |
| 6 | | | | |
| 5 | | | | |
| 4 | | | | |
| 3 | | | | |

974

ZAMBIA
(From 1965)

University of Zambia –
Projected Schools

| Student's Age | Year of Schooling | | | |
|---|---|---|---|---|
| 26 | 20 | HIGHER EDUCATION | | |
| 25 | 19 | | | |
| 24 | 18 | | | |
| 23 | 17 | | | |
| 22 | 16 | | | |
| 21 | 15 | | | |
| 20 | 14 | | | |
| 19 | 13 | | | |
| 18 | 12 | | | |
| 17 | 11 | SECONDARY | | |
| 16 | 10 | | | |
| 15 | 9 | | | |
| 14 | 8 | | | |
| 13 | 7 | ELEMENTARY | | |
| 12 | 6 | | | |
| 11 | 5 | | | |
| 10 | 4 | | | |
| 9 | 3 | | | |
| 8 | 2 | | | |
| 7 | 1 | | | |
| 6 | | | | |
| 5 | | | | |
| 4 | | | | |
| 3 | | | | |

Humanities
Phys. Scs.
Biol. Scs.
Soc. St.
Agric.
Med.
Admin.
Education
Tech. & Min.

**IV Form
III Form
II Form
I Form
VII Grade
VI Grade
V Grade
IV Grade
III Grade
II Grade
I Grade

(Senior Secondary)
(Junior Secondary)
(Upper Primary)
(Lower Primary)

Form VI Last entry –
Jan. '65
Form V
SECONDARY EDUCATION
PRIMARY EDUCATION

Technical
Training
Trade
Training

Teacher Tr.
Teacher Tr.
VIII Grade

Compulsory education:  None

School year:  January – December (3 terms, 10-12 weeks each)

Secondary grading:  Distinction – 75% and over

Credit   – 60% and over

Pass   – 40 – 59% and above

Fail   – below 40%

REPUBLIC OF ZAMBIA
(Formerly Northern Rhodesia)

Independence:  October 24, 1964.


BACKGROUND

The African population belongs to various Bantu tribes.  ("Bantu" is a
term which includes those peoples in whose language the root "ntu," with
appropriate prefix, means "man.")  Largest Bantu tribes in Zambia are
Bemba, Tonga, Chewa, Lamba, Lozi (of Baroteseland), Nsenga, Kaonde, Lala,
Chokwe, Ngoni.  Europeans are mainly of British origin, South Africans
are of Dutch descent.  There are also Italians, Asians (mainly Indians),
and persons of mixed races.

Forty different Bantu languages are spoken.  The 5 main languages for
administrative and educational purposes are:  Bemba (in various dialects
used widely in northern territory and is lingua franca in Copperbelt),
Lozi, Luvale, Tonga (widely used in southern province), and Nyanja.

David Livingstone explored the territory in 1851-1873.  1890, Cecil Rhodes'
British South Africa Company, already functioning in Southern Rhodesia,
extended its charter to areas north of the Zambesi, and from 1891-1923
the territory was ruled by the Company.  By an Order in Council, May 4,
1911, the two provinces of North-eastern and North-western Rhodesia were
joined under the name Northern Rhodesia, effective August 7, 1911.

In 1924, Southern Rhodesia became self-governing; Northern Rhodesia was
put under jurisdiction of the Colonial Office.  By an Order in Council,
February 20, 1924, the office of Governor was created, an Executive Council was initiated, with provision for a Legislative Council.

From 1925, discovery of Copperbelt mineral deposits brought European
settlers and riches to the territory.  From 1938-48, there was greater
emphasis on African responsibility in government.  In 1953, on the decision of the British government, Northern Rhodesia joined with Southern
Rhodesia and Nyasaland to form the Federation of Rhodesia and Nyasaland.
African opposition.  From 1953-63, Northern Rhodesia was a Protectorate
under the British Crown within the Federation of Rhodesia and Nyasaland.

In January 1959, by means of a new constitution there was an attempt to
structure a political system with greater cooperation between races.
1960, British government recommended greater African participation in
federal parliament and redistribution of federal and territorial functions.

1962, Nyasaland proposed to secede from Federation.  September 1962, a
new constitution for Northern Rhodesia; December 14, 1962, a new Executive Council initiated.  After break-up of Federation of Rhodesia and
Nyasaland, a new constitution for Northern Rhodesia, January 3, 1964,
assuring internal self-government in preparation for independence.
Independence attained October 24, 1964; name changed to Zambia.

Early Christian missions took responsibility for the education of Africans.  After 1953, federal government took over education for Europeans,
Asians and Coloureds; African education was assigned to territorial
government.  Thereafter, many mission schools grant-aided.

By 1958, 90% of children 8-11 years of age were in lower primary school,
less than 50% in urban areas.  After 11 years of age, only 50% continued
in upper primary.  Up to 1958, Manali Government School, Lusaka (boys'
boarding school), was the only secondary school offering complete matriculation course to Senior Cambridge Certificate.

1960, Rhodesian Selection Trust and Anglo-American Corporation, copper
mining companies, planned to make possible 6 years of compulsory lower
primary education in the Copperbelt, and a new secondary school for each
of the 4 main mining centers.


## COLONIAL ADMINISTRATION THROUGH FEDERATION OF RHODESIA AND NYASALAND

### (1924 - 1964)


### E U R O P E A N   E D U C A T I O N

European education was patterned largely after system in Southern Rhodesia.
The 1942 European Education Ordinance provided compulsory education for
European children between 7 and 15 years of age.  Children of the few
Europeans living in Northern Rhodesia starting at the age of 5 years re-
ceived primary and secondary training in private, government-aided schools.


### PRIMARY

All primary schools coeducational.

7-year program:  Infant - 2 years.

                 Primary - Standards I through V.

No examination required at end of program.

SECONDARY

Entrance until January 1964, non-selective.

Forms I through IV or V.
Courses for exceptional students, always of 4 years' duration.

Preparing for G.C.E. "O" level examinations.


# A F R I C A N   E D U C A T I O N

Educational system based on cooperation between government and voluntary agencies, normally missionary societies managing and maintaining large proportion of schools.  To these and to an increasing number of local authority schools government contributed grants-in-aid.  1925, Department of Education was created.


## PRIMARY EDUCATION

Entry Age:            6 - 8 years.

Duration of course: 8 years.

                    Primary - Lower  (  Sub-Standards A and B
                              Middle (  Standards 1 - 3
                              Upper  (  Standards 4 - 6

Curriculum:    English, Arithmetic, Religious Knowledge, Vernacular and
               Handwriting, Social Studies, Nature Study and Gardening,
               Crafts (boys), Domestic Science (girls), Art, Singing,
               Physical Education.

Certificate awarded:  Primary School Leaving Certificate
                      (Conclusion of full 8-year program).


## SECONDARY EDUCATION

Pupils selected on the results of Standard 6 (Grade VIII) examinations.


## JUNIOR SECONDARY COURSE, FORMS I - II

Curriculum:    Group A    English (oral and written), History, Geography,
                          General Science, Mathematics.

> Group B   Civics, Art, Woodwork, Housecraft, Latin, French,
> Needlework, Bookkeeping, African Languages (Bemba,
> Nyanja, Tonga, Lozi).

Examination:   Pass - fail examination on group basis.

Certificate awarded:   <u>Northern Rhodesia Junior Certificate</u>
(Junior Secondary School Leaving Certificate)
(Form II)


## SENIOR SECONDARY COURSE, FORMS III - IV OR V

Entrance requirements:                <u>Junior Certificate</u> (competitive basis)

Curriculum:                Must pass English and any 5 other subjects:
(2 or 3-year
 Secondary work,          English Language, English Literature, French/Afrikaans[+],
 approximate 5            Latin, Geography, History, Physics, Chemistry, Biology,
 hours each per           Mathematics, Additional Mathematics, Technical Drawing,
 week)                    Religious Knowledge.


Certificate awarded:       <u>School Certificate</u> and <u>G.C.E. "O"</u> level of
Associated Examining Board of London.


Curriculum:                Any 4 of the following subjects:
(2 or 3-year
 course)                  English Language, Afrikaans[+], History, Geography,
Mathematics, Physics and Chemistry, Biology, Latin,
Art.

Certificate awarded:       "M" level, G.C.E. of the Associated Examining
Board for South African Matriculation.


N.B.  Examinations for external students:  <u>G.C.E. "O"</u> level,
University of London.


[+]Afrikaans will be replaced by local vernacular languages (Bemba, Nyanja,
Tonga, Lozi) in areas where they are commonly spoken.


## HIGHER SCHOOL

Manlai Government School, Lusaka (boys' boarding) only school offering
complete matriculation course to Form VI in 1958.

1963 Form VI classes added to 4 more secondary schools:

> Gilbert Rennie (boys)
> Jean Rennie    (girls)        )      Sixth Form
> Canisius                      )        Programs
> Chipembi

Curriculum:          Any 3 or 4 of the following subjects:
(Sixth Form;         English, French, Afrikaans[+], Geography, History,
 approximately       Latin, Pure Mathematics, Pure and Applied Mathematics,
 5 hours each        Applied Mathematics and Mechanics, Physics and Chem-
 per week)           istry, Biology, Economics.

Certificate awarded:        Higher School Certificate and "A" level  G.C.E.
                            of the Associated Examining Board.

[+]Afrikaans will be replaced by local vernacular languages (Bemba, Nyanja,
Tonga, Lozi) in areas where they are commonly spoken.


## TECHNICAL AND VOCATIONAL EDUCATION

Previous to Independence technical training was provided by the following
program:

TRADE SCHOOLS:

Mostly run by local authorities and missions.


## GOVERNMENT TRADE SCHOOL, Soche

Entrance requirements:          Primary school leavers

Length of course:  3 years.

Curriculum:          Building trades:  Carpentry, Woodwork, Masonry, etc.


TRAINING SCHOOLS:

Operated by Government Departments (other than Ministry of Education).

Entrance requirements:          Primary school leavers;
                                tendency to require Junior Certificate
                                or Senior Secondary training.

Courses offered at:      Medical Training schools, Survey schools, Agricultural and Veterinary Training schools, and others.

## TECHNICAL TRAINING:

### COPPERBELT TECHNICAL FOUNDATION (Multiracial)

Established 1955 by Northern Rhodesia Chamber of Mines to provide theoretical technical training for apprentices.

Teaching centers opened 1958 at Kitwe (administrative headquarters); Chingola, Luanshya, Mulfulira.

Entrance requirements:      Primary School-Leaving Certificate. Some post-secondary.

Duration of course:  2 - 4 years.

Curriculum:      Mathematics, Physics, Trade Theories, Engineering, Drawing, Machine and Electrical Design, Heat Engines, Strength of Materials, etc. up to Advanced Technical Certificate standard.

Commercial subjects.

Adult classes:  African Languages, Technical subjects, Arts and Crafts.

### TEACHER EDUCATION

#### Teacher designations through 1964:

Grades of trained teachers:

T 5 teachers:  1-year course of training, post Standard IV (discontinued 1951).
T 4 teachers:  2-year training, post Standard VI.
T 3 teachers:  2-year training, post Standard VII or Form II.
T 2 teachers:  2-year training, post Form IV or School Certificate.
T 1 teachers:  2-year training, post Higher School Certificate.
HTC teachers:  2-year In-Service training - T 4 (discontinued 1962).
FTC teachers:  1-year In-Service training - T 3 (discontinued 1964).
Teachers of Handcraft - 1963, Handcraft and Junior Trade teachers trained instead as Primary class teachers.

T 5 and T 4 teachers teach Lower Primary School (Sub-Standards A, B and Standards I and II).

T 3, T 2, HTC and FTC teachers teach Upper Primary School (Standards IV, V and VI).

T 1 teachers teach Junior Secondary.

Postgraduate teachers for senior forms of secondary schools trained at University College of Rhodesia and Nyasaland.

## PRESENT SYSTEM

As of 1965, all education is multiracial.

Emergency Development Plan established early 1965 to expand capacity of primary and secondary education. Former Federal Government schools opened to students of all races.

Boarding schools decreasing as day school attendance increases at both former fee-paying and non-fee-paying primary and secondary institutions. As of 1965 many fee-paying secondary schools becoming non-fee-paying.

## PRIMARY EDUCATION

Plans for every 7-year old student to have 4-year primary course by 1970.

Nomenclature of both fee-paying and non-fee-paying schools changed from "Standard" to "Grade" as of January 1965. Terms "Sub-Standards A and B" and "Recpetion" no longer used. Henceforth, 1st class in both types of school now "Grade I."

Duration of course:  Grades I through VII.
                     7 years (replacing colonial 8-year program of Stan-
                        dards).

Language of instruction:  Grades I through IV - Local Vernaculars
                                                (English used partly)
                          Grades V through VII - English

### Fee-paying System

Entry age:     5 to 7½

Curriculum:    English, Arithmetic, History, Geography, Music, Physical
               Education, Religious Knowledge, Botany, French (final year).

Certificate awarded:  None.

## Non-fee-paying System

Entry age:        Approximately 7.

Curriculum:       English, Vernacular Languages, Social Studies, History,
                  Geography, Health Science, Religious Instruction, Physical
                  Education, Arts and Crafts, Singing, Domestic Science and
                  Gardening.

Certificate awarded:       Primary School-Leaving Certificate (formerly at
                           end of Standard VI, now Grade VII).

                           Students also take secondary selection examina-
                           tion in:  English, Arithmetic and General Paper.
                           50% pass qualifies for junior secondary school.


## SECONDARY EDUCATION

"Secondary" now replaces the term "High" school.

Entry age:   Under 17 years of age as of March 1965 (temporary).
             Proposed age - 13+.

Entrance requirements:             Primary School-Leaving Certificate and
                                   secondary selection examination.

Language of instruction:   English.

Duration of course:        Full secondary program.
                           Forms I through IV  (replacing colonial Forms I
                           through IV+).

                           Fee-paying secondary schools continue a 4-year
                           course for most able pupils.

                           In non-fee-paying schools, the course will gen-
                           erally be of 5 years' duration.

Curriculum:  See previous section.

Certificate awarded: University of Cambridge School Certificate and G.C.E.
                     "O" level (replacing former A.E.B.).

                     For external students:  G.C.E. University of London.


Higher School discontinued:  last entry into Lower Sixth, January 1965.
Last examinations for advanced level subjects given in November/December
1966.  Change effected in view of 1966 opening of University of Zambia
offering 4-year degree program.

Students requiring G.C.E. "A" level qualification as prerequisite to degree courses not planned at University of Zambia, will be found places for advanced preparation in other countries.

## HIGHER EDUCATION

### UNIVERSITY OF ZAMBIA, Lusaka

Open, March 1966.

Minimum Entrance Requirements:     Cambridge School Certificate, G.C.E. "O" level, University of London (external students).

Projected Schools of Study:

| | |
|---|---|
| School of Humanities: | History, Geography, English, French, Philosophy, Religious Studies, Archaeology, Classics. |
| School of Physical Sciences: | Physics, Chemistry, Mathematics, Statistics, Geology. |
| School of Biological Sciences: | Botany, Zoology, Biochemistry, Genetics. |
| School of Social Studies: | History, Geography, Economics, Political Science, Social Service, Philosophy, Law, International Relations, Statistics. |
| School of Agriculture | |
| School of Medicine | |
| School of Administration: | Will include Commerce and Accountancy. |
| School of Education | |
| School of Mining and Technology | |
| Institute of African Studies | |
| Extension Services | |
| Part-time and Extra-mural and Correspondence Studies. | |

## TECHNICAL AND VOCATIONAL EDUCATION

As of 1965 technical training accelerated for demands of industry, mining, commerce, and government in following programs:

Trade schools, colleges, government departments, and on-the-spot training or apprenticeship by employers.

I.  CRAFT AND OPERATIVE TRAINING:

Entrance requirements:          Standard VI (formerly)
                                Grade VII (Elementary)

Duration of course:  3-year scheme including 1 year full-time at Trade school, 2 years combined industrial and educational training.

Curriculum:     Construction Industry and other courses:  Brickwork, Carpentry, Electrical Wiring, Motor Vehicle Mechanics, Plumbing, Sheet Metal Work, Painting and Spraying, Woodwork and Cabinet Making, and also liberal studies.

Prospective construction industry employers to sponsor students and guarantee them further in-service training.  Mining industry provides own programs to train own operatives for branches of mine maintenance.

Certificates awarded:  Government Certificate of Industrial Training; City and Guilds of London Institute Craft Certificate (for advanced candidates).

II.  TECHNICIAN TRAINING:

Entrance requirements:          Grade VII (formerly Standard VI) and Form II.

Duration of course:  2 to 3-years block release on 5-year apprenticeship training.

Curriculum:     Mechanical, Electrical, Automobile Engineering, Applied Science (for metallurgical technicians, laboratory technicians, etc.)

Certificates awarded:  City and Guilds of London Institute Ordinary and Advanced Craft and Technician Certificates in the various subjects.

Government departments training more of their own technical assistants in Agriculture, Forestry and Survey.

NORTHERN TECHNICAL COLLEGE

Established in 1964.

This institution designed to provide a network of centers at:

    Ndola (headquarters) offering higher practical technical courses
    Kitwe (main outside center) offering technological courses
    Broken Hill Center   )
    Chingola Center     )    Satellite centers run junior
    Luanshya Center     )    technical schools feeding into
    Mufulira Center     )    technical and technological courses.

Academic courses offered:

    1.  Lower Secondary Education      Forms I - II

          Entrance requirements:    Grade VII
                                       Primary School-Leaving Certificate

          Curriculum:          English and Mathematics through Form II

          Certificate awarded: Zambia Junior Secondary Certificate.

    2.  Full Secondary Education      Forms III - IV - V

          Curriculum:          Geography, Mathematics, English, General
                              Science, Technical Drawing, Principles of
                              Accounts, Physics, Additional Mathematics,
                              French, Biology.

          Certificate awarded: G.C.E. "O" level of Associated Examining
                              Board.

    3.  Higher School Education

          Curriculum:          Pure Mathematics, Applied Mathematics, Pure
                              and Applied Mathematics, Physics.
                              (3 hours per week per subject)

          Certificate awarded: G.C.E. "A" level of Associated Examining
                              Board.

Apprentice courses offered:

Block courses conducted at Ndola Center for apprentices in following
trades; courses and syllabuses of the City and Guilds of London Institute
are followed:

## Mechanical Trades

### Mechanical Craft Course - Ordinary and Advanced Craft

Subjects:          Workshop Practice, Workshop Technology, Engineering Drawing, Mathematics, Science.

### Mechanical Technician Course

Subjects Part I:   Workshop Practice, Workshop Processes, Engineering Drawing and Materials, Engineering Science, Mathematics.

Subjects Part II:  Additional subjects selected from:  Control Systems Technology, Plant Maintenance and Works Services, Press Tool Technology, etc.

## Automobile Engineering

### Mechanics Course
### Technicians Course

Subjects:          Workshop Practice, Motor Vehicle Technology, Drawing, Calculus, Science and Laboratory Work.

## Fabrication of Steelwork Course

### Ordinary and Advanced Craft

Subjects:          Workshop Practice, Materials and Processes, Workshop Drawing and Development, Calculations.

## Electrical Trades

### Electrical Installation - Ordinary and Advanced Craft

Subjects:          Workshop Practice, Installation Work and Regulations, Electrical Science, Drawing, Calculations.

### Electrical Technicians

Subjects Part I:   Workshop Practice, Mathematics, Electrical Engineering Principles, Engineering Drawing and Materials.

Subjects Part II:  Electrical Power or Industrial Electronics and special techniques in branches of Electrical Engineering.

Subjects for Full Technological Certificate and Endorsement courses may be taken.

Commercial courses offered:

2 years intermediate, 2 years final full time.

Full-time Day Commercial

      Entrance requirements:        Minimum Form II pass
                                    15 years or older
                                    Fluency in English

      Subjects:       Shorthand, Typewriting, Commercial Correspondence,
                      Principles of Accounts, Private Secretarial Work,
                      Office Practice.

Part-time Evening Commercial

      Subjects:       Shorthand, Typewriting, Bookkeeping.

      Examinations for both above courses:  Pitman Examinations at end of
                                          each term.

Chartered Institute of Secretaries

      Course intended for students preparing for Intermediate Examination.

      Subjects:       Economics, Bookkeeping, English, Secretarial Knowledge.

      Certificates awarded:   Intermediate and Final Certificate of Pro-
                            fessional Institutions. G.C.E. "A" and
                            "O" level.

Royal Society of Arts

      Subjects:       Mathematics, Geography, English, General Science,
                      Engineering Drawing, Principles of Accounts.

                      3 subject  passes necessary for award of Certificate.

Above and following courses vary at different centers of the Northern
Technical College:

    Home Crafts
    Miscellaneous
    Languages: Chinyanja, Chibemba, French, German, English for Foreign
                     Students.

III.  HIGHER TECHNOLOGICAL TRAINING:

UNIVERSITY COLLEGE OF ZAMBIA

Proposed for 1966; Pure and Applied Science and Engineering courses.

DAVID KAUNDA SECONDARY SCHOOL

Established in 1964, secondary technical.

This newly opened institution planned to provide candidates for technical training.

Entrance requirements:          Primary School-Leaving Certificate
                                 Secondary examination

Duration of course:  5 years.

Curriculum:          English, Mathematics, Physics, Chemistry, Technical
                     Drawing, Woodwork, Metalwork.

Certificate awarded:    G.C.E. "O" level of Associated Examining Board.

THE EVELYN HONE COLLEGE OF FURTHER EDUCATION, Lusaka.

This institution provides general, vocational and professional courses and serves as a center for community and cultural activities.

Department of Commerce

(1)  Professional Studies

     Entrance requirements:          G.C.E. "O" level or Cambridge School
                                      Certificate in English and at least 2
                                      other approved subjects.

     Duration of course:  1 to 2 years.

     Examinations taken:  Intermediate Accountancy (A.C.C.) or Company
                          (C.I.S./C.S.S.)

ZAMBIA
989

(2)  Commercial Studies

Entrance requirements:    Good Form II Certificate; preference to those producing evidence of further study.

Duration of course:    3 years.

Examinations taken:    G.C.E. "O" level in 5 subjects at end of 2nd year.  Intermediate Accountancy or Company Secretarial Examination at end of course.

(3)  Secretarial Studies

Entrance requirements:    G.C.E. "O" level or School Certificate.

Duration of course:    1 year.

Examinations taken:    Royal Society of Arts or Pitman examinations in Shorthand, Typewriting and other commercial subjects.

(4)  Secretarial Studies

Entrance requirements:    Form II.

Duration of course:    2 years.

Examinations taken:    As above.

(5)  Bookkeeping/Clerical

Entrance requirements:    Form II.

Duration of course:    1 year.

Examinations taken:    Institute of Bookkeepers Intermediate Examinations.

Department of Communication

(1)  Advanced course in Communication and Journalism

Entrance requirements:    Form V.

Duration of course:    1 year.

Examination taken:    College Certificate of Studies.

(Same course)

    Entrance requirements:      Form II.

    Duration of course:    3 years.

    Examinations taken:    College examinations.

(2)   Special Reporters Course (Newspaper and News Agency)

    Entrance requirements:      Form V or VI.

    Duration of course:    3 months.

    Examinations taken:    College examinations.

(3)   Sub-Editing and Make-Up

    Entrance requirements:      Form V.

    Duration of course:    3 months.

    Examinations taken:    College examinations.

(4)   Film and T.V. New Technician Course

    Entrance requirements:      Form V.

    Duration of course:    4 months.

    Examinations taken:    College examinations.

(5)   Film Projectionists

    Entrance requirements:      Standard VI  (Grade VII)
                                   Form II.

    Duration of course:    1 month.

    Examinations taken:    College examinations.

## Department of Technology

(1)   Telecommunication and Technicians

    Entrance requirements:      Form II.

Duration of course:          2½ years.

Examinations taken:          Intermediate City and Guilds Institute.

## Department of Hotel and Catering

(1)  Basic Catering

Entrance requirements:          Standard VI or Grade VII.
                                Preference to Form II.

Duration of course:          1 year.

Examinations taken:          City and Guilds Institute.

## Department of Home Economics

(1)  Home Economics Certificate

Entrance requirements:          Grade VII.
                                Preference given to Form II.

Duration of course:          3 years.

Examinations taken:          College examinations plus G.C.E. "O" level
                             in relevant subjects.

(2)  Home Management

Entrance requirements:          Standard VI or Grade VI.

Duration of course:          1 year.

Examinations taken:          College examinations.

## MONZE AGRICULTURAL SCHOOL

Entrance requirements:          Form II

Duration of course:  2 years.

Curriculum:          English Language, Mathematics (at G.C.E. "O" level),
                     Animal Husbandry, Botany, Crop Husbandry, Agricul-
                     tural Economics and Marketing, Soil Conservation.

## MAZABUKA VETERINARY SCHOOL

Entrance requirements:                Form II.

Duration of course:  1½ years.

Curriculum:          Animal Husbandry, Tsetse Control, and other veterinary
                     subjects.


## THE RHODES-LIVINGSTONE INSTITUTE FOR SOCIAL RESEARCH, Lusaka

## THE OPPENHEIMER COLLEGE OF SOCIAL SERVICE

Established in 1961.



## TEACHER EDUCATION

Due to rapid expansion of student population as of 1965, duration of training courses reduced from 2 to 1 year.  During same year no School Certificate holders were trained.  Courses for Junior Secondary School teachers
discontinued until training becomes available at University of Zambia (1966).


11 teacher training colleges 1965, including:

|              |              |
|--------------|--------------|
| David Livingstone | Charles Luanga |
| Chalimbana   | Kitwe        |
| Robert Moffat | Mufulira (1962) |

2 more colleges schedules to open 1966 at Kasama and Fort Jameson.


Eventually 1 training college planned in each province of the Republic.
Following courses available, each of 1-year duration (a second year sometimes spent in attachment to school):

 (i)  L I  (through 1964)

          Entrance requirements:        Post-Primary

          Teaching area:     Lower primary classes.
                             Sub-Standards A - B
                      or     Grades I through IV.

(ii)  <u>LII</u>

    Entrance requirements:    Form II (<u>Junior Secondary Certificate</u>)

    Teaching area:   Grades I through IV.

(iii)  <u>U I</u>

    Entrance requirements:    Form IV (<u>School Certificate</u>)
                          <u>or</u>  Form II (<u>Junior Secondary Certificate</u>)

    Teaching area:   Grades V - VI - VII.

Curriculum:

    English - Methods of teaching English
    Arithmetic - Methods of teaching Arithmetic
    Social Studies - Methods of teaching Social Studies
    General Science - Methods of teaching General Science
    Nature Study - Methods of teaching Nature Study
    Vernacular - Methods of teaching Vernacular
    Religious Knowledge - Methods of teaching Religious Knowledge
    Physical Education - Practical methods
    Art - Practical methods
    School Organization
    Elementary Psychology
    Education and Principles of Education
    Visual Education

SPANISH AFRICA

# S P A N I S H   A F R I C A

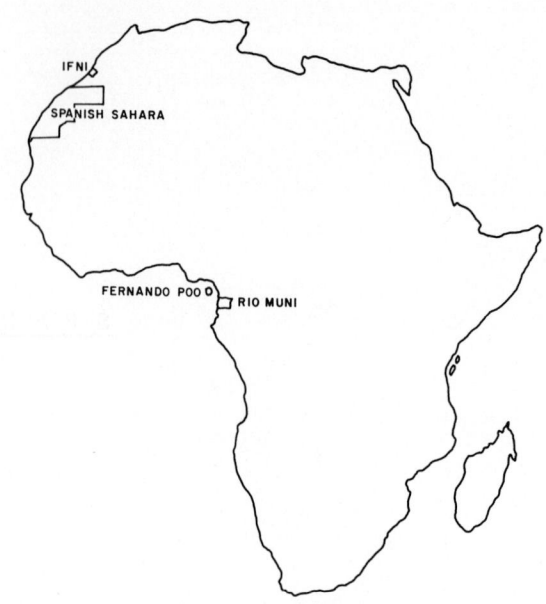

| Country and Capital | Area (sq. miles) | Est. Population | Independence Dates or Political Status | Official Language |
|---|---|---|---|---|
| SPANISH GUINEA<br>   Santa Isabel de<br>   Fernando Poo | 10,825 | 244,574 | Two Spanish provinces, Rio Muni and Fernando Poo, jointly administered | Spanish |
| IFNI<br>   Sidi Ifni | 580 | 49,889 | Spanish province | Spanish |
| SPANISH SAHARA<br>   El-Aaiún | 102,681 | 23,793 | Spanish province | Spanish |

SPANISH AFRICA

Periodo de iniciación profesional

Periodo de perfeccionamiento

Periodo de enseñanza elemental

SECONDARY EDUCATION
(estudios de grado medio)

PRIMARY EDUCATION

Compulsory education: 6-14 years of age

School year:

Grading:   10-1
10-9  Outstanding
8-7   Distinguished
6-5   Pass
4-1   (Held back)

Matricula de honor  (Honors)
Sobresaliente (Very good)
Notable (Good)
Aprobado  (Pass)
Suspenso  (Fail)

NONE

*

Infant school  (escuela de párvulos)

Nursery school  (escuela maternal)

HIGHER EDUCATION

SECONDARY

PRIMARY

Year of Schooling

| 20 | 19 | 18 | 17 | 16 | 15 | 14 | 13 | 12 | 11 | 10 | 9 | 8 | 7 | 6 | 5 | 4 | 3 | 2 | 1 |

Student's Age

| 26 | 25 | 24 | 23 | 22 | 21 | 20 | 19 | 18 | 17 | 16 | 15 | 14 | 13 | 12 | 11 | 10 | 9 | 8 | 7 | 6 | 5 | 4 | 3 | 2 |

SPANISH AFRICA

BACKGROUND

Spanish Africa comprises:   IFNI

                              SPANISH SAHARA    (Saguia Hamra
                                                               (Río de Oro

                              SPANISH GUINEA    (Fernando Poo
                                                               (Río Muni

The territory of Spanish West Africa was divided into 2 provinces of Ifni and Spanish Sahara, January 1958, both under the supervision of the commanding officer of the Canary Islands.

The Province of IFNI (580 sq. miles) with a population of 49,889 (1960) has its capital of Sidi Ifni. Morocco ceded Ifni to Spain in 1860; occupation was nominal until April 6, 1934. Most of population are Ait Ba Amarán, a Berber group.

The desert Province of SPANISH SAHARA (102,681 sq. miles) includes the zones of Río de Oro and Saquia Hamra, with a seminomadic Islamic population of 23,793 (1960), having its capital in El Aaiún. The strip between 27° 40' N. and Wad Draa was ceded by Spain to Morocco on April 10, 1958. Organized as a Province in 1958, it is divided into 3 districts with their centers at El Aaiún, Villa Cisneros and La Aguera. Population belongs to 4 main groups:  Chorfa, Tecna, Zuaga, Arabs.

The equatorial region of SPANISH GUINEA consists of the Provinces of Río Muni and Fernando Poo. Río Muni comprises the continental zone (10,040 sq. miles) and the islands of Corisco, Elobey Grande and Elobey Chico (6.6 sq. miles), with the capital of Bata; total population is 183,377 including 2,864 Europeans (1960). Fernando Poo comprises the islands of Fernando Poo (778.5 sq. miles) with 61,197 inhabitants including 4,220 Europeans, and Annobon (6.5 sq. miles) with 1,415 inhabitants. The capital is Santa Isabel which is also the capital of the region. Fernando Poo, discovered by Portuguese sailor, Fernao de Po, was first named Formosa. Portuguese ceded it to Spain, 1778, and Spain named it that year. It was a British anti-slavery base from 1827-43. With Río Muni it was organized as the West African Territories in 1904, later known (collectively) as Spanish Guinea. Provincial status, 1960. Río Muni was ceded by Portuguese to Spain, 1778. Spain did not occupy until 1900. Spanish Guinea is composed of at least 9 ethnic groups speaking more than 15 languages and dialects: Pamués (or Fang on mainland); Bubis on Fernando Poo; Fernandinos (on Fernando Poo) of Kru, Gambian, Cuban and Sierra Leone descent; Nigerians; Moslem Hausas; Europeans of 5 or 6 nationalities.

## PRE-PRIMARY EDUCATION

Ages 2 - 4, in escuela maternal (nursery school).

Ages 4 - 6, in escuela de párvulos (infant school).


## PRIMARY EDUCATION

Entry age:  6 years.

Ensenanza primaria (primary education):  3 stages.

    (1)  periodo de enseñanza elemental -  - 4 years
    (2)  periodo de perfeccionamiento      - 2 years
    (3)  periodo de iniciación profesional - 2 years

In Province of Ifni:  2 schools, racially integrated:  1 for boys, 1 for girls.

In Province of Sahara:  30 primary schools:

    "unitarias" - (niños) schools for boys
             (niñas) schools for girls
    "mixtas"     - coeducational

No racial discrimination, students separated only for teaching and practice of their respective religions.  (Native professors of Arabic and Koran.)

Certificado de estudios primarios awarded at close of 8-year program.


## SECONDARY EDUCATION

Entry age:  10 years.

Entrance requirements:       10 years of age, entrance examination (exámen de ingreso) in subjects taught at 4-year primary level (2 parts: written and oral).

| | |
|---|---|
| Bachillerato elemental: | grades 1 - 4. |
| Bachillerato superior: | grades 5 - 6. |
| Preuniversatario: | grade 7 |
| Prueba de madurez: | a post-pre-university year where higher level study may be taken and validated for exemption from first year university or higher technical school. |

6-year program (enseñza media):  academic training, and vocational training.
1-year preparatory course (preparatoria de ingreso) for entrance into
academic secondary studies.

In Province of Ifni, academic training offered in Centro de Enseñza
Media General Diaz de Villegas, in Sidi Ifni (affiliated with Instituto
Nacional de Enseñanza Media, Las Palmas, Canary Islands).  Vocational
training in Escuela de Artes y Oficios, established 1955, offering manual
arts.

Ifni, 6-year academic program.

Subjects:

1st yr:   Religion, Spanish Language, Geography and History, Mathematics,
          Drawing, Homemaking, National Indoctrination, Physical Educa-
          tion.

2nd yr:   Religion, Spanish Language, Geography and History, Mathematics,
          Drawing, Homemaking, National Indoctrination, Physical Educa-
          tion, French.

3rd yr:   Religion, Mathematics, Drawing, Homemaking, National Indoctrin-
          ation, French, Natural Sciences, Latin.

4th yr:   Religion, Language and Literature, Geography and History, Mathe-
          matics, Homemaking, Politics (Spanish National), Physical Educa-
          tion, Physics and Chemistry.

5th yr:   Religion, Mathematics or Greek, Drawing, Homemaking, National
          Indoctrination, Physical Education, French, Natural Sciences,
          Latin, Physics and Chemistry.

6th yr:   Religion, Mathematics, History, Literature, Greek, Homemaking,
          National Indoctrination, Physical Education, Latin, Physics,
          Philosophy.

In Province of Sahara, 6-year secondary program offered in Colegio Superior
Reconocido "General Alonso" in Aaium, and Colegio Elemental Reconocido in
Cisneros.

### COLEGIO SUPERIOR RECONOCIDO "GENERAL ALONSO"

#### SECONDARY PROGRAM (6-day week)

| Subjects      | Years: 1 | 2     | 3      | 4 | 5     | 6 |
|---------------|----------|-------|--------|---|-------|---|
| Mathematics   | 7 1/2    | 3 3/4 | 2 1/2  | 5 | 3 3/4 | 2 |
| Language      | 7 1/2    | -     | -      | - | -     | - |
| Geography     | 7 1/2    | 3 3/4 | -      | - | -     | - |
| Rep. Geography| -        | -     | 1 1/4  | - | -     | - |

| | | | | | | |
|---|---|---|---|---|---|---|
| Religion | 2 1/2 | 2 1/2 | 2 1/2 | 2 1/2 | 2 1/2 | 2 1/2 |
| Drawing | 3 3/4 | 2 1/2 | 2 1/2 | - | 2 1/2 | - |
| E. Physics | 3 3/4 | 3 3/4 | 7 1/2 | 3 3/4 | 3 3/4 | 2 1/2 |
| Physics | - | - | - | 7 1/2 | 2 1/2 | - |
| Greek Physics | - | - | - | - | - | 3 3/4 |
| Politics | 1 1/4 | 1 1/4 | 2 1/2 | 1 1/4 | 1 1/4 | 1 1/4 |
| French | - | 5 | 6 1/4 | - | 5 | - |
| Grammar | - | 7 1/2 | - | - | - | - |
| Rep. Grammar | - | - | 2 1/2 | 3 3/4 | - | - |
| Latin | - | - | 7 1/2 | - | 3 3/4 | 1 1/4 |
| Sciences | - | - | 2 1/2 | - | 7 1/2 | - |
| Rep. Sciences | - | - | - | 1 1/4 | - | 1 1/4 |
| Literature | - | - | - | 5 | - | 7 1/2 |
| Rep. Literature | - | - | - | - | 1 1/4 | - |
| History | - | - | - | 7 1/2 | - | 3 |
| Greek Chemistry | - | - | - | - | 5 | - |
| Philosophy | - | - | - | - | - | 7 1/2 |
| Homemaking | 3 3/4 | 3 3/4 | 3 3/4 | 3 3/4 | - | 2 1/2 |
| | 37 1/2 | 33 3/4 | 41 | 41 1/4 | 38 3/4 | 44 |

In Spanish Guinea, secondary program offered in Instituto Nacional de Enseñanza Media "Cardenal Cisneros", Santa Isabel de Fernando Poo.

At close of all 4-year secondary programs, an examination given (examen de grado elemental) for the bachillerato elemental, giving the title "Bachiller Elemental."

At the close of the subsequent 2-year program (in letters or science), *an examination given (examen de grado superior) for the bachillerato superior, giving the title "Bachiller Superior."

(Examinations given at the University of La Laguna, Tenerife, and the Instituto de Las Palmas, Canary Islands.)

VOCATIONAL EDUCATION

Vocational training offered in Escuela Laboral "Carrero Blanco" and in Escuela de Artes y Oficios, Sidi Ifni. Separate sections for boys and girls.

Boys

2 classes:  Iniciación Profesional:  14 - 16 years of age
            Formación Profesional:   16 - 20 years of age

General Mechanics        Soldering
Automobile Mechanics     Carpentry
Turning                  Electricity
Fitting                  Bookbinding
                         Shoemaking

Girls

Embroidery               Cooking
Dressmaking              Shorthand
Quilting                 Typing

# PORTUGUESE AFRICA

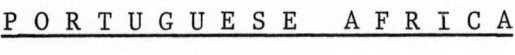

P O R T U G U E S E   A F R I C A

| Country and Capital | Area (sq. miles) | Est. Population | Independence Dates or Political Status | Official Language |
|---|---|---|---|---|
| ANGOLA<br>    Luanda | 481,351 | 4,840,719 | Portuguese overseas province | Portuguese |
| CAPE VERDE ISLANDS<br>    Praia | 1,557 | 201,549 | Portuguese overseas province | Portuguese |
| PORTUGUESE GUINEA<br>    Bissau | 13,948 | 544,184 | Portuguese overseas province | Portuguese |
| MOZAMBIQUE<br>    Lourenço Marques | 297,731 | 6,482,000 | Portuguese overseas province | Portuguese |
| SÃO TOMÉ and PRINCIPE<br>    São Tomé | 372 | 63,676 | Portuguese overseas province | Portuguese |

1005

PORTUGUESE AFRICA

Estudios Gerais Universitários de Angola e Moçambique

Primary Teacher Training

Industrial & Com. Institutes

Adaptation Teacher Training

Schools of Arts & Crafts

Vocational and Technical Train.

Preparatory cycle

SECONDARY EDUCATION

PRIMARY EDUCATION

Iniciacão (Kindergarten)

3rd cycle

2nd cycle

1st cycle

** 

*

| Student's Age | Year of Schooling | |
|---|---|---|
| 25 | 18 | HIGHER EDUCATION |
| 24 | 17 | |
| 23 | 16 | |
| 22 | 15 | |
| 21 | 14 | |
| 20 | 13 | |
| 19 | 12 | |
| 18 | 11 | |
| 17 | 10 | SECONDARY |
| 16 | 9 | |
| 15 | 8 | |
| 14 | 7 | |
| 13 | 6 | |
| 12 | 5 | |
| 11 | 4 | ELEMENTARY |
| 10 | 3 | |
| 9 | 2 | |
| 8 | 1 | |
| 7 | | |
| 6 | | |
| 5 | | |
| 4 | | |
| 3 | | |

Compulsory education: For native population, through adaptation education – 3yrs.
For Portuguese and others – 7-12 years of age

School year: Same number of days as in Portugal – 3 terms
Differences of climate govern distribution of year.

Secondary grading: 0-20

PORTUGUESE  AFRICA

<u>BACKGROUND</u>

Portuguese Africa is composed of:

Angola (Portugal's largest overseas Province)
Mozambique (second largest overseas Province)
Portuguese Guinea
Cape Verde Islands (10 islands and 5 islets)
São Tomé and Príncipe (2 volcanic islands)

Angola's population is 90% African, including several thousand Bushmen.
Portuguese navigator, Diogo Cão discovered mouth of Congo River, 1482.
Later, there were explorations of Angola and principal rivers.  Luanda
was established, 1575.  At Berlin Conference, 1884-85, an international
treaty fixed Angola's boundaries.

Mozambique's population is 90% African.  Approximately 100,000 Europeans,
60% living mainly in Lourenço Marques.  Also, mestiços, Indians and Chinese.

Portuguese Guinea has an indigenous population of Balantes, Fulani,
Manjakos, Mandingos, and Papels.  45% are Muslims.  Portuguese sailors
arrived in 1446; subsequently, trading posts established.  Until 1879,
territory was a dependency of the Cape Verde Islands.

Cape Verde Islands have a population of 60% mestiços (those of mixed
Portuguese and African background).  Islands uninhabited until Portuguese
arrived, 1456.  By end of 16th century, São Tiago and Fogo were well
settled.  18th century, British established coaling station at São Vicente.
The territory's main function is as a fueling station.  Highest rate of
literacy, 20%-25% in 1960.

São Tomé and Príncipe have a population largely composed of descendants
of original Portuguese colonists and Africans from Gabon and other parts
of Guinea coast.  Most of them live in the town of  São Tomé and villages
in eastern half of São Tomé island.

Schooling in Portuguese Africa follows the plan of national education
which includes all Portuguese territories.  It comprises the same grades
and branches of education with identical curricula, but adapted to the
particular conditions of the provinces.  In each school there is usually
a center of the Portuguese Youth under the supervision of the Director of
the School District.

2 types of schools:

(1)  Roman Catholic mission schools educating Africans through primary education.
(2)  Government schools for whites, Asians and children who have absorbed the Portuguese language and culture (<u>civilizados</u> in Angola, <u>assimilados</u> in Mozambique).

Prior to 1940, curricula for African schools were fixed by Department of Education and Instruction in territory; examinations were conducted by the state, and certificates were awarded by Director of Education. 1940-60, Roman Catholic Church took official charge of curricular matters. 1960, with reorganization of African colonies into Portuguese provinces, educational control was transferred to the Ministry of Education in Lisbon.


## PRESENT SYSTEM


## PRE-SCHOOL EDUCATION

Kindergarten education (<u>inicicão</u>) is given in government schools and other institutions of a private character.


## PRIMARY EDUCATION

Entry age:  6-7 years.

4-year program for standard primary (<u>ensino primário</u>).
5-year program for adaptation education (<u>ensino de adaptacão</u>).

Primary "adaptation education" for pupils of native population who do not have "sufficient knowledge of the Portuguese language and further indispensable conditions for entering standard education." Adaptation education, so called from Act of August 5, 1960, formerly called "rudimentary education" (<u>ensiño primário rudimentar</u>). Almost all adaptation education entrusted to Portuguese Catholic Missions.

In adaptation education, subjects taught through 2nd class of standard courses are distributed over 3 classes. 1st class, predominantly teaching of Portuguese.

Curriculum for adaptation education:

Portuguese, Arithmetic, Geography and Natural History, Drawing, Handwork, Ethics and Religion, Physical and Musical Education.

For girls, Domestic subjects:  Sewing, Embroidery, Knitting, and Cooking.

The transition from education for adaptation to standard primary education requires a Pass in an examination which takes place at the end of the 3rd adaptation education class.  A Pass enables a pupil to enroll in the 3rd class of standard education if he is not over 13 years of age.

Standard primary schools, 4-year program:

Primeira classe  (1st grade)
Segunda classe  (2nd grade)
Terceira classe  (3rd grade)
Quarta classe  (4th grade)

Standard curriculum:

Portuguese, Arithmetic, Geographical and Natural Science, Drawing, Handwork, Ethics and Religion, Physical Education, Musical Education, Domestic Training, Geometry, and History of the Mother-Country (2 latter, limited to last 2 years).

Carta de ensino primário elementar (lower elementary certificate) awarded upon successful examinations at close of 3-year program.

Carta de ensino primário do segundo grau (elementary certificate) awarded upon successful examinations at close of  4th year.

SECONDARY EDUCATION

Three branches:       Lyceum
                      Technical
                      Agricultural

LYCEUM PROGRAM

Entrance requirements:              At least 10 years of age.  Carta de ensino primário do segundo grau  and entrance examination.

7 forms, divided into 3 cycles:

Primeiro ciclo - 2 years  )
Segundo ciclo  - 3 years  )    general education
Terceiro ciclo - 2 years
(3rd year modified to university courses to which they give
   access.)

Lyceum education may be given in official or private establishments, or under individual or home tuition.

<u>Carta do curso géral dos liceus</u> (certificate of general education) awarded upon successful examinations at close of 2nd cycle (5 years).

<u>Carta do curso complementar liceus</u> (certificate of secondary education) awarded upon successful examination at close of 3rd cycle (7 years).

## HIGHER EDUCATION

October examinations given for matriculation at the Universities of Combra, Lisbon, Oporto and Technical University of Lisbon, and Higher Schools of Fine Arts at Lisbon and Oporto (course of Architecture).

Subjects to be taken for university entrance examinations:

    Classics:  Portuguese and Latin
    Romance studies:  Portuguese and French
    Germanic studies:  English and German
    History and Philosophy:  History and Philosophy
    Geography:  Natural Science and Geography
    Law:  Philosophy and Latin
    Medicine, Veterinary Medicine, Biology, Geology, Pharmacy, Agronomy, Forestry:  Physics and Chemistry and Natural Science
    Mathematics, Physics and Chemistry, Geophysics, Civil, Mining, Mechanical, Electrotechnical, Chemical and Industrial and Geopraphic Engineering:  Mathematics, Physics and Chemistry
    Economics and Business Administration:  Mathematics and Geography
    Overseas Administration:  Portuguese and Geography
    Architecture:  Mathematics, Physics, Chemistry, Art

## ESTUDIOS GERAIS UNIVERSITARIOS DE ANGOLA E DE MOCAMBIQUE (UNIVERSITY COLLEGE)

Centers for higher studies created at Angola and Mozambique (under same legislation as continental universities).

Level of courses same as that of identical courses existing in Portugal, and reciprocal transfers of students are allowed.

Courses in:

    Medicine, Civil Engineering, Mining Engineering, Mechanical Engineering, Electrotechnical Engineering, Chemical and Industrial Engineering, Agriculture, Forestry, Veterinary Science, and Education (pedagogical course for training secondary teachers, both for lyceums and for technical schools).

Parts of the courses have to be taken on the mainland.

Attached to the General College is a Centre of Humanistic Studies.


## VOCATIONAL AND TECHNICAL EDUCATION

In Mozambique, 13 schools of technical education:  1 industrial, 3 commercial, 4 industrial and commercial, and 5 elementary technical.

Entrance requirements:              4 years, elementary school and entrance examination.

2 sections:  commercial and industrial.
Preparatory cycle - 2 years.
3-year programs.

Commercial training:

General Commercial Course, Girls' Business or Industrial Training Course, Shorthand-Typists' Course, and preparatory section for admission to the Commercial Institutes.

Industrial training:

Fitters' Course, Motor Mechanics, Electrician/Monteur, Artistic Cabinet Making, Carpenter/Joiner, Laboratory Assistant, Decorative Painting, Decorative Sculpture; preparatory sections for admission to Industrial Institutes and Colleges of Fine Arts.


## SAMPLE OF SECONDARY TECHNICAL COURSES:

### Chemical laboratory assistant:

Portuguese, Portuguese History, Geography, Introduction to Natural Science, Elements of Physics, General Chemistry, Technological Chemistry, Notions of Chemical Analysis, Drawing, French (not required), Religion and Morals, Laboratory Work.

### Machinist:

Portuguese, History of Portugal, Geography, Introduction to Natural Science, Physics and Chemistry, Mathematics, General Mechanics, Technology and Estimating, Electricity, General Drawing, Projection and Perspective Drawing, Technical Drawing, Religion and Morals, Workshop (optional).

Electrician:

> Portuguese, History of Portugal, Geography, Introduction to Natural Science, Elements of Physics and Chemistry, Mathematics, General Mechanics, Electricity (classroom and laboratory), Technology and Estimates, General Drawing, Projection and Perspective Drawing, Technical Drawing (industrial and blueprints), Religion and Morals, Workshop (optional).

Carpenter and Joiner:

> Portuguese, History of Portugal, Geography, Introduction to Natural Science, Elements of Physics and Chemistry, Mathematics, Technology and Estimates, Drawing, Projection and Perspective Drawing, Technical Drawing, Modelling (joiners only), Religion and Morals, Workshop (optional).

Decorator Painter:

> Portuguese, French, Portuguese History, Elements of History of Art, Introduction to Natural Science, Physics and Chemistry, Applied Chemistry, Mathematics, General Drawing, Observation and Decoration Drawing, Projection and Perspective Drawing, Lettering, Human Figure Drawing, Decorative Composition, Interior Architecture, Religion and Morals, Workshop and Technology (optional).

Decorator Sculptor:

> Portuguese, French, Portuguese History, Elements of History of Art, Introduction to Natural Science, Mathematics, General Drawing, Observation and Decoration Drawing, Human Figure and Attire Drawing, Decoration Modelling, Human Figure Modelling and Elements of Sacred Sculpture, Decorative Composition, Religion and Morals, Workshop and Technology (optional).


SCHOOLS OF ARTS AND CRAFTS

Entrance requirements:            Completion of primary education.  (Open to all adolescents of any given origin.)

3-year course.

Success in final examination entitles to continuation of studies in Commercial or Industrial Schools.

## AGRICULTURAL TRAINING

Partly under the services of Agriculture and Forests, and of Veterinary
Science, and, for the pedagogical side, on the services of Education.

3 grades:       (a)   Elementary agricultural education
                (b)   Practical agricultural education
                (c)   Intermediate education

3 elementary schools created in Mocuba, in Ribaué, and in Inhamussua for
the training of Agricultural Foremen.

In Angola, 1963, courses created for the Diploma of Agricultural Foremen
(regente agricola) in Tropical Agriculture, in Tropical Forestry, in Animal Husbandry and Veterinary Nursing.  First 2 at Institute for Agricultural Research, 3rd at Central Laboratory for Veterinary Pathology.

Duration:  1 year.


School for Agricultural Assitants, at the Settlers' Colony of Limpopo.


School for Agricultural Technicians, coordinated with a Practical School
of Agriculture in the district of Manica e Sofala.  This school trains
its students for admission to the Institute of Agronomy (university level)
and for Veterinary Science (university level).

Practical School of Agriculture of the secondary grade is functioning in
the Supervision Department of the Technical Brigade for the Development
and Population of Limpopo.




## INDUSTRIAL INSTITUTES

Entrance requirements:              2nd cycle of liceu or preparatory indus-
                                    trial course, in which case entrance
                                    examination consisting of Mathematics,
                                    Physics, Chemistry and Drawing.

                                    If candidates possess only 1st cycle of
                                    liceu, preparatory examination on:
                                    Portuguese, French or English, Geog-
                                    raphy and History, Natural Science,
                                    Physics and Chemistry, Mathematics,
                                    Drawing.

Basic courses in:   Electrotechnics and Machinery, Building and Mines,
                    Laboratory and Industrial Chemistry.

4-year programs.

Electrotechnics and Machinery:

> Mathematics, General Physics, Special Physics, General Chemistry, Topography, Electricity, Measurements and Tests in Electrical Machines, Electrical Circuits, Electrical Machines, Weak Currents, Lighting Techniques, Technology and Machine Tools, Technical Mechanics, Machine Parts, Machines, Heating and Ventilation, Industrial Organization, Portuguese Political Administration and Corporative (i.e., "New State" as the present regime is called) Economy, Descriptive Geometry, Industrial Drawing, Carpentry Workshop, Mould Carpentry Workshop. Locksmith and Blacksmith Workshop, Casting Workshop.

Building and Mines:

> Mathematics, General Physics, Special Physics, General Chemistry, Mineralogy and Geology, Topography, Mechanics and Materials Resistance, Buildings, Materials and Building Techniques, Concrete, Building Stability, Bridges, Highways and Railroads, General and Applied Hydraulics, Mine Prospection and Exploration, Minerals and Metals Technology, Mining Analysis, Elements of Electrotechnics and Machinery, Heating and Ventilation, Budgeting, Portuguese Political Organization and Corporative Economy, Descriptive Geometry, Construction Drawing, Carpentry Workshop and Practical Work in Building.

Laboratory and Industrial Chemistry:

> Mathematics, General Physics, Special Physics, General Chemistry, Inorganic Chemistry, Organic Chemistry, Analytical Chemistry, Physics/Chemistry-Electrochemistry, Industrial Chemistry, Biological and Bromatologic Analysis, Mineralogy and Geology, Minerals and Metals Technology, Machine Parts, Elements of Electrotechnics and Machinery, Industrial Organization, Portuguese Political Organization and Corporative Economy, Descriptive Geometry, Industrial Drawing, Locksmith Workshop.

Grading:  0 - 20.

After course, 180 days in-service training (on-the-job training) in public services or private firms. Report must be presented on this. Then, a professional aptitude examination is given. Diploma granted after completion of professional aptitude examination.

For basic courses, 3 kinds of diplomas: Technician (agente tecnico) in Electromechanic Engineering, in Civil Engineering and Mines and in Chemical Engineering.

Other titles programmed: Machine Technician, Electricity Technician, Building Technician, Mining Technician, and Analyst.

COMMERCIAL INSTITUTES

Training for accountants, customs officers, administrative assistants and correspondents in foreign languages.  These schools give access to university level institutes:  Higher Institute of Economics and Finance, and Naval and Military Administration in the naval and military academies.

Entrance requirements:                    Entrance examination.  (Has no credit
                                           value except for matriculation.)

3 courses:        Accountant
                  Customs Inspector
                  Foreign Language Correspondent

3-year programs.  Specializations for accountant, customs inspector and foreign language correspondent in 3rd year.

Teaching parallels the 3rd cycle of liceu in general academic, and special, subjects.

Subjects:

        Mathematics, Business and Finance Calculus, General Chemistry and
        Analytical Methods, Raw Materials and Merchandise, Customs Technology,
        General and Economic Geography, Economic Geography of Portugal and
        Overseas Provinces, General and Economic History, Political Economy,
        Elements of Civil and Administrative Law, Elements of Commercial and
        Maritime Law, Customs Fiscal Law, Portuguese Political Organization
        and Corporative Economy, General Accounting, Organization and Indus-
        trial and Agricultural Accounting, Banking Operations and Their
        Accounting, Social Security Institutions and Their Accounting, Public
        Accounting and Overseas Administration, French (practical course),
        English (practical course), German (practical course), Penmanship,
        Typing, Shorthand.

Maximum of 18 class hours per week; 20 in special cases.
Grading:  0 - 20.  Final grade of yearly averages:  1st year counts as 1,
          2nd as 2, 3rd as 3.

On completion of certain subjects (approximately 2 years) students may transfer to the Higher Institute of Economics and Finance (in Portugal, part of Technical University) or to the military and naval academies (also in Portugal).

Diplomas awarded on completion of 3-year program:  Banking Accountant, Social Security Accountant, French Correspondent, English Correspondent, German Correspondent.

## ORIENTAL AND AFRICAN LANGUAGE INSTITUTE

A research and teaching center:  Arabic, Sanskrit, Concanim, some sub-Saharan languages, Creole languages.

## INSTITUTE OF EDUCATION AND SOCIAL SERVICE (INSTITUTO DE EDUCACAO E SERVICO SOCIAL DE MOCAMBIQUE, Lourenço Marques)

Established 1963.  Trains social workers, kindergarten teachers.  Specialization and refresher professional courses; research.

1st yr. (social workers):

> Medical Science, Overseas Sociology, Sociology, Psychology, Social Philosophy, Roman Catholic Theology, auxiliary techniques, Social Investigation, in-service training.

1st yr. (kindergarten teachers):

> Religion, Portuguese Culture, Oral and Written Expression, Morals and Culture for Educators, Social Preparation, General Psychology, Overseas Studies, Christian Education for Children, Child Psychology, Health Education, Children's Literature, Workshop, Physical Education, student teaching.

## OTHER PROFESSIONAL TRAINING

Board of the Services of Health and Hygiene maintains a technical school with the following courses:

> Regular nursing course, elementary nursing course, courses for assistant nurses and midwives, course for laboratory assistants, for assistant-radiologists, for assistant-radiotherapists,  for hospital nurses, for assistant hospital nurses, for microscopists.

Landsurveying Services maintains a Landsurveyors' Training School with landsurveyors'  courses, complementary landsurveying courses, courses for technical operators, map draughtsmen and calculators.

Services of Civil Aeronautics trains controllers.

Meteorological Services trains assistant-observers.

Harbours and Railways trains apprentices and telegraph operators.

Private bodies maintain courses for art and music education; others for teaching of Gujerati and Urdu and Chinese.

## TEACHER EDUCATION

### SCHOOLS FOR THE TRAINING OF PRIMARY EDUCATION TEACHERS

Entrance requirements:                 Completion of 2nd secondary cycle
                                       (5th form of Lyceum) or the equiva-
                                       lent, or diploma for adaptation edu-
                                       cation with 5 years' service classified
                                       as "Good."

2-year program, identical to that of Mother-Country.

### SCHOOLS FOR TEACHERS FOR ADAPTATION

Entrance requirements:                 Graduation from primary education.

3-year program.  Diploma awarded at close of program.

(Secondary teachers trained in Portugal.)

# SOUTHERN AFRICA

S O U T H E R N   A F R I C A

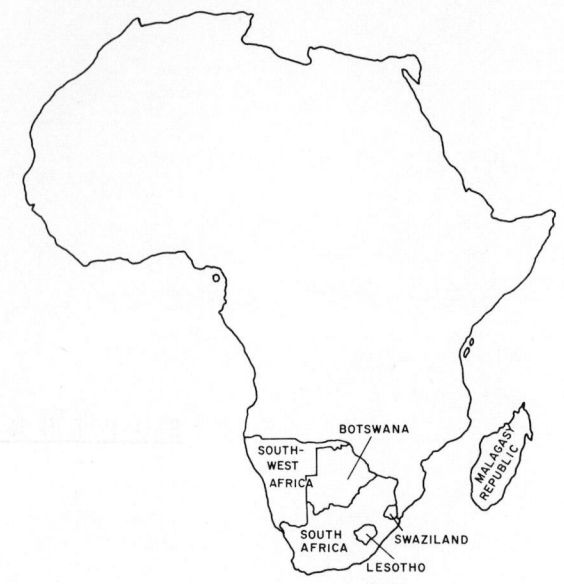

| Country and Capital | Area (sq. miles) | Est. Population | Independence Dates or Political Status | Official Language(s) |
|---|---|---|---|---|
| BOTSWANA<br>Gaberones<br><br>Formerly: Bechuanaland<br>(Mafeking, S.A.) | 275,000 | 542,000 | 30 September 1966 | English |
| KINGDOM OF LESOTHO<br>Maseru<br><br>Formerly: Basutoland<br>(Maseru) | 11,716 | 658,000 | 30 September, 1966 | English |
| MALAGASY REPUBLIC<br>(Madagascar)<br>Tananarive | 227,900 | 6,000,000 | 26 June 1960 | French and Malagasy |
| REPUBLIC OF SOUTH AFRICA<br>Capetown<br>(parliamentary)<br>Pretoria<br>(administrative) | 472,685 | 16,122,000 | 31 May 1910 | English and Afrikaans |
| SOUTH-WEST AFRICA<br>Windhoek | 317,887 | 554,000 | Republic of South Africa mandate | English and Afrikaans |
| SWAZILAND<br>Mbabane (Moabane) | 6,705 | 280,260 | British Protectorate Independence not later than 1969 | English |

BOTSWANA
( Bechuanaland )
(From January 1964)

Prior to January 1964

Technical
and
Vocational
Training

Teacher
Training

SECONDARY EDUCATION

PRIMARY EDUCATION

None

** V Form
IV Form
III Form
II Form
I Form

** V Form
IV Form
III Form
II Form
I Form

* III Form

7 Standard
6 Standard
5 Standard
4 Standard
3 Standard
2 Standard
1 Standard

6 Standard
5 Standard
4 Standard
3 Standard
2 Standard
1 Standard
B Sub
A Sub

**

| Student's Age | Year of Schooling | | |
|---|---|---|---|
| 26 | 20 | | HIGHER EDUCATION |
| 25 | 19 | | |
| 24 | 18 | | |
| 23 | 17 | | |
| 22 | 16 | | |
| 21 | 15 | | |
| 20 | 14 | | |
| 19 | 13 | | |
| 18 | 12 | | SECONDARY |
| 17 | 11 | | |
| 16 | 10 | | |
| 15 | 9 | | |
| 14 | 8 | | |
| 13 | 7 | | ELEMENTARY |
| 12 | 6 | | |
| 11 | 5 | | |
| 10 | 4 | | |
| 9 | 3 | | |
| 8 | 2 | | |
| 7 | 1 | | |
| 6 | | | |
| 5 | | | |
| 4 | | | |
| 3 | | | |

Compulsory education: None

School year: January – December

Grading: See SECONDARY and TEACHER EDUCATION

BOTSWANA
(Formerly Bechuanaland)

Independence:    September 30, 1966

## BACKGROUND

Western two-thirds of territory lies largely within the Kalahari Desert.
Main centers of population are concentrated on eastern border region.

Population composed of African tribal groups, Europeans, Eurafricans,
Asians.  There is also an Indian community.  The Bechuana are a Bantu
people.  The Batswana, main racial group, although racially homogeneous
are divided into 8 main tribes, each with its own African Authority,
Tribal Treasury, and defined tribal boundaries.  Other comparatively small
groups, such as the Damara, Bakalanga, Mampukushu, and Hottentots live
either in tribal territory or areas specially allocated to them.  These
groups differ from the Batswana and from one another in language and customs.

The country became British Protectorate, 1885, at request of Bechuana
chiefs, after clashes between Bechuana and the Boers.  1891, boundaries
defined.  From 1909-61, administered as a High Commission Territory by a
High Commissioner of Great Britain, resident in the Union of South Africa.
May 1961, constitutional recommendations for more democratic rule.
March 1961, self-government under a ministerial system.  With 1966 independence, the country changed its name from Bechuanaland to Botswana
(meaning "the land and its people"), and the capital, formerly in Mafeking,
S.A. was transferred to Gaberones.

First schools established about 1840 by London Missionary Society.  One of
the first, in the country of Bakwena at Kolobeng (one of Livingstone's
bases of operation).  Two schools in north by 1860.  In 1876, Hermannsburg
Mission opened a school for the Bamalete at Ramoutsa.  Dutch Reformed
Church started work among the Bakgatla.  Later, other missions of Roman
Catholics, Anglicans, and Seventh Day Adventists opened schools.

In 1910, by a joint request of London Missionary Society and chief of the
Bangwaketse Tribe, there was general adoption of a committee system of
management of education (by the Tribe, the Mission, and the District
Administration).  This led to the formation of similar committees in other
districts and to formal ratification of the system by Proclamation in 1938.
Thus, control of schools became secular.

## PRESENT SYSTEM

## PRIMARY EDUCATION

Entry age:  6 years.  Upper limit of age in January 1965, 10 years.

Of the 240 primary schools, one-third offer full 7-year primary course.
Remainder offer either 6 or 4 year courses.  (The number of students
completing more than 4-year primary course is little more than one-sixth
of total enrollment.)

Prior to January 1964, primary program was 8 years, classified as:  Sub A,
Sub B, Standard 1, Standard 2, Standard 3, Standard 4, Standard 5, Standard 6.

From January 1964, 7-year primary program:  Standards 1-7.

Primary school certificate examination at close of 7-year program.
Standard 7 Certificate awarded on successful examination.  Selection for
entry to secondary school is based on the results of this examination.

## SECONDARY EDUCATION

Prior to 1944, the Territory relied upon assistance from the neighboring
territories, notably the Republic of South Africa, for all forms of
secondary and post-primary vocational education.

1944, junior secondary course at Catholic St. Joseph's College.
1949, secondary school opened at Moeng in Bamangwato Tribal Territory.
1954, first full 5-year secondary course at St. Joseph's College and
      Bamangwato College.

At present, 8 secondary schools, entirely non-government.

| School | Type | Range of classes, 1965 |
|---|---|---|
| Moeng College (formerly Bamang- wato College) | Independent boarding.  Adminis- tered by Governing Council and financed mainly by government | Forms I-V |
| St. Joseph's College | Aided boarding-Catholic Mission | Forms I-V plus small commercial |
| Mater Spei | Aided day-Catholic Mission | Forms I-III to extend to Form V by 1967 |

| Moeding College | Aided boarding-London Missionary Society | Forms I-IV to extend to Form V by 1966 |
| Seepasito | Day school at tribal head-quarters in Kanye | Forms I-III |
| Isang | Day school at tribal head-quarters in Mochud. | Forms I-III |
| Kgari Sechele II | Day school at tribal head-quarters in Molepolole | Forms I-III |
| Swaneng Hill | Private day school in Serowe. Unaided | Forms I-III planning to extend to Form V by approximately 1966/67 |

Seepapitso, Isang, and Kgari Sechele II schools are administered and financed by Tribal Administrations.

All schools are co-educational.

Five years' secondary:

| 9th | Form I | |
| 10th | Form II | |
| 11th | Form III | High Commission Territories Junior Certificate |
| 12th | Form IV | Examination |
| 13th | Form V | Cambridge School Certificate Examinations |

Selection from Primary to Secondary School is by competition on the results of the Standard 7 Examination and is made by a committee of all Secondary School heads with a senior officer of the Education Department presiding.

All students sit for the H.C.T. Junior Certificate Examination at the end of Form III. This examination serves two purposes:

  (a) It is a leaving examination providing entry to certain civil service posts, to teacher training at Primary Higher level, and to employment in business and industry.

  (b) It is a selection test for students wishing to complete the full 5-year secondary program.

*Cambridge School Certificate Examinations at close of Form V. On success-ful completion, Cambridge School Certificate awarded, with Division I, II, III grading in descending merit.
No school yet offers the 7-year course leading to the Cambridge Higher School Certificate Examination.

Proposed comprehensive plan, which might begin in 1965 and be completed in 1969, realigning the present pattern of facilities for a better use of skilled staffs and laboratory and library facilities in 6 of the main centers where conditions are most favorable.

| School | Proposed Forms | | | | | Proposed No. of Teachers |
|---|---|---|---|---|---|---|
| | I | II | III | IV | V | |
| St. Joseph's | 2 | 2 | 2 | 2 | 2 | 12 |
| Moeding | 3 | 3 | 3 | 3 | 3 | 18 |
| Gaberones | 3 | 3 | 3 | 3 | 3 | 18 |
| Serowe | 3 | 3 | 3 | 3 | 3 | 18 |
| Mater Spei | 2 | 2 | 2 | 2 | 2 | 12 |
| Seepapitso | 2 | 2 | 2 | 2 | 2 | 12 |

Three schools would be converted to higher primary or possible agricultural schools after progressive reduction of classes: Isang, Kgari Sechele II, and Moeng College. Two new schools to be built at Serowe and Gaberones. With the above plan there would be 15 streams to School Certificate with 90 teachers.

Sample of School Program from:

ST. JOSEPH'S COLLEGE, Khale

Entrance requirements:    For Junior Secondary Department:
                          Department of Education Standard VII
                          Examination.

                          For Senior Secondary Department:
                          High Commission Territories Junior
                          Certificate.

Subjects taken:

High Commission Territories Junior Certificate Examination:

English, Tswana, Latin, French, General Mathematics, General Science, Geography, History.

Cambridge School Certificate Examination:

English Language, English Literature, Latin, Tswana, Mathematics, Principles of Accounts, Commercial Studies (Shorthand, Typewriting, and Elements of Commerce), History. Physics and Chemistry introduced in 1965.

Commercial Course:

> Post J.C. 2-year course.  Subjects include Shorthand, Typewriting, Commerce, Bookkeeping.

Certificates awarded:

> High Commission Territories Junior Certificate
> Cambridge School Certificate
> Royal Society of Arts Commercial Certificate
> Pitman Commercial Certificate
> (All public Examinations)

### TIMETABLE
#### (Hours per week)

| Subjects | Forms I | II | III | IV | V |
|---|---|---|---|---|---|
| English | 4 | 4 | 4 | 4 | 4 2/3 |
| Latin | 2 2/3 | 2 2/3 | 2 2/3 | 2 2/3 | 2 2/3 |
| French | 2 2/3 | | | | |
| Tswana | 2 2/3 | 3 1/3 | 3 1/3 | 3 1/3 | 3 1/3 |
| Science | 3 1/3 | | | | |
| Mathematics+ | 4 | 4 | 3 1/3 | 3 1/3 | 3 1/3 |
| History | 2 2/3 | 2 2/3 | 3 1/3 | 3 1/3 | 2 2/3 |
| Geography | 2 2/3 | 2 2/3 | 2 2/3 | | |
| Singing | 2/3 | | | | |
| Biology | | 3 1/3 | 3 1/3 | 3 1/3 | 2 2/3 |
| Bookkeeping | | | | 3 1/3 | 3 1/3 |
| Typewriting | | | | 2 | 2 |
| Shorthand | | | | 2 2/3 | 3 1/3 |
| Commerce | | | | 1 1/3 | 1 1/3 |
| Religion | 2½ | 2½ | 2½ | 2½ | 2½ |

+Form III.  Arithmetic 3 1/3 hrs.

## HIGHER EDUCATION

None.
Formerly a few students went to University College of Pius XII in Basutoland, University College of Fort Hare in South Africa, or overseas. Scholarship program launched 1961 to place maximum number of students overseas.

With the conversion of Catholic Pius XII University College into the University of Basutoland, Bechuanaland and Swaziland, more students will be drawn to this institution.

## VOCATIONAL AND TECHNICAL EDUCATION

### BECHUANALAND TRAINING CENTRE

Developed in 1964 from the Gaberones Trade School opened by the government, April 1962. The Trade School offered post-primary courses in Building and Carpentry, and post-junior secondary courses in Motor Mechanics.

In addition to these courses, the Centre now provides training courses of many different kinds ranging over the whole field of government service.

### HOMECRAFTS CENTRE

Home Economics taught at Homecrafts Centre, a Dutch Reformed Church institution in Mochudi. Grant-aided.

    2-year course for adolescents.
    1-year course for teachers already qualified, wishing to specialize
            in homecrafts subjects.
    2-year post-primary course gives general training in practical
            home management.

Homecrafts Certificate awarded at close of program.

Homecrafts Teachers' Certificate awarded to qualified teachers at close of 1-year course.

### COMMERCIAL COURSE

Commercial subjects taught at St. Joseph's College. Grant-aided. Courses in Bookkeeping, Commercial Arithmetic, Typewriting, Business Methods, English. 1960-61, additional year added.

### RAMATHLABAMA VETERINARY RESEARCH

6-months' course for cattle guards and veterinary assistants, restricted to employees of the Veterinary Department.

### AGRICULTURAL TRAINING

Agricultural training at the Agricultural Department's Training Centre at Mahalapye.

TEACHER EDUCATION

LOBATSI TEACHER TRAINING COLLEGE, Lobatsi

Opened 1956 (replacing former establishment at Kanye).

Primary Lower Course:    3-year post-primary program, training teachers
                         for the lower classes of the primary school.

   Entrance requirement:    Standard 7 Certificate (primary school
                            leaving certificate).

Higher Primary Course:   2-year post-junior secondary course, training
                         mainly for higher classes.

   Entrance requirement:    Junior Certificate (1st 3 years of
                            secondary school).

## TIMETABLE
(Hours per week)

| Subject | Primary Lower Course | | Primary Higher Course |
|---|---|---|---|
| | 1st Year | 2nd and 3rd Year | 1st and 2nd Years |
| Theory of Education (including demonstration and criticism lessons) | | 5 1/3 | 5 1/3 |
| English (including library period) | 6 2/3 | 5 1/3 | 5 1/3 |
| Setswana | 3 1/3 | 2 2/3 | 2 2/3 |
| Mathematics | 4 | 3 1/3 | 3 1/3 |
| History | 2 | 2 | 2 |
| Geography | 2 | 1 1/3 | 1 1/3 |
| Science or Nature Study | 2 | 1 1/3 | 2 |
| Health Education (including first aid) | 2 | 1 1/3 | 1 1/3 |
| Religious Education | 1 1/3 | 1 1/3 | 1 1/3 |
| Music | 1 1/3 | 1 1/3 | 1 1/3 |
| Physical Education | 1 2/3 | 1 2/3 | 1 2/3 |
| Blackboard and Teaching Aids | 2 2/3 | 2 | 2 |
| Handwork, Craft Work, etc. | 2 2/3 | 2 2/3 | 2 2/3 |

Year begins in January and contains 2 sessions of 19 weeks each (late
January-early June, late July-early December).  Several of these weeks must
be deducted for continuous teaching practice and examinations, the time
varying in different classes as follows:

| | Teaching Practice Weeks | Examinations Weeks | Total Weeks |
|---|---|---|---|
| Primary Lower, 1st year | - | 4 | 4 |
| Primary Lower, 2nd year | 2 | 4 | 6 |
| Primary Lower, 3rd year | 5 | 5 | 10 |
| Primary Higher, 1st year | 2 | 4 | 6 |
| Primary Higher, 2nd year | 5 | 5 | 10 |

(The number of weeks available for routine work in each class can be obtained by deducting the total figure in the above table from 38, and the number of hours devoted to teaching each subject in each class by multiplying the resulting figure by the number of hours given for the subject in the first table.)

Grading system:    Examination percentage (including practical examinations in teaching, oral work, blackboard word, and handwork) with 40% as the minimum pass-mark (in certain subjects and groups as well as aggregate). Aggregate of 60% gains first-class Pass; subject Distinction is gained by 75%.

Primary Lower Teachers' Certificate examination at close of 3-year program, conducted by the Bechuanaland Protectorate Education Department, which issues the Certificate.

Primary Higher Teachers' Certificate examination at close of 2-year program is conducted by an inter-territorial body known as the High Commission Territories Examination Council, which issues the Certificate.

Student obtaining Partial Passes on the Higher Teachers' Certificate can qualify for the award of a full Certificate by passing supplementary examinations.

## TEACHER TRAINING COLLEGE, Serowe

Offers same Primary Lower Teachers' Certificate as Lobatsi College.

## CORRESPONDENCE COURSES

Teachers may enroll in training college, remain on job and study during evenings through correspondence courses. From time to time they enter one or another training college for brief periods of instruction.

# KINGDOM OF LESOTHO
( Basutoland )

Commercial Training

Technical Training

Higher Primary Teacher Tr.

Primary (lower) Teacher Training

Agric. Training

SECONDARY EDUCATION

PRIMARY EDUCATION

(Secondary)

(Junior Secondary)

(Higher Primary)

(Lower Primary)

Law
Science
Education
Administration
Economics
Arts

** V Form
** IV Form
III Form
II Form
I Form
VI Standard
V Standard
IV Standard
III Standard
II Standard
I Standard
Grade B
Grade A

HIGHER EDUCATION
SECONDARY
ELEMENTARY

| Year of Schooling | Student's Age |
|---|---|
| 21 | 26 |
| 20 | 25 |
| 19 | 24 |
| 18 | 23 |
| 17 | 22 |
| 16 | 21 |
| 15 | 20 |
| 14 | 19 |
| 13 | 18 |
| 12 | 17 |
| 11 | 16 |
| 10 | 15 |
| 9 | 14 |
| 8 | 13 |
| 7 | 12 |
| 6 | 11 |
| 5 | 10 |
| 4 | 9 |
| 3 | 8 |
| 2 | 7 |
| 1 | 6 |
| | 5 |
| | 4 |
| | 3 |

Compulsory education: None

School Year: Late January – December

Grading: See SECONDARY and TEACHER EDUCATION

KINGDOM OF LESOTHO
(Formerly Basutoland)

Independence:   September 30, 1966.

## BACKGROUND

Previous to independence, Basutoland was a British-protected enclave with-in the Republic of South Africa.  Population almost entirely African. Europeans number approximately 2,000.  Some Asians and persons of mixed races.

Between 1815-1831, Basuto tribes united in the area.  Clashes occurred with advancing Boers until a British expedition in 1852 brought a tempo-rary truce.  1867, Basutos, defeated by Boers, asked British protection.

British sovereignty, 1868.  Three years later, territory awarded to Cape Colony.  1884, country restored to the Queen through the United Kingdom High Commissioner for South Africa.  Day-to-day government conducted by a Resident Commissioner in Basutoland.  With 1966 independence, the country was renamed Kingdom of Lesotho.

Mid-18th century, education started by missionary bodies:  French Protes-tant, Roman Catholic, and English Church (in order of arrival).  Primary and teacher training schools established; later, secondary schools.

1929, first government schools established:  5 higher primary schools. 1939, first government high school created, offering 5 years post-primary education, qualifying students for university entrance.  Subsequently, junior secondary schools established, offering 3-year post-primary edu-cation; also a technical school.

Presently, all lower primary schools and teacher training schools run by missions, and a large number of higher primary and secondary schools; government helps by grants-in-aid.

## PRESENT SYSTEM

### PRIMARY EDUCATION

Entry age:  Above 5 years plus; maximum, 14 years, to be reduced to 10 years by January, 1969.

8-year program:  6 years - lower primary
                 2 years - higher primary

Converting from 8 to 7 years of primary education, 1967.

## LOWER PRIMARY SCHOOL

Language of instruction is mother tongue with English gradually introduced as medium of instruction in 5th year. 6th year, English is language of instruction.

First 2 years:   English, Vernacular, Arithmetic, Moral Instruction, Arts and Crafts, Writing, P.T.

Next 4 years:    English, Vernacular, Arithmetic, History, Geography, Hygiene, Nature Study and Gardening (Needlework for girls), Moral Instruction, Arts and Crafts. P.T. Science as such is introduced in 6th year.

In some schools the 6th year is incorporated into the Higher Primary School. Promotion from Grades A to B to Standard I is by attendance; thereafter, by internal examination from Standard to Standard. No certificate is awarded at the close of lower primary program.

## HIGHER PRIMARY SCHOOL

Language of instruction:        English.

Two-year course; sometimes three.

Curriculum: Compulsory:      English
                             Arithmetic
                             Sesotho
                             Agricultural Theory OR Home Nursing and
                                  Mothercraft
                             Agriculture Practical OR Needlework

and any 4 of the following:

                             History
                             Geography
                             General Science and Nature Study
                             Hygiene
                             Housewifery and Laundry
                             Cookery

Lesotho Education Department Standard VI Certificate, previously Basutoland Education Department Standard VI Certificate, awarded at close of program.

## SECONDARY EDUCATION

Entry age:  Any age up to a maximum of 18 years.

Entrance requirements:  A pass in Standard VI with particular emphasis on a good pass in English, Sesotho (vernacular) and Arithmetic.

Language of instruction:   English.

Length of course:   A total of 4 or 5 years, divided as follows:

|  |  |
|---|---|
| Junior Secondary Schools: | 2-3 years post-primary schooling leading to <u>High Commission Territories Junior Certificate</u> examination. |
| Secondary Schools: | 2 years beyond junior secondary schools leading to <u>Cambridge School Certificate</u> examination. |

## <u>JUNIOR SECONDARY SCHOOLS</u>

2-3 years post-primary training.

### <u>TIMETABLE (JUNIOR CERTIFICATE)</u> - LESOTHO (Basutoland) HIGH SCHOOL

| | |
|---|---|
| English (i) Language | 5 hours |
| (ii)Literature | 5 hours |
| Sesotho | 2 hours |
| Biology | 3 hours |
| Introductory Science | 4 hours |
| Geography | 3 hours |
| History | 3 hours |
| Latin | 3 hours |
| Mathematics | 4 hours |
| Domestic Science | 4 hours |

| (N.B. | Biology | alternates with | Introductory Science |
|---|---|---|---|
| | Geography | " " | Domestic Science |
| | History | " " | Latin) |

Every student preparing for the <u>Junior Certificate</u> examination must take 6 subjects grouped as follows:

    I.English (i) Language
           (ii)Literature

    II.Afrikaans or French or Latin or a South African Language

    III.Elementary Mathematics (including Arithmetic)

IV.    Introductory Science or Biology

V.    Two of the following subjects:

   A third language taken under II above
   Agricultural Science
   Art, Craft, Arts and Crafts
   Bookkeeping and Commerce
   Domestic Science
   Geography
   History
   Leatherwork
   Metalwork
   Music
   Needlework
   Physiology and Hygiene
   Shorthand and Typewriting
   Typewriting
   Woodwork

Grading:    A.    80% and over         )
            B.    75% - 79%            )
            BB.   70% - 74%            )
            C.    60% - 69%            )     of the maximum marks
            D.    50% - 59%            )
            E.    40% - 49%            )
            F.    33 1/3% - 39%        )

Lowest grade:   40% aggregate and at least 4 subjects passed.

Highest grade:  Class I with merit.  Not frequently given.

High Commission Territories Examinations Council Junior Certificate
awarded on successful examination at close of junior secondary program.

SECONDARY SCHOOLS

Secondary schools cover the same course as the Junior Secondary Schools
but go 2 years further, ending with the Cambridge School Certificate,
an entrance Qualification to the University.

TIME TABLE (SCHOOL CERTIFICATE) - LESOTHO (Basutoland) HIGH SCHOOL

   English Language             3 1/3 hours

   English Literature           3 1/3 hours

   Sesotho (vernacular)         3 1/3 hours

   Biology                      4 hours

| | |
|---|---|
| Geography | 4 2/3 hours |
| Mathematics | 4 2/3 hours |
| History | 3 1/3 hours |
| Latin | 3 1/3 hours |
| Physics-with-Chemistry | 4 2/3 hours |
| Cookery | 4 2/3 hours |

(N.B.  Geography    alternates with   Mathematics
        History        "        "        Latin
        Cookery        "        "        Physics-with-Chemistry)

For the <u>Cambridge School Certificate</u>, which is taken 2 years after <u>Junior Certificate</u>, all candidates must sit for at least 6 subjects, which must include English Language and subjects taken from at least <u>3</u> of the following groups:

   I.    English Language (compulsory).

   II.   General Subjects:  English Literature, Bible Knowledge, History, Geography.

  III.  Languages:  Latin, Greek, French, German, Spanish, other approved languages (in the case of Basutoland, African).

   IV.  Mathematical Subjects:  Mathematics, Additional Mathematics.

    V.  Science Subjects:  General Science, Additional General Science, Agricultural Science, Physics, Chemistry, Biology, Physics-with-Chemistry, Botany.

   VI.  Arts and Crafts:  Art, Music, Woodwork, Metalwork, Metalwork (Engineering), Needlework and Dressmaking, Cookery and General Housecraft.

 VII.  Technical and Commercial Subjects:  Engineering Science, Surveying, Geometrical and Mechanical Drawing, Geometrical and Building Drawing, Commercial Studies, Commerce, Principles of Accounts, Health Science.

N.B.   The 5 other subjects are chosen from at least 3 of Groups II to VII.

       The Mathematics Course includes Algebra, Plane Geometry, Trigonometry, and Arithmetic.

       Laboratory work is an essential part of the Physics and Chemistry courses.

Grading:   Excellent
           Very Good
           Good              Divisions I, II, III in descending merit
           Credit
           Pass

Lowest grade:   One pass with credit and five ordinary passes including
                English Language.

Highest grade: All _Very Good_ passes.  Not frequent.

**_Cambridge School Certificate_ awarded upon successful examination.


## HIGHER EDUCATION

### UNIVERSITY OF BASUTOLAND, BECHUANALAND PROTECTORATE, AND SWAZILAND, Roma

Independent, non-denominational university, established by Royal Charter,
January 1, 1964.  Supported by the governments of the three territories.
Replaced University College of Pius XII, established in Roma, 1945,
directed by the Oblates of Mary Immaculate.  Probable change of name after
independence:  University of Botswana, Lesotho, and Swaziland.

Entrance requirements to degree and diploma courses:

> _Cambridge School Certificate_ in the
> 1st or 2nd Division, with a credit in
> English Language.

Recognized equivalent qualifications:

   (i)   A _General Certificate of Education_ provided that
        (a)   the candidate has taken examinations at ordinary
            level in at least 6 subjects in not more than 2
            sittings, and
        (b)   has passed at ordinary level in at least 4 subjects
            including English Language and not including more
            than one of the following:

> Domestic subjects
> Music
> Art
> Geometrical and Mechanical Drawing

  (ii)   A Matriculation Certificate or a Matriculation Exemption of
        the Joint Matriculation Board of the Republic of South Africa,
        provided that the candidate has passed in English at higher
        grade level.

There may be special requirements for entry to particular courses.
A pass in Mathematics at _C.S.C._ credit level or _G.C.E._ ordinary
level or equivalent is required for entry to courses leading to B.Sc.

The University is divided into Schools of Study.  Following are the Schools and the distribution of subjects in the various Schools:

| SCHOOLS | MAJOR SUBJECTS | MINOR SUBJECTS |
|---|---|---|
| School of African Studies | African Languages | |
| School of Biological and Earth Sciences | Botany Zoology Physical Geography | Agriculture |
| School of Education | Education | Psychology |
| School of Historical Studies | History | |
| School of Language and Literature | English | |
| School of Law, Economics and Administration | Economics Government and Administration Human Geography Law | Sociology Theology |
| School of Mathematical Sciences | Mathematics (Pure and Applied) | |
| School of Physical Sciences | Chemistry Physics | |

## DEGREES AND DIPLOMAS

Degrees:  The general B.A. (Bachelor of Arts)
B.A. (Econ.) (Bachelor of Arts in Economics)
B.A. (Admin.) (Bachelor of Arts in Administration)
B.Ed. (Bachelor of Education)
B.Sc. (Bachelor of Science)
B.Sc. (Ed.)  (Bachelor of Science with Education)
LL.B. (Bachelor of Laws)

Diplomas:  Diploma in Law
Postgraduate Certificate in Education
Certificate in Education concurrently with the B.A. or B.Sc. degree
Certificate in Education with Special Reference to Secondary Education

## LENGTH OF STUDY

Bachelor's degree requires 4 years of study, except where student has been admitted to the University with an approved qualification above that of 'O' level or equivalent.

GENERAL STUDIES

A program of General Studies (Foundation Studies) is part of every student's work in his first year at the University, consisting of one lecture and one seminar on each of the following topics:

Background to Modern Society

    1) The Universe and the Solar System (Physics)
    2) The Earth and its Formation (Physical Geography)
    3) The Nature of Matter (Physics)
    4) The Emergence of Life: What is a Living Being? (Botany and Zoology)
    5) The Origin and Evolution of Man (Botany and Zoology)
    6) What is Mind? (Psychology)
    7) The Origin of Civilization and the Ancient World (History)
    8) Christianity and the Western World (History)
    9) Europe and the World (History)
   10) The Age of Revolutions (History)
   11) Europe and Africa (African Studies)
   12) Africa Today (African Studies)

Modern Society

   13) The Organization of Society (Sociology)
   14) The Rule of Law (Law)
   15) Foundations of Government (Government)
   16) Economic Basis of Society (Economics)
   17) Agriculture and Society (Agriculture)
   18) The Education of the Community (Education)
   19) Language and Literature (English)
   20) Art and Music, with special reference to Africa (African Studies)
   21) Reason and Revelation (Philosophy)
   22) The Nature and Method of Science (Philosophy)
   23) The Nature of Mathematics (Mathematics)
   24) Problems of the Modern World
      a) International Relations (Government)
      b) Other Problems (Symposium)

COURSES OFFERED FOR THE GENERAL B.A. AND B.SC. DEGREES

   I. Major subjects:

      (i) Four courses:

         African Languages, English, Human Geography, Physical Geography, History, Law, Politics and Administration, Botany, Chemistry, Mathematics, Physics, Zoology.

(ii)   Three courses:

Economics, Philosophy.

II.   Minor Subjects:

Theology (1 or 2 courses)
Applied Mathematics (1 course)
Psychology (1 course)
Sociology (1 course)


STRUCTURE OF CURRICULUM

Curriculum for the Bachelor's degree is divided into Part I and Part
II.  Part I must be passed before Part II is begun.

The 12½ or 13 courses constituting the curriculum are built up in
this way:

| | | | | | |
|---|---|---|---|---|---|
| Part I | Year | I | 4½ | 4 | 4½ |
| | | | | or | or |
| | Year | II | 4 | 4½ | 4½ |
| Part II | Year | III | 2 | | |
| | Year | IV | 2 | | |


A course extends over a full year of instruction and study.  A
half-course may cover half the academic year or be distributed over
one whole academic year.

Bachelor of Arts (B.A.)

Combinations of Major Subjects with Ancillaries

| Majors | | Ancillaries |
|---|---|---|
| English | - History | |
| English | - African Studies | |
| English | - Human Geography | ½ course in Economic Statistics |
| English | - Philosophy | |
| History | - African Studies | |
| History | - Economics | ½ course in Ec. Statistics, and ½ course in Accountancy |
| Human Geography | - Economics | ½ course in Ec. Statistics, and ½ course in Accountancy |
| Human Geography | - African Studies | ½ course in Ec. Statistics |
| Human Geography | - History | ½ course in Ec. Statistics |
| History | - Philosophy | |

| Human Geography | - Physical Geography | Physics |
|---|---|---|
| Mathematics | - Philosophy | Applied Mathematics |
|  |  | Physics |
| Government | - Economics | ½ course in Ec. Statistics, and |
|  |  | ½ course in Accountancy |
| English | - Economics | ½ course in Ec. Statistics, and |
|  |  | ½ course in Accountancy |
| Government | - History |  |
| Government | - English |  |
| Government | - Human Geography | ½ course in Ec. Statistics |
| Government | - African Studies |  |
| Government | - Philosophy |  |
| Government | - Law |  |
| Law | - History |  |

## B.A. (Economics)

Part I:    The following courses must be included in the Part I curriculum:

English I, Economics I, Business I, Mercantile Law I, Accountancy ½ course, Economics Statistics ½ course, Foundation Studies ½ course, Special Topic ½ course, plus 2½ or 3 free courses chosen after consultation with the Department of Economics.

Recommended courses are:  Mathematics, Sociology, Government, Human Geography, History, Mercantile Law II (½), and Education.

Part II: Year III:       Two courses from:     Economics II
                                                Business II
                                                Accountancy II

         Year IV:        Two courses from:     Economics III
                                                Business III
                                                Accountancy III

## B.A. (Administration)

Year I:        Government I, Law I, English I, Economic Statistics ½ course, Foundation Studies (½ course), Foundation Studies Special Topic (½ course).

Year II:       Government II, Administration I, Economics I, Accountancy I.

Year III:      Government III, Administration II, Economics II.

Year IV:       Government IV, Administration III.

Diploma in Law

Internal students of the university may complete the Diploma in a minimum
of 2 years.

Program:   6 Law courses.   Internal students take 3 courses in each of
           their 2 years.   In addition, English I in 1st year.

Diploma awarded at a pass level or with a higher level.   Only those
students who have passed at the higher level may proceed to the degree
curriculum, leading to the LL.B.


Bachelor of Laws (LL.B.)

Candidate for this degree must follow the same curriculum as a candidate
for the Diploma and must pass those courses at the higher level.   Candidate entering the degree course with two 'A' level passes needs to take
only 4 of the Diploma courses, to be selected by the university.

Students with the above entrance qualifications must:

   (a)   Successfully complete 2 years of full-time study in prescribed
         legal subjects at the Faculty of Law in Edinburgh University,
         or do equivalent studies elsewhere.

   (b)   Successfully complete an approximate half-year period of full-
         time study at the University of Basutoland, Bechuanaland Pro-
         tectorate and Swaziland after concluding the studies mentioned
         in (a) above.


Bachelor of Science (B.Sc.)

Entrance requirements:          General requirements to university, and in
                                addition, a pass with credit in Mathematics
                                in the Cambridge School Certificate or its
                                equivalent.

Major Subjects Offered:

Major subjects selected from one of the following groups:

| Group A | Group B | Group C | Group D |
|---------|---------|---------|---------|
| Chemistry | Botany | Botany | Human and |
| Mathematics | Chemistry | Physical | Physical |
| Physics | Zoology | Geography | Geography |
| Physical Geography | | | |

(First year courses in Human Geography and Physical Geography are
identical and count as one course.)

## Approved Combinations of Majors

The following ancillary courses are required with major subject.  (Last column gives highly recommended courses.)

| Major Subject | Ancillary | Highly Recommended |
|---|---|---|
| Botany | Chemistry I, II | Physics I |
| Chemistry | Mathematics I, Physics I | Mathematics II |
| Human Geography | Economic Statistics | - |
| Mathematics | Physics I, Applied Math. | - |
| Physical Geography | Physics I | Chemistry I |
| Physics | Math. I, Appl. Math. I | Mathematics II |
| Zoology | Physics, Chemistry I, Botany | - |

(No student permitted to take Applied Mathematics unless he has taken Mathematics I and Physics I.)


## Education Degrees and Certificates

### Postgraduate Certificate in Education

Entrance requirements:   An approved degree of a recognized University, with a secondary school subject as one of the major or principal subjects of the degree.

Length of course:   1 academic year of full-time study.  (In special cases, the University may approve of part-time study over a period of 2 years, which would include at least 4-weeks residence at the University.)

Program:  (a)  Teaching Practice
         (b)  Courses in
            1) Educational Policy
            2) Educational Psychology
            3) The teaching of at least 3 subjects
         (c)  Special study of an approved educational topic
         (d)  Other activities as prescribed by the Department


### Bachelor of Education

Entrance requirements:  (a)  An approved degree.
                    (b)  An approved teacher's certificate.
                    (c)  At least 3 years' teaching experience (2 years, if undertaking the program part-time).

Length of course:   1 academic year of full-time study or 2 years of part-time study.

Program:   (a)  Courses in
                1) Educational Theory and Practice.
                2) <u>Either</u> Primary Education <u>or</u> Secondary Education <u>or</u>
                   Teacher Education.
           (b)  A thesis on an approved educational topic.


## Certificate in Education (concurrently with General B.A./B.Sc.)

Entrance requirements:   Candidate must first be qualified for admission
                         to a general B.A. or B.Sc. program.

Certificate program extends part-time over 4 years, concurrently with
the program for a general B.A. or B.Sc.

Curriculum:
           (a)  2 courses in Education, usually taken respectively in the
                1st and 2nd years of the degree program.
           (b)  Series of seminars in Education, 1 period per week in the
                3rd year, and the first term of the 4th year.
           (c)  2 periods of teaching practice, usually during the long
                vacations preceding the 2nd and 4th years of study.
           (d)  Special study of an approved educational topic.

<u>Certificate not awarded until student has completed the degree require-
ments as well as the certificate requirements.</u>


## B.Sc. (Education)

Two science subjects taken as majors; one subject taken for 4 years, the
other subject taken for 3 years (in the 1st, 2nd, and 4th years).

Education component of the degree:
           (a)  ½ course in Education, taken in either 1st or 2nd year.
           (b)  Course in Education, taken during the 3rd year.
           (c)  Series of seminars in Education, 1 period per week in the
                first term of the 4th year.
           (d)  2 periods of teaching practice during the long vacations
                preceding <u>either</u> the 2nd <u>or</u> 3rd year of study and the 4th
                year of study.
           (e)  Special study of an approved educational topic.


## Junior Secondary Teacher's Diploma (discontinued after 1965)

Entrance requirements:   As for degree.

Length of course:   2 years.

Program:  1st year:  4 academic courses (first degree courses from the
                     following groups:
                     (i)  English, an African Language, History, Mathe-
                          matics, Sociology, Geography, and 1 Science
                          subject.
                     (ii) English Usage, Botany, Chemistry, Mathematics,
                          Physics, Zoology, Geography.
          2nd year:  Special professional course offered by the School
                     of Education.

No candidate admitted to second year program unless he has passed 3 of
his first year courses.

Final examination at close of second year includes a test of practical
teaching in each of the candidate's principal teaching subjects.


Certificate in Education, with special reference to Secondary Education

Entrance requirements:   Must have passed the Part I Examinations for the
                         general B.A. or B.Sc. of the University (or its
                         equivalent) in at least the following:
                         (a)  2 major subjects taken for 2 years and
                              examined at the end of the 2nd year, and
                         (b)  either a third major subject, as above, or
                              two single one-year subjects (the first
                              assessed at the end of the first year but
                              not formally examined, the other taken in
                              the 2nd year and formally examined at the
                              end of that year).

Length of course:   1 academic year of full-time study.

Program:  (a)  Teaching Practice.
          (b)  Courses in
               1)  Educational Policy
               2)  Educational Psychology
               3)  The teaching of at least 3 school subjects
          (c)  A special study of an approved educational topic.
          (d)  Such activities as are prescribed by the School of Education.
          (e)  A candidate with 3 passes in the Part I Examination must
               complete in his third year a further course in a secondary
               school subject.


VOCATIONAL AND TECHNICAL EDUCATION

LEROTHOLI ARTISAN TRAINING CENTRE, Maseru

Run by government.  Prepares students as apprentices in:

Building                               Cabinet-making
Engineering (Mechanics)                Carpentry

Programs lead to the intermediate examinations of the City and Guilds
Institute, London.

## LELOALENG TECHNICAL SCHOOL, Moyeni, Quthing

Run by the French mission.  Similar programs to those listed above at the
Lerotholi Artisan Training Centre, plus Leatherwork and Tailoring.

## AGRICULTURAL TRAINING SCHOOL, Maseru

Run by the Department of Agriculture.

Entry age:  Minimum of 18 years.

Entrance requirements:   Junior Certificate, Lesotho Primary Teachers' Course,
                         previously Basutoland Primary Teachers' Course, Primary
                         Higher.

Programs in Agricultural Education and Rural Domestic Economy - 2½ years.
6½ months of pre-instructional training, mainly practical, in any of the
4 Training Farms (Farm Institutes) in the Territory, and 2 years academic
and practical training at the Agricultural Training School.

| Agricultural Education Program | Rural Domestic Economy |
| --- | --- |
| Field Husbandry | Cookery |
| Animal Husbandry | Needlework |
| Dairying | Housewifery |
| Pigs and Poultry | Laundrywork |
| Elementary Economics | Physiology and Hygiene |
| Soil Science | Food Chemistry |
| Plant Biology | Handicrafts |
| Animal Biology | Field Husbandry |
| Soil Conservation | Animal Husbandry |
| Advisory Methods and Extension | Tree Planting |
| Ecology | Gardening |
| Veterinary Science | Dairying |
| Land Utilization and Map Reading | Poultry Husbandry |
| Wool and Mohair | Extension and Advisory Methods |

Agricultural Diploma (Certificate Level) awarded at close of 2½-year program.

Diploma in Rural Domestic Economy (Certificate Level) awarded at close of
2½-year program.

SACRED HEART COMMERCIAL HIGH SCHOOL, Leribe

3-year Commercial Junior Certificate program:

| | | |
|---|---|---|
| English | Science/Agriculture | Arithmetic |
| Sesotho | Mathematics | Bookkeeping and Commerce |
| | | Typewriting and Shorthand |

Cambridge School Certificate program:

| | | |
|---|---|---|
| English Language | Scripture | Commerce |
| English Literature | Mathematics | Geography |
| Sesotho | Principles of Accounts | History |

## TEACHER EDUCATION

A certified teacher is one who holds one or more of the certificates or diplomas listed below (and issued in Lesotho (Basutoland)), or an equivalent certificate or diploma approved by the Permanent Secretary:

Infant Teachers' Certificate          )     Discontinued when 2 following
Elementary Vernacular Certificate )     Certificates were adopted and
                                                               required
Lesotho(Basutoland) Primary Teachers/ Certificate
High Commission Territories Primary Higher Certificate
Junior Secondary Teachers' Diploma
Post-graduate Certificate or Diploma in Education

Minimum qualifications:

Lower Primary Schools:          Infant Teachers' Certificate or the Elementary Vernacular Teachers' Certificate (formerly awarded), Primary Teachers' Certificate, or equivalent.

Higher Primary Schools:          High Commission Territories Primary Higher Teachers' Certificate, or equivalent.

Junior Secondary Schools:          Minimum qualification for any assistant teacher is a Senior School Leaving Certificate or equivalent and in addition the High Commission Territories Primary Higher Teachers' Certificate.

The headmaster or headmistress must be a graduate of a university approved by the Permanent Secretary, and hold a teaching certificate.

High Schools:                    Minimum qualification for an assistant
                                 teacher in the first three forms of a
                                 high school is the same as for Junior
                                 Secondary Schools.

                                 Minimum qualification for an assistant
                                 teacher in fourth and fifth forms is a
                                 degree approved by the Permanent
                                 Secretary, and a teaching certificate.

                                 The headmaster or headmistress must be
                                 a graduate of a university approved by
                                 the Permanent Secretary and hold a
                                 post-graduate teaching certificate.

## LESOTHO (Basutoland) PRIMARY TEACHERS' COURSE

Primary Teachers' Course, open to male and female students, qualifies for
teaching in Lower Primary Schools.
Primary Teachers' Course (Housecraft), open to female students only,
qualifies for teaching Domestic Science subjects and Art and Handwork
through the Primary School and other subjects in Lower Primary School.

Entrance requirements:   A pass in Standard VI.

Language of instruction:  English.  (Sotho, medium of instruction in Sotho.)

3-year programs.

### TIMETABLE
(40-minute periods per week)

| Subjects | 1st Year | 2nd Year | 3rd Year |
|---|---|---|---|
| **Group A** | | | |
| Class Teaching (including ) | | | |
| observation, criticism, ) | | | |
| and demonstration lessons)) | 4 | 6 | 11 |
| Methods of Teaching and ) | | | |
| School Organization ) | | | |
| Blackboard work and | | | |
| Teaching Apparatus | 3 | 3 | 3 |
| **Group B** | | | |
| English (oral and written) | 8 | 6 | 6 |
| Sotho (oral and written) | 3 | 3 | 3 |
| **Group C+** | | | |
| Arithmetic | 2 | 2 | 1 |

| | | | |
|---|---|---|---|
| Hygiene | 2 | 2 | 1 |
| Science and Nature Study | 2 | 2 | 1 |
| Geography | 2 | 2 | 1 |
| History | 2 | 2 | 1 |
| Housewifery and Laundry | 2 | 2 | 1 |
| Home Nursing, First Aid, and Mothercraft | 2 | 2 | 1 |
| Cookery | 2 | 2 | 1 |
| Mathematics | - | 2 | 1 |

(Students taking Mathematics must follow the Arithmetic syllabus in the 1st year.)

+Hygiene, Arithmetic and 3 other subjects to be selected from this group.

### Group D

| | | | |
|---|---|---|---|
| Agriculture or Needlework | 6 | 6 | 6 |
| Music | 2 | 2 | 2 |
| Handwork and Art | 3 | 3 | 3 |
| Physical Training | 2 | 2 | 2 |
| Religious Instruction | 2 | 2 | 2 |
| | (to be taken in half-periods) | | |
| Writing | 2 | 2 | 2 |
| | 45 | 45 | 45 |

### TIMETABLE (Housecraft Course)
#### (40-minute periods per week)

| Subjects | 1st Year | 2nd Year | 3rd Year |
|---|---|---|---|
| **Group A** | | | |
| Class Teaching (including observation, criticism, and demonstration) ) Methods of Teaching and School Organization ) | 4 | 6 | 10 |
| Blackboard Work and Teaching Apparatus | 3 | 3 | 3 |
| **Group B** | | | |
| English (oral and written) | 7 | 5 | 4 |
| Sotho (oral and written) | 2 | 2 | 2 |
| **Group C** | | | |
| Arithmetic | 2 | 2 | 1 |
| Hygiene | 2 | 2 | 1 |
| Housewifery and Laundry | 2 | 2 | 2 |

| Home Nursing, First Aid and Mothercraft | 2 | 2 | 1 |
|---|---|---|---|
| Cookery | 4 | 4 | 4 |

#### Group D

| Needlework | 6 | 6 | 6 |
|---|---|---|---|
| Music | 2 | 2 | 2 |
| Handwork and Art | 3 | 3 | 3 |
| Physical Training | 2 | 2 | 2 |
| Religious Instruction | 2 | 2 | 2 |
| | (to be taken in half-periods) | | |
| Writing | 2 | 2 | 2 |
| | 45 | 45 | 45 |

## EXAMINATIONS

### Conditions for a Pass:

First Year:   Internal examination.

> Group B:   40% in English and 40% in Sotho.
> Group C:   40% in Arithmetic and 40% in each of 3 other subjects.
> Group D:   40% in Agriculture or Needlework.
> For the whole examination:  40% aggregate.

Second Year:   Internal examination.

> Group A:   40% in Class Teaching and Methods of Teaching (in the event of failure, 50% in the two combined).
> Group B:   40% in English and 40% in Sotho.
> Group C:   40% in Arithmetic and 40% in each of 3 other subjects.
> Group D:   40% in Agriculture or Needlework and 40% in the Group aggregate.

Third Year:   External examination.

> Group A:   40% in each of the 3 subject areas.
> Group B:   40% in English (oral and written combined).
>           40% in Sotho (oral and written combined).
> Group D:   40% in Agriculture or Needlework.
>           40% in Handwork and Art.

### Conditions for a Pass - Housecraft Course:

First Year:   Internal examination.

> Group B:   40% in English and 40% in Sotho.
> Group C:   40% in each of 4 subjects.
> Group D:   40% in Needlework.
> For the whole examination:  40% aggregate.

Second Year:   Internal examination.

    Group A:   40% in Class Teaching and Methods of Teaching (in the event of failure, 50% in the two combined.)
    Group B:   40% in English, 40% in Sotho.
    Group C:   40% in each of 4 subjects.
    Group D:   40% in Needlework and 40% in Group Aggregate.

Third Year:   External examination.

    Group A:   40% in each of the 3 subject areas.
    Group B:   40% in English (oral and written combined).
          40% in Sotho (oral and written combined).
    Group C:   40% in Practical Domestic Science (Cookery, Housewifery and Laundrywork).
    Group D:   40% in Needlework
          40% in Handwork and Art

EXAMINATION MARKS

## INTERNAL

| | Marks |
|---|---|
| **Group A** | |
| Class Teaching | 100 |
| Methods of Teaching and School Organization | 150 |
| Blackboard Work and Teaching Apparatus | 50 |
| **Group B** | |
| English (including oral) | 150 |
| Sotho (including oral) | 150 |
| **Group C** | |
| 100 marks per subject (5 subjects) | 500 |
| **Group D** | |
| Agriculture or Needlework | 100 |
| Handwork and Art | 100 |
| Music | 50 |
| Physical Training | 50 |
| Religious Instruction | 50 |
| Writing | 50 |
| Total | 1,500 |

EXTERNAL

## Group A

| | |
|---|---:|
| Class Teaching | 150 |
| Methods of Teaching | 150 |
| School Organization | 150 |
| Blackboard Work and Teaching Apparatus | 50 |

## Group B

| | |
|---|---:|
| English - written | 150 |
|         - oral | 50 |
| Sotho   - written | 150 |
|         - oral | 50 |

## Group D

| | |
|---|---:|
| Agriculture or Needlework | 75 |
| Handwork and Art | 75 |
| Total | 1,000 |

HOUSECRAFT COURSE                    INTERNAL

## Group A

| | |
|---|---:|
| Class Teaching | 100 |
| Methods of Teaching and School Organization | 150 |
| Blackboard Work and Teaching Apparatus | 50 |

## Group B

| | |
|---|---:|
| English (including oral) | 150 |
| Sotho (including oral) | 150 |

## Group C

| | |
|---|---:|
| 100 marks per subject (5 subjects) | 500 |

## Group D

| | |
|---|---:|
| Needlework | 100 |
| Handwork and Art | 100 |
| Music | 50 |
| Physical Training | 50 |
| Religious Instruction | 50 |
| Writing | 50 |
| Total | 1,200 |

Lesotho Primary Teachers' Certificate (L.P.T.C.), previously Basutoland
Primary Teachers' Certificate (B.P.T.C.), awarded upon successful examinations.

L.P.T.C., (B.P.T.C.), certified teachers teach in the lower primary schools,
from preparatory to Standard IV.

## HIGH COMMISSION TERRITORIES PRIMARY HIGHER TEACHERS' COURSE

Higher Primary Teachers' Course qualifies for teaching in higher primary schools.

Entrance requirements:   A pass in the <u>Junior Certificate</u> examination to include the following:

        English

        Sesotho (excepting special circumstances approved by the Education Department)

        Elementary Mathematics (from 1966)

        Introductory Science <u>or</u> Biology

        History <u>or</u> Geography <u>or</u> a third language

        Candidates holding the <u>Cambridge School Certificate</u> are admitted.

Language of instruction:  English.

2-year program.

### TIMETABLE
### (40-minute periods per week)

| Subjects | Periods |
|---|---|
| **Group A** | |
| Class Teaching, and the Making and Use of Teaching Aids) | |
| Theory of Education ) 11 | |
| School Organization and Regulations ) | |
| **Group B** | |
| English:  Language and Comprehension ) | |
|         Composition ) | |
|         Literature ) 6 | |
|         Oral ) | |
| Vernacular:  Language and Comprehension ) | |
|         Composition ) | |
|         Literature ) 4 | |
|         Oral ) | |
| **Group C** | |
| Mathematics | 4 |
| History | 2 |
| Geography | 2 |
| Science | 2 |
| Health Education | 1 |
| Religious Education | 2 |

Group D

Compulsory:
   Music                                                        2
   Physical Education and Games                                 2
At least 2 of the following:
   Arts, Craft and Handwork        )
   Woodwork                        )
   Agriculture                     )                            6
   Needlework                      )
   Home Nursing and Mothercraft    )
                                             44 periods

## EXAMINATIONS

First and Second Years:  Internal examinations.

Final Examinations:  External examination.

Conditions for a Pass:

      Group A:  40% in Class Teaching, and the Making and Use of
               Teaching Aids, and in each of the external written
               subjects (Theory of Education, School Organization and
               Regulations, English, Sesotho, and Mathematics).

      Group B:  In each language:  40% in the aggregate.  (Marks for
               the internal paper are taken into consideration in
               borderline cases.)

      Group C:  40% in at least 5 of the subjects including Mathematics,
               and 40% in the aggregate for the whole group.

      Group A, B, C, D:  40% aggregate.

Conditions for a Distinction:

      Candidates who pass External Subjects with 70% or more are awarded
      a Distinction in each particular subject.  (Distinctions are
      rarely awarded.)

## EXAMINATION MARKS

|                                          | Marks | Duration of Paper |
|------------------------------------------|-------|-------------------|
| **Group A**                              |       |                   |
| Class Teaching                           | 200   | -                 |
| The Making and Use of Teaching Aids      | 100   | -                 |
| Theory of Education                      | 200   | 2½ hrs.           |
| School Organization (60) and Regulations | 100   | 2½ hrs.           |
|   (40)                         |       |                   |

Group B

English:

| | | | |
|---|---|---|---|
| 1st Paper: | Language, Comprehension and Method | 150 | 2½ hrs. |
| 2nd Paper: | Composition | 100 | 2 hrs. |
| 3rd Paper: | Literature | 100 | 2 hrs. |
| Oral | | 100 | - |

Vernacular:

| | | | |
|---|---|---|---|
| 1st Paper: | Language, Comprehension and Method | 150 | 2½ hrs. |
| 2nd Paper: | Composition | 100 | 2 hrs. |
| 3rd Paper: | Literature | 100 | 2 hrs. |
| Oral | | 100 | - |

Group C

| | | |
|---|---|---|
| Mathematics | 100 | 2 hrs. |
| History | 100 | 1½ hrs. |
| Geography | 100 | 1½ hrs. |
| Science | 100 | 1½ hrs. |
| Health Education | 100 | 1½ hrs. |
| Religious Education | 100 | 1½ hrs. |

Group D

| | | |
|---|---|---|
| Music | 100 | - |
| Physical Education and Games | 100 | - |
| Arts, Craft and Handwork | 100 | - |
| Woodwork | 100 | - |
| Agriculture | 100 | - |
| Needlework | 100 | - |
| Home Nursing and Mothercraft | 100 | - |

Minimum total of Marks    2,500

N.B.   20% of the maximum marks allocated for the 1st Paper in English, the 1st Paper in the Vernacular and to each of the subjects in Group C are reserved for a section dealing with the methods of teaching each of these individual subjects.

High Commission Territories Primary Higher Teachers' Certificate awarded upon successful examinations.

P.H. certified teachers are qualified to teach in the Higher Primary classes:  Standards V and VI.

MALAGASY REPUBLIC

Compulsory education:  6 years primary education

School year:  Primary and secondary – Sept. 1 to June 15

Higher education – October 1 to June 30

Secondary grading:  20 Perfect

10/20 pass mark

MALAGASY REPUBLIC
(République Malgache)


Independence:   June 26, 1960


BACKGROUND


The ethnic groups in Malagasy Republic are linguistically and culturally homogeneous.  The major ones are:  Merina (Tananarive Province, in center of island), Betsimisaraka (along east coast in Tamatave and Fianarantsoa Province), Betsileo (in southern Fianarantsoa Province), Tsimihety (in Majunga and Diégo-Suarez Provinces), Antaisaka (along east coast in Fianarantsoa Province), Sakalava (in west in Tuléar and Majunga Provinces), Antaimaro (along east coast in Tamatave Province), Bara (in Tuléar and Fianarantsoa Provinces), Antanosy (in Tuléar Province), Sihanaka, Mahafaly, Makoa, Antaifasy, Bezanozano, Antakarana, Antambahoaka, and Saint-Marianeans.  The Malagasy are an outcome of ancient intermingling of various immigrations, including Africans, Arabs, and Indonesians.  There are approximately 6000 French, some Indians, Greeks, and Chinese.

Official language, French.  All  Malagasy speak a single language (belonging to Indonesian group), but there are regional dialects.

Immigrations from Indonesia by first century, A.D.; followed by Arabs from Persian Gulf and Zanzibar.

In 1500, Portuguese Explorer, Diego Diaz, sighted island.  On returning to Portugal and informing the King, the King decided it must be the island of "Madagascar" about which he had read in Marco Polo's Voyages.  Marco Polo had not been to the island but had taken his information from Arabs who had told him of the "Kingdom of Mogadisho."  In misspelling the name he had coined the word "Madagascar," by which the island had subsequently been known.  Portuguese explorers landed on island, 1506; French, Dutch, and British followed.

In 17th century, French trading companies tried to establish colonies on south of island, but gave up efforts.  Island became base for pirates, especially English, including Captain Kidd.

Three main kingdoms of Malagasy, Merina in central plateau, Sakalave in West, and Betsimisaraka in East, warred with each other throughout 18th century, each becoming dominant at some period.

Radama I, leader of Merina Kingdom welcomed Europeans in early 19th
century in modernization of island.  London Missionary Society began
activities; Malagasy language transcribed into Latin alphabet.

After Radama's death, 1828, Rainilaiakivony, the prime minister and con-
sort of three succeeding queens, attempted to keep Madagascar independent,
in the face of interest in the island by British and French.  1883, war
between British and French.  Island became French Protectorate, 1885.
British recognition of French possession of Madagascar, 1890, in exchange
for French recognition of the British possession of Zanzibar.

From 1942-43, Vichy Government of France permitted occupation of island
by British troops to prevent use of naval facilities by Japanese.  Toward
end of World War II, Malagasy leaders requested that Madagascar become a
free state within the French Union.

Colonial reforms of 1956-67 abolished system of dual electorates and
established universal suffrage.  Referendum, September 28, 1958, Madagascar voted for new French constitution, and became an autonomous state in
the new French Community.  June 26, 1960, as the Malagasy Republic, it
became an independent state, remaining a member of the Community.

In 19th century, under Merina state, schools created by Christian missions.
First government public schools (écoles officielles) established 1896-1905,
in which Malagasy was the language of instruction in primary schools,
French in secondary schools.  In primary rural schools:  reading, writing,
the metric system, French, history and geography, gardening for boys,
embroidery for girls; 1903, drawing and hygiene added.  Regional schools
(one per district or province) accepted the best students from rural primary; each school had an experimental farm (terrain de culture) and workshop (atelier d'apprentissage).  Ecoles supérieures admitted graduates
from regional schools and private schools with similar standards; 1905-
1910, all of these schools merged into the single Ecole le Myre de Vilers
in Tananarive.  Académie Malgache established 1902.

All private schools (écoles privées or écoles libres) run by missions.
1898 ordinance codified Separation of Church and State; forced instruction
in private schools to conform to secular curriculums in public schools.

Education Reform Ordinance of 1951 brought the educational system as close
as possible to that of metropolitan France.  After 1952, all schools
modeled directly on those in France.

By 1952, 5 secondary schools:

> Lycée Gallieni (boys), Tananarive
> Lycée Jules-Ferry (girls), Tananarive
> Collège Moderne et Technique (co-educational), Tananarive
> Cours Complémentaire (co-educational), Tamatave
> Cours Complémentaire (co-educational), Diego-Suarez

By 1952, 3 levels of technical education:

Rural:              _Atelier de district_ for training village artisans.

Provincial:         _Centres d'apprentissage_, specialized training in
                    skills most needed in 6 national provinces.

National:           _Ecole industrielle_ and _collège technique_ prepar-
                    ing for positions in management, commerce, teaching,
                    printing, and other professions and trades.

Center for Advanced Studies (Institut des Hautes Etudes) established in
Tananarive, 1955.

By 1958, 5 _lycées_ and 18 _collèges classiques_ and _modernes_.  A higher percentage of Malagasy girls in school than in any other French-speaking area
in Africa.  By 1962, 2500 primary schools, 125 complementary schools, 28
secondary schools, 150 technical and vocational schools.


## PRESENT SYSTEM


## PRE-SCHOOL EDUCATION

No public pre-school education.  However, private and mission schools
provide education for children 3 to 6 years.


## PRIMARY EDUCATION

Entry age:  6 years.

Language of instruction:        Malagasy in first 2 years (_cours préparatoire_).
                                Both French and Malagasy used in last 4 years.

Length of primary education:    6 years.

                                _Cours préparatoire_,  2 years
                                _Cours élémentaire_,   2 years
                                _Cours moyen_,         2 years

Program:        French program same as in France.
                Malagasy program same for rural and urban schools.

Certificate awarded:    _Certificat d'études primaires élémentaires_
                        _(C.E.P.E.)._

## SECONDARY EDUCATION

Entrance requirements:     Pass <u>concours d'entrée en sixième</u>, consisting of
dictation of 80 words, study of a text, arith-
metic (4 sums, 1 problem).

Language of instruction: French.

Length of courses:        4-year short cycle (<u>enseignement court</u>)

7-year long cycle (<u>enseignement long</u>)

Programs:      Similar to French programs.  First foreign language
included in 1st cycle.  2 languages may be studied,
choice of English, German, Greek, Latin, Malagasy.

### SECONDARY TIMETABLES
(Hours per week)

#### Classes 6 and 5

| Subjects | Classique | Moderne et Technique |
|---|---|---|
| Mathematics | 3 | 3 |
| Observational Sciences | 1½ | 1½ |
| History and Geography | 2½ | 2½ |
| Experimental Scientific Work | - | 1 |
| Civics | ½ | ½ |
| French | 4 | 6 |
| Latin | 5 | - |
| Modern Language | 3 | 5 |
| Art | 1 | 1 |
| Music | 1 | 1 |
| Manual Arts | 1 | 1 |
| Physical Education | 2 | 2 |
| Total | 24½ | 24½ |

#### Class 4

| Subjects | Classique A | Classique B | Moderne |
|---|---|---|---|
| French | 3½ | 3½ | 5½ |
| Latin | 3½ | 3½ | - |
| Greek | 3 | - | - |
| Civics | ½ | ½ | ½ |
| Modern Language I | 3 | 3 | 3 |
| Modern Language II | - | 3 | 4 |
| History and Geography | 2½ | 2½ | 2½ |
| Mathematics | 3 | 3 | 3 |
| Observational Sciences | 1½ | 1½ | 1½ |

| Subjects           |       |       |       |
|--------------------|-------|-------|-------|
| Physical Education | 2     | 2     | 2     |
| Art                | 1     | 1     | 1     |
| Music              | 1     | 1     | 1     |
| Manual Arts        | 1     | 1     | 1     |
| Total              | 25½   | 25½   | 25½   |

## Class 3

| Subjects               | Classique A | Classique B | Moderne |
|------------------------|-------------|-------------|---------|
| French                 | 3½          | 3½          | 5½      |
| Latin                  | 3½          | 3½          | -       |
| Greek                  | 3           | -           | -       |
| Civics                 | ½           | ½           | ½       |
| Modern Language I      | 3           | 3           | 3       |
| Modern Language II     | -           | 3           | 4       |
| History and Geography  | 3           | 3           | 3       |
| Mathematics            | 3           | 3           | 3       |
| Observational Sciences | 1           | 1           | 1½      |
| Physical Education     | 2           | 2           | 2       |
| Art                    | 1           | 1           | 1       |
| Music                  | 1           | 1           | 1       |
| Manual Arts            | 1           | 1           | 1       |
| Total                  | 25½         | 25½         | 25½     |

## Class 2

| Subjects                 | Série A  | A'       | B        | C     | M     | M'    |
|--------------------------|----------|----------|----------|-------|-------|-------|
| French                   | 4        | 4        | 4        | 4     | 4     | 4     |
| Latin                    | 3        | 3        | 3        | 3     | -     | -     |
| Greek                    | 4        | 3        | -        | -     | -     | -     |
| Civics                   | ½        | ½        | ½        | ½     | ½     | ½     |
| Modern Language I        | 3        | 3        | 3        | 3     | 3     | 3     |
| Modern Language II       | -        | -        | 4        | 2     | 4     | 2     |
| History                  | 2        | 2        | 2        | 2     | 2     | 2     |
| Geography                | 1½       | 1½       | 1½       | 1½    | 1½    | 1½    |
| Mathematics              | 3        | 5        | 3        | 5     | 5     | 5     |
| Physical Sciences        | 2 3/4    | 3 3/4    | 2 3/4    | 4½    | 4½    | 4½    |
| Natural Sciences         | -        | -        | -        | -     | -     | 3     |
| Physical Education       | 2        | 2        | 2        | 2     | 2     | 2     |
| Art                      | 1        | 1        | 1        | 1     | 1     | 1     |
| Music (optional)         | 1        | 1        | 1        | 1     | 1     | 1     |
| Manual Arts (optional)   | 1        | 1        | 1        | 1     | 1     | 1     |
| Total                    | 28 3/4   | 30 3/4   | 28 3/4   | 30½   | 29½   | 30½   |

## Class 1

| Subjects | Série A | A' | B | C | M | M' |
|---|---|---|---|---|---|---|
| French | 4 | 4 | 4 | 4 | 4 | 4 |
| Latin | 3 | 3 | 3 | 3 | - | - |
| Greek | 4 | 3 | - | - | - | - |
| Civics | ½ | ½ | ½ | ½ | ½ | ½ |
| Modern Language I | 3 | 3 | 3 | 3 | 3 | 3 |
| Modern Language II | - | - | 4 | 2 | 4 | 2 |
| History | 2 | 2 | 2 | 2 | 2 | 2 |
| Geography | 2 | 2 | 2 | 2 | 2 | 2 |
| Mathematics | 3 | 5 | 3 | 5 | 5 | 5 |
| Physical Sciences | 2¼ | 3¼ | 2¼ | 4½ | 4½ | 4½ |
| Natural Sciences | - | - | - | - | - | 3 |
| Physical Education | 2 | 2 | 2 | 2 | 2 | 2 |
| Art (optional) | 2 | 2 | 2 | 2 | 2 | 2 |
| Music (optional) | 1 | 1 | 1 | 1 | 1 | 1 |
| Manual Arts (optional) | 1 | 1 | 1 | 1 | 1 | 1 |
| Total | 29 3/4 | 31 3/4 | 29 3/4 | 32 | 31 | 32 |

## Terminal Classes

| Subjects | Philosophy | Exp. Sciences | Elem. Math. |
|---|---|---|---|
| Philosophy | 9 | 5 | 3 |
| Letters | 1 | 1 | - |
| Civics | ½ | ½ | ½ |
| Modern Language I | 2 | 2 | 2 |
| Classical Language or Modern Language II | 1½ | 1½ | 1½ |
| History | 2 | 2 | 2 |
| Geography | 2 | 2 | 2 |
| Mathematics and Cosmography | 1½ | 4 | 9 |
| Physical Sciences | 2 | 5 | 6 |
| Natural Sciences | 2 | 4 | 2 |
| Physical Education | 2 | 2 | 2 |
| Art (optional) | 2 | 2 | 2 |
| Music (optional) | 1 | 1 | 1 |
| Manual Art for Girls (optional) | 1 | 1 | 1 |
| Total | 29½ | 33 | 34 |

Grading: To pass into next class, student must have a general yearly average of at least 10/20.

Diplomas awarded:

Brevet élémentaire (B.E.) at end of 4-year enseignement court.
The B.E. is being retained in Madagascar and is required to enter
a collège normal.

Brevet d'études du premier cycle (B.E.P.C.) after 4 years but in
the enseignement long section.

The above two Brevets give access to the medium range of the
Malagasy public service.

Examen probatoire de fin de première at end of 6 years.  Formerly
the first part of Baccalauréat.

Baccalauréat at end of terminal class.

Cours complémentaires:

Continuation classes after primary education for those failing examination
to lycées or collèges, and those with some secondary education lacking the
B.E. or B.E.P.C.  Short modern curriculum.  Cours complémentaires have
been rapidly increasing since 1957.


HIGHER EDUCATION

UNIVERSITY OF MADAGASCAR, Tananarive

Established in 1955 as Center for Advanced Studies (Institut des Hautes
Etudes); formally renamed November 1961.  Closely allied with Université
d'Aix-Marseille.

Entrance requirements:    Hold the Baccalauréat and pass the examen
                          probatoire.

Language of instruction: French.

Faculties (since October 1964):

                Letters and Human Sciences
                Law and Economic Sciences
                Medicine and Pharmacy
                Sciences

        Ecole Pratique des Hautes Etudes, devoted solely to Malagasy affairs.

        Department of International Affairs.

## Faculty of Law

Has special institute with correspondence courses and night classes to train administrative officers for the Madagascan civil service.

Department of Malagasy Jurisprudence created 1959.  Graduates of 4-year licence program can study an additional year to become magistrates.


## Faculty of Letters and Human Sciences

Places great emphasis on Madagascan culture and history, and also language.


## Faculty of Science

Prepares for certificates in General Mathematics and Physics (M.G.P.), Mathematics, Physics, Chemistry (M.P.C.), Physical, Chemical, and Natural Sciences (S.P.C.N.).

After one of these certificates, candidate may sit for entrance examination into the Ecole Nationale des Travaux Publics (public works), preparing engineers, or Ecole Supérieure d'Agronomie, preparing agricultural engineers (ingénieurs d'agronomie).

Candidates preparing for medicine must take the certificate in Physics, Chemistry, Biology (P.C.B.).


## INSTITUTE OF SCIENTIFIC RESEARCH OF MADAGASCAR (I.R.S.M.)

Departments in Pedology and Soil Sciences, Hydrology, Geography, Geophysics, Botany, Animal Biology, and Human Sciences.

Diplomas awarded:

Licence ès lettres,  Doctorat ès lettres

Licence ès sciences,  Doctorat ès sciences

Licence en droit,  Doctorat en droit

Doctorat en médecine


## INSTITUT NATIONAL SUPERIEUR DE RECHERCHE ET DE FORMATION PEDAGOGIQUE

Created January 1963.  Prepares for teaching both secondary and higher education.

4 categories:        (1)  Chargé d'enseignement or professeur de collège
                          d'enseignement général

                     (2)  Professeur licencié

                     (3)  Professeur certifié

                     (4)  Inspecteur de l'enseignement primaire

Language of instruction: French

Length of courses:   (1)  To become chargé d'enseignement, 2 years with
                          final examination.  Admittance with Baccalauréat.
                          After 3 months teaching in C.E.G. they take the
                          Certificat d'aptitude professionnelle des collèges
                          d'enseignement général (C.A.P.-C.E.G.).  Teach in
                          classes 6, 5, 4, 3.

                     (2)  To become professeur licencié, 1 year of profes-
                          sional training.  Must hold at least 1 licence
                          certificate in letters or sciences.  Teach in
                          lycées classes 2, 1, and terminal.

                     (3)  To become professeur certifié, 1 year of profes-
                          sional training.  Recruited from professeurs
                          licenciés with at least 2 years' professional
                          experience.  After 3 months pass the Certificat
                          d'aptitude au professorat de l'enseignement
                          secondaire (C.A.P.E.S.).  Teach in terminal class
                          of lycée and at university level.

                     (4)  To become inspecteur de l'enseignement primaire,
                          1 year leading to Certificat d'aptitude à l'inspec-
                          tion primaire (C.A.I.P.).  Recruited from chargés
                          d'enseignement and professeurs licenciés with at
                          least 5 years' service, and instituteurs bacheliers
                          with at least 10 years' service.  Teach in écoles
                          normales preparing instituteurs bacheliers.


ACADEMIE MALGACHE

Also known as Centre d'Etudes et d'Informations sur la Langue et la
Civilisation Malgaches.  Official institution attached to Ministry of
National Education.

2 sections:     Language:  particular study of Malagasy grammar.

                Civilization:  study of the arts, fauna, archaeology;
                               human, economic, and social sciences.

Administered by a Council chosen by the President of the Republic, from
specialists in each field.

HIGHER PROFESSIONAL SCHOOLS:

School of Medicine and Pharmacy, Befelatanana

State School of Midwifery

State School for Male and Female Nurses

School of Agriculture

School of Forestry

School of Animal Husbandry

School for Advisers in Farming

National Administration School

## VOCATIONAL AND TECHNICAL EDUCATION

School workshops attached to certain primary schools.

## APPRENTICESHIP CENTERS (Centres d'apprentissage)

Offer 3 to 4-year courses, curriculum corresponding in part to local needs. Many private centers, some administered provincially.

Courses in Housecrafts, General Mechanics, Automobile Mechanics, Garage Mechanics, Electricity, Carpentry, Printing, leading to Certificat d'aptitude professionnelle (C.A.P.).

Rural ateliers prepare village artisans.

## INDUSTRIAL AND COMMERCIAL TRAINING

Entrance requirements:  Pass concours d'entrée en sixième.

Industrial training given in:

(a) Collège d'enseignement technique:  4 years leading to Brevet industriel.

(b) Lycée technique industriel:  7 years leading to Baccalauréat technique.

Simplification of scientific programs:  no Chemistry; deletion of Optical Notions in 2nd year Physics; Resistance of Materials, Metallurgy, and Electricity in 3rd year.

Commercial training given in:

(a) Collège d'enseignement commercial:  4 years leading to Brevet commercial.

(b)  Lycée commercial:  7 years leading to Baccalauréat commercial.

Courses in Teaching, Management, Commerce, Printing, and other professions and trades.


TEACHER EDUCATION

COLLEGES NORMAUX

Entrance requirements:   Brevet élémentaire.

Length of course:        1 year of professional training.

Program:        Theoretical Pedagogy, Psychology, School Administration, Practical Teaching.

Certificate awarded:     Certificat d'aptitude à l'enseignement dans les écoles primaires (C.A.E.).  Holders teach in primary schools as instituteurs-adjoints.


ECOLE NORMALE D'INSTITUTEURS LE MYRE DE VILERS, Tananarive

Entrance requirements:   Baccalauréat.

Length of course:        1 year of professional training in Pedagogy, Psychology, etc.

Certificate awarded:     Certificat de fin d'études normales (C.F.E.N.). Holders teach in primary schools as instituteurs.


ECOLE NORMALE POUR LA FORMATION DES PROFESSEURS TECHNIQUES-ADJOINTS, Tananarive

Entrance requirements:   Baccalauréat technique.

Length of course:        2 years.  Professeurs techniques-adjoints teach in collèges d'enseignement technique.

At present some students are being recruited by special examination at the Brevet industriel level.  3-year course including 1 preparatory year.


INSTITUT NATIONAL SUPERIEUR DE RECHERCHE ET DE FORMATION PEDAGOGIQUE

Prepares teachers for secondary and higher education.  See Higher Education.

## ADULT EDUCATION

1959-60 adult literacy campaign in 150 centers.

Radio, motion picture and library facilities in constant use as adult
education.

1066

REPUBLIC OF SOUTH AFRICA
White, Coloured, Asiatic

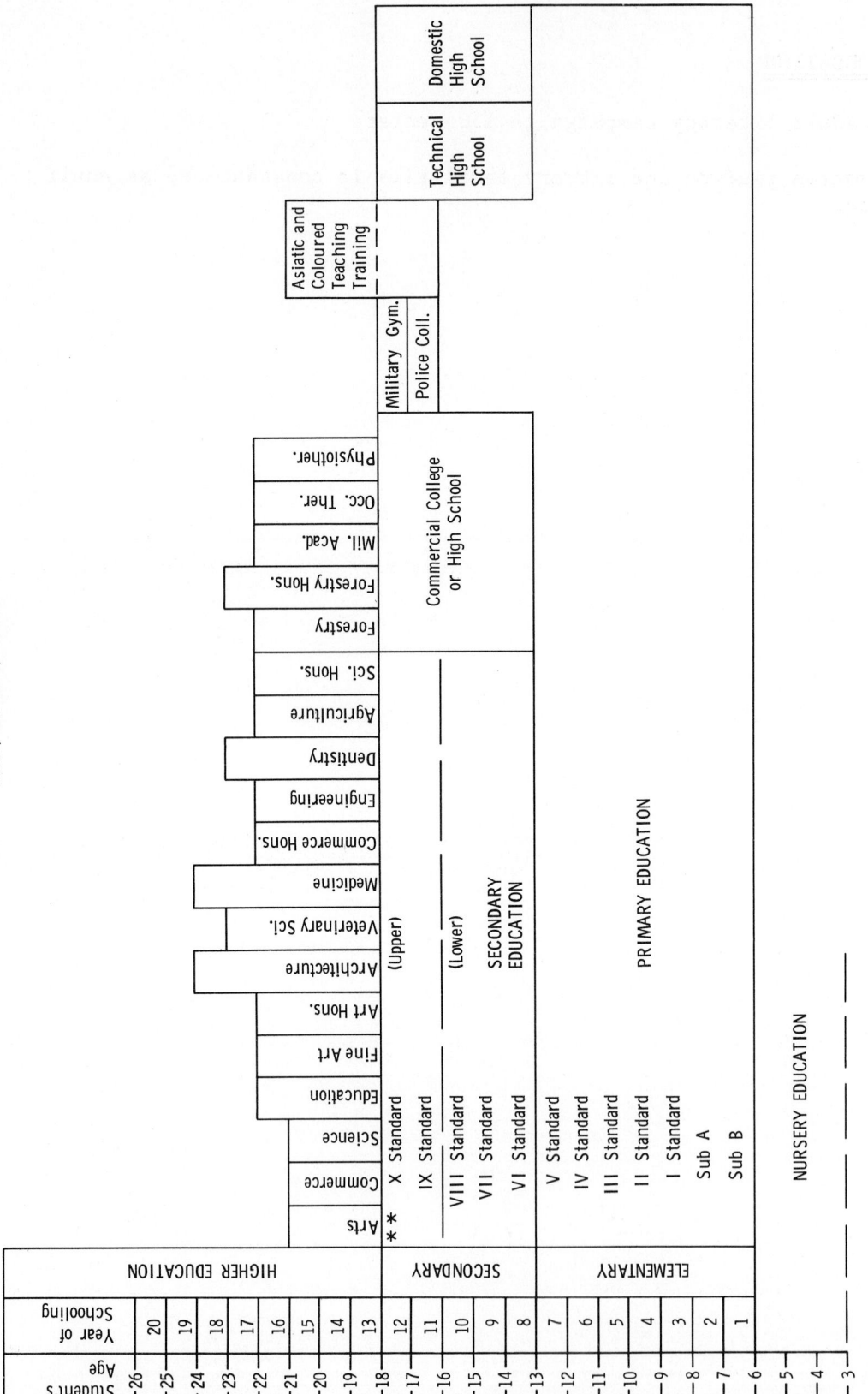

Compulsory Education: 7-16 years
School Year: February to November
Secondary grading: 100% with 33.3% passing

1067

REPUBLIC OF SOUTH AFRICA
(Bantu)

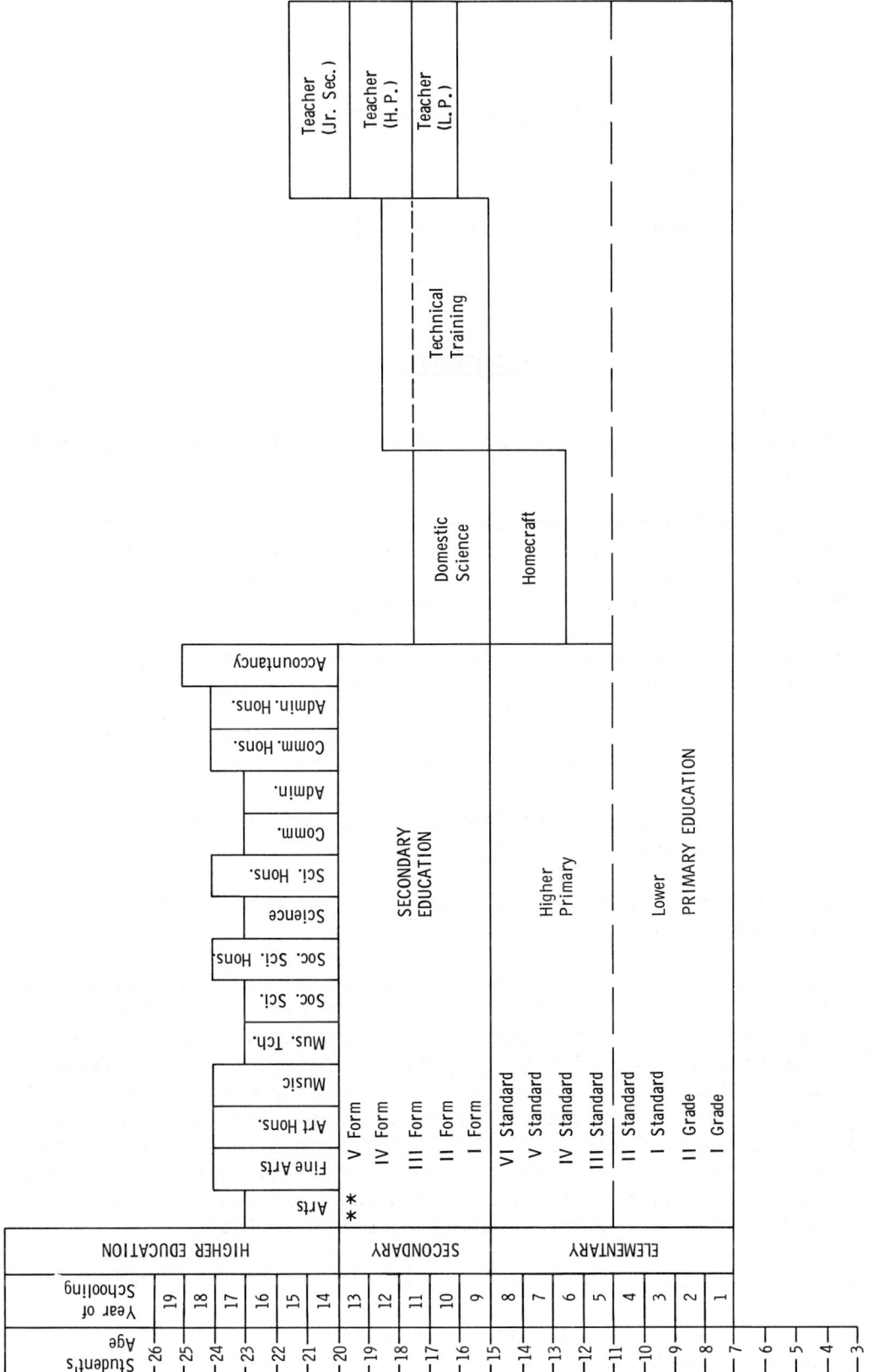

Compulsory Education: None

School Year: February to November

Secondary Grading: 100% with 33.3% passing

# REPUBLIC OF SOUTH AFRICA

Independence: May 31, 1910.
Withdrew from Commonwealth membership: May 15, 1961.

## BACKGROUND

Country composed of 4 provinces: Cape Province, Transvaal, Orange Free State, and Natal.

Country has one of the most complicated ethnic patterns. Indigenous negroid Africans belong to many tribes: Xhosa (29.4%), Zulu (25.7%), North (11%), South Sotho (10.7%), Tswana (8.2%), Tsonga (4.5%), Swazi (3.4%), Ndebele (2.5%), Venda (1.7%), others (2.9%).

Whites are divided between Afrikaners (descendants of the original Dutch, German and French Huguenot settlers) and Europeans of English descent.

Coloureds are a racial mixture of Hottentot, White and African blood, including Malayans (brought originally from the Dutch East Indies).

Asians include Hindus and Muslims from Indian subcontinents and the East Indies, and some Chinese.

60% of Africans live outside the African territories (Bantu reserves); many are migratory workers.

Each ethnic group has its own language. Afrikaners speak Afrikaans, derived from the Dutch of the 17th-century colonists, into which have been absorbed words and phrases from English, French, German, Portuguese, Malay, Bantu, Hottentot and other African languages. Coloureds speak Afrikaans; in Cape Town are bilingual. Asians in towns speak English as well as their own languages: Tamil, Gujerati, Hindi or Chinese. Africans speak their own tribal languages: Xhosa, Zulu, Pedi (Northern Sotho), Sesotho (Southern Sotho), Tswana, Tsonga, Swazi, Venda, and others. In white areas, they have learned the language of those for whom they worked. Before 1953, the 40% trained in missionary primary schools learned English.

In general, English is predominant in cities; Afrikaans in rural areas.

Settlers in 15th century found Bushmen, nomadic hunters of the western desert uplands, and Hottentots, in pastoral southern and eastern coastal areas. Bantu population at about the same time settled in North and East.

1488, Portuguese discovered Cape of Good Hope; 1497, Natal.  First
European settlement at Cape of Good Hope, 1652 for Dutch East India
Company.  Huguenots came in 1688.

1778, Dutch authorities set first boundaries between colonists and Africans.
1779-1812, 3 Kaffir wars.
1795, British occupied Cape.
1814, Netherlands ceded area to United Kingdom by Treaty of Vienna; first
British settlers, 1820.  Free Coloureds of Cape given same political and
legal status as Whites; 1834, slavery abolished.

1836, Dutch families started the Great Trek into the present Transvaal,
Orange Free State, and Natal.
British annexed Natal, 1843; extended rule over Kaffraria, 1847; Grigua-
land West, 1873, Bechuanaland, 1885; Zululand and Tongoland, 1887.  Orange
Free State annexed, 1848, but restored to independence, 1854.

Transvaal recognized as independent, 1852; annexed 1877, returned to
independence, 1881.  1881, Swaziland declared independent.  After a war
between the Boers and Basutos, Britain made Basutoland a British territory; 1884, it became a British Protectorate.

Cape Colony granted representative government, 1852; Natal made a Crown
Colony, 1856.  1872, Cape granted local self-government; Natal granted
the same, 1897.

1860, indentured Indians brought to Natal for work on sugar cane plantations; most remained.
1868, diamonds discovered along Orange and Vaal rivers; in the Kimberley
district, 1871.  This attracted a large number of foreigners, bringing
prosperity to Orange Free State and Cape.

1886, gold discovered on the Witwatersrand brought more foreigners,
making Transvaal, formerly the poorest of the states, the richest.

1899-1902, Anglo-Boer war arising from conflict between Boers (Dutch
farmers) and newcomers to Transvaal.  2 Boer republics relinquished independence by Treaty of Vereeniging, May 31, 1902; soon after, granted
self-government by British.

Between October 1908 and February 1909, leaders of Afrikaners (name replacing "Boers") and representatives from Natal and Cape drafted a
constitution for a united South Africa.  1909, British passed this constitution as South Africa Act:  effective May 31, 1910, as a union of 4
provinces.

1926, South Africa granted national autonomy, with equal status with Great
Britain, and with the right of free association  with the sovereign states
in the Commonwealth of Nations.

December 25, 1947, the Union formerly took possession of Prince Edward
Island; December 30, of Marion Island (1000 miles southeast of Cape Town).

Since 1948, the Nationalist Afrikaners political party has been in power,
enforcing through legislation racial separation (apartheid).

October 5, 1960, by referendum, republican form of government voted.
Became Republic, May 31, 1961.

March 15, 1961, at the Commonwealth Prime Ministers' Conference in London,
South Africa withdrew its application for continued Commonwealth membership; remained a member of the sterling area.

Prior to 1953, African education limited mostly to missionary schools,
some of which were government-aided.

Bantu Education Act, 1953:  native education placed under the Department
of Native Affairs (renamed Department of Bantu Administration and Development).  Schools transferred from missionary to government control;
revision of curricula.  By 1960, Bantu languages used as language of
instruction through Standard 6, eventually to extend through secondary and
higher education.  (The Department of Bantu Administration and Development
is one of the "State Departments."  There is also the Department of
Coloured Affairs.)

Control of teacher training taken over by government, 1956, making training
colleges instruments of legal separation.  Some institutions limited
enrollment to members of a particular language group.

Until 1959, higher education for non-whites under control of English-
language universities.  Many non-whites enrolled in Universities of South
Africa, Cape Town, Witwatersrand, Rhodes and Natal; each institution
having its own pattern of instruction for non-whites.  Cape Town and Witwatersrand taught non-Europeans with Europeans (withholding some social
privileges).  Natal admitted them to Non-European Medical School and
segregated classes at Durban Branch.  Rhodes supervised Fort Hare University College.

In 1959, extension of University Education Bill and University of Fort
Hare Transfer Bill:  barred all non-Europeans not registered by January 1,
1959, from entering any "white" institutions except Medical School at
Natal and correspondence classes at University of South Africa.  Fort Hare
taken over and new institutions for non-Europeans projected.

March 1960, first Bantu colleges opened.  Bantu language to be medium of
instruction (though not suited to many academic disciplines).  Fort Hare,
located at Ciskei, to be relocated in Umtata as Xhosa College; University
College of Zululand, Ngoya, for Zulus; University College of the North,
Turfloop, for Sotho, Tsonga and Venda Africans.

Western Cape University College for Coloureds, Belleville.  Indian College,
Durban.

## PRE-PRIMARY EDUCATION

Pre-primary education extends from approximately age 3 to 6, and is found in subsidized nursery schools for European pupils.


## PRIMARY EDUCATION

### W H I T E ,   C O L O U R E D ,   A N D   A S I A T I C

Sub A and B, Standards I-V.

Compulsory entry age:    7 years.
Permissive entry age:    5 years and 6 months.
(Coloured and Asiatic may not enter until 7 years old).

In all provinces, except Natal, Coloured and Asiatic children are grouped together for education.  The Cape has a special curriculum for them; the other provinces follow the white curriculum.  Asiatic children in Natal usually spend an extra year in the sub-standards learning English which is used as the medium of instruction.

Curriculum:           English, Afrikaans, Arithmetic, Social Studies
                      (History and Geography), Nature Study, Hygiene, Hand-
                      writing, Religious Instruction, Physical Instruction,
                      Music, Art, and Handicrafts.

Language of instruction: English or Afrikaans.

The student then goes directly to secondary education.


### B A N T U

#### LOWER PRIMARY SCHOOL

4 years:   Grade I (Sub-Standard A)
              II (Sub-Standard B)
           Standard I
           Standard II

Curriculum:           Reading, Writing, Arithmetic, official languages,
                      Religious Instruction, Handicrafts, Practical Hygiene,
                      Nature Study, Music, Environmental Study, Physical
                      Training.

Language of instruction: Mother tongue.

Promotion is automatic if attendance is satisfactory.

## TIMETABLE

| Subjects | Sub-Standards A and B (20-minute periods) | Std. I and II (30-min. per.) |
|---|---|---|
| Religion | 5 | 5 |
| Afrikaans | 5 | 9 |
| English | 5 | 9 |
| Home Language | 8 | 7 |
| Arithmetic | 7 | 7 |
| Environmental Studies | - | 3 |
| Health Education | 3 | 5 |
| Writing | 5 | 3 |
| Music | 2 | 3 |
| Arts and Crafts | - | 2 |
| Gardening | - | 2 |

## HIGHER PRIMARY SCHOOL

4 years after successful completion of lower primary.

Standards III-VI.

Curriculum:     More intensive study of lower primary subjects, plus the following:

Social Studies (History, Geography, Civics), Practical Knowledge of English and Afrikaans, Manual Training, Soil Conservation, Tree-planting, Gardening.

School hours:   27½ per week.

Assembly (50 min.), Religious Instruction (100), Afrikaans (205), English (205), Mother Tongue (180), Social Studies (150), Hygiene and Physical Training (100), Nature Study (60), Forestry and Soil Conservation - for boys (120), Arts and Crafts (120), Gardening (120).

Bantus must take external examination after completion of Standard VI. Pass in first or second class (50 average) required for admission to secondary school.  Average between 40 and 49 for third class pass giving School-Leaving Certificate.  (May not proceed to secondary school.)

## TIMETABLE
### (30-minute periods per week)

| Subjects | |
|---|---|
| Religion | 5 |
| Afrikaans | 8 |
| English | 8 |

| | |
|---|---|
| Home Language | 6 |
| Arithmetic | 7 |
| Social Studies | 5 |
| Health Education | 4 |
| Nature Study | 2 |

Practical Subjects
  (i)  Needlework (girls) Stds. III-VI
 (ii)  Homecraft (girls) Stds. V-VI
(iii) Gardening Stds. III-VI
 (iv)  Handwork: Arts and Crafts Stds. III-VI
  (v)  Handwork: Woodwork and Metalwork
               (Boys) Stds. V-VI         4 + 4

## SECONDARY EDUCATION

### W H I T E ,   C O L O U R E D ,   A N D   A S I A T I C

5-year program. Course is divided into 2 parts on a 3-2 year basis. After 3 years of successful schooling a Standard VIII Certificate (Junior Certificate) is generally obtained.

A 2-year post-Standard VIII course leads to the Senior Certificate, Secondary School-Leaving Certificate or Matriculation Certificate, which ends the secondary school course.

### JUNIOR SECONDARY LEVEL (Standard VIII)

#### Natal

Natal is the only province which has an external examination leading to the award of a Junior Certificate.

7 examination subjects are taken as follows:

    1 of the official languages on the higher grade
    The other official language on the higher or lower grade
    Arithmetic or General Mathematics
    4 additional subjects selected from an approved list.

The minimum mark required for a pass in any one subject is 33 1/3%.

In order to obtain the Junior Certificate, a candidate must pass in 1 of the official languages on the higher grade, pass in 4 other subjects and obtain a minimum aggregate of 40%.

Religious Education, Health Education, Music, Arts, Crafts, and Guidance are compulsory non-examination subjects.

Orange Free State

Internal examinations are conducted by schools for the Standard VIII
Certificate.  The requirements for a Junior Certificate are the same as
in Natal (see above).

Compulsory non-examination subjects include Religious Instruction,
Physical Education, Singing and Art Appreciation, Handicraft, and Guidance.


Cape of Good Hope

Internal examinations are conducted  with a view to certification at the
end of the 3-year junior secondary course.

The compulsory minimum for the 3rd year is:

    (a)  Religious Instruction, Physical Education, Music (as class
        subject).

    (b)  First official language, second official language, General
        Science, either General Mathematics or Social Studies.

    (c)  2 of the following:  General Mathematics, Social Studies, Art,
        Woodwork, Agriculture, Needlework, Domestic Science, Music (as
        examination subject), Typewriting, Bookkeeping and Commercial
        Arithmetic, a third language.

To pass the examination, a candidate must offer 6 subjects and pass in
both official languages, of which 1 must be on the higher grade, in 3
other subjects, and in the aggregate.

To pass in a subject a candidate must obtain 33 1/3% of the possible
number of marks, and to pass in the aggregate, 40% of the total number of
marks is required.


Transvaal

Certificates of attainment may be issued at the end of Standard VIII.
Differentiated education is applied, and pupils follow one of 3 courses at
the secondary school level.

In Standard VIII, pupils take their home language, the second language,
History, Arithmetic (or General Mathematics), General Science, Industrial
Arts or Home Economics, and a minimum of 2 optional subjects.

Conditions for school leavers to pass Standard VIII are as follows:

    (a)  University Entrance Course (A-Stream).
        Pupils must obtain a pass mark of 40% in their home language;
        a pass mark of 40% in each of 4 other subjects and an average
        percentage mark (inclusive of failing subjects) of 45%.

(b)  Standard X Course (B-Stream) and Standard VIII Course
     (C-Stream).
     Pupils must obtain a pass mark of 40% in their home language;
     a pass mark of 35% in each of 4 other subjects and an average
     percentage mark (inclusive of failing subjects) of 40%.

Compulsory non-examination subjects include Religious Instruction,
Physical Education, Singing and Art Appreciation, Handicrafts, and Guidance.


## SENIOR SECONDARY LEVEL

6 subjects are selected for the Cape Senior Certificate, the Orange Free
State (O.F.S.) School-Leaving Certificate and the Transvaal Secondary
School Certificate.

These subjects include 1 of the official languages on the higher grade,
the other official language on the higher or lower grade and any 4 other
approved subjects.  In the Cape, a science subject and 3 other subjects
are prescribed in addition to the 2 official languages.

The requirements for a pass are generally as follows:

(a)  In individual subjects 33 1/3%.

(b)  In the examination as a whole:

      (i)  a pass in 1 of the official languages on the higher grade.
     (ii)  a pass in 4 other subjects.
    (iii)  a minimum aggregate of 40%.

For the Cape Senior Certificate, a candidate must pass in 5 major subjects,
including the 2 official languages, one of which must be on the higher
grade.  In addition, a pass mark of 40% is required in this official
language.

The Cape Senior Certificate, the Natal Senior Certificate and the O.F.S.
School-Leaving Certificate do not admit holders to a degree course at a
university.  However, if a prescribed combination of subjects is taken,
full exemption from the Matriculation examination may be granted by the
Joint Matriculation Board, and this qualifies candidates for admission to
a university.

In the Transvaal, 2 separate examinations are written at the end of
Standard X, the Transvaal Secondary School Certificate examination which
does not permit holders to a degree course at a university and the Transvaal University Entrance Certificate which is accepted by the Joint
Matriculation Board for this purpose.


## Transvaal University Entrance Certificate

Not less than 6 and not more than 7 subjects are selected, at least 1 subject being chosen from each of the following 4 groups of subjects:

Group I:    English A
            Afrikaans A

    II:     English or Afrikaans, Latin, French, German, Hebrew

    III:    Physical Science, Biology, Mathematics

    IV:     History, Geography, Xhosa, Zulu, Northern Sotho, Southern
            Sotho, Tswana, Venda; or a subject from Group II; or Mathematics.

To pass the examination, a candidate must:

(a)  Pass in 1 subject in each of the groups mentioned above,
     obtaining at least 40% in each.

(b)  Pass in at least 1 other approved subject provided that if the
     candidate has not offered either Mathematics or German or Latin
     or French or Hebrew under (a) above, this 5th subject must be
     either 1 of the above mentioned subjects or Xhosa or Zulu or
     Northern Sotho or Southern Sotho or Tswana or Venda.

(c)  Obtain an aggregate of at least 44.4%.


## Natal Senior Certificate

(a)  6-subject Senior Certificate.

   (i)    English A or Afrikaans A
  (ii)    Afrikaans or English A or B grade (different language
          from above)
 (iii)    4 of the following:  (not chosen above)

| | |
|---|---|
| English A | Afrikaans A |
| English B | Afrikaans B |
| History | Geography |
| Latin | Mathematics |
| Greek | Additional Math. |
| French | Physical Science |
| German | Physics |
| Hebrew | Chemistry |
| Biology | Botany |
| Agriculture | Health Education |
| Art | Housecraft |
| Biblical Studies | Music |
| Bookkeeping and | Shorthand and |
|   Commercial Arithmetic |   Typewriting |
| General Science | Typewriting and |
| Geometrical Drawing |   Office Routine |
| Handicrafts | Zulu B |

(b)  7-subject Senior Certificate.

   (i)    English A or Afrikaans A

(ii)   Afrikaans or English A or B (different language from above)
(iii)  5 of the following:   (not chosen above)

| | |
|---|---|
| English A | History |
| Afrikaans A | Geography |
| English B | Mathematics |
| Afrikaans B | Additional Math. |
| Latin | Physical Science |
| Greek | Physics |
| French | Chemistry |
| German | Biology |
| Hebrew | Botany |

Oral tests in Afrikaans B, English B, French, German, and Zulu B form part of the examination.

Marks are assigned according to the following:

| | |
|---|---|
| English A or Afrikaans A | 400 |
| All other subjects | 300 |

provided that if Additional Mathematics is taken with Mathematics, the combined subject contains 400 marks.

The approximate standards for a pass and classification are:

(a)   In individual subjects, a minimum of 33 1/3%.

(b)   In the examination as a whole, passes in either English A or Afrikaans A, and 4 other subjects and a minimum aggregate as below:

| | 6 subjects | 7 subjects |
|---|---|---|
| Pass with Merit | 1,140 | 1,250 |
| Pass | 760 | 850 |

A candidate who takes 2 languages on the A grade and fails in 1 of them will be considered to have passed in that language on the B grade if he obtains at least 30% of the marks in that subject.

In the 7-subject examination, if a candidate obtains less than 25% of the maximum marks in 1 or more subjects, the marks in the subject in which the lowest marks are obtained will be excluded from the aggregate.

Natal Senior Certificate with Matriculation Exemption

Pass marks 860 (6 subjects) or 950 (7 subjects).

A candidate must obtain at least 40% in each of 4 subjects in each of the following groups:

(i)   English A or Afrikaans A
(ii)  The second official language or Latin or Greek or French or German or Hebrew or Zulu A or Southern Sotho A.

       (iii)   A Science subject or Mathematics
       (iv)   A subject chosen from (ii) not already taken, or
                Mathematics if not taken under (iii), or History or
                Geography

and have _either_ (i) included among those 4 subjects Mathematics or Latin
or French or Greek or German _or_ (ii) taken as a 5th subject, at least 1
of the subjects Mathematics, Latin, French, Greek, or German, and have
obtained not less than 33 1/3% of the total marks therein;

and (from December 1963) have passed _either_ in 2 languages plus Mathematics
_or_ 3 languages.

Candidates who obtain a minimum aggregate of 1140 marks (6 subjects) or
1250 marks (7 subjects) will be designated as having passed with merit.
All other successful candidates will be classed as passed.

## B A N T U

Primary and secondary work originally combined.  Present policy is separate
schools with the primary program ending at Standard VI.  Limited number of
high schools leading to Standard X with most schools leading to new Junior
Certificate course--3 years after Standard VI.

Form I (1st year) - Preparatory year leading to:

    (a)   Junior Secondary work, commencing in Form II

    (b)   Bantu lower teachers' course

Pupils wishing to take _Senior Certificate (Standard X)_ must conform to
regulations of Joint Matriculation Board if matriculation exemption is
desired.

5-year secondary course.

First 3 years are devoted to the Junior Certificate course (Forms I-III);
the next 2 years (Forms IV and V) end with the _Matriculation_ or _Senior
Certificate_.

## Junior Certificate Course (Forms I-III)

Provide for training in an academic direction, or in a more practical
direction.

## Form I:

Curriculum includes the following:

(a) Compulsory--not for examination purposes, Religious Instruction, Physical Training, Music and Singing.

(b) Compulsory--for examination purposes, Bantu Language, English, Afrikaans, Arithmetic, General Science, Social Studies.

(c) Optional--one of the following:  Agriculture, Arts and Crafts, Homecraft, Woodwork.

## Forms II and III:

General Junior Certificate Course.

(a) Compulsory--not for examination purposes, Religious Education, Physical Education, Music and Singing.

(b) Compulsory--for examination purposes, Bantu Language, Afrikaans, English, Social Studies, Arithmetic or Mathematics or General Mathematics, 2 of the following:  Latin or German or other approved language, Mathematics or Arithmetic, a Natural Science (General Science, Physical Science or Biology), Agriculture, Woodwork, Arts and Crafts, Homecraft.

Commercial and Clerical Junior Certificate Course.

(a) Compulsory--not for examination purposes, Religious Instruction, Physical Education, Singing and Music.

(b) Compulsory--for examination purposes, Bantu Language, Afrikaans, English, 4 of the following:  Bookkeeping, Commerce, Type-writing, Shorthand, Commercial Arithmetic, a Natural Science (General Science, Physical Science, or Biology), Social Studies, Mathematics.

## Forms IV and V:

Two-Year Matriculation Course.

Preparing for Senior Certificate.

Makes provision for educational streams so that pupils may choose an academic course in preparation for the university or one with an occupational bent, e.g. Commerce.  Schools may choose to follow the syllabus of the Joint Matriculation Board or the Departments of Education, Arts and Science.

After passing Form I differentiation begins (Academic, commercial or vocational).

After passiong Form III Junior Certificate is issued.  Then student may proceed to academic or commercial Senior Certificate course. For Junior Certificate, 40 required for pass in the vernacular and 33 1/3% in other subjects.  An aggregate of at least 40 and pass in at least 5 subjects including vernacular and one official language is required for pass in whole examination.

## JONGELIZWE COLLEGE

Founded in 1960 for sons of chiefs in the Transkei and Ciskei. Preliminary 3-year post-Standard VI course. Those who obtain 50 aggregate in final examination may proceed to further 2-year course taking the syllabus of the Joint Matriculation Board in addition to Bantu Administration, Traditional and Common Law, Statutory Laws in South Africa and adjoining countries, policies of other African territories, and Commercial Arithmetic.

A 2-year diploma course with Matriculation as entrance qualification is also offered.

## NATIONAL CERTIFICATES

May be taken by all races.

## National Standard VI Certificate

A candidate must pass in 4 subjects selected from:

| | |
|---|---|
| Group I | Afrikaans A or English A |
| Group II | Afrikaans A or B or English A or B (different language from I) |
| Group III | 2 of the following: Arithmetic, Geography, History, Mathematics, Physical Science |

Non-examination subjects for full-time students:

    (i)   Religious Instruction

  (ii)   Singing and Appreciation of Music or Drama and Speech Training

(iii)   Physical Education

Any candidate obtaining an aggregate of at least 60% in the full examination is awarded a first-class certificate, provided he qualifies for this certificate at one and same examination.

## National Standard VII Certificate

A candidate must pass in 5 subjects selected from:

| | |
|---|---|
| Group I | Afrikaans A or English A |
| Group II | Afrikaans A or B or English A or B (different language from I) |

Group III          3 of the following:  Arithmetic, Civics, Commerce,
                    French, Geography, German, History, Mathematics,
                    Physical Science, Physiology and Hygiene, Portuguese

Non-examination subjects for full-time students:

   (i)   Religious Instruction

  (ii)   Singing and the Appreciation of Music or Drama and Speech
       Training

 (iii)   Physical Education

Bookkeeping and Commerce are compulsory for full-time students at
commercial vocational schools.

The maximum number of languages that may be taken is 3.

Any candidate obtaining an aggregate of at least 60% in the full examination is awarded a first-class certificate, provided he qualifies for
this certificate at one and same examination.

## National Junior Certificate (Standard VIII)

A candidate must pass in 6 subjects selected from:

Group I          Afrikaans A or English A

Group II         Afrikaans A or B or English A or B (different
                 language from I)

Group III        4 of the following:

   (a)   French, German, Latin, Portuguese

   (b)   Agricultural Science, Biology, Botany, Chemistry,
       Physical Science, Physiology and Hygiene, Physics

   (c)   Shorthand, Snelskrif (Afrikaans Shorthand),
       Bookkeeping, Civics, Commerce, Commercial Arith-
       metic, Geography, History, Mathematics, Type-
       writing

Non-examination subjects for full-time students:

   (i)   Religious Instruction

  (ii)   Singing and Appreciation of Music or Drama and Speech
       Training

 (iii)   Physical Education

Full-time students at commercial vocational schools must take at least
3 commercial subjects.

The maximum number of languages that may be taken is 4.

The maximum number of subjects that may be taken under Group III (b) is 2.

A 5-subject certificate is awarded to a candidate who sits at the same examination for 6 or 7 subjects and who obtains at least 40% in each of 4 subjects, at least 35% in a fifth subject, and a grand total of at least 240 marks in the 6 or 7 subjects, provided that both official languages are included in the 5 subjects. A candidate who passes in 5 subjects but who does not qualify for the certificate or who sits for fewer than 6 subjects, must eventually pass in 6 subjects to qualify for the certificate.

Any candidate obtaining an aggregate of at least 60% in the full examination is awarded a first-class certificate, provided he qualifies for this certificate at one and the same examination.


National Senior Certificate (Standard X)

The National Senior Certificate is awarded to a candidate who has satisfied the requirements for any of the following groups:

        Commercial and General Group
        Matriculation Exemption Group
        Art Group

A.    National Senior Certificate (Commercial and General Group) is awarded to a candidate who has passed in at least 6 subjects, selected as follows:

Group I        Afrikaans A or English A

Group II       Afrikaans A or B or English A or B (not taken under I)

Group III      4 of the following:

    (a)  French, German, Latin, Portuguese, Northern Sotho-Lower, Southern Sotho-Lower, Shona-Lower, Tsonga-Lower, Tswana-Lower, Venda-Lower, Xhosa-Lower, Zulu-Lower

    (b)  Biology, Botany, Chemistry, Geology, Physical Science, Physics

    (c)  Shorthand, Snelskrif, Bookkeeping, Commerce, Economics, Mercantile Law, Typewriting

    (d)  Agricultural Science, Commercial Arithmetic, Common Law, Criminal Procedure, Geography, History, Introduction to Criminology and Ethnology, Mathematics, Physiology and Hygiene, Statute Law

Non-examination subjects for full-time students:

    (i)  Religious Instruction

(ii)   Singing and the Appreciation of Music or Drama and Speech
        Training

(iii)  Physical Education

The maximum number of languages that may be taken is 4.

The maximum number of subjects that may be taken under Group III (b)
is 2.

Full-time students at commercial vocational schools must take at
least 3 commercial vocational subjects under Group III (c).

The National Senior Certificate, Commercial and General Group, is
not recognized by the Joint Matriculation Board for purposes of
exemption from the Matriculation examination and will not admit
holders to a degree course at a South African university.

The National Senior Certificate, Commercial and General Group, is
accepted by the Department for purposes of admission to its teachers'
courses.

Any candidate obtaining an aggregate of at least 60% in the full
examination is awarded a first-class certificate, provided he qualifies for this certificate at one and the same examination.

B.   National Senior Certificate (Matriculation Exemption Group) is not
     accepted by the Joint Matriculation Board for exemption from the
     Matriculation examination and does not admit holders to a degree
     course at a South African university.  However, if a prescribed
     combination of subjects is taken, exemption may be obtained from the
     Matriculation examination and this qualifies the candidate for
     admission to a university.

     6 or 7 subjects from the following:

     Group I       Afrikaans A or English A

     Group II      1 of the following:  Biology, Botany, Chemistry,
                   Geology, Mathematics, Physical Science, Physics

     Group III     1 of the following:  Biology, Botany, Chemistry,
                   Geology, Mathematics, Physical Science, Physics

     Group IV      1 of the following:  Subject not taken from Group II,
                   Economics, Geography, History, Mathematics, Northern
                   Sotho-Lower, Southern Sotho-Lower, Shona Lower,
                   Tsonga-Lower, Tswana-Lower, Venda-Lower, Xhosa-Lower,
                   Zulu-Lower

     Group V       2 of the following:

                   (a)  Subjects not already taken under Groups II, III
                        and IV

(b)  Afrikaans Shorthand, English Shorthand, Bookkeeping, Commerce, Mercantile Law, Typewriting

(c)  Agricultural Science, Commercial Arithmetic,
Common Law, Criminal Procedure, Introduction to
Criminology and to Ethnology, Physiology and
Hygiene, Statute Law

(d)  Applied Mechanics, Building Construction and
Drawing, Electronics, Electrotechnics, Electrical
Construction and Drawing, Heat Engines, Machine
Construction and Drawing, Mining, Navigation,
Seamanship, Surveying, Telegraphy, Telephony

(e)  Armature Winding, Motor Body Repairing, Motor
Electricians, Bespoke Tailoring, Blacksmithing,
Boatbuilding, Boilermaking and Structural Steelwork, Bricklaying, Cabinetmaking, Carpentry and
Joinery, Drawing for Plumbers, Electricians,
Fitting Turning and Machining, Furniture Polish-
ing, Masonry, Motor Mechanics, Moulding, Painting
and Decorating, Patternmaking, Plastering, Radio-
tricians, Refrigeration, Sheetmetalwork, Sign-
writing, Upholstering, Welding, Woodcarving or
any other approved trade

Non-examination subjects for full-time students:

(i)  Religious Instruction

(ii)  Singing and the Appreciation of Music or Drama and Speech
Training

(iii)  Physical Education

Both official languages must be selected.

At least 1 of the following must be selected:  French, German, Latin,
a Bantu Language, Mathematics.

Not more than 4 languages may be taken.

Full-time students at commercial vocational schools must take at
least 3 commercial vocational subjects.


The Joint Matriculation Board Examination

Maximum number of marks assigned to each subject of the examination:

English (higher grade), Afrikaans (higher grade), Nederlands (higher
grade), German (higher grade), Bantu Languages (higher grade), and
Mathematics                                                    each 400

English (lower grade), Afrikaans (lower grade), Nederlands (lower
grade), Latin, Greek, French, German (lower grade), Portuguese,
Hebrew, Bantu Languages (lower grade), other languages, History,
Geography, Physical Science, Physics, Chemistry, Biology, Botany,
Zoology, and Geology                                              each 350

All other subjects                                                each 300

The following symbols are employed on the certificate to indicate the
standard attained:

A - 80% and over
B - 70% to 79%
C - 60% to 69%
D - 50% to 59%
E - 40% to 49%
F - 33 1/3% to 39%

A pass in any individual subject is a minimum of 33 1/3%.

## School-Leaving Certificate

A School-Leaving Certificate is awarded to a candidate who has taken no
fewer than 6 and not more than 7 subjects selected from Sections A and B
of the subjects prescribed for the Matriculation Certificate (see following section) at one examination, and who has passed in at least 5 subjects,
2 of which must be languages, one being English or Afrikaans on the higher
grade:

Provided that a candidate whose home language is a Bantu language may substitute a recognized Bantu language (higher grade)for Afrikaans (higher
grade) or English (higher grade), and a candidate whose home language is
German may substitute German (higher grade) for Afrikaans (higher grade)
or English (higher grade).

A candidate who enters for 6 or 7 subjects and passes in 5, obtaining the
minimum aggregate, but fails in 1 compulsory subject, may obtain the
School-Leaving Certificate by gaining, at any subsequent examination, not
less than 1/3 of the maximum marks in the subject in which he failed, or
in any other subject which satisfied the same compulsory requirement.
The class of certificate is determined by the original aggregate.

No candidate may take more than 4 languages.

The approximate standards for a pass and for classification are:
(a)  In individual subjects:  a minimum of 33 1/3%.
(b)  In the examination as a whole:  passes in each of 5 subjects,
     and a minimum aggregate as below:

|  | candidates taking | |
|---|---|---|
|  | 6 subjects | 7 subjects |
| For a pass in Class III | 800 | 800 |

|                        |      |      |
|------------------------|------|------|
| For a pass in Class II | 1040 | 1120 |
| For a pass in Class I  | 1350 | 1450 |

If a candidate takes 7 subjects and obtains less than 25% of the maximum marks in one or more of these subjects, the marks in the subject in which the candidate obtains the lowest number of marks shall be excluded from the candidate's aggregate. In the case of a candidate taking 6 subjects, all marks shall be included in the aggregate.

If a school-leaving candidate takes 2 of the subjects English (higher grade), Afrikaans (higher grade), Nederlands (higher grade), German (higher grade) at one and the same examination and obtains at least 40% in 1 of these subjects, he shall be considered to have passed with 40% on the lower grade in the other if his mark falls between 30 and 40%.

A candidate who enters for the Matriculation examination and obtains the prescribed aggregate for the School-Leaving Certificate but fails to obtain the Matriculation standard in one or more of the compulsory subjects or the prescribed aggregate for the Matriculation Certificate, may be awarded a School-Leaving Certificate.

A candidate who enters for 6 or 7 subjects and obtains at least 33 1/3% in 5 subjects including at least one of the prescribed languages, and who also obtains the minimum aggregate for a School-Leaving Certificate, may qualify for a School-Leaving Certificate by gaining at any subsequent examination not less than 33 1/3% of the maximum marks in the compulsory subject(s) in which he failed to obtain at least 33 1/3%, or in any other subject(s) which satisfy the same requirements.

## Matriculation Certificate

A candidate selects his subjects from the following list of subjects approved for the examination:

Section A:

    (1) Afrikaans (higher grade), English (higher grade).

    (2) Afrikaans (higher or lower grade), English (higher or lower grade), Nederlands (higher or lower grade), German (higher or lower grade), all Bantu languages (higher grade) in which the Board conducts an examination (Xhosa, Zulu, Northern Sotho, Southern Sotho, Tswana, Tsonga, and Venda), Latin, Greek, French, Hebrew, Portuguese, Italian.

    (3) Mathematics, Physics, Chemistry, Physical Science, Biology, Botany, Zoology, Geology.

    (4) Geography, History, Bantu languages (lower grade).

Section B:

> Agriculture, Housecraft and Hygiene, Bookkeeping, Bookkeeping and
> Commercial Arithmetic, Typewriting, Shorthand and Typewriting,
> Additional Mathematics, Mechanics, Art, Music.

(a)  A Matriculation Certificate is awarded to a candidate who has
taken 6 or 7 subjects, including not more than 4 languages.
The candidate must pass in at least 5 subjects, obtain the
minimum aggregate prescribed below, and

    (1)  have obtained a minimum of 40% in each of 4 subjects from
section A(1), at least 1 from section A(2), at least 1
from section A(3), and at least 1 from section A(4) or
another subject from sections A(1) or A(2) or Mathematics;

    (2)  have included among the subjects passed _either_ 2 languages
and Mathematics _or_ 3 languages, 1 of which is French or
German or Greek or Latin or a Bantu language;

    (3)  have included not more than 1 Bantu language in the 4 sub-
jects in which 40% must be obtained, and

    (4)  not have taken the same language on both higher and lower
grade.

(b)  A candidate whose home language is a Bantu language may take a
recognized Bantu language (higher grade), that subject being
considered as added to the subjects in section A(1) for this
purpose.  Such a candidate must also pass both Afrikaans (higher
or lower grade) and English (higher or lower grade).

(c)  A candidate whose home language is German may take German (higher
grade), that subject being counted as added to the subjects in
section A(1) for this purpose.  Such a candidate also enters
both Afrikaans and English, 1 of which shall be on the higher
grade, and passes in both Afrikaans and English on at least the
lower grade.

(d)  A candidate who obtains a School-Leaving Certificate with the
prescribed minimum aggregate for the Matriculation Certificate
but fails to obtain 40% in one or more of the subjects, may
complete the requirements for a Matriculation Certificate at a
subsequent examination, and if he is successful in completing
these requirements, he shall be awarded the Matriculation Certificate of the same class as his original School-Leaving Certificate.

(e)  If a matriculation candidate takes 2 of the subjects Afrikaans
(higher grade), English (higher grade), Nederlands (higher grade),
German (higher grade), and a recognized Bantu language (higher
grade), at one and the same examination, and obtains at least 40%
in 1 of these subjects, he shall be considered to have passed
with 40% in the lower grade in the other if his mark falls
between 30 and 40%.

(f)   A candidate who enters for 6 or 7 subjects, and obtains at
      least 33 1/3% in 5 subjects, including at least 1 subject from
      section A(1) and A(2) and who also obtains the minimum aggre-
      gate for a Matriculation Certificate, may qualify for the
      Matriculation Certificate, by obtaining at any subsequent
      examination or examinations not less than 40% of the maximum
      marks in the compulsory subject(s) in which he failed to obtain
      at least 40%, or in any other subjects which satisfy the same
      requirements.

The approximate standard for a pass in the examination as a whole is:

|  | candidates taking | |
|---|---|---|
|  | 6 subjects | 7 subjects |
| For a pass in Class III | 1000 | 1000 |
| For a pass in Class II | 1040 | 1120 |
| For a pass in Class I | 1350 | 1450 |

In the case of a candidate taking 7 subjects and obtaining less than 25%
of the maximum marks in one or more of these subjects, the marks in that
subject in which the candidate obtained the lowest number of marks is
excluded from the candidate's aggregate.  In the case of a candidate taking 6 subjects all marks are included in the aggregate.

Full exemption on the grounds of the National Senior Certificate of the
Department of Education, Arts and Science, and the Senior Certificate
of the Department of Bantu Education.

The Board may grant a certificate of full exemption to:

A bona-fide part-time candidate who obtained a minimum of 45% of the
aggregate for the National Senior Certificate, or the Senior Certificate of the Department of Bantu Education which included a minimum
of 6 approved subjects selected in accordance with the grouping requirements of the Board for the Matriculation Certificate, if, at
the first examination, he obtained a minimum of 40% in each of the
remaining subjects:  provided that if at the 2 examinations together,
he passed with a minimum of 40% in each of 5 approved subjects and
failed 1 subject at the second examination, but obtained not less
than 25% of the maximum possible marks, he may complete the examination conducted, in the case of the National Senior Certificate, by
the Department of Education, Arts and Science or by the Board and,
in the case of the Senior Certificate of the Department of Bantu
Education, by the Department of Bantu Education or by the Board:
provided further that a National Senior Certificate or a Senior Certificate of the Department of Bantu Education is not considered for the
purpose of exemption if the holder has been granted exemption from
any subject(s) by reason of success at any other examination.

A full-time or part-time candidate who obtained a minimum of 45% of
the aggregate for the National Senior Certificate or the Senior

Certificate of the Department of Bantu Education and if at one and the same examination for the certificate he

(a)    wrote a minimum of 6 approved subjects;

(b)    obtained at least 40% in each of the 4 compulsory subjects;

(c)    obtained at least 35% in 1 of the remaining subjects; and

(d)    passed in either Mathematics or a 3rd language.

A candidate who obtained a minimum of 45% of the aggregate for the National Senior Certificate or the Senior Certificate of the Department of Bantu Education by passing all the subjects at one and the same examination, but did not obtain 40% in 1 or more of the compulsory subjects or did not complete the requirements with regard to Mathematics or a 3rd language, if at a subsequent examination(s) he obtained at least 40% in any subject(s) from the required section(s) including Mathematics or a 3rd language.

The Board may issue a certificate of full exemption to any candidate who has, after examination by the department concerned or by a school approved by the Board on the recommendation of such department, obtained 1 of the following South African school certificates with the minimum aggregate indicated:

The Transvaal University Entrance Certificate with 1300 marks obtained in or after 1961.

The Cape Senior Certificate with 860 marks obtained in or after 1923.

The O.F.S. School-Leaving Certificate with 900 marks obtained in or after 1939, or

The Natal Senior Certificate with 860 marks obtained in or after 1953.

The Board may grant a certificate of full exemption from the Matriculation examination to an applicant from any country other than the Republic of South Africa or South-West Africa if he is in possession of a certificate which entitles the holder to unconditional admission as a candidate for an approved degree or diploma at an approved university or other recognized institution in the country of origin, and if the subjects in which he passed at the recognized examination include 4 subjects, 1 from each of the 4 sections prescribed for the Matriculation Certificate; and if in each of these 4 subjects the applicant has attained a standard which the Board deems equivalent to the Matriculation standard; and if the applicant has passed in either Mathematics or a 3rd language.

## Mathematics curriculum

Arithmetic:

Knowledge of the difference between the following types of numbers: integers, fractions, rational and irrational numbers, real numbers.

Representation of real numbers by points on a straight line.  The
four fundamental operations.
Problems in connection with lengths, areas and volumes in the cases
of the triangle, parallelogram, trapezium, circle, cylinder, prism,
pyramid, cone and sphere.
Simple and compound interest with simple applications using formulae
and calculations involving logarithms.

Algebra:

Algebraic notation.  The four fundamental processes.  Subtraction and
division as inverse processes of addition and multiplication respectively.
Inadmissibility of division by zero.  Use of brackets.  Bracket and
sign rules.  Meaning of the expression term, factor, coefficient.
The functional concept.  Independent and dependent variables.  Linear
quadratic and cubic expressions in one variable.  Polynomial and
degree of a polynomial in one variable.  Homogeneous expressions in
two variables.  Functional notation.  Evaluation of functions for
numerical values of the variables.  The use of rectangular axes to
visualize the change of a function.  Elementary deductions from
graphs, including inequalities.
Resolution into factors in simple cases.  Identities and their properties.
The Remainder theorem and application.  Equations, roots of equations.
Elimination and application to solving simple simultaneous equations
in 2 or 3 unknowns.  Simultaneous equations in 2 unkowns, 1 of 1st
degree and 1 of 2nd degree.  Expressing in a given functional relation
any one quantity in terms of the remaining quantities.  Like and unlike root-forms, and reduction to like forms.
Fundamental properties of logarithms.  Use of log and anti-log tables.
Simple ratio and proportion.
The n-th term and sum to n terms of the Arithmetic and Geometric
progression.  Arithmetic and Geometric mean of 2 numbers.

Synthetic Geometry:

The following concepts and results are introduced intuitively:
Point, straight line, angles, right angle, straight angle, revolution,
degree, acute angle, obtuse angle, reflex angle, adjacent angles,
supplementary and complementary angles, equality of lines and angles,
parallel lines, triangle, circle.

Trigonometry:

Definitions of the trigonometrical ratios  for an acute angle.  Elementary relations between them.  4-figure tables of the ratios and
their logarithms.  Solution of right-angled triangles.
Rectangular cartesian coordinates. Definitions of the trigonometric
functions for angles between $0^{\cup}$ and $360^{\circ}$.  Elementary relations
between them.  Simple identities using the relationships connecting
the trigonometrical functions.  Solution of simple trigonometric

equations.  Addition formulae for sine and cosine, where proofs are
restricted to the cases when the angles are acute.

Analytical Geometry:

Distance between 2 points whose coordinates are given.  Midpoint of
join of 2 points.  Gradient of a straight line.  Conditions that 2
lines should be parallel or perpendicular.  Equation of a straight
line

(a)  through a given point on the y-axis with given gradient;

(b)  through any given point with given gradient;

(c)  through 2 given points.

## HIGHER EDUCATION

### W H I T E S

#### English Media

Rhodes University
University of Natal
University of the Witwatersrand
University of Cape Town

#### Afrikaans Media

The Potchefstroom University for Christian Higher Education
University of the Orange Free State
University of Stellenbosch
University of Pretoria

#### English and Afrikaans Media

University of Port Elizabeth

### C O L O U R E D S

University College of the Western Cape

### B A N T U S

University College of the North
University College of Zululand
University College of Fort Hare

### I N D I A N S

University College for Indians

N O N - R A C I A L   C O R R E S P O N D E N C E
E X T E R N A L   D E G R E E - A W A R D I N G   U N I V E R S I T Y

University of South Africa

\*   \*   \*

RHODES UNIVERSITY, Grahamstown

Founded in 1904 as a university college.  Became constituent college of
University of South Africa in 1918.  Became Rhodes University in 1949.
Division opened in Port Elizabeth in 1959.

General entrance requirements:    Matriculation Certificate of the Joint
                                  Matriculation Board of the University of
                                  South Africa, or the Board's Certificate
                                  of Full Exemption from the Matriculation
                                  examination.

Faculties:

        Arts                    Divinity
        Science                 Law
        Education               Social Science
        Commerce

Language of instruction:        English

Degrees awarded:

| Faculty | Degree | Duration of Course (years) |
|---------|--------|----------------------------|
| Arts | Bachelor of Arts | 3 |
|  | Bachelor of Arts with Honours | 4 |
|  | Bachelor of Music | 4 |
|  | Doctor of Philosophy | 2-3 |
|  | Doctor of Literature |  |
|  | Bachelor of Fine Art | 4 |
|  | Master of Fine Art | 1 |
|  | Bachelor of Music | 4 |
|  | Master of Music | 1 |
|  | Doctor of Music |  |
|  | Licentiate Diploma in Music | 3 |
|  | Diploma in Fine Art | 4 |
|  | Diploma in Physical Education | 1 |

| | | |
|---|---|---|
| Science | Bachelor of Science | 3 |
| | Bachelor of Science with Honours | 4 |
| | Bachelor of Science in Pharmacy | 3 |
| | Master of Science | 1 |
| | Doctor of Philosophy | 2-3 |
| | Doctor of Science | |
| | Diploma in Leather Science | 1 |
| Education | Bachelor of Education | 1 |
| | Master of Education | 1 |
| | Doctor of Philosophy | 2-3 |
| | Doctor of Literature | |
| | University Education Diploma | 1 |
| | University Art Teacher's Diploma | 4 |
| | Lower Secondary Teacher's Diploma | 3 |
| | Higher Primary Teacher's Certificate | 3 |
| | University Art Teacher's Certificate | 4 |
| | Primary Teacher's Art Certificate | 1 |
| Commerce | Bachelor of Commerce | 3 |
| | Bachelor of Commerce with Honours | 4 |
| | Master of Commerce | 1 |
| | Bachelor of Economics | 3 |
| | Bachelor of Economics with Honours | 4 |
| | Master of Economics | 1 |
| | Doctor of Philosophy | 2-3 |
| | Certificate in the Theory of Accountancy | 3 |
| | Certificate in Secretarial Practice | 2 |
| Divinity | Bachelor of Divinity | 3 |
| | Doctor of Philosophy | 2-3 |
| | Doctor of Divinity | |
| | Diploma in Theology | 3 |
| | Certificate in Religious Knowledge | 2 |
| Law | Bachelor of Laws | 3 |
| | Master of Laws | 1 |
| | Doctor of Laws | |
| | Diploma in Law | 3 |
| | Diploma in Law (Public Service) | 3 |
| Social Science | Bachelor of Social Science | 3 |
| | Bachelor of Social Science with Honours | 4 |
| | Master of Social Science | 1 |
| | Doctor of Philosophy | 2-3 |
| | Doctor of Social Science | |
| | Diploma in Social Work | 1 |
| | Diploma in Social Studies | 2 |
| | Diploma in Personnel Welfare and Management | 1-2 |

Master's Degrees:

A candidate is not admitted to the degree of Master in the Faculty
of Arts (except the degree of Master of Music and Master of Fine
Art), or of Science, Commerce, or of Social Science until at least
2 years after admission to the degree of Bachelor, or 1 year after
admission to the degree of Bachelor with Honours, in such Faculty,
or, in the case of the degrees of Master of Education, Master of
Law, and Master of Music, until at least 1 year after admission to
the degree or status of Bachelor.

The examination for the degree of Master consists of

(a)   a thesis on a subject approved in advance by the Head of the
      department concerned, prepared under the direction of a super-
      visor appointed by the Senate;

or    (b)   such written or oral examination as may be prescribed by the
      department concerned.

The degree may be awarded with distinction.

Doctor of Philosophy

A candidate is not admitted to the degree of Doctor of Philosophy
until at least 3 years after admission to the degree of Bachelor
with Honours, or of Bachelor of Education, or of Bachelor of Divinity;
or until at least 2 years after admission to the degree of Master if
the candidate has not taken the Honours degree.

A candidate submits a dissertation on the results of his special
study or research.

A candidate may be required by the Senate to take a written or oral
examination on the subject of his dissertation and on the whole field
of study which it covers.

Degree of Doctor, other than Doctor of Philosophy:

A candidate is not admitted to any degree of doctor other than Doctor
of Philosophy, until at least 5 years after admission to the degree
of Bachelor with Honours, or of Bachelor of Education, or of Bachelor
of Laws, or of Bachelor of Divinity, or until at least 4 years after
admission to the degree of Master.

A candidate for the degree of doctor, other than Doctor of Philosophy,
submits, for the approval of the Senate, published work dealing with
some subject falling within the scope of the studies represented by
the University.

## Faculty of Arts

## Bachelor of Arts

A candidate for the ordinary degree must obtain credit in not less than 10 courses.

A candidate must obtain credit in all the required courses in at least 2 subjects, to be known as major subjects, which are selected from the following:

| | |
|---|---|
| Afrikaans/Nederlands | Philosophy |
| Biblical Studies | Physical Education |
| Economics | Public Administration |
| English | Mathematical Statistics |
| Fine Art Studies | Systematic Theology |
| French | Psychology |
| Geography | Sindebele |
| German | Sociology |
| Economic History | Southern Sotho |
| Roman-Dutch Law | Xhosa |
| Politics | Zulu |
| Greek | Another approved Bantu |
| Hebrew | language |
| History | Ecclesiastical History |
| Latin | Social Anthropology |
| Mathematics | Speech and Drama |
| Music | |

A candidate must obtain credit in at least 1 course in English or Afrikaans/Nederlands.

## Bachelor of Arts with Honours

A candidate who has been awarded the Ordinary degree may be admitted to the courses for the Honours degree.

Duration of course:  1 year.

## Bachelor of Fine Art

A candidate for the degree obtains credit in:  Special English or English I or Afrikaans/Nederlands I, to be taken in the first year.  A second course in English or Afrikaans/Nederlands, or a standard Arts course, other than Fine Art Studies and General History of Art, to be taken in the 1st or 2nd year.  The following courses, taken in the 1st year:  Theory of Art I, Basic Art.

All the courses set out in 1 of the following 3 groups:

|  A (Painting)  |  B (Graphic Design)  |  C (Sculpture)  |
|---|---|---|
|  | 2nd year |  |
| Theory of Art II | Theory of Art II | Theory of Art II |
| Painting I | Graphic Design I | Sculpture I |
|  | 3rd year |  |
| Theory of Art III | Theory of Art III | Theory of Art III |
| Painting II | Graphic Design II | Sculpture II |
|  | 4th year |  |
| Theory of Art IV | Theory of Art IV | Theory of Art IV |
| Painting III | Graphic Design III | Sculpture III |

## Bachelor of Music

1st yr:  History of Music I                  Ensemble I
         Theory of Music I                   Practical Subject I
         Orchestration and Instrumentation I

2nd yr:  History of Music II                 Ensemble II
         Theory of Music II                  Practical Subject II
         Orchestration and Instrumentation II

3rd yr:  History of Music III                Ensemble III
         Theory of Music III                 Conducting I
         Orchestration and Instrumentation III   Practical Subject III

4th yr:  History of Music IV, Theory of Music IV

         2 of the following:

         Afrikaans/Nederlands                Mathematics
         English                             Philosophy
         French                              Physics
         German                              Psychology
         History                             Social Anthropology
         Latin                               Sociology

## Licentiate Diploma in Music

A candidate obtains credit in all the courses (other than the practical
subject) for the first 3 years of the degree of Bachelor of Music.  In
addition, he must obtain credit in all the courses in 1 of the following
groups:

| | 1st yr: | 2nd yr. | 3rd yr. |
|---|---|---|---|
| Performers of an Instrument or Singing | Instrument I or Singing | Instrument II or Singing II Music Literature I | Instrument III or Singing III Music Literature II |
| Teachers of an Instrument or Singing | Instrument I Singing I Teaching Method I Music Literature I | Instrument II or Singing II Teaching Method II Music Literature II | Instrument III or Singing III School Music |
| Teachers of School Music | Method and Practice of School Music I Choral and Instrumental Ensemble I Recorder and other School Instruments I | Method and Practice of School Music II Choral and Instrumental Ensemble II Recorder and other School Instruments Choral and Instrumental Arrangements | Method and Practice of School Music III Choral and Instrumental Ensemble III Choral and Instrumental Arrangements II; Elements of Vocal Training |
| Choirmasters | Conducting and Choir Training I Choir I Elements of Vocal Training | Conducting and Choir Training II Choir II Choral Arrangements Music Literature Score Reading | Conducting and Choir Training III Choral Arrangements Music Literature II Score Reading II |
| Church Organists | Church Organ Playing and Choir I Elements of Vocal Training Modulation | Church Organ Playing and Choir Training Choral Arrangements Music Literature Improvisation | Church Organ Playing and Choir Training III Choral Arrangements Music Literature II Improvisation |

## Diploma in Fine Art

Eligibility:            School-Leaving Certificate Examination of the Joint Matriculation Board.

Duration of course:  4 years.

Curriculum:            1st year, Theory of Art I and Basic Art, and following years, all courses in 1 of the 3 groups (Painting, Graphic Design, Sculpture) listed above for Bachelor of Fine Art.

## Diploma in Physical Education

Eligibility:            Bachelor's degree.

Duration of course:  1 year.

## Faculty of Science

### Bachelor of Science

Eligibility:            Pass in Mathematics at Matriculation examination.

A candidate for the ordinary degree obtains credit in not less than 9 courses.

A candidate obtains credit in all the required courses in at least 2 subjects (majors) selected from the following:

| | |
|---|---|
| Applied Mathematics | Mathematics |
| Botany | Physics |
| Chemistry | Psychology |
| Geography | Zoology |
| Geology | Astronomy |
| Physiology | Entomology |
| Mathematical Statistics | |

### Bachelor of Science with Honours

A test in French or German is required.

Duration of course:  1 year.

### Bachelor of Science in Pharmacy

Eligibility:            Pass in Mathematics and in _either_ Botany, Biology, Chemistry, Physics, Physical Science, _or_ Zoology at the Matriculation examination.

### Curriculum:

| | | |
|---|---|---|
| 1st yr: | Botany I | Zoology I |
| | Chemistry I | Elementary Mathematics |
| | Physics I | |
| 2nd and | Chemistry II and III | Physiology and Pharmacology |
| 3rd yrs: | Pharmacy I and II | Forensic Pharmacy |
| | Pharmacognosy | Pharmaceutical Chemistry |

### Diploma in Leather Science

Eligibility:            Bachelor of Science with Chemistry as major subject.

Duration of course:  1 year.

Curriculum:

Principles of Leather Manufacture  Physical Chemistry (Leather)
Methods of Leather Manufacture    Practical Chemistry (Leather)
Analytical Chemistry (Leather)

A thesis is required.


## Faculty of Education

### Bachelor of Education

Eligibility:          Bachelor's degree and University Education Diploma.

Duration of course:  1 year.

The degree may be awarded with distinction.


### University Education Diploma (Graduate)

Eligibility:          Bachelor's degree.

Curriculum:

General Educational Method, Principles and History of Education,
Psychology of Education.

A method course in 2 of the following:

Biological Science              Latin
Bookkeeping                     Mathematics
Botany                          History
Chemistry                       Music
Classics                        Physical Education
Commerce                        Physical Science
Commercial Arithmetic           Religious Education
Fine Art                        Vocational Guidance
French                          Zoology
German                          Geography
Language and Literature of the  Greek
  mother tongue
Language and Literature of the second official language

For graduates in Arts and Science, a course in 1 of the following:

School Art                      Woodwork
Musical Appreciation and        Needlework
  School Music                  Shorthand
Organization and Coaching of    Typewriting
  Games and Sports              Librarianship
Play Production in Schools      Content and Method of
                                  Religious Instruction

For graduates in Commerce, advanced courses in Shorthand and Type-writing.

For graduates in Fine Arts, a course in Craft work.

## University Education Diploma (Non-graduate)

Eligibility:           2 years of study towards Bachelor's degree.

Same curriculum as for University Education Diploma (Graduate).

## University Art Teacher's Diploma

Duration of course:  4 years.

Candidate must earn the Bachelor of Arts in Fine Arts concurrently with the following additional courses:

|  |  |
|---|---|
| English and Afrikaans/Nederlands | Special Method Course in |
| General Education Method | Fine Art |
| Psychology of Education | Craftwork |
| Speech Training | Teaching Practice |
| Principles and History of Education | |

## Lower Secondary Teacher's Diploma

Eligibility:           School-Leaving Certificate examination.

Duration of course:  3 years.

## Curriculum:

7 of the following:

|  |  |
|---|---|
| Afrikaans/Nederlands | Botany |
| An approved Bantu language | Chemistry |
| English | Physics |
| Fine Art | Zoology |
| French | Geography |
| German | Greek |
| History | Latin |
| Mathematics | Music |
| Physical Education | |

## Alternative curriculum:

1st yr:   Accounting I, Economics I, English I or Special English or Afrikaans/Nederlands I

1 of the following:

| | |
|---|---|
| Elementary Theory of Finance | Mathematics I |
| Introductory French | Psychology I |
| French I | Typewriting I |
| Introductory German | Shorthand I |
| German I | |

2nd yr:   Accounting II or English II or Afrikaans/Nederlands II, Commerce

2 of the following:

| | |
|---|---|
| Economics II | Afrikaans/Nederlands II |
| Economic Geography | Mathematics I |
| Economic History | Elementary Theory of |
| Mathematics II |    Finance and Statistics |
| English I or Special English | Psychology I |
| Afrikaans/Nederlands I | Typewriting II |
| English II | Shorthand II |

3rd yr:   General Education Method, Principles and History of Education, Psychology of Education

Special Method courses in at least 3 of the following:

| | |
|---|---|
| Bookkeeping | Mathematics |
| Commercial Arithmetic | Typewriting |
| English or Afrikaans | Shorthand |
| Typewriting III | Language Work, oral and |
| Shorthand III |    written, in 1 of the |
| Secretarial Practice |    official languages |
| Speech Training | Teaching Practice |

## Higher Primary Teacher's Certificate

Eligibility:          School-Leaving Certificate examination of the Joint Matriculation Board

Duration of course:   3 years.

## Curriculum:

1st yr:   Physical Education, School Method, Teaching Practice (3 weeks)

3 of the following:

| | |
|---|---|
| Special English | History |
| Afrikaans/Nederlands | Geography |

2nd yr:   A 4th subject chosen from:

| | |
|---|---|
| Special English | School Art |
| Afrikaans/Nederlands | School Music (optional) |
| History or Geography | Woodwork or Needlework |

Psychology                          Speech Training
School Method                       Teaching Practice
English and Afrikaans/Nederlands

3rd yr:   Principles and History of          School Music (optional)
            Education                         Woodwork or Needlework
          Psychology of Education             Speech Training
          School Hygiene                      Nature Study
          Primary School Method               Teaching Practice
          English and Afrikaans/Nederlands    Content and Method of
          School Art                            Religious Instruction
                                               (optional if Music taken)

## University Art Teacher's Certificate

Eligibility:          School-Leaving Certificate examination.

Duration of course:  4 years.

Candidate must earn the Diploma in Fine Art concurrently with the following additional courses:

English and Afrikaans/Nederlands    Special Method Course in
General Educational Method            Fine Art
Psychology of Education             Craftwork
Speech Training                     Teaching Practice
Principles and History of Education

## Primary Teacher's Art Certificate

Eligibility:          Primary Teacher's Certificate of the Department of
                      Public Education of the Cape of Good Hope or equi-
                      valent certificate.

Duration of course:  1 year.

## Curriculum:

Painting, Design and Lettering, General Drawing, General History
of Art, Fine Art Teaching Method, Craftwork.

## Faculty of Commerce

## Bachelor of Commerce

Curriculum A (for students who wish to enter commerce, industry, or
teaching):

1st yr:   Accounting I, Economics I, Special English or English I or
          Afrikaans/Nederlands, Mathematics I or Elementary Theory of
          Finance and Statistics or Elementary Mathematics and Statistics

          1 of the following:

          Afrikaans/Nederlands I          Psychology I
          An approved Bantu language      Geology I
          Economic History I              German I
          Elementary Mathematics and      History I
            Statistics                    Latin I
          English I or Special English    Mathematics I
          French I or Introductory French  Philosophy I
          Geography I or Economic         Politics I
            Geography                     Sociology I

2nd yr:   Accounting II, Commerce I, Economics II

          1 of the following:

          Economic History I, Auditing I, Mathematical Statistics I,
          A course listed for 1st yr.

3rd yr:   Commerce II, Economics III

          2 of the following:

          Accounting III                  Mathematics III
          Actuarial Mathematics           Mercantile Law II
          Auditing II                     Statistics II
          Auditing I                      Public Finance
          Industrial Organization and     A course listed for 1st yr.
            Management

Curriculum B (for pre-legal students):

1st yr:   Accounting I, Economics I, Special English or English I or
          Afrikaans/Nederlands I or French or German

          2 of the following:

          An approved Bantu language, Afrikaans/Nederlands I, English I
          or Special English, Latin I, Roman Law I, Social Anthropology

2nd yr:   Accounting II, Commerce I, Economics II, Roman-Dutch Law I,
          Roman Law I or Roman Law II or Native Law

3rd yr:   Commerce II, Constitutional Law, Economics III, Roman-Dutch Law II.

Curriculum C (for accounting students):

1st yr:   Accounting I, Economics I, Elementary Theory of Finance and
          Statistics, Special English or English I or Afrikaans/Nederlands
          I, Mercantile Law I

2nd yr:   Accounting II, Auditing I, Commerce I, Economics II, Mercantile
          Law II

3rd yr:    Accounting III, Auditing II, Commerce II, Cost Accounting

## Bachelor of Commerce with Honours

Duration of course:  1 year.

A language examination is required.

## Bachelor of Economics

### Curriculum:

1st yr:    Accounting I, Constitutional Law, Economics I

2 of the following:

English I, Afrikaans/Nederlands I, Economic History I

2nd yr:    Economics II, Politics I, Public Administration I or Social
Anthropology I

2 of the following:

| | |
|---|---|
| Accounting II | Bantu Law |
| Economic History II | Philosophy I |
| French I or Introductory French | Psychology I |
| German I or Introductory German | Public Administration I |
| Geography I or Economic Geography | Public International Law |
| | Social Anthropology I |
| History I | Sociology I |
| Latin I | An approved Bantu language |
| Mathematics I or Elementary Theory of Finance and Statistics | |

3rd yr:    Economics III, Politics II, Public Administration II or Social
Anthropology II or History II

1 of the following:

History I, Bantu Law, Public Administration I, Public International Law, Social Anthropology I

## Certificate in the Theory of Accountancy

Eligibility:              Pass or exemption from the Matriculation examination
of the Joint Matriculation Board.

### Curriculum:

Accounting I, II, and III, Mercantile Law I and II, Auditing I and
II, Elementary Theory of Finance and Statistics, Cost Accounting,
Income Tax Practice, Accounts of Executors, Liquidators and Trustees

## Certificate in Secretarial Practice

Eligibility:          School-Leaving Certificate examination of the Joint
                      Matriculation Board.

## Curriculum:

1st yr:   Special English or English I or Afrikaans/Nederlands I or French
          or German, Accounting I, Economics I or another language, Short-
          hand I, Typewriting I

2nd yr:   Secretarial Practice, Commerce I, Shorthand II, Typewriting II

          1 of the following:

          Language, Accounting II, Mercantile Law, Economic Geography


## Faculty of Divinity

## Bachelor of Divinity

Eligibility:          Bachelor's degree.

## Curriculum:

Philosophy I                          History I
Introductory Greek or Greek I         Old Testament Language,
  or Hebrew I                           Literature and History
New Testament Language,               Comparative Religion
  Literature and History             Ecclesiastical History
Dogmatics                             South African Ecclesiastical
Apologetics                             History

A thesis is required.


## Diploma in Theology

Curriculum:

1st yr:   Biblical Studies I, Ecclesiastical History I, English I or
          Special English or Afrikaans/Nederlands I

2nd yr:   Biblical Studies II, Systematic Theology I, Ecclesiastical History
          II, Sociology I or Social Anthropology I or Psychology I or
          Philosophy I

3rd yr:   Biblical Studies III, Systematic Theology II

## Certificate in Religious Knowledge

### Curriculum:

1st yr:   Biblical Studies I, Ecclesiastical History I, English I or Special
          English or Afrikaans/Nederlands I

2nd yr:   Biblical Studies II, Systematic Theology I, Ecclesiastical History
          II, Sociology I or Social Anthropology I or Psychology I or
          Philosophy I


## Faculty of Law

### Bachelor of Laws

Eligibility:          Bachelor's degree.

### Curriculum:

1st yr:   Roman Law I, Roman-Dutch Law I, Constitutional Law, Criminal
          Law, Criminal Procedure

2nd yr:   Roman Law II, Roman-Dutch Law II, Succession and Husband and Wife,
          Property, Conflict of Laws or Bantu Law, Insolvency and Negotiable
          Instruments

3rd yr:   Jurisprudence, Contract, Delict, Company Law, Civil Procedure,
          Evidence


### Diploma in Law

1st yr:   Roman-Dutch Law I, Criminal Law, Roman Law or Mercantile Law I

2nd yr:   Roman-Dutch Law II, Law of Evidence, Criminal Procedure, Roman
          Law or Mercantile Law (not taken above)

3rd yr:   Roman-Dutch Law III, Mercantile Law II, Civil Procedure, Inter-
          pretation of Statutes,Bantu Law and Administration or Constitutional
          Law and Administrative Law


### Diploma in Law (Public Service)

1st yr:   Roman Dutch Law I, Criminal Law, Roman Law I or Mercantile Law I

2nd yr:   Roman Dutch Law II, Law of Evidence, Criminal Procedure, Roman
          Law or Mercantile Law (not taken above)

3rd yr:   Roman-Dutch Law III, Civil Procedure, Interpretation of Statutes,
          Mercantile Law II or Bantu Law and Administration

Faculty of Social Science

Bachelor of Social Science

Curriculum:

Sociology I, Economics I or Economic History I, Psychology I

7 of the following:

Afrikaans/Nederlands I            Elementary Mathematics and
A Bantu language                     Statistics
Economic History I and II         English or Special English
French                            Politics I
German                            Psychology II and III
History I                         Public Administration I and II
Mathematics I                     Social Anthropology I and II
Philosophy I and II               Social Work I and II
Physical Education I, II,          Sociology I and II
  and III                         Economics I, II, and III

Bachelor of Social Science with Honours

The Honours degree may be taken in Economics, Psychology, Social Anthropology, or Sociology.

Eligibility:         Bachelor of Social Science.

A foreign language test is required.

Diploma in Social Work (Post-Graduate)

Eligibility:         Bachelor's degree.

Curriculum:

Social Work III, Personal and Public Hygiene, Vital Statistics,
Advanced Social Pathology, Social Legislation and Administration

1 of the following:

Criminology and Penal Systems      Research Methods in Social Work
Psychopathology and Clinical       Social Group Work
  Psychology                       International Social and Health
Child Psychology and Child           Agencies
  Welfare                          Social Security and Insurance
Housing Problems and Family          Systems
  Welfare                          Community Organization and
Industrial Relations and Labour      Development
  Problems                         Comparative Social Work
          Recent Advances in Personality Theory

Diploma in Social Studies

Eligibility:              School-Leaving Certificate examination of the Joint
                          Matriculation Board.

Curriculum:

1st yr:    Sociology I, Psychology I

           2 of the following:

           Ecclesiastical History I
           Economic History I
           Economics I
           General History of Art
           History I
           History and Appreciation of Music
           Philosophy I
           Physical Education I
           Politics I
           Principles of Classical Culture
           Public Administration
           Social Anthropology I

2nd yr:    Sociology II, Social Work I

           2 courses chosen from above.


Diploma in Personnel Welfare and Management

Eligibility:              Bachelor's degree.

Curriculum:

           Economics I
           Economic History I or Economics II
           Psychology I
           Psychology II
           Social Problems
           Social Law and Administration
           Industrial Physiology and Hygiene
           Industrial Management
           Social Statistics
           Industrial Sociology
           Industrial Law
           Native and Coloured in Industry
           Aptitude Testing and Industrial Psychology

UNIVERSITY OF NATAL, Durban and Pietermaritzburg

Founded as Durban Technical College in 1907.

Natal University College founded in 1910 awarding degrees of the University of the Cape of Good Hope.

In 1918 became constituent college of University of South Africa.  Joined with Durban Technical College in 1920-22.

In 1949 became the University of Natal.

General entrance requirements:        Matriculation Certificate of Joint
                                      Matriculation Board.

Faculties:

         Arts                    Commerce and Public Administration
         Social Science          Engineering
         Science                 Agriculture
         Education               Medicine
         Law

Language of instruction:              English.

Degrees awarded:

| Faculty | Degree | Duration of Course (years) |
|---|---|---|
| Arts | B.A. | 3 |
| | B.A. (Hons.) | 4 |
| | M.A. | 1 |
| | Ph.D. | 2-3 |
| | D.Litt. | |
| | B.A. Fine Arts | 4 |
| | B.A. Fine Arts (Hons.) | 5 |
| | M.A. Fine Arts | 1 |
| Social Science | B.Soc.Sc. | 3 |
| | B.Soc.Sc. (Hons.) | 4 |
| | M.Soc.Sc. | 1 |
| | Ph.D. | 2-3 |
| | D.Soc.Sc. | |
| Science | B.Sc. | 3 |
| | B.Sc. (Hons.) | 4 |
| | M.Sc. | 1 |
| | Ph.D. | 2-3 |
| | D.Sc. | |
| | B.Sc. Chem. Tech. | 4 |
| | M.Sc. Chem. Tech. | 1 |

| | | |
|---|---|---|
| Education | B.Ed. | 1-2 |
| | M.Ed. | 1 |
| | Ph.D. | 2-3 |
| | D.Litt. | |
| Law | LL.B. | 3 |
| | LL.M. | |
| | LL.D. | 2 |
| Commerce and Public Administration | B.Com. | 3 |
| | B.Com. (Hons.) | 4 |
| | M.Com. | 1 |
| | B.Econ. | 3 |
| | B.Econ. (Hons.) | 4 |
| | M.Econ. | 1 |
| | Ph.D. | 2-3 |
| | D.Econ. | |
| Engineering | B.Sc.Eng. | 4 |
| | B.Sc.Eng. (Hons.) | 5 |
| | M.Sc.Eng. | 1 |
| | Ph.D. | 2-3 |
| | D.Sc.Eng. | |
| | B.Sc.Sur. | 4 |
| | M.Sc.Sur. | 1 |
| | B.Sc. Eng. Agric. | 5 |
| | B.Arch. | 4 |
| | M.Arch. | 1 |
| | D.Arch. | |
| | B.Sc.Q.S. | 4 |
| | M.Sc.Q.S. | 1 |
| Agriculture | B.Sc.Agric. | 4 |
| | M.Sc.Agric. | 1 |
| | Ph.D. | 2-3 |
| Medicine | M.B., Ch.B. | 6 |
| | M.Med. | 3-4 |
| | M.D. | |

## Faculty of Arts

The following courses are offered:

(a) 3-year course leading to the degree of Bachelor of Arts.

(b) 4-year course leading to the degree of Bachelor of Arts in Fine Arts.

(c) 1-year post-graduate course for the degree of Bachelor of Arts (Honours).

(d)   1-year post-graduate course for the Diploma in Play Production.

(e)   1-year post-graduate course for the degree of Bachelor of Arts in Fine Arts (Honours).

(f)   1-year post-graduate course for the Diploma in Speech Therapy (Logopaedics).

The degree of Master of Arts in Fine Arts may be awarded after a minimum of 1 additional year of study or research.

The following degrees (in the nature of research degrees) may also be granted:

> Doctor of Philosophy
> Doctor of Literature

## B.A. Curriculum

Duration of course:        not less than 3 years.

A candidate for the degree must obtain credit for not fewer than 10 qualifying courses distributed among not fewer than 5 subjects chosen from the following list:

| | |
|---|---|
| Afrikaans-Nederlands | English |
| Fine Arts | French |
| Art History and Appreciation | Special French |
| General Introduction to Fine Art | Geography |
| Approved Bantu language | Geology |
| Special course in Bantu language | German |
| Biblical Studies | Special German |
| Botany | Greek |
| Chemistry | Hebrew |
| Classical Civilization | History |
| Economics | Economic History |
| Roman Law | Latin |
| Introduction to Roman-Dutch Law | Native Administration |
| Constitutional Law | Philosophy |
| Criminal Law | Introduction to Philosophy |
| Bantu Law | Physics |
| Education | Political Science |
| Mathematics | Psychology |
| Applied Mathematics | Native Law |
| Mathematical Statistics | Sociology |
| Social Anthropology | Speech and Drama |
| Theology | Zoology |

Every approved curriculum includes at least 2 subjects known as major subjects.

A candidate selects his major subjects from the following groups:

(a)  Major subjects in which 3 qualifying courses are taken: Afrikaans-
     Nederlands, approved Bantu language, Fine Art, Economics, English,
     French, Geography, German, Greek, History, Latin, Mathematics,
     Psychology, Sociology, Speech and Drama.

(b)  Major subjects in which 2 qualifying courses are taken: Biblical
     Studies, Economic History, Native Administration, Philosophy,
     Political Science, Roman Law, Social Anthropology, Theology.

Every approved curriculum includes:

(a)  2 subjects chosen from the following list in each of which at least
     1 qualifying course is taken: Greek, Latin, Afrikaans-Nederlands,
     English, French, Special French, German, Special German, an approved
     Bantu language, special course in an approved Bantu language, Hebrew.

(b)  At least 1 qualifying course in Biblical Studies, or Economics, or
     Mathematics, or Philosophy, or Introduction to Philosophy, or Politi-
     cal Science, or Psychology, or Social Anthropology or Sociology, or
     Theology.

A candidate who has passed the final examinations in a major subject is
placed in first class; second class, division one; second class, division
two; or third class.


## Bachelor of Arts (Honours)

Eligibility:            A candidate must have satisfied the requirements for
                        admission to the degree of Bachelor of Arts in the
                        University or been admitted to the status thereof.

A candidate for the degree attends the University as a registered student
for not less than 1 academic year after satisfying the requirements for
admission to the degree of Bachelor of Arts in the University, or after
admission to the status thereof, and pursues an Honours course of advanced
study in 1 subject selected from the following list:

        Greek, Latin, Classics, Afrikaans-Nederlands, English, French,
        German, Modern Languages, Philosophy, Mathematics, History, Geo-
        graphy, Political Science, Economics, Psychology, African Studies,
        Sociology, Fine Art, Divinity.

A candidate who has passed the examination for the Bachelor of Arts
(Honours) is placed in one of 3 classes: first, second, or third.


## Master of Arts

Eligibility:            Any B.A. (Honours) who has been a registered student
                        of the University for not less than 1 academic year
                        after satisfying the requirements for that degree.

The examination for the degree consists of a dissertation, or of 2 or more written papers, or of a dissertation together with a written paper or papers.

The degree of Master of Arts may be awarded with distinction.


## Doctor of Philosophy

Eligibility:               Any M.A. and any M.A. in Fine Arts of the University of not less than 2 years' standing.

A B.A. (Hons.) and a B.A. in Fine Arts (Hons.) of the University of not less than 3 years' standing who has been specially exempted from the master's examination.

A B.A. in Fine Arts of the University of not less than 4 years' standing.

A candidate for the degree is required to pursue an approved course of special study or research on some subject connected with Language, Literature, Philosophy, Pure Mathematics, History, Geography, Economics, Political Science, Divinity, Psychology, Sociology, Social Anthropology, Archaeology, or Fine Art.


## Doctor of Literature

Eligibility:               Any B.A. (Hons.) and any B.A. in Fine Arts (Hons.) of the University of not less than 5 years' standing.

A candidate for the degree submits published work, or a thesis in a form suitable for publication which is a record of original and independent study or research by the candidate on some subject connected with Language, Literature, Philosophy, Pure Mathematics, History, Geography, Economics, Political Science, Divinity, Psychology, Sociology, Social Anthropology, Archaeology or Fine Art.


## Diploma in Play Production

Eligibility:               Candidate must have obtained a degree or been admitted to the status of a degree in the University, and must have completed courses substantially satisfying the requirements prescribed for Speech and Drama offered as a major subject in the University.

Duration of course:  1 academic year.

The examination for the Diploma consists of the following parts:

(1)  Written papers in the following subjects:

A general study of the theatre and drama.
A detailed study of two periods in the History of the Theatre.
The Principles and Application of Dramatic Criticism.

(2)  A practical test on the interpretation of drama in terms of speech
and movement.

(3)  A report on an approved subject intended to test the candidate's
capacity for independent creative work in the theatre.

(4)  The direction of an approved play and submission of the materials
giving a detailed record of the production, including execution of
scenery and costumes, supervision of make-up of characters and
lighting of the play.

The Diploma may be awarded with distinction.


## Diploma in Logopaedics

Eligibility:            Candidate must have obtained a degree or been
admitted to the status of a degree in the University,
and must have completed courses substantially satisfying the requirements prescribed for Speech and
Drama offered as a major subject in the University.

Duration of course:  2 academic years.

Candidate is required to complete Psychology I and Psychology II either
before entering upon or during the work for the Diploma, and Sociology I
or Social Anthropology I either before entering upon or in the 1st year
of the work for the Diploma.  At the end of the 1st year candidates
complete Anatomy, Physiology, Speech Pathology, and Therapeutics I.  At
the end of the 2nd year, candidates complete Neurology, Speech Pathology,
and Therapeutics II.

The Diploma may be awarded with distinction.


## Bachelor of Arts in Fine Arts

Duration of course:  4 academic years.

Curriculum:

1st yr:  Afrikaans/Nederlands I or English I

1 of the following:  Afrikaans/Nederlands I, English I (if not
taken above), Special French, French I, German I, Special
German, History I, Introduction to Philosophy.

General Introduction to Fine Art
Art History and Appreciation

2nd yr:    Painting I or Sculpture I
           Drawing from Life I
           History of Art I

3rd yr:    Painting II or Sculpture II
           Drawing from Life II
           History of Art II

4th yr:    Painting III or Sculpture III
           History of Art III

A candidate who has passed the final examinations in major subjects is placed, for those subjects only, in one of 3 classes, described as first, second, and third.

## Bachelor of Arts in Fine Arts (Honours)

Eligibility:         A candidate must have satisfied the requirements for admission to the B.A. in Fine Arts in the University, or been admitted to the status thereof.

Duration of course:  1 academic year.

The degree may be awarded with distinction.

## Master of Arts in Fine Arts

Eligibility:         Any B.A. in Fine Arts (Hons.) of the University who has been a registered student of the University for not less than 1 academic year after satisfying the requirements for that degree.

                     A graduate of another recognized university who has been admitted to the status of B.A. in Fine Arts of the University, and who has attended as a registered student of the University an approved course of study for not less than 2 academic years.

The degree may be awarded with distinction.

## Faculty of Social Science

The following courses are offered:

  (a)  3-year course leading to the degree of Bachelor of Social Science.

  (b)  1-year post-graduate course leading to the Post-Graduate Diploma in Social Welfare.

(c)  1-year post-graduate course leading to the degree of Bachelor
     of Social Science (Honours).

The following degrees, which are in the nature of research degrees, may
be conferred:

        Master of Social Science
        Doctor of Philosophy
        Doctor of Social Science


## Bachelor of Social Science (B.Soc.Sc.)

Duration of course:  not less than 3 academic years.

A candidate for the degree attends and completes not fewer than 11 full
qualifying courses chosen from the following list:

|  |  |
|---|---|
| Bantu Law | Mathematics |
| Constitutional Law | Methodology in the Soc.Sciences |
| Criminal Law and Procedure | Native Administration |
| Economic Geography | Philosophy |
| Economic History | Introduction to Philosophy |
| Economics | Political Science |
| Education | Psychology |
| Geography | Public Administration |
| History | Social Anthropology |
| Industrial Organization and | Social Work |
|    Management | Sociology |
| Industrial Psychology | Statistics A |
| Jurisprudence | Statistics B |
| Labour Economics | Mathematical Statistics |

Other subjects may be included in the curriculum.

Every approved curriculum contains at least 2 major subjects selected from
the following:

        Economics, Sociology, Social Work, History, Psychology, Political
        Science, Social Anthropology, Native Administration, Mathematical
        Statistics.

The degree may be awarded with distinction in one or more subjects.


## Post-Graduate Diploma in Social Work

Eligibility:        A Bachelor of Social Science who is qualified as a
                    social worker.
Duration of course:  at least 1 academic year.

Every candidate completes Sociology III, Genetic Psychology and Psycho-
Pathology, and Social Work.

The Diploma may be awarded with distinction.

## Bachelor of Social Science (Honours)

Eligibility:           Bachelor of Social Science.

Duration of course:  at least 1 academic year.

An Honours course of advanced study is pursued in 1 of the following:

>    Economics, Native Administration, Political Science, Psychology,
>    Sociology, Social Anthropology, Social Work.

The degree may be awarded with distinction.

## Master of Social Science

Eligibility:           Bachelor of Social Science (Honours) or Post-Graduate
                       Diploma in Social Work.

Duration of course:  at least 1 academic year.

The examination consists of a dissertation, or of 2 or more written
papers, or of a dissertation together with a written paper or papers.

The degree may be awarded with distinction.

## Doctor of Philosophy

Eligibility:           Master of Social Science.

Duration of course:  3 years

>    or  3 years with a Bachelor of Social Science (Honours)
>        or Post-Graduate Diploma in Social Work.

## Doctor of Social Science

Eligibility:           Bachelor of Social Science (Honours) or Post-Graduate
                       Diploma in Social Work of not less than 5 years'
                       standing.

Candidate is required to present published work or a thesis, some portion
of which shall already have been published.

## Faculty of Science

The following courses are offered:

(a) 3-year course leading to the degree of Bachelor of Science.

(b) 4-year course leading to the degree of Bachelor of Science (Honours).

(c) 1-year post-graduate course for the degree of Bachelor of Science (Honours).

(d) 1-year post-graduate course for the degree of Bachelor of Science (Chemical Technology).

The following degrees, which are in the nature of research degrees, may be conferred:

Master of Science
Master of Science (Chemical Technology)
Doctor of Philosophy
Doctor of Science

Eligibility:          Matriculation with Mathematics.

1st-year courses leading to degrees in Medicine, Dentistry, Veterinary Science, Forestry, and Agriculture.

Students who have passed 1st-year courses in the subjects of Physics, Chemistry, Botany, and Zoology, may be credited with the 1st year of study for the above degrees at other South African universities, and at overseas universities.

Students who wish to proceed to degrees in Agriculture must complete their 1st year in the Faculty of Science and are required to complete 1st-year courses, as for the degree of B.Sc., in Botany, Chemistry, Physics, and Zoology.

## Bachelor of Science

A course in any subject consists of not fewer than 60 separate class meetings.

A candidate obtains credit for not fewer than 9 courses distributed as follows:

(a) Not fewer than 8 courses from the following:  Applied Mathematics, Botany, Chemistry, Geography, Geology, Mathematics, Mathematical Statistics, Physics, Psychology, Zoology.

(b) Not more than 2 courses chosen from other subjects included in a curriculum for the degree of Bachelor of Arts.

Passes in examinations in all courses are graded first, second, or third class.

## Bachelor of Science (Honours)

Eligibility:          Bachelor of Science.

Duration of course:  at least 1 academic year.

Passes in the examinations for the degree are graded first, second, or third class.


## Master of Science

Eligibility:          Bachelor of Science or Bachelor of Science (Honours).

Duration of course:  2 years with Bachelor of Science.
                      1 year with Bachelor of Science (Honours).

The degree may be awarded with distinction.


## Doctor of Philosophy

Eligibility:          Any Master of Science or Master of Science (Chemical Technology) of the University of not less than 2 years' standing, who has attended the University as a registered student for at least 3 years.

Any Bachelor of Science (Honours) or Bachelor of Science (Chemical Technology) of the University of not less than 3 years' standing who has attended the University as a registered student for at least 3 years.

A graduate of another university who has been admitted to the status of Master of Science or of Master of Science (Chemical Technology) and who has attended as a registered student for at least 2 years.

A graduate of another recognized university who has been admitted to the status of Bachelor of Science (Honours) or of Bachelor of Science (Chemical Technology) who has attended the University as a registered student for at least 3 years.

A candidate for the degree is required to pursue an approved course of special study or research on some subject connected with the Mathematical, Physical, Natural, or Applied Sciences.


## Doctor of Science

Eligibility:          Bachelor of Science (Honours).

Duration of course:   3 years.

A candidate is required to present a thesis or published work which shall be a record of original and independent research on some subject connected with the Mathematical, Physical, Natural, or Applied Sciences.


## Bachelor of Science (Chemical Technology)

Eligibility:              Bachelor of Science or Bachelor of Science in Engineering.

Duration of course:   at least 1 academic year.

The degree may be awarded with distinction.


## Master of Science (Chemical Technology)

Eligibility:              Bachelor of Science (Chemical Technology).

Duration of course:   1 year.

The degree may be awarded with distinction.


## Faculty of Education

The following post-graduate courses are offered:

(a)   1-year course of professional training leading to the University Education Diploma.

(b)   2-year course of study leading to the degree of Bachelor of Education.

In addition, the following degrees, which are in the nature of research degrees, may be conferred:

Master of Education
Doctor of Philosophy
Doctor of Literature

Also a 2-year part-time course is offered, leading to the Certificate in Remedial Education.


## University Education Diploma

Eligibility:              B.A., B.Sc., B.A. Fine Arts, B.Com., B.Sc.Eng., B.Sc.Agric.

The Diploma is issued in the following forms:

(a)  University Education Diploma (graduate).

(b)  University Education Diploma (non-graduate), open to non-graduate
     candidates who have completed all but the final year of study for a
     degree, and intended more for the primary than for the middle school.

Duration of course:  not less than 1 academic year.

A candidate for the University Education Diploma completes the following
curriculum:

>   Principles of Education, Educational Psychology
>
>   1 of the following:  History of Education, Comparative Education,
>   Educational Sociology.
>
>   General Principles of Teaching
>   Methods of teaching a selected group of primary school subjects
>   Methods of teaching 1 or 2 secondary school subjects
>   Health Education
>   Organization and Administration of Education in South Africa
>
>   1 of the following:  School Librarianship, Vocational Guidance,
>   Audio-visual Techniques, Coaching and Supervision of Games,
>   Play Production
>
>   English or Afrikaans (unless exempted by test)
>   Speech Training (unless exempted by test)
>   Teaching Practice

The University Education Diploma may be awarded with distinction.


## Certificate in Remedial Education

Eligibility:          Natal Teacher's Diploma or equivalent plus 3 years
                      of suitable experience.

Duration of course:  1 academic year.

The curriculum includes:      Subnormality and Mental Defects
                              Educational Backwardness
                              Mental and Scholastic Testing
                              and practical remedial work.

The examination consists of 3 writen papers.

The Certificate in Remedial Education may be awarded with distinction.


## Bachelor of Education

Eligibility:          Bachelor of Arts or Science.

Duration of course:  2 academic years.

Curriculum:

1st yr:    Same as for University Education Diploma.

2nd yr:    Education Theory, General Educational Psychology

           Any 2 of the following:
           Social and Political Theory
           Educational Backwardness and Juvenile Delinquency
           Educational and Vocational Guidance
           Comparative Education
           Educational Administration and Supervision
           Prescribed texts from the History of Education
           Statistical Methods in Education

The degree may be awarded with distinction.


Master of Education

Eligibility:        Bachelor of Education.

Duration of course:  1 year.

Dissertation is required.


Doctor of Philosophy

Eligibility:        Master of Education of not less than 2 years'
                    standing.  Bachelor of Education of not less than 3
                    years' standing.

Duration of course:  2 years.


Doctor of Literature

Eligibility:        Bachelor of Education of not less than 5 years'
                    standing.

Thesis is required.


Faculty of Law

The following degrees are conferred:

Bachelor of Laws (LL.B.)
Master of Laws (LL.M.)
Doctor of Laws (LL.D.)

The following certificates are awarded:

Natal Law Certificate (N.L.C.)
Natal Public Service Law Certificate (N.P.S.L.C.)


## Bachelor of Laws

The LL.B. degree, together with the Bachelor's degree of some other
faculty that must precede it, qualifies its holder for admission as an
advocate of the Supreme Court of South Africa.

A candidate is not admitted to the LL.B. degree unless he has completed
a course in Latin.

Duration of course:  not less than 3 years.

A candidate for the degree attends and completes the following courses:

Roman Law
Introduction to Roman-Dutch Law
Constitutional Law

1 of the following:  Native Law, Bantu Law, Native Administration.

Accounting
Criminal Law
Roman Law II
South African Private Law I
Private International Law
South African Private Law II
Jurisprudence
Civil Procedure
Evidence

At the end of each year of study an examination embracing all the courses
taken during the year is held as follows:

1st yr:   Preliminary LL.B. examination

2nd yr:   Intermediate LL.B. examination

3rd yr:   Final LL.B. examination

The degree may be awarded with distinction.


## Master of Laws

Eligibility:          Bachelor of Laws of not less than 2 years' standing.

Candidate is required to submit a thesis embodying the results of his special study or research.


### Doctor of Laws

Eligibility:            Master of Laws of not less than 5 years' standing.

Duration of course:  2 years.

Published work or thesis required.


### Natal Law Certificate and Natal Public Service Law Certificate

A student who has obtained the Natal Law Certificate and who has served a period of 5 years of clerkship qualifies for admission as an attorney.

Eligibility as candidate for the Natal Law Certificate:

      (a)  A graduate of a university.

      (b)  A person who has obtained the Matriculation Certificate of the Joint Matriculation Board.

Eligibility as candidate for the Natal Public Service Law Certificate:

          Every person who, at the time of his first entry, is in the permanent employ of the government, including any Provincial Administration, the Railways and Harbours Service, and the Administration of the Mandated Territory of South West Africa;

    or  is in the permanent employ of the South African Reserve Bank, the Land and Agricultural Bank of South Africa, or any other body constituted by Parliament, for the main purpose of administering funds voted or authorized by Parliament by which it is wholly or partially financed.

Subjects of the examinations are as follows:

1st yr:   Roman-Dutch Law
          Roman Law
          Criminal Law

2nd yr:   Roman-Dutch Law II
          Mercantile Law I
          Criminal Procedure
          Evidence

3rd yr:   Natal Law Certificate candidates:

          Roman-Dutch Law III
          Civil Procedure

Interpretation of Statutes
Mercantile Law II or Native Law

Natal Public Service Law Certificate candidates:

Roman-Dutch Law III
Civil Procedure
Interpretation of Statutes
Native Law
Native Administration


## Faculty of Commerce and Public Administration

The following courses are offered:

 (a) 3-year course leading to the degree of Bachelor of Commerce.

 (b) 3-year course leading to the degree of Bachelor of Economics.

 (c) 1-year post-graduate course for the degree of Bachelor of Commerce (Honours).

 (d) 1-year post-graduate course for the degree of Bachelor of Economics (Honours).

 (e) 4-year course for the Certificate in the Theory of Accountancy.

The following degrees, which are in the nature of research degrees, are also awarded:

   Master of Commerce
   Master of Economics
   Doctor of Philosophy
   Doctor of Economics

The degree of Bachelor of Economics may be taken in either Industrial Administration or Public Administration.


## Bachelor of Commerce and Bachelor of Economics

Duration of course:  3 years.

Curriculum:

1st yr: Accounting I, Economics I, Economic History I, Statistics A, Elementary Finance, English I or Afrikaans-Nederlands I.

   1 of the following:

   Afrikaans-Nederlands I or English I (not taken above)
   Latin I         French I
   German I       Speech and Drama I

A qualifying course in an approved Bantu language

| | |
|---|---|
| Mathematics I | Psychology I |
| Economic Geography | Sociology I |
| Geography I | Social Anthropology I |
| History I | Philosophy I |
| Political Science I | Introduction to Philosophy |

2nd yr:   Accounting II, Commerce I, Economics II, Mercantile Law IA and IB.

1 of the following:

| | |
|---|---|
| Auditing | Economic History II |
| Industrial Organization and Management I | Economic Geography |
| Mathematical Statistics I | A second course in a subject taken in the 1st year |

3rd yr:   Commerce I, Economics II

2 full courses from the following:

| | |
|---|---|
| Accounting III | Statistics B |
| Auditing I and II | Cost Accounting |
| Accounts of Executors, Trustees and Liquidators | Income Tax |
| | Advanced Company Law |
| Industrial Organization and Management | Labour Economics |
| Advanced Statistics | Public Finance |
| Actuarial Mathematics | Welfare Economics |
| Banking | Agricultural Economics |
| | Economics of Transport |

The degrees may be awarded with distinction.

## Bachelor of Economics (Industrial Administration)

Curriculum:

1st yr:   Accounting I, Economics I, Economic History I, Psychology I, English I or Afrikaans-Nederlands I

1 full course from the following:

| | |
|---|---|
| Afrikaans-Nederlands I or English I | History I |
| | Political Science I |
| Latin I | Sociology I |
| French I | Social Anthropology I |
| German I | Philosophy I |
| Speech and Drama I | Introduction to Philosophy |
| A qualifying course in an approved Bantu language | Statistics |
| | Elementary Finance |
| Mathematics I | Methodology in the Social Sciences |
| Economic Geography | |
| Geography I | |

2nd yr:   Economics II, Industrial Organization and Management I, Industrial and Social Psychology, Mercantile Law IA, Industrial Law

1 of the following:

| | |
|---|---|
| Accounting II | Social Anthropology I |
| Mathematical Statistics I | Native Administration I |
| Economic History II | Social Work in Industry |
| Sociology I | |

3rd yr:  Economics III, Industrial Organization and Management II,
Labour Economics

1 full course from the following:

| | |
|---|---|
| Accounting III | Elementary Finance |
| Advanced Statistics | Methodology in the Social |
| Economic History II |    Sciences |
| Native Administration I | Public Finance |
| Social Work in Industry | Welfare Economics |
| Cost Accounting | Agricultural Economics |
| Statistics | Economics of Transport |

## Bachelor of Economics (Public Administration)

## Curriculum:

1st yr:  Accounting I, Economics I, Economic History I, Political
Science I, English I or Afrikaans-Nederlands I

1 full course from the following:

| | |
|---|---|
| Afrikaans-Nederlands I | History I |
| English I | Psychology I |
| Latin I | Sociology I |
| French I | Social Anthropology I |
| German I | Philosophy I |
| Speech and Drama I | Introduction to Philosophy |
| A qualifying course in an | Statistics |
|    approved Bantu language | Elementary Finance |
| Mathematics I | Methodology in the Social |
| Economic Geography |    Sciences |
| Geography I | |

2nd yr:  Economics II, Public Administration I, Native Administration I,
Constitutional Law or Municipal Law and Administration

1 of the following:

| | |
|---|---|
| Accounting II | Sociology I |
| Mathematical Statistics I | Social Anthropology I |
| Economic History II | Sociology II |
| Political Science II | Social Anthropology II |

3rd yr:  Economics III, Public Administration II or Native Administration II

2 of the following:

Native Administration II or Public Administration II

| | |
|---|---|
| Political Science II | Public International Law |
| Municipal Accounting | Municipal Law |
| Accounting III | Criminal Law |
| Auditing I | Labour Economics |
| Advanced Statistics | Welfare Economics |
| Economic History II | International Trade and |
| Sociology II | Foreign Exchanges |
| Social Anthropology II | Agricultural Economics |
| South African Bantu Law | Economics of Transport |

### Bachelor of Commerce (Honours) and Bachelor of Economics (Honours)

Eligibility:          Bachelor of Commerce or Bachelor of Economics.

Duration of course:  1 year.

A candidate for the degree of Bachelor of Commerce (Honours) pursues advanced study in 1 of the following branches:

| | |
|---|---|
| Accounting and Auditing | Economics |
| Commerce | Mathematics and Statistics |

### Curriculum:

Accounting and Auditing:

Advanced Theory and Practice of Accounting
Advanced Theory and Practice of Auditing
Theory and Practice of Costing and Cost Accounts

1 of the following:

Income Tax Practice
Law and Accounts of Executors, Trustees and Liquidators

The Accounts (and their audit) of one of the following:  holding company, mining company, municipal corporation, transport undertaking, insurance company or society, building society, undertaking working under the double account system.

Commerce:

Advanced Commerce
Advanced Economic Theory or Advanced Monetary Theory

1 of the following:

| | |
|---|---|
| Produce and Stock Exchanges | Labour Economics |
| Advertising and Market Research | Economics of Transport |
| Agricultural Economics | Essay |

Economics:

Advanced Economic Theory

Advanced Monetary Theory or an approved course in Applied
Economics

1 of the following:

Agricultural Economics
Economics of Transport
Labour Economics
South African Public Finance
The Economics of Under-
    developed Areas
South African Economic
    Problems
Essay

South African Economic
    History
A topic in the History of
    Economic Thought
Welfare Economics
An approved aspect of the
    study of Mathematical
    Economics or of Econometrics

Mathematics and Statistics:

Advanced Theory of Statistics
Advanced Actuarial Mathematics

A candidate for the degree of Bachelor of Economics (Honours) pursues
advanced study in 1 of the following branches:

Economics
Industrial Administration
Political Science

Public Administration
Native Administration

Curriculum:

Economics:

Same as for Bachelor of Commerce (Honours)

Industrial Administration:

Special Aspects of Industrial Organization and Management
Theory and Practice of Costing and Cost Accounts
Advanced Economic Theory or Advanced Monetary Theory

1 of the following:

Personnel Management
History of Scientific Management
Welfare Economics

Social Work in Industry
Economics of Transport
South African Economic
    Problems

Political Science:

A detailed study of a selected period in Political Philosophy
A selected topic in International Relations or the Public
    International Law of Peace
A more advanced study, historical and analytical, of the South
    African Constitution, including the party system and external
    relations

Problems of administration in the modern state, with special
reference to the needs of the Welfare State
A translation test from French or German or any other modern
language

Public Administration:

A detailed comparative study of the South African Constitution
and the constitutions of 2 other countries
Special aspects of Public Administration
Native Administration II

1 of the following:

| | |
|---|---|
| Municipal Finance | A special branch of Native Law |
| Municipal Accounting | Public International Law |
| Municipal Law and Administration | South African Public Finance |
| Municipal Law | Any other subject approved |
| South African Bantu Law | by the Senate |

Native Administration:

Comparative study of Colonial Native Policies and Practices
Detailed study of Native Administration in an approved African
territory and comparisons with the Republic of South Africa
Administration of Justice in Africa, with special reference to
the principles and applications of Bantu Law
Study on a comparative basis of an approved special topic in
the field of African Native Administration

1 of the following:

Study of a second special topic
Culture Contact and Applied Anthropology
A report of an approved selected subject of Native Administration

The degrees may be awarded with distinction.


## Master of Commerce

Eligibility:          Bachelor of Commerce or Bachelor of Commerce (Honours).

Duration of course:   2 years with Bachelor of Commerce.
                      1 year with Bachelor of Commerce (Hons.)

The examination for the degree consists of a dissertation.

The degree may be awarded with distinction.


## Master of Economics

Eligibility:          Bachelor of Economics or Bachelor of Economics (Honours).

Duration of course:   2 years with Bachelor of Economics.
                      1 year with Bachelor of Economics (Hons.)

The examination for the degree consists of a dissertation.

The degree may be awarded with distinction.

## Doctor of Philosophy

Eligibility:          Master of Commerce or Master of Economics of not less
                      than 2 years' standing.

                      Bachelor of Commerce (Hons.) or Bachelor of Economics
                      (Hons.) of not less than 3 years' standing.

## Doctor of Economics

Eligibility:          Bachelor of Economics (Honours) or Bachelor of
                      Commerce (Honours) of the University of not less than
                      5 years' standing.

A candidate for the degree is required to present published work or a
thesis.

## Certificate in the Theory of Accountancy

Eligibility:          Matriculation Certificate of the Joint Matriculation
                      Board.

Duration of course:   4 academic years.

## Curriculum:

1st yr:   Accounting I, Elementary Finance or Elementary Mathematics,
          Statistics, Mercantile Law IA

2nd yr:   Accounting II, Auditing I, Mercantile Law IB, Law of Executors,
          Trustees and Liquidators

3rd yr:   Mercantile Law II, Advanced Company Law, Accounts of Executors,
          Trustees and Liquidators, Accounting IIIA

4th yr:   Accounting IIIB, Auditing II, Cost Accounting, Income Tax

## Faculty of Engineering

Eligibility:          Pass in Mathematics of Matriculation standard.

Duration of degree courses:

| | |
|---|---|
| Engineering (Civil, Electrical, Mechanical and Chemical) | 4 years |
| Land Surveying | 4 years |
| Agricultural Engineering | 5 years |
| Architecture | 6 years |
| Quantity Surveying | 5 years |

The following degrees and diplomas are conferred:

  (i)   Engineering:

       Bachelor of Science in Engineering (B.Sc.Eng.)
       Master of Science in Engineering (M.Sc.Eng.)
       Doctor of Philosophy (Ph.D.)
       Doctor of Science in Engineering (D.Sc.Eng.)

  (ii)  Surveying:

       Bachelor of Science in Surveying (B.Sc.Sur.)
       Master of Science in Surveying (M.Sc.Sur.)

 (iii)  Agricultural Engineering:

       Bachelor of Science in Agricultural Engineering (B.Sc.Eng.Agric.)

  (iv)  Architecture:

       Bachelor of Architecture (B.Arch.)
       Master of Architecture (M.Arch.)
       Doctor of Philosophy (Ph.D.)
       Doctor of Architecture (D.Arch.)

   (v)  Quantity Surveying:

       Bachelor of Science in Quantity Surveying (B.Sc.Q.S.)
       Master of Science in Quantity Surveying (M.Sc.Q.S.)
       Diploma in Quantity Surveying (Dipl.Q.S.)

  (vi)  Town Planning:

       Diploma in Town Planning (Dipl.T.P.)

Curriculum:

1st yr:   All Engineering candidates:

       Mathematics I, Applied Mathematics I, Physics I, Chemistry I, General Engineering.

2nd yr:   All Engineering candidates except Chemical:

       Mathematics II, Applied Mathematics II, Physics II, Engineering, Engineering Drawing, Surveying.

Chemical Engineering candidates:

Chemistry II, Physics II, Mathematics II, Engineering C, Engineering Drawing.

3rd yr:   Civil Engineering candidates:

Civil Engineering I, Civil Engineering Drawing and Design I, Electrical and Mechanical Engineering, Elements of Geology, Surveying I, Mathematics and Applied Mathematics III, Sources of Technical Information.

Electrical Engineering candidates:

Electrical Engineering I, Telecommunications I, Electrical Engineering Drawing and Design I, Mechanical Engineering I, Mathematics and Applied Mathematics III, Sources of Technical Information.

Mechanical Engineering candidates:

Mechanical Engineering I, Mechanical Engineering Drawing and Design I, Metallurgy, Graphics, Electrical Engineering I, Mathematics and Applied Mathematics III, Sources of Technical Information.

Chemical Engineering candidates:

Physical and Analytical Chemistry IIIE, Chemical Engineering I, Electrical Engineering IC, Mechanical Engineering IC, Mechanical Engineering Drawing and Design IC, Mathematics IIIC.

4th yr:   Civil Engineering candidates:

Civil Engineering II, Civil Engineering Drawing and Design II, Surveying II.

Electrical Engineering candidates:

Electrical Engineering II, Electrical Engineering Drawing and Design II or Telecommunications II, Engineering Economics and Works Organization and Management.

Mechanical Engineering candidates:

Mechanical Engineering II, Mechanical Engineering Drawing and Design II, Engineering Economics and Works Organization and Management.

Chemical Engineering candidates:

Chemical Engineering II, Physical Chemistry IVE, Engineering Economics and Works Organization and Management.

The degree of Bachelor of Science in Engineering may be awarded with distinction.

## Master of Science in Engineering

Eligibility:            Bachelor of Science in Engineering.

Duration of course:  1 year.

A dissertation is required.

The degree may be awarded with distinction.

## Doctor of Philosophy

Eligibility:            Master of Science in Engineering of not less than 2
                        years' standing.

                        Bachelor of Science in Engineering of not less than
                        3 years' standing.

A thesis is required.

## Doctor of Science in Engineering

Eligibility:            Bachelor of Science in Engineering of the University
                        of not less than 6 years' standing.

The degree is awarded for independent published work.

## Bachelor of Science in Surveying

## Curriculum:

1st yr:   Mathematics I, Physics I, Geology I or Geography I, Surveying I.
2nd yr:   Mathematics II, Physics II, Geology II or Geography II,
          Surveying II.
3rd yr:   Mathematics III, Astronomy, Town Planning I, Surveying III,
          Community Studies, Electronics.
4th yr:   Town and Regional Planning II, Surveying IV, Legal Aspects of
          Surveying.

## Master of Science in Surveying

Eligibility:            Bachelor of Science in Surveying.

Duration of course:  1 year.

A dissertation is required.

A Bachelor of Science in Surveying who has completed the requirements for
the Diploma in Photogrammetry is awarded the degree on presentation of a
dissertation.

The degree may be awarded with distinction.

## Bachelor of Science in Agricultural Engineering

### Curriculum:

1st yr:   Mathematics I, Applied Mathematics I, Physics I, Chemistry I,
          General Engineering.

2nd yr:   Mathematics II, Applied Mathematics II, Physics II, Engineering,
          Engineering Drawing, Surveying.

3rd yr:   Building Construction I, Mechanical Engineering I, Elements of
          Geology, Civil Engineering I, Civil Engineering Drawing and
          Design, Surveying I, Hygiene and Sanitation.

4th yr:   Agricultural Engineering I, Agricultural Engineering II, Agri-
          cultural Engineering III, Biometry I, Agronomy I, Agricultural
          Chemistry I, Pasture Management and Soil Conservation III.

5th yr:   Agricultural Engineering IV, Agricultural Engineering V, Agri-
          cultural Economics, Agricultural Legislation.

## Bachelor of Architecture

Eligibility:          Pass in Mathematics in the Matriculation examination.

Duration of course:   6 years including 12 months of practical experience.

### Curriculum:

1st yr:   Design I, Building Construction I, History of Architecture I,
          Reading, Writing and Speech, Introduction to the Arts.

2nd yr:   Architectural Design II, Building Construction II, History of
          Architecture II, Architectural Science I, Land Surveying.

3rd yr:   Architectural Design III, Building Construction III, History of
          Architecture III, Architectural Science II.

4th yr:   Architectural Design IV, Building Construction IV, History of
          Architecture IV, Professional Practice I.

5th yr:   Architectural Design V, Building Construction V, Professional
          Practice II, Design Thesis.

## Master of Architecture

Eligibility:          Bachelor of Architecture or Matriculation Certificate
                      and Diploma in Architecture.

Duration of course: 1 year.

A thesis is required.

The degree may be awarded with distinction.


## Doctor of Architecture

Eligibility:           Bachelor of Architecture

A thesis is required.


## Bachelor of Science in Quantity Surveying

Eligibility:           Pass in Mathematics in the Matriculation examination.

Duration of course: 5 years.

## Curriculum:

1st yr:   Quantities I, Architectural Drawing I, Building Construction I, Reading, Writing and Speech, Introduction to Architecture.

2nd yr:   Quantities II, Building Construction II, Architectural Science I, Land Surveying, Architectural Drawing II.

3rd yr:   Quantities III, Building Construction III, Architectural Science II, Architectural Drawing III.

4th yr:   Quantities IV, Building Construction IV, Professional Practice I, Field Surveys of Buildings.

5th yr:   Quantities V, Professional Practice II, Analysis of Prices, Building Costs Research.

The degree may be awarded with distinction.


## Diploma in Quantity Surveying

Eligibility:           Matriculation Certificate.

Duration of course: 5 years.

## Curriculum:

1st yr:   Quantities I, Building Construction I, Architectural Drawing I, Reading, Writing and Speech, Introduction to Architecture.

2nd yr:   Quantities II, Building Construction II, Architectural Science I, Land Surveying, Architectural Drawing II.

3rd yr:  Quantities III, Building Construction III, Architectural Science II, Architectural Drawing III.

4th yr:  Quantities IV, Building Construction IV, Professional Practice I, Field Surveys of Buildings.

5th yr:  Quantities V, Professional Practice II, Analysis of Prices, Building Costs Research.

## Diploma in Town Planning

Eligibility:  Candidate must hold an approved degree, a professional qualification in Architecture, Civil Engineering or Land Surveying, or some other qualification acceptable to the Senate, or be eligible for registration with the Institute of S.A. Architects, or be eligible for corporate membership of the Institution of Civil Engineers, or have been admitted to practice as a Land Surveyor under the Land Survey Act.

Duration of course:  3 years.

## Curriculum:

1st yr:  Historical Development of Planning, Economics and Economic Geography, Sociology, Elements of Town Planning.

2nd yr:  Theory and Practice of Town Planning I, Civic and Landscape Design, Engineering Aspects of Town Planning, Elements of Geology.

3rd yr:  Theory and Practice of Town Planning II, Legal Aspects of Town Planning, Land Surveying in Relation to Town Planning, Town Planning Thesis.

## Diploma in Photogrammetry

Eligibility:  An approved degree, a professional qualification in Civil Engineering or Surveying.

Duration of course:  1 year.

There is an examination in the Theory and Practice of Photogrammetry.

## Faculty of Agriculture

## Bachelor of Science in Agriculture

Eligibility:  Matriculation with pass in Mathematics.

The usual 1st-year course consists of:  Botany I, Chemistry I, Physics I or IB, and Zoology I.

## Agricultural Economics Option:

2nd yr:   Agricultural Economics I, Agronomy I, Animal Husbandry I, Pasture Management and Soil Conservation I, Soil Science.

3rd yr:   Agricultural Economics II, Agronomy II, Animal Husbandry A, Biometry I, Economics II.

4th yr:   Agricultural Economics III, Agricultural Legislation, Biometry II.

## Agronomy Option:

2nd yr:   Agronomy I, Biochemistry I, Genetics I, Microbiology I, Pasture Management and Soil Conservation I, Plant Physiology and Anatomy, Soil Science I.

3rd yr:   Agronomy II, Agricultural Engineering A, Biometry I, Pasture Management and Soil Conservation II, Soil Science II.

      1 of the following:

      Biochemistry A, Genetics II, Animal Husbandry A.

4th yr:   Agronomy III, Agricultural Economics A, Entomology II.

## Animal Husbandry Option:

2nd yr:   Agronomy I, Anatomy and Physiology, Animal Husbandry I, Biochemistry I, Genetics I, Microbiology I, Pasture Management and Soil Conservation I.

3rd yr:   Animal Husbandry II, Agricultural Engineering A, Agro-Meteorology, Biochemistry II, Biometry I, Pasture Management and Soil Conservation II.

4th yr:   either   Animal Husbandry III, Animal Diseases, Population Genetics.

      or   Animal Husbandry IIIB, Agricultural Economics B, Agricultural Legislation, Agronomy III, Animal Diseases.

## Biochemistry Option:

2nd yr:   Biochemistry I, Chemistry II, Microbiology I, Plant Physiology and Anatomy or Anatomy and Physiology.  And

      either   Mathematics I or any 2 of the following:

      Agronomy I, Animal Husbandry I, Genetics I or Soil Science I.

3rd yr:   Biochemistry II, Biometry I, Chemistry III, 1 other course.

4th yr:   Biochemistry III, Organic Chemistry IV.

Biometry Option:

2nd yr:   Agronomy I, Animal Husbandry I, Genetics I, Mathematics II, Microbiology I.

Any 2 of the following:

Biochemistry I, Horticulture I, Pasture Management and Soil Conservation, Plant Pathology I, Soil Science I.

3rd yr:   Biometry I, Mathematics III, Mathematical Statistics.  And either Genetics II or Soil Science II.

4th yr:   Biometry II, Mathematical Biometry, Population Genetics.

Dairy Industry Option:

2nd yr:   Anatomy and Physiology, Animal Husbandry I, Biochemistry I, Dairy Industry, Microbiology I.

3rd yr:   Dairy Industry II, Agricultural Engineering B, Biometry A, Dairy Chemistry, Dairy Microbiology.

4th yr:   Dairy Industry III, Agricultural Legislation, Dairy Company Administration.

Entomology Option:

2nd yr:   Biochemistry I, Entomology I, Genetics I, Microbiology I, Plant Physiology and Anatomy.

3rd yr:   Entomology II, Agro-Meteorology, Biometry I, Biochemistry II, Organic Chemistry.

1 of the following:

Agronomy II, Horticulture II, Plant Pathology II.

4th yr:   Entomology III, Biometry II, Cytology.

Genetics Option:

2nd yr:   Agronomy I, Biochemistry I, Genetics I, Mathematics I, Microbiology I, Plant Pathology I, Plant Physiology and Anatomy or Anatomy and Physiology.

3rd yr:   Genetics II, Biochemistry II, Biometry I, Chemistry II, Microbiology II.

## Horticulture Option:

2nd yr:    Biochemistry I, Genetics I, Horticulture I, Microbiology I,
           Plant Physiology and Anatomy, Soil Science I, Plant Pathology I.

3rd yr:    Horticulture II, Agricultural Engineering A, Agro-Meteorology,
           Biochemistry A, Biometry I, Entomology II, Soil Science II.

4th yr:    Horticulture III, Agricultural Economics A, Agricultural
           Legislation.


## Microbiology Option:

2nd yr:    Biochemistry I, Genetics I, Microbiology I, Plant Physiology and
           Anatomy or Anatomy and Physiology, Soil Science I.

3rd yr:    Microbiology II, Biochemistry A, Biometry A, Chemistry II.

4th yr:    Microbiology III, Chemistry IIIB.


## Pasture Management and Soil Conservation Option:

2nd yr:    Agronomy I, Animal Husbandry I, Biochemistry I, Genetics I,
           Plant Physiology and Anatomy, Pasture Management and Soil
           Conservation I, Soil Science I.

3rd yr:    Pasture Management and Soil Conservation II, Agricultural
           Engineering A, Agro-Meteorology, Agronomy II, Animal Husbandry
           A, Biometry I, Soil Science II.

4th yr:    Pasture Management and Soil Conservation III, Agricultural
           Economics A, Agricultural Legislation, Silviculture.


## Plant Pathology Option:

2nd yr:    Biochemistry I, Genetics I, Microbiology I, Plant Pathology I,
           Plant Physiology and Anatomy, Soil Science I.

3rd yr:    Plant Pathology II, Agro-Meteorology, Biochemistry A, Biometry
           A, Genetics II.

           either Agronomy II or Soil Science II.

4th yr:    Plant Pathology III, Cytology, Microbiology II.


## Poultry Husbandry Option:

2nd yr:    Anatomy and Physiology, Animal Husbandry I, Biochemistry I,
           Genetics I, Microbiology I, Poultry Husbandry.

3rd yr:    Poultry Husbandry II, Agricultural Economics A, Animal Husbandry
           III, Poultry Diseases.

Soil Science Option:

2nd yr:   Agronomy I, Biochemistry I, Microbiology I, Plant Physiology and Anatomy, Soil Science I.

3rd yr:   Soil Science II, Agronomy II, Biometry I, Chemistry II.

4th yr:   Soil Science III, Chemistry III or IIIB.

Medium of instruction:   Instruction will be through the medium of both official languages.

The degree of Bachelor of Science in Agriculture may be awarded cum laude.

Master of Science in Agriculture

Eligibility:         Bachelor of Science in Agriculture.

Duration of course:  1 year.

The examination consists of:

(a)  A dissertation embodying the results of research conducted by the candidate.

(b)  1 or more written papers, or an oral examination, or both.

The degree may be awarded cum laude.

Doctor of Philosophy

Eligibility:         Master of Science in Agriculture of the University of not less than 2 years' standing who has attended the University as a registered student for at least 3 years.

Bachelor of Science in Agriculture of the University of not less than 3 years' standing who has attended the University as a registered student for at least 3 years.

A graduate of another recognized university who has been admitted to the status of Master of Science in Agriculture, and who has attended as a registered student for at least 2 years after obtaining the qualification by virtue of which such admission has been granted.

A candidate for the degree passes a written or oral translation test, or both, in at least 1 prescribed foreign language as a prerequisite for admission to the final examination for the degree.

Doctor of Science in Agriculture

Eligibility:           Bachelor of Science in Agriculture of the University
                       of not less than 5 years' standing.

A thesis is required.


Faculty of Medicine

M.B., Ch.B.

The University of Natal offers a 7-year course leading to the medical
practitioner's general qualification, the degrees of M.B., Ch.B. (Bachelor
of Medicine and Bachelor of Surgery).

The courses are as follows:

Preliminary year:     English I or Afrikaans, History I, Sociology I.  And
            Introductory Chemistry and Physics courses.

1st yr:    Botany I, Physics I, Chemistry I, Zoology I.

2nd yr:    Anatomy, Physiology, Psychology.

3rd yr:    Psychology, Pharmacological Physiology, Pathology.

4th, 5th,
6th yrs:   Medicine, Surgery, Obstetrics and Gynaecology, Special Subjects.


The South African Medical and Dental Council prescribes a "Minimum Medical
Curriculum" of 6 years.  The 1st year comprises the study of Botany,
Chemistry, Physics and Zoology.

The University of Natal adds to this course a "Preliminary year."  This
provides an introduction to the science subjects and includes a full 1st-
year course in English or Afrikaans, and full 1st-year courses in History
and Sociology.

The years of study in the Faculty of Medicine are referred to as "Preliminary", "First", etc. to "Sixth" in order to keep the terminology in line
with other faculties of medicine in the Union.

Admission to preliminary year:       Matriculation Certificate of the Joint
                                     Board of the Universities of South
                                     Africa, with a pass in Mathematics.

Promotion or admission to 2nd year:
                             either Satisfactory completion of the work of
                             the preliminary and 1st years.

                    <u>or</u>    An approved degree which includes
                            credits in Botany **I**, Chemistry **I**,
                            Physics **I**, and Zoology **I**.

A candidate is not permitted to enter upon the work of the 2nd year of the curriculum for the degrees until he has obtained credit for all of the following courses:

| | |
|---|---|
| English **I** or Afrikaans-Nederlands **I** | |
| History **I** | Chemistry **I** |
| Sociology **I** | Physics **I** |
| Botany **I** | Zoology **I** |

**2nd yr:**   Human Anatomy (including Embryology and Physical Anthropology),
                Human Physiology (including Experimental Physiology, Histology
                  and Biochemistry)
                Psychology

**3rd yr:**   Pathology (including Morbid Anatomy and Morbid Histology,
                Bacteriology, Parasitology, and Chemical Pathology)
                Pharmacological Physiology (Pharmacology)
                Psychology

**4th and**
**5th yrs:**   Medicine (including Child Health, Acute Infectious Diseases,
                Diseases of the Skin, Venereal Diseases and Tropical Diseases)
                Surgery (including Anaesthetics, Diseases of the Eye, Diseases
                of the Ear, Nose and Throat, Urology and Orthopaedics)
                Obstetrics and Gynaecology
                Clinical Pathology
                Preventive and Promotive Medicine
                Radiology
                Psychological Medicine
                Forensic Medicine
                Toxicology

**Final**
**year:**    Medicine, Surgery, Obstetrics, Gynaecology.

Passes in examinations in all subjects may be graded first, second or third class.


## Master of Medicine

The degree may be conferred on candidates who have obtained the M.B., Ch.B.

The degree may be taken in the following branches:

| | |
|---|---|
| Medicine | Radiology |
| Surgery | Diagnostic Radiology |
| Children's Diseases | Therapeutic Radiology |

                    Obstetrics and Gynaecology        Diseases of the Eye
                    Pathology                         Diseases of the Ear, Nose
                    Dermatology                           and Throat
                    Anaesthetics

Candidates for the M.Med. degree must have obtained the M.B.,Ch.B. at
least 2 years before being admitted to the M.Med. degree course, and they
must have been registered with the South African Medical and Dental
Council as medical practitioners for at least 1 year.

Duration of course:  3-4 years.

## Doctor of Medicine

Eligibility:              Candidates with any M.B.,Ch.B. of not less than 2
                          academic years' standing.

A thesis is required.

## UNIVERSITY OF THE WITWATERSRAND, Johannesburg

Founded as South African School of Mines in 1896.  Became Transvaal
Technical Institute in 1904, Transvaal University College in 1906, South
African School of Mines and Technology in 1910, and University College,
Johannesburg, in 1920.  In 1921 became University of the Witwatersrand.

General entrance requirements:    Matriculation Certificate or Exemption
                                  Certificate of the Joint Matriculation
                                  Board.

## Faculties:

            Arts
            Science
            Medicine
            Engineering
            Commerce
            Law
            Dentistry
            Architecture

Language of instruction:  English.

Degrees awarded:

| Faculty | Degree | Duration of course (years) |
|---------|--------|----------------------------|
| Arts | B.A. | 3 |
| | B.A. (Hons.) | 4 |
| | M.A. | 1 |
| | Ph.D. | 2 |
| | D.Litt. | |
| | B.A. (Fine Arts) | 4 |
| | B.A. (Social Work) | 4 |
| | M.A. (Social Work) | 2 |
| | M.A. (Clin. Psych.) | 2 |
| | B.A. (Logopaedics) | 4 |
| | B.A. (Public Admin.) | 4 |
| | B.Mus. | 3 |
| | M.Mus. | 1 |
| | D.Mus. | |
| | B.Ed. | 1 |
| | M.Ed. | 1 |
| | Diploma in Librarianship | |
| | Diploma in Native Affairs | 2 |
| | Diploma in Education of the Deaf | 2 |
| Science | B.Sc. | 3 |
| | B.Sc. (Hons.) | 4 |
| | M.Sc. | 1 |
| | Ph.D. | 2 |
| | D.Sc. | |
| | Diploma in Applied Geophysics | 1 |
| Medicine | M.B., B.Ch. | 6 |
| | M.Med. (Path.) | 4 |
| | M.D. | |
| | B.Sc. (Physiother.) | 4 |
| | Diploma in Anaesthetics | |
| | Diploma in Paediatrics | |
| | Diploma in Physical Medicine | |
| | Diploma in Psychological Medicine | |
| | Diploma in Public Health | |
| | Diploma in Radiological Diagnosis | 3 |
| | Diploma in Radiotherapy | 3 |
| | Diploma in Tropical Medicine and Hygiene | |
| | Diploma in Industrial Health | |
| | Diploma in Nursing | 18 mos. |
| | Diploma in Occupational Therapy | 3½ |
| | Diploma in Physiotherapy Education | 12-18 mos. |

| | | |
|---|---|---|
| Engineering | B.Sc. (Eng.) | 4 |
| | M.Sc. (Eng.) | 1 |
| | Ph.D. | 2 |
| | D.Sc. (Eng.) | |
| Commerce | B.Com. | 3 |
| | B.Com. (Hons.) | 1 |
| | M.Com. | 1 |
| | Ph.D. | 2 |
| | D.Sc. (Econ.) | |
| | Diploma in the Economics of Local Government and Public Administration | 2 |
| | Certificate in the Theory of Accountancy | |
| Law | LL.B. | 2 |
| | LL.M. | |
| | LL.D. | |
| | Diploma in Law and Diploma in Law (Public Service) | 3 |
| | Certificate in Law (Public Service) | 3 |
| Dentistry | B.D.S. | 5½ |
| | M.D.S. | |
| | D.D.S. | |
| | Higher Diploma in Dentistry | |
| | Diploma in Anaesthetics | |
| | Diploma in Public Dentistry | |
| | Diploma in Orthodontics | 2 |
| | Diploma in Maxillo-Facial and Oral Surgery | |
| Architecture | B.Arch. | 6 |
| | M.Arch. | 2 |
| | Ph.D. | 2 |
| | D.Arch. | |
| | B.Sc. (Q.S.) | 5 |
| | B.Sc. (Town and Regional Planning) | 4 |
| | M.Sc. (Town and Regional Planning) | |
| | D.Sc. (Town and Regional Planning) | |
| | Diploma in Quantity Surveying | 5 |
| | Diploma in Town Planning | 3 |
| | Graduate Diploma in Engineering | 1 |

## Faculty of Arts

### Bachelor of Arts

A candidate for the ordinary degree completes not fewer than 10 qualifying courses.

Duration of course:  3 years.

### Bachelor of Arts with Honours

A candidate for this degree complies with all the requirements for the ordinary degree of Bachelor of Arts and also completes an Honours course.

Duration of course:  4 years.

### Master of Arts

Duration of course:  1 year.

Dissertation required.

### Doctor of Philosophy

Duration of course:  2 academic years.

Thesis required.

### Doctor of Literature

Candidate must present published work.

### Bachelor of Arts in Fine Arts

#### Curriculum:

1st yr:   History of Art I, Theory and Practice of Art I, 2 other
          subjects.

2nd yr:   History of Art II, Drawing from Life I, Painting and Composition
          I, 1 other subject.

3rd yr:   History of Art III, Drawing from Life II, Painting II, Composition II.

4th yr:   Painting III, Composition III, Special study.

## Bachelor of Arts in Social Work

### Curriculum:

1st yr:   Social Work I, Sociology I, Psychology I, Afrikaans I or English I.

2nd yr:   Social Work II, Sociology II, Psychology II.

        1 of the following:

        Social Anthropology I, Economics I, Economic History I, Introduction to Philosophy.

3rd yr:   Psychology III, Social Work III, Sociology III.

4th yr:   Social Work IV.

        1 of the following:

        Advanced Sociology, Psychiatry and Mental Hygiene for Social Workers, Social Anthropology II, Introduction to Philosophy, African Administration.

## Master of Arts in Social Work

Duration of course:   2 years.

Dissertation required.

## Master of Arts in Clinical Psychology

Duration of course:   2 academic years.

Dissertation required.

## Bachelor of Arts in Logopaedics

### Curriculum:

1st yr:   Afrikaans I, Anatomy, Physiology and Histology for Speech, Voice and Hearing, English I, Phonetics and Linguistics I, Psychology I.

2nd yr:   Logopaedics I, Pathology of the Speech, Voice and Hearing Organs, Phonetics II, Psychology II, Theory of Education.

3rd yr:   Audiology I, Logopaedics II, Neurology of Speech, Voice and
          Hearing Organs, Psychology III.

4th yr:   Applied Neurology, Audiology II, Interviewing and Case Recording,
          Logopaedics III, Psychological Techniques in Clinical Practice.


## Bachelor of Arts in Public Administration

## Curriculum:

1st yr:   Public Administration I, Political Science I, Economics I or His-
          tory I or Sociology I or Psychology I, English I or Afrikaans I.

2nd yr:   Public Administration II, Political Science II.

          2 of the following:

          Economics I or II, Economic History I, African Administration I,
          Social Anthropology I, History I or II, Sociology I or II,
          Psychology I or II, a Bantu language, Problems of Modern Industry.

3rd yr:   Public Administration III, Political Science III.

          1 of the following:

          Public Finance, Constitutional Law, African Administration I or
          II, Economic History of South Africa, Economic History I or II.

4th yr:   Public Administration IV, Group Psychology or optional subject
          listed for 3rd year.


## Bachelor of Music

## Curriculum:

1st yr:   History of Music I, Counterpoint, Harmony and Composition I,
          Practical Music Study I, Form I, 1 other subject.

2nd yr:   History of Music II, Counterpoint, Harmony and Composition II,
          Practical Music Study II, Orchestration and Instrumentation I,
          Form II, 1 other subject.

3rd yr:   History of Music III, Counterpoint, Harmony and Composition III,
          Music Study III, Orchestration and Instrumentation II, Conducting
          I, 1 other subject.


## Master of Music

Duration of course:  1 year.

Dissertation required.

## Doctor of Music

An original published work is required.


## Bachelor of Education

Eligibility:          Bachelor's degree plus experience in education.

Duration of course:   1 year.

### Curriculum:

Philosophy of Education, Psychology of Education.

1 of the following:

Comparative Education, Educational Administration and Supervision, Statistics and Psychometrics, History of Education,
Remedial Education, Sociology of Education.


## Master of Education

Duration of course:   1 academic year.

Dissertation is required.


## Diploma in Librarianship

Eligibility:          Bachelor's degree is required.

Proficiency in English, Afrikaans, and 2 other languages.  2 years of
full-time library service.  A satisfactory bibliography on an approved
subject must be compiled.

### Curriculum:

Book Selection and Reference Methods, Cataloguing, Classification, Bibliography and Book Production, Library Administration,
Organization and Routine, Special Studies.


## Diploma in Native Affairs

Duration of course:   2 years.

### Curriculum:

1st yr:   Bantu Language I, African Administration.

1 of the following:

Economic History of South Africa, Sociology, Economic and Social
Development of South Africa, The Native in Economic Life.

2nd yr:   Bantu Language II, 2nd Bantu Language, Social Anthropology.


<u>Diploma in Education of the Deaf</u>

Eligibility:          Teacher's Diploma.

<u>Curriculum:</u>

1st yr:   Anatomy, Physiology, and Histology for Speech, Voice and Hearing;
          Audiology I, Education of the Deaf and Hard-of-hearing I, Logo-
          paedics I, Phonetics and Linguistics I.

2nd yr:   Audiology II, Child and Clinical Psychology, Education of the
          Deaf and Hard-of-hearing II, Logopaedics III, Phonetics II.


<u>Faculty of Science</u>

<u>Bachelor of Science</u>

A candidate for the degree completes at least 9 qualifying courses.

Major subjects for the degree are:

Anatomy                            Micro-Anatomy
Applied Mathematics                Physics
Botany                             Physiological Chemistry
Chemistry                          Physiology
Geology and Mineralogy             Psychology
Geography                          Zoology
Mathematics                        Mathematical Statistics


<u>Bachelor of Science with Honours</u>

Major subjects for the degree are:

Anatomy                            Psychology
Applied Mathematics                Zoology
Botany                             Biochemistry
Geography                          Chemistry
Mathematical Statistics            Geology
Mathematics                        Geophysics
Micro-Anatomy                      Physics
Physiological Chemistry            Theoretical Physics
Physiology

## Master of Science

Duration of course:  1 year.

Dissertation is required.

## Doctor of Philosophy

Duration of course:  2 years.

Thesis is required.

## Doctor of Science

Original published work is required.

## Diploma in Applied Geophysics

Eligibility:            Bachelor of Science.

Duration of course:  1 year.

## Faculty of Medicine

## M.B., B.Ch.

Eligibility:            Pass in Mathematics in the Matriculation examination.

Duration of course:  6 years.

## Examinations:

| | |
|---|---|
| 1st examination: | Botany, Chemistry, Physics, Zoology. |
| 2nd examination: | Anatomy, Physiology I. |
| 3rd examination: | Pathology and Microbiology, Physiology II. |
| 4th examination: | Forensic Medicine, Preventive and Social Medicine, Clinical Pathology, Psychiatry, Pharmacology. |
| Final examination: | Medicine, Obstetrics and Gynaecology, and Surgery. |

## Curriculum:

1st yr:   Botany, Chemistry, Physics, Zoology.

2nd yr:   Anatomy, Physiology I.

| 3rd yr: | Pathology and Microbiology | |
|---------|----------------------------|--|
| | Pharmacology | |
| | Introductory Medicine (Systematic and Clinical) | |
| | Introductory Surgery (Systematic and Clinical) | |
| | Physiology II | |

| 4th yr: | Anaesthetics | Obstetrics and Gynaecology |
|---------|--------------|----------------------------|
| | Clinical Anatomy | Preventive and Social Medicine |
| | Clinical Medicine | including Sociology |
| | Clinical Pathology | Forensic Medicine |
| | Clinico-Pathological Discussions | Psychiatry |
| | Clinical Surgery | Psychology |
| | Dentistry in relation to the | Therapeutics |
| | Practice of Medicine | Pharmacology |

| 5th yr: | Acute Infectious Fevers | Obstetrics and Gynaecology |
|---------|-------------------------|----------------------------|
| | Clinical Medicine | Paediatrics |
| | Clinical Surgery | Practical Anaesthetics |
| | Psychiatry | Radiodiagnosis and Radio- |
| | Diseases of the Ear, Nose, | therapy |
| | and Throat | Therapeutics |
| | Diseases of the Eye | Tropical Diseases |
| | Diseases of the Skin | Venereal Diseases |

| 6th yr: | Medicine | Conduct of Medical Practice |
|---------|----------|------------------------------|
| | Obstetrics | Surgery |
| | Paediatrics | Gynaecology |
| | Orthopaedics | Urology |
| | Neurosurgery | Social Medicine |
| | Physical Medicine | Neurology |
| | Clinico-Pathological Discussions | Therapeutics |
| | Plastic and Maxillo-Facial | Clinical Pathology |
| | Surgery | |

## Master of Medicine in Pathology

Eligibility:          Bachelor of Medicine and Bachelor of Surgery (M.B., B. Ch.).

Duration of course:  4 years.

## Doctor of Medicine

Eligibility:          M.B., B.Ch.

Thesis is required.

## Master of Surgery

Eligibility:          Diploma in Surgery or Diploma in Obstetrics and Gynaecology.

Thesis is required.


## Bachelor of Science in Physiotherapy

Eligibility:              Pass in Mathematics in the Matriculation examination.

Duration of course:  4 years.

## Curriculum:

1st yr:   Chemistry, Physics, Psychology, Zoology.
2nd yr:   Anatomy, Physiology.

## Final Professional Examination:

Theory and Practice of Massage, Theory and Practice of Medical
Gymnastics, Theory and Practice of Electro-therapy, General
Medicine, Surgery and Obstetrics, and Gynaecology.


## Diploma in Anaesthetics (D.A.)

Eligibility:              Attainment of a registrable qualification in Medicine,
Surgery and Obstetrics, or in Dentistry.

## Examination:

Part I:         Anatomy, Physiology, and Pharmacology in relation to
Anaesthesia.
Part II:        The History, Theory, and Practice of Anaesthesia.


## Diploma in Paediatrics (Dip. Paed.)

Eligibility:              Medical practitioners in Medicine, Surgery and
Obstetrics.

## Examination:

Part I:         Developmental Anatomy and Histology of Childhood,
Physiology of Childhood, Pathology of Childhood.
Part II:        Development and Training, Physical and Mental, of
the Child
Hygiene and Dietetics of Infancy and Childhood
Affections of the New Born and the Care of the
Premature Infant
Diseases in Infancy and Childhood, Medical, Surgical,
and Infectious
Therapeutics of Infancy and Childhood, including
Remedial Treatment, Physical and Mental

> Legislation and Public Administration in regard to
> the care of children, including the methods and
> conduct of infant welfare centers, child guidance
> clinics, nursery schools and speech clinics.

## Diploma in Physical Medicine (D.Phys.Med.)

Eligibility:        Practitioners in Medicine, Surgery and Obstetrics.

Examination:

    Part I:        Anatomy, Physiology and Pathology in relation to
                Physical Medicine.

    Part II:       Electrotherapy and Electrodiagnosis
                Heat Therapy, Hyperthermy, Hypothermy, and Acino-
                    therapy.
                Mechanotherapy, including Hydrotherapy and Occupational
                    Therapy
                Clinical Medicine and Clinical Surgery including Ortho-
                    paedics
                Psychological Medicine
                Rehabilitation Medicine

## Diploma in Psychological Medicine (D.P.M.)

Eligibility:        Practitioners in Medicine, Surgery and Obstetrics.

Examination:

    Part I:        Anatomy and Histology in relation to the Nervous
                System, Physiology in relation to the Nervous System,
                Psychology.

    Part II:       Pathology of the Nervous System, Neurology, Psycho-
                logical Medicine.

## Diploma in Public Health (D.P.H.)

Eligibility:        Practitioners in Medicine, Surgery and Obstetrics.

Examination:

    Part I:        Bacteriology, including Serology and Immunology,
                Parasitology, including Protozoology, Helminthology
                and Medical Entomology.

    Part II:       Hygiene, Preventable Diseases and Epidemiology,
                Health Legislation and Administration; Inspection of
                and report on premises, Practical and oral examination.

Diploma in Radiological Diagnosis - D.M.R.(D)

Duration of course:  3 years.

Curriculum:

>       Physics in relation to Radiology
>       Theoretical and Practical Radiology and Radiobiology


Diploma in Radiotherapy - D.M.R.(T)

Duration of course:  3 years.

Curriculum:

>       Physics in relation to Radiotherapy
>       Theoretical and Practical Radiotherapy and Radiobiology


Diploma in Tropical Medicine and Hygiene

Examination:

>       Parasitology, Tropical Pathology and Tropical Chemical Pathology,
>       Tropical Bacteriology and Immunology, Tropical Medicine,
>       Tropical Sanitation and Hygiene.


Diploma in Industrial Health

Examination:

>       Industrial Toxicology          Occupational Pathology
>       Medical Statistics             Epidemiology
>       Industrial Hygiene             Medical Jurisprudence
>       Chemistry, Physics, and the Physical Environment
>
>       Occupational Physiology, Occupational Health Services and
>       the Structure and Social Functions of Industry.


Diploma in Nursing (D.N.)

Eligibility:          Matriculation examination of the Joint Matriculation
                      Board.

Duration of course:  18 months.

Examination:

>       Elements of Anatomy and Histology
>       Elements of Physiology and Physiological Chemistry

Elements of Preventive Medicine
Elements of Educational Psychology and the Principles of Teaching
The Principles and Practice of Nursing

## Diploma in Occupational Therapy (D.O.T.)

Duration of course:  3½ years.

### Curriculum:

| | |
|---|---|
| Chemistry | Physics |
| Psychology | Theory of Occupational Therapy |
| Zoology | Crafts |
| Physical Training | Practice of Occupational |
| Anatomy | Therapy |
| Physiology | |

Symptomatology of Medical and Surgical Diseases and Disorders
Symptomatology of Mental and Nervous Diseases and Disorders
Theory and Application of Occupational Therapy
Crafts and Craft Application

## Diploma in Physiotherapy Education (D.P.E.)

Duration of course:   18 months, with the exception of a Bachelor of Science
in Physiotherapy, 12 months.

### Examination:

Anatomy, Physiology, Electromechanics, Educational Psychology,
Principles of Physiotherapy, Applied Physiotherapy, Practical
Teaching.

## Faculty of Engineering

### Bachelor of Science in Engineering

Eligibility:          Pass in Mathematics at the Matriculation examination.

Duration of course:  4 years.

### Chemical Engineering:

1st yr:   Applied Mathematics, Chemistry, Mathematics, Descriptive
Geometry, Physics.

2nd yr:   Applied Mechanics, Chemical Engineering, Chemistry, Mathematics,
Elements of Mechanical Engineering Design, Physics.

3rd yr:   Chemical Engineering, Chemical Engineering Thermodynamics, Electrical Engineering, Mathematics, Physical Chemistry.

4th yr:   Chemical Engineering, Chemical Engineering Design, Chemical Process Principles, Engineering Materials, Physical Chemistry, Numerical Analysis.

Civil Engineering:

1st yr:   Applied Mathematics, Chemistry, Descriptive Geometry, Physics, Mathematics.

2nd yr:   Applied Mathematics, Civil Engineering, Electrical Engineering, Mathematics, Mechanical Engineering, Elements of Mechanical Engineering Design, Physics.

3rd yr:   Applied Mathematics, Civil Engineering, Civil Engineering Design, Geology, Mathematics, Surveying.

4th yr:   Civil Engineering Design, Civil Engineering Practice, Hydraulic Engineering, Soil Mechanics and Foundation Engineering, Statistics for Engineers, Structural Engineering.

Electrical Engineering:

1st yr:   Applied Mathematics, Chemistry, Mathematics, Descriptive Geometry, Physics.

2nd yr:   Applied Mathematics, Electric and Magnetic Circuits, Fluid and Thermodynamics, Mathematics, Elements of Mechanical Engineering Design, Physics.

3rd yr:   Applied Mathematics, Electric Circuits, Electrical Machines I, Electronics I, Field Theory, Measurements and Materials, Metallurgy, Physics.

4th yr:   Communication, Electrical Engineering Design, Electrical Engineering Laboratory, Electrical Machines II, Electrical Networks, Electrical Systems, Electronics II.

          2 of the following:

          Control Engineering, Electric Power Transmission, Electromechanical Energy Conversion, Microwave Electronics, Pulsed Power Systems.

Land Surveying:

1st yr:   Applied Mathematics, Chemistry, Mathematics, Descriptive Geometry, Physics.

2nd yr:   Geology, Mathematics, Optics, Physics, Surveying, Topographical Drawing.

3rd yr:   Field Astronomy, Map Projections, Photogrammetry, Surveying, The Law Relating to Survey Practice, Statistics.

4th yr:   Field Astronomy, Geodesy, Surveying, Town Planning.

## Mechanical Engineering:

1st yr:   Applied Mathematics, Chemistry, Mathematics, Descriptive Geometry, Physics.

2nd yr:   Applied Mechanics, Electric and Magnetic Circuits, Fluid and Thermodynamics, Elements of Mechanical Engineering Design, Mathematics, Physics.

3rd yr:   Applied Mathematics, Electrical Machines, Electric Circuits and Transmission, Metallurgy, Physics, Fluid Mechanics, Graphical Analysis, Industrial Engineering, Mechanical Engineering Design, Numerical Analysis, Strength of Materials, Theory of Machines, Thermodynamics.

4th yr:   Advanced Mechanical Engineering Laboratory, Fluid Mechanics, Industrial Engineering, Mechanical Engineering Design, Strength of Materials, Theory of Machines, Thermodynamics.

        2 of the following:

        Advanced Strength of Materials, Gas Dynamics, Heat and Mass Transfer, Nuclear Engineering, Numerical Analysis, Production Engineering, Refrigeration and Air Conditioning, Statistical Methods.

## Metallurgy:

1st yr:   Applied Mathematics, Chemistry, Mathematics, Descriptive Geometry, Physics.

2nd yr:   Applied Mechanics, Chemistry, Geology, Mathematics, Physics, Assaying.

3rd yr:   Chemical Engineering, Electrical Engineering, Fuels and Furnace Technology, Geology, Intro. Phys. Metallurgy, Physical Chemistry, Non-Ferrous Metallurgy, Metallurgy of Iron and Steel, Ore Dressing, Refractories.

4th yr:   Electro-Metallurgy, Metallurgy of Iron and Steel, Non-Ferrous Metallurgy, Ore Dressing, Physical Metallurgy, Heat Treatment.

## Mining Engineering:

1st yr:   Applied Mathematics, Chemistry, Mathematics, Descriptive Geometry, Physics.

2nd yr:   Applied Mathematics, Civil Engineering, Electrical Engineering, Mathematics, Mechanical Engineering, Elements of Mechanical Engineering Design, Physics.

3rd yr:   Geology, Metallurgy, Mining Engineering, Mining Methods, Mining
          Plant, Statistics, Surveying, either Ore Dressing and Assaying
          or Coal Preparation and Fuel Analysis.

4th yr:   Geology, Mine Administration, Mine Design, Mining Economics and
          Valuation, Mining Methods, Surveying, Mining Engineering or Coal
          Mining Engineering.

## Mining Geology:

1st yr:   Chemistry, Geology, Mathematics, Physics.

2nd yr:   Chemistry, Descriptive Geometry, Geology, Mining Engineering,
          Mining Methods.

3rd yr:   Geology, Mining Methods, Ore Dressing and Assaying, Surveying.

4th yr:   Geology, Geophysics, Mining Economics, Surveying.

## Master of Science

Eligibility:        Bachelor of Science.

Duration of course:  1 year.

Dissertation is required.

## Doctor of Philosophy

Eligibility:        Bachelor of Science.

Duration of course:  2 years.

Thesis is required.

## Doctor of Science

Eligibility:        Bachelor of Science.

Original published work is required.

## Faculty of Commerce

## Bachelor of Commerce

A candidate selects Group I, II, or III.

Group I:

1st yr:  English I
         Elementary Theory of Finance and Statistics or Mathematics I
         Economics I
         Accounting I
         Mercantile Law I

2nd yr:  Business Organization and Technique I
         Economic History I
         Accounting II
         Economics II
         Mercantile Law II
         Company Law I

3rd yr:  Business Organization and Technique II
         Economics History II

         Any 2 from (a) to (d):

         (a)  Economics III or Public Finance
         (b)  (i)  Accounting III
         or  (ii)  Cost Accounting
         or (iii)  Income Tax and Accounting of Trustees, Liquidators
                   and Executors
         (c)  Mercantile Law III and Company Law II
         (d)  Any 2 courses selected from List X

Group II:

1st yr:  English I
         Elementary Theory of Finance and Statistics or Mathematics I
         Economics I
         Business Organization and Technique I
         Economic History I

2nd yr:  Accounting I
         Mercantile Law I
         Business Organization and Technique II
         Economic History II
         Economics II

3rd yr:  Accounting II
         Mercantile Law II
         Company Law I

         Any 2 from A(a), (b), and (c) or B(a), (b) and (c):

         A.   Any 2 of the following:
              (a)  Economics III
              (b)  Economic History III or Public Finance
              (c)  Any 2 courses from List X

         B.   (a)  Local Government
              (b)  Public Administration

    (c)  (i)  Constitutional and Administration Law and any 1
              of Economic History III, African Administration,
              Political Institutions
    or  (ii)  Local Government Finance and either Public
              Finance and 2 of the following, or 4 of the
              following:
              Banking and Monetary Policy
              Economic Fluctuations
              Financing of Economic Activity
              Industrial Organization and Management
              Modern Economic Problems

Group III:

1st yr:    English I
           Elementary Theory of Finance and Statistics or Mathematics I
           Economics I
           Accounting I
           Introduction to the Study of Law
           The Law of Contract

2nd yr:    Business Organization and Technique I
           Economic History I
           Accounting II
           Economics II
           Constitutional and Administrative Law
           Public International Law

3rd yr:    Business Organization and Technique II
           Economic History II
           Law of Corporations and Insolvency
           Roman Law

           Any course from (a) to (d):

    (a)  Economics III
    (b)  Public Finance
    (c)  Accounting III
    or    Income Tax and Accounts of Trustees, Liquidators and
          Executors
    (d)  Any 2 courses from List X

List X:

           Banking and Monetary Policy
           Economics of Transport
           Economic Fluctuations
           Financing of Economic Activity
           Industrial Organization and Management
           Industrial Trade and Tariffs
           Marketing
           Modern Economic Problems
           Stock Exchange Theory and Practice

## Bachelor of Commerce with Honours

Eligibility:            Bachelor of Commerce.

Duration of course:  1 year.

An Honours course in 1 of the following fields of study must be completed:

> Accounting, Applied Economics, Commercial Law, Economic History, Economics, Industrial Law, Local Government and Public Administration, Statistics.

## Master of Commerce

Duration of course:  1 academic year.

Dissertation is required.

## Doctor of Philosophy

Duration of course:  2 academic years.

Thesis is required.

## Doctor of Science in Economics

Published work is required.

## Diploma in the Economics of Local Government and Public Administration

Duration of course:  2 years.

## Curriculum:

> Economics I, Economic History I, Public Administration, Elements of Local Government, Economics II, Public Finance, Economics of Public Utilities, Local Government Law.

## Certificate in the Theory of Accountancy

Eligibility:              Matriculation Certificate of the Joint Matriculation Board.

Curriculum:

1st yr:   English I, Elementary Theory of Finance and Statistics <u>or</u>
          Mathematics I.

2nd yr:   Accounting I, Mercantile Law II, Company Law I,
          Principles of Applied Economics.

3rd yr:   Accounting II, Mercantile Law III, Auditing I.

4th yr:   Accounting III, Accounts of Trustees, Liquidators and Executors,
          Company Law II, Income Tax.

5th yr:   Accounting IV, Auditing II, Cost Accounting.


## Faculty of Law

### Bachelor of Laws

Eligibility:            Bachelor's degree.

Duration of course:  2 years.

Curriculum:

Introduction to the Study          Special Contracts I and II
  of South African Law             Law of Corporations and
Roman Law I and II                   Insolvency
Constitutional Law                 Jurisprudence
Criminal Law and Procedure         Law of Delict
Public International Law            Conflict of Laws
History of South African Law       Civil Procedure
Law of Persons                     Law of Evidence
General Principles of Contract     Law of Property


### Master of Laws

Eligibility:            Bachelor of Laws.

Dissertation is required.


### Doctor of Laws

Eligibility:            Bachelor of Laws.

Original work is required.

## Diploma in Law and Diploma in Law (Public Service)

### Curriculum:

1st yr:  Introduction to the Study of South African Law and
         South African Law of Persons, Criminal Law, Criminal Procedure,
         Constitutional and Administrative Law.

2nd yr:  General Principles of Contract, Interpretation of Statutes,
         Mercantile Law I, Law of Property and Law of Succession,
         Special Contracts.

3rd yr:  Roman Law, Law of Delict, Mercantile Law II, Civil Procedure,
         Law of Evidence.

## Certificate in Law (Public Service)

### Curriculum:

1st yr:  Introduction to the Study of Law and South African Law of Persons,
         Criminal Law, Criminal Procedure, Mercantile Law I.

2nd yr:  General Principles of Contract (including Agency),
         Interpretation of Statutes, Law of Property
         (including Mortgage and Pledge) and Law of Succession,
         Special Contracts.

3rd yr:  Roman Law, Law of Delict, Mercantile Law II, Civil Procedure,
         Law of Evidence.

## Faculty of Dentistry

## Bachelor of Dental Surgery (B.D.S.)

Duration of course:  5½ years.

### Curriculum:

1st yr:  Botany, Chemistry, Physics, Zoology.

2nd yr:  Anatomy, Physiology I.

3rd yr:  General Pathology, Physiology II, Pre-Clinical Prosthetic Dentistry

4th yr:  Special Anatomy and Physiology          Orthodontics
         Pharmacology and the Properties         Prosthetic Dentistry
            Dental Materials                     Anaesthetics
         General Medicine                        Pre-Clinical Operative Dentistry
         General Surgery                         Conservative Operative Dentistry
         Dental Surgery

5th yr:   Pathology and Histo-Pathology of the Teeth and Oral Cavity
          Oral and Maxillo-Facial Surgery
          Prosthetic Dentistry
          Orthodontics
          Conservative Operative Dentistry
          Oral Medicine
          Dental Ethics, Jurisprudence and Conduct of Dental Practice
          Public Health Dentistry
          Special Oral and Applied Anatomy


## Master of Dental Surgery (M.D.S.)

Dissertation is required.


## Doctor of Dental Surgery (D.D.S.)

Thesis is required.


## Higher Diploma in Dentistry (H.Dip.Dent.)

Eligibility:        Bachelor of Dental Surgery.

## Curriculum:

        Anatomy, Pathology, Physiology


## Diploma in Anaesthetics (D.A.)

Eligibility:        Bachelor of Dental Surgery.

## Examination:

        Anatomy and Physiology in relation to Anaesthesia
        History, Theory and Practice of Anaesthesia
        Pre-operative investigation, preparation and medication;
          the recognition of post-operative complications and
          their treatments as related to Anaesthesia
        The Pharmacology and Elementary Chemistry of Drugs
          used for or in association with Anaesthesia.


## Diploma in Public Dentistry (D.P.D.)

Eligibility:        Bachelor of Dental Surgery.

Examination:

        Microbiology, including Serology and Immunology
        Parasitology, including Protozoology
        Helminthology and Medical Entomology
        Preventive Orthodontics
        Pathology of Teeth and Oral Cavity and Oral Medicine
        Hygiene including Preventive Dentistry and Applied Dietetics
        Preventable Diseases and Epidemiology
        Health Legislation and Administration

## Diploma in Orthodontics

Eligibility:        Bachelor of Dental Surgery.

Duration of course:  2 years.

Examination:

        The Science of Dentistry (Anatomy, Physiology and Pathology)
        The Principles and Practice of Orthodontics

## Diploma in Maxillo-Facial and Oral Surgery (Dip. M.F.O.S.)

Eligibility:        Bachelor of Dental Surgery.

Curriculum:

        Anatomy, Physiology, Pathology, The Principles and Practice of
        Maxillo-Facial and Oral Surgery.

## Faculty of Architecture

## Bachelor of Architecture

Eligibility:        Pass in Mathematics at the Matriculation examination.

Duration of course:  6 years.

Curriculum:

1st yr:    Architectural Design I, Geometrical Drawing, Building
          Construction I, Mathematics, Physics.

2nd yr:    Architectural Design II, Building Construction II, Theory of
          Structures, I, History of Architecture I, Land Surveying.

3rd yr:   Architectural Design III, Building Construction III, Theory of
          Structures, II, History of Architecture II, Building Materials,
          Mechanical Equipment of Buildings I.

4th yr:   12 months' work in the office of an architect.

5th yr:   Architectural Design IV, Building Construction IV, History
          and Appreciation of Art, Specifications, Theory of Structures
          III, Mechanical Equipment of Buildings II.

6th yr:   Estimates and Quantities, Professional Practice, Town Planning
          and Landscape Design, Building Construction V.


## Master of Architecture

Duration of course:  2 years.

Dissertation required.


## Doctor of Philosophy

Duration of course:  2 years.

Thesis required.


## Doctor of Architecture

Original published work is required.


## Bachelor of Science in Quantity Surveying

Eligibility:        Pass in Mathematics at the Matriculation examination.

Duration of course:  5 years (2 yrs. full-time and 3 yrs. part-time).

## Curriculum:

1st yr:   Building Construction I, Geometrical Drawing, Mathematics I,
          Physics I, Quantities I.

2nd yr:   Building Construction II, Economics I, Land Surveying, Quanti-
          ties II, Theory of Structures I.

3rd yr:   Building Construction III, Building Materials, Quantities III,
          Sanitation and Hygiene, Theory of Structures II.

4th yr:   Analysis of Prices, Building Construction IV, Field Notes for
          Working Drawings, Quantities IV.

5th yr:   Building Finance, Valuations and Estimates, Professional
          Practice, Quantities V, Specifications.

## Bachelor of Science in Town and Regional Planning

Duration of course:  4 years.

## Curriculum:

1st yr:   Geography I, Economics I, Sociology I, Town and Regional
Planning Theory I, Town and Regional Planning Practice I.

2nd yr:   Civil Engineering in relation to Planning, Elements of Surveying and Cartography, Statistics in relation to Planning, Town
and Regional Planning Theory II, Town and Regional Planning
Practice II.

3rd yr:   Geography II, Land Economics, Town and Regional Planning Theory
III, Town and Regional Planning Practice III.

1 of the following:

Introduction to Philosophy, Philosophy of Science, English I,
French Special, Italian Special, German Special.

4th yr:   Town and Regional Planning Law and Public Administration,
Professional Practice and Procedure, Town and Regional Planning
Theory IV, Town and Regional Planning Practice IV.

## Master of Science in Town and Regional Planning

Dissertation or memoir is required.

## Doctor of Science in Town and Regional Planning

Original published work is required.

## Diploma in Quantity Surveying

Eligibility:          Pass in Mathematics at the Matriculation examination.

Duration of course:  5 years.

## Curriculum:

1st yr:   Building Construction I, Quantities I, Geometrical Drawing,
Mathematics, Physics.

2nd yr:   Building Construction II, Quantities II, Theory of Structures I,
Land Surveying.

3rd yr:  Building Construction III, Quantities III, Theory of Structures
         II, Building Materials, Sanitation and Hygiene.

4th yr:  Analysis of Prices, Field Notes for Working Drawings, Building
         Construction IV, Quantities IV.

5th yr:  Building Finance, Valuations and Estimates, Professional
         Practice, Specifications, Quantities V.


## Diploma in Town Planning

Eligibility:           Degree in Architecture, Civil Engineering or Land
                       Surveying.

Duration of course:  3 years.

## Curriculum:

1st yr:  Historical Developments of Planning, Economic Geography and
         Economics in relation to Town Planning, Elements of Sociology,
         Town Planning Theory I, Town Planning Practice I.

2nd yr:  Town Planning Theory II, Town Planning Practice II, Civic and
         Landscape Design, Civil Engineering in relation to Planning.

3rd yr:  Town Planning Theory III, Town Planning Practice III, Law in
         relation to Planning, Surveying in relation to Planning.


## Graduate Diploma in Engineering (G.Dip.E.)

Eligibility:           Bachelor of Science in Engineering or Bachelor of
                       Science with Honours.

Duration of course:  1 year.


## UNIVERSITY OF CAPE TOWN, Rondebosch

Founded as the South African College in 1829, became a university in 1918.

Prior to University Education Act, 1959, admitted students on basis of
academic qualifications only.  In all academic matters non-white students
treated on equal footing with white students.  Academic apartheid introduced with University Education Act of 1959.

General entrance requirements:      Matriculation Certificate or Exemption
                                    Certificate of Joint Matriculation Board.

Degrees awarded:

| Faculty | Degree | Duration of course (years) |
|---|---|---|
| Arts | Bachelor of Arts | 3 |
| | B.A. (Hons.) | 4 |
| | Master of Arts | 1 |
| | Doctor of Philosophy | 2 |
| | Doctor of Literature | |
| | Teachers' Diploma in Speech and Drama | 3 |
| | Performer's Diploma in Speech and Drama | 3-4 |
| | Certificate in Speech and Drama | 3 |
| | Diplomas in African Administration | 1-2 |
| | Certificate in Librarianship | 1 |
| | Higher Certificate in Librarianship | 1 |
| | Diploma in Librarianship | |
| Commerce | Bachelor of Commerce and Diploma in Commerce | 3 |
| | Master of Commerce | 1-2 |
| | Ph.D. | |
| | Certificate in Theory of Accountancy | |
| | Master of Business Administration | 2 |
| | Certificate in Business Administration | 15 mos.(part-time) |
| | Diploma in Business Administration | 3 (part-time) |
| Education | Bachelor of Education | 2 |
| | Master of Education | 2 |
| | Doctor of Philosophy | 2 |
| | Secondary Teachers' Diploma | 1 |
| | Higher Primary Certificate Course | 3 |
| Engineering | B.Sc. | 4 |
| | M.Sc. | 1 |
| | Ph.D. | 2 |
| | Doctor of Science | |
| Fine Art and Architecture | B.A. (Fine Art) | 4 |
| | M.A. (Fine Art) | |
| | B.A. (Art) | 3 |

|  |  |  |
|---|---|---|
| | Bachelor of Architecture and | |
| |   Diploma in Architecture | 6 |
| | Master of Architecture | 1 |
| | Degree in Quantity Surveying | 2 (full-time) |
| | | + 3 (part-time) |
| | Diploma in Quantity Surveying | 5 (part-time) |
| | Diploma in Fine Art | 3 |
| | Certificate in Fine Art | 3 |
| | Higher Primary Teacher's | |
| |   Diploma in Fine Art | 3 |
| | Certificate in Commercial Art | 3 |
| Law | Bachelor of Laws | 5 |
| | Master of Laws | |
| | Doctor of Laws | |
| | Diploma in Law | |
| Medicine | Bachelor of Medicine and | |
| |   Bachelor of Surgery | 6 |
| | Master of Medicine | |
| | Master of Surgery | |
| | Doctor of Medicine | |
| | Doctor of Philosophy | |
| | Diploma in Public Health | 2 (part-time) |
| | Diploma in Nursing - Sister | |
| |   Tutor | 2 |
| | Diploma in Physiotherapy | 3 |
| | Diploma in Physiological | |
| |   Medicine | |
| | Diploma in Therapeutic | |
| |   Dietetics | 1 |
| Music | Bachelor of Music | 4 |
| | Bachelor of Arts (Music) | 4 |
| | Master of Music | 1 |
| | Doctor of Music | |
| | Teacher's Licentiate Diploma | |
| |   in Music | 3 |
| | Performer's Diploma in Music | 3 |
| | Performer's Diploma in Opera | 3 |
| | Teacher's Certificate in | |
| |   Ballet | 3 |
| Science | Bachelor of Science | 3 |
| | Bachelor of Science (Honours) | 4 |
| | Master of Science | 1 |
| | Doctor of Philosophy | 2 |
| | Doctor of Science | |
| | Diploma in Analytical Chemistry | 1 |
| | Certificate in Exploration | |
| |   Geochemistry | |

| Social Science | Bachelor of Social Science | 3 |
| | Master of Social Science | 1 |
| | Doctor of Philosophy | 2 |
| | Doctor of Social Science | |
| | Certificate of Qualification as Professional Social Worker | |
| | Diploma in Social Science | 3 |
| | Advanced Diploma in Social Administration | 1 |
| | Certificate in Social Work | 1 |

## Faculty of Arts

### Bachelor of Arts

Duration of course:  3 years, with not less than 9 courses.

Examination at end of each course.

1-year courses usually entail about 100 meetings of 45 minutes each.

Exclusion from Faculty if student fails to pass 3 qualifying courses in any 2 consecutive years.

At least 1 major subject chosen from the following:

3-year courses:

African Languages
Applied Mathematics
Botany
Chemistry
Economics
English
French
Geography
Geology
German

Greek
Hebrew
History
Latin
Nederlands en Afrikaans
Physics
Psychology
Pure Mathematics
Sociology
Zoology

2-year courses:

Archaeology
Constitutional History and Law
Economic History
Logic and Metaphysics
Political Philosophy
Social Anthropology

Comparative African Government and Law
Ethics
Music
Roman Law

Mathematics compulsory for Applied Mathematics, Chemistry, Mathematical Statistics, Physics.

Chemistry compulsory for Botany, Geology, Physiology, Zoology.

Physics compulsory for Chemistry, Geology, Zoology.

Latin I necessary for Roman Law II.


## Bachelor of Arts (Honours)

Duration of course:  1 year for graduates.

### Subjects:

| | |
|---|---|
| African Languages | Greek |
| Archaeology | Hebrew |
| Classics | History |
| Comparative African Government and Law | Latin |
| | Mathematics |
| Economics | Nederlands en Afrikaans |
| English Language and Literature | Philosophy |
| French | Psychology |
| Geography | Social Anthropology |
| German | |

No second try after failure at examination.

Awarded in first, second or third class Honours.


## Master of Arts

Eligibility:          B.A. (Hons.) or graduate with equivalent courses.

Same subjects as for B.A. (Hons.).

At least 1 year's study after admission.

Examination by thesis.  Following are exceptions:

| | |
|---|---|
| Classics | Dissertation plus orals and written if required. |
| Economics | Dissertation plus orals and written if required. |
| English Language | Either thesis or special course. |
| English Literature | Thesis and course of study. |
| German | 4 papers and thesis. |
| Mathematics | Reading  knowledge of French, German or Russian, examination by written papers, thesis, or both, oral if required. |
| Philosophy | Thesis and oral. |

## Doctor of Philosophy

Research degree, open to bachelors of at least 3 years' standing.

At least 2 years of post-graduate work plus thesis.

## Doctor of Literature

Open to post-degree candidates of at least 8 years' standing.

Thesis or substantial published work not already presented to another university or for another degree.

## Teachers' Diploma in Speech and Drama

Eligibility:            Matriculation or exemption.

Duration of course:     3 years or may be combined with B.A. degree over 4 years.

## Performer's Diploma in Speech and Drama

Eligibility:            Matriculation or exemption.

Duration of course:     3 years or may be combined with B.A. degree over 4 years.

Same curriculum as Teachers' Diploma for first 2 years, practical qualifying examination and higher standard of performance required.

## Certificate in Speech and Drama

Eligibility:            Without Matriculation or School-Leaving Certificate.

Not recognized for teaching purposes.

Duration of course:     3 years.

Curriculum:             Same as for diploma.

## Diplomas in African Administration

Eligibility:            Matriculation, Senior School-Leaving Certificate or equivalent.

Duration of course:       Lower Diploma      1 year.
                          Higher Diploma     2 years.


## School of Librarianship

### Certificate in Librarianship

Eligibility:              Matriculation or exemption.

Duration of course:       At least 1 year full-time or 2 years part-time.

Curriculum includes:      Book Production, Book Stock and Assistance to
                          Readers, General Literature, Library Practice,
                          Practical Cataloguing and Classification,
                          practical field work.


### Higher Certificate in Librarianship

Eligibility:              Bachelor's degree or equivalent qualification.

Duration of course:       At least 1 year full-time or 2 years part-time.

Curriculum includes:      Bibliography, Book Selection and Reference Work,
                          Cataloguing, Classification, Library Administra-
                          tion, Principles of Librarianship, practical
                          field work.


### Diploma in Librarianship

Eligibility:              Higher certificate plus 2 years of practical
                          experience.


## Faculty of Commerce

### Bachelor of Commerce and Diploma in Commerce

Mathematics recommended at Matriculation.

Duration of course:       3 years in daytime.
                          5 years evening.
                          May be combined with B.A. or LL.B. over 5 years.

Minimum of 10 courses.  Compulsory courses in:
        Business Administration, Economics, Economic History, Statistical

Method, Preliminary Commercial Law or Roman-Dutch Law, Commercial or Municipal Law, Accounting.

Students with professional qualification in Accountancy may attend for 3 years in the evening.

Curriculum includes: Economics, Economic History, Business Administration, Economics of Accounting.

## Master of Commerce

Awarded by thesis (at least 2 years, for all candidates), or examination (1 year, if B.Com. with distinction).

## Doctor of Philosophy

Regulations as for Faculty of Arts.

## Certificate in Theory of Accountancy

Examinations by Public Accountants' and Auditors' Board.

Subjects may be recognized as subjects for the B.Com. degree.

Post-Graduate School of Business Administration and Applied Economics

## Master of Business Administration (M.B.A.)

Eligibility: Graduates only. Must hold Certificate in Business Administration or exemption.

Duration of course: At least 2 years approved courses plus minimum of 3 years' practical experience.

Curriculum includes: Functions and Principles of Management, Management Practices and Techniques, Application of Management Practices and Techniques, Managerial Personnel.

## Certificate in Business Administration

Eligibility: Graduates of Arts, Science, Engineering, Law, Social Science.
Holders of B.Com. not eligible.

Duration of course: 15 months part-time study.

Diploma in Business Administration

Eligibility:                Non-graduates with approved qualification plus 3
                            years of approved practical experience in
                            administration.

Duration of course:         3 years part-time.


Faculty of Education

Bachelor of Education

Eligibility:                Bachelors with at least 2 teaching subjects (3
                            courses in one, 2 courses in another).

Duration of course:         2 years.  During 1st year must complete require-
                            ments for a master's degree, or a second bachelor's
                            degree, or equivalent.  2nd year devoted entirely
                            to professional study and practice.

                            Also offered to part-time students over 2 years.
                            Open to bachelors with teaching certificate and at
                            least 2 years' approved teaching experience.


Master of Education

Eligibility:                Masters or equivalent, or holders of 2 bachelors
                            or a bachelor's Honours degree, plus teaching
                            certificate or diploma and Bachelor of Education.

Duration of course:         2 years with thesis.


Doctor of Philosophy

Eligibility:                Bachelors of at least 3 years' standing.

At least 2 years of post-graduate work.


Secondary Teachers' Diploma

Eligibility:                Open to approved graduates.

Duration of course:         1 year, purely professional.

Higher Primary Certificate Courses

Eligibility:              Matriculation or Senior Certificate or equivalent.

Duration of course:       3 years.

Courses in general primary education, or specialized in Fine Art, Music, or Speech and Drama.


Post-Certificate Studies:

    Special courses for specialization after Teacher's Certificate.


Special 1-year courses for holders of Teacher's Certificate:

    Special classes:    Children Handicapped in Speech and Hearing
                        Problem Children in European Primary Schools


Faculty of Engineering

Bachelor of Science in Chemical Engineering, Engineering or Land Surveying

Duration of course:       4 years.

Engineering:

1st yr:   Pure Mathematics, Applied Mathematics, Physics, Engineering
          Geometry and Workshop Practice.

2nd yr:   Civil, Mechanical and Electrical Engineering:
          Pure Mathematics, Applied Mathematics, Chemistry, Mechanical
          Engineering, Civil Engineering, Electrical Engineering.

          Electrical Engineering:
          Pure Mathematics, Applied Mathematics, Physics, Civil Engineer-
          ing, Mechanical Engineering.

3rd yr:   Civil Engineering:
          Civil, Electrical, Mechanical Engineering, Pure and Applied
          Mathematics, Geology, Land Surveying.

          Electrical Engineering:
          Heat Engines, Fluid Mechanics, Theory of Machines, Strength of
          Materials and Design, Metallurgy and Fuels, Pure and Applied
          Mathematics.

4th yr:   Specialized courses in Civil, Electrical or Mechanical Regular
          Workshop Practice.

With theses.

Approved First-Aid Certificate required.


Chemical Engineering:

1st yr:    Physics, Chemistry, Applied and Pure Mathematics.
2nd yr:    Chemical Engineering, Pure Mathematics, Chemistry, Physics.
3rd yr:    Division into 2 streams with options of Civil and Mechanical,
           or Chemical Engineering Science.
4th yr:    Specialization in above 2 streams with thesis.

Regular workshop practice compulsory.


Land Surveying:

1st yr:    Pure and Applied Mathematics, Physics, Geometrical Drawing.
2nd yr:    Pure and Applied Mathematics, Civil Engineering, Geology, Geo-
           metrical Optics and Optical Instruments, Land Surveying.
3rd yr:    Pure and Applied Mathematics, Astronomy, Land Surveying, Town
           Planning, Survey Law.
4th yr:    Land Survey, Photogrammetry, Field Astronomy.

Workshop and field practice compulsory.

Reading knowledge of German recommended.


Master of Science in Chemical Engineering, Engineering or Land Surveying

Eligibility:              B.Sc. in chosen field.
                          Also for graduates of not less than 2 years'
                          standing with at least 2 years of practical
                          experience in chosen field.

Duration of course:       1 year.

Thesis required.


Doctor of Philosophy

Eligibility:              Bachelor's degree of 4 years.

Duration of course:       2 years.

Thesis required.

Doctor of Science in Engineering, Chemical Engineering or Land Surveying

Eligibility:                Bachelor's degree of at least 5 years' standing.

Published papers or thesis showing original research.


Faculty of Fine Art and Architecture

Bachelor of Arts (Fine Art)

Duration of course:        4 years.

Subjects:

1st yr:    History of Art, Studio Work.

2nd yr:    History of Art, Anatomy, Evolution of Applied Design or History
           of Architecture, and Studio Work.

3rd yr:    History of Art, Theory of Fine Art, Studio Work.

4th yr:    Studio Work.

In addition 3 B.A. courses must be taken, not more than 1 in any year.


Master of Arts in Fine Art

Eligibility:                Admission to B.A. (Fine Art) with at least 1 year
                            post-graduate work in the practice of Fine Art,
                            or B.A. with 2 qualifying courses in Fine Art,
                            plus 2 years post-graduate work in the Theory and
                            Practice of Fine Art.

Duration of course:         At least 1 year's work is required.

Examination in the Theory and Practice of Fine Art, plus a thesis.

May be awarded with first or second class Honours or as a pass degree.


Bachelor of Arts (Art)

Primarily for teachers of Art in secondary schools.

Duration of course:        3 years.

Subjects:

1st yr:    History of Art, Studio Work.

2nd yr:   History of Art, Anatomy, History of Architecture, Studio Work, Psychology of Art   Education and Practice Teaching.

3rd yr:   History of Art, Theory of Fine Art, Studio Work, Psychology of Art Education and Practice Teaching.

3 qualifying B.A. or B.Sc. courses required; one must be a 2nd course in a teaching subject.


## Bachelor of Architecture and Diploma in Architecture

Eligibility:                    Mathematics at Matriculation necessary, and Science subject recommended for admission to all Architecture and Quantity Surveying courses.

Duration of course:             6 years full-time.
                                Full-time attendance in Studio Work each year.

## Subjects:

1st yr:   Studio Work, Building Construction and Materials, Theory of Construction, Draughtsmanship, History of Architecture, Theory of Architecture, Colour and Decoration, Surveying.

2nd yr:   Studio Work, Building Construction, Theory of Construction, History of Architecture, Hygiene and Sanitation, Theory of Architecture, Colour and Decoration, Building Materials, Measured Drawings.

3rd yr:   Studio Work, Building Construction, Theory of Construction, History of Architecture, Materials, Theory of Architecture, Colour and Decoration, Measured Drawings, Acoustics.

4th yr:   External experience under University supervision.

5th yr:   Studio Work, Advanced Construction, Specification, Professional Practice, Evolution of Applied Design, Equipment of Buildings.

6th yr:   Studio Work, Civic Design, Thesis Research, Thesis Design.

Since 1964, an additional year of practical experience required after the degree to qualify for registration as architects in South Africa.


## Master of Architecture

Eligibility:                    B.Arch. and at least 1 year's work in the Theory and Practice of Architecture subsequent to graduation.

Duration of course:             At least 1 year's work in School of Architecture plus thesis.
                                Oral on the subject of thesis may be required.

May be awarded with first or second class Honours or as a pass degree.

## Degree in Quantity Surveying

Offered from 1965.

Duration of course:        2 years full-time plus 3 years part-time.

### Subjects:

1st yr:    Building Construction, Quantities, Theory of Structures, Geo-
           metrical Drawing, History of Architecture, Physics, English or
           Afrikaans.

2nd yr:    Building Construction, Quantities, Theory of Structures, Sur-
           veying, Drainage and Sanitation, Economics, Accounting.

3rd yr:    Building Construction, Quantities, Materials and Specifications,
           Equipment of Buildings, Accounting.

4th yr:    Building Construction, Quantities, Analysis of Prices, Building
           Finance and Reports, Commercial Law, Thesis Research.

5th yr:    Quantities, Building Plant and Procedure, Professional Practice,
           Estimating and Cost Analysis, Arbitration, Thesis.

## Diploma in Quantity Surveying

Duration of course:        5 years part-time.

### Subjects:

1st yr:    Building Construction, Quantities, Theory of Structures, Geo-
           metrical Drawing, History of Architecture.

2nd yr:    Building Construction, Quantities, Theory of Structures, Survey-
           ing, Drainage and Sanitation.

3rd yr:    Building Construction, Quantities, Valuations, Building Materials,
           Equipment of Buildings.

4th yr:    Building Construction, Quantities, Specifications, Analysis of
           Prices, Thesis Research.

5th yr:    Quantities, Building Plant and Procedure, Professional Practice,
           Estimating and Cost Analysis, Thesis.

## Diploma in Fine Art

Eligibility:               Matriculation or exemption.

Duration of course:        3 years full-time.

Subjects:

1st yr:   History of Art, Studio Work.

2nd yr:   History of Art, Anatomy, Evolution of Applied Design or History
          of Architecture, Studio Work.

3rd yr:   History of Art, Theory of Fine Art, Studio Work.


## Certificate in Fine Art

Curriculum:     3 years full-time consisting solely of Studio Work in:

          Drawing, Painting, Modelling, Elementary Design including
          Geometry, Sculpture, Design and 1 Design or Craft subject.


## Higher Primary Teacher's Diploma in Fine Art

Eligibility:              Matriculation, Senior Certificate or equivalent.

Duration of course:       3 years full-time.

Curriculum:

1st yr:   2 or 3 B.A. or B.Sc. courses, 1 to be an official language
          (English I), and Art.

2nd yr:   Education subjects including Practice Teaching and Art.

3rd yr:   Teaching Practice for 1st term, Education subjects, and Art.


## Certificate in Commercial Art

Eligibility:              Matriculation, exemption or equivalent.

Duration of course:       3 years full-time.

Curriculum:

1st yr:   History of Art and Studio Work.

2nd yr:   Anatomy, Evolution or Applied Design, and Studio Work.

3rd yr:   Printing Processes and Studio Work.


## Special 1-year Course in Fine Art for holders of the Primary Teacher's Certificate

Curriculum:     History of Art, Studio Work, Method of Class Teaching (Art),
          and Practical Art Teaching.

<u>Faculty of Law</u>

<u>Bachelor of Laws (LL.B.)</u>

LL.B. is a post-graduate degree.

Latin at Matriculation a prerequisite.

Minimum of 5 years if certain courses of the LL.B. taken as part of the curriculum for the B.A. or B.Com. degree.

Candidate must have previously been or at the same time be admitted to an approved bachelor's degree, i.e. B.A. or B.Com.

May proceed to 3 degrees B.A., B.Com., and LL.B. at the same time over a minimum period of 6 years and at least 28 full qualifying courses. Of these at least 5 must be B.A. courses, other than first qualifying courses.

(1)  B.A., LL.B.

    <u>Curriculum</u>:

    1st yr:    Latin I, Constitutional History and Law I, Comparative African Government and Law I, plus any one first qualifying course from the following:

        (a)  Languages.
        (b)  Economics and Philosophy.
        (c)  Nederlandse Kultuurgeskiedenis, Social Anthropology, Pure Mathematics, Physics, Botany or Geology.

    2nd yr:    Roman Law I plus any 2 second qualifying courses chosen from (a), (b), or (c), except Physics, Botany or Geology; and Constitutional History and Law II, Comparative African Government and Law II or Latin II.

    3rd yr:    Roman Law II, Roman-Dutch Law, Jurisprudence A, plus one 3rd qualifying course chosen from above, thus completing B.A. degree.

    4th yr:    Law of Contract and Property, Commercial Law B, Comparative Law, Criminal Law and Procedure, Public International Law.

    5th yr:    Final LL.B. courses.

(2)  B.Com., LL.B.

    <u>Curriculum</u>:

    1st yr:    Latin I, Constitutional History and Law I, Comparative African Government and Law I, Economics I.

    2nd yr:    Roman Law I, Economics II, Economic History I, Commerce Preliminary, Statistical Method.

3rd yr:     Roman Law II, Roman-Dutch Law, Jurisprudence A, Commerce.

4th yr:     Law of Contract and Property, Commercial Law B, Comparative
            Law, Criminal Law and Procedure, Public International Law,
            Accounting 1B.

5th yr:     Final LL.B. courses.


## Master of Laws (LL.M.)

Eligibility:              LL.B.

Duration of course:       Not less than 2 years.

Thesis, with written or oral examination on subject of thesis, if required.


## Doctor of Laws (LL.D.)

Duration of course:       Not less than 4 years after LL.B., or 2 years
                          after LL.M.

Thesis or published work, with oral or written examination on subject of
thesis, if required.


## Diploma in Law

Eligibility:              Matriculation, exemption or equivalent.

Duration of course:       3 years full-time.  Does not exempt from degree
                          course.

## Curriculum:

1st yr:     Elements of Roman Law, South African Law, Criminal Law, Criminal
            Procedure.

2nd yr:     South African Law, Companies and Partnership, Law of Evidence,
            Constitutional and Administrative Law.

3rd yr:     South African Law, Mercantile Law, Civil Procedure, Interpretation
            of Statutes, Bantu Law and Administration.

Pass mark in all examinations:  50%.

All examinations classified as follows:

             75% and over    First Class
             65% - 74%       Second Class
             50% - 64%       Third Class
             Under 50%       Fail

## Faculty of Medicine

## Bachelor of Medicine and Bachelor of Surgery (M.B., Ch.B.)

Eligibility:            Mathematics at Matriculation.

Duration of course:     At least 6 years.

## Curriculum:

1st yr:  Botany Special (not fewer than 60 hrs. lectures and practical
         work).
         Zoology (at least 100 hrs. lectures and practical work).
         Physics (at least 120 hrs. lectures and practical work).
         Chemistry (at least 150 hrs. lectures and practical work).

2nd yr:  Anatomy (including Principles of Genetics, Embryology and
         Physical Anthropology).
         Physiology (including Biochemistry and Histology).

3rd yr:  Pathology, Pharmacology, Medical Psychology, Medical Sociology,
         Vaccination, Introductory Course in Medicine, First-Aid.

4th yr:  Medicine, Clinical and Systematic (including Infectious Diseases),
         Paediatrics, Obstetrics, Chemical Pathology, Physiology, Venereal
         Diseases, Applied Genetics, Introductory Course in Surgical
         Anatomy.

5th yr:  Surgery (Clinical and Systematic), Clinical Medicine, Practical
         Obstetrics, Gynaecology, Medical Jurisprudence, Public Health,
         Psychiatry, Pathology, Applied Anatomy, Anesthetics, Radiology,
         Ophtalmology, Dermatology, Ear, Nose and Throat, Venereal
         Diseases.

6th yr:  Coordination of already completed work and further clinical
         experience including Dentistry.  Also Medical Ethics and Methods
         of General Practice.

Degree may be given with first or second class Honours, or as a pass degree.

## Master of Medicine (M.Med.)

Offered in General Medicine, or in Anaesthetics, Dermatology, Obstetrics
and Gynaecology, Ophtalmology, Orthopaedics, Otorhinolaryngology,
Paediatrics, Pathology, Radiodiagnosis, Radiotherapy, Surgery.

Eligibility:            Prescribed intern year followed by registration
                        as a medical practitioner by the South African
                        Medical and Dental Council.

                        3 years' approved experience with at least 1 year
                        in approved clinical work other than the specialty,
                        and at least 1 year in the specialty.

Examination:                    Written, oral and clinical and/or practical
                                Essay or report may be required.


## Master of Surgery (Ch.M.)

Eligibility:                    At least 4 years after graduation.
                                At least 3 years in approved surgical appointment.

Thesis or published work.  Written examination in speciality, general
surgery and related subjects.


## Doctor of Medicine (M.D.)

Eligibility:                    At least 3 years after graduation.
                                Must have medical or Honours Science degree.

Thesis or published work.


## Diploma in Public Health

Eligibility:                    Medical qualification registered by South African
                                Medical Council.

Duration of course:             Before 1963, 1 year full-time; attendance of not
                                less than 480 hours.
                                Now part-time over 2 years.

Examinations:
    Part I:                     Bacteriology, Virology, Immunology and Parasito-
                                logy, Chemistry and Physics in relation to Public
                                Health, Geology as applied to water supplies,
                                Physiology and Biochemistry in their application
                                to Nutrition and Hygiene.

    Part II:                    Principles of Hygiene, Sanitation and Public
                                Health, Epidemiology, Vital Statistics, Public
                                Health Law and Administration, Industrial Hygiene,
                                Town-Planning, House-Planning, Sanitary Construction
                                and Interpretation of Plans, Principles of Genetics,
                                Radiation Hazards.

In addition, 3 months' regular attendance at clinical practice of hospital
for infectious diseases, and not less than 6 months in acquiring a practical
knowledge of public health administration.

## Diploma in Nursing - Sister Tutor

Eligibility:                      Post-registration qualification in order to teach
                                  medical and surgical nurses.
                                  At least 2 years' experience as registered nurse,
                                  at least 1 year being practical nursing experience.

Duration of course:      2 years.

## Curriculum:

1st yr:     Special courses in Physics, Chemistry, Biology and Bacteriology,
            Theory of Education, Educational Methods, Clinical Medicine,
            Surgery, Obstetrics and Gynaecology, Practice Teaching.

2nd yr:     Anatomy, Physiology and Pharmacology, Psychology of Education,
            Audio-Visual Methods, Public Health and Infectious Diseases,
            History of Education, History of Nursing and Nursing Administra-
            tion, Clinical Medicine, Surgery, Obstetrics and Gynaecology,
            Practice Teaching.

## Diploma in Physiotherapy

Eligibility:                      Women only.  Matriculation with Mathematics,
                                  exemption or equivalent.

Duration of course:      3 years.

## Curriculum:

1st yr:     Biology, Anatomy, Physiology, Physics and Chemistry, Techniques
            of Physiotherapy, Elementary Nursing Procedures and Hospital
            Etiquette.

2nd and     Medical and Surgical Conditions treated by Physiotherapy, Theory
3rd yrs:    and Practice of Physiotherapy, Clinical Practice of Physiotherapy,
            Physiology, Applied Anatomy.

## Diploma in Psychological Medicine

Eligibility:                      Medical qualification registered by South African
                                  Medical Council.

Duration of course:      At least 4 years after graduation.

Must show evidence of:

            Completion of internship
            Not less than 12 months in general medical and surgical wards
               while a resident or not less than 2 years general practice
            At least 2 years full-time psychiatric practice

6 months clinical practice of Neurology
6 months clinical practice of Child Psychiatry

No formal attendance at lectures is required.

Examinations:

Part I:            Anatomy of the Nervous System, Physiology of the
                   Nervous System, Psychology.

Part II:           Psychiatry, Neurology.


## Diploma in Therapeutic Dietetics

Eligibility:       Open to Science graduates with Physiology and
                   Microbiology or Chemistry, or other approved majors,
                   and graduates in Home Economics and Dietetics.

Duration of course:    1 year.


## Teacher Training Course for Qualified Physiotherapists

Eligibility:       At least 2 years' experience in the practice of
                   Physiotherapy in a clinic or hospital after
                   registration.

Duration of course:    2 years full-time.

Course covers the basic sciences, educational methods, and clinical
instruction in modern trends in treatment as affecting physiotherapy
procedures.


## Faculty of Music

## Bachelor of Music

Eligibility:       Matriculation or exemption.  Evidence of piano
                   proficiency.

## Curriculum:

1st yr:   First qualifying courses B.A. in
             (i)   English or Nederlands-Afrikaans
            (ii)   Music
           (iii)   Any other approved subject

2nd yr:   Second qualifying B.A. course in Music, special work in Harmony
          and Counterpoint and in Instrumental Study or Singing, General
          Musical Knowledge, Elementary Composition or Method of Class
          Teaching.

3rd yr:   Instrumental Study or Conducting or Singing, Harmony and Counter-
          point, History of Music, Composition, Teaching Method, Additional
          Composition or Method of Class Teaching and School Music.

4th yr:   Instrumental Study or Conducting or Singing, Composition,
          Orchestration, Analysis and Criticism (Orchestral and Choral),
          Harmony and Counterpoint.

## Bachelor of Arts (Music)

Primarily for teachers of Music.

Student qualified to teach 1 other B.A. or B.Sc. subject.

## Curriculum:

> 3 years covering B.A. or B.Sc. subjects (one 3-year course plus
> one 1-year course, or two 2-year courses), and Music.

> 1 additional year covering Principles and Practice of Education
> in the Faculty of Education, and Instrumental Study or Conducting
> or Singing in the Faculty of Music.

## Master of Music

Eligibility:              Open to Bachelors of Music, after at least 1
                          year's attendance at approved courses.

Courses:  Instrumental Study or Conducting or Singing
          More advanced Contrapuntal Forms
          Instrumentation, Score Reading and Conducting
          Works of the Great Composers
          Composition of a complete work in sonata style and a choral
           work or a thesis

## Doctor of Music

Eligibility:              Bachelors of not less than 4 years' standing.

Original work as a composer, theorist or historian of music.  Examination
is required.

## Teacher's Licentiate Diploma in Music

Eligibility:              Matriculation, exemption or equivalent.

## Curriculum:
          3-year program.

Principal and second subjects chosen from Piano, Orchestral
  Instrument, Conducting or Singing

| | |
|---|---|
| History of Music | Harmony and Counterpoint |
| Methods of Class Teaching | Aural Training |
| General Musical Knowledge | Interpretation Class |
| Repertoire Class | Quick Study and Sight |
| Choral | Reading |

## Performer's Diploma in Music

Eligibility:               Matriculation, exemption or equivalent.

## Curriculum:

3-year program.

Study of a principal and second subject chosen from Piano,
  Orchestral Instrument, Conducting or Singing
2 years in Harmony and Counterpoint, History of Music, General
  Musical Knowledge, Aural Training, Chamber Music, and
  accompanying classes.
1 year in Elements of Music and Elementary Harmony
3 years in classes in Repertoire, Quick Study and Sight Reading,
  Interpretation, and Choral

## Performer's Diploma in Opera (Singing)

Eligibility:               Senior School-Leaving Certificate or equivalent.

Duration of course:     3 years.

Courses:  Singing and Voice Training
          Practical Stagecraft and Acting Technique
          Practical Speech Training
          History of Opera
          General Musical Knowledge
          Aural Training
          History of Costume
          Theory and Practice of Operatic Production

## Teacher's Certificate in Ballet

Duration of course:     3 years.

Includes:  Ballet and Spanish Dancing, Dance Composition, History of Ballet
           and Ballet Music, General Ballet Knowledge, and Theory of Ballet.

One-year Post-Certificate Course in Ballet

Eligibility:              Certificate in Ballet.

Courses in Ballet, Spanish Dancing and National Dancing, and Elementary
Choreography.


Also available are special music endorsement programs for the Primary
Teacher's Certificate and the Higher Primary Teacher's Certificate.


Faculty of Science

Bachelor of Science

Eligibility:              Matriculation with Mathematics, or exemption.

Duration of course:       3 years.

Curriculum:     At least 8 courses.

3-yr. majors:   Applied Mathematics, Botany, Chemistry, Geography, Geology,
                Physics, Psychology, Pure Mathematics, Zoology.

2-yr. majors:   Mathematical Statistics, Physiology.

Other Science subjects (not allowable as majors):  Astronomy, General
                Physiology, Geochemistry, Microbiology.

To complete 2nd or 3rd year courses:

|  |  |  |
|---|---|---|
| Applied Math. I | needed for | Astronomy |
| Physics I | needed for | Astronomy, Chemistry, Geo-chemistry, Geology, Physiology |
| Chemistry I | needed for | Botany, Geology, Physio-logy, Zoology |
| Chemistry II | needed for | General Physiology, Geo-chemistry, Microbiology |
| Zoology I | needed for | General Physiology, Micro-biology |
| Geology II | needed for | Geochemistry |

May be given with distinction in individual major subjects.

The B.Sc. (Pure Science) and B.Sc. (Chemical Engineering) may be taken in
5 years, providing that regulations for both degrees are satisfied.

Syllabuses for first 2 years in Science courses:

Applied Mathematics

I    Elementary dynamics, statics, hydrostatics.

II   Rigid dynamics in two dimensions, particle dynamics including
     central orbits.  Statics including equilibrium of chains and
     virtual work.  Vector algebra and calculus, potential theory,
     differential equations of mathematical physics and simple
     applications of Fourier analysis.

Chemistry

I    General and inorganic chemistry, elementary organic chemistry.
     6 hours laboratory work per week.

IIA  Inorganic chemistry, organic chemistry, physical chemistry.
     (For students majoring in chemistry and for others not majoring
     in biological subjects.)

IIB  Physical chemistry, organic chemistry, introduction to bio-
     chemistry.  (For students majoring in biological subjects, but
     not in chemistry.)

     Both courses, 6 hours laboratory work per week.

Physics

I    General physics, heat, sound, light, electromagnetism, modern
     physics.  45 minutes practical work per week consisting of
     experiments testing principles of the theoretical course.

II   More advanced work on subjects of Course I.  General physics and
     properties of matter, heat and elementary thermodynamics, physical
     optics, magnetism and electricity, introduction to atomic physics.
     90 minutes practical work per week.

Pure Mathematics

I    Trigonometry, analytic geometry of the plane, algebra, elementary
     differential and integral calculus.

II   Further work on differential and integral calculus, functions of
     several variables, differential equations, complex numbers,
     analytic geometry of three dimensions, convergence.

Mathematical Statistics

I    Elementary probability, most common discrete and continuous dis-
     tributions, measures of location and dispersion, elementary
     hypothesis testing and estimation, association and contingency,
     correlation and simple regression, analysis of variance, elementary
     sampling theory.

II   Probability, special distributions, moments, theory of estimation,
     hypothesis testing and confidence limits, multiple regression and

covariance, design and analysis of experiments, sampling theory,
probit analysis, time series, non-parametric tests, relevant
mathematical methods.

## Bachelor of Science (Honours)

Duration of course:        1 year after B.Sc. or other bachelor's degree
                           with required number of Science courses.

Following subjects available:

| | |
|---|---|
| Applied Mathematics | Mathematics |
| Astronomy | Physics |
| Botany | Physiology |
| Chemistry | Psychology |
| Geochemistry | Theoretical Physics |
| Geography | Zoology |
| Geology | |

Degree awarded in first, second or third class.

## Master of Science

Preparatory training for research.

Eligibility:               Open to B.Sc. (Hons.) or equivalents as approved
                           by the Senate.

At least 1 year after admittance.

Awarded on thesis and/or lectures and written examination.

Reading knowledge of French, German or Russian is advisable.

Degree may be awarded with distinction.

## Doctor of Philosophy

Research degree, open to bachelors of at least 3 years' standing.

Duration of course:        Not less than 2 years' post-graduate work under
                           University supervision required.

Thesis or published work.

## Doctor of Science

Eligibility:               Open to bachelors of at least 5 years' standing.

Published work constituting an original and important contribution to learning.


Diploma in Analytical Chemistry

Awarded to B.Sc. graduates with 3 qualifying courses in Chemistry.

At least 1 year may be begun after 2nd Chemistry qualifying course for B.Sc. completed.


Certificate in Exploration Geochemistry

Elegibility:                    Open to B.Sc. graduates with high standards in
                                Geology and Chemistry.

Extends over whole of 2nd University term.

Designed to provide a thorough training in the basic theoretical principles, and both the laboratory and field techniques used in modern exploration Geochemistry.


Faculty of Social Science

Bachelor of Social Science

Eligibility:              Matriculation or exemption.

Curriculum:      3 years.

   (a)   3 courses in Sociology.
   (b)   3 courses in Social Administration or alternative combination:
         3 courses in any 1 of the following:

              Bantu Languages           History
              Economics                 Psychology
              Geography                 Pure Mathematics

         2 courses in Pure Mathematics and 1 in Mathematical Statistics.

         2 courses in Roman Law and 1 in Roman-Dutch Law.

         2 courses in each of any 2 of the following:

              Bantu Languages           History
              Comparative African Govern-  Logic and Metaphysics
                ment and Law            Political Philosophy
              Economics                 Psychology
              Economic History          Pure Mathematics

                    Ethics                    Social Administration
                    Archaeology               Social Anthropology
                    Geography

    (c)  Further courses to complete total of not less than 9:

         Any subject with qualifying courses in Faculty of Arts.
         Any subject with qualifying courses in Faculty of Science.
         Criminal Law and Procedure in Faculty of Law.
         Social Administration.


B.A. and B.Soc.Sc. :

    May be taken in not less than 4 years.  Candidate must satisfy
    regulations for both degrees.

    Not fewer than 12 qualifying courses.


Master of Social Science

Eligibility:                Open to B.Soc.Sc. or B.A. with at least 2 full
                            qualifying courses in Social Science.

Duration of course:         At least 1 year full-time or 2 years part-time.

Subjects: Sociology, Applied Sociology, Social Administration, Social
          Work, Social Legislation.

Research reports or theses on supervised work as prescribed.

May be awarded with first or second class Honours or as a pass degree.


Doctor of Philosophy

Research degree.

Eligibility:                Open to bachelors of at least 3 years.

Not less than 2 years post-graduate work under University supervision.

Thesis or published work.


Doctor of Social Science

Eligibility:                Open to bachelors of not less than 8 years, masters
                            of not less than 7 years, Ph.D.'s of not less than
                            6 years, provided that degrees gained through
                            Faculty of Social Science, or others if approved.

Published work showing original and important contribution to knowledge.

### Certificate of Qualification as Professional Social Worker

Awarded on bachelor's or diploma level for previous or subsequent passing of courses in Sociology, Social Administration and Human Relations, plus 2 professional examinations.


### Diploma in Social Science

Eligibility:                 Senior School-Leaving Certificate or equivalent.

Same regulations as B.Soc.Sc.


### Advanced Diploma in Social Administration

Eligibility:                 Open to B.Soc.Sc. or Dip.Soc.Sc. or other
                             approved qualifications.

Available in Housing Management, Medical Social Work, Personnel Management, Welfare Administration, Social Surveying.

Academic year with field work and intern experience.


### Certificate in Social Work

Curriculum:     at least 1 year.

              Sociology I, Social Administration I, Prescribed branch of Social
              Legislation, Selected field and laboratory study.



### THE POTCHEFSTROOM UNIVERSITY FOR CHRISTIAN HIGHER EDUCATION, Potchefstroom

Founded in 1869 by Dutch Reformed Church.

1904, its literary department transferred from Burgersdorp, Cape Province, to Potchefstroom, Transvaal, where the establishment was opened in 1905, to prepare young men for the degrees of the Cape University.

In 1921 the College was incorporated into the University of South Africa as The Potchefstroom University College; the title "for Christian Higher Education" was added in 1933 by Act of Parliament.

As a result of its growth and the high standard maintained since that time, it became an independent university in 1951.

General entrance requirements:     Matriculation Certificate or a School-
                                   Leaving Certificate which grants exemption
                                   from the Matriculation requirements.

Faculties:

Letters and Philosophy       Education
Natural Science              Economic Science
Theology

## The University and the Theological School of the Dutch Reformed Church

Theological students write their B.A. examination at the University, after which they proceed to a 4-year course of the Theological School.

During this course students do the Th.D. examination at the University.

## The University and the Potchefstroom Teachers' College

Various teachers' courses are offered at the Potchefstroom Teachers' College, e.g. a diploma following the degrees B.A., B.Sc., or B.Com. Candidates for this diploma take their degree at the University.

Language of instruction:     Afrikaans-Nederlands.

Degrees awarded:

| Faculty | Degree | Duration of course (years) |
|---|---|---|
| Letters and Philosophy | B.A. | 3 |
| | Honns. B.A. | 4 |
| | M.A. | 1 |
| | D.Litt. | |
| | D.Phil. | |
| | B.Mus. | 3 |
| | Honns. B.Mus. | 4 |
| | M.Mus. | |
| | D.Mus. | |
| | LL.B. | 3 |
| | LL.D. | |
| | B.A. (Bibl.) | 4 |
| | Honns. B.A. (Bibl.) | 5 |
| | M.A. (Bibl.) | 1 |
| | D.Phil. (Bibl.) | |
| | Church Organist's Diploma | 3 |
| | Licentiate in Music (Performance) | 3 |
| | Diploma in Library Science | 1 |
| | Lower University Diploma in Library Science | 2 |

| | | |
|---|---|---|
| Natural Science | B.Sc. | 3 |
| | Honns. B.Sc. | 4 |
| | M.Sc. | |
| | D.Sc. | |
| | B.Sc. (Huish.) | 4 |
| | Honns. B.Sc. (Huish.) | 5 |
| | M.Sc. (Huish.) | 1 |
| | B.Sc. (Farm.) | 3 |
| | Honns. B.Sc. (Farm.) | 4 |
| | M.Sc. (Farm.) | 1 |
| | D.Sc. (Farm.) | |
| | B.Sc. (Ind.Chem.) | 4 |
| | Diploma in Hospital Dietetics | 1 |
| Theology | Th.B. | 4 |
| | Th.M. | 1 |
| | Th.D. | |
| Education | B.Ed. | 2 |
| | M.Ed. | 1 |
| | D.Ed. | |
| | B.Sc. (Huish.OK.) | 4 |
| | Honns. B.P.Ed. | 1 |
| | M.P.Ed. | 1 |
| | D.P.Ed. | |
| | University Teacher's Diploma (U.O.D.) | 1 |
| | University Teacher's Diploma (Counseling) (U.O.D. Voorl.) | 1 |
| | University Primary Teacher's Diploma (U.L.O.D.) | 3 |
| | University Teacher's Diploma in Music (U.D.M.) | 1 |
| | Licentiate in Music Teaching (P.U.L.M.) | 3 |
| | Teacher's Diploma in Domestic Science | 3 |
| Economic Science | B.Comm. | 3 |
| | Honns. B.Comm. | 4 |
| | M.Comm. | 1 |
| | D.Comm. | |
| | Diploma in Business Administration (U.D.B.A.) | 1 |
| | Certificate in Theory of Accountancy (S.T.R.) | 5 |
| | Lower Certificate in Cost Accounting (L.S.K.) | 2 |
| | Higher Certificate in Cost Accounting (H.S.K.) | 2 |

A degree may be awarded with distinction.

GENERAL REGULATIONS:

The course <u>Studium Universale</u> is obligatory for all students wishing to obtain a first bachelor's degree, certificate or undergraduate diploma.

The course is divided into two disciplines:

    (1)  Studium Universale A I or II, obligatory for all students proceeding to a first baccalaureate.
    (2)  Studium Universale B I and II, obligatory for all undergraduate diploma students except those taking the Lower Diploma in Library Science or the Lower Certificate in Cost Accounting, for whom only B I is required.

<u>Studium Universale - A brief summary</u>

Part I (for 2nd year students):

    (a)  Conception of life:  Calvinistic, Roman Catholic, Existentialist, etc.
    (b)  Study of a particular aspect of the Calvinistic view of life.
    (c)  The Calvinistic life, world philosophy, and science concerning knowledge and science, scientific method, etc.

Part II (for 3rd year students):

The world as God's creation, universal and natural law, man's place in the world, man and history, etc.

<u>Examinations:</u>

Every candidate for a degree must take a written or oral examination, or both, in every course taken.

<u>First Bachelor's Degree</u>[+]

Eligibility:          Matriculation Certificate or Exemption Certificate of the Joint Matriculation Board.

Duration of courses: Every candidate for a first degree must attend a recognized course of study as a registered

[+]In these regulations, unless otherwise stated, "first bachelor's degree" means a bachelor's degree other than an Honneurs degree or a baccalaureate (<u>Baccalaureus</u>) in Education, Theology, or Law.
    "Post-graduate degree" means an Honneurs baccalaureate and a bachelor's degree in Education, Theology or Law for which a previous degree is required.
    "Advanced degrees" means a master's or doctor's degree.

matriculated student of the University, for the
period stated below:

B.A., B.Sc., B.Sc. (Farm.)
or B.Mus.                                                    3 years

B.Sc.(Huish.), B.Sc.(Huish.Ok.),
B.A.(Bibl.) or B.Sc.(Ind.Chem.)                              4 years

## Exemption:

The Senate may recognize a student's attendance at courses as a matriculated
student at another university, or may recognize certain examinations taken
at another university, in order to exempt him from taking the University's
examination in a specific subject; on the understanding that no student may
obtain the first bachelor's degree unless he has taken recognized courses
at the University during at least 2 of the final years in a 4-year bachelor's
course, or half the ancillaries in any other bachelor's degree course.

## Post-Graduate Degrees

Eligibility:              Baccalaureate degree.
                          Candidate must have knowledge of a third modern
                          Western language.

Duration of courses:      Every candidate for a post-graduate bachelor's
                          degree must reside as a registered student at the
                          University for the requisite period, namely:

                          (a)  For an Honneurs degree, at least 1 year after
                               the completion of the bachelor's requirements.
                          (b)  For B.Ed., at least 2 years after the
                               completion of the first baccalaureate.
                          (c)  For Th.B., at least 4 years after the
                               completion of the first degree.
                          (d)  For LL.B., at least 3 years after the
                               completion of the first degree.

## Master's Degrees

Eligibility:              Honns. baccalaureate or baccalaureate.

Duration of courses:      At least 1 year after an Honns. or 2 years after a
                          bachelor's degree, except for Theology and Education,
                          for which the period is 1 year after the bachelor's
                          degree.

## Examination:

The master's examination consists of a question or questions, and a
dissertation.

Except in unusual circumstances, with the Senate's consent, a candidate may only attempt the examination once.


## Doctoral Degrees

Eligibility:               The candidate must fulfill the requirements for the master's degree in that faculty, except in the case of Law, where the LL.B. is required.


## Examination:

A thesis is required which is the result of the candidate's study and research.


## Faculty of Letters and Philosophy

### B.A. Degrees

A student for the B.A. degree may choose to be examined in subjects selected from the following groups:

### Group A

    I.    Majors and ancillaries

        (1)  Afrikaans-Dutch, Bantu languages, German, English, English IB, French, Greek, Latin, Semitic languages.
        (2)  Philosophy.

    II.   Supplementary majors and ancillaries

        Geography, Bible Study, History, Art History, Social Welfare, Native Administration, Ethnology, Psychology, Sociology, Political Science, Journalism, Music History, Mathematics, Physical Education.

    III.  Supplementary ancillaries

        Library Science (2 courses), Special German, Greek History and Culture, Roman History and Culture, Music History, Harmony and Counterpoint (2 courses, only taken with Music History), Elocution and Drama, Economics (1 course), Economic History (2 courses), Physiology I, Hygiene I (only taken with Physical Education III).

### Group B - Social Sciences

    I.    Majors and ancillaries

        Geography, Bible Study, History, Social Welfare, Native Administration, Journalism, Political Science, Psychology, Sociology, Ethnology, Economics, Philosophy, Physical Education, Music History, Art History.

II.    Supplementary ancillaries

        Library Science (2 courses), Greek History and Culture, Roman
        History and Culture, Economic History, Commerce, Banking and
        Finance, Statistical Mathematics, Latin (1 course), Physiology I,
        Hygiene I (only taken with Physical Education III), Statistical
        Methods.

## Group C - Law

    I.    Majors

        Roman-Dutch Law, Roman Law.

    II.    Supplementary ancillaries

        History of Roman Dutch Law and Roman Law, Constitutional Law
        (1 course), Latin, Political Science, Philosophy, Economics,
        Native Administration.

A student must pass in at least 11 courses, the courses being distributed
in such a way that at least 5 are taken from the prescribed groups as
follows:

A student selects his majors and 1 more course from Groups A, B, or C,
with the proviso that:

    (a)  In Group A
        (i)  1 subject must be taken from Group A I(1),
      (ii)  At least 6 language courses must be chosen from Group
            A I(1),
    (iii)  At least 2 courses are to be completed from Groups A I(2),
            II and III, and

    (b)  In Group B, 2 language courses from Group A I(1) must be taken.

The course for the B.A. degree leading to the 2nd-year course of the LL.B.
degree must include Roman-Dutch Law and Roman Law as major subjects,
History of Roman and Roman-Dutch Law, Latin I, English I, and Constitutional Law.

## Honns. B.A.

General regulations for post-graduate degrees apply.

Unless the Senate rules otherwise, a subject for an Honneurs course is one
which a student completed as a major for the B.A. degree. Under exceptional circumstances, a student who is in possession of a bachelor's degree in
another faculty may be permitted to write the Honneurs examination in any
section of the Faculty of Letters and Philosophy.

Subjects: Geography, Afrikaans-Dutch Language and Literature, Bantu
          languages, German Language and Literature, Economics, English
          Language and Literature, French Language and Literature,
          History, Greek, Classical Languages, Art History and

Appreciation, Latin, Physical Education, Social Work, Native
Administration, Journalism, Semitic Languages, Psychology,
Sociology, Political Science, Ethnology, Mathematics, Philosophy.


## M.A.

General regulations for post-graduate degrees apply.

The degree may be awarded in the subjects listed for Honneurs B.A.


## D.Litt. and D.Phil.

D.Phil. is awarded in the case of Philosophy, Economics, Mathematics, Geography or related subjects; in other cases, the degree is D.Litt.


## B.Mus.

Eligibility:          At the beginning of his 1st year a student must
                      establish, in a practical test, his performing
                      proficiency, musicianship, and general knowledge of
                      music.  He will be expected to reach a standard
                      similar to that of the Advanced Certificate of the
                      University of South Africa.

In the case of a student taking Singing as major, or if the instrument
of his choice is not piano, he must take Piano as an additional subject.
The required standard of proficiency in piano playing will not be as high
as that demanded in Singing or in the chosen instrument.

Subjects: Music History, Harmony, Counterpoint, General Musical Studies,
          Musical Performance, German I or Special German, Afrikaans I,
          English I or French I, Composition, Orchestration, Art History
          and Appreciation I.

In addition,to enter for the final examination a student must offer a
composition exercise, prepared under the supervision of the Head of the
department.  The exercise is part of the 3rd-year examination; the
examiner's approval is required before the degree may be obtained.


## Honns. B.Mus.

General regulations governing post-graduate degrees apply.

Courses are as follows:

          3 special subjects chosen from Musical Studies.

          A detailed study of an approved subject is presented as a
          dissertation, or the performance of an approved concert

performance, <u>or</u> an additional question, <u>or</u> an original composition.

A student may not be enrolled simultaneously for the Honns. B.Mus. and the Teacher's Licentiate in Music, or the Church Organist's Diploma.


## M.Mus.

General regulations for post-graduate degrees apply.

The examination consists of a dissertation, <u>or</u> 4 questions from the area of musical science.


## D.Mus.

General regulations for doctoral degrees apply.


## Church Organist's Diploma

Eligibility:        (a)  Matriculation Exemption Certificate or equivalent, <u>and</u>
                    (b)  Certificate of the intermediate organist's exami-nation of the University of South Africa, or student must have reached the standard required for the examination, <u>and</u>
                    (c)  Certificate of the advanced piano examination of the University of South Africa, or an equivalent standard.

A student may study simultaneously for the Diploma and for the B.Mus. degree or the Licentiate in Music Teaching.

Duration of course:    3 years.

The following courses are offered:

> Organ, Music History, Harmony and Counterpoint, Organ Construction, General Musical Studies, Liturgy, Repertoire, Choir Conducting, Organ Method, Afrikaans or English or French.
>
> In Addition, Studium Universale B I and II are required.

Diploma may be awarded with distinction.


## Licentiate in Music (Performance)

Eligibility:            Licentiate in Music Teaching from any South African University.

Duration of course:    3 academic years.

The examination consists of a full concert recital.

Admission to the examination rests with the Head of the Conservatoire.

Licentiate may be awarded with distinction.

## LL.B.

The general rules concerning post-graduate degrees apply.

Duration of course:    3 academic years.

The following courses are taken:

> Roman-Dutch Law, Roman Law, History of Roman Law and Roman-Dutch
> Law, Constitutional Law, Latin, English, Equity, South African
> Private Law, Criminal Law, Conveyancing, Native Law, Exposition,
> Law of Evidence, Law of Procedure, International Law, Common
> Law, Forensic Medicine.

Without special permission of the Senate no student may proceed to the 2nd
year of study until he has passed in all the courses of the 1st year; nor
may he proceed to the 3rd year until he has passed at least 4 courses
including International Law and Law of Procedure.

Except for unusual circumstances, a student must pass in at least 4 courses
simultaneously in the 3rd year.

## LL.D.

General regulations for doctoral degrees apply.

The degree may only be awarded after the LL.B. has been held for 3 years.

Duration of course:    2-year program of special study and research.

Examination:           Final in languages, legal material and literature.

## B.A. (Bibl.)

The duration of this Library Science course is at least 4 years.

A candidate must pass in at least 15 courses, with Library Science I-IV
as major.

If a student should decide after his 1st or 2nd year not to continue
studying for this degree, the courses in Library Science may be accredited
towards a B.A. degree.

Students who intend taking Library Science III must spend 3 weeks doing practical library work in a recognized library under supervision.

Students taking Library Science IV must spend an additional 3 weeks in a library doing practical work.


## Honns. B.A. (Bibl.)

General regulations for post-graduate degrees apply.

Library Science as major for the B.A. (Bibl.) is a prerequisite for the Honneurs course in Library Science.


## M.A. (Bibl.)

General regulations for post-graduate degrees apply.

The subjects in which the degree may be taken are the same as for Honns. B.A. (Bibl.).


## Diploma in Library Science

Eligibility:            A recognized degree in Letters and Philosophy, Natural Science, Economics, or in any special or technical subject recognized by the Senate for this purpose.

Duration of course:     1 academic year.  A student who already holds the Lower University Diploma in Library Science may take the examination after 1 semester.

The following courses are taken:

> Library Organization and Administration, Cataloguing, Research and Bibliography, Book Selection and Supply, History of the Book, and Librarianship.

During his period of study a student must spend at least 4 weeks doing practical work in a recognized library.

Diploma may be awarded with distinction.


## Lower University Diploma in Library Science

Eligibility:            Matriculation Certificate or its equivalent or First-class pass in the National Senior Certificate.

N.B.    A student who has not fulfilled the Matriculation

exemption requirements may not, on acquiring the
Lower University Diploma, be exempted from any
requirements of the bachelor's degree, nor be
admitted to the University Diploma in Library Science.

Duration of course:    2 years.

The following courses are taken:

Afrikaans-Dutch I, English I, 3 other 1st-year courses chosen
from Groups B and C, Library Organization and Administration,
Cataloguing and Classification, Research and Bibliography,
Acquisition and Supply, History of the Book and Librarianship.

In addition, Studium Universale B I is required.

During his period of study, a student must spend at least 4 weeks doing
practical work in a recognized library.

Lower Diploma may be awarded with distinction.


## Faculty of Natural Science

## B.Sc. Degrees

Eligibility:            Pass in Mathematics in the Matriculation examination.
                        Physical Science strongly recommended.

9 courses are chosen from the following list:

Geography, Chemistry, Dietetics, Zoology, Physics, Geology,
Hygiene, Physiology, Physical Education, Microbiology, Botany,
Psychology, Statistical Mathematics, Theory of Statistics,
Applied Mathematics, Mathematics and 1 course in a modern
Western language, as for B.A.

In Addition, Studium Universale A I and II.

Note:   Hygiene II offered only until the end of 1964, and Hygiene
        III until the end of 1965.

A course of study consists of at least 2 majors, in each of which 2 or 3
courses must be followed.

A.   Majors with 3 courses:

Geography, Chemistry, Dietetics, Zoology, Physics, Geology,
Physiology, Physical Education, Botany, Psychology, Statistical
Mathematics, Applied Mathematics, Mathematics.

B.   Majors with 2 courses:

Microbiology, Theory of Statistics

A student choosing a major from column A below must follow the ancillary
courses in column B:

| A (Majors) | B (Ancillaries) |
| --- | --- |
| Geography | 1 course in Geology and 1 in Chemistry |
| Chemistry | 1 course in Physics |
| Dietetics | 1st year, Chemistry I and Hygiene I or Zoology I<br>2nd year, Chemistry II and Microbiology I<br>3rd year, Psychology (Special) |
| Zoology | 1 course in Chemistry |
| Physics | 2 courses in Math. and 1 Applied Math, except where Physics III and Geology III are taken together, when only Math. II required |
| Physiology | 1 course in Chemistry and a 1st course in Hygiene or Zoology |
| Geology | 1 course in Chemistry and 1 in Physics |
| Hygiene | 1 in each of Chemistry, and either Botany or Zoology or Physics or Physiology |
| Physical Education | 1 course in one of the following: Zoology, Physiology, Hygiene |
| Microbiology | 2 courses in Chemistry and 1 in each of Physics and Botany |
| Botany | 1 in Chemistry |
| Psychology | 1 course in two, or 2 courses in one of the following:  Zoology, Physics, Physiology, Hygiene, Statistical Mathematics |
| Applied Mathematics | 2 courses in Mathematics |
| Mathematics | 1 course in Applied Math. |

A student taking Dietetics as major must, from his 2nd year onwards, do
3 weeks of practical work each year during vacations in a hospital and/or
with the Ministry of Food.


Honns. B.Sc.

General regulations for post-graduate degrees apply.

The degree may be taken in the following:

> Geography, Biochemistry, Chemistry, Dietetics, Zoology, Entomo-
> logy, Physics, Physiology, Geology, Microbiology, Botany,
> Psychology, Applied Mathematics, Mathematics.
>
> Physiology and Biochemistry may be taken only after a 1st course
> in Physics.
>
> Chemistry may be taken only after a 1st course in Mathematics
> or Statistical Mathematics.
>
> Dietetics may be taken only after completing Physiology as a
> major and a second course in Chemistry.

## M.Sc.

General regulations for post-graduate degrees apply.

Subjects are the same as for Honns. B.Sc.

## D.Sc.

General regulations for doctoral degrees apply.

Subjects are the same as for Honns. B.Sc.

## B.Sc. (Huish.) (Domestic Science)

Duration of course:   4 years.

Subjects: Physics, Chemistry, Physiology, Botany, Microbiology, Housekeeping, Cookery, Dressmaking, Diet.

Students in Dietetics take a B.Sc. degree with Dietetics and Physiology
as majors and with Chemistry I and Hygiene I or Zoology in the 1st year,
Chemistry I and Microbiology I in the 2nd year, and Psychology Special
in the 3rd year as ancillaries.

A student who has completed the 1st year of the Diploma in Domestic Science
may switch to 2nd year B.Sc. (Huish.). Studium Universale A I and II are
required.

## Honns. B.Sc. (Huish.) (Domestic Science)

General regulations for post-graduate degrees apply.

Degree may be taken in Cookery and Dietetics.

### M.Sc. (Huish.) (Domestic Science)

General regulations for post-graduate degrees apply.

Subjects in which the degree may be taken are the same as for Honns. B.Sc. (Huish.).

### B.Sc. (Farm.) (Pharmacy)

Eligibility:             Matriculation or the equivalent examination with
                         pass in Mathematics and 1 of the following:  Physics,
                         Nature Study, Physical Science, Biology, Botany or
                         Zoology.

The following courses are taken:

Physics I, Botany I, Zoology I, Chemistry I-III, Pharmacy I and II, Pharmacology, Physiology I, Dispensing, and Pharmaceutical Practice.

In addition, Studium Universale A I and II.

### Honns. B.Sc. (Farm.) (Pharmacy)

General regulations for post-graduate degrees apply.

The degree may be taken in the pharmaceutical subjects.

### M.Sc. (Farm.) (Pharmacy)

General regulations for post-graduate degrees apply.

The degree may be taken in the pharmaceutical subjects.

### D.Sc. (Farm.) (Pharmacy)

General regulations for doctoral degrees apply.

Subjects in which the degree may be taken are the same as for M.Sc. (Farm.)

### B.Sc. (Ind.Chem.)

Eligibility:             Pass in the Matriculation examination in Mathematics
                         and Chemistry or Physical Science.

The following courses are taken:

Physics, Chemistry, Mathematics, Applied Mathematics, Engineering

Design, Chemical Technology, Industrial Economic and Business Administration.

Vacation work in Chemical Technology must be done during the 2nd and 3rd years.  A minimum of 2 calendar months are required at a recognized chemical factory, and a certificate confirming this must be submitted to the Head of the department.

A First-Aid Certificate is a prerequisite to the awarding of the degree.

## Diploma in Hospital Dietetics

Eligibility:            B.Sc. degree of this University with Dietetics as major, or equivalent.

Diploma is awarded to students who have completed a year's full-time service under supervision in a hospital recognized by the University, and who have subsequently passed the examination.

Diploma may be awarded with distinction.

## Faculty of Theology

### Th.B.

Eligibility:            B.A. degree.  The following courses must have been taken:  Hebrew II, Greek II (including New Testament Greek), Latin I, Philosophy II.  In his B.A. course a student may not include 1 or more courses in Bible Studies.  A reading knowledge of German is required.

Duration of course:    4 years.

### Courses:

4-year subjects:

Canon Law, Dogma, Apologetics, Revealed History (New and Old Testament).

3-year subjects:

Exegesis (Old and New Testament), Church History, Canonical Scripture.

1-year subjects:

Biblical Archaeology, Homiletics, Liturgy, Symbolism, Pastoral Practice.

## Th.M.

General regulations for post-graduate degrees apply.

Duration of course:    1-2 years.

The course of study consists of the following groups of subjects:

1.    Old Testament subjects:

Exegesis, Canon, Sacred History, Cultural Historical Background.
A student who takes this as the major group must satisfy the
Head of the department of his knowledge of Hebrew and at least
1 other Semitic language.

2.    New Testament subjects:

A student who takes this as the major group must satisfy the
Head of the department of his knowledge of Greek and of Aramaic-
Syrian.

3.    Church History, Canon Law.

4.    Dogma, History of Dogma.

5.    Apologetics, Evangelism.

6.    Missionary Study and History of Missions.

7.    Homiletics and Liturgics, Catechesis and Pastoral Practice.

Examination:    A candidate chooses:

(a)  1 of the 7 groups as major group.

(b)  1 of the subjects in the major group as major subject.

(c)  1 ancillary from each of 2 remaining groups.

## Th.D.

Regulations for doctoral degrees apply.

The subjects are the same as those for the Th.M.

## Faculty of Education

## B.Ed.

Eligibility:            University Teacher's Diploma or its equivalent from
                        another university, in the 1st study year.    The

Senate may recognize for this purpose a teacher's
certificate acquired after 2 years' post-matriculation study.

Duration of course:    3 years.

In the 2nd year of study, the student must pursue a full academic year's
course.

The final year's study consists of the following courses at Honns. level:
Theoretical Education, Comparative Education, Empirical
Education, Historical Education.

The examination in Empirical Education may involve a practical test.


## M.Ed.

General regulations for post-graduate degrees apply.


## D.Ed.

General regulations for doctoral degrees apply.


## B.Sc. (Huisch. Ok.)  (Domestic Science and Dietetics)

Eligibility:            A minimum of 33% in Mathematics or Physical Science
                        in the Matriculation examination.

Duration of course:    4 years.

The following courses are taken:

1st to     Chemistry I and II, Physics A, Physiology I-III, Cookery I-III,
3rd yrs:   Microbiology I and II, Botany I, Housekeeping I and II, Dress-
           making I and II, Dietetics I.

4th yr:    Dressmaking III or Dietetics II and courses as for University
           Teacher's Diploma (U.O.D.).


## Honns. B.P.Ed.

General regulations for post-graduate degrees apply.

Duration of course:    1 year.

The following courses are taken:

> Theoretical Physical Education, Empirical Physical Education, Historical Physical Education, Practical Physical Education.

The examination in Practical Physical Education may involve a practical and an oral test.


### M.P.Ed.

General regulations for post-graduate degrees apply.


### University Teacher's Diploma (U.O.D.)

Eligibility:            A recognized degree in Letters and Philosophy, or Natural Science, or Economics, or in any special or Technical branch of knowledge.

Duration of course:    1 year.

The following subjects are taken:

> Geography, Afrikaans-Dutch, Bantu Languages, Scripture, Chemistry, Zoology, English, Physiology, Physics, French, History, Greek, Art History and Appreciation, Latin, Physical Education, Music History, Botany, Statistical Mathematics, Ethnology, Mathematics.

The course of study is as follows:

> Majors:
>
> Theoretical Education, Empirical Education, Historical Education, Practical Education, Student-teaching.
>
> Ancillaries:
>
> Beginning and Methods of Primary School Teaching, Beginning and Methods of Secondary School Teaching.
>
> Practical Subjects:
>
> One or both official language(s), Elocution, School Health, Woodwork.
>
> At least 2 and not more than 3 of the following:
>
> Physical Education, Art, School Library Science, Typing, Afrikaans Linguistics, English Linguistics.


### University Teacher's Diploma (Counseling) - U.O.D. (Voorl.)

Eligibility:            B.A., B.Sc., or B.Comm. degrees with Psychology as major.

Duration of course:    1 year.

In place of Beginning and Methods of Primary School Teaching, the following are taken:

> Problems in Child Psychology, Psychometry, Career Guidance
> and its Methods, Socio-Pathological Educational Phenomena,
> Practical Work.

## University Primary School Teacher's Diploma (U.L.O.D.)

Eligibility:            Matriculation Certificate, Secondary School-Leaving
                        Certificate or National Senior Certificate.

Duration of course:    3 years.

Subjects as above with the addition of Needlework, Hygiene, Harmony and
Counterpoint.

## University Teacher's Diploma in Music (U.D.M.)

Eligibility:            B.Mus. degree.

Duration of course:    1 year.

Courses:  Method - The practical subject
          Method - Harmony and Counterpoint
          Method - School Music
          Method - Music History

Diploma may be taken with distinction.

## Licentiate in Music Teaching (P.U.L.M.)

Eligibility:            Matriculation Certificate or equivalent.

Duration of course:    3 years.

Subjects: Piano, Organ, Violin or Singing, Teaching Methods, Harmony and
          Counterpoint, General Music Studies, Afrikaans, French or
          English, Choral Conducting, School Music, and a practical
          subject.

## Teacher's Diploma in Domestic Science

Eligibility:            Matriculation Certificate or equivalent.

Duration of course:    3 years.

Subjects: Physiology, Physics, Chemistry, Microbiology, Empirical
          Education, Housekeeping, Cookery, Afrikaans and English
          Linguistics, Dressmaking, Practical and Theoretical Education,
          Dietetics.


## Faculty of Economic Sciences

### B.Comm.

Duration of course:   3 years.

Courses:   Economics, Accountancy, Industrial Economy, Statistics or
           Elementary Theory of Finance and Statistics, Afrikaans I or
           English I, Mercantile Law, Banking, Cost Accounting, Industrial
           and Personnel Psychology, Economic History, Income Tax, Auditing.

           In addition, Studium Universale A I and II.


A course of study for the B.Comm. degree to be credited towards the 2nd
year of LL.B. must include:

           Roman-Dutch Law III, Roman Law, History of Roman-Dutch Law and
           Roman Law, Constitutional Law I, Latin I, English I.


### Honns. B.Comm.

General regulations for post-graduate degrees apply.

Duration of course:   4 years

Further study in one of the following disciplines must be pursued, provided
that the examinations in the subjects in parentheses are passed before the
following courses are completed:

           Economics-Industrial Economy (Economics III, Industrial Economy
           III, and Commerce and Banking II).

           Accountancy (Accountancy III, Auditing I, Cost Accounting I,
           Income Tax I).

           Cost Accounting (Cost Accounting II, Accounting III).

           Industrial Economy-Cost Accounting (Industrial Economy III,
           Cost Accounting II).

           Statistics, Industrial and Personnel Psychology

           Economics, Commerce and Banking (Economics III, Commerce and
           Banking II).

Honns B.Comm. (Accountancy)

The following courses, which are also required for the Certificate in Theory of Accountancy (S.T.R.), are taken:

Accountancy IV A and V A, Income Tax II, Cost Accounting II A and III A, Auditing II and III, Executor's Accountancy, Industrial Economy.

Honns. B.Comm. (Cost Accounting)

The following courses are taken:

Management I and II, Income Tax II, Cost Accounting III and IV, Accounting IV B and V B, Production Methods, Industrial Law.

Honns. B.Comm. (Industrial Economy-Cost Accounting)

The following courses are taken:

Industrial Economy, Cost Accounting III and IV, Production Methods, Industrial Law.

M.Comm.

General regulations for post-graduate degrees apply.

Subjects are the same as for Honns. B.Comm.

D.Comm.

General regulations for doctoral degrees apply.

Subjects are the same as for Honns. B.Comm.

Certificate in Theory of Accountancy (S.T.R.)

Duration of course:    5 years.

The following courses must be taken:

Accountancy I-V A, Economics I, Statistics I, Mercantile Law I, Cost Accounting I-III B, English I A, Auditing I-III, Executors', Liquidators' and Curators' Accounting.

In addition, Studium Universale B I.

Lower Certificate in Cost Accounting (L.S.K.)

Eligibility:              Matriculation Certificate or a Secondary School-
                          Leaving Certificate, or equivalent.

Duration of course:   2 years.

Certificate is granted only to candidates who have completed 2 years'
recognized practice.

Subjects: Cost Accounting, Production Methods, Organization and Methods,
          Accountancy, Business Ethics, Electronic Computors.

          Studium Universale B I.

Certificate may be awarded with distinction.


Higher Certificate in Cost Accounting (H.S.K.)

Eligibility:              Recognized degree in Letters and Science or Natural
                          Sciences or Economics or any specialized techno-
                          logical science.
                          L.S.K. is acceptable.

Duration of course:   2 years.

Courses:  Cost Accounting, Advanced Organization and Methods, Advanced
          Production Methods, Modern Industrial Problems of Mechanization,
          Management or Economic Political Science, and an essay.

Practical work:           At least 2 weeks' practical work must be undertaken
                          at a recognized plant.

Certificate may be awarded with distinction.


University Diploma in Business Administration (U.D.B.A.)

Eligibility:              H.S.K.

Duration of course:   1 year.

Subjects:

     A.   (1)   2 of the following:

                Advanced Managerial Accountancy, Administrative Automation,
                Advanced Standard-and-Norm-Accounting, Cost Accounting IV,
                Expense Variability and Prediction of Expense-Variables.

          (2)   2 of the following:

Administrative Organization, Advanced Industrial Finance,
Analysis and Interpretation of Finance Accounts and
Conditions.

(3)  1 of the following:

Mercantile Law I, Industrial Law.

B.   A report on a subject in which the candidate has specialized.

Diploma may be awarded with distinction.

## UNIVERSITY OF THE ORANGE FREE STATE, Bloemfontein

The only establishment for higher learning in this province, founded as
Grey College (secondary school), in 1855. From 1904, the senior classes
of the college developed in such a way as to become the nucleus of a
university college. In 1918, it became a constituent college of the
University of South Africa, the name being changed from Grey University
College to the University College of the Orange Free State in 1935. In
1950, the College received its charter as an autonomous and independent
university.

Official languages:    English and Afrikaans. Matriculation examinations
                       in these languages set at 2 levels, ordinary and
                       higher. It is customary to take the mother tongue
                       at the higher level and the second language at the
                       ordinary level.

General entrance requirements:

(a)  Matriculation Certificate awarded by the Joint
     Matriculation Board, or Exemption Certificate.

     The University may in addition prescribe, as a pre-
     requisite for admission to a particular course, the
     attainment of a specified standard in a particular
     subject of the Matriculation examination or of an
     examination recognized by the Joint Matriculation
     Board for this purpose.

(b)  A student who passes, with good grades, a School-
     Leaving examination of one of the examining bodies
     of the Union of South Africa (Matriculation Board,
     Education Department of the Orange Free State, Cape
     Province, Transvaal, or Natal; or the Department of
     Education, Arts and Science) which does not grant
     him full exemption from the Matriculation exemption,
     must obtain conditional exemption. With this
     exemption, he will be admitted to the University,

and if he fulfills the requirements of the
conditional exemption within a year, the work done
at the University for credit will be recognized.

(c)   A student who has been admitted to the University in
respect of a conditional certificate of exemption
and who, at the end of this first year's course,
satisfied the University's examination requirements
but fails to fulfill the conditions for exemption
from the Matriculation examination, forfeits all
class and examination marks for credit.

Faculties:

| | |
|---|---|
| Arts and Philosophy | Law |
| Social Sciences | Economics and Administrative |
| Natural Sciences | Sciences |
| Agriculture | Education |

Teacher's College

Language of instruction:        Afrikaans-Nederlands

Degrees awarded:

| Faculty | Degree | Duration of course (years) |
|---|---|---|
| Arts and Philosophy | B.A. | 3 |
| | B.A. (Hons.) | 4 |
| | M.A. | |
| | D.Litt. | |
| | D.Phil. | |
| | B.Mus. | 4 |
| | B.Mus. (Hons.) | 4 |
| | M.Mus. | |
| | D.Mus. | |
| | Performer's Diploma | 3 |
| | U.O.V.S. Teacher's Diploma in Music | 3 |
| | Diploma in Church Music | 3 |
| | Diploma in Bantu Studies | 3 |
| | Undergraduate Diploma in Library Science | 2 |
| | Post-graduate Diploma in Library Science | 1 |
| Social Sciences | B.Soc.Sc. | 3 |
| | B.Soc.Sc. (Hons.) | 4 |
| | M.Soc.Sc. | |
| | D.Soc.Sc. | |
| | B.Soc.Sc. (Nursing) | 4 |
| | Diplomas in Social Welfare and Nursing | 1 |

| | | |
|---|---|---|
| Natural Sciences | B.Sc. | 3 |
| | B.Sc. (Hons.) | 4 |
| | M.Sc. | |
| | D.Sc. | |
| | B.Arch. | 6 |
| | M.Arch. | 2 |
| | D.Arch. | |
| | B.Sc. (Q.S.) | 5 |
| | M.Sc. (Q.S.) | 2 |
| | Diploma in Q.S. | 5 |
| | Diploma in Building | 3 |
| | Diploma in Diagnostic Radiography | 2½ |
| Agriculture | B.Sc. Agric. | 4 |
| | B.Sc. Agric. (Hons.) | 5 |
| | M.Sc. Agric. | |
| | D.Sc. Agric. | |
| Law | LL.B. | 3 |
| | LL.D. | |
| | Diploma Juris | |
| | D.R.S. (Diploma in Jurisprudence for Government Offices) | 3 |
| Economics and Administrative Sciences | B.Com. | 3 |
| | B.Com. (Hons.) | 4 |
| | M.Com. | |
| | D.Com. | |
| | B.Admin. | 3 |
| | B.Admin. (Hons.) | 4 |
| | M.Admin. | |
| | D.Admin. | |
| | Certificate in the Theory of Accountancy | 5 |
| | Diploma in Municipal Administration | 3 |
| | Diploma in Business Administration | 3 |
| Education | B.Ed. | 2 |
| | M.Ed. | |
| | D.Ed. | |
| | Teacher's Diploma in Business (O.D.H.) | 3 |
| | Teacher's Diploma in Physical Education (O.D.L.O.) | |
| | University Teacher's Diploma (U.O.D.) | 1 |

Examinations:

At the end of each year examinations are held in all subjects, including ancillaries.

Year-end marks:  A student's year-end mark for any subject is based
on his written, oral and practical work during the year.

With the exception of subjects for the B.Ed. degree and subjects in
which the regulations of the faculty concerned require a higher mark,
the minimum year-end mark for all subjects is 40%.

Pass requirements:

(a)  In order to pass in a subject a student must score the prescribed
     minimum in his year-end mark, in his examination mark, in
     addition to subminima in separate questions, if required.

(b)  A student is granted a first class pass if he achieves the
     relevant prescribed minimum.

(c)  Distinction:  A degree or diploma is awarded with distinction in
     a major subject if a student gains a first class pass in the
     final course in that major.

Pass in major subjects:

(a)  To have his majors recognized, a student must simultaneously pass
     his final courses, and he may not do so before the end of the
     3rd year of study.

(b)  A student who passes his majors simultaneously but fails 1 or
     more ancillaries, gets credit for the grades in the majors but
     not before he has passed the ancillaries.


## Honors Baccalaureate (Honneurs-Baccalaureus)

Eligibility:              Ordinary bachelor's degree.

A student may only offer as major a subject which he offered as major for
the ordinary baccalaureate, except by special permission.

Duration of course:    At least 1 year after the requirements of the
                       ordinary degree have been fulfilled.

## Examinations:

A student must take a university examination at the end of the course
and pass the whole examination simultaneously.


## Master's Degree

Eligibility:              An Hons. baccalaureate degree.

A subject which was not taken as a major for the bachelor's degree can
only be offered for the master's course with the Senate's special permission.

Examinations:

An examination for the master's degree consists of 2 parts:

Part I    A written examination which may not be taken before the end
          of the 1st year.
          Student may be wholly or partially exempted if he already
          holds the Hons. baccalaureate in the subject.

Part II   A written examination or a dissertation or both, according
          to departmental requirements.
          An additional oral examination may be required.

    (a)   Dissertation:
          The dissertation may not be submitted less than 18 months
          after completion of the bachelor's degree.

    (b)   Examination:
          A student passes or passes cum laude in the final exami-
          nation when he fulfills, individually and collectively, all
          the requirements of Parts I and II of the examination.

Doctorate

Eligibility:          Master's degree.
                      No student may be admitted to the doctorate until
                      the prescribed period following the attaining of the
                      master's degree.

Duration of course:

        (a)   In the case of the degrees D.Phil., D.Ed., D.Litt.,
              D.Com., D.Admin., 4 years or 3 years, of which at
              least 1 year shall be devoted exclusively to research.
        or    2 years which are fully devoted to research at the
              University.

        (b)   In the case of the D.Sc., at least 2 years which shall
              be devoted exclusively to research.

        (c)   In the case of the D.Arch., at least 2 years after
              obtaining the degree M.Arch.

        (d)   In the case of the LL.D., 4 years after the LL.B. or
              3 years of which at least 1 year shall be devoted
              exclusively to research.
        or    2 years fully devoted to research.

Faculty of Arts and Philosophy

B.A.

Duration of course:    3 years.

A candidate must take at least 11 courses, except where Physical Education
is 1 of the majors, when only 10 courses are necessary.

A candidate must complete at least 2 major subjects, with prescribed
ancillary courses.

<u>Major subjects</u>:

| | |
|---|---|
| English | Music |
| Afrikaans-Dutch | Ethnology |
| German | Physical Education |
| Latin | Civil Law |
| Greek | Roman Law and History of Law |
| Philosophy | Political Science |
| Bantu Languages | Bantu Administration |
| History | Company Law |
| Mathematics | Criminal Law |
| Economics | French |
| Geography | Hebrew |
| Sociology | |

<u>Ancillaries</u>:

A student who follows a final course in 1 of the subjects listed in
column A must take the ancillaries in column B:

| <u>A</u> | <u>B</u> |
|---|---|
| Latin | Classical Culture or Greek I |
| Greek | Classical Culture or Latin I |
| English | 1 course in Latin I or French I |
| Civil Law | Roman Law and History of Law |
| Roman Law and History of Law | Latin I |
| French | Special Latin or Latin I |

A degree course must have at least 1 course in English or Afrikaans-Dutch.

Courses of study:

From the following groups must be included:

(i)   At least 2 courses from A.
(ii)  At least 1 course from B or C.  <u>And</u>
(iii) Another course from B, or C, or D.

<u>Group A - Linguistics</u>

Bantu Languages, Latin, Greek, English, Afrikaans-Dutch, French
German, Hebrew.

## Group B - Jurisprudence

Roman Law and History of Law, Civil Law, Constitutional and Administrative Law, Bantu Law and Administration, International Law, Criminal Law.

## Group C - Philosophical Science

Mathematics, Philosophy, Political Science, Psychology, Ethnology, Economics, Education, Sociology, Social Welfare, Criminology.

## Group D - Social Science

History, Geography, Classical Culture, Bantu Administration, Musical History and Appreciation, Physical Education, Art History and Appreciation.

## Group E - Natural Sciences

Physics, Chemistry, Botany, Zoology, Geology, Biology, Applied Mathematics.

## Examinations:

(a)  Pass minimum:  at least 35% and an average of at least 40%. A sub-minimum of 25% in every question.

(b)  First class:  70%.

## B.A. Hons.

Subjects in which the Hons. baccalaureate may be taken:

| | |
|---|---|
| Afrikaans-Dutch | English |
| German | Latin |
| Greek | Classics |
| History | Mathematics |
| Economics | Geography |
| Sociology | Philosophy |
| Political Science | Ethnology |
| Bantu Languages | Music |
| Bantu Administration | Physical Education |
| Criminology | Psychology |

## Examinations:

An average of 50% and at least 40% in each of the prescribed questions are required in order to pass.

An average of 70% is required in order to pass cum laude.

M.A.

The following subjects may be taken:

| | |
|---|---|
| Afrikaans-Dutch | English |
| German | Latin |
| Greek | Classics |
| History | Psychology |
| Mathematics | Economics |
| Sociology | Geography |
| Political Science | Ethnology |
| Bantu Languages | Bantu Administration |
| Music | Physical Education |
| Education | |

Examinations:

50% average in the total marks of all oral and written examinations, provided that examination marks for individual examinations in Part I and Part II are not less than 40%.

Cum laude: 70%.

B.Mus.

Eligibility:

| Major subject | Requirement |
|---|---|
| Piano | Advanced certificate of the University of South Africa (or equivalent). |
| Organ | Final certificate for Piano and higher certificate for Organ of the University of South Africa (or equivalent). or Intermediate certificate for Organ in the same institution. |
| Singing | Intermediate certificate for Piano of the University of South Africa (or equivalent). |
| Stringed Instrument | Advanced certificate of the University of South Africa (or equivalent). |
| Composition | Advanced certificate in Harmony of the University of South Africa (or equivalent). |

Duration of course:  4 years.

Courses:  There are no majors, but the following count as preferred subjects:  History of Music, Performance.

1st year of B.Mus. includes:  Afrikaans-Dutch I or English I. 1 of the following:  German I, French I, Latin I, Art History, or Classical Culture.

4th year:   there is a choice between 2 directions of study, Academic, or Practical.

## Examinations:

The practical examinations consist of aural tests, chamber music, sight-reading, and the rendering of prescribed works.

Minimum pass mark:  45%, and an average of 50% in the combined year-end and examination marks.

Pass with distinction:  average for the combined year-end and examination mark, 70%.

## Performer's Diploma

The 3-year course is as follows:

(a)  Practical:

   (i)   Continuation of the 2 practical subjects of the 3rd year.
  (ii)   Repertory.
 (iii)   Literature.
  (iv)   Participation in choral works.
   (v)   Accompaniment.
  (vi)   Chamber Music.

(b)  Harmony IV.

## University of the Orange Free State (U.O.V.S.) Teacher's Diploma in Music

A student proceeding to the B.A. may, at the end of his 3rd year, acquire the Teacher's Diploma in Music if, in the 2nd and 3rd years he took the courses in method of the diploma course and passed the examinations.

## Diploma in Church Music

Eligibility:                 Matriculation Certificate or School-Leaving Certificate of the Joint Matriculation Board, or Senior Certificate of the Department of Education.

     and  (a)  Final standard of the University of South Africa or a similar examination in Piano.

     or   (b)  A pass in the intermediate Organ examination.

        (c)  Evidence of a knowledge of diatonic harmony and elementary modulation (at approximately the higher standard of the University of South Africa or Senior Certificate in Harmony).

Duration of course:   3 years.

Examinations:

       Pass-minimum and distinction as for B.Mus.


## Diploma in Bantu Studies

Eligibility:            School-Leaving Certificate or Senior Certificate of provincial education department, or Matriculation Certificate.

Duration of course:   3 years.

General regulations for the B.A. are applicable to this diploma.


## Undergraduate Diploma in Library Science

Eligibility:            School-Leaving Certificate or Senior Certificate of provincial education department, or Matriculation Certificate.

Duration of course:   2 years.

General regulations for the bachelor's degree are applicable to this diploma.

Courses of study:

       Library Science I and II, Bibliography I and II, Afrikaans-Dutch I, English I or Special English.

       1 other course selected from the B.A. list to be taken for the 2 years.

       Practical Librarianship.


## Post-graduate Diploma in Library Science

Eligibility:            At least a B.A.

Duration of course:   1 year.

Courses of study:

       Fundamentals and History of Librarianship, History and Development of the Book, Book Selection, Library Stock and Reference Work, Library Organization and Administration, Cataloguing and Classification.

       Practical work.

General regulations for the B.A. are applicable to this diploma.

## University of the Orange Free State (U.O.V.S.) Teacher's Diploma in Physical Education (O.D.L.O.)

Eligibility:           School-Leaving Certificate or Senior Certificate of provincial education department, or Matriculation Certificate, together with a medical certificate such as is required for the Physical Education degree course.

Courses:    At least 8 courses are chosen from the following: Physical Education II as well as at least 2 courses chosen from 1 of the following subjects: Geography, Afrikaans, Bantu, German, English, History, Latin, Mathematics; plus another 4 courses chosen from the above subjects or from other recognized B.A. courses, with the proviso that every course of study must include at least 1 course in Afrikaans/Dutch or English.

## Faculty of the Social Sciences

### B.Soc.Sc.

Duration of course:    3 years.

Course of study:

At least 11 courses, and practical work.

Majors:

At least 2 major subjects must be taken from the following:

Sociology                          Bantu Administration
Social Welfare                     Criminology
Psychology

Practical courses:

First-Aid and Home Nursing.

Female students must also take practical courses in Office Administration, Housekeeping, Needlework and Mothercraft.

Male students must take practical courses at the discretion of the department head.

Examinations:

At the end of each year there is an oral examination.

At the end of the 2nd or 3rd year, student must prove his proficiency in both English and Afrikaans.

### B.Soc.Sc. (Hons.)

General regulations for honors degrees apply.

The following subjects may be taken:

>    Sociology, Social Welfare, Psychology, Bantu Administration, Criminology.

### M.Soc.Sc.

General regulations for master's degree apply.

The following subjects may be taken:

>    Sociology, Social Welfare, Psychology, Bantu Administration, Criminology.

Examination regulations for the master's degree are the same as in the Faculty of Letters and Philosophy.

### B.Soc.Sc. Nursing

Duration of course:   4 years.

Majors:

>    At least 2 major subjects must be taken from the following:
>
>    Nursing                              Sociology
>    Social Welfare                       Psychology

Courses:

>    Nursing                      - 4
>    Sociology                    - 3
>    Psychology                   - 3
>    Anatomy and Physiology       - 5
>    Social Welfare               - 3
>    Practical duties             - 36 hours per week
>
>    Leave:   30 days annually.

Examinations:

>    Minimum pass and other regulations as for Faculty of Letters and Philosophy.

### Diplomas in Social Welfare and Nursing

Eligibility:            A recognized university diploma in Welfare Work.

Duration of course:     1 year.

Courses:

> As for B.Soc.Sc. (Hons.) except that the following choice of
> courses is added:
>
> Child Welfare, Youth Welfare, Family Welfare, Physical Hygiene.
> _and_   Company Organization and Welfare Action, Administration in
> Social Welfare, Questions of Sex-Relations and Social Welfare,
> Recreation and Social Welfare, Divine Worship and Social Welfare.
> _or_    An enquiry of limited extent into some phenomenon from the field
> of Social Welfare.

Examinations:

> Same regulations as for B.Soc.Sc. (Hons.)

## Faculty of Natural Sciences

### B.Sc.

Eligibility:              Pass in Mathematics at Matriculation examination.

Duration of course:       3 years.
                          A student who only takes 2 courses in his 1st year
                          must take at least 4 years for the degree course.

Courses of study:

> At least 9 qualifying courses must be taken.  Except in unusual
> circumstances, at least 5 of the 9 courses should be non-
> elementary courses.  Mathematical Statistics I, Astronomy I,
> Genetics I and Physiology I count as non-elementary courses.
>
> Courses must include at least 2 major subjects with the prescribed
> ancillary courses.

_Majors_ in which 3 qualifying courses are required:

| | |
|---|---|
| Mathematics and Applied Mathematics | Physics |
| Geology | Chemistry |
| Zoology | Botany |
| Geography | Psychology |
| | Statistics |

_Majors_ in which 2 qualifying courses are required:

> Mathematical Statistics (following a prior course in Math.)
> Astronomy (following a prior course in Mathematics)
> Physiology (after a 1st course in Chemistry, Physics and Zoology
> of which at least 2 are completed)

Genetics (after 4 first courses from the following are chosen
and at least 3 completed:  Botany, Zoology, Mathematics)
Statistics, Psychology, Chemistry (on the understanding that 1
of the 4 courses must be Botany or Zoology and another)
Mathematics or Statistics.  The other major to be taken together
with Genetics may be selected only from the above subjects.

Mathematics and Geography may only be combined as majors for the B.A.

A student who takes 1 of the major courses in column A must also take the
ancillary courses set out in column B:

| A | B |
|---|---|
| Applied Mathematics | At least 2 courses in Mathematics |
| Physics | At least 2 courses in Mathematics |
| Chemistry | Mathematics or Statistics |
| Botany | At least 1 course in Chemistry |
| Physiology | At least 2 courses in Chemistry and 1 course in each of Physics and Zoology |
| Geology | At least 1 course in Chemistry |
| Geography | At least 1 course in one of the following:  Mathematics, Physics, Botany, Zoology, or Geology |
| Psychology | At least 1 course in one of the following:  Mathematics, Physics, Zoology, or Statistics |
| Astronomy | At least 2 courses in Mathematics |
| Zoology | At least 1 course in Chemistry |
| Genetics | At least 1 course in Botany or Zoology and at least 1 course in Mathematics, Statistics, or Physics IB (an alternative course to Physics I) |
| Mathematical Statistics | At least 2 courses in Mathematics |

## Examinations:

In order to pass or to pass in the first class, a student must
fulfill the prescribed requisites for the subjects concerned.

Except for courses in Architecture and Quantity Surveying, the
following requisites apply:

| Subminima in | | Minimum | Combined year-end |
| Practical | Theory | Examination Mark | Examination Mark |
| 35% | 35% | 35% | 40% |

First class pass:  Combined year-end and examination mark, 70%.


## B.Sc. Hons.

General regulations for honors baccalaureates apply.

The following subjects may be offered:

> Mathematics, Applied Mathematics, Physics, Chemistry, Botany, Zoology, Geology, Geography, Psychology, Microbiology, Mathematics1 Statistics, Genetics, Physiology.

### Examinations:

> Except where the Senate requires a sub-minimum in stipulated subjects, the pass mark for the Hons. baccalaureate is an average for all the questions of 50%.

> The degree may be granted with distinction if a student obtains an average of at least 70%.


## M.Sc.

General regulations for master's degrees apply.

Degree is granted in the following divisions:

> Mathematics, Applied Mathematics, Physics, Chemistry, Geology, Botany, Zoology, Psychology, Geography, Microbiology, Mathematical Statistics, Genetics, Physiology.

### Examinations:

> If there is no dissertation, the average pass mark is 50% for the whole examination.

> If the candidate does not hold the B.Sc. Hons. and takes the master's examination in 2 parts, the average pass mark is 50% for each part.

> If a dissertation is prescribed, a candidate passes with 50% in the written questions, provided that he satisfied the examiners.

> Cum laude:     (i)  Written examination only, 70%.
>                (ii) With dissertation, 65% in the written examination where this is required apart from the dissertation and where, in the opinion of the examiners, he has earned the degree cum laude in the whole examination.

### Department of Architecture and Quantity Surveying

Eligibility:                    Matriculation Certificate or Matriculation Exemption
                                of the Joint Matriculation Board.

                                Mathematics of Matriculation standard are required
                                and also a natural science.

For diploma studies:  Matriculation Certificate of the Joint Matri-
                                culation Board or a recognized secondary School-
                                Leaving Certificate or equivalent.

                                Mathematics and a natural science of Matriculation
                                standard are required.

Exemption:                    Special qualifications and recommendations from the
                                Central Board of the Institute of South African
                                Architects.


Part-time attendance:  Only for those employed in the office of an
architect or quantity surveyor.


### B.Arch.

Attendance:                    A candidate must devote his full attention to the
                                study for the degree, but must simultaneously ful-
                                fill the prescribed period in an architect's office
                                (a period of at least 12 months).

Duration of course:    6 years.

Course of study:

                                Draughtsmanship, Building Construction, History of Architecture,
                                Applied Mathematics, Afrikaans or English, French or German,
                                Freehand Drawing, Theory of Building, Physics, Field Survey,
                                Acoustics, Town Planning, Specifications, Plan Drawing, and the
                                completion of a Plan.

                                The Plan consists of 4 parts:

(i)    Research concerning the recognized building types, municipal
        and other prescriptions and structural aspects.
(ii)   A report on the experiences encountered in the planning,
        and a full program of accommodation.
(iii)  The plan drawings (to accepted scale and which need not
        necessarily be work-drawings, but in which all practical
        aspects must nevertheless be explicit) must be complete
        with clear annotations indicating materials, etc.
(iv)   At least 1 sheet of drawings showing a subsection of build-
        ing in progress, worked out in detail.  Ground and elevation
        of this work must be submitted to and approved by the Head
        of the department.

Also to be submitted is a plan of actual terrain in
Bloemfontein in accordance with town planning and other
municipal regulations.  The terrain need not necessarily
be an empty one.

Examinations:

In order to pass, 50% required both in year-end and examination mark
and at least 50% combined average.

First class:  75%.

Candidate must pass a bilingual test before the beginning of his 4th
year of study.


M.Arch.

Eligibility:            B.Arch. and 3 years' practice.

Duration of course:    2 years.
                       Work under supervision of the Head of the department
                       while registered as graduate student for the M.Arch.

A dissertation is required.

Degree may be obtained cum laude when candidate has earned a first class
pass in the dissertation and oral examination.


B.Sc. (Q.S.)

Duration of course:    5 years.
                       During the 1st and 2nd years, a candidate must
                       devote his full time to study for the degree.
                       During the long winter and summer vacations of the
                       1st year and during the following 3 years, he must
                       work full-time in the office of a quantity surveyor.

Courses:  Quantities, Building Construction, Applied Mathematics, Geo-
          metrical Drawing, Survey Measurement, Building Theory, Physics,
          Terrain Measurement, History of Architecture, Price Survey,
          Building Costs and Specifications.

A candidate who passes in all the prescribed subjects and passes first
class in the main subjects of Quantities, Building Costs and Specifications
may receive the degree with distinction.


M.Sc. (Q.S.)

Eligibility:            Bachelor's degree in Quantity Surveying.

Candidate must:

(1) Pursue the theory and practice of Quantity Surveying for at
least 3 years after obtaining the baccalaureate.
(2) Work under the supervision of the Head of the department for 2
years while a registered student for the M.Sc.
(3) Complete a dissertation.

Degree may be obtained cum laude when candidate has earned a first class
pass in the dissertation and the oral examination.


## Diploma in Quantity Surveying

Eligibility:              Candidate must be employed full time in the office
of a quantity surveyor.

Duration of course:  5 years.

Course of study:     Subjects the same as for the B.Sc. (Q.S.).

## Examinations:

A candidate may be exempted from the examinations of the first and/or
second and/or third years by the Senate under exceptional circumstances.

Distinction:         As for B.Sc. (Q.S.).


## Diploma in Building

Eligibility:              Candidate must be employed full time in the building
trade throughout the course.

Duration of course:  3 years.

Course of study:

Building Construction, Applied Mathematics, Geometrical Drawing,
Quantity Costing, Building Theory, Trade Practice and Building
Organization, Equipping of Buildings, Price Survey, Specifi-
cations and Building Finance.

General regulations for the Architecture and Quantity Surveying degrees
apply.


## Diploma in Diagnostic Radiography

Eligibility:              Senior Certificate with Mathematics.

Duration of course:    2½ years.
                       Pursued in cooperation with National Hospital.

Courses:  Physics, Apparatus Construction, Photography, Anatomy and Physio-
          logy, First-Aid and Nursing (attendance), Practical Radiography,
          Radiographic Developments, Clinical Therapy, Radiation-Physics.

Admission to examinations:    Year-end mark of 40%.

Pass mark:    35% subminimum in each subject and 50% average.


## Faculty of Agriculture

### B.Sc. Agric.

Eligibility:            Matriculation Certificate or equivalent with a pass
                        in Mathematics.
                        All 1st-year students must attend at least 75% of the
                        lectures in conjunction with instruction in various
                        agricultural developments.

Duration of course:  4 years.

Main divisions of courses:

| | |
|---|---|
| Agronomy | Microbiology |
| Genetics | Plant Conservation |
| Soil Science | Sheep Husbandry and Wool |
| Agricultural Chemistry | Science |
| Agricultural Economics | Dairy Science and Technology |
| Agricultural Meteorology | Cattle Breeding |
| | Pastural Science |

Together with the above, the following are taken in requisite groupings:

| | |
|---|---|
| Chemistry (including Organic) | Agricultural Engineering |
| Physics | Geology |
| Botany | German or French |
| Zoology | Soil Microbiology |
| Mathematics | Poultry Breeding |
| Mathematical Statistics | Soil Physics |
| Biometry | Dairy Chemistry and Dairy |
| Plant Pathology | Engineering and Technology |
| Entomology | Fruit and Vegetable Develop- |
| Animal Pathology | ment |

Student must take the prescribed ancillaries with each major.

To obtain credit for any course in which he has passed in a particular
year, a student must have passed simultaneously in the minimum ancillary
courses and met the following requirements:

> A minimum of 1 and a maximum of 2 months' practical work in
> the field during vacation time, in the 3rd and 4th years, are
> required.

Examinations:

| Subminima in | | Minimum | Combined year-end |
|---|---|---|---|
| Practical | Theory | Examination Mark | Examination Mark |
| 35% | 35% | 35% | 40% |

First class:   70% in the combined year-end and examination mark.

Distinction:   In a major, during the last 2 study years, an average
of at least 70% and 60% in ancillaries.


B.Sc. Agric. (Hons.)

General regulations for honors baccalaureates apply.

Duration of course:   5 years.

Examinations:

> Minimum pass mark:  Average of 50% over the whole examination with a
> subminimum in certain questions prescribed by the department from
> time to time.

> Distinction:  Average of 70%.


M.Sc. Agric.

General regulations for master's degrees apply.

Examinations:

> Unless a student obtains exemption from Part I of the master's
> examination on the grounds of holding an Hons. baccalaureate, he is
> required to pass Part I, which is the same examination as for the
> Hons. baccalaureate.

> For Part II, a dissertation is required.

> Cum laude:  At least 65% in Part I, and in the dissertation of Part
> II, a standard.

## D.Sc. Agric.

This degree is mainly intended as recognition for independent research of merit and distinguished scientific knowledge.

## Faculty of Law

### LL.B. (Baccalaureus Legum)

Eligibility:          Bachelor's degree of a faculty other than that of Law.
                      Completion of the requirements concerning the non-legal subjects as determined by the University.

A candidate for the degree must have passed at least 3 language courses recognized as degree courses by a South African university, of which a course in Latin and a course in Afrikaans-Dutch or English are obligatory, on the understanding that a student who has matriculated in Afrikaans at the higher level must take English and one who has matriculated in English at the higher level  must take Afrikaans, and a student who took both Afrikaans and English at the higher level may choose between Afrikaans-Dutch and English.

A student holding the B.Comm. or B.Admin. degrees with at least Civil Law III need not (with the single exception of the prescribed course in Latin or Afrikaans or English) fulfill the language requirements of the LL.B.

Duration of course:   3 years.
                      Can be shortened to 2 when the bachelor's degree held by candidate has a combination of Law subjects prescribed by the University.

Courses:

| Major | Ancillary |
|---|---|
| Civil Law | Bantu Law and Administration |
| Law of Procedure | Common Law |
| Company Law | International Civil Law |
| Criminal Law | Conveyancing |
| Roman Law | |
| History of Law | |
| Constitutional and Administrative Law | |

Examinations:

The examinations in Criminal Law, Common Law, International Civil Law and Interpretation of Laws are held at the end of the 1st semester.

The examinations in Criminal and Common Law are taken after a course of 1 year and a course of 1 semester in each have been completed.

Minimum pass mark:

> (i) To pass in a 1st-year course or to obtain exemption therefrom, a combined year-end and examination mark of at least 50% is needed, and individual marks of at least 40%.
>
> (ii) To pass a 2nd or 3rd-year course a student must obtain at least 40% in each of the oral and written examinations with a combined minimum of at least 50%.

Distinction: At least 75% in the combined oral and written examination marks.

Cum laude: A pass with distinction in the following courses:

Civil Law V, Company Law II, Criminal and Administrative Law II, International Law, Law of Procedure II, Conveyancing and if 70% in a further total combined mark in all courses is attained.


## LL.D. (Doctor Legum)

General regulations for doctoral degrees apply.

Thesis:   A subject chosen from jurisprudence.

## Doctoral examination:

Apart from taking the examination mentioned in the general regulations for doctoral degrees, every candidate for the LL.D. who is not exempted by the Senate on the recommendation of the Faculty Board, is obliged to take a doctoral examination at least a year before submitting the thesis.

This examination consists of a major and 1 or more ancillaries chosen by the student with the approval of the Faculty Board.


## Dipl.Jur. (Diploma Juris)

General regulations for baccalaureates apply.

Eligibility: Matriculation Certificate or Matriculation Exemption of the Joint Matriculation Board.

Duration of course: 3 years.

Courses:

    Civil Law, Roman Law (special), Criminal Law.

    1 of the following:  Latin, English, Afrikaans-Dutch, Bantu Languages, Bantu Administration, History, Ethnology, Sociology, Psychology, Accountancy, Government Administration, Economics, Criminology, International Law, Interpretation of Laws, Criminal Procedure, Law of Evidence, Company Law.

    1 of the following:  Auditing, Administration of Estates, Income and Revenue, Civil Procedure.

Examinations:

    To pass in a course or to obtain exemption from it a student must obtain at least 50% in the combined year-end and examination mark, and at least 40% in individual marks in each subject.

    Cum laude:    Pass in 1 and the same examination in all the prescribed courses of the 3rd year with a grand total of at least 75%.

## D.R.S. (Diploma in Jurisprudence for Government Offices)

Eligibility:    As for Dipl. Jur.

Duration of course:    3 years.

Courses:  Civil Law, Roman Law, Criminal Law, Criminal Procedure, Law of Evidence, Company Law, Civil Procedure, Interpretation of Laws.

Examination:

    Pass mark and cum laude:  As for Dipl. Jur.

## Faculty of Economics and Administrative Science

### B.Com. and B.Admin.

Duration of course:    3 years.

At least 14 courses must be taken.

A course of study must consist of at least 2 major subjects with prescribed ancillaries.

    B.Com. majors:

        Economics, Industrial Economics, Accountancy, Statistics, Agricultural Economics, Industrial Psychology, Civil Law.

<u>B.Admin. majors:</u>

1 of the following:
Political Science, Economics, Industrial Psychology, Bantu
Administration, Civil Law.

A student who takes 1 of the courses in column A for the B.Com. as a 3rd
year course <u>must</u> take the corresponding course in column B:

| <u>A</u> | <u>B</u> |
|---|---|
| Agricultural Economics II or III | Economics III |
| Industrial Psychology II or III | Industrial Economics III |
| Auditing II | Accountancy III |
| Actuarial Science | Statistics III |
| Special Subject in Economics | Industrial Economics III |

Economic History is compulsory for the B.Com.

If the course Special Subject in Economics is taken concurrently with Agricultural Economics III and Industrial Psychology III, the Special Subject
has to be Soil Economics and Labor Problems respectively.

Compulsory subject combinations for B.Admin.:

| | | |
|---|---|---|
| Economic History | with | Economics |
| Ethnology I and Bantu Languages | with | Bantu Administration |

Municipal Administration may be taken only after Government Administration
I and Political Science I have been completed.

All students must be enrolled in the General Science course during their
studies.

<u>Examinations:</u>

Pass minimum.

For Accountancy, Auditing, Cost Accounting, Income and Revenue,
Estates Administration:  an examination mark of 50% and a combined
year-end and examination mark of 45%.

For Economics, Industrial Economics, Industrial Psychology, Municipal
Administration, Government Administration, Special Subject in
Economics, Statistics, Elementary Theory of Finance, Statistical
Methods, Actuarial Science and Economic History:  an examination mark
of 35% and a combined year-end and examination mark of 40%.

For Company Law (for B.Com. and B.Admin. students) the Faculty of Law
regulation is operative.

For all other subjects, the pass minimum is that of the faculty
concerned.  Unless otherwise stipulated, a subminimum of 25% in every
question is required.

First class:        Minimum of 70% in the combined year-end and exami-
                    nation mark, except in the case of law subjects,
                    where the regulation of that faculty applies.

It is not expected of a student to pass simultaneously in his chosen
subjects.


## B.Com. (Hons.) and B.Admin. (Hons.)

The following subjects may be taken:

| B.Com. (Hons.) | B.Admin. (Hons.) |
|---|---|
| Economics | Government Administration |
| Industrial Economics | Bantu Administration |
| Accountancy | Political Science |
| Statistics | Economics |
| Agricultural Economics | Industrial Psychology |
| Industrial Psychology | |

Ancillaries:

Economic History and Statistics I (or Statistical Methods A and
1 of Elementary Theory of Finance or Statistical Methods B) are
a requirement for Hons. degree in Economics and Industrial
Economics. A student who did not take 1 or both of these subjects in his undergraduate course of study must complete the
necessary courses during his honors studies.

Examinations:

Except where the Senate recommends subminima in certain subjects, the
pass mark for Hons. baccalaureates is an average examination mark of
50% for all papers.

Distinction:     Combined examination marks of at least 70%.


## M.Com. and M.Admin.

The subjects which may be taken are the same as for B.Com. (Hons.) and
B.Admin. (Hons.).  See above.

Examinations:

In the case of a written examination, 40% in each paper and 50%
aggregate.

In the case of a dissertation, student passes on satisfying the
examiners.

Cum laude:      In a written examination, an aggregate of at least
                70%. With dissertation, if it is in the opinion
                of the examiners of first class standard.

## Certificate in the Theory of Accountancy

Eligibility:                    Matriculation Certificate or Matriculation Exemption
                                Certificate.

Duration of course:    5 years.

Courses:    Afrikaans-Dutch or English, Theory of Finance, Company Law,
            Statistical Methods, Auditing, Economics, Accountancy, Cost
            Accounting, Income and Revenue.

## Examinations:

Pass requirements for all courses are 50% examination mark and 45%
aggregate except in Elementary Theory and Finance and Statistical
Methods (35%-40%) and in law subjects where the rules for that
faculty apply.

First class pass:  At least 70% aggregate except in law subjects
                   where the rules for that faculty apply.

## Diploma in Municipal Administration

Eligibility:                    School-Leaving Certificate of an education department.

The course of study is the same as for the B.Admin. degree except that
Municipal Administration I and II must be taken.

## Teacher's Diploma in Business (O.D.H.)

Eligibility:                    School-Leaving Certificate or equivalent, with or
                                without Matriculation Exemption, but with Accountancy
                                as school subject.

                                School examinations in Typing and Shorthand are not
                                a requirement.

Duration of course:    3 years.

Courses:    Accountancy, Industrial Economics, Afrikaans or English, Typing,
            Shorthand, Economics, Economic History, Economic Geography,
            Company Law, Philosophy of Education, General Method, Educational
            Psychology, History of Education, Practical Pedagogy, Public
            Health.  And 1 course from the Faculty of Education's offering.

## Diploma in Business Administration

Eligibility:                    A degree in another faculty or evidence that
                                candidate will be able to benefit by the course.

Duration of course:    3 years.

Courses:  Business Administration, Economic Policy, Financial Accountancy.


Faculty of Education

B.Ed.

Eligibility:              Ordinary Bachelor's degree, University Education
                          Diploma, and 2 years' teaching experience.

Duration of course:    At least 2 years.

Courses:  Philosophy of Education, General Method, General Educational
          Psychology, History of Education, History and Administration of
          Education in South Africa.

Examinations:

    Yearly mark:      40% in each separate subject and 50% average in the
                      subjects taken together before proceeding to the
                      examination.

    Final examination:  Combined year-end and examination mark of 40%
                        in each separate paper, provided that no examination
                        mark falls below 40%.  Average combined year-end and
                        examination mark of at least 50%.

    Distinction:      Combined year-end and examination mark of 70% in the
                      final examination in the 5 papers.


M.Ed.

Examinations:

    Dissertation on a subject in Education, to be presented no sooner
    than 1 year after the B.Ed. examination.

    Final:            At least 50% for the dissertation.

    Cum laude:        At least 70% for the dissertation.


D.Ed.

General regulations governing doctoral degrees apply.

Eligibility:              M.Ed. for at least 4 years, or M.Ed. for at least 3
                          years of which at least 1 was devoted to research
                          in a field approved by the University.

Every candidate for the D.Ed. degree must submit for the approval of the University a thesis on a subject in the field of Education.

## Teacher's Diploma in Business (O.D.H.) and Teacher's Diploma in Physical Education (O.D.L.O.)

Regulations for these diplomas follow those of the relevant faculties.

Duration of course:    3 years.

## University Teacher's Diploma (U.O.D.)

Eligibility:                B.A., B.Sc., B.Sc. Agric., or B.Com. in which at least 1 of the following subjects on a 3-year basis and a 2nd subject from the following list on a 2-year basis are chosen:

Afrikaans, English, Latin, Dutch, French, a Bantu language, Ethnology, History, Geography, Physical Education, Music, History of Music, Art, Art History, Geology, Industrial Psychology, Industrial Economics, Accountancy, Mathematics, Statistics, Physics, Chemistry, Botany, Zoology, and any other subject which the University may set from time to time.

or    B.Sc. Agric. with the above conditions for subjects or which has any 1 of the following on at least a 2-year basis:  Agronomy, Breeding, Cattle and Sheep Husbandry, Wool Science.

or    Bachelor's degree in Fine Arts with the following: Method of Art and Method of Art History.

or    Bachelor's degree in Engineering or any other such specialized or technical degree which the University may recognize from time to time.

Duration of course:    1 year.

## Major courses (all required):

Philosophy of Education, General Method, Educational Psychology.

Method in at least 2 but not more than 3 main secondary school subjects.

Practical teaching.

For students holding the B.Com., the following count as main subjects:  Method of Accountancy, and 2 of the following: Method of Business and Administration, Typing, Shorthand.

Ancillaries:

> Obligatory: Language study in both official languages, Public Health, Religious Instruction.
>
> 2 of the following: Singing or Elocution, Physical Exercise or Art History, Woodwork or Needlework, Geometrical Drawing.
>
> A student with a B.Com. or Engineering degree is exempt from the above.

Examinations:

For Majors, Ancillaries, Languages:

A student must obtain 40% in the yearly mark before being allowed to proceed to the examination.

A student must pass in a higher grade at least 1 of the 2 official languages to be used as a medium of instruction. Such an examination consists of 3 parts.

(i) A written test consisting of an essay.
(ii) An oral test.
(iii) An educational test.

For a pass in the final examination, the following are requirements:

(i) At least 60% in 1 of the official language media at higher level. If candidate scores less than 40% in the 2nd medium at lower level, he will only be issued a single-language (as distinct from bilingual) U.O.D. certificate.
(ii) At least 40% in every main subject, with a subminimum of 35%.
(iii) An average mark of 40% in the ancillaries in the class and examination mark, considering all the ancillaries as a group. Subminimum: 35%.

For Practical Teaching:

Students must submit a full report of a minimum of 50 specimen lessons which they have themselves given in school during the specimen teaching periods at the beginning of the academic year. The final mark in this subject is based on the whole year's practical work.

First class pass:
(i) Every main subject counts for 3 points if the candidate attains 70% in the combined class and examination mark, and 1 point for 60%-70%.
(ii) Each ancillary counts for 1 point, for 70% or more in the combined class and examination mark.
(iii) A candidate passes first class if he gets 11 out of 22 points.

Teacher's College

Primary Teacher's Certificate

Eligibility:                    Only women are eligible.
                                Matriculation, Orange Free State School-Leaving
                                Certificate or equivalent.

Duration of course:    2 years.

Courses:  Afrikaans-Dutch I, English I, History I.


Higher Primary Teacher's Certificate

Duration of course:    3 years.

In order to proceed to the 2nd year of this course, the candidate must
show that he has attended at a recognized university a 1st-year course
with at least 3 of the following subjects:

            Afrikaans, English, History, Geography, Religious Instruction,
            Biology, Botany, Zoology, Chemistry, Nature Study, Mathematics,
            or any other subject at the Director's discretion.



UNIVERSITY OF STELLENBOSCH, Stellenbosch

After Cape Town, Stellenbosch is the oldest town in South Africa, and as
early as 1685 scholastic teaching had its inception here with the building
of the Dutch Reformed Church.  Within the system of public schools
developed by Sir John Herschel, Stellenbosch was recognized as an
educational center.  In the 1860's the public school was re-organized as
the Stellenbosch Gymnasium, and here in 1874, an Arts Department of the
University of the Cape of Good Hope was brought into being.  Ten years
later the Arts Department was incorporated as the Stellenbosch College,
and in Queen Victoria's jubilee year, it was named the Victoria College of
Stellenbosch.  In 1918, Victoria College became the University of Stellenbosch.

General entrance requirements:     Matriculation Certificate of the Joint
                                   Matriculation Board.

                                   Mathematics for the Matriculation is
                                   compulsory for admission to the follow-
                                   ing courses:

                                   B.Sc.; B.Mil.; M.B., Ch.B.; B.A. (with
                                   Special Math. or Theory of Finance and
                                   Statistics); L.S.O.D. (with biological

subjects), and O.D.L.O. (with Math. or Physics or Chemistry as one of the subjects).

For admission to diploma courses a student must hold at least a School-Leaving Certificate of the Joint Matriculation Board or a Senior Certificate of one of the departments of education.

General requirements for doctoral degrees:

No one may be admitted

(a) To the degree of Doctor in the Faculties of Letters and Philosophy, Natural Sciences, Education, Agriculture, Commerce, Forestry or Military Science unless he has held the master's degree for at least 2 years.

(b) To the degree of Doctor in the Faculty of Law unless he has held the bachelor's degree in Law for at least 2 years.

(c) To the degree of Doctor in the Faculty of Divinity unless he has held the bachelor's degree in Divinity for at least 2 years.

(d) To the degree of Doctor in the Faculty of Engineering unless he has held the bachelor's degree in Engineering.

(e) To the degree of Doctor in the Faculty of Medicine unless he has held the bachelor's degree in Surgery.

Faculties:

| | |
|---|---|
| Letters and Philosophy | Commerce |
| Natural Sciences | Engineering |
| Education | Medicine |
| Agricultural Science | Forestry |
| Law | Military Science |
| Divinity | |

Language of instruction:          Afrikaans-Nederlands.

Degrees awarded:

| Faculty | Degree | Duration of course (years) |
|---|---|---|
| Letters and Philosophy | B.A. | 3 |
| | Hons. B.A. | 4 |
| | M.A. | 1 |
| | D.Litt. | |
| | D.Phil. | |
| | B.Mus. | 4 |
| | M.Mus. | 2 |

|                         |                                                                |     |
|-------------------------|----------------------------------------------------------------|-----|
|                         | B.A. (Law)                                                     | 3   |
|                         | B.A. (Soc. Work)                                               | 3   |
|                         | B.A. (Fine Arts)                                               | 4   |
|                         | B.A. with Art                                                  | 3   |
|                         | B.Dram.                                                        | 4   |
|                         | B.A. with Com. Subjects                                        | 3   |
|                         | B.A. (Bibl.)                                                   | 4   |
|                         | Hons. B.A. in African Studies                                  |     |
|                         | Lower Diploma in Library Science                               | 2   |
|                         | Higher Diploma in Library Science                              | 1   |
|                         | Diploma in Social Work                                         | 3   |
|                         | Primary Teacher's Certificate (Special) in Drama               | 1   |
| Natural Sciences        | B.Sc.                                                          | 3   |
|                         | Hons. B.Sc.                                                    | 4   |
|                         | M.Sc.                                                          | 1   |
|                         | D.Sc.                                                          |     |
|                         | B.Sc. Domestic Science                                         | 4   |
|                         | Hons B.Sc. Domestic Science                                    | 5   |
|                         | M.Sc. Domestic Science                                         | 1   |
|                         | Diploma in Domestic Science                                    | 2   |
| Education               | B.Ed.                                                          | 1-2 |
|                         | M.Ed.                                                          |     |
|                         | D.Ed.                                                          |     |
|                         | Secondary Teacher's Diploma (S.O.D.)                           | 1   |
|                         | Lower Secondary Teacher's Diploma (L.S.O.D.)                   | 3   |
|                         | Teacher's Diploma in Commercial Subjects (O.D.H.)              | 1   |
|                         | Teacher's Diploma in Domest. Science and Needlework (O.D.H.N.) | 1   |
|                         | Higher Primary Teacher's Diploma (H.P.O.D.)                    | 3   |
|                         | Diploma for Teachers of Special Classes (D.O.S.K.)             | 1   |
|                         | B.A. (Phys. Ed.)                                               | 3   |
|                         | B.Sc. (Phys. Ed.)                                              | 3   |
|                         | B.Ed.Ph.                                                       | 1-2 |
|                         | M.Ed.Ph.                                                       | 1   |
|                         | D.Ed.Ph.                                                       |     |
|                         | Teacher's Diploma in Physical Education (O.D.L.O.)             | 3   |
| Agricultural Science    | B.Sc. Agric. Science                                           | 4   |
|                         | Hons. B.Sc. Agric. Science                                     | 5   |

|                  |                                           |      |
|------------------|-------------------------------------------|------|
|                  | M.Sc.                                     | 1    |
|                  | D.Sc.                                     |      |
|                  | Diploma Course in Agric.                  | 2    |
| Law              | LL.B.                                     | 5    |
|                  | LL.D.                                     |      |
| Divinity         | B.D.                                      | 3    |
|                  | D.D.                                      |      |
|                  | Candidate's Diploma in Theology           | 3    |
|                  | Licentiate in Theology                    | 4    |
| Commerce         | B.Comm.                                   | 3    |
|                  | Hons. B.Comm.                             | 4    |
|                  | M.Comm.                                   | 1    |
|                  | D.Comm.                                   |      |
|                  | Certificate in the Theory of Accountancy (S.T.R.) | 5    |
| Engineering      | B.Sc., B.Ing.                             | 5    |
|                  | M.Ing.                                    | 1    |
|                  | Ph.D. Ing.                                |      |
| Medicine         | M.B., Ch.B.                               | 6    |
|                  | M.Med.                                    | 2    |
|                  | M.D.                                      |      |
|                  | Ph.D. Med.                                |      |
|                  | B.A. Nursing                              | 4    |
|                  | Diploma in Physiotherapy                  | 3    |
|                  | Diploma in Hospital Dietetics             | 1    |
|                  | Diploma in the Teaching of Nursing        | 1½   |
| Forestry         | B.Sc.                                     | 4    |
|                  | Hons. B.Sc. in Forestry                   | 5    |
|                  | M.Sc. in Forestry                         | 2    |
|                  | D.Sc. in Forestry                         |      |
| Military Science | B.Mil.                                    | 3    |
|                  | Hons. B.Mil.                              | 4    |
|                  | M.Mil.                                    | 1    |

## Faculty of Letters and Philosophy

## Diplomas giving admission to B.A. courses:

Students in possession of Matriculation Certificate or an Exemption Certificate of the Joint Matriculation Board who have thereafter obtained the Higher Primary Schoolteacher's Certificate (H.P.O.D.) are exempted from the first-year courses of the B.A.

The same applies to holders of the Diploma for Teachers of Special Classes (D.O.S.K.) and the Primary Teacher's Certificate.


## B.A.

Duration of course:    3 years.

Subjects are arranged in the following groups:

- A.   Languages:  Greek, Latin, Afrikaans-Dutch, English, German, French, Semitic Languages, Bantu Languages.

- B.   History, Geography, Philosophy, Psychology, Sociology, Social Work, Economics, Ethnology, Personal Law, Native Administration, Classical Culture.

- C.   Statistics, Theory of Finance, Physiology, Mathematics, Physical Education, Music, Drama, Library Science, Art, Industrial Psychology, Roman Law, History of Roman-Dutch Law.


## Hons. B.A.

At least 1 year after completion of B.A. degree.


## M.A.

Eligibility:          Hons. B.A.

A course of recognized research and/or directed study for at least 1 year after gaining the Hons. B.A.

Dissertation is required.


## D.Litt. and D.Phil.

See general regulations for doctoral degrees.


## Degree courses in Music:

A student will only be admitted to a degree course in Music if the standard he has already reached is considered adequate by the Director of the Conservatoire.


## B.Mus.

Duration of course:    4 years.

Curriculum:

> Practical Musical Studies - Piano or Organ or Violin or Violoncello or Singing.
> Acoustics, Harmony, Counterpoint, Theory of Music, History of Music, Teaching Methods, Form, Composition, School-music, Orchestration.
> Afrikaans or English or German.
> A paper on an acceptable subject.

M.Mus.

Eligibility:          B.Mus.

Duration of course:   2 years.

Curriculum:

> 2 of the following, 1 from each group, must be selected:

Group A    Advanced History of Music, Composition.

Group B    Practical Music Studies, Advanced Theory of Music.

Dissertation or composition is required.

B.A. (Law)

Duration of course:   3 years.

The following courses lead to the 4-year LL.B. degree:

> English, Latin.
>
> 2 of the following:  Philosophy, Economics, French, German, Sociology, Ethnology, Bantu Languages, Psychology, Native Administration, Industrial Economics, Mathematics.

and  History of Roman-Dutch Law, Roman Law.

B.A. in Social Work

Duration of course:   3 years.

Courses:  Social Work, Sociology, Psychology.

and  2 of the following:  Afrikaans, Economics, History, Ethnology, Native Administration, Geography, Philosophy, Personal Law, Foundations of Church Support, German, English.

B.A. in Fine Arts

Duration of course:    4 years.

Courses:   Drawing, Art History, Design, Perspective, Portraiture, Modelling,
           Special Anatomy, Photography, Ceramics, Graphic Technique, Teach-
           ing Methods, Museum Science.


B.A. with Art

Duration of course:    3 years.

The course consists of the first 3 years of the B.A. (Fine Arts) degree
above.


B.Dram.

Duration of course:    4 years.

In addition to the usual courses, Drama and an additional language may be
taken.

A student who holds the B.Dram. degree may be admitted to the course for
Secondary Teacher's Diploma (S.O.D.).


B.A. with Commercial Subjects

Duration of course:    3 years.

Shorthand and Typing (2 years) are recognized subjects.


B.A. (Bibl.)

Duration of course:    4 years.

Courses:   Library History, Library Administration, Foundations of Library
           Science, Reference-work, Cataloguing and Classification,
           Historical Bibliography.

     and   5 B.A. subjects at 1st-year level
           2 B.A. subjects at 2nd-year level
           2 B.A. subjects at 3rd-year level (major)

           One of the 5 1st-year B.A. subjects must be a language.

           Students must demonstrate their proficiency in both official
           languages.

           3 weeks of practical work required.

## Hons. B.A. in African Studies

Eligibility:          B.A. in 1 of the following:  Economics, Geography, History, Native Administration, Personal Law, Sociology, Ethnology - on a 3-year basis.

          and   those who have passed in at least 2 of the following at 1st-year level:  Bantu Languages, Economics, French or another language, Geography, History, Native Administration, Personal Law, Sociology, Ethnology.

The course is given by the departments of Bantu Languages, Economics, Geography, History, Native Administration, Sociology, Ethnology, and the Faculty of Law, on an inter-departmental and inter-disciplinary basis.

## Lower Diploma in Library Science

Duration of course:   2 years.

Courses:  5 1st-year B.A. subjects, as for B.A. (Bibl.) (see above), of which 2 must be Afrikaans and English.
Fundamentals and History of Library Science, Bibliography, Arrangement and Reference Work, Library Organization and Administration, Cataloguing and Classification.
At least 4 weeks of practical work.

## Higher Diploma in Library Science

Eligibility:          B.A. degree, with Afrikaans, English, and if possible, another language.

Duration of course:   1 year.

Subjects as for Lower Diploma above.

## Diploma in Social Work

Entrance requirements and content of the course are the same as for the B.A. degree, but it is not possible to proceed to the Hons. B.A., M.A., or Ph.D.

Duration of course:   3 years.

## Primary Teacher's Certificate (Special) in Drama (in English or Afrikaans)

Eligibility:          Primary Teacher's Diploma (P.O.D.)

Duration of course:    1 year.


## Faculty of Natural Sciences

### B.Sc.

Eligibility:              Matriculation with Mathematics.

Duration of course:    3 years.

Courses:    2 majors and 7 ancillaries.
            For the study of certain subjects, certain other subjects are
            required:

| Subject | Requisite |
|---|---|
| Botany | Chemistry |
| Anatomy | Botany, Zoology, Chemistry, Physiology |
| Chemistry | Physics, Mathematics I |
| Physics | Mathematics, Chemistry |
| Physiology | Chemistry, Zoology, Physics |
| Geology | Chemistry I, Mathematics I |
| Entomology | Zoology, Chemistry |
| Microbiology | Chemistry, Botany, Zoology |
| Zoology | Chemistry I |

### Hons. B.Sc.

Eligibility:              Bachelor's degree for at least 1 year.

Duration of course:    1 year.


### M.Sc.

Eligibility:              Honors degree.

A course of research and/or directed studies for at least 1 year.

A thesis is required.


### D.Sc.

General regulations for doctoral degrees apply.

## Department of Domestic Science

### B.Sc.  Domestic Science

Duration of course:    4 years.

Degree is awarded with the following 3 emphases:

> General Domestic Science
> Dietetics
> Teaching

There is a 3-year B.Sc. course with Dietetics and Physiology as majors.

### Courses A, B and C:

> Chemistry, Physics, Zoology, Cookery, Household Management.

### Course A (General):

> Physiology, Dressmaking and Needlework, Microbiology, Special
> Psychology, Special English.

### Course B (Dietetics):

> Chemistry, Physiology, Cookery, Dressmaking and Needlework,
> Microbiology, Household Management, Special English, Insti-
> tutional Management, Special Psychology, Special Applied
> Psychology.

### Course C (Teaching):

> Chemistry, Physiology, Cookery, Dressmaking and Needlework,
> Microbiology, Household Management, Teaching Administration,
> Educational Psychology, English and Afrikaans, Teaching
> Methods, Philosophy of Education, Practical Teaching.

A faculty course in Divinity may also be taken.

### Hons. B.Sc. Domestic Science

Eligibility:          B.Sc. Domestic Science.

Duration of course:   1 year.

### M.Sc. Domestic Science

Eligibility:          Hons. B.Sc. Domestic Science.

Duration of course:   1 year.

Dissertation is required.


## Diploma in Domestic Science

Eligibility:          School-Leaving Certificate of the Joint Matriculation
                      Board (minimum).

Duration of course:   2 years.

Courses:  Cookery, Household Management, Domestic Science, Physics,
          Physiology and Hygiene, Dressmaking and Needlework, First-Aid.


## Faculty of Education

### B.Ed.

Eligibility:          A university degree and a post-graduate secondary
                      teacher's diploma (e.g., S.O.D., O.D.H., U.O.D.).
                 or   a lower secondary teacher's diploma (J.S.O.D.).
                 or   a primary teacher's certificate and at least 5
                      years' teaching experience.

Duration of course:   1-2 years.

### M.Ed.

Eligibility:          B.Ed. degree.

Duration of course:   1 year.

In addition to dissertation, there is an oral examination.
Afrikaans and English required.


### D.Ed.

General regulations for doctoral degrees apply.


### Secondary Teacher's Diploma (S.O.D.)

Duration of course:   1 year, post-graduate.

Subjects:  Philosophy of Education, General Teaching Methods, Practical
           Teaching, Teaching Administration, History of Teaching in South
           Africa, Educational Psychology, Afrikaans and English.

At least 1 of the following:
Sunday-school Teaching, Handicrafts, Art, School Music, Youth
Movements, Library Science, Typing, Elocution, Physical
Education, Educational Clinical Psychology.

## Lower Secondary Teacher's Diploma (L.S.O.D.)

Duration of course:    3 years.

Courses selected from B.A. or B.Sc. groupings and from S.O.D.

## Teacher's Diploma in Commercial Subjects (O.D.H.)

Eligibility:          Diploma Comm.

Duration of course:    1 year.

Courses as for H.P.O.D. and S.O.D.

## Teacher's Diploma in Domestic Science and Needlework (O.D.H.N.)

Eligibility:          Diploma in Domestic Science.

Duration of course:    1 year.

Courses as for H.P.O.D. and S.O.D.

## Higher Primary Teacher's Diploma (H.P.O.D.)

Duration of course:    3 years.

Courses:  Afrikaans, English, Introduction to Education, Educational
          Psychology, Nature Study, Blackboard Work and School Art.
          Handicrafts (Needlework, Woodwork or Bookbinding), School
          Hygiene and Physiology, Mathematics, Physical Education,
          History, Geography, School Music, Philosophy of Teaching,
          History of Teaching.

## Diploma for Teachers of Special Classes (D.O.S.K.)

Eligibility:          L.S.O.D. or H.P.O.D.

Duration of course:    1 year.

Courses:  Teaching Exercises in Special Classes, Philosophy and History
          of Special Education, Special Educational Psychology and

Sociology (major), Handicrafts (major), Divinity Teaching (facultative).

## Department of Physical Education

### B.A. and B.Sc.

With Physical Education as one of the majors.

Duration of courses:  3 years.

### Courses for B.A.:

Physical Education, Afrikaans, and 1 of the following: English, German, History, Geography.

### Courses for B.Sc.:

Physical Education, Mathematics, Chemistry or Botany or Zoology.

### Majors for both:

Practical Physical Education, General Theory of Education, and another subject which may be counted as major for B.A. or B.Sc.

The subject Physical Education consists of 2 parts:

(a)  General Theory of Physical Education, which includes Method and Theory, History of Physical Education, Anatomy, Organization and Administration, Sociology and Physiology.

(b)  Practical Physical Education, which includes Athletics, various sports.  Folk Dancing, Rhythmic Athletics.

### B.Ed.Ph.

Eligibility:            The 3-year B.A. or B.Sc. with Physical Education and the S.O.D.
            or  The 4-year B.Sc. with Physical Education as major and competence in teaching Physical Education, Biology, and Physiology.

Duration of course:  1-2 years.

Courses:  Physical Education (major), 2 subjects from the B.Ed. list, Psychological Aspects of Recreation, Sociological Aspects of Recreation.

M.Ed.Ph.

Eligibility:          B.Ed.Ph. or equivalent.

Course consists of research and/or directed study for at least 1 year
after attaining the B.Ed.Ph.

A paper is required.


D.Ed.Ph.

Regulations for doctoral degrees apply.


Teacher's Diploma in Physical Education (O.D.L.O.)

Eligibility:          Matriculation Certificate.

Duration of course:   3 years.

Courses:        B.A. subjects              B.Sc. subjects

                Physical Education         Physical Education
                English                    Mathematics
                German                     Chemistry
                Geography          or      Botany
                History            or      Sociology
                English
                Afrikaans

A choice of subjects selected from the S.O.D. and H.P.O.D. lists.


Faculty of Agricultural Science

B.Sc. Agricultural Science

Duration of course:   4 years.

Before commencing the 4th year all students must have spent 2 months of
practical work on farms, research stations, etc.

Courses:  Physics, Chemistry, Botany, Zoology, Special Mathematics,
          Agricultural Chemistry, Biometry, Plant Physiology, Micro-
          biology, Horticulture, Viticulture, Animal and Poultry
          Husbandry, Animal Physiology, Geology, Applied Radiology,
          Breeding Methods, Plant Pathology, Agricultural Economics,
          Electrotechnics, Machine Maintenance, and various mechanical
          and technical allied subjects.

## Hons. B.Sc. Agricultural Science

Eligibility:            B.Sc. Agric.

Duration of course:   1 year.


## M.Sc.

Eligibility:            Hons. B.Sc. Agric.

Duration of course:   1 year.

A course of research and/or directed study, a written examination, and a dissertation.


## D.Sc.

General regulations for doctoral degrees apply.


## Diploma Course in Agriculture

Eligibility:            Standard 8.

Duration of course:   2 years.

The course is offered on the Experimental Farm at Elsenburg. Particulars may be had from the Principal, Stellenbosch-Elsenburg Agricultural College of the University of Stellenbosch.


## Faculty of Law

## LL.B.

Eligibility:            Bachelor's degree from another faculty.

Duration of course:   5 years.

An examination in English and Latin is obligatory.

A bachelor's degree in another faculty gives exemption from the first 2 years of the LL.B. course. The B.A. and B.Comm. degrees with Law subjects give exemption from the first 3 years.

Courses:  English, Latin.

   2 years of the following: Bantu Languages, German, French, Economics,
Industrial Economics, History, Native Administration, Psychology,
Sociology, Ethnology, Mathematics, Philosophy.

   History of Roman-Dutch Law, Economics, Roman Law, General
Jurisprudence, International Law, Constitutional Law, Mercantile
Law, Criminal Law and Procedure, Legal Interpretation.

LL.D.

A thesis is required.  Regulations for doctoral degrees apply.

Faculty of Divinity

Admission Courses to Theological Training:

The following courses of this University lead to admission to the
Candidate's Diploma in Theology and the Faculty of Divinity:

   (i)  The B.A. degree in which 5 subjects from the following groups
        are taken:

        A.  Afrikaans, English, German, Latin, Greek, Hebrew.
        B.  History, Ethnology, Bantu Languages, Psychology, Philosophy,
            Sociology, Social Work, or a Natural Science subject.

   (ii) Another bachelor's degree on the understanding that the candid-
        date has, as part of that degree, passed the University's
        examination in:

        A.  Afrikaans I, Greek II, or Hebrew II.
        B.  2 of the following, at least at 1st-year level:  German,
            Latin, History, Ethnology, Bantu Languages, Sociology,
            Philosophy, Psychology, Social Work, or a Natural Science
            subject.

B.D.

Eligibility:           B.A. with the following subjects:  Greek, II,
                       Hebrew II, Latin I or German I.

                       2 of the following at 1st-year level:  Afrikaans,
                       Sociology, Psychology, History, Ethnology, Philo-
                       sophy, Bantu Languages.

Duration of course:    3 years.

D.D.

Eligibility:            B.D.

Candidate must pass a written examination, submit a thesis not earlier than 2 years after obtaining the B.D., and may be required to pass an oral examination.

Candidate's Diploma in Theology

Eligibility:            B.A.  See admission courses to Theological Training, above.

Duration of course:    3 years.

Courses:  Old and New Testament Exegesis, Biblical Archeology, Textual Criticism, General Church History, South African Church Doctrine, Canon Law, Encyclopedics, Symbols, Church Doctrine, Theological Ethics, Apologetics, Homiletics, Evangelism, etc.

Licentiate in Theology

Students who have obtained the Candidate's Diploma in Theology may proceed to the Seminary for the Licentiate.

Duration of course:    4 years.

Courses:  As above.

Faculty of Commerce

B.Comm.

Eligibility:            Matriculation Certificate.

Duration of course:    3 years.  4 years for external students.

Courses:  Economics, Industrial Economics, Mathematics, Industrial Psychology or Economic Geography or Theory of Finance and Statistics.

2 of the following:  Company Law, Actuarial Science, Conveyancing, Shorthand-Typing.

Cost Accounting, Auditing, Income Tax, Mercantile Law.

Mercantile Law is a required subject if Industrial Economics or Conveyancing are taken.

Special Science is a prerequisite if Statistics or Actuarial Statistics are taken.

B.Comm. course with Law subjects:

The following B.Comm. course may be taken, leading to the 4th year LL.B.:

> Private Law, Economics, Industrial Economics, Mathematics, Latin, English, History of Roman-Dutch Law, Roman-Dutch Law.

Hons. B.Comm.

Eligibility:             B.Comm.
                         If the courses Theory of Finance and Statistical Science were not taken for the B.Comm. course, 1 of them must be completed before the Hons. B.Comm. may be awarded.

Duration of course:    1 year.   2 years for external students.

The course may be taken with emphasis in the following sub-disciplines:

    A.   Economics
    B.   Industrial Economics
    C.   Conveyancing
    D.   Industrial Psychology
    E.   Statistical Science

Courses for A:

> Advanced Economic Theory, International Finance and Banking, State Finance, International Trade, Econometric Problems, Advanced Demography, The Economics of Underdeveloped Communities, Socio-economic Systems, History of Economic Thought.

Courses for B:

> Advanced Theory of Industrial Economics, Organization and Technics in Trade, Industrial Administration, Cooperative Concepts, Finance of Underwriting and Investment, Advanced Cost Accounting, Marketing, Labor Questions.

Courses for C:

> Advanced Conveyancing, and a choice from A and B above.

Courses for D:

> Advanced Industrial Psychology and 2 of the following:  Labor Questions, Industrial Administration, Advanced Costing, Co-operative Concepts, Marketing.
> 1 or 2 subdivisions of Advanced Conveyancing.

Courses for E:

     The course is individually arranged.

External courses:

     As above, except that the student must spread the course over a minimum of 2 years. The examination for the Hons. B.Comm. degree may be taken in 2 parts provided that not more than 1 year elapses between the parts.

M.Comm.

Eligibility:          Hons. B.Comm.

Duration of course:   1 year.

Research and/or directed course of study must be pursued for at least a year after obtaining the Honors baccalaureate.

Dissertation is required.

D.Comm.

Regulations for doctoral degrees apply.

Certificate in the Theory of Accountancy (S.T.R.) External Division

Eligibility:          Matriculation with Mathematics.

Duration of course:   5 years.

Courses: Accountancy (major), Theory of Finance, Statistics, Afrikaans, Mercantile Law, Economics, Insolvency, Auditing (major), Income Tax, Cost Accounting (major), Advanced Accountancy (major).

Faculty of Engineering

B.Sc., B.Ing.

Eligibility:          Matriculation with Mathematics.

Duration of course:   5 years.

Divided into Civil, Mechanical, Electrotechnical, and Agricultural Engineering.

(1)  Civil:                 Includes Mathematics, Applied Mathematics, Physics,
                             Chemistry, Mechanical subdivisions of subject,
                             Machine Design and Construction, Metallurgy, Build-
                             ing, Land Survey, Geology, Agronomy, Town Planning,
                             and a thesis.

(2)  Mechanical:            1st 3 years as above with additional choice of:
                             Aerodynamics, Technical Thermodynamics, Electronics,
                             Graphics, inter al.

(3)  Electrotechnical:      1st 3 years as in (1) above.  Subjects from (2)
                             where relevant, and inter al., Telecommunications,
                             Electrical Measuring Techniques, High-Tension
                             Techniques, Geophysics, et al.

(4)  Agricultural:          1st 3 years as above.
                             Agronomy, Hydrology, Reinforced Concrete and Build-
                             ing Materials, Agricultural Chemistry, Special
                             Biometry, et al.

All divisions:              Practical work during each long vacation at the end
                             of the 2nd, 3rd and 4th years.

During the 5th year, students must submit an independent written assign-
ment.

English, and 1 of French, German or Dutch required.


M.Ing.

Eligibility:               B.Ing.

Courses and research for at least 1 year.

Dissertation and possibly an oral examination.


Ph.D. Ing.

The degree is not awarded less than 4 years after the baccalaureate in
Engineering, or 3 years after the master's degree in Engineering.

Written and oral examinations, and a thesis.


Faculty of Medicine

M.B., Ch.B.

Eligibility:               Matriculation with Mathematics.

A degree in another faculty before the commencement of medical studies is highly recommended.

1 year premedical (Physics, Chemistry, Botany, Zoology).

and  2 years preclinical (Anatomy, Physiology, Pathology, Microbiology, and Pharmacology).

Registration as student by the South African Medical and Dental Board, a year's internship following final examination.

Duration of course:   6 years.

The M.B., Ch.B. degrees are awarded cum laude:   75% final marks in all courses.

## M.Med.

Duration of course:   2 years, post-graduate.

Awarded in the following specializations:

| | |
|---|---|
| Surgery | Pathology |
| Internal Medicine | Roentgenology |
| Gynecology and Obstetrics | Ophthalmology |
| Pediatrics | Ear, Nose and Throat |
| Anaesthetics | Dermatology |

Written, oral and practical clinical examinations.

## M.D.

Eligibility:          After a period of at least 5 years from the obtaining of the M.B., Ch.B., or after having been registered for 1 year as M.D. or 3 years as M.Med.

Awarded in the following subjects:

| | |
|---|---|
| Surgery | Anaesthetics |
| Internal Medicine | Pathology |
| Gynecology and Obstetrics | Roentgenology |
| Pediatrics | |

Thesis and examination.

## Ph.D. (Med.)

Eligibility:          4 years after M.B.,Ch.B.

Subjects as for M.D.

Dissertation, written and oral examinations.


## B.A. Nursing

Eligibility:              Matriculation Certificate.

Duration of course:    4 years.

Courses:   Nursing, Psychology, Sociology, Social Work.
           Nursing includes History and Ethics of Nursing, Hygiene, Nature
           Study, Bacteriology, Anatomy, Physiology.

Over the 4-year period, total practical hours:   6226.


## Diploma in Physiotherapy

Eligibility:              Matriculation Certificate.

Duration of course:    3 years.

Courses:   Physiotherapy, Psychology I, Social Work I, First-Aid, Elementary
           Nursing, Physiology I, Special Anatomy, Special Surgery (includ-
           ing Neuro- and Plastic-Surgery), Special Abnormal Psychology,
           Therapeutic Activities (Handicrafts, etc.), Special Internal
           Medicine (including Infectious Diseases, Tuberculosis, and Psycho-
           somatic Diseases), et al.


## Diploma in Hospital Dietetics

Eligibility:              B.Sc. in Domestic Science or Dietetics.

Duration of course:    12 months of practical work in a recognized hospital,
                       followed by an examination.


## Diploma in the Teaching of Nursing

Eligibility:              Matriculation Certificate, Certificate of Registration
                          of the South African Nurses Board, and 2 years'
                          experience as a registered nurse.

Duration of course:    1½ years.

Courses:   Special Anatomy, Special Physiology, Special Cookery, Educational
           Psychology, Teaching Methods.

At least 50 hours' practical teaching.

Special Psychology, Special Sociology, Public Health, Biology, Physics, Elementary Chemistry.

and  The following Special Subjects:
Microbiology, Chemical Pathology, Pharmacology, Roentgenology, Physiotherapy.

History and Ethics of Nursing, Nurses' School Administration.


## Faculty of Forestry

### B.Sc.

Eligibility:              Matriculation Certificate.

Duration of course:   4 years.

Courses:  Botany, Chemistry, Physics, Special Science, Arboriculture, Land Reclamation, Management, Forestry-Engineering, Biometry, Conservation, Hydraulics, Technology, Economics, Photogrammatry, Special Industrial Psychology, Special Electronics.

Practical work during vacations.

Specimen collections.

A paper, in addition to final examinations.


### Hons. B.Sc. in Forestry

Eligibility:           B.Sc. in Forestry.

A course of directed study for at least 1 year.


### M.Sc. in Forestry

Eligibility:           B.Sc. in Forestry.

Duration of course:   A course of research and/or directed study for 2 years after Hons. B.Sc.

Examination and dissertation required.

## D.Sc. in Forestry

Regulations for doctoral degrees apply.

## Faculty of Military Science

### B.Mil.

Eligibility:              Matriculation Certificate.

Duration of course:    3 years.

1 year's study in an Army, Air Force or Naval Gymnasium.

Courses:  Economics, History, Geography, Martial Law or Constitutional
          Law, Physics, Special Mathematics, Air Science, Naval Science,
          Industrial Economics, Roman-Dutch Law, Mercantile Law.

### Hons. B.Mil.

Eligibility:              B.Mil.
                          An extension of the above, each application being
                          considered on its merit.

Duration of course:    1 year.

### M.Mil.

Eligibility:              Hons. B.Mil.

A course of research and/or directed study for at least 1 year.

Dissertation required.

## UNIVERSITY OF PRETORIA, Pretoria

Founded in 1908 as Transvaal University College (headquarters in Johannesburg since 1906) and began instruction in Letters and Philosophy, Law,
and the Sciences, towards higher examinations of the University of the
Cape of Good Hope.

In 1910 received recognition by the Governor-General of Pretoria as a
separate institution from the South African College of Mining and Technology in Johannesburg.

In 1930 the University of Pretoria became an independent university.

In 1932 came the decision that the services of the University should in the first place further the ideals of the Afrikaans-speaking section of the nation.

General entrance requirements:     Matriculation Certificate or Exemption Certificate of the Joint Matriculation Board of the University of the Cape of Good Hope.

Faculties:

|  |  |
|---|---|
| Letters and Philosophy | Veterinary Science |
| Science and Natural Science | Education |
| Agriculture | Medicine |
| Law | Dentistry |
| Divinity | Engineering |
| Commerce and Public Administration | |

Language of instruction:     Afrikaans-Nederlands.

Degrees awarded:

| Faculty | Degree | Duration of course (years) |
|---|---|---|
| Letters and Philosophy | B.A. | 3 |
| | B.A. (Bantu Languages) | 3 |
| | B.A. Law | 3 |
| | B.A. (S.W.) (Soc. Sc.) | 3 |
| | B.A. (Political Science) | 3 |
| | B.A. (Bibl.) | 3 |
| | B.A. Fine Arts (B.A.B.K.) | 4 |
| | B.A. (Nursing) | 4 |
| | B.A. (Physical Education) | 3 |
| | B.A. (Log.) | 4 |
| | B.Mus. | 4 |
| | B.A. (Hons.) | 4 |
| | B.A. (Hons.) Bantu Lang. | 4 |
| | B.A. (Hons.) S.W. | 4 |
| | B.A. (Hons.) Political Science | 4 |
| | B.A. (Hons.) (Bibl.) | 4 |
| | B.A. (Hons.) Phys. Ed. | 4 |
| | B.A. (Hons.) Class. Lang. | 4 |
| | M.A. Bantu Languages | |
| | M.A. (S.W.) | |
| | M.A. Political Science | |
| | M.A. (Bibl.) | |

M.A. Fine Arts (M.A.B.K.)
M.A. Physical Education (M.A.L.O.)
M.A. Logopedics
M.Mus.

D.Litt.
D.Phil.
D.Mus.

Diploma in Social Science
Higher Diploma in Social Science
Lower Diploma in Library Science
Diploma in Fine Arts
Diploma in Music
Certificate in Music

| | | |
|---|---|---|
| Science and Natural Science | B.Sc. | 3 |
| | B.Sc. (Hons.) | 4 |
| | M.Sc. | |
| | D.Sc. | |
| | B.Sc. (Huish.) (Domestic Sc.) | 4 |
| | M.Sc. (Huish.) | |
| | B.Sc. (Dieetk.) | 4 |
| | B.Sc. (Dieetk.) (Hons.) | 5 |
| | M.Sc. (Dieetk.) | |
| | B.Sc. (Verp.) (Nursing) | 4 |
| | B.Sc. (Mynb. Geol.) | 4 |
| | B.Arch. | 6 |
| | M.Arch. | |
| | B.Sc. (Q.S.) | 5 |
| | M.Sc. (Q.S.) | |
| | Diploma in Quantity Surveying | 5 |
| Agriculture | B.Sc. (Agric.) | 4 |
| | B.Sc. (Ing.) | 5 |
| | M.Sc. (Agric.) | |
| | M.Sc. (Agric. Ing.) | 2 |
| | D.Sc. (Agric.) | |
| | D.Sc. (Agric. Ing.) | |
| Law | LL.B. | 5 |
| | LL.M. | |
| | LL.D. | |
| | B.Iur. | 3 |
| | Dip. Iur. | |
| | Dip. Proc. | 3 |
| Divinity | B.D. | 3 |
| | D.D. | |

| | | |
|---|---|---|
| Commerce and Public Administration | B.Com. | 3 |
| | B.Com. (Hons.) | 4 |
| | B.Com. (Rek.) (Accountancy) | 3 |
| | M.Com. | |
| | M.Com. (Rek.) | |
| | M.B.A. | 3 |
| | D.Com. | |
| | D.B.A. | |
| | B.Admin. | |
| | B.Admin. (Hons.) | |
| | M.Admin. | |
| | D.Phil. | |
| | Dip. in the Business of Public Administration | 3 |
| | Diploma in Business Admin. (Dip. B.A.) | |
| | Certificate in Theory of Accountancy | 4 |
| Veterinary Science | B.V.Sc. | 5 |
| | D.V.Sc. | |
| Education | B.Ed. | 3 |
| | M.Ed. | |
| | D.Ed. | |
| | Higher Teacher's Diploma (H.O.D.) | 1 |
| | Higher Teacher's Diploma for B.Com. students (H.O.D. - B.Com.) | |
| | Higher Primary Teacher's Diploma (H.P.O.) | 3 |
| | Diploma in Youth Education | 3 |
| | 1-Year Diploma in Youth Ed. | 1 |
| | Diploma in Youth Education with B.A. (S.W.) | |
| | Diploma in Special Teaching (D.S.O.) | 1 |
| | Diploma in Phys. Ed. (D.L.O.) | 3 |
| | Teacher's Diploma in Physio. therapy | 1 |
| Medicine | M.B., Ch.B. | 6 |
| | M.Med. | 3-4 |
| | M.D. | |
| | Diploma in Radiographic Therapy | 2 |
| | Diploma in Radiographic Diagnosis | 2 |
| | Nurse's Diploma in Radio- Protection | 1 |

|  |  |  |
|---|---|---|
| | Diploma in Psychiatric Nursing | 1-2 |
| | Diploma in Medical Physics (D.M.F.) | 2 |
| Dentistry | B.Ch.D. | 5 |
| | M.Ch.D. | |
| Engineering | B.Sc. (Ing.) | 5 |
| | M.Sc. (Ing.) | |
| | D.Sc. (Ing.) | |
| | B.Sc. Surveying | 4 |
| | M.Sc. (S. and S.) (Town Regional Planning) | 3 |
| | Master in Land Surveying | 2 |
| | Doctor in Land Surveying | |
| | Dip. (S. and S.) | 3 |

## Examination symbols:

Applicable to all baccalaureate (baccalaureus) degrees:

| Marks % | Symbol | |
|---|---|---|
| 90 - 100 | A plus | ) |
| 80 - 89 | A | ) Pass cum laude |
| 75 - 79 | A minus | ) |
| 65 - 74 | B plus | ) |
| 55 - 64 | B | ) Pass |
| 50 - 54 | B minus | ) |
| 45 - 49 | C plus | ) |
| 40 - 44 | C | ) Re-examination allowed |
| 0 - 39 | D | ) Failure |

## Master's degrees

2 years after a **3**-year baccalaureate in the Faculties of Letters and Philosophy, and Science and Natural Science.

or   3 semesters after any other 3-year baccalaureate.

or   2 semesters after a 4-year (or more) baccalaureate.

Examination and dissertation, or examination alone, at the Senate's discretion.

## Doctor's degrees

|        Faculty        |    |                        Duration                        |
|-----------------------|----|--------------------------------------------------------|
| Letters and Philosophy |    | 4 years after bachelor's                              |
|                       | or | 3 years after master's                                 |
| Science and Natural Science |    | as above                                         |
| Agriculture           |    | 3 years full time                                      |
|                       | or | 4 years part-time study after completing bachelor's    |
| Law                   |    | 2 years after LL.B.                                    |
| Divinity              |    | 3 years after B.D.                                     |
| Commerce and Public Admin. |    | 4 years after bachelor's                          |
|                       | or | 3 years after master's                                 |
| Veterinary Science    |    | 3 years after bachelor's                               |
| Education             |    | as in Letters and Philosophy                           |
| Medicine              |    | 5 years after bachelor's                               |
| Engineering           |    | 4 years after bachelor's                               |

Thesis, written and oral examinations.

## Faculty of Letters and Philosophy

### B.A.

11 subjects including 2 majors from Groups I-III below.

Group I:   Afrikaans, German, English, French, Greek, Hebrew or another
           Semitic Language, Latin, Sotho, Zulu.

Group II:  Geography, Afrikaans Cultural History, Archaeology, Library
           Science, Bible Studies, Economics, Banking and Finance, His-
           tory, Criminology, History of Art, Physical Education, Music,
           History of Music and Musical Appreciation, Mathematics, Psy-
           chology, Sociology, Logopedics, Elocution, Civil Administra-
           tion, Political Science, Applied Sociology, Applied Ethnology,
           Statistics, Philosophy, Nursing, History of Pedagogy, Dramatic
           Art, Public Administration.

Group III: Bantu Law, Jurisprudence, Roman-Dutch Law, Roman Law, Consti-
           tutional and Administrative Law, Criminal Law, International
           Law.

Group IV:  Biology, Chemistry, Zoology, Physics, Physiology, Geology,
           Botany, Statistical Methods, Applied Mathematics.

| Special B.A. degrees:<br>(see list above) | Must include: |
|---|---|
| Bantu Languages | 2 Bantu languages, Applied Ethnology, Bantu Law, Roman-Dutch and Criminal Law. |
| Law | Roman-Dutch Law, Latin, Afrikaans or English, Roman Law, and 2 of the following: German, French, Greek, Criminology, Ethnology, Philosophy, Sociology, 1 Bantu language. |
| Social Science | 3 courses in Sociology, 2 courses in Applied Sociology, 1 course in Criminology, and at least 2 of the following: Economics, Criminology, Roman-Dutch Law, Psychology, Applied Ethnology, Political Science, Philosophy, Physical Education, 1 language. |
| Political Science | Sociology, Economics, History, Ethnology, Constitutional Law, 1 of the following: Criminology, Roman-Dutch Law, Psychology, Statistics, Philosophy, English, Afrikaans. |
| Bibl. (Library Science) | French or German. |
| Fine Arts | History of Art, Painting, Drawing, Anatomy, Graphic Art, English, Afrikaans, History of Music or Drama. |
| Nursing | 1 language, Elementary Physics, Chemistry, Biology, Anatomy, Physiology, Sociology, Psychology, Nursing Science (3 courses), and 1 of the following: Ethnology, Economics, Philosophy. |
| Physical Education | Physiology, 1 language, and 1 of the following: Physics, Psychology, History of Education, Chemistry, Philosophy. |
| Logopedics | Afrikaans, English, Physiology, Anatomy, Elocution, Psychology, Neurology and Pathology of Speech, Social Pathology. |

| Music | In addition to the final examination, a composition-exercise and a paper. |
|---|---|
| B.A. for Normal College Students | 6 courses in school subjects. |
| B.A. for future Higher Teacher's Diploma (H.O.D.) Students | History of Education, Educational Psychology |

## B.A. (Hons.)

Eligibility:        B.A. of this University, or one who has been granted status thereof.

Subjects: Geography, Afrikaans and Dutch, Afrikaans and Dutch Culture, History, Bantu Languages, German, Economics, English, French, History, Greek, Semitic Languages, Criminology, History of Art, Latin, Psychology, Sociology, Political Science, Applied Ethnology, Mathematics, Mathematics and Statistics, Philosophy.

The course consists of seminars and/or practical work and is followed by a written and/or oral examination.

## Master's Degrees

Eligibility:        After completion of Hons. B.A.

Subjects: As for B.A. Hons.

## Doctor's Degrees

Eligibility:        B.A. and fulfillment of M.A. requirements.

## Diplomas awarded:

        Diploma in Social Science
        Higher Diploma in Social Science
        Lower Diploma in Library Science
        Diploma in Fine Arts
        Diploma in Music

Certificate awarded:   Certificate in Music

## Faculty of Science and Natural Science

### B.Sc.

Eligibility:            Matriculation Certificate.

Subjects: 11 including 2 majors from list below (* denotes major).

       *Chemistry, *Zoology, *Entomology, *Physics, *Geology, *Botany, *Applied Mathematics, *Mathematics, *Geography, Biochemistry, Biology, *Physiology, Genetics, Microbiology, Statistical Methods, Nursing.

### B.Sc. (Hons.)

Eligibility:        B.Sc.

Subjects: Geography, Chemistry, Dietetics, Geology, Applied Mathematics, Mathematics, Statistics.

### M.Sc.

Eligibility:            Afrikaans with Dutch, a reading knowledge of French, German, or another foreign language.

Subjects: Geography, Anatomy, Biochemistry, Chemistry (Inorganic and Analytical, Physical, and Organic), Zoology, Entomology, Physical Chemistry, Physics, Physiology, Geology, Microbiology, Mathematics, Statistics.

### D.Sc.

General regulations for doctoral degrees apply.

### B.Sc. (Huish.)(Dieetk.) - Domestic Science and Dietetics

Subjects: Chemistry, Zoology, Physics, Cookery, Microbiology, Household Management, Dressmaking, Biochemistry, House Furnishing, Diet Therapy, Large-scale Cookery, and Management.

### B.Sc. (Hons.) (Dietetics)

Subjects: Organic Chemistry, Biochemistry, Advanced Dietetic Therapy, Statistical Methods.

An independent study of some aspect of one of the above.

<u>M.Sc. (Huish.)(Dieetk.) - Domestic Science and Dietetics</u>

Regulations as for other subjects in the Faculty.  Courses planned according to need.

Examination and dissertation.


<u>B.Sc. (Nursing)</u>

Eligibility:              Matriculation with Mathematics, or exemption.

Duration of course:   4-year program plus 6 months of practical nursing.

Subjects: Physics, Chemistry , Anatomy, Bacteriology, Physiology, Pathology.


<u>B.Sc. (Mining Engineering and Geology)</u>

Subjects: Geology, Chemistry, Physics, Mathematics, Applied Mathematics,
          Survey, Applied Geophysics, Metallurgy, Mining Law and Planning,
          Mining Economics, <u>et al</u>.

At least 20 weeks' vacation work.


<u>Diploma in Hospital Dietetics</u>

Eligibility:              B.Sc. (Dietetics)

Duration of course:   1 postgraduate year in Pretoria or Johannesburg
                      Hospital, and an examination.


<u>Department of Architecture and Quantity Surveying</u>

Eligibility:              Matriculation.

No candidate may be enrolled in the part-time sections unless he is
simultaneously employed in the office of an architect or quantity surveyor.


<u>B.Arch.</u>

Duration of course:   6 years full time, 8 years part time.

Subjects: Design Building Construction, History of Architecture, Applied
          Mathematics, Mathematics, Physics, Theory of Building, Geology,
          Building Finances, Electrotechnics, Acoustics, Specifications,
          Town Planning, Industrial Psychology, Arbitration, Economics,
          <u>et al</u>.

A practical exercise in the form of a Plan, to be submitted to the Head of the department, in addition to final examination.


## M.Arch.

Not less than 2 years after the B.Arch.

Oral examination and thesis.


## B.Sc. (Q.S.)

Duration of course:    5 years.

Subjects: Choice of relevant subjects from B.Arch. list and Construction Planning, Advanced Public Health, Cost Accounting, Building Equipment, Trade Practice, Building Costs, Quantity Prediction.

Full-time vacation work in employment of a surveyor is required.


## M.Sc. (Q.S.)

Eligibility:              B.Sc. (Q.S.) and 2 years' practice as quantity surveyor after obtaining baccalaureate.

Duration of course:    2 years.

2 years' work under supervision of the Head of the department during the period of study for the master's degree.

Thesis and oral examination.


## Diploma in Quantity Surveying

Duration of course:    5 years.

Throughout the course the candidate must be working full time in the office of a quantity surveyor.

Subjects: Quantity, Building Construction, Applied Mathematics, Planning, Afrikaans or English, Architecture, Building Theory, Pricing, Specifications, Building Finances, et al.


## Faculty of Agriculture

Eligibility:              Matriculation with Mathematics.

## B.Sc. (Agric.)

Courses:   Agronomy, Biochemistry, Entomology, Genetics, Soil Science, Agri-
           cultural Economics, Microbiology, Plant Pathology, Poultry
           Breeding, Sheep Breeding and Wool Tech., Dairying, Horticulture,
           Cattle Breeding, Livestock Exhibition.

Courses selected from the General Science lists.


## B.Sc. (Agric. Ing.)

See Engineering.

## M.Sc. (Agric.)

Courses as above.


## M.Sc. (Agric. Ing.)

Courses: Agricultural Information, Agricultural Business Economics,
         Educational Psychology, Theory of Education and Teaching,
         Educational Sociology, Research Techniques.

Examination and thesis.


## D.Sc. (Agric.) and D.Sc. (Agric. Ing.)

1 year before submission of thesis, an entrance examination must be taken.

The Faculty may prescribe directions of study in any faculty that will
integrate the doctoral course.

In addition to the thesis there is a final examination.



## Faculty of Law

## LL.B.

Eligibility:            Bachelor's degree in another faculty.

Duration of course:   3 years.

Subjects: Roman-Dutch Law, Roman Law, Law Latin, Mercantile Law, Bantu Law,
          Criminal Law, Criminal Procedure, Civil Law, Administrative Law,
          International Law.

## LL.M.

Eligibility:          LL.B.

Consists of further study in at least 2 sub-disciplines in Law studies above.

Examination and dissertation.

## LL.D.

Eligibility:          LL.B.

Comprehensive examination and thesis.

## B.Iur.

Duration of course:    3 years.

Subjects: Roman-Dutch Law, Roman Law, Criminal Law, Afrikaans or English,
          Company Law, Law of Criminal Procedure, Civil Law.

          1 of the following:  Latin, Economics, Sociology, Bantu Law or
          Advanced Ethnology, Ethnology.

## Diploma Iuris

Eligibility:          Matriculation.

Duration of course:    3 years.

Subjects: Roman-Dutch Law, Roman Law, Afrikaans or English.

          1 of the following:  Latin, Economics, Sociology, Political
          Science, Ethnology.

          Company Law, Criminal Process, Civil Law, Bantu Law.

## Diploma Proc. (Attorney's Diploma)

Eligibility:          Matriculation or exemption.

Duration of course:    3 years.

## Civil Service Examination in Law

Eligibility:          Anyone permanently or temporarily employed by the State,
                      the Provincial Administration, the South African
                      Reserve Bank, or other agencies.

Duration of course:    3 years.

Subjects: Same as for Dip. Iur.


## Senior Civil Service Examination in Law

Eligibility:              Open to all persons employed as above and who have
                          passed the above examination or the Lower or Junior
                          Civil Service Examination.

Duration of course:    2 years.

Subjects: Same as for LL.B.   General legal subjects.


## Faculty of Divinity

### B.D.

Eligibility:              B.A. in Latin, Greek, Hebrew, Philosophy, History,
                          Psychology, Afrikaans and Dutch Culture History
                          including 3 years of Greek, 2 of Hebrew, 1 each of
                          Latin and Philosophy.

Duration of course:    3 years.

Subjects: Old and New Testament Exegesis, Theology, Church History,
          History of Dogma, Canon Law, Phenomenology, Psychology of Worship,
          Missionary Theory, Missionary History.


### D.D.

Written and oral examination, and thesis.


## Faculty of Commerce and Public Administration

### B.Com. and B.Com. (Rek.)

Duration of course:    3 years.

Subjects: Economics, Banking and Finance, Accountancy, Industrial Psychology,
          Company Law, Statistics, Income Tax, Cost Accounting, Property
          Administration.

### B.Admin.

Duration of course:    3 years.

Subjects: Political Science, Economics, Civil Administration, Banking and
          Finance, Municipal Administration.

          1 of the following:  Accountancy, Roman-Dutch Law, a Bantu
          language.

          1 of the following:  Industrial Economics, Ethnology, Sociology.

          1 of the following:  History, German, French, English, Afrikaans.

### Honors Degrees

Eligibility:            Baccalaureate.

Duration of course:    1 year.

Subjects: General study of Economics, Trade, Finance and Banking,
          Industrial Economics.

          1 of the following:  Economic History, Agricultural Economics,
          Economic Statistics, Accountancy, Mathematics, various aspects
          of Civil, Municipal and International Administration, Political
          Science.

          A reading knowledge of French or German.

### M.Com. (Economics), M.Com. (Statistics), M.Admin. and M.B.A.

Eligibility:            B. (Hons.)

Duration of course:    3 years.

Courses:  A selection from the following, relevant to the specialization:

          Advanced Estate Accountancy and Insurance, Econometry, Time
          Analysis Demography, Variation Analysis, Political Science and
          Public Administration, Economics, Advanced Accountancy, Advanced
          Auditing, Production Administrative Practice, Financing, Labor
          Studies.

### D.Com., D.B.A.

Candidates submit a thesis on a subject passed in the master's examination
or B.Com. Hons. examination.

## D.Phil.

Candidates submit a thesis on a subject connected with Economics, Political Science or Public Administration.

## Diploma in the Business of Public Administration

Eligibility:              Matriculation.

Duration of course:   3 years.

Regulations as for B.Com. and B.Admin.

## Diploma in Business Administration (Dip. B.A.)

Eligibility:              Bachelor's degree.

Regulations as for M.B.A.

## Certificate in Theory of Accountancy

Eligibility:              Matriculation.

Duration of course:   4 years.

Subjects: Accounting, Auditing, Mercantile Law, Capita Selecta from Company Law, Financial Administration, Income Tax, Cost Accounting, Advanced courses in the last 3.

## Faculty of Veterinary Science

## B.V.Sc.

Eligibility:              Matriculation with Chemistry, Biology or another science, Latin or German or French, and Mathematics.

Duration of course:   5 years.

The course of study is parallel with that of all South African (and, for the matter, British Commonwealth) medical and dental courses, i.e.:

1st yr:   Premedical (Physics, Chemistry, Botany, Zoology).

2nd yr:   Preclinical, including Anatomy, Physiology, Histology, Embryology.

Thereafter, clinical subjects and practical work.

During the vacations students must undertake prescribed periods of professional work.

## D.V.Sc.

Thesis and examination.

## Faculty of Education

### B.Ed.

Eligibility:          Bachelor's degree.

Duration of course:   3 years.

Subjects: Philosophy of Education, Educational Psychology, Experimental Psychology, Social Pedagogics, Didactics, General Historical Pedagogics, South African History of Education, Clinical Child Psychology, Physical Education.

### M.Ed.

Eligibility:          B.Ed.

Advanced study in courses from the above.

Examination and paper.

### D.Ed.

Thesis and ancillary subjects from the following (with examinations): Historical Pedagogics, Philosophy of Education, Empirical Education.

### Higher Teacher's Diploma (H.O.D.)

Eligibility:          Bachelor's degree with school subjects recognized by the Department of Education.

Duration of course:   1 year.

Courses:  (1)  Educational subjects:

Philosophy of Education, Educational Psychology, Educational Sociology, Historical Pedagogics, General Didactics.

    (2)   Technical subjects:

         Blackboard Work, Elocution, Technical Aids in Modern
         Education, etc.

    (3)   Practical work:

         Demonstration sessions and visits to schools.

## Higher Teacher's Diploma for B.Com. Students - H.O.D. (B.Com.)

Eligibility:               B.Com. including at least 2 years in each of the
following: Accountancy, Economics, Banking and
Finance, Mercantile Law, Proficiency in Typing and
Shorthand.

Subjects as for H.O.D., exemption from technical subjects except Elocution.

## Higher Primary Teacher's Diploma (H.P.O.)

Eligibility:               School-Leaving Certificate and 3 weeks of practical
teaching.

Duration of course:   3 years

Subjects: Afrikaans or English, 4 subjects from the B.A. list, 3 subjects
from the B.Sc. list, and 9 school subjects.

Historical Pedagogics, Method in English, Afrikaans, and Divine
Worship, Elocution, Blackboard Work, Theory of Education and
Teaching, School Organization and Administration, Educational
Sociology.

16 weeks of experimental teaching.

## Diploma in Youth Education

Eligibility:               Matriculation.

Duration of course:   3 years.

Subjects: Theory and History of Youth Education, Sociology, English Youth
Culture, Afrikaans Youth Culture, Youth Orchestras, Woodwork,
Educational Psychology, Educational Sociology, National Health,
Public Health, Art, Organization and Theory of School Practice,
Child Welfare, Corrective Physical Education, Nature Study,
Mental Health.

## One-Year Diploma in Youth Education

Eligibility:        A recognized teacher's certificate and evidence of 2 years' post-matriculation teaching.

Subjects: As above.

## Diploma in Youth Education with B.A. (S.W.)

The diploma may be gained concurrently with the above degree course.

Requirements:  3 courses in Sociology, 3 courses in Applied Sociology, Educational Psychology, 1st-year courses in Afrikaans, English, Criminology, Philosophy.

A choice of subjects from the Diploma in Youth Education, above.

## Diploma in Special Teaching (D.S.O.)

Eligibility:        A recognized teacher's certificate and 2 years' teaching in junior school.

Duration of course:   1 year.

The course is subdivided into the following main groups:

      The Psychology of the Deviant Child
      Educational Sociology
      Organization and Practice of Special Education

Other subjects:      Corrective Physical Education, History of Special Teaching, Handicrafts, Art and Music.

## Diploma in Physical Education (D.L.O.)

Eligibility:        Matriculation.

Duration of course:   3 years.

Subjects: Physiology, and 1-year school subject from the following:

      Afrikaans, English, History, Geography, Biology, History of Art, Afrikaans Culture History, Ethnology, Theory and Practice of Physical Education, Educational Psychology, Applied Sociology, History of Physical Education, Sport Hygiene, Public Hygiene, Sport Massage, and Practice of Gymnastics, various sports.

9 weeks of experimental teaching.

Teacher's Diploma in Physiotherapy

Eligibility:            Matriculation.
                        A qualification in Physiotherapy recognized by the
                        South African Medical Dental Association.
                        At least 2 years' practice in a recognized hospital
                        as a qualified physiotherapist.

Duration of course:    1 year.

Subjects: Physics, Chemistry, Physiology, Pathological Anatomy, Physical
          Development, History and Ethics of Physiotherapy, Educational
          Psychology and Theory and Practice of Teaching, Organization and
          Administration, Supervision and Guidance in the Clinical Field.


Faculty of Medicine

M.B., Ch.B. (Baccalaureus in Medicine and Surgery)

Eligibility:            Matriculation with Mathematics.

Duration of course:    6 years.

Subjects: The customary premedical year of Physics, Chemistry, Botany,
          Zoology, followed by 2 preclinical years of Anatomy, Physiology,
          Biochemistry, Pathological Anatomy, Microbiology, Pharmacology,
          Toxicology, etc.

          3 clinical years.


M.Med.

Eligibility:            2 years after obtaining M.B., Ch.B. and after 1 year's
                        registration as qualified practitioner with the South
                        African Medical and Dental Association.

Duration of course:    3-4 years.

The degree may be taken in the following subjects:

                Internal Medicine                M.Med. (Int.)
                Surgery                          M.Med. (Chir.)
                Pediatrics                       M.Med. (Paed.)
                Obstetrics                       M.Med. (O et G.)
                Pathology                        M.Med. (Path.)
                Dermatology                      M.Med. (Derm.)
                Radiological Diagnosis           M.Med. (Rad.-D.)
                Radiological Therapy             M.Med. (Rad.-T.)
                Ear, Nose and Throat             M.Med. (L. et O.)

                Ophthalmics                M.Med. (Ophth.)
                Anesthetics                M.Med. (Anaes.)
                Psychiatry                 M.Med. (Psych.)
                Neurology                  M.Med. (Neur.)

Courses and basic subjects:

|  | Major | Ancillary | Basic Subjects | Duration |
|---|---|---|---|---|
| Internal | Int. Med. | Path. | Anatomy and Phys. | 4 |
| Surgery | Surg. | Path. | Anatomy and Phys. | 4 |
| Obstet. | Obstet. | Path. | Anatomy and Phys. | 4 |
| Pediat. | Pediat. | Path. | Anatomy and Phys. | 4 |
| Pathol. | Pathol. | Path. | 2 of: Pathology, Anatomy, Microbiol., Chem. Path. | 4 |
| Dermat. | Dermat. | Path. | Anatomy and Phys. | 4 |
| Radiol. | Radiol. | Path. | Anatomy, Phys., Physics | 3 |
| Ear/Nose/Throat | Path. | Anatomy and Phys. | -- | 3 |
| Ophthal. | Path. | Anatomy and Phys. | -- | 3 |
| Anesth. | -- | Anatomy and Phys. | Pathology, Pharmacology | 3 |
| Psych. | Psych. | Anatomy and Phys. | Psych. | 4 |
| Neurol. | Neurol. | Anatomy and Phys. | -- | 3 |

## M.D.

Eligibility:          5 years after M.B., Ch.B.
                      Must hold M.Med.

Thesis and examination.

Courses:  Bacteriology, Serology, Immunology, Parasitology, Chemistry and
          Physics, Hygiene, Mother and Child Care, Infectious Diseases,
          Venereal Diseases, Dental Hygiene, Medical Sociology, Industrial
          Diseases, School Hygiene, Genetics, Mental Hygiene, Epidemiology,
          Population Statistics, Public Health.

Diplomas

Eligibility:            Matriculation and, for nurses, registration with the
                        South African Medical and Dental Association and at
                        least 3 months' qualified experience in nursing.

    Diploma in Radiographic Therapy              2 years

    Diploma in Radiographic Diagnosis            2 years
        (Physics, Photography, Radio-
        isotopes, Instruction in
        Protection and Equipment
        Maintenance, etc.)

    Nurse's Diploma in Radio-Protection          1 year
        (as above)

    Diploma in Psychiatric Nursing               1 or 2 years

    Diploma in Medical Physics (D.M.F.)          2 years
        (Prerequisite:  M.Sc. in Physics;
        Radiobiology, Radiophysics,
        Statistical Methods, and subjects
        above)


## Faculty of Dentistry

### B.Ch.D.

Eligibility:            Matriculation with Mathematics.

Duration of course:   5 years.

Subjects: Physics, Chemistry, Botany, Zoology, Anatomy, Biochemistry,
          Physiology and Anthropology, 3 years of clinical subjects.


### M.Ch.D.

Eligibility:            B.Ch.D.

Duration of course:   2 years' professional practice.

Subjects: Major -      Jaw, Facial and Oral Surgery
          Ancillaries-Pathology and Bacteriology of the Mouth and Radiology
                       of the Head and Neck
          Others -     Plastic and General Surgery

## Faculty of Engineering

### B.Sc. (Ing.)

Eligibility:            Matriculation with Mathematics.

Duration of course:    5 years.

The degree is awarded in the following specializations:

>       Electrotechnical Engineering
>       Civil Engineering
>       Agricultural Engineering
>       Industrial Engineering
>       Chemical Engineering
>       Metallurgical Engineering
>       Mining Engineering

Practical work:        Compulsory excursions, and two 8-week full-time
                       periods of vacation work.

Subjects common to all divisions:

>       Mathematics, Physics, Applied Mathematics, Economics,
>       Metallurgy, Chemistry, Engineering Drawing.

Summary of subjects (major and basic) for specialized courses above:

Electrotechnical Engineering:

>       Machine Science, Thermodynamics, Electromagnetics, Electronics,
>       Radiation, Telecommunications.

Civil Engineering:

>       Building Construction, Graphics, Hydraulics, Surveying, Structure,
>       Industrial Economics, Planning, Railways and Harbors.

Agricultural Engineering:

>       Machine Science, Building Construction, Agronomy, Hydraulics,
>       Structural Science, Agricultural Economics, Industrial Economics,
>       Farming-Building Construction.

Industrial Engineering:

>       Electrotechnics, Machine Science, Industrial Psychology, Labor
>       Schedules, Chemical Thermodynamics, Factory Laws and Organization,
>       Production.

Chemical Engineering:

>       Subjects from Electrotechnical and Industrial Engineering,
>       Explosives, Special Scientific Functions of Chemical Engineers.

Metallurgical Engineering:

     Geology, Physical Metallurgy, Metal Production, Subjects from Industrial Engineering.

Mining Engineering:

     Geology, Graphics, Surveying, Metallurgy, Subjects from all the preceding.

## M.Sc. (Ing.)

Eligibility)          B.Sc. (Ing.)

Duration of course:   2 years.

May be taken in the following branches:

| | |
|---|---|
| Electrotechnical | Mechanical |
| Agricultural | Civil |

## D.Sc. (Ing.)

May only be taken 4 years after obtaining the B.Sc. (Ing.).

The thesis, or part thereof, must be published.

## B.Sc. Surveying

Full-time study only.

Duration of course:   4 years.

Subjects: Mathematics, Physics, Engineering Drawing, Applied Mathematics or Geography, Land Surveying, Astronomy, Optics, Geology, Photogrammetry, Town Planning.

Fieldwork is obligatory.

## M.Sc. (S. and S.)

Eligibility:        Bachelor's degree in Engineering, Surveying, or Architecture.

Duration of course:   3 years.

Subjects: Theory and Practice of Planning, Elementary Architecture and Landscaping, Urban Development in Historical Times, Geography, Urban Sociology, Statistics and Demography, Aerial Photography, Housing, Economics, Traffic Engineering, Agricultural Economics.

## Master in Land Surveying

Eligibility:            Bachelor's degree in Land Surveying.

Duration of course:    2 years.

Subjects: At the discretion of the relevant departmental head.

## Doctor in Land Surveying

May be awarded 4 years after obtaining the baccalaureate.

Candidate must have the necessary experience.

## Dip. (S. and S.)

Eligibility:            Surveyors who do not possess a degree but who have
                        passed the Surveyors Examination of the Joint
                        Committee for Professional Examinations.
                        Architects without a degree but with Diploma in
                        Architecture.

Duration of course:    3 years.

Subjects as for M.Sc. (S. and S.)

## UNIVERSITY OF PORT ELIZABETH, Port Elizabeth

Founded in 1965.

Courses are offered for the B.A., B.Com., B.Sc., and B.Ed. degrees, the
Lower Secondary Teacher's Diploma, and the Certificate in the Theory of
Accounting.

## Departments:

| | |
|---|---|
| Afrikaans-Nederlands | Bantu Languages (Xhosa) |
| English | Psychology |
| History | Sociology and Social Work |
| Geography | Mathematics |
| Latin | Economics and Economic History |
| Greek | Physics |
| Semitic Languages | Chemistry |
| German | Accounting |
| French | Commercial Law |
| Social Anthropology | Business Economics |

       Industrial Psychology         Philosophy of Teaching
       Educational Psychology

Language of instruction:     English and Afrikaans-Nederlands.

## UNIVERSITY COLLEGE WESTERN CAPE, Kasselsvlei

Founded in 1960 for Coloured students.

### Faculties:

       Arts
       Science
       Education

General entrance requirements:

       For degree courses -     Matriculation Certificate of the Joint
                             Matriculation Board.

       For diploma courses -    Senior Certificate.

### Faculty of Arts

Every curriculum contains a minimum of 11 qualifying courses.  Every curriculum contains at least 2 major subjects.

Candidates may present themselves for examination in the following subjects:

Group A:  Geography, Afrikaans-Nederlands, Afrikaans, English, Economics, History, History of Philosophy, Latin, Psychology, Sociology, Mathematics, German.

Group B:  German (Special), Principles of Greek Culture.

Group C:  South African Private Law.

Group D:  Zoology, Botany, Chemistry, Physics.

Every curriculum contains the following:

       At least 6 courses from Group A.
       Not more than 1 course from Group B.
       Not more than 1 course from Groups C and D.

### Degrees and diplomas awarded:

       B.A.         - Bachelor of Arts
       B.A. (S.S.) - Bachelor of Arts (Social Science)
       Hons. B.A. - Honours Bachelor of Arts
       M.A.         - Master of Arts

D.Phil.     - Doctor of Philosophy
Diploma in Librarianship
Diploma in Social Science


## Faculty of Science

Every curriculum contains 9 qualifying courses.

Candidates may present themselves for examination in the following subjects:

Group I:  Applied Mathematics, Botany, Chemistry, Geography, Geology, Mathematics, Physics, Psychology, Zoology.

Group II: Afrikaans/Nederlands, Afrikaans, English.

Not more than 1 course from Group II may be included in any curriculum.

## Degrees awarded:

B.Sc.          - Bachelor of Science
B.Sc. (Pharmacy) - Bachelor of Science (Pharmacy)
Hons. B.Sc. - Honours Bachelor of Science
M.Sc.          - Master of Science
Ph.D.          - Doctor of Philosophy
D.Sc.          - Doctor of Science


## Faculty of Education

## Lower Secondary Teacher's Diploma

Duration of course:   3 years.

1st yr:   4 of the following:
Afrikaans-Nederlands I, Bible Study, English I, Geography, German, Latin, History, Mathematics, Afrikaans, Professional English.

2nd yr:   3 subjects of which 2 must be continuations of 1st-year courses.

3rd yr:   Group A - Major subjects

Philosophy of Education, Educational Psychology, History of Education, Method and Administration, Method of the 2 major teaching subjects.

Group B

Afrikaans, English.

Group C

Practical teaching in both major subjects.

Group D - Additional subjects

Speech, Training, Afrikaans or English, School Librarianship, Blackboard Work, School Hygiene.

Course with B.Sc. subjects:

1st yr:   4 of the following:
          Applied Mathematics, Botany, Chemistry, Geography, Mathematics, Physics, Zoology.

2nd yr:   3 subjects of which 2 must be continuations of 1st-year courses.

3rd yr:   As above.

Course with B.Comm. subjects:

1st yr:   Business Economics I, Accounting I, Afrikaans or Afrikaans-Nederlands, Professional English, Snelskrif, Typing and Shorthand I.

2nd yr:   Business Economics II, Accounting II, Commercial Arithmetic, Snelskrif, Typing and Shorthand II.

3rd yr:   See above.

UNIVERSITY COLLEGE OF THE NORTH, Turfloop

Founded in 1960 for Bantus.

General entrance requirements:      Matriculation Certificate or Certificate from Joint Matriculation Board.

Faculties:

        Arts
        Science
        Education

Degrees awarded:

| Faculty | Degree | Duration of course (years) |
|---|---|---|
| Arts | Bachelor of Arts | 3 |
| | Bachelor of Administration | 3 |
| | Bachelor of Arts in Social Science | 3 |

| | | |
|---|---|---|
| Bachelor | Bachelor of Commerce | 3 |
| | Diploma in Commerce | 2 |
| | Diploma in Commerce for Teachers-in-service | |
| | Diploma in Social Work | 3 |
| | Diploma in Administration | 2 |
| Sciences | Bachelor of Science | 3 |
| | Bachelor of Science (Pharm.) | 3 |
| | Diploma in Pharmacy | |
| Education | Bachelor of Education | 1 |
| | Master of Education | 1 |
| | South African Teacher's Diploma | 2 |
| | University Education Diploma (Non-graduate) | 1 |
| | University Education Degree | 1 |

## Faculty of Arts

### Bachelor of Arts

The following subjects are offered:

Afrikaans-Nederlands
Praktiese Afrikaans
Bantu Languages:
  Sotho Languages
  Venda
  Tsonga
Biblical Studies
English
Preliminary Latin
Latin
Hellenistic Greek
Economics
Philosophy
Education
Sociology
Social Work
Principles of Greek Culture

Criminology
Anthropology
Native Administration
South African Bantu Law
South African Native Law
History
Political Science
Public Administration
Geography
Psychology
Mathematics
Biology
Zoology
Botany
Physics
Chemistry

### Bachelor of Administration

See University of South Africa.

### Bachelor of Arts in Social Science

See University of South Africa.

## Bachelor of Commerce

Candidates qualify for the Bachelor of Commerce degree under 1 of the following 5 headings:

General                          Statistics
Administration                   Law
Accounting

See University of South Africa.


## Diploma in Commerce

Eligibility:            Senior Certificate.

Duration of course:     2 years.

The following subjects are offered:

Bookkeeping                  Commercial Arithmetic
Economics                    Native Administration
Commerce                     Salesmanship
Mercantile Law


## Diploma in Commerce for Teachers-in-service

See Diploma in Commerce.


## Diploma in Social Work

Eligibility:            School-Leaving Certificate or a Junior Certificate
                        plus an approved professional diploma.

Duration of course:     3 years.

The 3rd year is full-time practical work.

Curriculum:     Sociology I and II, Social Work I and II, Native Law I.

                3 of the following: Economics I and II, Anthropology I and
                II, Psychology I and II, Criminology I and II.

                Social Work (practical work), Study of Cases, Group Work
                (singing and music; organized games and first-aid; work-
                therapy and handiwork), Community Organization, Typing
                Exercises.


## Diploma in Administration

2-year course in preparation.

## Introduction to Hellenistic Greek

Eligibility:            Matriculation Certificate, Senior Certificate, School-
                        Leaving Certificate, or Junior Certificate
              plus      2 years' further study which has been approved by the
                        Senate.

Duration of course:     1 year.

Courses:  Morphology and Syntax of Hellenistic Greek, Basic Vocabulary and
          Idioms, Translations of easy portions of the New Testament into
          Afrikaans or English.


## Faculty of Natural Sciences

## Bachelor of Science

The following subjects are offered:

| | |
|---|---|
| Biology | Applied Mathematics |
| Zoology | Mathematical Statistics |
| Physics | Geography |
| Botany | Psychology |
| Hygiene I | Afrikaans-Nederlands |
| Chemistry | Practical Afrikaans |
| Mathematics | English |

See University of South Africa.


## Bachelor of Science (Pharmacy) and Diploma in Pharmacy

See University of South Africa.


## Faculty of Education

## Bachelor of Education, Master of Education

See University of South Africa.


## South African Teacher's Diploma

Purpose of course:      Training of teachers for the first 3 classes (Forms
                        I-III) of the Secondary School.

Eligibility:                    Senior Certificate.
                                Candidates who have not obtained the Matriculation
                                Certificates <u>shall not</u> have their academic courses
                                credited towards a degree.

Duration of course:    2 years.

Curriculum:

1st yr:    <u>Group I</u> - Academic degree courses

           A full 1st-year course of subjects as for the B.A., B.Sc., or
           B.Com. degrees will be followed by:

           B.A.   -1st-year courses of which 1 course in the mother tongue
                   and 1 in either of the official languages will be compulsory.

           B.Sc. -4 1st-year courses of which at least 3 courses are in
                   Natural Sciences.

           B.Com.-A 1st-year degree course as prescribed by the University of
                   South Africa.

2nd yr:    <u>Group II</u> - Professional subjects

           Principles of Education, Empirical Education, School Organization,
           History of Education, Practical Teaching.

           <u>Group III</u> - Method and content

           4 of the following:
           General Science, Physical Science, Biology, Arithmetic, Mathematics,
           Commerce, Commercial Arithmetic, Bookkeeping, Afrikaans, English,
           Mother Tongue, Latin, Social Studies, Religious Instruction.

           <u>Group IV</u> - Compulsory practical subjects

           Teaching Aids, Blackboard Work, School Hygiene.

           <u>Group V</u> - Additional subjects

           Music and Singing, Physical Education.

## University Education Diploma (Non-graduate)

Eligibility:            Matriculation Certificate.

A candidate who has completed a full 2-year course for a bachelor's degree
can be admitted to the final year of professional training.

See University of South Africa.

## University Education Degree

See University of South Africa.

UNIVERSITY COLLEGE OF ZULULAND, Empangeni

Founded in 1959 for men and women students who belong to the Zulu or Swazi
language groups.  Degrees and diplomas awarded by the University of South
Africa.

General entrance requirements:        The requirements for admission to any
                                      specific degree or diploma offered by
                                      the University of South Africa are
                                      applicable.

Regulations for degrees in Arts

Candidates for the degree Baccalaureus Artium may enroll for the following
subjects:

Group A:   Afrikaans, English, Zulu, Latin, Mathematics, Psychology,
           Economics, Sociology, Anthropology, Philosophy, History, Geography.

Group B:   Practical Afrikaans, Practical English, Education, Criminology,
           Statistics, Economic Geography, Native Administration, Economic
           History.

Group C:   Roman Law, Private Law.

Group D:   Biblical Studies

Group E:   Physics, Chemistry, Botany, Biology, Zoology.

Regulations for degrees in Social Science

For the degree B.A. (S.S.) the 2 compulsory major subjects are Social Work
and Sociology.

Every curriculum includes at least 2 courses in Psychology.

Regulations for degrees in Theology

Same regulations as published in the "Calendar" of the University of South
Africa.

Regulations for degrees and diplomas in Education

Same regulations as the University of South Africa.

Regulations for degrees in Natural Sciences

Tuition in the following subjects is provided:

Zoology, Physics, Botany, Chemistry, Biology, Mathematics, Geography, Psychology, Applied Mathematics, Mathematical Statistics.

Regulations governing the degree Baccalareus Scientiae are the same as in the University of South Africa.

"B-courses" in Mathematics, Chemistry, and Physics.  These B courses may be taken by students who wish:

(a) to improve their knowledge of Mathematics and/or Chemistry and/or Physics before taking the normal B.Sc. degree courses in these subjects;

(b) to qualify as teachers by taking the 2-year diploma course;

or (c) to improve their qualifications as teachers by taking a special 1-year course.

It should be emphasized that "B-courses" are not degree courses but are designed to prepare the student for degree courses.

## Regulations for degrees in Commerce and Administration (B.Com. and B.Admin.)

Tuition for the first 2 years of the above degrees can be arranged at the College, including such subjects as Economics and Economic History, Business Economics, Accounting, Mathematics, Elementary Theory of Finance, Statistical Methods A and B, Economic Geography, Economic History; as well as a variety of ancillary subjects provided by the Faculty of Arts.

The regulations governing degrees in Commerce and Administration are the same as the University of South Africa.

DIPLOMA COURSES:

## Secondary Teachers' Diploma

The aim of this course is to train teachers for the first 3 years of the Secondary School.

Eligibility:          Matriculation Certificate or other acceptable entrance qualification.
                      Candidates who have not obtained the Matriculation Certificate or exemption may not have their courses credited towards a degree.

Duration of course:   2 years.

Subjects:

Group I:  Academic courses.  During the first year of study every candidate fulfills the requirements of 1 of the following curricula:
          B.A.   - 5 first-year courses towards a B.A. degree of which the mother tongue and 1 official language are compulsory.

B.Com.  - A first-year course prescribed by the University of
          South Africa.

B.Sc.   - <u>either</u>
          (i)   4 first-year B.Sc. courses of which at least 3
                shall be Natural Sciences.
       or (ii)  Mathematics B, Physics B, Chemistry B and either
                Biology I or Botany I or Zoology I.
       or (iii) Zoology I, Botany I, Chemistry B and Physics B.

Group II: Professional Subjects.
          Principles of Education, Empirical Education (Educational Psycho-
          logy), School Organization, Practical Teaching, History of
          Education with special reference to the History of Education in
          South Africa.

Division of teaching time, examination time, and marks:

| Subjects | Teaching Time | Examination Time | Maximum Marks |
|---|---|---|---|
| Principles of Education | 2 hrs. | 3 hrs. | 100 |
| Empirical Education | 2 hrs. | 3 hrs. | 100 |
| School Organization | 2 hrs. | 3 hrs. | 100 |
| Practice Teaching | -- | -- | 100 |
| History of Education | 2 hrs. | 3 hrs. | 100 |
| Four School Subjects | 4x2 hrs. | 4x3 hrs. | 400 |
| Teaching Aids | 1 hr. | 3 hrs. | 100 |
| Blackboard Work | 1 hr. | 2 hrs. | 100 |
| School Hygiene | 1 hr. | 2 hrs. | 100 |
| Music and Singing | 1 hr. | 2 hrs. | 100 |
| Physical Education | 1 hr. | 2 hrs. | 100 |

## Commercial Teachers' Diploma

Course of 1 year's duration intended primarily to train teachers who are in
possession of a Matriculation/High School-Leaving Certificate and a Teachers'
Certificate, to teach commercial subjects in secondary and high schools.

The following subjects are offered for the courses:

     Bookkeeping, Commerce, Office Routine, Economics, Typewriting,
     Practice Teaching

The official languages and other auxiliary subjects are included in the
course.

## Diploma in Commercial Subjects

Course of 1 year's duration intended to train students in possession of a
Matriculation or High School-Leaving Certificate to qualify for positions

as clerks, bookkeepers, etc. in the civil service or in the business world.

Curriculum is the same as for Commercial Teachers' Diploma, above.


Diploma in Social Work

Eligibility:              High School Leaving Certificate or equivalent.

Duration of course:    3 years.

The 3rd year is spent in practical work at an approved welfare organization.

Curriculum:    Sociology, Social Work, Psychology, Criminology.

               1 of the following:
               Social Anthropology, Native Law, Native Administration,
               Economics or a language.

               Sociology, Social Work and Psychology are studied during the
               1st and 2nd years.


Diploma in Social Work (Nursing)

Special diploma for qualified nurses who desire training in Social Work
has been instituted.


Special One-year Diploma Course for Teachers of the Official Languages,
    Mathematics and Science

Eligibility:              Teacher's Certificate and Matriculation or High
                          School Leaving Certificate, or equivalent.

Duration of course:    1 year.

Offered in the following subjects:

               The official languages
               Science and Mathematics

The purpose of these courses is to enable teachers to improve their knowledge
of these subjects and to enable them to teach them up to Junior Certificate
standard.

The following alternative curricula are offered:

    (a)  Official languages:  Candidates must have reached Matriculation
         or High School Leaving Certificate standard in 1 official language
         and at least Junior Certificate standard in the other.

or  (b)  Mathematics I or B, Physics I or B, Chemistry I or B, plus 1
         subject chosen from the following:  Biology, Botany, Zoology.

or    (c)   Zoology I, Botany I, Chemistry I or B and Physics I or B.


UNIVERSITY COLLEGE OF FORT HARE, Fort Hare

Founded as Fort Hare University College in 1916.  Incorporated as institution of higher education under Education Act of 1923.  In 1951, became
allied to Rhodes University.  From 1960 University College of Fort Hare
for Xhosa-speaking Bantu.  Students awarded external degrees of University
of South Africa.


Faculties:

| | |
|---|---|
| Arts | Law |
| Science | Commerce |
| Divinity | Education |

Degrees awarded:

| Faculty | Degree | Duration of course (years) |
|---|---|---|
| Arts | B.A. | 3 |
| | Hons. B.A. | 4 |
| | M.A. | 1 |
| | D.Litt. et Phil. | |
| Science | B.Sc. | 3 |
| | Hons. B.Sc. | 4 |
| | M.Sc. | |
| | Ph.D. | |
| | Advanced Diploma in Agriculture | 3 |
| Divinity | B.A. | 3 |
| | Diploma in Theology (Post-graduate) | 2 |
| Law | LL.B. | 4 |
| Commerce | B.Com. | 3 |
| | Hons. B.Com. | 4 |
| | M.Com. | |
| | D.Phil. | |
| Education | B.Ed. | 1 |
| | M.Ed. | 1 |
| | D.Ed. | |
| | U.E.D. | |
| | S.A.T.D. | 1 |

Faculty of Arts

Candidates for the B.A. degree may present themselves for examination in
the following subjects:

Group A - Linguistic Studies:

    Latin, Hellenistic Greek, Hebrew, English, Afrikaans-Nederlands,
    Bantu Language.

Group B - Legal Studies:

    Roman Law, Roman-Dutch Law, Native Law, Constitutional Law.

Group C - Philosophical Studies:

    Mathematics, Political Science, Psychology, Systematic Theology,
    Education, Economics and Economic History I, Philosophy of
    Religion, Economics, Anthropology, History of Philosophy,
    Systematic Philosophy

Group D - Historical and Cultural Studies:

    Mediaeval and Modern History, Ecclesiastical History, Geography,
    Economic History II, Principles of Greek Culture, Native
    Administration.

Group E - Natural Sciences:

    Physics, Chemistry, Applied Mathematics, Botany, Zoology.

Group F - Theological Studies:

    Biblical Studies, Missiology.


Every curriculum includes:

    (1)  At least 2 qualifying courses from Group A (either 2 courses in
         1 subject, or 1 course in each of 2 subjects), 1 of which must
         be in 1 of the official languages.

    (2)  At least 1 qualifying course from either Group B or Group C.

    (3)  At least 1 further qualifying course from Group B or C or D.

The major subjects of the curriculum are selected from the following:

    (a)  Major subjects in which 3 qualifying courses are taken:
         English, Afrikaans-Nederlands, Bantu Languages, Latin, History,
         Roman-Dutch Law, Geography, Economics, Political Science, Anthro-
         pology, Philosophy, Native Administration, Systematic Theology.

    (b)  Major subjects in which 2 qualifying courses are taken:
         Roman Law, Public Administration: provided that, except as other-
         wise allowed by the Senate, every curriculum for the B.A. degree
         shall include at least 4 non-initial courses.

Every curriculum for the degree contains at least 1 qualifying course in English or Afrikaans-Nederlands.


## Faculty of Science

Candidates for the B.Sc. degree may present themselves for examination in the following subjects:

Group I:   Mathematics, Applied Mathematics, Physics, Chemistry , Botany, Zoology, Geography, Psychology.

Group II: English, Afrikaans-Nederlands, a Bantu Language, Philosophy.

Major subjects of the curriculum are selected from the following:

Major subjects in which 3 qualifying courses are taken:
Pure Mathematics, Applied Mathematics, Physics, Chemistry, Botany, Zoology, Geography, Psychology.


## Hons. B.Sc.

Eligibility:              B.Sc.

Degree may be conferred in the following departments:

| | |
|---|---|
| Mathematics | Botany |
| Applied Mathematics | Zoology |
| Mathematical Statistics | Anatomy |
| Physics | Physiology |
| Chemistry | Geography |
| Geology | Psychology |
| | Entomology |

Examination:       Examination papers and/or practicals, with, in addition, such oral test or translation test as may be prescribed in an individual department.


## M.Sc.

Eligibility:       Hons. B.Sc. in chosen department.

Degree may be conferred in the following departments:

| | |
|---|---|
| Mathematics | Botany |
| Applied Mathematics | Zoology |
| Mathematical Statistics | Anatomy |
| Physics | Physiology |
| Chemistry | Geography |
| Geology | Psychology |
| | Entomology |

Examination:                    Either 2 or more examination papers or a dissertation.
                                Or a combination of examination papers and a
                                dissertation.


## Advanced Diploma in Agriculture

Curriculum:

1st yr:    Botany, Chemistry, Zoology, and Geography.

2nd yr:    The first half of the 2nd year is spent at Fort Hare.  The course
           of study includes:

   (1)  Field Husbandry:  Crops and their production; field crop
        trials; Veld and Veld management.

   (2)  Animal Husbandry:  Breed of cattle; management of beef and
        dairy cattle; the bull, cow, heifer and the calf.

   (3)  Soil Conservation:  Types, causes, control.

   (4)  Practical demonstrations and practical work on the Fort
        Hare Farm.

   The second half of the year will be spent in practical work.

3rd yr:    (1)  Field Husbandry:  Soil science; fertility and husbandry,
                soil conservation.

           (2)  Annual Husbandry:  Genetics; breeding, feeding and management.

           (3)  Agricultural Economics.

           (4)  Practical instruction on farm work.


## Faculty of Divinity

The following courses may be taken for the B.A. (Divinity) degree:

   (a)  Systematic Theology is a 3-year major course.
   (b)  Biblical Studies is a 3-year major course.
   (c)  Ecclesiastical History is a 2-year course but may be taken on
        a 1-year basis.
   (d)  Missiology I.
   (e)  Either Hellenistic Greek or Hebrew I.
   (f)  English and Afrikaans-Nederlands compulsory.
   (g)  A choice of 1 of the following:  Religious Philosophy I, Funda-
        mental Practical Theology I, Comparative Religious Studies,
        Ecumenical Studies I, Anthropology I, History I, Philosophy I.

## Diploma in Theology (Post-graduate)

Eligibility:          Bachelor's degree.

Duration of course:   2 academic years.

Curriculum:

> Biblical Studies I, II, III, Systematic Theology I, II,
> Ecclesiastical History I, Ecclesiastical History II or Systematic
> Theology III, English I or Afrikaans-Nederlands I, Hellenistic
> Greek or Hebrew I or Social Anthropology I or Psychology I or
> Philosophy I.

Diploma may be awarded with distinction.


## Faculty of Law

Candidates for the LL.B. degree must previously have been admitted to the
degree or status of Bachelor in some faculty other than Law.

No candidate is admitted to the 2nd year LL.B. examinations unless he has
completed a qualifying course in each of 3 languages, of which Latin I and
at least 1 of Afrikaans-Nederlands I and English I are compulsory.

Curriculum:

1st yr:   Roman-Dutch Law I, Roman-Dutch Law II, Roman Law I, Constitutional
          Law I, Public International Law.

2nd yr:   Roman-Dutch Law III, Roman Law II, Commercial Law, Constitutional
          Law II, Interpretation of Statutes and Conflict of Laws.

3rd yr:   Roman-Dutch Law IV, Commercial Law II, Procedure I (Evidence),
          Criminal Law I, South African Bantu Law or Comparative Law.

4th yr:   Roman-Dutch Law V, Jurisprudence, Procedure II, Criminal Law,
          Commercial Law III or South African Native Law.


## Faculty of Commerce

### B.Com.

Duration of course:   3 years.

Candidates may earn the degree under the following headings:   General and
Law.

General

1st yr:    Economics and Economic History I, Business Economics I, Accounting
           I, Mathematics, English I or Practical English or Afrikaans-Neder-
           lands I.

2nd yr:    Economics II, Business Economics II, Accounting II, Mercantile
           Law IA and IB.

           1 of the following:
           Psychology, History, Sociology, Mathematics, Economic Geography,
           General Introduction to Philosophy, History of Philosophy,
           Systematic Philosophy, Political Science, Economics History II,
           English I, Practical English, English II, Afrikaans-Nederlands I,
           Afrikaans-Nederlands II, Latin, Bantu Language.

3rd yr:    Economics III, Business Economics III.

           2 of the following:
           Accounting III, Auditing I, Cost Accounting, Economic History II,
           Mercantile Law IIA, IIB, IIC, Income Tax I, Income Tax II,
           Transportation.

Law

1st yr:    Economics and Economic History I, Business Economics I, Accounting
           I, Roman-Dutch Law I.

           1 of the following:
           English I, Latin I, Afrikaans-Nederlands I.

2nd yr:    Economics II, Business Economics II, Accounting II, Roman-Dutch
           Law II.

           1 of the following not taken in first year:
           English I, Latin I, Afrikaans-Nederlands I.

3rd yr:    Economics III, Business Economics III, Roman Law I, Roman-Dutch
           Law III.


Hons. B.Com.

Duration of course:    1 year after B.Com.

Examination is conducted by papers with, in addition, such oral test or
translation test as may be prescribed in an individual department.


M.Com.

Eligibility:           Hons. B.Com.

Examination for the degree consists of a dissertation and/or papers.

Degree awarded after submission of a thesis on an approved topic.

### D.Phil.

Eligibility:              M.Com. of not less than 2 years' standing.

Thesis is required.


## Faculty of Education

### B.Ed.

Eligibility:              Bachelor's degree and U.E.D.

Examination consists of 6 papers:

> Philosophy of Education, General Empirical Education, Special
> Empirical Education, History of Education, Method, Administration.


### M.Ed.

Eligibility:              B.Ed.

Dissertation required.


### D.Ed.

Eligibility:              M.Ed.

Thesis required.


## University Education Diploma (U.E.D.)

Eligibility:              Bachelor's degree.

Subjects of the examination are:

(1) Major subjects:
Philosophy of Education, Empirical Education, History of
Education, Method and Administration, Method of 2 principal
teaching subjects, Practical Teaching.

(2) Subsidiary subjects:
Blackboard Work, School Hygiene, School Librarianship or
Religious Instruction, Construction of Teaching Aids.

(3) Additional subjects:
Physical Education, Music and Choral Singing.

## University Education Diploma (Non-graduate)

Eligibility:             2 years' study towards a bachelor's degree.

Curriculum same as U.E.D. (graduate).


## South African Teachers' Diploma (Junior Secondary)

Trains teachers for the first 3 years of secondary school.

Eligibility:             Senior Certificate or equivalent.

Subjects:

<u>B.A.</u>:      5 first-year degree courses of which the vernacular and at least
          1 official language are compulsory, and 3 other courses of which
          2 must be school subjects and of which 1 may be the 2nd official
          language.

<u>B.Sc.</u>:     4 courses of which at least 3 must be school subjects.

<u>B.Com.</u>:    5 courses of which at least 3 must be school subjects, including
          Afrikaans-Nederlands I or Practical Afrikaans or English I or
          Practical English.

Subjects to be taken in the Professional Year:

<u>Group I:</u>   Principles of Education and Educational Psychology, School
          Organization, History of Education, Practical Teaching.

<u>Group II:</u>  Methods of teaching and content of the following school subjects
          in the first 3 years of the Secondary School Course:
          A modern language, 4 subjects from the following:
          Afrikaans, English, Vernacular, Latin, Social Studies, General
          Science, Biology, Physical Science, Agriculture, Arithmetic,
          Mathematics, Bookkeeping, Commerce and Commercial Arithmetic,
          Typewriting, Shorthand, Snelskrif.

<u>Group III:</u>  Compulsory subjects:
          Blackboard Work and Construction of Teaching Aids, Hygiene.
          Additional subjects:  Religious Instruction, Physical Culture,
          Gardening and Music.


## UNIVERSITY COLLEGE FOR INDIANS, Durban

Founded in 1961.

General entrance requirements:    <u>Either</u>  Matriculation Certificate of the
                                          Joint Matriculation Board
                                  <u>or</u>      A graduate of a university.

Faculties:

        Arts
        Science
        Commerce and Law

Language of instruction:      English

Degrees awarded:

| Faculty | Degree | Duration of course (years) |
|---|---|---|
| Arts | B.A. | 3 |
| | B.A. (S.S.) | 3 |
| | B.A. (Fine Arts) | 4 |
| Science | B.Sc. | 3 |
| | B.Sc. (Pharm.) | 3 |
| | B.Sc. (Hygiene) | 3 |
| Commerce and Law | B.Com. | 3 |
| | B.Admin. | 3 |
| | B.Ed. | 1 |

Diplomas awarded:

    Diploma Iuris
    Examination for Candidate Attorneys
    Diploma in Librarianship
    Diploma in Social Science
    Higher Primary Teachers' Diploma
    Junior Secondary Teachers' Diploma
    Secondary Teachers' Diploma (U.E.D.)

Faculty of Arts

B.A.

Candidates may qualify for a B.A. degree for 1 of the following: General, Education, Law.

Every B.A. curriculum must include at least 11 qualifying courses (a maximum of 5 in the 1st year, 4 in the 2nd year, and 3 in the 3rd year).

Examples of B.A. curriculum for General and Educational purposes:

I.   1st yr:   English I, Latin I, Geography I, History I, Sociology I.

      2nd yr:   English II, Latin II, Sociology II, Principles of Greek Culture.

3rd yr:    English III, Latin III.

II.   1st yr:    Mathematics I, Psychology I, Afrikaans-Nederlands I, Latin
                 I, Sociology I.

      2nd yr:    Mathematics II, Psychology II, Sociology II, English I.

      3rd yr:    Mathematics III, Psychology III.

III. 1st yr:     Geography I, History I, Practical Afrikaans I, English I,
                 Sociology I (or History of Art I).

      2nd yr:    Geography II, History II, English II, History of Art II.

      3rd yr:    Geography III, History III (or History of Art III).

Example of B.A. course with Law subjects leading to LL.B. degree:

      1st yr:    Private Law I, English I, Latin I, Afrikaans, Economics I.

      2nd yr:    Private Law II, Roman Law I, English II, Criminology I.

      3rd yr:    Private Law III, Roman Law II.

## B.A. (Social Science)

Duration of course:      Normal period of training is 3 years, but it can be
                         extended to cover 4 years if in the 4th year a
                         specialized course in Social Work is taken, e.g.
                         Cripple Care, Marriage Guidance and Counselling.
                         Degree certificate will be endorsed accordingly.

Curriculum consists of 11 or 12 courses and practical social work arranged
as follows:

   (1)   The 2 compulsory major subjects are Social Work and Sociology.

   (2)   Every curriculum includes at least 2 courses in Psychology, 1
         course in Social Law and 1 course in Criminology.

   (3)   The remaining courses are selected from the following:
         Psychology III, Economics I, II, and III, Criminology II and III,
         Politics I, General Introduction to Philosophy, History I,
         Mathematics I and a language course from Afrikaans-Nederlands I,
         Practical Afrikaans, English I, Practical English, French, German,
         or a special course in French or German.

Students must do practical social work with an institution or organization.

## B.A. (Fine Arts)

Duration of course:    4 years.

This course includes a teaching subject as a major in addition to the Fine Arts major.

1st yr:    (a)  Any 2 of the following courses:
                English, History, Latin, Afrikaans, Mathematics, History
                of Music, (Education and Psychology).
           (b)  Art Appreciation and History.
           (c)  General Drawing and Design.

2nd yr:    (a)  A 2nd course of (a) above.
           (b)  History of Art I.
           (c)  Either Painting I or Modelling I, or Design I.
           (d)  Drawing from Life I and Anatomy of the Human Figure.


## Faculty of Science

### B.Sc.

Candidates may qualify for a B.Sc. degree for 1 of the following directions:

        General
        Education
        Admission:  Medical, Dentistry, Pharmacy, Engineering*

(*Drawing must be taken in addition over the period.)

Every B.Sc. curriculum includes at least 9 qualifying courses over a period of 3 years (4 subjects in the 1st year, 3 in the 2nd year, and 2 in the 3rd year).

Candidates for the degree may present themselves for examination in the following subjects:

Group I:  Mathematics, Applied Mathematics, Physics, Chemistry, Botany, Zoology, Physiology, Hygiene, Geology, Geography, Psychology.

Group II: English I, Practical English, Afrikaans-Nederlands I, Practical Afrikaans, Latin I, Greek I, German I.

No candidate may obtain credit towards the B.Sc. degree for more than 1 course from Group II.

Example of a B.Sc. curriculum for General and Educational purposes:

    1st yr:  Chemistry I, Physics I, Mathematics I, Geography I (or
             English I, or Practical English, or Afrikaans I, or
             Practical Afrikaans).

    2nd yr:  Chemistry II, Physics II, Mathematics II.

    3rd yr:  Chemistry III, Physics III.

Example of a B.Sc. curriculum for Engineering (admission):

    1st yr:    Mathematics I, Applied Mathematics I, Physics I, Chemistry I.
    2nd yr:    Mathematics II, Applied Mathematics II, Physics II, Drawing.
    3rd yr:    Mathematics III, Applied Mathematics III, Drawing.


## B.Sc. (Pharmacy)

Curriculum includes the following courses:

    Chemistry (3 courses), Physics I, Botany I, Zoology I, Pharmaceutics
    I and II (including Forensic Pharmacy), Physiology, Pharmacology,
    Pharmacognosy and Pharmaceutical Chemistry.


## B.Sc. (Hygiene)

Main subjects:  Physiology, Hygiene.


## Faculty of Commerce and Law

## B.Com.

Candidates may qualify for the B.Com. degree under any one of the following
5 headings:

    General                         Statistics
    Administration                  Law
    Accounting

I.   General
    1st yr:    Economics and Economic History, Business Economics I,
               Accounting I, Mathematics or the separate part-courses,
               Elementary Theory of Finance and Statistical Methods A;
               English I or Practical English or Afrikaans-Nederlands
               or Practical Afrikaans.

    2nd yr:    Economics II, Business Economics II, Accounting II.
               2 separate part-courses:  Mercantile Law IA and Mercantile
               Law IB.

               1 of the following:
               Industrial Psychology, History, Sociology, Mathematics I,
               Economic Geography.

    3rd yr:    Economics III, Business Economics III.

               2 of the following:
               Accounting III, Auditing I, Economic History II.

Separate part-courses:  Mercantile Law IIA, Mercantile Law
IIB, Mercantile Law IIC.

## II.  Administration

1st yr:   Economics and Economic History I, Business Economics I,
Industrial Psychology I.
2 separate part-courses:  Statistical Methods A and
Statistical Methods B.
English I, or Practical English or Afrikaans-Nederlands I
or Practical Afrikaans.

2nd yr:   Economics II, Business Economics II.
2 separate part-courses:  Mercantile Law IA and Industrial
Law.
Industrial Psychology II, Accounting I.

3rd yr:   Economics III, Business Economics III, Industrial Psychology
III.

1 of the following:
Accounting II, Economic History II.

## III.  Accounting

1st yr:   Economics and Economic History I, Business Economics I,
Accounting I.
2 separate part-courses:  Elementary Theory of Finance and
Statistical Methods A.
English I or Practical English or Afrikaans-Nederlands I
or Practical Afrikaans.

2nd yr:   Economics II, Business Economics II, Accounting II.
2 separate part-courses:  Mercantile Law IA and Mercantile
Law IB.
Auditing I.

3rd yr:   Economics III, Business Economics III, Accounting III.

1 of the following:
Auditing II.
Separate part-courses:  Mercantile Law IIA, IIB, and IIC.
Cost Accounting.

## IV.  Statistics

1st yr:   Economics and Economic History I, Business Economics I,
Accounting I, Statistics I, English I or Practical English
or Afrikaans-Nederlands I or Practical Afrikaans.

2nd yr:   Economics II, Business Economics II, Statistics II, Accounting II.
2 separate part-courses:  Mercantile Law IA and Mercantile
Law IB.

3rd yr:   Economics III, Business Economics III, Statistics III.

          1 of the following:
          Accounting III, Auditing I, Cost Accounting, Mercantile
          Law IIA, IIB, and IIC.

## V.   Law

1st yr:   Economics and Economic History I, Business Economics I,
          Accounting I, Private Law I.

          1 of the following:
          Afrikaans-Nederlands I, English I, Latin I.

2nd yr:   Economics II, Business Economics II, Accounting II, Private
          Law II.

          1 of the following:
          Afrikaans-Nederlands I, English I, Latin I.

3rd yr:   Economics III, Business Economics III, Private Law III,
          Roman Law I.

## B.Admin.

Curriculum:

1st yr:   Accounting I, Political Science I, Economics and Economic
          History I, English I or Practical English or Afrikaans-Nederlands
          I or Practical Afrikaans.

          1 of the following:
          Private Law I, Industrial Psychology I, German I.

          2 of the separate part-courses:  Elementary Theory of Finance,
          Statistical Methods A, Statistical Methods B, French.

2nd yr:   Political Science II, Public Administration I, Economics II.

          2 of the following:
          Constitutional Law I, Public International Law, Industrial
          Psychology II, Accounting II, Statistics I.

3rd yr:   Political Science III, Public Administration II, Economics III.

          1 of the following:
          Industrial Psychology III, Municipal and Rural Administration,
          Transportation.

## Bachelor of Education

Eligibility:          Bachelor's degree and the University Education
                      Diploma, or B.P.Ed. degree, provided that a certifi-
                      cated teacher who does not possess the U.E.D. may be

admitted to the course of studies on the following conditions:

(a)  If he has had post-matriculation training he must

either  (i)  produce evidence of 5 years' satisfactory teaching experience;

or     (ii)  pass at one and the same examination a test in the 4 subjects Philosophy of Education, Empirical Education, History of Education, and Method and Administration.

(b)  If he has had pre-matriculation training, he must

(i)  produce evidence of 5 years' satisfactory teaching experience, and

(ii)  pass at one and the same examination a test in the 4 subjects Philosophy of Education, Empirical Education, History of Education, and Method and Administration:  Provided that the test mentioned above consists of the Papers for the examination for the University Education Diploma, and that no supplementary examinations shall be allowed.

Curriculum  extends over a period of at least 1 year and consists of the following subjects:

Philosophy of Education, General Empirical Education, Special Empirical Education, History of Education, Method, Administration.

## Regulations for Diploma Courses

### Diploma Iuris

Eligibility:     Matriculation or Matriculation Exemption Certificate
or  a certificate of conditional exemption issued to students from foreign countries.

Curriculum:

1st yr:   Private Law I, Mercantile Law I, Criminal Law, Practical Afrikaans or Afrikaans-Nederlands I or Practical English or English I.

2nd yr:   Private Law II, Criminal Procedure, Law of Evidence, Civil Procedure, Constitutional and Administrative Law.

3rd yr:   Private Law III, Roman Law, Mercantile Law II, South African Bantu and Native Law, South African Bantu Administration, Interpretation of Statutes.

Examination for Candidate Attorneys and Public Servants

The following persons are entitled to be registered as candidates for the Candidate Attorneys' Examination:

(a)  Any graduate by examination of a University.

(b)  Any person who has obtained the Matriculation Certificate of the Joint Matriculation Board or a certificate of full exemption from that Board.

Curriculum:

1st yr:   Private Law I, Mercantile Law I, Criminal Law.

2nd yr:   Private Law II, Criminal Procedure, Law of Evidence, Civil Procedure.

3rd yr:   Roman Law III, Private Law III, Mercantile Law II, Interpretation of Statutes, either Constitutional and Administrative Law or South African Bantu and Native Law and South African Bantu Administration.


Diploma in Librarianship

Candidates for this diploma shall hold a Matriculation or Matriculation Exemption Certificate.

The following subjects are prescribed:

1st yr:   Librarianship I, English I or Practical English, Afrikaans-Nederlands I or Practical Afrikaans.

          2 of the following:
          Economics and Economic History I, History I, Latin I, Psychology I, Sociology I, Systematic Philosophy.

2nd yr:   Librarianship II.

          1 of the following:
          German I or Special German, French I or Special French, Any 2nd course in a subject taken in the 1st year.

Candidates who complete the Diploma in Librarianship are exempted from 5 courses towards the B.A. degree.


Diploma in Social Science

Same requirements as for B.A. (Social Science) except that students will be accepted with a School-Leaving Certificate.

## Higher Primary Certificate

A candidate who has been successful in the Senior Certificate examinations will be admitted to the Higher Primary Teachers' Certificate course.

Each curriculum must include the following:

3 teaching subjects (minimum) selected from either the B.A., B.Com. or B.Sc. curriculum or a combination thereof. English I is compulsory.

2 years' professional training for full-time students and 3 years for extra-mural students.

## Junior Secondary Teachers' Diploma

A candidate who has been successful in the Senior Certificate examinations will be admitted to a Junior Secondary Teachers' Diploma course.

Each curriculum must include the following:

8 courses according to the B.A. or B.Com. or 7 courses for the B.Sc. curriculum, or combination thereof.

At least 2 of the above courses must be 2nd-year courses in teaching subjects.

1 year professional training (2 years extra-murally).

## Secondary Teachers' Diploma (U.E.D.) and Non-graduate Teachers' Diploma

This course is a full-time 1-year post-graduate course for students whose degree course included at least 1 major in a subject taught at school.

A non-graduate Secondary Teachers' Diploma course may be followed by students who require 1 academic year to complete the degree.

## UNIVERSITY OF SOUTH AFRICA, Pretoria

Bilingual university offering high quality correspondence courses leading to first and higher degrees.

Founded in 1919 as successor to University of Cape of Good Hope (founded in 1873). Gained autonomy 1946. Located in Pretoria since 1918, it is now to be transferred to Johannesburg. The government has not yet announced whether it will become an Afrikaans-medium residential university or continue its present correspondence program for external students.

The University Colleges for Coloureds, Bantus, and Indians award external
degrees of the University of South Africa. Their curriculums are determined
by examinations given by the University. Their relationship is similar to
that of extension divisions and parent institutions in the United States.

General entrance requirements:      Matriculation or Matriculation Exemption
                                    Certificate from Joint Matriculation
                                    Board.

Faculties:

        Arts                                  Science
        Divinity                              Law
        Social Science                        Commerce and Administration
        Education

Degrees awarded:

| Faculty | Degree | Duration of course (years) |
|---------|--------|----------------------------|
| Arts | B.A. | 3 |
| | Hons. B.A. | 4 |
| | M.A. | 1 |
| | D.Litt. and D.Phil. | |
| | B.A. in Fine Arts | 4 |
| | M.A. in Fine Arts | 2 |
| | B.Mus. | 4 |
| | M.Mus. | 1 |
| | D.Mus. | |
| | B.Bibl | 4 |
| | Certificate in School Librarianship | 2 |
| | Music Teacher's Diploma (S.A.) | 3 |
| | Diploma in Journalism | 2 |
| Divinity | B.A. (Theol.) | 3 |
| | B.D. | 3 |
| | M.Div. | |
| | D.D. | |
| | Lower Diploma in Theology | 2 |
| Social Science | B.A. (S.S.) | 3 |
| | Hons. B.A. (S.S.) | 4 |
| | M.A. (S.S.) | |
| | D.Phil. | |
| | Diploma in Social Work | 2 |
| Education | B.Ed. | 1 |
| | M.Ed. | 1 |
| | D.Ed. | |
| | University Education Diploma | 1 |

| | | |
|---|---|---|
| Science | B.Sc. | 3 |
| | Hons. B.Sc. | 4 |
| | M.Sc. | |
| | Ph.D. (Science) | |
| Law | LL.B. | 4 |
| | LL.M. | |
| | LL.D. | |
| | Diploma Iuris | 3 |
| | Alterum Diploma Iuris | 2 |
| | Attorneys' Admission Exam. | 3 |
| | Public Service Law Exam. | 3 |
| | Public Service Senior Law Exam. | 2 |
| Commerce and Administration | B.Com. | 3 |
| | Hons. B.Com. | 4 |
| | M.Com. | 1 |
| | D.Com. | |
| | B.Admin. | 3 |
| | Hons. B.Admin. | 4 |
| | M.Admin. | 1 |
| | D.Admin. | |
| | Diploma in Banking | 2 |
| | Diploma in Market Research and Advertising | 2 |
| | Certificate in Theory of Accountancy | 5 |

## Faculty of Arts

### Bachelor of Arts

Pass degree.

Duration of course:   3 years.

At least 11 qualifying courses, with at least 2 majors (i.e. 3 years' study in each major).

Major subjects chosen from the following:

| | |
|---|---|
| Afrikaans-Nederlands | History of Philosophy |
| Anthropology | Italian |
| Bantu Languages | Jewish Studies |
| Biblical Studies | Latin |
| Criminology | Mathematics |
| Economics | Native Administration |
| English | Political Science |
| French | Portuguese |
| Geography | Private Law |

German                          Psychology
Greek                           Russian
Hebrew                          Sociology
History                         Systematic Philosophy
History of Art                  Systematic Theology
History of Music

Majors requiring only 2 qualifying courses:

Roman Law                       Public Administration

Distinction in final course (i.e. 3rd year) gains pass with distinction.


Hons. Bachelor of Arts

Duration of course:   1 year after B.A.

Reading knowledge of French or German or sometimes Italian required in the
following:  African Studies, Classics, History (recommended), History of
Art, Political Science (recommended).

Latin I required for French and Italian.

Mathematical Statistics requires Mathematics III and Mathematical Statistics II.

Philosophy requires both Systematic and History of Philosophy in the B.A.,
one as a 3-year and one as a 2-year course.

Psychology has compulsory attendance at seminars and demonstrations, plus
original case-study.

Oral examinations in French, Italian, German, Physics (sometimes).

Pass in examination as a whole with minimum of 40% in every paper.

Distinction only with distinction aggregate.


Master of Arts

Eligibility:          Hons. B.A.

Duration of course:   At least 1 year after Hons. B.A.

Usually by dissertation.  Following are exceptions:

    (1)  Applied Mathematics:  3 papers or dissertation.
    (2)  Classics (Latin or Greek):  Dissertation and pass at least 1
         qualifying degree course in the other language.

(3)  French:  6 mos. in French-speaking country plus dissertation.
(4)  Italian:  6 mos. in Italy advised, plus dissertation.
(5)  Mathematics:  3 papers or dissertation.
(6)  Mathematical Statistics:  2 papers or dissertation.
(7)  Philosophy:  2 examinations and dissertation.
(8)  Physics:  4 papers, or 2 papers and dissertation.
(9)  Social Work:  Treatise and oral.

## Doctor of Literature and Philosophy

Eligibility:            M.A. in the subject.

Duration of course:    At least 2 years after M.A.

Thesis shall be an original work and a contribution to knowledge.

Oral or written examinations may be prescribed.

Degree in Classical Languages requires both Latin III and Greek III.

## Bachelor of Arts in Fine Arts

Admittance on special permission from Senate.

Permission to take examinations only after 6 months of practical work.

Curriculum:

1st yr:   Afrikaans or English, Modern Language or Latin or Greek or
          History or History of Music I, General Drawing and Design.

2nd yr:   Painting I or Design I or Modelling I, Drawing from Life I,
          History of Art I, Anatomy.

3rd yr:   Painting II or Design II or Modelling II, Drawing from Life II,
          History of Art II.

4th yr:   Painting III or Design III or Modelling III, History of Art III.

## Master of Arts in Fine Arts

Eligibility:            B.A. in Fine Arts.

Duration of course:    Minimum of 2 years.

Dissertation plus practical examination comprising 12 six-hour sessions.
50% of marks given to dissertation and practical each.

## Bachelor of Music

Eligibility:              Advanced Grade (VII) of the Music examinations of
                          the University of South Africa or another recognized
                          institution.
                          Pass in Music at Senior Certificate or Matriculation.
                          Approval of Head of Department of Music if practical
                          music standard equivalent to above.

Duration of course:    4 years.

1st yr:    Pass in at least 2 theoretical subjects and in principal practical
           subject.

Final yr: Original composition.


## Master of Music

Duration of course:    1 year after B.Mus.

Dissertation or original compositions.

Pass in French, German or Italian qualifying course or pass in a translation test from 1 of these into English or Afrikaans.

May be conferred with distinction.


## Doctor of Music

Duration of course:    At least 2 years after master's.

Either a thesis or an original set of compositions.


## Bachelor of Library Science (B.Bibl.)

Duration of course:    4 years.

At least 15 courses required.

3 fields:  Arts, Natural Science, Commerce and Administration.

2 foreign languages (1 modern) required unless passed at Matriculation.

If already in possession of a B.A. degree, may obtain B.Bibl. over 2 years
with at least 8 courses.

A certificate may be had after completion of 2 years of B.Bibl. for non-
graduates and after 1 year of B.Bibl. for graduates.

Bibliography compiled at end of 4th year, part of final examination.

3 months' practical library service.

## Certificate in School Librarianship

Eligibility:              School-Leaving Certificate and Teacher's Diploma.

Duration of course:   2 years.

## Music Teacher's Diploma (S.A.)

Eligibility:              Matriculation or Matriculation Exemption Certificate.

Duration of course:   3 years.

## Diploma in Journalism

Eligibility:              Degree with at least 1 qualifying course in Afrikaans-
                          Nederlands, English and a 3rd language.

Duration of course:   2 years with practical experience in the second.

## Diplomas in Bantu Studies (Higher and Lower), Native Administration, Police

Eligibility:              School-Leaving Certificate or equivalent.

    Lower Bantu Studies:              7 courses, not more than 5 in 1 year.

    Higher Bantu Studies:             Lower Diploma plus 5 courses.

    Higher Native Administration:     Lower Diploma (or exemption) plus 5
                                            courses.

    Police:                           3 years.

## Faculty of Divinity

## B.A. Theology

Duration of course:   3 years.

11 courses required:

```
Biblical Studies I, II and III       )
Systematic Theology I, II and III    )      2 majors
Ecclesiastical History I and II
Hebrew I
Greek I or Hellenistic Greek
Afrikaans-Nederlands I or English I
```

## Bachelor of Divinity

Eligibility:               B.A. and completion of Greek II, Hebrew II, Latin I.

Duration of course:   3 years.

May be conferred with distinction.

## Master of Divinity

Minimum of 2 years after Bachelor of Divinity.

Dissertation and study of a major and a subsidiary subject.   Examination has four 3-hour papers in major, two 3-hour papers in subsidiary.

Subjects to be chosen from:

```
Old Testament Language, Literature and Theology
New Testament Language, Literature and Theology
Systematic Theology
History of the Christian Church
```

## Doctor of Divinity

Eligibility:               M.Div. or B.D. plus oral doctoral examination in a major and 2 subsidiary subjects.

Duration of course:   At least 3 years after B.D. or 2 years after M.Div.

Submission of thesis.

## Lower Diploma in Theology

Eligibility:               School-Leaving Certificate or equivalent.

Duration of course:   2 years.

Curriculum:    Biblical Studies I and II, Systematic Theology I and II, Pastoral Theology.

1 of:  Afrikaans-Nederlands or Practical Afrikaans, English or Practical English.

2 of:   Ecclesiastical History I and II, Greek I or
Hellenistic Greek, Hebrew I.

## Faculty of Social Science

### B.A. in Social Science

Duration of course:    3 years or 4 years if specialized field studied.

11 or 12 courses:   3 courses in Social Work and 3 courses in Sociology or
Psychology.  At least 2 courses in Psychology or Sociology.  Remainder of
courses to be chosen from General Arts subjects.

Practical work each year in recognized welfare organization, obtaining
50% average for year's practical work.  Each year with different organization.

4th-year specialization in either Cripple Care or Marriage Guidance and
Counselling.

### Hons. B.A. in Social Science

May be taken in following departments:  Anthropology, Criminology,
Economics, Psychology, Social Work, Sociology.

Duration of course:   1 year after B.A. in Social Science.

Pass mark required in examination as a whole with a minimum of 40% in each
paper.

### M.A. in Social Science

Eligibility:           Hons. B.A. in Social Science.

Duration of course:    At least 1 year after Hons. B.A. in Social Science.

Same departments as Hons. B.A. in Social Science.

Dissertation required in all departments.  Social Work requires treatise
and oral.

### Doctor of Philosophy

Eligibility:           M.A. in Social Science.

Duration of course:    At least 2 years after master's.

Thesis dealing with subject in Social Science.


## Diploma in Social Work

Eligibility:               Degree and pass in at least Sociology I or Psychology
                           I.

Duration of course:    2 years.

Practical work each year in recognized welfare organization.


## Faculty of Education

## Bachelor of Education

Eligibility:               Bachelor's degree and University Education Diploma
                           (U.E.D.).
                    or     B.P.Ed.
                           May be admitted with U.E.D. with sufficient teaching
                           experience plus examinations normally given for U.E.D.

Duration of course:    At least 1 year.

Curriculum:        Philosophy of Education, General Empirical Education,
                   Special Empirical Education, History of Education, Method,
                   Administration.


## Master of Education

Duration of course:    At least 1 year after B.Ed.

Dissertation on Education.


## Doctor of Education

Eligibility:               Master of Education of at least 4 years' standing,
                    or     Master of Education of 3 years' standing including
                           at least 1 year devoted entirely to approved
                           research work.

Thesis in field of Education.

## University Education Diploma (U.E.D.)

Eligibility:        Degree and teacher's certificate, equivalent training for certificate or 2 years' employment as teacher, plus degree courses as follows:
1 third, 2 second courses (principal teaching subjects)
    or    1 third, 1 second and 2 first courses.

Duration of course:   At least 1 year.

Curriculum:    Philosophy of Education, Empirical Education, History of Education, Method and Administration, Method of the 2 principal teaching subjects for secondary school, Practical Teaching.

## Faculty of Science

## Bachelor of Science

Duration of course:   Minimum of 3 years.

At least 9 qualifying courses with at least 2 majors, required.

Major subjects (with 3 qualifying courses):

| | |
|---|---|
| Applied Mathematics | Hygiene |
| Astronomy | Mathematics |
| Botany | Physics |
| Chemistry | Physiology |
| Geography | Psychology |
| Geology | Zoology |

Major subject (with 2 qualifying courses):

Mathematical Statistics

## Syllabuses for first 2 years of Science subjects:

Applied Mathematics

    I.   Dynamics, Statics.

   II.  Two-dimensional motion of a particle, a rigid body and of a system. Generalized coordinates with applications. Three-dimensional vector algebra and analysis. Forces in three-dimensional virtual work. Stability of equilibrium, with applications.

Astronomy

    I.   Spherical trigonometry and astronomy, moon, stars, planetary system, refraction, radial velocity and proper motion.

    II.  More physical part of astronomy, together with the required basis of physics itself.

Botany

    I.   External morphology of the seed plants, different forms of stem, leaf and root. The plant cell. Internal structure of the seed plants. Principles of plant physiology.
Ecology of South African seed plants. Bacteria. General characteristics of Dicotyledons and Monocotyledons. Economic botany. Genetics.
Practical work (6-hour examination) deals with all above sections including interpretation of experiments.

    II.  Morphology, ecology and taxonomy of Thallophyta, Bryophyta, and Pteridophyta. Internal morphology of vascular plants. Cytology. Genetics.
Practical (6-hour examination) deals with all above sections.

Chemistry

    I.   General and physical, inorganic, organic.
Practical (7-hour examination) includes simple preparations, elementary trimetric analysis, simple qualitative analysis, simple gravimetric analysis.

    II.  Inorganic and analytical, physical and organic.
Practical two(7-hour dxaminations) in analytical and inorganic, and organic and physical.

Geography

    I.   Introduction to physical geography and human geography.
Practical exercises and making and use of maps (4-hour examination).

    II.  Regional geography, climatology and meteorology and biogeography.
Practical exercises on above (4-hour examination).

Geology

    I.   Crystallography, mineralogy, petrology, physical, structural, historical and economic geology.
Practical (6-hour examination) on description and identification with use of maps and section drawing.

    II.  Crystallography, crystal optics and mineralogy, and petrology.
Practical (two 6-hour examinations) identification and description with preparation of rock sections.

Hygiene

I.  The cell, growth, man, coordination, personal hygiene, bacteria,
    communicable diseases of school children, parasitism, principles
    of heredity.
    Practical (6-hour examination).  Use of microscope, dissection,
    anatomical models.

II.  Environmental factors affecting health, maternity, child and
     school hygiene, environmental hygiene, public health principles.
     Practical (6-hour examination).

Mathematics

I.  Trigonometry, algebra, geometry, calculus.

II.  Linear algebra, geometry, complex numbers, convergence,
     differential calculus, partial differentiation, differential
     equations.

Physics

I.  Mechanics, properties of matter, heat, optics, sound, electricity
    and magnetism, magnetostatics, current electricity, electronics
    and nuclear physics.
    Practical (6-hour examination).

II.  Mechanics, properties of matter, heat, light, electricity and
     magnetism, electrostatics and magnetostatics, current electricity,
     atomic and nuclear physics, sound.
     Practical (6-hour examination).

Physiology

I.  Microscopy of tissues and chief organs of the body, general
    physiology of muscles and nerves, the heart, blood, digestion,
    urinary system, senses, respiration, basal metabolism, endocrine
    glands, reproduction.  Biochemistry.
    Practical (6-hour examination), histology, experimental physio-
    logy and chemical investigations.

II.  Course I in more detail, compositions of foods, biochemistry,
     blood tests, hormones, and energy metabolism.
     Practical (6-hour examination).

Psychology

I.  The science psychology, animal behaviour, brain and nervous
    system, maturation and development, remembering and learning
    process, imagination and thinking, motivation, feeling and
    emotion, frustration and conflict, attention and perception,
    vision, hearing and lower senses, intellectual abilities,
    personality.

II.  Developmental psychology and social psychology.
     Practical work:  Introduction to interviewing techniques, studies
     in connection with above.

Zoology

   I.  Taxonomy, anatomy and physiology of various life forms.
       Introduction to study of cytology, histology and early embryo-
       logy of frog.  Mendel's laws of heredity.
       Practicals (two 3-hour papers), microscopic studies and
       dissections.

   II.  Anatomy, development and mutual relationships of certain phyla.
        Practicals (two 4-hour papers), microscopic studies and
        dissections.

Mathematical Statistics

   I.  Probability theory, frequency distributions, practical appli-
       cations.

   II.  Probability theory, frequency distributions, practical appli-
        cations.


40% total marks awarded to practical work, except in Physics where 30%.

To be admitted to Physics I, must have at least 33 1/3% at Matriculation.


## Hons. Bachelor of Science

Duration of course:   At least 1 year after bachelor's.

Awarded in following:

        Anatomy                          Mathematics
        Applied Mathematics              Mathematical Statistics
        Botany                           Physics
        Chemistry                        Physiology
        Geography                        Psychology
        Geology                          Zoology


## Master of Science

Duration of course:   At least 2 years after Hons. B.Sc.

Awarded in same departments as Hons. B.Sc.

## Doctor of Philosophy (Ph.D. Science)

Duration of course:   At least 2 years after master's.

Thesis in Mathematics, Natural Science or Applied Sciences.


## Faculty of Law

## Bachelor of Laws (LL.B.)

Eligibility:                Bachelor's degree of another faculty.  Must be at
                            least 21 when LL.B. conferred.

Duration of course:   4 years.

Curriculum includes:

          5 courses in Private Law, 2 courses in Roman Law, 2 courses in
          Constitutional Law, 2 courses in Criminal Law, at least 2 courses
          in Commercial Law, 2 courses in Procedure, 1 course in Inter-
          pretation of Statutes and Private International Law, 1 course in
          South African Bantu Law or Comparative Law, 1 course in Juris-
          prudence.

Prerequisite:               Latin I and 2 language courses.

Pass with distinction:  Distinction aggregate for 4th-year courses at
same examination and aggregate of 70% for 3rd-year courses.


## Master of Laws (LL.M.)

Duration of course:   At least 1 year after bachelor's.

Dissertation on subject in field of Law.


## Doctor of Laws (LL.D.)

Eligibility:                LL.M. or LL.B. plus doctoral examination in major
                            subject and 2 subsidiary subjects in field of Law.

Duration of course:   At least 4 years after LL.B.

Thesis is required.

## Diploma Iuris

Eligibility:                Matriculation or Matriculation Exemption Certificate.

Duration of course:     3 years.

15 courses required.  Matriculation standard in Latin required for Roman Law.

Distinction:  Pass in all 3rd-year courses simultaneously with aggregate of at least 70%.


## Alterum Diploma Iuris

Eligibility:              Diploma Iuris or equivalent.

Duration of course:     2 years.

9 courses required.

Distinction:  Pass in all 2nd-year courses simultaneously with aggregate of at least 70%.


## Attorneys' Admission Examination

Eligibility:              Matriculation or Matriculation Exemption Certificate.

Duration of course:     3 years.

12 courses required.  Matriculation standard in Latin required for Roman Law.

Distinction pass as for Diploma Iuris.


## Public Service Law Examination

Eligibility:              School-Leaving Certificate.

Duration of course:     3 years.

11 courses required.

Distinction pass as for Diploma Iuris.


## Public Service Senior Law Examination

Eligibility:              Diploma Iuris or Public Service Law Examination, or
                          equivalent.

Duration of course:     2 years.

8 courses required.

Distinction pass as for Alterum Diploma Iuris.


## Faculty of Commerce and Administration

### Bachelor of Commerce

Duration of course:    3 years.

Curricula offered in General, Administration, Accounting, Statistics or Law.

Economics, Business Economics and Accounting compulsory in all 5 programs.

Principal subjects:

Accounting                          Industrial Psychology
Auditing                            Private Law
Business Economics                  Statistics
Economics

Distinction pass if distinction mark in final course of principal subject.


### Hons. Bachelor of Commerce

Duration of course:    1 year after B.Com.

Following departments:

Accounting                          Economics
Auditing                            Industrial Psychology
Business Economics                  Statistics

Pass with minimum of 40% in each paper.

Distinction with distinction aggregate.


### Bachelor of Administration

Duration of course:    3 years.

Principal subjects:

Accounting                          Native Administration
Economics                           Political Science
Industrial Psychology               Public Administration

Distinction with distinction mark in final course of principal subject.

## Hons. Bachelor of Administration

Duration of course:    1 year after B.Admin.

Following departments:

| | |
|---|---|
| Economics | Political Science |
| Industrial Psychology | Public Administration |
| Native Administration | |

Pass and distinction as for Hons. B.Com.

Industrial Psychology Hons. requires practical work and case-study report.

## Master of Commerce and Master of Administration

Duration of course:    At least 1 year after Hons. Bachelor's.

Same departments as respective Hons. Bachelor's degrees.

Dissertation required, except Statistics:    3 papers, or 1 paper and dissertation.

## Doctor of Commerce and Doctor of Administration

Duration of course:    At least 2 years after master's.

Thesis in field of Economics, Commerce, Industrial Psychology, Political Science or Statistics.

## Diploma in Banking

Eligibility:          School-Leaving Certificate.

Duration of course:   At least 2 years.

13 courses required.

## Diploma in Market Research and Advertising

Eligibility:          A degree.

Duration of course:   2 years.

8 courses required.

Certificate in Theory of Accountancy

Eligibility:              Matriculation or Matriculation Exemption Certificate.

Duration of course:   5 years.

20 courses required.


VOCATIONAL AND TECHNICAL EDUCATION

COMMERCIAL TRAINING

        W H I T E ,   C O L O U R E D   A N D   A S I A T I C S

Commercial High Schools and Technical Colleges

Entrance requirements:        Completion Standard VII (9 yrs. of schooling).

National Junior Certificate (Commerce) is awarded after 1-year post-Standard VII course.  Pass in 6 subjects of which not more than 4 may be commercial and 2 must be the official languages.  The following non-examination subjects are also included:

            Religious Instruction, Singing or Speech Guidance, Physical
            Education and Civics.


National Commercial Certificate (Standard IX)

Candidate must pass in at least 6 subjects from the following:

Group I   -Afrikaans A or English A.

Group II  -Afrikaans A or B or English A or B (different language from I).

Group III-4 of the following:  Shorthand (English), Shorthand (Afrikaans),
        Bookkeeping, Commerce, Commercial Arithmetic, Economics,
        Mathematics, Mercantile Law, Typewriting.

Non-examination subjects for full-time students:

            Religious Instruction, Singing and the Appreciation of Music or
            Drama and Speech Training, Physical Education.

Full-time students at commercial vocational schools must take at least 3 commercial vocational subjects.

Any candidate obtaining an aggregate of at least 60% in the full examination will be awarded a first-class certificate, provided he qualifies for the certificate at one and the same examination.

## National Senior Certificate (Standard X)

See SECONDARY EDUCATION section for details.

## National Diploma in Commerce

Candidate must pass 5 subjects selected from the following:

Group I   -Afrikaans A or English A.

Group II  -Afrikaans A or B or English A or B (different language from I).

Group III-3 of the following:  Shorthand, Snelskrif, Bookkeeping, Commerce, Commercial Arithmetic, Economics, Mercantile Law, Typewriting.

Any candidate obtaining an aggregate of at least 60% in the full examination is awarded a first-class certificate, provided he qualifies for this certificate at one and the same examination.

## National Secretarial Certificate (Private Secretaries)

This course gives candidates an opportunity of obtaining a certificate in basic secretarial subjects after a period of full-time intensive study of at least 1 year after Standard X.

The examination is conducted at institutions under the control of the Department of Education, Arts and Science.

Entrance requirements:          Matriculation or School-Leaving Certificate of the Joint Matriculation Board or the National Senior Certificate or the Senior School-Leaving Certificate of the provincial education departments or a recognized equivalent certificate

Both official languages must be endorsed on the certificate.  Candidates for the certificate must have a minimum full-time attendance of 4 consecutive school quarters at the date of the 1st examination recognized for the certificate.

The following subjects are prescribed for the course.  Grades indicated are the minimum standard recognized.  The actual standard attained in a subject will be indicated on the certificate.

Group I   -Typewriting (senior), Shorthand or Snelskrif (senior), Afrikaans
           A or English A (Diploma), General Secretarial Practice or
           Commerce (Std. IX).

Group II  -1 of the following subjects, not taken under Group I:  Shorthand
           or Snelskrif, Afrikaans A or B (Diploma), different language from
           I, Bookkeeping (Std. IX) or Commercial Arithmetic (Std. IX).

Group III-The following non-examination subjects:  Office Routine, Speech
           Guidance and Deportment, Practical Elementary Bookkeeping if
           Bookkeeping or Commercial Arithmetic (from Group II) is not
           selected.

Any candidate obtaining an aggregate of at least 60% in the full examination will be awarded a first-class certificate, provided he qualifies
for this certificate at one and the same examination.


## National Teachers' Diploma in Commerce

Several full-time courses are provided for the National Teachers' Diploma
in Commerce:

   (1)   A 3-year full-time course for students with the National Senior
         Certificate.

   (2)   A 2-year full-time course for non-graduates with a recognized
         teachers' certificate.

   (3)   A 2-year full-time course for non-graduates with the National
         Diploma in Commerce.

   (4)   A 1-year full-time course for holders of a professional diploma
         in commerce or in accountancy.


## Secretarial Schools

A secretarial school is a separate entity within the Department of Commerce.

A full-time post-Standard X course leads to the National Secretarial
Certificate (Private Secretaries).

In addition, intensive secretarial, shorthand/typist and clerk/typist
courses as well as intensive courses in mechanized arithmetic or calculating
machine operation are offered.


## Evening and Part-Time Schools of Commerce

Courses offered in Commerce, Administration, Accounting, Modern Languages
and Adult Education.

Commercial Group Courses prepare students for the National Examinations of the Department of Education, Arts and Science. Individual subjects or complete groups may be taken for certificates ranging from the National Standard VI Certificate to the National Senior Certificate (with or without Matriculation Exemption) and the National Diploma in Commerce.

Intensive commercial, secretarial and language courses are provided from beginners' to diploma grades. Calculating Machine courses leading to National Certificates in Mechanized Arithmetic are also offered. Afrikaans courses leading to the following public examinations are offered:

(i)   Afrikaans (A or B).
      Standards VI, VII, VIII, IX and X and Diploma Grade.

(ii)  National Bilingual Certificate.

(iii) Taalbond.

Instruction is offered in the following professional examinations:

The Chartered Institute of Secretaries
The Institute of Bankers in South Africa
The Institute of Administration and Commerce of South Africa
The Institute of Industrial Administration
The Institute of Certified Bookkeepers of South Africa
The Office Management Society
The Institute of Municipal Treasurers and Accountants
The South African Accountants Societies General Examining Board
The Institute of Cost and Works Accountants
The Institute of Transport
The Corporation of Secretaries
Public Service Diploma in Accounting and Auditing
South African Institute of Management

## B A N T U

Commercial education is offered at the secondary level and is integrated in the general system.

A Junior Certificate course with a commercial bias is offered.

Subjects: A Bantu language, English, Afrikaans, History, Geography, and 2 of the following: Bookkeeping, Commerce, Typewriting, Shorthand, General Science, Chemistry, Biology.

A similar Senior Certificate course is offered.

Advanced commercial training is available at the University colleges, teacher-training or technical colleges, and through private correspondence colleges.

TECHNICAL TRAINING

## W H I T E ,   C O L O U R E D   A N D   A S I A T I C S

### Technical College or Technical High School

Minimum entrance qualification:     Passing of Standard V.

### National Junior Certificate

Restricted to pupils who have obtained the National Standard VII Certificate or a Standard VII Certificate of any of the provincial education
departments.

Full-time students follow a course comprising:

> Afrikaans, English, Mathematics, Physical Science, Machine
> Drawing or Building Drawing, Workshop Practice and Theory,
> Singing and Appreciation of Music, Religious Instruction and
> Physical Education.

### National Intermediate Certificate

Primarily for full-time students proceeding to the National Senior Certificate Course or to the National Certificate Course (Matriculation Exemption).

Entrance requirements:        National Junior Certificate.

Full-time students follow a course comprising:

> Afrikaans, English, Mathematics, Physical Science, Machine
> Drawing or Building Drawing, Applied Mechanics or Workshop
> Practice and Theory, Singing and Appreciation of Music,
> Religious Instruction and Physical Education.

### National Senior Certificate

Entrance requirements:        National Intermediate Certificate.

Course comprises the same subjects as that for the Intermediate Certificate.

### Matriculation Exemption

The National Senior Technical Certificate is not accepted by the Joint
Matriculation Board for purposes of exemption from the Matriculation

examination and does not admit holders to a degree course at a university. Full exemption from the Matriculation Certificate on the grounds of the National Senior Technical Certificate may be granted if a prescribed combination of subjects is taken and this qualifies the candidate for admission to a university.

## Technical Class Attendance of Apprentices

Where facilities are available all apprentices must, during the first 2 years of normal apprenticeship, attend technical classes 1 day per week during ordinary working hours, or, where facilities for attendance of classes up to the National Technical Certificate Part II do not exist, follow correspondence courses of the Witwatersrand Technical College.

## Part-Time Technical Courses

## National Technical Certificates

Entrance requirements:          Completion of Standard VII course.

3 years part-time study.

The National Technical Certificate (Part I) examination is conducted on the work of the 1st-year course, the National Technical Certificate (Part II) examination on that of the 2nd-year course, and the National Technical Certificate (Part III) examination is conducted on the work of the 3rd-year course.

Each certificate is awarded on a minimum of 3 subjects.

For the National Technical Certificate (Part III) Engineering course, a minimum of 3 subjects selected from the following:

> Aircraft Construction and Drawing II
> or Machine Construction and Drawing II
> or Electrical Construction and Drawing II
> or Drawing for Boilermakers and Structural Steelworkers III
> Mathematics III or Mathematics (Senior) or Workshop Calculations III (Engineers)
> Airconditioning II
> Applied Mechanics II or Elementary Strength of Materials
> Electronics II
> Electronics III
> Geology III or Senior Geology
> Heat Engines II or Internal Combustion Engines II
> Physical Science III or Physics III or Chemistry III or Senior Instrumentation III

For the National Technical Certificate (Part III) Building Course, a minimum of 3 subjects selected from the following:

Group I -Building Construction III or Mathematics III or Workshop Calculations III (Gen.).

Group II -At least 2 from the following:

Mathematics III, Applied Mechanics (Builders or Engineers) II or Elementary Strength of Materials, Chemistry III or Physics III or Physical Science III, Drawing and Decorative Design II, Drawing for Plumbers II, Brickwork III.

In addition to the National Technical Certificate (Parts I, II and III) courses in Building and Engineering, special courses for the National Technical Certificates are given in the following:

Aircraft Engineering
Baking
Boatbuilding
Boot and Shoe Manufacturing
Butchers
Chemistry
Furniture
Telecommunications
Hairdressing

Highway Engineering
Horticulture and Landscape Gardening
Production Engineering
Tailoring
Vehicle Building
Armature Winding
Instrument Mechanics
Electric Lifts

## National Technical Certificate (Mine Samplers)

May be taken part-time over a period of 1 or 2 years.

Candidate must produce evidence that he has been employed as a mine sampler for a period of at least 1 year immediately prior to the completion of the course.

## Advanced Part-Time Technical Courses

The Department of Education, Arts and Science has also instituted several courses at the post-matriculation or semi-professional level.

## National Advanced Technical Certificates (Parts I and II)

The course for this certificate extends over 2 years' part-time study.

Entrance requirements:      National Technical Certificate or National Senior Technical Certificate.

A minimum of 3 subjects must be selected for each grade.

The Advanced Technical Certificate (Part I) is awarded on the 1st-year
course and the Advanced Technical Certificate (Part II) on the 2nd-year
course.


## Technical High Schools

Technical colleges often have a technical high school attached which provides full-time vocational training for boys who intend to be apprentices
or proceed to Engineering training in a university.

Courses available from the National Technical Standard VI Certificate to
the National Senior Technical Certificate (Standard X) with or without
Matriculation Exemption.


## Apprenticeship Schools

Apprenticeship schools with part-time courses are offered by technical
colleges.  These provide courses specifically designed for indentured
apprentices but may be taken by others.  They provide training for the
Elementary Technical Certificate (Standard VII), the National Technical
Certificates Parts I, II and III, and the National Advanced Technical
Certificates, Parts I and II.


## Advanced and Professional Courses

Part-time advanced technical courses are intended primarily for students
who are preparing for the National Advanced Technical Certificates (2 yrs.
post-Standard X), for the National Diplomas in Building, Engineering,
Mining and other fields, for the National Diploma for Chemical Technicians,
for the National Diploma in Medical Technology and for Government Certificates of Competency.

Part-time courses leading to professional examinations of the following
are offered:

> Institutions of Civil, Electrical, Mechanical, Structural,
> Production and Automobile Engineering (London)
>
> Royal Society for the Promotion of Health
> (a)  Sanitary Health Inspectors
> (b)  Tropical Hygiene for Sanitary Inspectors
>
> Institute for Sewage Purification Ministry of Transport

Sandwich courses in Mechanical, Electrical and Radio Engineering, Telecommunications, Surveying, Draughtmanship and Sugar Technology leading to
National Diplomas for Technicians.

## National Certificate for Technicians (Mining)

This certificate is taken on a part-time basis over a period of 2-3 years.

3 courses are given:  Mine Assayers, Mine Surveyors, Metalliferous Mining.

Candidates must produce evidence of at least 1 year of applicable practical experience immediately prior to the completion of the course.

## National Certificate in Telecommunications (Civil Service)

This certificate is obtained in a 3-year sandwich course.

In the 1st year, pupil technicians do a $4\frac{1}{2}$ months' course at a technical college and during both the 2nd and 3rd years a $4\frac{1}{2}$ months' course of study is carried out at a departmental training center of the Engineering Division of the Post Office.  The rest of the time is spent on practical work.

9 specialized courses in telecommunications subjects are provided:

> Automatic Exchanges, Outstation Maintenance, Urban Subscribers'
> Maintenance, Outdoor Construction, Telegraphs, Radio, Mechanical
> Duties, Drawing Office Duties, Urban Carriers' Maintenance

## National Diploma for Technicians

Entrance requirements (for technician courses in general):

> Pass in Mathematics and Physics or Physical
> Science or an equivalent subject on the
> Senior Certificate level.

These requirements, however, do not apply to the first 4 courses in Mining and Metallurgy below.

## Mining and Metallurgy

Courses are taken on a part-time basis over a period of 3-4 years.

The National Diploma for Technicians is awarded in the following fields:

| | |
|---|---|
| Assaying and Metallurgical | Coal Mining |
| Analysis | Reduction Working |
| Metalliferous Mining | Metallurgy |

In the course in Metallurgy only, a pass in Mathematics and Physics or Physical Science or an equivalent subject on the Senior Certificate or National Technical Certificate III level is required.

## Engineering

Sandwich courses.

These courses are taken over 4 years. A period of 4½ months each year is devoted to full-time study. Students return to their employers for the remainder of the year for their practical training.

The National Diploma for Technicians is awarded in the following fields:

Civil Engineering
Electronic Engineering
Marine Engineering
Production Engineering
Signal Engineering
Electrical Engineering (heavy current)
Mechanical Engineering
Radio Engineering

## Chemical

The course for the National Diploma for Chemical Technicians consists of 2 parts which are taken over a total period of 3 years part-time study. There are 3 fields of study: Analytical Chemistry, Plant Operation, Bio-chemistry.

## Telecommunications (Public Service)

The National Diploma for Telecommunications Technicians (General) (Public Service) is obtained by following a 4-year sandwich course. Pupil technicians do a 4½ months' course at a departmental training center of the Engineering Division of the Post Office during their 3rd and 4th years. The rest of the time is devoted to practical training.

## National Certificate in Sugar Technology

Entrance requirements:       Standard VIII or Junior Certificate with Mathematics and Physical Science.

The Natal Technical College is the only institution offering a course in Sugar Technology. This 3-year sandwich course is conducted in cooperation with the South African Sugar Technologists' Association.

## Higher National Diploma for Technicians

After obtaining the National Diploma for Technicians in Mechanical or Electrical Engineering, technicians may follow a 2-year part-time course for the above diploma in one of two fields: Electrical Engineering or Mechanical Engineering.

## Correspondence Courses

The Cape Technical College conducts correspondence courses for the following
certificates:

        National Junior Certificate
        National Senior Certificate (General Group)
        National Senior Certificate (Matriculation Exemption Certificate)
        Institute of Administration and Commerce (S.A.)
        Shorthand Theory, Speed and Typewriting
        Special Language Courses:
          Afrikaans for Beginners
          Afrikaans Laer and Hoer Taalbond
          Xhosa Junior and Senior Courses
          German Junior and Senior Courses

The Witwatersrand Technical College has established a separate department
to deal with its correspondence courses.  The following courses are available:

        Introductory - equivalent to Standard V
        National Standard VI Certificate (General)
        National Standard VII Certificate (Commercial)
        National Senior Certificate (Matriculation Exemption)
        National Teachers' Diploma (Technical)
        National Teachers' Diploma (Workshop)
        National Technical Courses for Mechanical, Electrical and
          Building Trades
        National Technical Standard VI Courses
        Elementary Technical Certificate and National Technical Standard
          VII Certificate
        National Technical Certificate Part I and National Junior Certi-
          ficate (Technology) Standard VIII
        National Technical Certificate Part II and National Intermediate
          Certificate (Technology) Standard IX
        National Technical Certificate Part III and National Senior
          Certificate (Technology) Standard X
        Advanced Technical Certificate, Parts I and II
        National Engineering and Building Diplomas
        National Diploma in Draughtmanship
        National Diploma in Production Engineering
        National Technical Course-Mine Samplers:
          National Technical Certificate - Part I
          National Technical Certificate - Part II
          National Technical Certificate - Part III
          Special Mining Ventilation Course
        National Certificate for Technicians in the following fields:
          Mine Assayers
          Mine Surveyors
          Metalliferous Mining
        National Diploma for Technicians in the following fields:
          Assaying and Metallurgical Analysis

      Metalliferous Mining
      Reduction Workers
      Metallurgy
  National Technical Courses for Printers:
    National Printers' Certificate - Preliminary
    National Printers' Certificate - Intermediate
    National Printers' Diploma
  National Technical Courses for Hairdressers:
    National Technical Certificate - Part I
    National Technical Certificate - Part II
    National Technical Certificate - Part III
  National Diploma for Medical Technologists
    Intermediate Course
    Qualifying Course
  Course for Electrical Wiremen
  South African Railways and Harbours Promotion Courses
  Courses for Government Certificates of Competency:
    Mechanical and Electrical Engineers' Certificate of Competency
    Mine Manager's Certificate of Competency
    Mine Surveyor's Certificate of Competency
    Mine Overseer's Certificate of Competency
    Mine Assayer's Certificate of Competency
  Paper Manufacturers' Association Diploma:
    Preliminary
    Final
  Graphical Analysis of Optometric Findings
  Course for the Examination of the South African Institute of
    Valuers

Advanced part-time technical courses for the above certificates are given in:

| | |
|---|---|
| Engineering | Telecommunications |
| Building | Mining |
| Aircraft Engineering | Production Engineering |
| Boatbuilding | Structural Engineering |
| Building Inspection | Tailoring |
| Chemistry | |

In addition to the above A.T.C. courses a number of Diploma courses are offered:

| | |
|---|---|
| Engineering | Production Engineering |
| Building | Structural Engineering |
| Aircraft Engineering | Tailoring |
| Chemistry | |

# B A N T U

Boys obtaining Standard VII School-Leaving Certificate (3rd class pass)
may take 2-year trade course.  Girls may take 2-year courses in Dressmaking or Home Management.

3-year technical courses for boys with Standard VI continuation certificate
(1st or 2nd class pass) leading to Junior Certificate-Technical examination.

Advanced technical courses - entrance requirements:  Junior Certificate.

2-year course in homecraft - entrance requirements:  Standard IV.

## Junior Certificate - Technical

Curriculum:  Technical subject, Bantu language, Afrikaans, English,
             Arithmetic, Social Studies, Workshop Calculation or
             Mathematics.

## HOME ECONOMICS TRAINING

8 housecraft high schools conducted by the Department of Education, Arts
and Science.

Entrance requirements:        Passing of Standard V.

Courses are offered for the following certificates:

        National Standard VI Certificate (Domestic Science)
        National Standard VII Certificate (Domestic Science)
        National Junior Certificate (Domestic Science)
        National Intermediate Certificate (Domestic Science)
        National Senior Certificate (Domestic Science)

The subjects and curricula for the courses are, in many cases, the same,
the syllabuses naturally being graded, and the respective certificates are
awarded to candidates who have followed the prescribed courses and satisfied
the examination requirements of 6 of the subjects selected as follows:

Group I  - Official language (higher grade)

Group II - Official language (higher and lower grade)

Group III- Bookkeeping or Physiology and Hygiene

Group IV - (a)  Dressmakers' course:  Dressmaking, Drafting of Patterns,
                Needlework, and Art Needlework.

           (b)  General course:  Cookery and Nutrition, Institutional
                Management, Dressmaking and Needlework.

(c) Nursery School Helpers' course: Child Care, Cookery and Nutrition, Needlework applied to Children's Clothing.

Religious Instruction, Singing and Music, and Physical Education are also required.

The National Senior Certificate in Domestic Science is not accepted by the Joint Matriculation Board for exemption from the Matriculation examination and therefore will not admit holders to a degree course at a university, though it will admit holders to a diploma course.

## ART TRAINING

### High School Level Course

Certain technical colleges conduct a 2-year course leading to the National Senior Certificate in Art for students who have passed Standard VIII.

### National Senior Certificate (Standard X), Art Group

6 subjects from the following:

Group I   - Afrikaans A or English A.

Group II  - Afrikaans A or B or English A or B (different language from I).

Group III - Design, Drawing, History of Art.

Group IV  - Modelling or Painting.

Non-examination subjects for full-time students:

   (i)   Religious Instruction
  (ii)   Singing and the Appreciation of Music, or Drama and Speech Training
 (iii)   Physical Education

Only those candidates who have completed a course as full-time students at one of the institutions below will be allowed to enter for the examinations for the National Senior Certificate, Art Group.

        The Technical College, Bloemfontein
        The Technical College, Cape Town
        The Technical College, East London
        The Natal Technical College, Durban
        The Witwatersrand Technical College, Johannesburg
        The Technical College, Kroonstad
        The Technical College, Port Elizabeth
        The Technical College, Pretoria

Any candidate obtaining an aggregate of at least 60% in the full examination will be awarded a 1st-class certificate provided he qualified for
this certificate at one and the same examination.

The National Certificate in Art is not accepted by the Joint Matriculation
Board for exemption from the Matriculation examination, and will therefore
not admit holders to a degree course at a university.

The Johannesburg School of Art and the Technical College, Durban are
authorized to conduct a 2-year course leading to the National Senior Certificate in Ballet for students who have passed Standard VIII.

The National Senior Certificate in Ballet is not accepted by the Joint
Matriculation Board for exemption from the Matriculation examination, and
will therefore not admit holders to a degree course at a university.

Passes in 6 subjects selected from the following:

Group I   - Afrikaans A or English A.

Group II  - Afrikaans A or B or English A or B (different language from I).

Group III - History of Ballet and Theatre, Anatomy and Music, Practical
              Ballet and National Folk Dancing, Greek and Mime.

Religious Instruction is taken as a non-examination subject.


## Specialized Art Courses

A full-time 3-year course leading to the National Diploma in Art is also
offered by the institutions listed in the preceding section.  Students may
specialize in Fine Art, Commercial Art, Dress Design, and Industrial Art.

Entrance requirements:           16 years of age and Junior Certificate.

Students are required to take the Preliminary, Intermediate, and Final examinations at the end of each respective year and the Final Diploma is awarded
to successful candidates.

For the course in Industrial Art which is only given at the Johannesburg
School of Art, applicants must have passed the Matriculation or Senior
Certificate examination.

AGRICULTURAL TRAINING

W H I T E

## Facilities Provided by Provincial Education Departments

### Primary Schools

Nature study is compulsory in all primary schools.  It makes provision for
the teaching of the elementary principles of Agriculture, with emphasis on
the natural resources of soil, water, and vegetation.

### Secondary Schools

In a large number of secondary schools Agricultural Science is taught as an
optional subject.  One sixth of the normal school time is allowed for this
and the greater part of the teaching is theoretical.

### Agricultural High Schools

The 4 provincial departments control 17 agricultural high schools where
Agricultural Science is a compulsory subject for the School-Leaving Certificate.  1/3 of the normal school forenoon-time is allowed for theoretical
teaching and about the same time for practical training in the afternoons.
Pupils taking courses at agricultural high schools may qualify for exemption
from the Matriculation examination and qualify for admission to a university.

Most of the necessary practical facilities are available.  Hardly any
practical education is given outside the institutions.

Duration of course:    5 years, from Standard VI to Standard X, pupils
                       being admitted after they have passed Standard V.

### Agricultural Colleges

South Africa is divided into 6 main ecological regions, 5 of which have 1
agricultural college each, while the establishment of 1 in the sixth
region is being considered.

These colleges offer a 2-year diploma course intended to train future
farmers and technicians for State Departments as well as for private enterprise in the agricultural sphere.

The instruction embraces the broader needs of South African agriculture in
general.  Particular attention is paid to practical instruction, which

accounts for approximately half the student's time, the balance being
devoted to lectures and demonstrations. In addition to instruction in
subjects which are essentially of an agricultural nature, such as animal
and field husbandry, the engineering side of farming, such as the operation
and maintenance of farm machinery, blacksmithy and carpentry, receives due
recognition.

Entrants must have passed Standard VII as a minimum and be at least 16 years
of age. Preference is given to candidates with a Standard X Certificate
and to those who in addition have some farming experience.

In all the colleges English and Afrikaans are equally used as media.

In addition to the full diploma course, the colleges arrange special courses
and short courses in certain branches of farming, varying in length from 1
week to 3 months, e.g. Sheep and Wool, Dairying, Poultry Husbandry, Grain
Grading, Viticulture.

## Training Schools for Foresters

Entrance requirements:         Matriculation with pass in Mathematics.

Duration of course:            2 years.

A Diploma in Forestry is awarded.

## Veterinary Science

University of Pretoria offers a 5-year course leading to an initial degree
in Veterinary Science.

Courses leading to advanced degrees are offered at the Onderstepoort
Veterinary Research Institute by the University of Pretoria in conjunction
with the Department of Agricultural Technical Services.

## B A N T U

The Primary and Secondary programs are similar to the White programs given
above.

## Diploma in Agriculture

Offered at Fort Cox Agriculture College (Ciskei), Tsolo Agricultural School
(Transkei), and Arabie School (Northern Transvaal).

| Subjects | Duration (in years) |
|---|---|
| Animal Husbandry - cattle, horses, pigs, and dairying | 2 |
| Field Husbandry - dryland cropping, irrigation farming, veld management | 2 |
| Farm Management - agricultural economics, elementary statistics | 1 |
| Soil Conservation | 1 |
| Horticulture - vegetable gardening, fruit growing | 1 |
| Sheep and Wool | 1 |
| Poultry Keeping | 1 |
| Farm Handicrafts | 1 |
| Veterinary Science | $\frac{1}{2}$ |
| Forestry | $\frac{1}{2}$ |

The complete course covers a period of 400 hours of training, of which 50 hours are devoted to practical work.


## HEALTH TRAINING


### B A N T U

Entrance requirements:    17 years of age (minimum) and Junior Certificate with 50% pass in 6 subjects (Bantu language, English, Afrikaans, Domestic Science, Hygiene, and either Mathematics or Arithmetic).

Probationary period of 4 months' training (theory and practice) followed by Preliminary Training School Course.

Curriculum:  Diet Therapy, Hygiene, First Aid, Theory of Nursing, Anatomy and Physiology.

The student nurse's course can be completed in 3½ years when the Nursing Diploma is awarded.  The Diploma qualifies the student to become a staff nurse.  The usual order of progression is Staff Nurse Grade II, Staff Nurse Grade I, Sister, Matron.


### W H I T E


#### Pharmacists

Courses in preparation for the Diploma of the South African Pharmacy Board are offered by technical colleges in Cape Town, Durban, Johannesburg, Port Elizabeth, and Pretoria.

Entrance requirements:            <u>Matriculation Certificate</u> including Mathematics
                                  and 1 of the following:  Physical Science,
                                  Physics, Chemistry, Botany, Zoology or Biology.

3-year course plus 2 years' approved apprenticeship.

B.Sc. degrees in Pharmacy of 3 years' duration are offered at Rhodes
University and at Potchefstroom University for Christian Higher Education.


## TEACHER EDUCATION

Teacher training may be taken in one of 3 ways:  Through the Department of
Education, Arts and Science (National), through the various Provincial
Education Departments, or at the universities.


### W H I T E


### DEPARTMENT OF EDUCATION, ARTS AND SCIENCE

Teacher training courses are offered by the Department at 10 technical
colleges and teacher training institutions.  These courses lead to diplomas
or certificates in certain fields:  Art, Commerce, Home Economics, Technical
subjects and Nursery School Education.

Entrance requirements:            The courses for the examinations for the
                                  National Teacher's Diploma are conducted under
                                  the regulations of the Department of Education,
                                  Arts and Science.  The minimum qualification
                                  for admission to these courses is the <u>National
                                  Senior Certificate</u>.


### PROVINCIAL EDUCATION DEPARTMENTS

There are 15 provincial teacher training colleges in the Republic.

Entrance requirements:            In the Transvaal a Standard X with Matricu-
                                  lation Exemption is compulsory for the
                                  secondary teachers' course which consists of
                                  combined academic and professional training.
                                  For the primary teachers' course a Standard X
                                  certificate is required for entrance.

## UNIVERSITIES

Faculties of Education are attached to all universities in South Africa.
Generally, the universities cater more specifically to secondary teachers.
The majority also train primary school teachers, specialist teachers for
certain subjects in the primary and secondary school (Art, Physical Education, Domestic Science, Commerce), and teachers for certain sections of
primary and secondary education (nursery school education, junior work,
lower primary education, higher primary education, special education,
remedial education, and vocational education).

Entrance requirements:            Bachelor's degree is required for the
                                   secondary teachers' courses.  The entrance
                                   requirement for the primary teachers' course
                                   is a Standard X School-Leaving Certificate
                                   with Matriculation Exemption.

## SPECIALIZED TEACHER TRAINING

### Commerce

Training of teachers in Commerce is done in technical colleges.

Courses lead to the National Teachers' Diploma in Commerce.

(1)  A 3-year full-time course for students with the National Senior
     Certificate.

(2)  A 2-year full-time course for non-graduates with a Teachers'
     Certificate for which the prescribed course is of at least 2
     years' duration and for which the entrance requirement is the
     Matriculation Certificate.

(3)  A 2-year full-time course for non-graduates who have the
     National Diploma in Commerce.  This diploma must include
     both official languages and at least 3 commercial subjects.

(4)  A 1-year full-time course for holders of a professional diploma
     in Commerce or in Accountancy.

### Technical

#### DEPARTMENT OF EDUCATION, ARTS AND SCIENCE

### National Teachers' Diploma (Technical)

The National Teachers' Diploma (Technical) is a 1-year full-time course
for teachers which is offered at the Pretoria Technical College.

Entrance requirements:         1 of the following:

                               A degree in Engineering.
                               A degree in Pure Science.
                               A degree in Applied Science.
                               A National Diploma (with both languages
                                   senior grade).
                               A diploma in Pharmacy.

Graduate candidates for this course, unless in full-time teaching posts,
must have had 3 years' post-graduate industrial experience.


## National Teachers' Diploma (Workshop)

A 1-year full-time course for teachers (Workshop) offered at the Pretoria
Technical College.

Entrance requirements:         1 of the following:

                               The National Senior Certificate (Technical)
                                   and apprenticeship.
                               The National Technical Certificate, Part III,
                                   and the 2 official languages in the senior
                                   grade and apprenticeship.
                               A recognized equivalent and the 2 official
                                   languages (senior grade) and apprenticeship.

Both the National Teachers' Diploma (Technical and Workshop) may also be
taken by part-time study.  The course is then taken over 2 years.  Before
the diploma is granted, the student must have completed 100 hours of
teaching.


### UNIVERSITIES


## University of Natal:

    A 1-year course leading to the University Education Diploma (Technical)
    is provided for the holders of a degree  in Fine Arts (Commerce,
    Engineering or Agriculture.


## Home Economics

### DEPARTMENT OF EDUCATION, ARTS AND SCIENCE

A course leading to the National Teachers' Diploma in Home Economics is
offered to students who have obtained the National Senior Certificate.

Duration of course:                  3 years full-time study at one of the
                                     following institutions:

                                     The Johannesburg Teachers' College for Home
                                        Economics
                                     The Cape Technical College
                                     The Natal Technical College
                                     The Pretoria Technical College


## PROVINCIAL TEACHER TRAINING COLLEGES

In the Transvaal there is a 3-year general professional course with
specialization in Domestic Science.

Entrance requirements:          Transvaal Secondary School Certificate.

There is also a 1-year general professional course for graduates.

In Natal, a 1-year specialization course in Housecraft is provided for
holders of an initial teacher's diploma.

In the Orange Free State, a 1-year specialization course in Needlework is
provided for holders of an initial teacher's diploma.  A 3-year specialization course in Domestic Science and Needlework is provided in addition.

In the Cape Province two 1-year specialization courses are offered in
Needlework and Domestic Science to holders of the Primary Teachers' Certificate.


## UNIVERSITIES

A 4-year degree course in Housecraft subjects leading to the B.Sc. degree
in Domestic Science is provided by the Universities of Stellenbosch,
Pretoria and Potchefstroom.

Besides the ordinary degree in Domestic Science, these institutions offer
a B.Sc. degree in Domestic Science with a teacher's option.

A 3-year Teachers' Diploma in Domestic Science is offered by Potchefstroom.
The entrance qualification to this course is a Matriculation, a School-
Leaving or a National Senior Certificate.

The University of Stellenbosch offers a 2-year course for a Diploma in
Domestic Science.  The entrance requirement is the School-Leaving Certificate
of the Joint Matriculation Board or a Senior Certificate with a pass in
Mathematics or Science.

Students who have obtained the Diploma in Domestic Science may follow a 1-year
course leading to the Teacher's Diploma in Domestic Science and Needlework.

Art

## DEPARTMENT OF EDUCATION, ARTS AND SCIENCE

The National Teachers' Diploma in Art is open to persons holding the National Senior Certificate.

The courses offered are from 1 to 4 years' full-time training, depending on the candidate's qualifications.

## PROVINCIAL TEACHER TRAINING COLLEGES

In the Transvaal a 3-year general professional course with specialization in Art or in Arts and Crafts and a 4-year combined academic and professional course with specialization in Art is provided for students intending to become secondary teachers.

In the Cape Province and Natal a 1-year course of specialization in Arts is provided for persons holding an initial teachers' diploma.

In Natal there is in addition a 1-year specialization course in Handicrafts.

In the Orange Free State, a 1-year specialization course in 2 subjects, one of which may be Art, is provided.

## UNIVERSITIES

University of Cape Town:

A special 1-year course in Fine Art is offered to holders of a Primary Teachers' Certificate.

The Higher Primary Teachers' Certificate in Fine Art is a 3-year course for candidates who have obtained the Matriculation or Senior Certificate.

The degree of Bachelor of Arts (Art) is for students intending to become teachers of Art in high schools. Holders of this degree are eligible as teachers only after completing a course of professional study and training in the Faculty of Education leading to a recognized teaching certificate (Secondary Teachers' Certificate or Post-Graduate Primary Teachers' Certificate).

Rhodes University:

A 1-year course leading to the Primary Teachers' Art Certificate designed to enable a holder of a Primary Teachers' Certificate to specialize as a teacher of Art.

A 4-year course leading to the University Art Teachers' Certificate is equivalent to the Diploma in Fine Art (3 years) and the University Education Diploma (1 year) combined. Candidates must hold the School-Leaving Certificate.

In addition there is a 4-year course leading to the University Art Teachers' Diploma. This is equivalent to the degree of B.A. (Fine Arts) (3 years) and the University Education Diploma combined. Candidates must be matriculated.

## Agriculture

There is only 1 provincial teacher training college which offers a 1-year specialization course in Agricultural Nature Study to the holders of an initial teachers' diploma. In general, teachers acquire a B.Sc. degree in Agriculture (4 years) and then devote a year to an intensive course which leads to a professional teachers' diploma or certificate at a university or at a teacher training college.

A 1-year course leading to the University Education Diploma (Technical) is provided by the University of Natal to holders of a degree in Agriculture.

## Nursery Education

DEPARTMENT OF EDUCATION, ARTS AND SCIENCE

## National Teachers' Diploma in Nursery Education

Duration of course:          3 years.

Entrance requirements:       National Senior Certificate endorsed with 6 subjects of which 2 have to be the official languages.

A 1-year course is also offered.

Entrance requirements:       1 of the following:

An approved university degree or diploma involving not less than 3 years' full-time study.
A secondary or higher teachers' certificate involving not less than 3 years' full-time study.
An approved infants' or primary teachers' certificate involving not less than 2 years post-matriculation full-time training.
A registered nursing certificate.

# UNIVERSITIES

## University of Pretoria:

A diploma in Nursery Education may be taken over a period of 3 years'
full-time study.

Entrance requirements:  Matriculation or School-Leaving Certificate.

A 1-year diploma course in Nursery Education is provided for persons
holding a recognized teachers' certificate of 2 years' full-time
training after Matriculation, or the School-Leaving Certificate plus
at least 2 years' approved teaching experience.

A 4-year combined B.A. degree in Social Science and a Diploma in
Nursery Education is also offered.

Entrance requirements:  Matriculation Certificate.


## Special Education

At some special schools provision is made for teachers' in-service training.


# UNIVERSITIES

## University of Cape Town:

### Special courses for teachers

Holders of approved teachers' certificates are eligible for admission
to the following 1-year courses:

Training for teachers of special classes.
Training for teachers of children handicapped in speech and hearing.
Training for teachers of problem children.


### Diploma in Physiotherapy

The curriculum for the diploma extends over 3 years of full-time
training.

Entrance requirements:  Matriculation with pass in Mathematics.

### Teacher Training Course for Qualified Physiotherapists - Teachers'
### Certificate in Physiotherapy

This certificate is designed as a post-registration qualification to
fit the holder to undertake the teaching of student physiotherapists.

Every candidate for this certificate holds a Matriculation Certificate, has been registered with the South African Medical and Dental Council as a physiotherapist, and has had at least 2 years' experience in the practice of physiotherapy in a clinic or hospital.

The curriculum for the certificate extends over 3 academic terms of full-time study.

## University of Natal:

### Certificate in Remedial Education

A Certificate in Remedial Education may be taken over a 1-year period of full-time study or a 2-year period of part-time study.

Entrance requirements:    Graduates who hold recognized teaching qualifications.
Candidates who have had 3 years of approved experience and who hold a recognized teaching qualification obtained after at least 2 years' post-matriculation study.

## University of Pretoria:

### Diploma in Special Education (Pedotherapy)

A 1-year post-graduate diploma course is provided for persons with one of the following qualifications:

(a)  B.A. (Hons.) Psychology.

(b)  B.A. (Hons.) Sociology or B.A. (Social Work) and Psychology II.

(c)  B.A. with Psychology III and the Higher Education Diploma or another approved secondary teacher's diploma.

(d)  B.Ed. (Vocational Guidance) and Psychology II.

(e)  B.A. (Psychology III and Sociology II or Philosophy II) and secondary teacher's diploma.

### Diploma in Special Education (Education of the Deaf)

A 1-year extra-mural course is provided for persons who hold a recognized teacher's certificate obtained after 2 years of study, post-matriculation or post-school-leaving certificate level, and who have had at least 2 years' teaching experience.

## Teacher's Diploma in Physiotherapy

Duration of course:        1 year.

Entrance requirements:     Matriculation or an approved School-Leaving
                           Certificate.
                           Qualification in Physiotherapy.
                           At least 2 years' experience in a hospital
                           as a qualified therapist.

## Teacher's Diploma in Occupational Therapy

Duration of course:        1 year.

Entrance requirements:     Matriculation or an approved School-Leaving
                           Certificate.
                           Qualification in Occupational Therapy.
                           At least 2 years in a hospital as a qualified
                           occupational therapist.

## Degree of Bachelor of Arts in Logopaedics

The curriculum for the degree extends over 4 years of full-time study.

## University of Stellenbosch:

### Diploma for Teachers of Retarded Children

A 1-year course open to candidates holding an approved teachers'
certificate.

### Diploma in Occupational Therapy

Duration of course:        3 years.

Entrance requirements:     Matriculation Certificate.

## University of Witwatersrand:

### Diploma in Education of the Deaf

A 2-year Diploma in Education of the Deaf is provided for persons
holding a recognized teachers' diploma obtained after not less than
2 years' post-matriculation study.

Candidates complete a minimum of 200 hours of practical work in special
schools and institutions for the hard-of-hearing and the deaf in each
of the 2 years of study.

### Diploma in Occupational Therapy

The curriculum for the diploma extends over 3½ years of full-time study.

Entrance requirements:    Matriculation Certificate.

### Degree of Bachelor of Arts in Logopaedics and Diploma in Logopaedics

The curriculum for the degree course extends over 4 years of full-time study and that for the diploma over 3 years of full-time study.

Entrance requirements:    Matriculation Certificate.

### Degree of Bachelor of Science in Physiotherapy

Duration of course:        4 years of full-time study.

Entrance requirements:    Pass in Mathematics at Matriculation.

### Diploma in Physiotherapy Education

Entrance requirements:    A registrable qualification in Physiotherapy and 2 years' experience.

Duration of course:        18 months.  If candidate is a Bachelor of Science in Physiotherapy, he may complete the course in 12 months.

## PROVINCIAL TEACHER TRAINING COLLEGES

A 3-year general professional course with specialization in the teaching of mentally deviate children is offered by teacher training colleges in the Transvaal.

## C O L O U R E D

### Primary Teachers' Certificate

Trains teachers for primary school classes.

Duration of course:    2 years.

Entrance requirements:        Senior Certificate.

## Lower Primary Teachers' Certificate

Trains teachers for the junior primary school classes (sub-standard grades and Standards I and II).

Duration of course:              2 years.  Open to female students only.

Entrance requirements:           Junior Certificate.


## Higher Primary Teachers' Certificate

1-year course in a special subject such as academic subjects, infant school method, handwork, art, physical education, music.

Entrance requirements:           Primary Teachers' Certificate.


## University Education Diploma

For  secondary teachers.

1-year course of professional training after degree course.


## Lower Secondary Teachers' Diploma

Duration of course:              3 years - 2 years   academic training and 1
                                 year professional training.

Entrance requirements:           Senior Certificate.


## B.Educ. degree

2 years' post-graduate course in education.


## M.Educ. degree

3 years' post-graduate course.


## D.Educ.

2 years' post-master's degree course in Education.

## A S I A T I C S

### Natal Teacher's Senior Certificate

2 years' post-Junior Certificate.


### Natal Teacher's Diploma

2 years' post-matriculation.


### Natal Teacher's Senior Diploma

3 years' post-matriculation.


## B A N T U

### Lower Primary Teachers' Course

Duration of course:                2 years.

Women only are admitted.

Entrance requirements:             Form I.

Curriculum:      Principles of Education, Child Study and General Methods for
                 the Lower Primary School, School Organization, Practical
                 Teaching, Blackboard Work and Writing, Afrikaans, English,
                 Bantu language, Arithmetic, Religious Instruction, Hygiene
                 and Physical Training, Environmental Study, Music and
                 Singing, Needlework, Arts and Crafts.


### Higher Primary Teachers' Course

Duration of course:                2 years.

Entrance requirements:             Junior Certificate.

Curriculum identical to Lower Primary with stress on higher primary subject
matter.


### Junior Secondary Schools Course

2-year course at Bantu University College.

Entrance requirements:             Senior Certificate.

Curriculum: A 1st-year degree course consisting of 5 approved B.A. subjects or B.Sc. subjects, Bantu language, Afrikaans, English, Principles of Teaching, Empirical Education, School Organization, Practical Teaching, History of Education, modern language, method courses in 4 of the following:

General Science, Biology, Physical Chemistry, Agriculture, Arithmetic, Mathematics, Commerce, Commercial Arithmetic, Typewriting, Shorthand, Afrikaans, English, mother tongue, Latin, Social Studies.

1 of the following:  Needlework, Arts and Crafts, Music, Woodwork, Gardening.

<u>South African Teachers' Diploma</u> awarded on completion of course.


## Forms IV and V

Entrance requirements: Bachelor's degree.

Education Diploma of the University of South Africa.


## SPECIAL TRAINING

### Police

All new members of the police force take their initial training at the South African Police College, Pretoria.

Entrance requirements: Completion of Standard VIII.

Duration of course: 6-12 months.

The South African Police Force trains its experts at:

 The South African Police College, Pretoria, for detective probationers.

 The South African Criminal Bureau, Pretoria, for training of finger-print, ballistic, and handwriting experts.

 The South African Police Mechanical School Benoni, for police drivers.

 The South African Police Dog Depot, Pretoria, for dogmasters.


### Forestry

Lower skilled workers receive instruction at the Departmental Forestry College at Saasveld, near George, Cape Province.

2-year course with basic scientific subjects and elementary instruction in Forestry.

A Diploma in Forestry is awarded.

Higher skilled workers are chosen from graduates with degrees in Forestry.


## Department of Justice

2-3 months' courses for officers studying for the Public Service Law
Certificate.


## South African Railways

The Railway College at Esselen Park, Kaalfontein, Transvaal, a residential
college, was established in 1945.

Courses for various grades of staff and special courses for administrative
officers, supervisors, junior engineers, and instructors are conducted at
the College.

It also directs a number of part-time and full-time classes at important
centers for trainee firemen (stokers), electric drivers assistants, shunters,
and non-White ticket clerks.

Railway apprentices attend technical college classes until they have
obtained the National Technical Certificate, Part II.

Where technical college courses are not available, apprentices take the
correspondence courses of the Witwatersrand Technical College.


## MILITARY TRAINING

### W H I T E

## Army Training

Artillery, armour, infantry, mechanical and electrical engineering, field
engineering, signals, anti-aircraft, medical and administrative services.


## Air Force

Basic, advanced and operational flying, multi-engined and jet conversion,
air weapons, air navigation, radar, radio, aircraft engineering, and aerial
photography.

## Navy

Basic, seamanship, torpedo and anti-submarine, navigation, gunnery, electrical communications and operational training at sea.

## Gymnasia

A gymnasium for each of the 3 services is in existence.

The Army and Air Force Gymnasia are at Voortrekkerhoogte and the Naval Gymnasium is at Saldanha Bay.

Each offers a course of 12 months' full-time training.

Entrance requirements:        16-22 years of age and Standard VII (Navy) and Standard VIII (Army and Air Force).

## Academic

Academic training for Permanent Force candidate officers takes place at the Military Academy, Saldanha Bay.

The Academy functions with the University of Stellenbosch for academic training.

The academic courses followed by the candidate officers is of 3 years' duration on completion of which the B.Mil. degree and the rank of lieutenant are awarded.

## Staff and Administrative Training

The S.A. Military College, Voortrekkerhoogte undertakes staff, tactical and administrative courses for all Army officers and NCO's.

South African Air Force College, Voortrekkerhoogte undertakes staff and administrative courses for all Air Force officers and NCO's.

Specialized training of senior officers is taken in Great Britain and the United States.

SOUTH-WEST AFRICA

White and Coloured

Bantu

Compulsory Education: White and Coloured (10 years) –
7 years primary and 3 years junior
secondary

Bantu – none

School year: February to November

Secondary Grading: 100% with 33. 3% passing

Student's Age / Year of Schooling

SECONDARY / ELEMENTARY

**White and Coloured:**

SECONDARY EDUCATION
- Upper
  - X Standard
  - IX Standard
- Lower
  - VIII Standard
  - VII Standard
  - VI Standard

PRIMARY EDUCATION
- V Standard
- IV Standard
- III Standard
- II Standard
- I Standard
- Sub B
- Sub A

**Bantu:**

SECONDARY EDUCATION
- Teacher Training
- V Form
- IV Form
- III Form
- II Form
- I Form

PRIMARY EDUCATION
- Higher
  - VI Standard
  - V Standard
  - IV Standard
  - III Standard
  - II Standard
  - I Standard
- II Grade
- I Grade

SOUTH WEST AFRICA

BACKGROUND

The thousand-mile long Namib Desert along the coast of South West Africa is uninhabited except for the 3 towns of Luderitz, Walvis Bay and Swankopmund, and the diamond mining section at the mouth of the Orange River. The larger part of the country is a continuation of the high South African plateau. Extensive sand dunes lie along the eastern border beside the Kalahari Desert in Bechuanaland. The narrow Caprivi Zipfel (Caprivi Strip), 20-60 miles wide and 30 miles long, divides Angola from Bechuanaland.

The population groups in the country have maintained their individual identities. The various Bantu groups are divided into: Ovambos (239,363), inhabiting the reserve of Ovamboland in the north; Hereros (35,354), nomads living in the north-central and eastern areas; Okavangos (27,871) living in the east; East Caprivians,(15,840),and a small group of Tswana (linked ethnically to Bechuanaland) (9,992), and Kaokovelders (9,234). Other distinct population groups are: Damaras (44,353), who although Bantu in origin speak the Hottentot language; Namas (34,806), Hottentots living in the south; Bushmen (11,762), among the oldest inhabitants of the territory; Basters (11,257), living south of Windhoek in the Rehoboth Gebiet area; Coloureds (12,708), and Whites (73,464).

A proposal has been made for a stable and inalienable homeland for each of the 10 non-white groups: Ovamboland, Okavangoland, Kaokoveld, East Caprivi, Damaraland, Namaland, Hereroland, Rehoboth Gebiet, Bushmanland, and Tswana-land.

In 1483, Diego Cam, a Portuguese explorer, came to the coast. In 1487, Bartholomew Dias landed at Angra Pequena (now Lüderitz Bay). British, French, Dutch and German traders followed. In 1760, ivory hunter, Cacobus Coetse, was the first to enter the territory from the Orange River. London Missionary Society pioneered in mission establishments, followed by other British missionaries, mostly Wesleyan. German missionaries were mostly of the Rhenish order.

In 1867, islands off the coast were annexed by the United Kingdom and in 1878, Walvis Bay and an area of 400 square miles were annexed to Cape Colony. After negotiations with Britain and Cape Colony, Germany proclaimed a protectorate over the territory in 1885. In 1886 and 1890, Germany fixed the boundaries by agreement with the United Kingdom and Portugal. From 1903 to 1908 there were a series of native uprisings.

South African troops captured the territory from Germany in 1915. Administration was assumed by the Union of South Africa and a military government

was set up.  By the Treaty of Versailles, South West Africa became a
Class C mandate under the Union of South Africa, December, 1920.  August
4, 1961, a Deputy Minister for South West African Affairs was appointed.
Windhoek is the center of administration.  The country is divided into
21 districts controlled by magistrates.

Education of non-Europeans was first provided by missions in the last
of the 19th century.  The administration has fostered missionary effort
through subsidies, and has established schools in areas not served by
missions.  In the tribal areas such as Ovamboland and the Okavango section, the more than 150 mission schools are government-aided.  They
provide mainly fundamental and primary education.  There are a few Bantu
schools with secondary classes.  For the Coloured, there are 30 primary
schools, and high school facilities at Rehoboth.  Education for the
European population has been provided in 60 government schools with
almost a third of the pupils accommodated in hostels conducted by the
administration in cooperation with the government schools.  The Education
Proclamation of 1926 was amended in 1960 to initiate the Bantu system of
education.  The memorandum of May 2, 1960 brought application of apartheid
to education:  European education, Coloured education, Native education.

## PRESENT SYSTEM

Same primary and secondary programs as those in Republic of South Africa.
(See REPUBLIC OF SOUTH AFRICA, Primary and Secondary Education.)  For
Bantus, primary and secondary education, teacher training, technical
training and adult education within and without the Police Zone.  For
higher education and teacher training, European students may attend South
African higher institutions.  (See REPUBLIC OF SOUTH AFRICA, Higher Education.)  Bantus are not permitted to leave territory.

## PRIMARY EDUCATION

### W H I T E   A N D   C O L O U R E D

Entry age:                 7 years.

7-year program.

Language of instruction: English, Afrikaans, or German.

Curriculum:                Religious Instruction, Singing, Art, Physical
                           Education, 1st and 2nd Languages, Arithmetic,
                           Geography, History, Nature Study, Environment
                           Study, Hygiene, Handicrafts, and Writing.

Syllabus of Cape Province used.

### B A N T U

Until very recently education left to missionaries.  Mission schools still subsidized.  Program same as in South Africa.

Language of instruction is the mother tongue (1 of 9 African languages).

Most of native schools by Rhenish Mission, and offer only to Standard III. Higher Primary Schools (Standards III-VI) - 1 such school in each of the 17 reserves within the Police Zone.

Protestant  Unity Church conducts a school to Standard VI.


## SECONDARY EDUCATION

### W H I T E   A N D   C O L O U R E D

3-year Junior Secondary.  Continuation of basic primary subjects listed above with General Science, General Mathematics, Social Studies and Guidance added.

2-year Senior Secondary.

Students prepare for South African Joint Matriculation Board Examinations.

### B A N T U

4 Junior Secondary schools:  1 for Namas, 2 for Hereros and 1 for Ndongas and Kuanyamas.

Senior Secondary training only at institutions where teachers are trained: Augustineum  Training School and another in Ovamboland.


## VOCATIONAL AND TECHNICAL EDUCATION

Technical training for Coloured at Rehoboth.

Technical training for native children at Augustineum Training School.

Department of Bantu Administration and Development to add Carpentry, Building and Tailoring to agricultural training program in the Ovitoto Reserve and in Ovamboland.

<u>TEACHER EDUCATION</u>

<u>B A N T U</u>

2-year course at Augustineum Training School.

Entrance requirements:  Standard VI.

1381

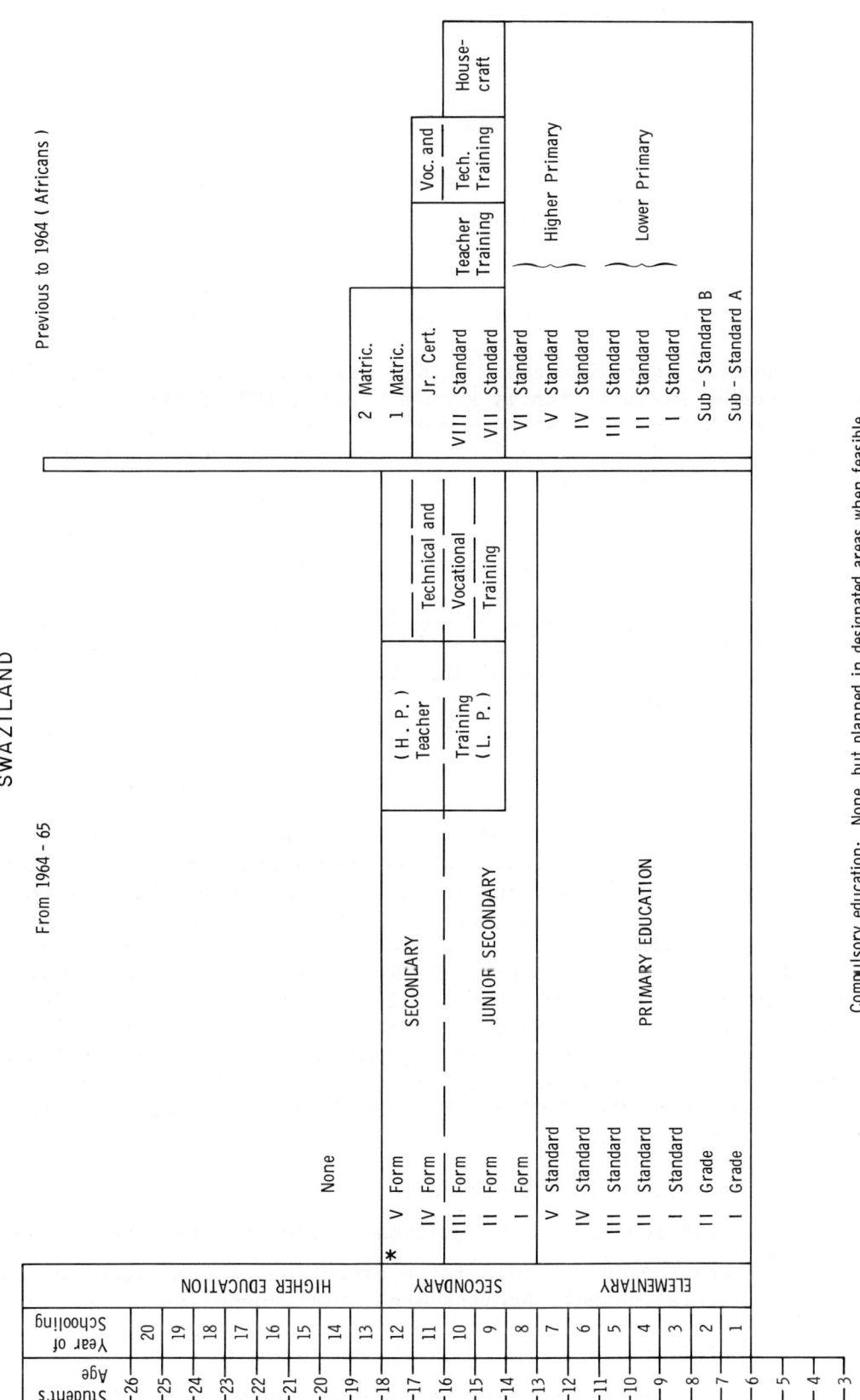

SWAZILAND

Compulsory education: None, but planned in designated areas when feasible ( Up to 1963, for Europeans, 7 - 16 years of age )

School year: January - December

Grading: See SECONDARY and TEACHER EDUCATION

SWAZILAND


BACKGROUND


The territory was settled in the early 19th century by a Bantu people, the Swazi, who had been driven from their home terrain, Northern Zululand.

The Swazis, numbering approximately 270,000, are a pastoral and agricultural people, living in small family kraals. About 60% of the land is owned by the Swazi Nation and has been set aside by the government for settlement purposes. "Swazi Nationland" is distributed in 35 separate blocks throughout the territory.

There are approximately 8,000 Europeans in Swaziland. A small Eurafrican population of 2,260 lives in the Hlatikulu district.

Swaziland protection was guaranteed by the United Kingdom in 1881, and by the South African Republic, 1884. Joint British-South-African-Swazi government set up, 1890. 1894, South African Republic assumed a Protectorate over the territory. After the Boer War, the country was administered by the Governor of Transvaal. 1907, placed under control of British High Commissioner for South Africa. Day-to-day government conducted by H.M. Commissioner resident in Swaziland. 1966, internal self-government.

Education for the Swazi was initiated by missionaries. The Methodist Church entered the territory in 1847, and by 1880 started educational work at Mahamba. Berlin Lutherans and Anglicans followed during the next 10 years: 1893, the Scandinavian Alliance and South African General Mission; 1904, the African Methodist Episcopal Church (a purely African denomination); 1909, Church of the Nazarene; 1910, Norway Free Evangelican Mission; 1914, Roman Catholics. Others which have since started evangelical and educational work include: the African Congregational Church, the Pilgrim Holiness Mission, the Swedish Zulu Mission, the Metropolitan Church Association of the Apostolic Church of Zion, and the Dutch Reformed Church. By 1924, there were over 100 mission schools. Today, most African schools are controlled by the Church.

Previous to 1964, education in 3 divisions:

African:  most schools run by missions, majority government-aided.

European:  grant-aided schools (with exception of Dominican Convent, girls' school, Bremersdorp), with compulsory education from 7-16 years of age or earlier passing of Junior Certificate (lower secondary) examination.

Eurafrican:  government-aided mission schools, education not compulsory.

For the education of Africans:

In 1906, at the kraal of the Chief Regent at Zombode, the government established a primary school, the forerunner of the Swazi national schools.  At
Matapha in 1928 a large school for sons of the reigning family and principal chiefs was founded which has since become the Swazi National High
School.  Government established the first teacher training center, 1936;
second teacher training school and a trades school, 1946.  Subsequently,
financial grants increased to missions, and secondary school facilities
expanded.

For the education of English-speaking children:

Provision for education dates from 1902.  Small 1-teacher schools begun
at different posts in the territory.  First schools at Goedgegun, Mbabane,
Manzini and Stegi.  After World War II, smaller farm schools closed in
the south and Goedgegun School (since re-named Evelyn Baring School)
developed into a large central school with primary and secondary divisions.
In the north, small schools centralized in the St. Mark's School at
Mbabane which had been opened in 1910 by Bishop Watts for children of
all races at his own personal expense; school  was transferred to the
government in November 1956.  A small but increasing number of African
and Eurafricans are now receiving English-medium instruction in these
schools.

For the education of Eurafricans:

First school started by Bishop Watts at Empolonjeni near Mbabane, 1914;
later transferred to Endlozana; closed 1931.  Anglican Church then opened
a boarding school for North Eurafricans at Manzina.  In 1921, Scandinavian Alliance (now the Evangelical Alliance) established the Florence
School for the southern areas; in 1934, school transferred to Hluti.
Third school established by the Roman Catholic mission, 1934; small
schools started at Mbabane and Stegi.  An increasing number of Africans
are now entering these schools.

By 1962, 12 schools for Europeans either government or government-aided
(9 primary, 3 high schools).  5 schools for Eurafricans, government-
assisted; 3 of them, boarding.  236 African schools under direct supervision of missions; 19 government-controlled schools, 36 small tribal
schools.  3 national schools maintained by the Swazi National Fund.  20
African schools offering secondary education.

In 1963, legislation prepared for a 1964 integration policy for the education of pupils of all races (repealing the Public Education Proclamation 1951, the African Schools Proclamation 1940, the Coloured Schools
Proclamation 1951, the Education Advisory Board Proclamation 1962).  By
1964, hitherto exclusively European schools admitting African and Eurafrican children.

Due to heavy pressures on the schools, the Education Advisory Board recommended that non-Swaziland pupils not be admitted into primary schools, and admitted into secondary schools only after eligible Swazilanders had been enrolled; to be effective 1965. Also, that the age of entry into the first grade of primary school be lowered to 10 years in 1964, 9 years in 1965 and 8 years in 1966, although certain schools (namely in the rural areas) may be designated as "over-age" schools permitted to accept older children.


## PRESENT SYSTEM


## PRIMARY EDUCATION

Admission to primary schools confined to children of parents resident in Swaziland.

342 primary schools are fairly well distributed over the high and middle veld regions; sparse in the low veld of Lubombo District.

Entry age:   6 years, as of 1966.  (7 years, 1964-66; 8 years previous to 1964.)

7-year program.

8-year program previous to 1964, in predominantly Swazi schools (because of the change in the medium of instruction, from vernacular to English, at Standard III level).

7-year program in English-medium schools.

Swazi schools in Grade I, 1963, all primary schools will be of 7-year duration.

Common syllabus reached Standard I, January 1964.

Previous to 1964:    Grade  I (Sub-Standard A)
                     Grade II (Sub-Standard B)
                     Standards I - VI
                     For Africans:  Elementary Vernacular, Standard I and II
                                    Lower Primary, Standard III and IV
                                    Higher Primary, Full Course
                     Standard VI examination at close of primary program

After 1964:          Standards 1 - 7.  Shortening of the primary course
                     will only be finalized by the end of 1968.

Curriculum:          English, Arithmetic, Geography, History, Health, Scripture,
                     Nature Study and Craftwork.  Previous to 1964 in English-
                     medium schools, Afrikaans was taught; in predominantly

Swazi schools, Zulu.  After 1964, both taught.  Domestic
Science and Carpentry taught in upper standards in some
schools.

Departmental (Standard 7) examination at close of primary program.


## SECONDARY EDUCATION


### FOR AFRICANS, PRIOR TO 1963-64

Little development in secondary education for Africans until 1964 when
South African government refused admittance of all extra-territorial
Africans to secondary and vocational schools.  Up to that time full edu-
cation for Africans leading to Matriculation had been available only at
Matapha National School (founded 1928, became government-aided, 1964),
Methodist Mission School, Mahamba and Catholic Mission School, Bremersdorp.
Several mission schools provided junior secondary classes.  After 1954,
secondary education expanded.

Secondary program:   3-year Junior secondary course
                     (Standard VII, VIII and Junior Certificate)

                     2-year upper cycle (Matriculation 1 and Matriculation
                     2)

Curriculum:    English, Zulu, Latin, Mathematics (Arithmetic to Junior
               Certificate), Physical Science, Biology, and Geography.
               Optional:  Bookkeeping, Typing and Shorthand.

External examination at close of Standard VII.  Successful candidates
received Continuation Certificate qualifying for entrance to Standard
VIII, or a Leaving Certificate qualifying for entrance to teacher, trade
or nurses' training.

Students continuing secondary education prepared for Junior Certificate
and Matriculation Examinations of the Joint Matriculation Board of the
University of South Africa.  Successful candidates in the Matriculation
Examination admitted to Pius XII College in Basutoland or post-matricu-
lation center in Rhodesia preparing students for entry to University
College of Rhodesia and Nyasaland.


### FOR EUROPEANS AND EURAFRICANS, PRIOR TO 1963-64

European full secondary education provided at St. Mark's School, Mbabane
(founded 1908 by Church of England, later independent, acquired by

government, 1956), Evelyn Baring School, Goedgegun (large central government school), and others. Junior secondary training in some mission
schools.

Eurafrican lower secondary education in 4 grant-aided mission schools.

4-year program:  2 cycles.

Curriculum:     English, Afrikaans, Latin, Mathematics, Physical Science,
                Biology, Geography. Optional: Agriculture, Domestic
                Science, and Bookkeeping.

Junior Certificate examination taken at end of 2nd year.

Matriculation examination of the Joint Matriculation Board of the University of South Africa at close of program.


### A F T E R   I N T E G R A T I O N   O F   S C H O O L S

Schools under classification of "secondary" range from full 5-year high
schools to those with only the first secondary class. Of 31 secondary
schools, 10 are full high schools offering matriculation (or equivalent)
facilities; 13 are junior secondary schools with first 3 years of junior
secondary up to Junior Certificate; 8 schools have first secondary class
only.

Full high schools are:    Matapha High School
                          St. Mark's Secondary School
                          Evelyn Baring High School
                          St. Christopher's High School
                          Salesian High School
                          St. Theresa's High School
                          Franson Christian High School
                          Manzina Nazarene High School
                          St. Michael's Secondary School
                          Our Lady of Sorrows High School

Schools with first secondary classes only are a peculiarity in the
Swaziland system as a Form I examination admits to teacher and other
forms of training.

Forms I - V:  full 5-year program.

High Commission Territories Junior Certificate Examination taken at end
of Form III. (In 1963, this replaced the South African Junior Certificate
Examination.)

General Certificate of Education Examination of the Associated Examining
Board or the Joint Matriculation Board Examination of the Republic of
South Africa at end of Form V.


Certificates awarded:

   High Commission Territories Junior Certificate
   *General Certificate of Education "O" level
   *Matriculation Certificate
   School Leaving Certificate


Beginning 1966, Form V students will write the Cambridge School Certificate Examination.  Only extra-mural candidates will enter for the University
of London Certificate of Education.


Sample 5-year program of the Evelyn Baring High School, Geodgegun, leading
to the Joint Matriculation Board Examination of the Republic of South Africa:

   Mathematics, Science or Biology; Geography/Bookkeeping; English,
   Afrikaans, Agricultural  Science or Domestic Science.  In addition,
   a commercial bias is offered with Bookkeeping and Typing as subjects;
   students following this program take an examination at a slightly
   lower level, the South African School Certificate.


TIMETABLE FOR FORMS IV AND V
(Evelyn Baring High School)

| Subjects | Hours |
|---|---|
| English | 4 |
| Afrikaans | 4 |
| Mathematics | 4½ |
| Science/Biology | 4 |
| Geography/Bookkeeping | 3½ |
| Agricultural Science/Domestic Science | 3½ |
| Extras | 2 |
|  | 25½ |


Grades used:    Pass      - 33%
                2nd Class - 55%
                1st Class - 65%

## HIGHER EDUCATION

Students may proceed to the University of Basutoland, Bechuanaland Protectorate and Swaziland.  (See BASUTOLAND, Higher Education.)

## VOCATIONAL AND TECHNICAL EDUCATION

Prior to 1964 vocational and technical training not available to Europeans.

3 vocational and technical schools (2 government, 1 voluntary agency, government-aided).

## SWAZILAND TRADE TRAINING CENTRE, Mbabane

Entrance requirements:           8 years of schooling.

Courses in:    Motor Mechanics, Electrical Installation, Building, Carpentry.  Fitting and Turning added in 1964.

Normally, 3-year courses, followed by 2-year apprenticeship in industry.

## MBULUZI TRAINING COLLEGE

College run by the South African General Mission with government grant-in-aid.

2 courses:  (1)  Housecraft
            (2)  Domestic Science Teaching

Housecraft course for equipping girls with the skills to run a home efficiently and economically.

2-year program:  Dressmaking, Cookery, Infant Care, Upholstery, General Housewifery.

Housecraft Certificate awarded.

Domestic Science Teachers' course open to qualified primary teachers. Training for specialist teachers in upper primary classes.

2-year program.

Domestic Science Teachers' Certificate awarded.

## CLERICAL TRAINING CENTRE

Attached to William Pitcher College (see Teacher Education for this College), pending provision of separate accommodations.

Entrance requirements:                  Junior Certificate, 1st or 2nd class
                                         pass and at least 40% in English.

2-year program:      English, Bookkeeping, Typewriting, Commercial Arith-
                     metic, Commerce and Office Routine, General Knowledge.

Pass mark:  45%.


## AINSWORTH DICKSON NURSING TRAINING SCHOOL

Attached to Bremersdorp Hospital under Director of Medical Services.

2-year nurse-aid course (post-primary) leading to Red Cross Certificates in First Aid, Infant Welfare and Home Nursing.

4-year course (post-primary) of the Swaziland Executive Nursing Committee.

4½-year course (post-Junior Certificate) leading to High Commission Territories Nursing Council Certificate.


## MDUTSHANE AGRICULTURAL TRAINING CENTRE

Conducted by the Department of Land Utilization.

1-year course for African cattle guards in Elementary Veterinary Science and Animal Husbandry.

1-year course for African Land Utilization Officers in Elementary Agriculture and Soil Conservation.


## TEACHER EDUCATION

Prior to 1964 no training for Europeans and Eurafricans.

3 teacher training colleges (1 government, 2 voluntary agency, government-aided):
          William Pitcher College, Manzini
          Nazarene Training College, Manzini
          Mbuluzi Training College (domestic science teacher training, see
              Vocational and Technical Education)

2-year programs training at:   post-Form I (Primary Lower), designated T4
                               post-Form III (Primary Higher), designated
                               T3


WILLIAM PITCHER COLLEGE, Manzini

Government institution.  Opened 1962 as Swaziland Teacher Training College;
renamed September 1963.

Subjects studied - T4

Primary Lower: English            Geography
               Zulu               Agriculture
               Arithmetic         Needlework
               Principles and Methods   Crafts and Handwork
                 of Education     Music
               Organization and   Physical Training
                 Management       Scripture
               Teaching Practice  Blackboard Work
               History            Applied Art and Teaching Aids

Grading:  1st Class, 75%; 2nd Class, 60%.  Pass Mark, 40% except Practical
          Teaching, 50%.

Primary Lower Teachers' Certificate (T4) awarded.


Subjects studied - T3

Primary Higher:     Class Teaching and the Making and Use of Teaching Aids
                    Theory of Education
                    School Organization and Regulations
                    English
                    Zulu
                    Mathematics
                    History
                    Geography
                    Science
                    Health Education
                    Religious Education
                    Music
                    Physical Education and Games
                    Art, Craft and Handwork
                    Woodwork
                    Agriculture
                    Needlework

Grading:  1st Class; 2nd Class.  Pass Mark 40%.

Primary Higher Teachers' Certificate awarded.


For clerical course offered at the college, see VOCATIONAL AND TECHNICAL
EDUCATION.

# A P P E N D I X   A

## CONTRIBUTORS

CONTRIBUTORS

NORTH AFRICA

ALGERIA

Dorothy LaGuardia, Head, Educational Placement
   Service
American Friends of the Middle East, Inc.

Ahmed Taleb, Ministre de l'Education Nationale
Ministère de l'Education Nationale, Algiers

M. Messaoudi, Chef du Service des Relations
   Extérieures
Ministère de l'Education Nationale, Algiers

P. Grandjean, Directeur
Ecole Normale Nationale d'Enseignement Professionnel
   et Collège d'Enseignement Technique d'Application,
   Algiers

Le Directeur
Ecole Nationale d'Architecture et des Beaux Arts,
   Algiers

Le Directeur
Ecole Normale Supérieure, Algiers

Mohamed Aberkane, Counselor
Embassy of the Democratic and Popular Republic of
   Algeria

David W. Mize
American Embassy, Algiers

MOROCCO

Virgil Crippin, Vice President, Program
American Friends of the Middle East, Inc.

Mustapha Mzabi, Cultural Attaché
Embassy of Morocco

M. El Machrafi, Directeur Général de l'Enseignement
Ministère de l'Education Nationale, Rabat

Ahmed Lakhdar, Recteur par interim
Université Mohammed V, Rabat

D. Amor, Directeur
Ecole Mohammadia d'Ingénieurs, Rabat

G. Benazzou, Directeur
Institut Nationale de Statistique et d'Economie
   Appliqué, Rabat

Le Directeur
Ecole Normale Supérieure, Rabat

Benouzekri Amor
Collège Ibn Wafid du Fouarat, Kénitra

REPUBLIC OF TUNISIA    Leo Fraenkel
American Friends of the Maghreb, Tunis

Secretariat d'Etat à l'Education Nationale
Tunis

Le Directeur
Ecole Supérieure d'Agriculture de Tunis

KINGDOM OF LIBYA    R. John, Inspector of English Studies
Ministry of Education, Eastern Region, Benghazi

Lily S. Johnson
Tripoli

A. R. Tayar, Registrar
University of Libya

F. Ashour
Embassy of Libya

## E A S T   A F R I C A

REPUBLIC OF THE SUDAN    Mutwakil A. Amin, Cultural Attaché
Sudan Embassy

E. G. Smith, Chief Inspector of Mathematics
Ministry of Education, Khartoum

A. S. Osman, Academic Secretary
University of Khartoum

Ahmed Ibrahim Idris, Principal
School of Hygiene, Ministry of Health, Khartoum

EMPIRE OF ETHIOPIA    Margaret Gillett, Associate Professor, Faculty
of Education
Macdonald College of McGill University, Quebec

J. C. Royds, Headmaster
The General Wingate School, Addis Ababa

T. N. Oommen, Assistant Director
Teacher Training Institute, Asmara

Alex G. Warren, Director of Instruction and
    Research
Jimma Agricultural Technical School

Mengesha Gebre Hiwot, Assistant Minister of
    Education
Ministry of Education and Fine Arts, Addis Ababa

Alemu Begashaw, Registrar
Haile Sellassie I University, Addis Ababa

REPUBLIC OF SOMALIA          R. Stanley Gex, Chief of Party
                             Somali Teacher Training Institute, US/AID
                             Mogadiscio

                             Mohamed Farah Salah, Director, Ministero Della
                                 Pubblica Istruzione
                             Scuola di Avviamento Professionale a Tipo
                                 Industriale, Mogadiscio

REPUBLIC OF KENYA            Gordon P. Hagberg, Institute of International
                                 Education
                             East African Regional Office, Nairobi

                             Jeremy J. White, Secretary
                             Strathmore College of Arts, Nairobi

                             G. Eustace
                             University College, Nairobi

                             Donald Schramm and Lloyd Sherman, Institute of
                                 International Education
                             East African Regional Office, Nairobi

                             K.V. Shah, Office of the Registrar
                             University College, Nairobi

                             Harold V. Smuck, Ag. Exec. Secretary
                             East Africa Yearly Meeting of Friends, Kisumu

                             F.R. Dain, Secretary/Executive Officer
                             The Christian Churches' Educational Association
                             Nairobi

                             Principal
                             Mombasa Technical Institute, Mombasa

UGANDA                     John Kisaka, General Secretary
                           Uganda Teachers' Association, Kampala

                           E.E. Oluo, Registrar
                           Uganda Technical College

                           Bernard Onyango, Deputy Registrar
                           Makerere University College

                           Gerald Moore, Director of Extra-Mural Studies
                           Makerere University College, Kampala

THE UNITED REPUBLIC        Dismas M.S. Mdachi, Registrar of Students
   OF TANZANIA             Ministry of Education, Dar es Salaam

                           J.I. Jackson, Registrar
                           The University College, Dar es Salaam

                           W.K. Chagula, Registrar
                           The University College, Dar es Salaam

                           S.G. Carlson, Senior Master
                           Lutheran Secondary School Ilboru, Arusha

                           Principal Secretary
                           Office of the Ministry of Education (Zanzibar)


E N G L I S H - S P E A K I N G   W E S T   A F R I C A

THE GAMBIA                 Alieu E.W.F. Badji
                           Crab Island Secondary Modern School, Bathurst

REPUBLIC OF GHANA          E. Bennett Caulley, Director, W.C.O.T.P.
                           Africa Regional Office, Accra

                           J.W.A. Sackeyfio
                           Ministry of Education, Accra

SIERRA LEONE               Hope Diffenderfer
                           US/AID, Freetown

                           H.E. Tucker, Chargé d'Affaires
                           Embassy of Sierra Leone

REPUBLIC OF LIBERIA        Laura Tucker, Cultural Attaché and Student Adviser
                           Embassy of the Republic of Liberia, Washington, D.C.

                           Martin Ruccius, Principal
                           Lutheran Training Institute, Monrovia

                           Albert Porte, Executive Secretary
                           The National Teachers' Association of Liberia
                           Monrovia

                           Richard R. Bond, Curriculum Supervisor
                           Cornell University Contract
                           University of Liberia, US/AID, Liberia

                           Emmanuel W. Johnson
                           B.W. Harris Episcopal School, Monrovia

                           George Londry, President
                           Maryland College of Our Lady of Fatima, Cape Palmas

                           Brother Austin Maley, C.S.C., Principal
                           St. Patrick's High School, Monrovia

FEDERATION OF NIGERIA      R.J. Smart, Inspector of Education
                           Ministry of Education, Kaduna

                           Stephen Awokoya, Permanent Secretary
                           Federal Ministry of Education, Lagos

                           Ben O. Akwukwuma, Secretary
                           Institute of Education, University of Ibadan

                           N.O. Ejiogu, Chief Inspector of Education
                           Eastern Nigerian Ministry of Education, Enugu

                           Alhaji M. Adelodun, Assistant Conservator of
                             Forests
                           Forest School, Naraguta

                           W.E. Iweama, Permanent Secretary's Office
                           Ministry of Education, Enugu

                           H.P. Elliott, for Permanent Secretary
                           Ministry of Agriculture, Enugu

                           A.E. Ekanem, Principal
                           School of Agriculture, Umudike

Kenyon T. Payne, Dean
Faculty of Agriculture, University of Nigeria

V. Chacwuemeka Ike, Registrar, and A.J. Okoroafo,
    Assistant Registrar
University of Nigeria, Nsukka

D.O. Somoye
Federal Ministry of Education, Lagos

Clarence Fieldstra
Department of Education, University of Lagos

D.T.R. Elsmore, for Permanent Secretary
Ministry of Agriculture, Kaduna

R.C. Musser
Ministry of Animal and Forest Resources, Kaduna

I.O. Onyeije

## F R E N C H - S P E A K I N G    W E S T    A F R I C A

ISLAMIC REPUBLIC OF       Mohamed Saïd, Bibliothécaire-Archiviste de
    MAURITANIA                1'Assemblée Nationale de Mauritanie
                          Nouakchott

REPUBLIC OF SENEGAL       M'Baye Mbengue, Directeur de 1'Ecole Faidherbe
                          Dakar

                          Alioune A. N'Doye, Chargé d'Affaires a.i.
                          Ambassade du Sénégal, Washington, D.C.

REPUBLIC OF MALI          Vera Zollberg
                          St. Xavier College

GUINEA                    T. Noel Stern, Professor of Political Science
                          Southeastern Massachusetts Technological Institute

                          Guinean Embassy
                          Paris

REPUBLIC OF IVORY          André Clerici, Directeur Général des Etudes
  COAST                        et Programmes
                           Ministère de l'Education Nationale, Abidjan

                           Vera Zollberg
                           St. Xavier College


REPUBLIC OF UPPER          Jacqueline Ki-Zerbo, Directrice de Publication
  VOLTA                    Syndicat National des Enseignants Africains de
                              Haute Volta, Ouagadougou

                           Sogossiro Sanon, Le Ministère de l'Information
                              Chargé de l'interim
                           Ministère de l'Education Nationale, Ouagadougou


REPUBLIC OF NIGER          Haïnnikoye Issa Mody, Directeur de l'Ecole Kalleye
                           Niamey


REPUBLIC OF DAHOMEY        M. Flavien Campbell, Directeur d'Ecole
                           Porto-Novo

                           Antoine André, Cultural Officer
                           Ambassade du Dahomey, Washington, D.C.


REPUBLIC OF TOGO           Didier d'Almeida
                           Ecole Bohn, Lomé

                           Ecole Togolaise d'Administration
                           Lomé

                           Collège Technique de Commerce
                           Lomé

                           Ecole Pratique
                           Sokodé


FEDERAL REPUBLIC OF        Mbarga Henri Bala, Directeur de l'Enseignement
  CAMEROUN                    du 1er degré
                           Yaoundé

                           Ralph Galloway, Directeur
                           Collège Protestant d'Edea, Edea

                           André Gwét, Directeur
                           Collège Evangélique de Libamba, Makak

Gwendolyn Charles, Directrice
College Moderne d'Elat, Ebolowa


# F R E N C H - S P E A K I N G   E Q U A T O R I A L   A F R I C A

REPUBLIC OF CHAD Félicien Adoum, Secrétaire Général du Syndicat
 des Instituteurs et Moniteurs de l'Enseignement
 Privé au Tchad
Fort-Lamy

Issaka Sako, Ministre de l'Education
Ministère de l'Education Nationale, Fort-Lamy

CENTRAL AFRICAN
REPUBLIC Le Secrétariat
Ambassade de la République Centrafricaine
Washington, D.C.

Institut d'Etudes Agronomiques d'Afrique Centrale
Wakombo

THE CONGO REPUBLIC
(Brazzaville) R. Paulian, Directeur
Centre d'Enseignement Supérieur de Brazzaville

REPUBLIC OF GABON Jean-Marc Ekoh, Responsable du Département
 d'Etudes et de Documentation, Eglise Evangélique
Libreville

Maurice Le Flem, Cultural Attaché
Ambassade de la République Gabonaise
Washington, D. C.

R. Barruel, Le Secrétaire Général
Ecole Gabonaise d'Administration, Libreville

Marc A. Trouillot, Directeur
Collège National d'Agriculture, Oyem


# C E N T R A L   A F R I C A

DEMOCRATIC REPUBLIC
OF THE CONGO
(Leopoldville) Basile Mabusa, Consultant Spécial
Leopoldville/Kalina

J. van Berkel, Directeur
Institut Congolais d'Enseignement Social
Leopoldville

J. Pongo, Chargé d'Affaires a.i.
Ambassade de la République du Congo (Leopoldville)
Washington, D.C.

G. Bogaert
Institut Supérieur de Commerce, Leopoldville

Le Directeur
Institut de l'Aviation Civile, Leopoldville

Agricultural and Technical Assistance Foundation
Los Angeles, California

REPUBLIC OF RWANDA    Pierre David, Adviser to Ministry of Education,
    Rwanda
    Montreal, Canada

    J. P. Crépeau, o.p., Secrétaire Général
    Université Nationale du Rwanda, Butare

KINGDOM OF BURUNDI    M. Lazare Ntawurishire, Directeur Général de
    l'Enseignement
    Ministère de l'Education Nationale, Bujumbura

    René Andrianne, Secrétaire de la Faculté des Lettres
    Université Officielle de Bujumbura
    Bujumbura

    P. O. Léon Bududu, Secrétaire de la Commission
    Nationale du Burundi pour l'UNESCO
    Ministère de l'Education Nationale et de la Culture,
    Bujumbura

RHODESIA    C. G. Msipa, General Secretary
    Rhodesia African Teachers' Association, Salisbury

    Mary Quick
    Bulaway

    M. Southwood, Academic Registrar
    University College of Rhodesia and Nyasaland
    Salisbury

    J. F. Gaylard, for Secretary of Education
    Ministry of Education, Salisbury

    Z. Gwanzura, Headmaster
    Hartzell High School, Umtali

A.B. Curtis, Headmaster
Ruzawi School, Marandellas

P.D. Taylor, Private Secretary to the Minister
   of Education
Salisbury

M.L. Hook, Bishop's Secretary for African Education
The Diocese of Mashonaland, Salisbury

J.D. Angus
University College of Rhodesia and Nyasaland

V. Otto, Headmistress
Nyadiri Centre Schools, Salisbury

Kenneth J.F. Skelton, Bishop of Matabeleland
Bulawayo

George J. Fleshman, Secretary, Board of Education
The Methodist Church, Salisbury

F.R. Snell, Rector
Peterhouse, Marandellas

Kenneth Thompson, Associate Dean
Berea College, Kentucky

Kingsley D. Dube, formerly First Secretary
Office of the Minister for Southern Rhodesia
   Affairs, British Embassy

ZAMBIA

Basile R. Kabwe, General Secretary
Zambia National Union of Teachers, Lusaka

S.A. Bottom, Headmaster
Kabulonga School for Boys, Lusaka

Office of Permanent Secretary
Ministry of Education, Lusaka

MALAWI

D.R. Singleton, for Secretary of Education
Ministry of Education, Zomba

John A. Carpenter, Director
Center for Intercultural Education
University of Southern California

I.C.H. Freeman, Registrar
University of Malawi

Martin P. Roseveare, Principal
Soche Hill College, Limbe

Michael E. Soulé, Lecturer in Zoology
University of Malawi

Bruce J. Hahn
Malawi Polytechnic, Blantyre

E. Kendall Clark
Colby School of Agriculture, Lilongwe


S P A N I S H   A F R I C A

José Díaz de Villegas
Instituto de Estudios Africanos
Madrid, Spain

Carlos M. Fernandez-Shaw, Cultural Counselor, and
Vizconde de Priego, Cultural Counselor
Embassy of Spain

Doña Magdalena Caballero, Secretaria del Instituto
Instituto Nacional de Enseñanza Media
Santa Isabel, Fernando Poo

Emilio Garcia Pozal, Maestro Nacional
Servicio de Enseñanza, Aaiún (Sahara)


P O R T U G U E S E   A F R I C A

ANGOLA                Sebastião a. Morão Correira, O Director dos Serviços
                      Direccão Provincial dos Serviços de Instrucão
                      Luanda

MOZAMBIQUE            Direccão Provincial dos Serviços de Educação e
                          Inspeccão de Ensino
                      Lourenço Marques

                      Louis Navega, Second Secretary
                      Embassy of Portugal

## S O U T H E R N   A F R I C A

| | |
|---|---|
| MALAGASY REPUBLIC | M. Pierre Rakotoson, Secrétaire National du Personnel Enseignant et Administratif de l'Education Nationale Malgache<br>Direction générale des Services académiques<br>Tananarive |
| LESOTHO | Evelly Selai Mohapi, Headmaster<br>Basutoland High School<br>Vice-President, Lesotho African National Teachers' Association<br>Maseru<br><br>Agricultural Officer (Education)<br>Department of Agriculture, Maseru<br><br>Brother Sarto J. Martel, s.c., Principal<br>St. Joseph's Training College, Maseru<br><br>J.M. Normand, Registrar<br>University of Basutoland, Bechuanaland Protectorate and Swaziland, Roma |
| BOTSWANA | C. Jack Smith, Deputy Director of Education<br>Department of Education,<br>Mafeking, Republic of South Africa<br><br>Leonard Devitt, Principal<br>St. Joseph's Catholic College, Gaberones<br><br>E.T. Grieveson, Principal<br>Teacher Training College, Lobatsi |
| SWAZILAND | Acting Director of Education<br>Department of Education, Mbabane<br><br>L.M. Arnold, Principal<br>William Pitcher College, Manzina<br><br>Robin Gaydon, Secretariat<br>Ministry of Education, Mbabane<br><br>Headmaster<br>Evelyn Baring High School, Goedgegun |

REPUBLIC OF SOUTH          Dr. Van der Ross
    AFRICA                 Battswood Training College, Wynberg

                           Department of Bantu Education
                           Pretoria

                           A.R. Hamilton, Secretary to the Archbishop of
                               Cape Town
                           Cape Town

                           J.D. Van Rooy, Cultural Attaché
                           Embassy of South Africa, Washington, D.C.

                           Department of Education, Arts and Science
                           Pretoria

                           Joint Matriculation Board
                           Pretoria

                                   *   *   *

FRANCE                     Jean Auba, Directeur de la Coopération
                           Ministère de l'Education Nationale, Paris

                           Edouard Morot-Sir, Cultural Counselor
                           Embassy of France, New York

ENGLAND                    G. Bruce, Secretary of the University Entrance
                               and School Examinations Council
                           University of London, London

                           T.S. Wyatt, The General Secretary
                           University of Cambridge Local Examinations
                               Syndicate, Cambridge

# APPENDIX   B

UNIVERSITY OF CAMBRIDGE LOCAL EXAMINATIONS SYNDICATE

Joint Examination for the School Certificate and General
Certificate of Education
(Overseas Centres Only)

Joint Examination for the Higher School Certificate
and General Certificate of Education
(Overseas Centres Only)

1965

UNIVERSITY OF CAMBRIDGE JOINT EXAMINATION FOR THE SCHOOL CERTIFICATE

AND GENERAL CERTIFICATE OF EDUCATION*

Regulations 1965**

This examination is designed primarily as a school examination.

## Subjects of Examination

Subjects grouped as follows:

I. English Language (compulsory subject for entry for the School Certificate).

II. General subjects: English Literature, Bible Knowledge, History, Geography.

III. Languages: Latin, Greek, French, German, Spanish, other approved languages.

IV. Mathematical subjects: Mathematics, Additional Mathematics.

V. Science subjects: General Science, Additional General Science, Agricultural Science, Physics, Chemistry, Biology, Physics with Chemistry, Botany.

VI. Arts and Crafts: Music, Woodwork, Metalwork, Metalwork (Engineering), Needlework and Dressmaking, Cookery, General Housecraft.

VII. Technical and Commercial subjects: Engineering Science, Surveying, Geometrical and Mechanical Drawing, Geometrical and Building Drawing, Commercial Studies, Commerce, Principals of Accounts, Health Science.

## Choice of Subjects

All candidates must sit for 6, 7 or 8 subjects. These must include English Language and subjects chosen from at least 3 of the groups II, III, IV, V, VI, and VII.

------------

*For background information on University of Cambridge Examinations, see Placement Recommendations, Appendix H.

**For Regulations booklet of the University of Cambridge Local Examinations Syndicate, write The Secretary, Syndicate Buildings, Cambridge, (Price, 1 sh.) Separate subject syllabuses are also available.

## Conditions for the Award of a School Certificate

All requirements must be satisfied at one and the same examination. To qualify for the Certificate candidates must:

(a)  reach a satisfactory general standard in their best 6 subjects, and

either  (b)  pass in at least 6 subjects (including English Language) with credit in at least one of them,

or  (c)  pass in 5 subjects (including English Language) with credits in at least 2 of them.

## Classification of Successful Candidates for the School Certificate

3 divisions. Division attained will be noted on the Certificate.

## First Division School Certificate

Pass in 6 or more subjects, which must include subjects from at least 3 of the groups II, III, IV, V, VI, and VII.

Pass with credit in at least 5 of these subjects, including English Language.

Reach a high general standard as judged by their performance in their best 6 subjects.

## Second Division School Certificate

Pass in 6 or more subjects, which must include English Language and subjects from at least 3 of the groups II, III, IV, V, VI and VII.

Pass with credit in at least 4 of these subjects.

Reach a certain general standard as judged by their performance in their best 6 subjects.

## Third Division School Certificate.

The remaining successful candidates.

## Two Kinds of School Certificates

School Certificate A, which records the name of the school, is issued only to those successful candidates who have been in attendance for at least 2 years continuously at one or more schools approved by the Syndicate and are still attending such a school at the time of taking the examination. Schools are normally approved for the issue of School Certificate A on the recommendation of the appropriate Education Authority.

School Certificate B is issued to all other successful candidates.

## Conditions of the Award of a General Certificate of Education on the Results of the Joint Examination

To qualify for a Certificate, candidates must obtain G.C.E. ordinary level passes (equivalent to School Certificate passes with credit) in at least 3 subjects.

Candidates who sit for, but do not qualify for, the award of a School Certificate receive a General Certificate of Education if they obtain G.C.E. ordinary level passes in at least 3 subjects.

Candidates who hold a Cambridge School Certificate or a General Certificate of Education with 3 passes, and who reach the standard of G.C.E. ordinary level pass (School Certificate pass with credit) in 1 or more subjects at a further examination will receive a General Certificate of Education.

Candidates who do not qualify for a certificate may apply for a statement of their results to be sent directly to a university or a public institution if they reach G.C.E. ordinary level pass in at least 1 subject.

## Grading System in the Joint Examination for the Cambridge School Certificate and General Certificate of Education

School Certificates and General Certificates of Education show subject grades from Grade 1 to 8, and indicate in which subjects candidates gained a G.C.E. ordinary level pass (School Certificate pass with credit). Grades 1 and 2 represent the Very Good standard.

|  School Certificate |  |  |  | G.C.E. |  |  |
|---|---|---|---|---|---|---|
| 1 - Very Good | ) |  |  | 1 | ) |  |
| 2 - Very Good | ) | 1 - 6 |  | 2 | ) |  |
| 3 - Credit | ) | Pass |  | 3 | ) | Ordinary |
| 4 - Credit | ) | with |  | 4 | ) | level |
| 5 - Credit | ) | credit |  | 5 | ) | pass |
| 6 - Credit | ) |  |  | 6 | ) |  |
| 7 - Pass | ) |  |  | 7 | ) |  |
| 8 - Pass | ) |  |  | 8 | ) | Fail |
| 9 - Fail |  |  |  | 9 | ) |  |

N.B.  Grading between 1951-1959:

    School Certificate                  G.C.E.

| School Certificate | | | G.C.E. | | |
|---|---|---|---|---|---|
| 1 - Very Good | | | 1 | ) | |
| 2 - Very Good | ) | 1 - 5 | 2 | ) | Ordinary |
| 3 - Credit | ) | pass | 3 | ) | level |
| 4 - Credit | ) | with | 4 | ) | pass |
| 5 - Credit | ) | credit | 5 | ) | |
| 6 - S.C. Pass | | | | | |
| 7 - S.C. Pass | | | | | |
| 8 - Fail | | | | | |
| 9 - Fail | | | | | |

## UNIVERSITY OF CAMBRIDGE JOINT EXAMINATION FOR THE HIGHER SCHOOL CERTIFICATE AND GENERAL CERTIFICATE OF EDUCATION[*]

Previous to 1964 only the Higher School Certificate examination was offered. From 1964 the General Certificate of Education was added. Following are the changes in the Regulations on which the Joint Examination now rests.

### 1964 Changes in the Regulations for the Higher School Certificate Examination.

(1)  The examination is re-named "Joint Examination for the Higher School Certificate and General Certificate of Education."

(2)  The G.C.E. equivalents of principal subjects and subsidiary subjects will be shown on all Higher School Certificates. (The equivalent of a pass at G.C.E. advanced level; that of a pass at Higher School Certificate subsidiary level is a pass at G.C.E. ordinary level.)

(3)  Candidates who enter for, but fail to qualify for the award of, a Higher School Certificate but who pass in at least 1 principal subject, or who pass in a subsidiary subject and have previously passed in a principal subject, will receive a General Certificate of Education.

(4)  Candidates who enter for a part of the examination and pass in at least 1 principal subject, or who pass in a subsidiary subject and

---

[*]For Regulations booklet of the University of Cambridge Local Examinations Syndicate, write the Secretary, Syndicate Buildings, Cambridge. (Price: 1 sh.) Separate subject syllabuses are also available.

have previously passed in a principal subject, will receive a General Certificate of Education.

(5)  In areas where private candidates (those not entitled to enter as "school" candidates) are accepted they will be eligible to receive Higher School Certificates and General Certificates of Education under the same conditions as school candidates (those entered by approved schools), but no entry will be accepted from a private candidate which does not include at least 1 principal subject.

## General Entrance Requirements for the Joint Examination

(1)  The Joint Examination for the Higher School Certificate and General Certificate of Education is limited to candidates who have gained a School Certificate or the equivalent or who, while not gaining a School Certificate, on one and the same occasion have passed with credit in at least 3 School Certificate subjects or have passed in at least 3 G.C.E. subjects.

Candidates are expected to have followed a 2-year advanced course beyond the School Certificate stage, and therefore are not normally allowed to enter for the examination in the year next following that in which they qualified to do so. Qualified candidates may, however, offer after 1 year not more than 2 principal subjects or 1 principal and 2 subsidiary subjects; they may also offer the General Paper.

(2)  Subjects may be offered at 2 levels, "principal" and "subsidiary," and there are 2 corresponding standards of success. A candidate who fails to reach "principal" level in a principal subject may be awarded a pass in it at "subsidiary" level.

The relationship, for exemption purposes, between the "principal" and "subsidiary" levels of this examination and "advanced level" and "ordinary level" in the General Certificate of Education follows:

It may be assumed that, for the purpose of exemption from University Entrance and Intermediate examinations and from the Preliminary or other examinations of professional bodies, a pass at principal level in a subject of the Joint Examination for the Higher School Certificate and G.C.E. will be considered the equivalent of a pass at advanced level in a corresponding subject of the General Certificate of Education in the United Kingdom. Similarly, a pass at subsidiary level in the examination will be considered the equivalent of a pass at ordinary level in the examination for the General Certificate of Education.

## Principal Subjects of Examination

English, Bible Knowledge, History, Geography, Economic and Public Affairs, Latin, Greek, French, Spanish, Mathematics, Pure Mathematics, Applied Mathematics, Physics, Chemistry, Biology, Botany, Zoology, Art, Music, Woodwork, Metalwork, Geology.

(The principal subject Physics-with-Chemistry is withdrawn as from the 1964 examination.)

## Subsidiary Subjects of Examination

English, Ancient History, Latin, Greek, French, Spanish, Mathematics, Physics, Chemistry, Biology, Botany, Geology, Music.

Parts of certain principal subjects may be offered as subsidiary subjects. No candidate may take a subject at both principal and subsidiary level nor take two subsidiary subjects from the same principal subject.

(A pass in the General Paper is recorded as a pass in a subsidiary subject.)

## Choice of Subjects

Each candidate for a <u>Higher School Certificate</u> must offer the General Paper and at least 3 principal subjects or at least 2 principal subjects and 2 subsidiary subjects.

No candidate may offer more than 4 subjects and the General Paper.

Entries for a General Certificate of Education which do not include a principal subject are not accepted from private candidates. School candidates who make such entries are not considered for the award of a certificate unless they have previously passed in a principal subject.

## Award of Certificates

(a) To qualify for a Higher School Certificate, candidates must at one and the same examination pass in the General Paper and

<u>either</u> (i) pass in at least 3 principal subjects
<u>or</u> (ii) pass in at least 2 principal subjects and 2 subsidiary subjects
<u>or</u> (iii) pass in at least 2 principal subjects and 1 subsidiary subject and reach a certain standard, as defined by the grades, in the 2 principal subjects in which they have been passed.

A Certificate may be awarded to a candidate who fails by a small margin in the General Paper but who satisfies the conditions stated in (i) or (ii) above.

(b)    To qualify for a General Certificate of Education, candidates must pass in at least 1 principal subject, or, provided they have previously passed in a principal subject, in 1 subsidiary subject. Candidates who enter for the full Higher School Certificate but fail to gain one, as well as candidates who do not enter for the full Higher School Certificate, will be considered for the award of General Certificates of Education.

Note:  A candidate who offers a subject at principal level and fails to reach that level may be allowed to pass at the subsidiary level. A candidate who reaches the pass mark in a modern language at the principal level while failing to attain a sufficient standard in the language (including the oral) tests or in Paper 3, or in a science subject while failing in the practical test, will normally be allowed to pass at the subsidiary level only.

System of Classification

For Principal Subjects

(Introduced 1963 for G.C.E. advanced level passes by all the approved Examining Bodies for the General Certificate of Education in the United Kingdom.)

        5 categories of "Pass":
            A
            B
            C
            D
            E
        Pass at Subsidiary level
        Fail

For Subsidiary Subjects and General Paper (as in past)

    Grades 1 - 9

        1 )                            7 )
        2 )                            8 ) (All)  Fail
        3 )                            9 )
        4 ) (All) Pass
        5 )
        6 )

The standard reached in each paper taken as part of a principal subject will also be stated in terms of these 9 grades.

A P P E N D I X   C


UNIVERSITY OF LONDON

General Certificate of Education Examinations
Held Overseas

June 1964 and January 1965

UNIVERSITY OF LONDON

GENERAL CERTIFICATES OF EDUCATION EXAMINATIONS*

Held Overseas June 1964 and January 1965


This examination is held primarily for <u>private</u> candidates. In certain instances the University is prepared to hold the examination in a school or college overseas.


## SPECIAL PROVISIONS FOR PRIVATE CANDIDATES

### Nigeria and Sierra Leone

See special <u>Nigerian Appendix</u> at close of main NIGERIA report. After January 1965 the supplementary conditions there listed to be abolished; however, candidates will choose their subjects from the listing under (8).


### Somali Republic

(1) Candidates who hold a General Certificate of Education, or a Matriculation Certificate of the University of London, or other certificate recording passes in subjects recognized by the University of London as equivalent to the G.C.E. may enter for one or more ordinary level or advanced level subjects and will receive certificates in respect of the subjects in which they pass.

(2) Candidates who do not hold one of the qualifications listed above will be required to enter at the ordinary level in not less than 4 and not more than 7 subjects, including English Language.

(3) A candidate who reaches the pass standard in any 3 subjects and at the same time achieves a certain minimum standard of attainment in English Language, or a candidate who reaches the past standard in 3 subjects including English Language, will be eligible for the award of a certificate.

(4) A candidate who fails to reach the pass standard in at least 3 subjects, or who fails to achieve a certain minimum standard in English Language, will not be eligible for the award of a certificate but will receive a statement of result.

---

\*For the <u>Regulations and Syllabuses</u> for the University of London G.C.E. examinations, write the Secretary, School Examinations Department, University of London, Senate House, Malet Street, London, W.C.1.

(5)  A candidate who fails to qualify for the award of a G.C.E. under
     paragraph (4) may count the subjects in which he is successful
     towards the fulfillment of the general entrance requirement for
     degree courses.


## Ghana and the Gambia

After January 1964 the supplementary conditions indicated below will be
abolished, but candidates must choose from the list of subjects listed
under (3).

(1)  Candidates who hold one of the following:

        a statement of eligibility,
        a General Certificate of Education
or  a Matriculation Certificate of the University of London
or  a Cambridge School Certificate
or  a West African School Certificate
or  a Nigerian Teacher's Certificate Grade I
or  a certificate recording passes in subjects recognized by the Univer-
        sity of London as equivalent to the ordinary level of the G.C.E.
or  who, at a Cambridge or a West African School Certificate Examination
        have gained credits in 3 subjects including English Language, or
        credits in 3 subjects together with a pass in English Language
        though failing to gain a certificate
or  who, at a previous G.C.E. examination of the University of London
        have gained at least 1 pass at the advanced level though failing to
        gain a certificate

        may enter for one or more subjects at the ordinary or advanced levels
        or both, subject to a maximum of 4 subjects at the advanced level or
        10 subjects in all, and will receive a certificate in respect of the
        subjects in which they pass. Subjects must be chosen from the lists
        in (3) below.

(2)  Candidates who do not hold one of the qualifications listed in para-
     graph above must enter at the ordinary level in not less than 4 and
     not more than 7 subjects chosen from the list in (3) below. One of
     the subjects offered must be English Language. They may not offer
     subjects at the advanced level. A candidate who reaches the pass
     standard in any 3 subjects and at the same time achieves a certain
     minimum standard of attainment in English Language, or who reaches
     the pass standard in 3 subjects including English Language, will be
     eligible for the award of a certificate stating the subjects in
     which he has passed. A candidate who fails to satisfy either of
     these requirements will not be awarded a certificate but will receive
     a statement of result. A candidate who fails to qualify for the
     award of a G.C.E. may count the subjects in which he is successful
     towards the fulfillment of the general entrance requirement for
     degree courses.

(3)   Subjects offered must be chosen from the following lists:

    (a)   <u>Ordinary Level</u>

| | |
|---|---|
| Art, Syllabus A | Hausa |
| Biology | History |
| Botany | History, Ancient |
| British Constitution | History of the British Common- |
| Chemistry |    wealth and Empire |
| Economics | History, British Economic |
| English Language | Igbo (Ibo) |
| English Literature | Latin, Syllabus A |
| Ewe | Mathematics, Pure |
| Fante | Mathematics, Additional |
| French | Music |
| Ga | Physics |
| General Science | Religious Knowledge |
| Geography | Spanish |
| Geology | Technical Drawing |
| German | Twi |
| Greek | Yoruba |

    (b)   <u>Advanced Level</u>

| | |
|---|---|
| Art, Syllabus A | Geography |
| Biology | Geology |
| Botany | German |
| British Constitution | Greek |
| Chemistry | History |
| Economics | History, Ancient |
| English Literature | History, British Economic |
| French | Latin |
| Mathematics, Pure | Physics |
| Mathematics, Applied | Religious Knowledge |
| Mathematics | Spanish |
| Music | Zoology |

<u>Kenya</u>

(1)   Only <u>bona</u> <u>fide</u> residents will be accepted for the examination.

(2)   Candidates who hold:

       a statement of eligibility of the University of London
<u>or</u>  a Cambridge School Certificate
<u>or</u>  a General Certificate of Education
<u>or</u>  a Matriculation Certificate of the University of London
<u>or</u>  a certificate recording passes in subjects recognized by the Univer-
       sity of London as equivalent to the ordinary level of the G.C.E.

       may enter for one or more subjects at the ordinary level or advanced
       level or both, subject to a maximum of 4 subjects at the advanced

level or 10 subjects in all, and will receive a certificate in respect of the subject(s) in which they pass. Subjects must be chosen from the lists in (5) below.

(3) Before entering the examination candidates who do not hold one of the qualifications set out in paragraph (2) above will be required to pass a qualifying test approved by the respective Ministries of Education.

(4) Candidates who do not hold one of the qualifications listed in paragraph (2), but have passed the qualifying test in paragraph (3) must enter at the ordinary level in not less than 4 and not more than 7 subjects chosen from the lists in paragraph (5) below. One of the subjects offered must be English Language. They may not offer subjects at the advanced level. A candidate who reaches the pass standard in any 3 subjects and at the same time achieves a certain minimum standard of attainment in English Language, or who reaches the pass standard in 3 subjects including English Language, will be eligible for the award of a certificate stating the subjects in which he has passed. A candidate who fails to satisfy either of these requirements will not be awarded a certificate but will receive a statement of result.

(5) Subjects offered must be chosen from the following lists:

(a) Accounts, Principles of
Afrikaans
Classical Arabic
Art, Syllabus A
Biology
Botany
British Constitution
Chemistry
Commerce
Economics
English Language
English Literature
French
General Science
Geography
German
Greek
Gujarati
Hindi
History
History, Ancient
History of the British Commonwealth and Empire
History, British Economic
Human Anatomy, Physiology and Hygiene
Italian
Latin
Logic
Mathematics, Pure
Mathematics, Additional
Physics
Physics with Chemistry
Religious Knowledge
Sanskrit
Spanish
Swahili
Technical Drawing
Urdu

(b) Advanced Level

Classical Arabic
Art, Syllabus A
Biology
Botany
British Constitution
History, Ancient
History, British Economic
History, Indian
Italian
Latin

Chemistry                          Mathematics, Pure
Economics                          Mathematics, Applied
English Literature                 Mathematics
French                             Physics
Geography                          Religious Knowledge
Geology                            Sanskrit
German                             Spanish
Greek                              Swahili
History                            Technical Drawing
                                   Zoology

## Tanzania (Tanganyika)

(1)  Only bona fide residents will be accepted for entry for the examina-
     tion.

(2)  Candidates who hold:

        a statement of eligibility of the University of London
     or a Cambridge School Certificate
     or a General Certificate of Education
     or a Matriculation Certificate of the University of London
     or a certificate recording passes in subjects recognized by the Univer-
        sity of London as equivalent to the ordinary level of the G.C.E.

     may enter for one or more subjects at the ordinary level or advanced
     level, or both, subject to a maximum of 4 subjects at the advanced
     level or 10 subjects in all, and will receive a certificate in re-
     spect of the subject(s) in which they pass.  Subjects must be chosen
     from the lists indicated in paragraph (7) below.

(3)  Candidates who do not hold one of the qualifications listed in para-
     graph (2) above, must enter for the one subject, English Language,
     at the ordinary level.

(4)  Any candidate who reaches Grade O or a better grade in English Lan-
     guage is entitled to a certificate for it and will then be eligible
     to take other ordinary level subjects of his own choosing at sub-
     sequent examinations.

(5)  Any candidate who reaches Grade F or G in English Language will not
     qualify for a certificate but will be eligible to take ordinary level
     subjects of his own choosing at subsequent examinations.

(6)  A candidate who holds a London G.C.E. indicating at least one ordi-
     nary level pass may enter for advanced level subjects in subsequent
     examinations.

(7)  Subjects offered must be chosen from following lists:
     Same as those shown in preceding KENYA section, with the exception
     of Ancient History, Logic and Sanskrit at ordinary level.

## Tanzania (Zanzibar)

(1) Except as provided for in (4) below, no candidate will be accepted who enters for less than 5 subjects, one of which must be English Language; at least one must be English Literature, History or Geography, and at least one must be Mathematics or a science subject (including Geography.)

(2) A candidate entering under (1) can not be eligible for the award of a certificate unless he reaches the pass standard in at least 3 subjects, one of which must be English Language or unless he reaches the pass standard in 3 subjects and at the same time achieves a certain minimum standard of attainment in English Language.

(3) A candidate who fails to qualify for the award of a G.C.E. under paragraph (2) may count the subjects in which he is successful toward the fulfillment of the general entrance requirement for degree courses.

(4) A candidate who holds a G.C.E. of the University of London or a Cambridge School Certificate or a certificate recording passes in subjects recognized by the University of London as the equivalent of the ordinary level of the G.C.E., will be permitted to enter for one or more subjects at ordinary or advanced level, and he will be eligible for the award of a certificate in respect of the subjects in which he reaches the pass standard.

(5) A candidate who does not hold one of the qualifications listed in (4) above must enter at the ordinary level. He may not offer subjects at the advanced level.

## Lesotho (Basutoland)

(1) No specific qualifications are required for admission to the ordinary level examination.

(2) A candidate must have passed in not less than 3 subjects at the ordinary level of which one must be English Language before proceeding to take 2 different subjects at the advanced level,

or  a candidate must have obtained one of the following certificates:

Cambridge School Certificate with credits in English Language, and 2 other subjects

School Leaving Certificate (J.M.B.) including a pass in English High Grade

National Senior Certificate (S.A.) including a pass in English Higher Grade

Cape (or other provincial) Senior Certificate including a pass in English Higher Grade.

## Republic of Cameroun

(1)   A candidate who holds one of the following qualifications may enter
      in any one or more subjects at any level up to a maximum of 4 sub-
      jects  at the advanced level and 10 subjects in all.  No subject may
      be offered at both levels at the same examination.
      (a)   A statement of eligibility (issued by a university).
      (b)   A G.C.E., irrespective of when gained, in 3 or more subjects.
      (c)   A G.C.E. gained not later than 1962.
      (d)   A Matriculation Certificate of the University of London.
      (e)   A Cambridge School Certificate with credits in 3 or more sub-
            jects.
      (f)   A West African School Certificate with credits in 3 or more
            subjects.
      (g)   A Cameroun or a Nigerian Teachers' Grade I Certificate.
      (h)   A statement of result in the Cambridge or West African School
            Certificate recording credits in 3 subjects, including English
            Language, or in 3 subjects and with a pass in English Language.

(2)   A candidate who has passed at the ordinary level in any subject may
      sit at the advanced level in that subject even though he does not
      satisfy any of the conditions in (a) to (h) above.

(3)   A candidate who holds one of the following qualifications may take
      the examination at ordinary level up to a maximum of 10 subjects:
      (a)   A G.C.E. in English Language.
      (b)   Grade 7 or 8 English Language at a G.C.E. examination (or Grade
            F or G with effect from the January 1964 examination).
      (c)   A pass in the qualifying test of the West African Examinations
            Council.
      (d)   A pass in one subject at the ordinary level at the G.C.E. exam-
            ination.
      (e)   A pass in English Language at Stage II (Intermediate) examina-
            tion of the Royal Society of Arts.
      (f)   Senior School Commercial Certificate of the Royal Society of
            Arts.
      (g)   A Cameroun or Nigerian Teachers' Grade II (Higher Elementary)
            Certificate.
      (h)   A pass in English Language at a School Certificate or a Cameroun
            or Nigerian Teachers' Grade II Certificate examination though
            failing to pass the whole examination.
      (i)   A valid testimonial for successful completion of at least form
            four in an approved secondary (grammar) school.
      (j)   A pass in English Language at the Preliminary Stage of the Cor-
            poration of Secretaries examination.

(4)   A candidate who does not hold any of the qualifications listed in
      (1) and (3) above must enter for the G.C.E. examination in English
      Language only.  Those who pass at the ordinary level qualify for a
      Certificate and may enter subsequently under (3,a) above.  Those who
      obtain Grades 7 or 8 will not qualify for a Certificate but may
      enter subsequently under (3,b) above.

(5) Candidates who hold the Cameroun or Nigerian Teachers' Grade II
    (Higher Elementary) Certificate and who are seeking to satisfy the
    academic requirements for the award of a Teachers' Grade I Certi-
    ficate may enter at the advanced level in one or more subjects
    chosen from the following list:

|  |  |
|---|---|
| English Literature | Pure Mathematics |
| French | Physics |
| Geography | Chemistry |
| History | Biology |
|  | Religious Knowledge |

Candidates in this category may also enter for the English Language
only examination.

## EXAMINATION SUBJECTS AVAILABLE

O = Ordinary Level            A = Advanced Level

| | |
|---|---|
| Accounts, Principles of | O |
| Art | O, A |
| Biology | O, A |
| Botany | O, A |
| British Constitution | O, A |
| Chemistry | O, A |
| Commerce | O |
| Domestic subjects (Cookery) | O |
| Domestic subjects (Needlework) | O |
| Economics | O |
| Elementary Surveying | O |
| English Language | O |
| English Literature | O, A |
| English Literature, Syllabus B | O |
| French | O, A |
| General Science | O |
| General Science, Additional | O |
| Geography | O, A |
| Geology | O, A |
| German | O, A |
| Greek (Classical) | O, A |
| Greek Literature in Translation | O |
| Handicraft | O |
| Handicraft (Metalwork) | O, A |
| Handicraft (Woodwork) | O, A |
| History | O, A |
| History, Ancient | O, A |
| History of the British Commonwealth and Empire | O |
| History, British Economic | O, A |

| | |
|---|---|
| History, Indian | A |
| History, Islamic | A |
| Human Anatomy, Physiology and Hygiene | O |
| Italian | O, A |
| Latin | O, A |
| Latin, Syllabus B | O |
| Logic | O, A |
| Mathematics, Pure | O, A |
| Mathematics, Pure, Syllabus B | O |
| Mathematics, Additional (O level) Further (A level) | O, A |
| Mathematics, Applied | A |
| Mathematics | A |
| Music | O, A |
| Physics | O, A |
| Physics with Chemistry | O |
| Religious Knowledge | O, A |
| Russian | O, A |
| Spanish | O, A |
| Technical Drawing | O, A |
| Zoology | A |
| | |
| Essay, British Guiana and Sierra Leone | A |
| English Literature for centers in Africa | A |
| Geography for centers in Africa | A |
| Economics for centers in West Africa | O, A |

## Specially Approved Languages

| | |
|---|---|
| Afrikaans | O, A |
| Albanian | O, A |
| Amharic | O |
| Arabic, Classical | O, A |
| Armenian | O |
| Armenian, Classical | A |
| Bahasa, Indonesia | O |
| Bengali | O |
| Bulgarian | A |
| Burmese | O |
| Chinese | O |
| Chinese, Classical | A |
| Czech | O, A |
| Danish | O, A |
| Dutch | O, A |
| Estonian | O |
| Ewe | O |

| | | |
|---|---|---|
| Fante | O | |
| Finnish | O | |
| Ga | O | |
| Greek, Modern | O, | A |
| Gujarati | O | |
| Hausa | O, | A |
| Hebrew, Classical | O, | A |
| Hebrew, Modern | O | |
| Hindi | O | |
| Hungarian | O, | A |
| Icelandic | O | |
| Igbo | O | |
| Irish | O, | A |
| Japanese | O | |
| Japanese, Classical | | A |
| Latvian | O | |
| Lithuanian | O | |
| Malayan | O | |
| Maltese | O | |
| Marathi | O | |
| Norwegian | O, | A |
| Pali | O, | A |
| Persian | O | |
| Persian, Classical | | A |
| Polish | O, | A |
| Portuguese | O, | A |
| Rumanian | O, | A |
| Samoan | O | |
| Sanskrit | O, | A |
| Scottish Gaelic | O, | A |
| Serbo-Croat | O, | A |
| Siamese | O | |
| Sinhalese | O, | A |
| Slovak | O, | A |
| Slovene | O, | A |
| Swahili | O, | A |
| Swedish | O, | A |
| Tamil | O, | A |
| Turkish | O, | A |
| Twi | O | |
| Ukrainian | O | |
| Urdu | O | |
| Vietnamese | O | |
| Welsh | O | |
| White Russian | O | |
| Yoruba | O | |

## Certificates

The General Certificates awarded record the name of the candidate, the school or center at which the examination was taken, and the subjects in which a pass at ordinary level was obtained. Certificates at advanced level record the grade of pass attained. A duplicate Certificate is not issued without satisfactory evidence of the destruction of the original.

## Grading

Results are issued in the form of grades.
Letter grades used for advanced level from 1963.

| Advanced Level | Grade 1962 | Grade 1963 | Scaled Mark |
|---|---|---|---|
| | 1 ) | A | 75+ |
| | 2 ) | | 70-74 |
| | 3 | B | 60-69 |
| | 4 | C | 55-59 |
| | 5 | D | 50-54 |
| | 6 | E | 40-49 |
| | 7 ) | O | 36-39 |
| | 8 ) | | 30-35 |
| | 9 | F | 0-29 |
| Ordinary Level | 1 | A | 75+ |
| | 2 | B | 70-74 |
| | 3 | C | 60-69 |
| | 4 | D | 55-59 |
| | 5 | E | 50-54 |
| | 6 | O | 45-49 |
| | 7 | F | 42-44 |
| | 8 | G | 35-41 |
| | 9 | H | 0-34 |

The marks referred to are scaled ones to equate the subjects (raw marks show inequalities: for example, many score high marks in mathematics and not so many in history).

In recording the certificates, in science subjects, the first grade shows the results for the subject as a whole and the next indicates the results in the practical examination. In French, German, Italian, Spanish and Russian, the first grade shows the results for the subjects as a whole, and the next the result for the oral test.

Three designations show attainment in the Special Papers. Grade 1 indicates "distinction," 2 "merit," and U "unclassified." No candidate may qualify for grade 1 or 2 on a Special Paper without attaining Grade A, B, or C on the basic advanced level papers in the same subject.

A P P E N D I X   D

THE WEST AFRICAN EXAMINATIONS COUNCIL

Joint Examination for the School Certificate and General
Certificate of Education in the Gambia, Ghana and Sierra Leone

Joint Examination for the West African School Certificate
and General Certificate of Education in Nigeria

1965

<u>THE WEST AFRICAN EXAMINATIONS COUNCIL</u>

Correspondence should be addressed to:

Headquarters Office:                 The Registrar
                                        The West African Examinations Council
                                        Private Post Bag
                                        Accra, Ghana

The Gambia:                        The Director of Education
                                        Bathurst

Ghana:                              The Deputy Registrar
                                        The West African Examinations Council
                                        P.O. Box 917
                                        Accra

Nigeria:                          The Senior Deputy Registrar
                                        The West African Examinations Council
                                        Private Mail Bag No. 1022
                                        Yaba

Sierra Leone:                    The Senior Assistant Registrar
                                        The West African Examinations Council
                                      P.O. Box 573
                                      Freetown

United Kingdom:                  The London Representative
                                        The West African Examinations Council
                                      41 Gordon Square, London, W.C. 1

<u>Joint Examination for the School Certificate and General Certificate
of Education of the West African Examinations Council - to 1965</u>[*]

This examination, held only in the Gambia, Ghana and Sierra Leone, was
designed primarily as a school examination. Candidates were accepted as
"school candidates" only if they were presented by a school which had
been recognized by the Council for the issue of the School Certificate.
Candidates not attending schools recognized for the purpose of taking
the examinations were accepted as "private candidates." There was no
age limit for candidates taking the examination.

---

[*]For <u>Regulations and Syllabuses</u>, write to appropriate office indicated above. Price: 5 sh.

N.B.  From 1965 the School Certificate ceased to be awarded and candidates
entered for the <u>General Certificate of Education Examination</u> of the
Council.  <u>See next section</u>.

## Subjects of Examination:

Subjects are grouped as follows:

|     |     |     |
| --- | --- | --- |
| I.   | Languages:        | English Language, Latin, Greek, French, German, Italian, Ewe, Fante, Ga, Twi, Arabic. |
| II.  | General subjects: | English Literature, Bible Knowledge, Islamic Religious Knowledge, History, Geography. |
| III. | Mathematics subjects: | Mathematics, Additional Mathematics. |
| IV.  | Science subjects: | General Science, Additional General Science, Physics, Chemistry, Biology, Agricultural Science. |
| V.   | Arts and Crafts:  | Art, Music, Woodwork, Metalwork, Needlework and Dressmaking, Cookery, General Housecraft. |
| VI.  | Technical and Commercial subjects: | Technical Drawing, Commercial subjects, Health Science. |

## Choice of Subjects

Normally, candidates must enter and sit for not less than 6 nor more than
9 subjects.  These must include subjects chosen from at least 3 of the
groups listed above.

## Grading

```
          1 - Excellent
          2 - Very Good
          3                    (1-6 pass with Credit)
          4
          5
          6
         ───
          7 - Pass
          8 - Pass
          9 - Failure
```

## Conditions for the Award of a School Certificate

All the requirements for the Certificate must be satisfied at one and the
same examination.  To qualify for the Certificate candidates must:

|        |     |     |
| ------ | --- | --- |
|        | (a) | reach a satisfactory general standard as judged by their aggregate performance in their best 6 subjects, and |
| <u>either</u> | (b) | pass in at least 6 subjects, with credit in at least 1 of them |
| <u>or</u>     | (c) | pass in 5 subjects, with credits in at least 2 of them. |

Two Kinds of Certificates

The form of Certificate, which records the name of the candidate at the time of entry and the name of the school(s) attended, is issued only to those successful candidates who have been in attendance for at least 3 years continuously at one or more schools recognized by the Council for the award of the School Certificate.

Other candidates, if successful, receive a modified form of Certificate.

Classification of Candidates Who Obtain a School Certificate

First Division Certificates awarded to candidates who:

    (a)  Pass in 6 or more subjects, drawn from not less than 3 of the Groups I - VI

    (b)  Pass with credit in at least 5 of these subjects, which must include credits in subjects from at least 2 of the Groups I, II, III, and IV, and

    (c)  Reach a high general standard as judged by their performance in their best 6 subjects.

Second Division Certificates awarded to candidates who:

    (a)  Pass in 6 or more subjects drawn from not less than 3 of the Groups I - VI

    (b)  Pass with credit in at least 4 subjects, and

    (c)  Reach a certain general standard as judged by their performance in their best 6 subjects.

Third Division Certificates awarded to the remaining successful candidates.

Conditions for the Award of a General Certificate of Education

A General Certificate of Education is awarded to candidates who:

    (a)  Enter for a full School Certificate and

    (b)  Pass with credit in at least one of the subjects offered.

Candidates who satisfy the conditions for the award of a School Certificate receive a combined School Certificate and General Certificate of Education on which it is made clear that in subjects in which they gained grade 6 or better they achieved a G.C.E. pass at ordinary level.

Exemption from Other Examinations

For the purpose of exemption from university entrance requirements, a pass with credit in a subject of the Joint Examination for the School Certificate and General Certificate of Education of the West African Examinations

Council will be considered the equivalent of a pass at ordinary level in a corresponding subject of the General Certificate of Education Examination by the Universities of Oxford, Cambridge, Durham and London and the West African Universities and University Colleges.

### Examination for the General Certificate of Education of the West African Examinations Council - from 1965[*]

This examination, held only in the Gambia, Ghana and Sierra Leone, is designed primarily as a school examination. Candidates can be accepted as "school candidates" only if they are presented by a school which has been recognized by the Council for the issue of the Certificate. Candidates attending schools which are not recognized for the purpose of taking the examination may enter as "candidates from unrecognized schools." "Private candidates," those not attending school, may make individual entries. There is no age limit for candidates taking the examination.

### Subjects of Examination

Languages:           English Language (a test in oral English is also available), Latin, Greek, French, German, Italian, Fante, Ga, Twi, Arabic.

General subjects:    English Literature, Bible Knowledge, Islamic Religious Knowledge, History, Geography.

Mathematics subjects: Mathematics, Additional Mathematics.

Science subjects:    General Science, Additional General Science, Physics, Chemistry, Biology, Agricultural Science.

Arts and Crafts:     Music, Woodwork, Metalwork, Needlework and Dressmaking, Cookery, General Housecraft.

Technical and Commercial subjects: Technical Drawing, Commercial subjects, Health Science.

### Choice of Subjects

Normally, candidates must enter for not more than 9 subjects. The Oral English test may be taken in addition to the 9 subjects chosen.

### Grading

See previous section on Grading.

---

[*]Write for:   Amendment Leaflet No. 2 to the Regulations and Syllabuses for 1965.

Two Kinds of Certificates

See previous section on Two Kinds of Certificates.

Conditions for the Award of a G.C.E.

To qualify for the Certificate, candidates must obtain at least Grade 6
(Credit) in one subject.

Standards in Subjects

Certificates awarded to successful candidates show the grades attained in
all the subjects in which the holder has obtained grade 8 or above.  Grade
6 is the lowest standard generally recognized for exemption from other
examinations.

For the purpose of satisfying the minimum entrance requirements of the
Universities of Oxford, Cambridge, Durham, London and all universities
and university colleges in the Commonwealth countries in West Africa,
Grade 6 in a subject of the Examination for the General Certificate of
Education of the West African Examinations Council is the equivalent of
a pass at ordinary level in the corresponding subject in the G.C.E. examinations of the British Examining Boards.

Interpretation of the subject grades in terms of the former Joint Examination for the School Certificate and G.C.E. of the West African Examinations
Council follows:


| GRADE | FORMER SCHOOL CERTIFICATE EQUIVALENT | | G.C.E. ORDINARY LEVEL EQUIVALENT |
|---|---|---|---|
| Grade 1 | Excellent | | ) |
| Grade 2 | Very Good | | ) |
| | | | ) |
| Grade 3 | Good | ) | ) |
| Grade 4 | | ) | ) |
| Grade 5 | | ) Credit | ) Pass |
| Grade 6 | | ) | ) |
| Grade 7 | ) Pass | | ) |
| Grade 8 | ) | | ) Fail |
| | | | ) |
| Grade 9 | Fail | | ) |

Joint Examination for the West African School Certificate
and General Certificate of Education - 1965*

This examination is taken in Nigeria only. The examination is designed
as a school examination. Candidates can be accepted as "school candidates"
only if they are presented by a school in Nigeria which has been recognized
by the Council for the issue of a Certificate. There is no age limit for
candidates taking this examination.

N.B.   Through 1964 this examination was known as the West African School
       Certificate Examination; no  G.C.E. was offered.

For details of examination, see Secondary Education, NIGERIA.

---

*For Regulations and Syllabuses, write the Nigerian office indicated
on page 1 of this section.  Price:  5 sh.

# A P P E N D I X  E


ROYAL SOCIETY OF ARTS

Ordinary Examinations

1964

ROYAL SOCIETY OF ARTS

Correspondence should be addressed to:

>   The Principal
>   Royal Society of Arts (Examinations Department)
>   18 Adam Street, Adelphi
>   London, W.C. 2

## SCHOOL CERTIFICATE (Commercial) EXAMINATIONS

Candidates take this examination after completing a 5-year course in a secondary commercial school. (See EASTERN NIGERIA for typical program.)

Examinations offered in following subjects:

| | |
|---|---|
| Accounts | History of the British Common- |
| Arithmetic | wealth |
| Biology | Human Biology and Hygiene |
| Chemistry | Italian |
| Civics | Mathematics I |
| Commerce | Modern British History |
| English Language | Physics |
| English Literature | Religious Knowledge |
| French | Shorthand (50/60 w.p.m.) |
| General Science | Spanish |
| Geography | Typewriting |
| German | |

Candidates must enter for minimum of 5 subjects, the choice of which must conform to requirements given below. Any number of subjects above the prescribed minimum may be taken. Candidates, may, if they wish, take papers in appropriate subjects at the Secretarial and Commercial Certificate examinations.

## Certificates awarded:

The Royal Society of Arts School Certificate (Commercial) is awarded to candidates who pass at 1 examination in:

|  |  |  |
|---|---|---|
| | (a) | English Language, |
| plus | (b) | At least 3 subjects selected from Accounts, Arithmetic, Commerce, Shorthand (50 or 60 words per minute), and Typewriting, |
| plus | (c) | At least 1 subject selected from the other subjects listed |

under "Examinations offered in following subjects" but not included in (b) above.

Consideration will be given to the award of the School Certificate (Commercial) to a candidate who passes in any 4 of the prescribed minimum of 5 subjects and who obtains not less than 40% of the marks in the fifth subject.

The certificate states the subjects in which the candidate has passed, or has passed with credit; in case of Shorthand, the Certificate states the speed in which the candidate has passed.

Candidates who are not awarded the School Certificate (Commercial) are issued with a certificate giving the subjects in which they have been successful.

Grade System - Marks awarded:

Maximum mark in each subject is 100; 50% required for a pass and 70% for a pass with credit. In Shorthand, at 50 and 60 words per minute 50-69 marks represent a speed of 50 words per minute and 70-100 marks represent a speed of 60 words per minute; a pass with credit is awarded only to candidates who obtain a high proportion of the marks allotted to the shorthand notes.

SECRETARIAL AND COMMERCIAL CERTIFICATE EXAMINATIONS, Stage II (Intermediate)

Candidates take this examination after completing a 2-year post School Certificate course.

Examinations offered in following subjects:

| | |
|---|---|
| Accounts | History of the British Common- |
| Arithmetic | wealth |
| Commerce | Italian |
| Economic History | Mathematics |
| English Language | Modern British History |
| English Literature | Office Practice |
| French | Shorthand (80/100 w.p.m.) |
| General Principles of | Shorthand - Typist's Certificate |
| English Law | Spanish |
| Geography | Statistics |
| German | Typewriting |

Candidates may enter for English Language only, or for English Language together with 1 or more other subjects offered in the scheme.

Special Secretarial and Commercial Certificates:

    A.    The Royal Society of Arts Secretarial Certificate, Stage II
          (Intermediate) is awarded to candidates who pass at 1 examin-
          ation in:

             (1)  English Language
plus    (2)  Office Practice, and Shorthand-Typist's Certificate
plus    (3)  At least 1 other subject selected from those given in
                  above Examination List, but not including Shorthand or
                  Typewriting. Candidates may, however, take Shorthand
                  and/or Typewriting as additional subjects for endorse-
                  ment on the certificate.

    B.    The Royal Society of Arts Commercial Certificate, Stage II
          (Intermediate) is awarded to candidates who pass at 1 examin-
          ation in:

             (1)  English Language
plus    (2)  At least 2 subjects selected from Accounts, Arithmetic,
                  Commerce, and Office Practice,
plus    (3)  At least 2 subjects selected from Economic History, English
                  Literature, French, General Principles of English Law, Geog-
                  raphy, German, History of the British Commonwealth, Italian,
                  Mathematics, Modern British History, Spanish, Statistics,
                  and Typewriting. Candidates may also take Shorthand and/or
                  Typist's Certificate as additional subjects for endorsement
                  on the certificate.

Grade System - Marks awarded:

Maximum mark in each subject is 100: 50% is required for a 2nd Class Pass
and 70% for a 1st Class Pass. In Shorthand, 50-69 marks represent a speed
of 80 words per minute and 70-100 marks represent a speed of 100 words per
minute; 1 class of pass only at each speed is awarded.

ORDINARY (Single-Subject) EXAMINATIONS

Examinations are held in Stage I (Elementary) (2 hours), Stage II (Intermediate) (2½ hours), and Stage III (Advanced) (3 hours), and in Shorthand
at 50, 60, 80, 100, 120, 140, 150, and 160 words per minute.

Candidates of any age may be examined. They may enter for single subjects
in any or all stages, and need not take the Elementary Stage of any subject before taking the Intermediate Stage, or the Elementary and Intermediate Stages before taking the Advanced Stage.

Candidates for the examinations in the Intermediate and Advanced Stages of
French, German, Italian, Russian, and Spanish are required to undergo an
oral test in the language.

## Subjects of Examination

| | | | |
|---|---|---|---|
| Accounting | Stage III | History (Modern British) | Stage I |
| Advertising | Stage III | | |
| Arithmetic | Stages I - III | History, Economic and Social | Stages II, III |
| Bookkeeping | Stages I - III | | |
| Cargo Insurance | Stage III | History of the British Commonwealth | Stages I - III |
| Central and Local Government | Stage II | | |
| Civics | Stage I | Income Tax Law and Practice | Stage III |
| Commerce | Stages I, II | Italian | Stages I - III |
| Commerce (Finance) | Stage III | Law of Evidence and Civil Procedure | Stage III |
| Commerce (International Trade) | Stage III | | |
| Commerce (Marketing) | Stage III | Law of Trusts | Stage III |
| Commercial Law | Stages II, III | Mathematics | Stage I |
| Common Law | Stage III | Norwegian | Stages I - III |
| Company Law | Stages II, III | Office Practice | Stages I - III |
| Costing | Stages II, III | Public Administration | Stage III |
| Danish | Stages I - III | | |
| Dutch | Stages I - III | Real Property and Conveyancing | Stage III |
| Economics | Stages II, III | | |
| English (with Literature) | Stages I - III | Russian | Stages I - III |
| | | Secretarial Duties | Stage II |
| English for Foreigners | Stages I - III | Shipping Law and Practice | Stage III |
| English Language | Stages I - III | Shorthand, 50 - 160 w.p.m. | |
| English Law, General Principles | Stage II | Shorthand-Typist's Certificate | Stages II, III |
| Esperanto | Stages I - III | Spanish | Stages I - III |
| French | Stages I - III | Statistics | Stages II, III |
| Geography | Stages I - III | Swedish | Stages I - III |
| German | Stages I - III | Typewriting | Stages I - III |
| | | Welsh | Stage I |

## Certificates:

The minimum percentages of marks for the award of certificates are as follows:

Stage I (Elementary):   Pass with Credit - 70%;        Pass - 50%.
Stage II (Intermediate):        1st Class - 70%;   2nd Class - 50%.
Stage III (Advanced):           1st Class - 75%;   2nd Class - 50%.

GROUP CERTIFICATES IN COMMERCIAL SUBJECTS

Stage I (Elementary)

Candidates must pass in the following 4 subjects in any Stage of the Society's examinations within 3 consecutive years:

(a)  Arithmetic or Mathematics
(b)  English (with Literature) or English Language
and (c)  2 of the other subjects in which an examination in the Elementary Stage is held, 1 of which must be either Bookkeeping or Commerce or Office Practice. All the subjects in which the candidate has passed will be endorsed on the Group Certificate.

Stage II (Intermediate)

Candidates must pass in at least 3 of the following subjects in the Intermediate Stage at any 4 consecutive series of examinations offered by the Society. Candidates must select 1 subject from group (a), 1 subject from group (b), and 1 other subject from either group (b) or group (c):

(a)  Commerce or Economics
(b)  Commerce or Economics - if not taken under (a); Arithmetic, Bookkeeping, Costing, Economic Geography, Economic and Social History, General Principles of English Law, Commercial Law, Company Law, Outlines of Central and Local Government, Statistics.
(c)  English (with Literature) or English Language or a foreign language.

Stage III (Advanced)

Candidates must pass in at least 3 of the following subjects in the Advanced Stage at any 4 consecutive series of examinations offered by the Society. Candidates must select 1 subject from group (a), 1 subject from group (b) and 1 other subject from either group (b) or group (c):

(a)  Either
     (i)   Commerce (Financial) or Commerce (International Trade) or Commerce (Marketing)
  or (ii)  Economics.
(b)  Either (i) or (ii) of (a) - if not already taken; Accounting or Bookkeeping; Arithmetic, Costing, Economic Geography, Economic and Social History, Commercial Law, Company Law, Cargo Insurance, Income Tax Law and Practice, Public Administration, Shipping Law and Practice, Statistics.
(c)  English (with Literature) or English Language or a foreign language.

## SPECIAL GROUP CERTIFICATES

### Clerk-Typist's Certificate

Candidates must pass in the undermentioned subjects at the same series of examinations:

|       | (a) | Typewriting, |
| plus  | (b) | English (with Literature) or English Language, |
| plus  | (c) | Bookkeeping or Arithmetic or Mathematics or Commerce or Office Practice. |

The prescribed subjects may be taken at any Stage, but for the award of the Clerk-Typist's Certificate the minimum requirement in Typewriting is a pass with credit in Stage I (Elementary).

### Group Certificate in Clerical Studies

Candidates must satisfy the examiners in the following subjects in Groups I and II:

Group I - Stage I (Elementary)

either  English Language, plus Commerce or Office Practice, together with Arithmetic or Mathematics, plus Bookkeeping,

or  Shorthand 50/60 w.p.m. plus Typewriting.

Group II - Stage II (Intermediate)

English Language, together with

|    | (a) | Arithmetic, Bookkeeping, and Commerce or Office Practice, |
| or | (b) | Secretarial Duties, Shorthand 80/100 w.p.m., and Typewriting, |
| or | (c) | Secretarial Duties and the Shorthand-Typist's Certificate. |

The examinations in each Group must be taken at one and the same series in any year. Candidates must satisfy the examiners in Group I before proceeding to Group II. Candidates failing in 1 subject only in a Group shall be allowed one further opportunity of passing in that subject within the following 12 months; such failure in 1 subject of Group I shall not debar a candidate from entering for Group II within the same period of 12 months. Certificates will be awarded to candidates each year in the subjects in which they have been successful, and such certificates will be exchanged for the Group Certificate in Clerical Studies when the regulations for the award of that certificate have been satisfied.

## Group Certificate in Secretarial Subjects

Candidates must pass in the following subjects at any 4 consecutive series of examinations offered by the Society:

    (a) Shorthand-Typist's Certificate, Stages II or III plus Secretarial Duties, Stage II,

or (b) Typewriting, Stages II or III, plus English Language or English (with Literature), Stages II or III, plus Secretarial Duties, Stage II,

or (c) Shorthand, 80 w.p.m. or more, plus Typewriting, Stages II or III, plus English Language or English (with Literature), Stages II or III, plus Secretarial Duties, Stage II.

## Group Certificate for Cost Clerks

Candidates must pass, within 2 consecutive years, in the Intermediate Stage of Arithmetic, English Language, Bookkeeping, and Costing.

## Group Certificate in Foreign Languages

Candidates must pass in 3 foreign languages, over any period of years. All the certificates must be in the Advanced Stage, and 1 at least must be a 1st class.

## Group Certificate in Law Subjects

Candidates must pass in 3 of the following subjects, over any period of years:

    (a) General Principles of English Law, Stage II;

    (b) 1 subject from Common Law, Law of Trusts, Real Property and Conveyancing, Stage III;

    (c) 1 of the subjects under (b) not already taken, or Company Law, Law of Evidence and Civil Procedure, Shipping Law and Practice, Stage III.

Passes in additional law subjects may be endorsed on the certificate.

## Group Certificate for Shipping Clerks

Candidates must pass in the following subjects in Stage III within 3 consecutive years:

    (a) Shipping Law and Practice,

    (b) Commerce (Finance) or Commerce (International Trade) or Commerce (Marketing),

and (c) Economic Geography.

They may also take a foreign language (Stage II), but this is optional.

A P P E N D I X   F

CITY AND GUILDS OF LONDON INSTITUTE

Courses Overseas

1964 - 1965

1442

# CITY AND GUILDS OF LONDON INSTITUTE

All correspondence should be addressed to:
    76 Portland Place, London, W.1.

Subjects offered overseas are listed below. In some cases, no specific approval of courses is required and candidates may be entered at any recognized examination center; in others, specific approval of a course is a prior condition of eligibility of candidates to take the examinations.

External candidates (those who have not attended courses of study at recognized colleges) must in some cases make special application for acceptance; in others, no formal application to the Institute is necessary.

Subjects in which examinations will be offered in 1965 or subsequent years:

Fuel Technology
Petroleum and Petroleum Products
Paint Technology, Paint Technologists' Course
Technology of Plastics
Gas Utilization
Gas Fitting
Metallurgy (last examinations 1964, except Advanced Section C - last
    examinations 1965
Iron and Steel Operatives' Course and Iron and Steel Operatives'
    Advanced Course
Metal Finishing (Practical Certificate only - last examinations 1965)
Leather Manufacture, Dyeing and Finishing and C. Craft and Technician's
    Certificate
Chemical Plant Operation
Coal Mining Certificate
Colliery Mechanic's Certificate
Colliery Electrician's Certificate
Steam Utilization Practice
Woolen and Worsted Raw Materials
Woolcombing
Worsted Spinning
Woolen Yarn Manufacture
Woolen and Worsted Weaving
Cotton Spinning
Plain Cotton Weaving
Cotton Weaving
Flax Spinning
Linen Weaving
Manufacture of Silk and Man-Made Fibres

Jute Spinning
Jute Weaving
Manufacture of Hosiery and Knitted Goods
Mill Engineering and Services
Industrial Organisation
Chemistry as applied to the Textile Industry
Appreciation of Colour and Design
Dyeing of Textiles
Electronics Servicing (Intermediate)
Radio and Television Servicing (Intermediate)
Telecommunication Technicians' Course
Electrical Installation Work
Electrical Engineering Practice
Radio Servicing Theory
Radio Amateurs' Examination
Industrial Radiography
Electrical Technicians' Course
Electrical Fitters' Course
Patternmaking
Foundry Practice
Machine Shop Engineering
Engineering Planning, Estimating and Costing
Boilermakers' Work
Sheet Metal Work
Railway Carriage and Wagon Construction (Final only)
Motor Body Work (Final only)
Refrigeration Practice
Science and Technology of Refrigeration
Welding
Boiler Operators' Certificate
Boiler-House Practice
Combustion Engineering
Instrument Maintenance
Carpentry and Joinery
Machine Woodworking
Brickwork
Masonry
Plasterers' Work
Painters' and Decorators' Work
Plumbers' Work (Ordinary Craft and Final Craft)
Plumbers' Work:  Plumbing Technology (Advanced Craft)
Ship Plumbing and Marine Sanitary Engineering (Old Scheme) (Final only)
Marine Plumbing (New Scheme)
Builders' Quantities
Welding in relation to Plumbers' Work
Structural Engineering
Mastic Asphalt Work
Concrete Practice
Stair Construction and Handrailing
Formwork and Shuttering for Concrete Construction

Roof Slating, Tiling and Cement Work
Furniture Industry (Cabinet-making)
Photography
Concrete Practice (Supervisory Level)
Flour Milling
Illuminating Engineering
Tailors' Cutting and Tailoring
Dental Technicians' Certificate
Dental Technicians' Advanced Certificate
Science Laboratory Technicians' Certificate and Advanced Certificate
Plumbing Design and Quantities
Wholesale Textile Distribution
Dress Manufacture
Clothing Technology
Leather Goods Manufacture
Goldsmiths' and Silversmiths' Work
Silversmiths' Work - Allied Crafts
Jewellery
Boot and Shoe Manufacture
Surgical Shoemaking
Boot and Shoe Repairing
Kiln Burners' Certificate
Basic Cookery for the Catering Industry
Metallurgical Technicians' Certificate
Metallurgical Technicians' Advanced Certificate (1st examination, 1966)
Cocoa, Chocolate and Sugar Confectionery Manufacture
Milk Processing and Control
Teachers' Certificate in Handicraft
Technical Teachers' Certificate
Domestic Subjects (Further Education Teachers' Certificate)
Paper and Board Making Practice
Science and Technology of Paper and Board Making
Power Plant Operation
Motor Vehicle Mechanics' Work
Motor Vehicle Electricians' Work
Motor Vehicle Technicians' Work
Aeronautical Engineering Practice
Aircraft Electrical Practice
Fabrication of Steelwork
Heating and Ventilating Technicians' Course
Shipbuilding
Ship Joinery
Yacht and Boat Building
Instrument Making
Solid Fuel Production, Distribution and Utilization
Colliery Mechanics' Advanced Certificate
Colliery Electricians' Advanced Certificate
Coal Mining Advanced Certificate
Steam Turbine Plant Operation
Mechanical Engineering Craft Practice

Iron Ore Operatives' Course
Iron Ore Quarrying Certificate
Iron Ore Quarrying Advanced Certificate
Coal Preparation
Typographic Design
Compositors' Work
Line Composition
'Monotype' Composition
Letterpress Machine Printing
Photogravure Machine Printing
Letterpress Rotary Machine Printing
'Monotype' Casters' Work
Electrotyping and Stereotyping
Photo-Engraving
Photogravure
Photolithography
Lithographic Artists' Work (Final exam only)
Lithographic Printing
Craft Certificate in Bookbinding and Printing Warehouse Practice
Advanced Craft Certificate in Bookbinding
Advanced Craft Certificate in Publishers' Edition Bookbinding
Advanced Craft Certificate in Printing Warehouse Practice
General Survey of the Printing Industry
Technical Processes of Printing
Appreciation of Design and Colour in Printing
Application of Science in Printing
Printers' Costing
Printers' Estimating
Printing Administration
Technical Illustration
Technical Authorship
Hand Embroidery
Advanced Hand Embroidery
Dress
Advanced Dress
Millinery
Advanced Millinery
Ladies' Tailoring
Advanced Ladies' Tailoring
Home Upholstery and Soft Furnishings
Advanced Home Upholstery and Soft Furnishings
Domestic Cookery
Advanced Domestic Cookery
Home Management
General Course in Science
Hand-Loom Weaving
Advanced Hand-Loom Weaving
Foundry Craft Practice
Sand, Gravel and Quarrying Operatives' Certificate
Sand, Gravel and Quarrying Certificate
Sand, Gravel and Quarrying Advanced Certificate

Heating and Ventilating Engineering Fitters' Course
Heating and Ventilating Fitter/Welders' Course (Oxy-Acetylene)
Heating and Ventilating Fitter/Welders' Course (Metal-Arc Welding)
Agricultural Mechanics' Work
Agricultural Engineering Fitters' Work (Old Scheme)
Agricultural Engineering Technicians' Certificate (New Scheme)
Farm Machinery Operation and Care
Aeronautical Craft Courses
General Course in Engineering
Structural Detailing
Shipbuilding Technicians' Certificate, Part I
Shipbuilding Technicians' Certificate, Part II
F.T.C. Qualifying Examination in Building Crafts
Mechanical Engineering Technicians' Course
Vehicle Body Work Craft Subjects
Shipbuilding Crafts, F.T.C. Qualifying Examination
Supplementary Studies in Telecommunications and Electronics
Instrument Maintenance Craft Certificate
Industrial Measurement and Control Technicians' Certificate
Instrument Production Craft Practice
Instrument Production Technicians' Certificate
General Course in Construction
Construction Technicians' Certificate (Part I)
Traffic Engineering Technicians' Certificate
Vehicle Body Engineering Technicians' Certificate
Computer Personnel (Certificate)
Foundry and Patternshop Technicians' Certificate
Welding Craft Practice

## Typical Examinations:  Welding

### Ordinary

(1)  A written paper of 3 hours' duration on general welding technology.

(2)  A written paper of 3 hours' duration on elementary welding science.
     Note:  The written papers may both include some questions involving
            sketching and calculations.

(3)  A practical test of 3 hours' duration in which the candidate will be
     required to perform practical tests in both techniques in mild steel
     only.

(4)  At the time of the practical test the local examiner will also mark
     specimen welds previously prepared as part of the course work.

### Advanced

(1)  A written paper of 3 hours' duration, either Paper 74/3 Electric-
     arc welding technology or Paper 74/4 Oxy-acetylene welding technology.

(2)   Paper 74/5, a written paper of 3 hours' duration on welding science.
      Note:  The written papers may both include some questions involving
             sketching and calculations.

(3)   A practical test of 3 hours' duration in either gas or arc techniques
      and including tests on non-ferrous metals.

(4)   At the time of the practical test the local examiner will also mark
      specimen welds previously prepared as part of the course work.

A candidate who has passed one Advanced examination may enter for the
other in a subsequent year and will not be required to answer again the
paper on Welding Science.


Certificates awarded

Certificates of the First or Second class are awarded to candidates who,
in the same year, satisfy the examiners in all sections of the examination taken, except in the case of candidates who, having passed one
Advanced examination in a previous year, are not required to take again
the paper on Welding Science.

Candidates whose specimen welds are judged unsatisfactory by the local
examiner fail the examination as a whole.


Full Technological Certificate

A full Technological Certificate in welding is awarded to a candidate
who has:

    (a)   obtained first class certificates in the Advanced examinations
          in both oxy-acetylene and electric-arc welding, or subsequently

    (b)   attained the age of 21 years,

    (c)   provided evidence of adequate industrial experience.

APPENDIX   G


FRENCH BACCALAUREAT

FRENCH BACCALAURÉAT

In Metropolitan France the Baccalauréat examination,[*] traditionally administered in two parts, Part I at the close of the classe de première, and Part II at the close of the classe terminale, has been revised.

On September 26, 1962 Part I became a probationary examination, called examen probatoire. In the summer of 1965 the examen probatoire was suppressed in favor of combining the two examinations at the close of secondary education, the examination was replaced by decisions of a council of teachers whose duty it is to pass on the academic performance of a student and determine which curriculum he will follow in the final year of secondary education.

The Baccalauréat examination, to be a new single examination by the summer of 1968, will mark the completion of secondary education. This examination, formerly national, will be drawn up by the local académie.

It is likely that most French-speaking African countries will retain some special examination at the close of the 6th year, such as the examen probatoire.

Following are the descriptions of the two parts of the examination:

For the title of Bachelier de l'enseignement secondaire (bachelor of secondary education) examinations are both written and oral. Written examinations are eliminative; they vary in duration according to the subject and the group.

Candidates for the Baccalauréat Part I or examen probatoire might choose from 8 groups: Série classique A, Série classique A', Série classique B, Série classique C, Série moderne M, Série moderne M', Série technique T, Série technique T'. The examination comprises compulsory tests (épreuves obligatoires) and one or two optional tests (épreuves facultatives).

The compulsory tests include:

(1) Written tests;
(2) An oral test in a modern foreign language (series B, M, M', T');
(3) A physical education test;

One of the optional tests deals with drawing, musical education or home economics. The other consists of an oral test in a modern foreign language not chosen by the candidate for his compulsory tests.

---

[*]For Les Examens du Baccalauréat: (Examen probatoire, Baccalauréat proprement dit): Programme des Matières pour 1964 (and subsequent issues) write Librairie Vuibert, Boulevard Saint-Germain, 63, Paris V.

Candidates for the <u>Baccalauréat</u> (Part II) may choose from 5 groups: <u>Série Philosophie</u>, <u>Série Sciences experimentales</u>, <u>Série Mathématiques élémentaires</u>, <u>Série Mathématiques et technique</u>, <u>Série Technique et économie</u>. The examination comprises compulsory tests and optional tests.

The compulsory tests include:

(1)   Written tests;
(2)   A physical education test;
(3)   For the series Technics and Economics, a test in a modern foreign language II;
(4)   For the series Mathematics and Technics, a practical, technical test.

One of the optional tests deals with drawing, musical education or home economics. The other consists of an oral test in a modern foreign language not chosen by the candidate for his compulsory tests.

Compulsory oral examinations for Parts I and II correspond to the compulsory written examinations and are affected by the same coefficients. Modern foreign languages for the written and oral examinations are: German, English, Arabic (literary, dialectical), Spanish, Portuguese, Italian, Modern Hebrew, Russian. Many others are included for the optional examinations in Part I.

Each separate test is graded on a scale from 0 - 20.

Grading on the examinations is done on the system of coefficients, set by the higher council of national education, which indicates the relative importance of each separate part of the examinations. For example, in the philosophy series, the examination in Philosophy carries 4 times as much weight as the examination in the Physical Sciences (Philosophy: coefficient 4; Physical Sciences: coefficient, 1). In the reverse, for the mathematical series, the ratio is 3 to 2 in favor of the physical Sciences (Physical Sciences: coefficient 3; Philosophy: coefficient 2). Computation of the final average grade is made in the following manner: the grade for each examination is multiplied by the coefficient assigned to the subject, totals are added, the sum is divided by the sum of the coefficients.

Certificates awarded to candidates carry the following mentions:

<u>Très bien</u>  - when the candidate has obtained an average mark at least equal to 16.

<u>Bien</u>       - when the candidate has obtained an average mark at least equal to 14 and less than 16.

<u>Assez bien</u> - when the candidate has obtained an average mark at least equal to 12 and less than 14.

<u>Passable</u>   - when the candidate has obtained an average mark less than 12.

### BACCALAUREAT PART I - EXAMEN PROBATOIRE

| SERIE A | Coeff. | Exam. Hours |
|---|---|---|
| Written tests: | | |
| French essay | 4 | 3 |
| Latin translation | 4 | 3 |
| Greek translation | 4 | 3 |
| Mathematics or Physical Sciences | 2 | 1 |
| History or Geography | 3 | 1 |
| Modern Foreign Language | 2 | 1 |
| Physical Education test: | 1 | |

| SERIE A' | | |
|---|---|---|
| Written tests: | | |
| French essay | 3 | 3 |
| Greek translation | 3 | 2 |
| Latin translation | 3 | 2 |
| Mathematics | 4 | 3 |
| Physical Sciences | 2 | 1 |
| History or Geography | 2 | 1 |
| Modern Foreign Language | 2 | 1 |
| Physical Education test: | 1 | |

| SERIE B | | |
|---|---|---|
| Written tests: | | |
| French essay | 4 | 3 |
| Latin translation | 4 | 3 |
| Mathematics or Physical Sciences | 2 | 1 |
| History or Geography | 3 | 1 |
| Modern Foreign Language I | 2 | 2 |
| Modern Foreign Language II | 2 | 2 |
| Oral test: | | |
| Modern Foreign Language I | 2 | |
| Physical Education test: | 1 | |

| Serie C | | |
|---|---|---|
| Written tests: | | |
| French essay | 3 | 3 |
| Latin translation | 3 | 2 |
| Mathematics | 5 | 3 |
| Physical Sciences | 2 | 2½ |
| History or Geography | 2 | 1 |
| Modern Foreign Language | 2 | 1 |
| Physical Education test: | 1 | |

## SERIE M

Written tests:

| | | |
|---|---|---|
| French essay | 4 | 3 |
| Mathematics | 4 | 3 |
| Physical Sciences | 4 | $2\frac{1}{2}$ |
| History or Geography | 2 | 1 |
| Modern Foreign Language I | 2 | 2 |
| Modern Foreign Language II | 2 | 1 |

Oral tests:

| | |
|---|---|
| Modern Foreign Language I | 1 |

Physical Education test:　　　　　　　　　　1

## SERIE M'

Written tests:

| | | |
|---|---|---|
| French essay | 4 | 3 |
| Mathematics | 4 | 3 |
| Physical Sciences | 3 | $2\frac{1}{2}$ |
| Natural Sciences | 3 | 2 |
| History or Geography | 2 | 1 |
| Modern Foreign Language | 2 | 1 |

Oral test:

| | |
|---|---|
| Modern Foreign Language | 1 |

Physical Education test:　　　　　　　　　　1

## SERIE T

Written tests:

| | | |
|---|---|---|
| French essay | 4 | 3 |
| Mathematics | 4 | 3 |
| Physical Sciences | 3 | 2 |
| History or Geography | 2 | 1 |
| Modern Foreign Language | 2 | 1 |
| Mechanical Construction | 4 | 4 |

Physical Education test:　　　　　　　　　　1

## SERIE T'

Written tests:

| | | | |
|---|---|---|---|
| French composition | 4 | | 3 |
| Mathematics | 2 | ) | |
| Statistical Mathematics or Problems of Economic Order | 1 | ) | 3 |
| Physical Sciences or Technology of Merchandising | 2 | | 1 |
| History or Geography | 3 | | $1\frac{1}{2}$ |

| | | |
|---|---|---|
| Modern Foreign Language I | 2 | 2 |
| Modern Foreign Language II | 3 | 2 |

Oral test:

| | |
|---|---|
| Modern Foreign Language I | 2 |

Physical Education test:                    1

## BACCALAUREAT - PART II

### SERIE PHILOSOPHIE

Written tests:

| | | | |
|---|---|---|---|
| Philosophy | 8 | | 4 |
| Mathematics | 2 | ) | |
| Physical Sciences | 2 | ) | 3 |
| Natural Sciences | 2 | | 1½ |
| History or Geography | 3 | | 3 |
| Modern Foreign Language | 3 | | 2½ |

Physical Education test

### SERIE SCIENCES EXPERIMENTALES

Written tests:

| | | |
|---|---|---|
| Philosophy | 6 | 3 |
| Mathematics | 3 | 2 |
| Physical Sciences | 4 | 3 |
| Natural Sciences | 3 | 2 |
| History or Geography | 3 | 1½ |
| Modern Foreign Language | 2 | 1½ |

Physical Education test

### SERIE MATHEMATIQUES ELEMENTAIRES

Written tests:

| | | |
|---|---|---|
| Philosophy | 2 | 3 |
| Mathematics | 7 | 3 |
| Physical Sciences | 6 | 3 |
| Natural Sciences | 1 | 1 |
| History or Geography | 2 | 1½ |
| Modern Foreign Language | 2 | 1½ |

Physical Education test

### SERIE MATHEMATIQUES ET TECHNIQUE

Written tests:

| | | |
|---|---|---|
| Test covering either Philosophy, History or Geography | 3 | 2 |
| Mathematics | 5 | 3 |

| | | |
|---|---|---|
| Physical Sciences | 4 | 3 |
| Modern Foreign Language | 2 | 1 |
| Mechanical Construction | 4 | 5 |

| | | |
|---|---|---|
| Practical technical test: | 2 | 5 |

Physical Education test

## SERIE TECHNIQUE ET ECONOMIE

Written tests:

| | | |
|---|---|---|
| Philosophy | 3 | 3 |
| Mathematics | 4 | 3 |
| History or Geography | 3 | $1\frac{1}{2}$ |
| Modern Foreign Language I | 3 | $2\frac{1}{2}$ |
| Economics | 5 | 3 |

Oral test:

| | |
|---|---|
| Foreign Language II | 2 |

Physical Education test

## TOTAL NUMBER OF POINTS NECESSARY FOR ADMISSION AND "MENTIONS"

### EXAMEN PROBATOIRE

| | With Phys. Ed. | Without Phys. Ed. |
|---|---|---|
| Admission | 200 | 190 |
| Admission by jury decision | 160 | 152 |
| Eligibility by examination | 160 | 152 |
| Eligibility by jury decision | 140 | 133 |

### BACCALAUREAT

| | Points gained | Points gained by jury decision |
|---|---|---|
| Eligibility examination | 160 | 140 |
| "Mentions" | | |
| Passable | 200 | 160 |
| Assez bien | 240 | |
| Bien | 280 | |
| Très bien | 320 | |

NEW CURRICULA OF CLASSES DE SECONDE (FROM SEPT. 1965)
ET CLASSES DE PREMIERE (FROM 1966-67)

At the level of classe de seconde, the studies are divided into 3 sections:
A, C, T.

Seconde A:  Literary

Classical or modern, includes 17 hours of literary teachings (Greek-Latin,
plus 1 living language or Latin and 2 living languages or 3 living languages) and 6 hours of scientific teaching.

7 options:

A 1     (corresponds to old section A).  Latin-Greek, 1 living language.
        Beginning in the school year 1965, it will only be offered in the
        schools having a traditional section A.

A 2     (corresponds to old section B).  Latin, 2 living languages (1st
        and 2nd language).

A 3     Latin, 1st living language, introduction to economics.

A 4     Two living languages and introduction to economics (specially
        open to students who want to drop Latin and can replace it with
        a 2nd living language).

        N.B.  A 3 and A 4.  These 2 options apply only for those schools
        (if technical or Lycées classiques or modernes) having a section
        T' (technique économique et commerciale).

A 5     Two living languages.  A special course of a 2nd living language
        is given 5 hours per week (2 hours more than the usual 3 hours
        per week).  This new way of teaching is meant for students with
        a literary bent who have not studied Latin and who know only 1
        living language, for instance, students coming from C.E.G.

A 6     Two living languages and translation of old Greek or Latin texts.

A 7     Three living languages.  This option will be offered only in
        schools provided with qualified teachers.

        N.B.  A 6 and A 7.  These options are for students with a literary
        bent who have not had Latin, but who have started the study of 2
        living languages.

There is not, at the moment, beginning Latin or Greek at the level of the
classe de seconde.

At the end of seconde A, students are divided into the following more
specialized classes:

1ère A.  Literary with option for Arts.

In terminale A, students have choice between 3 following groups:
  (i)   Latin, Greek, 1 living language
  (ii)  Latin, 2 living languages
 (iii)  3 living languages.

>    Section A is specially for students intending to enter the <u>Facultés de Lettres et Sciences Humaines</u>, the <u>Facultés de Droit et Sciences Economiques</u>, directed toward literary, artistic, juridical and economic studies and professions.

<u>1ère B</u>.  Literary, economic and social.

>    Introductory study of the essential instrument to humane sciences; statistical mathematics.

>    In terminale B the study of philosophy is mostly psychology and sociology.

>    <u>1ère économique</u> will lead to <u>baccalauréat</u> or to <u>brevet de technicien économique</u> replacing the present B.S.E.C. (<u>brevet supérieur d'enseignement commercial</u>).

<u>Seconde C:   Scientific</u>

10 hours of science and 14 hours of literature, including:  2 living languages or Latin, plus 1 living language or (optional) Greek or a 2nd living language.

Section C has 3 options:  1 compulsory option between Latin and a 2nd living language and electives as follows:

>    <u>C a 1</u>   corresponds to old seconde A' Latin, 1 living language with (<u>option facultative</u>) Greek.

>    <u>C a 2</u>   corresponds to old seconde C Latin, 1 living language compulsory, with <u>option facultative</u> of a 2nd living language.

>    <u>C b</u>    corresponds to old seconde M, 2 living languages (with additional 2 hours for beginners in 2nd language).  It is open to non-latinist students with a scientific bent.

At the end of seconde C, students are divided between the following classes:

>    <u>1ère C</u>:  Mathematics, Physical Sciences.  2 living languages or 1 living language and Latin or 1 living language and Greek optional.

>    <u>La terminale C</u> corresponds to old "<u>bac mathématiques élémentaires.</u>"

>    1ère D:  Natural and biological sciences, 2 living languages or Latin and 1 living language.

La terminale D includes the teaching of applied mathematics.

If they are gifted in Letters, students of seconde C can go towards classes de 1ère A or classes de 1ère B.

Section C is particularly convenient to students planning to enter the Faculties of Science, Medicine or Pharmacy, and to those intending to become science professors (mathematics, physical and natural sciences), scientific researchers, industrial and agricultural engineers, etc.


Seconde T:   Technical

10 hours of sciences; 6 hours of industrial drawing, technology and merchandising; 6 hours of workshop; 8 hours of literature including the study of a living language.

This section will only exist in 1956-66 in the Lycées previously having a section T (mostly the Lycées techniques).

At the end of the seconde T, students are divided between:

classes de 1ère 1:      Applied sciences leading to Bac T (old Bac mathematiques et techniques), 1 language

classes de 1ère T 1:    Technical sciences leading to Bac or Brevets de technicien industriel, 1 language.

This section T is for students wishing to enter the Faculties of Sciences or Ecoles Nationales Supérieures des Arts et Métiers, and les Instituts de formation supérieure, towards scientific and technical careers and the teaching profession.


In short, for students entering the seconde, there are 11 options divided into three sections:  A, C, T.

In classe de 1ère and in classe terminale, there are 5 sections:  A, B, C, D, T,  leading to Baccalauréats A, B, C, D, T, and 2 sections T 1.  Technique industrielle leading to Bacs de technicien will be replacing the Brevets de technicien).

On the other hand, special teaching remains, starting from the seconde, in 3 sections:  Technique hôtelière, technique sociale and the lycées agricoles.

BACCALAUREATS (FROM 1968)

S E C T I O N S

| | Bac A | Bac B | Bac Economic Technician | Bac C | Bac D | Bac T | Bac Industrial Technician |
|---|---|---|---|---|---|---|---|
| Terminale | Literature Linguistics and Philosophy with option in Arts | Economics and Social Sciences (beginning statistical Mathematics) | Economics | Mathematics and Physical Sciences | Natural Sciences and Biology | Applied Sciences | Sciences and Industrial Techniques |
| Première | Classical or Modern | Classical or Modern | Modern | Classical or Modern | Classical or Modern | Modern | Modern |

| | Seconde A Literary | Seconde C Scientific | Seconde T Technical |
|---|---|---|---|
| Seconde | Options of which 1 Economics (Classical or Modern) | 3 options (Classical or Modern) | Modern |

# A P P E N D I X   H


PLACEMENT RECOMMENDATIONS

by

Council on Evaluation of Student Foreign Credentials

PLACEMENT RECOMMENDATIONS BY THE
COUNCIL ON EVALUATION OF FOREIGN STUDENT CREDENTIALS
APPROVAL AUTHORIZED JULY 1965 AND APRIL 1966


The educational systems of the African countries are structured after

the educational systems of the European countries with which they have been

most closely associated. Systems organized along British lines include

Botswana, Gambia, Ghana, Kenya, Lesotho, Malawi, Nigeria, Rhodesia, Sierra

Leone, Sudan, Swaziland, Tanzania, Uganda and Zambia. Systems which follow

the French system include Algeria, Cameroun, Central African Republic,

Chad, Congo (Brazzaville), Dahomey, French Somaliland, Gabon, Guinea, Ivory

Coast, Malagasy Republic, Mali, Mauritania, Morocco, Niger, Sénégal, Togo,

Tunisia and Upper Volta. Systems developed after Belgian patterns include

Burundi, Congo (Leopoldville), and Rwanda. Systems which are composites of

several systems include Ethiopia, Libya, Somalia, South Africa and South

West Africa. In addition, the African territories of Spain comprising

Spanish Guinea, Spanish Sahara and Ifni follow the Spanish educational

system, while the Portuguese territories of Angola, Mozambique, Portuguese

Guinea, Cape Verde Islands, São Tomé and Principe conform to Portugal's

system. Lastly, the educational system of Liberia is patterned after that

of the United States. Placement recommendations are set forth in these

broad general groupings.

In the newly independent countries increasing modification of their

educational systems is apparent as each country seeks to develop in its own

way. Due to the numerous and rapid educational changes in Africa, the

placement recommendations here indicated can represent only tentative guide-

lines. The Council on the Evaluation of Foreign Student Credentials recog-

nizes the value and need for experimentation in admission of students from

the African countries. It suggests that institutions and organizations
in the position to apply selective techniques other than those defined
in the following pages be encouraged to do so.

## SYSTEMS ORGANIZED ALONG BRITISH LINES

As background to an understanding of the credentials held by African
students from countries having educational systems organized along British
lines, it is helpful to know something of the bodies which set the examinations and award the certificates.

There are nine examining bodies in England and Wales which offer a
General Certificate of Education, including the Cambridge Syndicate[1] and
the University of London[2] which are the two operating most extensively in
Africa. The Associated Examining Board[3] also has a substantial number of
candidates. This Board was constituted about ten years ago to deal with
the problems of technical and modern schools. It conducts examinations
in Africa in Malawi, Rhodesia and Zambia.

The Cambridge Syndicate offers its examinations directly through
schools. The University of London caters primarily to private candidates,
although London is prepared to examine in schools by means of the General
Certificate of Education examinations. The Cambridge Syndicate presently
offers the Joint Examination for the School Certificate and General Certificate of Education (taken at the close of Form V of secondary education

---

[1] University of Cambridge Local Examination Syndicate, Syndicate Buildings, 17 Harvey Road, Cambridge.

[2] School Examinations Department, University of London, The Senate
House, Malet Street, London W.C. 1.

[3] Associated Examining Board, Hesketh House, Portman Square, London, W. 1.

in England and West Africa, and at the end of Form IV in East Africa).  The General Certificate of Education (commonly referred to as the G.C.E.) in this instance is awarded at the ordinary ("O") level.

At the close of Form VI the Syndicate offers the Joint Examination for the Higher School Certificate and General Certificate of Education.  In this instance, the G.C.E. is awarded at the advanced ("A") level.

The University of London does not offer a School Certificate nor Higher School Certificate, it awards only General Certificates of Education.

The Cambridge School Certificate examination was introduced in England in 1923, replacing the Senior Cambridge examination.  The Joint Examination for the School Certificate and General Certificate of Education was introduced generally overseas in 1959.  The Joint Examination for the Higher School Certificate and General Certificate of Education was initiated in 1964.

The name "Oversea School Certificate" was created in 1951 when the G.C.E. replaced the School Certificate in England and was used through 1960.  In 1961, the word "Oversea" was deleted from the official title.[1]

Candidates for the Joint Examination for the Higher School Certificate and General Certificate of Education are accepted for the examination if they hold either a School Certificate or 3 G.C.E. subject passes (equivalent to School Certificate passes with credit) gained on one and the same occasion. Until 1964, candidates who did not qualify for the Higher School Certificate were awarded a form of certificate showing subjects in which they had passed.

---

[1] In a few African printed bulletins of 1964-65 and in some of the materials especially prepared for the  editors of this volume, the word "Oversea" was still found to be used in reference to the School Certificate; frequently the spelling occurred as "Overseas."  In whatever loose manner the word is now presently used, it will not be found in use by the Cambridge Syndicate after 1961.

In and after 1964 such candidates receive <u>General Certificates of Education</u>
showing the subjects in which they pass (see below for equivalences).

The <u>School Certificate</u> awarded to successful candidates is of two kinds:

(1)  <u>School Certificate A</u>

Records the name of the school and is issued to those successful
candidates who have been in attendance for at least 2 years continuously at one or more schools approved by the Syndicate and
are still attending such schools at the time of taking the examination.  (Schools are normally approved for the issue of <u>School
Certificate A</u> on the recommendation of the appropriate Education
Authority.)

(2)  <u>School Certificate B</u>

Issued to all other successful candidates.

Successful candidates are placed in 3 Divisions:  First, Second, and
Third.  (See descriptions of classifications and conditions for the award
of a G.C.E. on the Joint Examination, Appendix B.)

For the purpose of exemption from University entrance examinations and
from the Preliminary or other examinations of the professional bodies, the
system of equivalences[1] between the standards of the <u>General Certificate of
Education</u> in the United Kingdom and those of the Joint Examination for the
<u>School Certificate</u> and <u>General Certificate of Education</u> and for the <u>Higher
School Certificate</u> Examination are as follows:

A pass with credit, or since 1960, grades of 3, 4, 5 or 6, in a
subject of the Joint Examination for the <u>School Certificate</u> and
<u>General Certificate of Education</u> or a pass at subsidiary standard

---

[1] The University of London and the Cambridge Syndicate also endeavor to
ensure that all their grading standards are equivalent.

in a subject of the <u>Higher School Certificate</u> examination will
be considered the equivalent of a pass at ordinary level in a
corresponding subject of the <u>General Certificate of Education</u>
held in the United Kingdom.

Similarly, a pass in a subject at principal standard in the
<u>Higher School Certificate</u> examination will be considered the
equivalent of a pass at advanced level in a corresponding subject of the <u>General Certificate of Education</u>.

Regulations and Syllabuses are available from the examining bodies.  In
cases where mathematics and sciences play major roles as prerequisites to
mathematics, science, and engineering courses in U.S. institutions, evaluators may request syllabuses to ascertain correctly the levels of achievement
represented by the certificates under consideration.

With independence, some African countries or groups of countries have
developed their own leaving examinations and certificates, in cooperation
with representatives of the University of Cambridge Local Examination Syndicate.  The Sudan Examinations Council now administers examinations and
awards the <u>Sudan School Certificate</u> which can be equated to the <u>Cambridge
School Certificate</u> showing at least 5 passes, or a <u>General Certificate of
Education Examination Certificate</u> of one of the schools examining bodies of
England and Wales showing 5 passes at ordinary level.  Several years ago
the <u>Ethiopian School Leaving Certificate</u> began to replace the <u>University of
London General Certificate of Education</u> in Ethiopia.

In West Africa, the Cambridge Syndicate administered the examinations
for the <u>School Certificate</u> until the establishment of the West African
Examinations Council in 1950.  On the West African Examinations Council,
both the Cambridge Syndicate and the University of London are represented;

however, the Cambridge Syndicate has been the collaborator in carrying out some of the functions of the examining body and in awarding the certificates.

The main purpose in creating the Council was "to take over the responsibility for examining the pupils in the secondary schools of West Africa and progressively to adapt the schemes of examination and syllabuses to the emerging needs of the rapidly developing countries served by it."[1]

Until 1960 students completing the basic secondary course in Ghana, Sierra Leone, Gambia and Nigeria took the examination for the West African School Certificate. The examination was held in November and the certificate was awarded by the Cambridge Syndicate in collaboration with the West African Examinations Council. Students completing the sixth form in all four countries took the Cambridge Higher School Certificate.

In 1960 the West African Examinations Council offered the first examination for the new School Certificate of the West African Examinations Council. This Certificate was awarded by the Council alone. The examination was held in June. Ghana, Sierra Leone and Gambia shifted to this new School Certificate, while Nigeria continued with the West African School Certificate. The three countries also shifted from the Cambridge Higher School Certificate to the June University of London General Certificate of Education "A" level examinations, while Nigeria continued with the Cambridge Higher School Certificate examinations.

In 1963 a Joint Examination for the School Certificate of the West African Examinations Council and the General Certificate of Education was introduced in Ghana, Sierra Leone and Gambia and a Joint Examination for the West African School Certificate and the General Certificate of Education

[1] J. Deakin. "Changes in Examinations for West African Secondary Schools." West African Journal of Education, June 1964.

was introduced in Nigeria. Students who did not qualify for the School Certificate, but met certain other requirements, were awarded the General Certificate of Education.

English ceased to be a compulsory subject in the School Certificate examination in Ghana, Sierra Leone and Gambia, in 1963, and in Nigeria in 1964.

By 1965, the Council's responsibilities included "examining middle
school pupils in Ghana, conducting examinations for entrance to secondary
schools throughout West Africa and to teacher training colleges in Ghana,
providing part of the examinations used for the certification of teachers in
Ghana and Nigeria, and acting as an agent for numerous overseas bodies and
providing local facilities for the many thousands of candidates taking such
examinations as the London G.C.E., and the examinations of the Royal Society
of Arts and the City and Guilds of London Institute."[1]

In 1965 the School Certificate was eliminated in Ghana, Sierra Leone
and Gambia, and candidates were allowed to enter for the West African Examinations Council General Certificate of Education examinations in whatever
subjects they desired without any restrictions regarding minimum entry or
subject groupings. By that year, the major responsibility for awarding
School Certificates and General Certificates of Education had been transferred by the Cambridge Syndicate to the Council. Committees are now studying the need for a local "A" level or equivalent examination in the hope
that "with the assistance of the overseas bodies from which it has in the
past derived so much help, (the Council may) be able to mount its own sixth
form leaving examination by 1970 at the latest, and possibly by 1968."[2]

---

[1] Ibid.                                    [2] Ibid.

For some years the Associated Examining Board has conducted the "M"
Level Examination on behalf of the Zambia Ministry of Education. It should
be noted that a subject pass in this examination is the equivalent of a
pass in the <u>Matriculation Examination of the Joint Matriculation Board of
the Universities of South Africa</u>. The examination is taken at the end of a
five-year course of secondary education.

## Secondary Certificates

It is recommended that a student from an African country whose educational
system is organized along British lines, seeking admission to an institution
of higher education in the United States, in undergraduate status, should
present certificates showing that he has passed in examinations administered
by examining bodies in the United Kingdom or Africa, in at least five subjects representing a good range of fields and including English. Two of
these five subjects should be passed at one of the following levels:

<blockquote>
Principal standard in the <u>Cambridge Higher School Certificate</u>
examination
</blockquote>

<u>or</u>   Advanced level in a <u>General Certificate of Education</u> examination.
The remainder of the subjects should be passed at one of the following levels:

<blockquote>
Ordinary level in a <u>General Certificate of Education</u> examination
</blockquote>

<u>or</u>   Credit passes or higher in a <u>School Certificate</u> examination

<u>or</u>   Subsidiary standard in a <u>Higher School Certificate</u> examination.

It should be noted that certain sponsored students have done well in
U.S. colleges and universities with admission qualifications less than the
recommended standards. For example, the African Scholarship Program of
American Universities (ASPAU) has accepted some able students who had earned
only "O" level certificates. Institutions wishing to depart from the above

recommended standards should note carefully that other criteria such as
secondary school grades, test results, personal interviews and headmasters'
recommendations are part of the ASPAU selection process. As stated previously, the Council on the Evaluation of Foreign Student Credentials recognizes
the value and need for experimentation in admitting students from African
countries and suggests that institutions in a position to apply selective
techniques be encouraged to do so.

During the two years of sixth form in West Africa (fifth and sixth forms
in East Africa), students preparing for the <u>Cambridge Higher School Certifi-
cate</u> examinations or <u>General Certificate of Education</u> advanced level examinations devote most of their time to two or three subjects, thus developing a
considerable degree of specialization in these subjects while neglecting
other subjects considered important to a university preparatory program in
the United States. It is recommended that the person responsible for admission to the U.S. institution consider the strong and weak features of the
applicant's preparation as shown by the total record, including the <u>Higher
School Certificate</u> or <u>General Certificate of Education</u> "A" level examinations,
together with recommendations, school record, class rank when available, and
other relevant data. If the decision is favorable, the applicant should be
admitted as a freshman, but given the privilege of suitable advanced placement to be determined by appropriate examinations or other institutional
practices. In some cases, students will be able to enter second year courses
in the subjects they have passed at <u>Higher School Certificate</u> principal
standard or <u>General Certificate of Education</u> advanced level. If they do
this successfully, the institutions concerned should follow the practices
in granting or not granting credits that are used with U.S. students who
pass examinations and receive similar advanced placement.

Records of Students Coming from Universities as Undergraduates

It is suggested that caution be exercised in the case of an African student wishing to transfer to a U.S. institution after some period of attendance at a foreign university, but without completion of the degree, diploma, or certificate course which he started out to pursue. If there is any indication that the student was unable to continue at the university for scholastic reasons, the admissions officer should investigate this aspect fully and weigh the information carefully in reaching a decision concerning admission.

Holders of University Degrees

Variation is apparent in degree requirements of the universities in the African countries where the British educational system has been predominant. An examination of the distribution of subjects studied and length of time required for the bachelor's degree reveals a departure by some universities from the standard three-year general degree.

A number of the universities and university colleges admit students at "A" level and offer three-year bachelor's degree programs; however, others admit at "O" level and offer four-year bachelor's degree programs. Some institutions (e.g., University of Ghana, University College of Sierra Leone) offer two different types of degree programs (honours and general) which differ in the amount of specialization required, and may differ in the number of years needed to complete the program. Other institutions (e.g., University of Ibadan, University of East Africa) do not offer these two different types. They award an honours degree solely on the basis of performance, regardless of the structure of, or the amount of specialization in, the degree program.

Holders of an honours degree or a special degree with good rank (First Class or High Second Class) may be considered for graduate study in the same major field in the United States. Holders of other three-year and four-year first university degrees (such degrees may be called general, combined subjects, etc.) with suitable subject concentrations may be considered, also, for graduate admission, provided they have high rankings and strong recommendations. Holders of Pass or Third Division degrees are not recommended for graduate admission.

It may be assumed that the following degrees from universities in English-speaking Africa are three-, four- or five-year degrees in the meaning of the above paragraph:

(1) Various types of B.A. degrees

(2) Various types of B.Sc. degrees

(3) Various types of specialized first degrees such as B.Sc. (Agric.), B.Com., B.Sc.(Eng.), B.A.F.A., B.Pharm. or B.Sc. Pharm., B.Soc.Sc., and L.L.B.

The L.L.B. is given at most universities in English-speaking Africa as a first degree not requiring previous university study.

Mention must be made, also, of the B.Ed. which may or may not be a first degree. Makerere College of the University of East Africa, the University of Ibadan, and some other universities in English-speaking Africa offer the B.Ed. as a first degree, requiring three years of study. On the other hand, several South African universities, the University of Basutoland, Bechuanaland and Swaziland, and others, give the B.Ed. as a second degree, requiring one to three years of study after the Bachelor of Arts or Bachelor of Science.

Some of the universities in Africa do not as yet offer a wide variety

of specialization.  Faculties are being added each year and the number and
variety will increase rapidly.  Many of the universities in British-oriented
Africa started as university colleges whose degrees were awarded by the
University of London, or the University of Durham, or the University of
South Africa; two or three are still in such status.  Degrees of this sort,
when presented for evaluation, should be accepted as degrees of the parent
institution.

## Evaluation of Three- and Four-Year Degrees

In assessing an applicant's qualifications, the dean, department head,
and admissions officer must consider whether his degree required three years
or four, whether it contained the distribution and concentration expected as
foundation for the graduate program anticipated, whether it was a general or
honours type of degree, which division, rank or recommendation it carried.
A student presenting a general degree may be required to do additional work
before entrance to graduate study or extra work before completing a master's
degree.  If, as sometimes happens, a degree does not indicate, in any way,
the quality of the work done, institutions may be unwilling to admit or may
base their decisions on recommendations or other information obtained from
the African university.

## Longer First Degrees

Professional first degrees in architecture, usually B.Arch., in dentistry, usually B.D.S., in medicine, usually M.B.Ch.B., and veterinary medicine, B.V.Sc. or B.Vet.Med., normally require five or six years and are
available at some African universities.  Evaluation of these degrees, if
offered as a basis for further work in the United States, should be made by
appropriate professional school personnel.

Advanced Degrees

Advanced degrees from African universities which reflect the British educational system may be different in their requirements from degrees of similar name awarded by institutions in the United States. Quite a few masters and other advanced degrees are given to alumni of the institution concerned and sometimes to others on the basis of research and publications, or even as honorary degrees and do not, in such cases, imply resident study.

The master degrees in Africa, as in the United Kingdom, are of several types. They are all second degrees. A few of them require from one to two years' resident study (course work). Most are based on such additional work as thesis and/or examinations without course work. Some are entirely honorary. The same university may give the same degree as earned and also as honorary. It is recommended that the evaluator check on the requirements for each degree and discover from the record submitted and references the extent to which course work, research, and examinations were involved.

The Doctor of Philosophy degree, Ph.D., is not given at all English-speaking African universities as yet, since many have been in existence only a few years. At those institutions granting the degree, three years of attendance and research are required generally after the bachelor's degree. It is difficult to equate this degree to those granted by U.S. institutions, but it is definitely related to the research type master and doctor degrees of the United States.

Evaluation of Advanced Degrees

Holders of advanced degrees that require examinations or the completion of research, or both, should receive consideration for advanced placement in graduate studies much as would be done if similar work had been completed in our own country. Holders of advanced degrees that do not require examinations or the completion of research should, like the holders of honorary degrees in this country, receive appropriate title and honor, but advanced placement in graduate programs should not go with it.

### Holders of University Diplomas

Since diplomas vary in type and length of study required, it is difficult to evaluate them for credit. The shortest time in which a diploma may be earned is usually one year, though this may be on a part-time basis. Some schools offer diplomas which entail three, four, or even five years of study. Sometimes these are full time and sometimes part time. The evaluator can seldom be sure whether full time means full-time attendance for a session of three terms, or whether it means "sandwich," six months in school and six months in employment.

Careful distinction should be made between diplomas requiring a bachelor's or other degree as a prerequisite, and those which permit the General Certificate of Education or even lower qualification. Also, one should consider the content and purpose of the program since many are entirely different from customary degree course work, while others take the same subjects one would expect in a degree program, but take them up in a more limited way or with a specialized application. One should also distinguish diplomas given by universities from diplomas given by various technical and trade schools or professional associations, some of which have names that include the word "Institute" or the word "Institution."

## Evaluation of Diplomas

For a diploma from a university, if the evaluator is convinced the student has completed a full year on a full-time basis, and that the content is comparable to some part of the American degree program contemplated, credit up to a maximum of 30 semester (45 quarter) credits may be given, provided the courses taken are appropriate to the student's objective. It should be noticed that many diploma curricula are too narrow and highly specialized to justify so high an evaluation.

Diploma courses of two or three years' duration are given in a few universities and other higher educational institutions and may, where subject matter is appropriate to the applicant's degree objective, be recognized for undergraduate advanced standing in areas the applicant seems to have covered adequately.

Ordinarily credit should be withheld in the case of most diplomas and other certificates that are not given by universities, by other higher educational institutions or by schools and colleges directly affiliated with universities. If the applicant is found, after arrival in the United States, to have satisfactory proficiency in some part of his proposed curriculum, he may be given suitable placement or credit on the basis of validating examinations and/or satisfactory performance of work at a higher level in the United States.

## Certificates

The certificates awarded by universities sometimes seem to be much the same as diplomas, but more often than not a certificate course is shorter than a diploma course, or is offered at a lower level, or is less comprehensive in content.

### Holders of United Kingdom Vocational Certificates

Since persons studying for the Ordinary National Certificate and the City and Guilds of London Institute Certificates and Royal Society of Arts Certificate are in the main selected from candidates who do not hold qualifications for entering university study, it may be assumed that most of the work in the certificate courses is of a non-university type. Work for the Higher National Certificate is at a higher level, but includes a substantial amount of subject matter for non-academic and applied fields.

### Holders of Teacher's Qualifications
### University Diploma in Education--Non-Graduate

A Diploma in Education awarded by a recognized university may be accepted as a basis for advanced standing to the extent the subjects taken are applicable to the student's educational objective in a United States institution. Evaluators should make careful distinction between diplomas earned in classes open only to degree holders and diplomas earned in classes open to persons without degrees. Diplomas earned in classes open to persons without degrees should definitely be classed as undergraduate work.

### University Diploma in Education--Postgraduate

The Postgraduate Diploma in Education is in many ways more like a year course in undergraduate education than like graduate work, since students in this program have not previously had any coursework in education. The requirement of a full bachelor's degree in liberal arts or science for admission to the program, however, makes it somewhat comparable to the special "fifth year" programs in teacher education which a number of institutions in the United States are now offering. It may be given the same status creditwise as would be given to such a program.

Teacher Training College Qualifications

Teachers whose qualifications are based on work at a teachers college
that is not part of a university and whose diplomas and certificates are
not awarded through a university, may be accepted in a non-degree relationship for special programs. If they wish to enter U.S. institutions as degree
candidates, a careful evaluation of their previous work, in terms of U.S.
entrance and degree requirements, should be made.

Applicants who completed university entrance requirements, as outlined
above, before entering a teachers college, may be considered for advanced
standing on the basis of a subject-by-subject evaluation. Only that part
of their work which is comparable to degree courses in a U.S. college or
university should be accepted.

## SYSTEMS ORGANIZED ALONG FRENCH LINES

### The Baccalauréat

Up to September 1962, the Baccalauréat examination in France was given
in two parts:  Part I at the close of six years of secondary education,
classe de première (first class); and Part II at the close of seven years,
classe terminale (terminal class). On September 26, 1962, Part I became a
probationary examination, examen probatoire. The final Baccalauréat examination then dropped the Part II designation (see Appendix G).

It is evident that references to Part I of the Baccalauréat examinations
are quickly fading out of documentation and other references on secondary
school credentials in French related Africa. Students applying for admission to U.S. colleges and universities may present Part I records for some
years to come, however.

In 1965 plans were announced by the French Ministry of Education to suppress the examen probatoire, but at present they apply only to Metropolitan France itself. It is considered likely that most French-speaking African countries will retain some special examination at the end of the classe de première as a means of eliminating those students who are clearly incapable of going on to the terminal year. If such elimination were not to take place, terminal lycée classes throughout the area would have to contend with a very substantially increased number of students, far beyond their present capacity in classrooms and teachers.

The following placement recommendations apply both to the Baccalauréat of Metropolitan France and to the Baccalauréat of those French-speaking countries in Africa which have maintained full educational links with France: Sénégal, Ivory Coast, Cameroun, Malagasy Republic, Chad, Central African Republic, Dahomey, Gabon, Togo, Upper Volta, Niger, Mauritania and Congo (Brazzaville). It should be noted that Algeria, Guinea, Mali, Morocco and Tunisia have created their own Baccalauréat examinations patterned after those in France, but adapted to their own needs. Evaluation of these newly developed Baccalauréats will require special consideration.

Course grades, given two or three times during the academic year, for the penultimate and the final year, as well as during the examen probatoire and the Baccalauréat examinations derive their real value in the light of the coefficient attached to each course. The coefficient value varies in accordance with the student's field of specialization. It should be noted that students are apt to concentrate on high coefficient courses, especially during the final year, neglecting the low coefficient ones. Evaluators are advised to focus special attention on the high coefficient courses in appraising student performances (refer to Appendix G).

Students who have passed the Baccalauréat, Part I examination or the

examen probatoire should continue their education through the terminal year
and earn the Baccalauréat before coming to a college or university in the
United States.  Students from Africa may present either a Baccalauréat
(pre-1965 diplomas specifying Part II) issued by the French universities
(Paris, Bordeaux, etc.)  or by French universities in Africa (Dakar, Abidjan,
Tananarive, etc.) or a Ministry of Education attestation in lieu thereof to
the effect that they have duly obtained this diploma.

Each institution in the United States will have to establish by analysis, experience, and placement procedures the amount of advanced standing
which it can allow to students who have completed various final Baccalauréat
programs.  Advanced standing should be determined by means of a subject-by-
subject evaluation.  This can be done more reliably if some form of placement test or departmental interview is used after the student arrives.  Persons continuing subjects which they started abroad will benefit if they can
be given placement tests to assure correct levels of entrance.

As many as seven types of Baccalauréat Part I (Classical A, A', B, C,
M, M', and Technical) have been offered in a number of French related coun-
tries of Africa.  Some countries with less developed education have offered
only two or three types.  Four types of final Baccalauréat (Philosophy,
Experimental Science, Elementary Mathematics, and Technical) are typical.
(See Appendix G for details of Baccalauréat programs.)

Students who present certifications of having passed a former Baccalauréat I examination or an examen probatoire, and a final Baccalauréat
examination and who also present evidence of the type of curriculum followed,
including which language options were taken, may receive some advanced
standing credit in a college or university in the United States, provided
their preparation is suitable for the curriculums they expect to follow in

the United States. If the courses they have had appear to be comparable to those in colleges and universities in this country, it is recommended that they be granted up to one year of credit on the basis of subject-by-subject evaluation. Subject credit should be chosen according to the curriculum the student followed in the African school, the grades he made on the <u>Baccalauréat</u> or in placement tests after coming to the United States, and the degree requirements of the program he has chosen in the United States. In case of doubt about the award of credit, the institution may ask the student to submit to examinations. Frequently the languages will be the only area in which advanced placement or credit can be justified.

Students from the African countries which have followed the French tradition in education will have studied in many cases only one language other than French which is likely to be English. Advanced standing credit is not recommended for English studied as a foreign language in the secondary school. Credit for the French language and literature or native language and literature, such as Arabic, should be on the basis of examination or other institutional practices for the granting of transfer credit generally.

The <u>Technical Baccalauréat</u> curriculums in their present form are for the most part quite new, and recommendations made here are based on expectations rather than experience. It is suggested that careful investigation and placement procedures be used in the evaluation of each individual case.

### Undergraduate University Certificates

Any one of the certificates showing completion of preparatory studies or the propaedeutic year may be accepted as evidence of a year of college level work in the subjects studied.

Each <u>Certificate of Higher Studies</u> given for work toward the <u>Licence</u>

in a Faculty of Letters (four of these certificates, occasionally more, are required for the Licence) may be accepted as evidence of one semester (approximately 15 semester hours) of undergraduate, normally junior-senior level, study in the subject represented.  Similar certificates from a Faculty of Science (where five are often required) may be accepted for approximately 12 semester hours each.

### First Degrees--Licence

The Licence from the African countries which follow the French tradition in education may be accepted as a degree admitting to graduate classification. The four or more certificates earned in preparation for the Licence are ordinarily named on the Licence certificate and may be checked to see if the applicant for graduate study has completed work equivalent to a major in the field he wishes to enter; however, in some cases, he may be required to complete additional undergraduate work in his proposed field.

### Higher Professional School Diplomas

A 3-year diploma from an engineering or other higher professional school which requires the Baccalauréat or higher standing, for admission, may be accepted in lieu of a Licence if the subject matter covered is a suitable foundation for the line of work the applicant plans to undertake.  Applicants with certificates of studies constituting fewer than three years of higher education should be placed as undergraduates with possible advanced standing by the usual placement procedures.

### Advanced University Degrees

The Diplôme d'Etudes Supérieures may be accepted as representing work comparable to that of the master's degree in the United States.

The Doctorat du Troisième Cycle offered by the University of Algeria, the University of Rabat, and the University of Dakar, is granted for study and research in a special field.  Although not oriented toward teaching like the Doctorat d'Etat, the degree may be accepted as somewhere between the level of a U.S. master's and a U.S. Ph.D.

The Doctorat d'Etat and the Doctorat ès "spécialité" may be comparable to a U.S. Ph.D., and the holder may be considered for post-doctoral study.

### Certificates for Teachers in the Lower and Upper Secondary Schools

The Certificat d'Aptitude Pedagogue (CAP)  awarded at the close of a four-year teacher-training program may be considered for university entrance at the freshman level.  It usually represents 3 years of academic study based on the Brevet d'Etudes du Premier Cycle or Brevet Elémentaire, with an additional year devoted to professional training.  Credit for the final year of courses in educational theory, psychology, administration and practical pedagogy should be granted only by examination or on recommendation of the departments concerned.

The Certificat d'Aptitude au Professorat dans l'Enseignement Public du Second Degré (CAPES) may be accepted as representing preparation comparable to a master's degree.  It is held by some teachers in lycées and collèges and demands typically one year of study beyond the Licence.

The Agrégation, which is offered by the University of Dakar, represents completion of studies more advanced than CAPES and searching competitive examinations.  The program is available in fields in which secondary teachers are prepared.  It is a specialist's rating and will justify placement of the holder at a very high level of graduate work in his field.  The time spent in preparation, largely because of the keen competition for a few places, makes the Agrégation higher than the typical master's degree.

## CERTIFICATES NOT MENTIONED ABOVE

Certificates of attendance and assiduity should not be recognized for credit.  Certificates and diplomas other than those listed should be investigated carefully to prevent errors in identification and evaluation. African universities give many specialized certificates.  Also, the African countries which have followed the French tradition in education have a number of professional schools and colleges of university rank, as well as lower types of institutions for various sorts of specialized training.  It is suggested that in case of uncertainty the first thing to do is to identify the institution and try to make sure that it requires the Baccalauréat or equivalent for admission.  If it does, and there is sufficient information available to identify the length and type of course completed, and if such courses when taken in the United States on the same level would be accepted for credit in the institution concerned, then there exists a tentative basis for estimating the work covered and the credit that may be given either in a lump, or on a year and subject basis.

## COMPOSITE EDUCATIONAL SYSTEMS

### LIBYA

It is recommended that holders of the General Secondary Education Certificate, awarded to graduates of Libyan secondary schools be considered for admission to U.S. colleges and universities in freshman standing, provided they have attained superior marks on their final examinations.

Graduates of the Libyan University who have attained superior scholastic records may qualify for graduate admission in the United States provided preparation for the graduate objective is adequate.

## SOMALIA

Students who have completed their secondary schooling in the northern part of Somalia have studied for eleven years in schools which have followed the British tradition in education and are eligible to sit for the <u>University of London General Certificate of Education</u> ordinary level examinations. To be considered for admission to a U.S. college or university, the examination record should show at least five passes at ordinary level, covering a good range of subjects, including English, and all passes at a high standard and, in addition, satisfactory scores on such examinations or other devices as the admitting institution might use to validate suitable academic attainment.

Graduates of secondary schools in the southern portion of the country will have completed eleven or twelve years of study depending on whether they followed the Somali or Italian programs. Holders of the <u>Diploma</u> from the upper secondary school (Somali program) should be encouraged to continue their studies at the Istituto Universitario della Somalia for one or two years before coming to the United States for degree programs. Holders of the <u>Maturità Scientifica</u> may qualify for admission at a U.S. college or university in freshman standing, provided their examination records are well above average.

Credit for courses passed at the Istituto Universitario della Somalia may be allowed when evidence of final examinations passed with superior grades can be presented.

## ETHIOPIA

It is recommended that graduates of Ethiopian secondary schools who have successfully completed the Ethiopian School Leaving Certificate, with at least 5 passes at credit standard or better, or, prior to 1963, obtained the University of London General Certificate of Education, with at least 5 passes of good quality, at ordinary level, may be considered for admission at the freshman level. However, it is further recommended that institutions considering such admissions validate the achievement and ability of each applicant through examinations suitable for the purpose.

Graduates of Haile Sellasie I University or the former University College of Addis Ababa, who have attained superior scholastic records, may qualify for graduate admission in the United States, provided preparation for the graduate objective is adequate.

## SOUTH AFRICA
### Secondary Leaving Certificates

It is recommended that students from South Africa seeking admission as freshmen in U.S. colleges and universities present one of the following:

Cape Senior Certificate with Matriculation Exemption

Orange Free State School Leaving Certificate with
    Matriculation Exemption

Natal Senior Certificate with Matriculation Exemption

Transvaal University Entrance Certificate

Transvaal Secondary School Certificate

Joint Matriculation Board Matriculation Certificate[1]

---

[1] Students from South West Africa sit for the Joint Matriculation Board Matriculation Certificate.

The examinations should include an appropriate distribution of subject fields and a high standard should be attained overall.

## University Degrees

South African university degree requirements are not too dissimilar from those of British universities and African universities which have followed the British tradition.  The previous discussion of university degrees, certificates, and diplomas from the English-speaking African countries applies as well, in many respects, to South African university degrees. However, attention is called to some differences.

It is recommended that the three-year South African bachelor's degree based on five years of secondary school, be evaluated for credit toward the bachelor's degree at U.S. colleges and universities.  However, those students who have completed four-year or longer first degrees with high standing may be considered for graduate admission, provided the preparation for the graduate objective is adequate.

The South African master's degree is most frequently awarded on the basis of research, dissertation and/or examinations.  The Ph.D., on one hand, may be based on the master's degree and involve research and defense of a thesis; while on the other hand, it may be based on an honours beachelor's degree and will prove to be the usual research type degree.

The D. Litt. and D.Sc. are honorary degrees based solely on the recognition of published works.  Holders of honorary degrees should receive appropriate title and honor at U.S. colleges and universities, but advanced placement in graduate programs should not be granted.

## SYSTEMS ORGANIZED ALONG SPANISH LINES

Only very exceptional students from the territories comprising Spanish Africa are likely to qualify for freshman admission at U.S. colleges and universities, unless they have gone elsewhere for further study, since in most provinces only ten years of formal education, ending with the Bachillerato Superior are availalbe.  From the province of Ifni, however, students may qualify for admission at U.S. colleges and universities since the pre-universitario year is available there and, indeed, also a year of post pre-universitario studies.  Advanced standing credit may be allowed for this higher work when evidence of examinations passed with superior grades can be presented.

## SYSTEMS ORGANIZED ALONG PORTUGUESE LINES

Students who have completed the three cycles of secondary studies in the Portuguese African territories and received their Diplomas du curso complementar de licens (diplomas of secondary education) may qualify for admission to U.S. colleges and universities as freshmen, provided final examination records are superior.

Advanced standing credit toward the U.S. bachelor's degree may be allowed for courses studied at the centers for higher studies in Angola and Mozambique when evidence of final examinations passed with superior grades can be presented.

## SYSTEMS ORGANIZED ALONG BELGIAN LINES

Students who have completed the six years of secondary school in the Belgian oriented countries in Africa and earned the Diplôme d'humanités in Congo (Leopoldville) or Rwanda, or the <u>Diplôme homologué d'humanités</u>

in Burundi, or the <u>Diplôme d'humanités</u> ratified by a university faculty

or the certificate of completion for a one year pre-university course at

Lovanium University or one of the other official universities may qualify

for admission to U.S. colleges and universities in freshman standing,

provided they have obtained superior grades on final examinations.


The program of the National School of Administration and Law which

is open to students who have earned the <u>Diplôme d'humanités</u> may be evalu-

ated on a course for course basis toward requirements of a program desired

in the United States.

The three-year <u>Baccalauréat</u> from Rwanda and the two-year B.A. and

B.Sc. from Burundi may be accepted for credit toward a U.S. bachelor's

degree on a course for course basis, provided the examination grades are

superior.

The <u>Licence</u> from Congo (Leopoldville) based on the <u>Candidature</u> which

requires two years of study, followed by the first and second <u>Licence</u> exam-

inations, or the longer five-year <u>Licence</u> from Rwanda may be considered for

graduate admission at U.S. colleges and universities, provided superior

examination grades can be presented and preparation for the advanced degree

is adequate.


## <u>SYSTEM ORGANIZED ALONG UNITED STATES LINES</u>

### LIBERIA

It is recommended that graduates of secondary school in Liberia seek-

ing admission to institutions of higher education in the United States

should present transcripts of record showing superior grades and, in addi-

tion, satisfactory scores on such examinations as the admitting institution might use to validate suitable academic attainment.

Credit for courses completed at Liberian institutions of higher education level may be validated by examinations or advanced placement at U.S. colleges and universities.

Graduates of the University of Liberia may be considered for appropriate placement as advanced undergraduates to make up shortages in their preparation, provided their scholastic records are superior. Graduates of Cuttington College may be accepted on the same basis.

THE COUNCIL ON EVALUATION OF
FOREIGN STUDENT CREDENTIALS

Member Organizations and Representatives

American Association of Collegiate Registrars and Admissions Officers
    Inez H. Sepmeyer, University of California, Los Angeles
    Robert E. Tschan, Pennsylvania State University
    William H. Strain, Indiana University, Council Chairman; Coordinator,
      World Education Series
    Clifford Sjogren, University of Michigan, Council Secretary
    Ruth Arnold, University of Oklahoma, Editor, World Education Series

Association of American Colleges
    Herrick B. Young, Western College for Women

Association of Graduate Schools
    Robert S. Ford, University of Michigan

American Association of Junior Colleges
    W. Alan Jones, Florida State University

Council of Graduate Schools in the United States
    Gustave O. Arlt, Washington, D.C.
    Carroll Miller, Howard University

Institute of International Education
    James M. Davis, New York
    Lily von Klemperer, New York

National Association for Foreign Student Affairs
    J. Richard Toven, New York University
    Lee Wilcox, University of Minnesota


Observer Organizations and Representatives

African American Institute
    William Gaines, New York
    Julien Engle, Washington, D.C.

American Council on Education, Commission on International Education
    Elizabeth Shiver, Washington, D.C.

American Friends of the Middle East
    Orin Parker, Washington, D.C.
    Dorothy La Guardia, Washington, D.C.

College Entrance Examination Board
    Albert G. Sims, New York

U.S. Department of State, Agency for International Development
    Hattie Jarmon, Washington, D.C.

U.S. Department of State, Bureau of Educational and Cultural Affairs
    Marita T. Houlihan, Washington, D.C.

U.S. Office of Education
    Fredrika M. Tandler, Washington, D.C.
    Charles C. Hauch, Washington, D.C.

University of the State of New York, State Education Department
    James J. Fitzgibbons, Albany, N.Y.

A P P E N D I X   I


RESEARCH

# A PREDICTION STUDY OF AFRICAN STUDENTS SELECTED THROUGH THE AFRICAN SCHOLARSHIP PROGRAM OF AMERICAN UNIVERSITIES[1,2]

Lee Wilcox
University of Minnesota

## Introduction

The African Scholarship Program of American Universities (ASPAU) is a co-operative program of U.S. colleges and universities designed to enable well-qualified African undergraduates to study for a Bachelor's degree in the participating U.S. institutions. Begun in 1960 as a pilot project with Nigeria, ASPAU has, through 1965-66, selected 1,184 students from 32 African countries to study in 217 American colleges and universities. Students who survive ASPAU's rigorous screening (about 1 out of every 20 applicants is accepted) are assured of full financial support through tuition scholarships from the U.S. institution, maintenance support from the U.S. Agency for International Development, and round trip transportation from their home governments.

## ASPAU Selection Process

As already noted, ASPAU screening is a very selective process. Since this study is of ASPAU students who have been selected, the process of selection will be described in some detail as it relates to students from African

[1] Conducted under the auspices of the Committee on Research on International Education, American Association of Collegiate Registrars and Admissions Officers, through a sub-grant from the Ford Foundation grant to UCLA for this volume.

[2] Special appreciation is expressed to Janyce Anker and Marissa Chorlian for data collection.

countries whose educational systems generally follow the British pattern
(ASPAU students from French-speaking countries are not included).

There are five factors which are utilized, in combination, for selection purposes:

1.  School Certificate results (Cambridge, West African, or GCE ordinary
    level.

    The candidate's marks in his best six subjects are used for scoring
    purposes.  Individual subjects are scored 1 - 9 with 1 being the
    highest possible score.  The range on School Certificate results is
    generally from 10 to 35 for ASPAU candidates.

2.  Higher School Certificate results (HSC or GCE advanced level).

    For scoring purposes, 3 points are awarded for a principal level pass
    with distinction, 2 points for a principal level pass, and 1 point for
    a subsidiary level pass.  These points are doubled in the final formula
    and have a range of 0 to about 16.

3.  Special Scholastic Aptitude Test.

    Developed by the Educational Testing Service after experimentation
    with its regular Preliminary Scholastic Aptitutde Test,[1] the special
    SAT consists of a 70-item Verbal section and a 50-item Mathematical
    section.  The score used for males is V + 2M and for females, 1.5V +
    1.5M.

4.  Teachers' and Headmasters' ratings.

    From reports submitted by two teachers and the headmaster, the ASPAU

---

[1]W.D. Coffman, Evidence of Cultural Factors in Responses of African
Students to Items in an American Test of Scholastic Aptitude. The 20th
Yearbook, National Council on Measurement in Education (1963), pp. 27-37.

Scholarship Board (see 5) rates the reports and awards the candidate a score from 0 to 20. The reports assess the candidate both academically and personally.

5.    Interviewers' rating.

Each candidate who survives a preliminary screening based on School Certificate and SAT results is interviewed, in Africa, by a Scholarship Board comprised of two U.S. admissions officers, a field representative of the African-American Institute, and several nationals of the particular country (typically headmasters and college faculty members). The interviewing team is asked to consider the applicant mainly on non-intellective characteristics such as seriousness of purpose, potential for service to his nation, maturity, and adaptability. Each Board member assigns the candidate a score from 0 to 20 and the average of these scores is used for scoring purposes.

The scores on these 5 factors are combined, according to the following formulas recommended by the Educational Testing Service, to yield a composite score:

Males:    SAT - 75 - CSC + 2HSC + 2TR + 2IR = Composite

Females:  SAT - 60 - CSC + 2HSC + 2TR + 2IR = Composite

This composite is used to produce a rank-ordering of candidates which is a guide for selection decisions. It should be pointed out, however, that selection is not based solely on this composite as the country's manpower needs and the availability of indigenous educational opportunities are also important selection criteria.

## Purpose of the Study

Since considerable numbers of African students have studied in the
United States under the ASPAU program and, for most students, pre-admission
variables plus their grades were available in quantified form in ASPAU's
Cambridge office, the feasibility of this study seemed promising.  The basic
purpose is to assess the contribution of the variables used by ASPAU for
selection in predicting academic success in the ASPAU member institutions.
It has been noted by Coffman[1] that ". . . grade reports received from colleges confirm the exceptionally high validity of (the ASPAU) process as a
whole."  It is of interest, therefore, to analyze this process into its
components to determine their validity, both individually and in combination.  For this purpose, two different classes were selected to observe the
extent of their differences, if any.

## Sample

Data were collected on 443 ASPAU students, roughly one-half of whom
entered U.S. colleges in 1961 and one-half in 1963.  The data include
scores on the five variables described earlier (plus the composite), demographic variables such as age, sex, father's occupation, and rural-urban
background, and grade point average at the U.S. institution (total GPA for
1961 entrants; first year, second year, and total GPA for 1963 entrants).

## Results

Table 1 shows the means and standard deviations of the ASPAU variables
and the U.S. GPA's for the two groups (see page 1502).

---

[1]ASPAU Policy and By-laws (1965-66), p. 6.

Table 2 presents the inter-correlations of the six pre-admission variables and U.S. GPA. The lower left array is for the 1961 group; the upper right array is for the 1963 group (see page 1502).

Several comments may be made, at this point, concerning the data in Tables 1 and 2. Immediately apparent is the similarity between the 1961 and 1963 groups in terms of both means and intercorrelations. None of the differences between means is statistically significant at the .05 level (except the difference between SAT scores; a slightly different form was administered in 1963), nor are the differences between correlations statistically significant. All subsequent data, therefore, are for all students combined.

A second observation is that the correlations between predictors and U.S. GPA are rather minimal (although a correlation of $\pm.11$ is significant at the .05 level with an N of 200). This is to be expected in that an attempt is made in placement to match the student's capabilities with the demands of the college. To the extent that this matching is successful, the correlations will approximate zero since all students would have the same expected GPA. Another reason to anticipate low correlations with GPA is that this group of students constitutes a very select sample and hence the range of variability of the predictor variables is restricted. While this phenomenon cannot be corrected for within the data available, an attempt can be made to reduce the placement effects by dividing the total group of students into subgroups attending more or less homogeneous colleges. Ideally, one would consider students at a particular college as a subgroup. However, these 400 students are distributed among 200 U.S. colleges with no more than a few at any one college. Several methods were devised, therefore, to subdivide the total sample to analyze further the predictor-criterion relationships.

1.  ASPAU was asked to provide a subgrouping of their member institutions on the basis of the factors they consider in the placement process. Basically, the four subgroups arrived at in this way seem to represent a subjective breakdown based on the competitiveness of the institution.

2.  A more objective method of assessing the competitiveness of the ASPAU institutions is available in Astin's recent monograph.[1] He has catalogued an "Estimated Selectivity" score for over 1,000 U.S. colleges. This is expressed as a T score (mean of 50, standard deviation of 10) and is defined as "the total number of highly able students who want to enroll at the college divided by the number of freshmen admitted." The sample was subdivided into six subgroups based on this factor.[2]

| Subgroup | Est. Sel. |
| --- | --- |
| 1 | 69-81 |
| 2 | 61-68 |
| 3 | 57-60 |
| 4 | 50-56 |
| 5 | 45-49 |
| 6 | 37-44 |

3.  In addition to the scholastic demands of the college, it might be hypothesized that its size should be taken into account in defining less heterogeneous subgroups. A third breakdown was made by using

---

[1] Alexander W. Astin, Who Goes Where to College, Science Research Associates (1965).

[2] It is interesting to note that the correlation between this factor and the ASPAU grouping is .78.

both Estimated Selectivity and size (also in T score units from Astin).

A T score of 60 represents an enrollment of about 2,600 students.

| Subgroups | Est. Sel. | Size |
|-----------|-----------|------|
| 1 | 63-81 | 60 |
| 2 | 63-81 | 60 |
| 3 | 56-62 | 60 |
| 4 | 56-62 | 60 |
| 5 | 37-55 | 60 |
| 6 | 37-55 | 60 |

4.   Another potentially useful method of subgrouping would be on the student's field of study. Therefore, a fourth categorization combines selectivity and major field of study as follows:

| Subgroups | Est. Sel. | Major |
|-----------|-----------|-------|
| 1 | 60 | Engineering |
| 2 | 60 | Engineering |
| 3 | 60 | Humanities and Soc. Sci. |
| 4 | 60 | Humanities and Soc. Sci. |
| 5 | 60 | Science and Math. |
| 6 | 60 | Science and Math. |

Zero order correlations were computed between the six predictor variables and U.S. GPA and a multiple correlation was computed using the five individual predictors in an optimally weighted fashion. These correlations, by subgrouping, are shown in Table 3 with similar correlations from the total group for comparison purposes (see page 1503). Table 4, page 1503, summarizes the range and the median of these correlations.

## Discussion

A most striking characteristic of these African students is their excellent overall performance in U.S. colleges (many of which are highly competitive institutions). Their mean overall grade point average was 2.68 and only about five per cent had less than a C average. This further confirms the overall validity of the ASPAU selection process noted previously.

The placement process also seems to have been rather effective. Although the differences in mean GPA's between the students in the four
groups of colleges defined by ASPAU are significant (F=4.22, df 3,364),
students in all groups did well; when grouped on other dimensions (size and
major), the differences in mean performance are not significant. Of course,
students are not referred to colleges only on ability grounds. The student's major and sometimes his preference for type or location of college
are also considered. The correlation of .78 between ASPAU's groups and
Astin's objective estimate of selectivity, plus the fairly even performance
at all types of colleges, seem to validate ASPAU's placement procedures.

Another general observation that can be made is that the characteristics
of ASPAU students, both in terms of pre-admission data and their subsequent
performance in U.S. colleges, are rather stable. Their academic achievement,
as measured by the School Certificate and the Higher School Certificate, was
very similar for both the 1961 and 1963 groups, as were their ratings by
teachers, headmasters, and interviewers. Similarly, their U.S. grades are
nearly identical. Thus, there is no reason, from these data, to suppose
that ASPAU students as a whole are changing.

The intercorrelations of the ASPAU selection variables (Table 2) provide at least two interesting insights. First, it is apparent that the
overall ASPAU composite which combines the five variables could be estimated
with precision, for this group, from the SAT results (r=.91 (1961), r=.85
(1963)). This does not necessarily imply, however, that the other factors
are not important in the selection process. It could well be, for example,
that the usefulness of the other factors has been "used up" in selection--

e.g., that students with mediocre results on the School Certificate are not selected at all; therefore, students in the selected group will have School Certificate results more or less the same, resulting in little correlation with other factors.

Second, teacher and interviewer ratings do not correlate with the academic variables (although the correlation between the two ratings is about .60). This might be explained, especially for the interviewer ratings, in that the basis for rating is intended to be primarily on nonacademic grounds. Their moderately high inter-correlation could probably be accounted for because they are made at about the same time by the same people (the interviewing team).

The differential prediction of U.S. grades based on the data collected in Africa (Tables 3 and 4) is very limited. Even when students are divided into seemingly homogeneous college subgroups, correlations are not significantly improved. It may be that the range on the selection variables is so restricted that no subgrouping procedure would enhance their individual validities. To assess the full validity of the variables, one would need to have included candidates not selected by ASPAU who also attended the same or similar U.S. institutions. The multiple correlations are somewhat more promising although their values are rather low when compared with similar coefficients for domestic students (these probably should be compared, however, with multiple correlations derived from groups of superior domestic students--in this sense they are more typical).

The manner in which the five factors contribute to the multiple prediction varies considerably from sample to sample. A simple tally of the variables which have a significant (.05 level), positive weight in the 22 prediction equations shows: <u>School Certificate</u>--significant 11 times;

teachers and headmaster rating--significant 9 times; <u>Higher School Certi-</u>

<u>ficate</u>--significant 6 times, and SAT--significant 3 times.  Interestingly,

in the five samples in which the interviewer rating enters significantly

into the prediction equation, its weight is <u>negative</u> (i.e., the higher the

rating, the lower the grades).  This would seem to raise the question

whether the interviewing team ought not to call attention to students whose

personal characteristics and/or study objectives are not compatible with

the purposes of the ASPAU program rather than making a ranking which is

included in the composite.

## Summary

The ASPAU Program was the first attempt at full-scale <u>overseas</u> screening

and selection using a wide range of criteria in the rating of students.

These data tend to show that the students chosen by this method have

been well selected and that they have performed well.  Their performance, of

course, has been due in some measure to the skillful matching by the ASPAU

administrative staff of students with the most appropriate institutions.

The findings help to bring into focus the relative importance of the

several criteria in the selection process, but cannot be considered defini-

tive due to the selective nature of the sample and the lack of cross-valida-

tion.  Withal, the total selection criteria stand out as most effective.

U.S. admissions officers selecting non-ASPAU undergraduates may be en-

couraged by the findings of this study in that a careful analysis of <u>School</u>

<u>Certificate</u> and <u>Higher School Certificate</u> results, as well as reports of

school officials and such other data which may be available, should provide

sound criteria for assessing candidates' academic potential.

Table 1

## MEANS AND STANDARD DEVIATIONS OF ASPAU VARIABLES AND U.S. GPA

| Variable | Group | N | Mean | Std. Dev. |
|----------|-------|---|------|-----------|
| School Cert. | 1961 | 191 | 20.5 | 4.1 |
|              | 1963 | 219 | 20.1 | 4.2 |
| Total        |      | 410 | 20.3 | 4.1 |
| HSC/GCE-A | 1961 | 195 | 7.3 | 7.8 |
|           | 1963 | 219 | 6.7 | 7.3 |
| Total     |      | 414 | 7.0 | 7.5 |
| SAT | 1961 | 191 | 34.7 | 18.8 |
|     | 1963 | 216 | 27.4 | 17.5 |
| Total |    | 407 | 30.8 | 18.5 |
| Tch. Rating | 1961 | 170 | 30.6 | 3.2 |
|             | 1963 | 218 | 30.8 | 3.6 |
| Total       |      | 388 | 30.7 | 3.4 |
| Intv. Rating | 1961 | 170 | 30.9 | 3.4 |
|              | 1963 | 218 | 31.9 | 3.5 |
| Total        |      | 388 | 31.5 | 3.5 |
| Composite | 1961 | 162 | 81.6 | 25.2 |
|           | 1963 | 209 | 76.9 | 24.0 |
| Total     |      | 371 | 78.9 | 24.7 |
| 1st Yr. GPA | 1963 | 228 | 2.68 | .60 |
| 2nd Yr. GPA | 1963 | 220 | 2.63 | .61 |
| Total   GPA | 1961 | 211 | 2.71 | .51 |
|             | 1963 | 226 | 2.65 | .54 |
| Total       |      | 437 | 2.68 | .53 |

Table 2

## INTER-CORRELATIONS OF SIX PRE-ADMISSION VARIABLES AND U.S. GPA

|              | SC    | HSC  | SAT  | TR   | IR   | COMP | GPA  |
|--------------|-------|------|------|------|------|------|------|
| Sch. Cert.   |       | -.17 | -.34 | -.15 | -.03 | -.51 | -.18 |
| HSC/GCE-A    | -.24[1] |    | .22  | -.03 | .04  | .47  | .16  |
| SAT          | -.29  | .40  |      | .12  | .07  | .85  | .07  |
| Tch. Rating  | -.13  | -.03 | -.03 |      | .61  | .33  | .09  |
| Intv. Rating | -.11  | .07  | .05  | .60  |      | .25  | -.06 |
| Composite    | -.46  | .63  | .91  | .21  | .29  |      | .15  |
| U.S. GPA     | -.24  | .15  | .14  | .00  | -.07 | .20  |      |

[1]Since School Certificate results are expressed on a scale where low scores are best, negative correlations between School Certificate and other variables represent relationships in the expected direction.

Table 3

## CORRELATIONS WITH U.S. GPA

| | Mean GPA | SC | HSC | SAT | TR | IR | ASPAU COMP. | MULT. R | N |
|---|---|---|---|---|---|---|---|---|---|
| Total Group | 2.68 | -.20 | .16 | .11 | .06 | -.07 | .17 | .29 | 368-409 |
| 1961 Group | 2.71 | -.24 | .15 | .14 | .00 | -.07 | .20 | .33 | 169-192 |
| 1963 Group | 2.65 | -.18 | .16 | .07 | .09 | -.06 | .14 | .27 | 207-217 |
| ASPAU    -1 | 2.64 | -.38 | .28 | .27 | .13 | .01 | .41 | .48 | 94 |
| -2 | 2.68 | -.14 | .22 | -.03 | .18 | .05 | .13 | .35 | 113 |
| -3 | 2.57 | -.23 | .17 | .21 | .10 | -.10 | .28 | .36 | 104 |
| -4 | 2.87 | -.26 | .20 | .11 | -.10 | -.11 | .16 | .38 | 57 |
| Est. Sel. | | | | | | | | | |
| -1 | 2.64 | -.30 | .22 | .21 | .02 | -.16 | .29 | .41 | 64 |
| -2 | 2.66 | -.15 | .14 | .16 | .28 | .19 | .24 | .38 | 84 |
| -3 | 2.70 | -.29 | .27 | .22 | .06 | -.04 | .34 | .43 | 97 |
| -4 | 2.47 | -.23 | .22 | .04 | .21 | .02 | .24 | .41 | 50 |
| -5 | 2.67 | -.37 | .17 | .46 | .17 | -.06 | .60 | .65 | 31 |
| -6 | 2.88 | -.18 | .06 | -.33 | -.19 | -.15 | -.26 | .50 | 41 |
| ES and Size | | | | | | | | | |
| -1 | 2.63 | .02 | .14 | .10 | .00 | -.21 | .09 | .36 | 62 |
| -2 | 2.76 | -.38 | -.02 | .03 | .16 | .22 | .13 | .44 | 61 |
| -3 | 2.53 | -.33 | .28 | .16 | .35 | .09 | .33 | .52 | 39 |
| -4 | 2.63 | -.21 | .45 | .32 | -.01 | -.03 | .45 | .51 | 70 |
| -5 | 2.72 | -.27 | .11 | -.07 | -.12 | -.12 | .00 | .36 | 81 |
| -6 | 2.67 | -.19 | .06 | .16 | .20 | .20 | .21 | .43 | 55 |
| ES and Major | | | | | | | | | |
| -1 | 2.61 | -.22 | .33 | .40 | .24 | .06 | .50 | .56 | 61 |
| -2 | 2.73 | -.44 | .13 | .04 | .15 | -.13 | .18 | .56 | 35 |
| -3 | 2.60 | -.21 | .20 | .03 | .17 | .07 | .14 | .32 | 59 |
| -4 | 2.65 | -.23 | .01 | .00 | .02 | -.03 | .07 | .24 | 68 |
| -5 | 2.74 | -.21 | .02 | .03 | .13 | .10 | .10 | .22 | 53 |
| -6 | 2.73 | -.19 | .21 | .12 | -.18 | -.27 | .13 | .37 | 71 |

Table 4

## SUMMARY OF CORRELATIONS WITH U.S. GPA

| | No. Corr's | Range | Median r | N |
|---|---|---|---|---|
| Sch. Cert. | 22 | -.44/.02 | -.23 | 31-113 |
| H. Sch. Cert. | 22 | -.02/.45 | .19 | 31-113 |
| SAT | 22 | -.33/.46 | .12 | 31-113 |
| Tch. Rat. | 22 | -.19/.38 | .13 | 31-113 |
| Int. Rat. | 22 | -.27/.22 | -.03 | 31-113 |
| ASPAU Comp. | 22 | -.26/.60 | .20 | 31-113 |
| Mult. R | 22 | .22/.65 | .41 | 31-113 |

# A P P E N D I X  J

NATIONAL ADVISORY COMMITTEE

NATIONAL ADVISORY COMMITTEE

| Organizations | Representatives |
| --- | --- |
| American Council on Education | Robert Humphrey |
| Institute of International Education | Lily von Klemperer |
| American Association of Collegiate Registrars and Admissions Officers | Alfred Thomas, Jr. |
| American College Personnel Association, International Education Committee | Ivan Putnam |
| Association of Graduate Schools of the Association of American Universities | Robert Ford |
| College Entrance Examination Board | Edward Noyes |
| Council on Evaluation of Foreign Student Credentials | William Strain |
| Council of Graduate Schools | Gustav Arlt |
| National Association of Foreign Student Advisers | Richard Toven |
| University of California | Inez Sepmeyer |
| University of the State of New York, State Education Department | Helen McDermott |
| U. S. Department of Health, Education, and Welfare, Office of Education | Charles Hauch |
| U. S. Department of State, Cultural Affairs | Robert Richards |
| U. S. Department of State, Agency for International Development | Hattie Jarman |
| American Friends of the Middle East | Virgil Crippin |
| African Scholarship Program of American Universities | Richard Moll |
| African-American Institute | William Gaines |
| The Ford Foundation, International Training and Research Program | Melvin Fox--ex officio |

A SELECTED BIBLIOGRAPHY

A SELECTED BIBLIOGRAPHY

## BIBLIOGRAPHIES

Brembeck, Cole S. and John P. Keith. <u>Education in Emerging Africa--A Select and Annotated Bibliography</u>. East Lansing, Michigan: Bureau of Publications, College of Education, Michigan State University, 1962.

<u>Catalogues of the Collection of Education in Tropical Areas</u>. Catalogue of the University of London Institute of Education's Overseas <u>Lending Library</u>. Boston: G.K. Hall, 1964.

Couch, Margaret. <u>Education in Africa: A Select Bibliography. Part 1: British and Former British Territories in Africa</u>. Education Libraries Bulletin, Supplement 5. London: University of London Institute of Education, 1962.

_____. <u>Education in Africa: A Select Bibliography. Part 2: French Speaking Territories</u>. (Former French and Belgian Colonies, Portuguese and Spanish Territories, Ethiopia and Eritrea, Liberia.) London: University of London Institute of Education, 1964.

Dolan, Eleanor F. <u>Higher Education in Africa South of the Sahara: Selected Bibliography 1945-1961</u>. Washington: American Association of University Women, 1961.
    An annotated bibliography including periodical articles on Africa in general.

Drake, Howard. <u>A Bibliography of African Education South of the Sahara</u>. Aberdeen University Anthropological Museum Publication No. 2. Aberdeen, Scotland: Aberdeen University Press, 1942.
    Lists several thousands of documents, books and articles on education.

<u>Government Policy and International Education: A Selected and Partially Annotated Bibliography of Africa</u>. Draft by M. Datin, Sept., 1964. Obtained from Franklin Parker, Box 338, University of Oklahoma, Norman, Oklahoma.

Leyder, Jean. <u>Bibliographie de l'Enseignement Supérieur et de la Recherche Scientifique en Afrique Intertropicale</u>. 2 vols. Bruxelles: Centre de Documentation Economique et Sociale Africaine, 1959-1960.

Marais, Josef. <u>European Education in South Africa, 1944-1955</u>. A select bibliography. Cape Town, South Africa: University of Cape Town, 1956.

Rousseau, M.  A Bibliography of African Education in the Federation of
        Rhodesia and Nyasaland (1890-1958).  Cape Town, South Africa:


Shields, James J. Jr., comp.  A Selected Bibliography on Education in
        East Africa, 1941-61.  Makerere Library Publication No. 2.
        (Includes Kenya, Tanganyika, Uganda, Zanzibar.)  Kampala, Uganda:
        Makerere University College, 1962.


Talbot, Philipps, ed.  A Selected Bibliography:  Asia, Africa, Eastern
        Europe and Latin America.  New York:  American Universities
        Field Staff, Inc., 1960.


Tolman, L. E. and others, comp.  "Africa:  A Selected Bibliography with
        Related Instructional Aids for the Elementary and Secondary
        School," Journal of Education, No. 144 (Oct. 1961), pp. 1-90.


U.S. Dept. of State.  Bureau of Educational and Cultural Affairs.  Inven-
        tory of Recent Publications  and Research Studies in the Field
        of International Educational and Cultural Affairs.  Washington,
        D.C.:  CU Reference Service, Oct. 1964.


Yates, Barbara.  "A Bibliography on Special Problems in Education in
        Tropical Africa," Comparative Education Review, VIII, No. 3
        (Dec. 1964), 307-19.


_____.  "Educational Policy and Practice in Tropical Africa:  A General
        Bibliography," Comparative Education Review, VIII, No. 2 (Oct.
        1964), 215-28.

## BOOKS

Abraham, W. E.  The Mind of Africa.  Chicago:  University of Chicago
        Press, 1962.


Ashby, Sir Eric.  African Universities and Western Tradition.  Cambridge,
        Mass.:  Harvard University Press, 1964.


_____.  Patterns of Universities in Non-European Societies.  London:
        University of London, School of Oriental and African Studies,
        1961.


Becker, Herbert Theodor.  Das Schulwesen in Afrika.  Berlin:  de Gruyter,
        1943.
            A country-by-country study of colonial education.  Includes
        bibliography.

Bohannan, Paul. Africa and Africans. Garden City, N.Y.: Natural History Press, 1964.

Bouchard, Joseph. L'Eglise en Afrique Noire. Paris: La Palantine, 1958.
        A history of the educational work of Catholic missions in Africa.

Brace, Richard M. Morocco-Algeria-Tunisia: The Modern Nations in Historical Perspective. Englewood Cliffs, N.J.: Prentice-Hall, Inc., 1964.

Brelsford, W.V., ed. Handbook of the Federation of Rhodesia and Nyasaland. London: Cassell and Co., Ltd., 1960.

Campbell, J. McLeod. African History in the Making. London: Edinburgh House Press, 1956.
        A summary and assessment of the Jeffery and Binn's Commission Reports and the 1952 Cambridge Conference.

Carr-Saunders, M. M. New Universities Overseas. London: Oxford University Press, 1961.
        History and analysis of institutions of higher education in the Commonwealth, including Nigeria, Ghana, Sierra Leone, Rhodesia and Nyasaland, Kenya.

The Commonwealth Universities Yearbook. London: The Association of Commonwealth Universities Annual. (Distributed in the U.S. by the American Council on Education, Washington 6, D.C.)
        A Directory of the universities of the Commonwealth and the handbook of their Association.

Creighton, T.R.M. Southern Rhodesia and the Central African Federation. New York: Frederick A. Praeger, 1960.

Curle, Adam. Educational Strategy for Developing Societies; a Study of Educational and Social Factors in Relation to Economic Growth. London: Tavistock Publications, 1963.

Duffy, James. Portugal in Africa. Cambridge, Mass.: Harvard University Press, 1962.

Fletcher, B.A. The Building of a University in Central Africa. Leeds, England: Leeds University Press, 1963.
        Concerns University College of Rhodesia and Nyasaland.

Foltz, William J. From French West Africa to Mali Federation. New Haven, Conn.: Yale University Press, 1965.

Foster, Philip, <u>Education and Social Change in Ghana</u>. Chicago: University of Chicago Press, 1965.

Gagg, John Colton. <u>Modern Teaching in African Schools</u>. London: Evans Bros., Ltd., 1958.

Gallagher, Charles F. <u>The United States and North Africa</u>. Cambridge, Mass.: Harvard University Press, 1963.

Griffiths, Vincent Llewellyn. <u>An Experiment in Education: An Account of the Attempts to Improve Lower Stages of Boy's Education in the Moslem Anglo-Egyptian Sudan</u>, 1930-1950. London: Longmans, Green, 1953.
    A history of the development of the Institute of Education at Bakht er Ruda, a pioneering experiment in adapting western education to a rural environment, written by the Institute's founder and first principal.

Hailey, W. Malcomb (Lord). <u>An African Survey Revised, 1956</u>. London: Longmans, Green; New York: Oxford University Press, 1957.
    A compendium of social, economic and political developments in Africa based mainly on primary sources. Chapters cover education in British, French, Belgian, Portuguese, Spanish and "Independent" Africa.

Haines, Charles Grove. <u>Africa Today</u>. Baltimore: Johns Hopkins Press, 1959.
    Based on the proceedings of the Conference on Contemporary Africa which the Johns Hopkins University School of Advanced Studies sponsored in Washington, Aug. 1954. Bibliographical footnotes.

Hanna, A.J. <u>The Story of the Rhodesias and Nyasaland</u>. London: Faber and Faber, 1960.

Henderson, K.D.D. <u>Survey of the Anglo-Egyptian Sudan 1898-1944</u>. London, New York: Longmans, Green, 1946.
    A general sociopolitical and economic survey. About a quarter of the book deals with education in <u>five separate chapters</u> covering primary, secondary, technical, girls' education and education in the South.

Herskovits, Melville J. <u>The Human Factor in Changing Africa</u>. New York: Alfred A. Knopf, 1962.

Hilliard, Frederick H. <u>A Short History of Education in British West Africa</u>. London: Nelson, 1957.

Horner, Normar Aste. _Protestant and Roman Catholic Missions Among the_
    _Bantu of Cameroun: A Comparative Study_. Hartford, Conn.:
    Hartford Theological Seminary, 1956.

Hunter, Guy. _Education for a Developing Region: A Study in East Africa_.
    London: George Allen and Unwin, Ltd., 1963; New York: Oxford
    University Press, Inc., 1964.

_____. _The New Societies of Tropical Africa_. London: Oxford Univer-
    sity Press for the Institute of Race Relations, 1962.

Jowitt, Harold. _The Principles of Education for African Teachers in_
    _Training_. London: Longmans, Green, 1960.

_____. _Suggested Organization for the African School_. London: Long-
    mans, Green, 1960.

Junod, Violaine I. and Idrian I. Resnick. _The Handbook of Africa_. New
    York: New York University Press, 1963.

Keyes, H.M.R., ed. _International Handbook of Universities_. Paris:
    International Association of Universities, 1962.
        Distributed in the U.S. by the American Council on Education,
    Washington, D.C. (This is a companion volume to the _Commonwealth_
    _Universities Yearbook_ and therefore does not include Commonwealth
    countries.)

Kimble, George Herbert Tinley. _Tropical Africa_. 2 Vols. New York:
    Twentieth Century Fund, 1961.

Kitchen, Helen, ed. _The Educated African: A Country-by-Country Survey_
    _of Educational Development in Africa_. Compiled by Ruth Sloan
    Associates. New York: Frederick A. Praeger; London: William
    Heinemann, Ltd., 1962.

Lewis, Leonard John, ed. _Phelps-Stokes Reports on Education in Africa_.
    London, New York: Oxford University Press, 1962.

Lewis, William H., ed. _Emerging Africa_. Washington: Public Affairs
    Press, 1962.
        Papers by ten authors, originally presented at Georgetown
    University's second colloquium on Africa. The studies concen-
    trate on West and Northwest Africa.

Leys, Colin and Pratt Cranford. _A New Deal in Central Africa_. New York:
    Frederick A. Praeger, 1960.

Lucas, Eric. _English Traditions in East African Education_. London:
    Oxford University Press, 1959.

Mason, Reginald J. British Education in Africa. London: Oxford University Press, 1959.

McWilliam, H.O.A. The Development of Education in Ghana: An Outline. London: Longmans, Green, 1959.

Murdoch, George Peter. Africa: Its People and Their Culture History. New York: McGraw-Hill, 1959.

Okuma, Thomas. Angola in Ferment: The Background and Prospects of Angolan Nationalism. Boston: Beacon Press, 1962.
        Several chapters devoted to educational policy and practice.

Oliver, Roland and J. D. Fage. A Short History of Africa. Harmondsworth, Middlesex: Penguin Books, Ltd., 1962.

Olumbummo, Adegoke and John Ferguson. The Emergent University; with Special Reference to Nigeria. London: Longmans, Green, 1960.

Pankhurst, E. Sylvia. Ethiopia: A Cultural History. Woodford Green, Essex: Lalibela House, 1955.

Parker, Franklin. African Development and Education in Southern Rhodesia. Columbus, Ohio: Ohio State University Press, 1960.

Pells, Edward G. 300 Years of Education in South Africa. Cape Town, South Africa: Juta, 1954.

Read, Margaret. Education and Social Change in Tropical Areas. London: Thomas Nelson, 1955.

Sachs, Moshe Y., ed. Worldmark Encyclopedia of the Nations. Volume on Africa. New York: Harper and Row (Worldmark Press, Inc.), 1964.

Saunders, John Tennant. University College, Ibadan. Cambridge, Eng.: Cambridge University Press, 1960.

_____ and M. Dawouna, eds. The West African Intellectual Community. Ibadan, Nigeria: The Congress for Cultural Freedom and Ibadan University Press, 1962.

Scanlon, David G., ed. Traditions in African Education. New York: Bureau of Publications, Teachers College, Columbia University, 1964.

Sithole, N. African Nationalism. Capetown, South Africa: Oxford University Press, 1959.

Spencer, John, ed. Language in Africa. Papers of the Leverhulme Con-
        ference on Universities and the Language Problems of Tropical
        Africa, held at University College, Ibadan. Cambridge, Eng.:
        Cambridge University Press, 1963.

Steinberg, S.H., ed. The Statesman's Yearbook 1964-65. 101st ed.
        New York: St. Martin's Press, 1965.

Tabata, I.B. Education for Barbarism. Bantu Education in South Africa.
        London: Pall Mall Press, 1960.

Taylor, A., ed. Conference on Educational Selection in West Africa.
        University of Ghana, 1960. London: Oxford University Press,
        1962.

Thompson, Virginia McLean and Richard Adloff. The Emerging States of
        French Equatorial Africa. Stanford: Stanford University Press,
        1960.

UNESCO. World Survey of Education. Handbook of Educational Organization
        and Statistics. New York: International Documents Service, a
        division of Columbia University Press, 1955.

UNESCO. World Survey of Education - II: Primary Education. Paris: 1958.

UNESCO. World Survey of Education - III: Secondary Education. Paris:
        1961.

UNESCO. World Survey of Education - IV: Higher Education. Paris: 1966.


van den Berghe, Pierre L. South Africa: A Study in Conflict. Middle-
        town, Conn.: Wesleyan University Press, 1965.

Villard, Henry Serrano. Libya. Ithaca, New York: Cornell University
        Press, 1956.

Ward, William E.F. African Education. London: Oxford University Press,
        1953.

Wattenberg, Ben and Ralph L. Smith. The New Nations in Africa: 29
        Threshold Nations Making Headlines Throughout the World. New
        York: Hart, 1963.

Wilson, John. Education and Changing West African Culture. New York:
        Bureau of Publications, Teachers College, Columbia University,
        1964.
                A history of education in English-speaking Africa from 1923-
        1960 and a plan of development for the future.

Winter, Alban J.  African Education.  London:  Longmans, Green, 1960.

Wise, Colin.  A History of Education in British West Africa.  London,
          New York:  Longmans, Green, 1956.
                    Covers education in Nigeria, Ghana, Sierra Leone and Gambia
          from the beginning of the 19th century until 1950.

The World Almanac and Book of Facts for 1964.  New York:  New York World
          Telegram, 1964.

The World Almanac and Book of Facts for 1965.  New York:  New York World
          Telegram, 1965.

The World of Learning.  Directory of the World's Universities, Colleges,
          Learned Societies, Libraries, Museums, Art Galleries and Research
          Institutes.  London:  Europa Publications, Ltd.  (18 Bedford
          Square W.C. 1.)  Annual.  Fourteenth Edition, 1963-64.  Fif-
          teenth Edition, 1964-65.  Sixteenth Edition, 1965-66.


### ARTICLES IN BOOKS, PERIODICALS AND NEWSPAPERS

"Abidjan University,"  International Bureau of Education Bulletin, XXXVII
          (3rd quarter, 1963), 151.

Adamalekun, N.K.  "The University Curricula and National Needs,"  West
          African Journal of Education, VIII, Nos. 9-10 (1964).

"Adult Education in Ghana,"  London Times Educational Supplement, Jan.
          17, 1964, p. 90.

"Africa:  Its Educational Problems and Promises,"  Phi Delta Kappan, Vol.
          XLI, Jan. 1960.
                    Entire 200-page issue with 14 articles on the part education
          is playing in the changes taking place in Africa; published by
          Phi Delta Kappa, 8th and Union Ave., Bloomington, Indiana.

"Africa:  Symposium,"  Comparative Education Review, V (June 1961),
          39-58; VI (June, 1962), 58-77; VII (Oct. 1963), 149-62.

"African Education South of the Sahara,"  Journal of Negro Education,
          XXX, No. 3 (Summer, 1961), 173-364.

"African Higher Education,"  London Times Educational Supplement, Sept.
          21, 1962, p. 308.

"African Medical Training," London Times Educational Supplement, Aug.
        24, 1962, p. 194.

"African Ministers Meet; Follow-up to Addis Ababa," London Times Educa-
        tional Supplement, April 6, 1962, p. 676.

"African Student Credentials," Institute of International Education,
        Overseas, I (April, 1962), 31-32.

"African Teachers' Course," London Times Educational Supplement, July
        10, 1964, p. 56.

"African Women and Education: The Dakar Colloquium," Journal of Adult
        and Youth Education, V, No. 2 (1963), 81-88.

"Africanization of Higher Education in Africa," School and Society,
        XCII (April 4, 1964), 151, 174.

"The Afro-Anglo-American Conference, Salisbury, Rhodesia, March 23-28,
        1963," Teacher Education, IV, No. 2 (Nov. 1963), 93-147.

"Agricultural Education in Africa - the American Approach," Oversea
        Education, XXXIV, No. 1 (April 1962), 13-20.

Akrawi, Matta. "Educational Planning in a Developing Country - The
        Sudan," International Review of Education, VI, No. 3 (1960),
        257-84.

"Algeria Since Independence," London Times Educational Supplement, Dec.
        13, 1963, p. 875.

Amachree, G.K.J. "Education in the New Africa," American Association
        of College Teachers Education Yearbook (Terre Haute, Indiana),
        XVII (1964), 58-67.

Angarembga, A.G. "Teaching Problems in African Schools in Southern
        Rhodesia," New Era, XLV, No. 1 (1964), 14-17.

Ashby, Sir Eric. "Investment in Education," Progress, XLVIII, No. 268
        (March 1961), 61-70.

_____. "Wind of Change in African Higher Education," African Report,
        VII, No. 3 (March 1962), 5-6, 23.

Balogh, T. "Misconceived Educational Programmes in Africa," University
        Quarterly, XVI (June 1962), 243-49.

Biobaku, Saburi O.  "African Studies in an African University"   (Nigeria),
     Minerva, I, No. 3 (Spring, 1963), 285-301.

"Birth Pangs of a University - Addis Ababa University College," London
     Times Educational Supplement, Nov. 16, 1962, p. 634.

Bishti, M.  "Schools from Scratch," (Libya), London Times Educational
     Supplement, Aug. 25, 1961, p. 205.

Brickman, William W.  "Comparative Education:  Africa," Review of Edu-
     cational Research,   XXXIV (Feb. 1964), 51.

_____.  "Educational Scene in Africa," School and Society, XC (Nov.
     17, 1962), 389.

_____.  "Tendencies in African Education," Education Forum, XXVII
     (May 1963), 399-416.
          Based on content of the 1961 Addis Ababa conference on Afri-
     can education and the 1962 Tananarive conference on higher edu-
     cation in Africa, and the author's African experiences.  A
     summary of educational needs.

Bullington, R.H.  "African Education in Northern Rhodesia," Science
     Education, XLVIII (Oct. 1964), 320-26.

Caldwell, O.J.  "Africa and American Education," American Association
     of College Teachers Education Yearbook, 1961, pp. 75-82.

Carroll, Brendan J.  "The English Language Survey in West Africa,"
     English Language Teaching, XVI, No. 4 (July-Sept. 1962), 205-
     210.

Castagno, Alphonso A.  "Somalia," International Conciliation, March 1959.

Chaplin, B.H.G.  "Replanning of Junior Science Education in West Africa,"
     Science Editor, XLVIII (Oct. 1964), 366-70.

Clarke, Malcolm G.  "Secondary School Selection in Northern Rhodesia,"
     Oversea Education, XXXI, No. 3 (Oct. 1959), 99-109.

Clignet, R.P. and P.J. Foster.  "French and British Colonial Education in
     Africa," Comparative Education Review, VIII (Oct. 1964), 191-
     98.

"Comprehensive Schools; Questions of Adaptation" (Nigeria), London Times
     Educational Supplement, Feb. 7, 1964, p. 291.

"Conference of African States on the Development of Education in Africa,"
     International Journal of Adult and Youth Education, XIII, No. 4
     (1961), 175-89.

"Consolidating African Universities," Overseas, III (Nov. 1963), 30.

Constanzo, Giuseppe A. "L'educazione chiave di volta dello sviluppo della Somalia" (Education, Key to the Development of Somalia), Africa, XV, No. 3 (May-June, 1960), 139-45.

Cook, D. "Reflections After Visiting Some East African Secondary Schools," Makerere Journal, No. 8 (1963), pp. 57-64.

Cooper, William H. and John O.A. Herrington. "Ohio University Trains Nigerian Teachers," Oversea Education, XXXIII, No. 3 (Oct. 1961), 107-15.

Curle, A. "Nationalism and Higher Education in Ghana," University Quarterly, XVI (June 1962), 229-42.

Davidson, J.R. "The Work of the UNESCO Regional Centre for Education in Africa," Ghana Teacher Journal, XXXIX, No. 3 (1963), 8-11.

Dawson, G.G. "Education in Somalia," Comparative Education Review, VIII (Oct. 1964), 199-214.

"Development in Africa," London Times Educational Supplement, June 2, 1961, p. 1138.

"Development of African Education in Northern Rhodesia," Rhodesian Institute of African Affairs Monthly Bulletin, L (Nov. 1960), 3.

"Development of the University of Madagascar," International Bureau of Education Bulletin, XXXVI (2nd quarter, 1962), 77.

Doyle, L.A. "What's Happening at the University of Nigeria?" Adult Leadership, XIII (Summer, 1964), 76-78.

Duffy, J. "Portuguese Africa (Angola and Mozambique): Some Critical Problems and the Role of Education in Their Resolution," Journal of Negro Education, XXX, No. 3 (Summer, 1961), 294-301.

Edgington, D.W. "University at Large" (East Africa), University Quarterly, XVIII (Summer, 1964), 394-97.

Education in Africa: Symposium," Education Review, VI (June,1962), 58-77.

"Education in Ethiopia," Childhood Education, XXXVIII (April 1962), 381.

"Education in Nyasaland," Overseas, III (Jan. 1964), 30.

"Educational Aid for Africa:  Conference Report," School and Society,
        XC (Dec. 1, 1962), 426.

"Electrical Engineers in East Africa," London Times Educational Supple-
        ment, May 2, 1963, p. 923.

Emerson, R.  "Crucial Problems Involved in Nation-Building in Africa,"
        Journal of Negro Education, XXX, No. 3 (Summer, 1961), 193-205.

Evans, P.C.C.  "American Teachers for East Africa," Comparative Educa-
        tion Review, VI (June 1962), 69-77.

"Expansion of Education in Africa," School and Society, XXCIX (Dec. 2,
        1961), 410.

Fall, Bernard B.  "Education in the Republic of the Congo," Journal of
        Negro Education, XXX, No. 3 (Summer, 1961), 266-76.

Fletcher, Basil A.  "Building a University in Central Africa," Inter-
        national Association of Universities Bulletin, XI, No. 1 (1963).

_____.  "Educational Enterprise in Africa," School and Society,
        LXXXVII (May 23, 1959), 242-43.

Foster, P.J.  "Ethnicity and the Schools in Ghana," Comparative Educa-
        tion Review, VI (Oct. 1962), 127-35.

_____.  "Secondary School-leavers in Ghana:  Expectations and Reality,"
        Harvard Education Review, XXXIV (Fall, 1964), 537-58.

Frazier, E.F.  "Africa is Dead! Long Live Africa!" Teaching College
        Record, No. 63 (Nov. 1961), pp. 154-56.

Gagg, J.C.  "Starting a Second Language:  Trends in Africa," London
        Times Educational Supplement, Sept. 21, 1962, p. 319.

Gannon, Edmund J.  "Education in the Sudan," Comparative Education Review,
        IX, No. 3 (Oct. 1965).

"Ghana's Higher Education:  Two Universities," London Times Educational
        Supplement, July 14, 1961, p. 44.

Gillett, M.  "Western Academic Role Concepts in Ethiopian University,"
        Comparative Education Review, VII (Oct. 1963), 149-51.

Gillon, L.  "Lovanium:  The First University in the Congo," Progress,
        Spring, 1960, p. 277 ff.

"Girls' Education in Northern Rhodesia," Oversea Education, XXXII, No. 4
        (Jan. 1961), 178.

"Goals of an Educational Development Plan in Africa," School and
        Society, XC (Nov. 3, 1962), 379.

Gueye, Marie. "Education of Women in Rural Areas of Senegal," Inter-
        national Journal of Adult and Youth Education, XIII, No. 4
        (1961), 190-97.

Guilbeault, R.L. "University in Africa," International Journal of
        Adult and Youth Education, XIII, No. 3 (1961), 104-07.

Harbison, F.H. "Education and National Development," National Associa-
        tion of Secondary School Principals Bulletin, XLVIII (Jan. 1964),
        79-89.

Hawkridge, D.G. "Education and Technology in the African Context,"
        The Journal of Education of New Africa, I, No. 4 (Oct. 1963),
        14-15.

"Headway in Morocco," London Times Educational Supplement, Nov. 9, 1962,
        p. 598.

Hellmann, Ellen. "Some Comments on Bantu Education," Race Relations
        Journal, XXVIII, No. 3 (July 9, 1961), 35-49.

"Higher Education in Africa," Overseas, III (Dec. 1963), 31-32.

"Highest Priority in Nigeria; Investment in Education, 1961-70," London
        Times Educational Supplement, May 19, 1961, p. 1029.

Hutchison, Elmo H. "Sudan Looks to the Practical Side of the Education
        Picture," American Friends of the Middle East, Viewpoints, Dec.
        1963, pp. 20-24.

"The Inception of the Department of African Education in Northern Rhodesia,"
        Paedagogica Historica, IV, No. 1 (1964), 7-20.

Irvine, S.H. "African Education in Northern Rhodesia, the First Forty
        Years," Teacher Education, II, No. 2 (Nov. 1961), 36-50.

Jones, W.P. "Emerging Africa," National Education Association Journal,
        LII (May 1963), 38-41.

Jones-Quartey, K.A.B. "Adult Education and the African Revolution,"
        International Journal of Adult and Youth Education, XIII, No. 4
        (1961), 198-203.

Joyce, J.A. "Priorities in African Education," Saturday Review, XLVII
        (Aug. 15, 1964), 55-57.

Kaye, B.  "Task of an Education Department in a Developing Area" (Ghana),
    University Quarterly, XV (June 1961), 261-70.

Kehoe, Monika.  "Higher Education in Ethiopia:  A Report on Haile Sellassie
    I University,"  Journal of Higher Education, XXXIII (Dec. 1962),
    475-78.

_____.  "The Language Dilemma in Ethiopia,"  Oversea Education, XXXIV,
    No. 4 (Jan. 1963), 162-65.

_____.  "Teaching of English as a Third Language in Ethiopia,"  English
    Language Teaching, XVIII (April 1964), 125-29.

"Kenya After Independence,"  London Times Educational Supplement, Jan. 26,
    1962, p. 131.

Kibuka, K.  "Nursery Education in Uganda,"  Journal of Nursery Education,
    XVII (Summer, 1962), 157-59.

Kilby, P.  "Technical Education in Nigeria,"  Bulletin from the Oxford
    University Institute of Statistics, XXVI, No. 2 (May 1964),
    181-94.

Kinany, A. Kh.  "Problèmes d'Education dans le Monde  Arabe,"  Inter-
    national Review of Education, VIII, Nos. 3-4 (1963), 276-91.

Kintzer, F.C. and Z. Goodman, "Kenya Student Project,"  Junior College
    Journal, XXXIII (Jan. 1963), 22-24.

Klassen, F.  "Teacher Education in Ethiopia,"  School and Society, XCI
    (Feb. 23, 1963), 96-98.

Krisko, R.  "Teaching in Ghana,"  School and Community, XLIX (March
    1963), 24-25.

Lanier, O'Hara R.  "The Problems of Mass Education in Liberia,"  Journal
    of Negro Education, XXX, No. 3 (Summer, 1961), 251-60.

Larby, N.  "Nyasaland's Educational Future," London Times Educational
    Supplement, March 9, 1962, p. 448.

Lewis, L.J.  "Education and Political Independence in Africa,"  Compara-
    tive Education Review, V (June 1961), 39-49.

Lewis, W.H.  "North Africa,"  National Council of Social Studies Yearbook,
    XXXIV (1964), 437-53.

Lighton, R.E.  "Education of Teachers in the Republic of South Africa and
    the High Commission Territories,"  Year Book of Education, 1963,
    pp. 338-57.

Lingren, Vernon C. "Teacher Training in Libya," School and Society,
        Nov. 21, 1959.

Liveright, A.A. "Conference on University Adult Education in Africa,"
        International Journal of Adult and Youth Education, XIV, No. 2
        (1962), 101-06.

_____, H. Kaplan and C. Thomas "Layman's View of Adult Education in
        West Africa," Adult Education, XIII (Winter, 1963), 67-79.

Logan, Rayford W. "Education in Former French West and Equatorial Africa
        and Madagascar," Journal of Negro Education, XXX, No. 3 (Summer,
        1961), 277-85.

"Lovanium," La Revue de l'Association des Universités Entièrement ou
        Partiellement de Langue Française," Feb. 1963.

Low, Victor N. "Education for the Bantu: A South African Dilemma,"
        Comparative Education Review, Oct. 1958.

Luke, K.D. "U.S. Influence on East African Education," Overseas, III
        (Oct. 1963), 4-9.

Lystad, R.A. "Sub-Saharan Africa," National Council of Social Studies
        Yearbook, XXXIV (1964), 454-477.

MacMillan, R.G. "Education and Legislation in South Africa," Comparative
        Education Review, VI (June,1962), 58-62.

_____. "The Education of the South African Indian," International
        Review of Education, VII, No. 1 (1961), 97-104.

"Marking by Machines; West African Examinations Council," London Times
        Educational Supplement, Aug. 9, 1963, p. 169.

McLean, Drs. Helen and Frank. "Medical Education in Africa," Overseas,
        III (Feb. 1964), 4-10.

Mellanby, Kenneth. "Establishing a New University in Africa" (University
        College, Ibadan, Nigeria), Minerva, I, No. 2 (1963), 149-58.

Milne, F. Douglas and P.K. Stevenson. "Selection for African Secondary
        Schools in Northern Rhodesia," Oversea Education, XXXI, No. 2
        (July 1959), 61-69.

Morton, G. "Preschool Education in Ghana and Nigeria," Journal of Nur-
        sery Education, XVII (Summer, 1962), 191.

Muir, R.K. and R. Tonmur. "The Africans Strive for Education in South
        Africa," Comparative Education Review, IX, No. 3 (Oct. 1965),
        303-322.

Munroe, D. "Education of Europeans in South Africa," Comparative Education Review, V (Oct. 1961), 105-11.

"The National Apprenticeship in Ghana," International Labour Review, XXCV, No. 6 (June 1962), 612-21.

"National Educational Institute" (Leopoldville), International Bureau of Education Bulletin, XXXV (4th quarter, 1961), 207.

"New Baccalauréat," French Review, XXXVI (Feb. 1963), 394-401.

Nielsen, W.A., and others. "Our African Students," Overseas, I (Fall, 1962), 14-18.

"Nouvelle Réforme de l'Enseignement," French Review, XXXVIII (Jan. 1965), 402-05.

Nylander, C.T. "Ghana's Progress in Education," West Africa Review, XXVIII, No. 359 (1957).

Oberholzer, C.K. "Problems and Trends of Education in South Africa," International Review of Education, V, No. 2 (1959).

Osborne, D.G. "University Physics in Africa," International Review of Education, X, No. 3 (1964), 274-83.

Parker, Franklin. "The Addis Ababa Conference on African Education," Oversea Education, XXXV, No. 2 (July, 1962), 76-78.

_____. "British East Africa," The Negro History Bulletin, XXV, No. 4 (Jan. 1962), 74, 78-82, 95.

_____. "Education in the Federation of Rhodesia and Nyasaland," Journal of Negro Education, XXX, No. 3 (Summer, 1961), 286-93.

_____. "Federation of Rhodesia and Nyasaland"; "Nigeria," Collier's Encyclopedia 1964 Yearbook. New York: Crowell-Collier Publisher's Corp., 1964.

_____. "Malagasy (Malgache) Republic," The Americana Annual, 1964. New York: Americana Corp., 1964.

_____. "Malagasy Republic"; "Nigeria," The 1964 Compton Yearbook. Chicago: F.E. Compton and Co., 1964.

_____. "The Republic of the Congo," The Negro History Bulletin, XXV, No. 3 (Dec. 1961), 50, 60-61.

_____. "Schools for Africans in Southern Rhodesia," School and Society, LXXXVIII, No. 2171 (March 26, 1960), 154-55.

Partridge, W.G. McD.  "The Importance of a Teacher Training Forum,"
    The Journal of Education of New Africa, I, No. 2 (Oct. 1963),
    8-9.

"Pattern for Uganda," London Times Educational Supplement, Sept. 8,
    1961, p. 259.

Perry, G.W., comp.  "Problems of Underdeveloped Areas of the World with
    Special Focus on Africa," Journal of Education, No. 144 (Oct.
    1961), pp. 66-72.

Porter, D.B.  "First International Congress of Africanists," Journal of
    Negro Education, XXXII (Spring, 1963), 198-204.

"Progress in Morocco," London Times Educational Supplement, Oct. 27,
    1961, p. 559.

"Progress in Northern Rhodesia," Oversea Education, XXXII, No. 1 (April
    1960), 45.

Raum, O.F.  "Problems of Freedom in University Education in South Africa,"
    Yearbook of Education, 1959, pp. 4-6-432.

"Report on African Education on the Copperbelt," University College of
    Rhodesia and Nyasaland, Institute of Education, The Rhodes-Living-
    stone Journal, XXVIII (Dec. 1960), 69-70.

"Report on the Survey Team on Education in Malawi," Minerva, No. 3
    (Winter, 1965), pp. 233-44.

"Research in Ghana," London Times Educational Supplement, Nov. 9, 1962,
    p. 596.

Rongevin-Baville, M.  "The Organization and Content of Training for Public
    Administration in Africa," Journal Local Administration - Over-
    seas, II, No. 3 (1963), 123-36.

Rousseau, H.J.  "Rhodesian Comprehensive Schools," London Times Educa-
    tional Supplement, Feb. 23, 1962, p. 517.

Sawyerr, H.  "The University and the Sixth Form in West Africa," West
    African Journal of Education, VII, No. 3 (Oct. 1963), 159-162.

Scanlon, David.  "Church, State and Education in Sub-Saharan Africa:  An
    Overview," International Review of Education, IX, No. 4 (1963-
    64), 438-446.

"Secondary Education Reform" (Morocco), International Bureau of Education
    Bulletin, XXXVI (4th quarter, 1962), 214.

Shack, William A.  "Organization and Problems of Education in Ethiopia," *Journal of Negro Education*, XXVIII, No. 4 (Fall, 1959), 405-20.

Smyke, R.J.  "African Assignments for American Teachers," *National Education Association Journal*, L (May 1961), 27-28.

_____.  "Problems of Teachers' Supply and Demand in Africa South of the Sahara," *Journal of Negro Education*, XXX, No. 3 (Summer, 1961), 334-42.

Snyder, C.K.  "Africa's Challenge to American Higher Education; Final Report of the Tananarive Conference," *Higher Education*, XIX (June 1963), 7-19.

_____.  "Role and Importance of Africa South of the Sahara:  A Challenge to American Education," *High School Journal*, XLVII (Nov. 1963), 46-59.

Sparham, L.C.    "Secondary Education in Tanganyika," *East and West Review*," XXVII, No. 3 (July 1961), 87-90.

"Standards in Africa," *London Times Educational Supplement*, Nov. 2, 1962, p. 562.

Stratmon, David L.  "The Ghana Educational System," *Journal of Negro Education*, XXVIII, No. 4 (Fall, 1959), 398-403.

Stern, T.N.  "Political Aspects of Guinean Education," *Comparative Education Review*, VIII (June, 1964), 98-103.

Subarsky, Z.  "Science Education, East Africa," *Science Teacher*, XXXII (Feb. 1965), 32-40.

Sutton, Francis X.  "Education in Changing Africa," *Journal of Human Relations*, X, Nos. 2-3 (Winter-Spring, 1962), 256-65.

Taylor, O.W.  "Education in Tropical Africa," *High School Journal*, XLVII (Nov. 1963), 89-99.

*Teacher Education*.  Vol. III, No. 1 (May 1962).
        Includes a number of articles on teacher training and teaching methods in Africa.

"Teachers for East Africa:  1964," *Higher Education*, XX (May 1964), 15.

"The Teaching of Physics," *The Journal of Education of New Africa*, I, No. 2 (Aug. 1963), 36.

Thompson, C.H.  "African Education South of the Sahara," *Journal of Negro Education*, XXX, No. 3 (Summer, 1961), 173-79.

Thompson, P.D. "English in the Commonwealth: Nigeria," English Language Teaching, XVII (July 1963), 152-58.

Toynbee, Arnold J. "Africa: Birth of a Continent," Saturday Review, December 5, 1964.

Tregear, P.S. "The Primary Schoolleaver in Africa," Teacher Education, III, No. 1 (May 1962), 8-18.

Trent, W.J., Jr. "United Negro College Fund's African Scholarship Program," Journal of Negro Education, XXXI, No. 2 (Spring, 1962), 205-09.

Tukur, Bashiru. "Koranic Schools in Northern Nigeria," West Africa Journal of Education, VII, No. 3 (Oct. 1963), 149-52.

UNESCO. International Bureau of Education. International Yearbook of Education. Vol. XXV (1963); Vol. XXVI (1964).
        Brief reports on many African countries.

"UNESCO Program for Africa," School Life, XLIII (May 1961), 4.

"U.S. Educators Aid Africa; College of Further Education" (Northern Rhodesia), Higher Education, XIX (June 1963), 20.

"Université d'Elizabethville," La Revue de l'Association des Universités Entièrement ou Partiellement de Langue Française, Feb. 1963.

Wallin, P. "Rise of New Nations in Africa," Social Studies, LIV (Nov. 1963), 211-18.

Wangombe, M.T. "African Studies Our Schools," National Education Association Journal, LII (Feb. 1963), 21-22.

Weaver, E.K. "Science Education in Nigeria," Science Education, XLVIII (Oct. 1964), 351-61.

Weeks, S.G. "Education for Ugandans," West African Journal of Education, VIII, No. 1 (1964), 24-27.

West African Journal of Education, VIII, No. 2 (June 1964).
        The main themes of this issue cover the nature of school examinations and the steps taken to provide more suitable syllabuses and examinations for the secondary schools of English-speaking West Africa: Gambia, Ghana, Liberia, Nigeria, Sierra Leone. Published by the Institute of Education, University of Ibadan, Nigeria.

Wetmore, D., comp. "Africa at the Secondary School Level in the English Language Arts; the African Personality and Changing Africa," Journal of Education, No. 144 (Oct. 1961), pp. 82-90.

Wheeler, John H. "Apartheid Implemented by Education in South Africa," Journal of Negro Education, XXX, No. 3 (Summer, 1961), 241-50.

Williams, A.W. "Medical Education in East Africa," Journal of Medical Education, Sept. 1961.

Williams, C. "Educational Obstacles to Africanization in Ghana, Nigeria and Sierra Leone," Journal of Negro Education, XXX, No. 3 (Summer, 1961), 261-65.

Williams, G.F. "English for the Congo," Overseas, I (May 1962), 21-24.

Wilson, J. "Education and Cultural Change in Africa," Teachers College Record, LXIII (Dec. 1961), 189-95.

Wingard, P.G. "East Africa," Review of Educational Research, XXXII (June 1962), 294-97.

Wodajo, Mulugeta. "Ethiopia: Some Pressing Problems and the Role of Education in Their Resolution," Journal of Negro Education, XXX, No. 3 (Summer, 1961), 232-240.

World Confederation of Organizations of the Teaching Profession. "L'Education en Afrique," Panorama. Hiver, 1959/60.

Yates, B.A. "Structural Problems in Education in the Congo (Leopoldville)," Comparative Education Review, VII, No. 2 (Oct. 1963), 152-62.

SELECTED JOURNALS DEALING WITH AFRICAN
CULTURAL AND EDUCATIONAL MATTERS

Africa - Political, Social and Cultural. Africa Research Limited. 1 Parliament Street, City of Exeter, Devon, England. Monthly.

African Abstracts. International African Institute, London. Quarterly. In English and French.

African Digest. The African Bureau, 65, Denison House, Vauxhall Bridge Road, London, S.W.1. Bi-monthly.

African Report. African-American Institute, Suite 505, Dupont Circle Building, Washington, D.C. 20036. Monthly. Also publishes a yearly Index.

African Studies Bulletin. Stanford, Cal.: Hoover Institution. 3 times yearly.

Ghana Today. Ghana Office, Information Section, 13 Belgrave Square,
    London, S.W.1. Bi-monthly. Free.

Journal of Education of New Africa. Jena Publications, Salisbury,
    Rhodesia.

Nigerian Teacher. Government Printer, Lagos, Nigeria. Quarterly.

Overseas Education. A Journal of Educational Experiment and Research in
    Tropical and Subtropical Areas. Quarterly. Available from Her
    Majesty's Stationery Office, Cornwall House, Stamford Street,
    London, S.E. 1.

Oversea Quarterly. Department of Education in Tropical Areas, Univer-
    sity of London, Malet Street, London, W.C. 1.

South African Affairs. State Information Office, Pretoria, South Africa.

West African Journal of Education. Institute of Education, University
    of Ibadan, Nigeria. Quarterly.


                    FOR REFERENCE:   UNESCO Publications Center
                                     317 East 34th Street
                                     New York, N.Y. 10016

                    A Department of the National Agency for International
                    Publications, Inc. Distributor of the publications of
                    the United Nations Educational, Scientific and Cultural
                    Organization (UNESCO). Books, periodicals, art repro-
                    ductions, art slides, filmstrips, maps and all other
                    UNESCO-sponsored publications.

## DOCTORAL DISSERTATIONS

Coleman, Arthur Jame Kuscuiski. "A Survey of the Status of Teachers in
    Elementary and Secondary Schools of Liberia and a Suggested Plan
    for Improving Teacher Education." Unpublished Ph.D. disserta-
    tion, University of Pennsylvania, 1960.

Coleson, Edward Paul. "Educational Change in Sierra Leone." Unpublished
    Ph.D. dissertation, University of Michigan, 1956.

Dale, Gilbert R. "The History of Education in Liberia." Unpublished
    Ph.D. dissertation, University of Missouri, 1956.

Eels, Walter, C., comp. American Dissertations on Foreign Education,
    Washington, D.C. Committee on International Relations, National

Education Association, 1959. Listing dissertations prepared on 18 African countries.

Elliott, Dean A. "The Role of Agricultural Education in the Development of Agriculture in Ethiopia." Unpublished Ph.D. dissertation, Iowa State University, 1958.

Fafunwa, Alliu Babatunde. "An Historical Analysis of the Development of Higher Education in Nigeria." Unpublished Ph.D. dissertation, New York University, 1955.

Hoff, Advertus A. "Higher Education for a Changing Liberia; An Analysis of Emerging Needs, with Proposals for an Expanded, Strengthened Program." Unpublished Ph.D. dissertation, Columbia University, 1959.

Jester, David L. "Basic Considerations in Founding a College in Nigeria." Unpublished Ph.D. dissertation, Teachers College, Columbia University, 1959.

Kaypaghian, Fiametta P. "A Study of Elementary School Girl Dropouts and Non-Dropouts in Addis Ababa, Ethiopia." Unpublished Ph.D. dissertation, Harvard University, 1960.

Kessler, Jane S. "Educating the Black Frenchman." Unpublished Ph.D. dissertation, Harvard University, 1958.

McElligott, Therese E. "Education in the Gold Coast Colony, 1920-1949." Unpublished Ph.D. dissertation, Stanford University, 1950.

Moore, Malvin E. "A Survey of Education in the Belgian Congo." Unpublished Ph.D. dissertation, George Peabody College for Teachers, 1959.

Okeke, Uduaroh. "Education Reconstruction in an Independent Nigeria." Unpublished Ph.D. dissertation, New York University, 1956.

Ukeje, Onyerisara. "Nigerian Needs and Nigerian Education: A Study of the Critical Needs of an Emergent Nation and the Role of Education in Meeting Them." Unpublished Ph.D. dissertation, Columbia University, 1957.

Ukpaby, Ernest N. "American Education: A Critical Analysis of its Possible Implications for Nigerian Education." Unpublished Ph.D. dissertation, Bradley University (Illinois), 1956.

U.S. Library of Congress. African Section. A List of American Doctoral Dissertations on Africa. Washington, D.C.: U.S. Government Printing Office (Supt. of Documents), 1962.

World Confederation of Organizations of the Teaching Profession. African Education: A Partial Bibliography of U.S. Doctoral Dissertations. Washington, D. C., 1964.

## PUBLICATIONS OF GOVERNMENTS, INSTITUTIONS, LEARNED
## SOCIETIES AND OTHER ORGANIZATIONS

Aberkane, Mohamed. "Education in Independent Algeria." Unpublished
    Report. Embassy of the Democratic and Popular Republic of
    Algeria, 1963. (Mimeographed.)

Afrique Centrale. Enseignement d'Afrique Centrale. Bulletin de Liaison.
    Oct. 1964, Jan. 1965.

Allen, A.R. and William J. Miller. Education Terminology Guide for Nor-
    thern Nigeria. Research Memo Series. Zaria, Northern Nigeria:
    Ahmadu Bello University, Feb. 1965.

Alvarez Garcia, Heriberto Ramon. Historia de la acción cultural en la
    Guinea Española. Madrid: Instituto de Estudios Africanos, 1948.

Ambassade du Tchad, Washington, D.C. "General Information on Chad."
    Washington: 1964. (Mimeographed.)

Amin, Mutwakil A. "Education in the Republic of the Sudan." Unpublished
    mss. from Embassy of the Republic of the Sudan, 1964.

Angola. Anuário do Ensino. No. 2. Anos de 1960/1961. Luanda: Edicões
    do Centro de Informação e Turismo de Angola, n.d.

----. Direcção Provincial dos Serviços de Instrucão. Revista de Ensino.
    II Serie - No. 1, 1962. II Serie - No. 2, 1962. Luanda, n.d.

Annuaire de l'Enseignement Privé de l'Afrique Occidentale, Centrale,
    Orientale et de Madagascar, 1963. Paris: Edition Spéciale de
    l'Union Internationale (121 Rue de Grenelle).

Azevedo, Aliva de. Políticos de Ensino em Africa. Lisbon: Ministério
    de Ultramar, Centro de Estudos Políticos e Sociais, Estudos No.
    13, 1958.
        Part I is a general discussion of British, French, Belgian
    and UNESCO educational policies in Africa. Part II is a study
    of Portuguese educational policy and practice in Africa includ-
    ing a statistical appendix and bibliography.

Basic Facts on Libya. Washington: American Friends of the Middle East,
    Inc., 1963.

Basic Facts on the Sudan. Washington: American Friends of the Middle
    East, Inc., 1963.

<u>Basic Facts on Tunisia</u>.  Compiled by Erich W. Bethman.  Washington:
     American Friends of the Middle East, Inc., 1963.

Basutoland.  "Education Rules, 1965."  Government Notice No. 117 of 1964.
     3rd supplement to Gazette No. 3446.  Maseru:  1964. (Mimeographed.)

Bechuanaland.  Education Department.  <u>Annual Report for Year Ended Dec.
     31, 1963</u>.  Bechuanaland Press (Ptg.), Ltd., n.d.

Berea College.  <u>Nyatsime College, Salisbury (Rhodesia).  Feasibility
     Study</u>.  Berea, Kentucky:  1964.

Blood, Arthur G.  <u>The Fortunate Few.  Education in Eastern and Central
     Africa</u>.  London:  Universities' Mission to Central Africa, 1954.

Booker Washington Agricultural and Industrial Institute, Kahata, Liberia.
     <u>Bulletin, 1960-61</u>.

Burundi.  Ministère de l'éducation nationale.  <u>Programme des écoles pri-
     maires du Burundi, 1964</u>.  Bujumbura.

Calder, Rose.  <u>A Survey of English Teachers in the Provinces of Ethiopia
     (1963)</u>.  Addis Ababa:  Haile Sellassie I University.

Carr-Saunders, A.A.  <u>Staffing African Universities</u>.  London:  Overseas
     Development Institutes,
         Carnegie-sponsored study prepared as a background paper for
     the Tananarive conference in Sept. 1962.  Available through the
     Publications Division, American Council on Education, 1785
     Mass. Ave., N.W., Washington 6, D.C.

Central African Council.  <u>Commission on Higher Education for Africans in
     Central Africa.  A Report</u>.  London:  King, 1953.

Centre d'Enseignement Supérieur d'Abidjan.  <u>Livret de l'étudiant.  Année
     scolaire 1963-64</u>.  Abidjan:  Presses de l'Imprimerie de le Côte
     d'Ivoire, Jan. 31, 1964.

City and Guilds of London Institute.  <u>Regulations and Syllabuses Valid
     for Examinations, 1960, 1961, 1962, 1963, 1964, 1965</u>.  London:
     City and Guilds of London Institute (76 Portland Place, W1).

Cole, Henry B., ed.  <u>The Liberian Yearbook, 1962</u>.  Monrovia:  A Liberian
     Review Publication.

College of Technology, Yaba.  <u>Prospectus 1964-65</u>.  Summary of courses
     offered.  Yaba, Nigeria.

Conference of Representatives of the University of Cape Town and the
        University of Witwatersrand. The Open Universities in South
        Africa. Johannesburg: Witwatersrand University Press, 1957.

Congo Belge. Ministère des Colonies. Conseil Supérieur de l'Enseigne-
        ment. La Réforme de l'Enseignement au Congo Belge. Bruxelles:
        Imprimerie Louviéroise, 1954.

Cuttington College and Divinity School Suacoco, Liberia. Bulletins,
        Jan. 1964 and 1965.

Debeauvais, Michel. "Comparaison de plusieurs expériences de plans de
        développement de l'enseignement en Afrique." Paris: Centre de
        Perfectionnement pour le Développement et la Coopération Eco-
        nomique et technique. Ministère de la Coopération, 1962. (Mimeo-
        graphed.)

Dirección General de Plazas y Provincias Africanas e Instituo de Estudios
        Africanos. La Educación en la Region Ecuatorial de España 1949-
        1959. Madrid: Fenix, 1961.

Dubb, A.A., ed. "The Multitribal Society." Lusaka, Northern Rhodesia:
        Rhodes-Livingstone Institute for Social Research, 1962. (Mimeo-
        graphed.)
            Proceedings of the Sixteenth Conference of the Rhodes-Living-
        stone Institute for Social Research held at the Oppenheimer
        College for Social Service, Lusaka, Feb. 1962.

Dunwoody Industrial Institute. "Survey Report. The Khartoum Senior
        Trade School." Minneapolis: Feb.-March, 1963. (Mimeographed.)
            Submitted to U.S. Agency for International Development.

East Africa. Working Party on Higher Education in East Africa. Report.
        Nairobi: 1959.

East Africa High Commission. Higher Education in East Africa. Entebbe:
        Government Printer, 1958.

_____. Proceedings of the Conference on Muslim Education. Nairobi:
        Government Printer, 1959.

_____. Report by the Fact Finding Mission to Study Muslim Education
        in East Africa. Nairobi: Government Printer, 1958.

Education and Our Expanding Horizons. Durban: University of Natal Press,
        1962.
            Proceedings of the National Conference held in Durban at the
        University of Natal, July 9-21, 1960.

Education as an Instrument of National Policy in Selected Newly Developed
       Nations.  Vols. I-V.  Phase 2:  French Educational Strategies for
       Sub-Saharan Africa:  Their Intent, Derivation, and Development.
       Phase 3:  Formal Education in Congo-Brazzaville:  A Study of Edu-
       cational Policy and Practice.  Stanford:  Stanford University,
       Stanford International Development Education Center, 1965.

Education in Morocco.  A Survey.  Washington:  American Friends of the
       Middle East, Inc., April 1963.

Education in Morocco - Supplement.  Washington:  American Friends of the
       Middle East, Inc., 1964.

Education in Tunisia.  A Survey.  Washington:  American Friends of the
       Middle East, Inc., March 1963.

Ethiopia.  "Jimma Agricultural School Technological Bulletin."  An Agency
       for International Development Program of the United States of
       America Contracted to Oklahoma State University, Stillwater,
       Oklahoma, in cooperation with the Imperial Ethiopian Government,
       Ministry of Agriculture.  (Mimeographed, n.d.)

_____.  Ministry of Education.  Education in Ethiopia.  Addis Ababa:
       Communications Media Center, Ethiopia-U.S. Cooperative Education
       Program, 1961.

Les Examens du Baccalauréat de l'Enseignement du Second Degré.  (Examen
       probatoire, Baccalauréat proprement dit.)  Programme des Matières
       pour 1964.  Paris:  Librairie Vuibert.

Fondation de l'Enseignement Supérieur en Afrique Centrale.  "Enseigne-
       ments Dispensés au Cours de l'Année Universitaire 1963-64."
       Brazzaville, Congo.  (Mimeographed.)

_____.  "Guide de l'Etudiant, Année 1964-65."  Brazzaville, Congo.
       (Mimeographed.)

_____.  Notice sur l'Institut d'Etudes Agronomiques d'Afrique Centrale.
       Wakombo:  M'Baiki, Central African Republic.

Gabon.  Direction de l'Information de la République Gabonaise, Libre-
       ville.  L'Essentiel sur le Gabon.  Paris:  Editions Diloutremer,
       1960.

_____.  Ministère de l'Education Nationale.  Direction de l'Enseigne-
       ment.  Statistiques 1964.  Libreville.

Gambia.  The Education Ordinance, 1963.  Regulations.  Supplement "A" to
       the Gambia Gazette, No. 31, July 31, 1963.

Gambia. The House of Representatives. Education Policy 1961-65.
    Bathurst: Government Printer.

_____. Report of the Education Department for the Triennium 1961-1963
    with Statistical Tables for 1963. Sessional paper no. 17 of
    1964. Bathurst, 1964.

Georgis, Pol. Essai d'acculturation par l'enseigenemnt primaire au Congo.
    Bruxelles: Centre Scientifique et Médical de l'Université Libre
    de Bruxelles en Afrique Centrale, 1962.

Gouvernement Général de l'Afrique Equatoriale Française. Historique et
    Organisation Générale de l'Enseignement en A.E.F. Paris: Eco-
    nomique de AEF, 1931.

Government of Kenya. African Education in Kenya. Nairobi: Government
    Printer, 1949.

_____. Kenya Education Commission Report, Part I. Nairobi: Dec. 12,
    1964.

_____. Kenya Education Department. Syllabus for African Primary and
    Intermediate Schools, 1962. Nairobi.

_____. Ministry of Education. Curriculum in New Day Secondary Schools.
    Report INS/C/1/8/41. Nairobi: Dec. 10, 1962.

_____. _____. Secondary School Curriculum. Report INS/C/1/8/74.
    Nairobi: Jan. 13, 1965.

_____. _____. Triennial Survey, 1961-63. Nairobi: Government
    Printer, 1964.

_____. Report on Asian and European Education in Kenya, 1958. Nairobi:
    Government Printer, 1958.

Government Technical Institute, Enugu. Eastern Region, Nigeria. Prospectus.
    Senior Courses. 1962.

Groomes, Gwendolyn. Inventory of American Aid to Education in Africa.
    Washington: American Council on Education, Africa Liaison Com-
    mittee, Oct. 1962.
       A listing by geographical areas in Africa of 1961-62 educa-
    tional assistance projects supported by funds from public and
    private agencies in the U.S.

Hahn, Bruce J. Technical Education in Nyasaland. A Report to the Agency
    for International Development. Los Angeles: The School of Edu-
    cation, University of Southern California, Feb. 20, 1964.

Haile Sellassie I University. Department of Education. Conference on Secondary Education in Ethiopia (May 1-3, 1962). A Report. Addis Ababa.

Haile Sellassie I University Extension Information Bulletin (1964). Addis Ababa.

Haile Sellassie I University. "University Extension General Information, 1964-65." Addis Ababa. (Mimeographed.)

Hartshorne, K. Native Education in the Union of South Africa. Johannesburg: South African Institute of Race Relations, 1953.

Higher Education in East Africa. Issued by the Governments of Kenya, Tanganyika and Uganda and His Highness' Government of Zanzibar. Entebbe: Government Printer, 1958.

Horaires, Programmes, Examens, Instructions Officielles: Textes organiques du cycle d'observation et des collèges d'enseignement général. Paris: Editions S.U.D.E.L., 1964.

Horrell, Muriel. A Decade of Bantu Education. Johannesburg: South African Institute of Race Relations, 1964.

Imperial Ethiopian Government. Information Department. Ethiopia General Information. Addis Ababa: 1958.

_____. Ministry of Education and Fine Arts. Elementary Community School Curriculum (1958). Years I-VI (Experimental); Secondary School Curriculum (1958) (Provisional); Education in Ethiopia (1961); Junior Secondary School Curriculum (1961). Years VII-VIII (Experimental); Ethiopian Primary School Teachers Survey (1962); Secondary School Curriculum, Book 1, Book 2, Book 3 (1963); Education in Ethiopia (1964); School Census for Ethiopia, 1963-64; The Commercial School of Addis Ababa, Bulletin 1964-65. Addis Ababa.

Institute of International Education. Survey of the African Student, His Achievements and His Problems. New York: Nov. 1961.

International Council for Philosophy and Humanistic Studies. "Répertoire international des enseignements et des recherches africanistes et malgaches." (International Directory of African Studies, including Madagascar.) (Mimeographed (1962?))

Ivory Coast Republic. Ministère de l'Education Nationale. Année Scolaire 1963-64. Abidjan. (Mimeographed.)

_____. _____. "Arrêtés Nos. 00699 et 00700 du 23 juin 1964 fixant le fonctionnement administratif et l'organisation pédagogique de l'Ecole Normale Supérieure." (Mimeographed.)

Journal Officiel de la République Centrafricaine. Jan., Fev., 1964.
          Service du Journal Officiel, Bangui.

Kazimi, Ali Akbar. An Inquiry into Indian Education in East Africa.
          Nairobi: Government Printer, 1948.

Kenya Polytechnic. Prospectus 1965. Nairobi, Kenya. (P.O. Box 30214)

Kindell, Clyde R. "Agricultural Education at University Level: College
          of Agriculture, Haile Sellassie I University." Aug. 30, 1963.
          (Mimeographed.)

Kwame N'krumah University of Science and Technology, Kumasi. "Regula-
          tions for Matriculation Degrees and Certificates." Kumasi,
          Ghana: n.d. (Mimeographed.)

La Follette, Dr. Robert. Haile Sellassie I University - Reconnaissance
          Study (1964). Addis Ababa, Ethiopia.

Lewis, Arthur and L.V. Lieb. Report of the Conference on Institutes of
          Education, Jan. 27, 1964. Mombasa, Kenya.

Liberia "Annual Report of Dr. John P. Mitchell, Secretary of Education
          R.L. to the Honorable the Legislature of the Republic of Liberia
          in the Second Session of the Forty-Fifth Legislature of the Repub-
          lic of Liberia for the Year October 1, 1963 to September 30,
          1964." Monrovia. (Mimeographed.)

_____. The Cuttington College Program. Associated Colleges of the
          Midwest (20 North Wacker Drive, Chicago, Ill.), n.d.

_____. Department of Public Instruction. Curriculum Guides for Junior
          and Senior High Schools. 1961-64. Monrovia: n.d.

_____. Education in Liberia. Monrovia: National Teachers Association,
          1954.

Lovanium University. Catalog, 1961-62. Leopoldville, Congo.

Makerere University College. Department of Extra-Mural Studies. Extra-
          Mural Report, 1962-63. Kampala, Uganda, 1964.

Malawi. Annual Report of the Ministry of Education for the Year 1963.
          Zomba: Government Printer, 1965.

_____. The Blantyre Polytechnic School of the Ministry of Education,
          Malawi, Africa. Third Report Period, October 1964 to April 1965.
          Los Angeles: University of Southern California, School of Educa-
          tion, 1965.

Malawi (Nyasaland). Committee of Inquiry into African Education: Report.
    Professor J.F.V. Phillips, Chairman. Zomba: Government Printer,
    1962.

Marais, J. European Education in South Africa 1944-1955. Cape Town:
    University of Cape Town, 1956.

Ministère du Congo Belge et du Ruanda-Urundi. Teaching and Education in
    Belgian Congo and in Ruanda-Urundi. Brussels, 1958.

Morocco. The Educational Movement in Morocco During the School Year
    1959-60. Report submitted to the 23rd International Conference
    of Public Instruction, Geneva, July 1960 by the Ministry of
    National Education, Kingdom of Morocco.
        Conference sponsored by the International Education Bureau.

_____. Ministère de l'Education Nationale. "Arrêté du Ministre de
    l'Education Nationale No. 241-64 du 1er Juin 1964 fixant les
    conditions de délivrance des diplômes et certificats de l'Ecole
    Mohammadia d'Ingénieurs." Rabat: 11 Avril 1964. (Mimeographed.)

_____. _____. Division Pédagogique. Horaires de l'Enseignement
    Secondaire; Programmes de l'Enseignement Commercial Long, 4$^e$, 5$^e$,
    6$^e$ Années; Programmes des Classes d'Enseignement Commercial.
    Rabat: Oct. 1964.

_____. _____. Ecole Mohammadia d'Ingénieurs, Université Mohammed V.
    Rabat: 11 Avril 1964.

_____. _____. Plan Quinquennal 1960-1964. Rabat: 1960.

Mozambique. Board of Education. Panorama of Education in the Province
    of Mozambique. Laurenço Marques: Jan. 1964.

_____. Provincia de Mocambique, Instruçao Pública. Anuário do Ensino.
    Ano de 1963. Lourenço Marques: Imprensa Nacional de Moçambique,
    1964.

Nairobi Science Teaching Centre. Schemes of Work, 1964. Nairobi, Kenya.
    (P.O. Box 30231)

National Council for Social Research in South Africa. Registers of Cur-
    rent Research in the Humanities in South Africa. Pretoria:
    Annual.

Niger. "The Educational System of the Niger Republic." Niamey: Feb.
    1, 1964. (Mimeographed.)

Nigeria. Advanced Teacher Training College. "Academic Syllabuses of
        Studies." Owerri, Eastern Nigeria: Sept. 1963. (Mimeographed.)

_____. Commission on Post-School Certificate and Higher Education.
        Investment in Education. Lagos: Federal Ministry of Education,
        1960.
            The "Ashby Report," including a manpower survey by Frederic
        Harbison. This document has served as a guide for Nigerian edu-
        cational development since independence and a model for educa-
        tional planning in other countries.

_____. Eastern Nigeria Development Plan - 1962-68. Official Document
        No. 8 (1962). Enugu: Government Printer, 1962.

_____. Federal Ministry of Education. "Education Laws in Nigeria,"
        by D.O. Somoye. n.d. (Mimeographed.)

_____. _____. Our University College (University College, Ibadan).
        Lagos: 1960.

_____. _____. University Development in Nigeria. Report of the
        National Universities Commission, 1963. Apapa: The Nigerian
        National Press, Ltd.

_____. _____. Annual Report 1961. Official Document No. 30 (1963).
        Enugu: Government Printer, 1963.

_____. Ministry of Education, Eastern Nigeria. Directory of 1962
        Teachers' Colleges, Secondary Schools, Commercial Schools, Trade
        and Technical Schools. Official Document No. 1 Enugu: Govern-
        ment Printer, 1963.

_____. _____. Education Handbook 1964. Rev. to 31 July 1964.
        Official Document No. 26. Enugu: Government Printer, 1964.

_____. _____. Government Trade Centre, Enugu, Prospectus. Enugu:
        Government Printer, n.d.

_____. _____. Ministerial Broadcast on Education, January 1964, by
        Dr. S.E. Imoke, Minister of Education, Eastern Nigeria. Enugu:
        Government Printer, 1964.

_____. _____. Report on the Review of the Educational System in
        Eastern Nigeria. Enugu: Government Printer, 1962.

_____. _____. Report of the Conference on the Review of the Educa-
        tion System in Eastern Nigeria. Official Document No. 25 (1964).
        Enugu: Government Printer, 1964.

Nigeria. Ministry of Education, Eastern Nigeria. Syllabus for Elemen-
        tary Schools - Eastern Nigeria. Official Document No. 28. Enugu:
        Government Printer, 1963.

_____. Ministry of Education, Northern Nigeria. Classes, Enrollments,
        and Teachers in the Schools of Northern Nigeria, 1964. Kaduna:
        Ministry of Education, Planning and Development Division, 1964.

_____. _____. The Education Law, 1962 of Northern Nigeria. No. 43.
        Kaduna: Government Printer, 1962.

_____. _____. School Statistics of Northern Nigeria - 1963. Kaduna:
        Government Printer, 1964.

_____. _____. Teachers' Elementary Certificate Examinations.
        Syllabus of Subjects, Conditions of Award and Procedure. Kaduna:
        Government Printer, 1964.

_____. University of Nigeria Progress Report. Eastern Region Official
        Document No. 28. Enugu: Government Printer, 1963.

_____. Western Region. Report of the Committee Appointed to Review
        the Education System of Western Nigeria. Ibadan: Government
        Printer, 1961.
                The "Banjo Report," which extended the educational survey
        and planning work of the "Ashby Report" and made recommendations
        for immediate action to improve education.

_____. _____. White Paper on the Establishement of a University
        in Western Nigeria. Laid on the tables of the Western Nigerian
        Legislature as Sessional Paper No. 12, 1960. Ibadan: Govern-
        ment Printer, 1960.

Office de l'Information et des Relations Publiques pour le Congo Belge
        et le Ruanda-Urundi. Le Ruanda-Urundi. Brussels: 1957.

Parker, Dr. Franklin. "Report of a Conference on the Teaching of English
        in African Schools, 28-30 March, 1958." Salisbury, Southern
        Rhodesia: University College of Rhodesia and Nyasaland, 1958.
        (Mimeographed.)

Philosophical Society of Sudan. Education in the Sudan 1963. Khartoum:
        Philosophical Society of Sudan, 1964.

Potchefstroomse Universiteit vir Christelike Hoër Onderwys. Jaarboek
        1965. Potchefstroom.

Republic of the Congo. The Agricultural Program of the Congo Polytechnic
        Institute. 30 June 1961-29 June 1963. Los Angeles: Agricul-
        tural and Technical Assistance Foundation. (6333 Yucca St.)

Republic of the Congo. <u>Report on the Home Economics and Home and Family Life Program of the Congo Polytechnic Institute</u>. Los Angeles: Agricultural and Technical Assistance Foundation. (6333 Yucca St.)

Republic of the Sudan. "A New Plan for Education in the Sudan Presented by the Ministry of Education." Khartoum: 1961. (Mimeographed.)

_____. <u>Education under National Rule</u>. Presented by the Sudan Ministry of Education on the Second Anniversary of the Revolution (17 Nov.). Khartoum: n.d.

_____. Institute of Public Administration. "First Annual Report, March 1960 to March 1961." Khartoum: Aug. 1961. (Mimeographed.)

_____. _____. "Annual Report, 1961-62." Khartoum: 1962. (Mimeographed.)

_____. _____. "Background, Organization, Purpose, Program." Khartoum, n.d. (Mimeographed.)

_____. Ministry of Agriculture. <u>Forest Rangers College, Khartoum, Prospectus 1960</u>. Khartoum.

_____. Ministry of Education. <u>Annual Report 1957-58</u>. Khartoum: Min- of Education Publications Bureau.

_____. _____. <u>Report of the International Commission on Secondary Education in the Sudan</u>. Khartoum: Publications Bureau, 1957.

_____. <u>Regulations and Syllabuses for the Public Service Examinations</u>. Khartoum: Jan. 1964.

_____. <u>Sudan Almanac 1963</u>. An official handbook. Khartoum: Government Printing Press, 1963.

République Algérienne Démocratique et Populaire. Ministère de l'Education Nationale. "Recrutement des Elèves Professeurs de l'Enseignement Technique. Concours Féminins; Concours Masculins." Alger: n.d. (Mimeographed.)

_____. Ministère de l'Orientation Nationale, Direction des Enseignements de Second Degré. "L'Ecole Nationale Polytechnique." Alger: n.d. (Mimeographed.)

_____. _____. <u>Programmes et Instructions: Lycées, C.E.G., C.E.T.</u> Alger: Institute Pédagogique National, 1964.

_____. Ministère de l'Orientation Nationale, Direction des Enseignements Supérieurs. <u>Université d'Alger</u>. Alger: n.d. (Mimeographed sheets on each Faculty and Institute.)

République Centrafricaine.  Ministère de l'Education Nationale, Direc-
        tion Générale de l'Enseignement.  <u>Rapport Succinct sur le Mouve-</u>
        <u>ment Educatif en République Centrafricaine, 1962-63</u>.  Gangui.

République de Côte d'Ivoire.  Ministère de l'Education Nationale.
        <u>Statistiques - Situation de l'Enseignement au ler janvier 1964</u>.
        Abidjan.

République de Niger.  Ministère de l'Education Nationale.  "Situation
        de l'Enseignement au 1<sup>er</sup> janvier, 1964."  Niamey.  (Mimeographed.)

République du Congo.  Academie des Beaux Arts, Leopoldville.  <u>Programmes,</u>
        <u>1964</u>.

_____.  Ecole Supérieure de Commerce.  <u>Catalogue, 1965</u>.  Leopoldville,
        1965.

_____.  Ecole Nationale de Droit et d'Administration.  <u>Année Acadé-</u>
        <u>mique 1963-64</u>.  Leopoldville-Kalina.

_____.  Ministère de l'Education Nationale et des Affaires Culturelles.
        <u>Enseignement Secondaire.  5ème Direction/Programmes</u>.  <u>5ème Direc-</u>
        <u>tion/Etudes et Recherches Pédagogiques</u>.  Leopoldville:  1963.
            Series of booklets.

_____.  _____.  <u>5ème Secondaire.  5ème Direction Statistiques.  Liste</u>
        <u>des Etablissements du second degré recencés en 1962-1963</u>.  Leo-
        poldville.

_____.  _____.  <u>Enseignement Secondaire.  Cycle d'Orientation.  Pro-</u>
        <u>grammes et Livres et Manuels Recommandés - 1963 et 1964</u>.  Leo-
        poldville.
            Booklets for each year of the programs and for each subject.

_____.  Ministère de l'Education Nationale et des Beaux Arts.  <u>Institut</u>
        <u>National du Bâtiment et des Travaux Publics:  Catalogue</u>.  Leopold-
        ville:  n.d.

_____.  Ministère de l'Education Nationale.  <u>Programme National de</u>
        <u>l'Enseignement Primaire 1963</u>.  Leopoldville.

_____.  "Programmes des Ecoles Supérieures Pédagogiques de la République
        Démocratique du Congo."  Institut Pédagogique National:  n.d.
        (Mimeographed.)
            Series of course booklets.

République Tunisienne.  Secrétariat d'Etat à l'Agriculture.  <u>Ecole supéri-</u>
        <u>eure d'Agriculture de Tunis</u>.  Tunis:  n.d.

République Tunisienne. Secrétariat d'Etat à l'Education Nationale. "Situation de l'enseignement après quatre années d'application de la réforme." Tunis: 1962-63. (Mimeographed.)

Resources and Needs for Training Facilities for Africans in British Africa, Ethiopia and Liberia. Washington: Ruth Sloan Associates, 1955.

Rhodesia. Department of African Education. General Syllabus for Use in Standards 4, 5 and 6. Re-issue. Salisbury, Southern Rhodesia: 1960.

_____. Division of Native Education. Annual Report by the Director for the Year 1961. Presented to the Legislative Assembly, 1962. Causeway, Southern Rhodesia: Oct. 1962.

_____. _____. "Syllabus for Primary Teachers' Lower Certificate - Two Years Post Standard VI." Re-issue. Causeway, Southern Rhodesia: 1960. (Mimeographed.)

_____. _____, Training Syllabus for Primary Teacher's Higher Certificate (2 Years Post Junior Certificate). Causeway, Southern Rhodesia: 1961.

_____. Ministry of Education. Southern Rhodesia Junior Certificate Regulations and Syllabuses. Salisbury, Southern Rhodesia: 1963.

_____. Monthly Digest of Statistics, Oct. 1964. Compiled and issued by the Central Statistical Office, Salisbury, Southern Rhodesia.

_____. Report of the Native Education Inquiry Commission 1951. Bulawayo: Government Printer, 1952.
       The "Kerr Report."

_____. Report of the Southern Rhodesian Education Commission 1962. Salisbury: Government Printer, 1963.
       The "Judges Report."

_____. The Teachers' College, Bulawayo. "Revision of College Courses 1965." Bulawayo. (Mimeographed.)

Royal Society of Arts. Ordinary (Single Subject) Examinations. Regulations and Syllabuses (1964). London: Royal Society fof Arts Examination Dept., 1964.

_____. Regulations and Syllabuses for (a) School Certificate (Commercial) Examinations and (b) Secretarial and Commercial Certificate Examinations, Stage II (Intermediate). London: Royal Society of Arts Examination Dept., 1964.

_____. School Certificate (Commercial) Examinations 1963. Regulations and Syllabuses. London: Royal Society of Arts Examinations Dept., 1963.

Sierra Leone. Education Reports, 1954, 1955-57, 1958. Sessional Paper
    No. 4 of 1959. Freetown: Government Printer, 1959.

_____. Report of the Sierra Leone Education Commission. Freetown:
    Government Printer, 1954.
        The "Fulton Report," which surveyed primary, secondary,
    technical and higher education and teacher training and made
    recommendations.

_____. Sessional Paper No. 4 of 1959 - Government Statement on African-
    isation. Freetown: Government Printer, 1959.

Slade, Ruth. English-Speaking Missions in the Congo Independent State,
    1878-1908. Bruxelles: Académie Royale des Sciences Coloniales,
    1959.

Somaliland (Italian). Five Years Plan for the Development of Education
    in Somaliland 1951/52-1955/56. Mogadiscio: Stamperia A.F.I.S.,
    n.d.

South Africa. Department of Education, Arts and Science, National
    Bureau of Educational and Social Research. Education in South
    Africa. Information series no. 3. Pretoria: 1964.

_____. University College, Western Cape. Prospectus 1965. Kasselsvlei,
    C.P.

St. Joseph's Training College. "Syllabus for the High Commission Terri-
    tories, Primary Higher Teachers' Course." Maseru, Basutoland:
    1964. (Mimeographed.)

Sudan. University of Khartoum Calendar 1963-64. Khartoum: Government
    Printing Press.

Sumner, D.L. Education in Sierra Leone. Freetown: Government of Sierra
    Leone, 1963.
        A comprehensive history of education in Sierra Leone from the
    early mission beginnings in the late 18th century to 1950. The
    appendixes contain texts of major educational legislation since
    1867 as well as an extensive bibliography.

Swaziland. "Annual Report of the Director of Education, 1964." Mbabane.
    (Mimeographed.)

Tanganyika. The Basis for an Integrated System of Education. Government
    Paper No. 1, 1960. Dar es Salaam: Government Printer, 1960.

Tchad. Ministère de l'Information et du Tourisme. Les Treize Préfec-
    tures de la République du Tchad. Fort Lamy, 1962.

Togo.  "Rapport de fin d'année 1962-63." Lomé.  (Mimeographed.)

Tunisia.  Secrétariat d'Etat à l'Agriculture.  Ecole Supérieure d'Agriculture de Tunis.  Tunis, n.d.

_____.  Secrétariat d'Etat à l'Education Nationale.  Nouvelle Conception de l'Enseignement en Tunisie.  Tunis:  1958.

_____.  _____.  Perspective décennale de scolarisation (1959/60-1968/69).  Tunis.

_____.  _____.  Situation de l'Enseignement - après quatre années d'application de la réforme - 1962-1963.  Tunis.

_____.  _____.  Université de Tunis.  Livret de l'Etudiant, 1964.  Tunis.

Uganda.  African Education in Uganda.  Entebbe:  Government Printer, 1953.

_____.  Education in Uganda.  The Report of the Uganda Education Commission, 1963.  Entebbe:  Government Printer, 1963.

_____.  Memorandum by the Government on the Report of the Uganda Education Commission, 1963.  Sessional Paper No. 4 of 1963.  Entebbe:  Government Printer, 1963.

Uganda Technical College.  Prospectus 1965.  Kampala, Uganda.  (P.O. Box 181.)

UNESCO.  Africa and the United States.  Final Report of the 8th National Conference (UNESCO).  Prepared by Simon and Phoebe Ottenberg in cooperation with Boston University.  Boston:  1962.

_____.  Africa Calls.  Development of Education, the Needs and Problems, by Richard Greenough.  Paris:  1961.

_____.  The Development of Higher Education in Africa.  Report of the Conference on the Development of Higher Education in Africa, Tananarive, 3-12 Sept. 1962.  Paris:  1963.

_____.  "Education in the Belgian Congo,"  Education Abstracts, X, No. 3 (March 1958).

_____.  Field Staff Division.  Survey of Technical Training Needs and Facilities in the Gambia, by A.E. Snead.  Sessional Paper No. 4 of 1964.

_____.  Final Report of the Conference of African States on the Development of Education in Africa.  Addis Ababa, 15-25 May, 1961.  Paris:  1961.

UNESCO.  Final Report of the Meeting of Ministers of Education of African Countries Participating in the Implementation of the Addis Ababa Plan.  Paris:  1963.  (UNESCO/ED/191)

_____.  International Bureau of Education.  Compulsory Education and Its Prolongation.  Publication No. 133.  Paris/Geneva:  1951.

_____.  _____.  International Yearbook of Education.  XXV (1963); XXVI (1964); XXVII (1965).  Geneva.

_____.  Preparation and Issuing of the Primary School Curriculum.  Publication No. 194.  Paris/Geneva:  1958.

_____.  Preparation of General Secondary School Curricula.  Publication No. 216.  Paris/Geneva:  1960.

_____.  Primary Teacher Training.  Publication No. 117.  Paris/Geneva: 1950.

_____.  Report of the Educational Planning Group on Their First Mission to Somalia.  Paris:  1962.  (WS/0862.300)

_____.  Report of the UNESCO Educational Planning Mission for Tanganyika: June-October 1962.  Paris:  1963.  (WS/1262.136)

_____.  Secondary Teacher Training.  Publication No. 154.  Paris/Geneva: 1954.

_____.  UNESCO in the Congo, by Garry Fullerton.  Paris:  1964.

Université de Liège.  Le Problème de L'Enseignement dans le Ruanda-Urundi.  Bruxelles:  Fondation pour les Recherches Scientifiques au Congo Belge et au Ruanda-Urundi, 1958.

Université Libre de Bruxelles.  Institut de Sociologie Solvay.  L'Enseignement à dispenser aux indigènes dans les territoires non autonomes.  Bruxelles:  Editions de la Librairie Encyclopédique, 1951.

Université Officielle de Bujumbura.  Programme des Cours, 1964-65.  Bujumbura, Burundi.

Universiteit van die Oranje-Vrystaat.  Jaarboek 1964.  Bloemfontein.

Universiteit van Pretoria.  Jaarboek 1965-66.  Pretoria, South Africa.

Universiteit van Stellenbosch.  Jaarboek 1965.  Stellenbosch, South Africa.

University College, Durban.  General Prospectus 1964.  Pretoria:  The Government Printer.

University College of the North (Yunibesiti-Kholeji Ya Leboa).  Calendar 1965.  Pretoria, South Africa:  The Government Printer.

The University College of Sierra Leone.  Fourah Bay College.  Calendar, Session 1964-65.  Freetown, Sierra Leone.

University College of Zululand, Empangeni. Prospectus. Pretoria: The
    Government Printer, July 1963.

University of Basutoland, Bechuanaland Protectorate and Swaziland. Cal-
    endar, 1965. Maseru, Basutoland.

_____. "Information on Courses of Study Offered in 1965." Maseru,
    Basutoland. (Mimeographed.)

University of Cambridge Local Examinations Syndicate. Joint Examination
    for the School Certificate and General Certificate of Education
    (Overseas Centers Only). Regulations 1965. Cambridge: Univer-
    sity of Cambridge, Sept. 1963.

_____. Joint Examination for the Higher School Certificate and General
    Certificate of Education (Overseas Centers Only). Regulations
    1965. Cambridge: University of Cambridge, Sept. 1963.

University of Cape Town. General Prospectus 1965. With separate faculty
    bulletins, 1965. Cape Town: Cape and Transvaal Printers, Ltd.

University of Dakar. Livret d'Etudiant, 1963-64. L'Imprimerie Fabrègue
    a St. Yrieix-La-Perche (Haute Vienne), Jan. 1964.

University of East Africa. University College, Nairobi. Calendar, 1964-
    65. Nairobi, Kenya.

_____. The University College, Dar es Salaam. First Degree Courses,
    1964. Dar es Salaam, Tanzania.

_____. The University College, Dar es Salaam. Prospectus, Academic
    Year 1964-65. Dar es Salaam, Tanzania.

University of Ibadan, Nigeria. Calendar - 1963-64. Ibadan: Ibadan
    University Press, Jan. 1964.

University of Ife, Ibadan Branch. Calendar 1963-64. Ibadan, Nigeria.

University of Khartoum. Regulations Governing Admission to the Univer-
    sity, General Conditions. Khartoum, Sudan: Government Printing
    Press, 1963-64.

University of Lagos. Calendar 1964-65. Lagos, Nigeria.

The University of Liberia. Catalog and Announcement 1965-66. Monrovia.

University of London. School Examinations. Regulations and Syllabuses
    for the General Certificate of Education Held Overseas June 1964
    and January 1965. London: University of London, July 1962,
    June 1965 and Jan. 1966.

University of Malawi. "News Bulletin, June 1965." Zomba, Malawi.
        (Mimeographed.)

_____. "Notes on Policy and Plans." Zomba, Malawi. (Mimeographed.)

University of Natal. Calendar 1964. Durban, S.F.

The University of Nigeria, Nsukka. Eastern Region. Annual Report 1962-
        63. University of Nigeria Official Document Number 5 of 1963.
        Nsukka: Jan. 8, 1964.

_____. 1964-65 Calendar. C.M.S. (Nigeria) Press Port Harcourt.

University of South Africa. Calendar 1965. Pretoria.

University of Witwatersrand, Johannesburg. Calendar 1954. Pietermaritz-
        burg.

U.S. Department of Health, Education and Welfare. Office of Education.
        Educational Data: Algeria. Compiled by Anne N. Forrester in
        collaboration with Charles C. Hauch, Acting Director, Comparative
        Education Branch. Washington: March 1964. (OE-14034-74)

_____. _____. Educational Data: Libya. Washington: Feb.,1961.

_____. _____. Educational Data: Morocco. Compiled by Daira
        Barzdukas in collaboration with Abdul H.K. Sassani. Washington:
        April, 1962. (OE-14034-63)s

_____. _____. Educational Data: Republic of Tunisia. Compiled
        by Abdul H.K. Sassani. Washington: March, 1960. (No. 41-NE)

_____. _____. Education for Africans in Tanganyika - A Preliminary
        Study, by Betty George. Washington: 1960.
                In conjunction with this booklet, see also "A Guide to the
        Academic Placement of Students from Tanganyika in Educational
        Institutions in the U.S.A., 1961." Prepared by the Council on
        Evaluation of Foreign Credentials to be used with "Education
        for Africans in Tanganyika."

_____. _____. Education in Uganda, by David Scanlon. Washington:
        1964. (OE-14103)

_____. _____. Ministries of Education: Their Functions and Organ-
        izations. Washington: 1962. (OE-14064)

_____. _____. Recent Developments in Tanganyika. Washington:
        April 1961. (OE-14034-54.)

U.S. Department of State. <u>Africa</u>. African Series 34. Department of
     State Publication 7546. Washington:  May, 1963.

_____.  <u>Profiles of Newly Independent States</u>. Washington:  Government
     Printing Office, May 1963.

_____.  Bureau of Intelligence and Research.  Jacqueline S. Mithun,
     comp.  <u>African Programs of U.S. Organizations:  A Selective</u>
     <u>Directory</u>. Washington:  May 1965.

_____.  _____.  <u>A List of Current Social Science Research by Private</u>
     <u>Scholars and Academic Centers:  Completed Studies:  Africa (1965)</u>.
     External Research List 5.23-1964. Washington:  1965.

Van Zyl, H.  <u>A Practical Guide for Bantu Teachers</u>. Johannesburg:  A.P.B.,
     1958.

<u>Vocational Education in South Africa</u> . . . meeting the requirements of
     Industry, Commerce, and Agriculture. Fact Paper 45. Pretoria:
     Oct. 1957.

West African Examinations Council.  <u>Regulations and Syllabuses for the</u>
     <u>Joint Examination for the West African School Certificate and</u>
     <u>General Certificate of Education, 1965</u>. Oxford:  University Press.

_____.  <u>Regulations and Syllabuses for the Joint Examination for the</u>
     <u>School Certificate and General Certificate of Education in the</u>
     <u>Gambia, Ghana and Sierra Leone for 1965</u>. Oxford:  University
     Press.

_____.  <u>Teachers' Higher Elementary (Grade II) Certificate Examination -</u>
     <u>Nigeria. Syllabuses for Centrally Examined Subjects</u>. Oxford:
     University Press.

Williams, D.H.  <u>A Short Survey of Education in Northern Nigeria</u>. Kaduna:
     Ministry of Education, Northern Region of Nigeria, 1959.

World Confederation of Organizations of the Teaching Profession. <u>Handbook</u>
     <u>for Raising Teacher Status in Africa</u>. Washington:  1964.

_____.  <u>Survey of the Status of the Teaching Profession in Africa</u>.  A
     Field Report:  Study of recruitment and retention of teachers.
     Washington:  1961.

Zambia.  Ministry of African Education.  <u>Triennial Survey, 1958 to 1960</u>
     <u>Inclusive, Including Statistics for 1960</u>. Lusaka:  Government
     Printer, 1961.

_____.  Ministry of Education Circular No. 15 of 1964. Lusaka:  1964.

Zanzibar.  <u>Report of the Committee on Education</u>, 1959.